AMBULATORY PEDIATRICS

AMBULATORY PEDIATRICS

5th
Edition

Morris Green, MD
Perry W. Lesh Professor of Pediatrics
Indiana University School of Medicine
James Whitcomb Riley Hospital for Children
Indianapolis, Indiana

Robert J. Haggerty, MD
Professor of Pediatrics Emeritus
University of Rochester
School of Medicine and Dentistry
Rochester, New York

Michael Weitzman, MD
Professor and Associate Chair
Department of Pediatrics
University of Rochester
School of Medicine and Dentistry
Rochester, New York

W.B. SAUNDERS COMPANY
A Division of Harcourt Brace & Company
Philadelphia   London   Toronto   Montreal   Sydney   Tokyo

W.B. SAUNDERS COMPANY
A Division of Harcourt Brace & Company

The Curtis Center
Independence Square West
Philadelphia, Pennsylvania 19106

Library of Congress Cataloging-in-Publication Data

Ambulatory pediatrics / [edited by] Morris Green, Robert J. Haggerty, Michael Weitzman.—5th ed.

p.   cm.

Rev. ed. of: Ambulatory pediatrics IV / edited by Morris Green, Robert J. Haggerty. 1990.

Includes bibliographical references and index.

ISBN 0–7216–7401–1

1. Ambulatory medical care for children.   I. Green, Morris.   II. Haggerty, Robert J.   III. Weitzman, Michael.   IV. Ambulatory pediatrics IV.
[DNLM: 1. Pediatrics.   2. Ambulatory Care—in infancy & childhood.
WS 200 A497 1999]

RJ47.A433   1999   618.92—dc21

DNLM/DLC   98–50611

AMBULATORY PEDIATRICS   ISBN 0–7216–7401–1

Printed in the United States of America.

Last digit is the print number: 9   8   7   6   5   4   3   2   1

This book is affectionately dedicated to our wives,
Janice, Muriel, and Maggie,

and to our
children and grandchildren

CONTRIBUTORS

Henry M. Adam, MD

Professor of Clinical Pediatrics and Director, Pediatric Residency Training Program, Albert Einstein College of Medicine–Montefiore Medical Center, Bronx, New York
Pediatric Human Immunodeficiency Virus Infection

Hoover Adger, Jr., MD

Deputy Director, Office of National Drug Control Policy, Washington, DC
School Age and Adolescence: Substance Abuse Among Children and Adolescents

Henry W. Albers, MD

Assistant Professor, Wright State University; Orthopaedic Surgeon, Children's Medical Center, Dayton, Ohio
Injury Management: Musculoskeletal Trauma and Overuse Injuries

C. Andrew Aligne, MD

Instructor and Research Fellow, University of Rochester School of Medicine and Dentistry; Attending Physician, Rochester General Hospital, Rochester, New York
Environment: Children and Tobacco

Joel J. Alpert, MD

Professor of Pediatrics and Public Health (Health Law), Boston University School of Medicine and Public Health; Senior Pediatrician, Boston Medical Center, Boston, Massachusetts
An Overview of Childhood Mortality and Morbidity

Ellen L. Bassuk, MD

Associate Professor of Psychiatry, Harvard Medical School; Boston; President, The Better Homes Fund, Newton, Massachusetts
Homeless Children

Laurie J. Bauman, PhD

Professor of Pediatrics, Department of Pediatrics, Albert Einstein College of Medicine, Bronx, New York
Social Support

William R. Beardslee, MD

Gardner Monks Professor of Child Psychiatry, Harvard Medical School; Psychiatrist-in-Chief and Chairman of the Department of Psychiatry, Children's Hospital and Judge Baker Children's Center, Boston, Massachusetts
Children of Parents Who Have Major Mental Illness

Abraham B. Bergman, MD

Professor of Pediatrics, University of Washington School of Medicine; Director, Department of Pediatrics, Harborview Medical Center, Seattle, Washington
Child Advocacy: How Pediatricians Can Advocate Effectively

Jerry Bergstein, MD

Professor, Department of Pediatrics, Indiana University School of Medicine; Director, Section of Nephrology, James Whitcomb Riley Hospital for Children, Indianapolis, Indiana
Urinary Tract Infections

Stephen Berman, MD

Professor of Pediatrics and Director of Health Policy, University of Colorado Health Sciences Center; Attending Physician, Children's Hospital, Denver, Colorado
Acute Respiratory Infections, Otitis Media, Sinusitis, and Croup

Judy C. Bernbaum, MD

Associate Professor of Pediatrics, University of Pennsylvania School of Medicine; Director, Neonatal Follow-Up Program, Children's Hospital of Philadelphia, Philadelphia, Pennsylvania
Follow-Up Care of the Ex-Preterm Infant

David A. Brent, MD

Professor of Child Psychiatry, Pediatrics, and Epidemiology, University of Pittsburgh School of Medicine; Chief, Division of Child and Adolescent Psychiatry, and Director, Services for Teens at Risk (STAR), Western Psychiatric Institute and Clinic, Pittsburgh, Pennsylvania
School Age and Adolescence: Mood Disorders and Suicide

John G. Brooks, MD

Professor and Chair, Department of Pediatrics, Dartmouth Medical School, Hanover; Medical Director, Children's Hospital at Dartmouth, Lebanon, New Hampshire
Apparent Life-Threatening Events and Sudden Infant Death Syndrome

Ann B. Bruner, MD

Assistant Professor of Pediatrics, Johns Hopkins Hospital, Baltimore, Maryland
School Age and Adolescence: Substance Abuse Among Children and Adolescents

Robert S. Byrd, MD, MPH

Assistant Professor of Clinical Pediatrics, General Pediatrics, University of California, Davis, Sacramento, California
Maternal Literacy; School Age and Adolescence: School Readiness; School Age and Adolescence: School Avoidance

James R. Campbell, MD, MPH

Assistant Professor, Department of Pediatrics, University of Rochester School of Medicine and Dentistry; Attending Pediatrician, Rochester General Hospital, Rochester, New York
Environment: Childhood Lead Exposure

Richard F. Catalano, PhD

Professor and Associate Director, Social Development Research Group, University of Washington School of Medicine, Seattle, Washington
School Age and Adolescence: Delinquent Behavior

Robert W. Chamberlin, MD, MPH

Adjunct Professor of Pediatrics, Dartmouth Medical School, Hanover; Adjunct Professor, School of Health and Human Services, University of New Hampshire, Durham, New Hampshire
Community Organization for Ambulatory Pediatrics

Cynthia Christy, MD

Clinical Associate Professor, University of Rochester School of Medicine and Dentistry; Director, Inpatient Pediatrics, and Pediatric Clerkship Director, Rochester General Hospital, Rochester, New York
Sexually Transmitted Disease Syndromes

William Lord Coleman, MD

Associate Professor of Pediatrics, Center for Development and Learning, Department of Pediatrics, University of North Carolina School of Medicine, Chapel Hill; Assistant Consulting Professor of Pediatrics, Duke University Medical Center, Durham, North Carolina
School Age and Adolescence: Learning Problems of Children and Adolescents: Assessment and Management Techniques; School Age and Adolescence: Attention Deficits: Description, Diagnosis, and Management; School Age and Adolescence: Helping Children and Adolescents Make Friends: Social Skills

James Coplan, MD

Instructor, University of Pennsylvania School of Medicine; Director of Outpatient Services, Children's Seashore House, Children's Hospital of Philadelphia, Philadelphia, Pennsylvania
Speech and Language Disorders

Armando G. Correa, MD

Assistant Professor of Pediatrics, Baylor College of Medicine; Co-Director, Children's Tuberculosis Clinic, Ben Taub General Hospital; Attending Physician, Texas Children's Hospital, Houston, Texas
Tuberculosis

G. Paul DeRosa, MD

Executive Director, American Board of Orthopaedic Surgery, Inc.; Professor of Surgery/Orthopaedics, Duke University School of Medicine, Chapel Hill, North Carolina
Congenital, Developmental, and Nontraumatic Musculoskeletal Disorders

Thomas G. DeWitt, MD

Weihl Professor of Pediatrics, University of Cincinnati College of Medicine; Director, Division of General and Community Pediatrics, and Associate Chair for Primary Care Programs, Children's Hospital Medical Center, Cincinnati, Ohio
Vomiting and Diarrhea

William H. Dietz, MD, PhD

Director, Division of Nutrition and Physical Activity, National Center for Chronic Disease Prevention and Health Promotion, Centers for Disease Control and Prevention, Atlanta, Georgia
Obesity

Andrew S. Doniger, MD, MPH

Clinical Assistant Professor of Pediatrics and of Community and Preventive Medicine, University of Rochester School of Medicine and Dentistry, Rochester, New York
Public Health Services for Children and Families

Paul H. Dworkin, MD

Professor and Associate Chairperson of Pediatrics, Head, Division of General Pediatrics, and Assistant Dean for Medical Education, University of Connecticut School of Medicine, Farmington; Director and Chairperson of Pediatrics, Center for Children's Health and Development, St. Francis Hospital and Medical Center, Hartford, Connecticut
Behavior Problems of Toddlers and Preschool Children

Stanley I. Fisch, MD

President and CEO, Harlingen Pediatrics Associates, Harlingen, Texas
Immigrant Children

Marc Fishman, MD

Assistant Professor of Psychiatry, Department of Psychiatric and Behavioral Sciences, Johns Hopkins Hospital, Baltimore, Maryland
School Age and Adolescence: Substance Abuse Among Children and Adolescents

Carolyn H. Frazer, MD

Instructor in Pediatrics, Harvard Medical School; Assistant in Medicine, Children's Hospital, Boston, Massachusetts
School Age and Adolescence: Somatic Complaints in Children and Adolescents: Recurrent Headache; Abdominal, Chest, and Limb Pains

Frances Page Glascoe, PhD

Associate Professor of Pediatrics, Division of Child Development, Vanderbilt University Medical Center, Nashville, Tennessee
Developmental, Behavioral, and Educational Surveillance

Morris Green, MD

Perry W. Lesh Professor of Pediatrics, Indiana University School of Medicine, James Whitcomb Riley Hospital for Children, Indianapolis, Indiana
Health Supervision: Principles; Health Supervision: Goals and Content; Delirium; Fainting or Syncope; Tics

David Greenes, MD

Instructor in Pediatrics, Harvard Medical School; Assistant in Medicine, Children's Hospital, Boston, Massachusetts
Injury Management: Stabilization, Lacerations, Head Trauma, and Poisoning

David C. Grossman, MD, MPH

Associate Professor of Pediatrics, Harborview Medical Center, University of Washington School of Medicine; Co-Director, Harborview Injury Prevention and Research Center, Seattle, Washington
Injury Prevention

Robert J. Haggerty, MD

Professor of Pediatrics Emeritus, University of Rochester School of Medicine and Dentistry, Rochester, New York
Risks and Protective Factors in Childhood Illness; School Age and Adolescence: Conduct Disorders; Integrated Child Health Services; The Increasingly Global Village

Neal Halfon, MD, MPH

Professor, Pediatrics, School of Medicine, Community Health, and Public Health, and Director, UCLA Center for Healthy Children, Families, and Communities, University of California, Los Angeles, California
Foster Care

Robert H. A. Haslam, MD, FAAP, FRCP(C)

Professor of Pediatrics and Medicine (Neurology) and Chairman Emeritus, Department of Pediatrics, University of Toronto School of Medicine; Staff Child Neurologist and Pediatrician-in-Chief Emeritus, Hospital for Sick Children, Toronto, Ontario, Canada
The Diagnosis and Management of Seizures

J. David Hawkins, PhD

Professor, School of Social Work, Director, Social Development Research Group, and Chairman, Developmental Research and

Programs, University of Washington School of Medicine, Seattle, Washington

School Age and Adolescence: Delinquent Behavior

Charles Homer, MD, MPH

Assistant Professor of Pediatrics, Harvard Medical School; Director, Clinical Effectiveness Program, Children's Hospital, Boston, Massachusetts

Improving Quality in Your Practice

Barbara J. Howard, MD

Assistant Professor of Pediatrics, The Johns Hopkins University School of Medicine, Baltimore; Co-Director, Center for Promotion of Child Development Through Primary Care, Annapolis, Maryland

Behavior Problems in Infancy

Cynthia R. Howard, MD, MPH

Assistant Professor of Pediatrics, Department of Pediatrics, University of Rochester School of Medicine and Dentistry; Pediatric Director, Mother-Baby Unit, Rochester General Hospital, Rochester, New York

Breastfeeding

Michael S. Jellinek, MD

Professor of Psychiatry and of Pediatrics, Harvard Medical School; Chief, Child Psychiatry Services, Massachusetts General Hospital, Boston, Massachusetts

School Age and Adolescence: The Use of Psychotropic Medication in Children and Adolescents

Lorraine V. Klerman, DPH

Professor, Department of Maternal and Child Health, School of Public Health, University of Alabama at Birmingham, Birmingham, Alabama

School Age and Adolescence: When the Child's Mother Is a Teenager

Alan E. Kohrt, MD

Private Pediatric Practice, Rydal, Pennsylvania

Rural Health in the Context of Patient, Family, and Community

David Korones, MD

Assistant Professor of Pediatrics and Oncology, University of Rochester School of Medicine and Dentistry, Rochester, New York

Anemia

Richard E. Kreipe, MD

Associate Professor of Pediatrics, University of Rochester School of Medicine and Dentistry; Chief, Division of Adolescent Medicine, Children's Hospital at Strong, Rochester, New York

Health Supervision for Adolescents; Eating Disorders in Pediatric Practice

Richard D. Krugman, MD

Professor of Pediatrics and Dean, University of Colorado School of Medicine, Denver, Colorado

Physical and Sexual Abuse

Timothy Kutz, MD

Assistant Professor, University of Utah School of Medicine, Salt Lake City, Utah

Physical and Sexual Abuse

Philip J. Landrigan, MD, MSc

Ethel H. Wise Professor and Chairman, Department of Community and Preventive Medicine, and Professor of Pediatrics, Mount Sinai School of Medicine, New York, New York

Child Labor

Bruce P. Lanphear, MD, MPH

Associate Professor of Pediatrics, Children's Hospital Medical Center, University of Cincinnati School of Medicine, Cincinnati, Ohio

Environment: Indoor Pollutants and Toxins

Norma B. Lerner, MD

Clinical Associate Professor of Pediatrics, Division of Pediatric Hematology-Oncology, University of Rochester School of Medicine and Dentistry, Children's Hospital at Strong, Rochester, New York

Sickle Cell Disease

Gregory S. Liptak, MD, MPH

Associate Professor of Pediatrics, University of Rochester School of Medicine and Dentistry; Attending Pediatrician, Children's Hospital at Strong, Rochester, New York

Myelodysplasia; Cerebral Palsy

Mona Mansour, MD

Fellow, General Academic Pediatrics, Children's Hospital Medical Center, Cincinnati, Ohio

Vomiting and Diarrhea

John McBride, MD

Professor of Pediatrics, University of Rochester
School of Medicine and Dentistry; Chief,
Pediatric Pulmonary Division, Department of
Pediatrics, Children's Hospital at Strong,
Rochester, New York

Asthma

Paul L. McCarthy, MD

Professor of Pediatrics, Yale School of Medicine;
Head, Division of General Pediatrics,
Children's Hospital at Yale–New Haven, New
Haven, Connecticut

*Fevers and the Evaluation of the Child Who Has
Fever*

Jennie A. McLaurin, MD, MPH

Adjunct Clinical Faculty, Department of
Pediatrics, Wake Forest University, Bowman
Gray School of Medicine, Winston-Salem,
North Carolina

Health Care for Children of Migrant Farmworkers

Alan Meyers, MD, MPH

Associate Professor of Pediatrics, Boston
University School of Medicine; Attending
Physician, Pediatric Primary Care Center,
Boston Medical Center, Boston, Massachusetts

Food Assistance Programs for Children

Lyle J. Micheli, MD

Associate Clinical Professor of Orthopaedic
Surgery, Harvard Medical School; Director,
Division of Sports Medicine, Children's
Hospital, Boston, Massachusetts

*Injury Management: Musculoskeletal Trauma and
Overuse Injuries*

Tracie L. Miller, MD

Associate Professor of Pediatrics, University of
Rochester School of Medicine and Dentistry;
Co-Chief, Division of Pediatric
Gastroenterology and Nutrition, Children's
Hospital at Strong, Rochester, New York

Pediatric Nutrition

Lawrence F. Nazarian, MD

Pediatric Practitioner, Panorama Pediatric Group;
Clinical Professor of Pediatrics, University of
Rochester School of Medicine and Dentistry,
Rochester, New York

The Well-Equipped Office

Robert Needlman, MD

Assistant Professor, Case Western Reserve
University School of Medicine; Attending
Physician, Rainbow Babies and Children's
Hospital, Cleveland, Ohio

Failure to Thrive: Primary Care Interventions

Terry Nolan, MBBS, PhD

Associate Professor and Head of Clinical
Epidemiology and Biostatistics, University of
Melbourne, Department of Paediatrics; Senior
Specialist Physician, Continence Clinic,
Department of General Paediatrics, Royal
Children's Hospital, Melbourne, Victoria,
Australia

Encopresis

David L. Olds, PhD

Professor of Pediatrics, University of Colorado
School of Medicine; Director, Kempe
Prevention Research Center, University of
Colorado Health Sciences Center, Denver,
Colorado

Non-Physician Home Visits

Karen N. Olness, MD

Professor of Pediatrics, Family Medicine, and
International Health, Case Western Reserve
University School of Medicine; Co-Director of
Behavioral Pediatrics and Psychology,
Rainbow Babies and Children's Hospital,
Cleveland, Ohio

Self-Hypnosis, Self-Care

Craig C. Orlowski, MD

Assistant Clinical Professor, Department of
Pediatrics, University of Rochester School of
Medicine and Dentistry; Attending Physician,
Children's Hospital at Strong, Rochester, New
York

*Common Issues in Childhood Type I Diabetes
Mellitus*

Lee M. Pachter, DO

Associate Professor of Pediatrics and
Anthropology, University of Connecticut
School of Medicine, Farmington; Director,
Inpatient Pediatrics, Sickle Cell Service, and
Inner City Asthma Clinic, Center for
Children's Health and Development, St.
Francis Hospital and Medical Center, Hartford,
Connecticut

*Ethnic and Cultural Influences on Child Health and
Child Health Services*

Judith S. Palfrey, MD

T. Berry Brazelton Professor of Pediatrics, Harvard Medical School; Chief, Division of General Pediatrics, Children's Hospital, Boston, Massachusetts
Beyond the Office Door

Ellen C. Perrin, MA, MD

Professor of Pediatrics, University of Massachusetts Medical Center, Worcester, Massachusetts
School Age and Adolescence: Gay and Lesbian Issues in Pediatric Care

James M. Perrin, MD

Associate Professor of Pediatrics, Harvard Medical School; Director, Division of General Pediatrics, Massachusetts General Hospital, Boston, Massachusetts
State and Federal Programs for Children Who Have Chronic Conditions

Charles Poland III, DDS

Associate Professor, Pediatric Dentistry, Indiana University School of Dentistry and James Whitcomb Riley Hospital for Children, Indianapolis, Indiana
Oral Health in Children

Steven R. Poole, MD

Professor of Pediatrics and Vice Chair, Department of Pediatrics, University of Colorado School of Medicine; Medical Director, Children's Hospital Regional Health Care Network, Denver, Colorado
Pediatric Telephone Care

Neil S. Prose, MD

Associate Professor of Medicine (Dermatology) and Pediatrics, Duke University Medical School and Center, Durham, North Carolina
Common Skin Disorders

Susan H. Psaila, MD

Dermatology Resident, Duke University Medical Center, Durham, North Carolina
Common Skin Disorders

Leonard A. Rappaport, MD

Associate Professor of Pediatrics, Harvard Medical School; Associate Chief, Division of General Pediatrics, Children's Hospital, Boston, Massachusetts

School Age and Adolescence: Somatic Complaints in Children and Adolescents: Recurrent Headache; Abdominal, Chest, and Limb Pains

Kenneth B. Roberts, MD

Professor of Pediatrics, University of North Carolina School of Medicine, Chapel Hill; Director, Pediatric Teaching Program, Moses Cone Health System, Greensboro, North Carolina
The Role of the Practitioner in Pediatric Education

Sheryl Ryan, MD

Assistant Professor of Pediatrics, University of Rochester School of Medicine and Dentistry and Rochester General Hospital, Rochester, New York
School Health

Eric A. Schaff, MD

Associate Professor of Family Medicine and Pediatrics, and of Obstetrics and Gynecology, University of Rochester School of Medicine and Dentistry, Rochester, New York
School Age and Adolescence: Contraception

Stanley J. Schaffer, MD, MS

Assistant Professor of Pediatrics, University of Rochester School of Medicine and Dentistry; Attending Pediatrician, Children's Hospital at Strong, Rochester, New York
Environment: Childhood Lead Exposure

Neil L. Schechter, MD

Professor of Pediatrics and Head, Division of Developmental and Behavioral Pediatrics, University of Connecticut School of Medicine, Farmington; Director, Developmental and Behavioral Pediatrics, St. Francis Hospital and Medical Center, Hartford, Connecticut
Pain Management in Children

Lonnie K. Seltzer, MD

Professor of Pediatrics and Director, Pediatrics Pain Program, University of California, Los Angeles, School of Medicine, Los Angeles, California
The Primary Care Clinician's Role with the Child Cancer Patient

Paul M. Seltzer, MD

Department of Pediatrics, University of California, Irvine, School of Medicine and Medical Center, Orange, California
The Primary Care Clinician's Role with the Child Cancer Patient

Richard N. Shiffman, MD, MCIS

Assistant Professor of Pediatrics, Yale School of Medicine; Attending Physician, Yale–New Haven Hospital, New Haven, Connecticut
Informatics and Computers in Pediatrics

Joseph Shrand, MD

Instructor of Psychiatry, Harvard Medical School, Boston; Director, Child and Adolescent Ambulatory Services, McLean Hospital, Belmont, Massachusetts
School Age and Adolescence: The Use of Psychotropic Medication in Children and Adolescents

Constantinos G. Siafakas, MD

Instructor in Pediatrics, University of Rochester School of Medicine and Dentistry; Division of Pediatric Gastroenterology and Nutrition, Children's Hospital at Strong, Rochester, New York
Pediatric Nutrition

David M. Siegel, MD, MPH

Associate Professor of Pediatrics and Medicine and Co-Director, Pediatric Rheumatology, University of Rochester School of Medicine and Dentistry; Director of Adolescent Services and Associate Chief for Academic Affairs, Department of Pediatrics, Rochester General Hospital, Rochester, New York
Arthritis

Howard R. Spivak, MD

Professor of Pediatrics and Community Health, Tufts University School of Medicine; Vice President, Community Health, New England Medical Center, Boston, Massachusetts
Violence

Jeffrey R. Starke, MD

Associate Professor of Pediatrics, Baylor College of Medicine; Deputy Chief of Pediatrics and Director, Children's Tuberculosis Clinic, Ben Taub General Hospital; Attending Physician, Texas Children's Hospital, Houston, Texas
Tuberculosis

Ruth E. K. Stein, MD

Professor, Albert Einstein College of Medicine; Professor and Vice Chairman and Director of Office of Academic Affairs, Montefiore Medical Center, Bronx, New York
Home Care

Jeffrey J. Stoddard, MD

Clinical Faculty, University of Pennsylvania School of Medicine; Staff Physician, Children's Hospital of Philadelphia, Philadelphia, Pennsylvania
The Pediatrician and Managed Care

Laurence I. Sugarman, MD

Clinical Assistant Professor in Pediatrics, University of Rochester School of Medicine and Dentistry; Attending Pediatrician, Children's Hospital at Strong, Rochester, New York
Self-Hypnosis, Self-Care

Dale Sarah Sussman, MD

Visiting Clinical Instructor of Pediatrics, Center for Development and Learning, University of North Carolina School of Medicine, Chapel Hill, North Carolina
School Age and Adolescence: Attention Deficits: Description, Diagnosis, and Management

Peter G. Szilagyi, MD, MPH

Associate Professor of Pediatrics, Associate Chief of General Pediatrics Division, and Chief, Child Health Outcomes Research Division, University of Rochester School of Medicine and Dentistry; Director of Pediatrics Ambulatory Services, Children's Hospital at Strong, Rochester, New York
Childhood Immunizations

J. Lane Tanner, MD

Associate Professor of Pediatrics, University of California, San Francisco; Interim Director, Division of Behavioral and Developmental Pediatrics, Lucille Packard Children's Health Services, San Francisco, California
Crisis and Change in the Family: Divorce, Remarriage, Death, and Mobility

May L. Tao, MD, MS

Assistant Professor, University of California, Los Angeles, School of Medicine and UCLA Medical Center, Los Angeles, California
The Primary Care Clinician's Role with the Child Cancer Patient

Thomas F. Tonniges, MD, FAAP

Clinical Assistant Professor, University of Nebraska School of Medicine; Director, Department of Community Pediatrics,

University of Nebraska Medical Center, Omaha, Nebraska
The Medically Underserved

Deborah Klein Walker, EdD

Assistant Commissioner, Bureau of Family and Community Health, Massachusetts Department of Public Health, Boston, Massachusetts
School Age and Adolescence: Runaways; Assessment of Community Health Needs and Services

Linda F. Weinreb, MD

Associate Professor of Family and Community Medicine and Pediatrics, University of Massachusetts Medical School, Worcester, Massachusetts
Homeless Children

Michael Weitzman, MD

Professor and Associate Chair, Department of Pediatrics, University of Rochester School of Medicine and Dentistry, Rochester, New York
An Overview of Childhood Mortality and Morbidity; Immigrant Children

Esther H. Wender, MD

Clinical Professor of Pediatrics, Albert Einstein College of Medicine, Bronx, New York
Adoption

Paul H. Wise, MD, MPH

Associate Professor, Boston University School of Medicine; Lecturer, Harvard Medical School; Staff Physician, Boston Medical Center; Associate in Medicine, Children's Hospital, Boston, Massachusetts
Poverty and Racism

Mark L. Wolraich, MD

Professor of Pediatrics, Vanderbilt University School of Medicine, Nashville, Tennessee
Mental Retardation

Alan D. Woolf, MD, MPH

Associate Professor of Pediatrics, Harvard Medical School; Director, Program in Clinical Toxicology; Director, Massachusetts Poison Control System, Children's Hospital, Boston, Massachusetts
Injury Management: Stabilization, Lacerations, Head Trauma, and Poisoning

PREFACE

When the first edition of *Ambulatory Pediatrics* was published in 1968, it gave voice to an emerging discipline composed of pediatricians who provided care for children in outpatient departments. The field has matured so that most pediatric departments now have divisions of general pediatrics. Often the largest in the department, these divisions are responsible for patient care, teaching, and research in all out-of-hosptial settings—that is, outpatient departments, private office practices, community clinics—and for some inpatient settings, especially in caring for normal newborns and children who have numerous acute illnesses. These divisions are also responsible for the coordination of care both in the hospital and in the community for children who have complex chronic diseases. This new age of general pediatrics requires an integrative and contextual approach to personal and community pediatrics. It recognizes 1) that the environment or context in which children live has a large impact on their health and health care and 2) that providing optimal care requires the integration and coordination of the services provided by many disciplines in multiple settings.

Although this new edition of *Ambulatory Pediatrics* duplicates some topics in traditional pediatric texts, it does so less than in previous editions. Rather, it focuses much more on the clinician's role in health promotion, disease prevention, adaptation, early intervention, coordination of the care of children who have chronic illnesses, diagnosis and treatment of children who have psychosocial problems, and the role of the family and community in child health. It emphasizes the roles of pediatricians, whether in the private office, community center, or hospital outpatient clinic, as coordinators of care and promoters of the strengths of children and families.

This forward-looking book addresses what we judge to be currently underdeveloped areas of pediatrics and where we believe the future of pediatrics and the major issues of contemporary child health lie. Most other pediatric texts emphasize the physical diseases of children that often are the responsibility of subspecialists. Our decision on what clinical problems to include was based on their frequency in general pediatric practice or the need of children to receive integrated care rather than a single service. Thus, some chronic illnesses that are relatively rare are included because they require such coordination. Many common acute illnesses are not addressed here because they usually require only a single provider or are covered well in standard texts. For instance, we have omitted discussion of many acute infectious illnesses that were included in previous editions, either because these diseases now can be prevented effectively (e.g., measles or varicella) or because they are addressed well in such texts as *The Report of the Committee on Infectious Diseases of the American Academy of Pediatrics,* familiarly called *The Red Book.* Believing that the care of children who have a chronic physical illness is a "frontier" area for the general pediatrician, especially in the era of managed care, we emphasize that role in this text. As presented in the introduction to the section on chronic disorders, the general clinician's role in caring for children who have chronic physical diseases is generic to most of these illnesses; the clinician integrates care by medical subspecialists and often other human service personnel, and provides psychosocial as well as general pediatric care.

In an era of rapid changes in the organization and financing of health care in the United States, virtually all experts agree that primary care clinicians are the lynchpin of emerging systems, but their services need to be valued more highly, their numbers increased, and new roles developed and adapted for them. This text deals with the content of these services for children and with the relation of child health needs to organizational and financial issues. Thus, there are new chapters on informatics, expanding roles of telephone management, and issues about managed care.

With this edition we seek to define what consumes most of the time and effort of generalists today and what increasingly appears to be destined to do so in the future. At a time when children in economically favored families suffer few serious physical illnesses, general pediatricians are faced with many children who have biopsychosocial problems. The major social threats to children of today must be understood by child health professionals. These include restructured families, reduction in neighborhood cohesiveness, immigration, and poor education. On the other hand, immigrant children or those who travel abroad are exposed to unexpected diseases, and because such children are found in all communities, their health problems are included. Unfortunately, disadvantaged children who have lived their entire lives in our inner cities also suffer from disorders we assumed had long been controlled or eliminated in the United States, such as tuberculosis, infectious diarrhea, measles, and malnutrition. They also account for the majority of children and families suffering from the profound effects of the human immunodeficiency virus. In addition to a knowledge of these diseases and their management, the pediatric clinician needs to become even more skilled in working with other service agencies and in attending to the social and environmental aspects of these disorders. This edition, therefore, contains many new chapters. Information is provided regarding the role of the pediatrician and other health care professionals and community organizations; home visiting services; nutrition support programs; federal programs and public health services for children and families; migrant health; and new or newly recognized threats to children's health and functioning such as homelessness, effects of maternal illiteracy, and effects of cigarettes and other environmental exposures. Rural health, immigrant children, and child advocacy also are covered. We have tried also to cover new areas of pediatric activity, such as pain management, the use of imagery, and the role of the pediatrician in pediatric education.

The format of the book has been enhanced with more highlighted material, graphs, figures, and algorithms that will help the reader grasp and retain complex, multifactorial issues.

We seek in this edition to present our vision of the future of pediatrics—one in which general pediatricians working in out-of-hospital settings are destined to play the leading role as we enter a new millenium. This rapidly evolving era requires an enriched and broader educational vista. We hope that this text will help define the changing role of general pediatricians and provide information necessary for effective and satisfying practice.

MORRIS GREEN
ROBERT J. HAGGERTY
MICHAEL WEITZMAN

ACKNOWLEDGMENTS

We wish to express our heartfelt thanks to the authors who have contributed to this edition. Our secretaries, Mss. Judy O'Conner and Mary Ann Underwood in Indianapolis and Mss. Cindy Sutherland, Patricia Arnold, and Shirley D'Amore in Rochester, deserve our special commendation. We appreciate deeply their dedication and skill. Our editor, Judith Fletcher, of the W.B. Saunders Company has greatly facilitated our work. Finally, we wish to acknowledge our indebtedness to our colleagues, residents, and students for their stimulation and friendship.

MORRIS GREEN
ROBERT J. HAGGERTY
MICHAEL WEITZMAN

NOTICE

Pediatrics is an ever-changing field. Standard safety precautions must be followed, but as new research and clinical experience broaden our knowledge, changes in treatment and drug therapy become necessary or appropriate. Readers are advised to check the product information currently provided by the manufacturer of each drug to be administered to verify the recommended dose, the method and duration of administration, and contraindications. It is the responsibility of the treating physician relying on experience and knowledge of the patient to determine dosages and the best treatment for the patient. Neither the publisher nor the editor assumes any responsibility for any injury and/or damage to persons or property.

THE PUBLISHER

CONTENTS

SECTION I

CHILD HEALTH IN THE 21ST CENTURY

PART A

WHAT IS HEALTH?

Joel J. Alpert
Michael Weitzman

Chapter **1**

An Overview of Childhood Mortality and Morbidity

By most measures, children in the United States have never been healthier than they are today. Unfortunately, this optimistic view overlooks significant proportions of children who are not achieving the level of health that is possible in our society. Children today, no matter what their race or economic status, face a tidal wave of social, behavioral, and medical issues that contribute to a new morbidity and all too often to tragic mortality.

Approaching the 21st century, our advanced and highly developed democracy has attained an infant mortality rate unimagined a quarter century ago,

yet our world rank has worsened rather than improved. Because infant mortality rates are an index of a society's health, this paradox describes a warning concerning childhood morbidity and mortality for the United States. Far too many of our nation's children do not have health insurance and, as a result, do not have access to needed medical services.

Remarkable advances in immunization have prevented appreciable childhood morbidity and mortality caused by contagion. Measles, polio, mumps, diphtheria, and *Haemophilus influenzae* infection have become part of our pediatric past,

1

with a 98% decrease in incidence. Smallpox has been eradicated globally. Soon chickenpox, hepatitis, and other viral infections will be added to the list. Nutritional advances, public health measures such as fluoridation and the primary prevention of childhood lead poisoning, and effective antimicrobial agents also have improved child health greatly.

These advances did not occur overnight. The new morbidity began to emerge in the United States at the beginning of this century with the institution of public health programs that promoted a safer water supply and a recognition of the importance of basic nutrition. Even at this early date, the groundwork of our current failures began to appear. Although affluence was not protection against illness, having a higher socioeconomic status did improve the odds. Poor children in the United States were at greater risk; today, increased risks associated with poverty remain a major concern. In the 1990s, poverty is associated with prematurity, higher infant mortality, lead poisoning, drug abuse, teenage pregnancy, homicide, the acquired immunodeficiency syndrome (AIDS), and disorders of learning and behavior. These problems compromise the health of children. However, it would be a mistake to assume that the changing morbidity now occupying the attention of child health professionals is confined to the poor, because the changing morbidity strikes at every segment of our society, although most frequently among poor families. The best medical care in the world is available in the United States for those who can pay for it.

SOCIAL DIMENSIONS OF CHILDREN'S LIVES

Many children face significant adversity and disadvantage as a consequence of the social di-

mension of their lives. The following figures represent many of the most prevalent and well-recognized social risks to children's health in the United States: Approximately 25% of our children live in poverty; more than 30% are born to single mothers and 12% are born to teenage mothers; 33% of children live in households whose head has not completed high school, and 50% of these parents have not completed sixth grade; each year more than 1 million U.S. children experience divorce; 250,000 children live in foster homes and a somewhat larger number are in juvenile detention facilities; and families constitute 28% of all homeless people in the United States, as well as being the fastest growing segments of our population.

The effect of recent reforms in welfare and immigration policies on the social dimensions of children's lives are unknown, but many fear that they will increase the hardships and disadvantages of a significant percentage of children and families.

MORTALITY

Approximately 19,000 deaths of live-born infants in the United States occur in the first month of life from immediate perinatal conditions, congenital anomalies, birth asphyxia, and extreme prematurity (Fig. 1–1). Mortality then declines with age, with the period between 5 and 15 years being the healthiest decade of life in terms of mortality.

The infant mortality rate has declined for both whites and African-Americans more or less continuously since the mid-1960s, but a significant racial difference persists. In 1995, overall infant mortality in the United States ranked below that of 21 other countries. The present infant mortality rate for whites lags behind that of other countries. This relatively poor standing is for a country that has demonstrated dramatically reduced mortality and

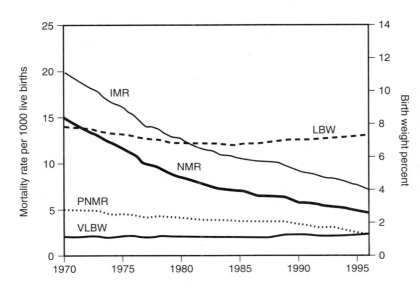

Figure 1–1. Infant mortality rate (IMR), neonatal mortality rate (NMR), postnatal mortality rate (PNMR), low birth weight (LBW) (<2500 grams), and very low birth weight (VLBW) (<1500 grams); United States, 1970–1995. (Redrawn from Guyer B, Martin JA, MacDorman MF, et al.: Annual summary of vital statistics—1996. Pediatrics 100:912, 1997. By permission of Pediatrics.)

morbidity at each birth-weight level and is among the best in the world in delivering technologically advanced services. The provisional infant mortality rate for 1995 was 7.5 per 1000 live births, the lowest ever recorded in the United States.

The speed of decline in the infant mortality rate for African-Americans and whites seemed relatively steady; the gap was possibly narrowing in the 1920s through the 1940s, but it began to widen again in the 1950s. The hope for equal progress in the 1960s proved temporary. In the largest U.S. cities, the infant mortality rate exceeded the state rate; in New York City the infant mortality rate rose from 12.8 per 1000 to 13.1 per 1000 from 1996 to 1997, the first increase in half a century. States and regions vary dramatically, with the lowest infant mortality rates in New England and the highest rates in the South Atlantic states.

The reason for our disappointing world rank is, in large part, our relatively high numbers of low-birth-weight infants and the correlation of infant mortality with birth weight. Death correlates with prematurity and very low birth weight (<1500 grams); the low-birth-weight (LBW) rate in the United States is high. The percent of LBW was 7.3% for all infants in 1993 and 13.2% in African-Americans. However, even postneonatal infant mortality in the United States is high, and deaths in this age group are much more influenced by access to medical care. High teenage pregnancy rates and tragically persistent gaps in the delivery of prenatal services also contribute to our poor standing regarding infant mortality.

After the first year of life, death from trauma assumes first rank and is the leading cause of death until age 45. In New York City in 1997, however, AIDS became the most common cause of death in 1- to 4-year-olds, replacing injury as the number one killer. Injury accounts for 50% of deaths from 1 to 25 years of age. Between the ages of 15 and 24, intentional violence makes a disturbing contribution, with homicide and suicide together equaling all of the remaining medical threats to adolescent health.

Childhood mortality also varies by gender and race. Death rates for males are 50% higher throughout childhood, with a threefold to fourfold difference during adolescence. The death rate for African-Americans less than 15 years of age is generally 1.5 to 2 times higher than that of whites. For males between the ages of 15 and 24, the homicide rate is more than five times greater for African-Americans than for whites, and homicide is the leading cause of death for African-American male adolescents. Only with regard to injury and suicide do death rates for whites exceed those for African-Americans. These racial differences in mortality reflect the disparity in economic status and quality of life between races in the United States.

MORBIDITY

From a historical perspective, the current state of child health is a triumph. Death rates have been reduced dramatically at all ages (except adolescence), providing an opportunity to face issues related to a well-established but changing morbidity.

A list of major contributions to children's morbidity provides us with a statement of important issues. Abnormalities and delays in development, asthma, hearing loss, visual limitations, otitis media, and family dysfunction are on the list. Maternal mental health includes significant unrecognized and untreated maternal depression, estimated at 5% in the middle class and 25% for those in lower socioeconomic classes.

Changing Morbidity

The socioeconomic dimensions observed in the mortality data are also found in the morbidity statistics. The poor are at greater risk for days lost from school, days of restricted activities due to illness, anemia, failure to thrive, lead poisoning, passive and prenatal exposure to tobacco smoke, homelessness, substance abuse, and AIDS. Because the poor have more LBW infants, they also contribute disproportionately to the survivors of the newborn intensive care unit who have chronic pulmonary disease, retinopathy of prematurity (ROP), and long-term complications as a result of intraventricular hemorrhage.

A number of disorders with causes related to the social dimensions of children's lives also contribute to childhood morbidity. One needs to recognize the dynamic relationship between social issues and illness and to recognize that the causes of morbidity can change. As AIDS illustrates, change can occur very quickly. For example, failure to thrive is associated etiologically with prenatal factors, recurrent infections, elevated lead levels, mother-child interaction problems, and chronic disease. Common to all of these are psychosocial factors, malnutrition, and family dysfunction. Failure to thrive accounts for 3% to 5% of admissions to pediatric teaching hospitals. Clinical audits in urban hospital emergency rooms demonstrate a 15% to 30% rate of growth deficits in the children admitted.

With increased technology, survival of LBW infants has increased markedly. In the United States, approximately 200,000 (6.8%) infants born each year are of low birth weight, and 41,000 are of very low birth weight (<1500 grams). These infants are subject to developmental delay, persistent neurologic injury, and long-term medical complications, including chronic lung disease (which occurs in 6% to 24% of infants who require mechanical ventilation) and ROP (59.5% of infants weighing <1000 grams at birth and 2.2% of those weighing 1000 to 1500 grams are reported as developing ROP).

Since 1972, more than 1 million children in the United States each year have had their lives affected by divorce. At present, an estimated 150,000 children of divorced parents enter foster care. Approximately 25% of children in foster care have disabilities, and 40% of them are from minority families.

Adolescents experience a broad range of risks. In 1994, more than 1 million women younger than 20 years of age became pregnant. Of these, nearly 470,000 gave birth, and more than 400,000 had abortions. More than 80% of pregnancies in unmarried women were unplanned.

Almost one in 12 adolescent girls becomes pregnant each year. These pregnancies pose significant medical and social risks for both the adolescent mother and her child: The younger the adolescent, the greater the risk. Adolescent birth rates are considerably higher in the United States than in other industrialized countries.

Many teenagers contract sexually transmitted diseases. Using barrier contraceptives inconsistently, they may experience pelvic inflammatory disease, infertility, ectopic pregnancy, cervical intraepithelial neoplasia, and spontaneous abortion. Neonatal morbidity is common in their offspring.

The number of injuries and deaths caused by violence is inordinately high among adolescents. For every death, 100 times as many intentional, nonfatal injuries may occur; the motor vehicle continues to be associated with enormous morbidity and substantial mortality.

Illicit drug use is common among adolescents. Current figures suggest lifetime substance use rates among high school seniors for alcohol at 92%; cigarettes, 69%; marijuana, 54%; stimulants, 26%; and cocaine, 17%. Drug abuse and accompanying mental disorders such as depression are leading contributors to adolescent mortality and morbidity. Drug use increased in the latter part of the 1990s, and cigarette smoking, especially among girls, has continued to increase.

AIDS is a known risk for children, and it is difficult to determine the full extent of pediatric human immunodeficiency virus (HIV) infection. Most infants and children acquire the infection congenitally, as a result of intravenous drug use by their parents. The children who have acquired

TABLE 1–1. Estimated Prevalence in 1980 of Chronic Diseases and Conditions in Children Aged 0–20 in the United States

Disorder	Prevalence Estimates, per 1000	Range of Prevalence Estimates, per 1000
Arthritis	2.2	1.0–3.0
Asthma	38.0	20.0–53.0
Moderate to severe	10.0	8.0–15.0
Autism	.44	.40–.48
Central nervous system injury		
Traumatic brain injury	.05	—
Paralysis	2.1	2.0–2.3
Cerebral palsy	2.5	1.4–5.1
Chronic renal failure	.08	—
Terminal	.01	—
Nonterminal	.07	—
Cleft lip/palate*	1.5	1.3–2.0
Congenital heart disease	7.0	2.0–7.0
Severe congenital heart disease*	.50	
Cystic fibrosis*	.20	—
Diabetes mellitus	1.8	1.2–2.0
Down syndrome*	1.1	
Hearing impairment	16.0	
Deafness	.10	.06–0.15
Hemophilia*	.15	
Leukemia		
Acute lymphocytic leukemia†	.11	
Mental retardation	25.0	20.0–30.0
Muscular dystrophy*	.06	
Neural tube defect*	.45	
Spina bifida*	.40	
Encephalocele*	.05	
Phenylketonuria*	.10	
Seizure disorder	3.5	2.6–4.6
Sickle cell disease*	.46	
Sickle cell anemia*	.28	
Visual impairment	30.0	20.0–35.0
Impaired visual acuity	20.0	—
Blindness	.60	0.5–1.0

*Estimated using prevalence at birth and survival data.
†Estimated using incidence and duration data.
From Gortmaker SL and Sapperfield W: Chronic childhood disorders: prevalence and impact. Pediatr Clin North Am 31:3, 1984. Reproduced by permission.

HIV during the school-age years have usually acquired it in the past as a consequence of contaminated blood products. Adolescents acquire AIDS by engaging in high-risk behaviors similar to those of the adult population. The contribution that HIV infection will make to childhood mortality and morbidity may be larger and out of proportion to the number of children actually infected.

Homelessness also is a problem for children in the United States. The fastest growing segment (estimated nationwide at 28%) of the homeless population consists of families, often with young children. A homeless child or adolescent, vulnerable to all recognized illness risks, has the added burden of inadequate medical care (see Chapter 5).

Abuse and neglect complete this overview of changing morbidity. The number of children affected by these problems, including sexual abuse, appears to have grown as a result of both increased occurrence and better reporting.

Traditional Biomedical Morbidity

The perception that the physical health of children in the United States has improved is correct, reflecting the decline in mortality described previously and the availability of effective medical and surgical interventions. The expected morbidity in children should be limited to common, acute, self-limited diseases; however, a wide variety of chronic disorders contribute to their illness experience (Table 1–1). The majority of these disorders are mild, but 10% are probably severe, and 80% of children who have severe chronic disease now survive into adulthood. The disorders include malignancies, juvenile rheumatoid arthritis, sickle cell disease, hemophilia, seizures, cystic fibrosis, and congenital heart disease. Long-term allergic disorders, such as allergic rhinitis and atopy with pulmonary and dermatologic manifestations, are common. Acne, psoriasis, obesity, anorexia, and other eating disorders are other persistent problems.

SUMMARY

The unmet challenges to child health now occupy center stage. Our optimistic outlook of a few years ago has been tempered. The United States is a heterogeneous nation with substantial regional differences in resources and availability and standards of care. The year 2000 health objectives for the United States include an ambitious list of child health goals. We continue to address the challenges of achieving optimal child health.

FURTHER READING

Better Health for Our Children: A National Strategy. Report of the Select Panel for the Promotion of Child Health. 4 vols. DHHS Publication No. 79-55071. Bethesda, MD, US Department of Health and Human Services, 1981.

Centers for Disease Control: Progress toward achieving the 1990 objectives for pregnancy and infant health. MMWR 37:405, 1988.

Death Before Life: The Tragedy of Infant Mortality. Report of the National Commission to Prevent Infant Mortality. Washington, DC, the Commission, 1988.

Gortmaker SL and Sapperfield W: Chronic childhood disorders; prevalence and impact. Pediatr Clin North Am 31:3, 1984.

Guyer B, Martin JA, MacDorman MF, et al.: Annual summary of vital statistics—1996. Pediatrics 100:905, 1997.

Haggerty RJ and Pless IB: Child Health in the Community. New York, John Wiley & Sons, 1975.

Hoekelman RA and Pless IB: Decline in mortality among young Americans during the 20th century: Prospects for reaching national mortality reduction goals for 1990. Pediatrics 82:582, 1988.

Hoekelman RA, Starfield B, McCormick M, et al.: A profile of pediatric practice in the United States. Am J Dis Child 137:1057, 1983.

National Center for Health Statistics: Monthly Vital Statistics Report. Vol 36, No. 5(Suppl), 1987.

US Public Health Service: Healthy people 2000: National Health Promotion and Disease Prevention Objectives. Washington, DC, US Department of Health and Human Services, 1991.

Zuckerman B, Weitzman M, and Alpert JJ (eds): Children at risk: Current social and medical challenges. Pediatr Clin North Am 35:1169, 1988.

PART B

PERSONAL FACTORS

Robert J. Haggerty

Chapter 2

Risks and Protective Factors in Childhood Illness

Most clinicians instinctively understand and determine personal risk and protective factors among their patients and families. During the past 30 years, a growing body of research has elucidated more precisely the risk factors that predispose children and their families to disease, and there is a beginning understanding of the mechanisms by which this occurs. The clinician of tomorrow will be compelled to determine specific risk factors for various disorders and to devise interventions for those children at risk, with the goal of preventing disease or reducing disability. This chapter deals with individual or personal factors; those that follow in this first section of *Ambulatory Pediatrics* are concerned with family and community risk factors. In later chapters dealing with specific disorders, such as substance abuse, the risk factors that predispose to a disorder are often presented.

Risk factors are those characteristics that when present in a person make it more likely that the individual rather than someone selected at random from the population will develop a disorder. Risk factors can be biologic (and in the future, specific genetic risk factors will be considered more and more in clinical medicine), psychosocial, or environmental. Some risk factors are causal for a disorder; others are merely markers of a disorder. Not everyone who has risk factors will develop a disorder. Therefore, there is a danger of labeling a child "at risk" and increasing the chances that he or she will develop a disorder or a psychologic reaction merely from the label. In the past, most research on this topic targeted the negative side of risk (i.e., the risk of

diseases' or disorders' occurring); more recently, however, researchers such as Garmezy and Rutter have focused on resilient children and the protective factors that make them so. Therefore, physicians need to assess protective factors as well as risk factors.

Many disorders have multiple risk factors. Insofar as these are causal, it is useful to identify those that can be targeted for interventions. It may not be necessary to reduce all risk factors. For example, Rutter has demonstrated that a single risk factor rarely increases the risk of a disorder, whereas an accumulation of several risk factors usually increases the probability of a disorder geometrically. Thus, reducing one of several risk factors may reduce the chance of disease without the need to reduce all risk factors.

BIOLOGIC RISK FACTORS

Genetic risk factors (Table 2–1) are determined largely by family history, although in the future there likely will be many genetic markers of specific disease risks available to the general clinician. Availability of these markers will raise many difficult ethical and legal issues to be resolved. Family history is an established part of any medical workup, although not always pursued with a precise understanding of risk. As a result, much parental anxiety is often engendered when, in fact, no increased genetic risk exists. For instance, in one family, the grandmother had adult-onset rheumatoid arthritis, her son had insulin-dependent diabetes

TABLE 2–1. Risk Factors Predisposing to Childhood Illness

Biologic
    Temperament, genetics
    Chronic physical disease
Environmental and Psychosocial
    Stressful life events
    Parental discord, illness, loss
    Poverty, inequality, racism
    Poor schools
    Lack of or poor child care
    Homelessness
    War and disaster
    Violence
    Lack of attachment
    Social isolation
    Lack of love and nurturance

mellitus, and her grandson was diagnosed with possible juvenile rheumatoid arthritis. The family was convinced that these three disorders were genetically linked, that they had "a bad gene."

Research, however, has demonstrated no genetic link between these three diseases. On the other hand, many disorders have an increased genetic risk, as with schizophrenia, depression, cystic fibrosis, and, of course, autosomal dominant genetic disorders. In the case of most behavioral disorders with "family loading," even identical twins experience different ages of onset or rates of occurrence of the disorder, indicating that environmental factors also play a role in disorders that have a clear genetic component.

Temperament is one biologic or genetic trait that clinicians now recognize as an important risk or protective factor. Clinicians and parents long have recognized that from birth some children are easy to soothe while others are irritable. Clinicians can help parents whose infants are more irritable understand that it is not their fault, that taking time to calm such babies helps reduce their irritability, and that becoming agitated and irritable themselves only reinforces the behavior.

Although originally temperament was studied in infants, this characteristic persists beyond infancy as a risk and protective factor. In older children, Kagan and his colleagues have demonstrated that a small group of children, perhaps 15% of the total, consistently withdraw, are shy, and show autonomic arousal when faced with a stressful environment. Very similar findings have been demonstrated by Suomi in monkeys. The interesting point is that if the shy and inhibited children who withdraw from challenge and have elevated heart rates and hormonal evidence of neuroendocrine arousal from stress are protected and helped to overcome their shyness, they often become leaders and very competent adults. Thus,

the focus should be on how different children respond to family and social environmental stresses and how clinicians can help them use their strengths and develop skills to overcome their risk factors.

Boyce and his colleagues have demonstrated the interaction of inborn biologic traits and exposure to stress as a factor in certain illnesses. Children who had exaggerated autonomic reactivity in the laboratory were found to have injury rates comparable to their minimally reactive peers under low stress conditions. However, under high stress conditions, increased injury rates were found only among the highly reactive group of children. Boyce also was able to study the reaction of children before and after a California earthquake. Those whose immune reactivity was high in the laboratory setting before the earthquake had more respiratory infections than those whose reactivity after the stress of the earthquake was low.

PSYCHOSOCIAL RISK FACTORS

Many of the environmental or psychosocial risks (see Table 2–1) such as poverty, poor schooling, parental discord, illness and loss, poor schools, homelessness, war and disaster, and environmental pollution are presented in the following chapters. Life stress is widely understood by the general public to be a psychosocial risk factor detrimental to one's health. Researchers have had a difficult time defining and measuring stress and correlating it with illness. The early experimental studies of Selye in animals gave a physiologic basis for the relation between stress and illness. Later studies have shown correlations of stress to reduced immunologic factors such as T lymphocytes and phagocytosis, reduced secretory immunoglobulin A in the pharynx, and increased catecholamines and norepinephrine, as well as cortisol. Several clinical studies have demonstrated statistical association between stressful life events and infections, myocardial infarctions, complications of pregnancy, problem behaviors, malignancies, and injuries. As with other risk factors, the more stressful life events that happen to a person, the more likely they are to develop disease. Nonetheless, the association between stress and illness has remained modest, and it now is clear that stress is neither a necessary nor sufficient cause of any specific disease. It is one risk factor among many that the clinician should ascertain. Research being directed at elucidating individual differences may help to explain the variable vulnerability and resilience to stress among different children.

PROTECTIVE FACTORS

Protective factors (Table 2–2) often are the obverse of risk factors, but specific protective factors have been demonstrated for some disorders. For example, membership in a structured, goal-directed peer group protects against substance abuse, and strong attachments to others and the presence of social supports generally are associated with a decreased risk of disorders. Resilience is another term sometimes used in place of protective factors. Across the life span, intelligence, attractive appearance, easy temperament, and the presence of supportive adults protect against a number of disorders. Many children and adults survive and even thrive after adversities, disasters, and family disruption that would seem to sink most of us. For instance, some of the survivors of the Nazi concentration camps demonstrated this capacity. The question facing researchers is the origin of this resilience. Undoubtedly, the major source of resilience is inborn or genetic. As noted, a child who has an easy-to-soothe temperament is often endowed with resilience against many problem behaviors. Some children seem especially resilient to infections, such as those in child care settings who are exposed to the same number of illnesses as their peers but appear to be resistant to most of them. Resiliency also is highly associated with a supportive environment. It has been said that "the penicillin of the 21st century will be social supports" (see Chapter 68).

RISK ASSESSMENT VERSUS UNIVERSAL SERVICES

This chapter implies that clinicians should always use risk assessment to target services to those in need. For some conditions, however, risk assessment is a poor strategy because it does not identify the majority of later-onset cases. This seems especially true for identifying newborn disorders. All children deserve access to basic services. In the course of this, some will be identified at greater risk and, therefore, at greater need for interventions. Risk assessment should not be used to ignore or diminish the need for basic services.

CLINICAL IMPLICATIONS

A key skill for child health clinicians is the ability to assess both risks and protective factors

TABLE 2–2. Protective Factors Against Childhood Illness

Personal
Temperament, genetics
Attractiveness to peers and adults
Problem-solving abilities
Self-esteem
Internal locus of control
Ability to plan and to aspire
Competence, intelligence
Religiosity
Ability to express feelings
Environmental
Stable family care
Competent role models
Social supports
Quality schools
Neighborhood resources

in their patients and families, to reduce the risk factors where possible, and to enhance protective factors. The clinician needs to help parents assess their child's temperament and alter their parental behavior to fit the individual child's inborn behavior. In addition, it is important to try to reduce those stressful life events that are associated, especially in reactive children, with disorders. For those stressful life events that cannot be avoided, such as school entry, tests and examinations, peer interactions, and the death of relatives, it is important that parents help children deal with them realistically and to learn coping skills, because such stresses will be a part of all of life. Although denial and avoidance may be successful under certain circumstances, helping children to master life stresses helps them grow and develop into more competent adults.

FURTHER READING

Boyce WT, Barr RG, and Zeltzer LK: Temperament and the psychology of childhood illness. Pediatrics 90 (Suppl):483–486, 1992.
Garmezy N, Master A, and Tellogen A: The study of stress and competence in children. Child Dev 55:97–111, 1984.
Haggerty RJ, Sherrod LR, Garmezy N, and Rutter M (eds): Stress, Risk, Resilience in Children and Adolescents: Processes, Mechanisms and Interventions. New York: Cambridge University Press, 1996.
Kagan J: Behavior, biology and the meaning of temperamental constructs. Pediatrics 90 (Suppl):510–513, 1992.
Offord DR, Bayle MH, and Racine F: Ontario child health study: Correlates of disorder. J Am Acad Child Adolesc Psychiatry 28:856–860, 1989.
Rutter M: Resilience in the face of adversity: Protective factors and resistance to psychiatric disorder. Br J Psychiatry 147:598–611, 1985.
Selye H: Stress: The Physiology and Pathology of Exposure to Stress. Montreal, Acta Medical Publishers, 1950.
Suomi SJ: Early stress and adult emotional reactivity in rhesus monkeys. *In* Bock GR and Whelan J (eds): The Childhood Environment and Adult Disease. Chichester, England, Wiley, 1991, pp 171–188.

PART C

FAMILY FACTORS: RISKS AND STRENGTHS

William R. Beardslee

Chapter 3

Children of Parents Who Have Major Mental Illness

Serious mental illness in a parent always affects the family, especially the children. Working with families who have youngsters at risk because of parental mental illness provides the pediatrician an important opportunity to help both parents and families.

It is essential for the primary care clinician to be able to recognize serious mental illness in parents and to develop an appropriate approach to evaluating and managing its effects on children. Family practitioners, internists, pediatricians, and similar health professionals who are not specifically trained to be mental health clinicians provide the care for nearly 75% of patients who have serious mental illness. There is clear evidence of high rates of psychiatric disorders in adults seen in general medical practices (Kessler, Cleary, and Burke, 1985). Furthermore, children of parents who have a serious disorder are likely to have higher rates of psychiatric disorders and other problems than are youngsters in families with no parental illness. **The pediatrician often may be the first and sometimes the only person to identify a serious parental disorder, to deal with its consequences, and to formulate a comprehensive approach.**

Because there are significant differences among the various major mental illnesses in terms of outcome, treatment, and risks to offspring, proper diagnosis is essential.

CHILDREN AT RISK

In the past 20 years, interest has been increasing in the study of children whose parents have expe-rienced major mental disorders, particularly in the diagnostic categories of alcoholism, depression, manic depressive disorder, schizophrenia, and severe anxiety disorder. This work has been influenced by advances in the understanding of the etiology, epidemiology, course, outcome, and treatment of major mental illnesses in adults and in the empirical study of rigorously diagnosed childhood psychopathology. The basic research approach has entailed identifying a group of children at higher risk for psychopathology than the general population because of serious parental mental illness and then evaluating all of the children at risk, whether or not they manifest the disorder. In general, risk research has shown that **during childhood, the outcomes for youngsters growing up with parents who have serious mental illness are heterogeneous: at any one point in time a higher percentage of these youngsters will manifest serious psychopathology than in comparison populations**, whereas some children manifest signs of disturbance without diagnosable illness, and many are functioning well. The findings of the heterogeneity of outcome from the risk research are similar to the clinical situations presented to a pediatrician. A range of possible adaptive and maladaptive outcomes will be evident in the youngsters whose parents have serious mental illness.

In terms of the empirical evidence for impairment in youngsters, serious mental illness during pregnancy may affect newborns adversely. In most

9

studies, serious maternal mental illness in the mothers of newborns and toddlers has been shown to be associated with disturbances in the early years of the child's life. Cognitive and other developmental impairments, difficulties in bonding, and diminished capacity to enter into symbolic play are some of the findings among toddlers.

In school-age and adolescent youngsters, the kind of disorder manifested depends more directly on the parental diagnosis and on the chronicity and severity of that disorder. Many parental diagnoses are represented in the offspring more commonly than in children with unaffected parents. In particular, **children of parents who have major long-standing depressions are at serious risk for developing depression during adolescence. In some studies, as many as 20% to 40% of these youngsters have serious depression at some time during their adolescence.** High rates of substance abuse disorders in the children of substance-abusing and alcoholic parents also have been described. However, there do not appear to be dramatically higher rates of schizophrenia in the offspring of schizophrenics during adolescence. This may be because the overall incidence of schizophrenia is so low during adolescence.

In addition to manifesting increased rates of the parent's disorder, these youngsters also manifest a range of other impairments, including diminished social functioning, symptoms that do not reach the level of diagnostic criteria, and in some instances, diminished school performance.

Much higher rates of serious parental mental illness have been identified from population and community studies that use epidemiologic techniques than from those that assess adults who present for clinical treatment. Whether or not parents have presented for treatment, serious illness in the parents is a risk factor for poor child outcome. A recent study of the children of parents recruited by random selection from a prepaid health plan demonstrated that mood disorders in these parents led to the same serious major effects in offspring that were evident in studies in which parents were identified through having sought psychiatric treatment for affective illness (Beardslee et al., 1993). This emphasizes the need for attention to all parental disorders in a practice rather than only those for which parents are receiving psychiatric treatment.

In most of the major empirical risk studies, a certain number of youngsters have proved unexpectedly to be functioning well and, indeed, are resilient in the presence of major stress. Resilient youngsters have been characterized by good interpersonal relationships, particularly with those other than the ill parent. Other characteristics have included constitutional factors such as certain temperamental characteristics, certain coping styles, and a positive sense of self-esteem. This area is being investigated because the characteristics of these resilient youngsters may lead researchers to effective interventions. From a clinical point of view, the presence of resiliency should be considered in the evaluation of youngsters.

MECHANISM OF TRANSMISSION OF DISORDER FROM PARENT TO CHILD

There is a genetic component to most of the serious major mental illnesses. This has been demonstrated both with monozygotic twin studies and by family studies demonstrating that relatives of those who have the illness are at greater risk themselves.

Psychosocial stress in families also contributes significantly to genesis of the disorder. On the one hand, in existing parental mental illness such stress factors increase or exacerbate the parental disorder. In some cases, severe stress actually may lead to the emergence of the disorder as a reaction to that stress—for example, alcoholism after job loss or depression after the breakup of a marriage. On the other hand, stress factors alone, apart from the impact on parental mental illness, have a serious negative effect on youngsters. Stress factors associated with serious mental illness in adults include increased rates of divorce and marital difficulties, frequent moves, diminished economic resources, and in psychologic terms, the inability of the parent to attend to and focus on the needs of the children. Analysis by Rutter and colleagues of the differences between a London borough and the Isle of Wight with respect to the rates of childhood psychopathology have highlighted the importance of such nonspecific factors. In addition, diminished economic resources in general and poverty in particular greatly exacerbate the effects of serious mental illness in parents on children, as do the effects of prejudice and discrimination.

Risk factors potentiate one another and are not simply additive. **Families that pose a number of risk factors—that is, serious mental illness in both parents, diminished economic resources, and divorce—have very high rates of serious disturbances in their youngsters.** The interaction of these risk factors has been described in general epidemiologic studies (Rutter, 1990), in studies of young children, and in the children of parents who have affective disorder. A number of researchers also have drawn attention to the fact that both parents are often impaired in families affected by mental illness, either through assortative mating or other mechanisms. This has particularly severe consequences for youngsters. It also is important to note that a much clearer understanding of the interaction between genes and environment will continue to develop through newer research techniques based on molecular biology.

IMPLICATIONS FOR PEDIATRIC PRACTICE

The clinician's first major task is to assess the parent and family situation. A parent may first speak to the clinician about symptoms he or she is experiencing or may bring the child in with unexplained symptoms that signal the onset of parental mental illness or family distress. The presence of serious changes in behavioral functioning or in worries, anxieties, or decreased self-esteem in the parent should be investigated, as should the possibility of suicidal thoughts and behavior. Serious parental mental illnesses often have their onset or exacerbation in the course of major family stresses; inquiry about such stresses is indicated—in particular, about divorce, recent moves, job loss, bereavement, or major physical illness, in addition to the presence of major mental illness. Both depression and alcoholism frequently are present in the same individual. Furthermore, occasionally the presence of disorder in one parent leads to the identification of a disorder in the other.

Assessment of parental illness should involve exploring the duration and intensity of symptoms and associated medical and physical problems. When possible, diagnosis should be made consistent with criteria as presented in the *Diagnostic and Statistical Manual of Mental Disorders*, fourth edition (DSM-IV). It is not the major role of the pediatrician to care for adults who have a psychiatric disorder, nor is it necessary to diagnose the parental disorder. Many clinicians may choose to take care of parents' uncomplicated mental disorders such as anxiety or depression in response to stresses. However, it is equally important for the clinician to recognize serious mental illness, and if he or she is not taking primary responsibility, to ensure adequate referral, treatment, and follow-up. If symptoms are serious or worsening or if suicidal thoughts are present, detailed inquiry and referral for help is indicated. Working with a mental health professional, most often a psychiatrist who can evaluate and treat the parent, will involve remaining in close touch with the professional and sharing information. For some disorders, for example alcoholism or substance abuse, the involvement of an intensive program to confront the abuse may be necessary. If at any time the clinician suspects that the parent's mental illness is so impairing as to require hospitalization, immediate action to evaluate this possibility should be taken.

Moreover, if the illness appears to be so impairing that the parent's ability to protect and nurture the child is in jeopardy, the clinician must ensure that there are other appropriate individuals in the home to care for the child or must arrange for placement outside of the home. This is rare, but the possibility always should be considered. Once the parent's serious illness has been identified and an appropriate referral has been made, the most important step is to determine the effects on the children. **How the youngsters are functioning at the time parents' conditions are identified, both in terms of any difficulties or impairments they may be encountering and also in terms of their strengths and resiliencies, should be assessed briefly.**

It is important to be able to assess the presence of a major mental illness in the child, such as substance abuse, alcoholism, major depression, or antisocial behavior. If such a disorder is present, referral and treatment should be instituted, with collaborative follow-up with the primary care clinician. Exploration of any such clinical signs of distress (e.g., diminished performance at school, lack of interest in friends by adolescents, or the presence of developmental delay or oppositional behavior in infants and toddlers) also is needed. The presence of symptoms that do not meet the criteria for diagnosis but interfere with normal functioning is serious and requires follow-up and sometimes referral for evaluation.

In any family in which there has been major disruption through serious mental illness, the lives of children will be affected. In many instances youngsters will not manifest serious disorders at the time of assessment. This provides an opportunity for the clinician to talk with the parents without having to treat a diagnosed disorder in the children and to inquire whether the parents have any questions or concerns. Parents generally appreciate this opportunity. In all cases, attention to how the youngsters understand the parent's disorder is indicated. A very common reaction of youngsters is to feel guilty or blame themselves for the parent's disorder. It is important to ensure that youngsters know they are not to blame. This probably can be accomplished best by careful discussion with the parents first and then by some discussion with parents and children together. Cognitive psychoeducational approaches are particularly helpful. Interest in the prevention of mental illness across the span of childhood has been increasing. **The presence of severe mental illness in the parents offers an important opportunity to consider taking preventive action for the child's mental health.** Recent work in the area of depression and its prevention and in family-based cognitive education for schizophrenia offers important leads.

SUMMARY

Serious parental mental illness is a family problem. In the case of serious disorder, the clinician's first role is as a diagnostician who will follow symptoms and make appropriate referrals for both parents and children. He or she should follow the referred individuals collaboratively with other caregivers and also with the other family members. Conditions change in families over time, and disorders worsen or remit. The presence of an ongoing, committed clinician will make a great difference to the family, one who will provide an opportunity for discussion, thought, and reflection as well as one who can respond at various points to the disorder as it presents. Thus, the primary care clinician's role is ongoing.

FURTHER READING

American Psychiatric Association: Diagnostic and Statistical Manual of Mental Disorders, ed 4. Washington, DC, Author, 1994.

Beardslee WR, Keller MB, Lavori PW, et al.: The impact of parental affective disorder on depression in offspring: A longitudinal follow-up in a nonreferred sample. J Am Acad Child Adolesc Psychiatry 32: 723–730, 1993.

Beardslee WR, Keller MB, Seifer R, et al.: Prediction of adolescent affective disorder: Effects of prior parental affective disorders and child psychopathology. J Am Acad Child Adolesc Psychiatry 35: 279–288, 1996.

Beardslee WR, Wright E, Salt P, et al.: Examination of children's responses to two preventive intervention strategies over time. J Am Acad Child Adolescent Psychiatry 36: 196–204, 1997.

Institute of Medicine: Reducing Risks for Mental Disorders: Frontiers for Preventive Intervention Research. Washington, DC, National Academy Press, 1994.

Kendler KS, Kessler RC, Neale MC, et al.: Alcoholism and major depression in women: A twin study of the causes of comorbidity. Arch Gen Psychiatry 150: 1139–1148, 1993.

Kessler LG, Cleary PD, and Burke J: Psychiatric disorders in primary care. Arch Gen Psychiatry 42: 583–587, 1985.

Merikangas KR, Weissman MM, Prusoff BA, and John K. Assortative mating and affective disorders: Psychopathology in offspring. Psychiatry 51:48–57, 1988.

Regier DA, Goldberg ID, and Taube CA: The defacto U.S. mental health service system: A public health perspective. Arch Gen Psychiatry 35: 685–693, 1978.

Reiss D, Plomin R, and Hetherington M: Genetics and psychiatry: An unheralded window on the environment. Am J Psychiatry 148: 283–291, 1991.

Richmond JB and Beardslee WR: Resiliency: Research and practical implications for pediatricians. J Dev Behav Pediatr 9:157–163, 1988.

Rutter M: Commentary: Some focus and process considerations regarding effects of parental depression on children. Dev Psychopathol 26: 60–67, 1990.

Rutter M, Yale B, and Quinton D: Attainment and adjustment in two geographic areas: Some factors accounting for area differences. Br J Psychiatry 4: 520–533, 1974.

Sameroff AJ: Transactional risk factors and prevention. In Steinberg JA and Silverman MM: Preventing Mental Disorders: A Research Perspective. Rockville, MD, US Department of Health and Human Services, 1987.

Tasman A, Kay J, Lieberman JA (eds): Psychiatry. Philadelphia, WB Saunders, 1997.

Tsuang MT and Faraone SV: The Genetics of Mood Disorders. Baltimore, The Johns Hopkins University Press, 1990.

J. Lane Tanner

Chapter 4

Crisis and Change in the Family: Divorce, Remarriage, Death, and Mobility

Major family changes are among the most prevalent and important influences on the developmental and psychologic well-being of America's children. Such changes include parental divorce, change to single-parent status, and remarriage; the death of a parent or other family member; and the move of the family home. These seismic events are common contextual influences on children and

TABLE 4–1. Living Arrangements of American Children Less Than 18 Years of Age—1996

Children living with:
  Two parents: 69% (11% in married stepfamilies)
  Single parents: 27%
    Divorced parent: 37%
    Separated parent: 23%
    Never-married parent: 36%
    Widowed parent: 4%
  Neither parent: 4%

From Marital Status and Living Arrangements, March 1996. Current Population Reports, P20-496, US Bureau of the Census, p. 36.

often become transformed into somatic and behavioral symptoms that can have long-term developmental outcomes. Table 4–1, which provides a profile of the living arrangements for American children in the 1990s, indicates the great number of children subject to the impact of family crisis and change.

FAMILY UPHEAVAL: PREVALENCE AND EFFECTS ON CHILDREN

Parental Divorce, Single-Parent Status, and Remarriage

Divorce

For most children, the divorce of their parents marks a wrenching end to the family they have known and the beginning of a new family constellation. Overall, the divorce rate in the United States, roughly constant since the mid-1970s, has resulted in **approximately 40% of children younger than age 16 experiencing the divorce of their parents.** In addition, the majority of divorced parents remarry, and second marriages carry some increased probability of ending in a second divorce.

Children in divorced families, on average, exhibit more problems and emotional distress than do children from continuously intact two-parent families. Lower academic achievement, more behavioral problems, more negative self-concept, more social difficulties, and more difficult parent-child relationships are significant sequelae for a portion of children who experience parental divorce. Some of these effects, such as a decline in academic achievement, are most dramatic during the first year or two immediately following the divorce. Others, including effects on social relationships, may have their most profound effects in later adolescence and adulthood.

Given the turmoil and sweeping changes that usually accompany divorce, it is a testimony to the resilience of children and families that the majority are able to cope successfully with both the crisis and the long-term adaptation required. Risk of seriously impaired developmental and psychologic well-being of the child in the wake of divorce has been shown to hinge on at least the following five parameters:

- *Parental absence.* To what degree does the child lose his or her relationship with the noncustodial parent?
- *The custodial parent's adjustment and quality of parenting.* How attentive, warm, and effective is the custodial parent?
- *Parental conflict.* How intense is the parental conflict, and how long has it persisted before and after the divorce?
- *Economic hardship.* How have household income, living place, and other material resources been affected by the divorce?
- *Accumulation of life stresses.* To what degree is the divorce a result of or a trigger for other significant stressors and changes, and what resources does the family possess for coping with the cumulative stress?

Single-Parent Status

The number of children living in homes headed by single parents has more than doubled in the past 2 decades. In addition to parental divorce, this increase is largely the result of more children living with a "never-married" parent. Thus, single-parent status may result from a major family change. Currently, 88% of children in single-parent homes live with their mothers. Single parents now head nearly two thirds of African-American families in which children reside, approximately one fourth of white families, and over one third of Hispanic families.

Evidence indicates that behavioral and developmental difficulties of children of single parents are related not so much to intrinsic qualities of parenting or family structure as to associated changes and conditions of living common to single-parent households. These include limitations of available resources—especially of family income (more than 50% live below the national poverty levels), time, and physical and emotional energy. An effective network of social support is vital in helping single parents meet the multiple demands and roles that confront them. Frequently, single parents must live with or rely on their own parents or extended family. The child's well-being depends on the parent's ability to provide a warm, authoritative, and predictable home and is most at risk when the parent becomes overwhelmed with her or his multiple tasks and responsibilities.

Remarriage

The majority of children who experience divorce will also experience the remarriage of at least one parent. Although remarriage frequently is accompanied by improved economic well-being, it also brings complex relational challenges for both the child and the step-parent, who may feel thrown together under circumstances influenced by distrust and conflicting loyalties. The age of the child, the prior relationship with the step-parent, and the circumstances of the family's life prior to the remarriage strongly influence the child's adaptation. Stepfathers who attempt to assume a disciplinary role early in the relationship have been shown to elicit more rejection and behavior problems from the child. Emotional adjustment generally has been shown to be more difficult for children living primarily with stepmothers than with stepfathers. The presence of half-siblings and step-siblings is associated with some increase in behavior problems and more distant step-parent–stepchild relationships.

Death and Bereavement

Approximately 5% of children in the United States will experience the death of a parent before their 16th birthday. More common is the experience of losing a grandparent, a classmate, or a pet. Some have had experiences with catastrophic events connected with war or natural disaster. Others have had very little experience with death or bereavement.

Children also have dramatically different developmental capacities for understanding the nature of death. Its irreversibility and finality are not fully grasped until well into school age. The realization of the inevitability of death comes, often as a blow, during the transition into adolescence. Not until adolescence is a mature understanding possible. The understanding of children and teenagers is influenced strongly by the cultural and religious beliefs about death that families and communities teach and model.

Although there is no set pattern to the bereavement process in children, certain common phases of children's reactions to the death of a parent have been identified. *A reactive phase of intense emotional grieving* is expected in the months immediately following the death. Responses of disbelief and denial, pain and sadness, and anger and protest frequently are accompanied by crying, sleep disturbances, and somatic symptoms. Preoccupation with thoughts about the deceased parent may interfere with school performance and daily activities. Confusion may be expressed about the reality, causes, and meaning of this major loss.

Several months to a year later, even as they come to greater acceptance of the reality of the death, children and adolescents frequently experience heightened anxiety regarding their own well-being and that of the remaining parent. Some children may regress into greater "clinginess," become fearful of the dark or of separation, and depend more on the surviving parent. Others may demand more attention and become more aggressive. Adolescents may become preoccupied with thoughts of their own vulnerability to disease and death. In these ways children may be thought of as *being preoccupied with the personal meaning of the event.*

Two to four years following the death, most children will get on with their lives. The *psychologic integration of the loss of the parent* might be thought of as a third general phase. Whether it is accomplished in a way that allows the child to proceed on a healthy developmental course depends on the support and security provided by the surviving parent and other significant adults, on the opportunity for open grieving, and on the accumulation of changes brought on by the death.

With the death of a parent, risk factors for a poorer psychologic outcome include circumstances in which the deceased is the mother; multiple children are in the family; the functional status of the surviving parent becomes chronically compromised; prior psychologic difficulties were present, or a conflict existed with the deceased; there is a social context of instability and lack of support; and the death was unanticipated or the result of suicide or homicide.

Family Mobility

Particularly for the young child, the primary locus of living—the "known world" to a great degree—is the family home. Leaving the familiar and adjusting to a new home is the norm rather than the exception for children in the United States. Census data have shown a fairly constant rate of mobility during the last decade, with approximately 17% of Americans moving each year. Multiple moves are made by many families, with estimates of 40% of children moving three or more times before reaching adulthood.

The available data regarding the effects of family moves on children suggest, in most cases, a pattern of successful coping and adaptation. For some children, however, the move presents special hardships connected to the conditions that prompted the move—for example, parental job loss or separation—or that result in significant losses difficult for the child to replace or rebuild in the new home. Whether in the short term or long term, preschoolers are likely to be especially sensitive to changes in child care arrangements and the availability of their parents after the move. They may have difficulty with a new bedroom or sleeping arrangement, have an increase in nightmares, and show some regression in behavior. School-age children, in the midst of developing social skills and important friendships, may have difficulty starting anew in an unfamiliar school or neighborhood.

With three or more family moves, some evidence exists for emotional, psychologic, school, and behavioral problems as sequelae. The moves may represent a significant stressor in themselves or may be a destabilizing influence on family life.

MAJOR FAMILY CHANGES FROM THE CHILD'S PERSPECTIVE

Family change is important to the extent that it affects the expected and predictable rhythms, the activities, and the supports of daily living. In the life of the child, the changes previously described are rarely understood as single events. More often, **they signify a connected sequence of events and an accumulation of changes that play out over years rather than weeks or months.** The valence of the change depends on what is gained and what is lost, as that is understood by the child. Change that may be minor to the parent may loom large for the child—for instance, change in bedroom arrangements, sleep time, household tasks, mealtime, or formerly established interactions with the absent parent. This understanding depends on the child's developmental stage, cognitive capacity, past experience and, especially, the adaptation by the family itself.

For the family, adaptation usually depends on four successive tasks or stages, as follows:

1. *A shared acknowledgment of the reality of the change.* This in turn assists the child's understanding and sense of inclusion—for example, having the child attend funeral or memorial services following a family death.

2. *A shared experience of the expression of feelings.* There is an acceptance within the family of complex feelings such as anger and protest, grief, helplessness, relief, and guilt.

3. *Reorganization of the family system.* With a new and realistic realignment of tasks, roles, and relationships, for example, changes in child care arrangements following parental divorce, the family can revitalize itself.

4. *Reinvestment in other relationships and life pursuits.* This is commonly not assumed by a parent until 1 to 2 years following a divorce or death.

FAMILY CHANGE AND THE PEDIATRIC CLINICIAN

The clinician's major tool for both assessment and intervention is a careful inquiry into the nature of the family change and empathic understanding of its meaning for the child and the family. Before advice can be given, the losses, gains, struggles, and demonstrated competencies that have attended the change must be appreciated by all involved. Frequently, it is this listening and understanding that is the clinician's most important "intervention."

For the pediatric clinician, the principal task usually is to identify the particular needs of the child, whose developmental and emotional needs are threatened by the change. In this situation, however, the family is truly the patient, and the experiences and needs of other family members, especially of the parent, must also be understood. A family meeting facilitated by the clinician can be a powerful method of furthering family dialogue that is stuck at any of the four adaptive stages described earlier. Arranging for new social supports through church, synagogue, or other religious communities, or through parent-teacher associations and other support groups, is an important intervention for families facing any important losses.

Pediatricians sometimes fear that delving into such complex psychosocial concerns may overwhelm their own available time, expertise, and emotional reserves. The key to "containing" this work in the pediatric context is the self-expectation for identifying, as opposed to resolving, maladaptive patterns and assisting the family in taking "just the next step" toward more successful coping. More focused psychologic assistance is available through individual and family psychotherapy and through group therapy programs with children and families affected similarly; however, this may well not happen without the recognition, understanding, and encouragement of the child's physician.

FURTHER READING

Behrman RE: Children and divorce. *In* Behrman RE (ed): The Future of Children, Vol 4. Los Altos, CA, Center for the Future of Children, The David and Lucile Packard Foundation, 1994.

Haggerty RJ, Sherrod LR, Garmezy N, and Rutter M (eds): Stress, Risk, and Resilience in Children and Adolescents:

Processes, Mechanisms, and Interventions. New York, Cambridge University Press, 1994.

Tanner JL (ed): Children, Families, and Stress. Report of the Twenty-Fifth Ross Roundtable on Critical Approaches to Common Pediatric Problems. Columbus, OH, Ross Products Division, Abbott Laboratories, 1995.

Walsh F, and McGoldrick M: Loss and the family life cycle. *In* Falicov CJ: Family Transitions: Continuity and Change over the Life Cycle. New York, Guilford Press, 1988, p 311–336.

Worden WJ: Children and Grief: When a Parent Dies. New York, Guilford Press, 1996.

Ellen L. Bassuk
Linda F. Weinreb

Chapter 5

Homeless Children

More than 20% of American children live below the poverty line. An estimated 100,000 children reside in shelters on a given night, and approximately 500,000 are homeless each year. These children are among the poorest and are the most stressed. Without the resources essential to foster basic development, they suffer more medical, socioemotional, and educational problems than their more advantaged peers but receive fewer services. To provide a basic level of health care, clinicians must understand the bleak reality of their lives and the barriers to comprehensive, coordinated, continuous care that they confront.

Overall, homeless children's adjustment is determined by their pathway into homelessness, the nature and severity of various stressors, such as sexual abuse or foster care placement, the mother's emotional symptoms and distress, and parenting practices. However, as children become older, their reaction to homelessness may be determined less by family relationships and their concept of family. School-age children are more aware of the stigma of living in a shelter and the trauma of losing their home. Many feel humiliated and embarrassed about being homeless and may be secretive with their peers about where they live. **Homeless children yearn for a real home and the stability, safety, and social connections it represents.**

Because experiences of homeless children are partly mediated by those of their mother, the clinician must complete a family-oriented medical and psychosocial assessment. **Most important, the basic need for emergency shelter, clothes, food, and immediate medical care must be evaluated and immediately addressed.** Once this has been accomplished, a more comprehensive family-oriented treatment plan can be formulated that is responsive to the experiences of homelessness, violence, and extreme poverty. Without an understanding of the reality of the mother's life, it is impossible to intervene effectively with the child.

THE NEEDS OF HOMELESS MOTHERS

The majority of homeless families are female-headed and extremely poor; more than 50% have annual incomes of less than $7000. The mothers are, on average, in their late twenties and have approximately two children—usually below age 6. These families are residentially unstable, profoundly disconnected from supportive relationships, and highly stressed. **Severe violent victimization is omnipresent in homeless families, with more than 90% of the mothers reporting sexual or physical abuse as children or battering as adults.** Not surprisingly, a disproportionate number of these mothers suffer from posttraumatic stress and associated psychiatric disorders (major depression and substance abuse) over their lifetime and have inadequate social supports.

PHYSICAL HEALTH PROBLEMS

Homeless children have more chronic illness than the general population: they experience an average of five acute illness symptoms (2 sick days and 1 bed day) each month. Seventeen percent of homeless children, compared with 7.5 percent in the general population, are judged to be in fair or poor health by their mothers. They suffer disproportionately from recurrent ear infections, asthma, scabies and lice, and acute gastrointestinal illnesses compared with their poor counterparts who are not homeless. Homeless children also are at high risk for poor nutrition and obesity. Not surprisingly, these children often fail to receive preventive medical services, including routine immunizations.

EMOTIONAL AND SOCIAL DIFFICULTIES

Most homeless children have experienced extreme adversity in their lives. Residential instability, lack of structure and routine, the pervasiveness of violence, and their mother's distress all contribute to their difficulties. Furthermore, by the time homeless children are preschoolers, almost 20% have been placed in foster care for varying periods (see Chapter 8). By the time they are of school age, almost one third have had a foster care placement. In response to multiple stressors, many of these children manifest developmental delays, anxiety, depression, and behavioral problems. Recent reports indicate that school-age homeless children have higher rates of emotional disorders with functional impairment than a comparable population of children who are not homeless.

EDUCATIONAL PROBLEMS

Homeless children attend school erratically or not at all. Timely school enrollment may be obstructed by immunization delays, problems in transferring school records, and lack of transportation. Furthermore, if a mother lacks child care and is responsible for transporting her child to school, she must take the entire family back and forth each day.

Because homeless families move frequently, many children often change schools, leading to disrupted relationships and learning. A recent study documented that 72% of homeless children changed schools during the year, a rate twice as high as among poor, home-dwelling children. Once homeless children are in school, their needs often are overlooked by a public system that is underfunded, overcrowded, and resource-poor. Thus, it is not surprising that many homeless children are doing below-average work or failing and are at high risk of dropping out.

CLINICAL AND PROGRAMMATIC RESPONSES

The desperate plight of homeless children calls for comprehensive medical and psychosocial assessment and treatment involving all family members. In addition to meeting basic needs, the clinician should try to identify obstacles to care (e.g., child care, transportation) and develop preventive strategies. An ongoing supportive relationship with the family is the key to effective care.

Pediatricians are increasingly being asked to provide primary medical care to homeless children. **Primary health care fosters comprehensive and ongoing medical treatment and, therefore, is an optimal setting for the provision of high-quality care to homeless children.** For many homeless families, the link with a caring clinician offers an excellent avenue for support and health education, as well as for managing medical needs.

The primary care clinician not only should treat poor children medically but should identify immunization gaps, assess for developmental problems, monitor growth, and routinely screen for lead poisoning. Because of poorly managed ear problems, these children also should be tested for hearing loss. Similarly, because of their disproportionately high rates of asthma and other upper respiratory infections, homeless children should be screened and receive early treatment for these problems. Whenever possible, environmental irritants, such as smoking, should be identified and eliminated.

In addition to a standard pediatric assessment, attention should be focused on evaluating the emotional and behavioral effects of environmental stressors, including frequent moves, foster care placement, physical and/or sexual abuse, and maternal depression. At a minimum, the majority of homeless children have witnessed violence and are likely to manifest various emotional symptoms. Additionally, the clinician should gather information about school readiness and performance.

The health issues of homeless children can be addressed adequately only within the context of the family's needs, especially the mother's. Studies have shown that, especially for younger children, the mother's negative emotional status is an important independent predictor of adverse outcomes in her children. Assessment of the mother's financial and social resources, mental health and substance use, violent victimization, and access to services should be routine, if prevention of adverse mental health outcomes for both mother and child is to be sought. Failure to address the mother's needs will limit the effectiveness of child-oriented interventions. Furthermore, whenever possible, appropriate educational opportunities for learning about children's normal growth and development, parenting practices, nutritional needs, and health supervision should be available.

Many communities have outreach programs for

homeless children. Unless the clinician has on-site social service or case management staff, collaborating with community-based agencies is critical for meeting the complex needs of these children. Although homeless children's needs are extensive and cannot be solved until the real causes of poverty are addressed, primary care clinicians can play a significant role in improving their health and well-being.

FURTHER READING

Bassuk EL, Weinreb LF, Buckner JC, et al.: The characteristics and needs of sheltered homeless and low-income housed mothers. JAMA 286:640–646, 1996.

Bassuk EL, and Weinreb LF: The plight of homeless children. *In* Blacher J (ed): When There's No Place Like Home: Options for Children Living Apart from Their Natural Families. Baltimore, Paul H. Brooks Publishing Co, 1994.

Bassuk EL, Browne A, and Buckner JC: Single mothers and welfare. Sci Am 275:60–63, 66–67, 1996.

Bassuk EL, Weinreb LF, Dawson R, et al.: Determinants of behavior in homeless and low-income housed preschool children. Pediatrics 100:92–100, 1997.

Buckner JC and Bassuk EL: Mental disorders and service utilization among youths from homeless and low-income housed families. J Acad Child Adolesc Psychiatry 36:890–900, 1997.

Wood D: Evaluation and management of homeless families and children. *In* Wood D (ed): Delivering Health Care to Homeless Persons. New York, Springer, 1992.

Robert S. Byrd

Chapter 6

Maternal Literacy

Many health problems faced by Americans are not solely medical. They have social underpinnings and consequences. Medicine is essential in the final resolution of many of these pressing health problems, but they must be dealt with in a social context. Some health problems will be responsive as much to social change as to medical interventions. These should go hand in hand; however, the medical profession must not only follow but help lead the way.
Cluff, "New Agenda for Medicine," 1987

SOCIETAL DIMENSION

Mothers who cannot read well may not tell their child's doctor that they are unable to read the information handout that was just given to them. They may not understand how to give medications to their child and may have trouble keeping appointments. In addition, their children are more likely to experience reading problems, to have problems in school, and to drop out of school, thus perpetuating the problem in the next generation.

A century ago, a literate person was one who could write his or her name. Such literacy would not permit full participation in the economic and social activities of today's society. Literacy, as defined in the 1991 National Literacy Act, is "an individual's ability to read, write, and speak in English, and compute and solve problems at levels

of proficiency necessary to function on the job and in society, to achieve one's goals, and develop one's knowledge and potential." **Low literacy is often hard to detect in clinical settings without specific screening tests.** Because low literacy is more common among those living in poverty, adverse health outcomes that are due in part to reading deficiencies may be attributed wholly to other factors, such as poverty, crowding, chaotic households, poor parenting, or inadequate resources.

In nonindustrialized countries, low maternal literacy has been linked to poor child health outcomes. For example, the female literacy rates in India and Sri Lanka (two countries that have similar gross domestic products) are 39% and 82%, respectively, and the infant mortality rates are 79 and 16 infant deaths per 1000 live births. For children living in the United States and other developed countries, health problems related to low maternal literacy have not been viewed as problems, because international studies typically use completion of the fourth grade as a proxy for literacy; by this measure, the United States is nearly 100% literate.

One major factor that heightened attention to literacy in the United States was a national survey of functional literacy conducted in 1992 that revealed high rates of problems (Kirsch and coworkers, 1993). Whereas only 4% of adults in the

United States are truly illiterate (reading below the fourth grade level), nearly 50% of U.S. adults struggle with printed materials typically encountered as part of their daily lives. Nearly one in five has extremely limited literacy skills, that is, reading only the most basic short text, determining where they need to sign their name on a Social Security card, and picking a date or time from an appointment card, for example. They are unable to synthesize information from various parts of a simple document, find an intersection on a map, or read a television program guide. At the next level of literacy, one in four adults can locate a single piece of information in text, compare easily identifiable information based on a criterion provided in a question and integrate two or more pieces of information, but cannot read materials that are dense, lengthy, or without headings or other organizational aids. Taken together, 48% of U.S. adults cannot make more than low-level inferences when using printed materials. In this survey, most people who had limited literacy skills described themselves as able to read and write well; few reported that they get a lot of help with everyday literacy tasks from family members or friends. Although one may conclude that most people who have low levels of literacy seem unaware of their limitation and do not use available help, other researchers have found that many adults feel ashamed of their inability to read and go to great effort to hide this from others, including never telling their spouses or children of their reading difficulties.

Although awareness has been heightened that many adults in the United States may have low reading skills, no study from a developed country has shown that low maternal literacy affects children's health directly and adversely, and such studies in adults are limited. One study has shown an association between low maternal reading skills and children's poor physical and psychosocial health; another study showed no relationship between literacy skills and health care costs among a Medicaid population (Weiss and associates, 1992, 1994). Most health and literacy studies highlight the gap between reading level and readability of written health information and demonstrate that patients who are of low literacy are less likely to follow the physician's instructions, keep appointments, and see a doctor early in the course of their disease. Thus, addressing literacy may yield added health benefits.

PATIENT EDUCATION

Patient and parent health informational materials often are written at a level that exceeds the reading skills of many families. Low literacy skills are more common among, but not limited to, those who fail to complete high school, those for whom English is a second language, and those who live in poverty. This presents special challenges to clinicians who serve low-income children. Literacy screening in such settings showed that parental reading skills are on average equivalent to a seventh or eighth grade reading level, despite a mean educational level of greater than the 11th grade. Evaluation of the reading level of parent education materials showed that only 25% of American Academy of Pediatrics' items and 19% of all materials evaluated were written at below the ninth grade level, and only 2% of all materials were below the seventh grade levels. Table 6–1 lists some pediatric health information materials and their assessed reading levels. Thus, in clinics serving low-income families, many of the available parent and patient education materials may be inaccessible to a significant proportion of families, especially those in the greatest need of health education. Furthermore, a high proportion of low-income patients are unable to read, and thus cannot understand, basic medical instructions, unless given by other means. Among patients attending two predominantly low-income clinics, 35% of English-speaking and 62% of Spanish-speaking patients had inadequate or marginal functional health literacy. Many lacked understanding of what it meant to take a medicine on an empty stomach or how to take a dosage of medicine four times a day. Many could not determine from an appointment card when their next appointment

---

TABLE 6–1. Reading Level of Health Educational Materials

American Academy of Pediatrics
    Protect Your Child ... Prevent Poisoning—12th grade
    Newborns: Care of the Uncircumcised Penis—12th grade
    Child Care: What's Best for Your Family—10th grade
    Healthy Kids, Zero Through Three—12th grade
Baby Books
    Caring for Your Baby and Young Child—12th grade
    Your Baby and Child from Birth to Age Five—12th grade
    Solve Your Child's Sleep Problems—14th grade
Centers for Disease Control and Prevention Immunization Pamphlets
    Diphtheria, Tetanus, and Pertussis: What You Need to Know—10th grade
    Measles, Mumps, and Rubella: What You Need to Know—12th grade
    Polio: What You Need to Know—10th grade

From Davis TC, Mayeux EJ, Fredrickson D, et al.: Reading ability of parents compared with reading level of pediatric patient education materials. Pediatrics 93:460–468, 1994. Reproduced by permission of Pediatrics.

was scheduled. Most had particular difficulty understanding informed consent forms.

To address child health problems related to low maternal literacy, the clinician must recognize that many parents have limited reading skills. Although low-literate adults are more likely to live in poverty, to have fewer years of education, or to be foreign born, reading problems are not limited to those groups or to persons whose difficulties are evident by their appearance or by speech. Interventions can be undertaken at a number of levels, including improvement of the delivery of health information, referral to community agencies to improve parental reading skills, and promotion of early literacy to prevent today's children from becoming tomorrow's "reading-challenged" parents.

Patient education should focus on transfer of needed information and need not be limited to written materials. Videotape, audiotape, and interactive multimedia computer teaching aids provide alternatives to the written information used to reinforce the advice that is part of the patient encounter, and these modes may be able to reach parents who read poorly or not entirely at all. Because these modes will not entirely replace written materials, attention needs to be directed at enhancing the readability of the printed materials that we use. Recommendations on how to prepare educational materials aimed at a low-literate audience include using simple words, short sentences, large type, generous margins, and graphics. Grammar-checking modules in some word processing programs can be used to estimate reading level. To ensure that written materials convey information effectively, they should be pilot tested with the target audience. When the reading level of patient materials is lowered, low-literate families find the materials more accessible and comprehension is improved among families of greater reading ability.

Clinicians are unlikely to identify every family with low literacy skills in their practices. Reading difficulties often are hidden because of shame. At times, however, these deficiencies become apparent. Through collaboration with community services, clinicians can to do more than just address health. Literacy programs, family resource centers, and adult education programs provide opportunities for adults to learn to read. The success of such programs varies, but a referral may transform individual families.

PREVENTION OF LOW LITERACY

Prevention of future reading problems begins during preschool years. Pediatric clinicians have multiple opportunities to assess children's development and intervene before the onset of reading problems, as discussed in Chapter 21. Children who are read to as preschoolers make better readers when they reach the early school years. Programs such as Reach Out and Read (Needlman and coworkers, 1991) and Head Start promote early literacy and may prevent reading problems later.

SUMMARY

Pediatricians do not take care of children in isolation from the family. Often the best treatment for children has to be directed to the family. Recognition that many parents in the United States have reading difficulties is a first step. **Interventions that enhance patient education, maternal literacy, or early literacy may improve health and probably will enhance the quality of life of children and their families.** Partnerships with community service agencies will only enhance these efforts.

FURTHER READING

Cluff LE: New agenda for medicine. Am J Med 82:803–810, 1987.

Davis TC, Mayeaux EJ, Fredrickson D, et al.: Reading ability of parents compared with reading level of pediatric patient education materials. Pediatrics 93:460–468, 1994.

Doak CC, Doak LG, and Root JH: Teaching Patients with Low Literacy Skills. Philadelphia: JB Lippincott, 1985.

Hertz E, Hebert JR, and Landon J: Social and environmental factors and life expectancy, infant mortality, and maternal mortality rates: Results of a cross-national comparison. Soc Sci Med 39:105–114, 1994.

Kirsch IS, Jungeblut A, Jenkins L, and Kovstad A. Adult Literacy in America. Washington, DC: US Government Printing Office, 1993.

Needlman R, Fried LE, Morley DS, et al.: Clinic-based intervention to promote literacy: A pilot study. Am J Dis Child 145:881–884, 1991.

Parikh NS, Parker RM, Nurss JR, et al.: Shame and health literacy: The unspoken connection. Patient Educ Couns 27:33–39, 1996.

Weiss BD, Blanchard JS, McGee DL, et al.: Illiteracy among Medicaid recipients and its relationship to health care costs. J Health Care Poor Underserved 5:99–111, 1994.

Weiss BD, Hart G, McGee DL, and D'Estelle S: Health status of illiterate adults: Relation between literacy and health status among persons with low literacy skills. J Am Board Fam Pract 5:257–264, 1992.

Williams MV, Parker RM, Baker DW, et al.: Inadequate functional health literacy among patients at two public hospitals. JAMA 274:1677–1682, 1995.

WHO Database on Monitoring and Evaluation of Progress in Implementing Strategies for Health for All by the Year 2000. Geneva, WHO, 1996.

Howard R. Spivak

Chapter 7

Violence

Until recently, the pediatric perspective of violence largely involved prevention, recognition, and treatment of child abuse. Although this remains an important concern, the range of violence now affecting the lives and health of children, unfortunately, is far broader. Interpersonal violence and its consequences of disability and death are prominent child health problems as we enter the 21st century.

Homicide has become the second leading cause of death for teenagers and young adults aged 15 to 24 years and the leading cause of death for African-Americans aged 15 to 34 years. Violent injuries increasingly are responsible for a growing proportion of serious physical disabilities among youth, with some urban areas reporting gunshot injuries as a more frequent cause of spinal cord injuries than automobile accidents. The Centers for Disease Control and Prevention project that if current trends continue, more children will die from handgun injuries than from automobile accidents within the next decade.

Although violent crime traditionally has been addressed by the criminal justice system, there is a growing need for the health care community to become more involved in both the prevention and treatment of violent injury. **Violent injuries are seen four times more frequently by the medical system—in emergency rooms and physicians' offices—than by the police.** The pediatric community has a particularly important role in this problem because there is growing evidence that serious risk factors are established in childhood and adolescence. Furthermore, above and beyond the human costs, the health care costs related to violent injuries are in the tens of billions of dollars annually. Finally, although the homicide rates for adults have been stable or declining in recent years, the homicide rates for teenagers have been rising, and the mean age at which the rate of homicide peaks has been falling. All of this underscores the importance for clinicians who take care of children to understand this issue better and know how to respond.

CONTRIBUTING FACTORS

For the development of effective strategies to identify and respond to risks for violence, it is important to understand the factors that contribute to risk for violent injury as a victim, an assailant, or both. A number of such factors give clear insight and direction for clinical interventions. These are reviewed in the following sections.

Poverty

The first factor associated with risk of injury due to violence is poverty. Homicide and violent injury rates are significantly higher in poor communities, both urban and rural. When socioeconomic factors are taken into account, racial differences in homicide rates disappear completely. Clinicians who work in low socioeconomic areas need to be aware that they are relating to a particularly high-risk population. It is important to point out, however, that all families and children living in poverty are not at high risk, and families who live in more affluent communities may be at very high risk. There is barely a community in this country that is not touched by violence or whose children are insulated from this issue.

Violence as a Learned Behavior

A second set of risk factors relates to violence as a learned behavior. Children exposed to violence and given the opportunity to learn to use violence to deal with conflict and anger are at increased risk for violent behavior and its consequences. A broad spectrum of exposures puts children at risk for violent injury later in adolescence and young adulthood. These identified exposures occur within the family context, at the community level, in schools, and in the media.

In the family, long-term risk for violent injury has been associated with child abuse, including verbal abuse and sexual abuse, the witnessing of spousal abuse and other forms of adult violence, and the use of corporal punishment. Some evidence suggests that the exposure to violence in the home early in life may be the most predictive factor for risk of violent injury later in life. This is of particular concern because as many as a third of families experience some form of family violence.

There also is evidence that growing up in a community that has high levels of violence is a risk factor—again, a red flag for clinicians who work in such communities. **Children also are being exposed to growing amounts of violence or threatened violence in schools. Some surveys of high school students report that as many as 25% of students claim to carry weapons to school at least on occasion.**

Last, there are the media, particularly television. Although policy makers continue to debate whether television influences behavior, an overwhelming amount of scientific evidence supports a strong association, if not explicit causality, between exposure to television violence and risk for violent behavior. Children who have average television viewing behavior are exposed to thousands of episodes of violence a year. This simulated violence often is portrayed as the first choice of approach to resolving conflict, is practiced by both heroes and villains, is almost always successful, has few apparent negative consequences such as pain, and is entertaining and engrossing.

Handguns

The presence of a handgun in the home has been associated with increased risk of both intentional and unintentional injury. The increased risk of intentional injury involves both homicide and suicide. Most handguns are purchased for protection, but they are more likely to be used in a family suicide or family homicide than for the originally intended purpose. There are approximately 80 million handguns in circulation in the United States, about a third of which are unregistered. If they are intended for protection, they are not likely to be locked up but rather to be in a night table drawer and, therefore, readily available to a child or teenager.

CONTEXT OF VIOLENCE

Contrary to popular belief, most violence in this country occurs between people who know each other rather than between strangers. Over 50% of homicides stem from arguments; only 15% occur in the course of a crime such as robbery or drug commerce. The typical homicide occurs between two people who know each other, are of the same race, are often young, have been drinking, get into an argument, and use a weapon, often a handgun. There is, in fact, no evidence that the severity of punishment from the criminal justice system affects these events.

A second contextual factor is adolescence. Although this developmental stage is not necessarily the point during which violence is learned, it is the stage during which risk greatly increases. Teenagers are extremely susceptible to insult, are prone to taking risks, are greatly influenced by peer pressure, and often identify with extreme characteristics of role models. This is true for both girls and boys and for young people in all geographic and socioeconomic circumstances.

THE ROLE OF PEDIATRIC CLINICIANS

This background gives considerable insight into strategies that clinicians may use in their practices and as advocates for child health in the community.

Screening for Risk

Several important risk factors for which clinicians can screen, if addressed, can reduce risk of violent injury. These include the presence of family violence and the ownership of handguns.

Although raising the issue of family violence can be awkward or uncomfortable, it is an increasingly accepted standard of practice to ask whether there is or has been any violence in the home. Pediatricians can raise this in the context of the potential effects on the child. In addition, because abused women may not seek care for themselves, the child's health care provider may be the only professional to whom they have access. When family violence is identified, care must be taken to contact someone experienced in dealing with this problem. Some inexperienced efforts to help may, in fact, exacerbate the risk. **Because there is significant concurrence between domestic abuse and child abuse, it is essential that children exposed to this circumstance receive evaluation and treatment.** There also are long-term consequences to the exposure itself, even without child abuse.

If handguns are identified in the home, parents need to be informed of the risks and encouraged to get rid of the gun. If they choose not to, then safe locked storage separating the gun and the ammunition is better than nothing.

Another area for screening is the identification of children who are exhibiting violent behavior, in terms of recurrent fighting, bullying, or recurrent victimization. If these circumstances exist, it is important to identify underlying issues and seek appropriate psychologic assessment and treatment. These children may be at risk for more serious violence in later childhood and young adulthood.

Anticipatory Guidance

As educators, pediatric clinicians play a key role in risk reduction. Areas of particular importance are disciplinary practices, conflict resolution strategies, television viewing, handgun ownership, as described previously, and child safety.

Although pediatricians may not be able to eliminate corporal punishment, they can introduce and encourage alternative strategies such as "time-outs." Evidence suggests that such advice from pediatricians can influence parents to try alternatives to spanking or hitting. Similarly, parents often need advice or assistance in dealing with sibling or peer conflict and in helping their children develop healthy strategies for dealing with anger and conflict.

Parents need to be aware of the effects of television viewing on children. They should be encouraged to limit television viewing time, to monitor and be aware of what their children are watching, and whenever possible to watch and discuss with their children what they are seeing. It is important to note that much programming labeled as "children's," particularly cartoons, is more violent than adult programming. Parents often are unaware of this. The less television the better, and what is watched should be appropriately violence-free.

Last, parents may need help identifying safe environments for their children. This is a particular concern of working parents who are unable to monitor their children's whereabouts, especially as the children get older. Advice in this area often is community-specific, and raising the issue can be useful in stimulating parents to think about their alternatives.

Treatment of Violent Injuries

Regrettably, when children or adolescents present with violent injuries, the treatment often is limited to addressing the physical injury and little else— the "stitch 'em up, send 'em out" method of treatment. For clinicians who treat such patients or provide follow-up care, it is important to do a more comprehensive evaluation and/or consider follow-up that addresses the possibility of risk for future injury. Many homicide victims have histories of previous nonfatal violent injuries. Underlying risk factors need to be identified, evaluated, and treated in the medical or a mental health setting.

Advocacy in the Community

It is important for clinicians to consider their role as child advocates in the community. **Violence is a situation in which interventions at the community level are as important as at the individual level.** The combination of individual and community strategies may be particularly valuable. Areas prime for advocacy of clinicians include school-based services such as conflict resolution curricula and after-school programs, handgun control or reduced accessibility to handguns, enhanced youth programs and services for youth, and efforts toward general public education and awareness of risk and contributing factors. Pediatricians and other clinicians who treat children are in a unique position to raise and speak credibly to these issues.

FURTHER READING

Farrell AD and Meyer AL: The effectiveness of a school-based curriculum for reducing violence among urban sixth-grade students. Am J Public Health 87:979–984, 1977.

Prothrow-Stith D and Weissman M: Deadly Consequences. New York, HarperCollins, 1991.

Spivak HR and Harvey B: The role of the pediatrician in violence prevention. Pediatrics 94:(Suppl):577–651, 1994.

Neal Halfon

Chapter 8

Foster Care

Children enter the foster care system for a variety of reasons, including physical and sexual abuse, parental neglect, and the consequences of drug use in many families. Pediatricians can play very important roles in the difficult decision making regarding whether a child should be placed in foster care and in identifying medical, mental health, and developmental problems of children in foster care. They also can help foster parents and social workers develop appropriate health care plans to address many important health needs.

The number of children in foster care was 494,000 in 1995, almost doubling from a decade earlier. The rising number of children in foster care parallels the rising number of child abuse reports, which also have doubled over the past decade to nearly 2 million reports involving 3 million children in 1995. In most states, the population of children in foster care is becoming younger, with the highest rates of placement for children less than 1 year old. The rising numbers and shifting demographics have been attributed partly to the growing numbers of young families living in poverty, combined with the devastating impact of drug use in families and the drug exposure of many infants.

Children in foster care have higher rates of acute and chronic medical, mental health, and developmental problems. Medical problems at the time of placement can include injuries secondary to physical abuse, sexually transmitted disease due to sexual abuse, and malnutrition as a result of general neglect. Prenatal exposure to alcohol and drugs, as well as the frequent occurrence of prematurity, can result in a range of neurodevelopmental problems and disabilities. Common medical problems abound: 65% to 75% enter foster care with uncorrected vision and hearing problems and untreated allergy and skin disorders. In 35% to 45% there are chronic health problems, with growth abnormalities, anemia, asthma, and neurologic disorders being the most common. The 20% to 40% of foster children with multiple chronic medical problems pose real challenges to pediatricians engaged in their care.

A wide range of studies has suggested that between 45% and 90% of foster children have a psychologic or behavioral problem, with 30% to 80% of them being moderately to severely impaired. Developmental assessment of children in foster care reveals that 30% to 60% of preschool children have evidence of developmental delay, and 45% to 75% of school-age children have problems in school.

As might be expected, children in foster care use health services at higher rates than do those in age- and income-adjusted comparisons. Several studies suggest, however, that irrespective of their comparatively high utilization rates, these children continue to be underserved relative to their needs. These are important considerations for clinicians in managed care environments, where risk-adjusted capitation reimbursement or a fee-for-service "carve-out" may be warranted.

The American Academy of Pediatrics and the Child Welfare League of America have developed standards for the assessment and treatment of children in foster care. These emphasize the importance of a comprehensive assessment that includes evaluation of physical, emotional, cognitive, and relational areas of functioning. These guidelines provide that children entering the foster care system should be screened within 72 hours of placement for medical and psychologic problems and should receive a comprehensive assessment within 30 days of placement.

One of the greatest challenges to the clinician attempting to assess these children comprehensively is the difficulty in obtaining appropriate health information from past health care clinicians, biologic parents, foster parents, child welfare workers, and schools. Some child welfare agencies have developed procedures and special forms to collect this needed health history and other relevant clinical information.

Given the very high rates of emotional, developmental, and behavioral problems in this population, an assessment of these domains of function is essential. Because many children in foster care have experienced disruptive relationships and many younger children have impaired emotional attachment in relationships, the socioemotional "scaffolding" necessary to support cognitive and language functioning is often severely compromised. Although it is relatively easy for a pediatrician to assess a child's development by using the Denver Developmental Screening Test (DDST), the Early Language Milestone Scale, or other readily available screening tools, it is somewhat more challenging to assess and understand the underlying emotional insults that many of these children have experienced. For this reason, pediatricians may find it useful to collaborate with a psychologist or other mental health provider in the evaluation of the specific emotional needs of foster children.

Because of the type of trauma and disruption that children have experienced before placement, their emotional and developmental response patterns often present a variable and changing picture over time. The 2-year-old who 2 weeks after placement appears docile and compliant often can demonstrate defiant and oppositional behaviors 2 months later. This behavioral change can be part of the normal adaptive response pattern of a frightened child placed into a loving foster home environment, who begins to test the limits of that environment once the child feels more secure.

These and other characteristics of the development of children in foster care suggest that the schedule of periodic supervisory health visits needs to be customized to meet each child's needs. Physicians might find that more frequent reassessments of the child's status are necessary to gain a more accurate understanding of the child's emotional and developmental capacities and needs. Again, this raises real challenges for clinicians who practice in capitated payment environments.

Care for children in foster care is a responsibility shared by foster parents, child welfare workers, and health professionals. Communication also is key. **Foster parents often need more information, advice, and counseling than do the biologic parents of the child.** Some foster parents will perceive the children in their care as especially vulnerable or as having certain underlying diseases or problems that require personalized responses. Foster parents may harbor unsubstantiated fears of underlying infectious diseases such as the human immunodeficiency virus or may attribute behavioral responses to the effects of drug exposure, when, in fact, the behavioral response patterns are part of the normal adaptive process accompanying a transition into a new family environment. Helping foster parents understand the nature of a child's problems, read the child's cues, and understand the child's capacities to adapt and change is an essential role of the pediatric clinician.

Since the quality of the foster home in which a child is placed is so important in determining the child's physical, psychologic, and social well-being, the physician can play an important role in supporting foster parents as the primary therapists in the child's often difficult rehabilitation process. For children with one or several special medical needs, or for those with severe emotional and behavioral problems, the physician–foster parent relationship is an important support for the foster family as well as for the child.

Major challenges for clinicians caring for children in foster care are not only finding the time necessary for complete and adequate assessment but also identifying appropriate services, making necessary referrals, guaranteeing appropriate follow-up, and assuming responsibility in communicating important information to the child's social worker. All of these case management functions place additional burdens on physicians, especially in the managed care environment.

In many parts of the United States, the foster care program has been carved out of the Medicaid–managed care process and is maintained in a fee-for-service system. This type of arrangement often allows the physician to bill more appropriately for the time and effort necessary to provide essential services to the child and family. In addition, several jurisdictions throughout the United States have begun to employ public health nurses and other allied health care personnel to assist with health care case management, which often is necessary to ensure that the children receive appropriate and timely care.

Physicians who intend to care for children in foster care often need additional information about how the foster care system functions; specially developed assessment tools that can help focus their evaluation of emotional, developmental, and behavioral issues; and other information and support about providing care to this at-risk population. Children in foster care require more comprehensive and coordinated care, and the pediatrician has a unique role to play in providing a health care home to this special group of children.

FURTHER READING

American Academy of Pediatrics, Committee on Early Childhood, Adoption and Dependent Care: Health care for children in foster care. Pediatrics 93:1–4, 1994.

Battistelli ES: Making Managed Care Work for Kids in Foster Care: A Guide to Purchasing Services. Washington, DC, Child Welfare League of America, 1996.

Blatt SP and Simms M: Foster care: Special children, special needs. Contemp Pediatr 14:109–129, 1997.

Child Welfare League of America: Standards for Health Care Service for Children in Out-of-Home Care. Washington, DC, Child Welfare League of America, 1988.

Halfon N, Berkowitz G, and Klee L: Children in foster care in California: An examination of Medicaid reimbursed health services utilization. Pediatrics 89:1230–1237, 1992.

Halfon N, Berkowitz G, and Klee L: Mental health service utilization by children in foster care in California. Pediatrics 89:1238–1244, 1992.

Halfon N, Mendonca A, and Berkowitz G: Health status of children in foster care: The experience of the Center for the Vulnerable Child. Arch Pediatr Adolesc Med 149:386–392, 1995.

Hochstadt NJ, Jaudes PK, Zimo DA, and Schachter J: The medical and psychosocial needs of children entering foster care. Child Abuse Neglect 1:53–62, 1987.

Rosenfeld AA, Pilowsky DJ, Fine P, et al.: Foster care: An update. J Am Acad Child Adolesc Psychiatry 448–457, 1997.

Schor EL: Foster care. Pediatr Clin North Am 35:1241–1252, 1988.

Simms MD: The foster care clinic: A community program to identify treatment needs of children in foster care. J Dev Behav Pediatr 10:121–128, 1989.

Spar K: Foster Care and Adoption Statistics: a CRS Report for Congress. Washington, DC, Congressional Research Services, 1997.

Standards for Health Care Service for Children in Out-of-Home Care. Washington, DC, Child Welfare League of America, 1988.

US Department of Health and Human Services, Administration for Children and Families, Administration on Children, Youth, and Families, and National Center on Child Abuse and Neglect: Child Maltreatment, 1995. Report from the States to the National Child Abuse and Neglect Data Systems. 1997.

Esther H. Wender

Chapter 9

Adoption

DEFINITION

The term *adoption* refers to the social and legal process that gives full family membership to children not born to the adopting parent(s). This process particularly affects three parties: the biologic parents, the adopted child, and the adoptive parent(s), a group often referred to as the "adoption triad." Others affected include siblings and other relatives, friends, and the community. The primary care clinician has an important role in promoting a healthy adoption process.

NUMBER AND TYPES OF ADOPTION IN THE UNITED STATES

Currently no comprehensive national data on adoption are kept by the federal government. However, the National Council for Adoption, one of several private organizations that collect adoption data from a variety of sources, reported the following information for 1986 (Table 9–1). These figures demonstrate that there are a number of different adoption arrangements and a variety of different backgrounds of children involved in adoption. These variations lead to different issues for the clinician who provides health care and counseling. The most important differences in adoption arrangements are described in the next sections.

TABLE 9–1. Numbers of Adoptions and Adoption Arrangements, 1986

Total international adoptions	10,019
Total domestic adoptions	104,088
Related adoptions	52,931
Unrelated adoptions	51,157
Public agency	20,064
Private agency	15,063
Individually arranged	16,040
Infant adoptions	24,589

Adapted from Adoption Factbook: United States Data, Issues, Regulations and Resources. Washington, DC, National Council for Adoption, 1989.

Related Adoptions

Although the figures vary markedly from year to year, a significant number of U.S. adoptions are by relatives, usually by step-parents adopting a stepchild. In this situation the children and their health history usually are known to the adopting parent(s). The primary issues are likely to relate to the preceding divorce and the interests of the noncustodial parent. Any special involvement by the primary care clinician would likely be related to these issues.

Unrelated Adoptions

As the figures show, unrelated adoptions may be arranged by public or private agencies. In recent years such adoptions have been frequently of children placed in foster care and subsequently released for adoption once parental rights were terminated. Such children range in age from infancy to adolescence, and many have significant health and/or emotional problems stemming from the circumstances of their initial foster placement. The involvement of agencies in adoption permits the availability of agency-based support services, although the collection and transfer of important health information may be difficult. The comprehensive assessment of the adopted child, including developmental and behavioral evaluation, is the physician's primary role.

Voluntary Placement of Infants for Adoption

Voluntary placement of infants for adoption, often thought of as the "typical" adoption, actually is becoming increasingly less common as social change has made it much more acceptable to raise children born out of wedlock. This type of adoption most frequently is carried out through individual arrangements involving physicians and attorneys, although private agencies also are frequently involved. The independently arranged adoption lacks the support services provided through agencies, although the absence of procedural restrictions is appealing to many involved.

International Adoptions

The adoption of infants and toddlers from other countries has become an increasingly popular option for parents who wish to adopt. Usually these adoptions are handled by private agencies that deal exclusively with the complex legal and social issues involved. The health status of these infants and children varies widely depending on the conditions in the country of origin and the circumstances surrounding such adoptions. The primary care clinician's role as a health consultant may be extensive.

HEALTH ASSESSMENT AND ONGOING HEALTH MANAGEMENT

Depending on the circumstances of the adoption, **the primary care physician may be involved in any or all of three phases of the provision of health care: (1) the consultation to the adopting parents regarding health risks or medical care issues prior to adoption; (2) the initial medical evaluation of the adopted child,** consisting of a brief evaluation at the time of adoption and a more comprehensive assessment once records are available; and/or **(3) the ongoing management of health issues as the adopted child grows and develops.** The important components of the initial medical evaluation are listed in Table 9–2.

Initial consultation regarding health risks or the medical management of already identified medical problems is complicated by the adopting family's expectations regarding these issues. The clinician should scrupulously avoid making recommendations regarding the decision to adopt. Clinicians should, however, provide information to the best of their knowledge regarding health risks based on known information, such as family history or the social circumstances of the child prior to adoption. If medical conditions have been identified previously, the clinician should provide information about prognosis and medical care needs in the future. There is always a risk that the family and/or the clinician will perceive a need to make guarantees about future health risks when no certainty exists.

TABLE 9–2. Initial Medical Evaluation

Relevant family and health history (when available)
Physical examination
  Growth parameters
  Developmental/behavioral assessment
  Dental evaluation
  Vision and hearing screens
Laboratory examination
  Hemoglobin
  Lead
  Urinalysis (if age-appropriate)
  Additional tests for international adoptees
    Newborn screening (if not done)
    Tuberculin skin test
    VDRL or RPR
    Hepatitis B serology
    Stool for ova and parasites
    CBC with differential
    HIV
    G6PD and/or Hb electrophoresis (for high risk)
Immunizations (if status uncertain, immunize child)

CBC, complete blood count; G6PD, glucose-6-phosphate dehydrogenase; Hb, hemoglobin; HIV, human immunodeficiency virus; RPR, rapid plasma reagin test; VDRL, Venereal Disease Research Laboratory (test for syphilis).

COUNSELING REGARDING ADOPTION ISSUES

The primary health care clinician has an important role in providing ongoing counseling regarding adoption issues. This role, however, is shared with specialized support services associated with public and private adoption agencies. Table 9–3 lists the most important counseling issues.

Adoption communication refers to the issue of how much and when to reveal the facts of the adoption to the adopted child. This, in turn, depends on the circumstances of the adoption, particularly the degree to which adopted children will be exposed to their biologic relatives. For example, in recent years the voluntary release of the infant for adoption has increasingly involved an "open adoption" procedure whereby the adopting parent(s) and the biologic parent(s) meet before adoption and may have ongoing contact as the child grows and develops. Also, if the adoption involves an older child, there may be continuing contact with the biologic parent.

TABLE 9–3. Counseling Issues in Adoption

Guidance in adoption communication
Routine behavioral/developmental guidance, including referrals
Information regarding specific, identified diseases and risks
Evaluation and/or referral for emerging problems
Guidance regarding legal issues, including referrals

TABLE 9–4. Causes of Developmental and Behavioral Problems in Adopted Children

Biological risks based on
  Genetic factors in biologic family
  Preadoption environmental issues
Psychologic factors related to
  The adoption process and its effect on the child
  The adoptive parents' psychologic problems
  Poor temperamental fit between adopted child and parents

If an infant is adopted by unrelated parents, the explanation of the adoptive status to the developing child may be difficult for many adoptive parents. However, the vast majority of adoption experts agree that **the child's adopted status should be conveyed, in developmentally appropriate ways, beginning with the earliest stages of verbal development and throughout childhood and adolescence.** The clinician should be prepared to help the parents provide this type of guidance to their adopted child.

The provision of guidance regarding developmental and behavioral issues requires an understanding of the complex issues involved. Table 9–4 lists the multiple factors that may be causally related to the adopted child's developmental or behavioral problems. The clinician must not make assumptions about the causes of the child's difficulties without evaluating all of these possibilities.

The resilience of the young child also must be appreciated. Many children adopted from neglectful or abusing environments thrive once placed in a stable and supportive environment. However, the clinician also must be sensitive to the adoptive parents whose enthusiasm may cloud their ability to acknowledge real and persistent problems.

Finally, clinicians should cultivate resources in their community that may provide assistance for adoptive families. The goal of pediatric practice is to promote optimal health and development of all children. Adoption provides one opportunity to promote that goal, especially in the case of children who are in need of a nurturing and stimulating environment.

FURTHER READING

Adoption Factbook: United States Data Issues, Regulations and Resources. Washington, DC, National Committee for Adoption, 1989.

American Academy of Pediatrics: Initial medical evaluation of an adopted child. Pediatrics 88:642–644, 1991.

American Academy of Pediatrics: Families and adoption: The pediatrician's role in supporting communication. AAP News 8(2):21, 1992.

Barnett ED and Miller LC: International adoption: The pediatrician's role. Contemp Pediatr 13:29–46, 1996.

Hostetter MK, Bennish ML, and Neumann K: Immigration, traveling, and internationally adopted children. American Academy of Pediatrics Update Tape, Vol 17, No. 10, 1997.

Philip J. Landrigan

Chapter 10

Child Labor

Child labor is defined as the paid employment of children younger than 18 years old. According to the U.S. Department of Labor, more than 4 million children and adolescents in the United States are legally employed. Illegal child labor also is widespread. Despite the common belief that the problem of illegal child labor was remedied long ago, it has persisted in the United States and appears to be on the rise. An estimated 1 to 2 million American children are employed under unlawful, often exploitative conditions—working under age, for long hours, at less than minimum wage, or with dangerous machinery. Tens of thousands of children are employed in illegal farm labor. **Four million American children and adolescents work legally. Another 1 to 2 million work under illegal and exploitative conditions.**

THE CURRENT RESURGENCE OF CHILD LABOR

Until the 1980s, child labor outside of agriculture was not a widespread problem in the United States. That picture reflected strong federal enforcement and generally favorable economic conditions. In the past 2 decades, however, a combination of economic and social factors have been responsible for a major increase:

- Increased child poverty
- Massive immigration
- Relaxation in enforcement of federal child labor laws. There are fewer than 1000 federal labor inspectors today for 113 million workers of all ages in the United States.

Sweatshops have become a particular concern. Data from the U.S. Department of Labor and the Government Accounting Office document the re-emergence of sweatshops in all areas of the United States. A sweatshop is defined as an establishment that routinely and repeatedly violates wage, hour, and child labor laws as well as the laws protecting occupational safety and health. Traditionally, sweatshops have been concentrated in large cities in the garment and meat-packing industries. Increasingly, however, restaurants and grocery stores, many of them in the suburbs, are fulfilling the definition of sweatshops and are employing children under unlawful and dangerous conditions. Much agricultural employment of children, albeit in the open air, takes place also under sweatshop conditions. **In 1997, 42% of high school seniors were employed. They worked an average of 24 hours per week for 25 weeks of the year.**

THE HAZARDS OF CHILD LABOR

Although work can encourage the development of discipline, teach a child the meaning of money, and provide valuable role models, employment during childhood and adolescence carries significant risks. These risks are magnified when employment is illegal or exploitative.

Health Risks

INJURIES. Work-related injuries to children are a significant health problem. In 1993, child and adolescent workers in the United States sustained an estimated 21,620 injuries involving lost workdays. In each of the years between 1992 and 1995, an average of 180 work-related traumatic deaths occurred among children and adolescents. Young farm workers had the largest number of deaths. Workers in jobs that interact with the public, such as retail sales clerks, also had high numbers of fatalities; homicide accounted for over 70% of deaths in these occupations. **Each year, over 20,000 teens are injured at work in the United States. Each year, 180 children and ado-**

lescents die of work-related trauma. Injuries occur 10 times more frequently among children employed illegally.

A recent review of adolescent visits to emergency rooms in Massachusetts found that work accounted for 7% to 13% of all emergency visits for 14- to 17-year-olds and for 14% to 26% of visits among 17-year-olds; the number of adolescent injuries that were work-related exceeded the number related to sports. **Work-related injuries account for 15% to 25% of all visits by adolescents to emergency departments—significantly more than sports injuries. Pediatricians should take a work history in the clinical assessment of every case of traumatic injury in a child or adolescent.**

In the years 1980 to 1987, workers' compensation awards were made to 10,047 children younger than age 18 in New York State for work-related injury—an average of over 1100 per year; 44% of these injuries resulted in some degree of permanent disability. They included lacerations, fractures, burns, scalds, scalpings, amputations, and eye loss. There were 35 deaths (Table 10–1).

CHRONIC ILLNESS. Children are known to experience a variety of toxic and carcinogenic exposures at work. These include formaldehyde and dyes in the garment industry, solvents in paint shops, organophosphate and other pesticides in agricultural work and lawn care, asbestos in building abatement, and benzene in pumping unleaded gasoline. It appears likely that such exposures contribute to later development of cancer and other chronic diseases.

HEALTH RISKS OF AGRICULTURAL LABOR. Rural children are employed extensively in agriculture, both on family farms and commercially. The hazards associated with agricultural work include lacerations, amputations, and crush injuries from farm machinery; blunt trauma from large animals; motor vehicle accidents, especially tractor rollovers; suffocation in grain elevators and silos; and exposures to pesticides. Small physical size and inexperience superimpose additional risks for very young farm workers. **Agriculture is the single most dangerous occupation for working children.**

TABLE 10–1. Injuries to Working Children in New York State

Fractures	Lacerations
Sprains and strains	Thermal burns
Amputations	Chemical burns
Gunshot wounds	Electrocutions

From Belville R, Pollack SH, Godbold JH, and Landrigan PJ: Occupational injuries among working adolescents in New York State. JAMA 269:2754–2759, 1993. Copyright 1993, American Medical Association.

TABLE 10–2. Major Provisions of the Fair Labor Standards Act

- Established standards for minimum wages and overtime pay
- Made record keeping on wages and hours mandatory
- Set limits on the number of hours that children may work
- Prohibited children from working in dangerous occupations (*except* in agriculture)
- Raised the age limit for full-time work to 16 years
- Established the work permit system

DEVELOPMENTAL RISKS. Interference with school performance is a second major hazard of child labor. Employed children risk having too little time for homework and being overtired on school days; teachers of children in areas where preholiday employment is common or where industrial home piece-work is escalating have reported declines in the academic performance of previously adequate students. Work also can increase the exposure of adolescents to drugs and alcohol. Obtaining a work-related history should be part of the evaluation of school difficulties in this age group.

LEGAL CONTEXT

Legislative efforts to control child labor in the United States extend back over 200 years. In 1938, after several unsuccessful attempts, the federal Fair Labor Standards Act was enacted. It remains the major legislation governing child labor in the United States today. This law establishes uniform standards for minimum wage, overtime pay, and

TABLE 10–3. Permitted Working Hours for Minors Under 18 Years of Age in New York State

Age of Minor (Girls and Boys)	Industry or Occupation	Maximum Daily Hours
Minors Attending School When school is in session		
14 and 15	All occupations except farm work, newspaper carrier, and street trades	3 hours on school days 8 hours on other days
16 and 17	All occupations except farm work, newspaper carrier, and street trades	4 hours on days preceding school days (i.e., Mon., Tues., Wed., Thurs.) 8 hours on Fri., Sat., Sun., and holidays
When school is not in session (vacation)		
14 and 15	All occupations except farm work, newspaper carrier, and street trades	8 hours
16 and 17	All occupations except farm work, newspaper carrier, and street trades	8 hours
Minors not Attending School		
16 and 17	All occupations except farm work, newspaper carrier, and street trades	8 hours
	Farm Work	
12 and 13	Hand harvest of berries, fruits, and vegetables	4 hours
14 and older	Any farm work	—
	Newspaper Carriers	
11 to 18	Delivers, or sells and delivers newspapers, shopping papers, or periodicals to homes or business places	4 hours on school days 5 hours on other days
	Street Trades	
14 to 18	Self-employed work in public places selling newspapers or work as a bootblack	4 hours on school days 5 hours on other days

From State of New York, Department of Labor, Division of Labor Standards. Albany, NY, 1992.

maintenance of records on wages and hours for employees of all ages (Table 10–2).

Under the Fair Labor Standards Act, no child younger than age 16 may work during school hours, and a ceiling is set on the number of hours of employment permissible for each school day and each school week (Table 10–3). Employment in any hazardous occupation outside of agriculture is prohibited for anyone younger than age 18. No child under the age of 18 may work in mining, logging, brick and tile manufacture, roofing, or excavating as a helper on a vehicle or on power-driven machinery. Meat processing machinery, delicatessen slicers, and supermarket box crushers are specifically prohibited.

In agriculture, legal restrictions are much less stringent; hazardous work is prohibited only until age 16, and all work on family farms is exempted. According to the law, however, no child younger than age 16 working on a nonfamily farm is allowed to drive a tractor that has an engine over 20 horsepower or to handle or apply category I or II pesticides or herbicides. The differences in legal protection between agricultural and other employment undoubtedly contribute to the high rates of injury and deaths among children working on farms.

Work permits are a central aspect of the administration of the Fair Labor Standards Act. Permits are issued to children by state and local school systems. School authorities may exercise discretion in issuing work permits, based on a student's academic performance. Also, in most states, a physician's signature is required on the work permit certifying that the child is fit for work. **Work-related injuries to children and adolescents should be made legally reportable.**

PREVENTION

Pediatricians are central to efforts to prevent hazardous child labor and to mitigate its harmful consequences. Both in their care for individual children and in their concerted action through the American Academy of Pediatrics, pediatricians are in an excellent position to advocate for working children.

Pediatricians need to recognize that many children and adolescents now work. They need to become knowledgeable about the industries in their area that employ children and adolescents and about the hazards associated with those industries.

When performing pre-employment physical examinations on children and adolescents, physicians should inquire about the type of work intended. If the work is in clear violation of the law or involves toxic or hazardous exposures, the physician should advise against such employment and recommend against issuance of a work permit.

Pediatricians need to bear in mind that every case of traumatic injury to a child or adolescent may be work-related. A brief history of possible occupational exposure needs to be obtained on every injured child. Moreover, pediatricians must note that an injured child may be reluctant to reveal that work was the source of trauma because of fear of job loss, reprimand, or even deportation.

FURTHER READING

Child labor and sweatshops. Congressional Q 6:721–744, 1996.

Centers for Disease Control and Prevention: Work-related injuries associated with child labor—United States, 1993. MMWR 45:464–468, 1996.

Brooks DR, Davis LK, and Gallagher SS: Work-related injuries among Massachusetts children: A study based on emergency department data. Am J Industr Med 24:313–324, 1993. This issue is devoted entirely to articles on child labor.

Belville R, Pollack SH, Godbold JH, and Landrigan PJ: Occupational injuries among working adolescents in New York State. JAMA 269:2754–2759, 1993.

Rivara FP: Fatal and nonfatal farm injuries to children and adolescents in the United States. Pediatrics 76:567–573, 1985.

Stanley I. Fisch
Michael Weitzman

Chapter 11

Immigrant Children

*W*hen a stranger resides with you in your land, you shall not wrong him. The stranger who resides with you shall be to you as one of your citizens; you shall love him as yourself, for you were strangers in the land of Egypt.

Leviticus 19:33–34

We are a nation of immigrants, and we are in the midst of the largest wave of immigration ever experienced in the United States. Immigrants contributed one third of all growth in our population during the past decade, and first- and second-generation immigrant children are the fastest growing segment of the U.S. population less than age 15. Their origins are so diverse that in the school systems of our largest cities (e.g., New York and Los Angeles), more than 100 different languages are spoken.

Immigrant children enter the United States under three defined categories: legal immigration, humanitarian admission (as legally admitted refugees and asylees), or illegal entry (as visa overstayers or undocumented immigrants) (Table 11–1). Most (85%) immigrants residing in the United States are here legally.

The ethnic and racial mixture of immigrants to the United States has changed from the earlier waves of European-dominant immigrants to newer waves originating in Asia, Latin America, and the Caribbean. Most recent immigrant children and their families live in the metropolitan areas of California, Florida, Illinois, New Jersey, New York, and Texas.

All new immigrants have been met with ambivalence about their likely effects on those who came before. Arguments focus on their impact on the economy and on whether immigrants contribute economic benefit or create a drain on public and private resources. The concerns also include threats to health from infectious diseases, such as tuberculosis, leprosy, or the acquired immunodeficiency syndrome, and threats to public order from increased crime. Although most of these concerns are unfounded, immigrant children present special challenges to health professionals who serve them.

HEALTH PROBLEMS OF IMMIGRANT CHILDREN

Health professionals should be aware of the special health problems for which immigrant children are at risk. These include vaccine-preventable diseases, tuberculosis, syphilis, hepatitis B, and parasitic infestations; poor nutritional status; delayed growth and development; poor dental health; and mental health and school problems.

Immigrant children may harbor infectious diseases with which U.S. practitioners are unfamiliar: malaria, amebiasis, schistosomiasis, and other helminthic infections; congenital syphilis, for which foreign-born children are not necessarily screened at birth; hepatitis B, particularly in immigrants from Southeast Asia; and tuberculosis. These must be considered in the differential diagnosis in any unusual disease state of a foreign-born child.

The evaluation and treatment of tuberculosis may be complicated by the administration of the bacille Calmette-Guérin (BCG) vaccine (usually manifested as a scar on the right upper arm) in a child's country of origin. Most infectious disease authorities recommend evaluating and treating a positive purified protein derivative (PPD) test in immigrant children in the same manner as all other children, without reference to the BCG. Contacts should be carefully and thoroughly evaluated.

Dental and nutritional problems among immigrant children can be significant. Their lack of access to care or poor socioeconomic circumstances in the country of origin may cause them to arrive in the United States with failure to thrive and rampant dental caries. Similar problems of lack of access to care and poverty may allow these ills to continue, unless health professionals make special efforts to overcome barriers to care.

One important barrier to care is limited proficiency in the English language. "Linguistically isolated households" were identified for the first time in the census of 1990. These are households in which no one older than age 12 speaks English; 4% of U.S. households overall; 30% of Asian language households; and 23% of Hispanic households are linguistically isolated. In five states,

TABLE 11–1. Immigration Terms

Asylee: a noncitizen in the United States (U.S.) or at a port of entry who is unable or unwilling to return to his or her country of nationality or to seek the protection of that country because of persecution or a well-founded fear of persecution

First-generation immigrant: an immigrant to the U.S. who has not been preceded by his or her parents or other family members

Humanitarian admission: the process by which immigrants are admitted to the U.S. for humanitarian reasons, such as suffering human rights abuses in the country of origin; usually involves asylees and refugees

Illegal immigrant: an immigrant who enters the U.S. illegally (i.e., without an invitation) or without inspection, or who enters legally (as a visitor, student, or temporary employee) but then fails to leave when his or her visa expires (see visa overstayer); also called undocumented immigrant

Immigrant children, children of immigrants: individuals from birth to age 18 who come to the U.S. with their parents or other family members, and U.S.-born children of parents who emigrated to the U.S. before those children were born

Legal immigrant: an immigrant who enters the U.S. as a legal permanent resident and who, after 5 years of continuous residence, is eligible to apply for citizenship

LEP: limited English proficiency, used to describe the linguistic ability of students who have difficulty reading, writing, speaking, and/or understanding English

Refugee: any person outside his or her country of nationality who is unable or unwilling to return to that country because of persecution or a well-founded fear of persecution (persecution or the fear of persecution may be based on the person's race, religion, nationality, membership in a particular social group, or political opinion); refugees are exempt from numerical limitation and eligible to adjust to lawful permanent status after 1 year of continuous presence in the U.S.

Second-generation immigrant: the U.S.-born child of a first-generation immigrant; as a U.S. citizen, eligible to receive certain benefits on the same basis as citizens

Undocumented immigrant: see illegal immigrant

Visa overstayer: a noncitizen who enters the U.S. on a visa that allows him or her to stay for a limited period of time, then overstays that limit; considered an undocumented, or illegal, immigrant

From Immigration and Naturalization Service, U.S. Department of Justice, 1994.

more than 20% of school-age children do not speak English at home. This has significant implications for physicians, teachers, and others who serve these families, including difficulties in understanding and communicating basic concerns and instructions, and possibly infringements on rights to privacy, confidentiality, and informed consent when translators must be used.

SPECIAL PROBLEMS OF INTERNATIONAL ADOPTEES AND REFUGEES

International adoptees have increased in recent years, to a current rate of 8000 per year. These children originate largely from Korea and South America but have included children from Romania, Russia, and the Balkans in recent years. Studies of these children have found that more than 50% have at least one important health problem on arrival; that 75% of these problems are infectious diseases such as tuberculosis, hepatitis B, and helminthic infections; and that as many as 80% of these problems may not be evident by history and physical examination and thus require laboratory screening for identification.

International adoptees should have an immunization update, serology for syphilis, hepatitis B surface antigen and antibody, and a PPD. If the PPD is negative, it should be repeated in 3 to

4 months. Consensus regarding the need for an assessment of stool for ova and parasites is less clear. Routine screening for human immunodeficiency virus or cytomegalovirus is not indicated.

Some refugees have been catastrophically uprooted, fleeing persecution or feared persecution. Many of these children and families have experienced terrible losses and witnessed atrocities. Health screening for these children before entry into the United States is rigorous, and many need continuing health supervision and mental health and social services.

Clinicians should be aware of and attentive to the unique stresses that immigration places on child and family adaptation and functioning. History taking from the family should include questions about the language spoken at home and attitudes toward the parents' and child's use of English; food habits; health practices, folk remedies, and understanding and perception of illness and use of health care services and medications; family structure and roles; life stresses, including separation from support systems; disparity between social, professional, and economic status in the country of origin and the United States; ongoing depression, grief, or anxiety resulting from traumatic events in the country of origin; and future hopes and plans.

Essentials of care for immigrant children include an awareness of the child and family's culture and health beliefs and the avoidance of

culturally offensive practices. The office staff should be familiar with the child and family's names and forms of address. Office staff can be instrumental in making timely referrals to appropriate community resources and making interpretative services available when needed. Health professionals should tolerate differences in attitudes and approaches to child rearing, respecting different cultures and traditions, but educating on safety and health to complement existing beliefs and practices rather than to supplant them.

FURTHER READING

Advisory Committee for the Elimination of Tuberculosis: Tuberculosis among foreign-born persons entering the United States: Recommendations of the Advisory Committee for the Elimination of Tuberculosis. MMWR 39:1–21, 1990.

American Academy of Pediatrics, Committee on Community Health Services: Health care for children of immigrant families. Pediatrics 100:153–156, 1977.

American Academy of Pediatrics, Committee on Infectious Diseases: Active and passive immunization: Refugees. *In* Peter G (ed): Report of the Committee on Infectious Diseases, 23rd ed. Elk Grove Village, IL AAP 1994, pp 66–67.

American Academy of Pediatrics, Committee on Infectious Diseases: Medical evaluation of internationally adopted children. *In* Peter G (ed): Report of the Committee on Infectious Diseases, 23rd ed. Elk Grove Village, IL, AAP, 1994, pp 111–114.

Emanuel B, Aronson N, and Shulman S: Malaria in children in Chicago. Pediatrics 92:83–85, 1993.

Hernandez DJ and Charney E (eds): National Research Council, Institute of Medicine. From Generation to Generation: The Health and Well-being of Children in Immigrant Families. Washington, DC, National Academy Press, 1998.

Hostetter MK, Iverson S, Thomas W, et al.: Medical evaluation of internationally adopted children. N Engl J Med 325:479–485, 1991.

Institute of Medicine, Board on Children, Youth, and Families: Immigrant children and their families: Issues for research and policy. The Future of Children 5(2):72–89, Summer-Fall 1995.

Iseman MD and Starke J: Immigrants and tuberculosis control. N Engl J Med 332:1094–1095, 1995.

Lequerica M: Stress in immigrant families with handicapped children: A child advocacy approach. Am J Orthopsychiatry 63:545–552, 1993.

Wolfe MS: Tropical diseases in immigrants and internationally adopted children. Med Clin North Am 78:1463–1480, 1992.

RESOURCES

National Conference of State Legislatures maintains a web site with current information about federal and state activities pertaining to immigrants: http://www.ncsl.org/statefed.

National Immigration Law Center actively monitors changes in federal and state laws and regulations affecting immigrants. Address: 1102 S. Crenshaw Blvd #101, Los Angeles, CA 90019; phone: 213-938-6452.

Resources for Cross-Cultural Health Care is a clearinghouse for information on how language and culture impact on the use and perception of health care services. Address: 8915 Sudbury Road, Silver Spring, MD 20901; phone: 301-588-6051; web site: http://www.milcom.com/diversityrx.

The Parent Network for the Post-Institutionalized Child provides information and publishes a newsletter about the problems of children adopted from hospitals, orphanages, institutions, or the streets of economically deprived countries. Address: PO Box 613, Meadow Lands, PA 15347; phone: 412-222-1766.

PART D

COMMUNITY FACTORS

Paul H. Wise

Chapter 12

Poverty and Racism

UNDERSTANDING POVERTY AND RACISM

Poverty and race are the most important general determinants of child health and survival in American society. The exploration of how race and poverty influence child health is best begun by examining what these terms mean. Poverty is defined most commonly as a measure of subsistence—that level of resources that permits the maintenance of physical efficiency. An example of this absolute definition of poverty is the official "poverty line" for the United States, in which calculation of subsistence (roughly three times the amount needed for a basic family diet) changes only in response to changes in food prices. Such absolute definitions have no direct relationship to the distribution of wealth in society. Alternatively, some have proposed definitions of poverty based on the concept of relative deprivation. Poverty in this schema implies a level of resources so inadequate that participation in expected, customary, community, or societal activities is not possible. Although more difficult to use at a policy level, this relativist concept recognizes that beyond subsistence, poverty can threaten health by distorting human interactions and precluding participation in even the most fundamental of societal activities.

For the purposes of understanding its influences on health, **racism is defined as a system of domination in which harmful or degrading beliefs and actions are linked to membership in a perceived racial group.** This definition stresses the social nature of race and reflects the mainstream view of population biologists and anthropologists that long has discounted any biologic basis for racial distinctions. Although selected race-related genetic disorders exist, the primary influence of race operates through the maldistribution of societal resources, including wealth and health care services. Therefore, racial differences in child health outcomes should be seen as highly interactive with issues of poverty.

The social meaning of race, however, is not confined to poverty alone. For virtually all causes of child death, racial differences in mortality persist even after income is controlled. This is due primarily to social factors, including racism, that in American society are related more closely to race than to income. Not only can the alienation and daily indignities that accompany racism enhance stress-related factors of risk, but also subtle differences in provider decisionmaking can create racial disparities in the use of crucial medical procedures and effective new therapies.

SOCIAL DISPARITIES IN MORTALITY AND MORBIDITY

The influences of race and poverty can be viewed as increasing the likelihood of poor health through two broadly defined mechanisms: the enhancement of risk for poor health and the reduction of access to effective interventions. Elevated risk can affect health by increasing the probability that an illness or traumatic event will occur and by increasing the severity with which the illness or injury affects the child. When a capacity to alter the impact of risk exists, disparities in access to this capacity can create inequities in outcomes. The interaction of elevated risk and reduced access is manifested in a variety of health conditions and defines, in tragic terms, the clinical expression of poverty and racial discrimination.

From birth, poor children are at higher risk of death than the nonpoor, although the dimensions of this disparity and the implications for clinical intervention vary considerably by age and cause of death. Infant mortality has long been associated with race and social class. Social factors elevate infant mortality primarily by increasing the risk of premature birth and, in some settings, by reducing access to intensive perinatal care, thereby increasing the mortality rate of premature newborns once they are born.

Because the occurrence of life-threatening trauma is so deeply linked to the activities of daily life, the adequacy of social conditions plays an important role in shaping childhood patterns of injury, the most common cause of death in childhood. The risks associated with inadequate housing and parental cigarette use as well as a reduced use of smoke detectors have created sharp social disparities in childhood fire mortality. Motor vehicle occupant mortality tends to be higher among children living in poverty, although this may not be the case in certain urban environments where poor children may have less exposure to riding in cars. Because poor neighborhoods often are located in seriously congested inner city areas, the risk of pedestrian injury to children in this setting is likely to be elevated substantially. In some urban communities, homicide is the leading cause of injury-related mortality among children from birth through adolescence.

Although preventable death may be the ultimate expression of poverty and race, a variety of emotional, developmental, and health problems also may affect poor children negatively. They are, for example, at increased risk for problems of cognitive and behavioral development, particularly when poverty is prolonged. When low social status is combined with biologic impairment, developmental and health outcomes may be particularly compromised. This is an important consideration because poor children suffer from high rates of serious chronic conditions, including the sequelae of premature birth, hearing loss, visual impairment (particularly due to reduced levels of corrective therapy), obesity, and the burden of asthma.

THE ROLE OF THE CLINICIAN

A socially diverse patient population presents child health clinicians with a challenging array of professional and personal responsibilities. First among these is the provision of clinical care of high quality. The central importance of clinical health care services stems from the many capabilities of clinical science coupled with the fundamental premise that all those in need deserve medical care given with compassion and respect for the patient's dignity. It is essential, therefore, that clinicians examine their own prejudices and skills in interacting with persons of diverse social backgrounds. Of particular interest is the completeness with which standard clinical protocols are followed and new and effective interventions and therapies are used. Beyond clinician sensitivities and decision making, however, the assurance of high quality care for all social groups must include examination of the organization and performance of the system of care within which the clinician practices. Office hours should be available to parents who work during the day. Mechanisms to overcome inadequate insurance coverage should be established by all practices to ensure access to care. Language capabilities should conform to those prevalent in local communities. Care should be exercised in selecting and training appointment, office, financial, and other nonclinical personnel, as they may shape a family's experience with the health care system.

Beyond direct care, clinicians can play an important role in fashioning a range of community public services and programs to meet local needs. Clinicians have served as local advocates, providing the technical expertise and professional legitimacy to help build effective community-based programs. Clinicians also have helped evaluate and disseminate the experiences of local programs and initiatives that can be adapted and used in other community settings.

A third arena of clinician capability lies in addressing the fundamental issues of poverty and racism in American society directly. The public deliberation of these issues and the public policies that have been developed to confront them require the expertise, political strength, and humane commitment of all those who care for children. Because social policies concerned with race and social stratification are likely to be the focus of continued public debate and legislative revision for years to come, it is essential that this often fractious public discourse be guided by the insights and experience of those who witness the clinical expression of poverty and racism in the daily lives of children.

FURTHER READING

Finkelstein JA, Brown RW, Schneider LC, et al.: Quality of care for preschool children with asthma: The role of social factors and practice setting. Pediatrics 95:389–394, 1995.

Gould SJ: The Mismeasure of Man. New York, WW Norton, 1981.

Greenberg J and Zuckerman B: State health care reform in Massachusetts. Health Affairs 16:188–193, 1997.

Kreiger N, Rowley DL, Herman, AA, et al.: Racism, sexism, and social class: Implications for the study of health, disease, and well-being. Am J Prev Med 9 (Suppl): 82–123, 1993.

Lewit EM: Child indicators: Child poverty. The Future of Children 3:176–182, 1993.

National Center for Health Statistics: Health—United States, 1995. Hyattsville, MD, Public Health Service, 1996.

Parker S, Greet S, and Zuckerman B: Double jeopardy: The impact of poverty on early child development. Pediatr Clin North Am 35:1227–1240, 1988.

Wise PH: Confronting racial disparities in infant mortality: Reconciling science and politics. Am J Prev Med 9 (Suppl): 7–16, 1993.

Chapter *13*

Environment

Stanley J. Schaffer
James R. Campbell

Childhood Lead Exposure

EFFECTS OF LEAD

Lead has been known for many years to have adverse health effects. Table 13–1 lists some of these effects and the blood lead levels at which they may occur. Most recent research has focused on the neurocognitive effects of lead exposure. Longitudinal studies have reported inverse associations between blood lead levels in toddlers and intelligence measurements at school age. These and multiple other studies led to the National Academy of Science to conclude that **"[i]n children,**

blood lead concentrations around 10 µg/dL are associated with disturbances in early . . . mental growth and in later intellectual functioning and academic achievement."

Over the years, researchers have ascribed adverse physiologic or neurocognitive effects to progressively lower blood lead levels. As a result, the Centers for Disease Control and Prevention (CDC) has repeatedly lowered the threshold blood lead level considered elevated (Table 13–2). Since 1991, the CDC has specified 10 µg/dL as the threshold blood lead level of concern.

LEAD SCREENING

Beginning in 1991, the CDC recommended universal screening of children under the age of 6. The CDC also recommended that risk assessment be performed at every regular office visit using a set of standard questions to determine the child's risk of lead exposure. Children whose parents respond negatively to all questions are considered to be at low risk for lead exposure; a positive response to any question places the child in the high-risk category. The 1991 guidelines suggested that low-risk children be screened at ages 12 months and 24 months, whereas high-risk children

TABLE 13–1. Threshold Blood Lead Levels Above Which Adverse Effects May Occur

Blood Lead Level	Toxic Effect
≥10 µg/dL	Decreased IQ
	Decreased hearing acuity
	Decreased growth
≥20 µg/dL	Decreased nerve conduction velocity
≥30 µg/dL	Decreased vitamin D metabolism
≥40 µg/dL	Decreased hemoglobin synthesis
≥90 µg/dL	Nephropathy
	Encephalopathy

Adapted from Centers for Disease Control: Preventing Lead Poisoning in Young Children. Atlanta, US Department of Health and Human Services, 1991.

TABLE 13–2. Blood Lead Levels Considered Elevated by the Centers for Disease Control

Years	Blood Lead Level
Prior to 1971	$\geq$60 µg/dL
1971–1975	$\geq$40 µg/dL
1975–1985	$\geq$30 µg/dL
1985–1991	$\geq$25 µg/dL
1991–present	$\geq$10 µg/dL

Adapted from Schaffer SJ, Campbell JR: The new CDC and AAP lead poisoning prevention recommendations: Consensus versus controversy. Pediatr Ann 23:592–599, 1994.

should be screened more frequently. A blood lead level is the preferred screening test owing to the insensitivity of the erythrocyte protoporphyrin level to diagnose blood lead levels in the 10 to 25 µg/dL range. Blood obtained by fingerstick phlebotomy may be contaminated by lead on the skin surface; thus a fingerstick blood lead level $\geq$15 µg/dL requires venous confirmation. Contamination can be minimized by adequate cleaning of the skin.

Future Directions of Screening Efforts

Studies report that the 1991 CDC risk-assessment questionnaire has a poor specificity while having a sensitivity for identifying children with blood lead levels $\geq$10 µg/dL and $\geq$15 µg/dL of about 70% and 85%, respectively. However, community-specific questionnaires, which inquire about risk factors common to a particular community, can have higher sensitivities. For example, a public clinic in Santa Clara County, California, which serves a Mexican-American population at risk for lead exposure resulting from the use of ceramic containers, improved the sensitivity of the risk assessment from 30% to 90% when questions regarding ceramics were included in a revised questionnaire. In 1997, the CDC revised the risk-assessment questionnaire to simplify it and make it more community-specific (Table 13–3). **Clinicians should be aware of risk factors specific to the population they serve and inquire about such factors when performing risk assessment.**

Epidemiologic studies report that the high prevalence of elevated blood lead levels documented in the late 1970s has dramatically decreased over the past 2 decades. The Second National Health and Nutrition Examination Survey (NHANES II) survey, conducted from 1976 to 1980, found that 88.2% of children aged 1 to 5 years had blood lead levels $\geq$10 µg/dL. In contrast, the NHANES III survey (Part 2), conducted from 1991 to 1994, found that only 4.4% of children aged 1 to 5 years

had blood lead levels $\geq$10 µg/dL. In response, **the CDC has revised their 1991 guidelines so as to allow targeted screening of high-risk children instead of universal screening in populations in which the prevalence of blood lead levels $\geq$10 µg/dL is below 12% or less than 27% of housing was built before 1950.** In practices having a higher prevalence of children with elevated blood lead levels or a higher concentration of children living in pre-1950 housing, universal screening continues to be recommended. Candidates for individual screening include

- All 1- and 2-year-olds in areas where more than 12% have blood lead levels of 10 µg/dL or higher or where more than 27% of homes were built before 1950
- Any child living in pre-1950 housing
- Children in low-income families (those whose families participate in the Special Supplemental Nutrition Program for Women, Infants, and Children [WIC] or are insured by Medicaid)
- Children in certain minority groups
- Children whose parents respond "yes" or "don't know" to questions about living in a pre-1950 house or regularly visiting a pre-1978 house that is in poor repair or is being or recently was renovated; or who respond "yes" or "don't know" to other questions pertaining to locally specific exposures.

MANAGEMENT OF ELEVATED BLOOD LEAD LEVELS

The objective in the management of children who have blood lead levels of 10 to 19 µg/dL is

TABLE 13–3. The 1997 CDC Lead Exposure Personal-Risk Questionnaire

1. Does your child live in or regularly visit a house that was built before 1950? This question could apply to a home child care center or the home of a babysitter or relative.
2. Does your child live in or regularly visit a house built before 1978 that is being or has recently been renovated or remodeled (within the last 6 months)?
3. Other questions relating to applicable individual or locally specific exposures, such as
   - Personal or family history of lead poisoning
   - Occupational, industrial, or hobby exposures to lead
   - Other sources of lead exposure
   - Cultural exposures to lead
   - Poverty
   - Predisposing behavior
   - Associated medical problems

Adapted from Centers for Disease Control and Prevention: Screening Young Children for Lead Poisoning: Guidance for State and Local Public Health Officials. Draft. Atlanta, US Department of Health and Human Services, 1997.

secondary prevention, that is, the early detection and implementation of interventions to prevent the sequelae of higher blood lead levels. Children with blood lead levels ≥20 µg/dL require frequent retesting, an environmental investigation, and more intensive management which, depending on the blood lead level, may include the provision of appropriate social services and medical treatment.

Dietary Interventions

Less lead is absorbed in the gastrointestinal tract of individuals who are replete in iron and calcium than in individuals who are iron- or calcium-deficient. Therefore (1) children with elevated blood lead levels should be tested for iron deficiency (see *Laboratory Testing*); (2) parents should be advised to provide foods that are rich in calcium and iron; and (3) children should be offered frequent, small snacks.

Dust Control

Toddlers expose themselves to lead by getting their hands dirty with lead-contaminated dust or dirt, followed by ingestion of the lead through normal hand-to-mouth behavior. For children with blood lead levels of 30 to 49 µg/dL, dust-control measures along with lead-based paint abatement are more effective in reducing blood lead levels than is lead-based paint abatement alone. Therefore, parents of children who have blood lead levels ≥15 µg/dL should be advised regularly to wet-mop floors and wet-wipe window sills with phosphated detergents to decrease levels of household dust and thus limit lead exposure.

Medical Evaluation

Children who have blood lead levels ≥20 µg/ dL confirmed by venipuncture should undergo a thorough medical evaluation. The medical provider should inquire about (a) the presence of symptoms attributable to lead exposure; (b) mouthing activities and pica; (c) previous blood lead levels; (d) nutritional status; (e) environmental history regarding the child's primary residence and other secondary sites (e.g., child care center); (f) occupational and hobby history of family members; (g) other sources of lead such as nonpharmaceutical medications; and (h) developmental history, with attention to language development. A physical examination should focus on neurologic and psychosocial/language development. Addi-

tionally, a home inspection is recommended to identify sources of lead exposure.

Advice for Parents on Deleading

Lead-based paint is the major source of lead among most children with blood lead levels ≥20 µg/dL. Abatement is the primary treatment for such children. Unfortunately, improperly performed abatement can also cause an elevation in blood lead levels. This occurs, for example, when dust is created by sanding or grinding surfaces containing lead-based paint, and children are then exposed through inhalation or ingestion. Parents should be advised (a) to have lead-based paint violations abated by a properly licensed contractor or with the close supervision of public health officials; (b) to relocate children and pregnant women to another site while the abatement is being conducted; and (c) to conduct a thorough cleanup of dust before allowing children to reinhabit the home.

Laboratory Testing

Iron deficiency is common among children who have elevated blood lead levels. Children who have blood lead levels ≥20 µg/dL should be tested for iron deficiency. Because anemia is not present in the early stages of iron deficiency, a ferritin level should be drawn or the iron saturation should be determined. Ferritin, a storage protein for medullary iron, is diagnostic for iron deficiency at levels ≤12 µg/L. An iron saturation (the ratio of the serum iron to the total iron-binding capacity) below 20% is also generally diagnostic of iron deficiency. An erythrocyte protoporphyrin level may be useful during follow-up to determine whether re-exposure has occurred (see Chelation).

PHARMACOLOGIC TREATMENT

Challenge Test

The calcium disodium edetate ($CaNa_2EDTA$) challenge test should be considered for children who have blood lead levels between 25 and 44 µg/dL. The test identifies children who will have an adequate lead diuresis when administered $CaNa_2EDTA$. Children are administered a single dose of 500 mg/m² of $CaNa_2EDTA$ followed by an 8-hour urine collection; the urine is subsequently assayed for total lead excretion. A $CaNa_2EDTA$

challenge test is considered positive, indicating that chelation would be beneficial, if the total urine lead (in micrograms) to CaNa$_2$EDTA administered (in milligrams) ratio is ≥ 0.6.

Chelation

Chelation, the use of pharmacologic agents to increase lead diuresis, is recommended for children who have venous blood lead levels ≥ 45 μg/dL or who have venous blood lead levels of 25 to 44 μg/dL and a positive CaNa$_2$EDTA challenge test. Venous lead and erythrocyte protoporphyrin levels should be obtained immediately before chelation to compare to postchelation values. The most commonly used pharmacologic agents for chelation are CaNa$_2$EDTA and succimer.

CaNa$_2$EDTA is administered parenterally at a dose of 1000 mg/m^2 per day for 5 days. Maintenance hydration should be administered during treatment to prevent CaNa$_2$EDTA-related nephrotoxicity. Urine should be monitored for protein and blood.

Succimer (2,3-dimercaptosuccinic acid) is a recently approved oral chelating agent administered at a recommended dose of 10 mg/kg three times a day for 5 days, followed by administration twice a day for an additional 14 days. It should be administered only to children living in lead-safe environments. Succimer has a sulfurous taste and smell and its most common side effects are nausea, emesis, and anorexia. A transient elevation of liver transaminases occurs in about 4% of cases but returns to normal after the medication is discontinued.

Venous blood lead and erythrocyte protoporphyrin levels should be obtained 2 to 4 weeks after chelation with either agent to allow the lead in the bony and soft tissue compartments to equilibrate with the blood compartment. A rising blood lead level or erythrocyte protoporphyrin in comparison with prechelation values suggests re-exposure to lead.

The optimum setting in which to perform chelation largely depends on the individual child's circumstances. **Children should never have continued lead exposure during chelation.** Hospitalization for chelation has some advantages, including assurance of compliance, easy monitoring for side effects, and removal of the child from a lead-contaminated home until abatement is completed; the disadvantages are the expense and inconvenience of hospitalization. In some cases, outpatient chelation may be a viable alternative if performed under close supervision in a lead-safe environment.

FURTHER READING

American Academy of Pediatrics, Committee on Drugs: Treatment guidelines for lead exposure in children. Pediatrics 96:155–160, 1995.

Brody DJ, Pirkle JL, Kramer RA, et al.: Blood lead levels in the US population—Phase I of the Third National Health and Nutrition Examination Survey (NHANES III, 1988 to 1991). JAMA 272:277–283, 1994.

Centers for Disease Control: Preventing Lead Poisoning in Young Children. Atlanta, US Department of Health and Human Services, 1991.

Centers for Disease Control and Prevention: Screening Young Children for Lead Poisoning: Guidance for State and Local Public Health Officials. Draft. Atlanta, US Department of Health and Human Services, 1997.

Harvey B: New lead screening guidelines from the Centers for Disease Control and Prevention: How will they affect pediatricians? Pediatrics 100:384–388, 1997.

National Academy of Science: Measuring Lead Exposure in Infants, Children, and Other Sensitive Populations. Washington, DC, National Academy Press, 1993.

Snyder DC, Mohle-Boetani JC, Palla B, and Fenstersheib M: Development of a population-specific risk assessment to predict elevated blood lead levels in Santa Clara County, California. Pediatrics 96:643–648, 1995.

C. Andrew Aligne

Children and Tobacco

"Tobacco" and "children" are two words that should never go together. Nevertheless, the exposure of fetuses, infants, and young children to tobacco smoke pollution remains rampant, and the nation's adolescents continue to join the ranks of nicotine addicts as if it were a "cool" thing to do. Over 25% of infants are born to smoking mothers; 42% of children are exposed to tobacco smoke *regularly*, and the proportion of children living in a household that has at least one adult smoker is well over 50%. Thirty-five percent of high school seniors are smokers, and smoking initiation rates among teens have been *increasing* during the past decade. If current trends continue, we can expect to see a rise in the number of today's children who will become victims of smoking-induced diseases such as lung cancer, heart attacks, and stroke. Moreover, there will be more smoking young parents and a resulting increase in the already significant disease burden associated with childhood passive smoking.

Tobacco smoke is a poisonous mixture of more than 4000 substances, including known carcinogens and toxins such as benzene and carbon monoxide. The literature on the hazards of both active and passive smoking is vast. The link between active smoking and adult disease is perhaps the most thoroughly investigated disease association in history. Similarly, the overwhelming evidence that passive smoking is a cause of death, disease, and disability in children comes from many types of studies, performed over many years, in nations all over the world. A recent review concluded that "the fact that children's health is at risk because of passive smoking is unquestionable." Despite its public denials, even the tobacco industry's own research shows that active and passive smoking are harmful.

EFFECTS OF TOBACCO EXPOSURE

The harmful effects of tobacco begin at the earliest ages. Cigarette smoking is the single most powerful determinant of poor fetal growth in the developed world; it is a much bigger problem than alcohol, cocaine, and all other drugs combined. Some authorities even speak of "fetal tobacco syndrome." Fetuses do not inhale smoke, but they are exposed to tobacco components that cross the placenta, and they are harmed by the effects of smoking on maternal physiology. Maternal smoking during pregnancy is associated with increased risk of fetal loss, prematurity, low birth weight, and perinatal death. Passive smoking also is a significant underlying risk factor for deaths caused by the sudden infant death syndrome, respiratory syncytial virus–induced bronchiolitis, asthma, and fire-related injuries. As a result, **it has been estimated that parental smoking kills more young children than motor vehicle crashes, poisonings, drownings, gunshots, bicycle accidents, and all other unintentional injuries combined.**

In addition, passive smoking has been found in various studies to be associated with an increased risk of other pediatric health problems, including cystic fibrosis exacerbations, pneumonia, acute and chronic otitis media, difficulty with breastfeeding (tobacco components are transmitted via breast milk), allergic rhinitis, atopic eczema, skin infections, cough, excess phlegm, irritation of the eye, nose, and throat, tonsillitis, chest pain, colds, sinusitis, reduced lung function, decrease in linear growth of 1 to 2 cm, cataracts, colic, and febrile seizures. Even minor ailments lead to

missed school days and to the child's feeling unwell when at school, perhaps contributing to the findings that children of smokers have lower scores on intelligence tests and are more likely to fail a grade in school. Moreover, they have an increased risk of behavior problems such as decreased attention span, hyperactivity, and aggressiveness.

Preliminary data suggest that prenatal and childhood exposure may have health effects not manifested until adulthood, such as cardiovascular disease and lung cancer. Furthermore, as part of a vicious cycle affecting future generations, parental smoking increases the risk that a child will become an adult smoker. Almost all smokers start the habit before adulthood, so that (adult) smoking is, in fact, a *pediatric* disease. The peak age of onset is 12 to 16 years, with the majority of smokers starting by age 14 and almost all by age 20. Thus, delaying initiation is probably equivalent to prevention of smoking.

SMOKING PREVENTION AND CESSATION

Primary pediatric clinicians are the only clinicians who routinely come into contact with nonsmokers at high risk of becoming smokers (i.e., preadolescents); thus, they are in the best position of anyone in the health care community to try to prevent smoking. They also may be the only health care professionals in routine contact with parents of young children, because young men and women rarely visit physicians for checkups. Thus, because of their regular contact with young children and their families, pediatricians and other pediatric clinicians have the opportunity and responsibility to intervene against both active and passive smoking.

The first step to reduce smoking is to simply ask about it. Unfortunately, most pediatricians are not doing this: Only 11% in a recent study routinely recorded smoking information on charts. There are numerous explanations for this failure to identify parents or adolescents who smoke. Many physicians have the impression that smokers do not welcome such questioning, that it is not the pediatrician's responsibility to discuss the parents' behavior, that there is no time for discussing smoking, and that there is nothing to offer if someone does say that he or she wants to quit. However, **studies of parental attitudes reveal that 90% of smoking parents hope to quit someday, and many not only welcome but expect pediatricians to discuss passive smoking.** Because of its potentially devastating effects, to-

TABLE 13–4. Correcting Adolescents' False Beliefs About Cigarettes

Myths	Truths
"Most people smoke."	Only one of three adults smokes.
"Successful people smoke."	People who have a college education are more unlikely to smoke.
"Glamorous people such as movie stars smoke."	Tobacco companies pay movie companies to put smokers in films.
"Healthy, athletic people smoke."	Smoking reduces athletic performance.
"Thin people smoke."	You can smoke and be fat; you can be thin and not smoke.
"Beautiful people smoke."	Smoking makes you less attractive because of "ashtray breath," stinky clothes, stained teeth, and wrinkles, etc.
"Smoking is a mature thing to do. Adults smoke and they like it."	The vast majority of adult smokers started as kids and would like to quit now.
"Smoking is a cool/rebellious thing to do."	Kids who smoke are suckers. Smoking is an addiction that the cigarette corporations con kids into so they can make money off of them.

bacco use needs to be addressed in anticipatory guidance. A variety of options are available for helping people to quit smoking, and merely suggesting that the smoker set a date for quitting, for example, takes less than a minute. Inquiries should be nonaccusatory. Any discussion of smoking should communicate that it is an addictive behavior harmful to the smoker and those around him or her and that you, the clinician, are offering encouragement and help to stop this habit. Congratulate nonsmokers, including quitters.

Once barriers to asking about smoking are overcome, smoking status should be recorded routinely, similar to a vital sign and in the problem list, starting with the prenatal visit. In addition, certain medical complaints represent "red flags" that should prompt the pediatrician to think of passive smoking. For example, a visit for recurrent otitis or a hospitalization for asthma constitutes an opportunity to reinforce the link between smoking and illness in the child. Preadolescents at highest risk to become smokers are those who are poor, white, female, or having trouble in school and who have relatives or friends who smoke. Another reason to target preadolescent girls for antitobacco interventions is that they are at high risk for acute complications of smoking related to oral contraceptive use and to pregnancy.

Moreover, the ideal solution to the problem of tobacco-related disease both in children and in adults would involve preventing initiation of smoking and focusing on preadolescent girls, because prevention is the best place to break the cycle of both active and passive smoking. **Discussing attitudes about smoking with preteens may reveal incorrect beliefs that can be countered with facts** (Table 13–4). Even brief contact with a pediatrician can have a profound impact on a child's life.

Public health interventions that include public service announcements (billboards, television, radio), increased cigarette taxes, school programs, and increased enforcement of laws restricting the sale of tobacco to minors have been shown to be effective in reducing teen smoking. Recent Food and Drug Administration regulations, as well as pending legislation and lawsuits seeking to restrict the tobacco companies' targeting of minors as new customers, also should help in this regard.* The American Academy of Pediatrics has recommended numerous steps that physicians can take to fight environmental tobacco smoke (ETS). Among these are the following: do not smoke, promote a smoke-free environment in the physician's office and other public places, do not display magazines that advertise tobacco, and support community antismoking programs.

For adolescents who have already started smoking, consider using concrete demonstrations of ill effects of smoking (e.g., measurement of carbon monoxide in expired air, chest radiographs of acute respiratory illness, peak flow) rather than abstract arguments. For adult smokers, try to sympathize rather than blame. Intensive programs organized specifically to help smoking parents of ill children have been used; however, it also is possible to increase quit rates by minimal interventions. **Because it is not uncommon for women to abstain from smoking during pregnancy but then resume the habit after the baby is born, critical times to intervene are at the prenatal visit or directly after a baby's birth.** Have information handy and be ready to refer to cessation programs. Consider recommending a nicotine replacement (gum, patch, or inhaler). Clinicians who wish to increase their skills in smoking cessation counseling can obtain additional information and training from the National Cancer Institute (see Resources at the end of the chapter).

---

*Although this chapter focuses on American children, it should be noted that the tobacco corporations' success in recruiting new smokers has been even more phenomenal in the rest of the world.

Once parents are smoking, if they are unwilling or unable to quit, then efforts must be directed toward reducing exposure of children to ETS. This can be accomplished best by not allowing smoking inside the home or other places where the child spends significant amounts of time (including automobiles); however, this is not easy to do, especially in areas that have harsh winters. The family member who insists on smoking indoors could be obliged to smoke as far away from the child as possible, perhaps going under a kitchen exhaust fan or by an open window; the efficacy of air cleaners that filter out tobacco smoke is under investigation.

Absorption of tobacco smoke by children is a function of the number of cigarettes smoked around the child and the proximity of the smokers; a dose-response relationship has been noted between exposure and health effects. Thus, while it has been found that maternal smoking (as opposed to smoking by fathers and other caretakers) is associated most strongly with pediatric morbidity, it is important to note that the risk of diseases increases with increasing total exposure from all sources (even prenatally).

Cigarette smoking is the number one cause of premature death in adults, yet it is a behavior that almost always starts during childhood. Children are innocent victims of environmental tobacco smoke, which contributes to a variety of health problems, beginning at the youngest ages. Parental smoking is perhaps the major preventable cause of death among infants and young children. Pediatricians and others who care for children must not only treat affected patients but also educate families and support educational, public health, and legal efforts to promote a tobacco-free environment for all children. No opportunity should be missed to prevent smoking-related disease or the initiation of smoking by children.

Noncigarette Forms of Tobacco

Smokeless tobacco comes in a confusingly named variety of forms, including "chewing" or "spit" tobacco, which goes in the mouth (plug, loose leaf, or "moist snuff" packaged in paper pouches that look like tea bags) and "snuff" or "dipping" tobacco, which goes in the nose (dry powder in a tin). The use of these products has nearly tripled in the past 20 years: Nationally, approximately 25% of white male high school students identify themselves as users. Relatively high use also is found among American Indians of both genders, who often start before kindergarten. Baseball players are a small but highly visible demographic group well known for spitting tobacco.

Despite the allure created by calculated advertisements, cultural customs, and celebrity worship, there is no safe form of tobacco. Although snuff and chew are smokeless, they still are delivery vehicles for the addictive substance nicotine, which they contain at even higher doses than in cigarettes. Moreover, smokeless tobacco use is associated with numerous health problems, including stained teeth, bad breath, gum damage, spots in the mouth (oral leukoplakia), and a fourfold increased risk of deadly oral cancers. Use of smokeless tobacco during pregnancy has been associated with increased perinatal mortality. Quitting may be abetted by nicotine replacement or substitution with chewing gum, herbal tea bags, sunflower seeds, or ground mint leaves.

Another noncigarette form of tobacco on the rise is the *cigar*. The sale of premium cigars in the United States has increased almost fourfold in the past 20 years. More than 25% of U.S. high school students have tried cigars. Cigars are less dangerous than cigarettes to the smoker, but those around the smoker are subjected to a more noxious smoke than that of cigarettes, so from the pediatric standpoint, the use of cigars is to be strongly discouraged.

Fortunately, one type of vehicle for tobacco use—the pipe—is becoming extremely rare. If only we could find out what made pipes "uncool" and make sure that happens to cigarettes, we might make progress in reducing smoking among children and youths.

FURTHER READING

Aligne CA and Stoddard JJ: Tobacco and children: An economic evaluation of the medical effects of parental smoking. Arch Pediatr Adolesc Med 151:648–653, 1997.

American Academy of Pediatrics, Committee on Substance Abuse: Tobacco-free environment: An imperative for the health of children and adolescents. Pediatrics 93:866–868, 1994.

Barnes DE, Hanauer P, Slade J, et al.: Environmental tobacco smoke; The Brown and Williamson documents. JAMA 274:248–253, 1995.

Breslow L and Johnson M: California's Proposition 99 on tobacco, and its impact. Annu Rev Public Health 14:585–604, 1993.

Charlton A: Children and passive smoking: A review. J Fam Pract 3:267–277, 1994.

DiFranza JR and Lew LA: Morbidity and mortality in children associated with the use of tobacco products by other people. Pediatrics 97:560–568, 1996.

Epps RP and Manley MW: A physician's guide to preventing tobacco use during childhood and adolescence. Pediatrics 88:140–144, 1991.

Kessler DA, Barnett PS, Witt A, et al.: The legal and scientific basis for FDA's assertion of jurisdiction over cigarettes and smokeless tobacco. JAMA 277:405–409, 1997.

The Smoking Cessation Clinical Practice Guideline Panel and Staff: Clinical practice guideline on smoking cessation. JAMA 275:1270–1280, 1996.

Spangler JG and Salisbury PL: Smokeless tobacco: Epidemiology, health effects and cessation strategies. Am Fam Physician 52:1421–1430, 1995.

RESOURCES

National Cancer Institute. Phone: 1-800-4-CANCER.
American Academy of Pediatrics. Phone: 1-800-433-9016.

American Cancer Society, American Lung Association, American Heart Association. Contact local chapters/coalitions.

Advocacy groups. DOC (Doctors Ought to Care), 5615 Kirby Drive, Ste. 440, Houston, TX 77005; STAT (Stop Teenage Addiction to Tobacco), 511 East Columbus Ave., Springfield, MA 01105.

Websites. There are many excellent resources on the web, featuring information, games, programs, and support groups. The Master Anti-Smoking Page includes links to many sites: www.autonomy.com/smoke.htm

Bruce P. Lanphear

Indoor Pollutants and Toxins

Pollutants and toxins found in residential dwellings are being recognized increasingly as major contributors to children's ill health. **A number of important diseases or conditions are linked to indoor pollutants, including asthma and lead poisoning.** Although less common, other toxins encountered in children's homes, such as pesticides and mercury, can be life threatening. Still other pollutants increase a child's risk of certain diseases in adulthood; exposure to radon or asbestos is associated with the development of lung cancer.

Unfortunately, it often is difficult for pediatricians to recognize and control pollutants and toxins found in and around children's homes. Some of the diseases associated with indoor pollutants typically have a latent period of 20 or more years and, therefore, are not encountered by pediatricians. Moreover, except for lead poisoning, exposures to indoor pollutants cannot be measured routinely in the clinic setting, and there is no pharmacologic therapy that can be administered in the clinic that will reduce exposures to toxins and pollutants. Nevertheless, **parents are increasingly concerned and knowledgeable about environmental hazards and often turn to their pediatricians for information and guidance.** Asbestos, indoor allergens, radon, and electromagnetic fields are discussed in this chapter. Lead poisoning and tobacco smoke exposure are addressed in the previous parts of this chapter.

ASBESTOS

Asbestos (from the Greek "unquenchable") is a generic term for a number of silicate minerals that have a fibrous, crystalline structure. The major types of asbestos used commercially are chrysotile, crocidolite, and tremolite, but chrysotile accounts for over 90% of asbestos used worldwide.

Asbestos has been used in thousands of products because of its high tensile strength and flexibility and its resistance to acidity and high temperatures. Likewise, because it does not evaporate, burn, or react with other chemicals, asbestos is not biodegradable and thus accumulates in the environment.

The development of asbestosis, lung cancer, and malignant mesothelioma, a rare neoplasm of the pleural lining of the lung or gastrointestinal tract, was first described among asbestos-exposed workers during the 1950s. The predominant route of entry was inhalation of dust, with ingestion playing a minor role. Since then, numerous studies have found that families of asbestos-exposed workers are also at risk for both asbestosis and asbestos-associated malignancies, primarily from dust brought to the home on the worker's clothing.

Exposure to asbestos does not lead to acute symptoms; instead, asbestos-related diseases typically develop over 20 or more years. The shortest reported latency period for malignant mesothelioma was observed in an 11-year-old child who was exposed to zeolite, a fibrous mineral found in the soil in certain parts of Turkey. Thus, because of the long latency period and the rare occurrence of malignant mesothelioma among children, the majority of pediatricians need to know only some basic information about how to prevent asbestos exposure.

Today, most exposures to asbestos occur during repair, renovation, or removal of asbestos in public schools or houses that were built before 1975. Common sources of asbestos in the home include ceilings (often described as cottage-cheese ceilings), pipe insulation, boiler coverings, and floor and ceiling tile. Building materials manufactured since 1975 do not contain asbestos. Still, indoor air may become contaminated from fibers released from existing building materials, especially if they are damaged or friable, and **homeowners should be instructed not to repair or**

remove any asbestos-containing materials without professional assistance.

INDOOR ALLERGENS

Asthma, a disease characterized by chronic inflammation of the airways and bronchial hyperreactivity, is a common chronic illness in the United States, affecting over 2.7 million children. It is the leading cause of hospital admissions among children (1.9 million hospital days annually) and accounts for over 10 million clinic and emergency department visits each year.

There is clearly a genetic predisposition to develop asthma, but numerous studies confirm that exposure to allergens or irritants, including pet and cockroach antigens, dust mites, and environmental tobacco smoke, is a risk factor for the development and exacerbation of asthma. Of children who have asthma, it is estimated that 80% to 90% also have an allergic disorder (see Chapter 48). For these children, asthma is a two-stage process. In the first stage, aeroallergen exposure above some threshold (e.g., > 2 μg/gram for settled dust mites and cat antigens and > 8 U/gram for settled cockroach antigen) is thought to cause immunoglobulin E–mediated inhalation sensitization, as measured by skin test reactivity. In the second phase, once sensitization has been established, continued exposure above an as-yet-undefined threshold is thought to cause asthma. Other mediators of asthma, such as viral infections and environmental tobacco smoke, acting separately or in combination with aeroallergens, increase bronchial hyperreactivity and exacerbations of asthma.

There are a number of environmental controls that have been promoted or tested in children who have asthma. Unfortunately, there are no uniform recommendations of proven effectiveness for children who have asthma, although a few studies suggest that controlling certain indoor allergens may be beneficial. For example, improvement in asthma symptoms has been observed consistently with the use of impermeable mattress covers for children who are sensitized to dust mites. There is other evidence that high-efficiency particulate air filters, carpet removal, and reduction in exposure to tobacco smoke may be beneficial for children who have asthma, but with the exception of reducing tobacco smoke exposure, the data are too sparse for any general recommendations.

RADON

Radon, a decay product of radium, is the major source of human exposure to alpha radiation. It is a tasteless, odorless, and colorless gas that produces no acute symptoms. Radon is thought to be responsible for the "wasting" disease of miners, first described in the 16th century, which later was shown to be lung cancer. Currently, the Environmental Protection Agency (EPA) estimates that 14,000 deaths annually (14% of all deaths caused by lung cancer) are due to exposure to indoor radon, second only to tobacco smoke.

Measurement of radon gas is expressed in picocuries per liter (pCi/L), and the EPA has recommended that remedial action be taken to lower the amount of radon in homes and schools if the measured level is 4 pCi/L or greater. For a lifetime exposure to radon at 4 pCi/L, the EPA estimates that the risk of developing lung cancer is 1% to 5%, but the risk is 10 to 20 times greater for cigarette smokers than for nonsmokers. The duration of exposure and the amount of time since initial exposure also are important factors in estimating risk.

Levels of radon exposure vary considerably in the United States, but nearly every state in the country has dwellings that have radon levels above acceptable limits, and 6 million (6%) homes are estimated to have dwellings that have radon levels above 4 pCi/L. Unfortunately, there is no way to predict exposure other than by testing. Testing kits or devices usually can be obtained in local hardware stores. Tests should be done in the lowest level of the house, approximately 20 inches above the floor and away from drafts, high heat, high humidity, and exterior walls. Windows and doors should be shut during testing. If excessive levels are found, simple remediation measures should be considered initially, including reducing the amount of time spent in the area that has levels above the acceptable limit and increasing ventilation. Then, if excess levels persist or if levels are especially high, the family should be instructed to contact a certified contractor.

ELECTROMAGNETIC FIELDS

Because electromagnetic fields surround us, it is not surprising that reports of increased risk of leukemia and brain cancer among children who lived in close proximity to electrical transformers captured the public's attention. Since the earliest study, published in 1979, numerous studies have been conducted. The majority indicate that exposure to electromagnetic fields is not a significant health hazard. In a recent review, the National Research Council concluded, **"The body of evidence . . . has not demonstrated that exposure**

to power-frequency electric and magnetic fields is a human-health hazard."

SUMMARY

Not all residential hazards deserve equal attention. Indeed, because the effects of tobacco smoke, in combination with asbestos or radon, are synergistic and because environmental tobacco smoke is a major cause of asthma and other respiratory diseases, perhaps the greatest contribution clinicians can make is to reduce children's exposure to tobacco smoke and prevent adolescents from starting to smoke tobacco. Pediatricians also need to be cognizant of signs and symptoms associated with other residential hazards, including asthma and lead poisoning, and to recommend, when appropriate, certain measures for asthmatic children who are sensitized to specific allergens, such as cat antigens or dust mites. Despite the increasing recognition of risks associated with residential pollutants and toxins, however, there is too little research available about how to control these hazards.

FURTHER READINGS

American Academy of Pediatrics, Committee on Environmental Hazards: Asbestos exposure in schools. Pediatrics 79:301–305, 1987.

American Academy of Pediatrics, Committee on Environmental Health. Environmental tobacco smoke: A hazard to children. Pediatrics 99:639–642, 1997.

Environmental Health. Report of the 27th Ross Roundtable on Critical Approaches to Common Pediatric Problems. Columbus, OH: Ross Products Division, Abbott Laboratories, 1996.

National Institute for Occupational Safety and Health: Workers Home Contamination Study. Publication No. 95-123. Cincinnati, OH, 1995.

National Research Council: Possible Health Effects of Exposure to Residential Electric and Magnetic Fields. Washington, DC, National Academy Press, 1997.

Pope AM, Patterson R, and Burge H (eds): Indoor Allergens: Assessing and Controlling Adverse Health Effects. Washington, DC, National Academy Press, 1993.

Pope AM and Rall DP (eds): Environmental Medicine: Integrating a Missing Element into Medical Education. Washington, DC, National Academy Press, 1995.

PART E

ROLE OF PEDIATRICIANS, OTHER CHILD HEALTH PROFESSIONALS, AND COMMUNITY ORGANI-ZATIONS

Judith S. Palfrey

Chapter **14**

Beyond the Office Door

As the 20th century draws to a close, pediatrics is at a turning point. On the one hand, economic pressures are pushing pediatricians to limit their practices to a small number of high-volume, biologically oriented interventions. On the other hand, the problems that face children and families demand new kinds of interventions that are multidimensional and address root causes rather than superficial signs and symptoms.

This chapter discusses child health initiatives that combine an appreciation for the complexity of the threats to children's health and safety with community-based approaches and focused interventions. To participate in these interventions, child health clinicians need to open the office door and walk outside. Many of these issues are discussed in detail in the chapters on school-based clinics, the care of children who have chronic conditions, the care of ex-premature children, early intervention, foster care, community organizations, community approaches, and child advocacy, among others.

WHAT'S HAPPENING TO OUR CHILDREN?

That walk in the community will be disconcerting. We will find one fifth of our children

living in poverty with all its attendant health risks and consequences. We will find that the infant mortality rate for our children of color still resembles that of a third world country. We will find that the children whose lives our medical technology has prolonged are struggling in a world that is only partially prepared to fulfill the promises made to them.

We will also encounter a new territory of family life with changing customs and interactions, altered concepts of time and space, and uncharted relationships. Increased ease of travel and electronic communication have simultaneously brought people together and pulled people apart in new and complex ways. The very cars and airplanes that allow people to get together over long distances also allow family members to leave neighborhoods and communities.

The communication revolution has confused our senses. The reality-unreality dimension of television allows us to be "in" the Gulf War. Children see Jackie Chan "pretend" to kill and maim and blow up his enemies. There is little sense of consequence when the same bad guy appears intact in the next episode.

The ability to do more has elevated levels of expectation and created a "busy day, busy people" world with few moments of calm and little space for reflection. Children are part of all the busyness. Their days start earlier and end later. They travel more and at younger and younger ages and interact with more and more people. Young children's experience now includes relationships in child care, with health care clinicians, play groups, and child care mates. School-age children's world is peopled by their classmates, but also by the many characters they encounter through media. Teenagers on the Internet now actually have access to the world.

As families confront these new realities, they expect their physicians to understand their daily life dimensions and to know the answers to questions such as "How do I protect Andrea from the Red Shirt Gang on "M" Street?" or "Can you help us find respite services to care for Susie? We have had no rest for 3 straight months." Another parent may confide: "I am scared to death—my husband and I just found a recipe for LSD downloaded on Sam's laser printer." Stethoscopes and reflex hammers may not be the only equipment we need to protect, to care for, and to cure the children of the new millennium.

HOW CAN WE RESPOND RESPONSIBLY?

To answer the questions families are posing requires the full use of community resources. In some communities, these are well developed and effective; in others they are rudimentary at best. In still others, no one has even acknowledged the need for them. Chapter 69 addresses the coalitions and political action required to establish community responsiveness. The types of services that exist in many (but not all) communities around the United States are delineated in this chapter. Additionally, the Bright Futures approach to child health care (see Chapter 18) is described as one way of involving pediatric practitioners to embrace a multifocal approach to the problems that confront the children and families in our care.

HEALTH AND EDUCATION

Pediatricians and educators have long acknowledged that they work for a common constituency of children. Together, schools and child care clinicians can augment each other's effectiveness. A pediatrician may see a child in the office and diagnose asthma, but it is at home and at school that the regimen of inhalers and pills is carried out.

Currently, there are three major ways that pedia-

tricians and other child health clinicians can interact with schools (see Chapter 74). These are (1) through traditional school health programs, (2) through special education, and (3) through school-based clinics. Each of these arenas is strengthened by the community linkage between health and education.

Traditional School Health Programs

Most schools in the United States have some type of school health program. The auspices, staffing, and extent of services of each program vary from state to state, county to county, and even town to town. The ratio of school nurses to pupils varies tremendously, with the average around 1500:1. School health programs, therefore, depend on the support of local community clinicians for assistance.

In general, traditional school health programs assure that the population of children in their charge have had adequate screenings and appropriate preventive measures (largely immunizations) and are learning about healthy habits for long-term health promotion. Because schools are responsible for all children, it has become traditional for them to be the public watchdogs that monitor children's health at least during the years from kindergarten to age 16—the age when most schools allow children to leave the school system.

Educators complain that they are serving many functions in the community beyond that of education. This is true and increasingly necessary. If there is to be any recourse to the problems of violence among youth, it will need to come through creative interagency interventions such as the ones that have been instituted in the Boston schools. Working with the schools, physicians have helped to establish "conflict resolution" training, which gives youngsters the skills they need to avoid harmful physical interactions while still acknowledging differences of opinion.

School health programs can assist in the care of children who have chronic illnesses. For instance, in Lexington, Kentucky, a CATCH (the American Academy of Pediatrics' Community Access to Child Health program) physician and an elementary school nurse have created "Nebulizer Ninjas" (see Chapter 73). Youngsters who have asthma become adept at their inhaler routines because it is fun to come to the nurse's office and participate in the "Nebulizer Ninja" games. The children work to beat yesterday's "personal best" on their peak flowmeters. Their compliance with medication regimens improves, and their visits to emergency departments decline.

Special Education

As professionals knowledgeable about a child's health and developmental status since birth, pediatricians are in an excellent position to help schools assess and plan for children who have a wide variety of special education needs.

The federal Individuals with Disabilities Education Act (IDEA) entitles all children who have disabilities to a free, appropriate public education. IDEA is composed of two major sections: Part B (school-age children) and Part C (early intervention).

Part B has four key components: identification, evaluation, services, and due process (parental involvement). Pediatricians can participate in each part of the program. Clinical input is increasingly important as schools are taking shortcuts with the identification and evaluation processes. For example, there is a critical need to correct the trend toward overly rapid diagnosis of attention-deficit hyperactivity disorder (ADHD). Re-evaluation by pediatricians should lessen the inappropriate use of both the diagnosis and the quick "fix" of medication. By involving themselves in the community and the schools, physicians can educate school personnel about the complex differential diagnosis that should be considered before settling on ADHD and medication. The possible diagnoses include specific learning disabilities, developmental delay, organizational difficulties, speech and language concerns, and sensory impairment, as well as a host of behavioral problems (e.g., post-traumatic stress disorder) and occasional physical disorders (e.g., hyperthyroidism).

Physicians also can help schools safely place children who have complex medical conditions that depend on technology for their management. Guidelines for the school care of such children have been developed and are in wide use throughout the country (Porter, 1997). Controversy often arises about the financing of these services. It is helpful for physicians to be aware of both the resources available in a given community and the particular financing mechanisms to cover community-based care. In many cases, for instance, Medicaid covers nursing and related services in schools.

Part C is the early intervention component of IDEA. Early intervention services are available to children at "established risk" of developmental delay, at "biologic risk," or at "environmental risk." The early intervention team evaluates the children and generates an Individual Family Service Plan (IFSP) to outline the suggestions for in-home and center-based interventions. Pediatricians provide an important link in early intervention as identifiers of children at risk and as part of the intervention team.

School-Based Clinics

In recent years, the number of school-based clinics (SBCs) has risen meteorically. The first such clinic opened in West Dallas, Texas, in 1970. By 1985, there were 32 SBCs in the United States; in 1996, there were 900. School-based clinics originally were designed to serve high school students who did not have access to other health care services. Although most clinics are still in high schools, junior high and elementary SBCs are beginning to appear.

The services offered in SBCs include sports assessments, employment physicals, health education, human immunodeficiency virus (HIV) prevention, contraceptive counseling, and occasionally, mental health and other services. Physicians in the community often provide backup consultation and 24-hour emergency coverage to these clinics so that the SBCs can function as full-service primary care sites for the youngsters in their care.

JUVENILE JUSTICE AND SOCIAL SERVICES PROGRAMS

Pediatricians can be very helpful to the juvenile justice and social services systems (see Chapter 65, subchapter on Runaways). Young people often become involved in criminal activity (including violence, drug abuse, prostitution) in response to a tangle of life events that has left them unsupported and poorly prepared for life. They turn to gangs for the social interactions that they are missing at home and in the community. In a bizarre way, they feel safer in that "community" than they do thrown out on their own.

The pediatrician's role with juvenile justice and social service organizations for high-risk youth includes the provision of health care and consultation from a developmental perspective. Youngsters who have declared themselves at high risk by one criterion (e.g., criminal activity) are at higher risk for a host of poor health outcomes—sexually transmitted diseases, HIV infection, substance abuse, violence perpetration, being the victim of violence, teen pregnancy, or teen fatherhood.

Multifactorial approaches to health and social needs are expensive and time-consuming but are the most effective. Feeling disenfranchised, the youngsters are unlikely to come to traditional health institutions; thus, the health institutions must come to them through outreach on the street—clinic location near the hangouts or blocks where the youth congregate. Probably, however, **the most important component of the pediatric work is a developmental perspective that acknowledges where the young person is in the life trajectory and helps to put together a support system that provides the educational, vocational, and counseling required for the young person to trust mainstream systems and to operate effectively as a young adult.**

FOSTER CARE AND ADOPTION

Foster care (see Chapter 8) and adoption agencies (see Chapter 9) frequently turn to pediatricians for consultation. Serving as a physician for this population of children can be challenging, but it also offers an opportunity to play a substantial role in securing a better situation for children who have suffered abuse or neglect or whose families simply cannot provide them with appropriate nurture.

Model medical systems for children in foster care have been developed in a number of cities and states. These systems emphasize consistency of health care, use of a medical passport, and timely follow-up and counseling for both the child and foster parents. Often the child has come from exceedingly trying circumstances with resultant problematic behaviors. The pediatric involvement at the beginning can be critical to assuring a developmentally appropriate response to a child's acting-out behavior. Children who have been sexually abused, for instance, behave in overstimulated ways as a cry for help. Referral to a well-trained pediatric psychologist or social worker can help in establishing tailored interventions.

Foster care parents also are called on frequently to care for children who have special health care needs, including congenital anomalies, assistance by medical technology, HIV infection, and so on. Pediatric consultation to the foster care program and to the parents about these conditions eases the burden and establishes useful health care delivery patterns for the families.

EARLY CHILDHOOD PROGRAMS

Two factors generally are said to contribute to the changes in early childhood programming. The first is that more women are entering the workforce, creating a heavier reliance on group child care arrangements. The second is a growing appreciation of the saliency of the early years (birth to age 3) in children's development. A third factor that rarely is discussed but may be increasingly recognized is the single-child family. More boys and girls are growing up as only children. For them, group child care offers the critical socialization provided in multiple-children households by playing with other children and by sharing toys and adult attention.

The child health concerns in group care include health screening for early disease detection and prevention, contagious disease control, immunizations, safety, nutrition, development, and socialization. Most child care and early childhood programs require consultation by a pediatrician in the development of their policies. In addition, pediatric consultation is advisable for infectious disease outbreaks, integration of children who have special health care needs, and expanded developmental intervention. Working with early childhood programs affords great opportunities for clinicians to promote healthy activities for individual children, groups of children, and families.

BRIGHT FUTURES

The challenge facing pediatricians at the turn of the new century is how to integrate the care of individual children and families with the care of children and families in general. Pediatric practice can meet this challenge by making a subtle but definite shift. Pediatricians always have realized that family and community factors shape children's health. The shift that is needed is the recognition that pediatricians can and should enter the area of family and community issues. Not to do so limits the possible interventions and robs the caregiver of valuable resources and allies.

The *Bright Futures National Guidelines for Health Supervision of Infants, Children and Adolescents* (Green, 1995) were developed to aid pediatricians in shifting to what Green terms "contextual pediatrics." The pediatric health team takes the pulse not just of the child but of the home, school, and community (see Chapter 18). The measurements look for both positive and negative contributors that determine the child's current health status and predict his or her future growth, development, and life fulfillment.

The Bright Futures guidelines emphasize a partnership between parents and professionals. Families have the 24-hour-a-day responsibility for their children's health. Preventive or health-promoting interventions will work only if they are incorporated into family and community life. Promoting healthy nutrition for a child is useless if the family's larder is filled with high-fat, high-caloric

TABLE 14–1. Community Service "Allies"

State/local public health MCH programs
American Academy of Pediatrics local chapters
University-based pediatric training programs
Local schools
Neighborhood health centers
Daycare centers
Head Start
Boys Clubs, Big Brother, YMCA, Boy Scouts
Girls Clubs, Big Sister, YWCA, Girl Scouts
Juvenile Justice Authority
Family court
Visiting nurses
Public health nursing
Child advocacy projects
Area Health Education Centers (AHEC's programs)
Job Corps (and other vocational programs)
Churches/synagogues
Fraternal organizations
Industry
Banks
Family groups

From Palfrey JS: Community Child Health: An Action Plan for Today. Westport, CT, Praeger Press, Greenwood Publishing Group, 1994.
MCH, maternal-child health.

snacks and no one in the household eats a balanced diet. Antismoking messages directed at individual teens fall flat if all members of the family smoke and smoking is viewed as a rite of passage into adulthood. The Bright Futures guidelines provide specific family preparation, trigger questions, and anticipatory guidance that involve the child's family in discussion of and decisions related to these health issues.

Bright Futures recognizes that the child health clinician belongs to a larger team that involves other professionals and community members. The contribution of the clinician involves growth, development, and health. This contribution is enhanced by the interaction with child care professionals and social service providers, as well as police, community businesspersons, and city or town officials. In essence, a major message of Bright Futures is that "health promotion is everybody's business." Table 14–1 lists many of the allies with which the pediatrician needs to work in the community.

The attitudinal shifts of the Bright Future's comprehensive vision of child health face an up-

ward climb against the forces that would constrain pediatrics and limit child health concerns to the biologic sphere. However, as the relationships among biology, environment, and lifestyle are becoming defined more clearly, the comprehensive child health approach takes on new meaning.

THE COMMUNITY PEDIATRICIAN AS ADVOCATE

Recognizing these interactions and limitations of the health care system, pediatricians who want to make a difference can become vocal in their communities as advocates and program developers (see Chapter 72). This evolving role for community pediatricians has been recognized by the American Academy of Pediatrics with the creation of the CATCH program. Chapter 73 delineates the many exciting roles that CATCH physicians are playing in the community, beyond the office door.

FURTHER READING

Green M (ed): Bright Futures National Guidelines for Health Supervision of Infants, Children and Adolescents. Arlington, VA, National Center For Education in Maternal and Child Health, 1995.

Haggerty R and Roghmann KJ: Child Health and the Community. New Brunswick, NJ, Transaction Publishers, 1993.

Halfon N and Klee L: Health and development services for children with multiple needs—the child in foster care. Yale Policy Rev 9:71–96, 1991.

National Center for Children in Poverty: Five Million Children: A Statistical Profile on Our Nation's Poorest Young Citizens. New York, School of Public Health, Columbia University, 1990.

Palfrey JS: Community Child Health: An Action Plan for Today. Westport, CT, Praeger Press, Greenwood Publishing Group, 1994.

Palfrey JS, Haynie M, Porter S, et al.: Project School Care: Integrating children assisted by medical technology into educational settings. J School Health 62:50–54, 1992.

Porter S: Children and Youth Assisted by Medical Technology in Educational Settings: Guidelines for Care, 2nd ed. Baltimore, Paul H. Brookes Publishing Co, 1997.

Prothrow Stith D: Deadly Consequences. New York, HarperCollins, 1991.

Simms MD: Foster children and the foster care systems. Curr Probl Pediatr 21:297–321; 345–369, 1991.

United Nations International Children's Emergency Fund: State of The World's Children. Geneva, UNICEF, 1995.

US Department of Health and Human Services: Child Health' 95. Maternal and Child Health Bureau Publication. Bethesda, MD, DHHS, 1995.

Wolfe A (ed): America at Century's End. Berkeley, University of California Press, 1991.

HEALTH PROMOTION AND DISEASE PREVENTION

PART A

PROCESS

David L. Olds   *Chapter 15*

Non-Physician Home Visits

In recent years, support has increased for home-visitation services as a way of augmenting office-based care for pregnant women and parents of young children. In principle, home visitors may contribute to the prevention of health and developmental problems, a reduction in hospital stays, a decrease in government expenditures for health and social services, and parents' effectively coping with the care of children with special needs.

From the standpoint of service provision, home visitors can link families with appropriate services, monitor the health status of vulnerable or sick populations, educate and counsel family members about disease prevention and health promotion, and (depending on their training) provide clinical services. Home visitors may be especially helpful in cases in which periodic visits to the office or health center are either impossible or insufficient to address the child's or family's needs. By reaching out to families that do not use office-based care, home visitors should be able to help families make better use of the formal health and human service system; and by observing conditions in the home, they should be able to gain a better understanding of families' needs and help them more effectively than can office-based personnel. **Empirical support, however, for the efficacy of different types of home-visitation programs is mixed.** In spite of this, they have been promoted widely by a variety of policy advisory groups.

PREVENTION OF MORBIDITY AND MORTALITY

In the early 1990s, both the National Commission to Prevent Infant Mortality and the U.S. Advisory Board on Child Abuse and Neglect advocated an increase in funding for home-visitation services as a means of preventing morbidity and mortality in children. The primary empirical foundation for these recommendations came from a randomized trial that tested a program providing prenatal and early-childhood home visitation by nurses to first-time at-risk mothers in a small, semirural community in central New York State. The advisory groups recommended that two state-level programs (the Hawaii Healthy Start program and the South Carolina Resource Mothers program) be disseminated on a national scale, in spite of their limited similarity to the program that was used as the empirical foundation for their recommendations. The Resource Mothers program focused primarily on pregnant women, while the Healthy Start program identified families in the newborn period thought to be at risk for child abuse or neglect. Both programs employed trained paraprofessionals. As a result of these recommendations, hundreds of home-visitation programs have been developed based on these models, with little empirical support for the particular program models employed.

Evidence from randomized trials of many different types of home-visitation programs has accumulated in recent years and can be used to guide policy and practice in these areas. Although there are very few trials that have directly compared different program components and types, it is possible to glean insight into essential program characteristics by comparing those programs that have produced large and/or broad-based effects and those that have failed to do so. **The evidence indicates that a few home-visitation programs have shown considerable promise in reducing adverse pregnancy outcomes, childhood injury, child abuse and neglect, and families' welfare dependence, but that most tested in randomized trials have failed to affect important aspects of maternal and child health.**

Table 15–1 shows the characteristics of home-visitation programs that have been most successful in improving pregnancy outcomes, reducing injur-

TABLE 15–1. Characteristics of Home-Visitation Programs That Produced the Largest and Most Broad-Based Improvements in Maternal and Child Outcomes

- Provided care to families with greater needs (e.g., low-income, unmarried mothers) and in which mother had had no previous live births
- Employed nurses
- Used a comprehensively designed model that focused on improving pregnancy outcomes, qualities of parental caregiving, and families' economic self-sufficiency
- Used detailed clinical protocols to guide nurses' work
- Began during pregnancy
- Followed up families at least through child's second birthday
- Had frequent home visits (scheduled at least two times per month)

ies, decreasing child abuse and neglect, and promoting family planning and economic self-sufficiency. The first program was studied in the context of a randomized trial conducted in Washington, DC, in the late 1960s and early 1970s. The second was studied in a series of randomized trials conducted in Elmira, New York, beginning in the 1970s and later in Memphis, Tennessee, beginning in the mid-1980s. It is noteworthy that these two programs shared remarkably similar characteristics: both programs employed nurses, both were grounded clinically in the primary care system, both focused on low-income families bearing first children, and both began their work with parents during pregnancy. Moreover, both employed a program model that focused explicitly on improving prenatal health, parent's care of their children, and parents' own economic self-sufficiency. Reviews of other randomized trials of home-visitation programs indicate that having any one of these characteristics by itself is insufficient. The likelihood of program success is increased if programs incorporate all of these characteristics simultaneously.

The greater success of programs that employed nurses is noteworthy in light of the rapid proliferation of programs that employ paraprofessionals and volunteers. In many communities paraprofessionals and volunteers are being employed to help link children and families with needed services and to serve as supports to the family. There are no published studies on the use of volunteers in this capacity. Moreover, the studies that have examined programs that hired trained paraprofessionals from the communities they serve are not promising. We have very little empirical evidence about the efficacy of non-nurse professionals, such as social workers or other visitors with completed college education (such as those with bachelor's degrees in education or child development) who work in similar home-visiting programs.

The absence of effect with paraprofessional visitors may be because the visitors do not have the professional training to deal effectively with the complex situations frequently presented by high-risk families, or it may be because the visitors in such programs have not been given appropriate clinical protocols, training, and supervision to guide them in their work. Research is currently being conducted to understand the reasons that paraprofessional programs have been relatively less successful.

Advocates of paraprofessional and volunteer programs contend that such programs cost less. If we assume that paraprofessional programs in the field are no more successful than those tested in research settings, the net monetary cost to government and society may, in fact, be much greater than well-designed community health nursing programs. Advocates for paraprofessional programs that hire staff from the communities that they serve often reason that these home visitors may be able to empathize more completely with families, and thus form more effective working relationships. To date, there is no evidence to support this position.

The specific outcomes affected by the two most successful home-visitation programs mentioned earlier (Washington, DC; Elmira, New York; and Memphis, Tennessee) are listed in Table 15–2. As this table indicates, these intensive programs of prenatal and early-childhood home visitation by nurses have been successful in improving women's prenatal health-related behaviors and qualities of infant caregiving; reducing child abuse and neglect, injuries, and behavioral problems; and decreasing the rates of subsequent pregnancy and welfare dependence among low-income families. Even when employing experienced, empathic nurses as home visitors, however, additional training, a manageable caseload, and high quality clinical supervision will be necessary to help nurses address successfully the wide range of risk factors that contribute to these adverse health and developmental problems.

REDUCING HOSPITAL STAYS

In addition to preventing problems, **early research indicates that home-visiting nurses can also cut health care costs by helping normal weight as well as very low birth-weight infants be discharged early from the hospital in safe and cost-effective ways.** Similarly, a government report has concluded that technology-dependent children can be provided care at home both safely and less expensively than in the hospital. The use of such arrangements assumes that the child's problems are manageable in the home, that the

TABLE 15–2. Illustrative Outcomes Effected by the Two Most Successful Home-Visitation Programs Examined in Randomized Trials

Outcome	Control	Nurse-Visited
Improvement in prenatal diet (change in % RDA over course of pregnancy)[a]	−0.33	4.14**
Reduction in prenatal cigarette smoking (change in number of cigarettes smoked per day over course of pregnancy)[a]	1.63	−2.54***
Pyelonephritis (%)[a]	3%	0%**
Pregnancy-induced hypertension[b]	20%	13%
Number of verified reports of child abuse and neglect (0–15 yr)[a]	0.54	0.20***
Emergency-department encounters for injuries and ingestions (1–2 yr)[a]	0.34	0.15*
All kinds of health care encounters for injuries and ingestions (0–2 yr)[b]	0.56	0.43*
Days hospitalized with injuries and ingestions (0–2 yr)[b]	0.18	0.04***
Children's self-confidence (exhibited during IQ testing[c] at age 3)	71%	88%*
Children's social confidence (exhibited during IQ testing[c] at age 3)	67%	91%**
Children's intellectual functioning (IQ testing at age 3)	91.2	99.3***
Reported behavioral problems (% with problems, age 6)[c]	79%	54%*
Maternal enrollment in school (during first 3 yr of child's life)[c]	49%	91%***
Paternal job stability (% with no job changes during first 3 yr of child's life)[c]	30%	64%*
Subsequent pregnancy (number of subsequent pregnancies, 0–15 yr)[a]	2.2	1.5*
Welfare dependence (number of months receipt of AFDC, 0–15 yr)[a]	90.3	60.4***
Government expenditures for welfare, child abuse and neglect, and health care (for low-income families, 0–4 yr post partum)[a]	$11,841	$8,343*

[a] Elmira, New York, study (see Olds et al. references).
[b] Memphis, Tennessee, study (see Kitzman et al. reference).
[c] Washington, DC, study (see Gutelius et al. references).
* $P < .05$. **$P < .01$. ***$P < .001$.
AFDC, Aid to Families with Dependent Children; RDA, Recommended Daily Allowances.

home is safe, that the parents demonstrate satisfactory caregiving skills, and that sufficient community services are available to support in-home care. These early studies need to be repeated in the context of managed care today, now that there is ever-increasing pressure to discharge children with chronic illnesses who require technologic support for survival.

HELP WITH CHILDREN WITH DISABILITIES AND CHRONIC ILLNESS

In addition to preventing health and developmental problems and cutting health care costs, there is some evidence from randomized trials that in-home care of children with chronic physical conditions can improve the parents' satisfaction with care and the child's psychologic adjustment and can reduce psychiatric symptoms on the part of the mother.

NEED FOR ADDITIONAL RESEARCH

Numerous additional questions remain to be answered about the efficacy of home-visitor programs. We know relatively little about the extent to which home-visitor programs can effectively serve populations that are at heightened risk because of particular parental characteristics, such as parents' being afflicted with mental illness, or their having neglected or abused their child in the past. Although the evidence suggests that beginning preventive home-visitation programs during pregnancy and serving families in which the mother has had no previous live births increase the likelihood of success, there are no published randomized trials that have systematically compared the relative efficacy of programs as a function of whom they serve and whether prenatal versus postpartum initiation of the service is as important as the evidence suggests. Some communities are now experimenting with teams of home visitors that include both nurses and paraprofessionals. Are there any benefits to such arrangements? In light of an increased emphasis on volunteerism, it is especially important to know how to identify and retain effective volunteers and to understand under what circumstances such volunteers can serve as useful adjuncts to office-based care.

FURTHER READING

Black M, Nair P, Kight C, et al.: Parenting and early development among children of drug-abusing women: Effects of home intervention. Pediatrics 94(4 Pt 1):440, 1994.

Brooten D, Kumar S, Brown LP, et al.: A randomized clinical trial of early hospital discharge and home follow-up of very-low birth-weight infants. N Engl J Med 315:934, 1986.

Combs-Orme T, Reis J, and Ward LD: Effectiveness of home visits by public health nurses in maternal and child health: An empirical review. Public Health Rep 100:490, 1985.

Gutelius M, Kirsch A, MacDonald S, et al.: Promising results from a cognitive stimulation program in infancy: A preliminary report. Clinical Pediatrics 11:585, 1972.

Gutelius M, Kirsch A, MacDonald S, et al.: Controlled study of child health supervision: Behavioral results. Pediatrics 60:294, 1977.

Heins HC, Nance NW, and Ferguson JE: Social support in improving perinatal outcome: The Resource Mothers program. Obstet Gynecol 70:2653, 1987.

Kitzman H, Olds D, Henderson CR, et al.: Effect of prenatal and infancy home visitation by nurses on pregnancy outcomes, childhood injuries, and repeated childbearing: A randomized controlled trial. JAMA 278:644, 1997.

Larner M and Halpern R: Lay home visiting programs: Strengths, tensions, and challenges. Zero to Three: Bulletin of National Center for Clinical Infant Programs 8:1, 1987.

National Commission to Prevent Infant Mortality: Home Visiting: Opening Doors for America's Pregnant Women and Children. Washington, DC, the Commission, 1989.

Olds D, Eckenrode J, Henderson CR, et al.: Long-term effects of home visitation on maternal life course and child abuse and neglect: 15-year follow-up of a randomized trial. JAMA 278:637, 1997.

Olds D, Henderson C, Chamberlin R, and Tatelbaum R: Preventing child abuse and neglect: A randomized trial of nurse home visitation. Pediatrics 78:65, 1986.

Olds D, Henderson C, and Kitzman H: Does prenatal and infancy nurse home visitation have enduring effects on qualities of parental caregiving and child health at 25 to 50 months of life? Pediatrics 93:89, 1994.

Olds D, Henderson C, Phelps C, et al.: Effects of prenatal and infancy nurse home visitation on government spending. Medical Care 31:155, 1993.

Olds D, Henderson C, Tatelbaum R, and Chamberlin R: Improving the delivery of prenatal care and outcomes of pregnancy: A randomized trial of nurse home visitation. Pediatrics 77:16, 1986.

Olds D, Henderson C, Tatelbaum R, and Chamberlin R: Improving the life-course development of socially disadvantaged mothers: A randomized trial of nurse home visitation. Am J Public Health 78:1436, 1988.

Olds D and Kitzman H: Can home-visitation improve the health of women and children at environmental risk? Pediatrics 86:108, 1990.

Olds D and Kitzman H: Review of research on home visiting for pregnant women and parents of young children. The Future of Children 3:53, 1993.

Resnick MB, Eyler FD, Nelson RM, et al.: Developmental intervention for low birth weight infants: Improved early developmental outcome. Pediatrics 80:68, 1987.

Stein REK and Jessop DJ: Does pediatric home care make a difference for children with chronic illness? Findings from the pediatric ambulatory care treatment study. Pediatrics 73:845, 1984.

US Advisory Board on Child Abuse and Neglect: Creating Caring Communities: Blueprint for an Effective Federal Policy on Child Abuse and Neglect. Washington, DC, US Government Printing Office, 1991.

US Congress, Office of Technology Assessment: Technology-Dependent Children: Hospital vs Home Care: A Technical Memorandum. Publication No. OTA-TM-H-38. Washington, DC, US Government Printing Office, 1987.

Yanover MJ, Jones D, and Miller MD: Perinatal care of low-risk mothers and infants. N Engl J Med 294:702, 1976.

Steven R. Poole

Chapter **16**

Pediatric Telephone Care

The telephone has long been an integral part of pediatrics. As much as one fifth of pediatric care has been provided by telephone during the fee-for-service era, and it is likely that the telephone will take on an even greater role in the managed care era. Pediatric telephone care has evolved in several ways during the past decade: (1) increasing delegation of telephone care to non-physicians both during and after office hours; (2) increasing reliance on telephone triage and advice protocols; (3) the consolidation of call groups; (4) the emergence of community-wide after-hours telephone care programs and pediatric call centers; (5) growing recognition of the importance of documentation; and (6) the incorporation of new telephone technologies into office practice. The emergence of managed care and capitation encourages increasing use of the telephone to provide (1) health education regarding self-care and appropriate use of resources; (2) triage to the lowest-cost, most appropriate resource 24 hours a day; (3) ongoing education and follow-up care for chronic illness; (4) routine practice information and communication in an automated fashion; and (5) use of other automated telephone systems that replace staff time on the telephone. Therefore, **the clinician will have to take responsibility for knowing not only how to provide telephone care, but also how to delegate, monitor, supervise, and evaluate other individuals and programs as they provide telephone care on his or her behalf.** The pediatrician will need to have an understanding of (1) telephone demographics and demand; (2) key elements of effective telephone care; (3) medical-legal risk reduction; (4) documentation; (5) telephone care protocols; (6) training and supervision of nurses using protocols to provide telephone care; (7) program evaluation and quality assurance; (8) the benefits and risks of call centers and service bureaus; and (9) the benefits and risks of new technologies.

TELEPHONE DEMOGRAPHICS AND DEMAND

Between 150 and 250 telephone calls each week are made to a pediatrician. Eighty-three percent are made during office hours, and of these, 50% are for administrative concerns and 50% are clinical. Eighty-nine percent of office telephone calls are regarding established patients, 90% are from parents (of which 95% are from mothers), and only 5% are truly emergent. Fifty percent are judged by the pediatrician to be necessary.

Seventeen percent of all calls are after-hours, with an average of three to four calls per pediatrician per weeknight and six to eight calls per weekend day and night with 85% to 90% occurring before 10:00 P.M. In the fee-for-service era, 15% of private-practice pediatric patients with an after-hours problem have been taken to an emergency department without calling their physician, and over half of children who receive care in a public clinic do not call. When parents call a pediatrician for after-hours care, at least 90% can be managed by the pediatrician over the phone.

Between 92% and 98% of parents are satisfied with their physician's telephone care, but as many as half of pediatricians feel that the telephone is the most annoying aspect of practice.

DELEGATION OF TELEPHONE CARE

Over 90% of pediatricians delegate office-hour telephone calls to non-physicians and in some urban settings 80% delegate at least some after-hours calls. During office hours, pediatricians delegate administrative calls to reception personnel, and 80% to 90% of clinical calls may be handled by a nurse, a medical assistant, or an office assistant without professional training. Ninety-seven percent of parents are satisfied with this arrangement. **Nurse practitioners can handle over 95% of clinical calls independently** and they score better than physicians on tests using simulated telephone calls. Although registered nurses have not been well-evaluated in comparison with physicians, it appears that when they receive thorough training and use pediatric telephone protocols, they can manage 80% to 90% of calls independently, safely, and effectively. Personnel without formal clinical training (i.e., with only in-office experience) over-refer 20% of the time and under-refer 10% of the time when handling illness calls. Particularly in managed care in which there are incentives to manage more care over the telephone with self-care advice, a nurse will become the expected standard as a substitute for the physician.

MEDICAL-LEGAL RISK

The legal responsibility for telephone care rests with the owner of the practice and/or the supervising physician. The duty to treat over the telephone does not begin until the clinician begins to give advice. However, once the practitioner begins to advise, he or she cannot back out of the duty to treat but must provide a complete response. **Once the duty to treat is accepted, the two most important elements of risk reduction are (1) complete documentation of the care provided, and (2) adherence to community standards of care. The most widely accepted and easily documented community standards are telephone care protocols.** Two additional means of reducing telephone liability are to ask the caller after advice has been given: (1) whether the caller has other questions or concerns and (2) whether the caller feels comfortable with the disposition and advice. If the caller is uncomfortable, then it is best to schedule the patient for a care visit or have the primary care physician speak to the caller.

Jurors in telephone care malpractice cases consider nurses acceptable substitutes for physicians in telephone care, but they expect that nurses are trained, use protocols, and are regularly evaluated. Other strategies to reduce medical-legal risk when care is delegated include (1) dated policies and procedures; (2) job descriptions defining duties, limitations, and expectations; (3) a requirement to use standardized protocols; (4) an organized system for documenting calls; (5) documentation of training and regular performance reviews for telephone care nurses; and (6) documentation of regular quality assurance activities. Whenever a physician is consulted by a non-physician regarding a telephone call, the case becomes the physician's. Therefore, the physician should be sure that he or she has enough information to render a decision, or the physician should talk to the caller personally.

DOCUMENTATION

Some simple calls do not require documentation; however, most do. The following types of calls require documentation: (1) when reported symptoms may be serious; (2) when a patient is advised to see a physician; (3) when significant medical advice is given; (4) when any advice regarding medication is given; (5) when a positive test is reported; and (6) when a change in treatment is recommended. Minimal documentation includes caller's name; patient's name; date; time; complaint, question or concern; protocol used; pertinent positive answers to protocol questions; disposition; summary of advice; and provider's signature. Documentation must be retrievable and therefore is best kept in the medical record. As practices consolidate in response to managed care and as call groups increase in size, there is increased need for complete documentation, improved communication, and a centralized, accessible record. The ideal solution is an automated telephone encounter record integrated with an automated medical record. An alternative is a two-part paper record that creates one telephone record for inclusion in the medical record and a copy that stays in an on-call book passed from one on-call provider to the next. This allows the clinician to view telephone care records at patient visits and allows the on-call physician to refer to recent calls and notice patterns.

TELEPHONE CARE PROTOCOLS

Training of physicians, midlevel practitioners, and nurses in telephone care has been limited. Skills, experience, and performance among all providers vary. Health care professionals at all levels make potentially serious errors when not using protocols. **Telephone care protocols have been shown to be safe and effective, to reduce medical-legal risk, and to improve documentation. For these reasons, protocols are recommended for all telephone care providers.** The process of creating protocols is time-consuming and difficult; therefore, most practices will purchase rather than create them. There are several books available that provide pediatric telephone protocols. When selecting protocols, the pediatrician should review and evaluate the protocols to be certain that they reflect his or her practice style and local standards.

TELEPHONE CARE BY NURSES USING PROTOCOLS

Nurses using protocols can manage 80% to 90% of all routine triage and advice calls in a safe, cost-effective manner during office hours or during after-hours. Physicians agree with the disposition made by nurses using telephone protocols 90% of the time. Parents comply with nurse triage 95% of the time, compared with 98% compliance with their pediatrician. When parents do not comply, it is usually because they wish to receive more convenient care or because they are uncomfortable with their child's symptoms. Caller satisfaction with nurse triage and advice is comparable to satisfaction with physician telephone care.

DEVELOPING A NURSE TELEPHONE TRIAGE AND ADVICE PROGRAM

The steps in developing a telephone triage and advice program are similar whether for a practice, a health plan, or an entire community: (1) write a brief description of the program and its objectives; (2) develop written policies and procedures; (3) select and adapt protocols; (4) select, train, and evaluate personnel; and (5) implement program evaluation and quality assurance.

POLICIES AND PROCEDURES

Policies and procedures define the expectations for staff in performing everyday activities as well as responding to special situations. The first step is to define the expectations for handling a routine triage and advice call: (1) pleasant greeting; (2) identify self, including title; (3) identify the caller and patient, including the patient's name, age, gender, and the relationship of the caller and the patient; (4) obtain sufficient information regarding symptoms to select the appropriate protocol and then follow the questions in the protocol; (5) use active listening, restate your understanding of the problems, and empathize with the caller; (6) select the appropriate disposition and provide the rationale for the recommendations; (7) determine what the caller (or patient) has already done for treatment, reinforce correct choices, and then provide appropriate advice; (8) ask if there are additional questions; (9) ask if the caller is comfortable with disposition and advice and will be able to follow it; (10) arrange and describe appropriate follow-up; and (11) document the encounter completely. Policies will be needed to describe how the practice prefers to handle a variety of types of calls: emergency calls, caller complaints, unhappy callers, deaf and speech-impaired callers, foreign language–speaking callers, prescription refills (urgent and nonurgent), and special requests. Policies are needed for calls that do not connect with the other party: no answer, busy line, wrong number, unidentified voice mail, and identified voice mail. A variety of other policy issues include how to handle insurance problems, answering service problems, telephone problems, and computer problems.

TELEPHONE CARE TRAINING

Ideally, training should include (1) a presentation on the basic steps, expectations, and key policies for telephone care; (2) instruction on the use of written protocols; (3) simulated cases for practice and review; (4) observation of an experienced telephone care provider; (5) close supervision by an experienced provider during an apprenticeship period; (6) regular review and critique; and (7) continuing education and updates. **All telephone staff (administrative and clinical) should be trained regarding policies and standards for issues such as response time for telephone calls, demeanor, courtesy, discretion, confidentiality, complete documentation, and the importance of caller satisfaction.** Formal nursing education courses on telephone triage and advice have dramatically increased in number and quality and are worth considering. Some sources recommend that physicians arrange simulated calls to the office to test how well policies and protocols are followed.

EVALUATION AND QUALITY ASSURANCE

The records of all calls by new personnel should be reviewed and suggestions discussed with the individual. Periodic review of telephone logs for all other telephone care providers should be conducted by the supervising physician or medical director. All complaints and adverse clinical outcomes should be thoroughly reviewed to determine what can be learned and whether protocols, policies, or procedures need to be changed. To decide which data to keep and how to evaluate the program, it is helpful to define what would constitute a successful call. For example, one large pediatric group defined a successful call as one which (1) is answered by a person within 4 rings (and fewer than 2% of callers hang up before the call is answered); (2) if the triage nurse is not available, a call back is made in less than 1 hour; (3) the caller is greeted in a very friendly manner; (4) the correct protocol is selected; (5) all appropriate questions are asked and answered; (6) the correct disposition is made;

(7) the caller is asked if there were any questions; (8) the caller is asked if he or she felt comfortable with the disposition (and if not, a satisfactory resolution was reached); (9) documentation is complete; and (10) the clinical outcome for the patient is good. From these 10 components of a successful call, the practice can establish 10 parameters to follow and evaluate: (1) call response time and abandonment rate (available from local telephone company); (2) call back time (available from documentation logs); (3) greeting assessment (simulated calls); (4) protocol selection error rate (logs); (5) protocol usage error rates (logs); (6) disposition error rates (logs); (7 and 8) caller questions and comfort assessment (observation); (9) documentation proficiency (logs); and (10) outcomes evaluation (track patients). In the managed care era, all practices will be expected by the health plans to conduct telephone quality review.

PEDIATRIC CALL CENTERS AND SERVICE BUREAUS

Large call centers are being developed to provide telephone triage and advice by hospitals to improve physician relations and by health plans to manage care. For-profit companies also are developing call centers as business ventures, called service bureaus. Nearly all are staffed by nurses using telephone protocols. However, the quality of triage and advice protocols, the experience of the nursing staff, the extent and quality of medical supervision, and the level of quality assurance vary greatly. In addition, at the present time, there is no licensure, regulation, accreditation, or national standards for these call centers. Therefore, before a clinician entrusts patients to a call center or service bureau, he or she should assess the protocols; the credentials, training, and evaluation of the nursing staff; the degree of medical supervision and backup; the completeness of documentation; the satisfaction rates of callers and subscribing physicians; the quality assurance process; and the philosophy underlying the protocols (i.e., increasing referrals to the sponsoring hospital versus reducing utilization of emergency departments by the sponsoring health plan).

The benefits of a call center arise from the economies of scale, which reduce the expenses of staffing, training, quality assurance, and telecommunications technology. The subscribing physician gives up some degree of personalization of care and control over the advice given.

THE TELEPHONE, MANAGED CARE, AND CAPITATION

In a managed care environment, rigorous telephone triage is needed after-hours to promote appropriate utilization of emergency services and to encourage self-care. When the proportion of the practice population that is capitated approaches 30%, it is financially prudent to begin to use telephone triage to promote self-care during office hours as well. Nurses using telephone protocols can manage 60% of office-hour calls with self-care and 80% of after-hours calls with self-care. **A physician can manage 70% to 80% of calls during office hours with self-care and 90% of after-hours calls without an after-hours visit.** Therefore, when very rigorous triage is required, a two-level triage process (with a physician taking over the calls when the nurse feels a visit may be necessary) can minimize unneeded visits.

Managed care brings additional malpractice risk to telephone care. Juries have made it clear that they disapprove of using telephone triage to cut health care costs, if there is a bad outcome. Therefore, the focus should be first on quality care, caller satisfaction, and safety.

TELEPHONE CASE MANAGEMENT

An increasing proportion of pediatric patients have chronic disease or are medically fragile. Managed care and capitation reduce reimbursement, encourage limitation of services, and increase paperwork and overhead for children with chronic illness. In response, the clinician must manage care more closely to reduce morbidity, but do so in a cost-effective manner. Telephone care can be helpful in several ways: (1) to provide ongoing health education about the disease; (2) to monitor disease status and adapt treatment; (3) to replace follow-up visits; and (4) to respond to questions or concerns as they arise. For common issues (like asthma, attention-deficit hyperactivity disorder, recurrent otitis media) telephone case management can be provided by nurses using telephone protocols. For less common chronic disease in a capitated population, the clinician will want to provide the telephone care (perhaps using protocols he or she receives from the pediatric subspecialist).

TELEPHONE TECHNOLOGIES FOR THE PRACTICE

A variety of telephone technologies are available, although little research has been published.

Automated attendant, voice messaging, interactive voice mail, and autopaging are technologies that can reduce staffing costs and improve efficiency. In selecting and implementing these technologies, the pediatrician must be sensitive to caller expectations and tolerances and each technology should: (1) have a fail-safe connection to a live person in case of emergency; (2) flag and expedite urgent messages; and (3) recognize and notify appropriate persons in case of malfunction.

Computer telephony refers to the systems that link computer and telephone technologies to improve efficiency in telephone communication. Two examples of computer telephony for which there is evidence of efficacy are auto-dialers and interactive voice response technology. Auto-dialers can be programmed to make automated outbound calls to remind parents of (1) upcoming established appointments; or (2) the need to make an appointment; or (3) the need to make an appointment for immunizations. Studies have shown that auto-dialers are effective in improving compliance in populations with low immunization rates or high no-show rates. They have not been well-studied in compliant, suburban pediatric populations. Interactive voice response technology can be used to provide prerecorded health information messages accessible by touch-tone phone. As costs of the technology decrease and pressure to promote self-care increases, this technology will become more attractive. When effectively promoted by the clinician and office staff, this automated telephone health education can provide information on minor problems and questions that will substitute for talking to a person and prevent a telephone call or an office visit over 60% of the time. The satisfaction rate among callers is 90%. As pediatricians evaluate each new technology, they will need to be certain that it has been shown to maintain or improve quality outcomes, reduce costs, and maintain caller satisfaction.

SUMMARY

The role of the pediatrician in telephone care has shifted from care provider to supervisor. The pediatrician now must oversee policy development, training, telephone care provider evaluation, documentation, protocol selection, call center selection, telephone case management, and the selection of new telephone technologies for the practice.

FURTHER READING

Brown JL: Telephone Medicine. St. Louis, CV Mosby, 1980.

Fox-Gliessman D, Poole SR, Schmitt BD, et al.: Pediatric Telephone Triage and Advice Manual. Denver, General Pediatric Publications, 1995.

Group Health Cooperative of Puget Sound: Nurses' Guide to Telephone Triage and Healthcare. Baltimore, Williams & Wilkins, 1985.

Katz BP: Telephone Medicine: Triage and Training—A Handbook for Primary Health Care Professionals, 2nd ed. Thorofare, NJ, Slack, Inc, 1991.

Katz H and Wick W: Malpractice, meningitis, and the telephone. Pediatr Ann 20:85–89, 1991.

Pext JC, Furth TW, and Katz HP: A 10-year experience in pediatric after-hours telecommunications. Curr Opin Pediatr 8:181–187, 1996.

Poole SR and Schmitt BD: After-hours telephone coverage: The application of an area-wide telephone triage and advice system for pediatric practices. Pediatrics 92:670–679, 1993.

Rosekrans J, Limbo D, Kaplan D, et al.: Training Manual for Pediatric Telephone Guidelines. Darien, CT, Patient Care Publications, 1979.

Schmitt BD: Pediatric Telephone Advice. Boston, Little, Brown & Co, 1985.

Schmitt BD: Pediatric Telephone Protocols. Littleton, Co, Decision Press, 1997.

Richard N. Shiffman

Chapter 17

Informatics and Computers in Pediatrics

At the dawn of the 21st century, the task of providing high quality health care has become one of the most information-intensive of all human endeavors. From the fruits of laboratory research to individual patient data, an overwhelming quantity of new information is generated every day, requiring skilled and efficient processing if it is to be used to enhance patient care. To address these prodigious information needs, the discipline of medical informatics has arisen at the intersection of medicine and computer science. Informatics is both a science—the study of medical knowledge and how it is used by skilled physicians—and an engineering discipline, which creates tools and technologies to enhance information management.

For more than 30 years, physicians have been actively involved in incorporating computers as tools in medical practice. In contrast to the successes of the commercial enterprise, where computers primarily process numeric data, developing computer solutions to medical problems has been a complex task, because clinical issues deal with symbolic constructs. Capturing, encoding, processing, and delivering clinical information represent the grand challenges of medical informatics.

This chapter provides an overview of several aspects of informatics activity—the computer-based patient record, computer-assisted clinical decision making, networking, and some of the challenges that remain to be resolved in clinical computing. Other topics, such as computer systems for practice management including billing and appointments and for professional and patient education, can be explored in Further Reading at the end of the chapter.

COMPUTER-BASED PATIENT RECORD

The term "computer-based patient record" (CPR) refers to electronically maintained information about an individual's lifetime health status and health care. The CPR has come to represent an ideal implementation—one not yet available for purchase from any vendor. Many components of the ideal CPR exist already and the systems that provide these transitional capabilities are termed electronic medical records (EMR).

Implementation of computer-based patient records promises to revolutionize medical practice but implementation of a full CPR will require more than simply replacing paper forms with electronic screens. Although the paper-based record is familiar and comfortable, the entire process of data collection, storage, and manipulation must be re-engineered if we are to realize the full potential of a computer-based patient record. The current paper record permits clinicians to record information flexibly and idiosyncratically—from detailed narrative descriptions of procedures to sketches of lesions. The paper record can be browsed by simply flipping pages and it never experiences downtime due to machine failure.

The current system, however, is far from perfect. Many users may need access to the information in the paper chart, including primary care physicians and subspecialists, therapists, social workers, financial and quality assurance managers, third party payers, and researchers. To access information about a particular patient, one must first locate the physical record, which can be present in only one place at a time. Records are frequently unavailable and, when they are found, specific information is often missing or illegible. Furthermore, the task of reviewing large charts is daunting. It is difficult and time-consuming for clinicians to organize information for efficient retrieval. Aggregation of information about many patients for quality assurance or research is arduous.

On the other hand, computer-based records are accessible 24 hours a day, from multiple sites. The same patient's record can be viewed by several users simultaneously. It can be organized to meet specific demands and displayed to show trends and meaningful summaries. Large charts can be searched efficiently for specific types of information (e.g., all serum lead determinations in 1997), and aggregation of information is almost instantaneous. Legibility is no longer a problem in printed reports. Sophisticated systems can use an individual patient's information to trigger reminders of appropriate care (such as immunizations for which a child is both due and eligible), can alert users to potentially critical events (such as drug interactions or critical laboratory results), and can provide on-line, consultative assistance. Safeguards can be implemented to protect the privacy of electronic records that are better than those applied to the current paper-based system.

In 1991, the Institute of Medicine defined the attributes of a fully functional computer-based record. In addition to the capabilities previously described, they recommended that the CPR should

- Include an individual's problem list that shows the status of each problem at each encounter and links individual problems to relevant test results and orders
- Indicate a patient's health status and functional level
- Indicate a logical basis for diagnoses and clinical conclusions
- Be capable of linking information from various settings (e.g., hospitals, outpatient laboratories, and home health agencies)
- Promote linkage to local and remote information sources, such as practice guidelines and bibliographic databases
- Support direct physician data entry since this will help to assure the accuracy of the information
- Support measurement of quality and costs of care

In many ways, development and deployment of ambulatory information management systems have lagged behind those of hospital-based systems. The knowledge substrate itself differs. Although hospitalized patients generate large quantities of data, these are all related to a single episode of care. On the other hand, ambulatory care deals with many—self-limited illnesses, risk assessment and screening, and preventive health interventions. Data from multiple distinct sources must be captured, integrated, organized, and effectively summarized to meet the needs of the clinician in ambulatory care. Longitudinal data must be stored and kept available over long time intervals to provide a lifelong history of health care. New data models are required and data integration capabilities must be developed.

The advent of managed care requirements has provided a new impetus to the implementation of computer-based records. Tremendous controversy exists about whether we can ever achieve a "paperless" office—and even whether this would be desirable. Physicians are being called on as never before to justify their activities with evidence of improved patient outcomes and responsible cost management. Automated clinical information systems will provide the data to demonstrate quality care and the means to implement quality improvement programs.

DECISION SUPPORT

The practice of pediatrics requires clinicians to make innumerable decisions accurately and efficiently. We decide what diagnosis best fits the constellation of signs and symptoms and the social context within which each child presents. We evaluate which other disease entities deserve consideration. We determine which tests provide the safest, most cost-effective discrimination among these alternatives. Should we hospitalize, or can the child be managed at home? Should we recommend treatment with a potentially risky medication, or should we pursue a course of watchful waiting? Few of these decisions are made with absolute certitude. **Computer-based decision support promises to improve the quality of decision making under conditions of uncertainty.**

E. H. Shortliffe, a pioneer informatics researcher, identified three general categories of decision support: (1) applications that facilitate access to clinical information to inform the decision-making process; (2) applications that focus attention and remind clinicians of issues that might otherwise be overlooked; and (3) systems that are designed to provide expert level consultation.

Decision Support Functionality

In examining decision support systems, it is useful to classify several dimensions of functional capability using a technology ladder. Ascending the ladder provides an increasing capability to inform the decision-making process with concomitantly higher technology requirements.

One dimension of decision support functionality relates to how much initiative is required in requesting assistance. A user may be required to initiate a request for help or assistance may be provided automatically. When busy clinicians must interrupt their work to actively seek help, they may choose to muddle along without potentially beneficial information. At the opposite extreme, providing too much unrequested information can lead to information overload. Thus, decision support systems must achieve a balance.

Second, the information provided by the system may be applicable generally to a population (e.g., immunization recommendations for 6-month-olds) or it may be specific to a particular patient (Johnny Doe, a 6-month-old who missed a scheduled immunization at 4 months and whose mother is receiving chemotherapy). **Applications that provide patient-specific information tend to be more useful and are perceived as being more "intelligent," but they require a high level of technology.**

Third, decision support may be made available immediately on an ad hoc basis or it may be delivered on a fixed schedule. Batch processing may allow certain efficiencies but real-time processing permits direct interaction between clinicians and knowledge resources.

Information Access Applications

Information access applications can provide user-initiated access to general knowledge sources to inform the decision-making process. **Clinicians can rapidly answer many of the questions that arise in day-to-day practice by querying the MEDLINE database, which contains more than 9,000,000 citations to the biomedical literature that have appeared in more than 4000 journals since 1966.** The database can be queried directly by a dial-up connection or indirectly through a subscription to a regularly updated CD-ROM–based product. The National Library of Medicine offers free access to the MEDLINE database via the World Wide Web (http://www.ncbi.nlm.nih.gov/PubMed).

An increasing number of journals (including *Pediatrics*, the *Journal of Pediatrics*, *Archives of Pediatrics and Adolescent Medicine*, *Journal of the American Medical Association,* and the *New England Journal of Medicine*) are available online with published abstracts or full-text articles. A plethora of reference textbooks and manuals are also available in digital format. The American Academy of Pediatrics offers its popular Pediatrics Review and Education Program (PREP) in a CD-ROM version that includes review articles and self-assessment exercises. A major advantage to having these references on-line is their accessibility. An entire virtual library can be made available at any computer terminal. Moreover, one can efficiently search for specific information simply by typing in keywords.

Users can obtain patient-specific information to enhance decision making through access to a computer-based record system or to laboratory or radi-

ology results reporting systems. In the hospital environment, it has been shown that having access to the most recent test results and the test fees at the time orders are being entered significantly decreases both duplicative test ordering and patient charges. Moreover, if a system can provide problem-oriented aggregation of data and graphing or flowcharting of results, it can help to assure that all relevant information is considered as interventions are planned.

Reminders

Reminders of appropriate care have been among the most effective implementations of computer-based decision support. The flood of patient-related data can overwhelm the abilities of well-intentioned clinicians to attend to critical details. A computer-based reminder system reviews online patient information and generates messages to physicians whenever particular clinical indications are noted.

A series of clinical trials has demonstrated that physicians who receive electronic reminders respond to the clinical situations that trigger them more often and more appropriately than physicians who are not reminded. Physicians adhere to preventive care protocols and recognize potential drug reactions and interactions more rapidly when computer-based reminders are provided. This has translated into improved outcomes for patients whose physicians receive electronic reminders. In analyzing one such study, McDonald and coworkers (1984) concluded that this difference was due to errors of omission on the part of the physicians deprived of decision support, that in fact they would have responded to these situations if they had been aware of them, and that computer reminders "improve the fidelity between physicians' intentions and their actions."

Reminders that are processed in real time are called *alerts*. They can remind a physician not to prescribe amoxicillin to a patient who is penicillin-allergic or they can make clinicians aware of critical laboratory test values.

Most reminder systems function automatically, processing vast quantities of on-line patient data against a set of carefully crafted rules. Rules are logical assertions—If-Then statements—that relate a set of clinical circumstances to an action. They may be quite simple, for example:

If the patient is 4 months old and the interval since the last immunization is at least 6 weeks, *Then* print a reminder that diphtheria, tetanus, pertussis, polio, and *Haemophilus influenzae* immunizations are due.

More complex rules may contain many decision variables and may trigger multiple actions.

The task of converting medical knowledge into rules can be quite demanding. System builders need credible knowledge sources and an understanding of both medicine and computing. Modern, evidence-based guidelines can provide a fertile resource for current recommendations on care that can be incorporated into rules.

Expert Consultation

A third category of decision support applications provides expert consultation in response to user-initiated requests about specific patients. These knowledge-based or "expert" systems apply artificial intelligence technologies to the resolution of clinical problems.

During the 1980s, several groups sought to create and refine diagnostic consultants. Some of the best known diagnostic systems include QMR (created at the University of Pittsburgh), DXplain (from the Massachusetts General Hospital), and Iliad (from the University of Utah). In general, diagnostic systems contain hundreds (or thousands) of disease profiles that include symptoms, signs, and laboratory findings. These diagnoses are compared with a set of patient observations using a variety of matching algorithms. Inferencing strategies vary and include probabilistic manipulations of disease prevalence and test sensitivity and specificity, causal reasoning based on understanding the relationships between presenting symptoms and pathophysiology, and neural networks that mathematically mimic the activities of neurons to evaluate input data. Most programs can construct a differential diagnosis list and query the user for additional information to help rank the possibilities.

Many of these diagnostic systems were designed to function like Greek oracles—all-knowing bestowers of wisdom about broad areas of medicine on a generally ignorant community of users. All required the physician to enter lists of findings and laboratory test results. Evaluations have shown that although the diagnoses these systems provide are often correct, diagnostic decision support programs are less useful in supplying the right diagnosis than in offering additional relevant diagnoses for consideration by the clinician. In a recent review of four of the best known systems, Berner and colleagues (1994) recommended that they be used by physicians "who can identify and use the relevant information and ignore the irrelevant information that can be produced."

Recently, the Greek oracle approach has been replaced by a model of assisted decision making in more restricted subject areas. Consultant systems can effectively provide advice about diagnosis of dysmorphic syndromes, coagulation disorders, prediction of neonatal acidosis, and metabolic defects. Others can assist with treatment planning in diabetes, the acquired immunodeficiency syndrome, and oncologic disorders. An immunization expert system can resolve complex issues of late starts, off-schedule immunizations, and mixed antigens, to provide immunization plans. The full potential of these consultant systems will be realized when they are integrated with a CPR, thereby eliminating onerous data entry requirements.

NETWORKING, THE WORLD WIDE WEB, AND TELEMEDICINE

Many of the greatest technologic advances of the last decade have been dedicated to enhanced communication and information sharing. Fax machines have enabled nearly instantaneous transmission of vital, complex documents from one site to another. Additionally, small groups of computers in an office or building can communicate via local area networks (LANs); likewise, information exchange is possible over greater distances via wide area networks (WANs) (e.g., between a pediatric office and the community hospital laboratory or between pediatricians in rural areas and consultants in medical centers). LANs and WANs provide enabling technologies for realization of the benefits of computer-based patient record and decision support systems.

The Internet is a global, interwoven, information-sharing array of LANs, WANs, and telephone and satellite links. Initially created in 1969 by the Defense Department, its structure is completely decentralized since it was intended to survive war and natural disasters. Because it uses a standardized addressing system and communication protocols, computers with different operating systems (e.g., Windows, Macintosh, and UNIX machines) can readily exchange information. Information transfer is free although users usually pay a fee for a connection to the network. Physicians can communicate directly with one another or with their patients via electronic mail (e-mail). They can also subscribe to community bulletin boards (called listserves) or sign on to various newsgroups to interact with users with similar interests.

The World Wide Web (WWW) refers to a segment of Internet activity that facilitates exchange of graphic information, text, sound, and hypertext linkages. A Web browser is a program that resides on an individual's personal computer and enables connection to various WWW sites and navigation through the information presented. A variety of search engines (e.g., Yahoo, Lycos, WebCrawler, Excite) can be used to find documents that relate to a particular topic. The PEDINFO site at the University of Alabama (http://www.uab.edu/ped-info) serves as a clearinghouse and pointer to hundreds of WWW sites that address issues of pediatric interest. The sites include general pediatric forums and information about specific diseases, pediatric subspecialties, institutions and organizations, health education, publications, and pediatric/medical software.

The next telecommunications frontier is telemedicine—the use of new technologies to diagnose and treat patients at a distance and the use of distant resources to care for patients who are close at hand. Technologic and economic obstacles are falling, enabling complex text, voice, and video information to be transmitted between clinical sites. Telemedicine permits broadcasting of continuing education sessions to groups of physicians who may reside in remote areas and provides a capability for individual patient consultation that allows a consultant to interview patients, examine video, and review x-ray prints, scans, pathologic slides, and other materials from hundreds or thousands of miles away.

INFORMATICS CHALLENGES

Despite this considerable progress, computers have not yet begun to influence the care provided by many physicians. Powerful computers have become available and affordable, but surprisingly strong sociocultural barriers inhibit their use by many clinicians. Although pediatricians may be quick to use other advanced technologies for patient care, some are disinclined and even antipathetic toward computers. **Except for enthusiasts and practitioners in a small number of showcase centers, relatively few clinicians are using computers in the routine care of their patients.** What factors are responsible for the disparity between the promise and the current status quo?

Until recently, efforts to provide computer support for medicine have emphasized financial and administrative systems. Several major technical issues exist in bringing computer-based clinical functionality to the primary care office. Many vendors offer software products that represent partial answers to the information needs of clinicians, but no single product effectively integrates information access, a computer-based patient record system, and decision support.

A significant obstacle is the issue of data entry. Although most pediatricians agree that *using* computer-based information would be beneficial, *entering* it can be sheer drudgery. The graphic user interface is intended to facilitate interactions between humans and computers. Mice, light pens, pen-based input, and voice-entry systems have been created to address these problems, but the computer keyboard continues to inhibit the interaction of many potential users.

Representation of medical information in a form that can be meaningfully processed by computers remains a major challenge. Standards for expressing and transmitting medical data between and among computers must be accepted widely. Simply encoding a full range of history and physical data, medications, diagnoses, laboratory test results, and radiographic findings requires a comprehensive, standardized vocabulary if the data are to be shared effectively. Although several vocabularies have been proposed (including SNOMED from the College of American Pathologists, the Read codes from the National Health Service of Great Britain, and the Unified Medical Language System of the National Library of Medicine), none has proved to be comprehensive and expressive enough to encode current clinical activity. Likewise, the medical knowledge to create decision support applications must be elicited from experts, must be structured on computer-accessible formats, and its currency must be maintained as new knowledge accumulates. The Arden syntax from the American Society of Testing and Materials is a proposed standard for expressing clinical rules in a format that facilitates sharing them interinstitutionally.

Finally, any computer implementation involves a cost to users. The cost results from a change from familiar work patterns and often a necessity for data entry. For a successful implementation with satisfied users, these costs must be balanced by a benefit—some new capability or functionality that didn't exist before.

Many pediatricians enjoy computing as an avocation. Local universities and community colleges offer courses that can enhance their education in computer topics. The Section on Computers and Other Technology (SCOT) of the American Academy of Pediatrics sponsors educational and research presentations at the Academy's annual and spring meetings. The Annual Meeting of the American Medical Informatics Association brings together thousands of informatics professionals and enthusiasts. The National Library of Medicine sponsors fellowships at 12 sites around the United States where advanced training in informatics can be obtained.

With the increasing complexity of the health care enterprise, it has become vital for multiple providers in a variety of settings to share clinical and administrative information in a manner never previously imagined. Widely accessible, reliable information is necessary to promote quality patient care in the increasingly cost-constrained health care environment. **Effective use of modern technologies should free clinicians from time constraints imposed by new organizational pressures.** Informatics research offers promising solutions for management of the explosive growth of information in contemporary health care.

FURTHER READING

American Academy of Pediatrics: Computers in the Primary Care Office. Elk Grove Village, IL, American Academy of Pediatrics, 1995.

Berner E, Webster G, Shugerman A, et al.: Performance of four computer-based diagnostic systems. N Engl J Med 330:1792–1796, 1994.

Degoulet P and Fieschi M: Introduction to Clinical Informatics. New York, Springer-Verlag, 1997.

Haggerty RJ: Child health 2000: New pediatrics in the changing environment of children's needs in the 21st century. Pediatrics 96(Suppl):804–812, 1995.

Institute of Medicine: The Computer-Based Patient Record: An Essential Technology for Health Care. Washington, DC, National Academy Press, 1991.

Johnson KB and Feldman MJ: Medical informatics and pediatrics: Decision support systems. Arch Pediatr Adolesc Med 149:1371–1380, 1995.

McDonald C, Hui S, Smith D, et al.: Reminders to physicians from an introspective computer medical record: a two year randomized trial. Ann Intern Med 100:130–138, 1984.

Van Bemmel JH and Musen MA: Handbook of Medical Informatics. New York, Springer-Verlag, 1997.

PART B

CONTENT

Morris Green

Chapter 18

Health Supervision: Principles*

1. Excellent care of patients is highly personal. Ideally, health supervision is individualized according to the structure and relationships in the family, cultural patterns, ethnicity, socioeconomic status, special health needs, educational background of the parents, psychosocial experiences, nutritional patterns, strengths, and risk status.

2. The child and adolescent are to be viewed in the context of their family and community.

3. The goal is to develop a partnership for disease prevention and health promotion among the clinician, the child, and the family.

4. When feasible, both parents should be encouraged to attend some of the health supervision sessions, especially the prenatal and infancy consultations.

5. Health supervision is a longitudinal process characterized by a continuing relationship with a physician, a nurse, or a health supervision team.

6. Health promotion is enhanced when it is integrated with community health and human services such as child care centers, early inter-

*The material in this chapter was adapted from Green M (ed): Bright Futures: Guidelines for Health Supervision of Infants, Children, and Adolescents. Arlington, VA, National Center for Education in Maternal and Child Health, 1994. Bright Futures was supported by the Maternal and Child Health Bureau and the Medicaid Bureau. Copies of this publication and a pocket guide are available from the National Maternal and Child Health Clearinghouse, 8201 Greensboro Drive, Suite 600, McLean, VA 22102.

vention programs, parent-child centers, developmental preschools, family support centers, mental health services, secondary and tertiary medical care, adequate housing, schools, and public health programs.

7. A diagnostic approach should apply to the appraisal of health. This includes the interview, developmental and educational surveillance, observation of parent-child interactions, the physical examination, screening tests, and an identification of family and community risks and strengths.

8. The health supervision agenda for children and adolescents includes the identification, monitoring, and containment of both biomedical and psychosocial risks.

9. Since family and societal changes have resulted in a dramatic effect on the chief causes of morbidity and mortality among children and adolescents, the prevention of the "new" morbidity and mortality is an important goal of health supervision.

10. The most successful sessions are those in which the interview is shaped, in part, by issues and questions raised by the parent, child, or adolescent.

11. The productivity of the health supervision consultation may be increased by asking parents to write down the questions, concerns, observations, and achievements they wish to discuss. Alternatively, a questionnaire or checklist may be completed at home or administered in the reception room.

12. In some instances, group health supervision sessions that complement or supplement individual visits can contribute to parent education.

13. Beginning with the middle childhood years, the child or adolescent should be included in the interview. Talking directly with older children and adolescents alone for a few minutes contributes to a therapeutic alliance and encourages responsibility for their own health.

14. The developmental status of infants and young children can generally be assessed through developmental surveillance consisting of appropriate questions, developmental questionnaires to be completed by the parents, and evaluation by the physician or nurse during the visit. Developmental landmarks have been included in Chapter 19 for the first 5 years of life as points of reference; however, they do not serve as adequate screening tests to determine the need for further assessment as discussed in Chapter 21, page 90, on developmental, behavioral, and educational surveil-

lance. School performance in middle childhood may be appraised through a review of report cards, school achievement records, and performance on psychoeducational tests when indicated.

15. Anticipatory guidance provides the family with information on what to expect next, including the promotion of healthy habits, injury prevention, good nutrition, oral health, reinforcement of constructive family relationships, encouragement of mutually enjoyable parent-child interactions, promotion of social competency, and support of community interaction.

16. Health supervision should be tailored to meet individual family needs. The periodicity of visits recommended in this chapter is intended to be appropriate for most children and families not judged to be at undue risk. Children and adolescents with chronic illness or disability, in foster care, living in chaotic households, or assessed at being at high risk medically, developmentally, or socially will require more health supervision or interventions. Augmented health supervision may also be needed during such critical periods of family transition as divorce, remarriage, death, parental mental or physical illness, unemployment, school entrance, adoption, or foster care placement.

17. More research is needed in relation to health supervision practices, currently based largely on expert opinion. Though challenging, measuring the outcomes of these interventions is essential.

18. When the clinician believes that additional information relevant to the present illness or development of the child would be useful, he or she may ask clarifying, or "trigger" questions. Parents and children who have a continuing relationship with a clinician are generally comfortable about asking questions, expressing concerns, and disclosing personal problems. Those less familiar with the physician or nurse may be uncomfortable and guarded in raising such issues. Without a clarifying trigger or prompting question, they may not mention negative feelings or report family problems such as violence, alcoholism, or personal illnesses such as depression. Parents often do not realize that such information would be helpful to the clinician.

Trigger questions are also helpful in prompting patients to report positive events and accomplishments. Awareness of such strengths are important in fostering health promotion and in increasing the patient's sense of efficacy.

Some trigger questions may apply broadly to infancy, childhood, and adolescence whereas others are more focused on chronologic or developmental periods. Such questions are to be used selectively and phrased tactfully so as not to appear interrogative or intrusive. Psychosocial screening questionnaires completed by the parent, child, or adolescent may also be useful in eliciting diagnostically useful information.

General Trigger Questions

How are you?

How is _____ doing?

What questions or concerns do you have for me today?

Have there been any major changes in your family since your last appointment? Any unexpected stresses, crises, or illnesses?

How is your family getting along?

What do you do as a family?

What do you most enjoy about _____?

What new things is he (she) doing?

How is communication going in your family?

Are there any aspects of _____'s behavior or development that are particularly worrisome or troubling?

Trigger Questions for Possible Periodic Inquiry

Because some issues arise in families these days that are difficult to talk about, I've come to ask a few questions routinely.

Have you even been in a relationship where you have been hurt, threatened, or treated badly?

Have you ever been worried that someone was going to hurt your child? Has your child ever been abused?

Do you think that smoking, drinking, or drug use is a problem for anyone in your family?

Do you have a gun in the house? Where is it kept? Is it locked up? Where is the ammunition stored?

Morris Green

Chapter **19**

Health Supervision: Goals and Content

This chapter includes a synopsis of developmental goals and the content of health supervision consultations during infancy, early childhood, and middle childhood. Health supervision in adolescence is discussed in Chapter 20 and immunizations in Chapter 27. A complete physical examination is recommended for each health supervision consultation. *Bright Futures: Guidelines for Health Supervision of Infants, Children, and Adolescents* and *Guidelines for Health Supervision III* may be consulted for further details.

---

*The material in this chapter was adapted from Green M (ed): Bright Futures: Guidelines for Health Supervision of Infants, Children, and Adolescents. Arlington, VA, National Center for Education in Maternal and Child Health, 1994. Bright Futures was supported by the Maternal and Child Health Bureau and the Medicaid Bureau. Copies of this publication and a pocket guide are available from the National Maternal and Child Health Clearinghouse, 8201 Greensboro Drive, Suite 600, McLean, VA 22102.

INFANCY

Developmental Goals

Family adaptation to the new infant

Mother-infant and infant-mother attachment

Development of a sense of trust

Achievement of a warm, nurturant parent-infant relationship

Optimal growth and development

Good nutrition

Injury prevention

Acquisition of self-comforting behaviors

PRENATAL VISIT

The chief purpose of the prenatal consultation is to foster a therapeutic alliance between the prospective parents and the health profes-

sional. It also can be used to inform the family about how this particular practice functions and how and when to call for help. These sessions are usually scheduled, optimally with both parents present, during the eighth or ninth month of pregnancy. The prenatal visit permits the recording of information about the course of the pregnancy, the family medical and social history, and other data for later reference. In addition to the questions that most parents have at this time, some of the following trigger questions may be appropriate.

Trigger Questions

How has your pregnancy been coming along?

What has been the most exciting aspect of this experience?

How are the preparations for your baby going?

Who will be helping you when you come home with your baby?

Have you had any concerns about your pregnancy?

How do you plan to feed your baby? Breast? Bottle?

What have you decided about circumcision if your baby is a boy?

How do you think the baby will change your lives?

How were things for you when you were growing up?

Do you plan to raise your baby the way you were raised or somewhat differently?

Do either of you drink? Smoke? Take drugs?

Do you plan to return to work? To school? What have you thought about child care arrangements?

Anticipatory Guidance

Obtain car seat.

Prepare older siblings for new baby.

Develop support system to help the mother after birth of her baby.

Offer supplementary information and suggest reading resources.

Provide parents with information about the practice, including how to arrange follow-up health care.

NEWBORN

Selected Components of the Health Supervision Consultation

Trigger Questions

Congratulations on your new baby. How are you feeling? How did the delivery go?

What are some of your questions this morning?

Is everything set for you to take your baby home?

Who will help you at home?

Observation of Parent-Infant Interaction and Family Communication

Complete Physical Examination

Plot length, weight, and head circumference
Red reflex
Palate
Cardiac murmurs
Femoral pulses
Jaundice
Abdominal masses
Genitalia
Orthopedic disorders, including developmental hip dysplasia

Screening Tests

Hereditary/metabolic screening

Anticipatory Guidance

Place the baby on his or her back to sleep.

Never leave the baby alone with a young sibling or pet.

Review with the parents the early signs of illness, and when to call the doctor.

Review what the parents are to do in case of an emergency.

Provide information about return appointment, office hours, call arrangements, night calls.

Review breast or bottle feeding.

Discuss the following:

Cord care
Circumcision care
Skin care
Vaginal discharge or bleeding
Crying
Sneezing and hiccups
Burping, spitting up
Change in stool characteristics
Sleep patterns
Postpartum "blues"
Injury prevention

Arrange to call the family in 24 hours after hospital discharge.

Schedule another health supervision consultation in 2 to 4 days if newborn is discharged less than 48 hours after birth; otherwise, in 4 to 5 days.

FIRST WEEK

Selected Components of the Health Supervision Consultation

Trigger Questions

How is _____ doing?
Who helps you with _____?
Has _____ been fussy?
How is feeding going?
Are you getting enough rest?
Have you been feeling tired or blue?

Observation of Parent-Infant Interaction and Family Communication

Complete Physical Examination

Plot length and weight
Red reflex, strabismus
Dacryocystitis
Cardiac murmurs
Developmental hip dysplasia
Abdominal masses

Anticipatory Guidance

Discuss baby's temperament.
Discuss possible fussy periods.
Promote maternal-infant attachment.
Discuss nurturing activities such as holding, cuddling, rocking, talking, and singing to infant, especially during his or her quiet, alert states.
Importance of the mother taking time to rest.
Mention that there will be times when the mother will feel tired, overwhelmed, inadequate, or depressed.

ONE MONTH

Selected Components of the Health Supervision Consultation

Trigger Questions

What do you enjoy most about _____?
Who helps you with _____?
How would you describe _____'s personality?
How is feeding coming along?
Have you been feeling tired or blue?

Observation of Parent-Infant Interaction and Family Communication

Complete Physical Examination

Red reflex
Strabismus

Developmental hip dysplasia
Torticollis
Metatarsus adductus
Neurologic examination

Developmental Surveillance

Fixates on human face and follows with eyes

Anticipatory Guidance

Discuss crying.
Do not leave baby alone in a tub of water or on a high place.
Always keep one hand on the baby.
Delay introduction of solid foods until infant is 4 to 6 months of age.

TWO MONTHS

Selected Components of the Health Supervision Consultation

Trigger Questions

How are you?
What do you enjoy most about _____?
How would you describe _____'s personality? How does he (she) respond to you?
Do you think _____ hears all right? Sees all right?

Complete Physical Examination

Red reflex
Strabismus
Developmental hip dysplasia
Torticollis
Metatarsus adductus
Neurologic examination

Observation of Parent-Infant Interaction and Family Communication

Developmental Surveillance

Coos and vocalizes reciprocally
Smiles responsively
In prone position, lifts head, neck, and upper chest with support on forearms

Anticipatory Guidance

Promote mutually enjoyable parent-infant interaction.

Encourage baby's vocalizations. Talk to him or her during dressing, bathing, feeding, playing, walking, and riding in the car.
Establish a bedtime routine.
Injury prevention.
If mother is returning to work, discuss child care arrangements.

FOUR MONTHS

Selected Components of the Health Supervision Consultation

Trigger Questions

How are you?
What new things is _____ doing?
What are you feeding _____ at this time?
How does _____ spend his (her) day?
Does _____ sleep through the night?
Do you think _____ hears all right? Sees all right?
What are your child care arrangements?
Have you been getting out as a couple without the baby?

Observation of Parent-Infant Interaction and Family Communication

Complete Physical Examination

Plot height, weight, weight for length, and head circumference

Developmental Surveillance

Babbles, coos, smiles, laughs, and squeals
In prone position, holds head erect and raises body on hands
Rolls from prone to supine
Opens hands
Looks at mobile

Anticipatory Guidance

Continue to breastfeed or use iron-fortified formula for the first year.
Do not put baby to bed with a bottle.
Encourage baby to learn to console himself or herself by putting him or her down awake.
Provide baby with the same transitional object, such as a stuffed animal or toy at bedtime.
Encourage play with toys.
Teach injury prevention.
Discuss babysitters and child care arrangements.

SIX MONTHS

Selected Components of the Health Supervision Consultation

Trigger Questions

How is _____ doing?
What do you and your family enjoy most about _____?
How does _____ spend his (her) day?
What is _____ eating?
Have you introduced solids?
Tell me about _____'s play?

Observation of Parent-Infant Interaction and Family Communication

Complete Physical Examination

Plot length, weight, weight for length, and head circumference
Neurologic examination, including tendon reflexes, muscle tone and use of extremities

Developmental Appraisal

Vocalizes single consonants
Babbles reciprocally
Rolls over
No head lag when pulled to sit
Sits with support
Bears weight in standing position
Grasps and mouths objects
Transfers cubes or other small objects from hand to hand
Rakes in small objects using fingers
Turns head to sounds

Anticipatory Guidance

Introduce solid foods, one food at a time; allow 3 to 4 days before adding another. Avoid foods that may be aspirated or cause choking.
Play social games such as pat-a-cake, peek-a-boo, so-big.
Put baby to bed while still awake.
Keep all poisonous substances, medicines, and other potentially toxic materials locked in a safe place.
Do not leave heavy objects or containers of hot liquid on tablecloths that the baby may pull down.
Keep a 1-ounce bottle of syrup of ipecac in the home.
Install gates at top and bottom of stairs.
Do not buy or use an infant walker.
Do not put baby to bed with a bottle.
Emphasize the importance of family communication.

NINE MONTHS

Selected Components of the Health Supervision Consultation

Trigger Questions

What are some of _____'s new achievements?

What is _____ eating?

Does _____ awaken at night?

Now that _____ is more active, what changes have you made in your home to ensure her safety?

What are your thoughts about discipline?

Observation of Parent-Infant Interaction and Family Communication

Complete Physical Examination

Plot length, weight, weight for length, and head circumference

Developmental Appraisal

Responds to own name
Understands "no-no" and "bye-bye"
Imitates vocalizations
May say "ma-ma" or "da-da" nonspecifically
Crawls, creeps, scoots
Sits independently
May pull to stand
Inferior pincer grasp
Pokes with index finger
Plays peek-a-boo and pat-a-cake
Feeds self with fingers
May show stranger anxiety

Screening Tests

Hematocrit or hemoglobin
Lead screening if at risk

Anticipatory Guidance

Encourage the baby's vocalizations.
Play social games such as pat-a-cake, peek-a-boo, and so-big.
Disciplinary measures at this age include distraction, stimulus control, proximal physical presence, and routines.
Limit the number of rules and consistently enforce them.
The need for parental authority and leadership.
Establish bedtime routine. Encourage baby to comfort himself or herself by putting him or her to bed awake.

Give infant table foods in order to increase the texture and variety of foods in his or her diet.

Developmental Goals: Early Childhood

Warm relationship and good communication with parents and siblings
Develops autonomy, independence, and assertiveness
Independence in eating
Completion of toilet training
Ability to separate from parents
Self-discipline
Intelligible speech
Demonstrates curiosity and initiative
Responds to limit-setting and discipline
Learns appropriate self-care
School readiness

TWELVE MONTHS

Selected Components of the Health Supervision Consultation

Trigger Questions

What do you do when _____ wants something he (she) should not have? Does _____ have a favorite object or toy he (she) uses to comfort himself (herself)?

Have you childproofed your home?

Do you have smoke alarms in your home?

Observation of Parent-Infant Interaction and Family Communication

Complete Physical Examination

Plot head circumference, length, weight and weight for length

Developmental Surveillance

Pulls to stand, cruises, may take a few steps alone
Has vocabulary of one to three words
Imitates vocalizations
Drinks from a cup
Waves "bye-bye"
Feeds self

Screening Tests

Tuberculin test if at risk

Anticipatory Guidance

Discipline means to teach and protect, not punish.

Disciplinary measures include distraction, gentle restraint of the child, removal of the object from the toddler or removal of the child from the stimulus, proximal parental presence, structure and routines.

The need for parental authority and leadership.
Although hitting and biting are common, the toddler should be taught not to hit or bite. "No hitting!" "No biting! Biting hurts!"

Praise the child for good behavior.
Pick up, cuddle, hold, and talk with the child.
Encourage exploration and initiative.

Establish a regular bedtime ritual.
Play games with the child.
Promote family communication.
Begin brushing the toddler's teeth with a tiny, pea-sized amount of fluoridated toothpaste.
Discuss initial dental referral.
Switch to a toddler car seat.
Supervise the toddler constantly when in or around water.
Keep toddler away from moving machinery, lawnmowers, overhead garage doors, driveways, streets.
As much as possible, let the toddler feed himself or herself.
If bottle feeding, change from formula to whole milk.

FIFTEEN MONTHS

Selected Components of the Health Supervision Consultation

Trigger Questions

What are you most proud of with _____?
Does _____ have any special things that he (she) likes to do such as look at a book or play a game?

Observation of Parent-Toddler Interaction and Family Communication

Complete Physical Examination

Plot weight, length, head circumference, and weight for length

Developmental Surveillance

Has vocabulary of three to six words
Can point to one or more body parts
Climbs stairs
Stacks two blocks
Listens to a story

Anticipatory Guidance

Encourage language development by reading books, singing songs, and talking about what you and he or she are seeing and doing together.
Teach injury prevention.
Discuss initial dental examination.
Support the child's emerging independence and autonomy while maintaining consistent limits.
Emphasize the need for parental authority and leadership.

EIGHTEEN MONTHS

Selected Components of the Health Supervision Consultation

Trigger Questions

Does _____ have any playmates?
What are some of _____'s favorite activities?
How much time do you spend playing with _____?
How does _____ assert himself (herself)?

Observation of Parent-Toddler Interaction and Family Communication

Complete Physical Examination

Plot weight, length, head circumference, and weight for length

Developmental Surveillance

Throws a ball
Has vocabulary of 15 to 20 words
Uses two-word phrases
Stacks three or four blocks
Listens to a story, looks at pictures, and names objects
Imitates a crayon stroke and scribbles

Anticipatory Guidance

Keep time-out or other disciplinary measures brief.
Do not expect toddler to share his or her toys.
Give child two to three nutritious snacks a day. Select snacks that are rich in complex carbohydrates. Limit sweets and high-fat snacks.
Discuss initial dental examination.
Emphasize the need for parental authority and leadership.
Limit quantity of television viewing.
Teach injury prevention.

TWO YEARS

*Selected Components of the Health
Supervision Consultation*

Trigger Questions

How are you disciplining and setting limits
for _____ ?

What are some of _____'s recent accomplishments?

How's toilet training going?

Does _____ have temper tantrums? How
do you deal with them?

*Observation of Parent-Child Interaction
and Family Communication*

Complete Physical Examination

Plot weight, height, head circumference, and
  weight for length

Developmental Surveillance

Can go up and down stairs one step at a time
Can stack five or six blocks
Has vocabulary of at least 20 words
Uses two-word phrases
Can follow two-step commands
Makes or imitates horizontal and circular crayon
  stroke
Uses cup, spoon, and fork

Screening Tests

Cholesterol screen if at risk
Lead screen if at risk

Anticipatory Guidance

Spend individual time with the child—playing,
  hugging or holding him or her, taking walks,
  painting, and doing puzzles together.
Start toilet training when child is dry for periods
  of about 2 hours. Child can distinguish between
  wet and dry, can pull his or her pants up and
  down, wants to succeed, and can indicate when
  he or she is about to have a bowel movement.
Discuss initial dental examination.
Teach injury prevention.
Emphasize the need for parental authority and
  leadership.
Limit television viewing.

THREE YEARS

*Selected Components of the Health
Supervision Consultation*

Trigger Questions

What are some of the new things
that _____ is doing?

How is toilet training going?

How is child care (preschool, early intervention) going?

Do family members understand _____'s
speech?

How are you dealing with _____'s greater
independence?

Are you able to set clear and specific limits
for _____?

*Observation of Parent-Child Interaction
and Family Communication*

Complete Physical Examination

Blood pressure determination

Developmental Surveillance

Jumps in place
Balances on one foot
Rides a tricycle
Speech is intelligible to strangers most of the time
Knows age and gender
Copies a circle and a cross
Can feed and dress self
Has bladder and bowel control
Fantasy play

Anticipatory Guidance

**Provide chance for child to participate in play
  groups, preschool.**
Limit television viewing.
Discuss initial dental examination.
**Encourage child to talk to you about his or her
  preschool, friends, or observations. Answer
  his or her questions.**
Expect normal curiosity about anatomic differences between boys and girls.
Use correct terms for genitalia.
Answer questions about where babies come from.
Emphasize the need for parental authority and
  leadership.
Teach injury prevention.

FOUR YEARS

*Selected Components of the Health
Supervision Consultation*

Trigger Questions

What are some of _____'s new skills?

What does his (her) preschool teacher say about
him (her)?

Observation of Parent-Child Interaction and Family Communication

Complete Physical Examination

Blood pressure determination

Developmental Surveillance

Draws a person with three parts
Knows first and last name
Describes a recent experience
Is aware of gender of self and others
Can sing a song
Hops, jumps on one foot

Anticipatory Guidance

Encourage interactive reading with the child.
Teach safety rules regarding strangers.
Have child wear a helmet when riding tricycle or bicycle.
Limit television viewing to average of 1 hour per day of appropriate programs.

FIVE YEARS

Selected Components of the Health Supervision Consultation

Trigger Questions

For the parents:
What makes you most proud of _____?
How does _____ feel about going to school?
What are your plans for _____'s after-school care?
For the child:
Tell me some of the things you do best.
Are you and your friends excited about going to school?
What do you do for fun?

Observation of Parent-Child Interaction and Family Communication

Complete Physical Examination

Developmental Surveillance

Knows own address and telephone number
Copies a square or triangle
Draws a person with a head, body, arms, and legs
Recognizes most letters of the alphabet
Prints some letters
Knows own address and telephone number
Dresses self

Screening Test

Urinalysis

Anticipatory Guidance

Praise child for cooperation and accomplishments.
Encourage child to talk with parents about his or her school or friends.
Expect child to follow family rules for bedtime, television, chores, etc.
Teach child to swim.
Teach child pedestrian and neighborhood safety rules.
Teach safety rules for interacting with strangers.
Promote physical activity.
Teach child to respect authority.
Teach difference between right and wrong.
Serve as an ethical and behavioral role model.
Handle anger constructively in the family.
Participate as a family in school and community activities.

Developmental Goals: Middle Childhood

Self-responsibility for good health habits
One or more close friends
Believe that they have the capacity for personal success
High self-esteem
School achievement
Self-responsibility for homework
Ability to express feelings
Understand right and wrong
Remain physically fit
Resolve conflicts and manage anger constructively
Social competence

SIX YEARS

Selected Components of the Health Supervision Consultation

Trigger Questions

For the parents:
What are you most proud of with _____?
What do you and _____ like to do together?
How is school going for _____?
Does _____ talk to you about what's happening in school?
Do you participate in activities at his (her) school?
For the child:
How is school going?

What do you like the most about school? The least?

Tell me some of the things you do best.

What do you like to do after school?

Do you have a best friend? Tell me about your friend.

Draw me a picture of your family. Tell me a story about your picture.

When you have a problem, to whom do you talk to about it?

Observation of Parent-Child Interaction and Family Communication

Complete Physical Examination

Screening Test

Cholesterol screen if family history

Anticipatory Guidance

Promote self-responsibility, e.g., for homework.
Encourage self-discipline and impulse control.
Encourage child to express his or her feelings.
Encourage reading.
Discuss after-school programs and activities.

EIGHT YEARS

Selected Components of the Health Supervision Consultation

Trigger Questions

For the parents:
What are some of the things you do together as a family?

How is _____ doing in school?

Does _____ have friends over? Does he (she) go to friends' homes?

For the child:
What do you do best?

What are you really proud of?

Tell me about your friends.

Do you stay home by yourself before or after school?

Have you ever been pushed to do things you didn't want to do?

Observation of Parent-Child Interaction and Family Communication

Complete Physical Examination

Examine for scoliosis
Tanner stage or sexual maturity rating

Anticipatory Guidance

Talk with parents about the importance of serving as role models by having healthy lifestyles.
Encourage regular physical activity.
Encourage child safety rules for the home.
Ensure that guns, if in the home, are locked up with ammunition stored separately.
Teach child to eat a balanced diet.
If child receives family life education at school, discuss it with him or her.

TEN YEARS

Selected Components of the Health Supervision Consultation

Trigger Questions

For the parents:
What are you most proud of with _____?

How is _____ doing in school?

Tell me about _____'s relationships with other children.

Does _____ share his (her) feelings and school experiences with you?

Do you talk to _____ about sensitive subjects such as sex, drugs, or drinking?

What sex education has _____ received? Who provided that? Did you discuss it with _____?

Does she know about menstruation?

Does he know about wet dreams?

For the child:
How is school going? How are your grades?

What do you do best?

Tell me about your friends. Do you have a best friend?

What education have you had about sex?

What are some of the questions that I can answer for you?

If you could, how would you change your life? Your home? Your family?

Do your friends smoke? Drink? Take drugs? Have sex? Do you?

What are some of the things that worry you? Make you happy? Make you sad? Make you angry? How do you handle that?

Complete Physical Examination

Determine the body mass index
Tanner stage or sexual maturity rating
Examine for scoliosis

Anticipatory Guidance

For the parents:

Anticipate such adolescent behaviors as the influence of peers, changes in communication between adolescent and parents, challenges to parental rules and authority, conflicts over issues of independence, refusal to participate in some family activities, moodiness, and risk taking.

Promote interaction with peers.

Help child develop ability to withstand peer pressure.

Prepare daughter for menstruation.

Prepare son for wet dreams.

Respect the child's need for privacy.

For the child:

Discuss body changes during puberty.

Discuss questions relating to sexuality.

Counsel not to smoke, use smokeless tobacco, drink alcohol, or use drugs.

Exercise regularly.

Importance of talking with physician if child feels angry much of the time, depressed, or hopeless.

Adolescent health supervision is discussed in Chapter 20.

FURTHER READING

American Academy of Pediatrics, Committee on Psychosocial Aspects of Child and Family Health: Guidelines for Health Supervision III. Elk Grove Village, IL, AAP, 1997.

Green M (ed): Bright Futures: Guidelines for Health Supervision of Infants, Children, and Adolescents. Arlington, VA, National Center for Education in Maternal and Child Health, 1994. A pocket guide is also available from the National Maternal and Child Health Clearinghouse, 8201 Greensboro Drive, Suite 600, McLean, VA 22102.

Richard E. Kreipe

Chapter 20

Health Supervision for Adolescents

CONTEMPORARY ADOLESCENCE AND HEALTH PROBLEMS OF ADOLESCENTS

Adolescence is the dynamic, developmental transition stage bridging childhood and adulthood. Causes of morbidity and mortality for adolescents now stem largely from life conditions and dangerous behaviors, rather than from natural causes: (1) injuries (including motor vehicle accidents, suicide, and homicide); (2) substance use and abuse; (3) reproductive health conditions ranging from sexually transmitted diseases (STDs) including the acquired immunodeficiency syndrome (AIDS) to unintentional pregnancy; (4) mental health problems, most notably depression and conduct disorders; and (5) nutritional and eating problems ranging from obesity to anorexia nervosa. Moreover, many lifestyle habits affecting the health of adults (both negatively and positively) are initiated as behaviors during the teenage years: more than 90% of adult smokers begin smoking before age 18, and healthy eating habits estab-

lished as an adolescent are likely to persist throughout adulthood.

The blurring of the interface between the biologic and psychosocial domains and between individual and public health concerns in this age group underscores the importance of health professionals' special training and experience in dealing with adolescents and their unique health issues. **Intervening during adolescence provides the opportunity not only to prevent the onset of health-damaging behaviors but also to modify health-compromising behaviors that may eventually become firmly entrenched in adult life.** Although adolescents have the lowest utilization of health care services and, as a group, remain relatively healthy, they report that their doctor is an important and respected source of information about their health. Table 20–1 lists the topics that adolescents and parents consider important to discuss with physicians. Thus, even though encounters between health care providers and adolescents tend to be few, episodic, unplanned, and based on a specific problem or need, they still provide excellent occasions to foster health promotion.

TABLE 20–1. Topics Adolescents and Parents Consider Important in Health Care Supervision Visits

Topic	Adolescent Preferences, %		Parental Preferences, %
	Desired Discussion at Visit	*Actually Discussed at Visit*	Topic Very or Somewhat Important
Exercise	86	42	92
Growth/nutrition	80	47	96
STDs	70	18	91
Contraception	66	22	85
Acne	64	30	90
Depression	59	16	88
Alcohol	52	23	94
Drugs	50	23	94
School	48	37	69
Smoking	47	30	92
Sexual abuse	36	6	—

STDs, sexually transmitted diseases.

Adapted from Malus M, LaChance PA, Lamy L, et al.: Priorities in adolescent health care: The teenager's viewpoint. J Fam Pract 25:159–162, 1987; and Cavanaugh RM, Hastings-Tolsma M, Keenan D, et al.: Anticipatory guidance for the adolescent parents' concerns. Clin Pediatr 32:542–545, 1993. Reprinted by permission of Appleton & Lange, Inc.

The purpose of this chapter is threefold: to stimulate interest in the clinician working with this challenging age group, to outline specific methods to address health promotion topics, and to improve the knowledge and skills of the clinician so that every visit with an adolescent can be an opportunity for valuable, preventive, and health-promoting services.

THEORETICAL CONCEPTS OF ADOLESCENT HEALTH SUPERVISION

Health supervision (previously known as "well adolescent care") consists of measures that promote adolescent health, prevent mortality and morbidity, and enhance subsequent development and maturation into healthy adulthood. It is an ongoing, interactive process, rather than an event, which includes regularly scheduled visits for anticipatory guidance, screening, brief counseling, and immunizations. Three complementary sets of guidelines (*Bright Futures: Guidelines for Health Supervision of Infants, Children, and Adolescents, 1995; Guidelines for Adolescent Preventive Services, 1994;* and *Guidelines for Health Supervision III, 1997*) that address the provision of such measures for adolescents have been published recently. The Bright Futures guidelines note that a major role of health supervision is the "periodic assessment and support of the adolescent's adaptation to new roles and risks that accompany growth and development." Health supervision is most likely to succeed when it fosters joint participation and shared responsibility of adults who have a personal or professional relationship with the adolescent (e.g., parents, teachers) and the adolescent himself or herself in a variety of settings and circumstances. Adolescents may require special efforts to engage them in regular health supervision and are most likely to do so when there is respect for their individuality, support of their emerging autonomy, a developmental approach, and a focus on their strengths in a therapeutic alliance characterized by mutual respect and trust.

In the Guidelines for Adolescent Preventive Services (GAPS), the goals of health supervision are to (1) deter adolescents from participating in behaviors that jeopardize health (such as smoking or dieting); (2) detect physical, emotional, and behavioral problems early and to intervene immediately; (3) reinforce and encourage behaviors that promote healthy living (such as regular exercise); and (4) provide immunizations against infectious disease. In contrast with traditional medical visits, in which diagnostic and therapeutic interventions are disease-oriented and the keystone of each encounter is the physical examination, health promotion stresses screening for comorbidities and targeting social morbidities in the context of the individual adolescent, focusing on practical solutions to common problems (see Tables 20–2 and 20–3).

Because physician counseling can help patients change behavior, the U.S. Preventive Services Task Force has concluded that **health education and counseling should have priority over conventional primary care clinical activities, such as laboratory screening.** Prochaska noted that the ability of adolescents to practice healthy behaviors requires three components: knowledge, resources, and motivation. Information is the central component of traditional health education, but numerous

TABLE 20–2. Comparison of Guidelines for Adolescent Preventive Services (GAPS) and Traditional Health Care

GAPS Recommendations	Traditional Health Care
Provider plays an important role in coordinating adolescent health promotion. This role complements health guidance that adolescents receive from their family, school, and community.	Provider role is considered to be independent of health education programs offered by schools, family, and the community.
Preventive interventions target social morbidities such as alcohol and other drug use, suicide, STDs (including HIV infection), unintended pregnancy, and eating disorders.	Emphasis is on biomedical problems alone, such as the medical consequences of health risk behaviors (e.g., STDs, unintended pregnancy).
Provider emphasizes screening for comorbidities, i.e., adolescent participation in clusters of specific health risk behaviors.	Emphasis is on the diagnosis and treatment of categorical health conditions.
Annual visits permit early detection of health problems and offer an opportunity to provide health education and develop a therapeutic relationship.	Visits are scheduled only as needed for acute care episodes or for other specific purposes (e.g., immunizations or an examination prior to participating in sports).
Provider performs three comprehensive physical examinations: one during early, middle, and late adolescence.	Current standards vary from as necessary to examinations every year during adolescence.
It is recommended that all parents receive education about adolescent health care at least twice during their child's adolescence.	Parents are included in the health care of the adolescent solely at the discretion of the provider, who also serves as the sole decision maker of what health education topics should be addressed with parents.

HIV, human immunodeficiency virus; STDs, sexually transmitted diseases.
Adapted from Guidelines for Adolescent Preventive Services, 3rd ed. Chicago, American Medical Association, copyright 1996. Reproduced by permission.

studies have shown that motivation is the stronger influence in changing behavior for adolescents. The stages of change model, in which motivation to change plays a central role, proposes five hierarchical stages of increasing readiness and motivation to modify (hopefully improve) health-related behaviors: (1) precontemplation, (2) contemplation, (3) preparation, (4) action, and (5) maintenance of healthy behavior.

Applied to adolescents and cigarette smoking, the stages of change model has clinical appeal. For example, consider a hypothetical 14-year-old adolescent male, Matt, who began smoking at 10 years of age and whose parents both smoke two packs per day, but who has already learned in health class in school the hazards of smoking. The combination of his perceived invulnerability to health problems ("I only smoke half a pack a day and don't always inhale"), combined with social benefits of smoking ("All my friends smoke and a lot of adults I know smoke without any problems") might place him at the precontemplation stage of smoking cessation. The most appropriate intervention would be for him to receive factual, personalized information, expressed with feelings of concern (avoiding nagging, pestering, or scare tactics), while soliciting his opinions and encouraging a therapeutic alliance as the foundation for advancing toward stages closer to smoking cessa-

tion): "I am concerned about your smoking, Matt. What are your thoughts about your habit?" The response to this trigger question could explain resistance to giving up smoking that he might have, or open up other areas of concern. Alternatively, it could also eventually increase Matt's receptivity to entering the stage of contemplation and would underscore the clinician's interest in facilitating such a movement toward health. The stage of contemplation would be evidenced by Matt's statement: "I know I should stop smoking, but it's so hard with my parents and friends all smoking. I've tried to cut back, but I can never go more than a day or two before I'm lighting up again."

Such a statement could be met with the clinician noting, "It sure is difficult, partly because nicotine is so addictive, and partly because you enjoy being with people who are smoking. However, my advice is still for you to stop smoking, and I'd like to help you do that. My hunch is that you're pretty popular with your peers. Do you think any of them might be interested in stopping, too? Also, it would help your parents' health if they stopped smoking. Have you ever talked to them about your wanting to stop? Maybe this could be a group effort, with everyone benefiting and everyone helping everyone else to stop smoking." This script could flow in different directions, but the

TABLE 20–3. Office Interventions for Adolescent Health Promotion

Identify those at risk
- Screening questions
- Family behaviors
- Peer behaviors

Clearly state desired behavior
- Personalize to patient
- Get patient commitment
- Set realistic goal, target date

Provide meaningful health information
- Stress immediate physical or social consequences (rather than long-term)
- Emphasize immediate benefits of desired behavior (health, performance, status or respect in eyes of peers)
- Give alternatives

Give resources for help
- Office handouts, how-to or self-help pamphlets
- Referrals to support groups and appropriate professionals
- Peer refusal skills

Join forces with other partners
- Families (role modeling, joint behavior changes)
- Schools (support strong interactive health education programs)
- Communities and organizations

Follow-up
- Reinforce at future visits
- Express continued interest
- Realize that behavior change is slow and incremental

Adapted from Beach RK: Priority health behaviors in adolescents: Health promotion in the clinical setting. *In* Adolescent Health Update: A Clinical Guide for Pediatricians, Vol 3. Section on Adolescent Health, American Academy of Pediatrics, Feb 1991. Used with permission of the American Academy of Pediatrics.

essential features for the clinician are to be interactive and to instill confidence in the adolescent's ability eventually to stop smoking.

When Matt advances to the third stage in the progression toward smoking cessation (preparation), he is motivated to stop smoking. At this stage, **the clinician needs to take a more active role in assisting the adolescent actually to stop smoking.** This could include interventions such as (1) providing self-help materials; (2) setting a quit-smoking date with the adolescent, noting it in the patient's record, and planning a follow-up visit soon after the quit date; (3) developing an individualized, written stop-smoking agreement, also placing it in the patient's record; (4) including the parents in smoking cessation efforts; (5) encouraging avoidance of settings in which smoking is likely; (6) encouraging the adolescent to ask for friends' help in smoking cessation; and (7) nicotine patch or gum.

Matt should be aware that smoking cessation might be difficult to attain and maintain: "Matt, quitting smoking can be hard, especially if you start to have withdrawal from the physical and social triggers to smoking. People who finally become nonsmokers may try five or six times

before they quit for good. I say that to let you know that I'm not going to give up as long as you don't." Likewise, if Matt stops smoking only briefly, one could explore how he was able to avoid smoking for a certain period of time, rather than focusing on his return to smoking. By helping him to determine what aided his efforts to stop smoking, as well as what triggered his relapse, Matt may be able to extend his next period of abstinence further. By avoiding situations that increase his risk of smoking and engaging in peer-related or family activities that do not involve smoking, he is more likely to become a nonsmoker.

The National Cancer Institute offers practical strategies in health promotion with respect to tobacco use, using a systematic approach of reminders that trigger more complete, frequent interventions and that prompt specific counseling strategies, based on the "5A's." These strategies include (1) *a*nticipating tobacco use before it occurs, and providing primary prevention messages about tobacco use; (2) *a*sking about tobacco use among friends, family, and the adolescent; (3) *a*dvising adolescents who are not using tobacco to continue nonuse and to avoid situations where smoking is likely to occur as well as *a*dvising adolescents who are using tobacco about the health risks associated with the form(s) of tobacco that they are using, and also *a*dvising them to decrease or eliminate their use; (4) *a*ssisting those who are interested in stopping tobacco use to do so with active encouragement and concrete decisions regarding change; and (5) *a*rranging follow-up visits for adolescents who are using tobacco, either to continue to advise them about cessation, or to assist them in attaining or maintaining cessation. The principles outlined in this method can be adapted to other adolescent health problems, such as weight reduction (Table 20–4).

UNIQUE FEATURES OF ADOLESCENT HEALTH SUPERVISION

Adolescents may be categorized into three stages: early (10 to 15 years of age), middle (15 to 17 years of age) and late (17 to 21 years of age). Likewise, various developmental tasks become focal points for young people as they proceed through adolescence. Four major tasks can be related to health and health care: undergoing and accepting the physical changes of puberty, achieving autonomy, acquiring a stable sense of identity, and attaining adult thinking skills. These developmental factors need to be kept in mind

TABLE 20–4. Centers for Disease Control and Prevention Priority Health Behaviors for Adolescents

1. Use seat belts.
2. Do not drink (or use drugs) and drive.
3. If you have sex, use condoms.
4. Do not smoke.
5. Eat a low-fat diet.
6. Get regular aerobic exercise.

These six "Golden Rules" are the most effective and achievable lifetime behaviors that will reduce years of potential life lost to the major killers: motor vehicle accidents, AIDS, cardiovascular disease, and cancer.

AIDS, acquired immunodeficiency syndrome.
Adapted from Beach RK: Priority health behaviors in adolescents: Health promotion in the clinical setting. *In* Adolescent Health Update: A Clinical Guide for Pediatricians, Vol 3. Section on Adolescent Health, American Academy of Pediatrics, Feb 1991. Used with permission of the American Academy of Pediatrics.

when interacting with an adolescent, since they can influence the health supervision consultation. For example, an early-adolescent female might be extremely self-conscious about her pubertal changes; she might benefit from being interviewed while her physical examination is being performed. Likewise, a late-adolescent male might present an adult appearance, but still might have concrete operational thinking. He would benefit from an approach focused on immediate consequences of health behaviors, rather than on abstractions.

Confidentiality is a critical element of health supervision for adolescents. Several unique features of confidentiality as applied to this age group deserve comment. First, providing confidentiality is crucial to the establishment of trust and engaging the adolescent as an active participant in health care. Fewer than one in five adolescents reports being willing to seek health care related to sexuality or drug use, if their parents knew. Second, confidentiality is based on a respect for privacy and autonomy in the developing adolescent, and not on keeping secrets from parents. All health supervision guidelines encourage open discussion between parents and adolescents. Likewise, parents are included in health guidance as part of routine visits for early adolescents. Confidentiality can be introduced by stating to the adolescent and parent(s) together, early in the visit, "When my patients grow into adolescents, they have an increasing need for confidentiality. By this, I mean what we talk about is kept private. By the time you become an adult, everything that you discuss with your doctor, whether it is me or someone else, is private. So it is a good idea to include

confidentiality as part of your care, now that you are an adolescent."

Third, confidentiality is relative. Continuing the comments previously made, one could raise this issue by saying, "Although most of what we talk about can remain confidential, it would not be in your best interest to keep some things private. Can you think of situations where we would need to share what we talk about with others?" When posed with this question, most adolescents identify having suicidal thoughts or intentions as circumstances in which confidentiality would need to be breached. One could then clarify when, why, and how breaches in confidentiality are handled: "If I think that you are in danger of hurting yourself, being hurt by someone else, or hurting someone else, then I might need to override confidentiality and let other people know what's going on—to prevent something bad from happening. However, to give you as much control over the situation as possible, we would discuss who should be included and how to do it. I wouldn't go behind your back, because the decisions would involve you."

A fourth feature of adolescent confidentiality is the legal rights of minors (generally those younger than 18 years of age). The general circumstances in which adolescents may seek health care without parental consent include being an emancipated minor (living independently or having served in the armed forces), or for care related to pregnancy, substance abuse, or mental health. If confidential health care is requested by an adolescent, the reasons should be documented and discussion with the parents encouraged (Table 20–5).

TABLE 20–5. Recommendations on Confidential Health Service for Adolescents

Confidential health care for adolescents is essential.
Physicians should allow emancipated and mature minors to consent for their own treatment.
Physicians should involve parents in the medical care of their adolescents when it is in the best interests of the adolescent. When it is not, parental consent or notification should not be a barrier to care.
Physicians should discuss their policies about confidentiality with parents and the adolescent patient.
State and county medical societies should play a more active role in supporting confidential services for teenagers. They also need to work to eliminate laws that restrict such care.
Medical schools and training programs need to educate students and residents about issues surrounding consent and confidential health care.
Health care financiers need to develop systems that preserve confidentiality for adolescents.

Adapted from American Medical Association Council on Scientific Affairs: Confidential health services for adolescents. JAMA 269:1420–1424, 1993. Copyright 1993, American Medical Association.

PROCESS OF INTERVIEWING ADOLESCENTS IN HEALTH SUPERVISION

Most practitioners find interviewing the adolescent the most difficult aspect of health supervision. Although questionnaires can facilitate fact-finding with respect to risks, there is no substitute for the clinical interview in obtaining information and developing a therapeutic relationship. Various mnemonic aids have been suggested, including HEADSS and PACES (Table 20–6). The latter is useful in health supervision, since it addresses issues relevant to the individual, family history, and the influence of the peer group. Using this format, the health supervision interview takes only several minutes but yields a large amount of data, while stimulating adolescents to think about how their behavior might affect their health.

The PACES interview begins with "P"—a focus on *peers and parents:* "The health problems of adolescents are different from either children or adults. To help me focus on the special needs of my adolescent patients, I have a reminder that I use—putting adolescents through the paces—with each letter of the word paces standing for an important area that I want to discuss during our visit. You can also bring up anything that you would like to discuss as we go along. The 'P' in paces stands for peers. What do you think are the health problems of people your age? What about *your* peers and friends? Do they do anything that might cause health problems for them? The 'P' also stands for parents. How is the health of your mom and dad? Do you worry about any of their health habits?"

With this questioning, it is clear that the interview is initiated with a focus on health, rather than on how things are at home. Moreover, it gives the provider a good sense of what health habits the adolescent may be at risk of encountering. Having a concept of the adolescent's peer group and parental behaviors gives the clinician a good understanding of the influences in an adolescent's environment, and can help one to focus on high-risk areas. This opening gambit is also less threatening than initially asking directly about his or her behavior, but naturally leads to such follow-up questions as "What's been *your* experience with using drugs at parties?" Finally, asking about parental health can lead to an updated family history.

The second element of the mnemonic is "A"—*alcohol, accidents, and other drugs*—and can be introduced with the question "What do you think is the leading cause of death in adolescents?" Most adolescents (if reminded, "It begins with the letter "A") answer either accidents or alcohol. Since half of fatal accidents involving adolescents are related to alcohol, patients can be told they are correct, regardless of which they answer. The astute clinician can individualize this aspect of the interview, based on the responses given up to that point. For example, for younger adolescents who do not use alcohol or drive, the focus on accidents may be on skateboarding safety or the need to use seatbelts when riding as a passenger in a car, and to never ride in a car being driven by someone who is impaired.

Tobacco has come under increased scrutiny recently owing to the lawsuits against the tobacco industry and the movement to reduce access to and use of tobacco products by children and adolescents. However, cigarettes continue to be seen as a "gateway drug" for numerous young people, since tobacco is often the first illicit substance to be used. Asking about *cigarettes and other forms of tobacco* as the third element of PACES gives the clinician an opportunity to identify the health beliefs and values of an adolescent. For adolescents who have not begun using tobacco products, the ways in which they have been able to resist pressures to smoke should be explored and positively reinforced.

By this stage, the adolescent is fully aware of the content and process of the exchange of information and the interview is often conversational. A practitioner who demonstrates interest can engage the patient as a therapeutic ally in health promotion. Thus, the transition to less traditional areas, represented in PACES by "E"—*exercise, eating, and emotions*—is facilitated. After exploring the health problems associated with substance use and abuse, the clinician could say, "We've talked a lot about health problems, but there are also things that you can do to keep healthy. Can you think of things that begin with the letter 'E' that you can do daily to make yourself healthy?" **The benefits of regular aerobic exercise (ranging from organized sports to**

TABLE 20–6. Interview Structures for Adolescents

Getting into Kids' HEADSS	Putting Adolescents Through the PACES
Home	**P**eers/parents
Education/vocation	**A**ccidents/alcohol and other drugs
Activities/ambition	**C**igarettes/other forms of tobacco
Drugs/DWI/delinquency	**E**xercise/eating/emotions
Sexuality/sexual abuse	**S**chool/sexuality/sleep
Suicide/safety	

DWI, driving while intoxicated.

TABLE 20–7. American Academy of Pediatrics—Health Care Visit for Preadolescents to Young Adults

	10 and 11 Years	12 and 13 Years	14 and 15 Years
Health Assessment	**Address questions to the child:** "How are things going for you?" "What would you like to discuss today?" School; recreation; problems discussed at the last visit **Address questions to the parents:** "What concerns do you have about your child?" Family stresses	**Address questions to the adolescent:** "How have you been?" "What concerns do you want to discuss today?" Status of problems discussed at the last visit **Address questions to the parents:** "What concerns do you want to discuss?" Family stresses; adolescent's emotional well-being	**Address questions to the adolescent:** "How is everything going for you?" "What questions do you have today?" Status of issues discussed at the last visit **Address questions to the parents:** "What questions do you have today?" "How are things going for your family?" "How is it parenting an adolescent?" "Do you have any concerns?"
Physical Examination (PE)	Height/weight/BP/body mass index[1] General PE: include scoliosis screen and sexual maturity rating (SMR) **Observations of behavior** **Testing:** Hgb or Hct, if menstruating[2] Dipstick urinalysis (UA) for leukocytes[2] Cholesterol, if indicated by history PPD, if indicated	Height/weight/BP/body mass index[1] General PE: include scoliosis screen, SMR, instruction in breast self-exam (BSE) or testes self-exam (TSE), pelvic examination if sexually active, assess vision/hearing at 12 yr **Observations of behavior/development** **Testing:** Hgb/Hct and dipstick UA for leukocytes[2] Cholesterol and PPD, if indicated Chlamydia, gonococci, syphilis and, in girls, Pap smear screening if sexually active HIV test if requested or if indicated by risk	Height/weight/BP/body mass index[1] General PE: include scoliosis screen, SMR, pelvic examination in sexually active girls, vision and hearing assessment at 15 years, and BSE or TSE instruction **Behavioral observations** **Testing:** Hgb/Hct and dipstick UA for leukocytes[2] Cholesterol and PPD, if indicated Chlamydia, gonococci, syphilis, and, in girls, Pap smear screening if sexually active HIV test if requested or if indicated by risk
Immunizations	Review immunization status Vaccine information sheets Td if indicated (usually 12–14 years); MMR #2 (if not yet given at 5–6 years); hepatitis B series may be started (if not given previously), schedule 2nd and 3rd doses; varicella vaccine if indicated	Review immunization status Vaccine information sheets Td if indicated; MMR #2 if indicated; varicella vaccine if indicated, schedule 2nd dose for 13-year-olds; hepatitis B (if not previously given), schedule 2nd and 3rd doses	Review immunization status Vaccine information sheets Td (if #5 dose not given in past 5 years); MMR #2 (if not previously given); hepatitis B series (if not yet given), schedule 2nd and 3rd doses; varicella vaccine if indicated, schedule 2nd dose

Anticipatory Guidance	**Nutrition** Balanced diet, limit junk food Fluoride, iron, calcium supplements if indicated **Good health habits** Regular exercise and dental care Avoid cigarettes, alcohol, other drugs **Injury prevention** Use of seatbelts Sports safety (helmets, protective gear) Gun safety **Good parenting practices** Show affection and interest Establish rules Encourage age-appropriate decision making (e.g., provide allowance, answer questions about sex)	**Good health habits, risk reduction** Nutrition, regular exercise Encourage sexual abstinence; if sexually active, discuss pregnancy prevention, STDs, including HIV prevention **Good parenting practices** Rules, supervision Interest and communication Promotion of independence, responsibility, self-esteem **Injury prevention** Use of seatbelts, helmets Hazards of drinking and driving Interpersonal conflict resolution without violence Gun safety	**Nutrition** Balanced diet, limit junk food, excess salt, fat **Sleep** **Social development** Encourage age-appropriate peer activities; resist harmful peer pressure **Good health habits, risk reduction** Regular exercise and dental care Cigarette, alcohol, and other drug use Encourage sexual abstinence; if sexually active, discuss pregnancy prevention, STDs, including HIV prevention **Good parenting practices** Rules formation and enforcement Promotion of adolescent's independence and acceptance of responsibility Communication, privacy, respect Role modeling, hazardous activity supervision
Closing the Visit	"Have we dealt with all of your concerns today?" Speak positively about the child's development Compliment parents on their parenting skills Schedule the next visit	"Have all your concerns been addressed?" Reinforce strengths of adolescent and parents Schedule the next visit Encourage the adolescent to contact you if an important concern arises	"Are there other questions we should discuss?" Talk positively and honestly about attributes of the adolescent and family Schedule the next visit, remind parents and adolescent that you welcome calls from the adolescent; have parents agree to visits initiated by the adolescent as necessary

Table continued on following page

TABLE 20–7. American Academy of Pediatrics—Health Care Visit for Preadolescents to Young Adults *Continued*

	16 and 17 Years	18 and 19 Years	20 and 21 Years
Health Assessment	**Address questions to the adolescent:** "How is everything going for you?" "What do you want to discuss today?" School, grades, dating, friends Status of concerns discussed at last visit **Address questions to the parents:** "Do you have questions or concerns about your son (or daughter)?" Changes in family or household? Stresses?	"How have you been since I saw you last?" "What do you want to talk about today?" School; work; long-term goals Family; friends; sexual activity Emotional well-being Alcohol or other drug use	"How are you doing?" "What would you like to talk about today?" Status of issues discussed at last visit Sexuality; menstrual history; sleep; school; work; friends; intimate relationships; relationship with parents Emotional well-being Cigarette, alcohol, or other drug use Family or household changes, stresses
Physical Examination (PE)	Height/weight/BP/Body mass index[1] General PE: include scoliosis screen, sexual maturity rating (SMR), pelvic examination in sexually active girls, and breast or testicle self-examination (BSE, TSE) instruction **Behavioral assessment:** Adolescent withdrawn or irritable? **Testing:** Hgb/Hct and dipstick UA for leukocytes[2] Cholesterol and PPD, if indicated

If sexually active: Females—annual gonorrhea/chlamydia screening and Pap smear Males—dipstick urinalysis for leukocytes Both—syphilis, HIV testing as indicated | Height/weight/BP/Body mass index[1] General PE: include scoliosis screen, SMR, pelvic examination in sexually active girls, and BSE or TSE instruction **Observation of behavior/development Testing:** Hgb/Hct and dipstick UA for leukocytes[2] Cholesterol and PPD, if indicated

Sexually active adolescents: Females—annual gonorrhea/chlamydia screening and Pap smear Males—urine dipstick for leukocytes Both—syphilis, HIV testing as indicated | Height/weight/BP/Body mass index[1] General PE: include scoliosis screen, SMR, pelvic examination in sexually active girls, and BSE or TSE instruction **Behavioral observations Testing:** Hgb/Hct, dipstick UA for leukocytes[2] Cholesterol and PPD, if indicated Pap smear

If sexually active: Females—test for gonorrhea/chlamydia Males—urine dipstick for leukocytes Both—syphilis, HIV testing as indicated |
| **Immunizations** | Check immunization status. Vaccine information sheets Td booster once every 10 years; MMR #2 (if not previously given); hepatitis B series (if not yet given), schedule 2nd and 3rd doses; varicella vaccine if indicated, schedule 2nd dose | Check immunization status; vaccine information sheets; contraindication of some immunizations during pregnancy Td booster once every 10 years; MMR #2 if not yet given; varicella vaccine if indicated, schedule 2nd dose; hepatitis B (if not yet given), schedule 2nd and 3rd doses | Check immunization status; vaccine information sheets; caution about immunizations and pregnancy Td booster every 10 years; MMR #2 (if not previously given); varicella vaccine if indicated, schedule 2nd dose; hepatitis B (if not previously given), schedule 2nd and 3rd doses |

Anticipatory Guidance	**Nutrition** Balanced diet; avoid junk food, excess salt/fat **Exercise** **Sleep patterns** **Social relationships:** Resist some peer pressure **Plans for college/vocational training** **Injury prevention:** Cigarette, alcohol, or other drug use Car safety; violence avoidance; gun safety **Sexual activity:** Encourage abstinence Prevention of pregnancy and STDs **Good parenting practices:** Rules; communication; privacy	**Nutrition:** Balanced diet **Good health habits:** Dental care; regular exercise **Social relationships:** Communication with family and friends; resolving conflicts without violence Sexual relationships; appropriate to say "no"; prevention of pregnancy and STDs **Injury prevention:** Cigarette, alcohol, or other drug use Seatbelts, driving safety Gun safety	**Nutrition:** Balanced diet; avoid junk food, excess salt and fat **Good health habits:** Regular toothbrushing and dental care Routine exercise **Sleep** **Plans for future employment** **Sexual activity:** Support choice to say "no." Pregnancy; STD prevention **Injury prevention:** Use of seatbelts; bicycle helmet Cigarette, alcohol, or other drug use Avoidance of violence
Closing the Visit	To parents and adolescent: "Have we discussed each of your concerns?" Note positive attributes of the adolescent Acknowledge positive aspects of the parent-adolescent relationship; schedule next visit Remind parents and adolescent that you welcome calls and self-initiated visits	"Are there other issues we should discuss?" Schedule the next appointment	"Do you have any other concerns that we should talk about?" Reinforce patient's positive attributes Schedule the next visit; this may be the time to arrange for transfer of patient and records to another health care provider

[1] Body mass index [weight in kg ÷ (height in m)[2]] is not specifically mentioned in AAP guidelines, but is a useful tool in determining over- and underweight.
[2] Hemoglobin (Hgb) or hematocrit (Hct) and dipstick urinalysis for leukocytes performed at least once between age 11 and 21 years.
BP, blood pressure; HIV, human immunodeficiency virus; MMR, measles/mumps/rubella; PPD, purified protein derivative; STDs, sexually transmitted diseases; Td, tetanus and diphtheria toxoid.
Adapted from American Academy of Pediatrics, Committee on Psychosocial Aspects of Child and Family Health: Guidelines for Health Supervision III. Elk Grove Village, IL, AAP, 1997.

walking) **recognized by the adolescent can be elicited and expanded, as needed.** In addition, the recommendation that adolescents engage in vigorous physical activity 3 or more times a week for 20 minutes or longer per session can be noted. This should be emphasized for sedentary adolescents, such as those who spend several hours in front of a computer or television screen. The next "E," eating, can be closely linked to exercise, since the balance between energy intake and output determines body weight: "Exercise helps build strength, fitness and endurance, helps improve moods and also helps you to maintain a healthy weight by burning energy. But the other side of energy, what you eat and drink, is also important in keeping yourself healthy. What's a typical breakfast, lunch, and dinner like for you? What about snacks and junk food? What do you think about your weight . . . would you like to lose, gain, or stay the same?" Depending on the answers to these questions, the clinician can shape the health supervision to fit the individual needs of the adolescent. For a more complete discussion of the approach to the adolescent with an eating disorder, see Chapter 54.

Depending on the flow of the interview up to that time, the final "E," emotions, may be touched on only briefly, or could be emphasized more than some of the other topics. Several approaches can be used to introduce this topic—for example, "Emotions, of course, also play a role in health, especially for adolescents. Emotional problems can lead to things like suicide. What would you do if a friend told you that he was thinking about killing himself?" The "correct" answer for an adolescent would be to tell a trusted, responsible adult, rather than try to solve the problem single-handedly. From that point, the clinician could ask, "Have *you* ever felt so down, depressed, or hopeless that you've thought about hurting yourself?" Depending on the answer, appropriate follow-up questions would be asked and responses documented. This problem-solving approach identifies strengths and vulnerabilities in the adolescent, and ensures that the adolescent has the knowledge to avoid suicide, a leading cause of death in America. For adolescents who seem well-adjusted, giving reinforcement for the positive aspects of their mental health may have a protective effect, helping them avoid high-risk behaviors.

The final letter in the PACES mnemonic, "S," represents *school or sexuality.* Taking a sexual history is often difficult for pediatricians. The process is often facilitated by letting the adolescent know that you routinely ask questions related to sexuality, because it is an important aspect of their developing identity and sexual behaviors can

lead to numerous health problems, even death (from AIDS). Without making any judgments or assumptions, the clinician states, "Some adolescents have sexual practices that put their health at risk. I need to ask you questions that I ask my other patients, because I am concerned about their health." Since males are more likely to be sexually active than females, this opener can lead to asking a boy straightforwardly, "Have you had sex with females, males, or both females and males?" Since it is sexual behavior (not sexual orientation) that affects health, one should avoid using labels such as homosexual or heterosexual. Adolescent male prostitutes often self-identify as being heterosexual but engage in homosexual practices for money, drugs, or shelter. If the patient seems offended by the question because he is not sexually active at all, emphasize the nonjudgmental purpose of the question and give positive reinforcement for his choice of abstinence.

Older adolescent males are more likely than not to have engaged in intercourse, requiring a more thorough sexual history as part of health supervision. The sexual history, for both males and females, should include (1) the number of sexual partners in the past 6 months; (2) whether partners were symptomatic or were diagnosed with (STDs); and (3) whether *any* sexual partner was at high risk for STDs (e.g., multiple partners, exchanging sex for drugs, intravenous drug users, sex without a condom). For adolescents who have a history suggestive of an STD, one needs to explore their specific sexual practices, to determine risk of certain complications: "It would be helpful to know the types of sexual practices between you and your partner(s). These include vaginal, oral, and anal sex. Which have you done in the last month?"

PHYSICAL EXAMINATION IN ADOLESCENTS

All guidelines recommend measurement of blood pressure, height and weight, and determination of body mass index to determine degree of over- or underweight at each visit. Bright Futures recommends a complete physical examination at each visit during early, middle, and late adolescence, whereas the American Academy of Pediatrics (AAP) considers a complete annual physical examination essential from 11 through 21 years of age (Table 20–7). Bright Futures suggests that the physical examination have an emphasis on conditions arising, or worsening, during the second decade of life, including detection and management of scoliosis, skin and dental problems, evidence of abuse, evaluation of sexual maturity, and gender-specific genital and breast examinations (including self-examination of the breast for females and of the testes for males). GAPS calls for annual visits but for only three comprehensive physical examinations in the asymptomatic adolescent—one each during early, middle, and late adolescence, with greater emphasis placed on gathering information and promoting health, screening, and immunization. All three guidelines recommend targeted physical examination for adolescents reporting symptoms during routine health supervision visits.

There is consensus regarding the value of pelvic examination and Pap smears for adolescent females, and of screening sexually active males and females for STDs (including AIDS). Several serious conditions, such as precancerous changes in the cervix, human immunodeficiency virus (HIV) infection, and many STDs may be asymptomatic, but can be effectively treated or cured if detected by screening. For patients requesting confidential care, arrangements must be made to ensure that a bill for the examination or laboratory tests is not sent to the parents.

SCREENING TESTS

There is uniformity, but not unanimity, in guideline recommendations for screening procedures. The AAP suggests assessment of vision and hearing during early, middle, and late adolescence by objective measures, whereas Bright Futures recommends screening for vision if it is not tested at school, and for hearing if the child is exposed to loud noises, or with recurring ear infections. GAPS makes no recommendations for screening of hearing or vision. On the other hand, Bright Futures recommends testing for tuberculosis once at 14 to 16 years of age, regardless of risk factors, whereas both GAPS and the AAP recommend a tuberculin test only if the individual was exposed or in a high-risk situation. Cholesterol screening in all three guidelines is recommended if family history is unknown, or if the patient is considered to be at risk for hyperlipidemia. Screening for anemia is recommended by the AAP for all menstruating females, whereas Bright Futures recommends such testing only with moderate to heavy menses, chronic weight loss, nutritional deficits,

or excessive athletic activity. The AAP also recommends screening urine for leukocytes by dipstick in both males and females. As noted above, there is consensus agreement to screen sexually active adolescents for gonorrhea, chlamydial infection, syphilis, and HIV infection (human papillomavirus added in GAPS).

ANTICIPATORY GUIDANCE

Anticipatory guidance follows the topics already addressed in this chapter. Preferably, the assessment and physical examination are sufficiently interactive that anticipatory guidance can be woven into the structure of the visit, rather than addressed as a separate process.

CONCLUSION

Health supervision for adolescents presents both a challenge and an opportunity. By helping the adolescent in the transition from being a child to being an adult, the clinician can assist the patient to become increasingly autonomous in taking responsibility for health, while parents take a less active and more supportive role in this regard. By following authoritative guidelines and using the techniques addressed in this chapter, the practitioner can assist adolescents in promoting their own health.

FURTHER READING

American Academy of Pediatrics, Committee on Psychosocial Aspects of Child and Family Health: Guidelines for Health Supervision III. Elk Grove Village, IL, AAP, 1997.

Elster AB and Kuznets NJ: Guidelines for Adolescent Preventive Services. Baltimore, Williams & Wilkins, 1994.

Green M (ed): Bright Futures: Guidelines for Health Supervision of Infants, Children, and Adolescents. Arlington, VA, National Center for Education in Maternal and Child Health, 1994.

Millstein SG, Petersen AC, and Nightingale EO (eds): Promoting the Health of Adolescents: New Directions for the Twenty-First Century. New York, Oxford University Press, 1993.

Ozer EM, Brindis CD, Millstein SG, et al.: America's Adolescents: Are They Healthy? San Francisco, University of California, San Francisco, National Adolescent Health Information Center, 1997.

Prochaska JO: An Eclectic and Integrative Approach: Transtheoretical Therapy. New York, NY, Guilford Press, 1995.

Chapter **21**

Developmental, Behavioral, and Educational Surveillance

THE CHALLENGES OF IDENTIFYING CHILDREN AT RISK

In many cases it is challenging to identify children with developmental, behavioral, and educational problems even though they comprise approximately 16% of pediatric patients. The reasons for this are numerous: Many children with problems have relatively mild symptoms that are not readily apparent in the absence of measurement. Primary care clinicians have limited time to devote to early detection. Reimbursement for screening is often negligible. The behavior of young patients may interfere with accurate assessment. Children most in need of screening—those who have numerous psychosocial risk factors—do not often seek well-child care. Finally, the length and accuracy of many popular measures also deter early detection. As a consequence, most physicians rely not on screening tests but on clinical judgment. **Unfortunately, research on clinical judgment shows that it identifies fewer than half the children with mild mental retardation and other developmental disabilities.** Similarly, clinical judgment is known to identify only about 30% of children with serious emotional and behavioral disturbances. These findings are especially troubling because early intervention greatly increases children's chances to have a productive life.

The indisputable benefits of early intervention depend entirely on early detection. So, a huge and pressing question is How can professionals quickly and accurately identify patients with disabilities, promote optimal development, and monitor carefully those who are at risk for difficulties? **WHAT NOT TO DO.** Checklists, such as those incorporated into patient encounter forms, may be one of the largest reasons for underdetection of disabilities in pediatric offices. For example, most checklists list four or five skills at each age level (e.g., child puts two words together, draws a circle, walks up stairs, and so on). Nowhere is there a system for scoring. If a child can

perform four of the five skills, should you refer? What about two of five? Or three of five? No one knows and that is absolutely wrong. It is essential to know which scores suggest the presence of a problem and to know the probabilities of making an accurate referral decision. Thus, validated and standardized screening tests with acceptable levels of accuracy are the only method of early detection with any established effectiveness.

WHAT TO DO: SCREENS RELYING ON INFORMATION FROM PARENTS. The most effective tools for use in primary care are those that rely on information from parents. These circumvent the challenges of trying to evaluate children who may be fearful, ill, or uncooperative. Parent-based measures can be administered by interview when illiteracy is known or suspected. For parents who are non-English-speaking, several measures are published in multiple languages. Parent-based screens are also far briefer than tools relying on direct elicitation of children's skills and can be equally as accurate. Six high quality tools relying on parent report (meaning descriptions of children's behavior, skills, and environments) are described in Table 21–1.

Also listed in Table 21–1 is a screen that helps identify psychosocial risk factors known to have an adverse impact on development and behavior. **Four or more parent/family risk factors are associated with a steep decline in intellectual and academic achievement (e.g., less than a high school education, single-parent household, more than three children in the home, frequent household moves, parental mental health problems including depression and anxiety, an authoritarian parenting style,** that is, the parents mostly issue commands to children with very little interactive communication focused on children's needs or interests). It is not clear that psychosocial risk factor screens can replace developmental and behavioral screens, but they can be used along with such screens to help focus referrals. For example, at-risk children will benefit from early stimulation programs such as good quality child care or Head Start, and their parents may need referrals for parent training, social work, or mental health services.

The Parents' Evaluations of Developmental Status (PEDS), one of the tools listed in Table 21–1, is relatively new and is particularly suitable for pediatric offices because it (1) capitalizes on typical aspects of a pediatric encounter (asking parents about their concerns); (2) takes about 2 minutes to administer and score; and (3) offers guidance not only on when to refer but also on when to counsel families versus watchfully wait or simply monitor developmental and behavioral progress. PEDS is presented in Figure 21–1. Although PEDs is simple to use, it is important to remember that PEDS is a standardized measure. The wording of questions is essential. For example, families do not respond well to questions such as, "Do you have any worries about your child's development?" apparently because the word "worries" is too ominous and only 50% understand the word "development." Further, parents are not always prepared to discuss their concerns and may not think about development in the same way as professionals, that is, as a series of domains. The parent who complains that his or her child does not obey may not have considered whether the child hears, has the memory or attention to execute commands, or has the language skills to understand in the first place. Thus, careful probing (PEDS questions 2 to 10 in Figure 21–1) and interpretation (as presented in Figs. 21–2 and 21–3) are essential to the effective use of this measure.

One interesting finding from research on PEDS is that parents, regardless of parenting experience or levels of education, are equally able to voice concerns when carefully questioned. The reason appears to be that parents derive concerns by comparing their children to others. Making comparisons is a relatively simple cognitive skill that is mastered even by parents who might be considered quite slow. Less experienced parents are certainly less confident about their concerns and often preface them tentatively, but research shows that they are as accurate as more experienced parents.

Interpreting parents' concerns is also challenging. Neither parents nor clinicians want to discover sometimes that a child has a problem. Parents, having come to their concerns prior to the encounter, often begin looking very carefully for developmental gains. As a consequence they may present concerns with such prefaces as, "I was worried but I think he's doing better now." Research shows that such responses must be categorized as a concern or else children with delays will be underdetected.

As with all screening tests, there will be over-referrals. One of the interesting findings in PEDS research is that most overreferrals are of families who have only a single significant concern. This leaves clinicians with two options. One is to refer families with a single concern for additional screening (e.g., through early detection programs, the public schools, and developmental evaluation centers). The second option is to administer a second and different screening test in the pediatric office. Thus, pediatricians with strong interests in developmental and behavioral issues can opt to do more, whereas those with less interest can refer for further screening. In either case, it is very important to follow up with families who have concerns but whose children do not fail a second screening test. Research shows that these children score significantly lower than the children of non-concerned parents—not so low that they qualify for public school special education services but low enough to consider other options such as private tutoring or speech therapy, community literacy programs, and the like. Their families will also benefit from counseling by the pediatrician (e.g., stimulation sheets on how to build language, social skills). It may be that their children have problems that are currently subclinical but may eventually become serious. For this reason pediatricians will want to watchfully wait and carefully monitor patients who pass screening but whose parents have significant concerns.

Only about 3% of parents are not able to respond well to PEDS. Research shows that language barriers are common in this group (e.g., the parent and clinician speak different languages or the parent appears to have language impairments or mental health problems that preclude meaningful dialogue). When such barriers are apparent, it is necessary to seek an interpreter or use a different kind of screen, for example, one that involves direct elicitation of children's skills. Although some parent-report screens can be administered directly to children, there are also a number of high quality direct screens, as shown in Table 21–2. These were selected because they met standards for screening test accuracy (sensitivity and specificity between 70% and 80%).

MAKING SCREENING TESTS WORK IN PRIMARY CARE. There are many approaches to organizing pediatric offices so that screening tests can be used effectively for detection as well as for monitoring and counseling families. Table 21–3 lists methods that some have found effective and efficient.

EDUCATIONAL SURVEILLANCE

There are many reasons why approximately 25% of children experience difficulties in school.

Text continued on page 98

TABLE 21–1. Screening Instruments Using Information from Parents

Developmental/Educational Screens	Age Range	Description	Scoring	Accuracy	Time Frame
Child Development Inventories (formerly Minnesota Child Development Inventories) Ireton H. (1992). Behavior Science Systems, Box 580274, Minneapolis, MN 55458 (Phone: 612-929-6220). ($41.00)	3–72 mo	Three separate instruments each with 60 yes-no descriptions. Can be mailed to families, completed in waiting rooms, administered by interview or by direct elicitation. A 300-item assessment-level version may be useful in follow-up studies or subspeciality clinics and produces age equivalent and cutoff scores in each domain	A single cutoff tied to 1.5 SD below the mean	Sensitivity in detecting children with difficulties is excellent (greater than 75% across studies) and specificity in correctly detecting normally developing children is good (70% across studies)	About 10 min
Parents' Evaluations of Developmental Status (PEDS) Glascoe FP. (1997). Ellsworth & Vandermeer Press, Ltd., 4405 Scenic Drive, Nashville, TN 37204 (Phone: 615-386-0061; fax: 615-386-0346). http://edge.net/≈express. ($38.00)	Birth–8 yr	Two questions eliciting parents' concerns. Waiting room, interview and Spanish versions. Written at the 5th grade level. Identifies when to refer; provide a second screen; counsel; or monitor development, behavior, and academic progress	Identifies significant versus nonsignificant predictors of problems	Sensitivity ranging from 74% to 79% and specificity ranging from 70% to 80% across age levels	About 2 min
Ages and Stages Questionnaire (formerly Infant Monitoring System) Bricker D. Squires J. (1994). Paul H. Brookes, Publishers, PO Box 10624, Baltimore, MD 21285 (Phone: 1-800-638-3775). ($130)	0–48 mo	Clear drawings and simple directions help parents indicate children's skills. Separate copyable forms of 10 to 15 items for each age range (tied to well-child visit schedule). Can be used in mass mailouts for child-find programs	Single pass/fail score	Sensitivity ranged 70% to 90% at all ages except the 4-mo level. Specificity ranged from 76% to 91%	About 5 min

Test	Age	Description	Scoring	Accuracy	Time
Behavioral/Emotional Screens **Eyberg Child Behavior Inventory** Eyberg S. (1998). Psychological Assessment Resources, PO Box 998, Odessa FL 33556 (Phone: 1-800-331-8378). (Price not yet available)	2½–11 yr (best used to age 4)	The ECBI consists of 36 short statements of common behavior problems. A score of more than 16 suggests referral for behavioral interventions. A score lower than 16 enables the measure to function as a problems list for planning in-office counseling and selecting handouts	Single refer/nonrefer score for externalizing problems: conduct, attention, aggression, etc.	Sensitivity 80%, specificity 86%	About 7 min
Pediatric Symptom Checklist Jellinek MS, Murphy JM, Robinson J, et al.: Pediatric Symptom Checklist: Screening school age children for psychosocial dysfunction. Journal of Pediatrics, 112:201–209, 1988 (the test is included in the article)	4–16 yr	Thirty-five short statements of problem behaviors including both externalizing (conduct) and internalizing (depression, anxiety, adjustment, etc.). Ratings of never, sometimes, or often are assigned a value of 0, 1, or 2. Scores totaling 28 or more suggest referrals. Item patterns can help decide whether mental health services (best for internalizing disorders) or behavior interventions (for externalizing disorders) are needed	Single refer/nonrefer score	All but one study showed high sensitivity (80% to 95%) but somewhat scattered specificity (68% to 100%)	About 7 min
Family Psychosocial Screening Kemper KJ, Kelleher KJ: Family psychosocial screening: Instruments and techniques. Ambulatory Child Health, 4:325–339, 1996 (the measures are included in the article)	Screens parents and best used along with the above screens	A two-page clinic intake form that identifies psychosocial risk factors associated with developmental problems, including (1) a four-item measure of parental history of physical abuse as a child; (2) a six-item measure of parental substance abuse; and (3) a three-item measure of maternal depression	Refer/nonrefer scores for each risk factor. Also has guides to referring and resource lists	All studies showed sensitivity and specificity to larger inventories greater than 90%	About 15 min

PEDS Response Form

Child's Name: __Billy Morris__   Parent's Name: __Linda Morris__

Child's Birthday: __4/17/94__   Child's Age: __3__   Today's Date: __4/27/97__

1. Please list any concerns about your child's learning, development, and behavior.

I don't think he talks as well as he should for his age. Otherwise he's just a great little boy, very loving, watches everything carefully. Figures things out quickly. Very bright!!

2. Do you have any concerns about how your child talks and makes speech sounds?

Circle one: No   Yes   (A little)   COMMENTS:

3. Do you have any concerns about how your child understands what you say?

Circle one: (No)   Yes   A little   COMMENTS:

He understands everything!

4. Do you have any concerns about how your child uses his or her hands and fingers to do things?

Circle one: (No)   Yes   A little   COMMENTS:

He's very coordinated

5. Do you have any concerns about how your child uses his or her arms and legs?

Circle one: (No)   Yes   A little   COMMENTS:

6. Do you have any concerns about how your child behaves?

Circle one: (No)   Yes   A little   COMMENTS:

Very helpful and cooperative

7. Do you have any concerns about how your child gets along with others?

Circle one: (No)   Yes   A little   COMMENTS:

Plays well, just too quietly

8. Do you have any concerns about how your child is learning to do things for himself/herself?

Circle one: (No)   Yes   A little   COMMENTS:

9. Do you have any concerns about how your child is learning preschool or school skills?

Circle one: (No)   Yes   A little   COMMENTS:

10. Please list any other concerns.

Figure 21–1. Parents' Evaluations of Developmental Status (PEDS) Response Form. (© Frances Page Glascoe, Ellsworth & Vandermeer Press Ltd., Nashville, Tennessee. Reproduced with permission.)

PEDS Score Form

Child's Name Billy Morris

Birthday 4/17/94

Find appropriate column for the child's age. Place a checkmark in the appropriate box to show each concern on the PEDS Response Form. See Brief Scoring Guide for details on categorizing concerns. Shaded boxes are significant predictors of difficulties. Nonshaded boxes are nonsignificant predictors.

Child's Age:	0-4 mos	4-6 mos	6-12 mos	12-15 mos	15-18 mos	18-23 mos	2 yrs	3 yrs	4-4 1/2 yrs	4 1/2-6 yrs	6-7 yrs	7-8 yrs
1. Global/Cognitive												
2. Expressive Language and Articulation							✓					
3. Receptive Language												
4. Fine Motor												
5. Gross Motor												
6. Behavior												
7. Social-Emotional												
8. Self-help												
9. School												
10. Other												

Count the number of checks in the small shaded boxes and place the total in the large shaded box below.

1

If the number shown in the large shaded box is greater than 1, follow Path A on PEDS Interpretation Form. If the number 1 is shown, follow Path B. Now count the number of small unshaded boxes and place the total in the large unshaded box below.

0

If the number shown in the large unshaded box is 1 or more, follow Path C. If the number 0 is shown, consider Path D if relevant. Otherwise, follow Path E.

©Frances Page Glascoe, Ellsworth & Vandermeer Press Ltd., 4405 Scenic Drive; Nashville, Tennessee 37204
Fax: 615-386-0346 Phone: 615-386-0061 web: http://edge.net/~evpress Please do not reproduce without written permission.

Figure 21–2. Parents' Evaluations of Developmental Status (PEDS) Score Form. (© Frances Page Glascoe, Ellsworth & Vandermeer Press Ltd., Nashville, Tennessee. Reproduced with permission.)

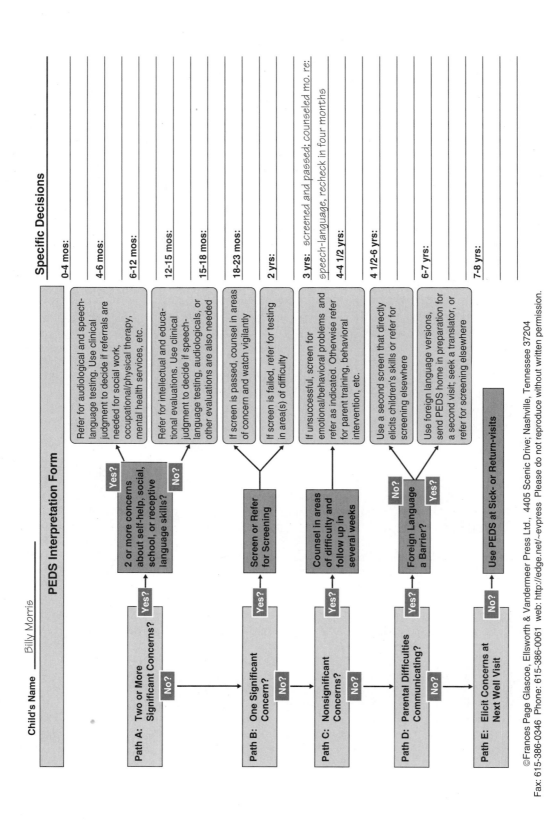

Figure 21–3. Parents' Evaluations of Developmental Status (PEDS) Interpretation Form. (© Frances Page Glascoe, Ellsworth & Vandermeer Press Ltd., Nashville, Tennessee. Reproduced with permission.)

TABLE 21–2. Highly Accurate Screens Involving Direct Elicitation of Children's Skills

Developmental/Educational Screen	Age Range	Description	Scoring	Accuracy	Time Frame
Brigance Screens Brigance AN. (1985). Curriculum Associates, 5 Esquire Road, N. Billerica, MA 01862 (Phone: 1-800-225-0248). ($248.55)	21–90 mo	Seven separate forms, one for each 12-month age range. Taps speech-language, motor, readiness and general knowledge at younger ages and also reading and math at older ages. Uses direct elicitation and observation	Cutoff and age equivalent scores for motor, language, and readiness and an overall cutoff	Good sensitivity and specificity to giftedness and to developmental and academic problems	10 min
Battelle Developmental Inventory Screening Test (BDIST) Newborg et al. (1984). Riverside Publishing Company, 8420 Bryn Mawr Avenue, Chicago, IL 60631 (Phone: 1-800-767-8378). ($99.00 + $270 if materials kit is purchased but test stimuli can be obtained for about $50 by shopping at discount department stores)	12–96 mo	Items use a combination of direct assessment, observation, and parental interview. The receptive language subtest may serve as a brief prescreen. Difficult to administer. Well standardized and validated	Age equivalents (somewhat deflated), cutoffs at 1.0, 1.5, and 2.0 SD below the mean	Good sensitivity and specificity	15 min (younger children); 35 min (older children)
Bayley Infant Neurodevelopmental Screen (BINS) Aylward GP. (1995). The Psychological Corporation, 555 Academic Court, San Antonio, TX 78204 (Phone: 1-800-228-0752). ($195)	3–24 mo	Uses 10 to 13 directly elicited items per 3- to 6-month age range to assess neurologic processes (reflexes, tone), neurodevelopmental skills (movement, symmetry), and developmental accomplishments (object permanence, imitation, and language)	Categorizes performance into low, moderate, or high risk via cutoff scores. Provides subtest cutoff scores for each domain assessed to focus referrals	Excellent specificity and sensitivity	10–15 min

TABLE 21–3. Organizing Pediatric Offices for Developmental/Behavioral Promotion and Detection

1. Ask parents to complete parent-report instruments while in waiting or examination rooms.
2. To avoid incomplete, incorrect, or nonreturned parent-report screens, ask parents if they would like to complete the measure on their own or have someone go through it with them. Almost all poor readers will select the latter.
3. Consider mailing parent-report tests in advance of well-child visits so that physicians need only score and interpret during the visit. This often improves the quality of parent report because families have sufficient time to respond more thoughtfully. Advance mailings are also helpful with families whose English is limited because they can usually find someone in the community to help translate items.
4. Set up a return visit devoted to screening when developmental concerns are raised unexpectedly toward the end of an encounter. A similar alternative is to have office staff call families after an encounter and administer a screen over the telephone.
5. Tape-record directions and items on parent-report instruments and use simplified answer sheets to circumvent illiteracy. This may be particularly helpful for parents whose primary languages are not spoken by office staff. Refugee resettlement workers may be able to assist in producing foreign language translations.
6. Train office staff to administer, score, and even interpret screening tests.
7. Pool resources with partners so that the practice can hire a developmental specialist to administer screening tests (and perhaps provide parent counseling, run parent training groups, and assist with group well-child visits, diagnostic evaluations, and referrals).
8. Recruit education majors or train volunteers to administer screening tests on a periodic basis (e.g., set a regular screening day in your office).
9. Maintain a current list of telephone numbers for local service providers (e.g., speech-language centers, school psychologists, mental health centers, private psychologists and psychiatrists, parent training classes). The availability of brochures describing services may promote parental follow-through on referral suggestions.
10. Encourage professionals involved in hospital-based care (e.g., child-life workers) to screen patients.
11. Collaborate with local service providers (e.g., child care centers, Head Starts, public health clinics, Department of Health and Human Services workers) to establish community-wide child-find programs that use valid, accurate screening instruments.
12. Keep parent information sheets handy. My clinic keeps them in plastic binders (so that originals are not lost). When an issue arises, I retrieve the original handout, copy it, read it on the way back to the examination room (in order to refresh myself on the contents) and then go through the highlights with parents. Good sources for parent information include
    • Barton Schmitt, Instructions for Patient Education (WB Saunders Co, Independence Square West, Philadelphia, PA 19106)
    • Wyckoff & Unell, Discipline Without Shouting or Spanking (Simon & Schuster, 1230 Avenue of the Americas, New York, NY 10020)
    • Downloadable handouts from the American Academy of Child and Adolescent Psychiatry: (http://www.aacap.org/web/aacap/factsFam/. These include 51 facts sheets written in Spanish, French, and English on such topics as divorce, disaster recovery, how to choose a psychiatrist, etc.
    • Downloadable handouts from the Ambulatory Pediatric Association for developmental promotion and other nonmedical issues: (http://www.ambpeds.org/ParentHandouts/APAHandoutsTOC.html)
13. Use screens as designed, adhering to standardized wording, scoring, and decision making. Violating test standardization decreases validity and increases the likelihood of underdetection.
14. It is possible that experienced pediatricians memorize test items and internalize norms. This may lead them to rely heavily on clinical judgment. Since human reasoning is not infallible and judgment can drift over time, professionals should test their decisions at least periodically by comparing them to the results of standardized screening tests. This should help keep clinical skills honed and provide an appropriate model for less experienced professionals such as residents and medical students.

Although parents may offer diverse complaints, as shown in Table 21–4, it is the similarity of parental complaints that makes triaging school difficulties especially challenging. For example, "short attention span" can be due to recent family problems, lack of motivation, undiscovered learning disabilities, poor teaching or inappropriate school environments, language impairments, emotional disturbance, health problems that interfere with school attendance and vitality, poor study skills, slow learning, or attention-deficit hyperactivity disorder. The task for pediatricians is to uncover the most likely cause and then select appropriate evaluations and treatments.

Despite the diverse reasons why children can have school difficulties, it is rarely necessary to administer direct screens in pediatric settings. It is far more practical to use two existing and readily available sources of information: (1) parents' and teachers' comments; and (2) the results of group achievement tests. These include the Iowa Test of Basic Skills, the California Achievement Test, and the Stanford Achievement Test, among many others. Such tests are standardized and validated on thousands of children in the same grade across the country. They are usually given annually or biannually by the public schools and take 3 to 9 hours to administer. As a consequence, group achievement test results offer much information on children's performance in such areas as reading vocabulary, word-attack skills, reading comprehension, math calculations, math concepts, handwriting, spelling, punctuation, capitalization, usage, science, social studies, humanities, and study skills.

TABLE 21–4. Warning Signs of School Problems

Inconsistent performance; does better one-to-one
Poor retention of information; has been retained
Excessive parental involvement in homework; takes too long
   to complete homework
Loss of self-esteem
Short attention span, hyperactivity
History of speech-language problems; otitis media with
   fluctuating hearing loss
Frequent school absences
Previously tested but not eligible for special education
Hates school; school phobic; psychosomatic symptoms
Hides schoolwork; lies about assignments
Trouble with letter sounds or letter naming

**TABLE 21–5. One Student's Group Achievement
Test Scores**

Subtest	Stanine	Percentile
Word study skills	4	23
Reading comprehension	6	64
Vocabulary	8	94
Listening comprehension	6	70
Spelling	6	69
Language	6	73
Concepts of number	8	95
Math computation	7	77
Math application	6	76
Social science	9	96
Science	5	48
Using information	7	85
TOTAL READING	5	41
TOTAL LISTENING	7	85
TOTAL LANGUAGE	6	74
TOTAL MATH	7	86

THE VALUE OF THE PEDIATRICIAN'S PERSPECTIVE ON SCHOOL DIFFICULTIES.

Why should pediatricians attempt to obtain and interpret school-administered group achievement tests? The reasons are many and compelling: (1) schools rarely use group achievement scores to screen individual children but instead to view the performance of entire schools, counties, and states; (2) diagnostic-prescriptive thinking is rarely a part of teacher training and teachers do not always know how to identify individual problems and devise treatment plans; (3) teachers do not have much opportunity to work with a child individually. Physicians can empathize by imagining a single examination room filled with 25 to 30 patients. How readily could those with problems be diagnosed?; and (4) teachers usually work with a child for 1 year at a time and rarely have longitudinal insight into children's medical and family histories. Such information is critical for interpreting test results.

GROUP ACHIEVEMENT TESTS. All group achievement tests provide a percentile and a stanine per subtest. Stanines (short for standard nine) are the most helpful statistic for screening because they divide the bell curve (the typical distribution of scores) into nine equal parts as shown in Figure 21–4. Stanines 1, 2, and 3 are below average; 4, 5, and 6 are average; and 7, 8,

and 9 are above average. Stanines 2 through 8 each represent 0.5 of a standard deviation (SD), whereas stanines 1 and 9 represent the assymptotes (the 98th percentile and above and the 2nd percentile and below). Stanines that differ by more than 2 SD represent significant scatter among scores.

The Six Common Problem Profiles

1. *Dyslexia and Other Learning Disabilities.* Table 21–5 shows group achievement scores on a sixth grader enrolled in a private school. Her pediatrician referred her for diagnostic testing due to parents' and teachers' complaints about her slow work rate, poor grades in a foreign language class, and diminished self-esteem. This student commented that she could not "read as fast as other students." Her achievement test scores show widely scattered stanines—spanning 2.5 SD with weaknesses in word-study skills, a measure of phonics (meaning decoding the sounds of letters), syllabification, and recognition of common prefixes, suffixes, and word roots. (In older students

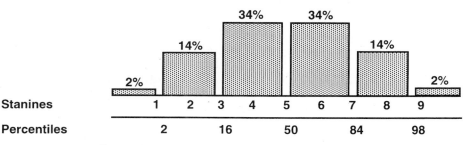

Figure 21–4. Normal distribution in stanines and percentiles.

the word-study subtest is not often included in the battery, and low scores in spelling can reflect word-attack deficits). This student's highest stanine of 9 suggests that she may be quite bright. Given that group achievement tests are timed, her average scores in science and other areas may be due to a slow reading rate secondary to difficulty decoding letter sounds.

These suppositions were supported by psychoeducational testing (meaning individually administered diagnostic measures of intelligence and academic achievement). The student was found to have an IQ of 128 and mild dyslexia—the most common type of learning disability in which basic reading processes are impaired due to deficits in phonics skills. Her intelligence enabled her to partially compensate by guessing at unfamiliar words based on visual appearance (e.g., substituting "curtain" for "curious"). However, when her guess failed to make sense in context, she had to reread the sentence and guess again. As a consequence, she took two to three times as long to complete reading assignments although her actual reading rate (on familiar words only) was grade appropriate.

Her treatment plan included tutoring two to three times per week in word-attack skills (had she been in a public school, participation in the resource class, a special education program available in each school, could have been an option). Tutoring was concluded after a few months because reading rate and comprehension improved dramatically. Achievement test scores the following year showed marked improvement in all academic areas. She continued to do well in school and eventually matriculated to a prestigious university.

It is worth noting that in some highly intelligent dyslexic students, dyslexia is not detected until college or even graduate school, when the heavy workload interferes with their ability to complete assignments. Modifying course loads, omitting foreign language requirements (it is hard to master the sounds of another language if those of English are not mastered first), and allowing extra time to complete examinations may be needed. It is important to note that students can have learning disabilities in written language, math concepts, and math reasoning. The profiles of such students are typically quite obvious (relatively consistent scores in all but the affected areas).

2. *Slow Learning.* These students have IQs that are between 74 and 85 and have substantial difficulties in school. They can be recognized by stanines of 1, 2, and 3 (and an occasional 4) on group achievement tests. A referral is warranted for psychoeducational and language assessments. These can be obtained privately or through the schools. Referrals to schools are expedited if pediatricians screen vision and hearing and include these results in a letter to the schools. Such letters should specify the kind of testing needed, that is, language and psychoeducational evaluations, and should be sent to the school's department of special education and to the principal in the child's school. Although schools have 40 days in which to legally comply with testing and special education placement if indicated, compliance is poor due to limited funding and high demand. As a consequence, parents (or office staff) should be encouraged to advocate for services by calling the principal and special education offices frequently until testing is provided.

Unfortunately, slow learners do not always qualify for special education assistance through the schools due to an omission in federal and state laws. For these students, it is helpful to recommend enrollment in Chapter I Reading and Math (federally funded remedial programs available to schools where the average family income is low), tutoring (which is often free from community centers and volunteer literacy programs), summer school, and vocational training during high school. Enrollment in supervised after-school youth programs is advised to promote competence in nonacademic areas such as sports and volunteerism and to prevent disenfranchisement and delinquency that may accompany chronically poor school performance. Many slow learners were at-risk children during their preschool years due to factors such as poverty, large family size, single parents with limited education, poor parenting style, and parental depression. It is advisable to identify young children with risk factors and make referrals to Head Start or other stimulation and parent training programs. This may prevent subsequent poor school performance, with its attendant risk for dropping out of high school, teen pregnancy, criminality, and unemployment.

3. *Academic Talent/Giftedness.* Students with superior intellectual capacity (IQs of 130 or greater) and/or extremely high achievement can be recognized by stanines of 7, 8, and 9. Schools offer services to these students, typically in the form of magnet schools, programs for academic acceleration, enrichment programs, parent groups, and community mentors. Access to these services usually requires psychoeducational testing. Pediatricians can also recommend extracurricular activities and parenting groups that focus on giftedness. There are numerous sites on the World Wide Web that can be helpful to families and children (e.g., http://www.eskimo.com/nuser.kids.htm/ has information on on-line gifted resources, enrichment

programs, talent searchers, summer programs, Odyssey of the Mind, and educational research on giftedness).

4. *Language Impairment.* These children can be recognized by low stanines in general information (sometimes referred to as "environment" in group tests). Reading comprehension deficits usually appear by the third grade when children stop just "learning to read" and begin "reading to learn." This is the first time in which written language equals the sophistication of oral language. Children with expressive or receptive language deficits will naturally have much difficulty understanding what they read. Sometimes math concepts, with their heavy dependence on vocabulary (e.g., more/less, before/after, backward/forward), will also be low. Children with language impairment profiles should be referred for psychoeducational and language evaluations. Pediatricians' knowledge of children's health and developmental histories are particularly helpful here: Children at risk for language impairment are those with more than four bouts of otitis media, those with fluctuating or stable monaural or bilateral hearing loss, and those with a history of speech-language difficulties. Even those identified and treated early may plateau after speech-language therapy is terminated and may fail to make continued progress. Interventions for children with language impairments typically include language therapy and resource services with consultation among the language therapist, parents at home, and the regular classroom teacher. Some school systems have self-contained classrooms for those with severe language problems. Private language therapy, if affordable, should further speed progress.

5. *Emotional and Family Difficulties.* This profile is characterized by deficits in math concepts and/or reading comprehension but not general information. This suggests that language is intact but that children are preoccupied (due to anxiety disorders, depression, post-traumatic stress disorder, and so on) and thus have substantial difficulties concentrating. They may ruminate about worries or escape into pleasurable fantasies. As a consequence, they have difficulties with tasks such as reading comprehension and applied math problems that require sustained, uninterrupted thought. Short attention span without hyperactivity is a common presenting complaint. The family history of these patients is usually known to the pediatrician and typically includes declining school performance over a period of years accompanied within the same time frame by a divorce, bereavement, family history of mental health or other psychosocial problems, frequent moves, or expo-

TABLE 21–6. How to Obtain Test Scores and Academic Screens When Scores Are Not Available

Ask parents to bring their copy to annual well-child visits during the school years.
Have parents sign a release and mail this to the school.
Have parents go by the school and pick up a copy.
With parents present and willing, call the school and ask for test results.

sure to traumatic events such as domestic violence. Appropriate referrals include family and/or individual counseling, as well as psychoeducational and language evaluations to assess needs for academic interventions. Medications and tutoring may be helpful.

6. *Attention-Deficit Hyperactivity Disorder (ADHD) with Learning Disabilities.* Attentional problems are characterized by wide, inconsistent scatter in scores over time (e.g., a jump from a 2 to an 8 in reading comprehension without intervention. This suggests that the student just happened to pay attention one year on the reading comprehension subtest). It should be noted that children with ADHD can pay attention some of the time to some things. It is the consistency of their attention that is the problem. Thus it is not surprising that many children with ADHD (especially the primarily inattentive type) also have written language learning disabilities, since competence with written language requires repeated attention—to content, usage, punctuation, capitalization, and spelling. Children with low scores in spelling, written expression, and/or language mechanics should be referred for psychoeducational testing. Use of ADHD rating scales can help confirm the diagnosis and offer direction for other needed interventions such as stimulant medication.

Table 21–6 shows methods for obtaining group achievement test scores. For practices within school systems that do not regularly administer group achievement tests there are direct screens that can be useful. Of particular merit is the Mini-Battery of Achievement (MBA).* Designed for ages 4 through adult, the MBA has four subtests that can be administered independently of each other: reading, math, writing skills, and factual knowledge. The MBA has excellent standardization and validation. It produces standard scores, grade and age equivalents, and percentiles. The MBA has extremely high correlations with more

*The MBA was constructed by Woodcock R, McGrew K, Werder J. (1994). Available from Riverside Publishing Company, 8420 Bryn Mawr Avenue, Chicago, IL 60631 (Phone: 1-800-767-8378). ($149 including computer scoring disk).

comprehensive academic measures and takes about 20 to 30 minutes to administer and score all four subtests.

When Achievement Scores Appear Adequate But Grades Are Poor

There are times when despite parents' and teachers' concerns, test results show at least average achievement. In these cases, parents usually complain about poor grades. How can students achieve well on standardized tests but have poor grades? Grades, unlike achievement test scores, reflect a student's effort, but do not always indicate whether he or she is learning. For example, a bright student who is not serious and fails to complete or turn in assignments or to study for tests may have an abysmal report card but superior test scores. He or she is learning but is not "performing up to potential." Although it is tempting to dismiss this problem as inconsequential, poor grades are not benign. They can limit opportunities for extracurricular activities, limit choices after high school graduation, and above all, contribute heavily to parent-child conflict, family distress, and poor self-esteem.

There are seven common reasons for poor grades but adequate group achievement scores. To assess these, it is again important to interview both the child and parent. It is also very beneficial to talk with the student's teacher(s).

1. *Are poor study skills and/or lack of motivation a problem?* Many children do not acquire adequate study and organizational skills. Often children are not taught how to organize their notebooks or lockers, manage their time, avoid distractions while studying, and so forth. Ask the student directly how he or she studies for tests, where and when homework is completed, the frequency and timing of extracurricular activities, whether assignments are always completed or ever lost, whether the correct books are brought home, whether assignment sheets used, whether study guides created, and the like. Children are typically quite candid about these issues. Equivocal answers should be construed as problematic (e.g., "Sometimes I forget my homework" may mean "often"). Brief tutoring in study skills can often rectify the problem.

Lack of motivation is more challenging and may reflect "power struggles" between the child's desire for autonomy and parents' high expectations and demands for accomplishment. Parents may provide excessive external structure and thus inadvertently reinforce dawdling and incomplete

work rather than initiative and promptness. Such a history may diminish children's interest in learning. Family counseling and parent training can help parents let children take more responsibility. A tutor can also help shift the responsibility from the parent and provide students a fresh start.

2. *Has the child had frequent school absences?* Children who miss more than 20 school days are at risk for school failure, and those who miss more than 30 are generally nominated for in-grade retention. Patients with chronic illness or trauma may miss a substantial amount of school but it will take a year or more for their problems to surface as lowered achievement scores. Primary care clinicians, as generalists on a medical team that may include various subspecialists, may be the only ones to consider the adverse consequences of school absence on school performance. It is advisable to initiate homebound services promptly and to refer these students for tutoring and summer school. Special education in the form of the resource classroom may be needed, and such children may be eligible under the category of health impairment.

Other reasons for excessive absence are a chaotic family life or truancy. Parents' own health problems can make children protective of their parents and thus reluctant to leave the house. Children experiencing such events will benefit from the services of a social worker who may be able to help families provide sufficient structure. Schools also have attendance officers who are usually skilled in a range of interventions that promote school attendance. Family and individual counseling is also advisable.

3. *Have recent life events adversely affected grades?* Sharp declines in grades may be the first indicator that a child is not coping well with recent life events such as divorce, a death in the family, or psychological trauma. Left untreated, poor grades may result in diminished learning and lowered achievement in subsequent school years. Prompt referrals for mental health services following a difficult life event can prevent a downward spiral in actual achievement. Services may include specialized support groups (e.g., on bereavement or divorce). Short-term tutoring may also be beneficial.

4. *Is the child an average learner in a school that demands above-average performance?* In most private schools and some public schools, the average achievement of enrollees is at the 6th to 7th stanine (65th to 80th percentile). Students in the most rigorous private schools often need to score even higher to be considered average relative to peers. Thus, a student whose achievement scores cluster in the average range may be per-

forming near the bottom of the class. Such children can sometimes remain in an overly challenging school with some of the following modifications: reduced course load (which may require summer school or an extra senior year), private tutoring, use of a tape recorder or word processor in class, and parental tolerance of B's and C's. Even with such modifications, children may spend an inordinate amount of time on homework, be excluded from worthwhile extracurricular activities due to poor grades, and develop secondary emotional problems—excessive anxiety or depression, or loss of self-esteem. In these cases, a change in placement is needed.

5. *Are test scores misleading because of retention in grade?* Norms for achievement tests are established by grade, not age. Older children who have been held back may have an automatic improvement in test scores (e.g., a rise from the 2nd to the 4th stanine). In such cases, adequate achievement scores may temporarily mask learning or language disabilities, slow learning, and so forth. Misinterpretation of scores can be avoided by obtaining scores from prior years and a good educational history from parents and teachers.

6. *Is the child younger than others in his or her grade?* In the early grades, children whose birthdays occur in summer and early fall and who have not been retained tend to perform near the bottom of their class because they are less mature and experienced. Generally such children are described as "immature" but as having mastered the essential skills. Far more disturbing are those who are not only immature but who have not learned letter sounds or even some of the names of letters of the alphabet. The latter are clearly in trouble and the former are probably not. However, in both cases, children are often recommended for retention in grade or for participation in transitional classes through which children are effectively retained although ostensibly without stigma.

Parents and pediatricians are usually quite troubled by retention recommendations. Retention is extremely controversial, and research on its outcome and value is equivocal. Nevertheless, there is some evidence that retention can be helpful for some children at certain times. Table 21–7 lists several guidelines that can help physicians, parents, and teachers make wise decisions about retention.

7. *Is ADHD (without learning disabilities) the cause?* By holding problems with attention and hyperactivity as the last consideration on the differential for school problems, pediatricians can avoid confusing attentional deficits as a *symptom of other problems* (e.g., slow learning, learning disabilities, or psychosocial problems) with attentional deficit *as the cause itself.* This sequence helps ensure that interventions are appropriate and that all other problems are ruled out. Given the latter, it is wise to ask parents and teachers to complete instruments that confirm this likely diagnosis. Behavioral intervention, parent training, classroom modifications, and medications should be used in consort for addressing ADHD without learning disabilities.

The entire differential for triaging school problems is presented in Figure 21–5. This is designed to serve as a helpful algorithm for working systematically through the wide range of causes for school difficulties.

TABLE 21–7. Helping Families with In-Grade Retention Issues

1. Children nominated for retention are often those with undiagnosed learning, language, or other disabilities. If children have not mastered critical skills, refer them for psychoeducational and language evaluations to be followed by special education or other services as indicated.

2. Whether children are enrolled in special education or not, retention in kindergarten or first grade is found in some studies to be helpful because it enhances mastery of critical reading and other skills.

3. Retention in higher grades is not known to be effective because nominees usually have gaps in learning (e.g., lack of mastery of first-grade skills that will not be readdressed by retention in a higher grade). Retention of older students is associated with dropping out of school in the higher grades.

4. Participation in summer school can be used to postpone retention decisions. Schools can be asked to screen chidren at the end of the summer to decide if they are ready for the next grade.

5. Retention is often traumatic for children and parents. This can be dealt with by having the child participate in the decision and by brief counseling for families.

6. Retention can be avoided altogether with reduced class sizes (approximately 15 students), teacher training that focuses on techniques for individualized instruction, and availability of a wide range of curricular materials. These observations may best be viewed as the subject of advocacy for pediatricians involved with school board funding decisions.

7. Retention prior to kindergarten (holding children out due to lack of readiness skills) is problematic because there are no guarantees that "more of the same" will ensure mastery of needed skills. The American Academy of Pediatrics' Committees on School Health, Early Childhood, Adoption and Dependent Care suggest that children who perform poorly on readiness testing (a type of screening test) should not be excluded from programs but rather referred for more thorough evaluations from which appropriate placement decisions can be made.

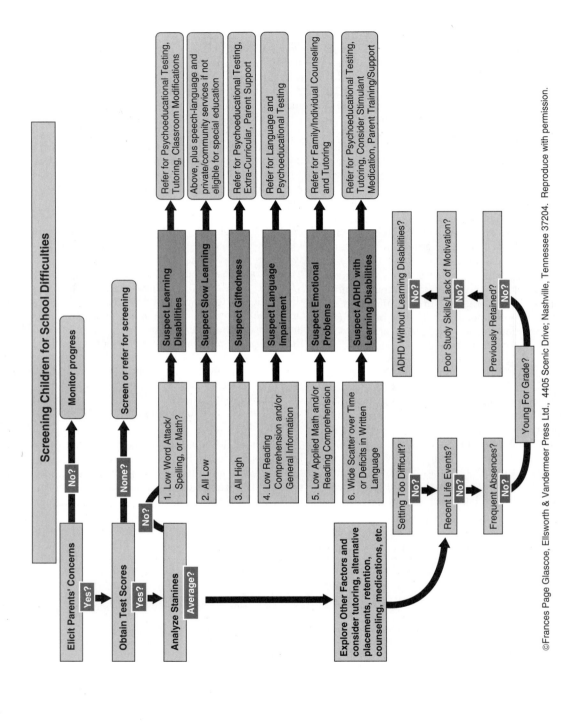

Figure 21–5. Screening children for school difficulties. ADHD, attention-deficit hyperactivity disorder. (© Frances Page Glascoe, Ellsworth & Vandermeer Press Ltd., Nashville, Tennessee. Reproduced with permission.)

FURTHER READING

Meisels SJ and Shonkoff JP (eds): Handbook of Early Child-hood Intervention. Cambridge, MA, Cambridge University Press, 1990.

Parker S and Zuckerman B (eds): Behavioral and Develop-mental Pediatrics: A Handbook for Primary Care. Boston, Little, Brown & Co, 1995.

Wender E (ed): Pediatric Roundtable on School Dysfunction. Columbus, OH, Ross Laboratories, 1993.

Wolraich ML (ed): Disorders of Development and Learning: A Practical Guide to Assessment and Management, 2nd ed. Chicago, Mosby–Year Book, 1996.

Lee M. Pachter

Chapter 22

Ethnic and Cultural Influences on Child Health and Child Health Services

As the population of the United States becomes more heterogeneous, health care practitioners are being called on to provide care to an increasingly diverse group of patients. This diversity is seen in domains such as family structure, socioeconomic status, parental age, sexual orientation, and ethnicity. It is the goal of "culturally sensitive" medicine to appreciate the relative role that ethnicity and culture play in an individual's approach to health, illness, and health care. The culturally sensitive clinician respects the beliefs, values, practices, and lifestyles of patients. He or she understands that health and illness are in large part molded by factors such as ethnic identity, cultural orientation, religious beliefs, and linguistic considerations. The culturally sensitive clinician realizes that in addition to the pathophysiologic aspects of disease, the socially defined and culturally relevant meanings and interpretations of illness to the patient and family are important clinical concerns. He or she understands the importance of acknowledging *intra*cultural variations in beliefs and practices, and avoids stereotyping individual patients based on any grouping such as ethnicity, class, or race. Many variables, including personal philosophy and psychology, family practices, as well as other social and socioeconomic factors that lie apart from "ethnicity," contribute to a person's health beliefs and practices.

"Culturally sensitive medicine" should be practiced not only with ethnic minority patients but also with every patient and family. Because of background, training, and life experiences, phy-sicians frequently approach health and illness from a different perspective than that of patients. **Each doctor-patient interaction may therefore be seen as a cross-cultural interaction between the "culture of medicine" and "the culture of the patient," regardless of the ethnicity of the doctor or patient.** These issues become even more important when the "cultural distance" between the doctor and patient increases (as it may when they come from different ethnic backgrounds), since chances for miscommunication increase. The clinician should be aware of this increased potential for misunderstanding and attempt to find ways to bridge the gap. **By attempting to understand the experience of illness from the patient's perspective, the clinician will have a better likelihood of effecting successful outcomes.**

This chapter presents an approach to clinical care that can be applied during interactions with *all* patients and families, since it defines "culture" in the broad context and shifts the focus of the clinical encounter from the biomedical-oriented view to the patient-oriented perspective.

FRAMEWORK FOR WORKING WITH DIVERSE PATIENTS AND FAMILIES: AWARENESS-ASSESSMENT-NEGOTIATION

Clinicians who work with patients and families who may have different approaches to health, illness, and health care use should

1. Become aware of commonly held health beliefs and practices in the communities in which they work (*awareness*).

2. Assess whether the specific patient or family that they are working with uses those beliefs and practices, and if so, under what circumstances (*assessment*).

3. Attempt to find ways to combine biomedical therapies, health education, well-child care, and illness management with the culturally relevant, patient-held beliefs and practices (*negotiation*).

Awareness—become aware of commonly held health beliefs and practices in the community that one works in.

Common approaches to health and illness within a community become evident through patient contacts, informal discussion, and experiences. The clinician may also find published resources pertaining to common traditional health beliefs and practices in specific ethnocultural groups, but the information in such sources often becomes outdated and, therefore, may not provide an up-to-date assessment of approaches to health and illness in a specific community. They should be used as "background material," the accuracy and relevancy of which needs to be established through discussion and communication with local community members.

The best source of local and up-to-date information about common health beliefs and practices in a particular community are *community members*—patients, office staff, community leaders, alternative health practitioners and healers, and social service representatives. Clinicians should be encouraged to ask these individuals about alternative health care practices. When approached in an open and positive manner, most people are not hesitant in discussing their beliefs, values, and customs.

Assessment—assess whether the specific patient or family that one is working with uses specific alternative beliefs and practices, and if so, under what circumstances.

The information obtained in the first step should be considered only as common ways in which members of a *community* may interpret health-related issues. Since the unit of measurement in clinical care is the *individual patient,* the clinician must assess to what extent a specific patient and family may act on certain culturally oriented beliefs, and under what circumstances. To assume that all members of a particular group subscribe to similar ethnomedical beliefs and practices would be incorrect.

The clinician should attempt to elicit the pa-

TABLE 22–1. The Health Beliefs History: Questions to Elicit a Patient's Explanatory Model*

What do you think is wrong with your child?
Why do you think he or she has gotten it (the illness)?
What do you think caused it?
Why do you think it started when it did?
What do you think is happening inside the body?
What are the symptoms that make you know he or she has this illness?
What are you most worried about with this illness?
What problems does this illness cause your child?
How long do you expect this to last?
How do you treat it?
What will happen if this is not treated?
What do you expect from the treatments?

*Adapted from Kleinman A, Eisenberg L, and Good B: Culture, illness, and care: Clinical lessons from anthropologic and cross-cultural research. Ann Intern Med 88:251–258, 1978.

---

tient's or parent's explanatory model for the illness episode by obtaining a *health beliefs history.* Table 22–1 describes some of the health beliefs questions that may help to elicit the patient's explanatory model.

The simultaneous use of physician-prescribed treatments and alternative therapies (such as folk remedies, nutritional supplements, spiritual practices, herbal therapies, and physical modalities) is common. This therapeutic pluralism may occur with any patient and family, not just those from ethnic minorities. Many clinicians feel uncomfortable asking patients about these practices and think that even if they ask, they will not get true answers. **One way of successfully eliciting information regarding folk and other alternative practices is to ask questions in a way that progresses from the general to the specific,** for example, first ask if they have ever *heard* of any other ways of treating the illness, then ask if they have ever *tried* them, and finally ask if they are presently using them. Table 22–2 gives examples of this approach.

TABLE 22–2. An Approach to Asking Questions About Folk and Other Alternative Remedies*

1. "People have told me that there are ways of treating (*specific illness*) that doctors don't know about, but people such as grandparents and older people know about. Have you heard of any of these remedies or treatments?"
2. "What are they?"
3. "Are they effective?"
4. "Have you ever tried (*specific remedy*) for your child's (*illness*)?"
5. "Are you using it now?"
6. "Is it helpful?"

*Progress from de-personal and general questions to specific questions.

Negotiation—attempt to find ways to combine clinicians' biomedical therapies, health education, well-child care, and illness management with the culturally relevant, patient-held beliefs and practices.

Once the patient's explanatory model is elicited and understood, the clinician should be able to assess the "fit" of this model vis-à-vis the biomedical model in an attempt to find areas of similarity between the two. Instead of replacing patient-held beliefs and practices, it is suggested that the areas of similarities be used to combine concordant aspects of the patient and biomedical models. For example, when asked about asthma, many individuals in the Puerto Rican community relate the belief that mucus retention is a major factor in the exacerbation of asthma symptoms. Instead of refuting that belief, one could incorporate it into health education by saying "Yes, it's true that during an asthma attack the body produces a lot of mucus, and that is one of the problems with asthma. *In addition to that,* the breathing tubes become inflamed and go into spasm . . ." This approach shows the patient that the clinician has listened to him or her and, after receiving positive feedback regarding health beliefs, the patient may be more open to listening to what the clinician has to say.

With regard to alternative treatments and remedies, the clinician should always assess the likelihood for adverse effects. Although there have been occasional reports of harmful or potentially harmful folk remedies, the vast majority of treatments and remedies are harmless if taken with standard precautions. **Once the clinician has determined that the remedy is not harmful, he or she should attempt to link the biomedical therapy to the remedy that the patient is already using.** If, for example, a suburban upper middle class mother is treating her child's urinary tract infection with a homeopathic remedy that purportedly "boosts the immune system," the clinician can encourage the mother to continue the practice while adding an antibiotic to "assist the immune system to fight off the infection through another mechanism." As another example, a Puerto Rican mother says that when her son has asthma symptoms she gives a syrup called *siete jarabe,* and if that doesn't work within an hour or two she then gives him a nebulized albuterol treatment. Instead of dissuading her from giving the syrup (which has no dangerous side effects if given as directed), one may say to the mother, "I'm not sure if the *siete jarabe* is effective in treating asthma, but I do know that it is not harmful if taken as directed, so if you think that it is helping your child, you

should continue to use it. I can tell you, though, that it will be much more effective if you give your child the albuterol right after the *siete jarabe,* instead of waiting an hour." This approach does no harm and increases the likelihood that biomedical therapy will be adhered to because the clinician has fit it within a context that is concordant with the patient's beliefs and practices.

It is the obligation of the clinician to recommend against the use of any harmful remedy or therapy. One may be more successful in doing this if an alternative therapy that fits within the patient's belief system is recommended. For example, one parent of a child with asthma mentioned in the health beliefs history that she prepares tea from the herb lobelia, which her naturopath said causes bronchodilation and removes mucus from the respiratory tubes. Although these effects have been noted for lobelia in the botanical literature, the risk to benefit ratio is high, especially since the amount of active ingredient is variable in tea preparations. After discussing these concerns with the mother, it was agreed that she would discontinue the use of this potentially harmful herb and instead try another herbal product that also has expectorant properties, but without the high risk to benefit ratio. The child was also started on standard biomedical therapy for asthma.

COLLABORATION WITH ALTERNATIVE HEALERS, FOLK HEALERS, AND OTHER COMMUNITY AGENCIES

Patients and families use varied resources for health and illness management. Under certain circumstances, alternative practitioners may be consulted in addition to the care provided within the biomedical health care system. The "Awareness-Assessment-Negotiation" approach can be applied to these issues as well. The culturally sensitive clinician should (1) become aware of the various alternative resources available to the patients in his or her community; (2) attempt to determine when and under what circumstances a particular patient or family may use these resources; and (3) try to develop collaboration between the biomedical health care system and the alternative practitioners.

Most alternative healers are open to collaboration with the biomedical doctor, and many patients feel comfortable discussing the alternative therapies with their doctor if they believe that the physician will accept this information in a nonpejorative fashion. It becomes important, therefore, to approach this area of discussion in an open and respectful way. If the patient mentions alternative therapies and remedies during the health beliefs history, the clinician should ask where he or she obtains the treatment or remedy. If consultations with alternative practitioners are mentioned, specific discussion regarding the treatments should be initiated. If the therapies received from the alternative practitioner appear to be nonharmful, the culturally sensitive clinician should not dissuade the patient from seeking this care, but should stress the importance of using *both* the biomedical and alternative care systems. One should also ask the patient or parent to contact you after meeting with the alternative practitioner, so you can discuss the specific therapies or plans that he or she recommended. This opens up communication between the patient and clinician, allows the clinician to have a fuller understanding of the overall health care activities of the patient, and also gives the opportunity to halt any potentially harmful therapies.

THE USE OF INTERPRETERS

When the clinician and patient do not share a common language, the use of a bilingual interpreter becomes necessary. Even patients who are partially fluent in English may prefer to have an interpreter available to help communicate complex and sensitive information to the clinician when they feel that their English abilities are limited. Different mechanisms for providing interpretation services are commonly used (Table 22–3). Each has its own advantages and disadvantages.

In offices and practices that see a large percentage of non-English-speaking or predominantly monolingual patients from a particular ethnic background, it would be advisable to have available a professional interpreter. This will allow for high quality and consistency in interpretation. The disadvantage is that of cost. The cost issue may be offset by defining the job description of the professional interpreter to include other related functions.

Office personnel such as nurses and secretaries acting as interpreters on an ad hoc basis has the advantage of utilizing existing resources, but there are a number of disadvantages as well. Interpretation is a professional level job that requires training in language as well as interpersonal skills. The abilities of nontrained persons vary. Also, pulling employees away from their regular work obligations to translate often creates inefficiency in the regular operation of the office, and they may feel that the role of interpreter is burdensome. If office staff are to be used as interpreters, this role should be built into the employee's job description, with other work responsibilities adjusted accordingly.

Often patients will bring in other family members or friends to assist in interpreting. On the positive side, that person is usually someone whom the patient feels comfortable enough with to be involved in discussions of private and sensitive matters (although this should not be assumed—always ask the patient in private if the person chosen is acceptable to him or her for interpreting). On the negative side, individuals who are closely affiliated with the patient may consciously or unconsciously editorialize or with-

TABLE 22–3. Options for Interpretation Services

Type of Interpreter	Advantages	Disadvantages
Professional interpreter	High quality Consistent interpretations	Cost
Office personnel on an ad hoc basis	Inexpensive Readily available	Burdensome Inefficient Nonprofessional quality
Family or friends of patient	Readily available Patient *may* feel comfortable with that person	Possibility of conscious or unconscious editorializing Nonprofessional, may not have knowledge of health concepts/medical terminology Patient may not feel comfortable (privacy issues)
Waiting room strangers; other nonmedical employees	Readily available	Patient confidentiality issues
Children	Readily available	Role issues (dependency of parent on child) Privacy and confidentiality issues Lack of knowledge of health concepts/medical terminology
Telephone interpretation services	Available 24 hours/day Wide variety of languages	Impersonal Inability to assess nonverbal metacommunication May not know local slang and dialects

TABLE 22–4. Guidelines for Effective Use of Interpreters

Ask the patient/parent if the interpreter is acceptable to him or her.

Even if you are "partially fluent" or have a good understanding of medical terms in the patient's language, use an interpreter so that subtle information is not lost.

Ask the interpreter not to paraphrase but to give a literal interpretation.

Look at the patient/parent, not the interpreter. You will pick up important nonlinguistic messages through intonation, body language, and expression.

Talk to the patient/parent, not the interpreter.

Use visual aids whenever possible.

Talk in short phrases, allowing the interpreter to effectively translate what you say.

When the patient/parent brings his or her own interpreter, have available a "third party" bilingual observer to make sure that the parent-designated interpreter is not editorializing, is not leaving out information, and is interpreting the information correctly. This is especially crucial during discussions regarding therapy, emergency or critical care issues, and other high risk/high emotion situations.

Document the use of interpretation services in the medical record.

---

hold sensitive information, and may not understand the medical issues that are discussed.

Strangers from the waiting room should never be used as interpreters, since this leads to concerns regarding patient confidentiality. The use of children as interpreters for their parents should also be avoided, due to issues regarding parent-child roles as well as the concerns regarding correct interpretation.

Professional interpretation services via telephone are available. The advantages of these systems are that interpretation services for a large number of languages and dialects are available, and the interpreters are professionals. The disadvantage is that the service may be seen as impersonal, and much of the important nonverbal communication that requires face-to-face interaction is lost over the telephone.

Regardless of how interpretation services are provided, one should always make sure that the identified interpreter is acceptable to the patient. Extra time should be allotted for visits that require

an interpreter. Key points in the optimal use of an interpreter are outlined in Table 22–4.

FURTHER READING

Barker JC and Clark MM (eds): Cross Cultural Medicine: A Decade Later. Special issue of The Western Journal of Medicine, Vol 157, No. 3, 1992.

Harwood A: Guidelines for culturally appropriate health care. *In* Harwood A (ed): Ethnicity and Medical Care. Cambridge, MA: Harvard University Press, 1981, pp 482–507.

Kleinman A, Eisenberg L, and Good B: Culture, illness, and care: Clinical lessons from anthropologic and cross-cultural research. Ann Intern Med 88:251–258, 1978.

Pachter LM: Culture and clinical care: folk illness beliefs and behaviors and their implication for health care delivery. JAMA 271:690–694, 1994.

Pachter LM, Bernstein BA, and Osorio A: Clinical implications of a folk illness: Empacho in mainland Puerto Ricans. Med Anthropol 13:285–299, 1992.

Pachter LM, Cloutier MM, and Bernstein BA: Ethnomedical (folk) remedies for childhood asthma in a mainland Puerto Rican community. Arch Pediatr Adolesc Med 149:982–988, 1995.

Woloshin S, Bickell NA, Schwartz LM, et al.: Language barriers in medicine in the United States. JAMA 273:724–728, 1995.

Cynthia R. Howard

Chapter 23

Breastfeeding

Breastfeeding is widely acknowledged as the optimal way to nourish an infant. **The Institute of Medicine recommends breastfeeding for all infants in the United States under ordinary circumstances, and recommends exclusive breastfeeding as the preferred method for feed-** **ing most infants from birth to age 6 months.** As women in the United States increasingly choose to breastfeed their infants, lactation management has become a common part of clinical practice for primary care clinicians. This chapter is written to provide essential information about the management of breastfeeding mother-infant dyads and the treatment of common problems associated with lactation.

BENEFITS OF BREASTFEEDING

Human milk is species-specific. Various aspects of breast milk composition are believed to be essential for optimal central nervous system and retinal development in infants. Human milk also reduces exposure to contaminated food sources, enhances the nutritional status of at-risk infants, and prevents infection via a number of anti-inflammatory, immunologic stimulating, and antimicrobial factors. The preventive effects of breastfeeding are especially evident in developing countries, where infant mortality rates are many times higher in artificially fed infants. In industrialized nations, breast-fed infants experience a decreased risk of gastrointestinal and lower respiratory tract disease, otitis media, and bacteremia and sepsis. Breastfeeding also appears to decrease the risk of sudden infant death syndrome and food allergies, and recent studies suggest that breastfeeding confers long-term protection against such chronic diseases as childhood-onset diabetes mellitus, lymphoma, and Crohn disease. Women who breast-feed also experience a number of health benefits including concurrent fertility reduction, lower risks of breast cancer, postpartum weight reduction, and probable protection against osteoporosis.

MANAGEMENT OF THE NURSING DYAD

PHYSIOLOGY OF THE LACTATING BREAST. Lactogenesis (the onset of copious milk secretion at parturition) is triggered by the decrease in progesterone after delivery. Prolactin and oxytocin provide the hormonal environment for maintenance of the milk supply. Prolactin is produced in response to the amount and frequency of an infant's suckling and controls milk synthesis and secretion. Suckling also promotes the release of pituitary oxytocin, which causes the myoepithelial cells in the breast to contract and milk ejection or "letdown" to occur (Fig. 23–1).

Most women who choose to can successfully breast-feed an infant. There are, however, a small number of women who experience lactation failure due to inadequate glandular tissue, neurohormonal disruption, or prolactin deficiency. Normal breast changes during pregnancy include an increase in breast size, increased pigmentation of

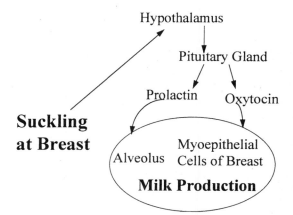

Figure 23–1. Prolactin is produced in response to the amount and frequency of an infant's suckling and controls milk synthesis and secretion. Suckling also promotes the release of pituitary oxytocin, which causes the myoepithelial cells in the breast to contract and milk ejection, or "letdown," to occur.

the nipple and areola, and hypertrophy of the Montgomery tubercles. *A lack of normal breast changes during pregnancy should alert the clinician to the possibility of primary lactation failure.* Women who have had surgical procedures that interrupt ducts and sever or damage nipple nerves may also produce inadequate supplies of milk. Close follow-up of infants of mothers with potential lactation problems is essential to ensure adequate nutrition and the institution of supplemental feedings if needed.

MILK PRODUCTION AND COMPOSITION. Milk production on the first postpartum day ranges from about 50 to 150 mL, with rapid increases in production occurring at about 36 hours post partum. Average milk production is approximately 750 to 800 mL/day and does not appear to be affected by maternal nutrition, body composition (adiposity), energy, or nutrient intake.

Infant characteristics such as ineffective or infrequent suckling by small infants can affect milk volume. **In the early postpartum period frequent suckling (10 ± 2 sessions per day) is important to the establishment of an adequate milk supply.** Mothers whose infants are hospitalized can develop an adequate supply by pumping their breasts (electric breast pump) five times or more per day (approximately 100 minutes total pumping time) in the first postpartum month.

Maternal factors that may contribute to inadequate milk production include pain, stress and fatigue, and the use of alcohol, cigarettes, or some oral contraceptives. Pain, stress, and fatigue inhibit oxytocin release and thus milk ejection. Progestin-only contraceptives have little effect on milk composition, volume, or breastfeeding duration. The American Academy of Pediatrics considers oral contraceptives to be compatible with breastfeeding. Smoking may decrease milk volume by decreasing prolactin and oxytocin response. Ethanol in sufficient amounts inhibits oxytocin release; for the average 60-kg woman (132 pounds) an alcohol dose of 0.5 gm/kg or approximately 2 to 2.5 ounces of liquor, 8 ounces of wine, or two cans of beer will inhibit oxytocin release despite the common belief that alcohol increases milk production. Fluids consumed in excess of thirst do not appear to increase milk volume.

Milk composition varies between women and with stages of lactation, although individual differences in well-nourished women are insignificant. There is good evidence that, by using their own body stores, women are able to produce milk with adequate amounts of protein, fat, carbohydrate, and most minerals even if their own supply of nutrients is limited. Milk composition is most likely to be affected by low maternal intakes of vitamins, especially vitamins B_6, B_{12}, A, and D. Women's needs are easily met by an average American diet containing 2700 kcal/day. At lesser energy intakes the nutrients most likely to be deficient are calcium, magnesium, zinc, vitamin B_6, and folate. Efforts should be made to increase nutrient intake in the diets of women who may be at risk for nutritional deficiencies during lactation, including adolescents, and dieting, impoverished, or completely vegetarian (vegan) women. Current evidence does not warrant recommending routine vitamin-mineral supplementation during lactation.

PRENATAL PREPARATION. The prenatal pediatric visit is an ideal time to discuss breastfeeding and address potential problems related to anatomic abnormalities, previous breast surgery, or the mother's ability to produce sufficient milk. In general, no special preparation of the breasts is necessary. Women should avoid the use of soap, alcohol, or other drying agents on the nipples. Nipple rolling and other manipulations are ineffective in preventing sore nipples and should be avoided owing to the risk of inducing uterine contractions and premature labor.

As many as 10% of pregnant women have inverted (nonprotractile) nipples that may make proper grasp of the breast by the infant difficult; flat or inverted nipples fail to protract when the areola is gently squeezed. No specific treatment is needed prenatally. Some mothers may require extra assistance in helping infants to latch onto the nipple and areola correctly after delivery. Compressing the areola between two fingers to allow the nipple to protrude as much as possible will help the infant grasp the breast. Expressing a small amount of milk before a feeding to soften the areola and entice the infant is also helpful. If needed, the nipple can be drawn out before breastfeeding with an electric pump. Inverted nipples often respond to these measures within the first 1 or 2 postpartum days.

EARLY LACTATION. **All labor and delivery, newborn nursery, neonatal intensive care, and postpartum nurses should be adequately trained to assist the nursing mother.** Although all women will benefit from a breastfeeding-supportive environment, those who become ill post partum, undergo difficult deliveries, or deliver multiple infants are at increased risk for breastfeeding problems. Problems commonly associated with these clinical situations include sleepy infants, late initiation of breastfeeding, increased needs for supplementation, less frequent night feedings, and delayed increases in milk supply. Excellent supportive care is essential for these at-risk mothers to successfully breastfeed. Table 23–1 lists factors that promote successful breastfeeding. Key factors in early management are as follows:

1. *Proper positioning at the breast.* It is essential that mothers are taught to properly position the infant at the breast (Fig. 23–2). The infant's abdomen should be against the mother's abdomen.

TABLE 23–1. Factors That Promote Breastfeeding

Prenatal	Immediate Post Partum	Infancy
General health information	Early maternal-infant contact First feeding within ½ hr of birth	Counseling and support
Breastfeeding education	Rooming-in	Avoidance of exposure to formula samples and advertising
Encouragement by health professional	"Demand" feeding schedules Avoidance of supplementation Supportive atmosphere for breastfeeding women	Information about breast pumping Counseling regarding return to work

Adapted from Kramer MS: Poverty, WIC, and promotion of breastfeeding. Pediatrics 87:399–400, 1991. By permission of Pediatrics.

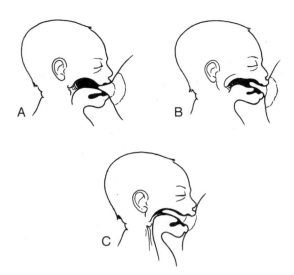

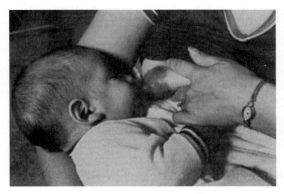

Figure 23–3. When the breast is offered to the infant, the areola is gently compressed between two fingers and the breast is supported to ensure that the infant is able to grasp the areola adequately. (From Lawrence RA: Breastfeeding: A Guide for the Medical Profession, 4th ed. St. Louis, CV Mosby, 1994, p 239.)

Figure 23–2. A, As the infant grasps the breast, the tongue moves forward to draw the nipple in. **B,** The nipple and areola move toward the palate as the glottis still permits breathing. **C,** The tongue moves along the nipple, pressing it against the hard palate and creating pressure. Ductules under the areola are milked and flow begins as a result of peristaltic movement of the tongue. The glottis closes, and swallowing follows. (From Lawrence RA: Breastfeeding: A Guide for the Medical Profession, 4th ed. St. Louis, CV Mosby, 1994, p 237.)

The infant's head should be well supported and kept in line with the infant's body. After eliciting a rooting response by stimulating the infant's lower lip with the nipple, the mother should bring the infant's head toward her breast by moving her arm or hand (Table 23–2).

2. *Supporting the breast.* The mother should support her breast using either a palmar or scissor grasp (Fig. 23–3). It is important that the mother's grasp of the breast not interfere with the infant's ability to latch on properly. The infant's lips should be everted and positioned on the areola about 1 or 1.5 inches from the base of the nipple.

3. *Detaching the infant from the breast.* The mother should break the suction at the breast by inserting her finger in the infant's mouth between the gums.

4. *Waking a sleepy baby.* Mothers should be taught ways to awaken a sleepy infant such as by diapering or gentle stimulation. Infants are usually alert for the first 1 to 2 hours after delivery and should be put to breast at this time. They then enter a period of deep sleep. Some infants may be difficult to awaken for the first 1 to 2 days after birth. Infants who are premature or lack sufficient fat stores may require close monitoring for possible hypoglycemia; however, healthy term infants should have adequate fat stores to avoid hypoglycemia. Parents should be reassured that the infant is well and will become increasingly alert over the first few days of life. Skin-to-skin contact between the mother and infant should be encouraged as much as possible. The mother should be taught to put the infant to breast as soon as feeding cues are noted and keep the infant awake at the

TABLE 23–2. Direct Observation of Breastfeeding

Infant	Mother
Infant roots and moves in to grasp breast well behind nipple	Appears comfortable and relaxed with feeding; arms and back are well supported
Tongue is over lower alveolar ridge of gums and forms a trough; peristaltic waves in the tongue effect milk delivery	Supports breast with scissor or palmar grasp
Jaw moves up and down, cheeks are full and rounded, audible swallowing is noted	Possible leaking from opposite breast as letdown occurs with feeding
Head is well supported and is in line with body	Breasts are full before, then soften with feeding
Infant's abdomen is against mother's abdomen	Mother reports minimal or no pain with feeding
Infant appears satisfied after feeding. Young infants will terminate feedings with sleep	When the infant is removed from the breast a teat is formed without ridges or other signs of trauma

TABLE 23–3. Indications for Supplemental Feedings

	Absolute Indications*	Probable Indications
Maternal	Severe maternal illness Contraindicated maternal medication; mother should temporarily pump and discard milk (most medications are compatible with breastfeeding)	Delayed lactogenesis (>5 days) Primary lactation failure: Inadequate glandular tissue, Sheehan syndrome, retained placenta Intolerable pain with feedings† Maternal-infant forced separation (e.g., infant or maternal illness, geographic separation)
Infant	Birth weight <1500 gm or gestational age <32 wk Small for gestational age, at risk for hypoglycemia Inborn error of metabolism (e.g., galactosemia)	Hypoglycemia after breastfeeding as documented by serum glucose Delayed lactogenesis resulting in dehydration or weight loss in excess of 8% Ineffective breastfeeding with adequate milk supply† Hyperbilirubinemia secondary to ineffective breastfeeding†

*Adapted from World Health Organization 27th World Health Assembly, United Nations Children's Fund: Protecting, promoting and supporting breastfeeding: The special role of maternity services (a joint WHO/UNICEF statement). Geneva, World Health Organization, 1989; and Powers NG and Slusser W: Breastfeeding update 2: Clinical lactation management. Pediatr Rev 18:147–161, 1997.

† When appropriate assessment of breastfeeding has occurred and subsequent management has been ineffective.

Supplements should preferably be pumped human milk, fortified human milk, or formula given by supplemental feeding system, cup, or finger feeding. (*Note:* It may be difficult to pump colostrum in the first few days post partum.)

breast with gentle stimulation (e.g., rub the infant's hands, feet, or back).

5. *Frequency and length of feedings.* Breastfeedings should be frequent, occurring every 2 to 2.5 hours. Equal stimulation of each breast is achieved by alternating the breast that is first offered. Some mothers benefit from general guidelines to nurse about 10 to 15 minutes per side in the first few days. Especially in the first week or two, infants will need to suckle about 2 or 3 minutes before letdown occurs.

6. *Supplements* (Table 23–3). **Care should be taken to avoid nonmedically indicated supplemental feedings.** Supplementation interferes with the supply and demand nature of breastfeeding. Additionally, the mechanical differences between breastfeeding and bottle feeding may cause some infants to refuse the breast or learn to suckle ineffectively. Supplements should preferably be given by supplemental nursing system, cup, or finger feeding.

7. *Postpartum support.* Early follow-up with the infant's clinician (5 to 7 days) by phone or home visit is essential to address problems and monitor the establishment of successful lactation (Table 23–4). If the infant is discharged before 48 hours, the infant should be examined within 1 to 2 days of discharge and again at 7 days. La Leche League representatives, hospital hotlines, and lactation consultants may also be useful to mothers in the early postpartum period.

SUPPLEMENTS IN THE BREASTFEEDING INFANT

Vitamin K prophylaxis should be administered to all newborns to prevent hemorrhagic disease of the newborn. Vitamin D levels in the breast milk of a well-nourished mother are adequate for the healthy term infant. However, if the mother's vitamin D nutritional intake or exposure to sunlight is inadequate, or if the infant does not experience adequate exposure, the mother's diet should be

TABLE 23–4. Clinical Criteria for Successful Breastfeeding at 5 to 7 Days

1. The infant is alert, active, and normally hydrated and has a vigorous coordinated suck.
2. The mother's milk has increased in quantity. Mothers will generally experience their milk "coming in" between postpartum days 2 and 4 and will note that their breasts become firm and full. The mother may report leaking of milk from the opposite breast with feeding and full breasts becoming softer after feeding.
3. The mother and infant have established an appropriate feeding schedule of every 2 to 3 hours with one longer sleep interval of about 5 hours. The infant should not be receiving any supplemental feedings (water or formula).
4. Any nipple tenderness the mother experienced in the first postpartum days should be mild and resolving.
5. The infant should be having at least 3 to 4 breast-milk stools (mustard-colored seedy stools) and after day 3 should be having 6 to 8 clear voids per day (at least one [cloth] diaper per day should be soaked).
6. The infant's weight loss since birth should be no more than 7%. After the mother's milk increases in quantity, the infant should gain between 15 and 30 grams/day. Birth weight should be regained by 10 to 14 days of age.
7. With direct observation of breastfeeding the infant is noted to root vigorously, latch easily, and have a rhythmic suck and swallow. The infant appears satisfied after breastfeeding.

improved or supplements of vitamin D provided. If this is not possible, the breast-fed infant should receive a vitamin D supplement.

Neonatal iron stores will meet the needs of a term infant for the first 3 to 4 months of life. Because iron in human milk is very bioavailable (approximately 50% is absorbed), breast-fed infants do not require supplemental iron until about 6 months of life, when other food sources such as iron-fortified infant cereal should be introduced. Fluoride supplements are no longer recommended for infants less than 6 months of age.

GROWTH OF THE BREAST-FED INFANT

Breast-fed infants experience a weight loss of 5% to 7% in the early postpartum period. After lactogenesis has occurred (by day 5 post partum), infants should gain between 15 and 30 grams per day. Birth weight should be regained by 10 to 14 days of age. The World Health Organization Working Group on Infant Growth is in the process of developing a new international reference for infant growth based on a worldwide sample of infants breast-fed for 12 months with introduction of solid food not beginning until 4 months of age. Thus far, only research findings have been published and final growth charts are not expected to be completed for several more years. Studies conducted in the United States have demonstrated that growth in length and head circumference is similar between breast-fed and formula-fed infants. Until about 3 months of life breast-fed infants parallel their formula-fed counterparts, at which time weight gain becomes slower, continuing so even with the introduction of solid foods. Thus **breast-fed infants tend to be leaner than formula-fed infants.** The slower growth rates and lower energy intakes of breast-fed infants are associated with normal development and decreased rates of infectious disease. Currently available growth charts are based on infants who were formula-fed and may lead to the false conclusion that the breast-fed baby is not gaining enough.

CONTRAINDICATIONS TO BREASTFEEDING

Contraindications to breastfeeding are rare and the assessment of any exposure must weigh potential risks against the many benefits of breastfeeding. Maternal medications are a common concern, although most are safe during breastfeeding. Contraindicated drugs include therapeutic radiopharmaceuticals, lithium, lactation-suppressing drugs, some antithyroid drugs, illicit or "street" drugs, and synthetic anticoagulants. Short courses of some medications may require mothers temporarily to pump their breasts and discard the milk. Other drugs may be contraindicated depending on the infant's age. For more specific information consult the sources listed in Further Reading at the end of the chapter.

Neither cytomegalovirus (CMV) nor hepatitis B or C is a contraindication to breastfeeding. Little information is available about hepatitis C transmission through human milk; however, the Centers for Disease Control and Prevention as of March 1997 has stated there is no reason to recommend against breastfeeding. Infants whose mothers are hepatitis B antigen positive may safely breast-feed if the infant is vaccinated and protected against infection with hepatitis B immune globulin (0.5 mL HBIG). If a mother requires rubella immunization after delivery she may still breastfeed. Mothers with active tuberculosis or active herpetic breast lesions should avoid breastfeeding.

Of more concern is the possible transmission of human immunodeficiency virus (HIV) infection through breast milk. Women who test seropositive for HIV antibody in the United States should be counseled not to breastfeed, thus avoiding postnatal transmission to an infant who may not be infected. Infants diagnosed with galactosemia should be fed a milk substitute with a nonlactose sugar source.

COMMON PROBLEMS

Assessment of a lactation problem should always include direct observation of the infant while breastfeeding.

JAUNDICED INFANTS. Infants who feed poorly, whether breast-fed or formula-fed, are at risk for hyperbilirubinemia due to delayed passage of meconium and an increase in the enterohepatic circulation of bilirubin. Efforts should be made to ensure that the infant is positioned and suckling effectively during breastfeeding (Table 23–1). Maternal pain, stress, and fatigue can contribute to delayed lactogenesis and must be addressed. Mothers should be encouraged to nurse frequently (10 to 12 times per day). Skin-to-skin contact with the infant and warm compresses before feeding will encourage milk letdown. The American Academy of Pediatrics (AAP) has published new guidelines that allow healthy term infants without evidence of hemolysis to be observed at increased levels of bilirubin (AAP, 1994). Close follow-up of these infants is essential to ensure successful establishment of lactation and resolution of hyperbilirubinemia.

FUSSY INFANTS, ACTING HUNGRY/ GROWTH SPURTS. Correction of any positioning or latch-on problem will ensure that the infant is breastfeeding effectively (Table 23–1). Skin-to-skin contact and warm moist compresses before breastfeeding will facilitate milk letdown. To encourage stimulation of the milk supply, infants should be allowed to feed as long as wanted, provided that the mother is comfortable. Pacifiers should be avoided. The mother of an infant undergoing a growth spurt may complain that her previously satisfied baby is always hungry. The mother should be encouraged to feed the infant frequently (on demand). Maternal milk supply will increase to meet the new demand within 5 to 7 days. Supplemental feedings are unnecessary. The mother may benefit from extra help at home.

SORE NIPPLES. Mothers commonly experience some discomfort in the early days of breastfeeding with the initial grasp and suckling of the breast. Caused by the negative pressure on empty ductules, the discomfort typically resolves as the mother's milk supply increases. Any nipple pain that persists throughout a feeding or fails to resolve within the first week requires further evaluation. The most common cause for nipple trauma and subsequent pain is poor positioning of the infant at the breast. Causes of trauma include infants who attach only to the nipple; suck in their lower lip and irritate the underside of the nipple; or are removed from the breast without first breaking suction.

The nursing style of the infant also can cause pain. Very vigorous infant suckling at the breast may result in temporary discomfort for the mother. Delicate tissues may benefit from air drying after nursing or from brief dry heat; a hair dryer set on warm and fanned across the breast for 2 or 3 minutes at 6 to 8 inches is helpful. Additionally, expressing a few drops of milk and allowing this to dry on the areola is beneficial.

Careful assessment of other factors that contribute to soreness is important. Soaps or self-prescribed treatments may lead to drying of the area and subsequent contact dermatitis. If the skin is particularly dry, the area may benefit from lubrication. The *routine* use of ointments, however, is not recommended because sebaceous and Montgomery glands are easily plugged. Vitamin A and D ointments are not harmful; however, vitamin E and local anesthetic creams should not be used. Purified lanolin ointments that are alcohol-free and "allergen-free" are safe if an ointment is indicated. Surface moisture due to milk or occlusive

plastic in nursing pads will aggravate the problem. Nipple shields reduce the amount of milk the infant receives and, in general, their use should be avoided.

Cracked, bleeding, or blistered nipples indicate the need for shorter, more frequent breastfeedings; the use of a short-acting analgesic before nursing also may be helpful. The mother should begin breastfeeding with the less sore breast, limiting the amount of non-nutritive sucking (that not associated with swallowing) by the infant. Cracks are often caused by poor positioning combined with excessive dryness. Pain is alleviated by proper breastfeeding positioning and by application of a therapeutic ointment such as vitamin A and D ointment, purified lanolin, or a synthetic corticoid (by prescription). When the nipple is severely affected and fungal and bacterial infections have been ruled out, 1% cortisone ointment, or a synthetic corticoid (halobetasol propionate, 0.05% or mometasone furoate, 0.1%) rubbed into the nipple and areola after each breastfeeding may be helpful. Usually a 2-day course of treatment is adequate.

ENGORGEMENT. Engorgement involves congestion, increased vascularity, and accumulation of milk in the breast. Treatment is directed at emptying the breast and frequent, effective breastfeeding is essential. Often, manual expression of a small amount of milk allows the infant to grasp the breast properly and nurse efficiently. Warm compresses applied to the breast before expression of milk facilitates letdown. Analgesics and a supportive brassiere are helpful. Milk production and vascularity stabilize over a few days of treatment. Between feedings, cool compresses may provide additional relief.

MASTITIS. Mastitis is an inflammation of the lactating breast, accompanied by cellulitis. It is commonly caused by *Staphylococcus aureus* or *Escherichia coli* and less commonly by *Streptococcus* and coagulase-negative staphylococci. A traumatized nipple leads to bacteria infecting a secreting lobule by way of the lactiferous ducts to the periductal lymphatics, or by hematogenous spread.

The clinical signs and symptoms of mastitis include fever of 101.3°F (38.5°C) or greater, systemic flulike illness (chills, aching, headache, nausea, malaise), and a pink, tender, hot, swollen, wedge-shaped area of the breast. Certain conditions may predispose a woman to mastitis, including milk stasis (engorgement or plugged ducts) and lowered maternal defenses secondary to fatigue and stress. Cracked or sore nipples may lead to milk stasis when a woman avoids nursing. Engorgement, plugged ducts, and sore nipples should be treated vigorously to prevent the development of mastitis. The onset of mastitis varies widely, from several days to several months post partum.

Early diagnosis and treatment are essential to prevent progression of the disease to abscess formation or chronic mastitis. Midstream cultures of milk and cell counts (bacteria $>10^3/mL^3$ and leukocytes $>10^6/mL^3$) may be helpful in diagnosis. Antibiotic therapy should, however, not await culture results. The affected breast should be regularly emptied by nursing or pumping. The woman may continue to nurse her infant beginning with the unaffected breast to enhance letdown on the affected side and lessen the discomfort when the infant latches on. The choice of antibiotics should be compatible with continued breastfeeding. Staphylococcal disease responds readily to dicloxacillin or nafcillin and streptococcal disease responds to penicillin. Acute uncomplicated mastitis presenting after 1 month post partum responds readily to dicloxacillin or erythromycin therapy. Antibiotics should be given for a minimum of 10 to 14 days. Adequate rest and stress reduction are essential. Warm compresses often hasten drainage of the involved area and provide additional pain relief. Analgesics and a supporting brassiere are also helpful.

MONILIAL INFECTION. Monilial infection of the breast typically presents as stinging, burning pain radiating throughout the breast during and after nursing. The infection is a common secondary complication of recent antibiotic treatment, maternal candidal vaginitis, or candidal infection (e.g., thrush) in the infant. The nipple may be normal or appear pink and shiny with typical satellite lesions. A 2-week course of treatment with a topical antifungal agent rubbed into the nipple and areola after breastfeeding is usually effective. Other sources of infection in the mother, such as vaginitis, should also be treated. The infant should always be treated simultaneously with oral nystatin to prevent recurrences.

COLIC AND BREAST REJECTION IN BREAST-FED INFANTS. Some breast-fed infants exhibit colicky symptoms believed to be associated with specific foods in the mother's diet, such as certain vegetables, fruits, strong spices, or teas. If a mother has questions regarding foods in her diet she should carefully document any effects in the 24 hours after ingestion of the suspected irritant. Caffeine, which appears in breast milk, may cause irritability. Most infants tolerate one to two cups of caffeinated beverage without problems. Smoking, which is known to decrease milk production, may also cause irritability since cotinine (a metabolite of nicotine) appears in breast milk.

Colic in breast-fed infants has also been attributed to cow's milk in the mother's diet. A positive family history of allergies, especially to cow's milk, is suggestive of this clinical entity and the infant may benefit from the mother eliminating cow's milk from her diet. A week-long trial of elimination is usually diagnostic.

FURTHER READING

American Academy of Pediatrics, Committee on Drugs: The transfer of drugs and other chemicals into human milk. Pediatrics 93:137–150, 1994.

American Academy of Pediatrics, Provisional Committee for Quality Improvement and Subcommittee on Hyperbilirubinemia: Practice parameter: Management of hyperbilirubinemia in the healthy term newborn. Pediatrics 94(Pt 1):558–565, 1994. (Published erratum appears in Pediatrics 95:458–461, 1995 [see Comments].)

Goldman AS: Review: The immune system of human milk: Antimicrobial, antiinflammatory and immunomodulating properties. Pediatr Infect Dis J 12:664–671, 1993.

Institute of Medicine: Nutrition During Lactation: Report of the Subcommittee on Nutrition During Lactation of the Committee on Nutritional Status during Pregnancy and Lactation. Washington, DC, Institute of Medicine, 1991.

Lawrence RA: Breastfeeding: A Guide for the Medical Profession. St. Louis, CV Mosby, 1994.

Powers NG and Slusser W: Breastfeeding update 2: Clinical lactation management. Pediatr Rev 18:147–161, 1997.

RESOURCE CENTERS

Lactation Study Center, University of Rochester School of Medicine and Dentistry (Phone: 716-275-0088). Provides information on medications and lactation, and lactation management issues. Maintains computer data bank regarding lactation literature.

Wellstart International (Phone: 619-295-5192). Provides educational programs and handouts and information regarding lactation management issues.

Constantinos G. Siafakas
Tracie L. Miller

Chapter 24

Pediatric Nutrition

Nutrition is central to the care of all infants and children. Successful nutrition involves not only adequate amounts of food but also appropriate composition of the diet and healthy eating behavior. For normal growth, intake must include water, carbohydrate, protein, fat, vitamins, minerals, and trace elements. The Recommended Dietary Allowances (RDA) published by the Food and Nutrition Board of the National Academy of Sciences are designed for the maintenance of adequate nutrition of healthy people (Table 24–1). The goal of RDAs is to ensure that the needs of all the population are met. Apart from energy requirements, RDAs usually exceed individual requirements.

NUTRITIONAL PRODUCTS AND INDICATIONS

BREASTFEEDING. Breast milk is the recommended feeding choice for full-term infants in the first 4 to 6 months of life (see Chapter 23). Breast milk has nutritional and antibacterial properties, while breastfeeding promotes the maternal-child bond. Compared with cow's milk–based formula, human milk contains more carbohydrate and fat but less protein. However, the protein consists

TABLE 24–1. Recommended Dietary Allowances (RDA) for Energy and Protein

Age	Energy (kcal/kg)	Protein (gram/kg)
0–6 mo	108	2.2
6–12 mo	98	1.6
1–3 yr	102	1.2
4–6 yr	90	1.1
7–10 yr	70	1.0
Males		
11–14 yr	55	1.0
15–18 yr	45	0.9
Females		
11–14 yr	47	1.0
15–18 yr	40	0.8

Modified from National Academy of Sciences, Food and Nutrition Board: Recommended Dietary Allowances, 10th ed. Washington, DC, National Academy Press, 1989.

mainly of whey (70% whey, 30% casein), which is easily digestible. It also contains bile acid–stimulated lipase, which complements the infant's immature pancreatic function. The lower concentration of vitamins and minerals, particularly calcium, iron and zinc, is compensated for by the higher bioavailability. Breast-fed infants should be supplemented with 10 μg of vitamin D and 0.25 mg of fluoride for infants living in areas with little sunshine and a fluoride water concentration less than 0.3 ppm, respectively. Strict vegetarian mothers should be counseled to take vitamin B_{12} supplements. All infants require vitamin K at birth.

Preterm human milk is higher in protein and electrolytes and lower in lactose compared with term milk. Calcium, phosphorus, and other nutrients in preterm human milk are not adequate for the needs of preterm infants; thus, supplementation with human milk fortifier (HMF; Mead-Johnson, Evansville, IN) is recommended. The HMF is discontinued when the infant approaches a post-conceptional age of 40 weeks or a weight of 2000 grams.

Contraindications to breastfeeding include infants with inborn errors of metabolism (e.g., phenylketonuria, galactosemia, urea cycle disorders), maternal infections such as *Mycobacterium tuberculosis,* human immunodeficiency virus (HIV) in the developed world, varicella, herpes simplex, or syphilitic lesions involving the breast, and certain drugs (e.g., alkylating agents, radioactive and antithyroid agents, gold salts, cimetidine, ergotamine).

MILK-BASED INFANT FORMULAS. Infant formulas are used when breastfeeding is contraindicated or the mother is unwilling or unable to nurse. Cow's milk–based formulas have been developed to approximate the composition of human milk. These formulas may be casein- or whey-predominant and provide a protein and energy content of 1.5 g/dL and 20 kcal/oz (67 kcal/dL), respectively. The major carbohydrate is lactose at a concentration close to 7 g/dL. The fat is a mixture of vegetable oils, which is more easily absorbed than the butterfat present in cow's milk. Water and micronutrients are added in amounts sufficient to meet the daily requirements of growing infants.

SPECIALIZED FORMULAS. Infants who are intolerant to cow's milk protein have problems with weight gain, vomiting, diarrhea, bloody stools, wheezing, skin rash, or even anaphylaxis. With these symptoms, if the infant is breast-fed and the mother is willing to continue to nurse, she should eliminate dairy products from her diet. If the infant is formula-fed or the mother wishes to discontinue nursing, formulas that are soy-based or hydrolyzed should be tried.

Soy-based protein formulas are lactose-free and are primarily indicated for infants with galactosemia or lactase deficiency. They can be given cautiously to infants with cow's milk protein allergy, yet there is a 30% to 50% cross-reactivity between cow's milk and soy protein. Soy formulas are also suitable for infants who require a strict vegetarian diet. They are not recommended for premature infants because they may result in decreased nitrogen retention and decreased absorption of minerals. For the latter, phytic acid, a contaminant in the processing of soy protein, which forms complexes with minerals, seems to be responsible.

Specialized formulas containing hydrolyzed whey or casein may be appropriate for formula-fed infants with allergies to milk and soy. Formulas composed of free amino acids are used for infants with more severe milk protein allergy, who have failed hydrolysate formulas. Hydrolyzed protein does not require pancreatic enzyme digestion and is efficiently absorbed in the proximal small bowel. Therefore, they are suitable for children with cystic fibrosis, short gut syndrome, and other disorders of maldigestion. Furthermore, the digestion of hydrolyzed protein leaves little residue, which results in a decrease of fecal production. This is helpful in situations in which fecal material should be minimized, such as perineal burns, abscesses, or rectal surgery. Elemental formulas in patients with Crohn disease are adequate treatment and lead to disease remission. The disadvantages of protein hydrolysate formulas include higher cost, unpalatability, and higher osmolality, which may result in osmotic diarrhea. Protein hydrolysate formulas are available for both infants and older children.

For infants with fat malabsorption, there are formulas with increased amounts of medium-chain triglycerides (MCTs), which are readily absorbed in the absence of bile acids and directly transported into the portal circulation. Pregestimil (Mead-Johnson, Evansville, IN) is an infant formula that combines both casein hydrolysate and increased amount of MCTs and is recommended for children with cholestasis and cystic fibrosis.

PRETERM INFANT FORMULAS. Preterm infant formulas are designed to meet the needs of rapidly growing premature infants, taking into consideration the immature intestinal and renal function. These formulas have a higher content of carbohydrate and protein compared with term infant formulas. Lactose, maltodextrins, and glucose polymers are the primary carbohydrate constituents and are well tolerated by premature infants. The whey-to-casein ratio approximates that of human milk. These formulas also contain a high percentage of MCT to reduce steatorrhea, which is commonly seen in low-birth-weight infants.

MISCELLANEOUS FORMULAS. Modular formulas are used to satisfy a specific nutrient requirement or to complement a limited dietary intake. Formulas such as Mono- and Disaccharide-Free Powder (Product 3232A) (Mead-Johnson, Evansville, IN) and RCF (Ross Carbohydrate-Free; Ross Laboratories, Columbus, OH) are carbohydrate-free and contain protein, fat, and minerals. The amount of added carbohydrate may vary according to the patient's tolerance (as in cases of short gut syndrome). Finally, there are formulas designed to fulfill the needs of patients with inborn errors of metabolism (e.g., phenylketonuria, tyrosinemia), and organ failure (kidney, liver, or lung). The composition of the different types of formulas available for infants and older children is shown in Tables 24–2 and 24–3.

MILKS. Follow-up formulas may be used from the age of 6 months, although they have no proven advantage over iron-fortified infant formulas. Whole milk is not recommended until after the end of the first year of life. Premature feeding of whole milk can lead to subclinical gastrointestinal bleeding and anemia. Supplementation with vitamins, minerals, and iron is advocated if it is to be given to an infant. The high concentration of sodium and saturated fat is another disadvantage. Recently, a link has been proposed between premature introduction of cow's milk and insulin-dependent diabetes mellitus. Goat milk is high in essential fatty acids but deficient in folic acid. In contrast to popular beliefs, it is as allergenic as cow's milk. Skim milk or partially skimmed milk, containing 1% to 2% fat, creates a high osmotic load because of the high concentration of protein and electrolytes. They are not recommended for the first 2 years of life. Although in normal conditions, the older infant's kidney concentrating ability is able to handle the osmotic load presented by skim milk, it cannot in situations of water deficit, leading to hypernatremic dehydration.

FRUIT JUICES. Fruit juices are popular

TABLE 24–2. Infant Formula Analysis per 100 mL

Formula	kcal/oz.	Protein gm	Protein Type	Protein %cal	Carbohydrate gm	Carbohydrate Type	Carbohydrate %cal	Fat gm	Fat Type	Fat %cal
Human milk mature	20	1.1	20% casein, 80% whey	6	7.2	Lactose	42	3.9	Human milk fat	52
Human milk premature	22	1.7	20% casein, 80% whey	9	8	Lactose	44	3.9	Human milk fat	48
Human milk fortifier (per packet)	3.5/mL	0.2	Reduced mineral whey and casein	10	0.7	Corn syrup solids, lactose	77	0.0		
Enfamil	20	1.5	Nonfat cow's milk, demineralized whey	9	6.9	Lactose	41	3.8	Coconut and soy oils, palm olein, sunflower oil	50
Similac	20	1.5	Nonfat cow's milk	9	7.2	Lactose	43	3.6	Coconut and soy oils	48
Enfamil Premature 20	20	2.0	Dimineralized whey, nonfat milk solids	12	7.4	Corn syrup solids, lactose	44	3.4	MCT, 40%; soy, 40%; coconut oil, 20%	44
Enfamil Premature 24	24	2.4	Dimineralized whey, nonfat milk solids	12	9.0	Corn syrup solids, lactose	44	4.1	MCT, 40%; coconut and soy oils	44
Carnation Good Start	20	1.6	Whey	9.8	7.4	Lactose 70%, maltodextrin	44	3.4	Palm olein, safflower and coconut oils	46
Isomil	20	1.8	Soy protein isolate	11	6.8	Corn syrup, sucrose	40	3.7	Soy and coconut oils	49
ProSobee	20	2.0	Soy protein isolate	12	6.7	Corn syrup solids	40	3.5	Coconut and soy oils, palm olein, safflower oil	48
Pregestimil	20	1.9	Casein hydrolysate, cysteine, tyrosine, tryptophan	11	6.9	Corn syrup solids, dextrose, cornstarch	41	3.8	MCT, 60%; corn oil, 20%; safflower oil, 20%	48
Nutramigen	20	1.9	Casein hydrolysate, amino acid premix	11	9.0	Corn syrup solids, cornstarch	54	2.6	Corn oil	35
Alimentum	20	1.9	Hydrolyzed casein	11	6.9	Sucrose, modified tapioca starch	41	3.8	MCT, 50%; safflower oil, 40%; soy oil, 10%	48
Neocate	21	2.0	Free amino acids	12	8.1	Corn syrup solids	47	3.2	Coconut oil, safflower oil, soy oil	41
Lactofree	20	1.5	Nonfat milk	9	7	Corn syrup solids	42	3.7	Palm olein, 45%; soy oil, 20%; coconut oil, 20%; sunflower oil, 15%	49

MCT, medium-chain triglycerides.

TABLE 24-3. Toddler and Young Child Formula Analysis per 1000 mL

Formula	kcal/oz	Protein			Carbohydrate			Fat		
		gm	Type	%cal	gm	Type	%cal	gm	Type	%cal
Cow's milk	19	34	Cow's milk	21	48	Lactose	30	34	Butterfat	49
Next Step	20	25	Nonfat milk	10	74	Lactose, corn syrup solids	44	33	Palm olein, 45%; soy oil, 20%; coconut oil, 20%; HO sunflower oil, 15%	45
Next Step Soy	20	22	Soy protein	13	78	Corn syrup solids, sucrose	47	29	Palm olein, 45%; soy oil, 20%; coconut oil, 20%; HO sunflower oil, 15%	40
Neocate One Plus	30	25	Free amino acids	10	146	Maltodextrins, sucrose	58	35	MCT oil, 35%; safflower oil; canola oil	32
Vivonex Pediatric	24	24	Free amino acids	12	130	Maltodextrins, modified starch	63	24	MCT oil, 68%; soy oil, 32%	25
Peptamen Junior	30	30	Hydrolyzed whey	12	138	Maltodextrin, sucrose, starch	55	38.5	MCT oil, 60%; soy oil, canola oil, lecithin	33
PediaSure	30	30	Sodium caseinate, whey protein	12	110	Hydrolyzed cornstarch, sucrose	44	50	Soy oil, 30%; HO safflower oil, 50%; MCT oil, 20%	44

HO, high oleic; MCT, medium-chain triglyceride.

among the pediatric population, especially in toddlers. Excessive intake, however, may limit the intake of other foods and cause diarrhea owing to increased osmotic load from their carbohydrate content. Juices are not necessary components of an infant's diet and need to be well diluted when they are given.

IRON SUPPLEMENTATION. The content of iron in human milk is low but is highly bioavailable. The breast-fed term infant should receive iron at the age of 6 months by supplement or by iron-containing solid food. The breast-fed preterm infant has insufficient iron stores and should leave the hospital nursery on an iron-supplemented formula. The bottle-fed infant should receive iron-containing formula for the entire first year. Iron-free or low-iron formulas are no longer recommended. Beliefs that iron-containing formulas cause gastrointestinal tract symptoms are erroneous. The risks of iron deficiency continue during the second year of life, especially for children consuming large quantities of whole milk.

NUTRITION OF THE OLDER CHILD. Beyond the first year of life, parents and caretakers are encouraged to feed their children a variety of foods so that the necessary amount of carbohydrates, protein, and fat is consumed. The major food groups should be offered, as given in the U.S. Department of Agriculture Food Guide Pyramid. The energy obtained from fat should be limited to 30% of the total calories; protein should provide 15% to 20%; and carbohydrates, 55%. With regard to calories from fat, 10% may come from saturated and polyunsaturated fatty acids and the remaining from monounsaturated ones. Awareness that atherosclerosis begins in childhood, especially with a family history, will help guide the dietary and screening recommendations.

Vegetarian diets are nutritious and promote excellent health, if they are accompanied by appropriate dietary counseling. There is substantial evidence that they decrease the risk of atherosclerosis, cancer, and obesity. Traditional vegetarians are categorized as lactovegetarians (consume only milk), ovovegetarians (consume both milk and eggs) and vegans (consume no animal products at all). Several nutritional hazards have been identified, especially among vegans. Growth failure may occur because the large volume of fiber required to meet the child's caloric need exceeds the absorptive capacity of the gastrointestinal tract and decreases the bioavailability of protein. Deficiencies of vitamin B_{12}, vitamin D, calcium, iron, and zinc can occur as well.

Adolescents require a diet high in calories and nutritious food, because of the altered body composition achieved during the growth spurt, change

in physical activity, and menstruation. Furthermore, adolescents are vulnerable to conditions that deteriorate nutritional status such as eating disorders (anorexia nervosa, bulimia), alcohol, tobacco and drug abuse, athletic activity, chronic degenerative disorders, accidents, and pregnancy. Increased requirements of calcium, vitamin A, vitamin C, iron, zinc, and folate during pregnancy deserve recognition.

NUTRITIONAL ASSESSMENT

Accurate assessment of the child's nutritional status is a valuable component of pediatric care. The early recognition of malnutrition is important but difficult to diagnose, since clinical signs and symptoms are not readily identified until the advanced stages. Longitudinal evaluation of growth and nutrition allows earlier detection of nutritional problems. Nutritional evaluation must include complete medical, psychosocial, and food intake history. Important aspects of the dietary history and clinical signs of nutrient inadequacies are shown in Tables 24–4 and 24–5.

TABLE 24–4. Information Needed for Accurate Nutritional Assessment

Diet

24-hour recall of food intake

3- to 7-day food record (requires weighing and measuring of consumed food)

Food frequency questionnaire (frequency and quantity of consumption of foods over a longer period of time)

Frequency of meals and snacks, variety of foods offered, and the amount consumed

For infants: formula type and preparation, volume and number of daily feedings, method of feeding

Psychosocial

Resources for food purchasing (food stamps, WIC, soup kitchens, food pantries, etc.)

Family eating patterns and cooking

Eating environment (at the table, alone or with other family members, in front of the television)

Medical

Food allergies or intolerance. In infants: history of formula changes

History of vomiting and diarrhea

Defecation pattern

Presence of diseases that interfere with feeding (e.g., cerebral palsy, cleft lip and palate) or affect nutrient absorption (e.g., cystic fibrosis, AIDS, short bowel syndrome, cancer, inflammatory bowel disease)

Feeding developmental milestones (oral and muscular development, dentition, weaning, texture progression of foods)

AIDS, acquired immunodeficiency syndrome; WIC, Special Supplemental Nutrition Program for Women, Infants, and Children.

TABLE 24–5. Clinical Findings Associated with Nutritional Derangement

System	Finding	Nutritional Derangement
General	Underweight, short stature	↓ Calories
	Overweight	↑ Calories
	Edema; apathy	↓ Protein
Hair	Hair loss; lack of luster and curl; depigmentation; ease of pluckability	↓ Protein
Skin (face)	Nasolabial seborrheic dermatitis	↓ Riboflavin
	Moon face; diffuse depigmentation	↓ Protein
Skin (general)	Generalized dermatitis	↓ Zinc, essential fatty acids
	Symmetric dermatitis of the skin exposed to sunlight, trauma, pressure points	↓ Niacin
	Follicular hyperkeratosis	↓ Vitamin A
	Scrotal, vulvar dermatitis	↓ Riboflavin
	Petechia; purpura; perifollicular hemorrhage	↓ Vitamins C and K
Eyes	Dry conjunctiva; keratomalacia; Bitot spots	↓ Vitamin A
	Circumcorneal injections	↓ Riboflavin
Lips	Angular stomatitis	↓ Riboflavin, iron
	Cheilosis	↓ Vitamin B-complex vitamins
Gums	Swollen; bleeding	↓ Vitamin C
	Reddened gingiva	↑ Vitamin A
Tongue	Red, swollen with loss of papillae	↓ Niacin, riboflavin, folate, vitamin B_{12}
Teeth	Caries	↓ Fluoride
	Mottled; pitted enamel	↑ Fluoride
Nails	Koilonychia	↓ Iron
Subcutaneous fat	Decreased	↓ Calories
	Increased	↑ Calories
Muscle	Decreased muscle mass	↓ Calories, protein
	Tender calves	↓ Thiamine
Skeletal	Epiphyseal enlargement	↓ Vitamins D and C
	Costochondral beading; bowed legs; craniotabes; frontal bossing	↓ Vitamin D
Neurologic	Ophthalmoplegia	↓ Thiamine, vitamin E
	Ataxia; loss of vibratory sense, deep tendon reflexes	↓ Vitamins B_{12} and E
Endocrine	Hypothyroidism, goiter	↓ Iodine
	Delayed puberty	↓ Zinc
Other	Altered taste	↓ Zinc
	Delayed wound healing	↓ Zinc, vitamin C
	Parotid enlargement	↓ Protein

Data compiled from several sources.

Anthropometry

Anthropometry is the measurement of physical dimensions of the human body at different ages and the comparison with reference standards. A recumbent length is measured when the child is younger than 2 years of age and standing height measurements are obtained after 2 years of age. Height and weight measurements are always corrected for age and sex. Weight is also interpreted in the context of height or length and is expressed as weight-for-height/length. All of these measurements can be expressed in percentiles, corrected for age and sex and plotted on the NCHS (National Center for Health Statistics) growth grids. Weight, height, and weight-for-height/length can also be expressed in percent standard, which is defined as actual height (weight)/standard height (weight) × 100. Alternatively, all growth requirements can be expressed as z-scores, where a z-score represents a unit of standard deviation from the median. Z-score measurements are more sensitive measures of movement of growth toward or away from the mean and allow for more accurate comparisons between chronologic observations in the same child or comparison of the same anthropometric value between children of different ages and sex. A z-score can be calculated using the following equation:

$$z\text{-score} = \frac{\text{Actual anthropometric value} - \text{Median reference value}}{\text{Standard deviation}}$$

Longitudinal assessment of growth patterns can give clues to the etiology of a nutritional disorder. Weight decrements out of proportion to decrements in height in early childhood suggest nutritional deprivation, with inadequate caloric intake. This pattern would yield below standard weight-for-length/height. With longer-term nutritional deprivation, linear length/height becomes depressed as well, thus yielding normal weight-for-length/height measurements. This condition is termed "nutritional dwarfism." In contrast, decrements in length/height prior to changes in weight suggest more endocrine-based disorders, and a symmetric decrease in weight and length/height may represent genetic disorders or normal familial growth trends. Children who have decreased weight-for-length/height should be evaluated further to determine which body compartment has been affected.

From a nutritional standpoint, a simple model of body composition includes the adipose tissue mass (fat) and the lean body mass (fat-free mass). The triceps skinfold thickness (TSF) and midarm muscle circumference (MAMC) are anthropometric measurements of body composition. The TSF, measured by a skinfold caliper on the arm midway between the acromium and olecranon, is highly correlated with subcutaneous fat stores. Nearly half of the body fat in humans is accumulated subcutaneously. The MAMC, which can be estimated by the midarm circumference and the TSF using a nomogram, correlates with muscle mass. In patients with liver, cardiac, pulmonary or renal disease, anthropometry may be more reliable than weight or height, since weight gain or loss may result from fluid shifts caused by the chronic illness.

Growth velocity, particularly valuable in detecting early malnutrition, assesses the rate of growth over a period of time and is usually expressed in centimeters per year. It is important that the parents' stature is taken into consideration when evaluating a child's growth. Another useful tool in the assessment of growth, especially when screening for obesity, is the body mass index [BMI = weight in kg/ (height in m)^2], which is well correlated with fat mass.

Head circumference, an index of brain growth, is influenced by nutritional status until 36 months of age. Decreases in head circumference due to nutritional compromise follow the changes in weight and height in chronologic order.

Laboratory Nutritional Evaluation

Serum albumin, prealbumin, transferrin, retinol binding protein, fibronectin, type I collagen, and somatomedin C (insulin-like growth factor-I) are used as indicators of visceral protein status. However, their values must be interpreted with caution, since liver and renal disease, infection, and inflammatory response affect them. Fibronectin, a nonimmune serum opsonin, seems to be less affected by these chronic conditions. Prealbumin is valuable because of its short half-life (2 days compared with albumin's half-life of 21 days), which allows for early detection of nutritional status alterations.

Bioelectrical impedance analysis (BIA) is an indirect determination of body fat and lean body mass that has attained clinical acceptance recently because of its ease and relatively low cost. It is based on the principle that a weak electrical current passes readily through mineral content of the body's fat-free mass rather than through fat. This method is dependent on the state of the patient's hydration.

Bone age provides an estimate of skeletal maturation and potential for catch-up growth. The determinations are made by hand and wrist x-ray films. A delayed bone age is defined as a value greater than 2 standard deviations below the mean bone age for chronologic age and sex. Bone age can be delayed in patients with malnutrition or other chronic illnesses, and bone age may be advanced in obesity.

Deficiencies of vitamins and minerals are common in protein-energy malnutrition and can impact on immune function. Deficiencies of specific nutrients such as vitamins A, C, and B$_{12}$, zinc or iron may alter delayed hypersensitivity skin responses and depress lymphocyte count, antibody production, and bactericidal capacity of neutrophils and macrophages. Vitamin E, riboflavin, vitamin B$_6$, zinc, copper, and selenium play a crucial role in the removal of oxygen radicals and levels can be low in protein-energy malnutrition. Demonstration of immune competence by skin test reactivity and a lymphocyte count above 1500 per milliliter is of particular prognostic value regarding the outcome of surgical procedures in malnourished patients. Several clinically recognizable states of nutrient deficiency or excess have been identified (Table 24–6).

PROTEIN-ENERGY MALNUTRITION STATES

Protein-energy malnutrition is a common problem in developing countries because of inadequate food intake. In developed countries, malnutrition occurs secondary to pathologic conditions that interfere with nutrient absorption and utilization. There are three clinical syndromes, that is, marasmus, kwashiorkor and cachexia, that represent extremes of the wide spectrum encompassed by protein-energy malnutrition. Marasmus is the result of inadequate calories in the diet. Kwashiorkor is

TABLE 24–6. Clinical Signs of Nutrient Deficiency and Excess

Nutrient	Deficiency Signs	Toxicity Signs	Food Sources
Vitamin A (retinol, β-carotene) Infants: 375 μg Children: 400–700 μg Adolescents: 800–1000 μg	Ocular manifestations: nyctalopia, xerophthalmia, Bitot spots, retinal degenerations	Headache (pseudotumor cerebri); vomiting; hepatomegaly/hepatic fibrosis; teratogenesis	Carrots, liver, green vegetables, breast milk, infant formula
Vitamin D (ergocalciferol D_2, cholecalciferol D_3) Infants: 7.5–10 μg Children: 10 μg Adolescents: 10 μg	Rickets/osteomalacia: epiphyseal enlargement, rachitic rosary, frontal bossing	Hypercalcemia; hypercalciuria; headache (pseudotumor cerebri); bone cortical hyperostosis	Fish, eggs, liver, sunlight, infant formula
Vitamin E (α-tocopherol) Infants: 3–4 mg Children: 6–7 mg Adolescents: 8–10 mg	Hemolytic anemia; neurologic changes: hypo- or areflexia, ophthalmoplegia, decreased proprioception and vibratory sense	Vitamin K antagonism: prolonged PT	Milk, eggs, oils high in fatty acid, breast milk, infant formula
Vitamin K (phylloquinone; menaquinone) Infants: 5–10 μg Children: 15–30 μg Adolescents: 45–65 μg	Coagulopathy (prolonged PT); hemorrhagic disease of the newborn	Large parenteral doses can cause anaphylaxis, hemolysis, hyperbilirubinemia, and kernicterus in the newborn	Fruits, green leafy vegetables, soy beans, cereals, breast milk, infant formula
Vitamin B_1 (thiamine) Infants: 0.4 mg Children: 0.7–1.0 mg Adolescents: 1.1–1.5 mg	Beriberi: muscle wasting, calf tenderness, polyneuropathy ("dry"), edema ("wet"), cardiac failure, Wernicke encephalopathy, Korsakoff psychosis Lactic acidosis	Anaphylaxis from excessive parenteral administration	Pork, nuts, breast milk, infant formula
Vitamin B_2 (riboflavin) Infants: 0.4–0.5 mg Children: 0.8–1.2 mg Adolescents: 1.3–1.8 mg	Nasolabial seborrheic dermatitis; glossitis; cheilosis; scrotal, vulval dermatitis; macrocytic anemia	None known	Liver, dairy products, almonds, lamb, pork, breast milk, infant formula
Vitamin B_3 (niacin) Infants: 5–6 mg Children: 9–13 mg Adolescents: 15–20 mg	Pellagra: diarrhea, dermatitis, dementia; cheilosis, glossitis; vaginitis	Flushing; peptic ulcer activation; excessive amounts of niacin result in increased utilization of muscle glycogen stores and decreased mobilization of fatty acid during exercise	Meat, liver, fish, poultry, breast milk, infant formula

Nutrient	Deficiency	Toxicity	Sources
Vitamin B₆ (pyridoxine) Infants: 0.3–0.6 mg Children: 1.0–1.4 mg Adolescents: 1.4–2.0 mg	Convulsions; dermatitis; anemia; abdominal distress, vomiting; personality changes	Neuropathy	Meat, fish, poultry, breast milk, infant formula
Vitamin B₁₂ (cyanocobalamin) Infants: 0.3–0.5 μg Children: 0.7–1.4 μg Adolescents: 2.0 μg	Megaloblastic anemia; peripheral neuropathy, demyelination, posterior column disease; decreased serum transaminases; acidosis, methylmalonic aciduria; dermatitis; glossitis; cheilosis	None known	Animal products, breast milk, infant formula
Biotin	Anorexia; nausea, vomiting; neurologic dysfunction: ataxia, seizures, depression; scaly dermatitis; alopecia; acidosis	None known	Liver, egg yolk, breast milk, infant formula
Vitamin C (ascorbic acid) Infants: 30–35 mg Children: 40–45 mg Adolescents: 50–60 mg	Scurvy: swollen, bleeding gums, petechial hemorrhages, follicular hyperkeratosis, joint pain; poor wound healing	Gastritis; oxalate and urate kidney stones	Broccoli, grapefruit, leafy vegetables, tomatoes, breast milk, infant formula
Pantothenic acid	Fatigue; headache; depression; slow growth; burning paresthesias; ↑ DTRs	Diarrhea; water retention	Meat, fish, poultry, legumes, breast milk, infant formula
Calcium Infants: 400–600 mg Children: 800–1200 mg Adolescents: 1200 mg	Osteomalacia, osteoporosis; tetany; seizures	Hypercalcemia, nephrocalcinosis; vomiting; lethargy	Dairy products, green vegetables, breast milk, infant formula
Phosphorus Infants: 300–500 mg Children: 800 mg Adolescents: 1200 mg	Weakness; anorexia; growth arrest; bone pain	Hypocalcemia; seizures	Dairy products, pork, fish, legumes, breast milk, infant formula
Magnesium Infants: 40–60 mg Children: 80–170 mg Adolescents: 270–300 mg	Neuromuscular hyperexcitability; cardiac arrythmias; hypocalcemia; hypokalemia; convulsions	Diarrhea; respiratory paralysis; hypotension; flaccid quadriplegia	Vegetables, breast milk, infant formula

Table continued on following page

TABLE 24-6. Clinical Signs of Nutrient Deficiency and Excess *Continued*

Nutrient	Deficiency Signs	Toxicity Signs	Food Sources
Chromium	Glucose intolerance; neuropathy; encephalopathy	No toxicity after oral ingestion has been reported	Brewer's yeast; meat; cheese
Copper	Hypochromic anemia, neutropenia; hyperlipidemia; skin depigmentation; bone disease	Diarrhea; hepatic necrosis; renal failure; hemolytic anemia; coma	Liver, oysters, nuts, legumes, corn oil margarine
Fluoride	Osteoporosis; dental caries	Mottled enamel; nausea, vomiting, abdominal pain; paresthesias; elevated transaminases	Fluoridated water
Iodine Infants: 40–50 μg Children: 70–120 μg Adolescents: 150 μg	Goiter; cretinism	Thyrotoxicosis	Iodized salt, fish, shellfish, breast milk, infant formula
Iron Infants: 6–10 mg Children: 10 mg Adolescents: 12–15 mg	Hypochromic microcytic anemia; pica; pallor; inability to concentrate	Hemosiderosis, hemochromatosis (chronic); GI bleeding, coagulopathy, shock (acute)	Infant cereals, red meat, liver, cereals, legumes, breast milk, infant formula
Manganese	Impaired growth; skeletal abnormalities; neonatal ataxia; dermatitis	In extremely high doses extrapyramidal central nervous system dysfunction	Nuts, grains, fruits, leafy vegetables
Molybdenum	Tachycardia, tachypnea; neurologic abnormalities	Antagonist of copper; goutlike syndrome	Meat, grains, legumes
Selenium Infants: 10–15 μg Children: 20–30 μg Adolescents: 40–55 μg	Myositis with elevated CPK; cardiomyopathy; macrocytic anemia; depigmented hair; osteoarthropathy; increased susceptibility to vitamin E deficit	Alopecia, brittle nails; garlic odor; dental caries; fatigue; irritability	Liver, kidney, meat, grains, seafood
Zinc Infants: 5 mg Children: 10 mg Adolescents: 12–15 mg	Acrodermatitis enteropathica; growth failure; delayed wound healing; hypogeusia; delayed puberty; immune dysfunction; diarrhea	Nausea, vomiting; anemia of copper deficiency; hypercholesterolemia; pancreatitis with IV zinc	Grains, legumes, pork, beef, chicken, nuts, seeds, eggs, breast milk, infant formula

CPK, creatine phosphokinase; DTRs, deep tendon reflexes; GI, gastrointestinal; IV, intravenous; PT, prothrombin time.
Adapted from Subcommittee on the 10th Edition of the RDAs, Food and Nutrition Board, Commission on Life Sciences, National Research Council Recommended Dietary Allowances, 10th ed. Washington, DC, National Academy Press, 1989.

TABLE 24–7. Manifestations of Protein-Energy Malnutrition

Feature	Marasmus	Kwashiorkor
Onset	Usually within the first year	Usually after the first year
Weight-for-age	Decreased	Mild decrease or increase when edema is present
Subcutaneous fat and muscle	Prominent loss of both	Minor or even no loss
Edema	None	Pitting edema in lower legs and face
Mental status	Normal	Irritability, apathy
Appetite	Good	Very poor
Hair	Normal	Thin, pale, fragile
Skin	Normal	Dermatitis
Liver	Normal	Hepatomegaly with fatty infiltration
Albumin	Normal	Low
Vitamin deficiencies	None or mild	Severe deficiencies secondary to low plasma carrier protein
Immune function	Moderate compromise	Severe compromise (impaired T-cell function and lymphopenia)

the result of a diet deficient in protein, independent of caloric content. The manifestations of both syndromes are shown in Table 24–7. Cachexia is a nutritional state characterized by weakness, anorexia, and loss of lean body mass with preservation of adipose tissue, in distinction to simple starvation in which lean body mass is preserved at the expense of fat. It has been proposed that proinflammatory cytokines such as interleukin-1, tumor necrosis factor, and interleukin-6, among others, appear to play a central role in the loss of lean body mass. Cachexia is seen in the context of chronic degenerative diseases such as cancer and the acquired immunodeficiency syndrome (AIDS).

Management of protein-energy malnutrition includes (1) initial rehydration since the patients are intravascularly depleted, correction of electrolyte abnormalities, and treatment of concurrent infections; (2) nutritional support (enteral or parenteral) to compensate for energy and protein loss and to potentiate catch-up growth and; (3) prevention of recurrent malnutrition. Cachexia is usually irreversible unless the progression of underlying disease is halted.

OBESITY

Obesity is the most prevalent pediatric nutritional disease in the United States. Parental obesity, higher socioeconomic class, small family size, and longer time spent viewing television are associated with higher incidence of childhood obesity. Clinical standards for obesity do not exist for children and adolescents. Diagnostic screening criteria that have been used include BMI greater than 85%; TSF greater than the 85th percentile; weight for height greater than the 95th percentile; and actual weight greater than 120% of that expected for height. Obesity is accompanied by both increased fat and lean body mass. When an obese child gains weight, he or she tends to gain more fat than lean body mass. In a state of negative energy balance, obese children tend to lose more fat, whereas adults lose more lean body mass. Primary obesity is associated with advanced bone age, increased height, and early menarche. Table 24–8 shows disease states associated with obesity.

Management of obesity includes parental education; a low-calorie and fat-balanced diet; increased physical activity and exercise; and behavioral modification. Family participation in weight reduction proves to be the most successful approach. There has been intense recent interest in leptin, a hormone that is encoded by the *ob* gene and synthesized and secreted by adipocytes. Leptin decreases appetite by acting at the center of appetite and satiety in the hypothalamus via specific receptors. Current research shows promising treatments in the near future.

ENTERAL NUTRITION

The intestinal tract is the preferred route of nutritional support because it is more "physiologic," has fewer complications, and cost is lower

TABLE 24–8. Disease States Associated with Obesity

Increased mortality
Cardiovascular disease; hypertension
Non–insulin-dependent diabetes mellitus
Hypoventilation (pickwickian syndrome)
Skeletal disorders (Blount disease: medial tibia fracture; slipped capital femoral epiphysis)
Liver disease (steatohepatitis, cirrhosis)
Social stress

compared with parenteral nutrition. Enteral nutrition is indicated in situations in which oral feedings are precluded or when the oral intake is not adequate (Table 24–9).

Supplementation with nasogastric or nasoduodenal feedings is preferred when the estimated course is shorter than 3 months. For longer courses, or for patients intolerant to nasoenteral feedings, gastrostomy or enterostomy tube feedings are indicated. Gastric feedings are preferable because of the antibacterial acid effect and digestive properties of the stomach as well as ease of feeding. Gastrostomy tubes are placed either percutaneously or surgically. Percutaneous endoscopic gastrostomy is most popular because of its lower cost, low postoperative morbidity, faster recovery, and earlier introduction of feedings. Gastrostomy tubes can be replaced in 2 to 3 months with low-profile gastrostomy devices, which cannot migrate through the pylorus and are less prone to accidental removal. When the risk for aspiration is high, as in conditions associated with abnormal swallowing function, severe gastroesophageal reflux, delayed gastric emptying, comatose patient, or intractable vomiting, transpyloric feedings are recommended. The complications and disadvantages of the different types of enteral feedings are shown in Table 24–10.

Enteral feedings can be administered intermittently or continuously. Intermittent feedings are preferable because they avoid the need for pumps, allow the child more mobility, and simulate physiologic feeding. Signs of intolerance include high gastric residua, diarrhea, vomiting, aspiration, and dumping syndrome (postprandial fullness, nausea, vomiting, diarrhea, pain, and sweating owing to rapid transit of food into the small intestine). Continuous infusions are required for transpyloric feedings and are also beneficial with malabsorption syndromes.

TABLE 24–9. Conditions That May Require Enteral Nutrition

Preterm infants
Congenital heart disease
Chronic lung disease (cystic fibrosis, bronchopulmonary dysplasia)
Gastrointestinal disease (e.g., short gut syndrome, inflammatory bowel disease, severe gastroesophageal reflux, severe allergic enteropathy, intractable diarrhea, immune deficiency disorders)
Chronic liver disease (especially before transplantation)
Chronic renal disease
Neurologic disease (e.g., cerebral palsy, muscular dystrophy)
Hypermetabolic states (e.g., burns, trauma, cancer, AIDS)
Anorexia nervosa

AIDS, acquired immunodeficiency syndrome.

TABLE 24–10. Complications and Disadvantages of the Different Types of Enteral Nutrition

Nasoenteral	Pharyngeal irritation and discomfort
	Sinusitis
	Easy displacement and risk for aspiration
Gastrostomy	Localized cellulitis at the ostomy site
	Gastroesophageal reflux and aspiration
	Migration of the tube through the pylorus
	Dumping syndrome
	Leakage of gastric contents
	Occlusion of the tube
	Perforation of the stomach on placement
Enterostomy	Need for general anesthesia on placement
	Perforation of the bowel
	Wound infection and dehiscence
	Intestinal obstruction
	Occlusion of the tube
	Inadvertent tube removal
	Need for continuous feeding

PARENTERAL NUTRITION

The decision to use parenteral nutrition (PN) is made after thorough assessment of nutritional status, nutrient requirements, function of the gastrointestinal tract, and risk associated with the parenteral route. Generally, an infant or a child is a candidate for PN if his or her gastrointestinal tract cannot be used or is incapable of supporting adequate maintenance, growth, and tissue repair.

Parenteral nutrition may be administered centrally or peripherally. Peripheral PN is infused using the veins in the extremities or scalp. However, the amount of carbohydrate infused is limited, since glucose concentrations in excess of 10 g/dL cause phlebitis. A higher concentration of glucose, and thus higher caloric administration, can be achieved via placement of central catheters, which terminate into one of the large veins entering the heart.

The constituents of PN include water, glucose, protein, lipids, electrolytes, minerals, vitamins, and trace elements. Compatible drugs can also be added to the solution. PN is initiated continuously at maintenance fluid rate and low glucose concentration (10 g/dL). The volume and glucose concentration are gradually advanced to avoid hyperglycemia and hyperosmolality. A gradual approach is also recommended for protein and lipid increases. Progression from continuous to cycled mode requires gradual increase of infusion rate during the night while increasing the time off PN during the day. Close laboratory monitoring is critical, especially when frequent changes in nutrient solutions are being made.

The complications of PN are catheter-related (e.g., sepsis, thrombosis, cardiac arrythmias, cardiac tamponade, pneumothorax) or metabolic (e.g., hypo- or hyperglycemia, electrolyte abnormalities, azotemia, hyperlipidemia, hyperosmolality, vitamin and trace element deficiencies).

SUMMARY

Nutrition during health and illness is an important aspect of every child's care. Breastfeeding is highly recommended for full-term infants because of its high nutritional value and immunologic properties. Human milk without supplementation is not sufficient to meet the nutritional needs of the premature infant. Cow's milk–based formulas, which have been designed to approximate human milk, are an alternative to breast milk in the first year of life. Cow's milk is allowed in the second year. Premature administration of cow's milk in infancy may lead to gastrointestinal bleeding and iron deficiency anemia. Specialized formulas are available for cow's milk protein allergy and other disorders of maldigestion.

Nutritional assessment is a necessary component in the evaluation of the pediatric patient. It is based on medical and dietary history, clinical examination, and anthropometric and laboratory values. Several clinical syndromes associated with deficiency or excess of energy and/or nutrients have been identified. Energy and/or nutrient repletion can be achieved via the enteral or parenteral route. The enteral route is more preferable because it simulates physiologic feedings and carries a lower risk for complications.

FURTHER READING

American Academy of Pediatrics: Pediatric Nutrition Handbook, 3rd ed. Elk Grove Village, IL, AAP, 1992.

National Academy of Sciences, Food and Nutrition Board: Recommended Dietary Allowances, 10th ed. Washington, DC, National Academy Press, 1989.

Pediatric Nutrition. Entire issue of Pediatric Clinics of North America, Vol 42, No. 4, 1995.

US Department of Agriculture, Human Nutrition Information Service: The Food Guide Pyramid. Washington, DC, USDA, Home and Garden Bull. 252, 1992.

Walker WA and Watkins JB (eds): Nutrition in Pediatrics, 2nd ed. Hamilton, Ontario, Canada, BC Decker, 1997.

Alan Meyers

Chapter 25

Food Assistance Programs for Children

THE NEED FOR FOOD ASSISTANCE

As in most countries, poor children in the United States are at risk of being undernourished, according to surveys of nutritional status that use a variety of different indicators. The best measure of the nutritional status of any community is the growth of young children, and **every national survey of the U.S. population to date has shown that, as a group, poor children are of shorter stature than their peers from higher socioeconomic strata.** This is a manifestation of chronic, mild undernutrition. Deficiencies of micronutrients, most notably iron, also are much more common among poor children. **Iron deficiency is of special importance because of its high prevalence (as much as 25%) among poor children in the United States and its well-documented adverse impact on cognitive function in children.** Dietary intake data from national samples show that low-income young children are less likely to achieve 100% of the Recommended Dietary Allowance (RDA) for a variety of nutrients than children in higher-income families, and it has been estimated from surveys of selected high-risk populations that nearly 20% of low-income U.S. families with children under 12 years of age have been hungry at some time in the prior year, and an additional 50% of these families are at risk for hunger.

Clinicians should be aware of the prevalence of hunger among the poor in general and in their communities in particular and should include questions on household food security (e.g., "Does your family always have enough to eat?") when assessing the child's environment, because some parents may not volunteer this information. The clinician also must be familiar with sources of support for families in need or be able to refer the family to a source of such information.

FEDERALLY FUNDED PROGRAMS OF FOOD ASSISTANCE

The federal government, through the Food and Consumer Service (FCS) of the U.S. Department of Agriculture (USDA), funds a variety of programs to provide food assistance to children in need (Table 25–1). These programs are operated jointly by the federal and state governments, with the federal government generally funding provision of the food and part of the administrative costs, the FCS establishing regulations and monitoring operations, and the states administering the program, including determining eligibility. Other sources of food aid are available in most communities, as well. The information presented in this chapter must be viewed in light of recent federal legislation having created major changes in these programs, further changes being likely, and the likely prospect of substantial regional and local variations in funding and administration of some of these programs.

Food Stamps

The Food Stamp Program is the major public program providing food to low-income families in the United States, with its origins dating to the Depression era of the 1930s. The modern program began as a pilot project in 1961, was authorized by Congress in 1964, and was expanded dramatically in 1974 when Congress required all states to offer the program to low-income households. The Food Stamp Program provides eligible low-income households with coupons (or electronic debit cards) that can be used as cash at participating food stores. Eligibility requirements include a gross household income of 130% or less of the federal poverty level ($20,280 per year for a family of four in 1997) and limits on assets. Public Law 104-193 (the Welfare Reform Act of 1996) made most noncitizens ineligible to receive Food Stamps, although the program has remained an entitlement, meaning that all eligible applicants will receive some benefits. Households are issued a monthly allotment of Food Stamps based on the Thrifty Food Plan, the USDA's low-cost model diet, adjusted for household size and net income. Purchases that may be made with Food Stamps include food or food products for human consumption and seeds and plants with which to produce food in a garden. Alcoholic beverages, res-

taurant food, pet food, vitamins, and nonfood items may not be purchased with Food Stamps. The program may be applied for at the local Food Stamp office, which usually is listed in the state or local government pages of the telephone book.

Research by the USDA has shown that families participating in the Food Stamp Program purchase more food and consume more nutrients than do nonparticipating low-income families and that Food Stamp shoppers obtain more key nutrients per food dollar spent than all other income groups.

In 1997 the Food Stamp Program served 23.5 million people monthly at an annual cost of $23.7 billion, with the average individual receiving $72 in Food Stamps per month, or approximately 80 cents per meal. Sixty-one percent of households receiving Food Stamps include children, and children comprise more than 50% of all participating individuals. It is estimated that 40% to 60% of eligible families do not participate in the Food Stamp Program. The Welfare Reform Act of 1996 will reduce federal Food Stamp expenditures by almost 20% ($27.7 billion) by the year 2002, with the average benefit falling from 80 cents per person per meal to 66 cents, with about two thirds of the reduction affecting families with children.

The Special Supplemental Nutrition Program for Women, Infants, and Children

The Special Supplemental Nutrition Program for Women, Infants, and Children (popularly known as WIC) provides food, nutrition education, and referral to health care and other services for low-income pregnant and lactating women and their children under age 5 years. WIC began as a pilot program in 1972 and was made permanent in 1974. Participants are provided with vouchers that may be redeemed at participating food stores for specified foods designed to supplement the diet, with different food packages provided for different categories of participants (pregnant women, lactating women, infants, and children). WIC foods include infant formula and cereal, juice, eggs, milk, cheese, peanut butter, and beans. Many states also offer coupons to participants to purchase fresh fruits and vegetables at participating farmers' markets through the WIC Farmers' Market Nutrition Program. Individual states negotiate rebates with formula manufacturers and limit WIC infant formula to that from the contracted manufacturer. When indicated, WIC provides therapeutic formulas for infants with a physician's prescription. Breastfeeding is encouraged as part of regular nutritional counseling.

TABLE 25–1. Federally Funded Food Assistance Programs for Children, 1997[a]

	Program Cost, $ Millions	Children Served, Millions	Average Benefit, $ per Person per Month	Income Eligibility	Categorical Eligibility
Food Stamps	23,673	12	73	≤130% poverty	U.S. citizens[b]
WIC	3,795	5.7	32	≤185% poverty	Pregnant and lactating women; infants; children <5 yr of age
School Lunch Program	5,720[c]	26[d]	42[e]	Free: ≤130% poverty; Reduced price: <185% poverty	All children attending participating schools
School Breakfast Program	1,198[c]	7[f]	26[g]	Same as Lunch Program	All children attending participating schools
Summer Food Service Program	271	2.6	41[h]	"Open": all children; "Enrolled": same as School Meals	All children <18 yr of age
Child and Adult Care Food Program	1,693	2	39[i]	Same as School Meals	All children attending participating programs
Special Milk Program	19	—[j]	3[k]	≤130% poverty	All children attending participating programs
Homeless Children Nutrition Program	3	.002	156[l]	All children in shelter	Children <6 yr of age

[a] USDA estimates.
[b] Exceptions include refugees and asylees, veterans, and immigrants who have 10 years' work history in the United States; eligibility may change if pending legislation is enacted.
[c] Federal expenditures only.
[d] Includes 13 million children receiving free and 2 million receiving reduced-price school lunch.
[e] Free lunch only; represents $1.99 federal subsidy for each lunch for a month (i.e., 21 school days).
[f] Includes 5.6 million children receiving free and 0.4 million receiving reduced-price school breakfast.
[g] Free breakfast only; represents $1.22 federal subsidy for each breakfast for a month (i.e., 21 school days).
[h] Based on lunch only; represents $1.97 for each lunch (21 meals per month).
[i] Based on $1.84 federal reimbursement for lunch at a child care center (21 meals per month).
[j] 151 million half-pints of milk served in 1995.
[k] Based on federal reimbursement of 12.25 cents per half-pint of milk (21 times per month).
[l] Reimbursement for 3 meals and 1 snack (30 days per month).

Eligibility requirements include an income standard (185% or less of the federal poverty level, or $28,860 per year for a family of four in 1997) and a state residency requirement, and applicants must be determined to be "at nutritional risk" by a health professional, such as a physician, nurse, or nutritionist. "Nutritional risk" may be based on a medical condition, such as failure-to-thrive, anemia, or chronic medical conditions, or on dietary risks, such as a history suggestive of an inadequate pattern of dietary intake. WIC is not an entitlement program, and because funding is not adequate to serve all eligible persons, when a local WIC agency reaches its capacity, participation is determined on the basis of a system of priorities. In descending order of priority, these categories include pregnant and lactating women and infants who have a nutrition-related medical condition; infants up to 6 months of age whose mothers were at nutritional risk during pregnancy; children who have a nutrition-related medical condition; pregnant and lactating women and infants who have an inadequate pattern of dietary intake; children who have an inadequate pattern of dietary intake; and postpartum women at nutritional risk. It should be noted that immigration legal status is not considered in determining eligibility for the WIC program, and the income threshold is higher than that for the Food Stamp program. The fact that infants and children are receiving regular primary care must be documented to enroll in the program as well as for recertification and ongoing participation. Local WIC offices may be located within health care facilities or elsewhere in the community; a list may be obtained by contacting the state WIC office, usually listed as an agency of state government.

The effects of WIC program participation have been studied extensively. The National WIC Evaluation, a major study commissioned by the USDA and published in 1988 (Rush and coworkers, 1988), found that prenatal WIC participation was associated with improved adequacy of prenatal care, longer duration of gestation, decreased preterm delivery, decreased fetal mortality, and increased birth weight. Children born to women participating in WIC prenatally also had significantly larger head circumference and better vocabulary and digit memory at 5 years of age than did children born to nonparticipants. Participating children had better immunization status and a more regular source of primary health care. These findings have been replicated in a number of subsequent studies; meta-analysis has shown that prenatal WIC participation was associated with a 25% reduction in low birth weight and a 44% reduction in very low birth weight, resulting in an estimated savings of $1.19 billion in infant medical costs in 1992. WIC participation also has been associated with decreased prevalence of iron deficiency among children.

In 1997, WIC served 7.4 million persons each month at a cost of $3.7 billion, with an average benefit of $32 per person per month. Approximately 50% of participants are children (aged 1 to 5 years), 25% are women, and 25% are infants (including over 45% of all infants born in the United States). Two thirds of families participating in WIC have incomes at or below the federal poverty level. The USDA estimates that about 60% of all eligible women, infants, and children (and 98% of eligible infants) are served by WIC.

School Meals

In response to the high rate of rejection of wartime draftees for reasons related to poor nutrition, Congress created the *National School Lunch Program* (NSLP) in 1946 "to safeguard the health of the Nation's children and to encourage the domestic consumption of nutritious agricultural commodities." The NSLP is administered federally by the Food and Consumer Service, at the state level by state education agencies, and locally by school districts, which are reimbursed in cash and donated commodities by the USDA, and for which they must serve meals that meet federal nutrition requirements, as well as offer free and reduced-price meals to eligible children. All elementary and secondary public and private nonprofit schools and residential child care institutions are eligible to participate. The NSLP is available in nearly 99% of public schools, and nationwide about 92% of all students have access to the program, of whom about 58% (26.2 million children in 1997) participate on an average day.

Children from families with incomes at or below 130% of the federal poverty level ($20,280 per year for a family of four in 1997) are eligible for free school meals, and those whose family incomes are between 130% and 185% of poverty are eligible for reduced-price meals, for which the school system may charge no more than 40 cents for lunch and 30 cents for breakfast. All other children may purchase a meal at full price, which may be set at any level by local school systems. Schools are reimbursed at a different rate for meals served at full price, reduced price, or free of charge. Parents of registered students receive information about the school meals programs and may apply for free or reduced-price meals. Although every child from a low-income family attending a participating school is eligible, parents are asked to submit a Social Security number and are warned of the possibility of federal audits.

The School Nutrition Dietary Assessment Study (Burghardt and Devaney, 1995), commissioned by the USDA and conducted in 1992, found that while the NSLP was providing adequate food energy, minerals, and vitamins, the meals contained an average 38% of energy from fat and 15% from saturated fat, well above the levels recommended by the Dietary Guidelines for Americans (30% and 10%, respectively), established jointly by the USDA and the U.S. Department of Health and Human Services (Kennedy et al., 1996). The Child and Adolescent Trial for Cardiovascular Health (CATCH), a randomized controlled field trial conducted in four states, showed that a coordinated program of school food service personnel training and classroom and home curricula could successfully reduce the percentage of calories obtained from fat and saturated fat to near the levels recommended, both at lunch and over 24 hours, without affecting participation in NSLP. In 1994, as part of the Healthy Meals for Healthy Americans Act (PL 103–448), Congress passed a major revision of the school meals legislation. USDA regulations now require that School Lunch provide one third of the RDA for all nutrients as a weekly average, and that beginning with the 1996–1997 school year, participating schools offer meals consistent with the Dietary Guidelines for Americans, including the recommendations for fat intake. The new law also permits schools that have a high proportion of low-income participants to offer free school meals to all students.

Congress established the *School Breakfast Program* (SBP) as a pilot program in 1966 and authorized it permanently in 1975. The intent of the legislation was to provide a breakfast in school, containing one fourth of the daily RDA for key nutrients, to children who, otherwise, would have none. Two thirds of schools offer the SBP, and although only about 20% of children at these schools participate (7 million children), over 86% of these children receive free or reduced-price breakfast. Although the availability of the SBP does not appear to increase the likelihood that a child will eat some breakfast on a school day, research suggests that those low-income children who do eat School Breakfast may perform better on certain cognitive tasks in school.

In 1997, Congress allocated $5.72 billion for the NSLP and $1.198 billion for the SBP.

Other Child Nutrition Programs

The *Summer Food Service Program* provides free meals to children who receive free or re-

duced-price school meals during school vacations. Schools and other community centers in areas where half or more of the households have incomes at or below 185% of the poverty level may operate as "open sites," where all neighborhood children receive free meals; other communities may operate as "enrolled sites," where only those children eligible for free or reduced-price school meals can receive a free meal. Most sites provide either one or two meals daily. Over 2.3 million children a day participated during the summer of 1997.

The *Child and Adult Care Food Program* provides meals and snacks in child and adult day-care facilities, including licensed nonprofit child care centers and family day-care homes, Head Start programs, after-school programs, group homes, and some adult day-care centers. Participants may qualify for free or reduced-price meals according to the same income guidelines used by the school meals programs; 82% of all meals are served free. The *Homeless Children Nutrition Program* provides free meals at 104 emergency shelters. The *Special Milk Program* provides milk to children in school programs and child care institutions who do not have access to other federally funded child food programs. Children can qualify for free milk under the school meals income criteria, and milk can be purchased for those children not qualifying.

OTHER SOURCES OF FOOD ASSISTANCE

Many children and adults, including many who participate in the federal food assistance programs described previously, must rely on other sources of food in an attempt to obtain an adequate diet. Community, religious, and charitable organizations in most U.S. cities operate food distribution services for the poor, either in the form of *food pantries,* which distribute packages of groceries, or *soup kitchens,* where meals are served on-site. One national survey found that 10% of the population used such emergency feeding programs.

There are two major sources for the food needed to operate these programs. The charitable organization Second Harvest collects surplus donations from the food industry and supplies a network of regional *food banks,* from which local agencies can obtain food to prepare and distribute at nominal cost. Over 1 billion pounds of food are supplied annually to nearly 50,000 feeding programs nationwide in this manner. In addition, the federal government, through the USDA, distributes food through its Commodities Assistance

Program (CAP); this includes The Emergency Food Assistance Program (TEFAP), which supplies commodities (both USDA and private-sector) and some administrative assistance to food banks and soup kitchens, and the Commodity Supplemental Food Program (CSFP), which provides commodities to low-income elderly persons and women, infants, and children not participating in WIC.

FURTHER READING

Avruch S and Cackley AP: Savings achieved by giving WIC benefits to women prenatally. Public Health Rep 110:27–34, 1995.

Burghardt JA and Devaney BL: The School Nutrition Dietary Assessment Study. Am J Clin Nutr 61(Suppl):173S–257S, 1995.

Kennedy E, Myers L, and Layden W: The 1995 dietary guidelines for Americans: An overview. J Am Dietetic Assoc 96:234–237, 1996. Also available on the web: www.usda.gov/agency/crpp/guide.htm.

Luepker RV, Perry CL, McKinlay SM, et al.: Outcomes of a field trial to improve children's dietary patterns and physical activity: The Child and Adolescent Trial for Cardiovascular Health (CATCH). JAMA 275:768–776, 1996.

Meyers AF, Sampson AE, Weitzman M, et al.: School Breakfast Program participation and school performance. Am J Dis Child 143:1234–1239, 1989.

Pollitt E: Does breakfast make a difference in school? J Am Diet Assoc 95:1134–1139, 1995.

Rush D, Alvir JM, Garbowski GC, et al.: The National WIC Evaluation: Evaluation of the Special Supplemental Food Program for Women, Infants, and Children. Am J Clin Nutr 48:389–519, 1988.

Wehler CA, Scott RI, Anderson JJ, et al.: Community Childhood Hunger Identification Project: A Survey of Childhood Hunger in the United States. Washington, DC, Food Research and Action Center, 1995.

Charles Poland III

Chapter 26

Oral Health in Children

The primary goal of pediatric dentistry is to establish preventive dental health habits that successfully guide the parent and child through childhood and into adulthood free of dental disease. This is an achievable goal since the most common diseases of the mouth, caries and periodontal disease, are entirely preventable. The strategies of prevention, early intervention, and anticipatory guidance used by the pediatrician and other primary care clinicians are the same used by the pediatric dentist to achieve similar successful preventive health outcomes.

Pediatricians play a significant role in initiating and determining the outcomes of preventive dentistry that lead to optimal oral health for the child.

The faith and trust parents have in their primary care clinician's advice provides a unique opportunity to break the cycle of oral disease that continues to be rampant in many young children. Educating parents about proper care of the infant's mouth and newly erupting teeth, good nutrition habits, and initiating appropriate systemic fluoride therapy emphasizes the importance of oral health and establishes the concepts of preventive dentistry within the family. To ensure that optimal oral health for the child continues, the pediatrician should help establish a dental "home" that will initiate an individualized preventive dental health program for the child and family, provide the parent with information about growth and development of the changing dentition and oral-facial complex, and provide for prevention and treatment of dental-facial trauma. Since dental disease continues to be frequent in many segments of our child population, the pediatrician needs to identify children in need of treatment and help families find dental care within their community. Restorative dentistry for young children can be expensive and difficult, often requiring sedation or outpatient general anesthesia. By understanding accepted dental treatment modalities and the behavioral challenges some children present, the pediatrician can help support and educate the family about treatment decisions.

Traditionally, the pediatrician has assumed the responsibility of oral health for children up to age 3 years unless a cavity was detected at an earlier age. Recent modifications to this tradition by the dental profession and others have confused many health professionals, health care administrators, and parents as to what is the appropriate age for the first dental visit. The basis for this modification is that it is not appropriate to have a child begin professional dental care after the caries process has been initiated. In addition, referring children for dental intervention at age 3 or older has not been successful in reducing the incidence or severity of dental decay in children.

The incidence of caries in young children has been well documented for many years. In 1981, Weddell surveyed children in 10 pediatric offices and found dental caries in 4.2% of 12- to 17-month-old children, 19.7% of 24- to 29-month-old children, and 36.4% of 30- to 36-month-old children living in a fluoridated community. Other studies have found up to a twofold increase in those figures in children living in nonfluoridated communities. Unfortunately, many health professionals have been misled into believing that dental caries is no longer a major health issue for children. Not surprisingly, the basis for much of this misunderstanding comes from highly publicized but incomplete conclusions of survey studies. For example, in 1994, the national press published summaries of a survey conducted by the National Institute of Dental Research in 1986–1987 and concluded that "50% of U.S. school children have never had a cavity." This "myth" as identified by Edelstein and Douglass (1995) failed to report dental disease in the primary dentition and averaged 5- and 6-year-old children with few permanent teeth into their permanent tooth data to arrive at their conclusions. In fact, the study showed that 50% of schoolchildren already had dental decay by 7 years of age. By the time children reached the age of 17 years, 84% had, on average, eight carious or filled tooth surfaces. Recent studies of the general childhood population continue to find the caries prevalence as high as 36% among children less than 3 years of age and up to 90% among children in some Head Start populations. Other studies confirm that children with restored dental decay remain at a higher risk to develop more cavities at a later age. The Centers for Disease Control and Prevention now define dental caries as the most common infectious disease in the U.S. population. Furthermore, a terminology change from baby bottle tooth decay to early childhood caries (ECC) to identify a specific dental disease found in young children is now suggested. Clearly, a different strategy to prevent the caries process in young children and the resultant destruction of teeth that establishes a pattern of decay throughout childhood must be implemented. The recommendation to start routine preventive dentistry at 12 months instead of 3 years of age is based on the present understanding of the caries process and current models of prevention, not on whether all deciduous teeth have erupted or the infant's possible crying.

It is no longer proper to delay the timing of the first dental visit after the caries process has begun or a cavity is detected. Rather, a risk-based assessment of the child's liability to the caries process should be completed before cariogenic bacterial colonization has begun, and this assessment is a prerequisite to initiate appropriate prevention or treatment options.

THE CARIES PROCESS

Dental "cavities" are the end result of the caries process that begins shortly after the eruption of the first tooth (6 to 9 months) and, if not adequately addressed, continues throughout the life of the child. The caries process is an infectious, chronic, multifactoral, bacterial disease initiated by the introduction of *Streptococcus mutans* (SM) and maintained by these and other related bacteria. Acquisition of SM is a necessary pathogenic event but not sufficient in itself to promote the caries process. The course of the disease is further modified by the virulence of the infecting organism, resistance of tooth structure to demineralization, the capacity of the host enamel to remineralize, and dietary and oral hygiene habits. Genetic and developmental factors play a much more limited role in the progression of the caries process.

The Bacterial Component

The infectious and transmissible nature of dental caries was described as early as 1960. Recent studies have identified a discrete "window of infectivity" that occurs between 19 and 33 months (26 months average) when the introduction of SM and related cariogenic organisms is most likely to occur. Other investigators have identified this "window" as early as 9 months of age (with *Streptococcus sanguis*), and the presence of caries in children 12 to 14 months of age confirms the existence of this early "window." The major source of these bacteria is a vertical transmission from the mother or close caregiver to the child. The fidelity (acquisition of specific strains of SM) of the transmission of the mother's SM bacteria to the child is known to be as high as 88% with race, gender, ethnic populations, and virulence of the organism being variables. Salivary SM colony counts in young children correlate with their mother's SM colony counts, and a young child's caries experience tends to correlate with that of the mother. The child's risk to acquire SM is determined by those factors that influence the maternal reservoir of SM. The mother's history of caries, her presence of active caries, defective dental restorations, poorly coalesced biting surface pits and fissures of molar and bicuspid teeth, and SM activity during the child's 6- to 33-month age period are the most critical factors. For optimal infant oral health, the introduction and colonization of the enamel with SM during this "window of infectivity" must be prevented until the other normal flora of the mouth can be established. Other "windows of infectivity" or opportunities to acquire the infecting bacteria in the mixed dentition or permanent dentition have not been identified, but most likely exist. For young preschool children, "Cavities are catching." All children are likely to harbor some SM as part of their oral flora, particularly as they get older. The caries process is then more likely to be modified by the influences of diet, fluoride exposure, and bacterial plaque control initiating the takeover of cariogenic bacteria from the normal oral flora rather than the colonization of one predominant organism from a caregiver.

Obtaining a preventive dental history identifies mothers with high SM counts. Counseling them on the risk they pose for their infants, and guiding them to appropriate dental care should start at the prenatal visits.

The Demineralization-Remineralization Phase

Mutans streptococci can be introduced and will begin to colonize the infant's mouth when the first tooth erupts. Once SM colonization of an infant's mouth has occurred, the caries process proceeds as a dynamic equilibrium process of demineralization and remineralization of enamel. Dental enamel is not an inert nonporous substance but rather a permeable structure composed of an inorganic hydroxyapatite crystal and an organic matrix that permits the exchange of the basic composition of the hydroxyapatite crystal with salivary calcium, phosphates, fluorides, and other dietary minerals. When the pH or ion concentration in the oral environment is altered, further demineralization or remineralization occurs. Fluorides particularly hasten the remineralization process, reduce the solubility of the enamel crystal, enhance the nucleation of calcium phosphate in the enamel crystal, and accelerate the maturation of the enamel surface. Newly erupted teeth, particularly deciduous teeth, are highly susceptible to caries. When fluorides are applied during the immediate posteruptive period, fluoride penetration into the enamel is increased by five times and significantly reduces enamel solubility and demineralization compared with enamel that matures without fluoride expo-

sure. Parents should be instructed to use small amounts of a fluoridated toothpaste on children as soon as teeth appear in the mouth to reduce the enamel solubility and promote the remineralization process. Many health professionals have mistakenly advised parents not to use fluoride toothpaste on young children for fear of enamel fluorosis. Small amounts of a fluoride toothpaste (¼ to ½ pea size) brushed on the child's newly erupted teeth and then wiped out with a cloth afford these susceptible young teeth the opportunity to resist demineralization and enhance remineralization.

The acid attack produced by the cariogenic bacteria and carbohydrate substrate do not produce a cavitation directly, but rather initiate this cycle of demineralization-remineralization of intact subsurface enamel. Advanced subsurface lesions, which may appear as a white chalky lesion, are commonly found along the gingival margin of deciduous anterior teeth and are reversible. Early subsurface lesions are not visible but are present at all times on the majority of tooth surfaces. In dynamic equilibrium, the caries process continues without destruction of enamel, but when the process reaches disequilibrium, cavitation of enamel occurs.

Nutritional Influences

As carbohydrate substrate is introduced into the mouth, bacterial plaque pH will fall within 2 to 3 minutes and initiate the demineralization process. Over the next 30 to 40 minutes, the saliva neutralizes and buffers the plaque pH and supports the remineralization phase. Parents need to be taught that a child's eating habits have a more significant influence on the caries process than restricting any one food or snack. The uncontrolled frequency of sugars and cooked starch ingestion maintains low plaque pH over a sustained time interval and promotes the demineralization process. Children who are "nibblers and sippers" are at the highest risk for caries versus those who are "whoofers and gobblers." **The most influential nutritional modifiers of the caries process in young children are the milk bottle in bed or used as a pacifier, or the uncontrolled use of the "traveling" sippy cup containing milk or fruit juice.** Parents who practice these inappropriate feeding and behavior practices may have children at high risk for ECC and should be counseled and referred to a pediatric dentist.

Historically, the bottle or nursing habits have been the focus of caries control in young children and remain major factors. However, recognizing that the **bacterial component transmitted from a caregiver is the basic etiology of the caries**

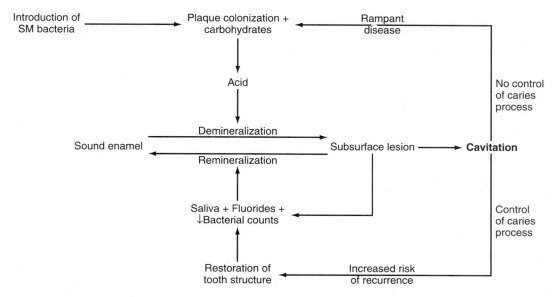

Figure 26–1. The dynamic process of caries formation and control. SM, *Streptococcus mutans.*

process in young children and is only modified by dietary habits (i.e., the bottle) is key to an accurate risk assessment to prevent caries in preschool children. This fact was well documented in a 1993 early caries study in Head Start children that found 86% of children with caries were reported to have taken the bottle to bed, but 69% of children with no caries also reported similar use of the bottle in bed. Understanding the timing of infectivity and the mechanism of demineralization-remineralization clarifies the rationale to initiate early preventive dental strategies and repair subsurface lesions before cavitation occurs. Figure 26–1 illustrates the dynamic nature of the caries process and control strategies.

THE FIRST DENTAL VISIT

The first professional dental visit is an opportunity for the pediatric dentist to establish a relationship with a family that will focus on wellness rather than disease. Parents need to view their child's dentist as a health supervisor instead of a "drill and fill" specialist. The goals of the first visit are to

1. Assess the risk for dental disease
2. Initiate a preventive dental program
3. Provide anticipatory guidance
4. Decide on the regularity of re-evaluation

Assessing the risk for dental disease includes a history of the parent's dental health, recent disease patterns, preventive dental habits, dietary and nutrition habits, and may include a dental examination of the parents, including salivary SM culturing. The clinical examination of the child identifies any abnormalities and provides the opportunity to evaluate the child's oral hygiene and demonstrate oral hygiene techniques to the parents. Salivary SM cultures of the child may also be done as part of the risk assessment. Anticipatory guidance provides information about developmental events about to happen and keeps the parents aware of changes in the child's oral health needs including advice on management of non-nutritive sucking habits. Regular re-evaluations and preventive visits are based on the risk assessment, preventive or treatment needs such as pit and fissure sealants, and expected developmental changes. This initial visit also allows the parent and child to view the dental facility, meet the dentist and staff, establish a protocol for emergency trauma, and become comfortable in the dental environment. Providing parents with behavior modification tips to make dental appointments a positive experience for the child are of the highest priority in pediatric dentistry and should be done early in a child's dental experience.

PREVENTIVE DENTISTRY IN THE PEDIATRIC OFFICE

INFANTS (6 to 12 Months of Age). **The most important strategy for the prevention of early childhood caries (ECC) is to prevent the colonization of SM into the child's mouth dur-**

ing the early years of tooth eruption. SM counts in mothers or close caregivers can be depressed temporarily or eliminated through professional dental care and the use of a chlorhexidine gluconate (0.12%) mouth rinse. Parents with high SM counts including those who do not follow a program of professionally supervised dental health should be given an explanation of the risks they pose for their child and referred for dental care.

Before teeth erupt, the parent should be instructed to clean the child's mouth once daily with a cloth or gauze. Toothbrushing with a small amount of fluoridated toothpaste (an amount less than the size of a pea for children under 18 months) should start with the eruption of the first tooth and be thoroughly done once a day. Several different novelty tools are available to clean a child's teeth, but the early introduction of a soft-bristled toothbrush helps the child develop the habit and accept the procedure later without resistance. Toothbrushes with large handles and wide bristle heads are easier for parents to use in removing the dental plaque from the gum line. Toothbrushing is easily accomplished in the bassinet or bed. Parents need a hands-on demonstration to learn how to brush an infant's teeth, not just a reminder that toothbrushing should be done.

Fluorides are one of the most effective preventive adjuncts to control the caries process. Systemic fluoride supplementation is indicated for children 6 months to 16 years of age living in areas with less than optimally fluoridated water and breast-fed infants over 6 months of age who do not receive significant amounts of fluoridated water (Table 26–1). Children exposed to multiple water sources including bottled or osmotically purified water make prescribing difficult. The pediatrician should attempt to identify the primary source of the child's water intake and prescribe on that basis. Supplemental fluorides should never be prescribed without testing the fluoride content of

TABLE 26–2. Risk Factors for Early Childhood Caries

Active caries in the mother or close caregiver	History of poor family oral health
High SM counts in mother	Previous ECC
High SM counts in child	Inadequate systemic fluoride
Visible decalcified lesions	High sugar intake
Inappropriate bottle use	Poor oral hygiene
Frequent snacks	Oral dysfunction
Physical handicaps	Children on free or reduced-price lunch programs
Poverty	
Frequent use of medicines containing sugars	Children with special health care needs

ECC, early childhood caries; SM, *Streptococcus mutans*.

the child's primary water supply unless identifying a primary water source is not possible. If this situation occurs, a risk-based assessment using the parent's dental health history is helpful and an early referral to establish the dental "home" may be appropriate. Children are now exposed to higher ambient levels of fluoride, especially through reconstituted fruit juices, sodas, and toothpaste. All of these sources contribute to increases in the incidence of mild dental fluorosis. Care should be taken not to overprescribe systemic fluorides. Many health professionals misunderstand the benefits of fluorides and believe that one type of fluoride adequately substitutes for any and all others. Use of multiple fluoride vehicles provides the patient an additive rather than a single benefit. Systemic fluoridation properly administered provides up to a 50% reduction in caries, while the topically applied fluorides (toothpaste, rinses, and professionally applied gels or varnishes) can add an additional 30% to 45% reduction in decay of the remaining portion.

CHILDREN (12 to 18 Months of Age). Establishing a dental "home" for a child before the "window of infectivity" opens ensures continuation of good oral health practices promoted by the pediatrician. Children with high caries risks should be referred to a pediatric dentist before their first birthday (Table 26–2). **All children should receive their first dental prophylaxis and topical fluoride treatment before 18 months of age.** Once the dental "home" is established, the pediatrician should periodically confirm that the child is receiving timely dental care. Table 26–3 summarizes the preventive dental health periodicity schedule that should be provided within the dental "home."

CHILDREN (18 Months to 18 Years of Age). During health supervision visits, the clinician should be alert to identify any signs of poor oral hygiene, abnormal growth and development of the teeth or occlusion, or signs of nonvital teeth.

TABLE 26–1. Systemic Fluoride Supplementation

Age	Fluoride Ion Level in Drinking Water, ppm*		
	<0.3	0.3–0.6	>0.6
Birth–6 mo	None	None	None
6 mo–3 yr	0.25 mg/day	None	None
3–6 yr	0.5 mg/day	0.25 mg/day	None
6–16 yr	1.0 mg/day	0.50 mg/day	None

*1.0 ppm = 1 mg/L; 2.2 mg sodium fluoride contains 1 mg fluoride ion.

Data from J Am Dent Assoc 126:195, 1995; and American Academy of Pediatrics: Flouride supplementation for children: Interim policy recommendations. Pediatrics 95:777, 1995.

TABLE 26–3. Periodicity of Examination, Preventive Dental Services and Oral Treatment for Children

Recommendations for Preventive Pediatric Dental Care*

Because each child is unique these Recommendations are designed for the care of children who have no important health problems and are developing normally. These Recommendations will need to be modified for children with special health care needs or if disease or trauma manifests variations from normal. The Academy emphasizes the importance of **very** early professional intervention and the continuity of care based on the individualized needs of the child.

Age[1]	Infancy 6–12 Months	Late Infancy 12–24 Months	Preschool 2–6 Years	School–Aged 6–12 Years	Adolescence 12–18 years
Oral Hygiene[2] Counseling	Parents/ Guardians/ Caregivers	Parents/ Guardians/ Caregivers	Child/Parent/ Caregivers	Child/Parent/ Caregivers	Patient
Injury Prevention Counseling[3]	•	•	•	•	•
Dietary Counseling[4]	•	•	•	•	•
Counseling for[5] Non-nutritive Habits	•	•	•	•	•
Fluoride Supplementation[6,7]	•	•	•	•	•
Assess Oral Growth[8] & Development	•	•	•	•	•
Clinical Oral Exam	•	•	•	•	•
Prophylaxis and Topical[9] Fluoride Treatment		•	•	•	•
Radiographic Assessment[10]			•	•	•
Pit & Fissure Sealants			If indicated on primary molars	1st permanent molars as soon as possible after eruption	2nd permanent molars and appropriate premolars as soon as possible after eruption
Treatment of Dental Disease/ Injury	•	•	•	•	•
Assessment and Treatment of Developing Malocclusion			•	•	•
Substance Abuse Counseling				•	•
Assessment and Removal of 3rd Molars					•
Referral for Regular and Periodic Dental Care					•
Anticipatory Guidance[11]	•	•	•	•	•

*American Academy of Pediatric Dentistry: Periodicity of examination, preventive dental services, and oral treatment for children. Pediatr Dent 18:28, 1996.

[1] First exam at the eruption of the 1st tooth and no later than 12 months.

[2] Initially, responsibility of parent; as child develops jointly with parents; then when indicated only child.

[3] Initially play objects, pacifiers, car seats; then when learning to walk; and finally sports and routine playing.

[4] At every appointment discuss the role of refined carbohydrates; frequency of snacking.

[5] At first discuss the need for additional sucking; digits vs. pacifiers; then the need to wean from the habit before the eruption of the first permanent front teeth. For school-aged children and adolescent patients, counsel regarding any existing habits such as fingernail biting, clenching, or bruxism.

[6] As per AAP/ADA Guidelines and the water source.

[7] Up to at least 16 years.

[8] By clinical examination.

[9] Especially for children at high risk for caries and periodontal disease.

[10] As per AAPD Radiographic Guidelines.

[11] Appropriate discussion and counseling, should be an integral part of each visit for care.

ORAL HYGIENE

Young children rarely develop advanced periodontal disease but a persistent gingivitis is a sign of poor oral hygiene and bacterial plaque control that will lead to caries activity. However, older teenagers with poor oral hygiene do show early signs of periodontal disease that becomes more difficult to control with increasing age, and they should be referred for dental care.

Oral hygiene for the preschool child needs to be performed at least once a day by a parent or caregiver. The family habit of sending children to brush after meals or before bedtime unsupervised will not be successful. Parents need to understand that the objective of toothbrushing is to remove the bacterial plaque from the gum line and in between the teeth, not just to remove food. Preschool and school-age children who have not developed fine motor coordination adequate to write their name in cursive require daily help from a parent. In addition, these children should be provided a toothbrush with a large handle and wide bristle head and asked to brush their own teeth twice each day to practice their skills and develop personal hygiene habits. Children should be encouraged to use the gross motor (back and forth) scrub brush technique until fine motor skills have matured (12 to 14 years of age). Dental flossing is a very difficult skill to master and should be provided by the parent at least three to four times per week in children over 3 years of age to remove the bacterial plaque that accumulates between the teeth where the toothbrush is ineffective.

In the presence of dental plaque–induced gingival inflammation, Dilantin and related drugs are known to produce gingival hyperplasia. Children receiving anticonvulsant drugs that can potentiate gingival hyperplasia should receive a dental prophylaxis the week anticonvulsant therapy is initiated and intense daily oral hygiene from a parent or caregiver thereafter to prevent the occurrence of gingival hyperplasia.

OCCLUSION DEVELOPMENT

The timing of the appearance of deciduous teeth in an infant's mouth is most variable. Slow or delayed eruption is common even in healthy children and should not be of concern until the child is 18 months or older. Any asymmetry in the normal eruption sequence, however, should be evaluated by a pediatric dentist if the condition persists for more than 3 months. Severely mobile neonatal teeth should be removed if there is a danger of aspiration, but they can be maintained and do not interfere with breastfeeding if the teeth are firmly attached to the alveolus.

Thumb sucking or pacifiers (non-nutritive sucking) and over-retained deciduous teeth are common problems that should not be allowed to complicate or interfere with the normal growth and development of the occlusion. Non-nutritive sucking is a normal activity in most children under the age of 2 years. Attempts to control these habits before the age of 24 to 30 months usually prove difficult and unnecessary; however, if continued they can alter the position of the teeth as well as interfere with growth and function of the mandible, depending on the frequency, duration, and intensity of the habit. The most commonly observed changes are

Flaring of the maxillary incisors (bucked teeth)
Development of an anterior open bite
Development of a posterior crossbite with a functional shift of the mandible

Flaring of the maxillary deciduous incisors and persistence of a small open bite have no abnormal effect on the position of the permanent incisors if the habit is stopped before the appearance of the erupting permanent incisors. Severe flaring of the deciduous maxillary incisors or large anterior open bite, particularly when combined with a retrognathic mandible, can interfere with speech development and mastication and should receive attention. The presence of a posterior crossbite (maxillary canines or molars inside the mandibular teeth) signals a potentially serious developmental disturbance when accompanied by a shift of the mandible laterally when the child bites the teeth together. These functional shifts of the mandible should be treated as early as possible (between 3 and 4 years of age) to prevent asymmetric growth of the temporomandibular joint and excessive unilateral growth of the mandible causing a lower facial asymmetry.

Thumb sucking habits that continue past 3 years of age and do not alter normal growth and development of the dental structures should not alarm the pediatrician or parents. Consulting with the child's established dental "home" should identify harmful digit habits that require treatment.

Over-retained deciduous teeth can be a common problem for children between 6 and 12 years of age. Deciduous teeth that have had an underlying permanent tooth visible for more than 3 weeks should be extracted to prevent the underlying permanent tooth from erupting into a position that would require later orthodontic treatment.

FRENUMS AND TONGUE-TIE

Frenums are bands of fibrous connective tissue running from the free mucosa of the inner surface of the lips or ventral surface of the tongue and attaching into the alveolar gingival mucosa. In the past, many physicians and dentists have aggressively clipped frenums (frenectomy) believing that they interfered with speech or alignment of teeth. Most clinicians now recommend a more conservative approach and agree that the vertical growth of the dental alveolar ridges that occurs with tooth eruption and facial growth will minimize the size and prominence of most frenums. Space between deciduous or permanent teeth (diastema) is normal before the eruption of the permanent maxillary canine teeth and should not be used as a criterion for a labial frenectomy. A broad heavy fanlike maxillary frenum that attaches into the palatine papilla and produces blanching of the papilla or a frenum that inserts into the gingival margin and produces gingival recession should be carefully evaluated for surgery by a pediatric dentist. If a child is able to advance the tip of the tongue over the mandibular incisors and touch the lower lip, there is adequate movement of the tongue for speech and mastication and a lingual frenectomy is not necessary.

AIRWAY ISSUES

Pediatricians are often placed in the position to approve or recommend a child for tonsil or adenoid removal based on the recommendation from a dentist that an obstructed airway is adversely affecting facial growth or an orthodontic outcome. Although a few dentists endorse these theories, there is little science to support or justify a surgical procedure based on these reasons alone. When pressed to agree to a surgical procedure based on dental outcomes, the pediatrician should request a consultation with the referring dentist, include the otolaryngologist, review the pertinent examination findings with them, critique any supporting science that is presented, and come to a consensus about the risk/benefit of the procedure.

NONVITAL TEETH

Young children frequently bump or injure their incisor teeth without the parents' knowledge. Some of these teeth will absorb enough energy to damage the pulp tissue causing the pulp to undergo liquefaction necrosis and loss of vitality. The clinical sign of this process is a dark tooth. Nonvital deciduous teeth have the potential to develop peripheral root resorption, chronic apical granulomas, and infection that can damage the underlying developing permanent tooth bud or spread to other tissues. Referral to a pediatric dentist should be done promptly.

MANAGEMENT OF DENTAL TRAUMA IN THE PEDIATRIC OFFICE

A traumatic injury to a child's mouth or teeth is unfortunately a common occurrence in young children and becomes a growing concern to parents as children become more active in sports or more independent in their play activities. **During health supervision visits or sports physical examinations, pediatricians should remember to recommend mouth guards for football, hockey, baseball, basketball, and soccer.** Custom-fitted mouth guards afford the best protection and allow for better comfort, retention, speech, breathing, and compliance.

Establishing a dental "home" for a child provides an action plan for emergency trauma that should be part of the 12-month health supervision visit. Frequently, however, in the parent's panic to find care for their child, pediatricians are called on to treat the child or give advice for a course of action. For most types of dental injuries in children, early diagnosis and treatment are key in retaining teeth, minimizing pain, and preventing infections. Pediatricians can play an important role by identifying those injuries that require immediate treatment to prevent the aesthetic disfigurement of tooth loss and minimize the cost of care and replacement of missing or broken teeth. Providing advice over the telephone without the benefit of a careful examination should be avoided unless an immediate dental referral is made.

When presented with a dental emergency, the pediatrician should review the child's medical history ensuring that the child has no special health care needs that would alter routine dental care. In addition, recording when, where, and how the injury took place will aid in identifying suspicions of child abuse.

Examining a child's mouth following a traumatic dental injury can be a challenging task but must be thorough to identify those conditions that require hemorrhage control, suturing, dental stabilization, and treatment to maintain a vital dental pulp.

Examining the lips, frenums, tongue, soft palate, and gingival and other mucosal surfaces will reveal any source of hemorrhage that should be controlled with pressure. Any lacerations or punctures should be cleaned, inspected for foreign bodies, and evaluated for suture closure if larger than 2 to 3 mm in length. Torn or lacerated gingiva that exposes alveolar bone should be sutured back in place. The need for a tetanus toxoid booster should be considered.

Observing the child for facial symmetry, bruising, and a full range of motion of the mandible aids in identifying fractures of the jaws. The teeth should be examined for mobility in both a labial and lingual/palatal direction identifying any tooth abnormally displaced from not only adjacent teeth, but also opposing teeth during function. Any fractured teeth should be identified, with the extent and position of the dental fractures and the presence or absence of dental pulp exposures noted.

When a missing tooth or tooth fragments cannot be found and identified, lateral soft tissue neck and thoracoabdominal radiographs for foreign bodies must be taken to ensure that no tooth fragments are lodged in the airway.

Since all types of dental trauma require follow-up care to ensure there are no long-term detrimental effects of pulp necrosis, subsequent infection, and peripheral root resorption, the pediatrician should not hesitate to involve a pediatric dental colleague at the earliest convenient time.

Traumatic dental injuries that require immediate attention and referral include

1. *Fractured jaw.* If a fractured jaw is suspected, the child should be sent immediately to the nearest hospital emergency facility.

2. *Dental alveolar bone fracture.* Fractures of isolated segments of alveolar bone alone are rare and identified by mobility of segments of teeth and bone rather than individual teeth within their sockets. Intra-arch dental stabilization is required.

3. *Dental crown fractures.* Vertical crown fractures that involve portions of the tooth beneath the gingiva are commonly associated with pulp exposures. Deciduous teeth with vertical fractures usually require extraction to prevent infection. Permanent teeth with vertical fractures require immediate endodontic attention to prevent pulp and apical abscess formation.

Horizontal crown fractures that involve extensive dentin or pulp exposure require immediate coverage to prevent the entry of microorganisms into the pulp tissues. The greater the length of time the dental pulp is exposed to the oral flora in the dental plaque and saliva, the less chance to maintain normal pulp vitality or achieve successful endodontic therapy.

4. *Root fractures.* Dental root fractures are identified only by radiographic examination of the dental tissues. However, any tooth that has been displaced from its socket or can be moved more than 2 mm in its socket should be suspected of having a root fracture. Immediate dental stabilization provides the only hope of maintaining these teeth.

5. *Intruded teeth.* Traumatic injuries that intrude or jam a deciduous incisor up into the alveolar bone are common occurrences in children under 3 years of age and may be so severe that the tooth is entirely dislodged into the alveolar process so as to appear to be missing.

Immediate attention is required for both intruded permanent and deciduous teeth to identify any alveolar bone or dental root fracture, confirm the position of the intruded tooth, and manage potential infections of the gingival tissues. Most deciduous teeth re-erupt and can be maintained in the child's dentition. Permanent tooth intrusions require orthodontic repositioning and endodontic treatment.

6. *Partial avulsions (extrusions).* Deciduous teeth that are so severely displaced that the tooth will not remain stable in its socket after repositioning or are in danger of being aspirated during sleep should be extracted immediately. Attempts to stabilize severely mobile deciduous teeth with intra-arch bonded splints to adjacent deciduous teeth carry a poor prognosis of pulp and root vitality and are not warranted.

Permanent teeth loosened from their bony socket more than 2 mm require immediate attention to rule out root fractures and should be stabilized to other teeth if their position in their socket cannot be maintained after manual repositioning. Immediate repositioning and stabilization allow for the reattachment process to begin without further damage to the alveolar bone and periodontal ligament and provide the best prognosis for retention of the tooth.

7. *Complete avulsions.* Deciduous teeth completely avulsed from their socket are usually not reimplanted. Although some dentists try to preserve the tooth in the child's mouth, the high frequency of root resorption, infection, and potential damage to the developing permanent tooth bud rarely justify putting the child through the procedure.

Reimplanting intact permanent teeth should always be attempted as long as the patient's medical history excludes diseases that compromise the immune system or increase the patient's susceptibility to systemic infection. To achieve long-term success, the tooth must be cleaned by careful patting of the root surface with a moist gauze, but not scraped. This preserves the periodontal ligament cell integrity and reimplantation back into the socket should be done as soon as possible. A direct relationship exists between the length of time the tooth is out of its socket and the failure of the tooth to reattach to alveolar bone without peripheral root resorption. Ideally the parent or pediatrician should clean and insert the tooth back into its socket and have the child or parent hold the tooth in place while on their way to a dental facility. When that cannot be accomplished, placing the tooth in cold normal saline or milk will preserve the intact periodontal cells for a short time. Bleeding from the dental socket is easily controlled with a pressure gauze.

8. *Toothaches accompanied by swelling.* A dental abscess in children that extends beyond the confinements of the tooth and alveolar bone into adjacent soft tissues of the face, floor of the

mouth, or neck can become life threatening if not resolved early and aggressively. Appropriate antibiotic and analgesic therapy should be started immediately, the source of the infection identified, and follow-up care closely monitored.

Traumatic dental injuries that require attention within 24 to 48 hours include

1. *Toothache not accompanied by swelling.* Most children do not complain of dental pain unless infection from the dental structures is spreading through alveolar bone to basal bone and adjacent soft tissues. To prevent a more serious infection, the pediatrician should prescribe analgesics and antibiotics in consultation with a pediatric dentist and insist the parents follow through with a dental appointment promptly.

2. *Simple fractures of crowns.* Most traumatic injuries to teeth involve only small fractures of enamel and dentin and do not endanger the pulp and underlying alveolar bone. These teeth may be sensitive to hot and cold stimuli and should be restored as soon as is convenient to comfort the child and return the tooth to function. Long-term follow-up care is necessary because any tooth that has received a traumatic blow is susceptible to pulp necrosis, alveolar abscess, and peripheral root resorption.

3. *Broken braces, wires, and dental appliances.* These are commonly seen as a result of the child's biting on an object such as a pencil or eating foods that are too coarse or sticky. It is very easy to overlook the fact that the loosened dental appliance is a result of trauma. A careful history and examination will guide the pediatrician to determine if immediate dental referral is neces-

sary. The pediatrician should feel free to remove any appliance that is causing pain or infection if an immediate dental referral is not accomplished.

4. *Minor bumps.* Minor trauma that causes loosening of deciduous and permanent teeth is common. When the mobility of the tooth is less than 2 mm and the tooth is positioned and stable in the socket, there is no need for an immediate referral but the child will need follow-up care to identify possible subsequent pulp necrosis and peripheral root resorption. The pediatrician should insist the child be seen by a pediatric dentist within a short period of time to establish the proper follow-up interval.

FURTHER READING

Caufield PW, Cutter GR, Dasanayake AP. Initial acquisition of mutans streptococci by infants: Evidence for a discrete window of infectivity. J Dent Res 72:37–45, 1993.

Edelstein BL: Case planning and management according to caries risk assessment. Dent Clin North Am 39:721–723, 1995.

Edelstein BL, Douglass CW: Dispelling the myth that 50% of U.S. schoolchildren have never had a cavity. Public Health Rep 110:522–530, 1995.

Green M (ed): Bright Futures: Guidelines for Health Supervision of Infants, Children, and Adolescents. Arlington, VA, National Center for Education in Maternal and Child Health, 1994.

Harris NO, Christen A (ed): Primary Preventive Dentistry, 4th ed. Norwalk, CT, Paramount Publishing, 1995.

McDonald RE, Avery AD: Dentistry for Child and Adolescent, 6th ed. St. Louis, Mosby–Yearbook, 1994.

Nowak AJ: Rationale for the first oral evaluation. Pediatr Dent 19:8–11, 1997.

Tinanoff N, O'Sullivan DM: Early childhood caries: Overview and recent findings. Pediatr Dent 19:12–16, 1997.

Weddell JA, Klein AI: Socioeconomic correlation of oral disease in six- to thirty-six-month-old children. Pediatr Dent 3:306–310, 1981.

Peter G. Szilagyi

Chapter 27

Childhood Immunizations

Childhood immunizations are one of the most cost-effective interventions in health care. The delivery of childhood immunizations has dramatically reduced the number of vaccine-preventable diseases in the United States by more than 98% (Table 27–1).

In addition to being correlated with incidence of vaccine-preventable diseases, childhood immu-

nization levels are often used as an index of the quality of health care of a population, a nation, an insurance plan, or a primary care practice. Since the implementation of school requirements in the United States, school-age immunization levels have been higher than 98%. The country also has reached a record high preschool immunization coverage level, with 78% coverage in 1997 for

TABLE 27–1. Number of Vaccine-Preventable Diseases: Maximum Cases per Year, and Cases in 1995

Disease	Maximum Cases per Year	Cases in 1995	Percent Change
Diphtheria	206,939	0	100%
Measles	894,134	309	99.97%
Mumps	152,209	906	99.40%
Paralytic polio	21,269	2	99.99%
Rubella	57,686	128	99.78%
Congenital rubella syndrome	20,000*	6	99.97%
Tetanus	1,560‡	41	97.37%
Pertussis	265,269	5,137	98.06%
Haemophilus influenzae invasive disease (<5 yr)	20,000*	290†	98.55%

*Estimated.
†Includes invasive disease due to non–type B *H. influenzae.*
‡Mortality.
Personal communication, National Immunization Program of the Centers for Disease Control and Prevention, (for data on maximum cases); and MMWR 45(34), 1996 (for data on cases in 1995).

four doses of diphtheria, tetanus toxoids, and pertussis (DTP) vaccine, three doses of poliovirus vaccine, and one dose of measles, mumps, and rubella (MMR) vaccine among children 19 to 35 months of age (according to the National Immunization Survey). Coverage levels for individual vaccines have risen to a high in 1997 of DTP_4, 81%; oral poliovirus vaccine (OPV_3), 91%; *Haemophilus influenzae* type b (Hib_{3+}), 92%; MMR_1, 90%; and hepatitis B_3, 83%.

Immunization levels are closely associated with other measures of preventive care. Studies have shown that children who are behind in immunizations are also likely to be behind in other preventive services. Thus, immunization levels are important both from the clinical and the policy perspectives. It is therefore important to examine factors affecting immunization delivery and current understanding of key aspects of immunization practice.

In spite of overall rising immunization rates in the United States, some major problems with respect to the delivery of childhood immunizations remain. First, immunization rates in preschool children, although rising, are still below the national goal of 90% coverage for all recommended immunizations. Immunization coverage has been lower for populations of children who are impoverished or uninsured, and rates in certain metropolitan areas are particularly low. Some patient risk factors for underimmunization include low educational level, large family size, low socioeconomic status, being a public clinic attendee, young

parental age, lack of prenatal care, and late start of the immunization series. Many of these risk factors coexist. Numerous studies have shown that most parents want their children to be fully immunized on time, but that there are barriers to accessing and receiving timely primary care and immunizations. One barrier is lack of knowledge about the immunization schedule; for example, most parents of underimmunized children do not realize that their children are behind in immunizations. Thus, it is critical for parents to understand the immunization schedule, and for them to know when to return for preventive visits or immunizations.

The majority of children in the United States receive immunizations in primary care offices, community health centers, or hospital outpatient clinics; however, a substantial proportion receive immunizations in public health clinics. Thus, primary care clinicians (both private and public) play a central role in immunizing children. Several provider factors often contribute to underimmunization (Table 27–2). First, some clinicians lack up-to-date knowledge about immunization schedules, contraindications, and how to respond to or tailor the schedule to specific clinical situations. This knowledge gap is compounded by the multiple changes in the recommended immunization schedule and the constantly evolving information about immunization delivery. Second, many clinicians overestimate their patients' immunization rates believing that most of their patients are up-to-date when, in fact, many remain underimmunized. Third, very few clinicians routinely assess immunization rates or barriers to immunization delivery within their own practice. Fourth, few providers can systematically identify underimmunized children. Fifth, **missed opportunities for vaccinations occur frequently in most health care settings.** Finally, cost to the clinician (purchasing and administering vaccines) and to the patient has, in the past, been a barrier to immunization delivery in many settings. Since the role of the primary care clinician is so crucial to immunization delivery, the next sections summarize some important information about childhood immunizations.

TABLE 27–2. Provider Factors Associated with Underimmunization

Insufficient knowledge about immunization practices
Overestimate of patients' immunization rates
Lack of regular assessment of practice's immunization rates
Inability to systematically identify underimmunized patients
Missed opportunities for vaccinations
Cost to provider and patients

INFORMATION ABOUT IMMUNIZATIONS

It is critical for primary care clinicians to have ready access to current information about immunizations. *The Report of the Committee on Infectious Diseases* of the American Academy of Pediatrics (AAP), commonly called the *Red Book,* is an indispensable reference, containing information about most issues and clinical situations pertaining to childhood immunizations. It is updated and published every 3 years. Other very useful references include updates published by and available from the AAP and the Advisory Committee on Immunization Practices (ACIP) of the Centers for Disease Control and Prevention (CDC); the 1997 *General Recommendations on Immunization* and *The Epidemiology and Prevention of Vaccine-Preventable Disease,* both published by the CDC; the *Standards for Pediatric Immunization Practices* published by the CDC; statements by the AAP published in *Pediatrics* and other journals; *AAP News* published monthly by the AAP; *Morbidity and Mortality Weekly Reports (MMWR)* published weekly; information distributed by state and local departments of health; official package inserts accompanying vaccines; and articles published in journal articles about new research in immunization delivery. An increasing amount of information is available on the Internet.

It is important also for clinicians to provide information to parents about childhood immunizations. The Vaccine Information Statement (VIS) forms, published by the CDC, provide useful information for parents including risks and benefits of individual vaccines. The CDC and state and local health departments also have pamphlets and informational packets to use for informing parents about immunizations.

TYPES OF VACCINES

There are two types of vaccines: live attenuated vaccines and inactivated vaccines. Live attenuated vaccines (e.g., MMR, OPV, varicella) produce an immune response similar to the natural infection by replicating within the vaccinated person. Inactivated vaccines include inactivated whole viruses (e.g., polio, influenza, hepatitis A), inactivated whole bacteria (e.g., pertussis), subunits (e.g., hepatitis B, acellular pertussis), toxoids (e.g., diphtheria, tetanus), pure polysaccharides (e.g., *H. influenzae* type b, pneumoccocal, meningococcal), and polysaccharide conjugates (*H. influenzae* type b). Inactivated vaccines generally require several doses to produce an adequate immune response,

and antibody titers usually fall over time. The type of vaccine affects the schedule, contraindications, and adverse events.

IMMUNIZATION SCHEDULES

Table 27–3 shows the Recommended Childhood Immunization Schedule for the United States, January to December 1998. This schedule represents a consensus by the ACIP, AAP, and American Academy of Family Physicians (AAFP), and is based on both the scientific knowledge about optimal immunologic response and understanding of the need to protect the child population from disease. The important changes since the 1997 immunization schedule include (1) revised recommendations for the polio vaccine, with a sequential schedule of IPV and then OPV being acceptable (and recommended by the CDC); (2) preference for acellular pertussis vaccine for both infants and toddlers; and (3) several new combined vaccines. The footnotes to Table 27–3 discuss recent developments and qualifications. It is important to check package inserts and the schedule's footnotes regarding the interchangeability of vaccines produced by different manufacturers. Since the Recommended Childhood Immunization Schedule will undoubtedly change over the years, all clinicians and office staff who immunize children should keep up with these changes and adopt the most current immunization schedule.

Table 27–4, from the 1997 Red Book, shows the recommended immunization schedule for children not immunized in the first year of life. Primary care clinicians may need to take into account individual circumstances and, at times, deviate from these schedules. In general, practitioners should attempt to vaccinate children as early as possible within the recommended ages and intervals between vaccinations.

USE OF VACCINES

Studies have shown that simultaneous immunization with any of the vaccines commonly administered in the United States produces adequate immunity. Thus, **there are no contraindications to simultaneous administration of vaccines (except for two unusual vaccines—cholera and yellow fever).** This has become increasingly important as recommendations for additional vaccines or new schedules (such as hepatitis B and the inactivated poliovirus vaccine [IPV]) require multiple injections. Studies have shown that most parents would prefer simultaneous injections to

TABLE 27–3. Recommended Childhood Immunization Schedule, U.S.: January–December 1998*

Vaccines are listed under the routinely recommended ages. Bars indicate range of acceptable ages for immunization. Catch-up immunization should be done during any visit when feasible. Ovals indicate vaccines to be assessed and given if necessary during the early adolescent visit.

Age ▶ Vaccine ▼	Birth	1 mo	2 mos	4 mos	6 mos	12 mos	15 mos	18 mos	4–6 yrs	11–12 yrs	14–16 yrs
Hepatitis B	Hep B-1		Hep B-2		Hep B-3					Hep B	
Diphtheria, Tetanus, Pertussis			DTaP or DTP	DTaP or DTP	DTaP or DTP		DTaP or DTP		DTaP or DTP	Td	
H. influenzae Type b			Hib	Hib	Hib	Hib					
Polio			Polio	Polio		Polio			Polio		
Measles, Mumps, Rubella						MMR			MMR	MMR	
Varicella						Var				Var	

*Approved by the Advisory Committee on Immunization Practices (ACIP), the American Academy of Pediatrics (AAP), and the American Academy of Family Physicians (AAFP).

Hepatitis B

- Infants born to mothers who are negative for hepatitis B surface antigen (HBsAg) should receive 2.5 μg of Merck vaccine (Recombivax HB) or 10 μg of SmithKline Beecham (SB) vaccine (Engerix-B). The second dose should be administered at least 1 month after the first dose. The third dose should be given at least 2 months after the second, but not before 6 months of age.
- Infants born to HBsAg-positive mothers should receive 0.5 mL of hepatitis B immune globulin (HBIG) within 12 hours of birth and either 5 μg of Merck vaccine (Recombivax HB) or 10 μg of SB vaccine (Engerix-B) at a separate site. The second dose is recommended at 1–2 months of age and the third dose at 6 months of age.
- Infants born to mothers whose HBsAg status is unknown should receive either 5 μg of Merck vaccine (Recombivax HB) or 10 μg of SB vaccine (Engerix-B) within 12 hours of birth. The second dose of vaccine is recommended at 1 month of age and the third dose at 6 months of age. Blood should be drawn at the time of delivery to determine the mother's HBsAg status; if it is positive, the infant should receive HBIG as soon as possible (no later than 1 week of age). The dosage and timing of subsequent vaccine doses should be based upon the mother's HGsAg status.
- Children and adolescents who have not been vaccinated against hepatitis B in infancy may begin the series during any visit. Those who have not previously received three doses of hepatitis B vaccine should initiate or complete the series during the 11- to 12-year-old visit, and unvaccinated older adolescents should be vaccinated whenever possible. The

second dose should be administered at least 1 month after the first dose, and the third dose should be administered at least 4 months after the first dose and at least 2 months after the second dose.

Diphtheria, Tetanus, Pertussis

- DTaP (diphtheria and tetanus toxoids and acellular pertussis vaccine) is the preferred vaccine for all doses in the vaccination series, including completion of the series in children who have received one or more doses of whole-cell DTP vaccine. Whole-cell DTP is an acceptable alternative to DTaP. The fourth dose (DTP or DTaP) may be administered as early as 12 months of age, provided 6 months have elapsed since the third dose and the child is unlikely to return at 15–18 months of age. Td (tetanus and diphtheria toxoids) is recommended at 11–12 years of age if at least 5 years have elapsed since the last dose of DTP, DTaP, or DT. Subsequent routine Td boosters are recommended every 10 years.

Haemophilus influenzae Type b

- Three H. influenzae type b (Hib) conjugate vaccines are licensed for infant use. If PRP-OMP (PedvaxHIB [Merck]) is administered at 2 and 4 months of age, a dose at 6 months is not required.

Polio

- Two poliovirus vaccines are currently licensed in the United States: inactivated poliovirus vaccine (IPV) and oral poliovirus vaccine (OPV). The following schedules are all acceptable to the ACIP, the AAP, and the AAFP. Parents and providers may choose among these options:

1. Two doses of IPV followed by two doses of OPV.
2. Four doses of IPV.
3. Four doses of OPV.

The ACIP recommends two doses of IPV at 2 and 4 months of age, followed by two doses of OPV at 12–18 months and 4–6 years of age. IPV is the only poliovirus vaccine recommended for immunocompromised persons and their household contacts.

Measles, Mumps, Rubella

- The second dose of MMR is recommended routinely at 4–6 years of age but may be administered during any visit, provided at least 1 month has elapsed since receipt of the first dose and both doses are administered at or after 12 months of age. Those who have not previously received the second dose should complete the schedule no later than the 11- to 12-year-old visit.

Varicella

- Susceptible children may receive varicella vaccine (Var) at any visit after the first birthday, and those who lack a reliable history of chickenpox should be immunized during the 11- to 12-year-old visit. Susceptible children 13 years of age or older should receive two doses, at least 1 month apart.

From Pediatric News, January 1998, p. 28. American Academy of Pediatrics.

TABLE 27–4. Recommended Immunization Schedules for Children Not Immunized in the First Year of Life*

Recommended Time/Age	Immunization(s)†‡§	Comments
Younger Than 7 Years		
First visit	DTaP (or DTP), Hib,‖ HBV, MMR, OPV¶	If indicated, tuberculin testing may be done at same visit. If child is 5 y of age or older, Hib is not indicated in most circumstances.
Interval after first visit		
1 mo (4 wk)	DTaP (or DTP), HBV, Var#	The second dose of OPV may be given if accelerated poliomyelitis vaccination is necessary, such as for travelers to areas where polio is endemic.
2 mo	DTaP (or DTP), Hib,‖ OPV¶	Second dose of Hib is indicated only if the first dose was received when younger than 15 mo.
≥8 mo	DTaP (or DTP), HBV, OPV¶	OPV and HBV are not given if the third doses were given earlier.
Age 4–6 yrs (at or before school entry)	DTaP (or DTP), OPV,¶ MMR**	DTaP (or DTP) is not necessary if the fourth dose was given after the fourth birthday; OPV is not necessary if the third dose was given after the fourth birthday.
Age 11–12 yrs	See Fig 1.1 in 1997 Red Book	
7–12 Years		
First visit	HBV, MMR, Td, OPV¶	
Interval after first visit		
2 mo (8 wk)	HBV, MMR,** Var,# Td, OPV¶	OPV also may be given 1 mo after the first visit if accelerated poliomyelitis vaccination is necessary.
8–14 mo	HBV,†† Td, OPV¶	OPV is not given if the third dose was given earlier.
Age 11–12 yrs	See Fig 1.1 in 1997 Red Book	

*Table is not completely consistent with all package inserts. For products used, also consult manufacturer's package insert for instructions on storage, handling, dosage, and administration. Biologics prepared by different manufacturers may vary, and package inserts of the same manufacturer may change from time to time. Therefore, the physician should be aware of the contents of the current package insert.

Vaccine abbreviations: HBV indicates hepatitis B virus vaccine; Var, varicella vaccine; DTP, diphtheria and tetanus toxoids and pertussis vaccine; DTaP, diphtheria and tetanus toxoids and acellular pertussis vaccine; Hib, *Haemophilus influenzae* type b conjugate vaccine; OPV, oral poliovirus vaccine; IPV, inactivated poliovirus vaccine; MMR, live measles-mumps-rubella vaccine; Td, adult tetanus toxoid (full dose) and diphtheria toxoid (reduced dose), for children ≥7 years and adults.

†If all needed vaccines cannot be administered simultaneously, priority should be given to protecting the child against those diseases that pose the greatest immediate risk. In the United States, these diseases for children younger than 2 years usually are measles and *Haemophilus influenzae* type b infection; for children older than 7 years, they are measles, mumps, and rubella. Before 13 years of age, immunity against hepatitis B and varicella should be ensured.

‡DTaP, HBV, Hib, MMR, and Var can be given simultaneously at separate sites if failure of the patient to return for future immunizations is a concern.

§For further information on pertussis and poliomyelits immunization, see the respective chapters (Pertussis, p 394, and Poliovirus Infections, p 424 in 1997 Red Book.

‖See *Haemophilus influenzae* Infections, p 220, and Table 3.9 (p 226) in 1997 Red Book.

¶IPV is also acceptable. However, for infants and children starting vaccination late (i.e., after 6 months of age), OPV is preferred in order to complete an accelerated schedule with a minimum of injections (see Poliovirus Infections, p 424 in 1997 Red Book).

#Varicella vaccine can be administered to susceptible children any time after 12 months of age. Unvaccinated children who lack a reliable history of chickenpox should be vaccinated before their 13th birthday.

**Minimal interval between doses of MMR is 1 month (4 weeks).

††HBV may be given earlier in a 0-, 2-, and 4-month schedule.

From American Academy of Pediatrics: *In* Peter G (ed): 1997 Red Book: Report of the Committe on Infectious Diseases, 24th ed. Elk Grove Village, IL, AAP, 1997. Copyright American Academy of Peadiatrics. Used with permission.

additional office visits. Hopefully, the continued development of combination vaccines will reduce the number of injections needed to vaccinate children in a timely manner.

The minimum interval between two doses of the same vaccination is outlined in Tables 27–3 and 27–4; however, it is important to note that these recommendations vary across countries. In general, administering two doses of the same multidose vaccine at intervals that are shorter than recommended might result in inadequate immu-nity; however, administering two doses at intervals greater than the recommended interval does not reduce immunity. Thus, a child who has had a lapse in the schedule does not need to start again.

It is important to handle and store vaccines properly. For example, vaccines require proper temperature storage (oral polio and varicella are stored in a freezer; most of the others are stored in a refrigerator). In addition, the MMR vaccine should be kept out of light at all times. Both MMR and varicella have to be reconstituted just before use. It is important to conduct regular verification of storage temperatures for vaccines as well as the vaccine expiration dates.

Vaccines have designated routes of administration, including oral (oral polio), subcutaneous (MMR) and intramuscular (the other commonly administered vaccines); check the package inserts if unsure of the route of administration. Although the site of injection varies with age (thighs versus arms), the buttocks should not be used for child immunizations because of potential damage to the sciatic nerve. In addition, reducing or dividing the dose of any vaccine is not recommended because this may reduce its effectiveness.

The Red Book and the other references stated earlier show the recommended timing of various vaccines for those children who have received immune globulin or other antibody-containing blood product.

RECORD KEEPING

It is critical for primary care clinicians to maintain and update an immunization history in each child's medical chart. **The National Childhood Vaccine Act of 1986 (and updated legislation) requires that the patient's medical record contain the following information for at least diphtheria, tetanus, pertussis, polio, measles, mumps, and rubella vaccines: date of administration, name, manufacturer, lot number, and expiration date of the vaccine, site and route of administration, and name and address of the clinician.**

It is recommended that parents keep portable immunization records and have practitioners update them with each vaccination. Portable immunization records are particularly important for families who move or switch clinicians. Ideally, the primary care office can review immunization records systematically of the entire preschool population to identify undervaccinated patients, determine the practice's immunization rates, and identify practice barriers to immunizations.

Although centralized computer immunization registries are being developed throughout the United States, currently the primary means to document individual children's immunization status involves written practitioner and patient immunization records.

ADVERSE EVENTS

Although vaccines are extremely safe, adverse events can occur. Side effects of vaccines are classified as major and minor. An extremely rare but serious consequence of OPV vaccination is the occurrence of paralytic poliomyelitis, which occurs in about 1 of every 1.5 million initial doses, and 1 of every 30 million subsequent doses. In addition, there is a small risk of paralytic poliomyelitis in close contacts who are immunodeficient. This extremely rare but serious adverse reaction from OPV precipitated the recent recommendation encouraging the use of IPV, which is not a live vaccine and does not result in this rare consequence.

Adverse events following administration of the whole cell pertussis vaccine have been the subject of much controversy. Local reactions (redness, swelling, pain, and tenderness at the injection site), fever ($< 105°F$ [$40.5°C$]), fretfulness, drowsiness, anorexia, and crying are relatively common following DTP vaccination. Interestingly, some practitioners have noted that these minor side effects are now less commonly seen, even with whole-cell DTP vaccine, perhaps in part due to the common practice of administering acetaminophen along with vaccinations. These minor side effects occur shortly following vaccination and resolve spontaneously. These side effects occur two to five times less frequently with the acellular pertussis vaccine (DTaP). More serious but transient adverse reactions following DTP vaccination include fever greater than or equal to $105°F$ ($40.5°C$; 1 in 330 doses of whole-cell pertussis DTP vaccine); seizures occurring within 72 hours of vaccination and generally associated with high fever (1 in 1750 doses), persistent inconsolable crying for over 3 hours (1 in 100 doses), and collapse or a shocklike state (1 in 1750 doses). These severe systemic reactions have only rarely been noted following DTaP vaccination.

The occurence of severe neurologic disease with permanent brain damage or death resulting from DTP vaccination is controversial. It is important to note that a temporal association of a severe reaction with a vaccination that is administered frequently does not prove causation. Although the evidence is still insufficient for a definitive statement, the 1997 Red Book notes that based on currently available data, pertussis vaccine "has not been proven to be a cause of brain damage" (Red Book, 1997, p. 404).

In general, side effects of live attenuated vaccines involve a minor form of the naturally occurring disease. For example, a fever and rash occurring 7 to 10 days after measles vaccination occurs in about 5% of cases. Side effects from inactivated vaccines do not resemble the naturally occurring disease, and are usually local reactions, with or without fever.

The National Childhood Vaccine Injury Act of 1986 requires health care clinicians to report certain adverse events that occurred within 30 days of receipt of a vaccination to the Vaccine Adverse Events Reporting System (VAERS). The Red Book and earlier-noted references list the specific adverse events that are reportable.

The National Vaccine Injury Compensation Program, effective since 1988, is a system that can compensate families for individuals who were injured or died after a vaccine-related event. Details of this program are available from the references to this chapter, from local departments of health, and from the National Vaccine Injury Compensation Program.

CONTRAINDICATIONS AND PRECAUTIONS

The two permanent contraindications to vaccination are severe allergy to a vaccine component or anaphylaxis following a prior dose, and idiopathic encephalopathy that occurred within 7 days of a pertussis vaccination. Hypersensitivity reactions to vaccines are very unusual, and methods to evaluate and manage children with allergic reactions are described in the Red Book. Table 27–5 shows vaccine contraindications for both live and inactivated vaccines. Short-term (< 2 weeks) corticosteroid therapy is not a contraindication for vaccination. Children with either asymptomatic or symptomatic human immunodeficiency virus (HIV) infection should receive the MMR vaccine but not other live vaccines (i.e., they should receive IPV instead of OPV, and should not have the varicella vaccine).

Table 27–6 shows many conditions that are *not* valid contraindications to vaccination. **Many children eligible for vaccinations have minor**

TABLE 27–5. *Valid* **Vaccine Contraindications**

Condition	Live Vaccine	Inactivated Vaccine
Severe allergy to component	Yes	Yes
Severe illness	Yes	Yes
Encephalopathy	—	Yes*
Pregnancy	Yes†	No
Immunosuppression	Yes	No
Recent blood product	Yes	No

*Applies only to pertussis vaccine.
†Except oral poliovirus vaccine, in certain situations.
From Atkinson W, Furphy L, Gantt, J, and Mayfield M: Epidemiology and Prevention of Vaccine-Preventable Diseases. Atlanta, US Department of Health and Human Services, 1997, pp. 33–38.

TABLE 27–6. *Invalid* **Vaccine Contraindications**

Minor illness
  Low fever
  Upper respiratory infection
  Otitis media
  Mild diarrhea
Antibiotic therapy
Exposure to disease or convalescence from disease
Pregnancy in the household
Breastfeeding infant
Premature birth
Allergies to products that are not in vaccine
Household member with seizures, SIDS*
Need for tuberculosis testing
Need for multiple vaccines

*A child with a household member having immunosuppression should not receive oral poliovirus vaccine.
From Atkinson W, Furphy L, Gantt J, and Mayfield M: Epidemiology and Prevention of Vaccine-Preventable Diseases. Atlanta, US Department of Health and Human Services, 1997, pp. 38–41.

illnesses such as upper respiratory infections, otitis media, or gastroenteritis—none of which are valid contraindications to vaccinations. Fever per se is not a contraindication unless the child has a moderate or severe illness along with the fever. Antibiotic therapy, exposure to an infectious disease, and the convalescent phase of an illness are all common conditions that are not contraindications to vaccination. All vaccines, including live vaccines, can be safely given to children who have close contact with pregnant women and to breastfeeding infants. For the increasing number of children born prematurely, it is important to remember that the vaccination schedule should follow the child's chronologic age, except that only IPV should be given in the hospital and hepatitis B should be given to infants who weigh more than 2 kg. There are no restrictions for vaccinations with respect to tuberculosis skin testing.

MISSED OPPORTUNITIES FOR IMMUNIZATIONS

A very important cause of underimmunization involves missed opportunities, which are defined as cases in which a child who is eligible for a vaccination does not receive all needed vaccinations. Missed opportunities have been shown to occur frequently in primary care offices, as well as in other health care settings. Missed opportunities can be caused by (1) nonsimultaneous administration of needed vaccines, (2) invalid contraindications, (3) bureaucratic or administrative obstacles (e.g., fees, appointment requirements), and (4) failure to screen for needed immunizations (particularly during acute or follow-up visits).

There are many ways that primary care clinicians can reduce or eliminate missed opportunities for vaccinations. First, practices should establish clear standards for assessing immunization status at all visits, and vaccinating children during visits other than scheduled well-child care visits. Second, practitioners should educate staff, parents, and each other about valid versus invalid contraindications to vaccination and follow the guidelines for simultaneous vaccination and vaccination during minor acute illnesses. Third, practices should determine the immunization levels of their own population and use this information to identify barriers and missed opportunities for vaccination. Practices that have poor immunization rates might wish to become more aggressive in vaccinating children and reducing missed opportunities. Fourth, practices should consider modifying office routines to minimize missed opportunities. For example, written guidelines can be established for nurses to screen and vaccinate eligible patients, and tickler files can be created to track undervaccinated children.

In 1992, the Standards for Pediatric Immunization Practices were published, and endorsed by key national organizations including the ACIP, AAP, and AAFP. Table 27–7 lists these standards. Although it is admittedly difficult in a busy office practice to adhere perfectly to all of these standards, they are useful reminders for clinicians and office staff to maximize immunization delivery to children.

COSTS

Studies have shown that for some populations of children, costs have been a barrier to timely vaccinations. Uninsured children have been found to have lower immunization rates than insured children, and provision of insurance coverage for immunizations and preventive care have been determined to increase immunization rates. Many primary care practitioners have found that vaccine costs were a barrier to their patients and that the purchase price of vaccines, combined with poor reimbursement from Medicaid and some insurance plans, was a major impediment to immunization delivery, resulting in referrals to public health clinics. Some legislative changes have been instituted in an attempt to reduce cost barriers to immunizations. Several states have adopted "First Dollar" vaccination laws that require most insurance plans to include the cost of preventive visits and vaccinations as part of the standard benefit package. A major part of the national Vaccines for Children (VFC) program involves free vaccinations to eligi-

TABLE 27–7. Standards for Pediatric Immunization Practices

Standard 1.	Immunization services are *readily available.*
Standard 2.	There are *no barriers or unnecessary prerequisites* to the receipt of vaccines.
Standard 3.	Immunization services are available *free* or for a minimal fee.
Standard 4.	Providers utilize all clinical encounters to *screen* and, when indicated, immunize children.
Standard 5.	Providers *educate* parents and guardians about immunization in general terms.
Standard 6.	Providers *question* parents or guardians about *contraindications* and, before immunizing a child, *inform* them in specific terms about the risks and benefits of the immunizations their child is to receive.
Standard 7.	Providers follow only true *contraindications.*
Standard 8.	Providers administer *simultaneously* all vaccine doses for which a child is eligible at the time of each visit.
Standard 9.	Providers use accurate and complete *recording procedures.*
Standard 10.	Providers *co-schedule* immunization appointments in conjunction with appointments for other child health services.
Standard 11.	Providers *report adverse events* following immunization promptly, accurately, and completely.
Standard 12.	Providers operate a *tracking system.*
Standard 13.	Providers adhere to appropriate procedures for *vaccine management.*
Standard 14.	Providers conduct semi-annual *audits* to assess immunization coverage levels and to review immunization records in the patient populations they serve.
Standard 15.	Providers maintain up-to-date, easily retrievable *medical protocols* at all locations where vaccines are administered.
Standard 16.	Providers operate with *patient-oriented* and *community-based* approaches.
Standard 17.	Vaccines are administered by *properly trained* individuals.
Standard 18.	Providers receive *ongoing education* and *training* on current immunization recommendations.

From the National Immunization Program. Washington, DC, Centers for Disease Control and Prevention. US Department of Health and Human Services, 1992.

ble children (currently children on Medicaid, Native American children, uninsured children, and those whose insurance does not cover immunizations), as well as improved reimbursement to providers for vaccines administered to these children. Although there has been some controversy about such legislation, there is general consensus among child health experts that costs of vaccinations should not be a barrier to timely receipt of childhood immunizations.

Much has been accomplished since 1796 when Edward Jenner inoculated James Phipps with cowpox, terming the procedure vaccination (after the word "vacca" for cow). The future is bright for children to live free of many vaccine-preventable diseases. By combining technologic advances of vaccines with aggressive delivery of immunizations by primary care clinicians and public health providers, our health care system will ensure healthier and disease-free lives for our children.

FURTHER READING

American Academy of Pediatrics: 1997 Red Book: Report of the Committee on Infectious Diseases. Elk Grove Village, IL, AAP, 1997.

Atkinson W, Furphy L, Humiston SG, Pollard B, Nelson JR, Wolfe C: Epidemiology and Prevention of Vaccine-Preventable Diseases. Atlanta, US Department of Health and Human Services, 1997.

Centers for Disease Control and Prevention: General Recommendations on Immunization: Recommendations of the Advisory Committee on Immunization Practices (ACIP). MMWR 43:(No. RR-1)1–37, 1994.

National Immunization Survey: National, state, and urban area vaccination coverage levels among children aged 19–35 months, U.S., July 1996–June 1997. MMWR 47:108–116, 1998.

Rodewald LE, Szilagyi PG, Shiuh T, et al.: Is underimmunization a marker for insufficient utilization of preventive and primary care? Arch Pediatr Adolesc Med 149:393–397, 1995.

Szilagyi PG and Rodewald LE: Missed opportunities for immunizations: A review of the evidence. J Public Health Management Practice 2:18–25, 1996.

US Department of Health and Human Services: Standards for Pediatric Immunization Practices. Washington, DC, DHHS, 1992.

SECTION III

MANAGEMENT OF DISEASE

PART A

COMMON ACUTE ILLNESSES, SYMPTOMS, TRAUMA, AND IMPAIRED FUNCTION

David C. Grossman

Chapter 28

Injury Prevention

Injuries represent the most important threat to the health of children and adolescents. Each year, close to 20,000 children and adolescents die, and a great many more are hospitalized as a result of unintentional and intentional injuries—the leading cause of death for children and adolescents over the age of 1 year. The prevention of injuries is definitely within the scope of pediatric practice. This chapter provides physicians and other child health clinicians specific guidance on effective injury prevention that can be advocated as part of health care to families or as a community health responsibility.

Injury, clearly, is a major public health problem.

Table 28–1 shows the leading causes of injury deaths for children and adolescents under 19 years of age in the United States in 1994. There are age-specific variations in injury rates among children. For example, pedestrian deaths are relatively concentrated among school-age children, whereas firearm injuries occur predominantly among adolescents. Mortality rates from unintentional injuries decreased by 39% between 1978 and 1991, whereas death rates for intentional injury rose by close to 50% during the same period. Thus, **the prevention of intentional as well as unintentional injury by pediatricians and other child health practitioners has become a growing priority.**

Health professionals are superbly placed to influence the risk of injuries to children by virtue of their frequent contact with families and their respected role in dispensing health-related advice. Potential opportunities for intervention include anticipatory guidance during well-child care, office or emergency department visits for injuries, and community child health projects.

ROLE OF OFFICE-BASED COUNSELING

Injury prevention strategies are likely to be most effective when they are passively introduced or integrated into the environment. The purest example of a passive intervention for injury prevention are airbags in motor vehicles. Airbag activation requires no action on the part of the driver and does not depend on behavioral compliance. However, there are few interventions in childhood injury prevention that do not require some degree of behavioral compliance. For example, bicycle helmets, smoke detectors, and handgun storage devices will only be effective when deployed. Hence, health care clinicians can teach families about effective injury prevention devices and behaviors during encounters for health supervision or illness. When giving information, clinicians need to provide clear, simple, specific, and developmentally appropriate advice. The Injury Prevention Program (TIPP) sponsored by the American Academy of Pediatrics is an example of a developmentally sequenced approach to injury prevention counseling in the office. Although the effectiveness of office-based counseling in changing risky behavior and preventing injuries is not fully proved, preliminary evidence suggests that this form of anticipatory guidance has positive outcomes.

INJURY PREVENTION STRATEGIES

Motor Vehicle Occupant Injuries

Motor vehicles cause the greatest number of injury deaths to children in the United States. These injuries can be divided into occupant, pedestrian, bicyclist, and motorcycle injuries. Occupant injuries have the highest incidence, although

TABLE 28–1. Leading Causes of Deaths from Injury Among Children and Adolescents—1994

	Age Group, yr							
	0–4		5–9		10–14		15–19	
	No.	Rate*	No.	Rate*	No.	Rate*	No.	Rate*
All Injuries	4286	21.72	1777	9.42	2696	14.38	12,257	69.57
All Unintentional Injuries								
Motor vehicle traffic	979	4.96	857	4.54	1096	5.84	3506	28.99
Occupant related	564	2.86	365	1.93	535	2.85	3506	19.90
Motorcycle	3	0.02	3	0.02	18	0.10	183	1.04
Pedal cyclist	15	0.08	91	0.48	146	0.78	72	0.41
Pedestrian	280	1.42	315	1.67	259	1.38	273	1.55
Drowning	548	2.78	189	1.00	221	1.18	358	2.03
Fire and flames	677	3.43	239	1.27	95	0.51	72	0.41
Falls	78	0.40	26	0.14	30	0.16	94	0.53
Unintentional firearm	34	0.17	25	0.13	126	0.67	327	1.86
Intentional								
Homicide	786	3.98	156	0.83	413	2.20	3532	20.05
Firearm	71	0.36	73	0.39	325	1.73	3150	17.88
Suicide	0	0.00	4	0.02	318	1.70	1948	11.06
Firearm	0	0.00	1	0.01	187	1.00	1377	7.82

*Rates expressed as deaths/100,000 persons.
From National Center for Health Statistics: Mortality Data Statistics. http//@www.edu.gov/ncipc/osp/usmort.htm

great progress has been made in the past decade. The single most important injury prevention intervention for children is the proper use of child car seats and lap-shoulder harnesses while in a moving vehicle. Despite great improvements, much more needs to be done to increase occupant safety for children. Car seats and seatbelts are highly effective, reducing serious injuries and fatalities by 71% and 45%, respectively. Despite laws mandating their use, compliance has not risen sufficiently compared with that in nations in which enforcement is stricter. Furthermore, car seat usage rates are highest in the first year of life but decrease to only 30% by age 3 years. In 1997, airbags were estimated to be present in over 50% of U.S. vehicles and represent a true life-saving measure for adults in driver and passenger seats. However, preliminary data suggest that children younger than 13 years of age and infants in car seats are at greater risk for serious injury and death when exposed to an airbag in the front passenger seat. If a rear seat is not available, counsel the family to install a deactivation switch for the front passenger airbag to prevent deployment when a child is seated there. Thus, **clinicians must emphasize the great importance of restraining all children younger than thirteen years in the *rear* passenger seat.** Another challenge is teaching parents and others the correct use of car seats. As many as 50% of car seats are used incorrectly with regard to positioning, buckle placement, and belt clips. The recent move toward universal anchorage systems for car seats should greatly facilitate proper use. Excellent parent education materials are available from the American Academy of Pediatrics (phone: 800-433-9016 or e-mail: http://www.aap.org), the National Highway Traffic Safety Administration (NHTSA), and other safety organizations.

Clinicians also can influence parents to purchase cars that have superior crash test performance. Both NHTSA (e-mail:http://www.nhtsa.dot.gov/cars/) and the Insurance Institute for Highway Safety (e-mail:http://www.hwysafety.org/) publish on-line information on crash testing outcomes for new vehicles exposed to front-end and side-impact crashes.

Adolescent drivers are at high risk for automobile crashes during their first years of driving, owing to driving inexperience and driving while alcohol intoxicated. To reduce these risks, parents may wish to do the following: (1) insist that adolescents drive heavier, safer vehicles to protect them in the event of a crash; (2) maximize their supervised driving experience to improve driving skills under different conditions; and (3) restrict driving privileges of adolescents who have alcohol-related problems.

Pedestrian and Cyclist Injuries

Pedestrian injuries, although an important cause of mortality and severe disability in preadolescents, offer very limited office-based prevention strategies. The most credible interventions to reduce this form of injury are engineering modifications such as crossing islands, traffic-calming measures, and narrower streets. School-based curricula to teach safe street crossing behaviors have had some effectiveness. Clinicians also can provide developmental information for parents regarding when children can learn to cross streets safely.

The most serious bicycle-related injuries are those that involve traumatic brain injuries. **Bicycle helmets are 70% effective in the reduction of brain injury and also have been shown to be efficacious in reducing maxillofacial injuries.** Helmets are equally effective in motor vehicle–related bicycle crashes. Clinicians need to reinforce the value of helmets, starting at an early age, and of modeling helmet use by parents. Success in convincing patients to wear helmets may be most effective in the context of a community-based effort that is reinforced by legislation. Proper helmet fit is a difficult challenge, particularly among children at a time when rapid head growth is occurring.

Motorcycle and off-road motorized bike injuries also represent a serious risk of head injuries to unhelmeted adolescents. Motorcycle helmets are 25% to 40% effective in the reduction of severe head injuries and are mandated by law in many states. However, off-road use of motorcycles remains a common practice, and helmet usage among participating adolescents must be stressed. Only those helmets meeting the specific federal Motor Vehicle Safety Standard No. 218 are legal and safe for use.

Drowning

Drowning is the second leading cause of death among children and adolescents, after motor vehicle injuries. The primary sources of exposure for drowning among young children are open water, swimming pools, and bathtubs. The measure most likely to reduce drowning in swimming pools is installing a fence that surrounds the pool and that has passively locking gates, preventing access to young children. Preliminary evidence suggests that such measures reduce the risk of drowning by about 50%. Other promising, but unproved, approaches to pool drownings are the use of pool alarms and swimming lessons. To prevent open-water drownings, personal flotation devices (PFDs), or lifejackets, have been promoted as the most protective strategy. The exact protective effect of PFDs has not been defined for either children or adults, but anecdotal evidence is highly suggestive of their protective value, although rates of use remain very low in most settings. A major source of drowning incidents is associated with boating mishaps; adolescents are particularly at risk for this type of injury. Adolescent drownings also are associated strongly with alcohol use and PFD nonuse. Hence, clinicians should discuss these concerns with families of adolescents who participate in recreational boating. PFD use has been promoted through loaner programs at the point of recreation, but little is known about whether these programs lead to increased use. Bathtub drownings should be completely preventable. Inadequate supervision of bathing toddlers and a history of seizure disorder both appear to elevate the risk of bathtub drownings. Children taking seizure medications should be supervised closely while in the bathtub.

Burns and Fire-Related Injuries

Mortality from fire-related injuries is attributable mostly to burns and asphyxiation from residential house fires, whereas most nonfatal burns (e.g., scalding injuries and other types of burns) are from other causes. The leading cause of residential fires is lighted cigarettes, which account for nearly one third of all fatal fires. Smoldering cigarettes ignite bedding and other furniture, leading to substantial smoke and carbon monoxide exposure before flames are ignited. Alcohol intoxication also is implicated frequently among smokers who ignite house fires. The main preventive maneuver available to families is the installation of smoke detectors on every floor of the house. Smoke detectors have been shown to be over 70% effective in the reduction of fire-related fatality. Although great strides have been made in the installation of home smoke detectors, barriers to proper use still exist. The main problem is that many detectors do not operate owing to battery failure or intentional disarming. The most common reason for disarming detectors is related to nuisance alarms; these frequently occur when the detector encounters smoke or vapors from the kitchen or bathroom. The use of photoelectric detectors may reduce these false alarms. Health care providers also should promote the use of flame-retardant sleepwear for young children. Although all child sleepwear sold in the United States must be flame retardant, many cotton clothes that are sold and used as sleepwear do not meet these requirements. Residential indoor sprinkling systems are effective in fire suppression; however, they are primarily an option for new housing only.

Scald burns represent a substantial proportion of nonfatal burn injuries, but there are few proven strategies to prevent their occurrence. Many of these injuries result from hot liquids being spilled and inadequate supervision or inattention. Scalding tap water also has been implicated frequently in scald burns, leading to new regulations requiring manufacturers of hot water heaters to set thermostats at no more than 120°F (48.8°C). An example of a purely passive approach to injury control, this has led to remarkable decreases in these types of burns. Because families may be unaware that the thermostat was reset to a higher temperature by a previous homeowner, they should be encouraged to check the water heater temperature.

Poisoning

The prevention of childhood poisonings is one of the earliest and most successful efforts to reduce unintentional injury among children. Much of the reduction in medication poisonings can be attributed to the Poisoning Prevention Packing Act of 1970, which required that medication containers be childproof. Consequently, mortality rates have fallen approximately 75%. Continued vigilance is needed by parents and pharmacists, because the latter may dispense nonchildproof containers on demand, especially to the elderly. The home-based use of ipecac, under physician direction, also has been promoted to parents to reduce the amount of poison absorbed, although more data supporting the efficacy of this common approach are needed.

Carbon monoxide is another relatively common, and potentially lethal, form of poisoning among children and adolescents, accounting for over 100 deaths in the United States each year. Such poisoning results from improper ventilation from a combustible fuel source and is related most frequently to faulty motor vehicle exhaust systems (especially in covered pickup trucks), faulty home heating devices, and indoor cooking with charcoal. Residential poisoning can be minimized with the use of household carbon monoxide detectors.

Poisoning also is one of the most common methods of suicide attempts and gestures, although few fatalities result from this method. Intentional poisoning is particularly common among adolescent females, reaching a peak at about 16 to 17 years of age and frequently involving the ingestion of medications, both prescription and nonprescription. It would be prudent for clinicians to recommend that parents of adolescents store only small quantities of potentially lethal prescription medications in the household.

Falls

Falls are another important source of injury morbidity and hospitalization among children, although they are not as important a cause of mortality as other injuries; however, children who fall from multistory buildings are at highest risk for serious injury or death. Installation of bars in windows above the first floor appears to reduce the incidence of this type of injury. Other common types of falls involve playground equipment and infant walkers. **Mobile infant walkers have been a source of concern because of their association with serious injuries during falls down stairways. Parents should be counseled to avoid these products.** Stationary infant walkers may prevent these falls but still allow young infants to reach potentially harmful items.

Firearms

Firearms are the leading cause of both homicide and suicide among children and adolescents and the second leading cause of injury among youth, after motor vehicle crashes, accounting for over 5000 deaths in the United States each year. Firearm injuries are about evenly distributed between suicides and homicides; handguns are implicated in over 50% of these deaths. Unintentional firearm injuries are less common, leading to about 500 deaths in youth each year. **Families that keep guns have a 5- to 10-fold risk of suicide and a 2.7-fold higher rate of homicide in the home.**

Because of the enormity of the firearm injury problem, clinicians should spend some anticipatory guidance time with families on prevention. Clinicians may wish to fashion their preventive message depending on whether the family already owns a gun. For young children, the main concern

is unintentional firearm injury related to handgun play or discovery. For adolescents, the major concern is access to guns by suicidal or delinquent youth.

Limiting access to firearms should be a key priority for gun-owning families. Families not owning firearms but contemplating a purchase should be informed of the risks associated with firearm ownership. Families currently owning a firearm should also be told of the risks and informed that the safest measure to reduce the risk of injury to their child is to remove the firearm from the home. Should they choose to keep a gun, they should store it unloaded, using a locking device. Several devices are available for the safe storage of guns. For rifles, the main choices are a full-size gun safe or a trigger lock. Gun safes are more resistant to theft but are expensive and may not be economical for an owner of one or two guns. Only trigger locks that use a key should be used; keyless trigger locks can be opened by older children and adolescents. For handguns, trigger locks are an inexpensive option, but because many handgun owners desire quick access to the gun for protection, they may not be acceptable to the owner. Trigger locks also do not shield the gun from view or protect against theft. Handgun lockboxes, small shoebox-size safes that have push-button combination locks, provide the owner with an enclosed container that can be bolted to a wall or floor. The boxes can be accessed within seconds by using a push-button combination code, thus eliminating the time required to search for a key. Clinicians can help families make these choices by explaining the relative merits and demerits of safe storage options and their availability.

REFERENCES

Baker SP, O'Neill B, Ginsburg MJ, and Li G: The Injury Fact Book. New York, Oxford University Press, 1992.

Bass JL, Christoffel KK, Widome M, et al.: Childhood injury prevention counseling in primary care settings: A critical review of the literature. Pediatrics 92:544–550, 1993.

Christoffel KK: Toward reducing pediatric injuries from firearms: Charting a legislative and regulatory course. Pediatrics 88:294–305, 1991.

Guyer B and Ellers B: Childhood injuries in the United States. Am J Dis Child 144:649–652, 1990.

Rivara FP and Grossman DC: Prevention of traumatic deaths to children in the United States: How far have we come and where do we need to go? Pediatrics 97:791–797, 1996.

Paul L. McCarthy

Chapter 29

Fevers and the Evaluation of the Child Who Has Fever

Children in the first 2 to 3 years of life have approximately four to six episodes of acute infectious illnesses per year, and these episodes often are associated with fever. As the child matures, the number of episodes per year decreases. The very young child who has fever caused by an acute infectious illness is a common problem. Moreover, these children more often have selected serious infectious illnesses, such as bacteremia, pneumonia, meningitis, and cellulitis associated with bacteremia, than do children in older age groups. Hence, it is worthwhile to review the pathophysiology, differential diagnosis, clinical and laboratory evaluation, and management of young children who have acute episodes of fever.

PATHOPHYSIOLOGY

Fever is a response to various inciting agents, such as viruses or pathogenic bacteria. The febrile response is regulated carefully by a central temperature-control mechanism located in the preoptic region of the hypothalamus. In response to an inciting agent, polymorphonuclear leukocytes and other phagocytic bone marrow–derived cells of the reticuloendothelial system release endogenous pyrogen, which acts on the thermoregulatory center through the mediation of prostaglandins. Usually the thermoregulatory center is set at approximately 98.6°F (37°C). During a febrile response, the thermoregulatory center is set to maintain a higher level of body temperature. This elevated temperature is maintained by increased heat production, especially through increased muscle activity, such as shivering; by increased heat conservation, especially through peripheral vasoconstriction; by decreased sweating; and by behavioral measures, such as covering oneself with blankets in response to chills even though the body temperature is elevated.

Fever should be differentiated from episodes of hyperpyrexia in which the thermoregulatory center has not been reset. In these episodes, body temperature may be elevated because of superheating by high ambient temperatures, and the physiologic responses recruited by the thermoregulatory center (e.g., sweating) are not able to compensate. An example of hyperpyrexia is that of an infant left in a closed automobile during warm summer months.

The thermoregulatory center during febrile episodes has an upper physiologic limit of 106°F (41.1°C). Temperatures beyond this should be considered potentially harmful to the host because of the possibility of damage to the central nervous system. In ranges of fever from 100° to 105.8° F (37.8° to 41.0°C), the data are conflicting regarding the value of an elevated temperature for the preservation of the host. Some types of microorganisms (e.g., treponemas) are destroyed; others (e.g., *Streptococcus pneumoniae*) grow poorly at higher temperatures. Some studies have documented an enhancement of selected immune responses if the temperature is elevated. However, other studies using different animal models have documented poorer survival during episodes of gram-negative sepsis when the body temperature is elevated. Thus, the question of the value of fever in host preservation during infectious episodes is far from resolved.

That fever places increased metabolic demands on the host is clear. Fever also exaggerates the pulmonary vasoconstriction induced by hypoxemia. The patient who is febrile is often tachycardic, uncomfortable, and because of irritability, difficult to assess for the underlying illness. Also, a strong correlation exists between height of fever and occurrence of febrile seizures in children who have fevers of 104° to 106°F (40° to 41.1°C).

DIFFERENTIAL DIAGNOSIS

An appreciation of serious infections that occur during acute illnesses has been gained in four prospective studies that have taken place in our Primary Care Center–emergency room and in private practice in New Haven, Connecticut. In these

TABLE 29–1. Diagnosis of Serious Illnesses During 996 Episodes of Acute Infectious Illnesses in Febrile Children Younger Than or Equal to 36 Months of Age

Diagnosis	No.	Percent
Bacterial meningitis	9	0.9
Aseptic meningitis	12	1.2
Pneumonia	30	3.0
Bacteremia	10	1.0
Focal soft tissue infection	10	1.0
Urinary tract infection	8	0.8
Bacterial diarrhea	1	0.1
Abnormal electrolytes, abnormal blood gases	9	0.9
TOTAL	89	8.9

From McCarthy PL: Acute infectious illness in children. Compr Ther 14(3):51, 1988. Reprinted with permission. © American Society of Contemporary Medicine and Surgery.

studies, 996 episodes of fever in children 36 months of age or younger were evaluated. The occurrence of serious illnesses documented in these patients can be seen in Table 29–1.

In one study, we followed two cohorts of patients whom we had recruited simultaneously: 225 patients from our Primary Care Center and 172 patients from one private practice. Each time these children had an acute infectious illness, they were to be seen by the study pediatrician. In the 32 months of the study, these children had a total of 1221 acute infectious illnesses, 761 in the cohort in the Primary Care Center and 460 in the cohort in the private practice. The occurrence of serious illnesses is shown in Table 29–2.

TABLE 29–2. Diagnosis of Serious Illnesses During 1221 Episodes of Acute Infectious Illnesses in 397 Children Followed for the First 32 Months of Life

Diagnosis	Primary Care Center (N = 761 Visits) No.	%	Private Practice (N = 460 Visits) No.	%
Bacterial meningitis	0	0.00	—	0.00
Aseptic meningitis	1	0.14	—	0.00
Pneumonia	9	1.27	1	0.19
Bacteremia	2	0.28	2	0.39
Focal soft tissue infection	1	0.14	1	0.19
Urinary tract infection	2	0.28	1	0.19
Bacterial diarrhea	5	0.71	0	0.00
Abnormal electrolytes, abnormal blood gases	3	0.42	0	0.00
TOTAL	23	3.24	5	0.96

From McCarthy PL: Acute infectious illness in children. Compr Ther 14(3):51, 1988. Reprinted with permission. © American Society of Contemporary Medicine and Surgery.

The data in Table 29–2 are a more accurate reflection of the occurrence of serious illnesses during episodes of acute infectious illness in young children followed in a primary care setting. The data in Table 29–1 probably represent a selection bias; that is, the data are not generated by a cohort of children followed over time but rather represent the subtle selection bias of children seen with acute illnesses at referral sites. The occurrence of serious illness was approximately three times greater in the latter group than in the cohort. Interestingly, no cases of bacterial meningitis were seen in the cohort, whereas meningitis occurred in one in 100 children in the four prospective studies. The bacterial diagnoses seen frequently in both studies were pneumonia, bacteremia, urinary tract infections (UTIs), and focal soft tissue infection. For unexplained reasons, bacterial diarrhea was more frequent in the cohort study.

GENERAL CONSIDERATIONS

The common serious illnesses in febrile children represent a diagnostic challenge. An optimal chest examination in young children is difficult because of noncooperation and respiratory rates more rapid than those of adults. Bacteremia, especially that caused by *S. pneumoniae,* often is seen in the febrile child as a minor illness, such as an upper respiratory tract infection (URI), a fever that has no apparent source, or a case of otitis media. Most patients who have a UTI may present with nonspecific findings such as fever, irritability, decreased feeding, or mild gastrointestinal symptoms (see Chapter 32). Bacterial meningitis may be an occult infection in a child. One study found that 11 of 152 patients who had bacterial meningitis did not have nuchal rigidity, Brudzinski sign, bulging fontanelle, or depressed sensorium. All of these children were younger than 16 months old and had a febrile seizure. Meningeal signs, therefore, may not be present in the age group at greatest risk for meningitis. Serious illnesses are special diagnostic challenges in children younger than 3 months. This group of patients is at risk for sepsis and meningitis, and the organisms causing these infections are often group B streptococcus or gram-negative organisms. Pneumonia may be caused by *Staphylococcus aureus* or gram-negative bacteria. Also, bacteremic UTIs occur more in these patients than in older children.

The diagnostic challenge in evaluating children who have acute infectious illnesses is to identify those who have serious illnesses by observing the child, taking a history, performing a physical examination, assessing age and temperature risk factors, and when necessary, using laboratory tests.

OBSERVATION

Observing a febrile child before noting the medical history and performing the physical examination is a key part of the diagnostic process. The observations that pediatricians make to judge the degree of illness of febrile children before the examination have been defined. The two most frequently noted observation variables concern the child's eyes: "looking at the observer" and "looking around the room." In fact, there are many ways in which eye function and appearance can be described. Normal eye appearance or behavior is described as "shiny," "bright," and "looks at observer." Infants who have severe impairment are described as "glassy," or "stares vacantly into space." These terms probably reflect what pediatricians mean by the term *alertness.*

Other observations that are used frequently by pediatricians include the child's "sitting," "moving arms and legs on table or lap," or "no movement in mother's arms." In fact, a variety of data describes and defines what is often referred to as *motor ability.* Again, some variables may describe normal motor ability ("sits without support)"; others describe severe impairment ("lies limply on table").

A number of the observation variables used most commonly, including "vocalizing spontaneously," "playing with objects," "reaching for objects," "smiling," and "crying with noxious stimuli," describe the child's characteristics that usually are referred to as *playfulness* or, when the child is impaired, *irritability.*

Another common observation is the response of a crying child to being held by the parent. A normal response is "stops crying when held by the parent"; severe impairment can be indicated, for example, by "continual cry despite being held and comforted." These data probably represent a more precise description of what is termed *consolability.*

Traditionally, one believed that as the pediatrician is forming a judgment of degree of illness by observation, he or she is assessing such organic variables as petechiae, bulging fontanelle, or nasal flaring. Certainly these organic variables are crucial, but a majority of observations concern the child's response to stimuli. In variables relating to eye appearance and function, for example, stimulus-response data about the eyes (e.g., "looks at pen being offered") are noted much more often than organic data about the eyes (e.g., sunken, red, glassy). More experienced pediatricians rely more heavily on stimulus-response data than do less experienced pediatricians.

Thus, the judgment of degree of illness by observation is based largely on the assessment of the interaction between the child and the environment. Often the extent of the interaction is apparent immediately. The child smiles at the observer and reaches for the proffered pen. At other times, the child cries and clings to the parent. After choosing a position of comfort for the child, usually on the parent's lap, the experienced examiner orchestrates the stimuli in an attempt to elicit normal responses from the child. To orchestrate this interaction, the pediatrician must be a developmentalist and know what an age-appropriate response would be. Thus, observation of febrile children is a complex process including both developmental skills and clinical skills; pediatricians must assess the child's responses to multiple stimuli and must also be alert to clinical clues, such as sunken eyes, cyanosis, and grunting.

Observation data have been examined further to identify those that are key predictors of serious illness in febrile children. Six items have been identified, and each has a three-point scale. These comprise the Acute Illness Observation Scales (Table 29–3). It should be noted that four of the six items concern the child's response to stimuli.

When these six items and their scales are used in practice, the best possible score is 6 (6 × 1 [1 = normal]); the worst possible score is 30 (6 × 5 [5 = severe impairment]). Nearly two thirds of the children who have acute illnesses had scale scores less than or equal to 10 (i.e., appear well); less than 3% of these children had serious illnesses. However, children appearing to be severely ill (scale score ≥16) were relatively uncommon, but if such a child were seen, the chance of serious illness was high (92% in one study). Approximately one in four children appeared moderately ill (score of 11 to 15), and even here the chance of serious illness was high (26% in the same study). The occurrence of serious illness in febrile children who appear moderately or severely ill as defined by a score greater than 10 was 13 times greater than the occurrence in children who appear well (score ≤10). It is not clear that these scales can be used in infants less than 2 months of age because response to social overtures may be difficult to evaluate in these patients.

HISTORY AND PHYSICAL EXAMINATION

What is the relationship between data gathered by observation and the results of the history and

TABLE 29–3. Acute Illness Observation Scales

(PLEASE CHECK BOXES THAT DESCRIBE YOUR CHILD'S APPEARANCE AND BEHAVIOR)

OBSERVATION ITEM	NORMAL	MODERATE IMPAIRMENT	SEVERE IMPAIRMENT
1. **QUALITY OF CRY**	STRONG WITH NORMAL TONE ☐ *OR* CONTENT AND NOT CRYING ☐	WHIMPERING ☐ *OR* SOBBING ☐	WEAK ☐ *OR* MOANING ☐ *OR* HIGH PITCHED ☐
2. **REACTION TO PARENT STIMULATION** (Effect on crying when held, patted on back, jiggled on lap, or carried)	CRIES BRIEFLY, THEN STOPS ☐ *OR* CONTENT AND NOT CRYING ☐	CRIES OFF AND ON ☐	CRIES CONTINUALLY ☐ *OR* HARDLY RESPONDS ☐
3. **STATE VARIATION** (Going from awake to asleep or asleep to awake)	IF AWAKE, THEN STAYS AWAKE ☐ *OR* IF ASLEEP AND STIMULATED, THEN WAKES UP QUICKLY ☐	EYES CLOSE BRIEFLY, THEN AWAKENS ☐ *OR* AWAKENS WITH PROLONGED STIMULATION ☐	WILL NOT ROUSE ☐ *OR* FALLS TO SLEEP ☐
4. **COLOR**	PINK ☐	PALE HANDS, FEET ☐ *OR* ACROCYANOSIS (BLUE HANDS AND FEET) ☐	PALE ☐ *OR* BLUE ☐ *OR* ASHEN (GRAY) ☐ *OR* MOTTLED ☐
5. **HYDRATION** (Moisture in skin, eyes, mouth)	SKIN NORMAL *AND* EYES, MOUTH MOIST ☐	SKIN, EYES NORMAL *AND* MOUTH SLIGHTLY DRY ☐	SKIN DOUGHY OR TENTED *AND* EYES MAY BE SUNKEN *AND* DRY EYES AND MOUTH ☐
6. **RESPONSE TO SOCIAL OVERTURES** (Being held, kissed, hugged, touched, talked to, comforted)	SMILES ☐ *OR* ALERTS ☐ (2 months or less)	BRIEF SMILE ☐ *OR* ALERTS BRIEFLY ☐ (2 months or less)	NO SMILE, FACE ANXIOUS ☐ *OR* DULL, EXPRESSIONLESS ☐ *OR* NO ALERTING ☐ (2 months or less)

Modified from McCarthy PL, Sharpe M, Spiesel SZ, et al.: Observation scales to identify serious illness in febrile children. Pediatrics 70:806, 1982.

physical examination? In one study, 36 of 350 children who had fever had a serious infectious illness. Ill appearance, abnormal history, or abnormal physical examination was each of equal efficacy in detecting serious illnesses. The history and physical examination taken together could detect approximately 78% (28 of 36) of the children who had serious illnesses, but a combination of observation, history, and physical examination had the highest sensitivity for serious illnesses and could detect 86% (31 of 36) of the children who had such illnesses.

The abnormalities found on history and physical examination have also been analyzed. Findings relating to the respiratory system or central nervous system (CNS) represent the majority of abnormalities; in addition, abnormalities of the respiratory system and CNS correlate the strongest with serious illnesses. This connection is not surprising because diseases of these systems represent many of the serious illnesses in children who have acute infectious illnesses.

Recent studies have reported on the ability of observation, history, and physical examination to predict selected serious illnesses. The ability to predict pneumonia has been studied in this way. One study gathered observation data that focused on a global impression of the severity of the child's illness as well as specific respiratory tract findings (respiratory rate, color, presence or absence of nasal flaring, grunting, retractions, and use of accessory muscles of respiration). Standardized items regarding the history were then recorded and included questions about the presence and duration of fever; the presence, duration, and quality of cough; sputum production; and rapid or noisy breathing. Features of the physical examination that were noted included findings from chest palpation, percussion, and auscultation as well as associated findings such as a pulse rate. This careful clinical data gathering was able to identify 93% of the patients who had pneumonia.

In summary, a combination of observation, history, and physical examination is a highly sensitive diagnostic maneuver for detecting serious illnesses in febrile children. Careful attention should be paid to abnormalities in the respiratory system and the CNS.

AGE AND TEMPERATURE RISK FACTORS

Children who have acute infectious illnesses can also be assessed for age or temperature risk factors. The occurrence of selected serious illnesses is greater in febrile children younger than 3 months old. There also is an association between degree of temperature and serious illnesses. As the degree of fever increases, so does the occurrence of bacteremia. The occurrence of bacteremia in young children is 7% when the temperature is 104°F (40°C) or greater, 13% when the temperature is 105° to 105.9°F (40.5° to 41°C) and 26% when the temperature is greater than or equal to 106°F (41.1°C). In addition, the occurrence of bacterial meningitis is higher when the temperature is greater than or equal to 106°F (41.1°C).

LABORATORY TESTS

Screening laboratory tests may help identify the child at increased risk for many of these common serious illnesses. For example, one study of children 3 to 36 months of age who had fever found that if the fever was 103°F (39.4°C) or greater and the leukocyte count greater than 15,000/mm³, 16% of the children had bacteremia; if the fever was the same but the leukocyte count was less than 15,000/mm³, the occurrence of bacteremia was

2.7%. Others have reported that the risk of any serious illness in febrile children is approximately twice as great if the leukocyte count is 15,000/mm³ or higher and/or the erythrocyte sedimentation rate is 30 mm/hour or more than if neither of these elevations is present. In children who had fever without an identified source by observation, history and physical examination, and urinalysis with microscopic tests should be considered; however, such screening examinations are not 100% sensitive for urinary tract infection, and a urine culture should be obtained simultaneously. Thus screening laboratory tests have limitations in detecting serious illnesses in febrile children but do point toward increased risk of these illnesses.

DIAGNOSTIC APPROACH

The basis of the diagnostic approach is a carefully performed observation period, followed by a medical history and physical examination. Appreciation of age and temperature risk factors is also important. If the child appears well, has no findings on history or physical examination to suggest serious illness, and has no age or temperature risk factors, no laboratory evaluation is indicated. If otitis media is present in such a child, it should be treated with appropriate antibiotics. The preceding profile is true of the majority of febrile children.

If, on the other hand, the child appears ill, abnormalities are discovered in the history or the physical examination, or both, laboratory studies appropriate for those findings are indicated. The child who has grunting and nasal flaring should at least have a chest roentgenogram. The child who has an acute onset of frequent watery stools flecked with blood should be presumed to have an enteric pathogen until proved otherwise, and a stool culture should be performed. Often, the presence of risk factors may indicate the direction in which the laboratory evaluation should proceed. The infant younger than 3 months old who appears ill without other findings should have a sepsis workup and be admitted for intravenous antibiotics. The irritable child who has a temperature of 106°F (41.1°C) but no other findings is at higher risk for CNS disease, and the workup should include at least a lumbar puncture and a blood culture.

These diagnostic recommendations are accepted readily by most physicians. **The area of greatest controversy concerns those situations in which the clinical impression after observation, history, and physical examination is that the febrile child does not have a serious illness but**

does have age or temperature risk factors. Although one can be fairly accurate in assessing the risk of sepsis-meningitis by clinical examination in infants less than 3 months old, most authors recommend a full sepsis workup. Infants who have fever in the first 30 days of life should have a full sepsis workup and be admitted to the hospital for intravenous antibiotics. Infants greater than 30 days of age who have fever should also have a full sepsis workup; generally, admission to the hospital is advisable thereafter, but in select and carefully considered circumstances, outpatient follow-up, either with or without the use of intramuscular ceftriaxone, has been advocated by some. In children older than 3 months, those without a focus of bacterial infection and with higher degrees of fever are candidates for blood cultures. The physician may obtain the blood cultures initially or screen the child first with a complete blood count and differential and then obtain a blood culture if the white blood cell count is elevated. Consideration also should be given to examining the urine. The use of expectant antibiotics, especially intramuscular ceftriaxone, on an outpatient basis before the results of the blood culture are obtained may be considered but is controversial. No study has demonstrated unequivocally that such an approach lessens the occurrence of subsequent focal soft tissue infections.

ADMISSION OR OUTPATIENT FOLLOW-UP

Children who have life-threatening infections should be admitted to the hospital for supportive care. This applies uniformly to children who have meningitis; to febrile infants younger than 3 months old (this category is the most controversial, as outlined previously); and to children who have more severe soft tissue infections, such as septic arthritis or buccal cellulitis. Children who have hypoxia due to lower respiratory tract disease or electrolyte abnormalities during gastroenteritis should also be managed as inpatients.

In other circumstances, clinical judgment is involved in the decision to hospitalize a child who has a serious infectious illness that is not life threatening, for example, a small lobar infiltrate without respiratory compromise in a 1-year-old child. In these circumstances, many factors will enter into the decision to hospitalize the child. Can the parents provide appropriate care for the child? Will the antibiotics be given as recommended? If the child's condition deteriorates, can the parents readily return to the hospital? Does the family have a phone in the home? Can follow-up be ensured? When the answer to all of these questions is yes, non–life-threatening serious infections can be managed on an ambulatory basis.

THERAPY

Antipyresis

If body temperature rises beyond the upper limit of physiologic thermoregulation—106°F (41.1°C)—lowering the temperature is mandatory. In the more usual range of fever, the indications for temperature control are less clear. In the febrile patient who is uncomfortable and irritable because of the elevated temperature, antipyresis is warranted. If, in the physician's judgment, fever control will assist in evaluating the patient's state of well-being, antipyresis is warranted. Generally, it seems wise to treat temperatures above 103°F (39.4°C).

The mainstay of antipyretic therapy is acetaminophen. Acetaminophen is an antiprostaglandin that acts to reset the thermoregulatory center toward normal by inhibiting prostaglandin synthesis and thus interfering with the action of endogenous pyrogen. Acetaminophen is well absorbed in the digestive tract, reaching peak plasma levels in 1 to 2 hours, and its antipyretic effect dissipates in 4 to 6 hours. Unlike other available antipyretics, acetaminophen is not a gastrointestinal irritant, nor does it have an antiplatelet effect. Unlike aspirin, it has not been associated with bronchoconstriction. The dosing schedule of acetaminophen for patients of various ages and weights is given in Table 29–4.

If fever does not respond to acetaminophen, the use of ibuprofen may be considered. The additional benefit, however, is small, and this benefit must be weighed against the antiplatelet, gastrointestinal irritant, and renal-vasoconstrictive effects of this agent. Acetaminophen remains the standard antipyretic because of its effectiveness, low cost, and minimal side effects.

External Cooling

The efficiency of external cooling during fever has long been a subject of debate. One study found no advantage to antipyretics plus external cooling versus antipyretics alone. It is essential in fever states that the thermoregulatory center be reset to normal by antipyretic use. Otherwise, the body will continue to produce and attempt to conserve heat even though external cooling is applied. If external cooling is applied in addition to

TABLE 29–4. Acetaminophen Dosage by Age and Weight

Age	0–3 mo	4–11 mo	12–23 mo	2–3 yr	4–5 yr	6–8 yr	9–10 yr	11 yr	12 yr–adult
Weight (lb)	7–11	12–18	19–27	28–35	36–47	48–59	60–71	72–95	≥96
Dose (mg q 4 hr)*	40†	80	120	160	240	320	400	480	640

*Dose every 4 hours but not more than five doses in 24 hours.
†All doses approximately 10 to 15 mg/kg/dose.
  Usual dosage forms: Drops: 80 mg = 0.8 mL; chewable tablets: 80 mg; elixir: 160 mg = 5 mL; junior tablets: 160 mg; adult tablets: 325 mg or 500 mg.
  From McCarthy PL: Fever. *In* Rakel RE (ed): Conn's Current Therapy, 1989. Philadelphia, WB Saunders, 1989.

antipyretics, it should be in the form of water at body temperature. As the water evaporates from the skin, calories are expended as the heat of evaporation, and thus heat is removed from the body. Because of these considerations, it usually is not necessary to use cold water, which may lead to shivering and increased heat production. A thin film of tepid water should be applied to the entire body, allowed to evaporate, and then reapplied.

Because isopropyl alcohol may be absorbed through the skin and because appreciable blood isopropyl alcohol levels may result, its use in sponging should be discouraged. Sponging with tepid water should be reserved for the few patients in whom a higher grade of fever (103° to 106°F [39.4° to 41.1°C]) does not respond to acetaminophen. External cooling also may be used in those hyperthermic patients whose elevated temperature is due not to a reset of the thermoregulatory center, as in acute infectious illnesses, but to increased heat production, as in malignant hyperpyrexia, or to high ambient temperatures. If the body temperature is quite high, a more vigorous attempt at external cooling is warranted, namely, sponging

with very cold water. A cooling mattress can be used in tandem with cold water sponging in these circumstances.

FURTHER READING

Baker MD, Bell LM and Avner JR: Outpatient management without antibiotics of fever in selected infants. N Engl J Med 329:1437–1441, 1993.

Baraff LJ, Bass JW, Fleisher GR, et al.: Practice guidelines for the management of infants and children 0 to 36 months of age with fever without source. Pediatrics 92:1–12, 1993.

Bass JW, Steele RW, Wittler RR, et al.: Antimicrobial treatment of occult bacteremia: A Multicenter Co-Operative Study. Pediatr Infect Dis J 12:466–473, 1993.

Fleisher GR, Rosenberg N, Vinci R, et al.: Intramuscular versus oral antibiotic therapy for the prevention of meningitis and other bacterial sequelae in young, febrile children at risk for occult bacteremia. J Pediatr 124:504–512, 1994.

Kramer MS, Tange SM, Drummond KN, Mills EL: Urine testing in young febrile children: A risk-benefit analysis. J Pediatr 125:6–13, 1994.

McCarthy PL, Fink H, Baron M, et al.: Observation, history, and physical exam in identifying serious illnesses in febrile children less than 24 months. J Pediatr 110:26–30, 1987.

McCarthy PL: The pediatric clinical evaluation and pneumonia. Curr Opin Pediatr 8:427–429, 1996.

Stephen Berman

Chapter **30**

Acute Respiratory Infections, Otitis Media, Sinusitis, and Croup

ACUTE RESPIRATORY INFECTIONS

CLASSIFICATION. Acute respiratory infections are the most frequent type of childhood illness. Although most are self-limited viral infections, a few progress to severe and even fatal illnesses. Acute respiratory infections are classified by clinical syndromes that reflect upper, mid-

dle, and lower respiratory tract involvement, as well as by viral and/or bacterial etiology.

Upper respiratory syndromes present with any combination of nasal congestion, coryza, nasal discharge, cough, earache, sore throat, headache, facial pain, bad breath, and fever. Viral infection causes acute rhinitis and pharyngitis. Acute otitis media and sinusitis develop when viral upper respiratory infections are complicated by bacterial infections of the middle ear and paranasal sinuses.

Middle viral respiratory syndromes include acute laryngitis, laryngotracheobronchitis (croup), and tracheobronchitis. Laryngitis presents with hoarseness; laryngotracheobronchitis presents with hoarseness, barking cough, and stridor; and tracheobronchitis presents with a cough that usually is difficult to distinguish from an uncomplicated upper respiratory infection. Auscultatory findings seldom are helpful because rhonchi or harsh expiratory breath sounds are quite similar to the transmitted sounds of nasal congestion. Middle bacterial respiratory syndromes include acute epiglottitis and tracheitis. Most often caused by *Haemophilus influenzae* type B infection, their incidence has declined dramatically with widespread immunization against this pathogen.

Lower respiratory syndromes include pneumonia and bronchiolitis, which usually present with tachypnea and/or retractions. The auscultatory sounds suggestive of pneumonia are called crackles, rales, or crepitations. Bronchiolitis presents with wheezing due to airway obstruction; crackles are heard when atelectasis is present distal to bronchiolar mucus plugging.

ETIOLOGY. The viral agents usually responsible for upper, middle, and lower respiratory infections are shown in Table 30–1. Although any respiratory virus can produce all of the syndromes, some have a predilection for certain areas of the respiratory tract. Rhinoviruses cause approximately 50% of upper respiratory infections or colds, but rarely, if ever, involve the lower respiratory tract directly. However, these infections can trigger acute respiratory distress in individuals who have reactive airway disease. Parainfluenza viruses and respiratory syncytial virus (RSV) are the most frequent pathogens associated with middle respiratory croup syndromes. RSV, parainfluenza viruses, influenza viruses, and adenovirus are responsible for the majority of lower respiratory infections.

TABLE 30–1. Viruses That Cause Acute Respiratory Infections

Upper Respiratory Infections	Middle and Lower Respiratory Infections
Adenoviruses	Adenoviruses
Coronaviruses	Enteroviruses
Enteroviruses	Influenza viruses
Herpes simplex virus	Parainfluenza viruses
Influenza viruses	Respiratory syncytial virus
Parainfluenza viruses	
Respiratory syncytial virus	
Rhinoviruses	

Likewise, a relatively small number of bacterial pathogens cause the majority of bacterial infections of both the upper and lower respiratory tract (Table 30–2). These include *Streptococcus pneumoniae, H. influenzae, Moraxella catarrhalis,* and *Streptococcus pyogenes.* Additional bacterial pathogens include *Staphylococcus aureus, Chlamydia,* gram-negative enteric organisms, and anaerobic organisms. *S. pneumoniae* and *H. influenzae* are the pathogens associated most frequently with both upper respiratory bacterial infections such as otitis media and sinusitis as well as pneumonia. *S. pyogenes* is the bacterial pathogen more often responsible for tonsillitis and pharyngitis.

PATHOGENESIS. The pathogenesis of acute respiratory infections involves interactions among host characteristics, the virulence of viral and bacterial pathogens, and environmental exposures. **Environmental factors that increase the frequency of respiratory infections include child care attendance, later birth order, passive smoking, and absence of breastfeeding.**

Viral infection initially involves the ciliated and nonciliated epithelial cells of the upper respiratory tract. Viral replication, which peaks at about 24 hours, may persist for up to 3 weeks. When the viral infection disrupts the upper airway epithelial barrier, bacteria are better able to attach, penetrate, and spread. When the nasopharynx becomes heavily colonized with these potential pathogens, children are predisposed to both upper and lower bacterial respiratory infections.

Otitis media usually develops several days after cold symptoms first appear. When the viral infection results in nasopharyngeal bacterial overgrowth, aspiration of a large infecting inoculum through the eustachian tube into the middle ear space becomes more frequent. Aspiration is promoted by both nasal obstruction that increases the positive pressure in the nasopharyngeal space and the eustachian tube dysfunction that produces a negative pressure in the middle ear space. Viral infection also alters mucociliary clearance, which contributes to stasis of contaminated middle ear fluid. Similar pathogenic mechanisms lead to obstruction of the sinus ostia and predispose to sinusitis.

The maturity and functional activity of the immune defenses, including T-cell, B-cell, complement, and phagocytic function, contribute importantly to the likelihood of respiratory infection. Bacterial respiratory infections are more common during the first 2 years of life because the immune response against bacterial polysaccharides is not yet as fully developed as it is later. Children who experience recurrent and/or persistent bacterial in-

TABLE 30–2. Most Common Bacterial Causes of Respiratory Infection

	Tonsillitis/Pharyngitis	Otitis Media	Sinusitis	Epiglottitis/Tracheitis	Pneumonia
Streptococcus pneumoniae	—	+ + + +	+ + + +	+	+ + + +
Haemophilus influenzae	—	+ + +	+ + +	+ + + +	+ +
Moraxella	—	+ +	+ +	—	—
Streptococcus pyogenes	+ + + +	+	+	—	+
Staphylococcus aureus	—	+	+	+	+
*Chlamydia**	—	+	—	—	+ + +
Gram-negative enteric	—	+	+	—	+
Anaerobes	+	+	+	—	+
Pseudomonas†	—	+	—	—	+

*In infants less than 3 months of age.
†More frequent in patients who have cystic fibrosis.
+ + + +, most common; −, least common.

fections may also have selective immune impairments to specific otitis pathogens.

Acute Viral Upper Respiratory Infection (Common Cold)

The common cold is the most frequent pediatric infectious disease. Children younger than age 5 have an average of six to 12 colds a year; those in child care or who have school-age siblings may have more.

DIAGNOSIS. The signs and symptoms of a cold include fever, nasal congestion, coryza, cough, and sore throat. In most cases, the clinical illness, in the absence of secondary bacterial infection such as sinusitis or otitis, resolves within 7 to 10 days. Fever, which usually resolves within 4 days, may be as high as 105°F (40.6°C) without superinfection. The findings on physical examination are nonspecific.

TREATMENT. Treatment is largely symptomatic. Acetaminophen or ibuprofen is symptomatically helpful for fever, sore throat, or muscle aches. A stuffy, congested nose can be treated with normal saline nose drops. Long-acting xylometazoline (Otrivin) or 0.05% oxymetazoline (Afrin) nose drops may be used when symptoms interfere with normal activities such as eating and sleeping; however, nose drops should be discontinued by 5 days to prevent rebound chemical rhinitis. Antihistamines are not effective in relieving cold symptoms. In infancy, a nasal bulb syringe is useful to remove nasal secretions. Antibiotics should not be administered without evidence of an associated bacterial infection. Codeine and dextromethorphan do not alleviate the symptoms of acute cough. Parents should be instructed that rapid or difficult breathing with retractions are signs of a lower respiratory infection such as bronchiolitis or pneumonia.

OTITIS MEDIA

DEFINITIONS. Otitis media is an inflammation of the middle ear associated with a collection of fluid in the middle ear space (effusion) or a discharge (otorrhea). *Acute otitis media* commonly is defined as the presence of a middle ear effusion with tympanic membrane inflammation presenting with a rapid onset of symptoms such as fever, irritability, or earache. These symptoms, however, are nonspecific and may result from an associated viral upper respiratory infection. *Unresponsive acute otitis media* is characterized by the continued presence of membrane inflammation, effusion, and clinical signs or symptoms after 48 hours of therapy. *Recurrent acute otitis media* is defined as three new acute otitis media episodes within 6 months or four in 1 year. *Otitis media with effusion,* defined as an asymptomatic middle ear effusion without membrane inflammation, can be categorized by the duration of the effusion. *Otitis media with residual effusion* is characterized by an effusion present 3 to 16 weeks following the diagnosis of acute otitis media. *Otitis media with persistent effusion* occurs when the effusion remains longer than 16 weeks. *Otitis media with complications* occurs when there is irreversible damage to the middle ear structures such as tympanosclerosis, retraction pockets, adhesions, ossicular erosion, cholesteatoma, perforations, or the presence of other intratemporal and intracranial complications.

DIAGNOSIS. Otoscopic findings with acute otitis media include decreased tympanic membrane mobility, a bulging tympanic membrane with impaired visibility of the ossicular landmarks, a yellow and/or red color, exudate on the membrane, or bullae. Other findings that suggest otitis media with effusion include a translucent or transparent membrane with visible landmarks; air-fluid levels; and amber; straw color, or clear middle ear fluid with diminished membrane mobility. Eustachian tube dysfunction producing negative middle ear pressure is suggested by prominence of the lateral process, shortening of the long arm of the malleus with a more horizontal orientation, and greater mobility of the tympanic membrane with negative than with positive pressure. Although tympanometry can be used to identify the presence of an effusion, it cannot determine whether the tympanic membrane is inflamed. In addition, tympanometry often is more difficult to accomplish in young crying patients than is pneumatic otoscopy.

Acute otitis media often is overdiagnosed. Failure to perform pneumatic otoscopy to assess tympanic membrane mobility also contributes to overdiagnosis. Using a pneumatic otoscope head, obtain an adequate view of the tympanic membrane. It is important to create an adequate seal with the speculum, have adequate light intensity, and avoid mistaking the ear canal wall for the tympanic membrane. A red membrane with normal mobility is not to be interpreted as evidence of acute otitis media. That finding can be caused by the viral upper respiratory infection, the child's crying, or efforts to remove cerumen.

MICROBIOLOGY. While viruses have been isolated as the single agent in less than 10% of middle ear aspirates with acute otitis media, bacterial pathogens can be isolated in 80% to 90%. The most common bacterial pathogens in acute otitis media and otitis media with effusion are *S. pneumoniae, H. influenzae,* and *M. catarrhalis.* Additional bacterial pathogens include *Streptococcus pyogenes, S. aureus,* gram-negative enteric organisms, and anaerobic organisms. The microbiologic causes of acute otitis media in early infancy differ from those in older children. The risk of gram-negative enteric infection is especially high in infants younger than 6 weeks of age who have been or are hospitalized in a neonatal intensive care nursery. In normal infants during the first 3 months of life, acute otitis media is caused by *S. aureus* and *Chlamydia trachomatis* as well as by *S. pneumoniae, H. influenzae,* and *M. catarrhalis.*

Penicillin-resistant *S. pneumoniae* has recently become a more frequent pathogen in otitis media. Children who have resistant strains are often younger than 18 months of age and have recently received antibiotics.

Acute Otitis Media

Antibiotic treatment of otitis media has become controversial because of questions about benefit and concerns about increasing the prevalence of drug-resistant microbes. A meta-analysis of the results of 33 randomized placebo-controlled clinical trials of the efficacy of antibiotics for the treatment of acute otitis media found that treatment increased the resolution rate by 13.7% (95% confidence interval [CI], 8.2 to 19.2); 81% (95% CI, 69 to 94) of patients who received a placebo became asymptomatic. The type of antibiotic administered had no effect on outcome regardless of whether the antibiotic had better coverage of β-lactamase organisms. Concerns, however, have been raised that the sample sizes of these studies are insufficient to determine the effect of treatment on the prevention of mastoiditis, an infrequent complication of acute otitis media. More rapid reduction in pain also may be a reasonable justification for therapy. In addition, studies using pre- and post-treatment tympanocentesis document that appropriate antibiotic administration eradicates the bacterial pathogen from the middle ear aspirate and that persistence of the pathogen correlates with continued signs and symptoms.

Although most clinicians routinely treat acute otitis with antibiotics, it also is reasonable in certain circumstances to individualize this decision and to include parental preference in determining whether to use antibiotics. The decision should be based on the tradeoff between the risks of antibiotic treatment (e.g., an allergic reaction, significant side effect, and possible subsequent colonization and infection with a multiple antibiotic-resistant pathogen) versus the benefit of a more rapid clinical response in about 14% of patients and possible reduction in the risk of mastoiditis. Children younger than 24 months of age should always be treated with antibiotics because of their relatively underdeveloped immune system and their higher risk of developing a complication. Untreated children who fail to improve within 48 to 72 hours should be reassessed and treated with antibiotics if the acute otitis still is present.

Amoxicillin is the first-line antibiotic for acute otitis media. The optimal duration of therapy is unclear but 7 days is reasonable. A dose of 60 to 75 mg/kg/day divided and given two or three times daily is recommended to provide better coverage for penicillin-resistant *S. pneumoniae.* For patients allergic to penicillin, the first-line alternatives are trimethoprim-sulfamethoxazole; erythromycin plus sulfisoxazole; or a newer macrolide, such as azithromycin or clarithromycin. When the physician is concerned about an associated bacteremia, the child's inability to take oral medications because of vomiting, or poor compliance, the patient can be treated with an intramuscular injection of ceftriaxone or procaine penicillin. Procaine penicillin is similar to amoxicillin in its coverage of non-β-lactamase-producing *H. influenzae*. Antihistamines with or without decongestants are of no benefit in treating acute otitis media.

Children who have ear pain may gain relief from acetaminophen, ibuprofen, or topical therapy with Auralgan ear drops. When pain is severe, tympanocentesis results in prompt relief.

The optimal timing for follow-up visits depends on the child's response to therapy. Children should be reassessed when symptoms continue beyond 48 hours or recur before the next scheduled visit. A follow-up visit for children who become asymptomatic should be scheduled in 3 to 6 weeks. Children younger than 15 months of age or who have a history of recurrent otitis media or antibiotic treatment of otitis media within the prior month should have a follow-up visit in 3 weeks. Follow-up visits in 6 weeks may be scheduled for other children.

Unresponsive Acute Otitis Media

It often is difficult to determine why a child has failed to respond to antibiotics. Concomitant middle ear viral infection, as well as failure to eradicate the middle ear bacterial pathogen, are associated with therapeutic unresponsiveness. Compared with other children presenting with untreated acute otitis media, there are more isolations of β-lactamase organisms (83% vs. 44% for *H. influenzae*) and resistant *S. pneumoniae* (18% vs. 8%). Because the bacterial pathogen is eradicated in about 50% of unresponsive cases, continuous symptoms may be related to an associated viral infection.

In areas where most strains of *H. influenzae* are still sensitive to trimethoprim-sulfamethoxazole, trimethoprim-sulfamethoxazole is recommended to treat acute otitis media unresponsive to high-dose amoxicillin; however, in areas where many strains of *H. influenzae* have become resistant to trimethoprim-sulfamethoxazole, treating unresponsive acute otitis media with amoxicillin plus clavulanate, a third-generation cephalosporin, or with a new macrolide, is recommended. The in vivo effectiveness of the newer macrolides (azithromycin and clarithromycin) against strains of *H. influenzae* is unclear. However, these macrolides do appear to provide better coverage of intermediate-resistant *S. pneumoniae* than do third-generation cephalosporins. Third-generation cephalosporins and the newer macrolides may provide improved coverage for *S. pneumoniae* with intermediate resistance, but they offer minimal advantage in covering highly resistant organisms. If unresponsive acute otitis media persists after a second course of antibiotics, a myringotomy or tympanocentesis in order to isolate the pathogen and drain the effusion should be considered.

Recurrent Otitis

The decision to administer antibiotic prophylaxis to children who have experienced three documented episodes of acute otitis media in a 6-month period should be individualized, taking into consideration parental preference. A meta-analysis of nine randomized controlled trials that had 958 subjects compared the difference in the rate of occurrence of acute otitis media per patient month while receiving antibiotic prophylaxis with placebo controls. Although antibiotic prophylaxis reduced the otitis rate by 44%, the mean rate difference was only about 1.33 fewer episodes per patient year for patients receiving antibiotics, compared with controls. These studies were carried out before the emergence of penicillin-resistant *S. pneumoniae* and *H. influenzae* resistant to trimethoprim-sulfamethoxazole. In areas that have a high prevalence of penicillin-resistant *S. pneumoniae* and β-lactamase-positive *H. influenzae*, amoxicillin prophylaxis does not appear to be effective. Although the risk of acquiring resistant *S. pneumoniae* on continuous prophylaxis appears to be increased, the sequelae of acquisition are not clear. Giving antibiotics at the onset of upper respiratory infection symptoms for 7 to 10 days rather than daily continuous therapy may have less of an effect on colonization with resistant *S. pneumoniae* and similar benefits as continuous therapy.

Another approach to preventing recurrent otitis episodes is active immunization. Clinical trials of the newly developed conjugate pneumococcal vaccine are under way. Children who have recurrent otitis should be given influenza vaccine, and if older than 2 years of age, 23-valent pneumococcal vaccine. Studies of both these approaches have reported encouraging results.

Children who have experienced five or more well-documented new episodes of acute otitis media within 12 months should be considered for possible referral for insertion of ventilating tubes. The decision to insert ventilating tubes for recurrent acute otitis should not be based solely on parental recall of the number of new episodes. The benefit of ventilating tubes to prevent new infection in controlled trials is similar to that of antibiotic prophylaxis; however, the duration of each episode is shortened markedly. The benefit of adenoidectomy to prevent recurrent acute otitis has not been well documented, but there is evidence that some children who have recurrent otitis have chronic adenoidal infection.

Otitis Media with Residual and Persistent Effusions

Residual middle ear effusions are part of the resolution continuum of acute otitis media, irrespective of antibiotic therapy. For example, about two thirds of children who have a history of acute otitis media had a middle ear effusion or high negative middle ear pressure 1 month after diagnosis of acute otitis media, regardless of antibiotic therapy.

The main reason to treat middle ear effusion is concern about the negative effects of prolonged conductive hearing impairments on language development and academic functioning. Although the available data document a causal relationship between severe congenital or acquired hearing loss (usually sensorineural) and language development, the data fail to establish a causal relationship between conductive hearing loss associated with otitis media and subsequent hearing-related development. Children diagnosed with a persistent effusion may have a slightly higher incidence of cholesteatoma, adhesive otitis, retraction pockets, membrane atrophy, or persistent membrane perforations compared with children who have no history of persistent effusion, but the insertion of ventilating tubes in children who have persistent effusion does not prevent these complications.

The management options for otitis media with residual effusion present for 3 to 16 weeks include observation, antibiotics alone, and combination antibiotic plus corticosteroid therapy. Considerable controversy exists about the use of combination therapy and the best way to manage these residual effusions because the spontaneous clearance rate during the subsequent month is about 20% to 25%. If combination therapy is tried in selected patients, a corticosteroid (prednisone, 1 mg/kg/day twice daily for 7 days) combined with an antibiotic effective against intermediate-resistant *S. pneumoniae* and β-lactamase-producing organisms for 10 to 14 days may be used. Unimmunized children who have no history of varicella and have been exposed in the prior month should not receive prednisone because of the potential risk of disseminated disease if on corticosteroid therapy. Prednisone side effects are similar to those noted in treating asthmatic episodes with short steroid courses: increased appetite, fluid retention, occasional vomiting and, in rare cases, marked behavioral changes. If the patient clears the persistent middle ear effusion unilaterally or bilaterally, he

or she should be followed monthly. Low-dose intermittent antibiotic prophylaxis for colds during the next 3 months with amoxicillin, 30 to 40 mg/kg/day to prevent a recurrence of otitis media may be considered.

Children of normal development should be referred for ventilating tubes and/or adenoidectomy after the effusion has persisted for at least 16 weeks and is accompanied by a documented bilateral hearing impairment of 20 dB or greater. Although it correlates with audiologic testing, tympanometry should be considered a screen and not a substitute for audiologic testing. The timing of ventilating tube placement or adenoidectomy should be individualized depending on the child's developmental and behavioral status, as well as parental preference. Adenoidectomy is not recommended for children younger than 4 years of age. Although adenoidectomy for otitis media without signs of upper airway obstruction usually is considered a second-line surgical intervention when a child has developed a complication from the ventilating tubes, such as persistent otorrhea, or requires multiple tube reinsertions, some surgeons advocate its use as the primary surgical therapy. Children who have a submucous cleft should not have an adenoidectomy because of the risk of velopharyngeal insufficiency and speech impairments. Because tonsillectomy in combination with adenoidectomy is no more effective than adenoidectomy alone in treating persistent effusions, it is not recommended.

ACUTE SINUSITIS

DEFINITIONS. Sinusitis is an acute bacterial infection within the paranasal sinuses. The ethmoidal sinus is the only one significantly developed at birth. The maxillary sinus is rudimentary at birth and visible on x-ray film by 6 months. The frontal sinus is not visible until 3 to 9 years of age.

DIAGNOSIS. Clinical ethmoiditis does not usually occur until 6 months of age. About 50% of cases occur between 1 and 5 years of age, with retro-orbital pain and/or periorbital cellulitis being the most common presenting signs. Maxillary sinusitis, seen clinically after 1 year of age, is associated with upper molar or zygomatic pain. Frontal sinusitis, associated with pain above the eyebrow, is unusual before 10 years of age. The clinical presentation of acute sinusitis in children may be either gradual or sudden. With the more sudden onset, the patient presents with a high fever, signs of systemic toxicity, and severe pain or periorbital inflammation. With a more gradual presentation, nasal discharge, postnasal drip, and daytime cough persist longer than 10 days. In addition, low-grade fever often is present in association with malodorous breath or intermittent, painless morning periorbital swelling. Older patients may complain of a headache, a sense of facial fullness, or pain overlying the involved sinus.

Physical examination reveals injected nasal mucosa, usually associated with nasal or postnasal mucopurulent discharge. Occasionally, percussion tenderness is present over the infected sinus. Periorbital swelling or mild discoloration also may occur. Transillumination of the sinuses is not helpful unless it is grossly asymmetric. Preseptal periorbital cellulitis secondary to ethmoiditis is the most frequent complication of paranasal sinusitis. Less frequently, orbital cellulitis or abscess develops associated with decreased extraocular movement, proptosis, edema, and altered visual acuity. The most common complication of frontal sinusitis is osteitis of the frontal bone, called Pott puffy tumor. Additional serious intracranial complications include cavernous sinus thrombosis, subdural empyema, brain abscess, and meningitis. The most common maxillary complication is cellulitis of the cheek. Rarely, osteomyelitis of the maxilla develops.

In most acute cases, radiographs are not needed. Radiographic studies are indicated mainly in children who have (1) facial swelling of unknown cause; (2) acute sinusitis unresponsive to 48 hours of therapy; (3) persistent or recurrent sinusitis; and (4) chronic asthma. Many clinicians believe that computed tomography (CT) scans rather than standard sinus radiographs should be obtained. Positive findings in children older than 1 year include opacification of the involved sinuses, air-fluid levels, or mucosal thickening of greater than 5 mm. Findings consistent with sinusitis may be found in asymptomatic patients who have colds or nasal allergies.

MICROBIOLOGY. The pathogens that cause acute sinusitis are usually *S. pneumoniae, H. influenzae* (nontypable), *M. catarrhalis,* and β-hemolytic streptococci. Rarely, anaerobic bacterial infections cause fulminant frontal sinusitis. Viruses can be isolated in 10% of sinus aspirates, but their pathogenic role is unclear.

MANAGEMENT. Patients who have evidence of periorbital or orbital cellulitis or any central nervous system complications should be hospitalized for intravenous therapy with nafcillin or clindamycin, plus a third-generation cephalosporin such as cefotaxime. Pending culture results, the first-line antibiotic for less severe cases of acute sinusitis is high-dose amoxicillin (60 to 75 mg/kg/day divided into three doses) for 10 days.

Antibiotic treatment is to be continued for another week if the patient has improved but is not yet totally asymptomatic. If the patient is allergic to penicillin, a third-generation cephalosporin, newer macrolide, or trimethoprim-sulfamethoxazole should be considered. Failure to improve after 48 hours suggests a resistant organism or potential complication. The usefulness of topical decongestants and oral antihistamine-decongestant combinations to promote drainage is not clear. Vasoconstrictor nose drops and sprays are associated with rebound edema if used for more than 5 to 7 days. Concern has been raised about potential adverse effects related to impaired ciliary function, decreased blood flow to the mucosa, and reduced diffusion of antibiotic into the sinuses. Patients who have underlying allergic rhinitis may benefit from intranasal cromolyn or corticosteroid nasal spray. Bulb syringe lavage with normal saline also may be of benefit.

SURGICAL TREATMENT. An otolaryngologist should be consulted for unresponsive and/or complicated cases because sinus aspiration and drainage may be helpful. For intraorbital or intracranial complications, external drainage of the abscess is as important as antibiotic therapy. The role of endoscopic sinus surgery in children is unclear.

RECURRENT AND/OR CHRONIC SINUSITIS

Chronic or frequent episodes of sinusitis occur in a small group of patients, most commonly caused by allergic rhinitis. Rarely, cases are caused by pressure against the ostia by a septal deviation, nasal malformation, polyp, or foreign body. In cases of chronic or recurrent pyogenic pansinusitis, poor host resistance (e.g., an immune defect, Kartagener syndrome, or cystic fibrosis) must be ruled out by immunoglobulin studies, cilia studies, and a sweat chloride test. Anaerobic and staphylococcal organisms often are responsible for chronic sinusitis. If allergies do not offer a sufficient explanation for the problem, the patient should be referred to an otolaryngologist for complete evaluation.

CROUP

Croup is a clinical respiratory syndrome characterized by acute stridor resulting from inflammation of the respiratory tract above the larynx (uvula, epiglottis, and arytenoid cartilages), the larynx (false vocal cords, aryepiglottic folds), or trachea. Although infection of the epiglottis is usually caused by *H. influenzae* type B, *S. pneumoniae* and *S. pyogenes* rarely can cause acute epiglottitis. Infections of the larynx and trachea (laryngotracheitis) usually are caused by viral agents.

DIAGNOSIS. Croup usually occurs in children younger than 5 years of age. Physical findings include hoarseness, a barky cough, and stridor. Most often the stridor is present while the child is crying or coughing. In more severe cases, the stridor is present when the child is calm. Patients who have croup who can be managed at home have intermittent stridor with crying or coughing, good air exchange, minimal or no retractions, no signs of dehydration, and are able to drink without drooling. Patients whose croup is more severe have stridor at rest, marked retractions with decreased air entry, signs of dehydration, an inability to drink, or an altered mental status. These more severe cases usually require hospitalization. Signs of impending upper airway obstruction related to croup include cyanosis, severe retractions with minimal air exchange, restlessness, agitation, or anxiety consistent with "air hunger."

MANAGEMENT. The overwhelming majority of patients with croup have moderate respiratory distress. Parents are encouraged to offer fluids to prevent the child from becoming dehydrated. Although scientific evidence is lacking, a cold mist vaporizer may be helpful. Antibiotics should be reserved for children who have an associated acute otitis media. Steroid treatment with dexamethasone, 0.5 to 1 mg/kg (up to 10 mg) given orally or parenterally as a single dose or repeated in 12 hours, appears to modify the course of croup. The use of corticosteroids in ambulatory patients reduces the progression of the inflammation and may prevent hospitalization. Racemic epinephrine reduces the respiratory distress in croup. Children who have croup or stridor resolving after treatment with racemic epinephrine in an ambulatory setting should be observed for at least 3 hours before returning home, because stridor and respiratory distress frequently recur. Patients who have severe respiratory distress should be hospitalized and managed with both racemic epinephrine and corticosteroid. Children may be discharged from the hospital when stridor at rest and respiratory distress have resolved.

FURTHER READING

Berman S: Current concepts: Otitis media in children. N Engl J Med 332:1560, 1995.

Berman S, Roark R, Luckey D: Theoretical cost effectiveness of management options for children with persisting middle ear effusions. Pediatrics 93:353, 1994.

Cruz MN, Stewart G, Rosenberg N: Use of dexamethasone in the outpatient management of acute laryngotracheitis. Pediatrics 96:220, 1995.

Dunham ME: New light on sinusitis. Contemp Pediatr 11:102, 1994.

Roark R, Petrofski J, Berson E, Berman S: Practice variations among pediatricians and family physicians in the management of otitis media. Arch Pediatr Adolesc Med 149:43, 1995.

Rosenfeld RM, Vertrees JE, Carr J, et al.: Clinical efficacy of antimicrobial drugs for acute otitis media: Metaanalysis of 5400 children from 33 randomized trials. J Pediatr 124:355, 1994.

Ruddy RM: Croup: Has management changed? Contemp Pediatr 133(10):21, 1993.

Stool SE, Berg AO, Berman S, et al.: Otitis Media with Effusion in Young Children. Clinical Practice Guideline No. 12. AHCPR Publication No. 94-0622. Rockville, MD: Agency for Health Care Policy and Research, July 1994.

Wald ER: Chronic sinusitis in children. J Pediatr 127:339, 1995.

Williams RL, Chalmers TC, Stange KC, et al.: Use of antibiotics in preventing recurrent acute otitis media and in treating otitis media with effusion. JAMA 270:1344, 1993.

Mona Mansour
Thomas G. DeWitt

Chapter 31

Vomiting and Diarrhea

Vomiting and diarrhea are common pediatric complaints. When they occur together, the most common diagnosis is acute gastroenteritis. However, both can occur independently and in association with each other in many other disorders. In the following discussion, the pathophysiology and evaluation of vomiting and diarrhea are addressed separately. Then rehydration therapy is discussed, as it is the key element in the management of most disorders involving vomiting and diarrhea.

Finally, other therapies and treatments specific to vomiting and diarrhea are presented.

VOMITING

Virtually all children will experience episodes of emesis at some point. In most instances, vomiting is self-limited and requires minimal intervention. Despite its usually benign etiology, vomiting causes significant parental concern and anxiety. The goal of the clinician is threefold: (1) to differentiate benign from potentially serious etiologies of emesis; (2) to assess the need for rehydration; and (3) when appropriate, to reassure parents and suggest supportive measures they can perform at home to provide appropriate and safe care for their child who has emesis.

Pathophysiology

Vomiting is controlled by two functionally distinct areas in the brain stem: the vomiting center and the chemoreceptor trigger zone (CTZ). The vomiting center regulates the actual act of vomiting. It receives afferent impulses from the gastrointestinal tract, as well as from other parts of the body. These include higher cortical centers such as the labyrinthine apparatus and the CTZ. Efferent impulses from the vomiting center travel to the phrenic nerve (diaphragm), the spinal nerves (abdominal musculature), and the visceral nerves (esophagus and stomach), resulting in emesis. The CTZ is incapable of initiating vomiting independently. A variety of exogenous and endogenous chemicals stimulate the receptors of the CTZ, which then sends efferent impulses to the vomiting center, resulting in emesis.

Evaluation

Vomiting is seen most commonly as part of a gastrointestinal illness. Obtaining a thorough history is critical in separating benign self-limited causes of vomiting from more serious, pathologic causes. Particular attention should be paid to the nature of the emesis as well as to the hydration status of the patient. **Emesis of a bilious nature indicates an obstruction in the gastrointestinal tract distal to the stomach.** Bilious emesis in the newborn period may signify a congenital abnormality or a malrotation-volvulus and requires further evaluation and intervention. In infants, simple regurgitation is associated more commonly with gastroesophageal reflux (GER), whereas more forceful, projectile emesis can signify hypertrophic pyloric stenosis (HPS). Presence of blood in the emesis should also be assessed. Small amounts of blood in the emesis may be found with forceful, persistent emesis and may signify a Mallory-Weiss tear. Larger quantities of blood suggest more serious conditions such as severe gastritis or hemorrhage due to erosion of an ulcer.

Knowing the frequency and quantity of emesis assists in determining the hydration status of the patient. The level of alertness and activity of a child also help determine hydration status. The frequency and amount of urine output should be assessed in all patients. Usually, children will urinate at least three times a day or every 8 hours. The index of suspicion for dehydration should increase if a child has had no urine output for 8 hours or if the child has had no urine output on awakening in the morning. The dietary history should include questions about the type and amount of food and fluids. Specifically inquire about formula preparation in infants because inappropriately made formula increases the risk for serum sodium abnormalities (both hypo- and hypernatremia).

The onset and timing of emesis also are helpful clues. **Recurrent, early morning vomiting warrants investigation for causes of increased intracranial pressure.** Emesis that occurs predominantly after feeding may suggest GER or overfeeding. The latter may be suggested if inappropriately large volumes are given. Forceful, recurrent, projectile vomiting after feeding occurs in infants who have HPS. In late fall and winter when gas heating sources are in use, carbon monoxide poisoning is a possible cause of emesis, especially if vomiting is not associated with diarrhea.

Associated symptoms may support certain diagnoses. Fever suggests infectious causes, both gastrointestinal as well as other infections that may trigger emesis, such as otitis media, pneumonia, urinary tract infection, meningitis, and sepsis. Cough or respiratory distress with post-tussive emesis suggests a pneumonic process. Abdominal pain that precedes vomiting is more suggestive of a serious organic problem than is pain that follows vomiting. Vomiting associated with bloody stools and intermittent abdominal pain suggests intussusception. Urinary frequency, dysuria, suprapubic pain, or lower back pain may signify urinary causes for emesis. Polyuria and polydipsia in association with emesis suggest the diagnosis of diabetic ketoacidosis. In young infants who are emetic and fail to thrive, one must consider inborn errors of metabolism, genetic abnormalities, and endocrine disorders (congenital adrenal hyperplasia [CAH], renal tubular acidosis [RTA], and cystic fibrosis). A history of perinatal deaths in the family may support the diagnosis of inborn errors or CAH. Pernicious vomiting after varicella or influenza infection with antecedent aspirin use suggests Reye syndrome. Female adolescent patients should be asked about their sexual history, and the possibility of pregnancy needs to be addressed. Where appropriate, questions regarding body image and diet need to be asked of both male and female adolescents to determine their risk for eating disorders, such as anorexia nervosa and bulimia. Suicide attempts with certain medications as well as intoxication with alcohol can result in emesis.

When performing the physical examination of a patient who is emetic, assessment of the patient's mental and hydration status should be emphasized. The general level of consciousness of the patient as well as presence of irritability, lethargy, and focal neurologic signs should be assessed. Watching the child interact with the parent before any intervention can help determine baseline neurologic status. Heart rate, pulses, blood pressure, capillary refill, and skin color all help in assessing circulation. Examining skin turgor, fullness of the fontanelle, presence of tears, and moistness of the mucous membranes helps assess hydration. Clinicians should distinguish between the doughy appearance of the skin in children who have hypernatremic dehydration and the loose, tented skin of children who have hypotonic or isotonic dehydration. Pediatric patients should have their growth chart reviewed, and the current weight should be compared with recent weights. If significant weight has been lost over time or if the growth chart indicates failure to thrive, chronic or persistent illness must be entertained. **Acute weight loss is the best indicator of the patient's current hydration status.** The current weight also can be compared with those weights obtained subsequently to monitor the patient's course of illness.

Table 31–1 lists the criteria for different degrees of dehydration.

A careful abdominal examination includes inspection for visible signs of obstruction, such as peristalsis and distention. A moribund infant whose abdomen is distended and who has a history of emesis suggests a malrotation with midgut volvulus. Palpation should include eliciting any peritoneal signs, such as rebound or guarding. A palpable "olive" just to the right of midline in the patient's right upper quadrant suggests HPS. A sausage-shaped mass in the right upper quadrant suggests intussusception. Suprapubic tenderness or costovertebral angle tenderness suggests urinary tract infection. Careful examination of other systems can determine other nongastrointestinal causes of vomiting. Table 31–2 has a more complete differential diagnosis of emesis, stratified by age.

Laboratory Evaluation

Laboratory tests should be guided by the history and physical examination. If the child has severe or protracted vomiting, blood should be drawn to determine electrolyte concentrations as well as blood urea nitrogen and creatinine. A low bicarbonate can result from poor peripheral perfusion and lactic acidosis or from an underlying condition that causes metabolic acidosis. Hypochloremic metabolic alkalosis is seen in children who have HPS and in children who have cystic fibrosis. Diagnostic imaging studies should be used judiciously. If obstruction of the gastrointestinal tract is suspected, plain abdominal films with two views can be performed. An upper gastrointestinal study can be especially helpful in diagnosing upper gastrointestinal obstructions, and pH probes are helpful in diagnosing GER. Skilled ultrasonographers can assist in the diagnosis of HPS and appendicitis. Air contrast or barium enemas can be used to

TABLE 31–1. Degree of Dehydration and Associated Clinical Signs and Symptoms

Mild, 3%–5%	Moderate, 6%–9%	Severe, ≥10%
Vital signs normal	Heart/respiratory rate increased	Heart/respiratory rate increased
Child alert, thirsty	Blood pressure normal	Blood pressure normal/decreased
Normal skin turgor	Child listless, irritable	Child lethargic/comatose
Normal capillary refill	Skin tents	Skin cold/clammy
Mucous membranes slightly dry	Capillary refill 2–3 sec	Skin tenting severe
Flat fontanelle	Lips/mucosa dry	Capillary refill >3 sec
Tears present	Fontanelle sunken	Mucous membranes very dry
Urine output slightly decreased	Tears absent	Fontanelle sunken
	Urine output decreased	Tears absent
		Urine output decreased significantly

Adapted from Limbos MAP, Lieberman JM: Management of acute diarrhea in children. Contemp Pediatr 12(12):68, 1995.

TABLE 31–2. Differential Diagnosis of Vomiting Stratified by Age

	Newborn and Infant	Child	Adolescent
Mechanical obstruction/ functional ileus	Congenital anomalies—intestinal atresia/stenosis Meconium ileus Malrotation–volvulus Hypertrophic pyloric stenosis Intussusception Hirschsprung disease	Malrotation–volvulus Appendicitis Intussusception Adhesions from previous surgery Meconium-ileus equivalent in CF patients	Appendicitis Adhesions from previous surgery Meconium-ileus equivalent in CF patients
Infectious	AGE-viral, bacterial, toxin-producing Extraintestinal Otitis media UTI Pneumonia Sepsis Meningitis	AGE-viral, bacterial, toxin-producing Extraintestinal Otitis media UTI Pneumonia Sepsis Meningitis	AGE-viral, bacterial, toxin-producing Extraintestinal Otitis media UTI Pneumonia Sepsis Meningitis
Metabolic, endocrine	Congenial adrenal hyperplasia Renal tubular acidosis Inborn errors of metabolism Adrenal insufficiency DKA	DKA	DKA Pregnancy
Toxins/drugs	Carbon monoxide poisoning	Carbon monoxide poisoning	Carbon monoxide poisoning Alcohol intoxication Suicide attempt with various drugs/substances
Gastrointestinal	Gastroesophageal reflux Overfeeding Hepatitis Reye syndrome	Hepatitis Inflammatory bowel disease Cyclic vomiting Pancreatitis Cholecystitis Reye syndrome	Hepatitis Peptic ulcer disease Inflammatory bowel disease Pancreatitis Cholecystitis Reye syndrome
Psychologic	Munchausen by proxy	Munchausen by proxy	Munchausen by proxy Bulimia Anorexia nervosa
Neurologic	Increased intracranial pressure	Increased intracranial pressure Migraines	Increased intracranial pressure Migraines

AGE, acute gastroenteritis; CF, cystic fibrosis; DKA, diabetic ketoacidosis; UTI, urinary tract infection.

evaluate intussusception. Computed tomography and magnetic resonance imaging are used infrequently in the evaluation of emesis in children.

DIARRHEA

Diarrhea is defined as the frequent passage of unformed watery bowel movements. Acute diarrhea usually has an abrupt onset, is self-limited, often is associated with vomiting, and most commonly is a result of a gastrointestinal infection by a virus, bacteria, or parasite. Chronic diarrhea, an increase in stool frequency and volume that lasts longer than 10 to 14 days, can be due to a variety of gastrointestinal and systemic diseases. This section addresses the evaluation and management of a patient who has acute diarrhea.

Pathophysiology

Understanding the underlying mechanisms of diarrhea and gastrointestinal function is important in determining the etiology and treatment of diarrhea. The gastrointestinal tract has age-related variations in the metabolism of fluids and electrolytes with the result that younger children are at greater risk for significant volume loss and dehydration with a given infection. The four primary mechanisms that cause diarrhea can operate alone or in combination. These four mechanisms are secretory, osmotic, cytotoxic, and inflammatory. Secretory diarrhea occurs when enterotoxins produced by an infectious, metabolic, or exogenous toxic agent stimulate secretion of fluid and electrolytes out of the cell and block reabsorption of fluid and electrolytes into the cell. The result is increased intestinal fluid. Osmotic diarrhea occurs when the intraluminal osmolarity increases due to undigested nutrients such as fat, proteins, and carbohydrates. Osmotic diarrhea is seen most commonly in the malabsorption syndromes but often occurs in combination with secretory and cytotoxic diarrheas. In cytotoxic processes, the mucosal cells of the intestinal villi are lysed, and the villi shorten and flatten. The result is a functional decrease in the absorptive and digestive surface. Inflammatory processes most often affect the mucosa and submucosa of the terminal ileum and colon. Inflammation is associated most commonly with invasion by a bacterial agent. Leukocytes and blood exude into the intestinal lumen. This inflammation leads to decreased fluid absorption by the colon and increased colonic motility. These processes also can cause decreased gastrointestinal motility, delayed gastric emptying, and functional ileus. The resulting luminal dilatation can lead to abdominal pain and vomiting. The same agent can cause diarrhea by multiple mechanisms. The causative agents of acute infectious diarrhea encountered most frequently are viruses; rotavirus is the most common. The most common cause of infectious, bloody diarrhea in the United States is Escherichia coli 0157. Table 31–3 lists common etiologic agents and the mechanisms by which they cause diarrhea.

Evaluation

The history and physical examination allow the clinician to narrow the diagnostic possibilities for acute diarrheal illnesses. Because the most common diagnoses associated with acute diarrhea are infectious in nature, a particular focus should be placed in this etiologic area. However, important historical and physical examination cues can suggest other gastrointestinal and systemic entities.

The history should include the onset, frequency, consistency, duration, and severity of the diarrhea. Questions to address hydration status are critical because most diarrheal illnesses are self-limited, and determining a specific cause is unnecessary when fluids and feedings are managed appropriately. (See Evaluation section under Vomiting for assessment of hydration status.) Special care must be taken in the assessment and treatment of infants under 2 months of age because they are at much greater risk of dehydration and morbidity from their illness. The presence of blood or mucus suggests nonviral infectious causes as well as other disorders associated with inflammation, such as inflammatory bowel disease (IBD). Associated gastrointestinal symptoms such as vomiting, abdominal pain, tenesmus, and anorexia should be addressed. Tenesmus is associated more often with bacterial processes. Intermittent abdominal pain associated with bloody stools and vomiting in young children is consistent with intussusception. Associated systemic symptoms such as fever help to support infectious causes but also are seen in inflammatory diseases. If contacts are ill with similar symptoms, viral infection is much more likely. Viral illness also is more common in winter months. Bacterial gastrointestinal illness occurs more frequently in the summer or warm months. Family history should include questions about gastrointestinal diseases such as IBD and food intolerance. Table 31–4 contains a list of questions that can be asked to assess risk for bacterial or parasitic infection.

The physical examination should begin with the assessment of the general appearance of the patient, with attention paid to the level of alertness, the degree of activity, and any presence of irritability and lethargy. Hydration status is assessed as discussed previously (see Evaluation section under Vomiting). An abdominal examination follows, with inspection for signs of distention as well as abdominal masses. Auscultation may reveal high-pitched "rushing" sounds that indicate increased motility. Palpation is performed to evaluate for presence of peritoneal signs as well as to deter-

TABLE 31–3. Common Etiologic Agents of Diarrhea

Secretory		Inflammatory	Osmotic	Cytotoxic
Escherichia coli	Bacillus cereus	Campylobacter fetus	Rotavirus	Rotavirus
Vibrio cholerae	Shigella	Clostridium difficile	Lactose	Norwalk agent
Clostridium difficile	Salmonella	Salmonella	Sorbitol	Crytosporidium
Campylobacter sp.	Yersinia enterocolitica	Shigella	Cystic fibrosis	E. coli
Clostridium perfringens	Giardia lamblia	Invasive E. coli	Malabsorption	Celiac disease (?)
Aeromonas hydrophila	Neuroblastoma	Yersinia enterocolitica	syndromes	
Plesiomonas shigelloides	Pheochromocytoma	Entamoeba histolytica	Small bowel	
Staphylococcus aureus	Carcinoid tumors	Inflammatory bowel	overgrowth	
Vibrio parahaemolyticus	Crytosporidium (?)	disease	Inflammatory bowel	
Rotavirus			disease	

Adapted from DeWitt TG: Acute diarrhea in children. Pediatr Rev 11(1):8, 1989. By permission of Pediatrics.

TABLE 31–4. Historical Assessment of Risk for Bacterial/Parasitic Infection

Question	Associated Infectious Agent
Does your child's diarrhea contain blood or mucus?	*Salmonella* *Shigella* *Yersinia enterocolitica* *Campylobacter* *Clostridium difficile* Toxigenic *Escherichia coli*
Have you and your children traveled to a foreign country recently?	Toxigenic *E. coli, Shigella, Entamoeba histolytica*
Are you or your children recent immigrants to this country?	Toxigenic *E. coli* (very recent immigrants) *Shigella* *Entamoeba histolytica* Multiple other parasitic diseases based on country of origin
Has your child gone camping recently?	*Giardia lamblia*
What type of water supply do you have in your home? Do you have well water?	*Giardia lamblia* *Cryptosporidium*
Does your child attend child care?	Rotavirus *Giardia lamblia* *Cryptosporidium* *Shigella*
Do you have any pet cats or dogs?	*Yersinia enterocolitica*
Do you have any pet reptiles (snake, turtle, iguana, etc.)?	*Salmonella*
Has your child eaten any of the following foods recently? Partially cooked or uncooked meats Raw seafood Dairy products/eggs	*Vibrio cholerae* (raw seafood) *Plesiomonas shigelloides* (raw seafood) *Salmonella* (dairy products/eggs) *Campylobacter* (dairy products)
Has your child recently eaten food at a picnic or place where food may have been without refrigeration for an extended period?	Toxin-mediated diseases—*Staphylococcus aureus, Bacillus cereus*
Has your child been on antibiotic therapy recently?	*Clostridium difficile*
Has your child had any seizures associated with this diarrheal illness?	*Shigella*
Does your child have an immune deficiency?	Increased risk for multiple agents—*Salmonella, Cryptosporidium*

mine the presence of hepatosplenomegaly. The perineal area is examined for fistulas or skin tags that may suggest IBD. Inspection of the stool and the use of a guaiac card help determine the presence of blood. Extraintestinal signs such as rash, lymphadenopathy, and arthritis also should be noted.

Laboratory Evaluation

In most acute diarrheal processes, laboratory evaluation is limited. Electrolytes, blood urea nitrogen, and creatinine will confirm and help quantify dehydration. The sodium level directs the selection of fluids and the rate of correction of dehydration. Because serum creatinine is low in infants, a creatinine level of 1 mg/dL may be double the patient's normal value. A high urine specific gravity supports dehydration. If bacterial pathogens are suspected, stool cultures should be sent. Some disagreement exists on whether stool leukocytes should be sent, even for patients at high risk for bacterial disease. Some argue that stool leukocyte tests, which now require processing by the laboratory, do not alter management when stool cultures are obtained simultaneously. However, those who recommend stool leukocyte tests suggest ordering these in patients at high risk for bacterial disease and in patients who have diarrheal disease persisting longer than 3 or 4 days. If leukocytes are present in the stool, there is an overall 70% chance of having bacterial infection. However, the actual percent chance varies widely with the individual pathogen, and the absence of white blood cells does not rule out bacterial processes. Tests for specific suspected agents should be requested (see Table 31–4). Knowledge of what a negative stool culture result means at your reference laboratory is critical.

MANAGEMENT OF VOMITING AND DIARRHEA

Hydration and Feeding Therapy

The goal of treating vomiting and diarrhea is to reduce clinical symptoms and to encourage return to the healthy state. **Correction of fluid and electrolyte imbalances is crucial in the treatment of vomiting and diarrhea.** Fluid and electrolyte losses are corrected in two phases: rehydration and maintenance. Rehydration in severely dehydrated patients or patients who have suspected surgical causes for vomiting and/or diarrhea should begin with intravenous infusion of 10 to 20 mL/kg of isotonic solution (lactated Ringer or normal saline). This should be followed by reassessment of the patient's clinical status. If still severely dehydrated, a repeat bolus should be administered. Once intravascular volume expansion has occurred, maintenance fluids can be initiated. Correction should occur over 16 to 24 hours in isotonic or hyponatremic dehydration. In hypernatremic dehydration, rehydration should occur over 24 to 48 hours to decrease the risk of seizures and neurologic sequelae. When surgical conditions are not being considered, nasogastric tube administration of fluid can be an alternative for patients who have no intravenous access.

In most patients who have mild to moderate dehydration, oral rehydration can and should be initiated. After the degree of dehydration from clinical signs and symptoms (see Table 31–1) is estimated, the deficit is replaced over 4 to 6 hours with a solution that has a sodium concentration between 50 and 90 meq/L and a glucose concentration of 2% to 3% (WHO-ORS, Rehydralyte, Infalyte). Maintenance therapy follows with an oral rehydration solution that has a slightly lower sodium concentration, 40 to 60 mEq/L (Pedialyte, Infalyte). Studies of patients who have noncholera diarrheal illness show that the same hydration solution with a sodium concentration of 45 to 90 mEq/L can be used for both the rehydration and maintenance phases in children who have mild to moderate dehydration. Table 31–5 lists appropriate therapy for different degrees of dehydration.

Liquids that have high carbohydrate concentrations (Jell-O water, soda, and Gatorade) should be avoided. Two more recently available items for assistance in rehydration are popsicles made from rehydration solutions and premeasured powder packets that can be mixed with 8 ounces of water. Small, frequent amounts of fluids in the maintenance phase are the key to success of oral rehydration therapy (ORT). ORT can be used to treat dehydration regardless of the age of the patient, the causative agent, or the type of dehydration (isotonic, hyponatremic, hypernatremic).

Standard glucose-based ORT solutions restore and maintain hydration; however, they have little effect on stool volume and frequency. Cereal-based ORT solutions have been developed recently to attempt to address these limitations of standard ORT. Polymers in cereal-based ORT are broken down rapidly at the intestinal cell surface. Osmolarity is not increased because the resulting glucose and amino acid components are quickly absorbed along with sodium and water. Cereal-based ORT can reduce stool volume by 20% to 30% but is not available commercially.

Early refeeding has been shown to decrease stool output, shorten duration of disease, and lessen the nutritional consequences of diarrhea. Children who are mildly dehydrated should be fed throughout their illness. Breast-fed infants can be nursed safely throughout diarrheal illnesses. Children who have moderate to severe dehydration should be fed as soon as possible after rehydration. Most formula-fed infants can return to full-strength cow's milk formulas. If diarrhea persists after reinstitution of the formula, the infant can be changed to a soy formula for 2 to 3 weeks. An older child's diet should include foods high in complex carbohydrates, such as the commonly recommended BRAT diet (bananas, rice, applesauce, and toast). However, this diet is low in energy, protein, and fat; therefore, the diet should be advanced as soon as tolerated.

Children who are severely dehydrated (>10%) often present with cardiovascular compromise and altered mental status and should be managed in the hospital. Patients who have 5% to 10% dehydration can be cared for at home if the clinician feels comfortable with the parent's ability to care for the child. Extreme parental anxiety or protracted vomiting by the child may necessitate hospital admission. For children who are less than 5% dehydrated, ORT can be given safely on an outpatient basis. Parents should be instructed on how to evaluate hydration status. In addition, parents should know to call or return for re-evaluation if signs or symptoms of dehydration do not improve or if they worsen.

Other Therapies

Antiemetics have no role in the treatment of infants and a very limited role in the treatment of older children. Promethazine (Phenergan) carries an increased risk for dystonic reactions and other central nervous system effects in children compared with adults. Indications for antidiarrheal

TABLE 31–5. Degree of Dehydration and Appropriate Rehydration and Maintenance Therapy

	Degree of Dehydration			
	None	*Mild*	*Moderate*	*Severe*
Rehydration therapy (replace existing loss)	None	Oral rehydration solution (50–90 mEq/L of sodium, 2%–3% glucose) 50 mL/kg (over 4–6 hr)	Oral rehydration solution (50–90 mEq/L of sodium, 2%–3% glucose) 100 mL/kg (over 4–6 hr)	Intravenous fluids 10–20 mL/kg boluses of LR or NS until vital signs stabilize, then 100 mL/kg IV fluids or oral rehydration solution (50–90 mEq/L of sodium, 2%–3% glucose)
Maintenance therapy (replace ongoing loss/ maintain adequate dietary intake)	Infants: Breast milk or full strength formula Older infants and children: Milk, juices, foods high in complex carbohydrates	Infants: Breast milk, regular strength cow's milk formula unless persistent diarrhea; then soy-based formula, oral rehydration solution (40–60 mEq/L sodium) Older children: Clear liquids, milk, foods high in complex carbohydrates Replace ongoing losses: 10 mL/kg for each stool, 2 mL/kg per episode of emesis	Infants: Breast milk, regular strength cow's milk formula unless persistent diarrhea; then soy-based formula, oral rehydration solution (40–60 mEq/L sodium) Older children: Clear liquids, milk, foods high in complex carbohydrates Replace ongoing losses: 10 mL/kg for each stool, 2 mL/kg per episode of emesis	Infants: Breast milk, regular strength cow's milk formula unless persistent diarrhea; then soy-based formula, oral rehydration solution (40–60 mEq/L sodium) Older children: Clear liquids, milk, foods high in complex carbohydrates Replace ongoing losses: 10 mL/kg for each stool, 2 mL/kg per episode of emesis

IV, intravenous; LR, lactated Ringer solution; NS, normal saline.
Adapted from Limbos MAP, Lieberman JM: Management of acute diarrhea in children. Contemp Pediatr 12(12):68,1995.

agents also are limited in pediatrics. Restricted use of these compounds has been suggested because of the limited studies that demonstrate improved outcomes in children taking medications as compared with controls. Pepto-Bismol (bismuth subsalicylate) has been successful in reducing stool volume and frequency. However, routine use may distract parents from focusing attention on the more important issues of hydration and feeding. Diphenoxylate and atropine sulfate (Lomotil) and loperamide (Imodium A-D) have no role in the treatment of infants and children; the risks of these medications outweigh their benefits. Both may decrease intestinal motility, resulting in increased length of illness and increased opportunity for certain organisms to cause invasive disease. These agents should *never be used in a patient who has bloody diarrhea*. No conclusive evidence is available to support the use of adsorbents such as attapulgite, cholestyramine, and mixtures of kaolin and pectin to reduce the duration of diarrhea or stool frequency. Recent studies of restoring intestinal microflora (*Lactobacillus casei, Bifidobacterium bifidum,* and *Streptococcus thermophilus*) with their associated immune properties to the intestine are encouraging, but further investi-

gation is warranted. The use of antimicrobials is also limited, even in diarrheal disease due to bacterial causes. *Shigella* infections should be treated with trimethoprim-sulfamethoxazole, ampicillin, or a third-generation cephalosporin because of the low inoculum necessary to transmit the infection. If *Shigella* is cultured from a patient in child care, the child should be excluded until cultures return negative. *Salmonella* infections only need to be treated if the child is at risk for invasive disease (immune-compromised children, infants younger than 3 to 6 months of age, and children who have hemoglobinopathies). Giardial infections should be treated with quinacrine, furazolidone, or metronidazole. *Cryptosporidium*, which can cause diarrheal outbreaks, has no uniformly effective treatment. In most immunocompetent children, no specific antimicrobial therapy is warranted.

The most effective management for all gastrointestinal illness is prevention. Simple practices such as good handwashing and hygiene can limit the spread of infection within households and child care settings. Avoidance of certain foods also decreases risk for certain pathogens (see Table 31–4). Hospitalizations and morbidity may be reduced if education about management of vomiting, diarrhea, and dehydration is included as part of anticipatory guidance at health supervision visits in the first year of life. Because many of the episodes of vomiting and diarrhea occur at this time, parents who have appropriate education can initiate treatment earlier in the course of disease. Researchers have developed rotavirus vaccines, and current trials to determine safety and efficacy are being undertaken. Although cholera is not a major causative agent of diarrhea in the United States, cholera vaccines would help to minimize the morbidity from infectious diarrhea worldwide. Until new preventive technologies are available, the cornerstone of successful management of de-

hydration in acute vomiting and diarrheal illness rests on ORT.

FURTHER READING

Limbos MAP, Lieberman JM. Management of acute diarrhea in children. Contemp Pediatr 12(12):68, 1995.

The management of acute diarrhea in children: Oral rehydration, maintenance, and nutritional therapy. MMWR, Vol 41, 1992.

Meyers A. Fluid and electrolyte therapy for children. Curr Opinion Pediatr 6:303, 1994.

Practice parameter: The management of acute gastroenteritis in young children. American Academy of Pediatrics, Provisional Committee on Quality Improvement, Subcommittee on Acute Gastroenteritis. Pediatrics, 97(3):424–435, 1996.

Jerry Bergstein

Chapter 32

Urinary Tract Infections

Treatment of symptomatic urinary tract infections (UTIs) is indicated because of the morbidity of the acute infection. Perhaps even more important, radiologic studies performed subsequent to the detection of infection may lead to the discovery of anatomic lesions (e.g., obstruction, reflux) whose management may prevent ongoing kidney damage.

CLINICAL MANIFESTATIONS

During the first 3 months of life, UTIs are more common among boys than girls due to a higher frequency of structural abnormalities, and the presence of a foreskin. Uncircumcised boys have a 10- to 20-fold higher rate of infection than circumcised boys because of a larger number of potentially pathogenic periurethral bacteria. Beyond 3 months, UTIs are much more common among girls. During infancy, UTIs may arise from bacteremia or fecal organisms ascending the urethra; after 2 months of age, ascending infections are most common.

The signs and symptoms of UTI in various age groups are listed in Table 32–1. **The symptoms of urinary tract infection in small children may not point to the urinary tract as the source of the child's illness.** Because the physical examination rarely is helpful in the diagnosis of UTI,

appropriate laboratory studies are required to confirm the diagnosis.

DIAGNOSIS

The best test to confirm the diagnosis of urinary tract infection is the urine culture. Thus, all children who have a febrile illness not explained by findings on the physical examination should have a urine culture performed. Because the results of the culture may not be available for 48 hours, other tests can be used that immediately will suggest any presence of a UTI.

The screening test used most frequently to detect infection is the microscopic examination of urine sediment for leukocytes (pyuria) and bacteria. Unfortunately, the correlation between the numbers of leukocytes and bacteria in the urinaly-

TABLE 32–1. Signs and Symptoms of Urinary Tract Infection

Newborn
Fever, irritability, vomiting, poor feeding, diarrhea, jaundice
Infants
Fever, irritability, diarrhea, abdominal pain, diaper rash, failure to thrive
Older Children
Urgency, frequency, dysuria, abdominal pain, enuresis

sis and a positive culture is not high, thus limiting the diagnostic value of the urinalysis. In general, a UTI is unlikely if a spun urine contains fewer than five white blood cells (WBC) per high-power field. On the other hand, a urine sediment that contains large numbers of WBCs and bacteria correlates sufficiently with a positive urine culture, so that therapy may be initiated on the basis of the sediment findings. It still is prudent to send for a urine culture to confirm the diagnosis and to obtain antibiotic sensitivities to the organism.

Certain studies, which usually can be done with the results of a urine dipstick test, have been promoted as rapid diagnostic tests for UTI. Examples include the leukocyte esterase test, which detects an enzyme derived from neutrophils, and the nitrite test. The accuracy of the leukocyte esterase test is compromised because there are many causes of pyuria (e.g., nonbacterial infections, local irritation, glomerulonephritis, interstitial nephritis) other than bacterial infection of the urine. The accuracy of the nitrite test is compromised by two factors: (1) Only certain of the gram-negative organisms (and none of the gram-positive organisms) have the metabolic capacity to reduce nitrate to nitrite, and (2) because it takes several hours for sufficient nitrite to accumulate in the urine to give a positive test, the test is most likely to be positive on the first sample taken in the morning. It is positive less commonly in the typical patient who comes to the office later in the day having voided frequently all day. Studies indicate that the sensitivity (a positive test is associated with a positive urine culture) and specificity (a negative test is associated with a negative culture) of these tests are variable (Table 32–2). Thus, they are of limited value in diagnosing urinary tract infection.

The quantitative bacterial colony count technique was developed originally to distinguish between contamination and infection of the urine. Initial studies suggested that in a clean-catch, midstream specimen, counts of 100,000 or more colonies per milliliter of a single organism yield a 95% chance of true infection. Subsequent studies reduced the accuracy to 80% to 85%. Thus, 15% to 20% of patients who have colony counts of 100,000 will have a contaminated specimen. **Recent studies indicate that in symptomatic patients, colony counts as low as 100 per milliliter indicate infection.** Because most microbiology laboratories will discard specimens that have such low colony counts as contaminants, be certain to write on the culture request of all symptomatic patients that sensitivity testing should be performed on any growth cultures.

Before toilet training, children's urine specimens for culture commonly are obtained by using bag devices. Because these devices are easily contaminated, such cultures are significant only if sterile, indicating that infection is absent. Growth of any number of organisms must be confirmed by catheterization or suprapubic aspiration cultures. Because urine obtained by suprapubic aspiration is rarely contaminated, growth of any number of bacteria suggests infection. Since catheterization may introduce small numbers of organisms into the bladder and contaminate the specimen, infection is indicated by a colony count of more than 100 per milliliter.

TREATMENT

At the initial evaluation of the patient who has a urinary tract infection, it is important to distinguish clinically between lower (bladder) and upper (pyelonephritis) tract infection. Clinical manifestations of pyelonephritis include fever, chills, vomiting, flank pain, and enlargement of the involved kidney(s). The urine will show many WBCs and may contain WBC casts. Renal function will be decreased in bilateral pyelonephritis. Patients who are diagnosed clinically with pyelonephritis should be hospitalized. Immediately after blood and urine cultures (a lumbar puncture also should be considered in infants) are obtained, ultrasound should be performed to rule out obstruction. The child then should be started on intravenous ampicillin and gentamicin until the culture results are available.

Most UTIs are bladder infections. The choice of a therapeutic agent is mandated by 90% of bladder infections being caused by *Escherichia coli*. **Cost and efficacy suggest generic trimethoprim-sulfamethoxazole as the agent of choice.** Should the child be allergic to sulfa, alternatives include nitrofurantoin, amoxicillin, and cephalexin. Although recent studies suggest than 1 to 3 days of antibiotic therapy may be sufficient in some children, **a full 10-day course of treatment is recommended in all children** until the merits of short-course therapy are confirmed.

During the course of therapy, no additional studies (e.g., urinalysis and/or culture) are necessary if sensitivity studies confirm that the of-

TABLE 32–2. Sensitivity and Specificity of Rapid Diagnostic Assays

Assay	Sensitivity	Specificity
Leukocyte esterase	74%–96%	71%–98%
Nitrate	22%–93%	70%–98%

fending organism is susceptible to the antibacterial agent being used. Another urine culture should be obtained approximately 1 week after completion of therapy to be certain that the infection has been cured. If the follow-up culture is sterile and subsequent radiographic studies are normal, surveillance cultures for asymptomatic infections are unnecessary (see Screening for Asymptomatic Bacteriuria further on). Additional cultures need be obtained only if symptomatic infection is suspected.

RADIOGRAPHIC STUDIES

Radiographic studies after the first urinary tract infection in a male at any age are needed because of the high frequency of underlying anatomic abnormality. This evaluation should consist of both a renal ultrasound and a voiding cystourethrogram.

The need for radiographic studies after the first infection in girls remains controversial. The argument that studies should not be performed until after the second infection because UTIs are so common in girls is no longer tenable because 80% of girls who have one infection will have another, usually within a year. The data available suggest that the chance of detecting a significant anatomic abnormality (reflux, obstruction) in girls correlates inversely with age. Infections during the first 5 years of life lead most frequently to renal scarring, perhaps due in part to this being the time of most rapid renal growth. Thus, for girls presenting with a first infection under the age of 5 years, we recommend both a renal ultrasound and a voiding cystourethrogram. Following a first infection in girls between the ages of 6 and 10 years, only an ultrasound is recommended. Granted, mild reflux will be missed, but such reflux generally is due to infection and will resolve in the absence of further infection. Girls suffering a first infection beyond age 10 do not require radiologic studies, because radiographic abnormalities are rare in this group. Should patients 6 years and older suffer recurrent UTIs, an ultrasound and voiding cystourethrogram should be performed to rule out structural abnormalities.

REFLUX

Reflux is defined as the regurgitation of urine from the bladder into the ureter. It is due to a defect in the valvelike mechanism created by the intramural portion of the terminal ureter. Reflux at any age is abnormal; there is no maturational component to the function of the valvelike mechanism.

The international classification of reflux is listed in Table 32–3. The subject of reflux is extremely controversial, and despite national and international studies on the subject, the significance of reflux remains to be determined. Reflux does not predispose to infection, but infection causes most reflux. Approximately 80% of reflux is due to infection, the remainder being associated with structural abnormalities of the urinary tract. Reflux due to infection usually falls within grades I to III and usually resolves in the absence of additional infections. Grades IV and V reflux rarely resolve. They frequently accompany other developmental anomalies of the kidneys and/or lower urinary tract and may be associated with decreased growth and progressive scarring of the kidneys in the absence of additional infections.

The optimal management of reflux is unknown. Recent studies comparing medical with surgical management in children who have grades III and IV reflux show no advantage to either form of therapy. **The initial treatment of grades I to IV reflux is suppressive therapy** (see next section) to prevent the development of a UTI while the reflux, it is hoped, resolves. Although reflux does not predispose to infection, should infection occur, the infected urine would be refluxed to the kidneys, placing the patient at risk for the development of pyelonephritis and renal scarring. At yearly intervals, a [99m]technetium-dimercaptosuccinic acid (DMSA) renal scan or renal ultrasound should be obtained (to monitor the kidneys for growth and scarring) and the voiding cystourethrogram repeated (to see if the reflux has resolved). If the reflux has resolved, suppressive therapy may be discontinued. Indications for antireflux surgery include (1) any grade of reflux with persistent infection; (2) grade IV reflux when associated with decreased growth or progressive scarring; and (3) the presence of grade V reflux (renal growth may improve after the correction of gross reflux).

A brief word about the role of cystoscopy in the evaluation of the initial urinary tract infection. If the appropriate radiographic studies are normal,

TABLE 32–3. International Classification of Vesicoureteral Reflux

Grade I	Ureter only
Grade II	Ureter, pelvis, calyces without dilatation
Grade III	Mild dilatation of ureter and pelvis
Grade IV	Moderate dilatation of ureter, pelvis, and calyces
Grade V	Gross dilatation of ureter, pelvis, and calyces

cystoscopy is not indicated. If reflux is detected in males, cystoscopy may be indicated to rule out posterior urethral valves. In females, cystoscopy may be indicated if a lower tract abnormality (e.g., ureterocele) is suspected. The possibility of urethral stenosis in females should not be invoked as a reason for cystoscopy, because this lesion is extremely rare.

SUPPRESSIVE THERAPY

Candidates for suppressive (also called prophylactic) therapy include patients who have reflux and those who, despite normal radiographic studies, suffer recurrent symptomatic UTIs. The latter are defined as three culture-proven symptomatic infections in a 12-month period. The purpose of long-term suppression is to prevent recurrent infections. Because most infections derive from fecal organisms ascending to the bladder, suppression is accomplished with an agent that will eradicate these organisms over the course of therapy. **Trimethoprim-sulfamethoxazole is the agent of choice** because it reduces or eliminates enterobacteriaceae from the fecal flora, and any remaining organisms remain susceptible to it.

Although the best regimen for suppression has not been defined, the following protocol is recommended. Before initiating suppression, existing infection must be eradicated and follow-up culture sterile. Trimethoprim-sulfamethoxazole is started at therapeutic dosage and continued at this dosage for 3 months. Patients allergic to sulfa may be treated with nitrofurantoin (Macrodantin). After 3 months of suppression, a urine culture is obtained. If this is sterile, the dosage is cut in half but continued twice daily (breakfast and bedtime). This reduced dosage is continued for the duration of suppression. During suppression, a culture should be obtained promptly if the patient develops symptoms of UTI or fever unexplained by findings on the physical examination. For patients treated for recurrent infections despite normal anatomy, the duration of suppression is 1 year. Following completion of suppression, further cultures are unnecessary unless symptoms arise. For the rare patient who again suffers recurrent symptomatic infections after 1 year of suppression, a second year is recommended. For patients who have reflux, suppression may be continued until the reflux resolves or is surgically corrected.

SCREENING FOR ASYMPTOMATIC BACTERIURIA

Several studies indicate that the prevalence of asymptomatic urinary tract infections in girls is between 1% and 3% and that 5% of girls will acquire an asymptomatic infection at some time during their school years (the prevalence in boys is too low to be considered). These data have been used to promote the screening of girls for asymptomatic infections in the hope that (1) early detection and treatment of asymptomatic infection will prevent the morbidity of symptomatic infection, and (2) the subsequent detection of anatomic abnormalities might prevent progressive upper tract damage.

However, **the results of recent studies militate against routine screening for asymptomatic infection.** *E. coli* found in girls who have asymptomatic infection differ from those found in girls who have symptomatic infection. These asymptomatic "infections" usually resolve spontaneously and rarely result in symptomatic infection. Treatment of asymptomatic infection leads to recolonization of the urinary tract with new bacteria that may be more virulent, leading to infection that can produce symptoms and upper tract damage. Thus, nontreatment actually may prevent symptomatic infection.

Asymptomatic infections occasionally may be associated with upper tract scarring. Yet this scarring, which usually begins before 5 years of age, is rarely progressive and does not lead to renal failure. Finally, the treatment of asymptomatic UTIs seems to have no effect on the clearing of reflux, the progression of renal scars, or the later development of hypertension. Thus, the screening of girls for asymptomatic infection cannot be recommended.

FURTHER READING

Kunin CM: Urinary tract infection in females. Clin Infect Dis 18:1–12, 1994.
Lindshaw M: Asymptomatic bacteriuria and vesicoureteral reflux in children. Kidney Int 50:312–329, 1996.
Roberts JA: Factors predisposing to urinary tract infections in children. Pediatr Nephrol 10:517–522, 1996.
Sherbotie JR, and Cornfeld D: Management of urinary tract infections in children. Med Clin North Am 75:327–338, 1991.
Stamm WE, and Hooton TM: Management of urinary tract infections in adults. N Engl J Med 329:1328–1334, 1993.

Cynthia Christy

Chapter 33

Sexually Transmitted Disease Syndromes

BACKGROUND AND OBJECTIVES

Sexually transmitted disease is the most common infection among sexually active adolescents. Of the 20 million cases of sexually transmitted diseases (STDs) reported each year, 30% occur in adolescents. From 1981 to 1991, 24% to 30% of the reported morbidity from gonorrhea and 10% to 12% of the reported morbidity from primary and secondary syphilis in the United States were in adolescents. **Because sexually transmitted diseases can present with or without symptoms, screening by history, physical examination, and appropriate laboratory tests are indicated for all adolescents and children at increased risk for STDs.** High-risk adolescents include those who are sexually active; are pregnant and undergoing therapeutic abortion; present with symptoms compatible with an STD; live in group homes; are suspected of being a victim of sexual violence; are prostitutes; are street youth; and are drug and/or alcohol abusers.

The management of STDs has been based on the causative agents responsible for the diagnosis, such as *Neisseria gonorrhoeae* and *Chlamydia trachomatis*; however, because more than one STD frequently coexist in a patient, a syndrome-based approach to the diagnosis and management of STDs has developed. Common syndromes are presented in this chapter; the tables detail the appropriate methods of diagnosis and treatment. A comprehensive review of STDs is available in the Centers for Disease Control and Prevention (CDC) guidelines and the *1997 Red Book* of the American Academy of Pediatrics.

CLINICAL SYNDROMES

Vaginitis; Cervicitis

Vaginitis, defined as infection or irritation of the vaginal mucosa and/or the cervix, follows exposure to chemical irritation or an STD agent and generally presents with vaginal discharge and vulvar irritation. In prepubertal girls, factors such as poor hygiene, the proximity of the rectum to the vagina, the presence of undifferentiated cuboidal vaginal epithelium, and the lack of protection by labial fat pads and pubic hair are believed to increase the chance of vulvovaginal irritation. With the onset of puberty and estrogenization, the vaginal epithelium shifts from cuboidal to a glycogen-containing, stratified squamous epithelium. An increase in growth of lactobacilli leads to the production of lactic acid, with a drop in the vaginal pH from 7.0 to 4.0 to 4.5. Because these changes make the vagina relatively resistant to infection by *C. trachomatis* and *N. gonorrhoeae,* cervicitis rather than vulvovaginitis occurs.

In the preadolescent, the causes of vaginitis can be grouped into allergic or contact reactions (such as to soap or bubble bath), physical factors (such as a foreign body), or specific microbiologic causes such as *Shigella,* other gram-negative enteric bacteria, *Staphylococcus aureus*, and group A streptococci. For the younger child, it is important to obtain specimens for culture, Gram stain, and suspension in 10% potassium hydroxide (KOH preparation). The evaluation also should include an evaluation for pinworms by the cellophane tape test immediately on awakening.

Vaginitis in the postpubertal girl usually is caused by *Candida albicans, Trichomonas vaginalis,* or bacterial vaginosis. Symptoms suggestive of vaginitis include a vaginal discharge, dysuria, and vulvar itching; signs include an abnormal vaginal discharge and vulvar or vaginal irritation. Sexually active females who have vaginitis should be evaluated for candidiasis, bacterial vaginosis, *T. vaginalis,* gonorrhea, and chlamydial infection. The cause of vaginitis usually can be identified by microscopic examination of fresh samples of vaginal discharge. The clinical characteristics and methods of diagnosis of the causes of vaginitis are listed in Table 33–1.

TABLE 33–1. Clinical Characteristics and Methods of Diagnosis of the Common Causes of Vaginitis

		Bacterial Vaginosis	Candidal Vaginitis	Trichomonal Vaginitis
Symptoms		Malodorous discharge, no dyspareunia	Discharge (usually not malodorous) Vaginal pruritus Dysuria, dyspareunia	Discharge (may be malodorous) Vulvar pruritus Dysuria, dyspareunia
Signs	*Discharge*	Thin, white, ± frothy, clings to vaginal wall	Thick, curdlike	Heavy, yellow-green, frothy
Laboratory Diagnosis	*pH*	>4.7	<4.5	>5.0
	KOH preparation	"Fishy" amine odor	Yeasts or pseudohyphae (70%)	
	Saline preparation	Clue cells (>90%) Few WBCs	WBCs and epithelial cells	Motile trichomonads (60%) WBCs
	Gram stain	Numerous mixed bacteria: small curved rods and cocci, few large gram-positive rods*	Hyphae and pseudohyphae	Trichomonads rarely visible
	Culture	Not useful	Useful if KOH is negative	More sensitive than wet mount preparation

*Consistent with lactobacilli.
KOH, potassium hydroxide; WBC, white blood cell.
Adapted from Centers for Disease Control and Prevention: 1998 Guidelines for treatment of sexually transmitted diseases. MMWR 47(No. RR-1):18–85, 1998; and MacDonald NE, Gully PR, Cameron DW, and Samson LM: Sexually transmitted disease syndromes, skin and mucous membrane infections and inguinal lymphadenopathy, urethritis, vulvovaginitis, and cervicitis and pelvic inflammatory disease. *In* Long SS, Pickering LK, and Prober CG (eds): Principles and Practice of Pediatric Infectious Diseases. New York, Churchill Livingstone, 1997.

Bacterial Vaginosis

CLINICAL MANIFESTATIONS. Bacterial vaginosis (BV), the most common vaginal infection among sexually active adolescents and adult women, is characterized by the presence of a profuse, malodorous, white discharge. It also may be asymptomatic. Bacterial vaginosis results from the replacement of the normal H_2O_2-producing *Lactobacillus* species in the vagina with anaerobic bacteria (e.g., *Bacteroides* species, *Mobiluncus* species), *Mycoplasma hominis*, and *Gardnerella vaginalis*.

DIAGNOSIS. The diagnosis of BV requires the presence of three of the following symptoms or signs: (1) a homogeneous, white, noninflammatory discharge that sticks to the vaginal wall; (2) clue cells; (3) a pH of vaginal fluid greater than 4.5; and (4) a fishy or "amine" odor of the vaginal discharge before or after the addition of 10% KOH (the "whiff" test). Clue cells are squamous vaginal epithelial cells covered with many vaginal bacteria that cause a stippled or granular appearance. In BV, clue cells make up at least 20% of the vaginal epithelial cells.

TREATMENT. Symptomatic patients should be treated with metronidazole (see Table 33–2). Lower-dose metronidazole (250 mg three times daily for 7 days), single-dose metronidazole (2 grams), or clindamycin (300 mg twice daily for 7

days) is recommended for the treatment of symptomatic pregnant women after the first trimester. Treatment of male sexual partners does not influence the relapse or recurrence rate of BV.

Candida albicans Vulvovaginitis

CLINICAL MANIFESTATIONS. Vulvovaginal candidiasis caused by *C. albicans* is very common: 75% of women experience at least one episode during their lifetime, and 40% to 45% experience two or more episodes. The typical symptoms of vulvovaginal candidiasis (see Table 33–1) include vaginal pruritus and discharge.

DIAGNOSIS. The diagnosis of candidal vaginitis, suggested by the nonspecific clinical symptoms in addition to a white vaginal discharge, is confirmed by the presence of yeasts or pseudohyphae on a wet preparation or Gram stain of the vaginal discharge (see Table 33–1). The ability to see the organism is improved by adding 10% KOH to the saline wet preparation. This addition disrupts cells that obscure the yeast forms.

TREATMENT. Topical treatments such as butoconazole, clotrimazole, miconazole, terconazole, and tioconazole are effective in 80% to 90% of patients who have candidal vaginitis. Because 10% to 20% of women are colonized with *Candida* species and other yeasts in the vagina, only

TABLE 33–2. Treatment of Sexually Transmitted Diseases (Based on 1998 CDC Recommendations)

		Drug	Dosage
I.	Bacterial vaginosis	Metronidazole*†	500 mg orally 2 times a day for 7 days, *or*
		Clindamycin cream, (2%)	One applicator (5 gm) intravaginally at bedtime for 7 days, *or*
		Metronidazole gel*†	0.75%, one applicator (5 gm) intravaginally 2 times a day for 5 days
II.	Candidal vaginitis	Butoconazole (2% cream)	5 gm intravaginally for 3 days, *or*
		Clotrimazole (1% cream)	5 gm intravaginally for 7–14 days, *or*
		Miconazole (2% cream)	5 gm intravaginally for 7 days, *or*
		Fluconazole	150 mg orally in a single dose
III.	Trichomonas vaginitis	Metronidazole†	2 gm orally in a single dose, *or*
			500 mg orally 2 times a day for 7 days, *or*
			15 mg/kg/day in 3 doses for 7 days for prepubertal children
IV.	Chlamydial infection Urethritis, endocervicitis, or proctitis (Because of the high rate of coinfection with *Neisseria gonorrhoeae,* presumptive treatment for gonorrhea is necessary)	Doxycycline	100 mg orally 2 times a day for 7 days, *or*
		Azithromycin	1 gm orally in a single dose, *or*
		Erythromycin base	50 mg/kg/day divided in 4 doses for 10–14 days for children <8 years old
	Chlamydial infection in pregnancy	Erythromycin base	500 mg orally 4 times a day for 7 days, *or*
		Amoxicillin‡	500 mg orally 3 times a day for 7 days
	Ophthalmia neonatorum or infant pneumonia	Erythromycin	50 mg/kg/day orally divided into 4 doses for 10–14 days
V.	Nongonococcal urethritis	Use same therapy as for chlamydial urethritis	
VI.	Gonorrhea Uncomplicated: urethritis, endocervicitis, proctitis, assuming possible coexisting chlamydial infection	Ceftriaxone	125 mg IM in a single dose, *or*
		Cefixime	400 mg in a single dose, *or*
		Ciprofloxacin	500 mg in a single dose, *plus*
		Azithromycin	20 mg/kg (maximum, 1 gm) in a single dose, *or*
		Doxycycline	100 mg 2 times a day for 7 days
	Complicated: meningitis or endocarditis	Ceftriaxone	1–2 gm IV every 12 hours; duration depends on illness
	Gonococcal conjunctivitis	Ceftriaxone	50 mg/kg (maximum, 1 gm) IM in a single dose
	Disseminated gonococcal infection	Ceftriaxone	1 gm IM or IV every 24 hours for 24–48 hours after improvement begins; then therapy should be switched to one of the following regimens to complete 7 days of therapy with:
		Cefixime	400 mg orally 2 times a day, *or*
		Ciprofloxacin§	500 mg orally 2 times a day
	Gonorrhea in pregnancy		**Do not** use quinolones or tetracyclines. Possibilities include the recommended alternate cephalosporin regimens, *or*
		Spectinomycin	2 g IM, *plus*
	(Plus a regimen effective against possible coinfection with *Chlamydia trachomatis*)	Erythromycin base	500 mg orally 4 times a day for 7 days, *or*
		Amoxicillin	500 mg orally 3 times a day for 7 days
VII.	Acute pelvic inflammatory disease Endometritis, salpingitis, parametritis Inpatient treatment		
	Regimen A	Cefoxitin	2 gm IV every 6 hr, *or*
		Cefotetan	2 gm IV every 12 hours (continued at least 24 hours until patient demonstrates clinical improvement), *plus*
		Doxycycline	100 mg IV or orally 2 times daily to complete a 14-day course
	Regimen B	Clindamycin	900 mg IV every 8 hours, *plus*
		Gentamicin	1.5 mg/kg IV every 8 hours (continued at least 24 hours after patient demonstrates clinical improvement), *plus*
		Doxycycline	100 mg 2 times daily to complete a 14-day course
	Outpatient treatment		
	Regimen A	Ofloxacin	400 mg orally 2 times a day for 14 days, *plus*
		Metronidazole*†	500 mg orally 2 times a day for 14 days
	Regimen B	Cefoxitin	2 gm IM plus Probenecid 1 g orally, *or*
		Ceftriaxone	250 mg IM, *plus*
		Doxycycline	100 mg orally 2 times a day for 14 days

TABLE 33–2. Treatment of Sexually Transmitted Diseases (Based on 1998 CDC Recommendations)

		Drug	Dosage
VIII.	Genital herpes simplex infections		
	First episode of genital herpes	Acyclovir	400 mg orally 3 times a day for 7–10 days, *or*
			200 mg orally 5 times a day for 7–10 days, *or*
		Famciclovir	250 mg orally 3 times a day for 7–10 days, *or*
		Valacyclovir	1 gm orally 2 times a day for 7–10 days
	Recurrent episodes	Acyclovir	400 mg orally 3 times a day for 5 days, *or*
			200 mg orally 5 times a day for 5 days, *or*
			800 mg orally 2 times a day for 5 days, *or*
		Famciclovir	125 mg orally 2 times a day for 5 days, *or*
		Valacyclovir	500 mg orally 2 times a day for 5 days
IX.	Syphilis		
	Primary and secondary		
	Adult	Benzathine penicillin G	2.4 million units IM in a single dose
	Child	Benzathine penicillin G	50,000 units/kg IM (up to the adult dose of 2.4 million units in a single dose)
	For penicillin allergy	Doxycycline	100 mg orally 2 times a day for 14 days, *or*
		Tetracycline	500 mg orally 4 times a day for 14 days
	Latent syphilis		
	Early latent syphilis	Benzathine penicillin G	2.4 million units IM in a single dose (for children: 50,000 units/kg/dose up to the adult dose)
	Late latent syphilis or latent syphilis of unknown duration	Benzathine penicillin G	7.2 million units total, given as 3 doses of 2.4 million units IM at 1-wk intervals (for children: 50,000 units/kg/dose up to the adult dose)
	Congenital syphilis	Aqueous crystalline penicillin G	100,000–150,000 units/kg/day (administered as 50,000 units/kg IV every 12 hr during the first 7 days and every 8 hr thereafter) for 10 days, *or*
		Procaine penicillin G	50,000 units/kg/dose IM a day in a single dose for 10 days
X.	Chancroid	Azithromycin	1 gm orally in a single dose, *or*
		Ceftriaxone	250 mg IM in a single dose, *or*
		Erythromycin base	500 mg orally 4 times a day for 7 days, *or*
		Ciprofloxacin§	500 mg orally twice a day for 3 days
XI.	Lymphogramuloma venereum	Doxycycline (for patients ≥8 years old)	100 mg 2 times a day for 21 days, *or*
		Erythromycin base	50 mg/kg/day (maximum 500 mg) orally 4 times a day for 21 days
XII.	Granuloma inguinale	Doxycycline (for patients ≥8 years old)	100 mg orally 2 times a day for a minimum of 21 days, *or*
		Trimethoprim-sulfamethoxazole (TMP-SMX)	1 double-strength (160 mg TMP, 800 mg SMX) orally 2 times a day for a minimum of 21 days

*Contraindicated in first trimester of pregnancy; consult 1998 CDC Guidelines for use in pregnancy.
†Patients should be advised to avoid alcohol during treatment with metronidazole and for 24 hours afterward.
‡If erythromycin is not tolerated.
§Contraindicated in patients ≤17 years old.
IM, intramuscular; IV, intravenous.
Adapted From Centers for Disease Control and Prevention: 1998 Guidelines for treatment of sexually transmitted diseases. MMWR 47 (No. RR-1):18–95, 1998.

symptomatic patients should be treated. Intravaginal preparations of butoconazole, clotrimazole, miconazole, and triconazole are available over the counter. Single-dose oral fluconazole (150 mg) is also effective in adolescents and adults who have mild to moderate disease. Treatment of sexual partners is not indicated because it does not prevent recurrences, and this infection is neither sexually acquired nor transmitted.

Trichomonas vaginalis Vulvovaginitis

CLINICAL MANIFESTATIONS. Trichomoniasis, which is caused by the flagellated protozoan *T. vaginalis*, is a sexually transmitted infection that frequently coexists with other STDs. Although most men infected with this organism are asymptomatic, many women experience symptoms, including vulvar irritation and a malodorous, yellow-green discharge. Dysuria (30% to 50%) and abdominal pain (in up to 12%) also may occur. Because the prepubertal vagina does not support the growth of *T. vaginalis*, this organism, if present, probably represents urinary tract infection or sexual abuse.

DIAGNOSIS. The diagnosis is suggested by the symptoms and confirmed by identification of the motile organism on a saline wet preparation (see Table 33–1); however, saline wet preparations correctly identify the protozoan in only 40% to 80% of cases. Culture of *T. vaginalis* (positive in

>95% of cases) and antibody tests using direct or indirect immunofluorescent antibody or enzyme-linked immunoassay tests, although more sensitive than wet preparations, usually are not needed for diagnosis.

TREATMENT. Oral single-dose metronidazole is the preferred therapy. Sexual partners also should be treated. Patients who have *T. vaginalis* infection should be evaluated for other STDs.

Cervicitis

CLINICAL MANIFESTATIONS. Mucopurulent cervicitis is characterized by a yellow endocervical exudate. This infection usually begins in the endocervix, where the columnar epithelium remains after the ectocervix develops squamous epithelium at puberty. Cervicitis is uncommon in prepubertal children. Some women may have no symptoms; others may experience an abnormal vaginal discharge, abnormal vaginal bleeding (e.g., after intercourse), or symptoms of an associated urethritis. The condition may be due to *N. gonorrhoeae* or *C. trachomatis,* although in most cases neither organism is identified. Other possible etiologies include herpes simplex virus (HSV), actinomycetes (associated with the presence of an intrauterine device [IUD], group B streptococci, and cytomegalovirus.

DIAGNOSIS. The clinical diagnosis is based on the presence of yellow, mucopurulent cervical discharge or the detection of white blood cells (WBCs) (from >5 to 30 WBCs per high-power field) under oil immersion. Cervical changes may be subtle or progress to an intensely erythematous and friable appearance. Organism-specific testing for *N. gonorrhoeae* or *C. trachomatis* is indicated in sexually active adolescents. Patients who have severe cervicitis or ulcerative cervicitis unresponsive to conventional therapy should have cultures for HSV obtained, because this organism has been found in 10% to 20% of cases.

The results of tests for *C. trachomatis* or *N. gonorrhoeae* determine the treatment needed. Empirical therapy may be indicated if the likelihood of infection is high and the patient may not return for follow-up (see Table 33–2). Sexual partners of women who have mucopurulent cervicitis should be evaluated and treated on the basis of their test results.

Urethritis

Urethritis is an inflammation of the urethra characterized by a purulent, mucoid discharge and/or pruritus and dysuria. Asymptomatic infections occur commonly. The two common bacterial agents causing urethritis among men are *N. gonorrhoeae* and *C. trachomatis*. Specific testing is recommended to determine the cause and to facilitate treatment of sexual partners.

Nongonococcal Urethritis

CLINICAL MANIFESTATIONS. Nongonococcal urethritis (NGU) is characterized by a purulent discharge and the presence of five or more polymorphonuclear leukocytes per oil immersion field on a fresh smear of a urethral exudate. *C. trachomatis* is the most common cause, accounting for 23% to 55% of cases. Complications of NGU due to *C. trachomatis* can include epididymitis and Reiter syndrome. Other causes include *Ureaplasma urealyticum* (20% to 30% of cases) and *T. vaginalis* (2% to 5% of cases). HSV occasionally causes NGU.

DIAGNOSIS. A Gram-stained smear of urethral exudate should be evaluated for WBCs and the absence of gram-negative intracellular organisms. Increasingly, the leukocyte esterase test (LET) is being used to screen urine for NGU from asymptomatic sexually active males. The diagnosis should be confirmed in males who have a positive urine LET by a Gram-stained smear of a urethral swab specimen and culture for *N. gonorrhoeae* and *C. trachomatis*.

TREATMENT. The recommended treatment of NGU is doxycycline or azithromycin (see Table 33–2). If patients do not respond to initial treatment, a wet mount examination for *T. vaginalis* and a culture for HSV should be performed. Sexual partners are at risk for chlamydial infection and its associated complications and should be treated after evaluation.

Chlamydial Infections

CLINICAL MANIFESTATIONS. **C. trachomatis infection is the most common sexually transmitted infection in the United States. The highest rates of infection occur in sexually active adolescents and younger adults.** It has a variety of clinical manifestations ranging from urethritis and vaginitis in prepubertal girls to cervicitis, perihepatitis, and pelvic inflammatory disease in postpubertal females. **Sexually active adolescents should be screened for C. trachomatis even if they are asymptomatic during annual examinations.** *C. trachomatis* causes epididymitis in males and Reiter syndrome in either sex. The infection can be chronic, and reinfection is common.

Infection in adolescents and adults is transmitted by sexual activity. Coinfection with *N. gonorrhoeae* is common, so presumptive treatment is indicated. In prepubertal children beyond infancy who have genital *C. trachomatis,* one should suspect child abuse, although perinatally acquired infection can be present up to 3 years of age. The diagnosis in prepubertal children must be by cell culture techniques because of their high specificity.

DIAGNOSIS. The definitive diagnosis of chlamydial infection is by tissue culture. Because these organisms are obligate intracellular pathogens, epithelial cells must be present in the culture specimen. The tests currently available for chlamydial antigen or nucleic acid include (1) direct fluorescent antibody staining for elementary bodies, (2) enzyme-linked immunofluorescent antibody, (3) nucleic acid amplification, and (4) DNA probe analysis. Tests for the detection of chlamydial antigen are useful from symptomatic males, symptomatic and asymptomatic women, and infants who have conjunctivitis (conjunctival specimens). When child sexual abuse is suspected, a culture of the organism is required for diagnosis.

TREATMENT. Uncomplicated genital infection in adolescents and adults is treated with oral doxycycline for 7 days or azithromycin in a single dose (see Table 33–1). Erythromycin or azithromycin is recommended for children aged 6 months to 12 years. Erythromycin is recommended for infants younger than 6 months.

Post-treatment cultures are recommended if the patient was treated with erythromycin, sulfisoxazole, or amoxicillin, but not after doxycycline, azithromycin, or ofloxacin unless symptoms persist or reinfection is a possibility. Sexual partners should be evaluated and treated if the last sexual contact was within 60 days of onset of the symptomatic index patient's symptoms or treated even if the last sexual contact was greater than 60 days before this time.

Gonococcal Infections

CLINICAL MANIFESTATIONS. Gonococcal infections usually are symptomatic in men; thus, treatment is begun before serious sequelae develop. Unfortunately, many women remain asymptomatic until complications develop. Screening of high-risk women is recommended as a primary method of controlling gonococcal infections in the United States. The symptoms of *N. gonorrhoeae* infection range from uncompli-

cated infections such as urethritis, vulvovaginitis, proctitis, and pharyngitis to pelvic inflammatory disease (PID), disseminated gonococcal infection, meningitis, arthritis, endocarditis, and conjunctivitis.

The organism is transmitted during intimate contact, whether by sexual activity or during parturition, and very rarely by household exposure in prepubertal children. **Sexual abuse must be considered in prepubertal children and nonsexually active adolescents who have gonococcal infection.** Coinfection with *C. trachomatis* is common.

DIAGNOSIS. Gram-stained smears of the exudate are helpful in the evaluation for *N. gonorrhoeae,* which are gram-negative intracellular diplococci. Gram stains of exudate from the endocervix of postpubertal women are less sensitive than culture, but they may be useful in the initial evaluation of a patient who has acute abdominal pain. Culture is performed on selective media, such as Thayer-Martin (chocolate agar with antibiotics), which inhibits most normal flora. Because *N. gonorrhoeae* is sensitive to drying and temperature changes, prompt inoculation of the specimen onto selective media or the transport medium is necessary.

Genital, rectal, and pharyngeal cultures should be obtained before treatment is begun, in addition to tests for other STDs (e.g., syphilis, human immunodeficiency virus [HIV] infection, hepatitis B, and *C. trachomatis* infection). Nonculture methods of diagnosis (such as Gram stain, DNA probes, or enzyme immunoassay) cannot be used alone for diagnosis in children because false-positive results occur.

TREATMENT. The treatment of gonococcal infections varies by whether the infection is complicated. Because of the prevalence of penicillin-resistant organisms, the initial therapy is an extended-spectrum cephalosporin (see Table 33–1). Patients who have gonococcal infection should also be treated for chlamydial infection.

For uncomplicated infections, a culture at the end of treatment is not recommended unless patients have persistent symptoms. Reinfection or coinfection is more likely than treatment failure.

Pelvic Inflammatory Disease

CLINICAL MANIFESTATIONS. PID is infection of the uterus and fallopian tubes due to ascending spread of organisms from the vagina and cervix to the endometrium, pelvic peritoneum, and contiguous structures. The risk of PID is highest in sexually active adolescents. Other risk factors include multiple sexual partners, previous PID, and the presence of an IUD. Ascending infection is uncommon in prepubertal girls.

The common clinical manifestations of PID include constant bilateral lower abdominal or pelvic pain and nonspecific signs such as fever, nausea, and vomiting. Mild or abnormal vaginal bleeding, vaginal discharge, and dyspareunia may be present. PID also may be asymptomatic. The symptoms of PID often occur within the week following the onset of menses.

Common findings on physical examination include lower abdominal, cervical motion, or adnexal tenderness and fever. However, only 30% to 35% of patients who have PID have fever. A mass may be palpable on bimanual pelvic examination or identified on ultrasound examination. Acute complications of PID include the Fitz-Hugh–Curtis syndrome (perihepatitis) in 15% to 30% of cases and tubo-ovarian abscess in 20% of cases. Tubal infertility occurs in 10% to 30% of cases after a single episode of PID. Other long-term complications include chronic pelvic pain and ectopic pregnancy.

N. gonorrhoeae and C. trachomatis often are suspected in PID; however, the cause is usually polymicrobial. The other organisms isolated from upper tract specimens in patients who have PID include multiple anaerobic organisms, facultative bacteria (e.g., G. vaginalis, Streptococcus species, and coliform bacteria), and genital tract mycoplasmas (e.g., M. hominis, U. urealyticum, and Mycoplasma genitalium). N. gonorrhoeae has been found from the upper genital tract of 25% to 50% of women who have PID, C. trachomatis in 10% to 43%, and anaerobic and facultative bacteria in 25% to 84%. Ten to 20 percent of women who have endocervical infection with N. gonorrhoeae and 10% to 30% of those who have C. trachomatis develop symptomatic PID.

DIAGNOSIS. PID is diagnosed on the basis of clinical findings (Table 33–3) supported by laboratory evidence of N. gonorrhoeae and C. trachomatis. Endocervical cultures for N. gonorrhoeae and C. trachomatis and rectal cultures for N. gonorrhoeae should be obtained before treatment. The cervical secretions may contain an increased number of leukocytes. Leukocytosis and an elevated erythrocyte sedimentation rate (ESR) and/or C-reactive protein also support the clinical diagnosis. Unfortunately, no single constellation of symptoms is both sensitive and specific for the diagnosis of PID. The positive predictive value for salpingitis with a clinical diagnosis of symptomatic PID is 65% to 90% when compared with laparoscopy. Laparoscopy can be used both to confirm the diagnosis and to obtain cultures but

TABLE 33–3. Criteria for Clinical Diagnosis of Pelvic Inflammatory Disease

Minimum criteria
  Lower abdominal tenderness
  Adnexal tenderness
  Cervical motion tenderness
Additional criteria*
  Oral temperature >38.3°C (101°F)
  Cervicitis
  Elevated ESR or C-reactive protein
  Culture or nonculture evidence of cervical infection with
    Neisseria gonorrhoeae or Chlamydia trachomatis
Definitive criteria
  Histopathologic evidence on endometrial biopsy of
    endometritis
  Tubo-ovarian abscess on sonography
  Laparoscopic evidence of pelvic inflammatory disease

*Presence of additional criteria increases specificity but decreases sensitivity.
ESR, erythrocyte sedimentation rate.
Adapted from Centers for Disease Control and Prevention: 1998 Guidelines for treatment of sexually transmitted diseases. MMWR 47(No. RR-1):18–95, 1998.

usually is not practical. A pregnancy test should be obtained in most cases.

TREATMENT. The treatment of PID (Table 33–2) **is empirical and broad spectrum to cover the most common etiologies. Antibiotic treatment should be started promptly, before waiting for culture confirmation.** Many experts recommend hospitalization of all adolescents who have PID to ensure compliance with treatment and follow-up. Criteria for hospitalization include (1) tubo-ovarian abscess, (2) pregnancy, (3) peritonitis or a suspected pelvic abscess, (4) immunodeficiency (i.e., patient has HIV infection), (5) failure to respond to outpatient therapy, (6) inability to comply with an outpatient regimen, (7) severe illness, high fever, or nausea and vomiting, or (8) unclear diagnosis and surgical ectopic pregnancy or appendicitis cannot be excluded.

Measures of control include evaluation and empirical treatment of male sexual partners for gonococcal and chlamydial infection. The patient should be instructed to abstain from intercourse until all her symptoms have subsided and treatment is completed. Patients also should be offered serologic screening for syphilis, HIV counseling and screening, and hepatitis B immunization if previously unvaccinated. Patients who have positive cultures for N. gonorrhoeae and C. trachomatis should be recultured within 7 to 10 days after therapy is completed, and a follow-up appointment in 4 to 6 weeks is useful owing to the high risk of reinfection. Education about STDs and the use of barrier contraceptives (they decrease the risk of PID) should be provided.

TABLE 33–4. Clinical Features of Genital Ulcer Syndromes Associated with Sexually Transmitted Diseases

	Herpes Simplex (Herpes)	Treponema pallidum (Syphilis)	Haemophilus ducreyi (Chancroid)	Chlamydia trachomatis (LGV)*	Calymmatobacterium granulomatis (Granuloma Inguinale)
Incubation period	2–14 days	2–4 wk (range 10–90 days)	1–14 days	3–42 days	8–80 days
First lesion	Vesicle	Papule	Tender red papule	Papule, vesicle	Subcutaneous nodule
Site of infection					
Male	At site of inoculation	At site of inoculation	Genital ulcer or inguinal pain	At site of inoculation	90% genitalia
Female	At site of inoculation	At site of inoculation	More variable†	At site of inoculation	90% genitalia
Ulcer	Small, clustered, round, superficial, painful	Medium size, superficial, raised edge, painless	Friable base coated with purulent exudate; painful	Small to medium size, round to oval, elevated edge	Variable size, elevated edge, irregular shape, single or multiple
Adenopathy	Bilateral, painful	Bilateral, not painful	Painful, unilateral inguinal adenitis (bubo)	Painful, unilateral	Regional lymphadenopathy, pseudobuboes
Induration	None	Firm	Soft	Firm	Firm
Diagnosis‡	Antigen detection, tissue culture, electron microscopy	Darkfield examination for spirochete, serology	Culture of H. ducreyi from ulcer or lymph node on semiselective media	Tissue culture of aspirate from bubo	Giemsa or Wright stain for Donovan bodies of crush preparation of lesion
Treatment§	Consider acyclovir	Penicillin	Ceftriaxone, azithromycin, or erythromycin	Doxycycline or erythromycin	Doxycycline or TMP-SMX¶

*Lymphogranuloma venereum.
†Dysuria, dyspareunia, vaginal discharge, pain on defecation, rectal bleeding.
‡Patients also should be evaluated for syphilis, hepatitis B, HIV, *Chlamydia trachomatis,* and *Neisseria gonorrhoeae.*
§See Table 33–2.
¶Trimethoprim-sulfamethoxazole.

Adapted from Centers for Disease Control and Prevention: 1998 Guidelines for treatment of sexually transmitted diseases. MMWR 47(No. RR-1):18–95, 1998; and MacDonald NE, Gully PR, Cameron DW, and Samson LM: Sexually transmitted disease syndromes, skin and mucous membrane infections and inguinal lymphadenopathy, urethritis, vulvovaginitis, and cervicitis and pelvic inflammatory disease. *In* Long SS, Pickering LK, and Prober CG (eds): Principles and Practice of Pediatric Infectious Diseases. New York, Churchill Livingstone Inc., 1997, pp 381–402.

Genital Ulcer Syndromes

Genital ulcers are present in infections with herpes simplex virus, *Treponema pallidum, C. trachomatis* serovars L1, L2, and L3 (lymphogranuloma venereum), *Haemophilus ducreyi* (chancroid), and *Calymmatobacterium granulomatis* (granuloma inguinale). An ulcer, by itself, is not a specific sign of genital infection. Classic findings of the genital ulcer syndromes are presented in Table 33–4.

The assessment of patients who have genital ulcers should include a careful physical examination, including a pelvic examination for women, with attention to the presence or absence of ulcer pain and regional lymphadenopathy. In the United States, most patients who have genital ulcers have genital herpes, syphilis, or chancroid. The frequency of each infection varies with location and specific population. Granuloma inguinale, caused by the gram-negative bacillus *C. granulomatis*, is rarely found in the United States but is common in New Guinea and parts of Africa, India, and the Caribbean. In 3% to 10% of cases, patients who have genital ulcer disease may be infected with more than one pathogen and are at increased risk for acquiring HIV infection, if exposed.

DIAGNOSIS. Initially, diagnostic testing for the two most common causes of genital ulcers, syphilis and herpes simplex virus, should be done (Table 33–4). Optimal therapy depends on specific identification of the cause.

TREATMENT. Treatment is specific for each disease process and is presented in Tables 33–2 and 33–4.

Genital Warts

CLINICAL MANIFESTATIONS. Genital and anal warts are benign epithelial tumors of the skin and mucous membranes caused by human papillomavirus (HPV), usually types 6 or 11 if the warts are visible. The clinical manifestations of anogenital HPV infection range from subclinical infection to condylomata acuminata, the skin-colored growths with rough surfaces. This infection can occur on the external genitalia of males. On women, common sites of HPV infection include the cervix, vagina, and external genitalia. Although most warts are asymptomatic, they occasionally can be pruritic, bleed, or cause local pain.

Human papillomaviruses are DNA viruses, and more than 70 types have been identified. Those causing nongenital infections are distinct from those causing infection of the anogenital area. A small number of the HPV types causing anogenital infection have been associated with malignancies.

Anogenital warts are transmitted for the most part by sexual activity or at delivery. Beyond infancy, the presence of anogenital warts should prompt consideration of sexual abuse. Up to 38% of sexually active adolescent females have evidence of genital HPV infection.

DIAGNOSIS. Genital warts are diagnosed by clinical appearance. To detect cervical HPV, the cervix is soaked in 3% to 5% acetic acid (vinegar), which turns the lesion white. Histologic examination of a biopsy also is diagnostic. Asymptomatic infection may be diagnosed by cytologic evidence on the Pap smear. No culture method is available for HPV.

TREATMENT. The optimal treatment for anogenital warts is not known; the choice should be guided by the preference of the patient. The local application of podofilox solution or gel (0.5%) by the patient or podophyllin resin (10% to 25%) by the clinician is often the first treatment of choice. Other treatments include cryotherapy, trichloroacetic acid, electrocautery, laser surgery, and surgical excision. Intralesional interferon and patient-applied podofilox have not been evaluated in children. Treatment of the visible lesion does not eliminate the HPV infection. Subclinical lesions are not treated. Relapses with all treatments are common, ranging from 5% to 20%. Spontaneous regression of genital warts has occurred in 20% to 30% of patients in placebo-controlled trials.

Evaluation of asymptomatic sexual partners is not indicated. Sexual transmission of anogenital warts can be reduced by the use of condoms. Appropriate investigation is necessary if child abuse is suspected.

FURTHER READING

American Academy of Pediatrics, Peter G (ed): 1997 Red Book: Report of the Committee on Infectious Diseases, 24th ed. Elk Grove Village, IL: American Academy of Pediatrics, 1997.

Centers for Disease Control and Prevention: 1998 Guidelines for treatment of sexually transmitted diseases. MMWR 47(No. RR-1):18–95, 1998.

Committee on Adolescence, 1994 to 1995: Sexually transmitted diseases. Pediatrics 94(4):568–572, 1994.

MacDonald NE, Gully PR, Cameron DW, and Samson LM: Sexually transmitted disease syndromes, skin and mucous membrane infections and inguinal lymphadenopathy, urethritis, vulvovaginitis, and cervicitis and pelvic inflammatory disease. *In* Long SS, Pickering LK, and Prober CG (eds.): Principles and Practice of Pediatric Infectious Diseases. New York: Churchill Livingstone Inc., 1997, pp 381–402.

Webster LA, Berman SM, and Greenspan JR: Surveillance for gonorrhea and primary and secondary syphilis among adolescents, United States 1981–1991. MMWR 42(SS3):1–11, 1993.

John G. Brooks

Chapter 34

Apparent Life-Threatening Events and Sudden Infant Death Syndrome

One of the most impressive public health successes of the 1990s is the greater than 50% reduction in the death rate from sudden infant death syndrome (SIDS) associated with a change in infant sleeping position to the nonprone position in this country and many other developed countries. Despite this relative success, approximately 1 of every 2000 live-born infants in the United States still succumbs to SIDS. The clinical scenarios with which the general pediatric clinician is faced in relation to SIDS and apparent life-threatening events include counseling families who are worried about SIDS, counseling all parents of newborn infants about avoiding risk factors for SIDS, supporting families at the time of a loss of an infant to SIDS, and managing infants who have experienced an apparent life-threatening event and other infants at possible high risk for SIDS. This chapter summarizes the most well established and current information about SIDS risk factors and SIDS prevention initiatives and suggests approaches to the management of these infants and their families.

SUDDEN INFANT DEATH SYNDROME

SIDS is defined as the sudden death of an infant under 1 year of age that remains unexplained after a thorough case investigation, including performance of a complete autopsy, examination of the death scene, and review of the clinical history. To establish the diagnosis of SIDS, an autopsy must be performed and the clinical circumstances of the death reviewed carefully and sensitively to rule out the 15% of sudden unexpected infant deaths due to other identifiable causes, such as infection, intracranial hemorrhage, metabolic inborn errors of metabolism, or trauma. Because findings on autopsy of a SIDS infant are nonspecific (e.g., pulmonary vascular congestion, intrathoracic pete-

chiae), the greatest importance of the autopsy is to diagnose or exclude other causes of death. Specialized autopsy studies have demonstrated group differences between SIDS and non-SIDS control infants compatible with but not diagnostic of episodes of recurrent hypoxemia before death. These findings, however, are not sufficiently sensitive or specific to be of any use in establishing the diagnosis of SIDS in an individual case.

Most cases of SIDS, especially in full-term infants, occur in the first 6 months of life, with a peak incidence between 2 and 4 months of age. The most typical history is of an infant who apparently is completely healthy and is found dead in bed, especially in the morning but also during naps.

Well-designed epidemiologic, case-control studies have identified and confirmed some maternal, infant, and environmental characteristics associated with an increased risk of SIDS (Table 34–1). The maternal risk factors for SIDS include maternal smoking (prenatal and/or postnatal), young maternal age (younger than 20 years of age), less prenatal care, social deprivation, and maternal use of illegal drugs during pregnancy. Infant factors

TABLE 34–1. Risk Factors for Sudden Infant Death Syndrome

Maternal
Maternal smoking
Young maternal age (<20 yr)
Less prenatal care
Maternal use of illegal drugs in pregnancy
Infant
Low birth weight
Prematurity
Male gender
Prone sleeping position
Side sleeping position
Environment
Soft bedding
Passive exposure to cigarette smoke

associated with increased SIDS risk include low birth weight, prematurity, multiple births, male gender, and sleeping prone or on the side. Environmental risk factors for SIDS include soft bedding, postnatal passive exposure to cigarette smoke, and under some circumstances, sleeping in the same bed with an older child or adult. Risk-scoring systems that have been developed based on this type of epidemiologic information, in the hope of identifying at birth those infants who are at high risk of SIDS, have been evaluated on multiple occasions and do not have sufficient sensitivity or specificity to be useful clinically. Likewise, searches for physiologic characteristics or markers of the infant at high risk for SIDS have yielded no clinically useful information.

By far the most successful application of epidemiologic data to decrease the incidence of SIDS has been associated with multiple national public education SIDS reduction campaigns. The most dramatic changes occurring in response to these campaigns have been a nearly 10-fold reduction in the prevalence of prone sleeping infants in many countries (in this country, the reduction of prone-sleeping infants has been less than fourfold to date). **In those countries where prone sleeping is now practiced by less than 10% of the infant population, the SIDS rates generally have fallen by at least 50%. In the United States in 1997, the prevalence of prone sleeping among infants was about 23%, but both the SIDS rate and the prone-sleeping prevalence rate were nearly twice as high in African-American as in other infants.** The risk of SIDS for infants usually put to sleep on their side is intermediate between that of prone- and supine-sleeping infants, probably due to some side-sleeping infants turning to prone sleeping during the night. The current recommendations of the American Academy of Pediatrics regarding infant sleeping position and co-sleeping are summarized in Tables 34–2 and 34–3. The mechanism by which prone sleeping increases the risk of SIDS is unknown but may relate to an increased risk of asphyxia due to a combination of partial airway obstruction and partial rebreathing of air in a pocket in the mattress around the face or actually rebreathing air in and out of the mattress when the infant's face is partly or completely into the mattress or other bedding surface. Normal infants would arouse and terminate the conditions of asphyxia, but the SIDS infant, perhaps because of a transient neurodevelopmental condition of high vulnerability, may not experience the self-protective arousal when such dangerous conditions develop.

The emotional impact of a SIDS death on the infant's family, caretakers, and pediatric

TABLE 34–2. American Academy of Pediatrics' Recommendation for Sleeping Position of Infants

1. Normal, healthy infants should be placed for sleep on the back or side. The supine position carries the lowest risk of SIDS.
2. This recommendation does not apply to infants who have
   • Upper airway anomalies or obstructions
   • Gastroesophageal reflux
3. The recommendation is for infants during sleep.
4. "Tummy time" when infant is awake and observed should be encouraged.
5. Soft bedding should be avoided.

SIDS, sudden infant death syndrome.
From American Academy of Pediatrics, Task Force on Infant Positioning and SIDS: Positioning and sudden infant death syndrome: Update. Pediatrics 98:1216–1218, 1996.

clinicians is enormous, deep, and long-lived. The clinician's responsibilities include supporting the family at the time of the death, providing the family accurate information about SIDS, offering to connect the family to SIDS information and support programs (e.g., the nationally based SIDS Alliance; phone: 1-800-221-SIDS), and seeing that a proper autopsy is performed and the results conveyed to the family promptly. Preliminary results should be available within 24 hours of the autopsy, but several months may pass before the final autopsy report is available.

Certain clinically identifiable infant groups may be at increased risk for SIDS (Table 34–4). Within the apparent life-threatening event (ALTE) group and the premature infant group, the SIDS risk for certain subgroups has been established. For example, the presence or absence of apnea of prematurity, or a history thereof, in premature infants does not affect the SIDS risk of that infant, although more premature infants generally are at higher risk of SIDS. Although the risk of SIDS is not increased among infants who have or have had bronchopulmonary dysplasia, those infants are at increased risk of post–hospital-discharge infant

TABLE 34–3. Bed Sharing and Sudden Infant Death Syndrome (SIDS)

1. No evidence exists that bed sharing reduces SIDS risk.
2. Bed sharing with a smoking adult increases SIDS risk.
3. Cribs do not cause SIDS.
4. If mothers choose to bed-share with an infant, they should avoid soft sleep surfaces.
5. Bed sharing is associated with
   ↓ Infant sleep time
   ↑ Touching and interacting
   ↑ Feeding

Data from American Academy of Pediatrics, Task Force on Infant Positioning and SIDS: Does bed sharing affect the risk of SIDS? Pediatrics 100(2):272, 1997.

TABLE 34–4. High Risk for the Sudden Infant Death Syndrome (SIDS)

Risk Factor	SIDS Incidence, per 1000 Live Births	% of SIDS
Birthweight <1.5 kg	4.3	2.6%
ALTE	1–100	5%
Sibling of SIDS	4	0.7%
Infant of addict	1–4	—

ALTE, apparent life-threatening events.

mortality from other causes. The risk of SIDS among infants who experience intracranial hemorrhage has not been established.

Subsequent siblings of SIDS victims are at a three- to five-fold increased risk of SIDS compared with the general population, but it is not clear whether this increased risk can be explained by the over-representation of adverse risk factors among families who have already lost one infant to SIDS. It is more likely that the **familial clustering of SIDS is due to common environmental and sociologic factors than to genetic mechanisms.**

APPARENT LIFE-THREATENING EVENTS

The management of infants who experience apparent life-threatening events (ALTE) can be challenging to the general pediatrician. An ALTE is defined as "an episode that is frightening to the observer and is characterized by some combination of apnea (central or occasionally obstructive), color change (usually cyanotic or pallid but occasionally erythematous or plethoric), and marked change in muscle tone (usually limpness), choking, or gagging. The observer usually feels that the infant was at high risk of dying or had actually died."

Two subgroups of the ALTE population have been identified as being at particularly high risk. First is those infants whose event occurs during sleep and is perceived to "require" resuscitation. These infants, despite the prescription of home monitors, may have a subsequent mortality as high as 10%. The infants from this high-risk group who have a subsequent severe event "requiring" resuscitation or vigorous stimulation are reported in one study to have a 28% subsequent mortality despite prescription of home monitors. Infants who have repeat episodes and develop a seizure disorder in association with the episodes are reported to be at a similar very high risk of subsequent mortality. In all but one of the reported cases, the repeat episode occurred within 3 weeks of the initial severe episode. Infants who have

severe episodes requiring resuscitation are a very small subgroup of the total ALTE population. It is important to explain to parents of ALTE infants that *while overall the risk of SIDS is usually increased only very slightly in the ALTE population,* **most SIDS victims have not been noted to experience ALTEs before their death.** Thus the overlap between the ALTE and the SIDS populations is relatively small. The incidence of ALTE in the general population is about 1% to 3%.

The management of ALTE infants is based on identification of high-risk subgroups and specific causes (Table 34–5). The first two decisions to be made are whether the infant's life is in imminent danger and whether the infant has experienced an abnormal event or merely excessive reaction by a caretaker to a normal event. The specific causes of ALTEs most likely to be identified are infection (5% to 40% depending on the season of the year), gastroesophageal reflux and other causes of stimulation of laryngeal chemoreceptors (approximately 20% of ALTE infants), and seizures and other neurologic disorders (15% to 20%), but no cause is found in about 50% of these infants (i.e., idiopathic ALTE). The most common infections to explain an ALTE include pertussis and, during the winter months, respiratory syncytial virus, but serious and acute infections such as septicemia or meningitis can present in this fashion, as well. The reflex response to stimulation of laryngeal chemoreceptors (e.g., by gastric acid or other flu-

TABLE 34–5. Differential Diagnosis of Apparent Life-Threatening Events (ALTE)

Laryngeal chemoreceptor apnea
Gastroesophageal reflux
Seizure disorder
Infection
Apnea of prematurity
Upper airway obstruction
Cardiac disease
Breathholding
Anemia
Hypoventilation syndromes
CNS tumor
Apnea of infancy (idiopathic)

CNS, central nervous system.

ids with non-normal chloride concentration) consists of apnea, bradycardia, and central pooling of blood (i.e., pallor). Because gastroesophageal reflux is so common in infants, those who have ALTE due to reflux must have extreme responses to this stimulation, so reflux per se is not enough to explain an ALTE.

The evaluation of an infant who has ALTE, once it is established that there is no immediate threat to the infant's life, consists of a careful history, physical examination, and limited laboratory evaluation to look for indirect evidence of recurrent hypoxemia, for example, increased intensity of the pulmonic component of the second heart sound, right ventricular hypertrophy by electrocardiography (ECG), metabolic acidosis, compensatory metabolic alkalosis suggesting chronic hypoventilation, and clues to a specific cause for the frightening event. If at all possible, the history should be obtained from the individual who discovered the infant in its abnormal state and should include a detailed description of the infant at the time of discovery (e.g., color, distribution of abnormal color, muscle tone, respiratory effort), the specific stimulation and resuscitation measures used, and the infant's response to the interventions. The infant's activities and state just before and after the episode also should be documented (e.g., time since feeding, any clinical symptoms, postictal state). The approximate duration of any reported apnea should be documented. Information about family history and other medical problems of the infant should be documented. In addition to a careful cardiac, respiratory, and neurologic examination, the infant's breathing during sleep and feeding should be observed.

Most infants who present acutely after an ALTE should be hospitalized, because such episodes may occur in clusters, thereby providing opportunities for professional intervention and resuscitation, if necessary, and for direct observation of the event by clinicians. In addition, the parents or other caretakers are likely to feel very frightened, often believing that their infant recently almost died; thus, time for reassurance, evaluation, and counseling can be most productive.

Unless the history or physical examination strongly suggests a specific etiology that warrants additional evaluation, assessment limited to a complete blood count, serum bicarbonate, and in-hospital cardiorespiratory monitoring is sufficient evaluation for most infants. Additional tests that may be helpful if suggested by the history or physical examination include electroencephalography (EEG), ECG, cultures, and additional imaging studies of the brain, airway, or heart. The 12- to 24-hour continuous recording of cardiorespiratory pattern (i.e., pneumogram) has no role in the evaluation of ALTE infants because the prognostic significance of the pneumogram findings is unknown. On rare occasions, a polysomnogram (i.e., multichannel recordings of respiration, ECG, pulse oximetry, nasal airflow, carbon dioxide, and/or EEG) may be helpful if there is a strong suspicion of apneic seizures, obstructive apnea, or central hypoventilation. A leukocytosis on CBC may suggest infection, and a lymphocytosis may suggest pertussis. A low serum bicarbonate level supports a recent asphyxic episode (i.e., resolving metabolic acidosis).

Some ALTE specialists who are less inclined to prescribe home monitors may be more likely to do additional in-hospital evaluations before discharge. It certainly is cost effective and medically valid to do very limited in-hospital evaluation of most ALTE infants if one quite liberally prescribes home monitors with the plan of additional evaluation if more "real" episodes occur. Both of these approaches are within the national standard of care for most ALTE infants as defined by the 1986 NIH Consensus Development Conference on SIDS and Infant Home Monitoring. This working group recommended that monitors be used in infants who have experienced severe episodes during sleep that were perceived to require resuscitation, and indicated that it was wrong to use monitors for normal infants and asymptomatic premature infants. There were insufficient data, a lack that persists today, to make evidence-based, specific recommendations for infants who experience less severe ALTEs.

Whenever monitors are prescribed, 24-hour technical and medical support must be readily available to the family, and the caretakers must be fully instructed in infant resuscitation and monitor use and troubleshooting. The specific reasons for monitoring, the expected duration of monitoring, and the indications for notifying the medical caretakers about any subsequent events must be clearly explained to the family before discharge. The monitor should be set to alarm for a respiratory pause of greater than 20 seconds and for a heart rate of less than 60 to 70 beats/minute, depending on the age of the infant. Although probably not necessary in all monitoring situations, "smart" or "documented" monitoring can be very helpful in infants whose caretakers report multiple alarms. These monitors have the capacity to record for brief periods before, during, and after each alarm and to store this information for "downloading" at regular intervals and transcription to hard copy. Often, examination of the hard copy can distinguish between false alarms due to movement artifact or a weak signal and real events. Most events reported by parents are not substantiated by simultaneous "smart monitoring."

Parents must understand the limitations of home monitoring before they embark on this course. For example, reports are only anecdotal that monitors have contributed to saving lives, and the caretakers must be within 10 seconds of the infant at all times. Noisy activities like showers or vacuuming must not be undertaken by the responsible caretaker. Occasionally, false alarms may disrupt sleep for both the infant and the family, although this usually should not be a major problem.

SUMMARY

Despite significant progress in reducing the incidence of SIDS, SIDS and the fear of SIDS and other infant deaths and ALTE remain a significant concern among parents of infants. Pediatric clinicians who are informed about SIDS and its relationship to certain risk factors and high-risk groups can be reassuring to such worried families and can ensure that appropriate steps are taken to minimize the risk of SIDS.

FURTHER READING

ALTE

Brooks JG: Apparent life-threatening events and apnea of infancy. Perinatal Clin North Am 19:809–838, 1992.
National Institutes of Health Consensus Development Conference on Infantile Apnea and Home Monitoring, Sept. 29 to Oct. 1, 1986: Consensus statement. Pediatrics 79:292–299, 1987.

SIDS

American Academy of Pediatrics Task Force on Infant Positioning and SIDS: Positioning and sudden infant death syndrome (SIDS): Update. Pediatrics 98:1216–1218, 1996.
American Academy of Pediatrics Task Force on Infant Positioning and SIDS: Does bed sharing affect the risk of SIDS? Pediatrics 100:272, 1997.
Guntheroth WG: Crib Death: The Sudden Infant Death Syndrome, 3rd ed. Armonk, NY: Futura Publishing, 1995.
Valdes-Dapena M, McFeeley PA, Hoffman HJ, et al.: Histopathology Atlas for the Sudden Infant Death Syndrome. Washington, DC: Armed Forces Institute of Pathology/American Registry of Pathology/National Institute of Child Health and Human Development, 1993.

Morris Green

Chapter 35

Delirium

Delirium represents a reversible toxic or metabolic encephalopathy characterized by a disturbance in consciousness that ranges from extreme hyperactivity to coma. Symptoms of delirium characteristically fluctuate widely but are generally worse at night. Since the sleep-wakefulness cycle is commonly disturbed, the child may be excessively alert and unable to fall asleep at night or unusually drowsy during the day.

The delirious patient's ability to sustain attention is limited, and his or her conversation may skip abruptly from one topic to another. At one moment the child may seem to be in complete contact with the immediate environment, while a few seconds later he or she obviously does not clearly perceive or understand what is going on. At times, the impairment in consciousness is persistent and does not fluctuate. The delirious child may demonstrate great excitement and hyperactivity—running about the examining room, trying to open the door, struggling and thrashing around the examining table or bed. Anxiety, fear, anger, depression, euphoria, and apathy may be displayed. The child may pull at his or her fingertips, reach for imaginary objects or pick at his or her clothes. Motor incoordination, incoherent speech, inability to write, tremulousness, and ataxia may be noted. Auditory and visual hallucinations and illusions lead the child to misinterpret shadows (e.g., he or she may see large bugs on the bed or on the walls). Cognitive function, short-term memory, and comprehension are impaired. The confused older child may be unable to answer orientation questions, attend to a task such as sequential subtraction, repeat backward a series of digits, or respond correctly to other components of a mental status examination (e.g., date, time, and place).

ETIOLOGIC CLASSIFICATION OF DELIRIUM

I. Infectious Disorders
   A. **Any acute, febrile disease, especially the exanthems, may cause delirium.**
   B. Pneumococcal or other bacterial pneumonia. In some instances, delirium and fever may be the only presenting symptoms.
   C. Inflammatory diseases of the central nervous system such as meningitis or encephalitis.
   D. Reye syndrome is characterized by a prodromal illness. Protracted vomiting, lethargy, disorientation, irrational behavior, hallucinations, combativeness, stupor, and coma may follow. Elevated levels of aspartate transaminase, alanine transaminase, and blood ammonia are found.
   E. Typhoid fever.
   F. Shigellosis.
   G. Rabies may be characterized by periods of hyperactivity, combativeness, and disorientation alternating with intervals of normal mental status.
   H. Toxic shock syndrome may be accompanied by confusion, disorientation, agitation, and somnolence.
   I. Infectious hepatitis may produce signs of delirium owing to impending hepatic failure.
   J. Infectious mononucleosis. The "Alice in Wonderland" syndrome (see VIIB).

II. Drugs and Poisoning
   A careful search for possible poisoning is indicated in all children with acute delirium, including a review of the contents of medicine cabinets, night tables, and all medications taken currently or in the past by the parents or other adults in the household. In the absence of a history of drug ingestion, a blood and urine screen for toxic substances should be pursued. The possibility of intentional poisoning of children should be kept in mind.
   A. Barbiturates.
   B. Antihistamines taken orally or contained in preparations for cutaneous application.
   C. Theophylline toxicity may lead to extreme restlessness and visual hallucinations.
   D. Corticosteroids.
   E. Isoniazid.
   F. Jimson weed poisoning may produce delirium. Convulsions are also a common complication. Symptoms, which may begin in minutes or a few hours, include visual illusions, dryness of the mouth, extreme thirst, incoherent speech, confusion, disorientation, combative behavior, stupor, coma, incoordination, and hyperactivity. The pupils are dilated and fixed, and the skin is flushed and dry. Opisthotonos may develop. A diffuse erythematous rash may be present. The temperature may be as high as 105°F (40.6°C). Imipramine poisoning may cause similar symptoms.
   G. Atropine and other anticholinergic poisonings.
   H. Amphetamine abuse.
   I. Hallucinogens. Lysergic acid diethylamide (LSD), psilocybin, mescaline, piperidine derivatives, or other agents that produce gross distortions in perceptions without loss of consciousness. Visual, tactile, auditory, olfactory, or gustatory hallucinations may occur. Delirium that persists for several days may be caused by phencyclidine ("angel dust") intoxication. Hypertension and urinary retention may also be present.
   J. Gasoline sniffing.
   K. Cocaine.
   L. Marijuana.
   M. Alcohol may produce manifestations of delirium.
   N. Hoigne syndrome, consisting of hallucinations, panic symptoms or seizures, may occur after an injection of procaine penicillin.
   O. The simultaneous administration of carbamazepine and erythromycin to the same patient may cause confusion, dizziness, ataxia, and atrioventricular block.
   P. Neuroleptic malignant syndrome.
   Q. Tricyclic antidepressant ingestion.

III. Hypoxemia (e.g., carbon monoxide poisoning or respiratory failure) may cause confusion.

IV. Metabolic disorders (e.g., uremia, hypoglycemia, hepatic failure, thyroid storm, nonketotic hyperglycinemia during febrile illness).

V. Burn encephalopathy, characterized by delirium, personality changes, seizures, or coma, may occur with acute burns owing to hypovolemia, sepsis, or hyponatremia.

VI. Head Trauma

Early sequelae include such symptoms of delirium as agitation, psychomotor retardation, aggressiveness, incoherent speech, muteness, hallucinations, and fearfulness.

VII. Complicated Migraine

A. Acute confusional state is characterized by restlessness, hyperactivity, confusion, combativeness, agitation, or stupor. Episodes may persist for hours.

B. "Alice in Wonderland" syndrome, occurring immediately or several days before a migraine headache, could simulate delirium, with aberration of time perception, distortions in body image, visual illusions, and trancelike states. This syndrome may also be a complication of infectious mononucleosis.

VIII. Heat stroke may produce incoherent speech, agitation, confusion, and disorientation before progressing to stupor and unconsciousness.

IX. Grief related to the death of a family member may cause hallucination of the deceased in nonpsychotic children.

MANAGEMENT

The treatment of delirium depends on its cause. Symptoms caused by a drug will subside with its discontinuation. Antibiotic therapy is indicated for bacterial infections. Children who are delirious should be kept in a dimly lighted room without shadows with a familiar person in attendance and with some orienting features such as pictures or a window. They should also be periodically oriented to place, time, and those who are present. Psychotropic medication or hospitalization may be necessary in some instances.

FURTHER READING

Drugs that cause psychiatric symptoms. Med Lett 31:113–118, 1989.

Rumach HB: Jimsonweed abuse. Pediatr Rev 5:141–145, 1983.

Takahashi A, Franklin J: Alcohol abuse. Pediatr Rev 17:39–46, 1996.

Werner MJ: Hallucinogens. Pediatr Rev 14:466–472, 1993.

Morris Green

Chapter **36**

Fainting or Syncope

Fainting or syncope refers to brief, usually sudden, periods of unconsciousness, loss of postural tone, and falling owing to cerebral ischemia. Generally, the history is the most helpful diagnostic tool. Special attention must be given to the circumstances in which the syncope occurred; the possible precipitating factors; the prodromal symptoms and signs; the suddenness of onset; the duration of the episode; and the occurrence of convulsive movements.

Vasodepressor or neurocardiogenic syncope due to a sudden and marked fall in blood pressure is the most common cause of fainting in adolescents. Fainting may occur when the patient becomes suddenly frightened or threatened by some real or imagined danger. It may also represent a reaction to severe pain or other unpleasant stimulus such as the sight of blood or a needle puncture. Syncope is especially likely to occur in hot, humid, close quarters; after prolonged motionless standing; when the patient is fatigued; and after fasting. In patients with emotionally induced syncopal attacks, anxiety may be overt or reported in frightening dreams. Psychologic factors may cause recurrent fainting spells, especially those not precipitated by apparent cause.

Simple faints almost always begin with the patient standing. Prodromal symptoms may include a feeling of great weakness, generalized numbness, pallor, nausea, excessive salivation, warmth, sweating, lightheadedness, yawning, sighing, blurring of vision, and epigastric discomfort. The antecedent complaints may either suddenly terminate in the faint or be aborted spontaneously or by assumption of the head-low position. Some patients have recurrent, sudden fainting episodes without prodromal symptoms. The interruption of consciousness in an episode usually lasts only a few seconds, but it may persist for several minutes. Clonic movements may ensue if the patient remains unconscious longer than 15 to 20 seconds. Symptoms may recur if the patient sits or stands up too quickly.

Head-upright tilt-table testing is often used in the evaluation of children and adolescents with recurrent, unexplained, or neurocardiogenic syncope.

As a conversion symptom, syncope may be a symbolic expression of unconscious, repressed instinctual impulses, usually of a sexual or hostile nature, and often directed toward a member of the family. Such episodes, most common in adolescent girls, may also be precipitated by a real or fantasized sexual experience. The patient may have a history of repeated episodes of syncope as well as other manifestations of a conversion disorder. It is postulated that conversion of the consciously unacceptable impulse to a syncopal episode permits a partial discharge of these feelings and helps avoid the accompanying anxiety.

Whereas overt anxiety is frequently noted with vasodepressor syncope, the patient with syncope on a conversion basis shows little concern. Characteristically, these episodes occur in the presence of others and are not preceded or accompanied by prodromal symptoms such as nausea, weakness, pallor, and sweating. Patients with conversion syncope may slump or fall in a dramatic fashion, but they avoid injury. They may faint while sitting or recumbent, an unusual sequence in vasodepressor syncope. During the episode, the patient's eyes may flutter or remain open or tightly closed. Moaning, groaning, or other sounds may be noted. Unusual positions and movements may be assumed. The patient may slip in and out of unconsciousness or have less impairment of consciousness. Interruption of consciousness may persist for seconds or hours.

Differentiation by history between vasodepressor syncope, breathholding spells, and epilepsy is occasionally difficult since the first two disorders may be accompanied by clonic movements. Syncope due to epilepsy usually lasts longer (generally over 30 seconds) and is more likely to occur with the patient recumbent than is characteristic of simple syncope. An electroencephalogram and other studies may occasionally be necessary for differentiation.

Syncope during exertion is a diagnostic red flag because it precedes at least 50% of sudden cardiac deaths in the pediatric age group. A history of fainting during exercise may be associated with an aberrant left coronary artery or other coronary artery abnormality. Occasionally, syncope occurs with exertion in patients who have isolated, marked pulmonic stenosis. Primary pulmonary hypertension may be characterized by episodes of syncope, especially on effort, and syncope may be the presenting complaint. Mitral valve prolapse may be characterized by precordial pain, palpitations, arrhythmias, or syncopal episodes. Congenital or acquired heart block or cardiac arrhythmias may decrease cardiac output sufficiently to produce unconsciousness. Symptomatic sinus node dysfunction may cause syncope and bradycardia. Other complaints that suggest a cardiac dysrhythmia include dizziness, palpitations, chest pain, and seizures. Electrocardiography, Holter monitoring, maximal exercise testing, and electrophysiologic studies may be indicated. Severe aortic stenosis may cause syncope, especially after physical exertion. Hypertrophic cardiomyopathy in adolescents may produce slight dyspnea and angina on exertion and syncope. A systolic ejection murmur is heard along the upper right sternal border. Attacks of paroxysmal dyspnea in infants with congenital heart disease (e.g., tetralogy of Fallot), may terminate in syncope. Episodes of palpitation, weakness, faintness, and syncope may occur with paroxysmal supraventricular tachycardia and with sudden obstruction of the mitral orifice by a left atrial myxoma.

Swallowing syncope owing to increased vagal tone on deglutition and a decrease in heart rate has been reported. Lightheadedness, confusion, headache, alteration of consciousness and syncope, usually of short duration and owing to cerebral hypoxia, may occur after severe paroxysms of coughing. Severe anemia, especially that caused by blood loss, may be accompanied by lightheadedness, giddiness and, occasionally, syncope. Although hypoglycemia does not lead to true syncope, the patient may complain of faintness and exhibit pallor and sweating.

Hyperventilation may cause a syndrome characterized by lightheadedness ("dizziness"), generalized weakness, chest pain, palpitations, tingling and numbness of the hands, tetany, or syncope. Adolescent patients are more likely to report "blacking-out" spells, seizures, and sensations of smothering, choking, or shortness of breath. A panic attack may be characterized by hyperventilation along with faintness, dizziness, vertigo, and "blackout" spells. Direct questioning or an attempt to replicate the symptoms by having the patient hyperventilate for a couple of minutes may be necessary.

Breathholding spells are common in infants, and they may uncommonly occur until 4 years of age. These episodes are triggered by some injury, often trivial, or by anger and frustration. Vigorous crying is usually the first manifestation followed after a variable period by the child suddenly gasping or holding the breath until he or she becomes blue, unconscious, and limp. Clonic, tonic, and tonic-clonic convulsive movements may occur. Pallid syncope and loss of muscle tone may follow breathholding. Patients with myelodysplasia and Arnold-Chiari malformation may experience prolonged breathholding spells, especially following crying or noxious stimuli.

Syncope lasting from a brief faint to unconsciousness for 5 to 10 minutes may occur in the prolonged QT-interval syndromes. The congenital form described by Jervell and by Lange-Nielsen are autosomal recessive disorders characterized by deafness, prolonged QT interval, large T waves on the electrocardiogram, and sudden death. The Romano-Ward syndrome is an autosomal dominant trait without deafness. A sporadic form of prolonged QT-interval syndrome also exists. Episodes may be precipitated by emotional stress, noise, or physical exertion.

Postural or orthostatic hypotension, an unusual cause of syncope in pediatrics, may occur when a child or adolescent has stood motionless for a long time in a military or parade formation. Orthostatic hypotension causing syncope may also occur in the toxic shock syndrome. Postural hypotension in patients with anorexia nervosa or bulimia may account for lightheadedness, dizziness and, occasionally, syncope.

Hyperventilation and syncope may occur after intense physical effort in an athletic contest. Heat exhaustion, another exercise-related disorder, is characterized by headache, weakness, muscle cramps, and syncope.

FURTHER READING

Braden DS, Gaymes CH: The diagnosis and management of syncope in children and adolescents. Pediatr Ann 7:422–426, 1997.

Terry Nolan

Chapter 37

Encopresis

Encopresis is defined as repeated, involuntary defecation into clothing by children 4 years of age and older and of at least 1 month's duration. Boys are three times more likely to have this condition. At age 8, about one in 50 boys are affected. Children who have acquired continence but then start to soil again have *secondary* encopresis; failure ever to have acquired continence is termed *primary* encopresis. Clinic-based studies report approximately equal numbers of children who have primary and secondary forms of this condition.

Constipation and encopresis are terms that describe symptoms. Constipation refers to the difficulty (i.e., straining, abdominal pain, perineal pain on defecation) associated with passage of stool. Chronic constipation is usually, though not always, associated with fecal retention. Encopresis is a term that describes fecal incontinence in the absence of structural abnormality. Encopresis usually, though not always, is associated with fecal retention. Constipation may precede encopresis, but most incontinent children do not have difficulty passing stool; indeed, it is effortless and usually frequent.

Fecal continence is achieved through a complex mix of physiologic and behavioral factors. Recent studies using manometry and surface electromyography of the external anal sphincter have demonstrated that up to 50% of children who have difficult-to-treat encopresis have an abnormal and prolonged external anal sphincter contraction during straining to defecate. This contraction, termed *anismus*, apparently leads to ineffective rectal evacuation and, thereafter, fecal accumulation. During subsequent play or relaxation, the increased rectal volume and pressure results in the extrusion of stool and the soiling episode. Studies also have documented a prevalence of rectal hyposensitivity of about 40% in children who have encopresis. Whether this is a cause or result of fecal accumulation has not been established. The combination of rectal hyposensitivity and anismus may be important contributory mechanisms that promote the continuation of the encopresis retention–extrusion cycle.

Encopresis, therefore, should be seen as an evacuation release disorder, rather than as a disorder of colonic motility or as the simple consequence of constipation. Nevertheless, a small number of children will have ongoing severe constipation, with small volume, hard stool, and sometimes a history of anal tears with bright blood in the stool. Although it used to be thought that children who had Hirschsprung disease never soiled, rare reports have appeared in the literature, making this an uncommon manifestation of a very rare disease.

Behavioral factors that are important for continence development or maintenance include the acquisition of a toileting routine that permits activation of the physiologic mechanisms described previously. Oppositional behavior or extreme negativism by a child locked in a struggle with parents over many aspects of daily living may include toilet refusal. Occasionally, harsh toilet training experiences, or pain from infant or toddler periods due to severe constipation, contribute to this unwillingness to sit on the toilet. A child who has a poor attention span and a high level of motor activity and an underlying rectal hyposensitivity or other physiologic defect may have particular difficulty establishing an adaptive toileting routine. An association exists between encopresis and enuresis, but the significance of this is not yet understood. It is possibly related, at least in part, to bladder compression by a distended rectum.

CLINICAL ASPECTS

A careful and sensitive history is necessary to determine the specific type and duration of the child's incontinence. This also has a therapeutic element in revealing to both the child and the parents that the symptoms are predictable and, to some extent, stereotyped. It frequently is enormously reassuring to the parent and child to see the physician recognize their "secret" symptoms. Initially, the child and parents should be interviewed separately, then together. Table 37–1 details the crucial elements of the history that describe the scope of the clinical problem. The most frequent associated event for children who have secondary encopresis is commencement of school, when new routines may result in less vigilance and attention to regular toileting and reluctance by the child to use the school toilet. Urinary tract infection also should be considered, especially if abdominal pain and urinary frequency are reported. Occasional patients will present with a history of sexual abuse, but this is most unlikely to be related causally to fecal continence. As with any patient, however, the clinician needs to consider this as a possibility during the history and physical examination.

TABLE 37–1. Critical Questions for an Informative Continence History

Soiling Details

Is encopresis primary or secondary? What is the duration of soiling?
Was there a precipitating event?
What is the frequency of soiling episodes?
What is the consistency and quantity of soiled stool?
Are there any nocturnal episodes?
Does soiling occur outside the underwear?
What is the child's awareness of soiling?

Toileting

Is there any spontaneous defecation?
What is the frequency of stool into the toilet?
Is there a toileting routine?
Is there any resistance to a toileting routine?
What is the type and size of stool in the toilet?
Is there any urinary incontinence?

Emotional and Social Adjustment

Is the child isolated, depressed, or anxious because of incontinence?

Family and School Impact

What is the pattern of parental reaction to soiling?
Is the child ostracized at school?

A comprehensive examination is important, with the focus on assessing the extent of fecal accumulation and ruling out rare causes of lower bowel dysfunction, especially disorders affecting the lumbosacral cord. Motor and sensory function in the lower limbs should be assessed and the sacral area should be inspected. Assessment of the child's emotional state is important in deciding whether further, more detailed investigation is required. A rectal examination need not be performed at the initial consultation if an abdominal radiograph is undertaken—as it should be in most cases to assess the extent of fecal accumulation adequately. However, if the response to treatment is suboptimal, a rectal examination should be performed to exclude a pelvic mass. Anorectal manometry and electromyography should be reserved, if available, for investigation of treatment-resistant cases. Similarly, rectal biopsy should occur only if there is a lifelong history of severe constipation (i.e., dating from delayed passage of meconium at birth).

TREATMENT

A structured toileting program together with the support of the pediatric clinician are the essential starting points for management (Table 37–2). In the past, the pervasive belief that encopresis was due simply to constipation led to the widespread use of laxative medication on its own, a prescrip-

TABLE 37–2. Encopresis Management Principles

Counseling and education of parents *and* child
Structured toileting program with daily diary
Laxative disimpaction and maintenance therapy
Physician commitment to follow-up
Sensitive palliative care for treatment-resistant cases

tion for inevitable relapse and continued incontinence.

Education and counseling represent the cornerstone of successful management, with close attention to those aspects of the history that characterize the likely basis for a particular child's incontinence. The use of a parent information sheet and treatment diary help legitimize the medical nature of the child's condition, providing direct information for a parent who may not have been present for the initial consultation and recording the details of the therapeutic plan. The diary is used to monitor compliance with the sitting program and success with stool deposition in the toilet, spontaneously initiated defecation episodes, and medication use.

It is crucial to address and motivate the child directly and to instill an earnest expectation for an optimistic outcome as the reward for all the hard work with the program. A "team and coach" approach works exceptionally well in many families.

The toileting program consists of timed sittings on the toilet three times every day, using an oven clock or egg timer. The prime target behavior is stool deposition in the toilet. The duration of the sitting depends on the likely compliance of the child, but 5 to 10 minutes most often is used. For younger children, or those who are markedly opposed to sitting, a less ambitious target behavior is employed initially, such as going into the bathroom, with advancement later to sitting on the toilet. Achieved targets are rewarded with check marks in the diary for sitting and accident-free days and with gold stars for stool in the toilet.

Laxative use has been shown to be a valuable addition to treatment. The way in which it is used depends on the radiographic assessment of fecal retention. For minor degrees of retention, oral laxative alone is adequate and may take the form of titrated combinations of a bowel stimulant (e.g., senna derivative or bisacodyl) and lubricant-softener (e.g., paraffin oil preparations). A regimen of alternating daily stimulant and lubricant-softener often is effective. For children who have more substantial levels of fecal accumulation, a preliminary disimpaction phase is administered easily at home by a parent, usually the mother. Three-day cycles of a commercial prepackaged enema (one

or two on day 1), rectal suppository (one or two on day 2), and oral bowel stimulant medication on day 3 may be repeated up to three times. **The immediate debulking of the rectum and colon produces a rapid diminution in soiling episodes and is a powerful early motivation for tackling the more arduous sitting program.**

Following this disimpaction phase, daily oral laxative treatment is continued. Only rarely is it necessary to admit a child for inpatient care, and then only for a short period. Home-administered enemas or suppositories, either by a parent or a community outreach nurse, are vastly superior to the frequently traumatic ritual of bowel washouts or nasogastric polyethylene glycol infusions in the hospital.

If the child has only minor retention and there is a good prospect of enthusiastic cooperation with the toileting program, a preliminary, time-limited trial of behavior modification, with or without the assistance of oral laxative medication, may be attempted. This approach may be useful for parents who are reluctant to use rectal medication. It should be remembered, however, that there is good clinical trial evidence that this approach is not as effective overall.

The total duration of this combined program varies depending on individual patient characteristics, but should not be discontinued until the child has developed a daily or second-daily pattern of self-initiated defecation in the toilet concomitant with the disappearance of soiling.

Similarly, if there is evidence of significant psychopathology, postponed assessment of the need for further investigation or management until acquisition of continence may avoid unnecessary referral. On the other hand, if very substantial behavior problems exist—especially severe oppositional behavior—establishing co-management with a competent behavioral specialist at the outset may be worthwhile. Direct liaison with the child's teacher or other school staff may be helpful in obtaining discrete assistance with special toilet privileges and washroom access at school. Encopresis may be only one of a number of other family problems that require assessment and management. Prompt and effective treatment of the encopresis should provide a firm base to address such problems, with the child and family confident after overcoming what might previously have been an apparently insurmountable difficulty for them.

FOLLOW-UP

Frequent and careful follow-up is an important role for the physician. Only too frequently, the encopretic child is sent away with a prescription for laxatives and some rudimentary advice about the importance of sitting on the toilet, without any follow-up. **The diary is a critical link between the physician and the child, and the follow-up interviews center around examining it with the child and giving due acknowledgment to the child's achievements in sitting and defecating into the toilet.**

Following successful early remission from soiling, later minor relapse is not uncommon and usually attributable to departure from the structured sitting program before adequate awareness of rectal filling has developed. A return to the original or slightly simplified version of the induction regimen usually is successful. The return or first appearance of rectal sensation and spontaneous toileting is the most reliable sign of a capacity for independent toileting. **There is good evidence of substantial improvement in child behavior and social adjustment following remission from encopresis.** Parents frequently report an overall improvement in the child's demeanor, appetite, and level of activity.

Within 6 months, the chance of complete and long-lasting remission is approximately 55%, with a further 35% being substantially improved. Despite this excellent outcome and good compliance with behavior modification and medication use, a number of children continue to have minor soiling—sometimes daily. The continued support of the clinician is even more important in these cases, together with further palliative care if necessary. The use of biologically active underwear deodorant sprays and panty liners often help minimize the social embarrassment suffered by the small numbers of children who have persistent symptoms. The assistance of an incontinence specialist (or nurse practitioner) may help in this regard. Unfortunately, a number of controlled trials have shown that although biofeedback training that teaches children to inhibit external sphincter contraction during straining produces transient improvement in continence, this improvement is not sustained.

FURTHER READING

Loening-Baucke V: Encopresis and soiling. Pediatr Clin North Am 43:279–298, 1996.
Loening-Baucke V: Biofeedback training in children with functional constipation: A critical review. Dig Dis Sci 41:65–71, 1996.
Nolan TM and Oberklaid F: New concepts in the management of encopresis. Pedr Rev 14:447–451, 1993.

Robert Needlman

Chapter 38

Failure to Thrive: Primary Care Interventions

Failure to thrive (FTT) presents a formidable challenge to the clinician. FTT is not a diagnosis but rather a clinical sign that requires further exploration. The causes, pathophysiology, and prognosis vary depending on the particulars of the case, making a "flowchart" of the course impractical. FTT is a risk factor for long-term cognitive and emotional problems. With a prevalence of 10% to 30% among children in lower income families, FTT is among the more common, serious pediatric conditions.

Many children who fail to thrive attain normal size by the end of adolescence. Cognitive and emotional development, however, may be permanently affected. **Failure to thrive in the first 2 years of life—and especially in the first 6 months—may prove particularly damaging, as this is a critical period for myelinization and synapse formation.** Biologic insults such as chronic undernutrition act synergistically with environmental risk factors such as family disorganization or parental mental illness to increase developmental risk. Conversely, the combination of nutritional rehabilitation and infant stimulation may improve the outcome significantly.

DEFINITION AND GRADING

The essential feature of FTT is inadequate weight gain during early childhood. Typically, this means weight below the 5th percentile on the National Center for Health Statistics (NCHS) growth charts, or slowed growth such that the weight curve crosses two major percentile lines. Universally agreed-on criteria are lacking. The weight-for-height curve is a better indicator of nutritional status than is weight-for-age growth data. For example, most well-nourished children who have trisomy 21 fall below the 5th percentile for both weight and height on the NCHS charts. They have short stature, not FTT.

FTT implies undernutrition. Chronic undernutrition results in loss of body mass (wasting), followed by slowed linear growth (stunting). When linear deceleration precedes slowed weight gain, a genetic or endocrine problem is likely. The degree of wasting in FTT can be expressed by calculating the weight as a percentage of the ideal (median) weight, either on the weight-for-age or weight-for-height curve. Similarly, the degree of stunting can be expressed by calculating the height as a percentage of the median on the height curve. A weight-for-height determination less than or equal to 80% of the median constitutes moderate wasting; at less than or equal to 70%, the wasting is severe.

The NCHS curves have been adopted by the World Health Organization for international use. However, a number of caveats apply. Although rapid crossing of percentiles is abnormal, infants who are large at birth may gradually drift down on the curves, reaching a steady percentile channel by 12 to 18 months. It is important to correct for gestational age until age 2 to avoid overdiagnosing FTT in premature infants. **For breast-fed babies, the NCHS curves (which were standardized on mainly bottle-fed babies) may create the illusion of excessive growth early in the first year with inadequate growth thereafter.**

ETIOLOGY AND SUBTYPES

Almost any severe chronic medical condition can cause FTT among its manifestations. When no such condition is evident, a psychosocial cause is commonly presumed and the diagnosis of non-organic FTT (NOFTT) given. The organic-nonorganic dichotomy helps to categorize children for research, but it can be misleading clinically. For one thing, organic conditions and psychosocial factors often are intertwined. For example, a child who has congenital heart disease may not only have increased caloric requirements, but also be difficult to feed and have highly stressed parents. Subtle organic factors such as oral-motor dysfunction may initiate frustrating mealtime interactions that lead to conflicts during feeding, which become increasingly entrenched. A typical history might reveal early reflux or gagging on solids, growth faltering, and a parent who tries to overcome these difficulties through force-feeding or who gives up and terminates meals early.

A second reason to question the organic FTT–NOFTT dichotomy is that undernutrition, regardless of the cause, leads to organic dysfunction. Chronic undernutrition is associated with impaired humoral (IgA) and cellular immunity. With each bout of illness, metabolic demands rise and food intake falls, worsening the child's nutritional status. In developing countries, this infection-malnutrition cycle often ends in death. Micronutrient deficiencies often complicate FTT. Iron deficiency impairs brain function and increases absorption of lead, which may decrease appetite further. Both low iron and high lead may affect parent-child interactions adversely. Zinc deficiency slows growth directly and impairs taste-bud function, reducing the attractiveness of food.

Multiple psychosocial factors have been associated with NOFTT. Family interactions may be less warm, more negative and conflict-ridden, and less responsive to the child's cues, both during meals and at other times. Mothers of children who have NOFTT are more likely to be victims of physical or sexual abuse or to have been victims during their own childhoods. Children who have NOFTT have an approximately fourfold risk of physical abuse. Poverty places children at higher risk for poor growth, in some cases simply by limiting the family's ability to purchase adequate food; in other cases, the quality of family relationships and organization limits the child's access to scarce family resources.

A clinically useful distinction focuses on the quality of the parent-child relationship. When FTT occurs in the context of parental preoccupation with stressors such as domestic violence or substance abuse, there often is early termination of feeding, a lack of warmth in the parent-child relationship, and delayed language development. By contrast, when FTT occurs in the context of an overly close parent-child relationship, mealtimes tend to be prolonged, as the child persistently rebuffs the parents' equally persistent attempts at feeding. The child's drive for autonomy overrules the biologic hunger drive, resulting in a "battle of the spoons." Language development often is age-appropriate or precocious, reflecting the high degree of parent-child interaction.

EVALUATION AND MANAGEMENT

The evaluation of a child who fails to thrive includes four areas: medical, nutritional, social, and developmental. A multidisciplinary team in-

TABLE 38–1. Workup of Medical Conditions Associated With Failure to Thrive

History	Diagnostic Consideration	Investigation
Spitting, vomiting	Gastroesophageal reflux	Upper GI series, pH probe, esophagoscopy
Abdominal distention, cramping, diarrhea	Malabsorption (e.g., cystic fibrosis, celiac disease, lactase deficiency	D-Xylose test, stool fat, antigliadin titer or biopsy, sweat chloride test*
Travel to or from developing country; homeless, overcrowded conditions, or living in a shelter	Parasitosis (especially *Giardia*), tuberculosis, inadequate access to cooking facility and refrigeration	Stool ova and parasite determination, duodenal biopsy, string test, PPD
Snoring; periodic breathing during sleep; restless sleep; noisy or mouth breathing	Adenoid hypertrophy	Lateral neck film (soft tissues and airway)
"Asthma"	Chronic aspiration, cystic fibrosis	Chest film, "milk scan," sweat chloride test*
Frequent (minor) infections	HIV, other immune deficiency	Serologic tests, immunoglobulins,* PPD with control for anergy*

*May be abnormal secondary to malnutrition.
GI, gastrointestinal; HIV, human immunodeficiency virus; PPD, purified protein derivative (tuberculin) test.
From Frank D, Silva M, and Needlman R: Failure to thrive: Myth and method. Contemp Pediatr 10:114–133, 1993.

cluding a pediatrician, nutritionist, social worker, and developmental specialist is ideal. Pediatricians may need to refer to clinicians in those professions, integrating their insights and coordinating their efforts.

Medical

Medical management entails identifying the risk factors, and treating the underlying conditions associated with growth failure (Table 38–1). Time of onset can offer important clues (Table 38–2). Special attention should be paid to perinatal risk factors, such as prematurity, small for gestational age, and prenatal exposure to drugs (e.g., antiseizure medications, alcohol, or cocaine). Neonatal head circumference is important, because symmetric intrauterine growth retardation (IUGR), in which height and head circumference as well as weight are below expected values, may carry a worse prognosis for later growth than asymmetric IUGR, in which weight is reduced, but height and head circumference have been spared. Any signs of malabsorption (frequent, soft, or acholic stools; distention; or flatulence) should be investigated. Frequent minor infections suggest immune deficiency (growth failure may be the first sign of the acquired immunodeficiency syndrome). Minor infections also may be a consequence of malnutrition-related immune dysfunction and should be treated aggressively.

As part of the review of systems, special attention should be paid to medical conditions that may cause loss of appetite as their first or only manifestation. This category includes infections (giardiasis, other parasites, chronic urinary tract infections, chronic sinusitis, dental caries), gastrointestinal conditions (e.g., gastroesophageal reflux, celiac disease, malabsorption, chronic constipation), mechanical obstruction (e.g., adenoid hypertrophy, vascular slings), neurologic impairment

TABLE 38–2. Age of Onset of Failure to Thrive: Diagnostic Considerations

Age of Onset	Diagnostic Considerations
Prenatal (IUGR, prematurity)	"Symmetric" IUGR: prenatal infections, congenital syndromes, teratogenic exposures (associated with oral-motor dysfunction)
Neonatal	Incorrect formula preparation; failed breastfeeding; metabolic, chromosomal, anatomic abnormalities; neglect
3–6 months	Inadequate monetary resources, improper formula preparation, milk protein intolerance, oral-motor dysfunction, celiac disease, HIV
7–12 months	Autonomy struggles, overly fastidious parent, rumination, oral-motor dysfunction, delayed introduction of solids
After 12 months	Acquired illness, new psychosocial stressor (e.g., divorce, job loss, new sibling), caries (especially, nursing bottle caries)

HIV, human immunodeficiency virus; IUGR, intrauterine growth retardation.
From Frank D, Silva M, Needlman R: Failure to thrive: Myth and method. Contemp Pediatr 10:114–133, 1993.

(e.g., oral-motor dysfunction, tactile hypersensitivity), and metabolic or toxic causes (e.g., lead toxicity, iron deficiency, zinc deficiency).

The family history may point to inherited conditions, such as inflammatory bowel disease. Parental size is important in explaining short stature, but is less relevant to FTT.

A thorough physical examination is essential. Any signs of intentional injury are critical, because the combination of food restriction and physical abuse is potentially life threatening. Laboratory tests should be limited, initially, to screening for relatively common conditions that may contribute to, or complicate, growth failure. Routine tests might include a complete blood count, lead level, urinalysis, urine culture, electrolytes, and a PPD (tuberculin) test with a control to detect anergy. More extensive testing, when not directed by history or physical findings, rarely yields useful information.

Nutritional

Nutritional assessment focuses on current intake, feeding behaviors, and the feeding history. Current intake is gauged best by a food log or a 24-hour diet recall interview by a nutritionist. As a first approximation, a description of a typical day's intake may identify obvious deficiencies. For young infants, a detailed description of formula preparation or a typical breastfeeding meal is important. The mother's impression that the child "eats a lot" is often erroneous. Excessive juice consumption is associated with FTT. Skim and 1% milk may also blunt the appetite, without providing sufficient calories. Any special restrictions (e.g., vegetarianism), food fads, and favorite foods should be noted.

The primary aim of dietary guidance is to increase the ingestion of calories and protein by raising the caloric density of the food. In practical terms, that means encouraging fatty foods because, ounce for ounce, lipids provide twice as many calories as proteins or carbohydrates. Vegetables need cheese sauce; apples and bananas need peanut butter. For infants, a 24 calorie per ounce formula can be made by mixing 1 can (13 ounces) of formula concentrate with 8 (not 13) ounces of water. One scoop of formula powder can be added to 4 ounces of strained fruit ("super fruit"). One cup of dry milk powder added to 4 cups of whole milk increases calories and protein ("super milk").

Awareness of the cultural meanings ascribed to different foods can be helpful. For example, green vegetables may signify health, but do not provide concentrated calories. A multivitamin that contains iron and zinc (only palatable in tablets) can address potential micronutrient deficiencies and allay parental concerns about vitamins, avoiding struggles over vegetables.

The history should include the timing, setting, tenor, and duration of meals. Young children need three meals and three snacks per day. Children who "graze," nibbling from an open dish at whim, may never develop enough appetite to eat a full meal and may consume fewer total calories. For young children, a highchair provides containment and a situational cue to eat. Offering small portions allows the child a sense of control by asking for more and prevents the child from being overwhelmed by the food on the plate. Meals should be social times, but not full of distractions that draw the child's attention away from the food. Parental attention normally accompanies eating. By contrast, parents of children who have FTT often pay attention only while the child is refusing to eat, thereby inadvertently reinforcing the food refusal. Normally, meals are completed successfully within about 20 to 30 minutes. A much shorter duration suggests premature termination; longer mealtimes suggest a protracted "battle of the spoons."

The feeding history is important in uncovering etiologic factors, such as late introduction of solids; frequent spitting, choking or gagging; or rejection of textured foods. Occupational therapy may be necessary to address oral-motor dyscoordination or hypersensitivity, particularly in children who have cerebral palsy or other identified conditions. An account of the parents' responses to these challenges (e.g., force-feeding, prolonged meals, or encouraging "grazing") can elucidate what the feeding problem has meant to the parent and allow the parent to visualize new, more effective mealtime strategies. Behavioral treatment may be necessary in cases of entrenched food refusal.

Social

In some families, the child's rate of weight gain can be a barometer of the severity of stress. For example, the weight gain may rise when an alcoholic mother "goes on the wagon," only to fall again after she relapses. Other relevant stressors include physical and mental illness among family members and domestic violence. Knowledge of financial resources and expenses can clarify the role of economic deprivation. Parents who are ashamed to admit that their children are hungry may acknowledge unavailability of preferred, high-calorie foods such as meats, particularly at the end of the month before the paycheck or food stamps arrive. Homelessness makes food preparation and storage difficult. Families that are "staying with" friends or relatives (the housed homeless) often face similar hurdles. Social work intervention entails shifting the balance of stressors versus supports through referrals to community resources (e.g., food kitchens). The therapeutic relationship with the social worker often constitutes a powerful intervention in itself. Involvement of county child-protection services may help if persistent parental noncompliance with medical recommendations undermines the child's recovery.

Developmental and Behavioral

Developmental assessment is crucial because cognitive and behavioral disorders are often the most serious long-term sequelae of FTT. Federally mandated early intervention laws in all 50 states provide free child and family evaluations for children 0 to 3 years of age. After age 3, the school system can provide developmental and educational evaluation and services.

Management Strategies

Assessments in all four areas—medical, nutritional, social, and developmental—must be carried out simultaneously, the results of the initial findings and interventions determining the next steps. For example at the first visit, a 9-month-old who has mild growth faltering might be found to have excessive juice intake and a "grazing" pattern, so dietary changes are recommended. At follow-up a month later, the child's progress is reviewed and the father's alcoholism is divulged, leading to a referral to Al-Anon.

Parents of children who have FTT may persist in believing that the problem is due to illness or genetics or deny that a problem exists at all. Some take the diagnosis as a personal indictment. It is important to understand such beliefs in order to help the parents take appropriate action. FTT demands that the clinician build a therapeutic alliance, while keeping in mind the possibility that the parents' behavior may be endangering the health of the child. Close follow-up care is necessary—weekly for young children who have moderate or severe wasting, less frequently for children who are older or less affected.

Hospitalization is indicated when concerted outpatient efforts have failed or when the child's age or severity suggests imminent danger. The goal of hospitalization is nutritional rehabilitation, quantification of intake, and observation of the parent-child interaction. The response to hospitalization, however, does not (as commonly believed) distinguish organic FTT from NOFTT, because of the overlap between these subtypes and because hospitalization itself may impair food intake. Placement in a foster home or specialized "medical placement home" may be necessary.

PREVENTION

Although the efficacy of primary and secondary prevention of FTT is unproved, it makes sense to educate parents about developmentally appropriate and effective feeding techniques as a part of anticipatory guidance. On introduction of solid foods, parents can be counseled about the dangers of coaxing, bribery, and force-feeding. The concept of a "division of responsibility" is helpful: The parent is responsible for providing nutritious food at regular intervals; the child is responsible for determining how much to eat. Relatively early introduction of different textures and flavors may prevent some food refusal. Frequent, smaller quantities may be less intimidating and allow the child to feel more in control of the volume. Anticipatory guidance about feeding problems may be particularly important for children at risk because of prematurity, developmental disability, physical anomaly, or temperament. At the first signs of growth faltering, the primary care physician can begin pulling together information about the various factors that relate to failure to thrive and can intensify guidance about feeding and nutrition. Early medical, nutritional, social, and developmental intervention may prevent the emergence of refractory problems. Children who have recovered from FTT in terms of body size may remain at heightened risk for developmental and behavioral problems. Ongoing close pediatric monitoring, therefore, is prudent.

FURTHER READING

Chatoor I and Egan J: Nonorganic failure to thrive and dwarfism due to food refusal: A separation disorder. Am J Acad Child Psychiatry 22:294–301, 1983.

Frank DA: Biologic risks in "non-organic" failure to thrive. *In* Drotar D (ed): New Directions in Failure to Thrive. New York, Plenum Press, 1986, pp 17–26.

Frank DA and Zeisel SH: Failure to thrive. Pediatr Clin North Am 35:1187–1206, 1988.

Green M: Failure to thrive; or loss of weight. *In* Green M (ed): Pediatric Diagnosis, 6th ed. Philadelphia, WB Saunders, 1988.

Satter E: Child of Mine: Feeding with Love and Good Sense. Palo Alto, CA, Bull Publishing Co, 1983.

Chapter 39

Injury Management

Alan D. Woolf
David Greenes

Stabilization, Lacerations, Head Trauma, and Poisoning

Although the developing subspecialty of pediatric emergency medicine has redirected the site of care for many injured children to the emergency department, the primary care clinician still often participates in both the triage and care of the injured child. Thus, the pediatrician must be familiar with the recognition and management of childhood injuries (see Chapter 28 for prevention). In this chapter, we discuss the initial stabilization of the injured child and the management of three common pediatric injuries: lacerations, head trauma, and poisoning.

STABILIZATION

The management of patients who have sustained a traumatic injury begins with the "primary survey," in which the clinician attends to the familiar "ABCs" of emergency assessment—evaluating the patient's Airway, Breathing, and Circulatory status. Traumatic injury to the face or neck may lead to airway difficulties because of anatomic obstruction of the airway or because the patient is unable to clear secretions. In order to maximize airway patency while still protecting the cervical spine, the injured patient should be placed in a supine position on the bed, with the neck stabilized in a neutral position (ideally with a hard cervical collar or with an assistant manually holding the head and neck). The clinician may attempt maneuvers to open the airway, such as the "jaw thrust," in which forward pressure is applied from behind the angle of the mandibles, or the "chin lift," in which the chin is pulled forward.

In some cases, especially with unconscious or semiconscious patients, oral or nasopharyngeal airways may be used as an adjunct. The clinician must avoid any manipulation of the neck that, in the case of an unstable cervical spine, may lead to spinal cord injury. Cervical spine precautions should be maintained until the clinician is certain that no cervical spine injury has occurred. Patients who cannot cooperate with a careful examination of the neck (because of altered mental status); who complain of pain, tenderness, or decreased range of motion of the neck; or who have suffered a high-force mechanism of injury (Table 39–1) should be assumed to have a possible injury to the cervical spine. Any patient whose airway is compromised or in whom there is a question of cervical spine injury should be transferred by ambulance to a trauma center as soon as possible.

Injured patients may have abnormalities of their breathing either because of neurologic injury (in which neurologic control of respiration is compromised) or because of direct injury to the chest, which may lead to pneumothorax, hemothorax, or pulmonary contusion. All seriously injured patients should receive 100% oxygen, accompanied by bag-mask ventilation if the patient is making inadequate or ineffective respiratory effort. Any patient whose respirations are inadequate or who has signs of respiratory distress (e.g., grunting, flaring, retractions, cyanosis, or stridor) should be transferred to a trauma center as soon as possible.

The patient's heart rate, pulses, and blood pressure should be measured to assess the circulatory status. Circulatory instability may result from external or internal hemorrhage or from cardiac pump failure (as may occur with cardiac contusions, cardiac tamponade, or pneumothorax). Any significant external bleeding should be tamponaded with direct pressure to the bleeding site. Patients who have circulatory instability after traumatic injury need to be transferred as soon as possible to a trauma center. If possible, intravenous access should be obtained and 20 mL/kg of normal saline or lactated Ringer solution infused for patients presenting with any signs of circulatory instability. However, transfer to a trauma center should not be delayed by attempts to begin intravenous fluid therapy.

The primary survey for traumatized patients extends past the "ABCs" to include an assessment of "D" and "E" as well. "D" stands for Disability, reminding the clinician to assess the patient's neurologic status. A mini-neurologic evaluation should consists of an assessment of the patient's mental status ("alert," "responsive to voice," "responsive to pain," or "unresponsive"), an assessment of the patient's pupils (symmetry of size and reactivity to light), and an assessment of strength of all four extremities. If any neurologic abnormalities are noted, it should be assumed that the patient has suffered a brain injury, and the patient should be transferred to a trauma center as soon as possible.

Finally, the "E" of the primary survey stands for "Exposure," reminding the clinician to remove the patient's clothing and to look quickly over all of the body for any life- or limb-threatening lesions. Any sources of bleeding should be tamponaded. Extremities that appear deformed, swollen, or tender should be assumed to be fractured and should be splinted. The patient should be rolled (maintaining cervical spine precautions) so that the back can be examined for any signs of injury.

Patients who have abnormalities noted on the primary survey should have resuscitation efforts begun immediately, and an ambulance should be called. In addition, any patient who has suffered any of the high-force mechanisms of injury listed in Table 39–1 should be assumed to be at risk for serious injury and should be transported to a trauma center.

If the patient does not meet these criteria for immediate transfer, a careful secondary survey should be performed. One should examine the patient systematically from head to toe, evaluating for any signs of injury to the head, neck, chest, abdomen, back, pelvis, or extremities. The clinician should have a low threshold for concern and for transfer, recognizing that many injuries that are only mildly symptomatic now may be life threatening within a couple of hours. Patients hav-

TABLE 39–1. Indications for Immediate Transfer to Trauma Center

High-Force Mechanisms of Injury

Motor vehicle collisions involving any of the following:
  Pedestrian struck by a car at a speed >20 mph
  High-speed collisions, especially with significant damage to the car
  Ejection of the passenger
  Rollover of the vehicle
  Death of any occupants of the car
  Prolonged extrication
Falls greater than 20 ft
Explosions or fires

Signs of Potentially Serious Injury on Secondary Survey

Head

  Depressed skull fracture
  Bulging fontanel
  Retinal hemorrhages
  Penetration or open injury
  Deterioration of mental status
  Abnormal neurologic examination
  Facial deformity or instability

Neck

  Posterior spine tenderness
  Decreased range of motion of the neck
  Shifting of the trachea away from midline
  Crepitus
  Penetration injury

Chest

  Chest wall tenderness or deformity
  Decreased breath sounds; unequal breath sounds
  Point of maximal impulse (PMI) of heart shifted
  Penetration injury
  Muffled heart tones

Abdominal

  Penetration injury
  Tenderness
  Distention or discoloration

Genitourinary/Rectal

  Blood at the urethral meatus
  Blood (gross or occult) noted on rectal examination

Extremities

  Signs of femur fracture (tenderness, deformity, swelling)
  Decreased or absent pulses
  Coolness or pallor of an extremity
  Complete or near-complete amputation

Back

  Spinous tenderness or deformity
  Decreased range of motion

ing any of the signs of symptoms listed in Table 39–1 should be assumed to have a potentially life-threatening injury and should be transported to a trauma center as soon as possible for definitive care.

Patients who have none of these symptoms or signs are at a lower risk for serious injury. For many patients, injuries will be limited to contusions of the soft tissue or perhaps to isolated extremity fractures. If the patient meets none of the criteria for urgent transfer previously described, definitive care may be able to be provided by the primary care clinician in the office or perhaps by a referral to an orthopedic surgeon. If there is any question about how a traumatized patient should be managed, it always is safer to refer the patient to an emergency department.

LACERATIONS

Lacerations are among the most common injuries suffered in childhood. Many children who have lacerations seek care from their primary care clinicians. Although some complicated lacerations require referral to an emergency department or to a surgeon, many can be managed well by a clinician in the office.

Assessment

History

When assessing a laceration, the mechanism of injury should be explored carefully. Lacerations caused by dirty objects and lacerations caused by human or animal bites are at especially high risk for infection. Lacerations involving particulate objects, especially broken glass, raise the risk of foreign bodies' being present in the wound. Blunt force injuries, such as falls or collisions, raise the possibility of bony injuries underlying the fracture or injuries to other body parts as well. In addition, it is important to note the timing of the injuries, because lacerations that are more than several hours old are at increased risk for wound infection.

The patient's immunization history should be ascertained, as should the presence of any drug allergies. Consideration should be made for any chronic medical conditions that may impede hemostasis (e.g., hemophilia) or wound healing (e.g., chronic steroid use).

Physical Examination

Assuming that the history and a rapid assessment of the patient's general appearance raise no concerns for major organ or multiple trauma, the physical examination can focus mainly on assessing the laceration and associated structures. The location, orientation, length, and shape of the wound should be assessed. The wound edges should be assessed for contour (regular or jagged), viability (shredded or severely contused tissue

may not be viable), and apposability. The wound should be examined for dirt, gravel, glass, or other foreign bodies. The depth of the wound should be assessed to determine which tissues are involved (e.g., epidermis, dermis, fatty subcutaneous tissue, fascia, muscle). The presence and integrity of other anatomic structures visualized in the wound—tendons, blood vessels, nerves, or bones—also should be noted.

Adjacent bones should be evaluated for signs of fracture, that is, tenderness, ecchymosis, or bony deformity. For lacerations involving the extremities, a careful examination of sensory, motor, and vascular function distal to the laceration needs to be performed to exclude the possibility of injuries to tendons, arteries, and nerves.

Radiographs

Radiographs should be obtained if there is concern for possible bony injury or if there is a possibility of radiopaque foreign bodies in the wound. Most wounds involving broken glass should be radiographed because glass may penetrate deeply into a wound while leaving minimal superficial signs of its presence.

Treatment

When to Refer

Wounds that are (1) grossly contaminated; (2) caused by animal bites; (3) more than 24 hours old on the face and scalp; or (4) more than 6 hours old elsewhere in the body are all at increased risk of infection, especially if the wound is sutured. Decisions about whether to suture these wounds will depend primarily on the degree of suspected contamination, the size and location of the wound, and the wound's cosmetic importance. If there is question about how an old or contaminated wound should be managed, referral to an emergency department is indicated. In addition, if the wound was caused by a wild animal or by a domestic pet who is acting ill or who cannot be located for observation, referral should be made for rabies prophylaxis. Other reasons to refer patients to an emergency department are listed in Table 39–2.

Preparing the Child and Family

The clinician should explain the process of repair to the family, with assurance that aside from minimal discomfort caused by the administration of local anesthesia, the repair should be painless.

TABLE 39–2. Lacerations That May Require Referral to a Surgeon or Emergency Department

Lacerations with any of the following:
  Wounds at high risk for infection (see text)
  Lacerations of nerves, tendons, blood vessels, or glands
  Devitalized tissue edges, requiring more than minimal
    debridement
  Suspicion of retained foreign body
  Cosmetically difficult wounds, including full-thickness
    wounds of the nose or ear or lacerations to the vermilion
    border of the lip
  Repairs that require sedation or immobilization beyond
    what can be done safely in the office

Many older children are able to cooperate and will hold still for the repair. For infants, toddlers, and younger children, an assistant generally is needed to immobilize the affected body part during the repair. Often, a papoose or a "mummy wrap" with a sheet is necessary to immobilize the child adequately.

For young children having delicate or cosmetically important repairs (e.g., of lips, eyelids, or eyebrows), sedating medications may be required. Patients receiving sedation should have continuous monitoring of their oxygen saturation, heart rate, respiratory rate, and blood pressure. An assistant should be ready to provide supplemental oxygen, suction of the oropharynx, and bag-mask ventilation, if necessary. If the child cannot be monitored safely during the sedation, the patient should be referred to an emergency department.

Before beginning the repair, the clinician should be assured that all necessary equipment is available. A list of required materials is shown in Table 39–3.

Local Anesthesia

Appropriate use of local anesthetics provides complete anesthesia for most patients during the suturing. Usually, 1% lidocaine (maximum dose 5 mg/kg) is injected with a 25- to 30-gauge needle, in a series of injections into the subcuticular surfaces of the wound edges, until the complete circumference of the wound has been anesthetized. Anesthesia is achieved within 2 to 5 minutes of administration. Buffering of the lidocaine with sodium bicarbonate (10% sodium bicarbonate with 90% lidocaine by volume) or warming of the lidocaine to body temperature makes lidocaine administration less painful.

Many physicians prefer using lidocaine in a solution premixed with epinephrine (1:10,000). The addition of epinephrine causes local vasoconstriction, which leads to decreased systemic absorption of the lidocaine and less bleeding in the surgical field. Lidocaine with epinephrine should be avoided in regions with end-arteriolar circulation (digits, tip of nose, and penis), in which there is a theoretical risk of severe vasoconstriction and tissue necrosis.

Cleaning the Wound

After the wound is anesthetized, pressure irrigation with normal saline should be performed to clear debris and bacteria from the wound. Pressure irrigation can be performed with a 30- or 60-mL syringe attached to an 18-gauge angiocath or to a commercially available splash guard. A total of 100 mL of saline for each centimeter of laceration length should be used as a minimum, with larger volumes for dirty wounds. The skin adjacent to the wound should be cleaned with 10% povidone-iodine solution (Betadine). Sterile drapes around the edges of the cleaned skin provide a larger sterile field.

Any shredded or devitalized tissue at the wound margin should be debrided, but the amount of debridement generally should be kept to a minimum. If extensive debridement appears necessary, referral to a surgeon or emergency department is indicated. Any foreign bodies visualized in the wound should be removed. Shaving of hair around a laceration is generally not recommended, because shaving is cosmetically undesirable and may increase skin irritation and inflammation.

Wound Repair

Very superficial wounds, with edges that appear well apposed, may be treated simply with a sterile

TABLE 39–3. Materials Needed for Laceration Repair

Local anesthetic
  1% lidocaine solutions, with and without epinephrine
  Small syringes (3–5 mL) and needles (25–30 gauge for
    injection)
Irrigation and wound cleaning materials
  Large syringes (30–60 mL) with Luer-Lok connectors
  Large-bore intravenous catheters or needles, or splash
    guards for pressure irrigation
  Sterile saline solution
  Sterile bowl
  Povidone-iodine solution
  Gauze pads (4 × 4)
  Sterile drapes
  Sterile gloves
Suturing equipment: scissors, toothed forceps, needle driver
Suturing material
  Absorbable sutures (Vicryl), sizes 3-0 to 5-0
  Nonabsorbable sutures, Ethilon or polypropylene, sizes 4-0
    to 6-0
  Steri-Strips

tape, such as Steri-Strips. This tape may be applied with tincture of benzoin solution to improve adhesion.

Lacerations that have some gaping of the wound edges heal best if the skin edges are apposed with sutures. In general, wounds should be repaired so that each layer of tissue involved in the laceration has its edges apposed and sutured sequentially, that is, fascia to fascia, dermis to dermis, and skin to skin. Superficial lacerations may require only skin sutures. Deeper lacerations may require several layers of closure.

Subcuticular layers should be repaired with absorbable suture, preferably polyglactin 910 (Vicryl), which provides good tensile strength for 3 to 4 weeks before absorbing. Fascia may be closed with 3-0 or 4-0 Vicryl. For subcuticular sutures of the dermis, 4-0 or 5-0 Vicryl generally is used. These subcuticular sutures should be inverted, so that the knot is buried deep in the wound and does not protrude into the healing skin. The main purpose of suturing the dermis is to eliminate the "dead space" that would exist deep in the wound if only the skin were sutured and to take the tension off the skin sutures to allow better healing of the skin. With well-placed subcuticular sutures, the skin edges are almost fully apposed before skin sutures are placed, so that there is a minimum of tension on the skin sutures.

For skin sutures, nonabsorbable suture material such as nylon or polypropylene are preferred, because, theoretically, they cause less inflammation and less scarring than the absorbable sutures: 6-0 sutures generally are used on the face, 5-0 sutures on the upper extremity, and 4-0 sutures on the lower extremity and scalp. Sutures should be perpendicular to the wound margin and should be spaced regularly, ranging from an interval of every 3 mm for facial lacerations to an interval of every 10 mm for larger lacerations in cosmetically unimportant areas. The ideal cuticular suture is tight enough to appose and evert the skin edges but not so tight as to strangulate the skin.

After the skin has been closed, a topical antibiotic (such as bacitracin) should be applied to the suture line. A sterile dressing or bandage should be applied, with attention to placing a bandage that will withstand the curious patient's attempts to remove it.

Aftercare

The family should be instructed to keep the wound covered and dry for 48 hours to allow re-epithelialization to begin. Thereafter, the wound may be gently cleaned daily with soap and water. The family should be instructed to watch carefully for any signs of wound infection and to return immediately if any of these signs arise. The length of time that sutures should be left in place depends on the body part involved, ranging from 5 days for facial lacerations to 7 to 10 days for upper extremity lacerations and 10 to 14 days for lower extremity lacerations.

Prophylactic antibiotics are not indicated for simple, clean lacerations repaired soon after injury. Prophylactic antibiotics should be considered for dirty wounds, for wounds closed later after an injury, and for bite wounds. Most authorities recommend prophylactic antibiotics for human bite wounds, and many recommend antibiotics for dog and cat bites as well. Antibiotics used for bite wounds should provide coverage for *Staphylococcus aureus*, streptococcal species, oral anaerobes, and *Pasteurella multocida*. Amoxicillin/clavulanate, 40 mg/kg/day divided into 3 daily doses, often is used in this setting. Nonbite wounds that require prophylaxis can generally be treated with a first-generation cephalosporin (such as cephalexin, 50 mg/kg/day, divided into 4 daily doses), which covers well for *Staphylococcus* and *Streptococcus*, the two most common pathogens in this setting. Usually, an antibiotic course of 3 to 5 days is sufficient for prophylaxis.

All lacerations should be considered potential risks for tetanus infection. The child should receive a "booster" immunization of 0.5 mL of tetanus and diphtheria toxoid (Td) if he or she has not completed the primary immunization series (three shots), has not had a tetanus immunization within the past 10 years, or has a contaminated or complicated wound and has not had a tetanus immunization within the past 5 years. For children whose wounds are contaminated or complicated and whose primary immunization series is incomplete, tetanus immune globulin (3000 to 6000 IU) also should be given.

Alternative Techniques

Increasing experience has been reported on using tissue adhesives such as the cyanoacrylates for laceration repair without sutures. These adhesives appear to be less painful and frightening for the patient and quicker to use than conventional sutures. The tissue adhesives are being used increasingly widely in other countries. Although not yet approved for use in the United States, the tissue adhesives probably will become an important tool for laceration repair in the coming years.

HEAD TRAUMA

Epidemiology

Head trauma is a common reason for consulting a pediatrician. It has been estimated that 12% of all children in the United States contact a physician with a complaint of some form of head trauma each year. Head injury is a leading cause of morbidity and mortality in pediatrics, accounting for 50% to 60% of all pediatric trauma-related deaths each year.

Most pediatric head injuries are not serious and can be well-managed by the primary care pediatrician. The challenge for the pediatrician is to recognize the warning signs in those few cases that are more serious and that require referral for further emergency management.

Pathophysiology

Most head injuries in pediatrics result from blunt impact, most typically from falls by younger children and from sports injuries or motor vehicle collisions involving older children. Shaking injuries, usually as a result of child abuse (the "shaken baby" syndrome), also may lead to serious brain injury. Penetrating trauma to the head (from bullets or from impalement) is a much less common form of head injury in pediatrics.

Blunt trauma or shaking injury to the head may cause direct neuronal injury, which in itself may lead to altered mental status, focal neurologic deficits, or seizures, and often is accompanied by cerebral edema and/or intracranial bleeding. Because the cranium can accommodate a fixed volume, the accumulation of blood or edema fluid in the brain leads to an increase in intracranial pressure, with a consequent increase in the resistance of blood flow to the brain. Brain perfusion is compromised, and neuronal injury worsens. This process continues until the cerebral edema and/or intracranial bleeding can be relieved through medical or surgical management.

Patients can be symptomatic after head injury in the absence of recognizable anatomic lesions visualized by computed tomography of the head (head CT). Persistent symptoms (such as headache, vomiting, or abnormality in mental status) after a head injury in a patient who has no recognizable anatomic lesions is termed a *concussion*. For patients who have a concussion, it is presumed that there has been some more minor degree of direct brain injury.

Clinical Assessment of Head Injury

The primary goal in the assessment of head-injured children is to detect those patients who have suffered intracranial injury, especially those who may have intracranial bleeding or edema. A secondary goal is to detect those patients who may have fractures of the skull, both because skull fractures indicate an increased risk for associated intracranial injury and because skull fractures themselves may need further management. Depressed skull fractures may need surgical elevation, and linear skull fractures in infants may enlarge over time if a leptomeningeal cyst or "growing fracture" develops. The clinician needs to be vigilant for any case in which the injuries observed do not appear to be in keeping with the mechanism described, in which case a diagnosis of child abuse needs to be considered.

Taking the History

The first issue to consider in the history is the reported mechanism of injury. Of course, higher force mechanisms of injury (such as a pedestrian struck by a motor vehicle or a child who falls from a great height) greatly increase the risk of serious injury. It should be noted, however, that even low-force mechanisms may lead to serious injury, especially in infants and toddlers. A number of researchers, for instance, have found that skull fractures in infants quite commonly result from household falls of less than 3 or 4 feet. It also is well known that even low-force blunt impact to the temporoparietal region of the head may lead to laceration of the middle meningeal artery and the development of an epidural hematoma.

The clinician should ascertain whether there was loss of consciousness (LOC) at the time of the initial impact. Serious brain injuries certainly may occur in the absence of LOC; conversely, brief LOC may occur even in minor head injury. However, as a general rule, a history of LOC (especially prolonged LOC) indicates a higher degree of impact to the brain and a greater risk for intracranial injury.

The clinician also should inquire about the child's behavior and activity since the injury. Lethargy, irritability, headache, and vomiting are not uncommon in the first few hours even after minor head injuries, but those patients who appear to have severely altered behavior or persistent or worsening symptoms 3 to 4 hours or more after an injury are especially worrisome for intracranial damage. Any child who has had seizures, depressed mental status, or focal neurologic symptoms after head trauma is at very high risk for an intracranial injury.

Finally, it is important for the clinician to note how long ago the head injury occurred. Some intracranial injuries (most notably epidural hematomas) may present with a "lucid interval" of 6 to 8 hours in which the patient appears relatively well before the intracranial bleeding accumulates to such an extent that it causes symptoms. The clinician who sees a child 2 hours after an injury, therefore, needs to realize that the child's condition may deteriorate later.

Physical Examination

The physical examination of the head-injured infant begins with a survey of the "ABCs" and vital signs. Next, a quick neurologic assessment should be performed to determine the patient's mental status (alert, arousable to voice, arousable to pain, or unarousable), behavioral state (lethargy or irritability should be noted), pupillary status (asymmetry or poor reactivity should be noted), and symmetry of strength and tone in the extremities. For children who have an open anterior fontanel, the fontanel should be assessed for fullness or bulging, which may indicate an increase in intracranial pressure. The eyes also should be funduscopically examined to evaluate for papilledema, which will be seen in some cases of increased intracranial pressure, or retinal hemorrhages, which are virtually pathognomonic for the shaking trauma common in child abuse.

Finally, the head should be examined carefully for any areas of swelling, ecchymosis, palpable depression of the skull, or palpable fracture lines. Signs of basilar skull fracture such as hemotympanum, bruising over the mastoid bone (Battle sign), periorbital ecchymoses ("raccoon eyes"), or cerebrospinal fluid rhinorrhea also should be noted.

The clinician should recognize the risk of cervical spine injury in any patient who has significant head trauma. The posterior spine should be palpated carefully for any tenderness or bony abnormality. If this examination is normal and the patient is alert and cooperative and has no complaints of neck pain, a test of *active* range of motion of the neck may be performed. If the patient is not alert, cannot cooperate, or has any complaint of neck pain or tenderness, range of motion testing should be deferred and the patient's neck immobilized, preferably in a hard cervical collar. If the patient does not have normal active range of motion, a cervical spine injury should be suspected and the neck immobilized.

Whom to Refer

Children who may have intracranial injury should be referred to the emergency department for head CT imaging and neurosurgical consultation. Included in this group are all head-injured children whose mental status is abnormal or who have focal neurologic dysfunction. Children who have penetrating trauma to the skull or any signs of skull fracture should be referred as well. In addition, children whose neurologic status is normal but who have persistent or progressing headache, lethargy, irritability, or vomiting should be referred. Any child who has post-traumatic seizures should be referred, as should children who have a history of any significant LOC. Some authors argue that brief LOC (less than 1 minute) may not be important in a child who now appears entirely well. If there is any question about how a patient who has a history of brief LOC should be managed, however, it probably is safer to refer the patient to an emergency department. In addition, any child who has a possible cervical spine injury should be transferred to an emergency department by ambulance, so that cervical spine immobilization can be safely maintained during transport. Finally, any child for whom the clinician suspects possible child abuse should be referred for a thorough medical and social investigation.

Management of Minor Head Injury

Children who do not meet these criteria likely have minor head injuries and can be managed safely at home. The clinician should consider observing these children in the office for a period of time, especially those who present soon after an injury. When children are discharged to home, the clinician should instruct the parents to watch for vomiting, seizures, changes in the child's behavioral state, or other complaints over the first 8 to 12 hours after the injury.

Children should be encouraged to rest until all symptoms associated with the head injury have resolved. Recent recommendations from the American Academy of Neurology suggest that if a child had LOC or has persistent concussive symptoms for greater than 15 minutes after an injury, he or she should be counseled to avoid any activities (such as sports) with a risk of reinjury for at least 1 week after symptoms resolve.

POISONING

Epidemiology

Although advances in the prevention of poisonings among children have been quite effective, toxic exposures continue to be a major pediatric health problem. More than 1.5 million poisonings are reported to poison control centers annually, approximately 60% of which involve children under 6 years of age. Table 39–4 presents the most common poisonings in young children living in the United States. Fortunately, the overwhelming majority of these episodes are trivial and result in few or no symptoms. However, about 1% of hospitalizations of children are for more serious poisonings.

The peak age in childhood for poisoning incidents is between 18 months and 3 years. There is a slight male predominance until adolescence, when girls attempt suicide by self-poisoning much more often. Although most pediatric poisonings take place in the home around mealtime, out-of-home poisonings most often take place in the homes of grandparents. Many poisonings in early childhood occur when medicines or products are in use and their safety caps have been removed. Profiles of children who suffer multiple episodes of poisoning reveal them to be negativistic, aggressive, hyperactive, difficult to control, and engaged in a power struggle with their parents. Parents of poisoning repeaters have been characterized as young and inexperienced at parenting skills, with few psychosocial supports.

First Aid

If the poisoned child is at home, the parent should call the regional poison center and administer appropriate first aid. For many trivial or nontoxic exposures, this involves simply watching the child closely for unusual allergic or other symptoms.

TABLE 39–4. Most Frequent Causes of Early Childhood Poisoning in Children <6 Years Old

Agent	Number	% Total
Cosmetics and personal care products	137,225	12.1
Cleaning substances	126,511	11.1
Analgesics	86,936	7.6
Plants	79,362	7.0
Cough and cold preparations	70,632	6.2
Foreign bodies	60,579	5.3
Topical agents	57,673	5.1
Pesticides (includes rodenticides)	45,897	4.0
Antimicrobials	40,220	3.5
Vitamins	37,932	3.3
Gastrointestinal preparations	37,027	3.3
Arts/crafts/office supplies	29,010	2.6
Hydrocarbons	27,632	2.4
Hormones and hormonal antagonists	21,161	1.9
Food products/food poisoning	20,143	1.8

Data from Litovitz TL, Smilkstein M, Felberg L, et al: 1996 Annual Report of the American Association of Poison Control Centers Toxic Exposure Surveillance System. Am J Emerg Med 15: 447–500, 1997.

Skin Exposures

For most skin or mucous membrane exposures, first aid involves washing the skin with lukewarm running water and soap or placing the victim in a shower. Some toxins, such as organophosphate pesticides, are absorbed directly through the skin. In such cases gloves and an apron must be worn to avoid contamination.

Eye Exposures

For ocular exposures, the parent should immediately hold the victim's head under lukewarm running water that is at low pressure but directed onto the eye to flush out and dilute the toxin as much as possible. Flushing with water for 15 to 20 minutes is recommended, although difficult to achieve. No ophthalmic drops or solutions should be used initially without consulting an ophthalmologist. If the toxin is a known corrosive or carries a known high risk of ocular damage, or if pain, redness, and periocular swelling continue beyond 30 minutes after flushing, the victim should be sent to a medical facility for ophthalmologic examination.

Inhalant Exposures

When a known noxious gas has been inhaled, the first priority of the rescuer is self-protection against becoming a second victim. Many unsuspecting good samaritans who enter an unventilated garage where a car's motor is running to "save" a comatose friend have themselves been overcome by carbon monoxide before being able to complete the rescue. When confronted with this scenario, the rescuer is well advised to get help, ventilate the building without going inside, or enter using appropriate precautions, including an approved, self-contained breathing apparatus. Moving the victim to fresh air is the first aid for inhalant exposures.

Oral Exposures

When a poisoning by mouth occurs, the rescuer should give nothing by mouth until the inherent toxicity of the compound can be determined. Because time is so important in determining whether lavage, charcoal administration, or both should take place, a poison center should be contacted immediately.

Clinical Assessment

History

The clinician's first contact with a family concerning a childhood poisoning usually is

over the telephone. **It is important to gather as much information as possible before deciding on the correct triage** (Can the child stay home? Is any action recommended in the home? Should the parent call an ambulance?) **Important points of the interview are summarized in Table 39–5.**

The physician must keep in mind that the history may not always be accurate. Parents may underestimate the dose of a poison to allay their own fears. Drugs of abuse frequently contain adulterants, of which the adolescent user may be unaware; for example, cocaine frequently is cut with inositol or phencyclidine. What is marketed as an amphetamine may, in fact, be phenylpropanolamine or caffeine. In addition, emotionally distraught teenagers attempting suicide or those who have a psychiatric illness such as anorexia nervosa may deliberately give misleading information about the time of ingestion or the quantity ingested or even about the type of drug or poison involved.

Physical Examination

The clinician's first responsibility is to assess the patient's airway, the adequacy of ventilation, and the stability of the cardiovascular system. Advanced cardiorespiratory life supports should be implemented as necessary to stabilize the patient's condition.

The child should then be examined quickly, with particular attention paid to the vital signs; skin; and cardiovascular, respiratory, and neurologic systems. The physician should assess the patient's level of consciousness and look for focal neurologic deficits, because many poisons exert selective effects on the central nervous system. Pupil size, deep tendon reflexes, and integrity of the higher cortical function should be determined. Frequently the patient's physical appearance and the examination can support the diagnosis of a particular poison. The patient's breath may have the characteristic garlic odor of organophosphate poisoning; the patient may be confused and tachypneic, as in salicylate intoxication; or the patient's skin may have a bluish tinge secondary to methemoglobinemia induced by nitrites or dapsone exposure.

Specific toxins may bind to receptors on specific target organs and produce predictable effects. For example, some poisons mainly affect the liver

TABLE 39–5. Important Points of History Taking in a Poisoning

Toxin identity
    Exact toxins involved
    Single toxin vs. polydrug overdose
Dose
    Drug/chemical/toxin's concentration
    Amount of toxin involved in the incident (worse case scenario)
Route
    Ingestion, inhalation, dermal or eye exposure, parenteral
Events
    Single episode (acute, one-time) of poisoning or one of several repetitive events (subacute)
    Chronic overdose
    Withdrawal (abstinence) syndrome
Duration
    Time and duration of exposure
    Span of time between exposure and presentation to medical facility
Victim
    Age and weight
Symptoms and tempo
    Symptoms*
    Progression of symptoms (rapidly improving or getting worse [tempo of progression])
Medical background
    Underlying relevant medical conditions
    Known allergies (either to the toxin or to a potential antidote)
    Current and past medications available to the patient
Circumstances of incident
    Location (e.g., home, grandparent's house, child care facility, school)
    Unintentional vs. intentional
    Other potential victims
    Suicide attempt vs. drug misuse
    Occupational or environmental exposure to the toxin
    Child abuse or neglect involved
    How many similar such injuries in child's past

*Note: Some toxins (e.g., acetaminophen, *Amanita* mushroom poisoning, oral hypoglycemics such as glipizide or glyburide, Lomotil, monoamine oxidase inhibitors, paraquat) are notable for a symptom-free period after exposure ranging from 6 to 12 hours to as long as a day or two before toxicity develops.

TABLE 39–6. Toxidromes of Symptoms and Signs in Poisoning

Amphetamines, sympathomimetics: Tachycardia, nausea, vomiting, hypertension, abdominal pain, diaphoresis, anorexia, tremulousness

Anticholinergic drugs: Disorientation, ataxia, psychomotor agitation, hallucinations, psychosis, seizures, coma, extrapyramidal symptoms, respiratory failure, ileus, urinary retention, mydriasis, hyperpyrexia, dry flushed skin, tachycardia

Cholinergic agents (e.g., organophosphate pesticides): Salivation, lacrimation, urination, defecation, gastrointestinal cramping, emesis (mnemonic: SLUDGE); also bronchorrhea, respiratory failure, seizures, miosis, bradycardia, fasciculations, seizures, coma

Iron: Nausea, hematemesis, hemorrhagic diarrhea, shock, hypotension, coma, hyperpyrexia, metabolic acidosis, coma, arrhythmias, hepatitis, respiratory failure (late)

Narcotics: Confusion, lethargy, ataxia, coma, respiratory depression, hypotension, miosis, bradycardia, pulmonary edema, seizures (specifically meperidine, propoxyphene)

Phencyclidine: Rotatory nystagmus, dissociative delusions, aggression, coma, seizures

Salicylates: Tachypnea, hyperpyrexia, nausea, vomiting, mixed acidosis, confusion, coma

Theophylline: Nausea, vomiting, tremulousness, tachycardia, arrhythmias, confusion, seizures, coma

Toxic alcohols (i.e., methanol/ethylene glycol): Intoxication, osmolar gap, metabolic acidosis, blindness (methanol), urinary crystals and renal failure (ethylene glycol)

(e.g., *Amanita phalloides* mushrooms, acetaminophen, carbon tetrachloride), the kidney (e.g., nonsteroidal anti-inflammatory agents, gold, mercury, ethylene glycol), the heart (e.g., β-blocking agents, calcium channel blockers, cardiac glycosides, tricyclic antidepressants, doxorubicin hydrochloride [Adriamycin]), the lungs (e.g., paraquat), and the central nervous system (e.g., opiates, barbiturates, carbon monoxide, isoniazid, camphor). Other poisons, including hydrogen sulfide gas, cyanide, iron, salicylates, antimetabolites, alkylating agents, and colchicine, are general cellular poisons that affect multiple organ systems. Table 39–6 presents some of the constellations of symptoms and signs (toxidromes) that are seen in pediatric poisonings.

Laboratory Tests

Although the diagnosis of a toxic exposure is suspected most often on the basis of the history and physical examination, it sometimes can be confirmed by the laboratory assessment of body fluids. Both blood and urine usually are sent for a "toxic screen" analysis. Some agents, such as cocaine, are cleared from the blood rapidly and are detected with more precision as the parent compound or metabolites in the urine. Although a toxic screen will detect common drugs and chemicals (e.g., acetaminophen, aspirin, ethanol, some drugs of abuse), the clinician is well advised to know the limits of the laboratory to which the specimen is sent. A negative toxic screen does not rule out a poisoning; many drugs and chemicals, including most pesticides, hallucinogens, and newer sedative-hypnotics and antidepressants, are not detected by routine screenings. The physician must rely on clinical skills and judgment, rather than on the toxic screen.

Once a drug has been detected, quantification of its concentration in the serum or urine may indicate the severity of the overdose. Most toxicologic laboratories should be able to perform an immediate quantitative level (if the clinician specifically requests it) of acetaminophen, carbamazepine, ethanol, iron, lithium, methanol, phenobarbital, phenytoin, salicylate, theophylline, or valproic acid. The more specific the physician can be in defining which drugs are to be ruled out, the better will be that laboratory's ability to perform the most precise assay.

Other laboratory tests can assist in diagnosis. A metabolic acidosis associated with an elevated anion gap, for example, can be seen in methanol, phenformin, isoniazid, iron, salicylate, cyanide, and ethylene glycol overdoses.

The clinician also can use simple chemical tests on blood or urine at the bedside to confirm a suspected diagnosis. Whole blood drawn from a patient who has significant methemoglobinemia appears chocolate-brown in color. Serum from a patient who has ingested nail polish remover or isopropyl alcohol turns Acetest tablets purple, indicating the presence of acetone. Boiled urine, when treated with fresh 10% ferric chloride solution, will turn color in the presence of salicylates (burgundy red) or phenothiazines (greenish purple).

Tests frequently ordered in a poisoning of unknown origin include arterial blood gas, electrolytes, blood urea nitrogen (BUN) and creatinine, liver enzymes, serum lactic acid, and urinalysis. A calculated serum osmolality ($2 \times Na + BUN/2.8 + glucose/18$) lower than the measured osmolality indicates the presence of a toxin with osmotic activity (e.g., ethanol, isopropranol, ethylene glycol, or methanol). If rhabdomyolysis is suspected, a serum creatine phosphokinase and serum and urine myoglobin levels can be helpful.

In assessing a patient who has overdosed on a warfarin-containing pesticide, clotting factors (prothrombin time, partial thromboplastin time) should be monitored for several days.

Patients who have ingested a volatile hydrocarbon or who have vomited while confused or comatose may require a chest radiograph so that an aspiration pneumonia can be ruled out. Chest radiographs also may be important in the assessment of patients who have taken a drug or chemical with known pulmonary toxicity, such as paraquat or iron. Carbon monoxide, ethchlorvynol, opiates, salicylates, and other agents can cause a noncardiogenic pulmonary edema that will be confirmed by chest radiograph. An abdominal film may pick up radiopaque tablets of chloral hydrate, heavy metals, iron and iodine, phenothiazines, and enteric-coated tablets (mnemonic: CHIPE).

Treatment

The management of poisoned patients includes resuscitation and supportive care, oral decontamination, elimination of the toxin, and antidotes, when they exist. The flow of diagnosis and management of the poisoned patient, based on both clinical judgment and pharmacokinetic principles, is illustrated in Figure 39–1.

The poisoned patient who presents in cardiopulmonary arrest must be resuscitated according to standard pediatric advanced cardiac life-support guidelines. Special attention should be given to clearing the airway, supporting respiratory function and air exchange, establishing intravenous access, and stabilizing the pulse and blood pressure. Dextrose, naloxone, and oxygen should be administered to all comatose patients or patients who have seizures whose history is unknown.

Oral Decontamination for Ingestions

Ipecac

When an alert child has recently ingested a large amount of a potentially harmful substance, it may be most expeditious to begin decontamination in the home. This process is accomplished by the administration of syrup of ipecac to the child to induce vomiting. Parents always should contact a poison center before giving ipecac. When it is indicated, parents are instructed to give a measured amount (2 teaspoons for children 9 to 12 months old; 1 tablespoon for children 1 to 12 years old; 30 mL for adolescents older than age 12) of syrup of ipecac, along with 6 to 8 ounces of water or juice. The child is spun around and walked or carried for 10 to 15 minutes until vomiting takes place. The dose of ipecac may be repeated if no vomiting occurs within 20 minutes; this regimen is effective in more than 90% of poisonings. General contraindications include the probability of a nontoxic ingestion or of a significant risk of aspiration (e.g., in the drowsy or comatose patient or when a hydrocarbon has been ingested). Ipecac-induced emesis also is contraindicated when the patient has swallowed a caustic compound or a neurotoxin capable of causing seizures or coma rapidly (e.g., isoniazid, camphor, strychnine, tricyclic antidepressants). Ipecac should not be administered if a vagal stimulus can worsen the agent's cardiotoxicity (e.g., calcium channel blockers, beta blockers, digitalis). Finally, syrup of ipecac should not be given to the patient who is bleeding from the upper gastrointestinal tract, who has uncontrolled hypertension or malignant cardiac arrhythmias, or who is younger than 6 months of age.

Lavage

Lavage of the stomach contents, using an orogastric tube, is an alternative to emesis in the oral

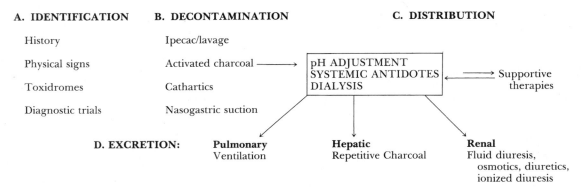

Figure 39–1. Approaches to diagnosis and clinical management for the poisoned patient.

decontamination of the patient. It is the preferred method for use in an emergency clinic, especially for the lethargic patient and also for children younger than 9 months of age. Once the tube has been inserted, 100 to 200 mL of fluid (normal saline or lacated Ringer solution) is given by syringe at each pass and then withdrawn until 1500 to 2000 mL has been exchanged or until the fluid is clear of tablets or the toxin. Frequently, the final pass is made by using activated charcoal, which then is left in the stomach.

Activated Charcoal

Activated charcoal is the adsorbent used most commonly in the oral decontamination of the poisoned patient. A finely graded, engineered charcoal that has a large surface area and specific pore-size characteristics, activated charcoal can perform three separate functions in the decontamination of the patient: (1) initial adsorption of toxin, (2) interruption of enterohepatic recirculation of toxic metabolites, and (3) gastrointestinal dialysis. Most common drugs and chemicals are adsorbed effectively by activated charcoal. The toxin is entrapped within the pores of the charcoal particle and held there until it is eliminated through defecation. The tremendous surface area of activated charcoal, at greater than 1000 m² per gram, increases its efficacy when it is given in excess of the amount of poison to be adsorbed. The usual pediatric dose is 1 gram/kg body weight to a maximum of 50 grams per dose.

Evidence suggests that repetitive doses of activated charcoal can affect osmotic gradients for some drugs, such that they are drawn across the semipermeable membrane of the intestinal blood vessels back into the lumen of the gut. There they are adsorbed by the charcoal, which in effect creates an "infinite sink" for the movement of molecules from a higher concentration in the blood toward a lower concentration in the gut lumen. Additionally, repetitive charcoal can interfere with hepatobiliary recirculation of toxic metabolites arising from the hepatic metabolism of a drug such as a cyclic antidepressant or an anticonvulsant.

There are some contraindications to oral-activated charcoal therapy. Some compounds (e.g., alcohols, caustic agents, cyanide, heavy metals, iron, lithium, and pesticides) are not appreciably adsorbed by charcoal. The presence of upper gastrointestinal bleeding, indicating that endoscopy may be needed, makes charcoal therapy inadvisable because the visual field is obscured. When a patient has been given oral medications as a part of therapy (e.g., anticonvulsants, antibiotics), char-

coal can inhibit the therapeutic drug's absorption and lower serum levels below effectiveness. Oral charcoal, especially repetitive doses, also may be contraindicated in those patients who have protracted vomiting or an abdominal ileus.

Enhanced Elimination

For those toxins whose parent compound, active metabolites, or both are excreted renally, establishing a brisk diuresis may enhance endogenous clearance. Exchange transfusion may be required to eliminate toxins in special circumstances. A few toxins, such as phencyclidine, have considerable enterogastric recirculation, so that continuous gastric suction may be beneficial to remove additional drug.

Catharsis and Whole-Bowel Irrigation

Cathartics are used to move (1) a toxin through the gastrointestinal tract before it can be absorbed or exert a corrosive local effect (e.g., an aspirin concretion), (2) charcoal-bound toxin out before it is desorbed off the charcoal, and (3) foreign bodies along the bowel before they can break down and release toxins (e.g., lead-containing paint chips, button batteries) or cause obstruction (e.g., large coins). Cathartics can reduce bowel transit time from 20 to 22 hours to 4 to 6 hours. Agents used commonly include sorbitol (3 to 4 mL/kg of a 35% solution up to 150 mL) and magnesium citrate (4 mL/kg up to 300 mL). Phosphate cathartics are associated with excessive salt absorption and calcium and electrolyte imbalances in children and are not recommended. During cathartic use, the child's stooling pattern and fluid-electrolyte status should be monitored carefully. For some toxins (e.g., iron tablets, lead-containing paint chips, sustained-released calcium channel blockers), whole-bowel irrigation with an isosmotic solution (e.g., polyethylene glycol) is given in large amounts (3 to 4 L) orally to cleanse the bowel of the offending toxin, literally washing pills out the rectum.

Ion Trapping

The fact that nonionized species of a small molecule can pass across membranes, whereas charged species cannot, forms the basis for the principle of ion trapping as an elimination strategy. Some drugs and chemicals change from ionized to nonionized species at a specific pH (known as the pKa). Through manipulation of the blood pH (usually alkalinizing the blood) and thereby

TABLE 39–7. Antidotes

Toxic Compound	Antidote	Dose	Route
Acetaminophen	N-Acetylcysteine	140 mg/kg load; 70 mg/kg q 4 hr × 17	PO
Arsenic	Dimercaprol (BAL)	3–4 mg/kg q 4 hr	IM
Benzodiazepine	Flumazenil	0.3 mg (see package insert)	IV
Beta-adrenergic blocker	Glucagon	50–100 μ/kg	IV
Calcium channel blocker	Calcium chloride	0.15–0.30 mL/kg (10% solution)	Slow IV
Carbamates	Atropine	0.02–0.05 mg/kg/dose (max 1 mg/dose)	IV
Carbon monoxide	Oxygen	100% or hyperbaric	Inhale
Cyanide	Amyl nitrite	1 ampule q 30 sec	Inhale
	Sodium nitrite	0.33 mL/kg (3% solution) to max 10 mL	IV
	Sodium thiosulfate	1.65 mL/kg (25% solution) to max 50 mL	IV
Digitalis	Digoxin immune Fab antibodies	5–10 vials (see package insert)	IV
Ethylene glycol/methanol	Ethanol	600 mg/kg load; 110 mg/kg/hr until toxic alcohol blood concentrations fall to less than 20 mg/dL	IV
Heparin	Protamine	See package insert	IV
Iron	Deferoxamine	15 mg/kg/hr	IV
Isoniazid (INH)	Pyridoxine (vitamin B[6])	1 gm/gm INH taken	IV
Lead	CaNa$_2$EDTA	50 mg/kg (max 1 gm/day)	IV
	Dimercaprol (BAL)	3–4 mg/kg q 4–6 hr (max 300 mg/dose)	IM
	Penicillamine	10–30 mg/kg/day	PO
	DMSA	See package insert	PO
Opiates	Naloxone	0.10 mg/kg/dose (max 2 mg/dose)	IV
Organophosphates	Atropine	0.02–0.05 mg/kg/dose (max 1 mg/dose)	IV
	Pralidoxime (2-PAM)	25–50 mg/kg (max 1 gm/dose)	IV
Phenothiazines (dystonic reaction)	Diphenhydramine	1–2 mg/kg/dose; max 25 mg	IV
Warfarin sodium (Coumadin)	Phytonadione (vitamin K)	1–5 mg	IM or slow IV (0.5 mg/min)

CaEDTA, calcium disodium ethylenediaminetetraacetic acid; DMSA, 2,3-dimercaptosuccinic acid; IM, intramuscularly; IV, intravenously

the urine pH (pH > 7.5), some drugs (e.g., aspirin and phenobarbital) can be trapped in their ionized form within the renal tubules and excreted rather than being reabsorbed through the tubular cells into the bloodstream.

Hemodialysis and Hemoperfusion

Hemodialysis and hemoperfusion are clearly hospital-based therapies and may be indicated in poisoning due to salicylates, ethanol, theophylline, isopropanol, methanol, ethylene glycol, and lithium.

Antidotes

An antidote is a "remedy"—a drug or chemical that combines with a poison to render it harmless. Most clinicians also include, in a broader although less precise definition, those remedies that counteract toxic effects or enhance a toxin's inactivation through metabolic processes. There are several mechanisms through which antidotes can work, including (1) alteration of the chemical or physical properties of the toxin; (2) chelation; (3) competitive receptor binding; (4) blocked metabolic activation of the toxin; (5) enhanced metabolic inactivation of the toxin; (6) specific antibody to the toxin; (7) counteraction of the toxin's physiologic effects; and (8) other or unknown mechanisms of action.

A representative list of antidotes for common pediatric poisons is given in Table 39–7. In addition, antisera are available for pit viper (Crotalidae) snakebites, coral (Elapidae) snakebites, and black widow spider (*Latrodectus mactans*) bites. A trivalent antitoxin (A, B, and E) also is available for the treatment of botulism.

FURTHER READING

Stabilization

American College of Surgeons Committee on Trauma: Advanced Trauma Life Support Course for Physicians. Chicago, American College of Surgeons, 1993.

Chameides L, Hazinski MF (eds): Textbook of Pediatric Advanced Life Support. Dallas, TX, American Heart Association, 1994.

Ruddy RM, Fleisher GR: An approach to the injured child. *In* Fleisher GR and Ludwig S (eds): Textbook of Pediatric Emergency Medicine, 3rd ed. Baltimore, Williams & Wilkins, 1993, pp 1079–1088.

Ziegler MM, Templeton JM: Major trauma. *In* Fleisher GR and Ludwig S (eds): Textbook of Pediatric Emergency Medicine, 3rd ed. Baltimore, Williams & Wilkins, 1993, pp 1089–1099.

Lacerations

Berk WA, Welch RD, Bock BF: Controversial issues in clinical management of the simple wound. Ann Emerg Med 21:95–103, 1992.
Lease JG: Office care of wounds. Pediatr Rev 13:257–261, 1992.
Rosenberg NM, Stewart GM, Quan L, Horton MA: Laceration management. Pediatr Emerg Care 9:247–250, 1993.
Templeton JM: Minor lesions. *In* Fleisher GR and Ludwig S (eds): Textbook of Pediatric Emergency Medicine, 3rd ed. Baltimore, Williams & Wilkins, 1993, pp 1299–1306.

Head Trauma

American Academy of Neurology, Quality Standards Subcommittee: Summary of recommendations for management of concussion in sports. MMWR 46:224–227, 1997.
Bruce DA: Head trauma. *In* Fleisher GR and Ludwig S (eds): Textbook of Pedatric Emergency Medicine, 3rd ed. Baltimore, Williams & Wilkins, 1993, pp 1102–1112.
Dietrich AM, Bowman MJ, Ginn-Pease MF, et al: Pediatric head injuries: Can clinical factors reliably predict an abnor-

mality on computed tomography? Ann Emerg Med 22:1535–1540, 1993.
Duhaime AC, Alario AJ, Lewander WJ, et al: Head injury in very young children: Mechanisms, injury types, and ophthalmologic findings in 100 hospitalized patients younger than 2 years of age. Pediatrics 90:179–185, 1992.
Goldstein B, Powers KS: Head trauma in children. Pediatr Rev 15:213–219, 1994.
Quayle KS, Jaffe DM, Kuppermann N, et al. Diagnostic testing for acute head injury in children: When are head computed tomography and skull radiographs indicated. Pediatrics 99:1–8, 1997.
URL:http://www.pediatrics.org/cgi/content/full/99/5/e11.

Poisoning

Litovitz TL 1996 Annual report of the American Association of Poison Control Centers Toxic Exposure Surveillance System. Am J Emerg Med 15:447–500, 1997.
Olson KR, Pentel PR, Kelley MT: Physical assessment and differential diagnosis of the poisoned patient. Med Toxicol 2:52–81, 1987.
Woolf AD: Poisoning in children and adolescents. Pediatr Rev 14:411–422, 1993.
Woolf AD, Lovejoy FH Jr: Epidemiology of drug overdose in children. Drug Safety 9:291–308, 1993.
Woolf AD, Shannon MW: Clinical toxicology for the pediatrician. Pediatr Clin North Am 42:317–333, 1995.

Henry W. Albers
Lyle J. Micheli

Musculoskeletal Trauma and Overuse Injuries

MUSCULOSKELETAL TRAUMA

Musculoskeletal injuries are a major reason for hospital admission and outpatient visits. Pediatric musculoskeletal injuries may be acute or result from chronic overuse or a combination of these mechanisms. This chapter outlines a few basic principles related to acute and chronic injury and describes the more commonly seen maladies by region.

TYPES OF INJURY

Fractures

Fractures in childhood can involve any part of the bone, including the growth plate, and may result from single-impact macrotrauma or repetitive microtrauma. Single-impact fractures can be classified on the basis of mechanism of injury. Rotation of the body about a planted extremity

can result in a *spiral fracture,* whereas a direct blow to a long bone can cause a *transverse fracture.* A *buckle* or *torus fracture* is specific to younger children and is a compression fracture near the metaphysis of a long bone. A *greenstick fracture* is an incomplete fracture, consisting of a disrupting of the tension side of the bone and bending of the compression side.

Open fractures disrupt the soft tissues at the level of the fracture, with exposure of the fracture site to the outside environment. **A high index of suspicion of an open fracture should be maintained for a fracture associated with any wound, including puncture wounds or abrasions.** If inadequately treated, these injuries can be limb- or life-threatening, with complications including osteomyelitis, gas gangrene, and tetanus. Appropriate treatment includes tetanus prophylaxis, intravenous antibiotics, and immediate surgical debridement in an operating room.

Growth plate (physeal) fractures are specific to children. The physis is an irregular, undulating cartilaginous layer located between the epiphysis and the metaphysis near the end of the long bones. It is responsible for the longitudinal growth of the bone; injury to this cartilage can result in abnormal growth. Growth cartilage is less resistant to deforming forces than either ligaments or bone, and fractures frequently occur through the growth plate. Growth deformity may result from injury to the physis or misalignment of the fracture fragments. If one portion of the growth plate is damaged, the remaining portion may continue to grow, leading to angular deformity. Injury to the entire growth plate may lead to complete growth arrest, with subsequent shortening of the bone at maturity. If the fracture fragments heal in a malaligned position, a "bony bar" may form across the physis, leading to abnormal growth. Additionally, if fractures enter joint surfaces, an incongruous joint may result. Therefore, **any fracture that may have associated growth plate involvement should be followed up after it has healed to permit early intervention if these complications occur.**

Growth plate fractures are classified into five types by Salter and Harris (Fig. 39–2). Type I fractures are injuries through the physis without displacement. They are suggested by local tenderness and soft tissue swelling. Radiographs often are normal or may show slight widening of the growth plate. Type II fractures generally are evident on radiograph, with a metaphyseal fragment attached to the epiphysis. Types III and IV fractures are intra-articular and may lead to joint incongruity and post-traumatic arthritis if accurate reduction is not achieved. Type V injuries involve a crush to the physis, with complete disruption of growth. The initial radiographs are normal, but growth disturbance arises over time.

The complications of growth plate fractures also are determined by the specific growth plate involved. Fractures of the proximal humeral physis rarely result in complications, whereas fractures of the distal femoral physis have a high incidence of growth disturbance and angular deformity.

The vascular status of a fractured limb must be carefully evaluated initially and during subsequent treatment. Arterial complications of fractures include complete transection, intimal tear, spasm, extrinsic compression, thrombosis, or aneurysm and may result in loss of the limb if not recognized and treated within a few hours. *Compartment syndromes* **consist of muscle ischemia resulting from a hemorrhage or swelling within a muscle compartment, from a tight circumferential cast or dressing, or from a transitory period of ischemia, with resultant muscle injury and swelling.** These syndromes must be recognized and treated immediately by loosening any tight casts or dressings and, if necessary, by surgical release of the muscle compartments (fasciotomy). Failure to recognize and treat compartment syndromes early may lead to muscle necrosis and ischemic (Volkmann) contracture, with severe loss of function.

Patients who have elevated compartment pressures complain of pain that seems out of proportion to the severity of the injury. A constellation of symptoms cited frequently is the "five P's." The earliest clinical finding is *pain with passive motion* (e.g., passively flexing and extending the fingers, toes, or ankle). This maneuver stretches the ischemic muscles, causing pain. Late findings (*pallor, pulselessness, paresthesia,* and elevated *pressure*) may indicate irreversible nerve and muscle damage.

The presence of *multiple fractures*, especially if they are of different ages, should raise the specter of child abuse. Any such possibility warrants hospitalization and social service evaluation. Akbarnia and Akbarnia et al. reported in 1974 a 35%

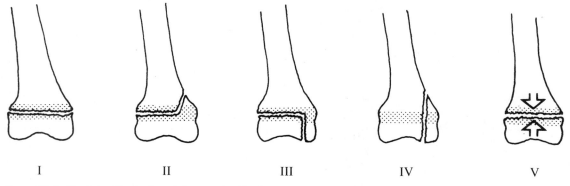

Figure 39–2. The Salter-Harris physeal fracture classification. Type I goes through the physis. Type II passes through the physis and out through the metaphysis. Type III extends across the physis and into the joint surface. Type IV passes through the metaphysis, physis, and epiphysis. Type V involves a crush injury to the physis.

risk of repeat abuse and a 5% to 10% chance of death if child abuse is missed in the emergency room.

Stress fractures begin as tiny cracks in the bone or growth plate and propagate faster than the body can heal them (Fig. 39–3). Diagnosis often is delayed because plain radiographs may be normal for 2 to 3 weeks after onset of symptoms. Subsequently, radiographs might show periosteal reaction as evidence of healing, or a frank crack. A high clinical index of suspicion is prudent if the patient has a history of repetitive activity, such as sports training or repetitive jumping. Tenderness may be elicited by direct palpation or application of a bending force to the site of pain. Bone

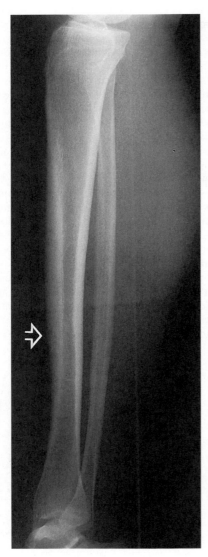

Figure 39–3. Stress fracture *(arrow)*. The cortex typically is thickened, and an overt transverse fracture line may be seen.

scintigraphy using technetium-99 may reveal stress fractures before plain radiographic changes are evident. The differential diagnosis includes osteomyelitis and bone neoplasms.

Pathologic fractures occur from normal stresses through abnormal bone. Bone may be weakened by benign or malignant neoplasms. A variety of metabolic diseases can disturb normal calcium metabolism or bone turnover. Osteomyelitis also weakens bone and can predispose to a pathologic fracture, although this would not typically be the presenting symptom.

Joint Injuries

Childhood injuries about the joints can include ligament sprains and strains, tendinitis of the major muscle-tendon units that insert near the joint, growth plate fractures, dislocations, and internal derangements of the joint itself. Internal derangements may include avulsion fracture, meniscus tear, osteocartilaginous fracture at the joint surface (osteochondritis dissecans), or loose bodies ("joint mice"). Joint incongruity and arthritis may result from intra-articular fracture or avascular necrosis of the epiphysis due to Legg-Calvé-Perthes disease or sickle cell disease. Corticosteroid use also has been associated with osteonecrosis.

Ligament sprains and tears in children may be more common than previously believed. The ligaments of children are stronger than the growth plate, and excessive forces often result in growth plate fracture or ligament avulsion. However, growth cartilage is stronger before the onset of puberty, and ligament tears in prepubescent children may occur without injury to the growth plate.

Dislocations of the shoulder, elbow, hip, or knee may be associated with serious vascular or neurologic injury. Intimal tears of the popliteal artery as a result of dislocation of the knee may present initially without any positive clinical signs but may lead to arterial thrombosis and amputation. Therefore, arteriography is indicated after tibiofemoral dislocation. The presence of gross instability of the knee may reflect a dislocation that reduced spontaneously or during transport before being seen by the physician and thus also may require arteriographic evaluation.

Evaluation of joint injury begins with a detailed history (mechanism of injury and subsequent symptoms), physical examination, and radiographic studies. Magnetic resonance imaging (MRI) is especially useful in the noninvasive evaluation of the knee and shoulder. However, some studies have shown that physical examination can be as sensitive and accurate as MRI and much less expensive. Plain films of the affected joint should be obtained as the initial imaging study. As with any second-stage imaging study, MRI should be reserved for cases in which the diagnosis is in doubt. MRI findings may dictate a different course of action. Ultrasonography has been used to evaluate the rotator cuff in the shoulder, but this technique is highly operator-dependent.

Arthroscopy is another excellent diagnostic technique. It provides direct visualization of intra-articular structures and often may allow treatment of any identified abnormality. Resection or repair of torn menisci, removal of loose bodies, and internal fixation of osteochondral fractures can be performed arthroscopically with less morbidity than in open surgery.

Muscle-Tendon Unit Injuries

The increased participation of children in organized sports activities has led to an increase in chronic overuse injuries. These injuries occur rarely in children engaged in free play. Rather, these injuries result from repetitive activities involved in training and competition and are specific to the type of sport in which the child is participating. They generally are curable with rest, stretching and strengthening programs, and modifications of the activity.

When a diagnosis of an overuse problem is considered, several key historical points must be elicited. Abrupt increase in training intensity, frequency, or duration does not allow the musculoskeletal system to adapt or to recover from the repetitive microtrauma induced by the activity. This may result in macroscopic, symptomatic overuse injury. These injuries often occur following sudden increases in activity level in a single sport, such as during an intensive summer camp program.

The stresses to specific anatomic structures also may be accentuated by malalignment, such as the increase in stress in the medial collateral ligament of the knee in runners with genu valgum (knock-knees).

Shoe characteristics, such as improper fit, inadequate impact absorption, or poor support, can be important factors in running injuries. Surface hardness also may result in increased impact forces that may contribute to overuse injury in runners and dancers. It often is useful to examine the footwear used during the activity for signs of uneven wear.

Previous injury, underlying disease state, or chronic pain also may contribute to overuse injury. These factors may alter the way the limb is used

or positioned, resulting in asymmetric stresses on specific structures. The associated muscle atrophy and weakness also may increase the risk of further injury.

The increase in soft tissue tightness or loss of flexibility associated with the adolescent growth spurt may exacerbate stresses that cause overuse injuries. Traction apophysitis and mechanical low back pain often appear with puberty.

Specific sports activities are associated with well-defined injury patterns. The repetitive shoulder motion of swimming contributes to the frequency of overuse syndromes of the shoulder with this sport. Gymnasts and dancers have a high incidence of spondylolysis, presumably secondary to the repetitive hyperextension of the lumbar spine.

Complaints of pain or limping by the child should never be taken lightly. They should be assessed thoroughly by detailed history, physical examination, radiographs, and other appropriate special tests. **Infectious processes and musculoskeletal neoplasms may be overlooked in their early stages if the complaints of an active child are attributed too readily to sports or recreational activities.**

SITES OF INJURY

Each section of the body is susceptible to generalized injuries (acute or chronic) and also injuries to that specific anatomic site. The more commonly encountered afflictions are described, starting at the top and working down.

The Head

Head injuries may occur during any type of sports activity. Concussions are categorized into three types, depending on the degree and duration of the injury. Type 1 is short-lasting confusion without amnesia. Type 2 also results in confusion, but with associated amnesia. Type 3 involves unconsciousness. Type 2 and type 3 concussions may be difficult to differentiate from intracranial hemorrhages, so a high level of suspicion must be maintained. *Postconcussion syndrome*, characterized by irritability, headaches, and difficulty concentrating, may develop.

The Spine

The Neck

GENERAL CONSIDERATIONS. Neck pain or injury always must be treated with caution.

A careful history should include localization of pain, paresthesia, dysesthesia, or weakness of the neck or upper extremities at the time of injury or afterward. The mechanism of injury should be determined as accurately as possible, including the details of the event (motor vehicle accident, sports injury, etc.) and the direction of the neck injury (flexion or extension, rotation, recoil). Any prior injury should be noted.

ACUTE INJURY. After an acute injury, the neck must be immobilized in a neutral position. A soft collar, rolled towels or sweat pants, or sandbags may be used as bolsters. The patient should be transported on a backboard if there is any suspicion of serious injury. Small children should be immobilized without flexing the neck. They have large heads in relation to their bodies. If they are placed in a supine position flat on a backboard, the neck is forced into flexion. Therefore, children should be placed on special headboards with a cutout for the occiput or placed on a pad to elevate the torso.

The physical examination should include a detailed neurologic examination. It is very important to complete and document a thorough examination at the first encounter, because the examination may be painful and repeated attempts resisted by the child. For the same reason, it is prudent to reserve examination of obvious injuries for last. This applies to injury in any part of the body. Evidence of associated head injury or facial fractures should be noted. Such injury must raise a high level of suspicion for a cervical spine injury. Radiographic evaluation consists of plain anteroposterior and lateral views of the entire cervical spine and an open mouth or odontoid view. All seven cervical vertebrae down to the C7–T1 junction must be seen. Often the patient has significant muscle spasm or guarding and the lower cervical vertebrae are not clearly visualized. In this instance a computed tomography (CT) scan through the area may be in order. If serious injury is suspected, the radiographs should be obtained before any range of motion of the neck is attempted. If flexion or extension elicits pain, lateral flexion and extension views should be obtained with a physician present to evaluate for ligamentous injury. However, these views typically are obtained a few days later after the initial muscle spasm has subsided.

Attention to detail is important in the radiographic evaluation of the cervical spine in children. Increase in the anterior excursion of C2 on C3 on lateral flexion radiographs may be a normal finding. Congenital anomalies, including failure of formation or segmentation, failure of ossification of the odontoid (*os odontoideum*), or spinal dys-

raphism, should be noted. Children also may incur a spinal cord injury without radiographic abnormalities. There may be profound neurologic deficit without any obvious injury on radiographs. Infantile spinal columns may stretch up to 2 inches without disruption, whereas the spinal cord is susceptible to rupture with more than a $\frac{1}{4}$ inch stretch.

Patients also may present with complaints of injury resulting in transitory pain or dysesthesia in one of the arms. These *"stingers"* or *"burners"* result from stretching of the brachial plexus as the neck is forced to the side. This usually results in burning pain passing down the arm, followed by transitory weakness. Occasionally the weakness may not become evident until several days after the injury. This condition generally resolves with time. If the patient suffers recurrent episodes, a thorough evaluation of the cervical spine is indicated.

If the cervical spine is stable and no major injury has occurred, treatment consists of initial rest, local heat, and mild analgesics to control muscle spasm and pain, followed by progressive rehabilitation, beginning with isometric exercises in the six directions of motion. Subsequently, dynamic range-of-motion and muscle-strengthening exercises are performed through the painless arc of motion in all directions.

NONACUTE NECK PAIN. Several nontraumatic conditions also may present with neck pain. Congenital lesions may result in stiffness and pain. Klippel-Feil syndrome is characterized by a short neck, limited motion, and vertebral anomalies in the cervical spine. This condition is associated with many other syndromes and may involve hearing, cardiac, and renal abnormalities. The most common associated musculoskeletal problem is scoliosis, which frequently requires treatment to control the curve progression. Torticollis in the infant may be secondary to cervical spine malformations or congenital muscular torticollis. The latter condition is thought to be secondary to fibrosis and contracture of the sternocleidomastoid muscle. If not treated, this may lead to severe facial asymmetry and plagiocephaly. Treatment consists of gentle stretching exercises, with surgical release of the contracted muscle reserved for recalcitrant cases. Cervical spine abnormalities must be ruled out before any stretching program is initiated. **Developmental dysplasia of the hips coexists in 20% of cases of congenital muscular torticollis; thus, the hips also must be evaluated.**

Torticollis in older children and adolescents may be due to inflammatory conditions. Grisel syndrome is torticollis secondary to rotatory subluxation in the cervical spine following an upper respiratory tract infection. This responds to appropriate treatment of the infection and immobilization of the neck with a soft collar. Subluxation greater than 7 to 10 days' duration may require traction to obtain reduction. Torticollis of more than 1-month's duration has a decreased chance of reduction and may require fusion of the affected portion of the spine.

Other conditions often include cervical problems; thus, the cervical spine must be evaluated before any problems arise. Down syndrome and Morquio syndrome are associated with an increased incidence of instability of the upper cervical spine. Children who have these conditions should have lateral radiographs in flexion and extension before participating in sports to rule out mechanical instability. If the odontoid is abnormal or if there is more than 4 to 5 mm of instability in the flexion-extension views, the patient should refrain from contact sports.

The Thoracic Spine

ACUTE TRAUMA. Injury to the upper back and thoracic spine is relatively uncommon. Strain of the back muscles, especially between the scapula and spinous processes, can be diagnosed by careful physical examination. Symptomatic disk herniations are rare and are diagnosed and treated the same as in adults.

Vertebral fractures result from high energy trauma. Fractures may occur from axial loading such as in falls. There is a high correlation between calcaneus fractures and spine fractures, so look for both. With significant posterior displacement of the vertebral body into the spinal canal, spinal cord injury may result. Therefore, a careful neurologic examination is mandatory. Treat simple compression fractures with rest, extension bracing (if needed), and gradual resumption of activities.

NONACUTE INJURY. Scheuermann kyphosis occurs in adolescents and leads to back pain and a gradual kyphotic or "round-back" deformity. This may be caused by repetitive microfracture of the vertebral end plates. This process may result in loss of anterior vertebral height, with "wedging" of the body on the lateral radiograph (Fig. 39–4) and kyphosis. Mild cases are treated with rest, heat, and analgesics, followed by progressive dorsal extension and lumbar flexion exercises for strength, flexibility, and pain control, although exercises have not been shown to correct the deformity. The patient should avoid lifting heavy weights. If kyphosis is marked (Cobb angle >50 degrees), extension bracing may result in permanent improvement of the deformity and symptoms.

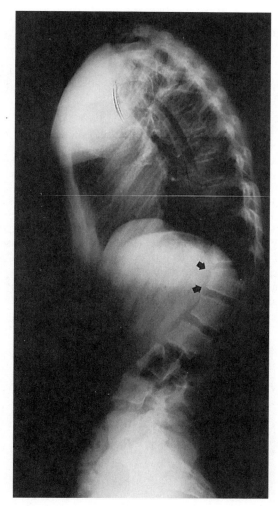

Figure 39–4. Scheuermann kyphosis *(arrows)* involves anterior wedging and end-plate irregularities of adjacent vertebral bodies in the thoracic or thoracolumbar spine.

The Lumbar Spine

ACUTE TRAUMA. Lumbar spine fractures also result from high energy trauma. Axial loading (e.g., falling from a height) is a common mechanism. The vertebral body is compressed anteriorly, without any injury directly around the spinal cord. However, the vertebral body is quite strong, and injury sufficient to fracture the body results most often in a burst fracture, with bone being retropulsed into the spinal canal. As mentioned previously, neurologic injury may occur, and a thorough examination is crucial. Fortunately, there is more room for the neural elements in the lumbar spine, and complete function is often maintained. These fractures are treated with extension bracing or surgical stabilization, depending on the degree of instability.

Another common mechanism of injury is flexion-distraction, such as occurs in a motor vehicle accident when the victim is wearing a lap belt. The vertebral body acts as a fulcrum and may be crushed, while the posterior spinal elements and ligaments are distracted and torn apart. These generally are unstable injuries and necessitate operative intervention.

Low back pain is seen in children and adolescents. Pain elicited with forward flexion or sitting may reflect injury to the anterior spinal elements. These syndromes include vertebral body end-plate fractures, as mentioned earlier, and intervertebral disk herniation. Localizing neurologic signs and sciatica may be present with lateral disk herniation because of specific nerve root impingement. However, a central disk bulge or herniation without nerve root impingement may occur with only localized low back pain or severe hamstring tightness. Diagnosis may be confirmed by MRI. These patients should be treated the same as adults, with

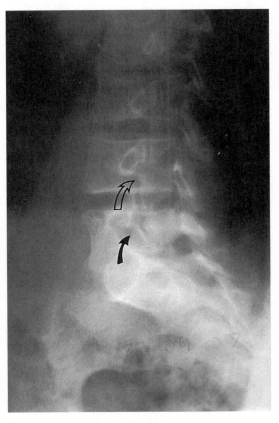

Figure 39–5. Spondylolysis is the result of a disruption of the pars interarticularis, which is well demonstrated in this oblique radiograph of the lumbosacral spine. The defect at the L5 level (*black arrow*) is distinguished from the normal anatomy above (*open arrow*).

relative rest and anti-inflammatory medications being the mainstay. Most improve over several weeks.

NONACUTE INJURY. Low back pain that is exacerbated by hyperextension may be a result of injury to the posterior elements. *Spondylolysis* **is a stress fracture of the pars interarticularis and may result from repetitive hyperextension of the low back, which commonly occurs in dancers and gymnasts.** The stress fracture may be demonstrated with oblique radiographs of the lumbosacral spine (Fig. 39–5). Occasionally the plain films are negative and single-photon emission CT (SPECT) bone scan is necessary to confirm the diagnosis. If the spondylolysis is of recent onset, bony healing may be attained by a program of antilordotic bracing in extension.

During the growth spurt, there may be an increase in the tightness of the lumbodorsal fascia and hamstrings and a weakness of the anterior abdominal muscles. **This combination of tightness posteriorly and weakness anteriorly may cause a tight lumbar lordosis or swayback, which may predispose to any of these low back disorders.** Mechanical low back pain is a syndrome associated with increased lumbar lordosis, tight lumbodorsal fascia, and tight hamstrings, but no other demonstrable anatomic lesions. Exercises that are useful in prevention and treatment include low back and hamstring stretching and abdominal strengthening. Activity modification and antilordotic bracing also are useful in treatment.

Spondylolisthesis, the forward displacement of one vertebra over another, usually occurs at the L5–S1 level (Fig. 39–6). Spondylolisthesis at the L4–L5 level is usually degenerative and is seen in adults. This condition may be asymptomatic, but severe displacement or progression may be indications for spinal fusion. Spondylolisthesis may produce a rapidly progressive scoliosis that typically resolves when the slip is fused. Severe slips may also result in neurologic deficits, which often resolve with stabilization of the spine.

An examination of a child's back should always include an assessment for scoliosis or other spinal deformity. **Persistent back pain in the child or adolescent may be due to infection or neoplasm and must never be dismissed simply as mechanical in origin without a thorough investigation.**

The Shoulder and Shoulder Girdle

ACUTE TRAUMA. Injuries about the shoulder in the child can involve the clavicle, the proximal humerus or glenohumeral joint, the acro-

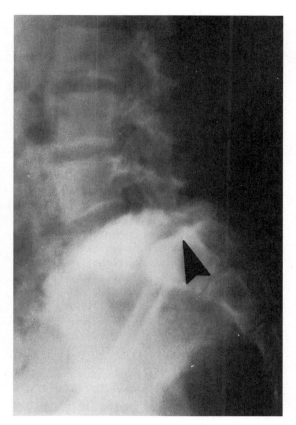

Figure 39–6. Spondylolisthesis involves the anterior translation of one verebral body over another. In the typical adolescent case, this occurs at L5–S1. In this example, L5 is displaced anteriorly in relation to S1 *(arrowhead).*

mioclavicular joint or medial clavicular growth plate, the rotator cuff, or the scapula.

Fractures of the clavicular shaft are common in children. These injuries can result from direct trauma, such as a blow or a fall, or from indirect trauma, such as a fall on an outstretched hand. If badly displaced, the fracture can be gently reduced and splinted with a figure-of-eight strap or a sling. Most patients find a sling to be more comfortable. The brachial plexus and axillary artery are just deep to the clavicle. Injury to these structures is uncommon but should be ruled out. Union of the fracture is usually rapid, and the patient and parents are instructed to expect a visible and palpable bony bump from the fracture callus. Open reduction rarely is required. If the proximal fragment is widely displaced superiorly or posteriorly, it may be "buttonholed" through the trapezius muscle. This blocks apposition of the fragments and may necessitate open reduction. In an even rarer circumstance, the proximal fragment is displaced inferiorly, becoming trapped under the coracoid pro-

cess or the biceps tendon. This also requires open reduction.

Fractures of the proximal humerus occur relatively more frequently in the child than in the adult. In contrast, glenohumeral dislocations are rare in children. Proximal humeral epiphyseal separations may result from a birth injury or trauma in the young child. A Salter-Harris type II fracture is more common in the adolescent. Dramatic remodeling may occur with both types of injury, despite displacement. Therefore, most of these injuries are treated with sling immobilization and pain medications. In preadolescents, up to 50% displacement and 45 to 50 degrees of angulation is acceptable. As the patient nears skeletal maturity (less than 2 years' growth remaining), less remodeling potential remains and, therefore, less deformity is accepted. Fractures that involve the articular surface of the humeral head should have open reduction and stabilization.

Acromioclavicular separation or dislocation rarely occurs in the child but may be more frequent among adolescents playing contact sports. This injury ranges in severity from the simple sprain to dislocation with complete disruption of the supporting ligament complex. Epiphyseal separation also is quite common. The distal clavicular physis closes in early adulthood (22 to 25 years). Therefore, what appears to be a shoulder separation in someone younger than this is more likely a physeal injury. Distal clavicle fractures, physeal separations, and acromioclavicular joint disruptions are classified similarly. Open reduction rarely is required. Initial treatment consists of icing and sling support for comfort, followed by early range-of-motion and muscle strengthening exercises when tolerated. Widely displaced injuries, as described previously, may require open reduction.

Sternoclavicular joint injuries may occur. These, too, are most often physeal injuries but can be frank dislocations. With anterior displacement, the medial clavicle is prominent. Reduction may be attempted, but these typically are unstable. Full functional recovery is to be expected. Therefore, treatment consists of comfort measures and early range of motion when tolerated. Posterior injuries can be life threatening because the clavicle may compress the upper mediastinal structures. Closed reduction should be performed in the operating suite with a thoracic surgeon available in case any mediastinal injury occurs during the reduction maneuver. Fortunately, once achieved, the reduction usually is stable.

NONACUTE INJURY. Overuse injuries of the shoulder occur in athletes involved in throwing or swimming. "Little League shoulder" is a stress fracture of the proximal humeral growth plate that results from repetitive throwing. This responds to rest until the injury is healed; then the throwing technique should be modified to avoid recurrence. Another common overuse injury of the shoulder is rotator cuff tendinitis and impingement syndrome, in which the inflamed rotator cuff muscles are caught between the humeral head and the coracoacromial ligament or acromion, particularly with overhead activity. Unlike in the adult, rotator cuff tears are rare in the child or adolescent. This, too, responds to modification of activity and conditioning of the shoulder. Surgical decompression is performed in refractory cases. Male gymnasts may develop "ringman's shoulder," a benign hypertrophy of the bony attachment of the pectoralis major. This may contribute to shoulder impingement. Female gymnasts suffer most commonly from supraspinatus tendinitis.

Shoulder pain in the young swimmer or thrower may be a sign of anterior subluxation of the glenohumeral joint. These athletes develop progressive laxity of the anterior joint capsule, demonstrated by an increase in external rotation on physical examination. This condition is associated with posterior capsule tightness, which can be confirmed clinically by a limitation of internal rotation at the 90-degree abducted position or limitation of adduction at the 90-degree forward-flexed position. A directed exercise program to restore full range of motion and strength may be helpful. This includes active resisted internal rotation, with the shoulder abducted to 90 degrees, and strengthening of the muscles about the scapula.

The Elbow

ACUTE TRAUMA. A painful swollen elbow in a child is an emergency that must be evaluated expeditiously. A nursemaid's elbow is a straightforward problem that is easily treated and has no adverse outcome. At the other extreme, a *displaced supracondylar fracture* can result in permanent disability or loss of the limb secondary to neurovascular compromise of the forearm and hand. Initial management includes evaluation of the distal neurovascular status, with examination of the radial pulse, capillary refill, and motor and sensory activity of the median, radial, and ulnar nerves. The elbow then is immobilized in a position of comfort. This position might *not* be at 90 degrees of flexion, a position that may worsen the swelling and neurovascular compromise. If available, ice packs and a gentle, loose compression dressing should be applied to minimize swelling. The limb should be observed closely to catch any signs of impending compartment syndrome.

Radiographs of high quality are necessary for diagnosis and treatment. Multiple views or comparison views of the contralateral elbow are often helpful. The adjacent joints (shoulder and wrist) are examined and radiographs obtained if injury is suspected. Ipsilateral fractures of the forearm can occur with elbow injuries. An orthopedist should be consulted and vigilance maintained to detect a compartment syndrome of the forearm.

Other fractures about the elbow may be less likely to cause vascular compromise than displaced supracondylar fractures but require careful assessment nevertheless. Circumferential bandages or casts should be avoided in any acute elbow injury associated with swelling; splints and slings may be equally effective and much safer for immobilization.

Elbow dislocations are potentially severe injuries that require rapid, skillful reduction. Nerve injury may occur and should be sought out. Fortunately, these usually are transitory stretch injuries that resolve over several weeks or months. Vascular injury is more rare but can occur. The elbow should be immobilized and the patient made comfortable until reduction can be accomplished.

Nursemaid's elbow is a fairly common and much less ominous injury involving a dislocation of the radial head at the elbow. This may occur after sudden longitudinal traction across the elbow as a child falls to the ground or an impatient adult lifts the child too forcefully. The radial head is reduced easily by gentle flexion of the elbow and supination of the forearm while direct lateral pressure is placed on the radial head. The reduction is stable, requiring no immobilization. It is very embarrassing to the physician and alarming to the patient to attempt one or two reductions of a supposed nursemaid's elbow, only to discover on subsequent radiographs that the child has a supracondylar humerus fracture. This also may cause or exacerbate any neurovascular injury.

NONACUTE INJURY. Little League elbow is a common chronic condition that includes several overuse injuries in the young throwing athlete. This may include stress fracture of the medial epicondylar physis, osteochondritis of the lateral condyle, and overgrowth or nonunion of the medial epicondylar apophysis. These injuries occur from repetitive throwing that causes valgus strain at the elbow and associated medial distraction and lateral compression. Lateral pain, catching, or locking may be a sign of osteochondritis dissecans of the capitellum, which may be associated with loose bodies in the joint. Lateral compression also may cause injury and premature closure of the proximal radial growth plate. Medial distraction may result in irritation or frank avulsion of the medial epicondyle.

Radiographic examination, including antero-posterior (AP), lateral, and both oblique views, may delineate the specific injury in Little League elbow. Arthrography or arthroscopy also may be helpful. MRI may allow early diagnosis, despite normal radiographs. If detected early, the process may be alleviated by relative rest and strengthening exercises. The child's throwing technique should be altered to reduce valgus stress at the elbow. If conservative treatment of capitellar osteochondritis fails, elbow arthrotomy and removal of loose bodies should improve pain and range of motion.

Gymnasts subject their elbows to chronic stresses. Tension across the medial side of the joint occurs when bearing weight on the hands. Hyperextension may lead to arthrosis in the posterior aspect of the elbow. These problems are treated as previously discussed.

The Forearm, Wrist, and Hand

With injuries to the forearm, wrist, and hand, as with any extremity injury, initial neurovascular assessment should be performed. Displaced fractures about the wrist may result in median nerve injury. Pain on rotation of the forearm, particularly supination, may be a sign of injury. Radiographic evaluation of a forearm injury should include views of the elbow and wrist. A Monteggia fracture is a fracture of the ulnar shaft associated with dislocation of the radial head; the latter component may be overlooked if the elbow is not included in the radiographic studies.

Fractures about the wrist and distal forearm follow an age-related pattern. In the younger child, a minimally displaced buckle or *torus fracture* may occur, and simple application of a short arm cast or splint for 3 to 4 weeks is usually adequate treatment. In the older child, metaphyseal fracture of the radius and ulna may be completely displaced and may require reduction under anesthesia. Adolescents sustain Salter-Harris type II fractures through the distal radial physis and also may require anesthesia for reduction to minimize injury to the growth plate.

Fractures of the carpal bones are relatively uncommon in children, owing to high relative cartilage content of the carpal bones. However, injuries such as scaphoid fractures do happen. A typical history (a fall backward onto a hyperextended wrist) and physical examination (snuffbox tenderness) should alert the physician to this possibility.

Even if radiographs are negative, it is prudent to assume that an occult injury is present. Treatment consists of a thumb spica cast and reassessment in 10 to 14 days. At that point, radiographs will demonstrate bony resorption at the fracture line, and cast immobilization is continued until healing is complete (up to 3 months). If radiographs are negative and the physical examination is benign, the immobilization is discontinued and the patient has suffered nothing other than a minor inconvenience. If the initial radiographs demonstrate a displaced fracture of the scaphoid, an anatomic reduction is required (often by open means) to reduce the risk of nonunion and avascular necrosis of the scaphoid. Such complications will result in chronic pain and early arthritis of the wrist.

A dislocated finger should be diagnosed with caution in a child. A fracture through the growth plate may mimic a dislocation, and an attempt at reduction may injure the growth plate further. Also, a "chip" fracture may represent an avulsion of a tendinous insertion. There is a very delicate balance between the intrinsic and extrinsic ligaments and tendons in the hand. Even presumably minor injuries may lead to major functional deficits. Also, there is limited capacity for remodeling in the hand, so reduction criteria are more stringent.

Applying sudden force to the tip of an extended finger, forcing it into flexion, and disrupting the extensor mechanism result in a *mallet finger*. In the skeletally mature, the extensor tendon is avulsed from the distal phalanx. Treatment consists of full-time extension splinting of the distal interphalangeal joint for 6 weeks. In skeletally immature patients, a fracture occurs through the physis, or a portion of the epiphysis pulls off with the tendon. If the nail bed is disrupted, this should be considered to be an open fracture and treated appropriately. Otherwise, treatment is extension splinting for 4 to 6 weeks. If, however, a large portion of the epiphysis displaces (>25% of the articular surface) and adequate closed reduction cannot be achieved, open reduction and fixation is necessary.

The same mechanism of injury also may cause disruption around the proximal interphalangeal (PIP) joint. A *jammed finger* involves sprains of the collateral ligaments of the PIP joint. The ligaments are intact, and treatment consists of splinting and rest, with gradual range of motion when tolerated. Joint stiffness and swelling may persist for months and, to a lesser degree, may be permanent. A more severe injury is the *boutonnière deformity*. This actually is a late change resulting from disruption of the central slip over the dorsum of the PIP joint caused by violent hyperflexion. The medial and lateral components of the extensor mechanism drop to the sides of the digit, thus acting as flexors rather than extensors. Treatment is by surgical repair and is best if done acutely.

Another common hand injury is the *skier's thumb*. This is an injury to the ulnar side of the metacarpophalangeal (MCP) joint of the thumb. The thumb is forced away from the hand. A sprain of the ulnar collateral ligament or a Salter-Harris type I or III fracture of the proximal phalanx epiphysis may occur. Minor sprains or undisplaced fractures are treated in a thumb spica cast. Displaced intra-articular fractures or complete ulnar collateral ligament tears should require operative repair.

The Pelvis and Hip

ACUTE TRAUMA. Injuries about the hip and pelvis are less common than other lower extremity childhood injuries, especially in the ambulatory patient. Fractures or dislocations of the pelvis or hip in children usually are a result of major trauma but may occur with sports or play activities. Pelvis fractures, of themselves, are of relatively minor concern unless the acetabulum is involved. The major concern is injury to the contents of the pelvis. Hips can be dislocated during sports or play. Emergent reduction is desirable to reduce the risk of avascular necrosis (AVN) of the femoral head. Obtain a CT scan to assess the reduction and to ensure that no loose bodies are trapped in the joint. If so, hip arthrotomy and debridement are necessary. Following reduction, the patient is treated with protected weight bearing and close long-term observation to detect evidence of AVN.

Apophyseal avulsions of the origins of major muscle-tendon units are another cause of acute pain and disability in the adolescent (Fig. 39–7). These injuries result from sudden distraction of the affected muscle, often with a simultaneous voluntary contraction. They may occur at the ischium (hamstrings), anterior superior iliac spine (sartorius), anterior inferior iliac spine (rectus femoris), iliac crest (abdominal muscles), or lesser trochanter (iliopsoas). Management includes rest and positioning to relax the affected muscle, followed by gradual restoration of motion and strength. Widely displaced avulsion fractures of the ischium may require early open reduction and fixation. Avulsion of the ischial tuberosity may heal by exuberant callus formation. This produces a large bony prominence that can interfere with normal sitting. In rare cases, excess bone is resected.

NONACUTE INJURY. *Slipped capital femoral epiphysis*, **which is a physeal separation of the proximal femur, occurs in active children, more frequently around puberty, in African-Americans, and in overweight children.** The problem may occur acutely with sudden pain, possibly with a previous history of symptoms for several weeks or months, or may present with chronic complaints only. The femoral and obturator nerves cross the hip joint, and patients may complain of knee rather than hip pain. Thus, the diagnosis may be delayed if the problem is attributed to a knee injury. **It is important to examine the hips of patients presenting with knee pain.** The diagnosis usually can be made from across the room, because the patient walks in with a limp and external rotation of the affected limb. Physical examination may reveal loss of internal rotation and obligatory external rotation of the hip with flexion. Forceful maneuvers should be avoided

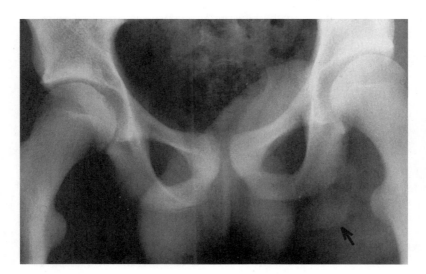

Figure 39–7. Apophyseal avulsion of the ischial tuberosity *(arrow)*. If the ischial tuberosity is widely displaced, it may result in a large bony prominence that interferes with sitting.

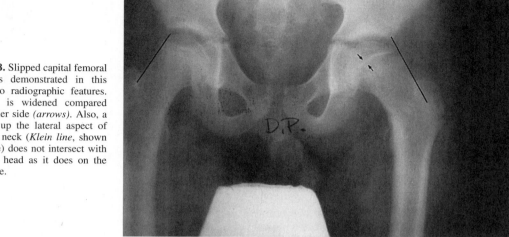

Figure 39–8. Slipped capital femoral epiphysis is demonstrated in this case by two radiographic features. The physis is widened compared with the other side *(arrows)*. Also, a line drawn up the lateral aspect of the femoral neck (*Klein line*, shown in the figure) does not intersect with the femoral head as it does on the opposite side.

during the examination. Excessive manipulation of the hip of a patient who has an acute slip (the patient is unable to bear weight on the affected limb) may predispose the hip to development of AVN. Diagnosis is confirmed by AP and frog-leg views of the pelvis (Fig. 39–8). The patient should have complete rest of the hip to prevent further slippage until internal fixation can be performed.

An activity-related limp and hip pain may be the first sign of *Legg-Calvé-Perthes disease*, or avascular necrosis of the femoral head (Fig. 39–9). A coincident history of sports injury may cause confusion or delay the diagnosis of these severe problems. Other causes of hip pain that must be included in the differential diagnosis are transient synovitis and septic arthritis.

An overuse injury occasionally encountered in

young athletes is apophysitis in the pelvis. In particular, young runners, hurdlers, and skaters may develop recalcitrant pain and tenderness of the iliac apophysis. Radiographs of the pelvis usually demonstrate widening of the apophysis. Treatment consists of relative rest and physical therapy to stretch and strengthen the hip abductors.

The Thigh

Injuries to the thigh include muscle-tendon unit injuries and stress fractures of the femur. Thigh contusions range in severity from minor to severe and occur with varying degrees of thigh pain, swelling, and limitation of knee motion. Treatment consists of immediate immobilization (bed rest for

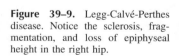

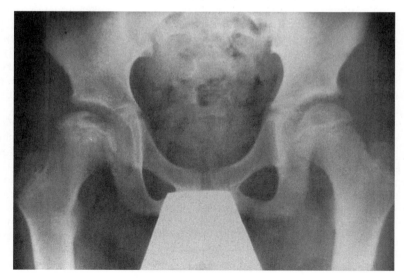

Figure 39–9. Legg-Calvé-Perthes disease. Notice the sclerosis, fragmentation, and loss of epiphyseal height in the right hip.

severe injuries), ice to control swelling, relative rest, and gentle compression. Heat or warm-water whirlpools are not used in the rehabilitation of thigh contusions. When strength and range of motion have been restored, sports may be resumed, with the use of a protective thigh pad to prevent reinjury. Disability from a thigh contusion may persist for a year or more, and recovery may be delayed further by the development of *myositis ossificans* in the damaged muscle.

Stress fractures of the femur may present with hip, thigh, or knee pain. Fractures of the midportion of the shaft are treated with protected weight bearing and rest. **Fractures of the proximal femur must be treated with great respect. These may displace and result in AVN of the femoral head.** Often these fractures are treated with internal fixation to stabilize the bone until healing occurs. Fractures of the distal femur present with knee pain.

The Knee

ACUTE TRAUMA. The knee is the most common site of both single-impact and overuse injury in the young athlete. The differences in tissue characteristics of the child compared with the adult account for the different patterns and types of injury. Ligaments are relatively stronger in children. Forces that result in a midsubstance tear of the anterior cruciate ligament (ACL) in the adult often cause an avulsion of the ACL at its insertion into the tibial spine in the child (Fig. 39–10). Epiphyseal separations also are more likely to occur than ligament tears, particularly in adolescents in the final stages of growth. Nevertheless, as noted previously, ligament tears have been observed in prepubescent children.

The initial evaluation of the knee injured by single-impact macrotrauma may be difficult. In some cases, ligament injury can occur without associated fracture. Swelling and effusion, combined with muscle spasm, may impart a false clinical stability. If the radiographs are unremarkable, the child might be splinted, and if a follow-up examination is delayed until 2 weeks later, satisfactory ligament repair may no longer be feasible.

Therefore, a careful history is imperative for proper diagnosis. A major disruption of the ACL complex may be caused by a severe twisting injury, such as violent rotation of the body about the knee, with the foot firmly planted. Hyperextension of the knee is another common mechanism of ACL injury. The medial collateral ligament (MCL) may be injured by a valgus stress, such as

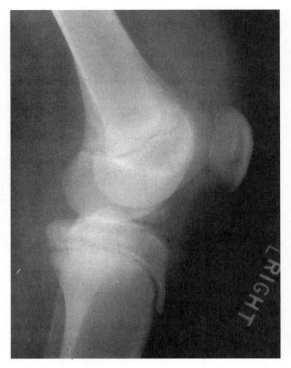

Figure 39–10. Avulsion fracture of the anterior tibial spine demonstrated on a lateral knee radiograph. The anterior cruciate ligament is still in continuity but likely is stretched.

an impact on the lateral side of the knee by another player with the foot planted. A "pop" and a sensation of the knee tearing or giving way should raise the suspicion of a possible ligament injury, as should the presence of giving way on weight bearing subsequent to the injury. Cruciate ligament injury precludes continuance of the activity, whereas less severe injury such as a sprain or even a meniscal tear may allow for resumption of the activity.

Early effusion, occurring shortly after the injury, is usually a hemarthrosis and results from an intra-articular ligament tear or avulsion or an intra-articular fracture. Fat droplets in the aspirate of an acute hemarthrosis usually result from bony injury, including ligament avulsion. The presence of blood in the knee reflects serious derangement in at least 90% of observed cases and, therefore, is a relative indication for acute arthroscopy. In contrast, knee swelling that occurs several hours after the injury may be a synovial effusion, a sign of a meniscal tear, or a low-grade sprain.

A detailed physical examination is important in localizing the anatomic structure or structures injured. Joint line tenderness and pain on loading of the medial or lateral tibiofemoral joint with varus or valgus stress (MacMurray test) suggest a meniscus tear. Pain on patellofemoral compression may indicate patellofemoral stress syndrome or chondromalacia. The Lachman and pivot shift tests are diagnostic of cruciate ligament injury and must be familiar to anyone treating knee injuries.

Radiographic evaluation should include AP, lateral, skyline, and tunnel views. The standard trauma series obtained in many emergency rooms does not include the latter two views and might miss patellar or femoral condylar pathologic lesions. The diagnostic accuracy of acute traumatic knee injuries has been improved greatly with the use of MRI. Unsuspected injuries, such as physeal fractures of the distal femur, also may be discovered.

Isolated *collateral ligament injuries* are treated with bracing and early range of motion. Isolated *posterior cruciate ligament tears* are infrequent and are treated with early conditioning and rehabilitation. Neurovascular injury may be associated and should be ruled out. These injuries respond best to acute repair of the damaged structures. Isolated *tears of the ACL* may be treated with rehabilitation or surgical reconstruction. If there is coincident meniscus tear, the meniscus should be repaired, if possible. The ACL should be reconstructed to decrease rotatory stresses on the repaired meniscus and thus maximize its chance of healing. Meniscus tears may result in mechanical symptoms such as locking of the knee. In these cases, arthroscopic debridement or repair should be done. *Popliteal (Baker)* or *meniscal cysts* may arise in the chronic setting and should point to intra-articular derangement of the knee.

Avulsion of the ACL at the anterior tibial spine (Fig. 39–10) occurs with sports activities involving sudden rotation of the body about the planted knee but also may occur with hyperextension. The traditional recommendation for closed reduction is by extension of the knee. However, we have noted by arthroscopic examination of these injuries that the fully extended position may result in partial displacement of the fragment. The best closed reduction usually is achieved with the knee flexed at 20 degrees. If the knee is unstable, as demonstrated by a positive Lachman test, an arthroscopic evaluation should be performed. If accurate closed reduction cannot be achieved or maintained, open reduction and fixation may be performed to achieve accurate healing of the fragment and restore stability to anterior translation of the tibia in relation to the femur. Even though this is a bony avulsion injury, there still is a component of stretch injury to the substance of the ACL. Therefore, the ligament will be slightly lax despite anatomic relocation or even recession of the anterior

tibial spine. Fortunately, patients rarely report functional deficit.

Patellar dislocation may present as an acute or recurrent problem. Often the patella reduces spontaneously with knee extension, so a frank dislocation is not evident at the time of examination. The patient will have an effusion, a positive apprehension sign (apprehension with lateral displacement of the patella), and tenderness along the medial aspect of the patella and over the adductor tubercle of the femur. The latter is secondary to tearing of the medial retinaculum and the patellofemoral ligament. Open repair may be indicated if radiographs reveal a bony avulsion off the side of the patella. Otherwise, the knee is immobilized in extension, with gradual range of motion and strengthening to follow. Recurrent dislocations are treated primarily with quadriceps strengthening. Refractory cases may require surgery to realign the pull of the extensor mechanism.

Rupture of the quadriceps or patellar tendons results in an inability to extend the knee. The quadriceps tendon may sustain a partial tear, leaving the medial and lateral retinacula intact, thus preserving weak extension against gravity. These remaining tissues may be completely disrupted by strong quadriceps contraction, resulting in complete extensor mechanism tear. **Physical examination of the knee always should include assessment of knee extension strength.** Both of these injuries require surgical repair for any expectation of functional recovery.

NONACUTE INJURY. During the growth spurt, the soft tissues about the knee become tighter as they elongate during the rapid bone growth. The relatively heavy fascia lata laterally, compared with the thinner medial structures, can result in lateral deviation of the quadriceps mechanism and the patella. Severe lateral tightness may lead to lateral subluxation or dislocation of the patella. Milder degrees of lateral tightness may cause low-grade aching pain of the knee, often anteriorly. This may be exacerbated by activities that increase patellofemoral pressure, such as climbing stairs or prolonged sitting. This *patellofemoral stress syndrome* may begin after a period of overuse, such as sudden increase in activity level, running on a hard surface, or hill running. The articular surface of the patella is normal on arthroscopic evaluation. However, the increase in patellofemoral joint pressure may eventually lead to chondromalacia patellae, which consists of softening, fibrillation, and erosion of the articular cartilage.

Patellofemoral stress syndrome is treated with an exercise program to strengthen the medial structures of the quadriceps and upper thigh and to stretch the tight lateral structures. This program includes progressive resisted adductor and quadriceps muscle strengthening, performed with the knee extended. Dynamic exercises (repetitive flexion and extension) are avoided, including running, but swimming with the knee extended or simulated cross-country skiing is not precluded. This activity is supplemented with stretching of the fascia lata and the hamstrings. In some children, an envelopment brace that leaves the patella open may relieve symptoms in the early stages of rehabilitation or during resumption of full activities.

This exercise program has resulted in resolution of symptoms after 6 months in 93% of the children in our practice. The others who do not improve may have their strength restored and resume painless activities after surgical release of the lateral patellar retinaculum, which may be performed as an open procedure (77% success rate) or arthroscopically (65% success rate).

Osgood-Schlatter disease is a traction apophysitis that appears during the adolescent growth spurt and is associated with tight quadriceps (positive Ely test). It presents with pain and tenderness at the tibial tubercle apophysis, where the patellar tendon inserts on the tibia. Jumping activities, such as gymnastics or figure skating, may exacerbate the symptoms because of repetitive vigorous knee extension and stress on the apophysis. Treatment includes static quadriceps strengthening, as discussed earlier, and quadriceps stretching exercises. Immobilization may worsen quadriceps weakness and tightness.

Osteochondritis dissecans consists of osteochondral fracture at the articular surface, which may be traumatic in origin or secondary to ischemia. The child may present with low-grade aching pain and intermittent swelling of the knee. Displacement of the fragment may lead to loose body formation and locking of the knee. Radiographs (particularly the tunnel view) are usually diagnostic. The most common location of this lesion is the lateral aspect of the medial femoral condyle (Fig. 39–11). MRI indicates the status of the articular cartilage. If the articular surface is broken, joint fluid will be seen deep to the lesion, as evidenced by a high signal intensity on T2-weighted images.

The likelihood of healing is higher in skeletally immature patients (growth plate still open). If the articular cartilage is intact, the knee is immobilized in extension and healing is expected by 6 to 12 weeks. If the lesion does not show evidence of healing by then, arthroscopic drilling of the subchondral bone may hasten the process. Loose fragments with some intact cartilage may be stabi-

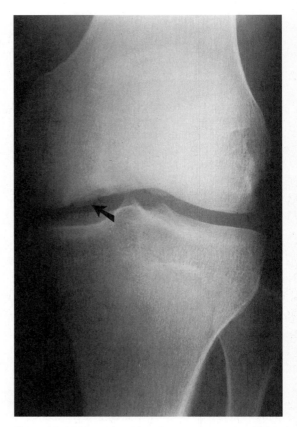

Figure 39–11. Osteochondritis dissecans most commonly involves the lateral aspect of the medial femoral condyle. This lesion is demonstrated clearly in the radiograph *(arrow)*. Often, a tunnel or notch view is necessary to show the defect.

lized with pins or screws until healing occurs. Acutely dislodged fragments can be excised, or replaced and stabilized if of sufficient size. Chronic loose bodies are removed. Autogenous osteochondral transplants harvested from a nonarticular area of the knee and the use of cultured chondrocytes transplanted into the defect are new techniques currently under evaluation.

Discoid lateral meniscus or the "popping knee" may present with chronic or acute pain. Symptomatic patients typically present in childhood; however, this may be discovered as an incidental finding at any age. Patients will complain of lateral knee pain and a click or clunk with full extension. In some cases there is a mechanical block to full extension secondary to the abnormal meniscus. This is a clinical diagnosis. Radiographic changes, if present, are subtle. MRI is not sensitive, owing to the small size of the meniscus in a child. Treatment is by resection, partial or complete, or by repair of the abnormal attachments.

The Ankle and Foot

Ankle sprain must be diagnosed with caution in the child. Inversion injuries result in tears of the lateral ligaments, as in adults, but also may cause a minimally displaced avulsion fracture or a fracture of the distal fibular physis. **Careful examination will differentiate among maximal tenderness over the ligaments, at the ligamentous insertion sites, and at the physis.** If examination is hindered by excessive swelling or if a physeal injury is likely, the ankle should be immobilized in neutral position in a short leg cast or brace for 3 weeks. At that point, the nature of the injury can be more precisely identified, and in most cases, immobilization discontinued.

Sprains may be treated with immobilization, ice, and compression, followed by protected motion and strengthening exercises. Third degree sprains (complete ligamentous rupture) may benefit from a short period of cast immobilization. Otherwise, rehabilitation may be facilitated by braces that protect the injured ligaments by blocking inversion or eversion but allowing dorsiflexion and plantarflexion.

Overuse injuries of the feet and ankles include stress fractures, osteochondroses (Kohler disease and Freiberg infraction), and tendinitis. Stress fractures arise in the metatarsals, especially after a sudden increase in activity. Occasionally, a bone scan is necessary to make the diagnosis. These fractures usually respond to activity modification and possibly the use of a stiff-soled shoe. *Kohler disease* involves AVN of the navicular bone. Patients complain of midfoot pain; radiographs show fragmentation of the navicular bone (Fig. 39–12). Treatment is symptomatic, and short leg walking-cast immobilization results in resolution of symptoms in 8 weeks. Long-term follow-up shows reconstitution of the bone without any sequelae. *Freiberg infraction* is an AVN of the second metatarsal head, which causes forefoot pain; this is common in dancers. Treatment consists of short leg casting for 4 weeks. A metatarsal pad used in the shoes afterward relieves pressure. If symptoms persist, the lesion may require bone grafting. *Heel pain* in the child may be due to calcaneal fracture or apophysitis (Sever disease). Etiologic factors in calcaneal apophysitis include tight heel cords, improper training, and shoes having a negative cant (heel lower than toebox). Treatment includes a program of directed heel cord stretching and dorsiflexion strengthening exercises and a temporary heel lift. Intermittent icing and anti-inflammatory medications may provide temporary symptomatic relief.

Osteochondritis dissecans of the talus may occur, especially in very active children such as gymnasts and runners. MRI is helpful in determining the size of the lesion. Treatment is similar to that for osteochondritis dissecans lesions of the distal femur.

Tendinitis most commonly involves the tibialis posterior or peroneal tendons. A patient also may have "snapping tendons" in which the peroneal tendons subluxate from their course behind the lateral malleolus. These conditions respond to rest, ice, and anti-inflammatory medications for symptomatic care and to strengthening and stretching exercises for prevention.

Another common cause of midfoot pain is a *tarsal coalition*. The tarsal bones may have incomplete separation, with a residual cartilaginous bridge. This is thought to be an autosomal domi-

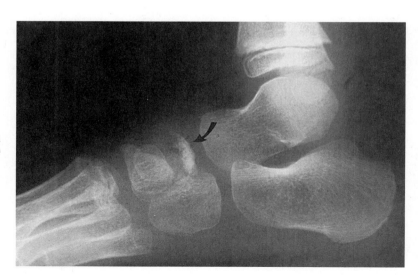

Figure 39–12. Kohler disease with sclerosis and fragmentation of the tarsal navicular *(arrow).*

nant trait with variable penetrance. Fifty percent of all patients have bilateral involvement. Calcaneonavicular coalitions usually become symptomatic in the 8- to 12-year-old age group; talocalcaneal coalitions become bothersome in the 12- to 16-year-old age group. As the cartilage begins to ossify, the midfoot becomes stiff. The classic presenting complaint is foot pain that is worse when walking on uneven surfaces. The patient may have flatfeet and spasm of the peroneal muscles. Symptomatic patients should be immobilized in short leg walking casts until asymptomatic. Shoe inserts may be helpful afterward. Surgical resection may be indicated if symptoms persist.

PREVENTION OF INJURIES IN THE CHILD

Knowledge of the risk factors that contribute to musculoskeletal injury is helpful in the clinical evaluation of the injured child. Patterns of overuse associated with a particular sport should raise the clinical index of suspicion for specific injuries. Early diagnosis is facilitated with this approach, and **ongoing injury and chronicity can be avoided with appropriate relative rest, directed exercises, and attention to other factors, such as technique and equipment.**

This knowledge also may be useful in the prevention of injury in the child. The maintenance of flexibility with a directed exercise program during the growth spurt may prevent traction apophysitis or back injury. As trainers and instructors become more aware of the association between technique and specific injury, modification of training methods can minimize the risk of injury. This approach is being used in dance training, in which directed exercises improve iliopsoas strength and efficiency of body mechanics and possibly decrease the risk of injury. Another example is the young pitcher, who may decrease the risk of Little League elbow by avoiding side-arm pitching.

Complete evaluation, including radiography, is important for the child who has pain or injury,

even if the patient associates the symptoms with an athletic injury. Sometimes the symptoms may stem from a neoplastic process, and the athletic injury is coincidental.

Attention to environmental factors, such as street and playground safety, decreases the incidence and severity of musculoskeletal injury in the child. Furthermore, the physician who intervenes on a suspicion of child abuse may help prevent further injury or loss of life.

FURTHER READING

Ahern DK and Lohr BA: Psychosocial factors in sports injury rehabilitation. Clin Sports Med 16:755–768, 1997.

Akbarnia B, Torg JS, Kirkpatrick J, and Sussman S: Manifestations of the battered-child syndrome. J Bone Joint Surg 56A:1159–1166, 1974.

Atlantoaxial instability in Down syndrome: Subject Review. Pediatrics 96:151–154, 1995.

Cohen WI: Atlantoaxial instability: What's next? Arch Pediatr Adolesc Med 152:119–122, 1998.

Cook PC and Leit ME: Issues in the pediatric athlete. Orthop Clin North Am 26:453–464, 1995.

Eiskjaer S, et al.: The significance of hemarthrosis of the knee in children. Arch Orthop Trauma Surg 107:96–98, 1988.

Fulkerson JP: Patellofemoral pain disorders: Evaluation and management. J Am Acad Orthop Surg 2:124–132, 1994.

Gerbino PG and Micheli LJ: Back injuries in the young athlete. Clin Sports Med 14:571–589, 1995.

Hulstyn MJ and Fadale PD: Shoulder injuries in the athlete. Clin Sports Med 16:663–679, 1997.

Ireland ML and Hutchinson MR: Upper extremity injuries in young athletes. Clin Sports Med 14:533–569, 1995.

Leadbetter WB: Anti-inflammatory therapy in sports injury. Clin Sports Med 14:353–410, 1995.

Metzl JD and Metzl K: Sports medicine and the primary care practitioner: Five illustrative cases. Curr Probl Pediatr 27:366–379, 1997.

Micheli LJ and Wood R: Back pain in young athletes: Significant differences from adult in causes and patterns. Arch Pediatr Adolesc Med 149:15–18, 1995.

Saperstein AL and Nicholas SJ: Pediatric and adolescent sports medicine. Pediatr Clin North Am 43:1013–1033, 1996.

Stanitski CL: Anterior cruciate ligament injury in the skeletally immature patient: Diagnosis and treatment. J Am Acad Orthop Surg 3:146–158, 1995.

Stanitski CL: Pediatric and adolescent sports injuries. Clin Sports Med 16:613–633, 1997.

Tria AJ, et al.: Conservative care for patellofemoral pain. Orthop Clin North Am 23:545–554, 1992.

Wiggins DL and Wiggins ME: The female athlete. Clin Sports Med 16:593–612, 1997.

Richard D. Krugman
Timothy Kutz

Chapter 40

Physical and Sexual Abuse

In 1962, C. Henry Kempe estimated that there were 749 battered children in the United States. Nearly 4 decades later, reported incidents of suspected abuse and neglect have exceeded 2.9 million reports per year according to the National Center on Child Abuse and Neglect. Approximately 25% of these cases are physical abuse, 14% are sexual abuse, and 53% are neglect. **Retrospective surveys indicate that at least 25% of females and 10% to 15% of males have had at least one episode of sexual abuse in childhood.** The latest incidence study, based on 1993 data, estimates that 0.5% to 0.9% of children (381,700 to 614,100) were physically abused, and 0.3% to 0.4% of children (217,700 to 300,200) were sexually abused that year. Children are abused and neglected in various ways in a number of settings and by different perpetrators. The forms of abuse include physical, sexual, and emotional abuse; emotional neglect (including nonorganic failure to thrive in infancy); physical neglect; medical care neglect; and other more unusual forms. These other forms include Munchausen syndrome by proxy and intentional poisoning. The settings in which children are abused include the home, child care center, child care facilities, schools, scouting locales, camps, and other settings in which children congregate. The perpetrators of abuse and neglect predominantly are parents (biologic or step-parents), grandparents, uncles, aunts, siblings, and cousins. Unrelated boyfriends of single mothers also have been implicated in numerous cases. Perpetrators outside the home usually are known to the child or family—for example, a neighbor—but a small percentage are strangers (particularly in cases of sexual abuse).

In the last several decades, primary care clinicians have found themselves confronted with an increasing number of requests for medical evaluations of children who either have been abused or are thought to have been abused. In addition to recognition, the role of the health professional in prevention and treatment also is discussed.

GENERAL CONSIDERATIONS

The recognition of any form of abuse depends on the physician's willingness to consider it in the differential diagnosis of the chief complaint. Many physicians believe that they do not have abused and neglected children in their private practices. They may have known certain families for many years and cannot accept that the parents, whom they have known for so long, could abuse their children. This presumption is dangerous for the reasons that follow.

1. **Any parent in any socioeconomic class may be physically, sexually, or emotionally abusive to one or more children.** Many communities have lived through the trauma of discovering that physicians, teachers, and mental health professionals, among others, have been convicted of physical or sexual abuse of their own children or the children of others. Although reports of abuse predominate from lower socioeconomic groups, higher stress levels in that population or decreased reporting by professionals serving higher socioeconomic groups, or both, could explain this observation.

2. Children are entrusted to many caretakers (babysitters, scout leaders, child care center employees, teachers, etc.) for much of the day, especially in single-parent homes or in those in which both parents are employed outside the home. At least 20% of reported abuse is extrafamilial; therefore, the physician who is seeing a possibly abused child in the office who has parents the physician knows and trusts might miss extrafamilial abuse because the parents are not aware of the cause of the injury and generally tend to trust their hired caretakers.

3. The influence of drugs and alcohol on abuse and neglect is substantial. Unless physicians understand the substance abuse habits of their patients' parents or designated caretakers, they neither can be sure of parental behavior nor predict it accurately.

In short, the individual who brings the child to the physician may be the abuser, may suspect someone of being abusive, or may have no idea that abuse has occurred. Thus, it becomes imperative for physicians, calmly and dispassionately, to explore the possibility of abuse with the parents of the child (e.g., "There are a number of possible causes for these symptoms, including . . . abuse. Have you considered that possibility?"). A report or investigation by social services or law enforcement agencies should be considered a routine part of the data needed to diagnose abuse and neglect properly in any suspected case. That it is routine and required by law to report *all* cases that have similar symptoms or injuries should be explained to the parents. Although it potentially is an inconvenience to the family, reporting is done in the best interest of all children in society. Most parents understand the need to report.

PHYSICAL ABUSE

History

The history of what has happened to the child is critical to being able to diagnose whether the child has been injured accidentally or is a victim of physical abuse. Presentations can include fractures, bruises, burns, abdominal injuries, and head injuries. A discrepant history—that is, a history presented to the physician that does not fit the medical findings in the case—is the cardinal feature in differentiating accidental from nonaccidental injury. For example, a physician may be told that the child fell off the couch; medical findings of skull and extremity fractures would indicate an obviously discrepant history. A cautionary note, however: As previously noted, the individual who brings the child to the office may not have been the caretaker at the time the child was injured or abused. Therefore, abuse should be considered as a possibility when a discrepant history is found, but the discrepancy will have to be corroborated by child protective service or law enforcement agencies. Other forms of discrepant histories can be less obvious. They can be partial histories, as when the physician is told that the child was found having seizures or not breathing in bed, whereupon resuscitation efforts were made and the child was brought to the hospital. In these cases, the individual often is telling the truth regarding the occurrence of a seizure but has not described the violent shaking or beating of the child that preceded the seizure. A third form of discrepant history is absolutely no history in a child presenting with evidence of major trauma. In addition to a discrepant history, which is the cardinal feature, there are other features commonly found in abuse cases; these are summarized in Table 40–1. Not all are present in all cases, but when they are, they make nonaccidental injury more likely.

TABLE 40–1. Features Differentiating Accidental and Nonaccidental Trauma

Discrepant history
Delay in seeking care
Crisis in abuser's life
Triggering behavior by child (e.g., crying, toileting)
History of abuse in childhood of abuser
Social isolation
Unrealistic expectations for the child
Pattern of increased severity of injury over time
Use of multiple hospitals or providers

Physical Examination

A comprehensive physical examination is necessary in all cases of physical abuse. Particular attention should be given to the height, weight, and head circumference of children younger than 2 years of age and the height and weight of children older than 2 years. A clear association has been noted between physically abused children and nonorganic failure to thrive, which may coexist in the same child. An examination of the head, ears, eyes, nose, and throat is important for evidence of Battle sign, hemorrhagic tympanic membranes, torn frenula in the mouth, chipped teeth, retinal hemorrhages, or other signs of ocular or other trauma. All bones should be palpated and extremities examined for clinical signs of injury. The genitalia should be examined carefully, because the triggering behavior for physical abuse often is related to toilet accidents and because children who are physically abused may also have been sexually abused. Signs of scarring or trauma to the genitalia and anus should be searched for.

Bruises, welts, lacerations, scars, and burns are the common external manifestations of physical abuse. The injuries may include grab marks on the arms or legs, multiple bruises over the buttocks of paddled or beaten children, bite marks, cigarette burns on the hands or feet, and welts from blows delivered by belts or electric cords. In general, bruises that occur over soft tissue parts of the body are more likely to be from abuse than those that occur over bony prominences; the latter usually are accidental. Bruises in any infant who is not yet ambulatory are very worrisome and indicate rough handling that potentially could be dangerous.

Certain burns are of extreme concern for physical abuse. Immersion scald burns of the buttocks in particular are seen commonly in children or infants who have soiled or wet their pants and are taken to a bathtub and immersed in very hot water. There may be a spared area (doughnut-hole effect) on the part of the body that was pressed against the tub, or there may be a stocking or glove distribution of the burn on the hands or feet.

The number, size, color, shape, and site of all bruises and burns should be carefully recorded in the physical examination of abused children.

Laboratory Data

Coagulation testing should be done in children who have multiple bruises about whom the parents claim "easy bruisability" or in children who have subdural or subarachnoid hemorrhage, retinal hemorrhage, or other manifestations of head trauma when the etiology is in doubt.

In addition to coagulopathies, various connective tissue and metabolic disorders have been mistaken for child abuse. Those encountered more commonly in this context include osteogenesis imperfecta, Ehlers-Danlos syndrome, epidermolysis bullosa, Menkes disease, methylmalonic aciduria, and glutaric aciduria, type I. In cases in which clinical features alone are not diagnostic, laboratory testing may be necessary. Skin biopsy is occasionally helpful regarding connective tissue disorders. However, not all connective tissue disorders are identified by biopsy. In cases in which there is enough suspicion to warrant protective service intervention, monitoring the child in a protected environment for evidence of further injury may actually be more sensitive than biopsy. If the child does not sustain injuries in a safe environment, it is most likely the injuries were secondary to a caretaker's abusive actions, regardless of the presence of a disorder. Laboratory evaluation for metabolic disorders should include assays for amino and organic acids. An inexpensive quantitative assay is available specifically for serum glutaric acid.

These tests are not mandatory in all cases and need not be done when the etiology of the injury is clear.

Radiologic Findings

When physical abuse is suspected in a child under 2 years of age, a radiologic "skeletal survey" consisting of radiographs of the skull, chest, vertebral column, and extremities should be obtained. Although not required in children older than 2 years, they often are obtained if abuse is suspected and the child is preverbal. Characteristic radiologic findings in abused children include (1) spiral fractures of the long bones in nonambulatory infants; (2) metaphyseal chip or buckethandle fractures in the long bones of infants and young children; (3) signs of multiple untreated fractures at different stages of healing; (4) asymmetric periosteal elevations; or (5) posterior rib fractures. These all have been associated with nonaccidental injury of children.

Management

When physical abuse of children is suspected, all 50 states require the physician to report that suspicion to the mandated child protective services agency. The reason for the report is to permit appropriately trained child protective services and law enforcement personnel to interview the family and investigate the home and other surroundings where the child has been, not to file charges against the parent. This multidisciplinary approach to assessment and case management is critical for both good diagnosis and protection of children.

The approach to the family should be calm and compassionate. It is not the physician's responsibility to "know who did it." The caretaker can be told that the possible causes of the injuries noted are numerous, and one of them is nonaccidental injury. Because it is suspected, it must be reported. Clearance should be obtained by the child protective services agency before the child leaves the office or clinic. The physician can maintain a helping posture with the caretakers and be available for further follow-up if need be. At a time when more than 60% of reports to child protective services agencies are not "substantiated," it becomes important that someone in the health care system be available to continue to monitor the child.

If the safety of the child cannot be ensured and the physician is concerned about the nature of the injury, the child should be hospitalized for further social and medical evaluation pending the county's or state agency's investigation. As of 1997, more than 500 pediatricians in the United States were available to primary care clinicians as regional consultants in the diagnosis and management of physical abuse. This network can be accessed through the Child Abuse and Neglect Section Manager at the American Academy of Pediatrics, Elk Grove Village, Illinois. The evaluation of siblings also may be helpful in an assessment of possible abuse.

Physicians should be prepared to testify in court. Most physical abuse cases are heard in a juvenile (civil) court; the juvenile court is designed to ensure the safety and protection of children. It relies on a lesser burden of proof and is not concerned with prosecution. Physicians will find that they will be less likely to appear in court if their medical records and written reports to the child protective services agency are complete and if they state their opinions clearly. In the small percentage of physical abuse cases that entail serious bodily injury or death, a criminal court proceeding also may be held, during which the state will attempt to prosecute the alleged abuser. Physician testimony usually will be required in these cases, and reports alone will not suffice to keep a physician out of court. Having good records, however, makes court appearances (often months to years later) more tolerable.

Treatment

Most primary care physicians are not involved in the subsequent treatment of abused children; nevertheless, in 1997 there were too few clinical treatment facilities for abused children in the United States. Nearly all chronically abused children, particularly those abused within their family, need some form of treatment. Treatment can be arranged through a multidisciplinary approach and can involve therapeutic child care, therapeutic Head Start programs, and individual therapy for the abused child. Physicians should pay careful attention to the classroom settings of abused children and try to ensure that the school system is aware of the nature of the child's problems so that the teachers assigned to the child will be helpful and not contribute to the problem.

Prevention

The primary care physician is in a strategic position to implement programs designed to prevent the serious physical abuse of children on an individual family basis as well as in his or her community. A number of studies have shown that it is possible to identify dysfunctional families early on, such as those who are socially isolated, burdened with acute and chronic stresses, those who have inappropriate or unrealistic expectations for their children, and those who had an individual or family history of abuse or neglect. The provision of a supportive "home visitor" to high-risk individuals has been shown to reduce the likelihood of serious physical abuse of children in these families. These studies, which have been conducted in numerous parts of the United States and around the world, have demonstrated that extra services provided for these families without labeling the families as abusive can be successful in preventing physical abuse. These extra services

should include prenatal classes, parenting classes, and ongoing contact and support to parents by either public health or lay home visitors. Community programs such as crisis nurseries, hotlines, arrangements for therapeutic child care, family planning programs, and home visitation have all played a role in preventing serious physical abuse of children.

SEXUAL ABUSE

Sexual abuse is defined as the engaging of a child in sexual activities that the child does not understand, to which the child cannot give informed consent, or that violate social taboos. Sexual abuse of children includes fondling; oral-genital, anal-genital, and genital-genital contact between adults and children; mutual masturbation; exhibitionism; frottage; and exploitation of children in the making of child pornography. The sexual abuse of children is a uniformly criminal offense (unlike physical abuse, which is generally dealt with only in the juvenile court). Sexual abuse can occur in both intrafamilial and extrafamilial settings. When it is intrafamilial, it is termed incest, and both social services and law enforcement agencies will be involved. When it is extrafamilial, it generally is handled only by law enforcement agencies.

Incidence

The incidence of sexual abuse is reported to be 0.3% to 0.9% per year during the lifetime of American children. It now is one of the more common reasons for a pediatric clinic visit at many hospitals in the United States, exceeded only by minor, acute illnesses and asthma. Most of the perpetrators of sexual abuse are known to the children, and many are within the extended family. Girls tend to be sexually abused more often within their families; boys more often are sexually abused in out-of-home settings. Recently there has been an increased recognition of adolescents as perpetrators. The majority of individuals who sexually abuse children have been sexually abused themselves. When sexual abuse occurs in the family, it often becomes a tight family secret, and adaptive behavior is learned by the sexually abused child (Table 40–2). It is impossible to know whether sexual abuse is increasing or just better reported; it has been described in children for hundreds of years. Retrospective surveys show similar percentages of adults who were sexually abused in their childhood 70 years ago as were

TABLE 40–2. Child Sexual Abuse Accommodation Syndrome

Helplessness
Secrecy
Entrapment and accommodation
Spontaneous or unconvincing disclosure
Recantation

sexually abused when they were children 20 and 30 years ago—that is, approximately 11% to 16% of men and 22% to 28% of women. Yet it also is true that with the changing demography of the American home, children now are at greater risk of being sexually abused by a step-parent, by a parent's paramour, on visitations with a parent, or in extrafamilial settings, such as child care.

Recognition

The recognition of sexual abuse of children depends almost entirely on the willingness of the physician to accept its existence. Sexually abused children can present to the physician in a variety of ways. (1) The child may be brought to a physician for a medical evaluation by a child protective services worker or law enforcement worker who has reason to believe that the child may have been sexually abused. (2) The physician may, as part of a differential diagnosis of a child's symptoms, entertain the possibility of sexual abuse and be the first person to suspect its presence. (3) A parent may request an "abuse examination" at a change in custody in a divorce or custody dispute. Whatever the presentation, the diagnosis of sexual abuse is fraught with many emotional as well as legal overtones.

Presentation

The presentation of children who are sexually abused differs from the usual pediatric presentation because sexual abuse typically is covert. Because the abuser enforces the child's secrecy, it is rare for children to complain of sexual abuse in the same way that they complain of sore throats or earaches. The presentations are listed in Table 40–3. Among these are statements, various behavioral problems, and medical presentations that often are masked. Among the nonspecific presentations of sexually abused children are abdominal pain; sleep disturbances, including nightmares; school problems; appetite disturbances; temper tantrums; fears; and anxiety. Some children may show signs of withdrawal, depression, guilt, or an

increased expression of anger over and above what is usual for them. Adolescents may present as suicidal, substance abusers, or runaways. These individuals should be asked directly about any history of sexual abuse. Medical presentations of sexual abuse include genital and anal trauma, sexually transmitted disease, recurrent urinary tract infections, enuresis, or encopresis. In adolescents, pregnancy may be the first presenting sign of sexual abuse in girls, and perpetration of sexual abuse on others may be the first presenting sign, particularly in boys.

Physical Examination

A sexually abused child should be examined physically in a coordinated manner with law enforcement and child protective services personnel involved in the case. Sexually abused children should not be interviewed and reinterviewed multiple times. The physician should talk to the agency individuals involved to make sure that an adequate history has been taken and then relay the medical findings. A comprehensive physical examination is important because sexually abused children may also show signs of physical abuse, neglect, or other problems. Under no circumstances should the physical examination be forced on the child, and care should be taken to establish

TABLE 40–3. Presentations of Sexual Abuse

General statements
Direct statements
Behavioral changes
    Sleep disturbances (e.g., nightmares, night terrors)
    Appetite disturbance (e.g., anorexia, bulimia)
    Atypical sexualized play
    Phobias, avoidance behavior
    Withdrawal, depression
    Guilt
    Temper tantrums, emotional lability, aggressive behavior, unusual anger
    School problems
    Promiscuity or prostitution
    Substance abuse
    Excessive masturbation
    Runaway behavior
    Suicidal behavior
    Hysterical or conversion reactions
    Perpetration to others
Medical conditions
    Genital or urethral trauma
    Genital infection or inflammation
    Sexually transmitted diseases
    Recurrent urinary tract infections
    Abdominal pain
    Enuresis, secondary
    Encopresis, secondary
    Pregnancy

rapport so that the child is not traumatized further. If the child is a victim of intrafamilial sexual abuse, it is better to interview the child away from the parents. In extrafamilial sexual abuse cases, the parents' presence may be reassuring.

If the history indicates that the sexual misuse has included penile contact, ejaculation specifically, within 72 hours, a forensic "rape kit" evaluation should be performed. In most cases of sexual abuse, this history is not obtainable because children delay disclosure. The physical examination should be done as completely as possible, leaving the genital and rectal examinations for last. In general, invasive examinations are unnecessary in prepubertal children. The vaginal, rectal, and perineal areas should be observed, and the anatomy of the hymenal tissue should be documented. The significance of genital and anal anatomic variations is debated in the literature: the clinician is referred to the current literature for guidance in this area. At this point, gonococcal, syphilitic, or human immunodeficiency virus (HIV) infection; significant acute genital or anal trauma; and the presence of sperm, semen, or semen-specific proteins or enzymes are the only findings specific for sexual abuse in the absence of an unacceptable history.

Laboratory and Other Studies

Cultures and serology should be performed in prepubertal children when penile contact is disclosed or suspected and in adolescents. Separate gonorrhea and chlamydial cultures usually are indicated and should be obtained from the oral cavity, vagina, and rectum in girls and from the oral cavity, rectum, and urethra (if there is a discharge present) in boys. When indicated epidemiologically, serologic tests for syphilis, HIV, and hepatitis B virus should be performed. Again, if the assault is acute, a rape kit should be obtained.

Management

Hospitalization of sexually abused children is becoming increasingly rare. In most communities the child protective services agency attempts to locate a safe environment for the child as soon as possible. Ideally, the alleged perpetrator should be excluded from the child's home if the case is intrafamilial rather than moving the child into foster care, which tends to suggest to the child that the child is at fault. All sexually abused children should be evaluated by a competent mental health professional, and most such children will

require ongoing therapy. The treatment sites available throughout the country, unfortunately, are inadequate to the task of dealing with all the children who are being identified. Sexually abused children need ongoing follow-up care, not only for their medical problems but also for the psychologic sequelae they may suffer as the legal and child protective services systems extend the disposition of their case over subsequent years. Physicians are likely to be called on for testimony in both civil and criminal cases regarding their medical findings. With the exception of the pathognomonic signs described previously, a direct history from the child, or both, most physicians will be able to say only, "The physical findings in this case are consistent with but not diagnostic of sexual abuse." Physicians may need to remind social workers, law enforcement officers, and prosecutors that medical examinations rarely "diagnose" sexual abuse.

Prognosis

There are few longitudinal studies on the outcomes for sexually abused children. It is clear from retrospective studies, however, that many sexually abused children have later difficulties, ranging from mild to severe, in many areas of interpersonal relationships. There may be subsequent difficulties in dating, marital life, and parenting. Follow-up for sexually abused children is an important ongoing concern. In general, a poorer prognosis is associated with earlier onset, closer relationship to the abuser, longer duration of abuse, and higher degree of coercion and penetration.

Prevention

There are a myriad of sexual abuse prevention programs throughout the United States. Few, however, have been evaluated adequately. Those that have been evaluated have shown that children retain the cognitive skills of safety around strangers, and two programs have shown positive behavioral change in participating children. Several programs discussing date rape have also been successful. These findings should not be extrapolated to all programs, and physicians should ensure that their community avoid placing the burden of prevention of sexual abuse of children on children alone.

A public health approach to the problem of sexual abuse has been used successfully. The Boy Scouts of America, as a case in point, received many complaints of sexual assaults involving scoutmasters. The organization assembled a panel of experts as consultants. As a result, a new section regarding child abuse was added to the Boy Scout Handbook, acknowledging its existence and allowing discussion. An analysis of the epidemiology of the assaults revealed that the majority occurred on overnight outings. Requiring more than one adult on all overnight trips significantly decreased the number of incidents.

Adequate attention must be paid to safety in child care, schools, and other settings in which children congregate. Safe and supervised facilities must be provided. The prevention of intrafamilial sexual abuse and all forms of sexual abuse in the next generation may well hinge on these efforts and our ability to provide treatment to the child victims of today.

FURTHER READING

Helfer ME, Kempe RS, and Krugman RD: The Battered Child, 5th ed. Chicago, University of Chicago Press, 1997.

Hymel KP and Jenny C: Child sexual abuse. Pediatr Rev 17:236–249, 1996.

Reese RM: Child Abuse: Medical Diagnosis and Management. Philadelphia, Lea & Febiger, 1994.

Sirotnak A and Krugman RD: Physical abuse of children: An update. Pediatr Rev 15:394–399, 1994.

PART B

MANAGEMENT OF CHILDREN WHO HAVE CHRONIC DISORDERS (GENERIC APPROACH)

Ruth E. K. Stein

Chapter 41

Home Care

New technologies now permit the long-term survival of seriously ill children and have made possible portable equipment that facilitates care outside the hospital. These advances have accelerated the development of care alternatives for children who have serious physical disorders. Pediatric home care provides health and related services in a noninstitutional setting to a medically fragile or technology-dependent child or one whose family is expected to monitor the child's special health needs and/or provide health care beyond that usually needed by healthy children. In other instances, it is a way of providing technical care at home that may in the past have been restricted to the hospital, thus reducing length of hospital stay.

The goals of home care are to normalize the child's life in a family and community setting, minimize the disruptive impact of the disorder and hospitalization, and foster the child's optimal growth and development. On a prolonged basis, this requires a fundamental change in both the site and focus of care, returning responsibility to the family and community as much as is possible and safe. Accomplishing this requires a package of services that emphasizes family values and full participation in community life, to the same extent that they are emphasized for healthy children. This requires a willingness to decentralize services and to form a partnership between professionals and families.

TYPES OF HOME CARE

In the past few decades, a variety of programs have been developed to transfer care to the community. There are programs for home transfusions of children who have hemophilia and for home dialysis of children who have end-stage renal failure, as well as for children who require intravenous medications or total parenteral nutrition. Comprehensive outreach programs for children have been developed that have a broad array of diagnoses, primarily for youngsters whose conditions are subject to frequent change or whose daily care requires special training of family members. Home care programs offered to seriously ill children who have a wide range of diagnoses generally provide medical and nursing supervision and care coordination as well as health education; social services; occupational, physical, and speech therapies; and many other related services. At one extreme, home care services exist to treat children who have short-term acute illnesses, such as those that provide parenteral antibiotics or traction; at the other extreme, such programs provide hospice services for terminally ill youngsters and their families.

Major program initiatives also exist around the country to discharge and maintain children who depend on ventilators in the home for long periods. These range from those that offer limited technical assistance to those that provide highly comprehensive multidisciplinary teams. Virtually all clinicians who care for children who depend on technology report that many other, nontechnology-dependent youngsters are not receiving the formal home care services they need. Moreover, they find that families whose children have a chronic condition need a large number of very similar noncategorical services regardless of the child's diagnosis or the intensity of the nursing requirements.

NECESSARY ELEMENTS FOR SUCCESSFUL HOME CARE

To succeed, a home care program must meet the needs of the community that it serves, build on existing strengths, capture the interest and support of influential health care and community leaders, and create ways to close gaps in existing systems of care. Whereas ideas, elements, and components of home care programs can be transplanted, whole programs cannot; **rather, programs must be adapted to the unique requirements of each site**.

Within this broad framework, every home care effort should include several ingredients. The family must be willing and able to care for the child at home. Families understandably may be ambivalent when first approached with the idea of home care. Many are fearful of the responsibility and its impact on their lives. They often need considerable help and support to provide a medically safe, nurturing environment and to learn new skills. To facilitate this transition, parental involvement should start as soon as possible. This means that planning should begin as soon as it is known that the child will require some form of ongoing care, even if the full extent of services needed is not yet entirely clear. **Such planning requires skillful inpatient staff who understand their roles as facilitators of a successful discharge plan and as parent trainers, rather than direct care providers who reinforce the family's uncertainty about their own expertise.**

Home care also requires a well-thought-out and flexible plan that covers a wide array of contingencies. This plan must be developed jointly with the family. Parents should participate in decision making about their child's care and must understand the child's condition, its implications, and the risks and benefits of home care. They have to be willing to live with uncertainty, know what their child's care entails, and be prepared to take on a great part of the care.

A central feature of the individual child's home care plan is the provision to each family of a designated care coordinator—one person who helps to pull all the pieces together. This may be a nurse, social worker, parent, lay advocate, physician, or any other member of the team, but it must be clear who the individual is and that the family is comfortable with the designated person. In some instances a family member may assume this role. Success in meeting a family's needs depends on each team member being willing to give up some independence in order to ensure that all the elements of care are coordinated. It also requires ongoing availability of the care coordinator and a single identified physician who will assume major responsibility for oversight and backup of the primary medical care. This may be provided by a community-based or hospital-based generalist or subspecialist.

Appropriate equipment and supplies must be in place and pretested in the home before hospital discharge. Family members and other caretakers should be trained using the child's own home equipment. Another essential element of the plan is a backup system for emergencies of all sorts. These include both medical and family emergencies, as well as those involving disruptions of power sources or mechanical failure of life support equipment. The financial resources for ongoing support of needed services, equipment, supplies, and medications also must be secured before hospital discharge.

Another key ingredient of every home care system is a mechanism for providing and ensuring continuing social and emotional support. Adequate educational and social opportunity for the child as well as for other family members must be ensured. Help may be forthcoming from parent groups, educators, social workers, visiting nurses, neighbors, extended family, or a combination thereof. Without support, parents and community-based helpers may experience burnout. This is a serious problem. Research on the care of chronically ill adults demonstrates unequivocally that **failure to support the care providers at home is the single most important determinant of readmission to hospitals or institutions**. It is logical to expect that the same will occur with home care of children who have a chronic illness. Optimally, families should have available respite and child care alternatives that will allow members to continue to function under the extra strain of caring for their child outside of the hospital. Support services should be financed, carefully monitored, and coordinated, but this often is difficult to ensure.

Finally, if home care does not appear to be working for the benefit of the child and family, every family should have an acceptable and appropriate alternative, such as respite care or long-term placement. When home care is provided for an acute illness, there often is less preparation and more likely the provision of direct services by an agency or vendor in the home. This agency may be available on call to solve problems. Such agencies often work under a physician's orders and merely execute the treatment in the home—often with a smaller degree of family responsibility.

ELIGIBILITY

The principal adult criterion for admission to home care is being homebound. This poses a major issue in considering home care needs of children because infants and children generally are not homebound in the traditional sense, and it is desirable to integrate them into the community as fully as possible. Therefore, this eligibility criterion is really inapplicable to most pediatric programs. Alternative definitions of home care eligibility are viewed as problematic by some policy makers because they tend to be more cumbersome administratively and do not distinguish clearly between those who are and are not eligible for home care. In addition, policy makers fear that other definitions will result in enrollment of children who now are managing without special arrangements. Several proposals to establish childhood eligibility based on the creation of a series of alternative care needs or functional impairments that would enable a child to qualify have been suggested. Although such functional criteria undoubtedly would be somewhat more difficult to administer than a single diagnostic requirement, they would provide a far more realistic approach to a complex problem. Moreover, they could be sufficiently flexible to provide incentives for promoting healthy adaptation and progressively normalizing life experiences as the child matures or improves.

Fostering positive adaptation and decreasing dependency is a more important issue for pediatric home care than for most adult home care services, because of the long-term impact of childhood experiences on the child's future and because most children who need home care survive into adulthood.

BENEFITS, RISKS, AND ETHICAL ISSUES

A few well-done studies have demonstrated that home care for children who have complex medical conditions is medically safe. Home care lowers the number of hospital days and decreases school absences through the prompt initiation of medical therapies that prevent longer-term complications. At the Bronx Municipal Hospital Center/Albert Einstein College of Medicine, a randomized controlled trial of a comprehensive home care program for children that had been operating for 10 years showed that home care has psychologic benefits for the child and for the mother and that it results in more satisfaction with care and more complete attention to the full range of recommended health care needs. At the very least, these data confirm that such programs can accomplish their primary habilitative mission. The home care program studied was beneficial across the whole range of burdensome conditions and a wide range of family situations. It played an important and powerful preventive role and appeared to be most effective for those who were not in crisis at the time the service was started. This has important implications because it suggests that the program should not be reserved for those families and children who already are having trouble. In this way, it is similar to many other interventions that are most effective when offered to those at risk before they manifest signs of crisis.

None of the studies of pediatric home care services has been conducted in circumstances in which there was a legislative or regulatory imperative that children be cared for at home. The importance of this point cannot be overemphasized. Until recently, many families and medical and nursing staff could choose to leave the child in a health care facility when home management seemed suboptimal for either medical or family reasons. However, past successes are being used to create policies that may impose home care on those who may not be equipped to provide it, forcing some children to be discharged without adequate training of family members, sufficient community backup for medical emergencies, and appropriate support services.

Cost-saving incentives threaten to drive much of current home care policy. In managed care, home care is used widely to shorten hospital stays for acute episodes. Long-term home care is less available through managed care or public programs unless it saves money for third party payers. If costs are even a fraction higher in the home, reimbursement usually is not available, regardless of the long-term savings potential. For example, several programs have suggested that some children are able to be weaned from a ventilator more quickly in the home than in the hospital. Home care payment may not be approved, however, unless expenditures are projected to cost less on a current monthly or semiannual basis. Such policies are shortsighted and may produce higher long-term expenditures and waste human resources by prolonging unnecessary institutionalization; however, long-term savings do not always accrue to the insurer, especially when there is the possibility of switching plans. **Given the importance of normalizing child development, it is essential that the economics of daily management not be the only consideration in assessing the usefulness and desirability of home-based services for children who have long-term conditions.** Present costs need to be weighed against the long-term costs of failing to invest in the habilitation and promotion of the child's optimal development.

Financial estimates of home care also have gen-erally failed to look at the implications for the economics of the family, such as out-of-pocket cost and the limitations this may place on the parent's ability to work outside the home. As families increasingly count on two incomes, this has become an issue of growing importance.

Home care policies may create difficult ethical issues and confusing levels of expectation for parents. For example, there have already been instances in which a parent's refusal or inability to provide home care to a child has resulted in the parent's loss of custody of the child. On the other hand, some children whose parents could not provide home care have been left in hospitals for indefinite periods of time, although it was not in their best interest. The need to weigh priorities for both the child and all family members may pose substantial moral dilemmas.

SUMMARY

Home care programs should be comprehensive, organized, and flexible; coordinate care; and should ensure access to support services. The American Academy of Pediatrics Task Force on Home Care and Committee on Children with Disabilities has developed useful sets of guidelines for such programs, which can help in designing home care services. They also may help to ensure that home care programs are implemented with an eye toward safety, as well as balance of the needs of the family and the best interests of the child.

FURTHER READING

American Academy of Pediatrics: Ad Hoc Task Force on Home Care of Chronically Ill Infants and Children. Pediatrics 74:434–436, 1984.

American Academy of Pediatrics, Committee on Children with Disabilities: Guidelines for home care of infants, children, and adolescents with chronic disease. Pediatrics 96:161–164, 1995.

Jessop DJ and Stein REK: Who benefits from a pediatric home care program? Pediatrics 88:497–505, 1991.

Jessop DJ and Stein REK: Providing comprehensive health care to children with chronic illness. Pediatrics 93:602–607, 1994.

Stein REK and Jessop DJ: Evaluation of a Home Care Unit as an Ambulatory ICU. Final Report to Maternal and Child Health and Crippled Children's Service Research Grants Program, June 1984.

Stein REK and Jessop DJ: Does pediatric home care make a difference for children with chronic illness? Findings from the pediatric ambulatory care treatment study. Pediatrics 73:845–853, 1984.

James M. Perrin

Chapter 42

State and Federal Programs for Children Who Have Chronic Conditions

The multiple sources that finance health care for children who have chronic conditions (Table 42–1) in the United States include federal-state partnerships (mainly Medicaid), parents' employers (group health coverage), insurance purchased directly by the family, out-of-pocket payment, and charity care resulting from nonpayment. The Title V programs for children who have special health care needs, another federal-state partnership, provide a variety of direct services along with support and maintenance of systems of care for children who have chronic conditions. In addition to these direct health care and insurance programs, many children who have chronic conditions receive health services and related treatments through public education programs (early intervention and special education). Still another program, Supplemental Security Income (SSI), provides direct cash payments to families who have children with relatively severe chronic conditions to help with the additional costs of caring for such children. This patchwork of state and federal programs supplements private health insurance but varies greatly from state to state because of state options to implement the programs in widely different ways, partly reflecting the states' different compositions and needs.

Despite these several programs (or perhaps because of this fragmented system of financing care), many children and adolescents lack access to health insurance. Even when they have insurance, many children lack coverage for essential services. Among the services that children who have

chronic conditions need (and that most other children rarely or never need) are specialized nursing services, educational services to improve these children's integration in schools, social services, and other specialized therapies (including physical, occupational, respiratory, and speech and language therapies, and nutritional services). They and their families also often benefit from preventive mental health services and respite care. Given the complexity and potentially conflicting nature of the many services they receive, many families need help with coordination of care. Children who have chronic health conditions may require habilitative services, especially home and community nursing and related services, over long periods of time, a model of care aimed more toward maintaining function or improving long-term outcome than toward a short-term rehabilitation model more suitable to older people who have acute events such as strokes. Many insurance plans, nonetheless, place stringent limits on the length of time during which children can receive these services.

PRIVATE HEALTH INSURANCE

Most American children receive health and related services paid for by a parent's employment-based family health insurance plan. However, the erosion of dependent coverage in many employment-based contracts over the last decade has led to a major decrease in the number of children in the United States who have health insurance from this source. Many companies have discontinued health benefits for dependents or made coverage available at relatively high cost to employees. To some degree, the growth of Medicaid financing over the past decade has counteracted this tremendous loss of coverage in the private health insurance market, but the total number of children

TABLE 42–1. Sources of Support for the Care of Children Who Have Chronic Conditions

Private (employer-based) health insurance
Medicaid
Maternal and Child Health (Title V) programs for children who have special health care needs
Special education and early intervention programs

lacking insurance grew by about 1 million between 1987 and 1995.

Even for those children who have stable employment-based health insurance, benefits may exclude many needed services. Most private insurance plans provide adequate coverage for hospitalization, physician services, and pharmaceuticals; however, few insurers offer satisfactory benefits for home or community-based care. Private health plans may exclude coverage for preexisting conditions, especially for smaller employers. The potential loss of coverage for a child who has cystic fibrosis when a parent changes employment diminishes job mobility for many households. This situation may improve since the passage of the Kassebaum-Kennedy bill in 1996, although the portability ensured by this act does not guarantee that available insurance will be affordable. Private plans also often include deductibles, co-insurance, and stop loss limits that families may be able to afford for occasional service but that can lead to major out-of-pocket expenses for families who have children who use services frequently. Finally, many plans include a lifetime ceiling on benefits, which children who have multiple or long-term hospitalizations can meet when still relatively young.

MEDICAID

The second most important source of health care coverage for children and adolescents who have chronic condition is Medicaid, the long-standing public health insurance program for lower income families (Table 42–2). Medicaid currently provides health insurance to a substantial minority of children in the United States. About one fourth of all U.S. children have Medicaid insurance; Medicaid covers the costs of about one third of all deliveries in the United States. Medicaid, which dates from 1965, has its roots in

earlier state welfare systems. As such, although derived from federal legislation, it is an amalgam of individual state programs that vary widely. Children and adolescents who have chronic health conditions become eligible for Medicaid through several mechanisms. First, most children who receive Medicaid do so because their households are supported through public welfare programs (e.g., Aid to Families with Dependent Children, now called Temporary Assistance to Needy Families). Since the early 1980s, Congress has mandated several expansions of Medicaid, serving in part to break the link between Medicaid and public welfare assistance. Legislation has increased the levels of family income for certain age groups, mandating levels of 100% or 133% of poverty for children of specified ages and also providing states the option of going beyond this level for certain older age groups. Even so, most children and adolescents eligible under these newer rules have not enrolled, leaving about 3 million Medicaid-eligible but unenrolled children. The second major source of Medicaid eligibility has come from the SSI program. This program, described further on, provides Medicaid coverage for SSI recipients in almost every state, even when the household income may be substantially higher than the state's usual income eligibility for Medicaid. A third mechanism for obtaining Medicaid eligibility for children who have chronic conditions, although used by relatively few children, is the so-called Medicaid spend-down provision. This provision specifies that when a family has income higher than Medicaid eligibility levels but accrues costs associated with caring for the child's health condition that lower the family income to the eligible level, that child too can receive Medicaid coverage.

In general, Medicaid benefits cover a broader array of services than do most private insurance plans. However, although states must offer certain basic health care benefits (subject to certain limitations), they have an option to provide many others that are particularly important to children who have chronic conditions. Required basic benefits include inpatient and outpatient hospital services, other laboratory and radiographic services, physician services, home health services, and Early Periodic Screening, Diagnosis, and Treatment (EPSDT) program services. Optional services include prescription drugs (although essentially all states currently cover drugs), transportation, personal care services, private duty nursing, eyeglasses, dental services, physical and occupational therapies, and speech, hearing, and language services. The EPSDT program, through both the treatment component and certain administrative

---

TABLE 42–2. Medicaid

Current enrollment
   Covers about 33% of children and adolescents in the United States
   Supports almost 40% of births
Eligibility
   Welfare recipiency (Aid to Families with Dependent Children, now Temporary Assistance to Needy Families) the main source of coverage
   Broader financial eligibility categories (beginning in 1980s), but only 33% of eligible children and adolescents enrolled
   Disability status
      Supplemental Security Income program

provisions, expands coverage and services beyond the limits of the regular Medicaid program. The 1989 Medicaid expansions required states to provide the full range of federally approved Medicaid services (even if these services are not covered in the state's Medicaid plan) when treating children whose conditions were identified through an EPSDT visit. The 1989 expansions also described in more detail the types of screening that must be available to children, along with the main elements of health supervision.

Over the past few years, women and children who have Medicaid insurance have experienced a rapid growth in managed care, increasingly including children who have major medical disabilities. This growth in managed care carries both opportunities and risks for children at high risk for health problems. Managed care offers improved access to primary care and coordination of services, but it also can provide incentives to limit access to needed services. The care of children who have chronic conditions in managed care systems has had little evaluation, and mechanisms to assess and ensure quality of care for Medicaid populations are only in the early stages of development.

In recent years, the Medicaid program has been the target of discussion for substantial revision, as have been the block grants proposed in 1995, which would have provided much greater state flexibility in determining eligibility (eliminating most federal eligibility requirements) and also much more leeway in the definition of benefit packages. Current trends toward state waivers and block grants suggest that these programs will have even more state variations in the future and that their eligibility and benefit structures will evolve.

MATERNAL AND CHILD HEALTH PROGRAMS

The federal-state Title V Maternal and Child Health programs provide a wide variety of services to families. Approximately one third of Maternal and Child Health funds support programs for children who have special health care needs, mainly focused on children with chronic health conditions and developmental disabilities, with less attention paid to children who have primary mental health conditions. These programs have existed for many decades; the major variation is in how states choose to employ their federal funds and matching state dollars. Some states provide direct health care services, both outpatient and inpatient; other states offer a variety of subspecialty medical and surgical care programs only; still others support a variety of services not usually

covered by public or private insurance; and finally some states put substantial amounts of their resources into the development of systems of care. Recent revisions to the Title V authorization required states to allocate resources for the development of systems of care, aiming to organize the complex variety of services that children who have chronic conditions need. An additional important component of the federal Maternal and Child Health program includes targeted grant programs (special projects of regional and national significance), which have led to major innovations in care for women and children and for training of professionals to work with these populations.

Although the enabling legislation for the Title V programs does not require an income test for eligibility, most states limit their services to low-income children, especially for direct services. The many options in the use of these funds have given states much flexibility, allowing them to target resources to fill gaps in the health care system. It also, however, creates inequities among states, such that a child who has a specific condition included in the Title V program in one state might be ineligible for services in another (nearby) state. States also may use different income eligibility standards for service. Yet, the mandates to develop systems of care and ensure that all children who have special health care needs have access to a wide and coordinated set of services in their communities have highlighted the central role of the Maternal and Child Health programs in each state. State programs have provided leadership in developing standards of care for children who have special health care needs, implementing systems for monitoring their care, and building an infrastructure that supports children's access to appropriate subspecialty services while receiving most needed services in their home communities. Many state programs for children who have special health care needs have also developed effective ties with the state Medicaid agency, especially with the transition of Medicaid to managed care and capitation. These ties have helped the development of standards of care for children who have disabilities and improved the ability of Medicaid agencies to monitor these children's care.

SUPPLEMENTAL SECURITY INCOME

The SSI program provides cash benefits for low-income people who have severe physical, developmental, or mental disabilities. As mentioned previously, in most states, children who receive SSI also receive Medicaid coverage even

when the household income may be higher than the state's usual eligibility levels for Medicaid. SSI application also provides links with Maternal and Child Health programs in most states. Although first implemented for children in the 1970s, the program provided benefits to relatively few children until major program changes that began in the late 1980s expanded the numbers of children receiving SSI benefits from approximately 275,000 in 1989 to over 1 million in 1997. This tremendous growth in numbers of child and adolescent recipients followed major efforts on the part of the federal Social Security Administration to identify eligible children and to expand the list of mental health conditions considered disabling, along with a Supreme Court ruling in 1990 that struck down the then-current guidelines for determining childhood disability as too restrictive and discriminatory against children. Despite this major growth, several estimates suggest that there still are many children who would meet clinical and financial criteria for the program but who do not yet receive SSI benefits.

To obtain SSI, children and their families apply through the Social Security system, which, after determining general financial eligibility, refers the case to the Disability Determination Service (a state agency). This unit then gathers clinical and related data about the child's presumed disability from physicians and others. Based on these data (but without any direct encounter or examination of the child), the disability determination staff (with limited supervision by clinically trained personnel) decides whether the child has substantial disability that meets criteria for SSI eligibility. **The Social Security Administration publishes their specific guidelines or "listings" of eligible conditions, most with indicators of severity thresholds. Child health professionals can refer to these guidelines (available from any state disability determination office) to help decide whether a child who has a disability will likely meet eligibility standards. These lists also provide guidance on the type of information needed to document a child's disability.**

Of children who receive SSI benefits, approximately 40% have a primary diagnosis of developmental retardation; 35%, a primary diagnosis of a physical disability; and the remaining 25%, diagnoses of mental conditions other than mental retardation. This last category has had the greatest growth over the last several years, especially in the numbers of child and adolescent recipients who have a diagnosis of attention-deficit hyperactivity disorder, in parallel with the major growth of this diagnosis in the general population. The Welfare Reform Bill of 1996 directed the federal government to develop a new and somewhat stricter definition of childhood disability that will likely make eligibility for children who have diagnoses in this last category more difficult.

The SSI benefit mainly covers cash assistance and public health insurance for eligible people. It does little to ensure that children who have coverage have access to specialized services, appropriate long-term planning, or the coordination of care needed by many families. Many state Title V programs for children who have special health care needs have collaborated with the state Disability Determination Service, such that when children are identified as eligible for SSI, the Title V programs work to integrate the child and family into other service systems.

SPECIAL EDUCATION

Two components of public special education programs provide important services to children who have disabilities, including for many in-school health-related services. The Education of the Handicapped Act of 1975 (PL 94-142) was landmark legislation whose purpose was to "assure the free appropriate public education of all handicapped children in the least restrictive environment." This legislation ensured that children who have disabilities and other health impairments receive education along with additional services required for them to benefit from participation in school. This act has been expanded several times and renamed the Individuals with Disabilities Education Act, with its most recent reauthorization in 1997. The most recent revisions of the act have given states a good deal more flexibility in the use of funds. Program expansions include provisions of resources to states to extend services to children aged 0 to 3 years in order to encourage early identification and prevention of conditions that may affect the child's later ability to be educated. Most communities now have early intervention programs, which typically provide in-home services for very young children who have potentially disabling conditions and group settings for slightly older children (1- and 2-year-olds). Many programs direct their efforts toward training parents to provide treatments or stimulation for their children and toward helping parents learn skills to encourage the child's best development.

Many older school-age children who would have had far more restricted educational opportunities without its implementation have benefited enormously from the Individuals with Disabilities Education Act. These benefits have helped children particularly who have mental retardation, learning disabilities, orthopedic conditions, and speech and language problems. The benefit of the act for children who have complex chronic conditions, especially physical disabilities, has varied, because many such children do not meet eligibility requirements when they are narrowly applied and because of variations in how states and communities have implemented the act. Many children who have chronic conditions are classified as having "other health impairments." When determined eligible, these children have access to a relatively broad array of school-based services, when it can be shown that the services are essential to the child's participation in school. These health-related services can include physical and occupational therapy, speech and language therapy, psychologic services, social work services, and recreational services.

States use different definitions for determining children eligible for both the early intervention programs and special education. A few states have included children in their early intervention programs who are considered to be "at risk" for developmental disabilities although lacking clear evidence of disabilities, and the 1997 reauthorization provides incentives to encourage states to expand programs for children "at risk." Local school districts implement these state and federal programs, and the numbers of children served and the services they receive vary tremendously among school districts.

SUMMARY

Clinicians working with families who have children with chronic conditions should know about these key financing and service programs and especially how their states and communities have implemented them. Child health professionals can help families access needed benefits through their public or private insurance or from SSI, including access to maternal and child health and special education programs. Pediatricians also can help states and communities develop monitoring plans for these programs and the care they provide to families.

FURTHER READING

American Academy of Pediatrics, Committee on Children with Disabilities: Why supplemental security income is important for children and adolescents. Pediatrics 95:603–608, 1995.

Fox HB and Newacheck P: Private health insurance of chronically ill children. Pediatrics 85:50–57, 1990.

Newacheck PW, Stein REK, Walker DK, et al.: Monitoring and evaluating managed care for children with chronic illnesses and disabilities. Pediatrics 98:952–958, 1996.

Perrin JM, Shayne MW, and Bloom SR: Home and Community Care for Chronically Ill Children. New York, Oxford University Press, 1993.

Rosenbaum S, Hughes D, and Johnson K: Maternal and child health services for medically indigent children and pregnant women. Med Care 26:315–332, 1988.

Gregory S. Liptak

Chapter 43

Myelodysplasia

OCCURRENCE AND PREVENTION

Myelodysplasias are a group of congenital malformations of the spinal cord, brain, and vertebrae that have variable manifestations (Table 43–1). Spina bifida occulta occurs in 5% to 10% of the general population. Other myelodysplasias occur in approximately 60 per 100,000 births in the United States. Although a minority of occurrences can be associated with a single factor, such as the use of valproic acid, excessive maternal use of alcohol during the pregnancy, or maternal diabetes, approximately 85% have multifactorial causes. The malformation begins approximately 23 to 28 days after gestation, when normal closure of the neural tube fails. The neural tube has multiple sites of closure, each of which may have its own genetic control and environmental sensitivity.

Maternal nutritional intake during early pregnancy has been associated with myelodysplasia. Women who previously have given birth to infants who have myelodysplasia have shown a 70% reduction in recurrence when treated prenatally with folic acid, 4 mg per day (at or before the time of conception and continuing for the first 3 months of the pregnancy). Daily supplemental doses of

TABLE 43–1. Types of Myelodysplasia

Condition	Pathophysiology	Effect on Functioning
Spina bifida occulta	Split vertebral arches	None
Meningomyelocele	The meninges, containing the malformed spinal cord and spinal nerves, protrudes from the split vertebral arches	Diminished motor function and loss of sensation
Meningocele	The meninges protrude through split vertebral arches	None—requires surgical closure
Encephalocele	Openings of the skull that allow the meninges and brain to protrude	Associated with hydrocephalus and developmental delay
Anencephaly	Absence of development above the brain stem	Fatal condition

folic acid, from 0.4 to 0.8 mg per day, can reduce the incidence of *new* cases of neural tube defects by at least 50%, which may be related to its ability to overcome a genetically controlled chemical block in the metabolism of homocysteine. Therefore, **the U.S. Public Health Service is recommending that women in the general population who are contemplating a pregnancy should take 0.4 mg supplemental folic acid per day while they are trying to conceive and for the first 12 weeks of pregnancy.** However, because many pregnancies are unplanned, certain staple foods such as bread, flour, and rice are being supplemented in the United States.

Other genetic influences can be seen in the incidence of myelodysplasia. **Couples who have had one child with myelodysplasia have a recurrence risk about 30 times higher than the general population.** Certain ethnic groups, such as people of Irish and Welsh extraction, have a much higher incidence. Finally, neural tube defects may occur as part of a complex genetic syndrome—for example, in trisomy 13 and trisomy 18. The incidence of myelodysplasia appears to be declining around the world, both because of prenatal diagnosis followed by therapeutic abortions and because of factors that are unclear.

PRENATAL DIAGNOSIS

A neural tube defect can be diagnosed prenatally in several ways. Most screening programs first measure levels of alpha-fetoprotein (AFP) in the mother's serum during weeks 16 to 18 of pregnancy. If the level of maternal serum AFP is elevated, high-resolution ultrasonography is performed. Abnormalities of the fetal spine and of the head (lemon and banana signs) can be detected in this fashion. If myelodysplasia still is suspected, amniocentesis should be considered to determine amniotic fluid levels of AFP and acetylcholinesterase, a chemical found in cerebrospinal fluid. Elevated levels of both chemicals, as well as ultrasonographic evidence of an abnormal head or spine,

confirm the diagnosis of myelodysplasia. Prenatal knowledge regarding the occurrence of myelodysplasia can be helpful to a family, even if they are not considering a therapeutic abortion, by allowing them to plan for the special needs of their child, including the consideration of cesarean section, which has been shown to decrease the severity of subsequent paralysis.

IMPAIRMENTS

The entire nervous system is affected by meningomyelocele (MM). For example, multiple disorders of the cranial nerve nuclei are found in children who have MM; the visual gaze centers of the brain can be affected, leading to strabismus; sections of the spinal cord and brain stem well above the primary lesion can be affected by excessive fluid in the central canal (syrinx) or other anomalies such as split cord (diplomyelia and diastematomyelia); and diffuse changes in the brain's cortex lead to problems such as visual-spatial impairments, which result in learning disabilities. Precocious puberty, due to a disorder of the hypothalamus, is a common occurrence in girls who have MM and hydrocephalus and can be treated with leuprolide, a synthetic analogue of gonadotropin-releasing hormone.

Paralysis and Loss of Sensation

The extent of paralysis and sensory loss in MM depends on the location of the primary defect in the spinal cord, with sensory and motor function below that point being impaired. Table 43–2 illustrates the level of lesion and its effects on mobility. The loss of motor and sensory function may not be symmetric in a child—one side may have higher function or sensation than the other.

Chiari Malformation and Hydrocephalus

Almost all children who have MM above the sacral level have Chiari type II (also called Ar-

TABLE 43–2. Level of Lesion in Meningomyelocele and Functional Implications

Level of Lesion	Percent with Hydrocephalus	Mobility Status	
		Childhood	Adulthood
Thoracic (T1–T12) or high lumbar (L1, L2)	90	Require extensive orthosis such as a parapodium, reciprocal gait orthosis, or HKAFO	Use wheelchairs; community ambulation is rare
Lumbar (L3, L4)	80	Will ambulate with less extensive orthotics, using crutches	Most use wheelchairs; community ambulation is uncommon
Low lumbar (L5) and sacral (S1–S4)	65	Will ambulate with minimal or no bracing, with or without crutches	Most continue to be community ambulators

HKAFO, hip, knee, ankle, foot orthosis.
Adapted from Charney EB: Myelomeningocele. *In* Schwartz MW, et al. (eds): Pediatric Primary Care: A Problem Oriented Approach, 3rd ed. St. Louis, Mosby, 1998, p 663.

nold-Chiari) malformation of the hindbrain, with the brain stem and part of the cerebellum displaced below the foramen magnum. Symptoms and signs of Chiari malformation include difficulty swallowing, choking, hoarseness, breathholding, poor respiratory effort with inadequate oxygenation, apnea, stiffness in the arms, opisthotonos, and sudden death from cardiorespiratory arrest. Treatment of symptomatic Chiari malformation includes posterior fossa decompression, in which the lower back of the skull and the arches of some of the cervical vertebral bodies are removed to provide additional space for the brain stem. Individuals who have symptomatic Chiari malformation may require tracheostomy, gastrostomy feedings, and supplemental oxygen.

Hydrocephalus develops in 60% to 95% of children who have meningomyelocele and is more common in higher-level lesions. In general, infants who have hydrocephalus require a ventricular shunt several days after the spinal defect is surgically closed. Shunts, however, often become blocked and occasionally become infected, especially during the first year of life. By the time children reach age 2 to 3 years, approximately 50% of the shunts inserted have failed and must be replaced. Signs and symptoms of a malfunctioning shunt include excessive head growth and a tense fontanel, lethargy, headache, vomiting, and irritability, paralysis of the seventh cranial nerve, and paralysis of upward gaze. Similar symptoms plus fever and elevated white blood cell count occur with an infected shunt. More subtle symptoms include change in personality, decline in school performance, weakness of the arms or legs, back pain, or symptoms of Chiari malformation. If a blocked shunt is suspected, the child should be evaluated by a computed tomography (CT) scan (or ultrasound in infants) as well as radiographs of the shunt system (shunt series). If the shunt is infected, intravenous antibiotics are indicated; it

often is necessary to remove an infected shunt and, after antibiotic treatment, replace it with a new one.

DISABILITIES

Mobility

Most infants who have MM, regardless of the level of their lesion, learn to crawl "commando style" as their first means of mobility. Infants who have strong voluntary hip flexion and some knee movement may eventually assume the all-fours crawl, but often not until after 1 year of age. Sensorimotor assessment during the child's first year should include evaluations of range of motion of joints, muscle tone, muscle strength, muscle bulk, sensation, movement skills, postural control, and sensory-integrative skills. Many infants who have MM have delayed rolling and sitting skills.

Children who have sacral (S1, S2) lesions learn to walk well generally by 2 or 3 years of age with bracing at the ankles or no bracing at all. Children who have midlumbar (L3) paralysis often require crutches and bracing up to the hip. Children who have thoracic or high-lumbar paralysis may eventually stand upright and walk, but only with support of the hips, knees, and ankles provided by extensive bracing and/or mobility devices such as the parapodium (an external flexible skeleton), reciprocal orthosis, or hip-knee-ankle-foot orthosis (HKAFO) used with crutches or a walker. Children who have L3 and L4 level involvement often are ambulatory during childhood but stop walking sometime during early adolescence; typically these individuals have strong quadriceps and hip adductors but have weak hip extensors. Children who have thoracic or lumbar level MM should be referred to early intervention programs after they are 6 months of age for physical therapy. Wheeled mobility devices, such as the wheelchair, offer the advantages of speed and attractiveness. Children should be offered both upright and wheeled mobility by the time they enter regular school.

Musculoskeletal Deformities

When partial or total paralysis occurs, muscle imbalance and lack of mobility lead to deformities around joints. For example, a clubfoot is often present at birth in infants who have midlumbar (L3) or higher-level paralysis. Treatment involves serial casting during the first 3 to 4 months of life to straighten the deformity gradually; corrective surgery follows at 4 months to 1 year of age. Other ankle and foot deformities may require surgical intervention to facilitate proper foot placement in shoes. Bracing is used to help maintain physiologic positions of joints but should be monitored to minimize the likelihood of a breakdown of the skin over bony prominences.

Muscle imbalance and lack of movement lead to hip deformities. Children who have high-lumbar or thoracic-level paralysis are vulnerable to developing hip contractures that interfere with walking and lead to hip dislocation. Surgical correction is controversial and may be appropriate only for those children who have low lumbar level paralysis and have the potential for ambulation. Loss of muscle strength and inactivity may predispose children who have MM to pathologic fractures.

Scoliosis and Kyphosis

Scoliosis and kyphosis occur in almost 90% of children who have MM above the sacral level and may be congenital or acquired. Scoliosis may result from both muscle imbalance and congenital anomalies of the vertebral bodies, which may be abnormally shaped or fused with each other, and most often is seen in children who have high-lumbar or thoracic-level paralysis. Congenital scoliosis and kyphosis usually are associated with spine and rib malformations. Kyphoscoliosis associated with anomalous vertebrae is rigid and usually gets worse early in childhood. In contrast, curvatures related to muscle imbalances are flexible until later in childhood and more amenable to correction.

If untreated, spinal deformities eventually may interfere with sitting and walking and may decrease pulmonary capacity. Scoliosis that is greater than 30 degrees is usually treated with an orthotic support (thoraco-lumbosacral orthosis [TLSO]).

Despite this, the curvature often progresses, and surgery may be necessary. Surgical correction involves a spinal fusion with bone grafts, often in two stages—one anterior and one posterior—and the use of metal rods (e.g., internal fixation with Luque instrumentation) for stabilization of the spinal column. Children who have congenital rather than developmental scoliosis generally respond poorly to orthotic treatment and may require spinal fusion at younger ages.

Kyphosis usually is located in the lumbar spine and may measure 80 to 90 degrees at birth. Kyphectomy often is performed in older children because a kyphectomy performed in the neonatal period at the time the lesion on the back is closed is often unsuccessful.

Urinary Dysfunction and Sexual Impairment in Males

Bladder and bowel dysfunction are present in virtually all children who have MM, regardless of their level of spinal cord lesion or paralysis. Children who have MM may have a urinary bladder that is flaccid or spastic; they may have a urinary outlet that is incompetent or spastic. Inability to empty the bladder of urine completely may predispose to infection of the bladder and/or kidneys. The combination of a tight sphincter and hypertonic bladder is most likely to produce serious kidney damage (hydronephrosis and kidney failure) because the high pressure generated in the bladder results in reflux of urine into the kidney.

In infancy, the urinary tract may be imaged by ultrasonography to evaluate the structure of the kidneys and bladder. (Malformations such as horseshoe kidneys are more common in children who have MM.) Evaluation of the bladder by using a cystometrogram or a test for leak pressure point is performed as well. If hydronephrosis or elevated pressure in the bladder (>40 cm H_2O) is found, the remedy is to minimize pressure by using either vesicostomy (a surgical opening from the bladder to the abdominal wall) or regular clean intermittent catheterization (CIC) to drain urine.

The infant should be monitored for the occurrence of urinary infections. If these occur frequently, daily oral antibiotics such as cefalexin (Keflex) or amoxicillin can be given prophylactically. If this fails, CIC is begun: antibiotics such as neomycin or gentamicin also can be instilled into the bladder through the catheter. The kidneys are studied with ultrasound at 6- to 12-month intervals to ensure that they remain normal. Attempts to achieve urinary continence are generally begun after 3 to 4 years of using CIC. In older children, prophylaxis for urinary tract infections may be provided with medications such as cotrimoxazole (Septra or Bactrim) or nitrofurantoin (Macrodantin).

Medications may be necessary if CIC does not result in continence. Medications such as oxybutynin chloride (Ditropan), which can be given orally or instilled into the bladder, often are used to diminish bladder wall contractions, and pseudoephedrine (Sudafed) or imipramine chloride (Tofranil) may be used to enhance storage of urine. By using a combination of CIC and medications, socially acceptable continence is achieved during the elementary school years in about 70% of children who have bladder dysfunction due to MM. Voiding cystourethrography by using conventional dye or radionuclide tracers may help to monitor or diagnose genitourinary reflux.

A surgical intervention such as bladder augmentation with appendico-vesicostomy, in which the bladder capacity is increased and the appendix is used as a conduit for catheterization through the abdominal wall, is considered for a well-motivated, mature child who has remained incontinent despite regular CIC and medication. Children who have bladder augmentation using a segment of small bowel may leak bicarbonate into the urine and become acidotic with long-term erosion of bone; those who have augmentation with a segment of stomach may become alkalotic with secondary hypokalemia and may even develop ulceration of the stomach segment used for augmentation.

Although 75% of postpubertal males who have MM can have erections, most do not have normal control of these; most also have retrograde ejaculation, whereby the semen is discharged into the bladder. Penile implants, injection or application of prostaglandin, and the use of vacuum devices prior to coitus can help males achieve erections. Females have normal fertility despite decreased genital sensation and should use the same precautions to prevent pregnancy and sexually transmitted diseases as do sexually active girls who have no MM. Frequent intercourse may lead to vaginal ulcers.

Bowel Dysfunction

Bowel problems in children who have MM are related to uncoordinated, ineffective function of the anal sphincters, combined with a lack of rectal sensation. Also, abnormal migration of neurons into the bowel can cause ineffective passage of stool through the intestines. Constipation is common and may be interspersed with periods of overflow diarrhea; fecal incontinence can be socially devastating. Attempts at bowel management are begun as soon as the child begins eating solids by encouraging foods that are high in fiber. When the child is between 2½ and 4 years of age, timed potty-sitting is tried after every meal to take advantage of the postfeeding gastrocolic reflex. If, after several months, bowel control has not been achieved by this method, parents may be instructed in the administration of a daily stool softener such as lactose or sorbitol, a laxative containing senna, a fiber supplement, or a nightly rectal suppository (e.g., bisacodyl [Dulcolax]), which will facilitate more complete bowel emptying. For older children who have low-level lesions, biofeedback may be used to improve rectal sensation. Daily enemas using water or saline have been successful. Several surgical procedures allow forward-flowing irrigation of the colon regularly. These include the cecostomy, whereby a plastic tube is inserted under fluoroscopy into the colon through the abdominal wall, and the antegrade colonic enema procedure, in which the appendix is reversed and serves as a conduit between the abdominal wall and the cecum. These are indicated for a select group of youth in whom more conventional bowel techniques have failed.

Achievement of bladder and bowel continence is both a realistic and critical part of the child's development. Competence in toileting, a basic activity of daily living, is necessary for normal emotional and social growth toward independence. Prevention of soiling, wetness, and odor also enhances the child's self-esteem.

Skin Sores (Decubitus Ulcers)

Skin sores or decubitus ulcers frequently occur in children who have MM, whose weight-bearing surfaces (e.g., feet, buttocks) are insensitive to pain. These sores become more frequent during adolescence and may require long-term treatment in a hospital. These ulcers can be prevented—for example, by using sunscreen to prevent sunburn, replacing tight-fitting shoes or braces, using foot protection such as aqua treads whenever swimming, and avoiding hot baths or crawling about on rough or hot surfaces. For children in wheelchairs, pressure sores on the buttocks or the coccyx can be prevented by modifying the wheelchair with an adaptive seating system and by having the child perform regular wheelchair situps to relieve pressure and change position. Existing sores should be treated by removing pressure, treating infections with antibiotics, ensuring that tetanus immunizations are up to date, and treating with dressings, including wet-to-dry saline-soaked gauze, or "artificial skin" such as tegaderm or duoderm. If ulcers do not heal in a reasonable amount of time, an underlying infection of soft tissue or bone may be the cause and will require diagnosis and treatment.

Seizure Disorders

Approximately 15% of individuals who have MM have seizures at some time in their lives. Seizures usually are tonic-clonic and respond well to anticonvulsant medication. They may be associated with a blocked or infected shunt.

Visual Deficits

Strabismus, or squint, is present in about 20% of children who have MM. This may result from abnormalities of the visual gaze center or from increased intracranial pressure from a malfunctioning ventricular shunt with increased pressure on cranial nerve VI. Paralysis of upward gaze (Parinaud phenomenon) may be associated with acutely increased intracranial pressure.

Cognitive Deficits

Approximately two thirds of the children who have MM and shunted hydrocephalus have intelligence within the normal range. The remaining one third are mentally retarded, usually in the mild range. The occasional children with MM who are moderately or severely mentally retarded usually have had a history of ventriculitis, often from an infected shunt, or have had prenatal hydrocephalus with a head circumference at birth that was well above the 95th percentile and a cortical mantle of less than 1 cm.

Children with MM who are not mentally retarded generally have difficulties in perceptual organizational abilities, attention, speed of motor response, memory, and hand function. Consequently, many of these children have learning problems in subjects such as arithmetic. These children should receive formal educational testing before entering kindergarten, with periodic reevaluation as they progress through school, in order to identify their strengths and weaknesses and develop customized academic plans and realistic expectations that optimize their learning.

Obesity

Children who have MM are at increased risk for obesity because they burn fewer calories. As a result, about two thirds of these children are significantly overweight in spite of what appears to be a normal or even reduced-calorie diet. Attention should be directed to increasing involvement in regular physical activities such as stretching, aerobic conditioning (e.g., wheelchair sports), strength training (such as the lifting of free weights), and limiting sweets and fats in the diet.

Progressive Neurologic Deterioration

MM is a nonprogressive condition. If a child's strength, bowel and bladder function, or daily living skills deteriorate, a reason should be sought. Common causes include malfunctioning ventricular shunt, tethered spinal cord (TSC), syrinx of the spinal cord, or other condition of the spinal cord (such as split spinal cord). Older children may lose function because they become depressed. TSC may be related to scarring at the site of the initial surgery to close the back or to a lipoma or dermoid of the spinal cord. In TSC, pressure or stretch on the spinal cord leads to areas of poor circulation, which results in diminished functioning. If a lipoma or other cause of TSC is found, surgery may help to relieve symptoms. TSC has been linked to rapidly progressive scoliosis; however, this connection is still uncertain. Table 43–3 outlines some common causes of neurologic deterioration and an approach to their evaluation.

Allergy to Latex

About 50% of children who have MM have allergies to latex. Although the reason for this is unclear, the allergies are more common in children who have had frequent surgical procedures. Children who have allergies to latex may develop fatal anaphylaxis during surgery. Thus, all surgical procedures, including dental procedures, should occur in latex-free settings. Early contact with latex should be avoided in all children who have MM in an effort to prevent the occurrence of allergies. Catheterization should be performed with nonlatex catheters; gloves used during care should be nonlatex; toys that contain significant amounts of latex, such as balloons and rubber balls, should be avoided, as should products that contact the skin, such as Band-Aids or Ace bandages.

PSYCHOSOCIAL ISSUES

The care of a child who has MM is extraordinarily expensive. Direct medical expenses have

TABLE 43–3. Evaluation of a Child Who Has Meningomyelocele Who Presents with Neurologic Deterioration

Symptoms	Evaluation	Possible Condition
Declining performance in school; change in personality	History Physical examination CT scan or ultrasound of head; shunt series	Depression Side effect of medication Ventricular shunt malfunction
Deterioration of gait; changes in bowel and bladder function	History Physical examination, including evaluation of strength CT scan or ultrasound of head; shunt series MRI scan of spinal cord Cystometrogram	Ventricular shunt malfunction Side effect of medication Tethered spinal cord; syrinx
Difficulty swallowing; hoarseness	History Physical examination, including evaluation of strength	Chiari II malformation; syrinx Ventricular shunt malfunction
Disordered breathing with sleep	CT scan or ultrasound of head; shunt series	
Deterioration of upper extremities	MRI scan of posterior fossa	

CT, computed tomography; MRI, magnetic resonance imaging.

been estimated to be $99,000 over the individual's lifetime, with total estimated costs—including indirect costs such as loss of parental income and decreased productivity—of $250,000. Therefore, one of the priorities of care is to provide financial counseling to families of an affected child. The disabilities associated with MM can interfere with the normal developmental goals of childhood. Failure in school may exacerbate a preexisting poor self-image that many of these children have as a result of their physical disabilities. The feeling of being different can impair the establishment of peer relationships in both the school and the community. The child's self-esteem also may be lowered if he or she must continue to wear diapers. As the child ages, lowered self-esteem also may relate to a poor body image and difficulty with the normal sexual changes. Increasing rejection by peers, realization that the disability is permanent, and the presence of impotence because of the spinal cord lesion may lead to depression.

MULTIDISCIPLINARY MANAGEMENT

Because of the complexities of myelodysplasia, a clinician cannot be solely responsible for the child and family (Table 43–4). Basic members of the health care team should include a physician (e.g., general pediatrician, neurodevelopmental pediatrician, pediatric neurologist, or physiatrist) who has a particular interest and expertise in the care of patients with MM, a nurse coordinator, physical and occupational therapists, a social worker, consulting orthopedic, urologic, and neurosurgical surgeons, and an orthotist. Other team members or consultants may include a psychologist, plastic surgeon, dentist, special educator, speech-language therapist, genetic counselor, and financial counselor. The services the child needs and receives should be coordinated by a designated care coordinator (case manager). Efforts should be made to empower the child and family by giving them the information and resources needed to provide optimal functioning. The child and family are presented with a management plan that is both appropriate and realistic for the child.

PROGNOSIS

The survival rate of children who have MM has improved dramatically over the past 40 years. In the 1950s, survival to adulthood occurred in fewer than 10% of children who had spina bifida. At present, survival to adulthood is about 85%. The change in the survival rate is attributable to many factors, including the use of ventriculoperitoneal shunts and prevention of kidney damage. Adults who have survived MM often experience problems with unemployment and social isolation. Integrated, high-quality health care in childhood and adolescence should allow individuals who have MM to reach their potential during adulthood.

TABLE 43–4. Factors of Concern to the Primary Care Physician Providing Care to the Child Who Has Meningomyelocele with Management Strategies

Factor	Management Strategy
Prevention of myelodysplasia	Recommend folic acid for all females of childbearing age
Prenatal counseling	Discuss cesarian section and location of delivery (tertiary level nursery)
Health maintenance	Provide immunizations, anticipatory guidance, routine visits; monitor growth; ensure dental care
Nutrition	High-fiber, low-fat diet; monitor for obesity
Brain malformations	
Cognitive problems	Monitor development; refer to early intervention program; arrange formal evaluation before school entry
Strabismus	Examine frequently eyes and vision; refer to ophthalmologist
Hydrocephalus	Monitor head circumference and signs and symptoms of shunt failure; refer to neurosurgeon
Chiari malformation	Monitor for neurologic deterioration; monitor activities of daily living; refer to neurosurgeon
Precocious puberty	Monitor sexual development; refer to endocrinologist
Soft tissue malformation	
Infection	Prevent infection in newborn—intravenous antibiotics and surgical closure of the defect
Tethering, lipoma, dermoid of spinal cord	Monitor gait, strength, bladder, and bowel function
Vertebral body malformation	Monitor back for scoliosis and kyphosis; refer to orthopedist
Altered sensation	Monitor integrity of skin; provide preventive counseling regarding skin care
Altered motor function	
Mobility	Monitor developmental milestones; refer to physical therapist and/or early intervention program
Contractures, deformities	Evaluate range of motion of joints; refer to physical therapist and/or orthopedist
Sexual functioning in males	Begin discussions of sexuality early; refer to urologist
Urinary tract dysfunction	Routine urinary cultures; routine renal ultrasonography; voiding cystourethrography as indicated; cystometrograms as indicated; refer to urologist; counsel regarding catheterization
Bowel dysfunction	High-fiber diet; timed toileting; stool softeners; refer to gastroenterologist, nurse clinician
Allergy to latex	Avoid contact with latex; preoperative prophylaxis
Psychosocial concerns	Counsel about finances; monitor family's functioning, child's self-esteem, and behavior; refer to social worker; provide assistance with transition to adulthood

FURTHER READING

Bannister CM and Tew B: Current concepts in spina bifida and hydrocephalus. Clin Dev Med 122:1–215, 1991.

Duncan CC and Ogle EM: Spina bifida. *In* Goldberg B (ed): Sports and Exercise for Children with Chronic Health Conditions. Champaign, IL, Human Kinetics, 1995, 79–88.

Mayfield JK: Comprehensive orthopedic management in meningomyelocele. *In* Rekate HL (ed): Comprehensive Management of Spina Bifida. Boca Raton, FL, CRC Press, 1991, pp 113–163.

Shurtleff DB, Luthy DA, et al.: Meningomyelocele: Management in utero and post natum. Ciba Found Symp 181:270–280, 1994.

Williamson GG (ed): Children with Spina Bifida: Early Intervention and Preschool Programming. Baltimore, Paul H. Brookes Publishing, 1987.

James Coplan

Chapter 44

Speech and Language Disorders

NORMAL SPEECH AND LANGUAGE DEVELOPMENT

Language consists of any symbol system for the storage or exchange of information. Speech is only one subset of language development (Fig. 44–1). Initially, an infant's vocalizations lack symbolic value and, therefore, are termed *prelinguistic.* In the auditory domain, prelinguistic milestones follow a highly predictable sequence, which begins with cooing (open, musical vowel sounds) and progresses to blowing bubbles (the "raspberry"), which in turn is succeeded by laughing, monosyllabic babbling ("ba," "da," "goo"), and polysyllabic babbling ("mama-mama," "lalalala," "nananana"). This sequence is universal in the normal infant's first 6 to 9 months of life. By 9 to 10 months, the infant begins to truncate the polysyllables "mama-mama" or "dadadada" into "mama" and "dada," initially without understanding, but eventually with understanding of the specific association between these sounds and the persons they represent. By 12 months, most infants will have one or two additional single words other than "mama," "dada," or the names of other family members or pets. Infants begin producing spontaneous, novel, two-word combinations around 22 months of age, "telegraphic" three- to five-word utterances around 30 months, and complete sentences by 36 months.

Auditory receptive development also may be divided into prelinguistic and linguistic phases. As with auditory expressive development, the prelinguistic phase extends from birth to about 9 months of age and is marked by "alerting" to voice or sound, recognizing familiar sounds, and orienting to sound progressively and more sophisticatedly. By about 9 months, infants begin to respond selectively to their own name and to the command "no" (although the parent's inflection and context may represent additional cues). By 12 months of age, an infant should follow at least a one-step command, such as "Give me. . ." or "Come here. . .," without an accompanying gestural cue on the adult's part. The normal infant should point to body parts on command starting around 15 months and should be able to follow two-step commands by age 24 months.

In addition to speech and language development, infants make extensive use of visual communication. Infants are born with a biologically determined preference for faces over other visual stimuli. Eye contact, social smile, responses to facial expressions, and participation in simple gesture games such as pat-a-cake or peek-a-boo form a regular sequence of prelinguistic visual milestones that spans the first 9 months of life. Between 9 and 12 months of life, a normally developing infant will reach for a desired object and perhaps cry in frustration; by 12 months, the infant will *point* to the desired object, while gazing imploringly at his or her caregiver. Under ordinary circumstances, index-finger pointing to desired objects represents the principal form of visual language, until the appearance of reading and writing around age 5. In deaf infants, however, or in normal-hearing infants exposed to sign language for some other reason (e.g., if another family member is deaf), signed vocabulary development and complexity of signed "utterances" parallel the development of verbal expression during the second year of life.

TYPICAL PRESENTATIONS OF SPEECH OR LANGUAGE DELAY

Difficulty with nursing, excess choking on liquids, delayed emergence of chewing (a 12-month skill), and excessive drooling are common features of oromotor dysfunction, which eventually may be manifest as delayed or unintelligible speech. This pattern of development is noted commonly in children who have *oromotor apraxia* (difficulty with motor planning) or *dysarthria* (typically encountered as one component of generalized upper motor impairment in cerebral palsy). Although speech may be severely or profoundly impaired in children who have oromotor apraxia or dysarthria, language comprehension and visual communication skills are *normal,* unless the child has an additional disability such as mental retardation or hearing loss.

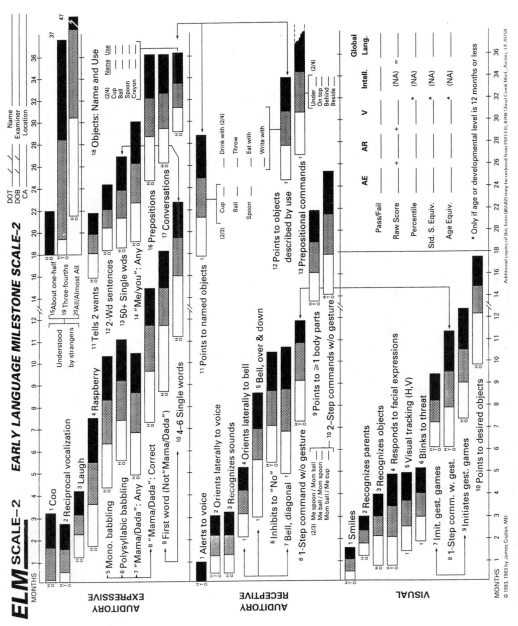

Figure 44-1. When assessing language development, one must evaluate auditory expressive, auditory receptive, and visual language domains separately, because different underlying disorders give rise to different patterns of speech and language delay. Auditory expressive language should be broken down further into *content* (e.g., cooing, babbling, single words, and two-word phrases) and *intelligibility* (the proportion of child's speech understood by others). Key milestones for each language domain are illustrated here. Shading of the horizontal bars corresponds to the ages by which 25%, 50%, 75%, and 90% of children achieve each milestone. (Score sheet from the Early Language Milestone Scale, 2nd ed. © PRO-ED, 8700 Shoal Creek Boulevard, Austin, TX 78758. Used by permission.)

Paucity of vocalization during the prelinguistic stage of development (0 to 9 months) is seen commonly in children who have global developmental delay, that is, *mental retardation (MR)*. Children who are mentally retarded manifest delayed auditory receptive and visual language development, in addition to delayed speech, including delayed ability to respond to verbal commands and delayed emergence of index-finger pointing to desired objects. Although the parent may express concerns regarding "delayed speech," in reality the child who is mentally retarded manifests delayed *language*. **Parental assertions that the child "understands everything" must be taken very cautiously,** because in many cases the child is relying on context or cueing rather than on genuine understanding. Alternatively, the parent may be breaking complex commands down into a series of one-step commands. This enhances the child's ability to function, but is not the equivalent of the ability to process complex commands. Adaptive skills, such as the use of tools (spoon or crayon), dressing and undressing skills, and play skills also are delayed in children who are mentally retarded. Gross motor development may be delayed but is just as likely to be normal.

Children who have *developmental language disorder (DLD)* typically manifest isolated speech delay or combined auditory expressive and auditory receptive delay. Visual language milestones (e.g., pointing) and adaptive skills (use of a spoon or crayon, dressing skills, etc.) are normal. DLD presumably reflects relatively focal impairment of those brain systems that serve language, in the absence of a generalized impairment of brain function (e.g., MR). Children who have DLD typically experience significant frustration because of their limited ability to speak. Often, children who have DLD will begin inventing their own sign language. Expressive language impairment usually dominates the clinical picture during the preschool years. However, many children who have DLD also have significant, although subtle, receptive language or auditory processing difficulties. These receptive language problems often come to light during elementary school, at a time when the expressive deficit has faded. Children who have DLD also are at increased risk for the emergence of learning disabilities, particularly in the areas of reading and writing.

Children who have autism or pervasive developmental disorder (PDD) have language development that is not merely delayed (i.e., typical of a normal but younger child, as in the case of a child who is mentally retarded), but "deviant" (i.e., not typical for a child of *any* age). Speech may be absent altogether or may be present but odd. "My child talks, but he doesn't communicate," lamented one parent, whose toddler had memorized the weather channel and a deck of playing cards, but could not carry on an ordinary conversation. Other "atypical" language features include echolalia (verbatim repetition of the utterances of others) and distortions of inflection, which may sound singsong or robotic. Children who have autism or PDD also manifest delayed or absent visual language, including poor eye contact and impaired use of gestures. The autistic child may point, but such pointing often has a rhetorical rather than communicative quality about it—the child is merely pointing things out, rather than using pointing as a means to request something from his or her caregiver. Rather than speaking or pointing, the child with autism may push or pull the adult's hand toward a desired object, stand in front of the desired object (e.g., the refrigerator), or simply get things without help or communicating his or her needs to others. Children who are autistic also manifest difficulty relating to other persons in the ordinary manner (not cuddly as an infant, no reciprocal play when older, difficulty responding appropriately to social cues), as well as a variety of repetitious behaviors with insistence on the maintenance of routines (e.g., watching the same videotape over and over or eating only a very narrow range of foods).

Infants who have profound *hearing loss* will coo and babble fairly normally in the first few months of life, although their repertoire of prelinguistic utterances is limited, and vocalization does not progress beyond the babbling phase. Children who have lesser degrees of hearing loss may develop speech, although intelligibility is impaired, and the total amount of speech may be reduced. **Hearing loss is virtually impossible to detect in infants or preschool children in an office setting.** Listening comprehension is nonexistent in the child who is profoundly deaf, but even in deaf infants, the parent or physician still may be fooled owing to the infant's reliance on visual cues.

Factors that do *not* give rise to speech or language delay include bilingual upbringing, birth order, and other members of the family's "talking for" the child.

EVALUATION

Speech and language delay are merely symptoms, not medical diagnoses. The pediatric clinician should do the following in the speech- or language-delayed child:

- Document auditory expressive, auditory receptive, and visual language skills.
- Document nonlanguage skills (adaptive, play, personal-social).

- Document hearing status. *All children who are speech- or language-delayed should be evaluated by an audiologist, no matter how well they seem to hear in the office.*
- Obtain consultation from a speech pathologist, psychologist, or developmental pediatrician, depending on level of concern and locally available resources. In most communities, the Health Department or local public school maintains a child study team that can provide a functional assessment of the toddler or preschool child's developmental status.
- Obtain additional medical diagnostic studies, as dictated by the particulars of the case.
- Obtain G-banded chromosomes, fragile X syndrome by DNA analysis, creatine phosphokinase (in males), metabolic screening, or human immunodeficiency testing, as needed. In the absence of specific craniofacial or other syndromic features suggestive of central nervous system malformation, brain imaging studies such as computed tomography or magnetic resonance imaging seldom are informative. Electroencephalography seldom is indicated, the exception being children whose autism is newly diagnosed, especially in those cases in which the parents are adamant that the child was previously normal.

TREATMENT

Treatment in most instances is educational in nature. Children who are mentally retarded need a general infant stimulation program, because their language delay is only one aspect of overall developmental delay. Children who have autism or PDD will benefit from a program that emphasizes language pragmatics, that is, the use of language as a medium for social interaction. Treatment for the autistic child usually is best offered in a social setting (e.g., in a classroom) because one of the goals of therapy for a child who is autistic is to learn how to interact appropriately with other children. Serotonin reuptake inhibitors may be helpful for autistic children who experience extreme difficulty with repetitious behaviors, and stimulant medication sometimes is helpful in the presence of impulsivity. No medication, however, is able to reverse the core language and social skills deficits of the autistic child. Manual sign language may benefit children who have DLD, MR, or autism, as well as children who have hearing loss. The introduction of sign language is often followed by a dramatic decrease in frustration and tantrums. Parents should be reassured that sign language does not delay the emergence of speech. Likewise, the introduction of sign language should not be taken as evidence that the child's parents or teachers have "failed" in their efforts to elicit speech. Children who have DLD may benefit from computer-assisted training programs focusing on auditory processing skills. Children who have hearing loss should receive amplification and aural rehabilitation under the supervision of an audiologist and speech and language pathologist. Cochlear implantation is now valid treatment for children older than 24 months who have severe to profound hearing loss. Children who have dysarthria may require a feeding and swallowing program and the introduction of an augmentative communication system, which may range from picture symbols to a laptop computer with speech synthesis and speech recognition capability.

PROGNOSIS

Speech and language in children who have DLD typically improve dramatically by the time of school entry. Many children who have DLD will go on to manifest some degree of language-based learning disability, however. Prognosis for speech and language development in the child who is mentally retarded is governed by the degree of MR itself. Typically, the child who has MR manifests language skills that would be normal for a younger child. Prognosis for speech and language development in autistic children is a function of the degree of autism, coupled with the degree of coexisting MR, if any. In the mildly autistic child of normal general intelligence, speech and language development may improve dramatically, to the point at which symptoms of the original language disorder all but disappear (although the older autistic child and the autistic adult may continue to manifest subtle features of verbal literalism and difficulty with verbal humor). Prognosis for language development in the child who has hearing loss depends on the age at which hearing loss occurred (before or following the acquisition of speech), the length of time the hearing loss went unrecognized before therapy was instituted, the presence of any coexisting cognitive impairment, and the degree of environmental support the child receives. Profoundly deaf infants born to deaf parents usually do well educationally, probably because they receive language stimulation (in the form of signing) from birth.

FURTHER READING

Rapin L: Autism. N Engl J Med 337:97–104, 1997.

Merzenich MM, Jenkins WM, Johnston P, et al.: Temporal processing deficits of language-learning impaired children ameliorated by training. Science 271:77–94, 1996.

Souliere CR, Quigley SM, and Lanhman AW: Cochlear implants in children. Otolaryngol Clin North Am 27:533–556, 1994.

Gregory S. Liptak

Chapter 45

Cerebral Palsy

OCCURRENCE AND ETIOLOGY

Cerebral palsy is defined as a group of disorders of movement and posture due to a nonprogressive lesion of the developing brain. Cerebral palsy occurs with a birth prevalence of 2 to 2.5 per 1000 live births in developed countries. **The prevalence has increased 15% over the past 20 years, coinciding with the increased survival rate of infants who are of very low birth weight.** In a recent survey of infants, 28% of cerebral palsy occurred in children born weighing under 1500 grams, and 20% occurred in children born weighing between 1500 and 2500 grams. Children born weighing less than 1000 grams make up 0.2% of neonatal survivors but comprise 8% of children who have cerebral palsy.

For decades, cerebral palsy was attributed to abnormal perinatal events. However, many factors operating in the prenatal, perinatal, and postnatal periods can damage the infant's brain. Neither sophisticated fetal monitoring nor an increased rate of cesarean sections has decreased the frequency of cerebral palsy. A definite cause for most cases of cerebral palsy is unknown; when it can be identified, it usually is of prenatal origin. A more accurate appraisal of the cause of cerebral palsy is "bad babies make bad deliveries." Intrapartum events play a limited role and frequently are influenced by a preexisting abnormality. Isolated risk factors such as fetal bradycardia, neonatal acidosis, intraventricular hemorrhage in the absence of periventricular leukomalacia, and low Apgar scores are poor predictors of cerebral palsy, especially in full-term infants. However, low birth weight (<2000 grams), periventricular leukomalacia (necrosis of white matter near the lateral ventricles), hydrocephalus, congenital malformations, prolonged need for ventilation, and newborn encephalopathy (recurrent seizures, hypotonia, coma) are all associated with later cerebral palsy.

In about 10% of cases, cerebral palsy has a postneonatal cause, including infections such as meningitis and encephalitis, asphyxia, and accidental injury. Cerebral palsy in some instances may be preventable by strategies that decrease the occurrence of accidents during childhood and by measures that minimize periventricular leukomalacia in premature infants, such as improving circulation and countering the effects of excitatory neurotransmitters, for example, by the administration of magnesium salts to women in labor.

CLASSIFICATION AND DIAGNOSIS

Cerebral palsies are classified according to the type and distribution of motor abnormalities (Table 45–1). This classification includes four categories: *spastic* (involving the pyramidal tracts), *dyskinetic* (involving the extrapyramidal tracts), *ataxic*, and *mixed*. Spasticity is velocity-dependent resistance of muscles to passive stretch (clasp-knife rigidity) and is associated with neurologic signs of upper motor neuron damage such as hyperreflexia, clonus, and extensor plantar response. These abnormalities impair normal movements, such as gait and the manipulation of objects. *Diplegia* is defined as greater involvement of the legs than the arms, *quadriplegia* as an equal involvement of all four limbs, *hemiplegia* as involvement of one side of the body, and *double hemiplegia* as greater involvement of the arms than the legs.

Dyskinesia is characterized by the involuntary movements of athetosis and chorea, as well as dystonia, which is most pronounced when the child initiates a movement. Dysarthria commonly occurs with dyskinesia. Ataxia involves incoordination of movement and impaired balance and may be associated with an intention tremor. Children who have mild ataxia may appear to have normal coordination but are apraxic, that is, they

TABLE 45–1. Classification of Cerebral Palsy

Spastic	Dyskinetic
Diplegic	Hyperkinetic
Quadriplegic	Dystonic
Hemiplegic	Ataxic
Double hemiplegic	Mixed

are unable to initiate acts such as hopping, skipping, or buttoning.

Because the fibers in the corticospinal tract that control the legs are closest to the ventricles, mild periventricular leukomalacia or hydrocephalus is most likely to lead to spastic diplegia. **Children who have spastic quadriplegia generally have more extensive lesions and are more likely to be mentally retarded (64% have an IQ <50) and have seizures (~50%) than children who have other kinds of cerebral palsy.** They also are more likely to have feeding difficulties, severe joint contractures, and scoliosis. Each form of cerebral palsy may be caused by a multitude of causes, and a single etiologic factor, such as meningitis, may lead to different forms of cerebral palsy.

Although the lesion of the brain in cerebral palsy is nonprogressive, the clinical signs change as the child develops, especially in the first several years of life. Abnormal patterns emerge as the damaged nervous system matures. For example, the child who is destined to have spastic quadriplegia is often hypotonic in early infancy. At 6 months of age, as tone increases, the child may develop adduction of the thumb (palmar thumb) followed in a month or two by scissoring of the legs when he or she is held upright. By 9 months of age, the child may have diffuse spasticity and hyperactive deep tendon reflexes. Dyskinetic patterns generally are not obvious until the child is about 18 months of age. Ataxia may not be apparent until even later. Cerebral palsy often is diagnosed when the child is around 10 months of age.

History and Physical Examination

Information obtained during the history of a child suspected of having cerebral palsy should include parental concerns regarding the child's development, current levels of developmental functioning, prenatal history, perinatal and neonatal events, family and social history, developmental milestones, visual and auditory functioning, nutrition, and feeding. A complete neurologic evaluation of the child should include assessment of cranial nerves, posture, muscle tone of the extremities, trunk and neck (head control), deep tendon reflexes, postural responses, and primitive reflexes including the asymmetric tonic neck response, truncal incurvation (Galant's reflex), plantar grasp, crossed extension, and truncal support. Typically, primitive reflexes appear in neonates, then disappear over time. Their absence or their persistence beyond a certain period may indicate

abnormalities of the central nervous system. The postural responses of "righting," protection, and equilibrium when the child is tilted to both sides require more integration of sensory and motor functions and are more sensitive to nervous system damage than are the primitive reflexes.

Cerebral palsy should not be diagnosed on the basis of a single physical finding. Also, a single evaluation of a child is not as useful in establishing a prognosis as is a series of examinations over time. Early signs that should raise suspicion of cerebral palsy include difficulty feeding due to abnormal oral-motor patterns (tongue thrusting, tonic bite, oral hypersensitivity), irritability, and delayed milestones, such as head control. The presence of delayed milestones, primitive or exaggerated reflexes, abnormal postural responses, abnormal muscle tone, and abnormal posture suggests the diagnosis of cerebral palsy.

A thorough orthopedic examination should be performed, including range of motion of all joints by using a goniometer. Ankle dorsiflexion should be determined with the knee extended and flexed. Hip flexion should be evaluated by using the Thomas test, and hip abduction performed both with the hips and knees flexed and with the legs extended. The presence of hip dysplasia can be ascertained by examining for asymmetry of skinfolds in the gluteal region, thighs, labia, and buttocks, by performing the Barlow and Ortolani maneuvers in young children and the Galeazzi maneuver in children of all ages, and by assessing for pistoning of the hips. The back should be assessed for kyphosis, excessive lordosis, and scoliosis. The forward bending test with a scoliometer should be used in children who are cooperative. Evaluation of the child's gait in the stance and swing phases can help determine structural problems such as tibial torsion and coxa valga as well as joint contractures and pain.

Because children who have cerebral palsy are at increased risk for nutrition and feeding problems, careful monitoring of their physical growth is critical. Reliable measures of height or length in children who have cerebral palsy are often impossible to obtain owing to scoliosis, fixed joint contractures, involuntary muscle spasms, and poor cooperation due to cognitive deficits. Tibial length has been used as a proxy for height. Evaluation of the child whose growth is impaired includes evaluation of dietary intake for calories and content.

The diagnosis of cerebral palsy implies that no active disease is present. The differential diagnosis includes neurodegenerative disorders, inborn errors of metabolism, developmental or traumatic lesions of the spinal cord, severe neuromuscular disease, movement disorders, spinocerebellar degenerations, neoplasms, hydrocephalus, and subdural hematoma. Repeated examinations are needed to rule out a degenerative condition. If a child diagnosed as having dyskinetic cerebral palsy has symptoms that worsen significantly as the day progresses, dopa-responsive dystonia should be considered. This rare form of dystonia may begin with toe-walking and difficulties with gait and responds dramatically to the administration of levodopa.

Imaging and Laboratory Studies

Neuroimaging techniques such as ultrasonography, computed tomography (CT), and magnetic resonance imaging (MRI) have increased the understanding of the structural abnormalities associated with cerebral palsy and may help clarify the timing of a lesion. Neuroimaging may demonstrate periventricular leukomalacia, postischemic necrosis, cerebral dysgenesis, hydrocephalus, porencephaly, tumor, prenatal ischemic injury, or leukodystrophy. The information gained with brain imaging, although usually not helpful in directing therapy, can be useful in explaining the specific cause of a child's cerebral palsy to the parents. The electroencephalogram (EEG) is useful for the diagnosis and management of associated seizures; continuous EEG monitoring with videography may help differentiate seizures from other movement disorders. Evaluation of disabilities such as an abnormal gait may require special diagnostic studies such as gait analysis by using video- and computer-assisted analysis. Children who have feeding disorders should have a clinical feeding evaluation that includes assessment of the child's seating and posture during meals as well as assessment of the swallowing mechanism, which can be aided by a video-fluoroscopic swallow study using foods of different consistencies. Evaluation for gastroesophageal reflux by using a barium swallow, a pH probe, a radionuclide gastric emptying study, or endoscopy with biopsy and evaluation for aspiration by using radionuclide swallow studies may be indicated. The assistance of feeding specialists is invaluable in this evaluation.

DISABILITIES

Table 45–2 lists disabilities that are associated with cerebral palsy. All types of language abnormality may be encountered, ranging from aphasia to poor articulation. Abnormal speech may be related to hearing, intelligence, experience, lan-

TABLE 45–2. Disabilities Associated with Cerebral Palsy in Children

Impaired communication
Impaired cognition
Impaired mobility
Impaired self-care and hygiene
Impaired nutrition/feeding
Dental caries, malocclusion
Seizures
Impaired vision or hearing
Impaired access to care
Adverse effects on family
Impaired transition to adulthood

guage development, the integration of motor mechanisms of the oropharynx, and coordination of breathing patterns. Nearly 75% of individuals who have cerebral palsy are cognitively impaired. About 60% are mentally retarded, mildly in about 33% and moderately or severely in 33%. In the remainder, who function in the normal range, specific learning disabilities such as visual-spatial impairment often occur.

Impaired mobility is a common occurrence and may result from spasticity with or without joint contractures, dyskinesias, and scoliosis. Self-care and hygiene can be impaired by gross motor and fine motor abnormalities and difficulties such as drooling. Defects in gastrointestinal function and growth are common. In general, physical growth is inhibited. Many children who have cerebral palsy fail to thrive, especially those who have dyskinesia or spastic quadriplegia. Feeding difficulties due to oropharyngeal incoordination and recurrent vomiting occur and may be associated with aspiration and gastroesophageal reflux. Dental disease (malocclusion and caries) is common. Seizures commonly occur, as do impaired vision and hearing. Roughly 40% develop seizures, which have their onset most often in the first 2 years of life. Oculomotor anomalies include strabismus, refractive error, and nystagmus. Sociocultural risk factors have a profound effect on development and interact with biologic risk factors. Perinatal and other biologic risk factors that can lead to intellectual impairment do not have the same detrimental consequences for middle- or upper-class children as they do for poor children.

INTERVENTION

In cerebral palsy, a pathophysiologic abnormality of the brain, for example, leukomalacia, leads to an impairment such as spasticity. Spasticity then leads to alterations in functioning, such as shortened stride length, which leads to disabilities, such as a slow gait. The disabilities may lead to adverse social consequences or handicaps, such as the inability to use public transportation. Adults who have cerebral palsy have identified *communication skills, self-care activities,* and *mobility* as the three most important functional outcomes of care. The goals of intervention, therefore, are to prevent adverse functional outcomes and to prevent disabilities and handicaps. For example, reducing muscle spasticity by using medications or performing surgery will not be worthwhile if they do not also improve the child's ability to function.

No single professional can fulfill the multiple medical, social, psychologic, educational, and therapeutic needs of a child who has moderate or severe cerebral palsy. Comprehensive management requires an expert multidisciplinary team whose members can instruct and support parents to enable them to achieve maximal potential for self-help and care for their child. As mandated by Public Law 99-457, physicians should refer children who have cerebral palsy to early intervention services. These services may include special education; physical, occupational, and speech therapies; adaptive equipment; training for mobility and living skills; and assistance with communication. Physical therapy does not change the basic disorder significantly. However, physical therapists and other professionals may provide support to families and enable them to learn how to position and handle their child, provide more opportunity for play and learning, and facilitate feeding and the parent-child relationship. Whether or not formal early intervention services are provided, early social support should be provided to the family to help them cope with the crisis of diagnosis.

The care provided should be integrated. For example, children whose legs are spastic often have dorsiflexion at the ankle, flexion at the knee, and flexion and adduction of the hip. Repair of one or two of these problems may leave the child unimproved or worse; all three areas must be addressed simultaneously. Gait analysis, using videography, electromyography (EMG), and computerized sensors, has improved the orthopedic care given to these children. Following orthopedic surgery, therapy to maximize range of motion and skills should be instituted.

Table 45–3 outlines the treatment for spasticity. Oral medications to decrease spasticity, such as diazepam, baclofen, and dantrolene, are used, but all have potential adverse effects with no documented improvement in functioning. Various casting and splinting techniques that may maintain muscle length and inhibit increased tone may be helpful. In many cases orthopedic procedures such

TABLE 45–3. Measures for the Treatment of Spasticity

Treatment	Comment
Orthopedic surgery to shorten muscles or lengthen/transfer tendons	All interventions in an extremity should be coordinated, e.g., Achilles tendon and hamstring lengthenings; heterotopic ossification or joint dysplasia may occur
Casting, splinting, and range of motion exercises	Traditional therapy; may lead to irritation of skin
Oral medications—baclofen, diazepam, dantrolene, tizanidine	Often associated with profound sedation
Intrathecal baclofen pump	Serious intra- and postoperative complications, especially infection
Selective dorsal root rhizotomy	Permanently weakens muscle; may lead to sensory deficit; may lead to unstable hips
Intramuscular botulinum toxin	Effect is transient; may be used to delay surgery

as tenotomies and tendon transfers are necessary. Selective dorsal rhizotomy and intrathecal baclofen can decrease spasticity and increase range of motion, and some patients may make functional improvements in sitting and gait. Intramuscular botulinum toxin has been used to decrease spasticity in individual limbs and demonstrates promise for future transient therapy.

Drooling has been managed with the transdermal scopolamine patch, oral glycopyrrolate, and surgical removal of the salivary glands. Treatment for the child who has difficulty feeding may include provision of special seating devices to maintain him or her in an upright, neutral position or insertion of a gastrostomy tube with or without fundoplication. This usually improves weight gain and general health but may not improve longitudinal growth. The physician who cares for the child who has cerebral palsy should advocate to ensure that the child has access to first-rate care as well as to ensure that the community provides access to services so that disabilities do not become handicaps.

PROGNOSIS

More than 90% of infants who have cerebral palsy survive into adulthood. Children with cerebral palsy who are so severely affected that they cannot move their extremities or bodies voluntarily and who require nonoral feedings are at increased risk for early death. Prognostication before the child's second birthday may be difficult, except at the extremes of involvement. In general, the prognosis is related to clinical type, rate of motor development, evolution of infantile reflexes, intellectual abilities, sensory impairment, and emotional-social adjustment. Those children who sit unsupported by 24 months of age and crawl by 30 months are more likely to walk independently. Most of those who first sit between 3 and 4 years of age will walk only with aids or braces. The retention of obligatory primitive reflexes at 18 months of age makes independent ambulation unlikely. Virtually all children who have hemiplegia will learn to walk, as will many who have athetosis or ataxia. Those who walk under the age of 2 years are more likely to have normal or borderline IQs.

Individual achievement is related to many factors such as intelligence, physical function, ability to communicate, and personality. The availability of training, jobs, sheltered employment, and counseling is a major factor in the adjustment of adults who have cerebral palsy. The presence of a supportive family and the availability of medical care by specialists are further important factors. Long-term planning and preparation to make the transition from adolescence to adulthood are required, particularly when the individual will have multiple needs.

A variety of assistive devices, such as switches, which improve the interface between individual and environment; computers; and small electric motors, which may replace some motor activities, are available. The use of speech synthesizers, symbol charts, or spelling boards can profoundly enhance an individual's ability to communicate effectively. Simple environmental enhancements such as ramps or accessible showers and assistive devices such as a pencil holder or mouth-activated switch can dramatically improve the quality of life of individuals who have cerebral palsy. Accessing these services requires coordination of care, knowledge of the resources available in the community, referral to experts, and financial assets. The physician caring for these individuals has the ability and the obligation to ensure that these services are available to the individual who has cerebral palsy and his or her family.

FURTHER READING

Cummins SK, Nelson KB, Grether JK, and Velie EM: Cerebral palsy in four northern California counties, births 1983 through 1985. J Pediatr 123:230–237, 1993.

Dammann O, Walther H, Allers B, et al.: Development of a regional cohort of very-low-birthweight children at six years: Cognitive abilities are associated with neurological disability and social background. Dev Med Child Neurol 38(Suppl 2):97–106, 1996.

dePaz AC Jr, Burnett S, and Bragga LW: Walking prognosis in cerebral palsy: A 22-year retrospective analysis. Dev Med Child Neurol 36:130–134, 1994.

Goldberg MJ: Measuring outcomes in cerebral palsy. J Pediatr Orthop 11:682–685, 1991.

Kuban KC and Leviton MD: Cerebral palsy. N Engl J Med 330:188–195, 1994.

Mark L. Wolraich

Chapter **46**

Mental Retardation

BACKGROUND

Mental retardation is the diagnosis employed with children who demonstrate significantly below average functioning in their general cognitive abilities and adaptive behavior. Because general cognitive abilities cover a broad range of mental skills and a broad range of severity, children who have this diagnosis constitute a very heterogeneous group in presentation, prognosis, and etiology.

Even children who have identical intelligence quotients may be vastly different in their abilities. Furthermore, not all the skills assessed by general intelligence tests reflect how well one is able to function independently in society. For this reason the American Association on Mental Retardation (AAMR) emphasizes the importance of adaptive skills when considering the diagnosis of mental retardation. These skills need to be considered separately because many skills included in general intellectual assessment are not associated with independent functioning; conversely, many skills important to independent functioning are not necessarily included in general intellectual assessment. One needs to look beyond a child's intelligence score or degree of mental retardation and identify his or her strengths and weaknesses to best help parents maximize their child's potential. Those who are interested in a more in-depth discussion of the theoretical issues of general intelligence and its assessment are encouraged to read *The Mismeasure of Man* by Stephen Jay Gould, an excellent discussion of the concept of general intelligence and its limitations and misuses.

How individuals who are mentally retarded are viewed and the practice of segregating large numbers of these individuals in large state institutions began to change in the 1960s following the disclosure that inadequate care was being provided to residents in many facilities. This led to a movement to deinstitutionalize individuals, to encourage families to care for their children at home, and to provide community and educational services that enable mentally retarded children to live at home and mentally retarded adults to remain in their communities. In the 1970s several federal laws were passed to ensure and provide individuals who have developmental disabilities, including mental retardation, with educational and community services. These laws include the Education for All Handicapped Act (Public Law 94-142), now called the Individuals with Disability Education Act (IDEA), which outlined procedures for evaluation and program planning as well as support for educational services, and the Civil Rights of Institutionalized Persons Act (CRIPA) of 1980, which required states to upgrade their community programs and move individuals out of institutions. Today, few individuals who have mental retardation remain isolated in institutions. In most communities there are an array of services and programs to enable such individuals to live lives within the mainstream of society, although more programs are still required to achieve this goal fully for all individuals. As a result, the role that primary care clinicians have in providing health care to these individuals has increased.

More recently, in the AAMR's attempt to deemphasize the importance of general cognitive abilities and increase the focus on adaptive functioning, they have proposed that an intelligence quotient less than 70 to 75 be required as a necessary but not sufficient criterion for the diagnosis. In addition, there need to be deficits in at least two of 10 adaptive behavior domains. The extent of limitation also is employed to define severity, which has been reduced to two levels—mild or severe. However, these new criteria have been criticized for not having good, formalized measures of adaptive behaviors and for identifying too

many people who have the necessary criteria. Most educational and clinical programs continue to use the previous categories of mild, moderate, severe, and profound. Therefore, this chapter organizes the presentation according to those categories.

MILD MENTAL RETARDATION

Children who have mild mental retardation may not present with any problems until 3 years of age; many times they actually do not present until they enter kindergarten at age 5. If they do not attend a preschool program, their parents may not notice the deficits until their child is seen in comparison with same-age peers. Often in the case of the kindergartner, the diagnosis is made by the school psychologist after referral from the teacher who describes the child as immature and delayed in acquiring academic skills.

Although the most frequent cause of mental retardation for these children is cultural-familial or idiopathic, it is important for the physician to rule out any underlying etiology. This function is one that none of the other professionals caring for children, such as psychologists or educators, is able to undertake. There are conditions that can have some associated intellectual impairment, for example, neurofibromatosis, fragile X syndrome, muscular dystrophy, or Klinefelter syndrome. It is important to obtain a careful family history and physical and neurologic examinations. Findings suggestive of a familial pattern or dysmorphic features are important to note and warrant further workup. Deprivation in the home also needs to be identified. Although most of the medical conditions have no specific corrective interventions, adverse environmental situations can benefit by interventions, such as removal in the case of abuse or severe neglect. **In less severe cases, educational and social interventions, such as the Head Start program, have been shown to have long-term beneficial effects on the children's abilities to function in school.**

An additional important role for the physician is to help ensure that the child has an adequate psychoeducational evaluation and that an appropriate educational program is developed. The evaluation should be comprehensive so that it categorizes the child's strengths and weaknesses and identifies associated problems. It also should assess the child's visual and auditory status and expressive and receptive language abilities. A child who has a hearing impairment and a language disorder may be misdiagnosed as being mentally retarded. Even if these deficits are not the major source of the child's disability, these impairments, as well as visual deficits, may limit the child's abilities further if the deficits are ignored. Furthermore, a child's intelligence level, determined at one assessment, may not always indicate a true or unchanging level. Abilities may change with appropriate programming, particularly in children who are culturally deprived, and the actual tasks assessed to determine intelligence change with the age of the child being tested. Thus, a child sometimes may appear more capable at an earlier age when intellectual assessment depends primarily on memory skills and less on associative skills and less capable at a later age, when the situation is reversed.

Physicians and other professionals frequently are asked by parents to provide some indication about the potential of their child. This may be difficult to assess. Additionally, **there is a tendency for primary care clinicians to have lower expectations than other professional groups** **when considering the prognosis of children who are mentally retarded.** General guidelines for all four levels are presented in Table 46–1.

Children who have mild mental retardation can grow up to be fairly independent adults. Although they usually do not attain high school level academic abilities, they can learn sufficient reading and arithmetic skills to function independently, including maintaining employment, living independently, marrying, and in a few cases, raising children. Most, however, will need some supervision to help them manage their daily activities.

As children who have mild mental retardation grow to adulthood, their parents should be encouraged to consider some important issues. Because of limitations in judgment, being taken advantage of or being physically or sexually abused becomes a serious concern for adolescents or adults who are mentally retarded. To assist parents, special education classes now provide programs to deal with these issues, but this problem will continue

TABLE 46–1. Developmental Characteristics, Potential for Education and Training, and Social and Vocational Adequacy According to the Four Levels of Mental Retardation

Level	Preschool Age (0–5) Maturation and Development	School Age (6–21) Training and Education	Adult (21 and over) Social and Vocational Adequacy
Profound	Gross retardation: minimal capacity for functioning in sensorimotor areas; needs nursing care	Obvious delays in all areas of development; shows basic emotional responses; may respond to skillful training in use of legs, hands, and jaws; needs close supervision	May walk, need nursing care, have primitive speech; usually benefits from regular physical activity; incapable of self-maintenance
Severe	Marked delay in motor development; little or no communication skill; may respond to training in elementary self-help, e.g., self-feeding	Usually walks (barring specific disability); has some understanding of speech and some response; can profit from systematic habit training	Can conform to daily routines and repetitive activities; needs continuing direction and supervision in protective environment
Moderate	Noticeable delays in motor development, especially in speech; responds to training in various self-help activities	Can learn simple communication, elementary health and safety habits, and simple manual skills; does not progress in functional reading or arithmetic	Can perform simple tasks under sheltered conditions; participates in simple recreation; travels alone in familiar places; usually incapable of self-maintenance
Mild	Often not noticed as retarded by casual observer but is slower to walk, feed self, and talk than most children	Can acquire practical skills and useful reading and arithmetic to third- to sixth-grade level with special education; can be guided toward social conformity	Can usually achieve social and vocational skills adequate to self-maintenance; may need occasional guidance and support when under unusual social or economic stress

From President's Panel on Mental Retardation: Mental Retardation, a National Plan for a National Problem: Chart Book. Washington, DC, US Department of Health, Education, and Welfare, 1963.

to be a concern for parents. Long-term supervision of the child's financial welfare also needs to be arranged as the child grows into adulthood.

MODERATE MENTAL RETARDATION

Physicians frequently are the first professionals to diagnose moderate retardation in a child. The diagnosis sometimes is made at birth, as when a child has Down syndrome, or may be strongly suspected, as in the case of a high-risk neonate. Other disorders that have mental retardation as a symptom may appear within the first 2 years of life. Thus, the primary care clinician is frequently the first professional to counsel the parents about their child's disability. The physician plays a crucial role in helping the parents understand the nature of the disability and the important aspects of development so that the parents can maximize their child's abilities. This counseling should, if at all possible, be undertaken with both parents present, in a nondisruptive environment, and with adequate time available. Sometimes the parents may want other family members or significant persons,

such as a member of the clergy, to be present. Those wishes should be granted if at all possible, although it may be helpful to restrict the size of the group. The physician should be as specific as possible about the child's condition. This information should be provided in detail after the parents have recovered from the immediate shock of learning that they have a child with a disability and frequently requires subsequent sessions. It usually needs to be repeated on several occasions. Providing written material about the condition or a tape recording of the informing interview can help the parents to review what they have learned about their child's condition.

The likelihood of an identifiable etiology is much greater for children who have moderate mental retardation. Table 46–2 provides a list of the broad groups of potential causes of mental retardation that should be considered in trying to identify an underlying cause. The first step in the search for an underlying cause for mental retardation in a patient is a complete history and physical examination. As part of the history, a detailed family history should be obtained to identify any possible hereditary disorders, such as phenylketonuria or tuberous sclerosis. Information

TABLE 46–2. Causes Contributing to Mental Retardation*

Category		Subgroups		Studies to Consider
I: Prenatal onset of problem in morphogenesis	44%	Single defect of brain	14%	Consider CT scan Pneumoencephalography
		Multiple defect, including brain		
		a. chromosomal	12%	Chromosome studies
		b. unknown	6%	Chromosome studies
		c. known syndrome, not chromosomal	6%	
II: Perinatal insult to brain	?3%	Traumatic		
		Metabolic		
		Infectious		
III: Postnatal onset of problem	?12%	Environmental		
		Metabolic disorders, including known inborn errors	4%	Indicated metabolic study
		Infectious		
		Other		
IV: Undecided age of onset of problem	41%			Consider metabolic studies, buccal smear for X-chromatin, chromosome study
Disorders that might present *clinically* in several of the above categories	?Very small %	Prenatal infectious disease		Appropriate culture and/ or antibody studies, PBI, or T_4
		Hypothyroidism, congenital		

*Categorization of patients who have mental deficiency, as an aid toward rational diagnostic evaluation. The percentage figures represent the approximate percent of each category and subgroup from the *total* of 1224 seriously mentally deficient patients in a study by Kaveggia et al: Diagnostic genetic studies on 1,224 patients with severe mental retardation. Proceedings of the Third Congress of the International Association for Scientific Study of Mental Deficiency, held at the Hague, Holland, September 4–12, 1973.

CT, computed tomography, PBI, protein-bound iodine, T_4, thyroxine.

Adapted from Jones KL: Smith's Recognizable Patterns of Human Malformation, 4th ed. Philadelphia, WB Saunders, 1988. Reprinted by permission.

about the gestational and birth history also is important. Although studies suggest that birth asphyxia plays less of a role in brain damage than was thought previously, identifying information, such as the infant being small for gestational age, could suggest a prenatal insult, for example, a congenital infection. Neonatal seizures also are a symptom of particular note. A careful physical examination can reveal anomalies suggesting a chromosomal or inherited disorder, and abnormal results from a neurologic examination may suggest other problems, such as cerebral palsy.

Some laboratory tests may be helpful. Most of the time, the appropriate tests can be selected based on the findings of the history and physical examination. These can include karyotyping, DNA testing, or biochemical studies to identify inborn errors of metabolism. Some tests such as thyroid screening and screening for phenylketonuria are worth obtaining if the history and physical findings give negative results. Although these tests are likely to have been done as part of newborn screening, false-negative possibilities warrant repetition of those tests for a child who has moderate retardation of no clear etiology.

Making a definite diagnosis is important for several reasons. In most cases it will not identify any treatable or reversible disorder, but it may provide the parents with a more specific answer to their question about why the condition occurred; it may help the physician to be more specific about the likely outcomes; and it also may provide useful information for genetic counseling for the parents and other family members. If there is any doubt, it is important to obtain consultation from other services, such as genetics or neurology.

At some point during the counseling process, although generally not at the initial session, it is helpful to connect the parents with parents of children who have the same or similar conditions. This works best if the physician personally knows parents who have similarly affected children in his or her practice, but it also can be done by making use of parent organizations such as the Association for Retarded Citizens (ARC).

The major source of treatment for children who are mentally retarded is educational programming. Because of federal legislation (see earlier), most communities now have programs for children from the time when the condition or developmental delay is first identified. These programs may enhance development and, equally important, provide parents with the opportunity to meet other parents and to understand and deal with their children better. In these programs and in subsequent special education programs, the physician

frequently serves as an independent third party to whom the parents can turn for support and advice.

It is important for physicians to become familiar with the process as defined in the Individuals with Disability Education Act. This process includes identifying, testing, and providing services and follow-up for the child who is mentally retarded. The process also encourages a good deal of parental participation throughout. School programs are expected to include parents in their deliberations (staffing) and must secure their written consent for both assessment and programming. The primary care clinician sometimes needs to provide information to the school staff to clarify medical issues, such as seizures. School personnel appreciate input from a child's physician, particularly if medical problems such as seizures or anticonvulsive medications may affect the child's performance. Frequently the physician also can enhance the communication between parents and school personnel before disagreements become adversarial. When school programming is inadequate, the physician should advocate for the child who has mental retardation to help the parents ensure that their child is receiving appropriate services.

Two other areas in which the physician should be involved are the issues of sexuality and independent living. As children who are mentally retarded grow into adolescence, most are faced with the same sexual maturation process as other individuals, which can be a concern to parents. Furthermore, parents of children who are moderately retarded need to have the same awareness as parents of children who are mildly retarded of the potential for sexual abuse and what can be done to prevent it. The second issue, alternatives to living with parents, needs to be considered on attainment of adulthood. This often is a difficult decision for many parents and should be considered with sufficient time to explore the possibilities. Many communities have developed supported living arrangements for adults who require supervision and assistance. These usually are apartments housing two to three individuals and a supervisor. A limited number of these facilities are available, so it is important to allow ample time for planning to ensure that the programs are both appropriate and adequate.

As stated previously, primary care physicians have a history of being unduly pessimistic about the prognosis for children who have mental retardation; 15 to 20 years ago, early institutionalization commonly was recommended in cases of Down syndrome. A more realistic set of prognoses presented in Table 46–2 (see earlier), provides rough guidelines for likely capabilities at different ages. Again, it is important to realize that these are only guidelines. Individual children will show a good deal of variation, and in recent years, societal changes have increased the opportunities for disabled individuals so that adults who are moderately retarded can work in gainful employment if they have sufficient social skills. Although creating unreal expectations can lead to unhappy parents later in life, it is important in this case to be as encouraging as possible as long as parents are aware that predictions about the future are difficult and may not be accurate.

Moderately retarded individuals also can live in supported-living supervised homes. They can learn to work at rote jobs, mostly in supervised conditions, but in some cases in the competitive job market. They generally can be independent in terms of public transportation as long as they are on familiar routes that they have been trained to use. Much of their success depends on their social skills and dependability.

SEVERE TO PROFOUND MENTAL RETARDATION

Most of the recommendations made about diagnosis and management of individuals who have moderate mental retardation also apply to the care of children who are severely and profoundly retarded. These children usually present in the first year of life. They frequently have multiple medical problems, including seizures, spasticity, and feeding problems.

Clinicians tend to be even more pessimistic about the outcomes for these children. A major cause for this pessimism is the generalized impression characteristic of children who are profoundly mentally retarded. Although children who have profound mental retardation may be in a vegetative state, children who have severe retardation are not. Their interactions are at a simplified level, but they do interact with their environment and the people in it.

Most of these children will live at home and attend special education classes in their community. They frequently are in greater need of medical attention because of a number of secondary conditions, such as seizure disorders, visual or auditory impairment, or physical handicapping conditions, such as cerebral palsy.

Although the degree of independence that these children attain is much more limited, many of their achievements such as independence in toileting, dressing, or feeding have major implications regarding the degree of supervision that they will require. These, in turn, translate into the eventual placements that will be possible and, ultimately,

what the cost of each individual's care will be. Most training programs attempt to provide each child with skills to maximize his or her potential to experience a full life, including vocational and recreational activities. Therefore, although the goals of educational programs for children who are severely retarded may be limited, they can have a major impact on the child's quality of life. Likewise, the more manageable the child and the more support services provided to the parents, the easier it is for them to raise their child in their own home. In almost all cases, this is a better arrangement than out-of-home placement, for both the child and the community. In these circumstances, a child's physician can contribute a great deal by providing advice and support to parents.

Adults who are severely retarded are still capable of living in supported-living placements unless they have difficult medical needs, such as ventilator assistance, or severely disruptive behavior. Many are capable of functioning in supervised employment activities. They can interact and establish meaningful relationships with people around them. Adults who are profoundly retarded, on the other hand, are more limited in their abilities and may be close to a vegetative state.

MANAGEMENT

Unfortunately, mental retardation rarely is cured. In an age of dramatic medical advances, this fact can be very frustrating to parents and can lead them to seek any form of therapy that promises a cure or a dramatic improvement. Such a response is particularly likely if the parents feel that their questions and concerns have not been addressed appropriately or if they have some unexpressed feelings such as guilt. It is possible to reduce their search for unproved cures if the clinician is careful in counseling and allows parents to bring up and discuss all potential therapies. Some parents are likely to seek out unorthodox therapies under any circumstances. In those situations, it is helpful if the clinician can still maintain a positive relationship. In all likelihood, the child still will require conventional care. However, if the activities the parents are pursuing can potentially cause harm, reporting possible child abuse or neglect should be considered if the parents continue with such activities.

Siblings can be affected adversely by a brother or sister who is mentally retarded. They can be placed in the ambivalent situation of feeling jealous of their retarded sibling, who demands more of their parents' time and receives more parental attention, and feeling sorry for that sibling. This ambivalence can lead to conscious or unconscious desires for the mentally retarded brother or sister to die or disappear. The sibling's social status at school also may be affected by having a brother or sister who is mentally retarded. Frequently, the sibling who has fewer apparent needs gets overlooked. The primary care clinician is in an excellent position to identify whether problems exist with siblings and to provide counseling or obtain help for them.

The clinician also is in a good position to work as an advocate in the community. That misinformation and negative attitudes still exist in communities has become evident as the mainstreaming of mentally retarded individuals into the educational system and the community has progressed. A supportive community physician can be particularly helpful with community issues, such as the acceptance of supported-living facilities. He or she also can play an important role as an educator in the community. As stated earlier, primary care clinicians can help teachers to understand the medical aspects of their students' problems so that the students become less challenging to manage in the classroom. They also can help to educate parent organizations about the causes

of mental retardation and about whether treatments are either helpful or controversial. Lastly, they can work to develop prevention programs for mentally retarded individuals, such as informing potential parents about the hazards of alcohol or tobacco use during pregnancy.

FURTHER READING

Gould SJ: The Mismeasure of Man. New York, WW Norton, 1981.

Luckasson R, Coulter DL, Polloway E, et al.: Mental Retardation: Definition, Classification, and Systems of Supports. Washington, DC, American Association on Mental Retardation, 1992.

MacMillan DL, Gresham FM, and Siperstein GN: Conceptual and psychometric concerns about the 1992 AAMR definition on mental retardation. Am J Ment Retard 98:325–335, 1993.

Wolraich ML (ed): Children with Disorders of Development and Learning: The Practical Assessment and Management, 2nd ed. Chicago, Mosby–Year Book, 1996.

Wolraich ML, Siperstein GN, and Reed D: The Prognostications of Physicians About Mentally Retarded Individuals. Advances in Developmental and Behavioral Pediatrics, Vol 10. Edited by Wolraich M and Routh D. London, Jessica Kingsley Publishers, 1992, pp 109–130.

Zorzi G, Thurman SK, and Kistenmacher ML: Importance and adequacy of genetic counseling information: Impression of parents with Down's syndrome children. Ment Retard 18:255–257, 1980.

Craig C. Orlowski

Chapter 47

Common Issues in Childhood Type I Diabetes Mellitus

The primary goals in the treatment of type I diabetes are to avoid the short- and long-term complications of diabetes through normalization of blood glucose while maintaining psychologic well-being and promoting normal growth and development. Unfortunately, none of the treatment regimens currently available allow complete normalization of blood glucose in all situations, and all regimens require significant effort on the part of the patient and family. For these reasons, diabetic children and their families are faced with many medical and psychosocial challenges. This chapter discusses some of the common issues facing the clinician caring for children who have diabetes.

In a nondiabetic child, the blood glucose level

is maintained within a narrow range by instantaneous secretion of insulin and counter-regulatory hormones in response to feeding and other stimuli. In a diabetic child, this process is prevented by the autoimmune destruction of the pancreatic beta cells, resulting in insulinopenia. Insulin injections are an attempt to correct this insulinopenia but can never reproduce perfectly the precise biologic effect and timing of endogenously secreted insulin. Instead, a predetermined dose of insulin is administered first, which then must be balanced by a given amount of food and activity. Anything that upsets this balance, such as variations in insulin absorption, exercise, food quantity, or types of food, will lead to variations in blood glucose levels, resulting in hyperglycemia or hypoglycemia.

Maintaining this tenuous balance requires predictability in daily routine, frequent self-monitoring of blood glucose, adherence to a meal plan, and other related tasks.

DIAGNOSIS

A history of several weeks of polyuria and polydipsia, often with weight loss, along with glucosuria and hyperglycemia usually is sufficient to diagnose type I diabetes. The presence of ketones supports the diagnosis of type I diabetes, but ketones may not be present if diabetes is diagnosed early in the clinical course. Diabetic ketoacidosis (DKA) in a lean child virtually assures the diagnosis of type I diabetes. Oral glucose tolerance tests generally are contraindicated and unnecessary in children who have elevated random blood glucose (bG) values of greater than 200 mg/dL. For children who have newly diagnosed type I diabetes, insulin treatment should be initiated as soon as possible. The reader is referred to the readings at the end of the chapter for details on initial treatment and teaching. Type II diabetes mellitus often is associated with increasing weight or obesity, a family history of type II diabetes, and a different, more indolent, clinical evolution. Although type II diabetes is encountered less frequently in children, its incidence is reported to be increasing along with that of childhood obesity. Measurement of anti–islet cell antibodies is not necessary routinely but can help distinguish between type I and type II diabetes in confusing cases.

Within several weeks after diagnosis, many children enter into the so-called "honeymoon" period in which there often is a marked decrease in insulin requirement and normalization of bG. It is important for parents and patients to be educated about this phase at the time of diagnosis to minimize the possibility of this period being misinterpreted as a spontaneous cure or as evidence of misdiagnosis.

GOALS FOR BLOOD GLUCOSE CONTROL

The Diabetes Control and Complications Trial (DCCT), a 9-year-long multicenter, prospective, randomized controlled clinical trial, compared intensive diabetes therapy with conventional therapy for both the development and progression of complications in type I diabetes. Conventional therapy consisted of one or two daily injections of insulin, including mixed intermediate- and rapid-acting insulins, daily self-monitoring of urine or blood glucose levels, and education about diet and exercise, and did not routinely include daily adjustments in insulin dosage. Subjects were examined every 3 months. Intensive therapy included the administration of insulin three or more times daily by injection or by external pump. Insulin dosage was adjusted according to the results of self-monitored bG levels measured at least four times per day, dietary intake, and anticipated exercise. Patients were seen every month and contacted between visits.

The results for the subgroup of subjects who were adolescents at the time of enrollment were similar to those seen in adults. Patients in the intensive therapy group had lower hemoglobin A_{1c} (HbA_{1c}) values and average measured bG values that were 80 mg/dL lower than the conventional treatment group. Intensive therapy resulted in a 53% and 70% drop in occurrence of retinopathy or progression of retinopathy, respectively. Microalbuminuria, an early indicator of diabetic nephropathy, was reduced similarly by 55% in the intensive therapy group. This decrease in complication rate was not without cost. Besides the additional effort of intensive therapy, the rate of severe hypoglycemic episodes in the intensive therapy group was 3.1 times the rate for the conventional therapy group. Few of the hypoglycemic reactions required hospitalization or resulted in injury. Neurobehavioral testing did not show any significant impairment in subjects who had recurrent severe hypoglycemic events. Thus, overall, **the risk-benefit ratio is in favor of encouraging tight control in adolescents, similar to that in adults.**

The risk-benefit ratio in the prepubertal child is not as clear. There is some indication that prepubertal children are relatively protected against the long-term complications of diabetes, although this conclusion is not accepted universally. The duration and control of diabetes before puberty may not be as important as the duration and control as an adolescent. Because severe hypoglycemia may be more harmful to the developing brain, it is likely that the most prudent course would be to tolerate somewhat higher average bG levels in prepubertal children while aiming for more intensive therapy in the adolescent and young adult. A reasonable target bG range for adolescents would be to have at least the majority of samples be in the 80 to 150 mg/dL range with HbA_{1c} values less than 8%, approximately the level achieved in the DCCT. In the prepubertal child, the target bG range of 80 to 180 mg/dL may be more reasonable, with HbA_{1c} values as close to the DCCT range as possible without excessive hypoglycemia.

More importantly, **any incremental improvement toward normalizing the bG level reduces** the long-term complication rate, irrespective of the original degree of control. That is, a reduction in HbA_{1c} from 13% to 11% seems to be as important in the reduction of complications as a reduction from 10% to 8%.

ROUTINE CARE

Good glycemic control requires attention to the details of daily diabetes management. Even the most vigilant clinician will be able to participate in only a small fraction of the daily decisions facing a patient who has diabetes. Thus, the central role of the primary care clinician or the subspecialist is to facilitate self-management through the provision of appropriate resources. The decision of the primary care clinician whether to manage a child who has diabetes or refer the child to a diabetes specialist depends on several factors. Remembering that each incremental decrease in average bG decreases the chance of long-term complications, it becomes apparent that all children, not just children having difficulties, deserve as intensive a treatment regimen as practical. Thus, optimally, the clinician who manages diabetes in children without referral to a diabetes specialist should provide resources to the patient similar to those provided by the diabetes specialist. These include sufficiently long office visits to address all problems, nurse educators familiar with issues of type I diabetes in children, dietitian support by a dietitian familiar with childhood diabetes, and rapid telephone access 24 hours per day. Additionally, the clinician needs to have sufficient experience with children who have type I diabetes to provide competent care. Particularly appropriate for referral to a diabetes specialist are (1) the child whose diabetes is poorly controlled, as indicated by recurrent DKA; (2) the child who has recurrent hypoglycemia or wide fluctuations in bG levels; (3) the very young child; and (4) the child who has unusual diabetes, such as the child receiving very large doses of insulin.

Table 47–1 gives an overview of a typical regimen for the routine care of a child who has diabetes.

INSULIN THERAPY

Despite the impossibility of mimicking endogenous insulin secretion perfectly, current regimens of subcutaneous insulin injections can result in reasonable glycemic control for most patients. Currently available insulins generally are categorized as rapid-acting (regular and lispro), interme-

TABLE 47–1. Typical Management of Childhood Diabetes

Daily self-management
Two or more insulin injections
SMBG 3–4 times
Meal plan
Anticipation of effects of variation in activity and meals on bG
Weekly self-management
Review bG records; decide if changes needed
Every 3-month visit to primary care clinician
Review bG record
Assess patient goals and progress
Problem solving
Anticipatory guidance and emotional support
Nutritional counseling (or every other visit)
Refer to other services as needed
Yearly
Urine for microalbuminuria determination
Ophthalmologic examination
Thyroid screening

bG, blood glucose; SMBG, self-monitoring of blood glucose.

diate-acting (NPH and Lente), or long-acting (Ultralente). Table 47–2 gives the typical kinetics of action for each of these insulins. Ideally, insulin would be infused at a diurnally varying background rate with boluses of insulin at the time of meals. Such therapy is possible with constant subcutaneous insulin infusion (CSII) therapy, using an insulin pump; however, very few children are sufficiently mature and motivated to use insulin pumps. Therefore, some combination of subcutaneous injections, utilizing intermediate- or long-acting insulin to provide the background level, along with a rapid-acting insulin to "cover" major meals, generally is used.

A "mixed-split" insulin regimen consisting of a combination of NPH (or Lente) and regular insulin is the most common routine currently used with children. Typically, total daily doses (although not in the honeymoon period) are 0.7 unit/kg for prepubertal children, 1.2 unit/kg for early and midadolescents, and 0.7 unit/kg for late adolescents and adults, although a fairly wide range

TABLE 47–2. Human Insulin Therapeutic Kinetics

Type of Insulin	Time, hr		
	Onset	*Peak*	*Duration*
Short-acting			
Lispro	<0.5	1–2	2–3
Regular	0.5	2–3	4–6
Intermediate-acting			
NPH	2–4	4–8	10–14
Lente	2–4	4–12	12–18
Long-acting			
Ultralente	6–10	Broad	18–24

of doses is seen. Usually the morning dose is about twice the evening dose, with the NPH representing about two thirds of the insulin within each injection. The morning injection is given 20 to 30 minutes before breakfast, with the regular insulin covering breakfast and the NPH providing coverage for lunch and the early afternoon. The evening injection is given 20 to 30 minutes before dinner, with regular insulin covering dinner and the NPH providing overnight coverage. Although some patients are managed on twice-daily injections of NPH only, this routine generally is associated with significant postprandial hyperglycemia and should be discouraged.

Given the typical peaks and duration of the various insulins, a simple approximation is that the lunch bG levels mostly reflect the action of the morning regular insulin and to a lesser degree, the morning NPH; the dinnertime bG levels reflect the morning NPH. The bedtime bG levels reflect the dinnertime regular insulin, and the morning bG levels, the dinnertime NPH. Using this guide, increases or decreases of 10% to 15% in each of the respective doses can be made until the desired glycemic control is achieved.

Several common problems occur with the twice-daily injection regimen. Fasting morning hyperglycemia may occur as the result of a combination of the waning of the effect of the evening NPH and the "dawn phenomenon," a decrease in insulin sensitivity caused by the nocturnal rise of counter-regulatory hormones. Attempts at correcting fasting hyperglycemia by increasing evening NPH may result in nocturnal hypoglycemia, an effect that can be tested for by 2 A.M. bG determinations. Shifting the NPH injection to bedtime may correct this situation by delaying the peak NPH action toward the waking hours. Use of Ultralente, in place of the NPH, may allow control of fasting morning bGs without the nocturnal low caused by the peak of the NPH action. Inclusion of uncooked cornstarch in the evening snack, by use of specially prepared commercially available snack bars or by use of homemade preparations, has also been shown to reduce nocturnal hypoglycemia. The uncooked cornstarch acts as a slow-release carbohydrate, providing a source of glucose throughout the night. Another common problem is hypoglycemia occurring before lunch or in the midafternoon as the result of the ongoing insulin (NPH plus residual regular) action at times of little carbohydrate intake. Providing or increasing the regular midmorning or afternoon snack may alleviate this problem. Use of the recently available lispro (Humalog [Lilly]) insulin, a more rapidly acting but shorter duration insulin, in place of regular insulin, also may help midmorning hy-

poglycemia. Lispro insulin gives the added advantage of not requiring the 20- to 30-minute wait before eating required for optimal action with regular insulin. As experience is gained, lispro insulin may replace or supplement regular insulin in many children.

Blood glucose levels sporadically vary out of the "target range," even in patients who adhere strictly to insulin and nutritional regimens. Use of a "sliding scale," which varies the dose of regular insulin up and down from baseline, using an empirically derived scale, may assist some children by normalizing these aberrant bG levels more rapidly.

MONITORING

Good glycemic control is impossible without detailed information regarding the effect of insulin, food, and activity on bG levels. Frequent self-monitoring of bG has become the norm in the management of type I diabetes. Many children perform three to four blood sugar determinations per day without major difficulty. However, as with all aspects of diabetes management, the frequency of bG sampling must be negotiated with the child and family. Typical times for bG sampling are before meals (breakfast, lunch, and dinner) and at bedtime. Other particular situations in which bG determinations are useful include before sports activities, immediately before the adolescent patient drives an automobile, at 2 A.M. when the nighttime dose of NPH is increased, and any time there is clinical suspicion of hypo- or hyperglycemia. bG determinations at lunchtime in school may prove impractical for some children but often can be accomplished by educating and collaborating with school personnel. If lunchtime bG sampling is not performed routinely at school, weekend lunchtime bG levels can give some guidance to insulin adjustments. Urine testing for glucosuria adds no information, but urine testing remains the only practical method of checking for the presence of ketone formation. Urinary ketones need not be checked routinely but should be checked if two or more consecutive bG determinations are greater than 300 mg/dL or if the patient is feeling ill.

Modern glucometers measure bG levels on as little as 3 μL of whole blood and often can store hundreds of values. However, the individual bG values should be written in a log, at least once weekly, to allow periodic review, analyzing for patterns across days and within days. Adolescents should be encouraged to review the blood sugar readings with their parents, taking care to explain that parental review does not suggest that the adolescent is untrustworthy or immature.

Glycated hemoglobin determinations (HbA$_1$ or HbA$_{1c}$) have made it possible to follow glucose control over time. Exposure of proteins to glucose results in a slow, nonenzymatic and concentration-dependent covalent linkage of the glucose to the protein. Assaying the percentage of hemoglobin, a conveniently obtained protein with a turnover rate of several months, linked to glucose provides an index of the approximate average bG values over the preceding 8 to 12 weeks. Glycated hemoglobin determinations should be performed three to four times yearly. The clinician needs to be careful not to overemphasize the "report card" nature of these periodic determinations but rather should emphasize their use by patient, family, and clinician as an important tool for assessing the impact of changes in self-management. Glycated hemoglobin values vary between laboratories, depending on the techniques used, but generally an HbA$_{1c}$ of 10% represents an average bG level of about 240 mg/dL. Each additional 1% above or below 10% represents an increase or decrease of about 30 to 40 mg/dL from 240 mg/dL. For example, an HbA$_{1c}$ of 9% equals an average bG level of about 200 to 210 mg/dL. Significant discrepancies between the recorded bG values and the glycated hemoglobin should alert the clinician to the possibilities of bG errors, unusual hemoglobinopathies resulting in glycated hemoglobin values, or most likely, confabulated bG results.

NUTRITIONAL MANAGEMENT

The nutritional requirement of children whose diabetes is well controlled does not differ significantly from that of a nondiabetic child; the goal is to provide sufficient nutrition to meet energy requirements and to achieve normal growth and development. However, because the diabetic child's insulin is given in anticipation of a given quantity and type of nutrition at a given time, bG levels will vary in direct relationship to changes in these nutritional factors. This balancing of food intake with insulin can be approached best through a meal plan that uses food "exchange lists." Foods that are similar in carbohydrate, fat, and protein content are grouped and equivalent portion sizes indicated. In this manner, for example, one "starch exchange" (15 grams of carbohydrate) could equal one half of a bagel, one tortilla, or one half cup of grits, chosen depending on patient preference. The food preferences of the family and child, as well as lifestyle considerations, form the basis for nutritional therapy. Insulin regimens should be adapted, as much as possible, to the child's preferred distribution of carbohydrates, rather than the converse. Although simple in concept, the details of meal planning are often confusing, and families often benefit from regular input from a registered dietitian familiar with nutritional issues of children who have diabetes. Dietary input is a very important part of the regular medical care and should occur every 3 to 6 months.

Caloric requirements can be estimated by several methods. One quick estimate is 1000 calories for the first year of life plus 100 additional calories for every year over 1 year of age until age 12. From 12 to 15 years of age, for females, the requirement is 1500 to 2000 calories plus 100 calories per year over the age of 12; for males, it is 2000 to 2500 calories plus 200 calories per year over the age of 12. Another estimate is 100 calories for the first 10 kg, then 50 calories for each kilogram between 10 and 20 kg, then 20 calories per kilogram thereafter.

A simplified version of the exchange planning, which emphasizes the carbohydrate content of foods, has gained in popularity, especially among adolescents. Meal planning using "carbohydrate counting" is based on the finding that the most important dietary influence on bG level is the amount, not the type, of carbohydrate consumed. That is, both simple and complex carbohydrates are absorbed into the bloodstream at about the same rate. One carbohydrate choice equals any starch, fruit, or milk serving with 15 grams of carbohydrate. This method can simplify dietary management greatly for active adolescent patients. Carbohydrate counting also allows limited amounts of "treats," such as candy or ice cream, to be incorporated into the meal plan.

ACTIVITY

Physical activity, whether it is spontaneous play or organized sports, is an integral part of childhood and should not be forbidden or restricted. Activity acts synergistically with insulin to increase muscle glucose use and generally is a helpful adjunct in controlling bG levels. However, activity can result in immediate or delayed hypoglycemia. Additionally, the increased blood flow in arms or legs associated with exercise can increase the rapidity of insulin absorption, leading to hypoglycemia. Pretreatment of anticipated activity immediately before activity with additional carbohydrate may be sufficient to prevent hypoglycemia. The athlete should, whenever possible, determine his or her bG level just before competition or rigorous practice to guide the additional amount of carbohydrate needed. Carbohydrate sources, such as juice or glucose tablets, should be available during the activity.

A reduction in insulin dosage also is often appropriate when the activity is anticipated and especially if the activity is rigorous. Necessary reductions can vary from 10% to 60% for extremely rigorous activity such as competitive long distance swimming or running. The family should be aware of delayed hypoglycemia that can occur at 2 to 5 A.M., hours after the activity. bG levels should be determined at 2 A.M. on several days after the initiation of a new aerobic sport or after significant increases in spontaneous activity, such as occurs with the onset of warm weather in northern climates.

HYPOGLYCEMIA

Symptomatic low bG levels can occur at any time and require prompt attention. For this reason the patient and select others, such as teachers, coaches, and close friends, should know how to recognize and treat low bG levels. Whenever possible, bG levels should be checked before treatment. Routinely, 15 grams of carbohydrate, equivalent to 4 to 6 ounces of juice or regular soda, should be given, although older children may require more. The child should wait 15 minutes before resuming activity. Glucagon emergency kits containing a 1-mg vial of lyophilized glucagon are available and are a useful backup in emergencies when the child is unconscious from hypoglycemia.

SICK DAY MANAGEMENT

Children who have type I diabetes are no more likely to develop viral or bacterial infections than are nondiabetic children. The autoimmunity implicit with type I diabetes should not be confused with immunodeficiency. Nor are children who have diabetes prone to the local infections associated with the peripheral vascular disease of long-standing diabetes. Management of diabetes during routine illnesses can be disconcerting for parents, physicians, teachers, and caretakers because bG levels sometimes vary in unexpected ways. However, most ill diabetic children can be managed via telephone or with a simple office visit and telephone follow-up.

As with the telephone management of any illness, the clinician needs to form an overall picture of the child's condition by inquiring about activity level, food intake, signs of localized infection, and

any vomiting and fever. Additional information required for the diabetic child includes recent bG values (with a current reading) and a urine ketone determination if the bG is greater than 300 mg/dL or if there is repeated vomiting. The goal during illness is to avoid symptomatic "lows" while preventing hyperglycemia severe enough to cause excessive glucosuria and, eventually, DKA. Thus, a bG level in the mid to upper 100s range during illness provides some "buffer" to hypoglycemia if the bG falls unexpectedly; it also prevents glucosuria, which might lead to dehydration and electrolyte imbalance. Some general rules are as follows:

1. For the nonvomiting child who has a significantly elevated bG reading but no urinary ketones, a 10% to 15% increase in insulin, usually as regular or lispro, may suffice.

2. Sick children who have moderate or severe ketonuria and no vomiting need more aggressive therapy to prevent DKA from occurring. Supplemental short-acting insulin should be given when ketonuria is found, either at the time of the usual dose or between usual doses. A general starting point is to give an additional dose of regular insulin equal to 0.1 unit/kg, or 10% of the child's total daily dose. The bG level should be rechecked in about 2 hours. If the desired drop in bG does not occur, the initial or a slightly increased dose can be repeated every 2 to 3 hours. Lispro insulin, by virtue of its rapid onset of action, may be particularly useful in this situation.

3. Vomiting children who have hyperglycemia and severe ketonuria usually require evaluation for the presence of DKA.

4. The vomiting child who has mild, asymptomatic hypoglycemia or borderline bG is particularly disconcerting. Although some insulin always is needed, the short-acting insulin (regular or lispro) usually should be deleted and the NPH decreased by 50%. Additional insulin always can be administered if this reduction proves excessive; however, insulin cannot be removed from the child once it is administered. The caretakers should be reminded to give room temperature, noncarbonated (or "defizzed") sugar-containing fluids in small amounts to help alleviate the hypoglycemia, aiming for approximately 15 grams of carbohydrate per hour. bG levels should be determined every 30 to 90 minutes, depending on the degree of hypoglycemia. If the child becomes symptomatic, if the child has a further bG decrease into an unsatisfactory range, or if the bG is not rising within an hour or two into an acceptable range, intravenous glucose therapy is warranted.

During any scenario, the primary care clinician

must be accessible to the child's caregivers quickly. Telephone follow-up every few hours is mandatory to monitor progress and advise the caregivers. In this manner, the vast majority of illnesses in diabetic children can be managed safely at home.

ADOLESCENCE

Virtually all adolescents demonstrate the typical teenage behaviors that reflect the "individuation–separation" process necessary to progress from childhood to adulthood. The diabetic adolescent is no different but has the additional burden of diabetes with which to contend. Some adolescents do extremely well and are able to maintain tight glycemic control without undue impact on their normal routine. Many adolescents, however, experience social, psychologic, and practical barriers to optimal diabetes management.

Many issues can become the focus of conflict between the adolescent and family. For the adolescent who has diabetes, adherence to the diabetes treatment plan, with its added demands of testing, injections, dietary routines, and so on, can easily become the focus of these conflicts. Although the parental concern usually is focused on ensuring compliance with the treatment regimen in order to avoid the long-term complications of diabetes, the adolescent may see diabetes as an impediment to the normal teenage lifestyle and peer acceptance. This may result in disinterest in diabetes care, anger, rebellion, and even denial and lead to poor control.

Three key concepts may help both parent and clinicians with the adolescent patient who is having difficulty coping with diabetes. First, the adolescent is a person with his or her own set of interests, concerns, beliefs, values, and skills. Second, flexibility is needed. No aspect of self-management is non-negotiable. Third, there should be an attitude of unconditionally accepting the adolescent. That is, **interventions should be aimed at problem solving and not at judging or assigning blame.**

Each of these concepts can be translated into clinical practice. Recognizing the adolescent's own interests and concerns is mandatory for integrating diabetes self-management into the patient's lifestyle. It rarely is productive to suggest a change in self-management if that change is perceived as interfering with an important aspect of the adolescent's life. For example, a patient-athlete who performs at a highly competitive level may be unwilling to "tighten" control if this change could lead to hypoglycemia during competition. **Failure to recognize the patient's uniqueness will doom the effectiveness of any intervention.** Surveys of diabetic adolescents reveal that their usual concerns parallel those of nondiabetic teens. That is, while parents may agonize about bG control and its relationship to long-term complications, adolescents are more concerned about peer acceptance, participation in normal activities, interpersonal relationships, and the typical teenage concerns. Helping the adolescent to find ways to manage his or her diabetes responsibly within the context of normal adolescent activities is essential.

Flexibility is essential in individualizing self-management routines. All aspects of management are negotiable. Although the clinician does not want to be perceived as encouraging suboptimal care, compromise between the ideal medical self-care regimen and what is acceptable to the adolescent is necessary. Evoking promises from the adolescent under pressure or by coercion rarely leads to long-term changes in behavior. This concept also must be emphasized to the parents.

The adolescent must perceive the clinician and parents as accepting of him or her as an individual. Many patients interpret review of bG logs and determination of HbA_{1c} values as a time of judgment: "bad" bG values reflect "bad" behavior, or even worse, "bad" bG readings reflect on the patient as a "bad" person. In this context, the natural tendency for the adolescent who has bG values outside the normal range is not to be entirely truthful by not recording undesirable bG values, by misrepresenting bG values, or simply by not performing self-monitoring at times when bG levels tend to be out of target. bG readings that are "too perfect" and do not seem to reflect HbA_{1c} values are indicators of misrepresentation. By taking a problem-oriented approach, the clinician can avoid being viewed as a surrogate parent; otherwise, the recommendations of the practitioner may be treated the same as those of the parents and rejected. Along these lines, the clinician also should have an understanding with the parents that the clinician may not always agree with the parents. Rather than adjudicate disputes between adolescent and parent, the clinician should facilitate communication between the two and help effect resolution.

COMPLICATIONS AND ASSOCIATED CONDITIONS

Fortunately, the long-term complications of diabetes are rarely a clinically significant problem during the childhood years. Retinopathy and nephropathy rarely occur prior to the fifth year of the disease and before puberty. Nevertheless, because these complications are serious and their progression can be favorably modified, it is incumbent on the clinician to remain vigilant.

The earliest changes in the eye are forms of nonproliferative retinopathy, such as microaneurysms and hard exudates. It is recommended that every child with diabetes of more than 5 years' duration who is pubertal receive an annual dilated eye examination by a qualified eye professional. Before that time, the primary care clinician should perform an annual direct funduscopic examination.

Early nephropathy can be detected by annual examination of urine for microalbuminuria once the diabetes has been present for 5 years and the child is pubertal. Microalbuminuria can be detected on 24-hour urine specimens or on a first-morning void by determining the albumin-creatinine ratio. The presence of microalbuminuria is a cause for concern and should prompt referral to an endocrinologist or nephrologist. Routine "dipstick" analysis for protein is not sufficiently sensitive to be clinically useful.

Hashimoto thyroiditis (chronic lymphocytic thyroiditis) is the most common autoimmune disorder associated with type I diabetes. The thyroid gland should be examined on every visit and a thyroid-stimulating hormone value obtained yearly or if the thyroid is abnormal to palpation. Other autoimmune conditions associated with type I diabetes are rare but include adrenal insufficiency, vitiligo, alopecia, chronic autoimmune hepatitis, and pernicious anemia.

FURTHER READING

DCCT Research Group: The effect of intensive treatment of diabetes on the development and progression of long-term complications in insulin-dependent diabetes mellitus. N Engl J Med 329:977–986, 1993.

DCCT Research Group: Effect of intensive diabetes treatment on the development and progression of long-term complications in adolescents with insulin-dependent diabetes mellitus: Diabetes Control and Complications Trial. J Pediatr 125:177–187, 1994.

Kaufman FR: Diabetes mellitus. Pediatr Rev 18:382–392, 1997.

Kostraba JN, Dorman JS, Orchard TJ, et al.: Contribution of diabetes duration before puberty to development of microvascular complications in IDDM subjects. Diabetes Care 12:686–693, 1989.

Plotnick L: Insulin-dependent diabetes mellitus. Pediatr Rev 15:137–148, 1994.

Santiago L (ed): Medical Management of Insulin-Dependent (Type I) Diabetes, 2nd ed. Alexandria, VA, American Diabetes Association, 1994.

John McBride

Chapter 48

Asthma

Despite the decreasing prevalence of many other pediatric diseases and the availability of effective new therapies, asthma is increasing in prevalence and severity in individuals of all ages throughout the world. In response to this challenge, the National Asthma Education and Prevention Program, sponsored in part by the National Heart, Lung and Blood Institute of the National Institutes of Health, has developed *Guidelines for the Diagnosis and Management of Asthma* published first in 1991 and revised in 1997. These Guidelines provide a basis for the approach to asthma outlined in this chapter. The original document is widely available in full and condensed versions and is a useful, well-referenced resource for those who care for children who have asthma (see Further Reading at the end of the chapter).

The fundamental contribution of recent asthma research has been the realization that inflammation rather than bronchospasm is the major underlying abnormality in individuals who have asthma. Airway inflammation contributes directly to airway narrowing through mucosal edema and mucus plugging and indirectly by increase in airway reactivity. Airway obstruction in asthma, whether related to edema, mucus plugging, or bronchospasm, usually is reversible, either acutely (minutes to hours) or gradually (days to weeks). Chronic inflammation occasionally may lead to airway remodeling and result in permanent airway narrowing, but the incidence of this presumably irreversible process is not known. The modern management of pediatric asthma is based on the concept that therapy should be directed not only to reversing bronchospasm but to eliminating or preventing airway inflammation.

DIAGNOSIS

The diagnosis of asthma usually is straightforward, based on recurrent episodes of wheezing and an acute response to a bronchodilator. It is important, however, to keep in mind both the difficulty of recognizing asthma in children who have atypical symptoms and the danger of failing to diagnose other disease processes in children who also have asthma. Asthma generally is underdiagnosed: Recurrent episodes of cough, chest tightness, or atelectasis (on radiograph) with or without wheezing almost always are due to asthma. For those children who seldom or never wheeze, the acute reversibility of symptoms with bronchodilators points to the diagnosis of "cough-variant" or "inflammatory" asthma, but the most helpful finding is a clinical response to a therapeutic trial of aggressive asthma therapy, including a short course of oral corticosteroids (1 to 2 mg/kg/day for 4 to 10 days) and a longer course of inhaled anti-inflammatory medication. Although a response to such a course of therapy is strong evidence for the diagnosis of underlying asthma, it does not rule out the presence of another process such as cystic fibrosis, chronic aspiration, or immune deficiency, because airway inflammation and hyperreactivity commonly complicate these conditions. Signs and symptoms of the conditions listed in Table 48–1 (e.g., coughing with eating, digital clubbing, failure to thrive, steatorrhea) should lead to additional investigations, particularly in children whose symptoms are not controlled easily.

In children or adolescents who have mild to moderate asthma that can be controlled easily, diagnostic testing usually is unnecessary. In children who have moderate to severe asthma whose symptoms do not respond to modest measures, a chest radiograph, spirometry, or formal pulmonary function testing and other studies should be considered.

Asthma in preschool children may differ from that in older children both pathophysiologically and in long-term prognosis. Infants whose exacerbations are related to viral infections, who are not

TABLE 48–1. Differential Diagnosis of Childhood Asthma

Foreign body aspiration	Bronchopulmonary dysplasia
Vocal cord dysfunction	Congestive heart failure
Vascular ring	Mediastinal adenopathy
Laryngeal web	Viral bronchiolitis
Laryngotracheomalacia	Sinusitis
Cystic fibrosis	Allergic rhinitis
Recurrent aspiration	Postnasal drip

TABLE 48–2. Factors That May Complicate or Contribute to Pediatric Asthma

Allergy
    Cow's milk allergy (in infants)
    Perennial inhaled allergens (dust mite, mold, etc.)
    Seasonal inhaled allergens (pollens, grasses, etc.)
Irritant exposure (especially to cigarette smoke)
Sinusitis
Gastroesophageal reflux
Allergic bronchopulmonary aspergillosis

atopic, and who have no family history of asthma are unlikely to have asthma later in childhood. On the other hand, many older children and adolescents who have moderate or severe asthma will first have manifested symptoms before 2 years of age. Atopy and a family history of asthma are the most reliable (but imperfect) predictors of the persistence of childhood asthma. Asthma in early childhood often responds less dramatically to therapy than does asthma in school-age children and adolescents.

CONDITIONS AND FACTORS THAT EXACERBATE ASTHMA

It is important to identify factors that may contribute to childhood asthma (Table 48–2). Of these, the most important is exposure to inhaled allergens or irritants, particularly in the home. Sensitivity to specific inhaled allergens is unusual in children younger than 3 years of age; in older children, sensitivity to specific allergens can often be elicited by history. Skin tests or radioallergosorbent testing (RAST) for perennial allergens (such as house dust mites, mold, and animal dander) has been recommended for atopic patients who have moderate or severe persistent asthma because sensitivity to these allergens can be more difficult to elicit by history than that to seasonal allergens. A firm diagnosis of sensitivity can be useful in justifying environmental control efforts. Of irritants, passive (or active) exposure to cigarette smoke is the most important. Studies for other medical conditions that exacerbate asthma (sinusitis, gastroesophageal reflux, etc.) are usually reserved for children who have atypical asthma or symptoms that are difficult to control.

When the clinical history or specific sensitivity testing suggests that environmental factors are contributing to a patient's asthma, steps to modify exposure should be recommended (Table 48–3). The effectiveness of exposure control should be re-evaluated regularly, particularly when symptoms are not controlled easily.

TABLE 48–3. Control Measures for Environmental Factors That Exacerbate Asthma

Environmental Factor	Control Measures
Animal dander	Remove animal from home. Keep animal out of bedroom. Filter or turn off air ducts to bedroom. Bathe animal weekly.
House-dust mites	Essential Encase mattress/pillow. Wash bedding in hot water weekly. Desirable Reduce humidity to <50%. Remove bedroom carpets.
Cockroaches	Use poison bait traps. Cover exposed food.
Indoor molds	Reduce indoor humidity (<50%). Fix leaky pipes. Clean moldy surfaces (consider heating ducts).
Cigarette smoke	Avoid passive or active exposure.
Wood-burning stoves, fireplaces	Reduce exposure.
Unvented stoves, heaters	Reduce exposure.
Other irritants (perfume, cleaning agents, etc.)	Reduce exposure.

MONITORING ASTHMA THERAPY

Goals of Therapy

The goals of asthma therapy extend beyond the control of episodes of airway obstruction (Table 48–4). It is helpful to review these goals with patients and families during each visit for asthma management. Failure to achieve these goals may reflect inadequate therapy, education, or adherence, but also should prompt the clinician to reconsider the diagnosis of asthma and the possible contribution of complicating conditions. Failure to meet the goals of asthma management is the primary indication for referral of a child or adolescent who has asthma to an asthma specialist. The goal overlooked most easily is meeting the patient's and family's expectations regarding asthma control.

TABLE 48–4. The Goals of Pediatric Asthma Therapy

Minimize acute and chronic symptoms.
Maintain "near-normal" pulmonary function.
Maintain normal activity, including physical exercise.
Prevent exacerbations.
Avoid side effects of therapy.
Meet patient and family expectations.

Classification of Asthma Severity

Some 5% to 7% of children have asthma. The majority have infrequent, mild, and self-limited episodes of bronchospasm often associated with viral infections; a smaller proportion have symptoms that regularly interfere with normal activities and school; and a tiny minority have life-threatening or corticosteroid-dependent disease. Regardless of severity, the goals of asthma therapy remain the same. Children and adolescents who have asthma can be categorized roughly into four groups of severity (Table 48–5). A child is assigned to the highest classification satisfied by any single criterion. This classification can be used as a rough guide for therapy (see further on).

Monitoring and Assessment

Effective asthma therapy requires that the patient, family, and primary care clinician recognize the presence and severity of airway inflammation and obstruction. Accurately identifying the presence and level of airway obstruction facilitates such steps as initiating therapy as early in an exacerbation as possible and recognizing the point at which consultation with a clinician or care in a medical facility is necessary. The ability to intensify or decrease chronic asthma therapy based on the presence or absence of changes in airway obstruction and inflammation may eliminate or reduce dramatically the number of severe exacerbations requiring hospitalization, improve the patient's ability to function normally, and minimize the risk of medication side effects.

Clinical Monitoring

Patients and families can be taught to recognize changes in airway inflammation and obstruction based on observations of wheezing, tightness, or the presence or absence of cough at night, with exercise, or with upper respiratory infections. The most important sign of impending severe obstruction is the failure of "rescue" bronchodilator treatment to reverse acute symptoms or the return of symptoms sooner than 4 hours after such a treatment. Many patients can be managed successfully on the basis of clinical observation alone.

Peak Flow Monitoring

Peak flow monitoring, an objective measurement that correlates well with the level of airway function in many children, can be of great benefit for patients over 5 or 6 years of age,

TABLE 48–5. Classification of Pediatric Asthma

Classification	Symptoms	Nighttime Symptoms	Lung Function, % of predicted
Severely persistent	Continual symptoms; limited activity	Frequent	FEV_1 <60%
Moderately persistent	Daily use of rescue therapy; activity often limited; exacerbations 2 times per week	>1 time per week	FEV_1 >60%, <80%
Mildly persistent	Exacerbations <2 times per week; many normal days	>2 times per month	FEV_1 >80%
Mildly intermittent	Symptoms <2 times per week; normal between exacerbations; exacerbations brief	<2 times per month	FEV_1 >80%

FEV_1, forced expiratory volume in 1 second.

particularly those who do not accurately perceive changes in airway function. In the early stages of asthma education, peak flow monitoring can help patients learn to appreciate the relationship between symptoms and airway function. It also provides an objective measurement that can facilitate communication with health care clinicians. Peak flow monitoring has limitations. The measurement is totally effort-dependent and must be performed correctly. The maneuver itself can precipitate bronchospasm in a few patients, and it should not be used in such individuals. In others, peak flow can fail to detect important changes in airway function. Many patients have difficulty adhering to regular peak flow monitoring and may simply report "made-up" values. For many patients, peak flow measurements do not add to the accuracy of symptom monitoring. Nevertheless, many individuals who have persistent asthma will benefit from learning this technique, and patients who have moderately or severely persistent asthma should be taught peak flow monitoring. It can be continued as a part of ongoing management in those patients for whom it proves valuable. Peak flow values always should be interpreted in conjunction with the other signs and symptoms of asthma.

There are a number of important principles of peak flow monitoring (Table 48–6). Patients must make a maximal effort from a full inspiration; improper or inconsistent efforts can lead to overtreatment. Measurements must be compared with each patient's "personal best"; predicted "normal" values based on height can be misleading. To identify a patient's "personal best" value, several weeks of intensive therapy, with or without a burst of systemic corticosteroids, may be necessary. Peak flowmeters are remarkably durable and reliable, but there may be important differences

among meters, so each patient should use only one type. Peak flow usually is lowest in the early morning. Increasing discrepancy of peak flow values between morning and evening is one indication of the degree of airway hyperreactivity, but therapy usually can be managed in terms of morning values alone. The response to bronchodilators when peak flow values are below the personal best are useful in monitoring airway hyperreactivity.

Therapeutic Action Plan

Whether airway inflammation and obstruction is monitored clinically or by peak flow measurements, the patient and family should have a clear idea of steps to take when asthma exacerbates or improves. These steps should be concrete and outlined in a written plan given to the patient. Typical plans are based on a three-zone system (see Table 48–9). Specific interventions are initiated when clinical symptoms or decreasing peak flows place a patient in the "caution" zone, and more aggressive interventions and consultation with a clinician are recommended when the "dan-

TABLE 48–6. Principles of Peak Flow Monitoring

Establish personal best (may require period of intensive therapy).
Predicted normal values may be misleading.
Each patient should use a single peak flowmeter; brands are not interchangeable.
Measure peak flow each morning or as indicated by symptoms.
Measure before and after bronchodilator unless at personal best.
Patient demonstrates technique on each visit.
Recognize spirometry-induced bronchospasm if present.
Patient has a written plan by which to respond to measurements.

ger" zone is reached. Conversely, long-term therapy can be tapered when a child has remained in the "normal" zone for a long period (usually months).

Long-term therapy can be regulated most effectively when a patient is able to keep a written daily diary of clinical symptoms and peak flow measurements and has the opportunity to review asthma management regularly with a clinician. It is unrealistic, however, to assume that all patients will maintain a diary over time, and asthma usually can be managed adequately on the basis of less complete information. Requiring patients where symptoms are easily controlled to maintain such records risks inappropriately emphasizing a mild disability. Whatever the case, clinician visits at intervals based on the severity of a patient's asthma provide an important opportunity to monitor progress and to reinforce teaching. Visits every 6 months for those whose asthma is mildly persistent and more frequent visits for those whose asthma is moderate or severe are reasonable.

ASTHMA MEDICATIONS

Asthma medications fall into two categories: those useful in the management of acute bronchospasm (rescue therapy) and those used for long-term maintenance treatment. It is important that patients and families understand the overall rationale for drug therapy and particularly the difference between these two categories of drugs. The specific medications and the route of administration are important considerations.

Medications for Management of Acute Airway Obstruction

Acute asthma symptoms usually are reversed effectively by administration of a $beta_2$-adrenergic agonist either nebulized or delivered by a metered-dose inhaler (MDI) (Table 48–7). Bronchodilator treatments for acute bronchospasm are called "rescue therapy." Although dosage based on body weight sometimes is recommended, it is equally appropriate to prescribe the same dose of inhaled bronchodilator for patients of all sizes because smaller breaths result in lower inhaled doses by smaller children. Patients usually are instructed to use bronchodilators as rescue therapy at home no more frequently than every 2 to 4 hours. In acute airway obstruction, however, this can result in undertreatment. In the hospital or emergency department, patients are managed quite safely with continuous delivery of a bronchodilator in a dos-

TABLE 48–7. Asthma Rescue Therapy*

Medication	Comments
Short-acting beta$_2$-adrenergic agonist (albuterol and others)	Aerosol or MDI; use q 2–4 hr at home or continuously in hospital setting with oxygen administration.
Anticholinergic medications (ipratropium bromide)	Aerosol or MDI. May provide additive benefit to beta$_2$ agonist. Use q 1–2 hr.
Systemic corticosteroids	Use for moderate to severe exacerbation to speed recovery and prevent recurrence.

*For treatment of acute asthma symptoms.
MDI, metered-dose inhaler.

age equivalent to two or more puffs of a bronchodilator MDI every 15 minutes. Although this approach is not appropriate when oxygen cannot be administered to correct hypoxemia, patients should be instructed to use a bronchodilator up to every 20 to 30 minutes for acute bronchospasm if they are on the way to a medical facility and are not responding to less aggressive therapy. Ipratropium bromide, an anticholinergic delivered by nebulization or MDI, may provide additive bronchodilation in patients who have acute bronchospasm treated with high doses of a beta$_2$ agonist and is a reasonable alternative bronchodilator for rare patients unable to tolerate beta$_2$ agonist therapy. For most patients who have acute severe bronchospasm, systemic (oral or intravenous) corticosteroid therapy equivalent to 1 to 2 mg/kg/day of methylprednisolone for 3 to 7 days improves the response to bronchodilators and helps prevent relapses; higher doses may be indicated for hospitalized patients.

Medications for Long-Term Therapy of Pediatric Asthma

Because the long-term therapy of pediatric asthma is directed primarily at resolving and preventing the chronic inflammation that underlies recurrent episodes of bronchospasm and airway obstruction, anti-inflammatory agents are central to most regimens for patients who have persistent asthma. Regular use of a long-acting bronchodilator also may provide improved long-term control (Table 48–8).

Cromolyn Sodium and Nedocromil. One or the other of these inhaled, anti-inflammatory agents, given by nebulization or MDI, is preferred by many clinicians as first-line therapy for chil-

TABLE 48–8. Medications for Long-Term Asthma Control

Medication	Comments
Cromolyn sodium, nedocromil	Nebulizer or MDI; little toxicity.
Inhaled corticosteroids	MDI with spacer; little toxicity at low doses; monitor linear growth and for oral candidiasis.
Long-acting beta$_2$ agonists (oral delayed-release albuterol or inhaled salmeterol)	MDI or PO; nighttime symptoms, steroid-sparing effect. *Do not use* for rescue therapy.
Methylxanthines	PO; corticosteroid sparing in low/moderate dosage; little toxicity at these doses.
Leukotriene modifiers	PO; ? alternative to low-dose corticosteroids.
Systemic corticosteroids	PO; burst therapy to regain control or cover high-risk periods; use lowest daily or alternate-day dose to control symptoms.

MDI, metered-dose inhaler; PO, by mouth.

dren who have persistent asthma, primarily because they often are effective and seldom are, if ever, associated with intolerance or side effects. They need to be used religiously, two to four times a day. Patients need to understand that they have no acute bronchodilator effect and that a response to therapy may not be evident for 3 or more weeks.

Inhaled Corticosteroids. Corticosteroids administered by an MDI with a spacer (to minimize oral deposition) are first-line therapy for persistent asthma in adults and usually are more effective than cromolyn sodium and nedocromil in children. Modest doses do not affect growth or bone density adversely in most children, but some children may be particularly sensitive to these effects. Side effects can be recognized and minimized by carefully monitoring height at each visit, using a spacer (even with good MDI technique), washing out the mouth after each dose, and decreasing the dose when symptoms have been well controlled for 2 or 3 months. When patients require larger doses for control (greater than 8 to 12 puffs per day of a regular-strength MDI), attempts to add corticosteroid-sparing medications (methylxanthines, cromolyn sodium, nedocromil, or long-acting beta$_2$ agonists) and to improve environmental control and adherence are indicated. Concomitant use of nasal corticosteroids increases the risk of side effects.

Methylxanthines. Theophylline and the other methylxanthines have both bronchodilator and anti-inflammatory effects. They are used less frequently than in the past because the control of acute bronchospasm requires levels sometimes associated with toxicity and because their acute bronchodilator effect is not additive to that of beta$_2$ agonists. Chronic therapy with modest doses of theophylline, however, appears to be effective in controlling airway inflammation and in allowing a decrease in the dose of inhaled corticosteroids. It is likely that methylxanthines will be used more commonly for this purpose in the future. It is important to monitor levels at doses greater than the equivalent of 10 mg/kg/day of theophylline. Theophylline levels may increase with viral infections or concurrent use of drugs, such as erythromycin, which inhibit hepatic metabolism. Levels should be measured when signs of toxicity appear. Erythromycin should be avoided or the dose of theophylline temporarily halved.

Long-acting Beta$_2$ Agonists. Salmeterol given as an MDI provides bronchodilatation for up to 12 hours and also has been shown to allow a decrease in the dose of inhaled corticosteroids required to maintain control in some patients who have asthma. It particularly is useful for patients who have bothersome nighttime symptoms. Toxicity that might ensue if patients use long-acting agents at frequent intervals for rescue treatment is an important concern. Patients and parents need to understand that this agent is not to be used for acute symptoms.

Leukotriene Modifiers. Zafirlukast and zileuton are oral anti-inflammatory agents that interfere with the action of leukotrienes, important mediators of airway inflammation. Their roles in pediatric asthma management are, as yet, not well defined. They may provide alternatives for patients who demonstrate corticosteroid side effects.

Systemic Corticosteroids. Oral corticosteroids are the most potent and reliable agents available for the rapid and chronic control of airway inflammation. Corticosteroid "bursts" (equivalent to 2 mg/kg/day of prednisolone in two or more doses for 3 to 7 days) is the standard approach for regaining control of asthma in the face of an acute exacerbation. Shorter and occasionally lower regimens (1 mg/kg/day) may be used at the first sign of symptoms or during high-risk periods (viral infections or unavoidable exposure to allergens) in patients who have had serious exacerbations. More aggressive systemic corticosteroid therapy is indicated for hospitalized patients. The side effects of isolated burst are modest, but more than two to four bursts per year suggests a suboptimal maintenance regimen and is an indication for referral to an asthma specialist. Corticosteroid "dependence," the chronic need for daily or every-other-day oral corticosteroids in any dosage, is nearly always associated with serious side-effects and should lead to additional intervention, including specialist referral.

Route of Administration

Inhaled medications have become the main-stay of pediatric asthma therapy. Most of these medications can be delivered by metered dose inhalers to children of all ages. Spacer devices are available with masks suitable even for infants. It is important, however, that parents learn how to deliver these medications. Ineffective aerosol delivery is a common cause of inadequate symptom control. Every asthma clinical visit should include demonstration of MDI technique by the patient or family. Although it is acceptable for older children to use bronchodilator MDIs without a spacer if they demonstrate good technique, it is preferable that spacers always are used with corticosteroid MDIs because oropharyngeal deposition and the risk of side effects are minimized. It also is important to check the spacer being used at every visit; spacer valves deteriorate over a period of months, and a valve that fails to seal completely on expiration can limit the delivered dose severely. Although inconvenient and time-consuming, nebulization still is reasonable for children who are unable to use a spacer and MDI effectively. Most medications, including cromolyn, beta$_2$ agonists and ipratropium, are available for delivery by nebulizer. A corticosteroid nebulizer solution is not available in the United States.

MANAGEMENT OF ACUTE ASTHMA EXACERBATIONS

Every patient should have a written plan describing how to manage an acute exacerbation. The plan is based on the patient's or family's ability to recognize the level of obstruction by symptom or peak flow monitoring and provides instructions for rescue therapy and changes in long-term therapy. A three-zone system recommended by many specialists is described in Table 48–9. An asthma exacerbation occurs when a standard dose of an inhaled bronchodilator fails to reverse acute obstruction, when relief lasts less than 4 hours, or when a patient begins to require more bronchodilator doses than usual. If a patient remains in the red (danger) zone despite rescue treatment at home or if bronchodilator treatments are required more frequently than every 2 to 4 hours or fail to provide relief, the patient should be referred to a medical facility for more intensive therapy, including oxygen. En route to such a facility, the patient should use the bronchodilator up to every 15 to 20 minutes as necessary to prevent severe airway obstruction. A short burst of corticosteroids taken as early as possible in the exacerbation is appropriate for patients who have had serious exacerbations in the past, those who are or recently have taken systemic corticosteroids, and those requiring intensive therapy in a medical facility. Well-documented protocols for treatment of acute airway obstruction in a medical facility are available. Once the acute exacerbation is resolved, intensification of maintenance therapy usually is appropriate (see next section).

LONG-TERM ASTHMA MANAGEMENT: STEP-UP AND STEP-DOWN THERAPY

A rational approach to long-term asthma therapy based on symptom or peak flow monitoring that is clearly understood by the patient and family is fundamental to modern asthma management. One useful approach involves four levels or steps of increasingly intense therapy (Table 48–10), each step corresponding to usual maintenance therapy for one of the previously mentioned

TABLE 48–9. Three-Zone System of Asthma Monitoring

	Symptoms	Peak Flow	Typical Response
Green zone (normal)	None	>80% of personal best	Maintain or taper long-term therapy
Yellow zone (caution)	Need for rescue treatments, or nighttime symptoms, or increased symptoms with exercise	50%–80% of personal best	Rescue treatment Step up long-term therapy Consider corticosteroid burst
Red zone (danger)	Failure to respond to rescue treatment or return of symptoms in <4 hr	<50% of personal best	Rescue treatment Corticosteroid burst Step up long-term therapy Call clinician

TABLE 48–10. Step-Up and Step-Down Long-Term Therapy of Pediatric Asthma

	Usual Long-term Therapy for Patients Who Have:	Usual Maintenance Therapy	Other
Step 1	Mild intermittent asthma	None	
Step 2	Mild persistent asthma	Inhaled cromolyn or nedocromil or low-dose inhaled corticosteroid	May substitute PO methylxanthine or leukotriene modifier
Step 3	Moderate persistent asthma	Medium-dose inhaled corticosteroid ± long-acting bronchodilator (beta$_2$ agonist or methylxanthine)	Many specialists add inhaled cromolyn or nedocromil
Step 4	Severe persistent asthma	High-dose inhaled corticosteroid + long-acting bronchodilator ± oral corticosteroid	Use alternate-day corticosteroid dose, if possible

asthma severity levels (see Table 48–5). Long-term asthma therapy can be broken down into two basic principles. The first is that when a patient has normal airway function, maintenance therapy should be tapered gradually (over months) or "stepped down" until the lowest level of therapy that maintains control is identified. Patients who have predictable exacerbations associated with respiratory infections, during particular seasons, or with other unavoidable exposures may need to intensify therapy intermittently or avoid stepping down therapy even in the absence of symptoms. The second principle is that when a patient develops an acute or chronic exacerbation, control should be re-established as quickly as possible. Control usually is re-established most rapidly with a burst of systemic corticosteroids. Once control is re-established, maintenance therapy is stepped up by one or two levels until long-term control is demonstrated, at which point therapy is tapered or stepped down again.

Therapy usually can be initiated for a particular patient based on the severity classification of that patient's symptoms (see Table 48–5) and therapy stepped up or stepped down over time based on symptom control. **Repeated exacerbations should stimulate efforts to reconsider the adequacy of environmental controls and identify complicating conditions or suboptimal adherence.**

ADHERENCE WITH THERAPY

Suboptimal adherence is one of the most frequent reasons for failure of asthma control. Indications of inadequate adherence include absence of apparent side effects or normal morning cortisol levels in patients on systemic steroids, failure to fill prescriptions for inhalers or oral medications at appropriate intervals, and inadequate serum levels in patients taking methylxanthines. Inappropriate use of MDIs or nebulizers is a related cause of treatment failure. Inhaler technique should be evaluated on each visit. Poor adherence in a patient who has moderate or severe asthma and psychosocial disruption is one indication for referral to a mental health professional. Arranging for regular supervised administration of asthma drugs at school, when possible, also may be useful.

EXERCISE-INDUCED ASTHMA

Maintaining normal activity, including participation in vigorous exercise, is an important goal of asthma therapy. Vigorous exercise can precipitate asthma symptoms in children who have suboptimally controlled asthma and in children who have "exercise-induced asthma" but rarely have problems at other times. Typically, symptoms develop after 5 or 10 minutes of exercise and occasionally with the cessation of vigorous activity. Exercise-induced symptoms usually are controlled by treatment with two puffs of a beta$_2$ bronchodilator, cromolyn sodium, or nedocromil, 10 to 15 minutes before exercise. For children who have underlying airway inflammation (chronic asthma), stepping up maintenance therapy may be helpful. Warming up gradually also may decrease symptoms for individual children.

ASTHMA SELF-MANAGEMENT

Patients, families, and other caretakers play pivotal roles in asthma management. Successful asthma control depends on patient and caretaker education so that everyone required to make judgments about management has a clear understanding of the rationale of therapy and the details of symptom monitoring, drug administration, and side effects. Asthma education begins with the initial evaluation of a child who has asthma and must be reinforced consistently with each subsequent visit. Nebulizer, MDI with spacer, and peak flowmeter techniques must be taught and re-evaluated regularly; the same applies to environmental controls, symptom perception, and appropriate responses to a change in symptoms. The period immediately following a serious exacerbation provides an opportunity to reinforce asthma education at a time that the patient and family may be particularly motivated. School personnel often play an important role in supervising medication administration, monitoring symptoms, and dealing with acute exacerbations during school hours and can provide important observations of the extent to which the child achieves normal levels of functioning. Written instructions on the appropriate response to changes in symptoms should be provided to the patient and family, to school personnel, and to any other individuals who assume responsibility for a child's care. Lists of sources for patient and provider education materials are readily available.

SPECIALIST REFERRAL

Children whose asthma is confusing or difficult to control often benefit from evaluation or ongoing supervision of therapy by a clinician who has

TABLE 48–11. Indications for Referral to a Specialist for Childhood Asthma

Inadequate symptom control
Frequent exacerbations
Need for systemic corticosteroid therapy
Need for more than two corticosteroid treatments in a year
Failure to maintain normal activity and function
History of a life-threatening asthma exacerbation
Atypical signs or symptoms or question of differential diagnosis
Possible presence of complicating condition
Additional diagnostic testing indicated (e.g., skin testing, complete pulmonary function tests)
Severe persistent asthma (referral can be considered for patients who have moderately persistent asthma)
Failure to meet patient family expectations
Need for additional education/adherence counseling
Significant psychosocial dysfunction (consider mental health professional referral)

special expertise in pediatric asthma diagnosis and management, usually a pediatric allergist or pulmonologist. The point at which referral is appropriate depends to some extent on the experience and comfort of the primary care clinician. One reason for referral is failure to achieve the goals of asthma therapy. Specific indications for specialist referral are listed in Table 48–11.

FURTHER READING

National Asthma Education and Prevention Program: Expert Panel Report II: Guidelines for the Diagnosis and Management of Asthma. Bethesda, MD, National Institutes of Health, 1997.

May L. Tao, Paul M. Seltzer, and Lonnie K. Seltzer

Chapter 49

The Primary Care Clinician's Role with the Child Cancer Patient

Childhood malignancy is a rare but emotionally charged diagnosis in the practice of general pediatrics. Earlier detection, more effective treatment including surgery, chemotherapy, and radiation therapy, and better supportive care have resulted in much success in the last 2 decades. Of the approximately 7500 children under 15 years of age who are diagnosed with cancer each year in the United States, about 80% will be cured.

Furthermore, it is estimated that the prevalence of childhood cancer survivors among young adults (15- to 45-year-olds) in the United States will reach 1 in 900 persons by the year 2000 and possibly 1 in 250 persons by the year 2010. Although the specific management of a child who has cancer is specialized and changing rapidly, a primary care clinician has an important role in the three phases of care: (1) when cancer is suspected,

(2) during diagnosis and primary treatment, and (3) in long-term follow-up. This chapter describes how a clinician can facilitate and enhance care at all three stages.

WHEN TO SUSPECT CANCER

Unlike adult cancer which typically manifests as carcinoma, childhood cancer more commonly originates from hematopoietic tissue (i.e., leukemias), neural tissue (i.e., brain tumors), and connective tissue (i.e., sarcomas). Information on the relative proportions of childhood neoplasms by age groups is provided in Table 49–1. Many neoplasms are associated with congenital anomalies or developmental defects, immunodeficiency states, or genetic and chromosomal disorders. Examples include malformations such as aniridia and hemihypertrophy, which are associated with Wilms tumors; ataxia telangiectasia, which predisposes to leukemias and lymphomas; and neurofibromatosis, which is associated with optic gliomas. Children who have preexisting conditions that increase their likelihood for developing cancer should be followed carefully and regularly for early signs and symptoms.

Warning signals of cancer in children differ from those in adults and typically include fever, an apparent infection, a mass, pain, pallor, purpura, changes in gait or balance, alterations in personality, and eye abnormalities. Although some complaints may seem nonspecific, an alert clinician often can differentiate an unusual situation from a more routine problem. Unrelenting fever, despite antibiotics or without signs of chronic infection, may be the result of an occult lymphoma. On the other hand, neurotropenia occurs in patients who have leukemia, predisposing them to infections. These patients may present similarly with fever that fails to respond to antibiotics. Fever also may be secondary to necrosis in an undetected abdominal tumor such as a neuroblastoma or Wilms tumor. Chronic ear drainage, mimicking a difficult to resolve middle ear infection, may represent a rhabdomyosarcoma or Langerhans cell histiocytosis.

Cervical lymph node enlargement that persists beyond 4 to 6 weeks or progresses after 2 weeks, particularly in an older child or an adolescent, should be investigated for lymphoma. Nontender, firm lymph nodes or nodes in unusual locations (e.g., supraclavicular), also should be considered suspicious for tumor. All masses in the abdomen should trigger immediate concern for malignancy and deserve prompt evaluation.

Limb pain is a frequent complaint of physically active children. It may be ascribed to minor trauma that often precedes the bone pain of bone tumors. Pain that is localized, persistent, or out of proportion to the sustained trauma warrants radiographic investigation. Persistent joint or bone pain also is often seen in children presenting with leukemia.

Purpura and pallor, particularly when associated with listlessness, may reflect thrombocytopenia and anemia from bone marrow failure due to leukemic infiltration. A peripheral blood count can quickly demonstrate cytopenia or leukocytosis, and a blood smear may show leukemic cells.

Changes in gait, balance problems, and head tilt are commonly seen in children who have posterior fossa tumors. Personality changes, which may be a more subtle presentation of a supratentorial brain

TABLE 49–1. Relative Proportions of Malignancies by Age Groups*

	0- to 4-Year-Olds	5- to 9-Year-Olds	10- to 14-Year-Olds
All leukemias	36%	33%	21%
All CNS tumors	18%	28%	20%
Neuroblastoma	14%	3%	<1%
Non-Hodgkin lymphoma	3%	8%	9%
Hodgkin lymphoma	<1%	4%	12%
Wilms tumor	9%	5%	1%
Rhabdomyosarcoma	3%	5%	2%
Germ cell	3%	2%	4%
Retinoblastoma	6%	<1%	<1%
Osteogenic sarcoma	<1%	2%	7%
Ewing sarcoma	<1%	2%	4%
Other	7%	7%	18%
All histologies (annual incidence rates)†	186.6	107.0	112.4

*Benign tumors are not included.
†Rates are per million.
Cumulative data from the Surveillance, Epidemiology, and End Results Program, 1988–1992 for ages 0 to 14.
Adapted from Gurney JG, Davis S, Severson RK, et al.: Trends in cancer incidence among children in the United States. Cancer 78:532–541, 1996. Copyright © 1996 American Cancer Society. Reprinted by permission of Wiley-Liss, Inc., a susbsidiary of John Wiley & Sons, Inc.

tumor often are recognized by parents. These may be associated further with headache, morning vomiting, and/or visual changes such as diplopia or blurriness. Changes in vision accompanied initially by squinting and associated with leukokoria (white reflex) suggest retinoblastoma and warrant a thorough ophthalmologic examination.

ROLE DURING DIAGNOSIS AND TREATMENT

Referral to Cancer Center and Initial Evaluation

When the warning signals, history and physical examination, and initial laboratory tests or imaging studies strongly suggest cancer, referral to a tertiary care center with pediatric cancer specialists rather than to a community hospital or to an adult oncologist is mandatory. Reasons for prompt referral, even before a biopsy or a surgical procedure, include (1) better survival rates if the child's initial workup and plan of treatment are developed in a children's cancer center in collaboration with the primary care clinician; (2) availability of sophisticated diagnostic and imaging studies; (3) availability of specialized tests (e.g., bone marrow typing analysis, immunophenotyping, and oncogene expression) that can be obtained only before therapy; (4) availability of surgical and pathologic expertise, which may be crucial both in proper diagnosis and in definitive treatment; and (5) availability of supportive care expertise (e.g., specialist nurses, neuropsychologic testing for brain tumor patients, and placement of indwelling venous access lines).

The two key principles of diagnosis are to identify the tumor and its extent (stage). Pediatric tumors, particularly solid tumors, can be a challenge, requiring specialized pathologic expertise. For example, the small, round blue cell tumors of childhood, which include neuroblastomas, lymphomas, rhabdomyosarcomas, and Ewing sarcoma, may be difficult to differentiate. They often require molecular or cytogenetic analyses. Studies done in a community hospital, such as a biopsy or bone marrow aspiration, often have to be duplicated at the cancer center because of inadequate sample for diagnosis or need for more tissue to perform specialized tests. Centralizing all diagnostic evaluations limits the trauma of multiple, painful procedures for a child. In some cases, baseline assays need to be performed before surgical procedures, such as alpha-fetoprotein and β-human chorionic gondadotropin hormone before a germ cell tumor is removed. Otherwise, important information that may have directed the treatment approach or be used in follow-up for recurrent disease is lost. Thorough staging to determine the local or distant extent of disease before surgery or biopsy not only can inform the surgeon about the procedure he or she should perform but also can affect the overall plan.

Children who have cancer should be treated in the context of an integrated pediatric oncology team, which usually includes surgeons, pediatric oncologists, radiation oncologists, radiologists, pathologists, psychologists, and other specialists and support staff, depending on the diagnosis and treatment. Whenever appropriate and possible, children should be placed on a study (such as those sponsored by the Children's Cancer Group or Pediatric Oncology Group, two collaborative research groups).

Referral to a pediatric cancer center, however, may remove the child and family from their social support system. The child and family may have difficulty understanding and negotiating the complicated tertiary care system (composed of housestaff, fellows, and protocols). They can become lost in the high-tech jargon and unfamiliar surroundings that replace the familiar relationship the family enjoyed with the primary care clinician. The primary care clinician can (1) mediate communication between the tertiary care center and the family; (2) explain to the family the reason for and the meaning of individual tests, ensuring that they understand the treatment goals and prognosis and discussing the significance of acute complications such as fever and possible late effects; (3) monitor appropriate evaluation and control of pain; and (4) attend to the child's and the family's emotional and psychologic needs. The primary care clinician's obligation is to not only facilitate the technical expertise of evaluation and therapy but also to attend to the humanistic aspect of cancer management, maintaining the overall well-being of the child and family.

To be effective in this role, the primary care clinician must promote effective communication with the tertiary center. For example, the primary care clinician should ensure that the referral institution has relevant past medical, developmental, and social history about the child. In turn, the primary care clinician should receive copies of hospital discharge summaries, clinic notes, and diagnostic reports. Most children are on a treatment protocol, and copies of the protocol along with the schedule or scheme outlining specific therapy and evaluation times should be obtained by the primary care clinician.

Children need to be told, in a way that they can understand, about their disease, treatment plans, and procedures. Withholding information, especially if the child is of school age, can be self-defeating and harmful, because children know when something is wrong, and the uncertainty usually is more frightening. It is the pediatrician's difficult job to encourage and help parents to explain to their child what is happening and what to expect. For example, if a procedure is likely to be painful, a child should be helped by the clinician to prepare for the event by reviewing the mechanisms of the procedure and the likely sensory experiences, using language the child can understand and accept (Table 49–2).

During Treatment

The duration of a child's treatment may range from a few months to several years, depending on the tumor type. Occasionally only surgery is required, for example in the case of a completely resected benign brain tumor. However, follow-up imaging studies and regular examinations by the cancer specialist and primary care clinician are required. For these children, immunizations, infections, growth failure, and behavioral changes must still be monitored by the primary care clinician so that appropriate support and information can be given to the patient and family.

For the family who lives far away from a cancer center, it often is possible to begin treatment at the referral center and then receive at least some of the treatments or evaluations closer to home under the care of a local oncologist or the primary care clinician. Indwelling Hickman lines and subcutaneous port devices for chemotherapy ease the administration and discomfort of receiving chemotherapy. Protocol schema outlining the timing of drugs, detailed descriptions of administration technique, precautions, and side effects should be available from the tertiary care center. Complications, such as allergic reactions and severe cytopenia following chemotherapy, need to be communicated promptly to the tertiary care center.

In almost all cases, radiation therapy for a child should be delivered at a tertiary cancer center. Most radiation oncologists in the community have little or no experience treating children. Technical concerns are involved in treating a child with radiation therapy to ensure that not only the tumor is treated adequately to reduce chances of recurrence but also that normal growth and development are perturbed as little as possible.

While the patient is on treatment (chemotherapy, radiation therapy, or both), the primary care clinician and the tertiary care center must agree and define who will have first-line responsibility should the patient become sick. For those families who live a long distance from the referral center, that responsibility often will fall on the primary care clinician. The patient's family also will need a continuing professional contact at the tertiary care center, that is, a physician who will be responsive to calls should an unexpected or an acute incident arise. For example, fever (temperature $\geq 38°$ C [100.4°F]) owing to both infectious and noninfectious causes, is encountered commonly in children undergoing treatment for cancer. When accompanied by neutropenia (defined as the percentage of polymorphonuclear cells times a white blood cell count less than or equal to $500/\mu L$ or below $1000/\mu L$ and falling), a fever may be a harbinger of serious infection and should prompt a meticulous physical examination and appropriate cultures (of blood, urine, and any other suspicious loci such as an intravenous access site), followed by initiation of empirical broad-spectrum antibiotics.

TABLE 49–2. Psychologic Interventions for Cancer-Related, Procedural Pain

Goals
Capture attention
Reduce distress
Reframe the pain experience
Help the child dissociate from the pain

Type	Explanation/Examples
Preparation	Explain mechanical and sensory aspects of procedure.
Desensitization	Practice procedure so that child may experience the mechanics and sensations of the procedure, e.g., using the alcohol swab without the needle.
Distraction	Blow bubbles, play favorite music, play video games.
Positive reinforcement	Give rewards such as stickers or prizes for having "made it through" the procedure.
Hypnotherapy	Suggest images of a favorite place or activity that encourage the child to notice sights, smells, sounds, textures, etc., to enhance imaginative involvement. For example, ask the child to imagine playing soccer, to notice the goal ahead and the ball in front of his or her feet, and to feel himself or herself running on the field.

During the treatment period, there are a number of cancer- and treatment-related medical problems with which the primary care clinician can and should be involved. For example, it is not uncommon for a child to lose 10% or more of body weight while undergoing therapy. Nutrition can suffer for a variety of reasons (e.g., anorexia, stress, treatment-related nausea, painful mucositis, and tumor effects such as mechanical obstruction or altered metabolism). The child may require dietary supplementation under the guidance of a registered dietitian, medications (e.g., antiemetics, appetite stimulants), or even tubal or parenteral alimentation if cachexia is severe enough.

Nausea and vomiting are common debilitating side effects experienced by cancer patients and include symptoms induced by treatment or the disease, as well as those that are anticipatory. Antiemetic therapy is most effective when administered prophylactically—that is, on a schedule to maintain effective levels. Establishing good control over these symptoms at the outset of emetogenic therapy is crucial and prevents escalation to unmanageable proportions. Ondansetron, a 5-hydroxytryptamine type 3 receptor antagonist, used alone or in conjunction with potentiators, has become the general first-line pharmacologic approach. Psychologic interventions, such as hypnosis and guided imagery for distraction, relaxation, and changing expectations, also have been useful adjuncts in reducing both anticipatory and post-therapy nausea and vomiting (also see Chapter 31).

Pain is another troublesome and debilitating side effect of cancer and its treatment. It typically is multifactorial and can be related to procedures or disease. The pediatrician should remain vigilant about inadequately treated or unrecognized pain and may want to consult with the referral center about how best to control it. Tylenol alone or with codeine may suffice for mild to moderate pain. Opioids with or without adjuvants, such as tricyclic antidepressants, should be used for moderate to severe pain without fear of addiction. These medications should be given in adequate doses to be effective and on a regular schedule if the pain is more than episodic. Some types of tumors (e.g., those that invade or compress nerves) and treatments (e.g., vincristine) can produce neuropathic pain. This type of pain often is not relieved by opioids and may require tricyclic antidepressants, gabapentin, clonidine, or other similar agents. Useful agents and their doses are summarized in Table 49–3. More than 50% of children who have cancer report pain that is underestimated by their physicians and, therefore, undertreated. Frequent monitoring and adjusting of pain management needs for the outpatient can prevent hospitalization for pain management.

Clinicians can prepare a child or adolescent for upcoming medical procedures, such as lumbar punctures or bone marrow aspirations, by initiating a dialogue about the child's anxieties, by understanding the level of distress the child experiences, and by eliciting helpful aspects of parental behaviors and responses. The clinician can arrange a few office visits to discuss strategies with the child and parents to reduce anxiety and pain, identifying potential problems before they become major stressors and result in disruption of treatment or more drastic intervention measures. In addition to pharmacologic measures to reduce cancer-related procedural pain, there are psychologic interventions that are useful (Table 49–2).

For younger children, separation anxiety during a long hospitalization, developmental regression or "acting out," and fear of physicians and procedures can occur and may require psychologic assistance for behavioral modification. For older children, fear of treatment, adjustment reactions to diagnosis and treatment, anger and depression, and strained relationships with peers and parents also may require special professional attention. These problems can exacerbate symptoms such as pain, nausea, and vomiting and result in noncompliance. The primary care clinician should consider psychologic interventions that can be used with or without psychotropic medications and family therapy. Most good cancer centers have psychologists, psychiatrists, or social workers who are integral to the oncology care team; the primary care clinician should seek out their guidance.

Follow-Up Period and the Long-Term Survivor

Once therapy is completed, it must be emphasized that the child or adolescent will require *lifetime* follow-up not only to screen for disease recurrence and second tumors but also to assess the adverse effects of therapy on physical, intellectual, and psychosocial development. There should be clear communication between the primary care clinician and the tertiary care center as to who will perform follow-up laboratory and radiographic assessments, which may be stipulated by treatment protocols. For example, children who have brain tumors might get computed tomography or magnetic resonance imaging scans every 3 to 6 months for the first 2 years after completion of treatment and then twice yearly after that. It is crucial that information on follow-up assessments continues to be exchanged between the primary

TABLE 49–3. Pharmacologic Agents for Cancer-Related Pain

Drug	Dosage (oral)	Comments
Mild Pain		
Acetaminophen	Usual dosages	
NSAID (e.g., ibuprofen, naproxen)	Usual dosages	Avoid use in a patient who has thrombocytopenia or platelet dysfunction (e.g., due to marrow suppression)
Mild to Moderate Pain		
Codeine PO$_4$ (± acetaminophen)	1 mg/kg/dose q 4 hr	Constipating; consider giving with stool softeners
Oxycodone (± acetaminophen)	0.1 mg/kg/dose q 4–6 hr	
Long-acting OxyContin available		Less constipating than codeine but requires a triplicate prescription
Moderate to Severe Pain		
Morphine sulfate (MSO$_4$) (Long-acting MS Contin available)	0.3 mg/kg PO q 2–4 hr; 0.03 mg/kg IV q 2–4 hr	Constipating; consider giving with stool softeners
Hydromorphone HCl	0.15 mg equivalent to 1 mg MSO$_4$	Useful if pain is expected to be prolonged
Methadone HCl	0.1 mg/kg PO q 6–8 hr	
	0.01 mg/kg IV q 6–8 hr	
Neuropathic Pain		
Amitriptyline	10–20 mg PO qhs, to 150 mg for effect	Useful if lancinating pain due to tumor compression or obstruction, vincristine toxicity, ulnar neuritis, etc.
Gabapentin	100–200 mg tid	
Muscle Spasm Pain		
Muscle relaxants (e.g., baclofen, cyclobenzaprine [Flexeril])	Dosage varies; see a drug therapy text	
Procedural Pain		
EMLA (eutetic mixture of local anesthetics)	Apply a half to a whole 5-gm tube (do not rub) ≥ 1 hour prior to procedure	Apply to intact skin an hour before procedure and cover with an occlusive dressing. Use EMLA with behavioral techniques, sedatives, and other analgesics as needed

NSAIDs, nonsteroidal anti-inflammatory drugs.

care clinician and the tertiary care center, and also that the primary care clinician understands the surveillance issues and the late sequelae risks specific to the malignancy and the treatment received.

Some tertiary cancer centers have dedicated late effects clinics that are important venues for both patients and their families to receive care and education, and for clinical specialists to learn about the effects of emerging or changing treatments. As the child or adolescent grows up and moves on to the care of an internist, obstetrician-gynecologist, or adult oncologist, the treatment history and potential late complications should be reviewed with the young adult patient and family. Correspondences with relevant records should be sent to the new clinician.

Our understanding of the long-term implications of childhood cancer and its toxic treatments are not known fully. Late tissue damage (months to years in onset) depends on the interplay of therapy received (i.e., surgery, chemotherapy, radiation); patient variables such as developmental status and genetic predisposition; and tumor factors such as location, extent of invasion, and systemic effects of tumor-induced organ dysfunction. Growth can be affected by radiation-induced spi-

nal foreshortening or pituitary damage after cranial irradiation for brain tumors (and to a much lesser degree for leukemia). As is generally the case with all radiation effects, the outcomes are accentuated in younger children and at higher doses. Increasingly, strategies are evolving to reduce these effects, such as reduction or replacement of radiation with chemotherapy, hyperfractionated schemes, and more sophisticated treatment planning and delivery that limit the volume of normal tissue irradiated.

Some chemotherapies, such as prednisone and methotrexate, if given in higher doses for a protracted period, can contribute to osteoporosis, necrosis of the bone, and fractures. Growth should be measured frequently by the pediatrician starting before therapy and after treatment (every 3 months during therapy and for the first year thereafter and then once or twice a year) until skeletal growth is complete. Pubertal development (delayed or precocious) also should be monitored carefully, especially in children who received higher-dose cranial irradiation (e.g., for brain tumors).

Fertility is a frequent concern of adolescents or parents for their children. Effects of radiation and alkylating agents (e.g., cyclophosphamide) on ovaries or testes are age- and dose-dependent. Children who are prepubertal at treatment, especially girls, have a lower risk of chronic toxicity.

Hormonal abnormalities include elevated thyroid-stimulating hormone (which should be suppressed with thyroid hormone supplement) after radiation for head and neck rhabdomyosarcomas and Hodgkin disease or hypothalamic-pituitary deficiencies resulting from brain irradiation. Other organ toxicities include cardiac dysfunction after mediastinal irradiation or anthracyclines, pulmonary damage secondary to bleomycin or lung irradiation, and renal abnormalities detected by urinalysis following cisplatin or nitrosourea chemotherapy.

A worrisome and potentially adverse outcome is a second tumor. Reasons for increased risk of second tumors in cancer survivors include genetic predisposition (substantiated by cancer family syndrome) and induction by previous cancer treatment. For survivors of childhood cancer, the average lifetime risk for developing a second malignancy is estimated to be about 10 to 20 times that of age-matched controls. The time to second malignancy is variable. Patients treated with agents such as cyclophosphamide and etoposide are most likely to develop leukemia within 5 years of exposure to the drug, in contrast to solid tumors, which generally are associated with radiation therapy and have a peak incidence of solid tumors at 10 years after therapy. Long-term survivors often are considered cured; however, primary care clinicians should keep in mind that tumor recurrence remains the greatest cause of death beyond 5 years after diagnosis.

The psychologic impact of childhood cancer is difficult to predict. Although some children and their parents restructure the experience in existential or religious terms to add positive meaning to their lives, the cancer experience also may create disruption for some, with psychologic sequelae for the survivor and other family members. Researchers have found that a substantial portion (15% to 66%) of long-term childhood cancer survivors display self-reported psychologic impairment, behavioral problems, and even psychiatric symptoms. There seem to be subsets of survivors who are particularly vulnerable. For example, among childhood leukemia survivors, female, minority, and unemployed survivors report the most psychologic distress compared with sibling controls.

These possible sequelae need to be explored with the child's family by the primary care clinician, including an assessment of the impact on the siblings who also have been shown to be negatively affected by the cancer experience. A large collaborative group study has shown that parents of siblings of children who have cancer were not only less likely to seek medical help for these siblings compared with parents of children who had no cancer, but also were more likely to underreport these siblings' health problems. In addition, those siblings who adapted dysfunctionally to their sick sibling's illness were more likely to have poor health outcomes themselves. Providing an opportunity to talk about the cancer experience and addressing current fears for survivors, while also remaining attentive to their apparently healthy siblings, is an important support function for clinicians.

Many of these children are at risk for difficulties in school reintegration, academic performance, and acquisition of social skills. With contemporary leukemia treatment and lower radiation doses (18 Gy), the results are more subtle, and specific learning problems (i.e., problems with attention and nonverbal cognitive processing skills) are seen in contrast with the global depression of IQ with higher-dose cranial radiation therapy (24 Gy). Evidence is accumulating that certain subgroups are particularly vulnerable to intellectual impairment. For example, girls seem to selectively experience the synergistic detrimental effects of high-dose intravenous methotrexate (18 Gy) and cranial irradiation. In addition, children who are younger (≤5 years old) at treatment are at greater risk for future cognitive deficits. Brain tumor patients, who often receive much higher doses of radiation and also undergo surgery and, less frequently, chemotherapy, are at significant risk for neurologic, endocrinologic, and neuropsychologic sequelae. It is important that even subtle cognitive impairments are recognized early, that these children undergo neuropsychologic evaluations, and that they receive appropriate special educational attention.

Finally, emphasis on health promotion and disease prevention behaviors is particularly germane in cancer survivors and should be a priority for primary care clinicians. Annual maintenance examinations should be scheduled to monitor for physical late effects, to ensure that psychologic and educational needs are being met, and to counsel about avoidance of tobacco use, excessive alcohol consumption, diet, exercise, and sexuality. Discussing risk reduction through good health habits and advice about regular cancer screening and early cancer detection not only will help prevent yet another cancer experience but enhance survivors' overall future health and well-being.

FURTHER READING

Bleyer WA: The impact of childhood cancer on the United States and the world. CA Cancer J Clin 40:355–367, 1990.

Herold AH and Roetzheim RG: Cancer survivors. Primary Care Clin 19:779–791, 1992.

Pizzo PA and Poplack DG (eds): Principles and Practice of Pediatric Oncology, 3rd ed. Philadelphia, Lippincott-Raven Publishers, 1997.

Schechter NL, Altman A, and Weisman S (eds): Report of the Consensus Conference on the Management of Pain in Childhood Cancer. Pediatrics (Suppl) 86(5):813–834, 1990.

Waber D and Tarbell N: Toxicity of CNS prophylaxis for childhood leukemia. Oncology 11:259–264, 1997.

Zeltzer LK: Pain and symptom management. In Bearison DJ and Mulhern RK (eds): Pediatric Psychooncology: Psychological Perspectives on Children with Cancer. New York, Oxford University Press, 1994.

Zeltzer LK, Dolgin MJ, Sahler OJZ, et al.: Sibling Adaptation to Childhood Cancer Collaborative Study: Health outcomes of siblings of children with cancer. Med Pediatr Oncol 27: 98–107, 1996.

Zeltzer LZ, Bush JP, Chen E, and Riveral A: Understanding and managing children's pain. Part I: History, physiology, and assessment strategies. Curr Probl Pediatr 27(6):225–253, 1997.

Zeltzer LZ, Bush JP, Chen E, and Riveral A: Understanding and managing children's pain. Part II: Prevention and treatment. Curr Probl Pediatr 27(7):264–284, 1997.

Zeltzer LZ, Chen E, Weiss R, et al.: Comparison of psychological outcome in adult survivors of childhood acute lymphoblastic leukemia versus sibling controls: A cooperative Children's Cancer Group and National Institutes of Health Study. J Clin Oncol 15:547–556, 1997.

Henry M. Adam

Chapter 50

Pediatric Human Immunodeficiency Virus Infection

Pediatric human immunodeficiency virus (HIV) infection is a family disease: The vast majority of children (among new cases, close to 100%) have been infected congenitally by a mother stricken with the virus. For the clinician, this reality creates an environment in which psychosocial and emotional issues often are as compelling, and as complex, as the more directly medical problems the children face. The family nature of HIV infection is true throughout the world, everywhere the virus occurs, but in its treatment and prognosis HIV-related disease in the United States has now moved into an entirely different sphere from what the illness means to children in the third world. The development of new but very expensive drugs that expand our arsenal against HIV, along with recent advances in our understanding of the pathophysiology of HIV infection, brings the United States to the brink of transforming pediatric acquired immunodeficiency syndrome (AIDS) from a fatal to a chronic illness. In Africa, it has been said, if the answer to AIDS were a glass of pure water, there would not be money enough to pay for the cure.

Already, around the world, 28 million people have been infected with HIV. Six million have died, 1.5 million of them children. Each day another 8500 people become infected, at least 40% of them women of childbearing age. By the year 2010, United Nations AIDS (UNAIDS) predicts, the life expectancy for entire nations in sub-Saharan Africa will have been virtually halved by the AIDS pandemic. For every child infected with HIV, another is orphaned by the virus.

In the United States, more than 20,000 children have been infected with HIV, nearly 8000 have developed pediatric AIDS as defined by the Centers for Disease Control and Prevention (CDC), and from 1000 to 2000 infants are born newly infected each year. Among children ages 1 to 4 years, HIV infection has become the number one cause of death in New York City, and nationwide it is among the five most common killers of preadolescents.

Overall, the rate of viral transmission from infected women to their infants is between 15% and 35%, averaging 25%. Some infections certainly occur in utero through exposure to transplacental blood, but the majority of infected infants acquire HIV during labor and delivery, from maternal blood and cervical secretions. Although some factors correlating with higher risk for transmission have been identified, such as the mother's viral load, the outcome of an individual pregnancy cannot be predicted accurately. **Breast milk also poses a significant danger to infants, with a 10% to 20% risk of viral transmission from an infected mother.** In the United States, women known to be infected with HIV, or at substantial risk for infection, should not breast-feed their babies. The relative risks and benefits of breastfeeding in developing countries, where 10% to 30% of pregnant women may be infected with HIV, are less clear.

Particularly since the identification of HIV as the etiologic agent responsible for AIDS made screening possible to protect the blood supply, **nonperinatal transmission of HIV to children has become unusual in the United States.** Tragically, a whole generation of hemophiliacs was devastated by HIV infection before the virus was identified, but **transfusion-associated cases are now rare,** with a risk of about 1 per 500,000 donations, and blood products such as factor VIII replacement no longer pose a threat. **Children are, of course, at the same risk as adults from sexual contact, and reports of abused children infected with HIV continue. A few children and adolescents also have been infected by using contaminated paraphernalia when injecting drugs.**

Virtually all recent cases of pediatric HIV infection have been congenital, and among the most significant recent developments relating to this epidemic was the AIDS Clinical Trials Group (ACTG) 076 protocol, which demonstrated that zidovudine given to women through the last two trimesters of their pregnancy, during labor and delivery, and then to their newborns for the first 6 weeks of life can reduce viral transmission from 25% to 8%—in effect, primarily preventing two thirds of congenital infections. With the adoption of the protocol as standard care, experience in several states has confirmed the effectiveness and safety of this preventive therapy, but questions remain: Will combination therapy, which has become the norm for treatment of established HIV infection, be even more effective in preventing transmission than zidovudine used alone? For women not identified as being HIV infected until the time of delivery, will postnatal treatment for their infants arrest infection, with or without intrapartum coverage?

Undetected infection among pregnant women, unfortunately, is not rare. Not only is pediatric **HIV infection** a family disease, but **in the United States it is a disease of particular families—impoverished and disenfranchised minority families who have a high risk for associated drug use.** Nationwide, African-American women are 15 times more likely, and Latino women are seven times more likely, than white women to be infected with HIV. Pediatric infection, being congenital, obviously follows the demographics of HIV infection among women: While less than 30% of all American children are of African or Latino descent, more than 80% of children infected with HIV belong to these minorities. For many poor, minority women living in American inner cities, access to good prenatal care is a problem, and distrust of the health care establishment is widespread. The result is that even in settings in which early screening for HIV infection is encouraged, many pregnant women who are infected go unidentified, either because they receive no prenatal care or they refuse testing for fear of the consequences, social as much as medical. Nor is it unusual for women who have known HIV infection to refuse preventive zidovudine therapy when they are pregnant. The conviction that zidovudine actually is a poison designed to kill minority people who have AIDS has real currency in inner-city communities, which is not so surprising in a country that produced the Tuskegee "experiment." If in the United States the prevention of mother-to-child HIV transmission by the use of antiretroviral therapy has its limits, in the developing world the cost of such drugs reduces discussion to irrelevance.

HUMAN IMMUNODEFICIENCY VIRUS INFECTION AS A FAMILY DISEASE

As a disease of families, pediatric HIV infection raises a variety of emotional, psychologic, and social issues integral to any attempt at comprehensive care. Particularly as advances in treatment have made early identification of infected infants more and more desirable, neonatal screening programs have become increasingly aggressive, and infected young women are more frequently identified initially through routine screening of their babies. In states such as New York, where newborn screening for HIV infection is now mandatory, clinicians need to be prepared for the wrenching situation of greeting an unsuspecting young woman bringing her 2-week-old child for a first postnatal visit with the news that the baby's test at birth was positive for HIV. Because the screening test (an enzyme-linked immunosorbent assay, or ELISA) looks for antibody against the virus rather than for HIV itself, a positive newborn "screen" actually reflects maternal IgG passed through the placenta to the child, meaning that the mother is certainly infected, whereas her baby may or may not be. In adults, the incubation period between the time of infection and the first onset of symptoms is commonly 10 or more years, so it is not surprising that many women are unaware of their infection until their babies are tested. The impact of this "double diagnosis" at what should be one of life's most joyous moments obviously must be overwhelming, and the normal process of grieving may well be aborted—the mother's grief for herself confounded by typical feelings of guilt at "what she has done to her baby" and grief for the baby muddled by the uncertainty of whether the child actually is infected. With the extensive availability now of polymerase chain reaction (PCR) testing, which directly identifies HIV, a definitive diagnosis almost always can be made in a child by 3 months of age, at least shortening a family's period of uncertainty from what in the past was sometimes as long as 18 months or more.

Yet another factor that contributes to the uncertainty of the outlook for infants born to HIV-infected women derives from the epidemiology of the infection: HIV exposure is not an isolated phenomenon. Impoverished minority women living in American inner cities are at high risk for sexually transmitted diseases other than HIV, as well as for the TORCH (toxoplasmosis, other infections, rubella, cytomegalovirus infection, and herpes simplex) infections and hepatitis; they are at risk for drug, alcohol, and tobacco use and certainly for poor nutrition and inadequate prenatal care. All these associated risks pose a threat to the developmental and physical integrity of the newborn, even if the child is fortunate enough to have escaped infection with HIV itself.

Disclosure

A devastating feature of HIV infection is that beyond its morbid medical implications, it often imposes a terrible social burden. Families faced with a child diagnosed as having a life-threatening illness, for example, leukemia or diabetes, usually have relatives, friends, and neighbors available as a support system. Often a young mother just told she and her baby are infected with HIV insists the diagnosis be kept secret. AIDS in our society carries a stigma that other diseases do not bear: The young woman knows that instead of the empathy she needs, she may rouse anger and hostility, that she may well be condemned for living a "degenerate" lifestyle and infecting her baby, and that she risks rejection and isolation if her diagnosis is exposed. Even without the moral (actually pseudomoral) backlash, AIDS evokes the kinds of fear typical of a "plague." Despite all the data to

the contrary, many parents cringe at the notion of having their children share a playroom or a classroom, a toilet, or a fountain, not to mention a hug or a kiss, with an HIV-infected child. Discretion is not a strength of most children, and the perceived need for secrecy contributes to the resistance so many families feel when they are encouraged to disclose the diagnosis of HIV infection to a stricken child—tell the child, and the whole neighborhood will know. **Although the pediatric literature, principally based on experiences with leukemia, generally reports that developmentally appropriate disclosure leads to psychologic and emotional benefits in children who have serious illnesses, many children infected with HIV are not allowed to come to their own terms with the disease that they almost surely suspect they have.**

As an aside, so widespread is publicity about HIV infection that it is worth considering in a general pediatric practice whether some children who have a chronic disease such as asthma, or even an acute illness such as influenza, might not fantasize that they really are sick with AIDS. Giving children the opportunity to reveal their suspicions can be important, allowing "negative" disclosure to let them know that they are not infected with HIV.

Disclosure more directly becomes an issue for the pediatrician when the time comes to fill out school medical forms. Many families ask their doctor not to specify that their child is HIV infected. **The conflict of interest for the pediatrician, between telling the truth and honoring the right to confidentiality, is complicated further by the benefit to an immunocompromised child of having school officials understand the importance of immediately reporting any exposure to contagious diseases.** In deciding how to respond to this dilemma, the pediatrician should at least be aware that almost 2 decades into the epidemic **there is no documentation of child-to-child HIV transmission in a classroom;** the only real risk to health runs the other way—from the otherwise healthy child who has, for example, chickenpox to the child who has AIDS.

Long-Term Planning

Another set of issues that HIV infection raises for clinicians relates to long-term planning. In a family infected with HIV, it often is not clear who will survive longer, parent or child. Parents need guidance in facing their own vulnerability and organizing custodial arrangements for their child in the event that they die first. If the child's disease is the more aggressive, parents need help in thinking through what their wishes are for terminal care. As discomforting as these discussions are, they best serve the interests of the child when they happen within the environment of a trusting relationship, with time to unfold rather than pressured by an impending crisis.

The early identification of infants infected with HIV is becoming more commonplace through a combination of more widely mandated pre- and postnatal screening programs and the availability of PCR testing to clarify the antibody screen. Together, family and physician can start coming to terms with the social and medical implications of the diagnosis. Besides relieving uncertainty and allowing grief to take its course, hearing the family's agenda and answering its questions, and arranging for whatever resources and services may be available to help meet the family's needs, the pediatrician has to begin addressing the many special issues involved in the care of a child who is HIV infected.

IMMUNIZATIONS

Although there is a theoretical concern that immunizing infected children stimulates their HIV to replicate, the effect appears to be transient and not clinically important enough to override the benefit of providing protection to immunocompromised hosts against potentially lethal pathogens. Evidence, as well as common sense, suggests that **the most benefit is gained when children infected with HIV are vaccinated early, while their immune systems are still capable of mounting a response: They should be immunized aggressively without delay.** As is routine for all children, they should receive hepatitis B vaccine; diphtheria, tetanus, and pertussis (DTaP) vaccine; *Haemophilus influenza* type b (Hib) vaccine; and even though it is a live viral vaccine, measles, mumps, and rubella (MMR) vaccine (except if the child is severely immunocompromised). Because measles poses a fatal threat to children whose T-cell function is diminished, MMR should be given at the earliest recommended time, the first birthday. For protection against polio, inactivated polio vaccine (IPV) is the clear choice. In addition to these standard immunizations, HIV-infected children should receive pneumococcal and influenza vaccines. Pneumococcus is by far the most common cause of bacterial disease in children who have HIV. Unfortunately, the currently available vaccine, with capsular polysaccharide antigens, does not reliably elicit an immune response until children are 2

years old. A new conjugate vaccine, apparently effective as early as 2 months of age, should be available soon; its limitation is that it will provide protection against fewer serotypes of pneumococcus than the 23-valent polysaccharide vaccine. The high prevalence of lung and heart disease with underlying HIV infection has led to the recommendation for influenza vaccine; although there is little evidence to prove its effectiveness in children who have HIV, the vaccine has been safe. With a vaccine against varicella now available, the prospect of immunizing at least asymptomatic HIV-infected children is tempting, but the safety of this live viral vaccine for such children is still to be proved. For the prevention of tuberculosis, the only vaccine currently available, bacille Calmette-Guérin (BCG), is a live attenuated product of questionable efficacy that is contraindicated in the presence of immunodeficiency: Annual Mantoux testing with purified protein derivative (PPD) of tuberculin for early identification must serve in place of vaccination.

SECONDARY INFECTIONS

Immunizations are a help, but secondary infections still account for substantial morbidity and mortality in children who have HIV, making prophylaxis an important strategy in their care. For years the leading cause of early death among these children was *Pneumocystis carinii* pneumonia (PCP), an opportunistic infection that trimethoprim-sulfamethoxazole (TMP-SMX) can prevent almost entirely. While about 50% of adults develop intolerable side effects from TMP-SMX, more than 90% of children can continue on the drug long-term. So devastating is PCP, and so relatively benign is prevention with TMP-SMX, that the CDC recommends routine prophylaxis beginning at 1 month of age for all infants born to HIV-infected women, whether or not the infants are known to be infected. Once a child is proved not to be infected, by remaining symptom-free and having two, or better three, negative PCRs, TMP-SMX can be stopped. For a child who becomes symptomatic or has a positive PCR, prophylaxis should continue throughout the first year of life irrespective of the CD4+ T-cell count. Beyond the first birthday, the CD4+ T-cell count is a reasonable predictor of risk for PCP: From 1 through 5 years, only children whose counts are below 500 μL routinely need TMP-SMX; from 6 years onward, a count below 200 μL becomes the threshold for prophylaxis. No matter what the CD4+ T-cell count, children who have had PCP infection or who have less than 15% CD4+ T cells should remain on TMP-SMX (Table 50–1).

With longer survival from the extensive use of prophylaxis against PCP, other opportunistic infections have become more common among children who have HIV. Atypical mycobacteria pose a significant threat once CD4+ T cells fall below 100 μL. Fortunately, effective prophylaxis is available with several well-tolerated agents: rifabutin, clarithromycin, and azithromycin. Fungal infections, particularly with *Candida,* remain a serious problem. Although the lower that CD4+ T cells fall the greater the risk, no particular count serves as a reliable marker for jeopardy. Children who have had recurrent thrush or an episode of more extensive mucocutaneous candidiasis benefit from prophylaxis, either with nystatin mouthwashes or fluconazole. Local herpes simplex infection, usually type 1, is likely to be recurrent, with the danger of systemic spread; prophylactic acyclovir for affected children often is useful.

Both varicella and measles can be overwhelming in immunocompromised children. As long as the varicella vaccine remains contraindicated, only passive protection with varicella-zoster immune globulin is available to HIV-infected children when they are exposed to chickenpox; acyclovir as prophylaxis following exposure has not been proved effective. Even if they have been immunized appropriately with MMR, when they are exposed to measles, HIV-infected children should receive additional passive protection with standard immune globulin, which has significant titers of antibody against measles.

Recurrent bacterial infections affect both the quality of life and the survival of children who have HIV. In addition to their T-cell deficiency, they have dysfunction of humoral immunity, often marked by a polyclonal hypergammaglobulinemia. Along with bacteremia, pneumonia, and otitis media, they are at increased risk for meningitis, sinusitis, lymphadenitis, parotitis, osteomyelitis, and skin infections. In a collaborative study that established the effectiveness of intravenous immune globulin (IVIG) in reducing the morbidity, if not the mortality, from bacterial infections, children who received placebo infusions but were taking TMP-SMX to prevent PCP did as well as children in the treatment group. This finding suggests that antimicrobial prophylaxis, particularly with an agent active against pneumococcus, may be an alternative to the more invasive measure of chronic intravenous therapy. The widespread emergence of resistant pneumococcal strains complicates the decision of how to intervene for a child who has recurrent bacterial disease, as does the finding that children who have CD4+ T-cell counts below 200 μL are not likely to benefit from IVIG.

Obviously, children who have HIV are at risk for many other secondary infections against which no prophylaxis is now available, among them cytomegalovirus, intestinal parasites, toxoplasmosis, cryptococcal meningitis, and unusual bacterial diseases. Careful clinical monitoring for the signs and symptoms of infection allows early detection when prevention is not possible. **Isolating a child who has HIV from peers and from the normal experiences of life is neither practical nor effective. Nor really is it desirable. Experience has shown that even in a preschool child care center, where the risk for spread of contagious diseases is particularly high, HIV-infected children can participate safely if reasonable precautions are taken.**

MANAGEMENT OF NONINFECTIOUS COMPLICATIONS

Besides secondary infections, HIV predisposes children to a myriad of complicating illnesses affecting virtually every system in the body. Most importantly, it affects growth and development, what childhood most fundamentally is about. More than 75% of HIV-infected children have central nervous system involvement, ranging from a devastating progressive encephalopathy to more subtle neurologic deficits. Early assessment and intervention to stimulate cognitive progress and motor skills are basic to their care. So, too, is aggressive attention to nutrition, with a calorically enriched diet critical to improve growth.

These children are at risk for anemia, leukopenia, and thrombocytopenia, as well as for a variety of neoplastic diseases, particularly lymphomas and leiomyosarcomas. Beyond the chronic effects of recurrent pneumonia on their lungs, with bronchiectasis an especially difficult complication, they

TABLE 50–1. *Pneumocystis carinii* **Pneumonia Prophylaxis**

Age	Criteria
1–6 mo	HIV+ mother
7–12 mo	HIV+ child
1–5 yr	CD4+ <500 μL
6–12 yr	CD4+ <200 μL
Always if: CD4+ <15%	
History of PCP	

TMP-SMX: 75 mg/m² bid Monday, Tuesday, and Wednesday

can be affected with lymphocytic interstitial pneumonitis (LIP), a pulmonary disease apparently unique to HIV infection that can lead to significant hypoxemia and exacerbate reactive airways. For reasons that are not clear, perhaps because of earlier and more aggressive antiretroviral therapy or a change in the epidemiology of a facilitating factor (Epstein-Barr virus has been suggested), LIP seems to be less common than it was a decade ago. Cardiomyopathy is a frequent complication of HIV infection; even when not severe enough to cause overt congestive heart failure, it may restrict cardiac reserves sufficiently to produce compromise in the face of other physiologic stresses, such as systemic infections. Not surprisingly, the gastrointestinal (GI) tract is particularly susceptible to the effects of HIV: The virus is lymphotropic, and the concentration of lymphoid tissue in Peyer patches makes the gut a prime target. Aside from direct HIV enteropathy, which can cause malabsorption and diarrhea, the immune compromise to the GI tract opens it to an array of viral, bacterial, amebic, and parasitic infections. The liver, too, is subject both to the immediate effects of HIV and to complicating infections by a host of other agents, most frequently any of the other viruses with a predilection to cause hepatitis. Renal tubular acidosis occasionally affects infants who have HIV, but a more common problem related to the kidneys is the HIV nephropathy that usually strikes children of school age. Although focal segmental glomerulosclerosis is the lesion most frequently, neither the histology of this disease nor its response to treatment is predictable, so early biopsy is indicated to avoid therapy that may do more harm than good. Like so many other organs, the skin may respond directly to HIV with a seborrheic or eczematous-like eruption, or it may manifest either a systemic or local infection or neoplasm. In part because disease of the skin is so obvious, it can play a peculiarly poignant role in the life of a child who has HIV. An example is molluscum contagiosum, a self-limited and relatively harmless infection for the vast majority of affected children. In a child, however, whose T-cell function is diminished, molluscum can become chronic, widespread, and even disfiguring. Not the least of its impact, it also can become a barrier to the social contact any child, but especially one who has HIV, cannot thrive without: How many child care centers or schools will allow a child covered with molluscum to remain in its rooms? Finally, neither the eyes nor the teeth are exempt from HIV's effects, most prominently from secondary infections. Children who have HIV should regularly visit an ophthalmologist and dentist attuned to the complications of their disease.

Further confounding the management of HIV-infected children, beyond the multitude of organ systems that can be involved in their disease, is the host of side effects associated with the many medications to which they may be exposed. Antiretrovirals, as well as antibiotics and agents directed against specific complicating illnesses, can cause anemia, leukopenia, neuropathies, diarrhea, hepatitis, and rashes, often making it difficult to know if the disease or the treatment is producing the symptom.

CLINICAL COURSE, PROGNOSIS, AND THE FUTURE

In general, children infected with HIV have followed one of three patterns in their disease. Up to 25% have become overtly sick very early, in the first months of life, and their course has been relentlessly progressive, marked by opportunistic infections, most typically PCP and candidiasis, by encephalopathy, and by a virulent wasting syndrome. Speculatively, these are children more likely to have been infected during fetal life. It is hoped that the early introduction of aggressive antiretroviral therapy will change the dismal prognosis this group has faced; already, the widespread use of prophylaxis against PCP has made a difference. **The majority of children have had more slowly progressive disease, often not developing any symptoms until after 6 months of age or even for several years.** Probably they represent the group of children more likely to have been infected intrapartum. Their illness characteristically has presented with generalized lymphadenopathy and hepatosplenomegaly; with recurrent bacterial infections, usually pneumonia, otitis, sinusitis, and adenitis; with LIP; and possibly related to it, with lymphocytic infiltration of their parotid glands. Their prognosis has been more mixed, with many surviving to school age or even into their teens, despite the limited treatment options available until recently. Finally, **a few children who have congenital HIV infection have had an "adultlike" pattern to their disease, remaining asymptomatic for as long as 10 years or so, then, once symptoms have appeared, going on to develop severe immunosuppression within a year or two,** at least in the days before newer therapeutic choices were at hand.

Along with more and new kinds of drugs, a basic change in our understanding of the pathogenesis of HIV infection has radically altered strategies for treating children. Until a few years ago it was widely believed that after the viremia accompanying initial infection, HIV went into a long period of latency, lying dormant in lymphoid tissue. It now is clear that HIV replicates actively from the outset, producing up to 10 billion particles a day. At first this avid viral activity is balanced by the immune system's ability to produce as many CD4+ T cells as are destroyed by replicating HIV. Eventually viral replication overtakes languishing T-cell renewal, and with compromise of the immune system, symptomatic illness begins. From this model comes the rationale for early therapy, even in the absence of significant symptoms.

Another innovation that has made earlier and more aggressive therapy clinically feasible is the ability to measure viral load in the blood and to follow it along with the CD4+ T-cell count as they each respond (or do not) to changes in treatment. If the CD4+ count suggests how far the train has traveled toward the end of the line, the viral load reflects how fast the train is moving. Not only can the train be slowed, its direction can be reversed. Together the two measures allow finer tuning of more options than has been possible in the past.

Three different classes of antiretroviral agents (Table 50–2) interfere with viral replication at two different steps in the process. Reverse transcriptase inhibitors, both the nucleoside analogues and the non-nucleosides, block the transcription of viral genomic RNA to DNA. The protease inhibitors keep a large precursor polyprotein from being cleaved into its functional units. With this variety of agents available for use in combination, as well as more sophisticated techniques for moni-

TABLE 50–3. Goals of Therapy

Normalize growth and development
Prevent secondary complications
Improve quality of life
Prolong survival
Cure ???

toring viral and immune system responses to treatment, it now is reasonable to propose more ambitious goals (Table 50–3) for the therapy of children who have HIV infection: normalize growth and development; prevent secondary complications by preserving immune competence; improve quality of life; prolong survival; and, optimistically, begin to think about eradicating infection, at least in some children.

The principles of therapy (Table 50–4) that may make these goals realistic are also becoming clearer: initiate therapy early to reduce viral load; counteract viral resistance, principally by using combination therapy; provide central nervous system penetration; and maintain therapy long-term.

There still are significant problems in implementing such treatment goals and principles, even in the United States, where it is at least possible to consider them. In the developing nations of Africa and Asia, obviously they remain as unreachable as the Holy Grail. Even in the United States, as more and more children receive aggressive combination therapy, cost will be an issue: The cost of the antiretroviral drugs themselves for a child on triple therapy is between $10,000 and $20,000 a year. Because the great majority of pediatric HIV infection in America strikes poor, minority children living in inner cities, often without access to adequate medical care, many will not receive the treatment they should. From an entirely different perspective, the treatment of children who have HIV is also handicapped by the paucity of data derived from the pediatric AIDS experience. Because there are so many

TABLE 50–2. Antiretroviral Medications

Reverse Transcriptase Inhibitors
 Nucleoside analogues
  Zidovudine (ZDV, AZT)
  Didanosine (ddI)
  Zalcitabine (ddC)
  Stavudine (d4T)
  Lamivudine (3TC)
  Abacavir, Adefovir, and PMPA
 Non-nucleosides
  Nevirapine
  Delavirdine*

Protease Inhibitors
 Saquinavir
 Ritonavir
 Indinavir
 Nelfinavir
 GW141W94 and ABT378*

*Not yet approved.

TABLE 50–4. Principles of Therapy

1. Initiate early to reduce viral load
Retard irreversible immune damage
Retard clinical progression
2. Counteract viral resistance
Consider previous drug exposure
Use combinations of drugs
Avoid introducing drugs one at a time
3. Provide CNS penetration
Include either zidovudine or stavudine
4. Maintain long-term therapy
Lymphoid tissue and CNS sanctuaries

CNS, central nervous system.

fewer infected children than adults, but also because of a persistent reluctance to initiate drug trials with children until long after studies have been under way with adults, much of the information guiding pediatric therapy is extrapolated from adult practice—a less than ideal situation.

Still, if not yet for the children of the developing world, there is for many children who have HIV in the United States a hope more tangible than could have been believed just a few years ago. Given the protean nature of this infection with all its medical, social, and emotional complexity, the involvement of the general pediatrician, trained to think about the whole child in the context of a family, will remain critical alongside the increasingly sophisticated specialized care that new drugs and techniques are offering.

FURTHER READING

American Academy of Pediatrics: HIV infection. *In* Red Book: Report of the Committee on Infectious Disease, 24th ed. Elk Grove Village, IL: AAP, 1997.

Centers for Disease Control and Prevention: AIDS among children—United States, 1996. MMWR 45:1005–1010, 1996.

Connor EM, Rhoda SS, Gelber R, et al.: Reduction of maternal-infant transmission of human immunodeficiency virus type 1 with zidovudine treatment. N Engl J Med 331:1173–1180, 1994.

Pizzo PA and Wilfert CM (eds): Pediatric AIDS: The Challenge of HIV Infection in Infants, Children, and Adolescents, 2nd ed. Baltimore, Williams & Wilkins, 1994.

Judy C. Bernbaum

Chapter 51

Follow-Up Care of the Ex-Preterm Infant

Over the past 25 years the number of low-birth-weight infants who survive has increased substantially. Of the estimated 3.9 million infants born during 1995, the percent of low-birth-weight (LBW; <2500 grams) infants rose to 7.3% and the incidence of very low birth weight (VLBW; <1500 grams) infants remained stable at 1.3%. As more infants of low birth weight enter the pediatric population, physicians must become expert in managing their unique medical conditions, in addition to monitoring their developmental progress and recognizing early signs of neurologic disorders. Physicians can play a major role in the identification of problems early in their evolution. Their efforts can have a major effect on the prevention or further progression of a child's disabilities.

This chapter reviews frequently encountered conditions experienced by preterm infants after discharge from a neonatal intensive care unit (NICU).

DISCHARGE

Discharge from an NICU to home is frequently viewed as the most difficult task for the hospital staff and is equally stressful for the family and their primary care physician. Effective discharge planning begins with communication during hospitalization among members of the staff caring for the infant, the family, and the physician who will become responsible for the child after discharge. The opportunity for families to become familiar with their child by frequent visiting in the unit will help them develop appropriate and realistic expectations for this process.

The primary care physician's role in discharge planning depends on the level of involvement in an infant's neonatal care. If the child requires intensive care in a tertiary care unit, frequently the care is under the direction of a neonatologist who most often will not be involved with providing primary care after discharge. Because this is the setting in which the greatest potential for breakdown in communication between the tertiary care center and the primary care physician can occur, it is crucial to maintain phone contact with the tertiary care center throughout the infant's hospital course or to review the events of the entire hospitalization just before the infant's discharge. If possible, the primary care physician should be available to meet with the family to answer questions that may arise throughout the hospital course or to review the infant's problems and follow-up needs before the first official outpatient visit. Most often, there is greater involvement of the primary care physician in a hospital with a level II or III nursery. In this setting he or she can participate in the care of the infant throughout the hospitalization or can get involved just before discharge, after the child is initially cared for by a neonatologist. The primary care physician is better able to participate in or organize the discharge planning process and there is less chance of breakdown in communication with the hospital staff. Table 51–1 details the suggested guidelines for predischarge testing based on birth weight.

Most preterm infants spend time after discharge recovering from their NICU experience. Their problems vary depending on the degree of prematurity and the impact their premature birth had on their delicate organ systems. Many infants are left with little in the way of residual problems. Many others, however, leave the nursery with continuing health problems and need treatment for weeks to months, which often affects many aspects of their growth and development. Although still requiring well-child care, many of these infants have needs that are far from routine. Special attention must be given to growth and nutrition, immunizations, vision and hearing, and the sequelae of illnesses experienced during the neonatal period. **It becomes the responsibility of the primary care physician or the designated special care follow-up program to provide the ongoing medical care and developmental surveillance that will enable each child to achieve his or her maximum level of health and development.**

TABLE 51–1. Suggested Guidelines for Predischarge Tests

Test	<1000 Gm	<1500 Gm	>1500 Gm	Other Considerations
Audiologic screening	√	√	√*	• Congenital infection • Anatomic malform. of head/neck • Family history of hearing loss • Hyperbili at exchange levels • Bacterial meningitis • Ototoxic medications • Severe birth asphyxia • Prolonged mechanical ventilation • Syndromes associated with hearing loss • ECMO or high-freq ventilation
Ophthalmologic examination	√	√	○	• <28 wk gestation • B.W. >1500 gm *and* unstable clinical course • First exam 4–6 wk of age
Car seat evaluation	√	√	○	• <37 wk gestation at birth • Any condition placing infant at risk for apnea/O₂ desaturation
Complete blood cell count with reticulocyte count	√	√	√	• All infants approaching discharge
Head ultrasound/MRI/CT	○	○	○	• If clinically indicated; to confirm either resolution or progression of previously identified process
Neonatal metabolic screening	√	√	√	• All infants once enterally fed
Nephrocalcinosis screening	√	○	○	• Preterm and/or on furosemide • Urine dipstick for blood/protein

Pneumogram/thermistor	○	○	○	• Perform if clinically indicated
				• Consider if:
				  -recent apnea or bradycardia
				  -receiving methylxanthines
				  -gastroesophageal reflux

Osteopenia screening (Calcium, phosphorus, alkaline phosphatase)	√	○	○	• Long-term total parenteral nutrition • GI malabsorption • Cholestatic liver disease
Drug levels	○	○	○	• On medications requiring blood levels (caffeine/phenobarbital)
Recent chest X-ray	○	○	○	• Any patient with BPD with a copy for parents to take to primary care physician

○ = Recommended   √ = Suggested if meets criteria in "Other Considerations."

*As per NIH consensus statement, recommended as part of universal screening of all newborns, especially those admitted to an NICU, using either brainstem auditory evoked responses or otoacoustic emission testing.

ECMO, extracorporeal membrane oxygenation; GI, gastrointestinal; BPD, bronchopulmonary dysplasia.

A mulltisystem evaluation of the preterm infant is necessary to identify potential areas of concern that may require further assessment after discharge. Guidelines for the tests vary from institution to institution.

GROWTH

The pattern of growth following discharge is a valuable indicator of an infant's well-being, particularly during the first 2 years of life. Aberrant growth may reflect a variety of disorders, including inadequate caloric intake, chronic illness, feeding difficulties, abnormalities in gastrointestinal motility, or social-emotional difficulties. Although these factors can affect all infants discharged from nurseries, the preterm infant is particularly vulnerable. It is crucial to monitor nutritional intake closely and to interpret growth rates, having a complete understanding of the infant's history, current problems, and expectations for growth.

Many factors affect the growth of a preterm infant, including gestational age, birth weight, severity of neonatal illness, caloric intake, ongoing illnesses, environmental factors in the home, and heredity. Caloric requirements for a healthy, preterm infant generally exceed those of a normal term infant, especially during rapid catch-up growth. Chronic illnesses, such as bronchopulmonary dysplasia, which increase caloric expenditure, add to an infant's daily requirements. Malabsorption after necrotizing enterocolitis and chronic emesis from gastroesophageal reflux (GER) may impair growth as a result of increased losses. In contrast, decreased intake may be caused by fatigue, hypoxemia, oral motor dysfunction, or esophagitis from GER. Neurologic complications, such as intraventricular hemorrhage (IVH) or periventricular leukomalacia (PVL), may also affect motor skills, which can result in feeding problems. Finally, infants with intrauterine growth retardation caused by congenital infections, chromosomal abnormalities, or other syndromes may never achieve normal growth.

Patterns of Growth

When one is evaluating the growth of an LBW infant, the gestational age should be considered. **Growth parameters should be plotted on preterm growth curves according to the infant's adjusted age until 2½ years of age.** Various patterns of growth emerge from different groups of patients.

Healthy LBW, appropriate-for-gestational-age (AGA) infants generally experience catch-up growth during the first 2 years of life, with maximal growth rates between 36 and 44 weeks after conception. Little catch-up growth occurs beyond a chronologic age of 3 years. More than 80% of preterm infants who were appropriately grown at birth achieve normal growth reflecting their family's genetic makeup. Head circumference usually is the first parameter that demonstrates catch-up growth and commonly falls at a higher percentile than either weight or length during the first several months after discharge. Increases in weight are commonly followed by linear growth increases within several months. Because rapid head growth may represent the onset of posthemorrhagic hydrocephalus, one should be cautious in interpreting rapid head growth as catch-up growth in the preterm infant who has suffered a grade III or IV intraventricular hemorrhage. An imaging study may be necessary if the infant's history or symptoms suggest increasing intraventricular pressure. In contrast, a head circumference that measures more than 3 standard deviations below the mean is often associated with significant developmental disabilities. **Head growth at 8 months of age is one of the best predictors of eventual growth and neurodevelopment. Slowing of head growth at 5 to 6 months of age is an ominous sign.**

It is important to evaluate an infant's growth velocity for weight and length. Some infants grow at a slow but progressive rate during this period. However, a low weight for length or a decline in all growth parameters suggests inadequate nutritional intake and may warrant further investigation. If a preterm infant's weight significantly exceeds length in percentiles, one should discuss the possibility of overfeeding with the family. Ironically, obesity may occur in a previously underweight preterm infant, owing to compensatory overfeeding or in a infant whose medical problems have resolved but whose diet remains high in calories.

Growth of the small-for-gestational-age (SGA) infant is strongly influenced by the cause of the intrauterine growth retardation. Overall, LBW-SGA infants demonstrate less catch-up growth than LBW-AGA infants, but when they do, it occurs by 8 to 12 months adjusted age. By 3 years of age, approximately 50% of SGA infants are below average in weight compared with 5% to 20% of LBW-AGA infants. Symmetric SGA infants with birth head circumference similar in percentile to birth weight are less likely to demonstrate catch-up growth than are those SGA infants whose head circumference at the time of birth exceeds the percentiles for length and weight. As with AGA infants, head circumference is normally the first parameter to demonstrate catch-up, followed by weight and then by length.

Because of the wide range of growth that is considered normal for preterm infants during the first several years of life, it is best to analyze trends rather than make assumptions based on single measurements. When abnormalities are noted in growth trends, investigation into the infant's nutritional status during hospitalization, the results of cranial sonography studies, and the status of continuing illnesses should be undertaken to identify a possible cause.

Nutritional Requirements

Traditionally, although somewhat controversial, the goal for preterm infants is to achieve a growth rate approximating the expected fetal growth rate at the same postconceptional age. Because weight gain is suboptimal during acute illness, all efforts should be made to promote catch-up growth once the medical condition is stable. The nutritional needs of the preterm infant during the first few months of life exceed those of a term neonate and may persist for the first year of life. Appropriate choices for most preterm infants include breast milk or either a term infant formula or one manufactured to meet the needs of the growing premature infant. Other infants continue to need more highly concentrated formulas, specialized formulas, or fortified breast milk because of increased caloric requirements or dysfunctional feeding. In addition, caloric supplements can be added to formula or breast milk to help improve caloric intake further (Table 51–2). Infants given feedings with caloric densities beyond 24 kcal/ounce should be monitored closely for symptoms suggestive of intolerance such as vomiting, diarrhea, or dehydration.

When caloric additives are used, care should be taken to maintain an appropriate caloric distribution of nutrients with a ratio among carbohydrates-fats-protein of approximately 40-50-10.

Caloric requirements for adequate growth vary. Healthy preterm infants generally require 110 to 130 kcal/kg/day, but some infants with chronic disease may require up to 150 or more kcal/kg/day. Caloric intake should be increased as tolerated until weight gain is satisfactory.

Feeding Problems

Although unusual in term infants, feeding disorders are relatively common in preterm infants. Most feeding problems occur in the neonatal period, but many infants demonstrate recurrent or chronic problems with sucking and swallowing during the first year of life. Unrecognized, these problems may lead to significantly impaired nutritional intake and cause stress in the parent-infant

TABLE 51–2. Follow-Up Care of the Ex-Preterm Infant

Guidelines for concentrating standard formulas (using concentrated liquid or powder)

20 kcal/oz	13 oz concentrate	+ 13 oz water
	or	
	3 scoops powder	+ 6 oz water
24 kcal/oz	13 oz concentrate	+ 9 oz water
	or	
	3 scoops powder	+ 5 oz water
27 kcal/oz	13 oz concentrate	+ 6 oz water
	or	
	5.5 scoops powder	+ 8 oz water

Guidelines for concentrating NEOCARE formula

20 kcal/oz	3 scoops + 5.5 oz water
22 kcal/oz (standard formulation)	3 scoops + 5 oz water
24 kcal/oz	3 scoops + 4.5 oz water
27 kcal/oz	3 scoops + 4 oz water

Guidelines for concentrating Enfamil 22 formula

22 kcal/oz (standard formulation)	1 scoop + 2 oz water
24 kcal/oz	2 scoops + 3.5 oz water

Guidelines for fortifying breast milk (using standard formula)

22 kcal/oz	1 tsp formula powder to 6 oz BM
24 kcal/oz	1 tsp formula powder to 3 oz BM
26 kcal/oz	1.5 tsp formula powder to 3 oz BM

Guidelines for fortifying breast milk (using NEOCARE formula)

24 kcal/oz	1 scoop Neocare powder to 10 oz BM

Some Common Dietary Supplements (generally add 1 ml of a supplement per oz of formula; not recommended to use more than one type of supplement at a time; can add supplements to concentrated formula as tolerated)

Microlipids	4.5 kcal/ml	Well-tolerated; can be difficult to obtain (order through pharmacies)
Vegetable oil	9 kcal/ml	Inexpensive; need to blenderize into formula
MCT oil	7.6 kcal/ml	Does not blend well into formula (order through pharmacies)
Polycose	2 kcal/ml	Low caloric density (order through pharmacies)
Karo syrup	4 kcal/ml	May cause loose stools (can use light or dark)

relationship. Infants at greatest risk for developing feeding problems include those whose oral feedings are delayed during the neonatal period and those who have immature oral motor skills related to prematurity. In addition, those with transient neurologic immaturity or more permanent neurologic deficits are at highest risk. Additional risk factors for the development of feeding dysfunction include chronic lung disease, tracheostomy, gastroesophageal reflux, frequent negative stimulation around the nose and mouth (such as repeated suctioning, prolonged intubation, or passage of a nasogastric tube), and inconsistent feeding techniques by multiple caregivers.

The evaluation of a possible feeding disorder includes a detailed history of feeding behaviors and nutritive intake, a physical examination including assessment of oral motor reflexes, and observation of a feeding. If an infant with chronic lung disease desaturates during feeding, increasing the supplemental oxygen during feeding can improve feeding. Evaluation of the type of nipple and its hole may show that the hole is too small, causing fatigue, or too large, making it difficult to control the flow. Indications for radiologic evaluation include suspected aspiration during feeding or an anatomic abnormality such as a tracheoesophageal fistula or delayed gastric emptying.

All of these conditions are amenable to therapy if identified early. Treatment of underlying medical problems often helps ameliorate the feeding problems. A pediatric speech pathologist or occupational therapist trained in feeding techniques can assess an infant and develop an appropriate feeding program. Feeding an infant is normally a relaxing, nurturing act that plays a role in parent-infant bonding. In the presence of a feeding disorder, feedings may become a major source of stress, frustration, and anxiety for the infant, parents, and physicians.

Immunizations

Preterm infants should receive the same immunizations as term infants and on similar schedules without correcting for their prematurity. The American Academy of Pediatrics Committee on Immunization Practices recommends that full doses of diphtheria, tetanus, pertussis (DTP, or DTa [acellular] P), *Haemophilus influenzae* type B (Hib), oral or inactivated polio, and measles-mumps-rubella (MMR) vaccines be administered to prematurely born infants at the appropriate postnatal (chronologic) age. With the approval for use of the acellular pertussis vaccine, the pertussis component of the DTP vaccine should not be withheld because of an infant's prematurity or underlying chronic disease. Oral polio vaccine should be used only after discharge from the hospital. Inactivated polio vaccine, enhanced potency, should be given to any child who remains hospitalized beyond 2 months of age, is immune-compromised, or lives with an immuno-deficient individual.

Hepatitis B vaccine should be withheld until approximately 2 months of age for preterm infants weighing less than 2 kg at birth. If the infant remains critically ill at 2 months of age, the initial vaccine can be administered once the child has become medically stable.

Infants with chronic pulmonary disease (e.g., bronchopulmonary dysplasia) or cardiac disease with pulmonary vascular congestion are at high risk for developing serious illness if infected with an influenza virus. To protect vulnerable infants, immunization with influenza vaccine is indicated for household contacts, including siblings, primary caretakers, and home care nurses as well as hospital personnel. For infants 6 months of age or older, two doses of split virus vaccine should be given 1 month apart between October and December followed by one annual dose. Adults and older siblings who have natural immunity or who have received previous immunizations need only one yearly dose.

Although a vaccine to protect against respiratory syncytial virus (RSV) disease is still unavailable, passive immunity can be provided in the form of intravenous (RespiGam) or intramuscular (Synagis) RSV immunoglobulin specially formulated to provide a high titer of anti-RSV antibodies. In 1996, the Food and Drug Administration approved RespiGam and, in 1997, approved Synagis for use in preterm infants at risk for the development of severe complications if they were to become infected with RSV. Because the half-life of these preparations is approximately 1 month, infants must receive treatment monthly during the RSV season (typically, November through March or April). Statistically, both RespiGam and Synagis usage has resulted in a significant decrease in the incidence and severity of RSV disease and the need for hospitalization in this high-risk group of children.

SPECIALIZED CARE

Retinopathy of Prematurity

ROP is a disorder that interrupts the normal vascularization of the developing retina. Most cases of ROP resolve spontaneously, but even with complete resolution, scarring of the retina may occur. The initial examination should not take place before 4 to 6 weeks' chronologic age, as a vitreous haze may interfere with visualization of the retina and the yield for identifying ROP is low. If only one examination is possible, it should be at 7 to 9 weeks of age to catch the peak period during which ROP occurs. A schedule of follow-up visits is based on the initial findings. All infants with immature fundi or any stage of ROP require close monitoring until the eyes have matured or the ROP has completely resolved. Thereafter, follow-up to assess for refractive errors should be at 1 year of age and before kindergarten or earlier if there are clinical signs.

Sequelae of ROP depend largely on the extent of retinal scarring. As much as 80% of stage 3 ROP resolves spontaneously without significant scarring, but there may be subtle retinal changes resulting in refractive errors, strabismus, or amblyopia. Early identification of a child with a visual handicap is essential to provide the child and family with the services for visually impaired children that are available on county and state levels.

Hearing Problems

The incidence of sensorineural hearing loss in preterm infants is generally reported to be between 1% and 3%. Several factors place these infants at particular risk for hearing loss, including birth weight less than or equal to 1500 grams, hypoxia, hyperbilirubinemia, prolonged mechanical ventilation, perinatal asphyxia, meningitis, and ototoxic drugs. Passing an initial hearing screening does not preclude the possibility of a later acquired hearing loss. Absent or abnormal responses to auditory stimulation, delays in speech development, poor articulation, or inattentiveness should raise the suspicion of a hearing loss that requires a more thorough evaluation. All infants who fail an initial hearing screening should be referred to an audiologist for further testing and intervention.

Intraventricular Hemorrhage

IVH is one of the most serious neurologic events encountered by neonates. It occurs in up to 50% of infants born weighing less than 1500 grams. There is an inverse relationship between gestational age and the incidence of hemorrhage. With the increase in survival of infants at lower gestational ages, an increase in the number of infants with IVH may be expected as well. Follow-up imaging studies should be performed to demonstrate resolution of hemorrhage and to diagnose any anatomic sequelae. The most common complications of IVH include hemorrhagic infarction, posthemorrhagic hydrocephalus, porencephalic cyst, periventricular leukomalacia, and ventriculomegaly without hydrocephalus (hydrocephalus ex vacuo).

In clinical practice, a common problem is distinguishing the onset of hydrocephalus from catch-up head growth when an infant's head circumference crosses percentiles. **Clinically, all premature infants with and without IVH should be monitored with at least monthly measurements of head circumference and documentation of neurodevelopmental progress.** If a child has greater than a 2-cm weekly increase in head circumference or demonstrates any symptoms suggestive of increased intracranial pressure or a change in neurologic status, hydrocephalus should be considered and evaluated by cranial imaging studies.

Most often, ventriculoperitoneal shunts for hydrocephalus continue to work without complication according to the principle of volume dependence. If complications occur, they are usually caused by mechanical malfunction or infection.

In general, the outcome in children with lesser grades of IVH is similar to that in children with no IVH. Infants with the more severe grades of IVH fare worse and are more likely to demonstrate abnormalities in neuromotor and cognitive functioning. However, even children with grade III or IV IVH can have overall normal neurodevelopmental outcome in the preschool years, depending on the location and size of the initial insult. The incidence of cerebral palsy is generally reported in the 3% to 6% range in the total preterm population. The incidence of cerebral palsy for those with higher grades of IVH ranges from 40% to 55%. Cerebral palsy can be seen without intellectual impairment.

Approximately 50% of children with grade III or IV IVH experience significant developmental delays and subsequent mental retardation. Evidence indicates that even children with these insults who attain average or below-average intellectual abilities may experience abnormalities in visual-perceptual and visual-motor coordination. These abnormalities may lead to learning disabilities in an academic environment. There are reports that even children with lesser grades of IVH are more likely to demonstrate learning disabilities compared with those preterm infants experiencing no bleed.

Periventricular Leukomalacia

PVL is a result of ischemic infarction and subsequent weakening of the white matter adjacent to the lateral ventricles. This is followed by either repair or the development of cysts. The reported incidence of PVL in infants with birth weight less than 1500 grams varies from 2% to 22%. Infants at risk for PVL are those whose perinatal course was complicated by severe hypoxia, ischemia, or both. In the weeks that follow a major insult leading to PVL, phagocytosis of the necrotic material occurs with development of fluid-filled, periventricular cysts. PVL and subsequently the presence and size of cysts can be determined using cranial ultrasonography, computed tomography, or magnetic resonance imaging scan. Resolution of the cysts is highly variable, and some never completely resolve.

Beyond the neonatal period, screening for the presence of PVL should be considered in any child with cerebral palsy without an apparent cause. Since there are no symptoms associated with the development of PVL, it can be easily missed during the neonatal period. If PVL is not associated with residual cysts, few if any sequelae develop. If PVL is associated with the loss of vital areas of neural tissue and formation of cysts greater than 3 mm in diameter, 80% to 90% of infants so affected are at risk for developing cerebral palsy, manifested as moderate to severe quadriplegia. The intellectual capacities of children with PVL and cyst formation are more variable. Mental retardation is more common in infants with residual cysts but ranges from mild to severe. If the cysts develop in the occipital region, visual impairment may result.

All infants with PVL, especially with cysts, should be closely monitored for neurodevelopmental sequelae. Parents of infants with PVL should be counseled on the importance of periodic neurodevelopmental assessments for early detection of any sequelae and intervention when appropriate.

Chronic Lung Disease

Bronchopulmonary dysplasia (BPD) is the most frequently diagnosed chronic lung disease in preterm infants, usually developing as a sequel to the acute lung injury experienced during the first few weeks of life. Infants who require supplemental oxygen beyond 36 weeks postconceptional age often carry this diagnosis.

Some infants with mild or minimal residual lung disease may come to the primary care provider's attention with their first viral respiratory tract infection. Those with more severe disease are often discharged with medication requirements, nebulizer treatments, and supplemental oxygen. Clinical manifestations are similar to those in the nursery and include tachypnea, tachycardia, retractions, rhonchi, bronchospasm, and poor air movement into the lungs bilaterally. More subtle signs of chronic respiratory distress include poor weight gain, feeding intolerance, decreased activity, and a reduced tolerance to exercise. Medical management of infants with BPD often includes a variety of therapies, including one or more of the following: fluid restriction, diuretic therapy, bronchodilator medications, steroids, and supplemental oxygen, even after initial hospital discharge. These therapies are altered depending on the infant's clinical status and potentially withdrawn as the infant matures and improves. How early withdrawal can be depends on the severity of lung disease at the time of discharge. Additionally, BPD may continue to worsen after discharge so that infants who tolerated either no medication or lower levels may begin to require aggressive intervention after discharge, especially if they experience respiratory-related intercurrent illnesses.

Minimizing the exposure of infants with BPD to environmental irritants and communicable diseases helps decrease the frequency of intercurrent episodes of bronchospasm and allows more time for the lung to heal. Some environmental irritants include cigarette or fireplace smoke, pet fur or dander, kerosene heaters, paint, and infectious agents. The less irritation the lung is exposed to, the quicker the recovery process will be.

Rehospitalization is a common occurrence in children with BPD, especially during the first year of life. Parents of these infants should be advised of this possibility before initial hospital discharge. Every effort should be made to treat an infant with intercurrent illnesses and associated bronchospasm as an outpatient, but if the infant does not readily respond, hospitalization is appropriate for more aggressive treatment. If the child requires an elective surgical procedure such as a hernia repair, admission should be avoided during epidemics of respiratory-related illnesses, such as during RSV season.

Developmental Outcome

As infants of increasingly earlier gestation and low birth weight survive, there is great concern that there not be a disproportionate increase in late mortality or other morbidities. Assessment of development is an essential part of any pediatric visit and is especially important with the preterm infant. Despite an improved outlook on the outcome of low-birth-weight infants, there remains a higher incidence of mental retardation, cerebral palsy, and learning problems in the preterm population. **The majority of infants who weigh between 1000 and 1500 grams at birth are intellectually normal after the first year of life; the remainder, approximately 10% to 15%, have moderate or major delays.** This percentage represents a major improvement over the 90% incidence of handicaps in these infants in the 1950s. The outlook for infants with birth weight less than

1000 grams is less positive. Approximately 15% to 20% of these infants have moderate to major delays in development. Of those infants weighing less than 800 grams at birth, approximately 25% are developmentally delayed.

In addition to the children who have moderate to major developmental delays, another large population of preterm children has been identified with learning problems. These are children of all birth weights who, despite normal intelligence as measured by IQ testing, have problems learning in school and often require special education. Deficits have been documented in perceptual-motor integration skills, impulse control, attention span, language skills, and integration of sensory stimuli. These learning disabilities are more difficult to identify before school age but can have a significant impact on the affected child and family.

The goals of tracking are early identification of disabilities and early initiation of therapeutic and educational services to prevent complications and to optimize the quality of their outcome. Screening by the community physician can be accomplished using standardized assessment tools. These tools, such as the Denver Developmental Screening Test, typically assess the acquisition of observable milestones. Adjustment of age for prematurity is recommended at least through 24 months. The adjusted age reflects the child's neurologic and biologic maturity and prevents the overidentification of developmental delays. When these tools are used correctly, they can guide the professional in the identification of children who need more in-depth evaluations. The results of the developmental examination must be interpreted in coordination with evaluation of vision and hearing abilities. Even mild deficits in hearing or vision can affect progress in other areas of functioning. Cognitive and language delays or disorders of behavior may be related to hearing loss. Delays in gross motor skills and perceptual motor or fine motor skills may be related to visual impairment.

Assessment of muscle tone and neurologic integrity and acquisition of motor milestones are also important. Cerebral palsy is rarely diagnosed until the second year of life, when the persistence of abnormalities is apparent, especially when the child has experienced a cerebral insult known to be associated with the development of residual muscle tone abnormalities. Those children who demonstrated suspect neurologic status in infancy but whose muscle tone normalizes, a condition often referred to as transient dystonia, remain at risk for other developmental disabilities, including learning disabilities.

Although motor milestones are significant in the first year, it is important that cognitive skills, including language milestones, be followed closely after the first year. Language acquisition and the pragmatic use of language allow an important opportunity for assessment. Children who begin to speak at a later-than-expected age are likely to demonstrate other delays within their language usage and language comprehension. To assess for more subtle delays in language usage, the language skills of these children should be evaluated even if verbal speech has been achieved. Language skills are strongly associated with later success in reading.

Although developmental assessment during infancy is not typically a good statistical predictor of later intelligence, these tests are accurate in describing a child's strengths and weaknesses and guiding therapeutic efforts. Standardized tests done in infancy and with toddlers are more predictive for children who are significantly delayed. Testing at the age of 3 or 4 can rule out significant deficits such as mental retardation but cannot rule out learning disabilities affecting academic learning.

For children with no risk factors during the neonatal period who demonstrate normal early development, short-term screening is appropriate. Children who exhibit delays in cognitive, language, or motor skills, who are suspect in their neurologic status during the early years, or who have significant neonatal risk factors should be tracked into school entry because of the increased risk of learning disabilities during the school-age years.

An additional part of developmental surveillance is to encourage the family to support and to optimize their child's development. Parents of LBW children are vulnerable to lowering their expectations of their child and limiting their experiences. Developmental screening is a vehicle for helping parents identify their child's strengths and weakness and to find ways to support his or her best growth and development.

SUMMARY

Care of the preterm infant after discharge is a challenge for the practicing physician. All premature infants should be followed through infancy and into preschool and school years because of their common ongoing medical concerns and the high risk of developmental disabilities. Although impossible to predict with great accuracy in the neonatal period, it is appropriate to select those preterm infants who have the highest risk for disabilities and provide them a closer degree of surveillance.

FURTHER READING

American Academy of Pediatrics and American College of Obstetricians and Gynecologists: AAP Guidelines for Perinatal Care, 2nd ed. Elk Grove Village, IL, AAP, 1988.

American Academy of Pediatrics Joint Committee on Infant Hearing: 1990 Position statement. ASHA (Suppl 5):3, 1991.

Bernbaum J and Hoffman-Williamson M: Primary Care of the Preterm Infant. St. Louis, Mosby–Year Book 1991.

Bernbaum JC, Daft AL, Anolik R, et al.: Response of preterm infants to routine DTP immunizations. J Pediatr 107:184, 1985.

Bozynski MEA, Nelson MN, Matalont AS, et al.: Cavitary periventricular leukomalacia: Incidence and short-term outcome in infants weighing <1200 grams at birth. Dev Med Child Neurol 85:572, 1985.

Clancy RR: Neonatal seizures. In Stevenson DL and Sunshine P (eds): Fetal and Neonatal Brain Injury: Mechanisms, Management and the Risk of Practice. Philadelphia, BC Decker, 1989.

Cooper A, Floyd TF, Ross AJ, et al.: Morbidity and mortality of short-bowel syndrome acquired in infancy: An update. J Pediatr Surg 19:711, 1984.

Cryotherapy for Retinopathy of Prematurity Cooperative Group: Multicenter trial of cryotherapy for ROP. Arch Ophthalmol 106:471, 1988.

DeVries LS, Regey R, Pennock JM, et al.: Ultrasound evolution and later outcome of infants with periventricular densities. Early Hum Dev 16:225, 1988.

Escobar GJ, Littenberg B, and Petitti DB: Outcome among surviving very low birthweight infants: A meta-analysis. Arch Dis Child 66:204, 1991.

Ford LM, Han K, Steichan J, et al.: Very low-birth-weight, preterm infants with or without intracranial hemorrhage. Clin Pediatr 28:302, 1989.

Graziani LJ: Intracranial hemorrhage and leukomalacia in preterm infants. In Spitzer A (ed): Intensive Care of the Fetus and Neonate. St. Louis, Mosby–Year Book, 1996.

Graziani LJ, Pasto M, Stanley C, et al.: Neonatal neurosonographic correlates of cerebral palsy in preterm infants. Pediatrics 78:88, 1986.

Guyer B, Strobino DM, Ventura SJ, et al.: Annual Summary of Vital Statistics—1995. Pediatrics 98:1007, 1997.

Hack M and Fanaroff AA: Growth patterns in the ICN graduate. In Ballard RA (ed): Pediatric Care of the ICN Graduate. Philadelphia, WB Saunders, 1988.

Hack M, Taylor G, and Klein N: School age outcomes in children with birthweights under 750 grams. N Engl J Med 331:753, 1995.

Halsey CL, Collin MF, and Anderson CL: Extremely low birthweight children and their peers: A comparison of preschool performance. Pediatrics 91:807, 1993.

McCormick MC: Long term follow up of NICU graduates. JAMA 261:1767, 1989.

Vohr BR and Garcia CT: Neurodevelopmental and school performance of very low birth weight infants: A seven year longitudinal study. Pediatrics 76:345, 1995.

Yeh TF, McClenan DA, Ajayi OA, and Pildes RS: Metabolic rate and energy balance in infants with BPD. J Pediatr 114:448, 1989.

Armando G. Correa
Jeffrey R. Starke

Chapter 52

Tuberculosis

Tuberculosis has received much attention in the United States over the past decade because of its increased incidence, recognition of miniepidemics in locations such as hospitals and prisons, and the development of drug resistance caused mainly by poor adherence to treatment. Approximately 22,000 cases of tuberculosis occur annually in the United States; 10 million cases and 3 million deaths occur annually throughout the world. Between 10 and 20 million persons living in the United States are infected with *Mycobacterium tuberculosis* and are at risk for developing tuberculosis in the future if they are not tested and adequately treated.

Although the majority of children in the United States have little risk of becoming infected with *M. tuberculosis,* there are large pockets of children who are at specific risk of coming into contact with an infectious person (Table 52–1). Recently, the American Academy of Pediatrics (AAP) and Centers for Disease Control and Prevention (CDC) have emphasized seeking out and testing children who have specific risk factors while severely limiting or eliminating "routine" tuberculin skin testing among low-risk children. Mass testing should be curtailed because **the only available test to determine the presence of tuberculosis infection—the tuberculin skin test—has a relatively low specificity, making the vast majority of "positive" results in low-risk children falsely positive.**

EPIDEMIOLOGY

Although the incidence of tuberculosis in the United States increased by approximately 18% in all age groups from 1988 to 1994, the number of

TABLE 52–1. Children at Increased Risk of Tuberculosis Infection in the United States

Children who were born or resided in countries that have a high prevalence of tuberculosis

Children from families that have a recent history of tuberculosis

Foster children

Children who have present or past contact with adults who are or were:

    Residents of high-prevalence countries

    Residents of correctional institutions or long-term care facilities

    Homeless

    Users of intravenous or other drugs of abuse

    Infected with the human immunodeficiency virus

annual cases among children less than 15 years of age increased by approximately 40%, from 1188 to 1695. Because most pediatric tuberculosis cases arise from rapid progression (over weeks to months) of recent infection, this increase implies a high rate of recent transmission in specific communities. Infection with *M. tuberculosis* during childhood is also important in the sense that it adds to the "pool" of infected individuals from which future cases of contagious adult tuberculosis will arise.

A child's risk of acquiring infection with *M. tuberculosis* depends almost entirely on the likelihood that the child will "share air" with an adult who has contagious pulmonary tuberculosis (Table 52–1). Most experts have cited four major reasons for the increase in tuberculosis infection and disease over the past decade: (1) the coepidemic of human immunodeficiency virus (HIV) infection, because immune suppression from HIV is the most potent risk factor for development of tuberculosis in a previously infected adult; (2) increasing numbers and rates of tuberculosis among foreign-born persons in the United States, most of whom had untreated tuberculosis before immigration; (3) increased transmission of tuberculosis among adults in congregate settings such as prisons and jails, nursing homes, homeless shelters, and health care facilities; and (4) a decline in the tuberculosis public health infrastructure in many regions and cities. All four of these issues also have affected rates of infection and disease among children, although the decline in public health infrastructure—with the resultant deleterious effect on contact investigations around new cases—probably has had the greatest impact on pediatric tuberculosis case rates.

High tuberculosis rates always have occurred among the socioeconomically deprived, especially recent immigrants. In 1994, 23% of U.S. childhood tuberculosis cases occurred among the for-

eign-born. Minority children accounted for 86% of childhood cases; the relative risk of tuberculosis for children younger than 15 years of age compared with white, non-Hispanic children was 11.08 for black and 13.36 for Hispanic children. Several studies also have shown increased rates of childhood tuberculosis associated with increased rates of tuberculosis among HIV-infected adults in the community. In many areas, the demographic groups that have the greatest tuberculosis morbidity also have large numbers of HIV-infected adults.

Transmission of *M. tuberculosis* is from one human to another, usually via infected airborne droplets of mucus that can remain suspended in the air for hours. Children who have pulmonary tuberculosis are rarely, if ever, contagious. This probably is related to the relatively sparse load of *M. tuberculosis* bacilli in the typical intrathoracic lesion in this age group, absence of a productive cough, and lack of a forceful cough mechanism. Adolescents who have tuberculosis can develop upper lobe infiltrates, cavities, and a productive cough that resembles disease in adulthood; these patients should be considered contagious until it can be shown otherwise.

PATHOGENESIS

Inhalation of infected droplets is the source of tuberculosis infection in the vast majority of children. Congenital infection by lymphohematogenous spread during pregnancy or aspiration of contaminated amniotic fluid is rare.

Symptomatic lymphohematogenous spread from a pulmonary focus, leading to tuberculous meningitis or miliary disease, occurs in only 0.5% to 3% of untreated infected children, usually 3 to 6 months after the initial infection. Most intrathoracic tuberculosis in children develops within 4 to 12 months of infection. In young children, the first year after infection is particularly "critical" for the development of the most serious complications of this disease. Lesions of the bones or joints usually do not appear for at least a year after the infection, and renal tuberculosis may take more than 5 years to develop.

In adults, the estimated risk for progression of the untreated infection to disease is 5% to 10% during their lifetime. This risk is increased markedly to 7% to 10% per year among those coinfected with HIV. Among children, the likelihood of an untreated infection developing into tuberculosis depends on the age at the time of the primary infection, with rates as high as 40% for those younger than 2 years of age, 15% to 25% for children 2 to 5 years of age, and 5% to 15% among older children and adolescents.

CLINICAL FEATURES OF TUBERCULOSIS IN CHILDREN

Stages of Tuberculosis

There are three basic stages of tuberculosis in children: exposure, infection, and disease. *Exposure* implies that the child has had significant contact with an adolescent or adult in whom contagious pulmonary tuberculosis is suspected or confirmed. The most frequent setting for exposure is the household, but occasionally it can be a school, child care center, or other environment. In this stage the tuberculin skin test is negative, the chest radiograph is normal, and there are no signs or symptoms of disease. At this time it is not possible to determine if the child is truly infected because it may take up to 3 months for a positive tuberculin skin test to develop after the organisms are inhaled. In children, particularly those younger than 6 years of age, severe tuberculosis can occur in less than 3 months because of the short incubation period of pulmonary, disseminated, and central nervous system tuberculosis. Although exposed adults usually are not treated but receive a second skin test 3 months after last contact with the contagious source case, young children (<5 years old) in the exposure stage should receive chemotherapy until infection has been excluded.

The hallmark of tuberculosis *infection* is a reactive Mantoux tuberculin skin test, with no signs or symptoms of tuberculosis and a chest radiograph that either is normal or reveals only granuloma or calcification in the lung parenchyma and/or regional lymph nodes. Although selected adults 35 years of age or older may not be treated, virtually all infected children should receive a course of chemotherapy to prevent future disease.

Tuberculosis *disease* occurs when signs or symptoms or radiographic manifestations caused by *M. tuberculosis* became apparent. In adults, the distinction between tuberculosis infection and disease is usually clear because disease often is the result of reactivation of previously dormant organisms years after infection. In the pediatric patient, this distinction is less clear because disease more often complicates the initial infection. Adults who have disease almost always have significant symptoms and radiographic abnormalities, whereas up to 50% of children who have disease may be asymptomatic and their radiographic abnormalities subtle. Most of these relatively asymp-

tomatic children who have tuberculosis are discovered by the contact investigation of an adult case.

Pulmonary and Intrathoracic Tuberculosis

The spectrum of pulmonary involvement caused by *M. tuberculosis* in children can range from none in an asymptomatic infection to progressive pulmonary tuberculosis. The beginning of the tuberculosis infection in children typically is asymptomatic. Occasionally, the child may have nonspecific symptoms such as low-grade fever, malaise, and cough. Every primary infection leads to lymphangitis and regional lymphadenitis, which can be enhanced by the development of tuberculin hypersensitivity. However, in most children these lymph node changes cannot be detected clinically or radiographically. The child remains asymptomatic and the radiograph remains normal more commonly among school-age children (80% to 90%) than among infants younger than 1 year of age (40% to 50%). In some children, as the hilar lymph nodes enlarge, bronchial narrowing caused by extrinsic compression may lead to air trapping. Partial bronchial obstruction also can occur when the infected node erodes into a bronchus, leading to deposition of caseous material within the lumen and a subsequent ball-valve effect (endobronchial tuberculosis). As the obstruction worsens, complete airway obstruction with reabsorption of air can occur, causing atelectasis and infiltrate (Fig. 52–1). These changes cause the appearance of a segmental lesion in one or more lobes of the lung. Other radiographic findings in pediatric pulmonary tuberculosis can include lobar infiltrates, adenopathy alone, or rarely, a cavity. **Even in the presence of extensive pulmonary disease, many children are asymptomatic at the time of diagnosis.** Infants, however, are more likely to present with localized wheezing, persistent cough, fever, anorexia, and weight loss.

Tuberculous pleural effusions arising from a subpleural focus are rare in children younger than 2 years of age and uncommon in children younger than 5 years of age. Symptoms usually are acute, with fever, chest pain, and shortness of breath. Tuberculous pleural effusion cannot be distinguished from any other cause of pleural infection solely on clinical or radiographic grounds.

Extrathoracic Disease

Miliary or disseminated tuberculosis is an early complication of the infection. It is caused by the release of a large amount of bacilli into the circu-

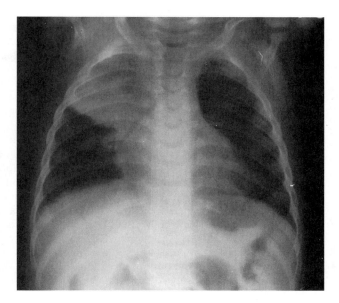

Figure 52–1. Typical appearance of a segmental lesion of tuberculosis in the chest radiograph of a child.

lation, leading to development of disease in two or more organs. Children, particularly infants, are more prone to develop miliary disease than are adults. The clinical presentation varies greatly depending on the number of bacilli discharged into the blood and where they lodge. The onset may be insidious or acute, and signs and symptoms include persistent fever, weight loss, hepatomegaly, splenomegaly, generalized lymphadenopathy, and eventually, respiratory distress. Approximately 30% to 50% of children who have miliary disease have meningitis at the time of diagnosis.

The most feared complication of tuberculosis is tuberculous meningitis. Up to 3% of children infected but not treated before 2 years of age develop this form of tuberculosis; the frequency drops to 1% or less later in life. Meningitis usually occurs within 3 to 6 months after the initial infection. The presentation usually is subacute, with nonspecific symptoms such as anorexia, weight loss, and fever followed by headache and neck stiffness, eventually leading to alteration in consciousness, stupor, seizures, and the emergence of focal signs. Typical cerebrospinal fluid (CSF) findings include a moderate lymphocytic pleocytosis, a low glucose level, and an elevated protein concentration. Hyponatremia due to inappropriate secretion of antidiuretic hormone is seen frequently. Abnormal chest radiographs are seen in most children who have tuberculous meningitis. The tuberculin skin test can be negative in 40% of children at the time of diagnosis.

Mycobacterial lymphadenitis, which occurs most often in the neck, usually causes a slow, nontender enlargement of one or several nodes, with an absence of systemic signs or symptoms. Of the mycobacteria isolated from lymph nodes of children younger than 12 years old, 65% to 80% are *Mycobacterium avium-intracellulare* complex, 10% to 20% are *Mycobacterium scrofulaceum,* and approximately 10% are *M. tuberculosis.* In most cases of nontuberculous mycobacterial lymph node disease, the children are young (<4 years old), the chest radiograph is normal, the tuberculin skin test reaction is less than 12 mm, and no adult family members have tuberculosis disease or even infection. By contrast, more than 90% of culture-proved mycobacterial lymphadenitis in children older than 12 years and in adults is caused by *M. tuberculosis.* Because the distinction between lymph node disease caused by *M. tuberculosis* and nontuberculous mycobacteria is frequently difficult on clinical grounds, surgical excision usually is necessary for both diagnostic and therapeutic (in the case of nontuberculous mycobacteria) reasons.

Bone and/or joint tuberculosis complicates 1% to 6% of untreated infections with *M. tuberculosis* in children. Spinal involvement is seen in 50% to 65% of pediatric cases of skeletal tuberculosis; other less common sites include the femur, tibia, and fibula. The clinical and radiographic presentation varies widely and depends primarily on the stage of disease at the time of evaluation. Skeletal tuberculosis may go unrecognized for months to years because of its indolent nature and the lack of specific signs or symptoms.

Other unusual sites for tuberculosis in children include the middle ear, gastrointestinal tract, skin, kidneys, and ocular structures.

DIAGNOSIS

Tuberculin Skin Test

Most experts agree that the Mantoux tuberculin skin test, using a standardized preparation of 5 tuberculin units of purified protein derivative (PPD) administered intradermally, is the only technique acceptable in the evaluation of children and that multiple puncture devices should no longer be used because of their inherent inaccuracy and limitations. Application of the Mantoux test becomes fairly simple with some practice and use of a special technique for children (Fig. 52–2). The injection of 0.1 mL of tuberculin should cause an immediate wheal of 5 to 8 mm, which is reabsorbed over the next hour. The test should be interpreted at 48 to 72 hours after placement *only by a trained health care professional;* parents never should be allowed to interpret the test because many studies have shown that they cannot do so with adequate accuracy. The diameter of the induration (not erythema) should be measured and recorded in millimeters in the medical record. Use of the words "negative" and "positive" is discouraged because interpretation can change if additional epidemiologic information becomes available.

The usual sensitivity and specificity of the Mantoux skin test is 90% to 95%. When a test that has a sensitivity and specificity of 90% is applied to a low-risk population—an incidence of true infection of *M. tuberculosis* below 5%—the vast majority of "positive" results will be falsely positive, created by biologic variability, nonspecific reactions, and infection by nontuberculous mycobacteria. Because the skin test is the only test to detect tuberculosis infection, true positives cannot be distinguished from false positives by further testing. These false-positive results lead to unnecessary treatment, costs, and anxiety for the patient, family, and clinician. The low sensitivity and especially specificity of the tuberculin skin test make it undesirable for use in low-risk persons and is why mass testing or universal screening is not helpful in tuberculosis control. The trend in the United States is to reduce or eliminate the routine testing (including school-based testing) of low-risk children, which has been shown to be neither effective nor cost-beneficial, but to target children who have risk factors for one-time or periodic testing.

The classification of the tuberculin skin test response must take into account epidemiologic and clinical factors. In recent years the CDC and AAP have recommended varying the size of induration considered positive in different groups of people (Table 52–2). This is an attempt to minimize false-negative results among children most likely to have rapid progression of tuberculosis infection to disease and minimize false-positive results in children who have no risk factors for tuberculosis. For children at the highest risk of infection and rapid progression, particularly those who have had exposure to contagious cases of tuberculosis, a reactive area ≥5 mm is classified as positive. For other high-risk groups, a reactive area ≥10 mm is positive. For children who have no discernible risk (older than 4 years of age), a reaction ≥15 mm is a positive result. **In general,**

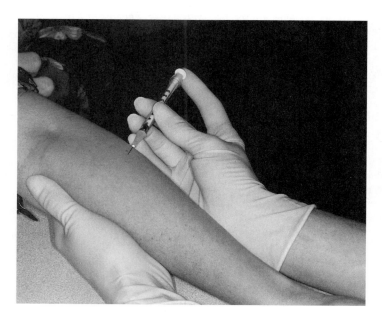

Figure 52–2. A useful technique for the application of the Mantoux tuberculin skin test on a small child. The placer anchors her hand on the side of the child's arm and injects the tuberculin in the transverse direction.

TABLE 52–2. Cutoff Size of Reactive Area for Positive Mantoux Tuberculin Reaction

≥ 5 mm	≥10 mm	≥15 mm
Persons in contact with infectious cases	Children born, or who have lived, in high-prevalence countries	Children ≥4 years of age who have no risk factors
Persons who have an abnormal chest radiograph	Residents of prisons or jails, nursing homes, institutions	
Persons who have HIV and other infections	Users of intravenous street drugs	
Children who are immunosuppressed	Those who have other medical risk factors, e.g., malnutrition, diabetes	
	Locally identified high-risk populations	
	Children in close contact with high-risk adults	
	Children <4 years of age	

Modified from American Academy of Pediatrics. Tuberculosis. *In* Peter G (ed): 1997 Red Book: Report of the Committee on Infectious Diseases, 24th ed. Elk Grove Village, IL, AAP, 1997, p 541. Used with permission of the American Academy of Pediatrics.

previous receipt of a bacille Calmette-Guérin
(BCG) vaccine should not influence whether a
child receives a tuberculin skin test and how
the initial skin test is interpreted.

Any child who has a reactive tuberculin skin
test should have a thorough physical examination,
a careful history taken for possible exposure to or
risk for tuberculosis, and a posterior-anterior and
lateral chest radiograph. It is crucial to search for
the possible source case for the child because the
drug susceptibility testing of the organism from
this source case is frequently the only information
available to determine the proper treatment for
that child. In some cases, the local health department will test family contacts, but in some cases
the clinician should perform this task.

Radiography

Although the presence of one or several small
granulomas or calcifications in the lung parenchyma or hilar or mediastinal lymph nodes is
common in reaction to the presence of *M. tuberculosis,* these findings are treated as tuberculosis
infection rather than disease. **Lymphadenopathy,
typically involving the hilar or paratracheal
nodes, is the hallmark of pulmonary tuberculosis disease in childhood.** However, if the atelectasis and/or infiltrate is extensive, it may be difficult
to visualize the enlarged nodes specifically. Radiographically, the hilar region may be difficult to
evaluate with a posterior-anterior view alone,
hence the importance of always including a lateral
view when evaluating a child who possibly has
tuberculosis.

Bronchial obstruction leading to a segmental
lesion is manifested by a fan-shaped lesion on a
radiograph (see Fig. 52–1). This lesion is characterized by atelectasis and consolidation of the involved area. Other radiographic pulmonary mani-

festations include linear, interstitial, and nodular
densities; thin-walled cavitation within consolidation; focal emphysema; bronchiectasis; or a focal
mass.

Tuberculous meningitis has a predilection for
the base of the brain. Computed tomography (CT)
or magnetic resonance imaging (MRI) can reveal
basal inflammation, hydrocephalus, and focal pa-
renchymal abnormalities such as tuberculomas or
infarction. If any of these findings are seen in a
child who has meningitis, treatment for tuberculosis should be started immediately while the diagnostic evaluation and contact investigation are carried out.

Microbiologic Methods

Because children 12 years of age or younger
rarely are able to produce sputum and expectorate
voluntarily, early morning gastric aspirates are
used for isolation of *M. tuberculosis.* This requires
the insertion of a nasogastric tube in an inpatient
setting because the sensitivity of outpatient gastric
aspirates has been extremely low. Acid-fast staining of these samples is rarely positive. The culture
yield of three consecutive morning gastric aspirates for *M. tuberculosis* in children is only 30%
to 50%, although the yield from infants can be as
high as 70%. The culture yield for other body
fluids from children who have extrapulmonary disease is usually less than 50%. Fortunately, it is
not necessary to obtain cultures from most children who have tuberculosis if the adult source
case has been identified and drug susceptibility
information on his or her isolate of *M. tuberculosis*
is available. In general, cultures are necessary only
when the source case is unknown or the diagnosis
is unclear, especially in an immunocompromised
child.

MANAGEMENT

Directly Observed Therapy

The major problem in the management of the stages of tuberculosis is poor adherence to drug therapy (Table 52–3) by the child and family. Giving antituberculosis medications to children is particularly difficult because, essentially, there are no practical, usable preparations designed for pediatric use. Pills must be crushed and messy suspensions concocted to allow an infant or young child to take the medications. It is important to try to keep the taking of medicine as positive an experience as possible by use of incentives and enablers for the child and parents.

Many studies have shown that in tuberculosis, as with all chronic diseases, at least 30% to 50% of patients will have significant difficulty following the prescribed drug regimen. Adherence worsens as the number of drugs increases. **Because nonadherence with antituberculosis treatment can lead to relapse and the creation and transmission to others of drug-resistant organisms, a system called** *directly observed therapy (DOT)* **should be used to treat virtually all patients who have tuberculosis disease and some high-risk patients who have tuberculosis infection or exposure.** DOT means that a third party—usually a health care worker from the health department, although it can be a school nurse, teacher, or other responsible adult—observes, in person, the administration of each dose of medication. Use of DOT also allows medications to be given twice a week instead of every day, a schedule that has been shown to be highly effective for the treatment of drug-susceptible tuberculosis.

Exposure to Tuberculosis

Every child who has had significant contact with an adult or adolescent who has suspected pulmonary tuberculosis should receive a skin test, physical examination, and chest radiographs. Exposed children 5 years of age or younger should begin treatment immediately. The decision to treat exposed older children is more controversial; some experts treat them, especially if younger siblings are to be treated, while others do not treat them, but repeat the skin test in 3 months.

Treatment is based on the established or likely drug susceptibilities of the organism from the source case. At the current level of isoniazid resistance in the United States, this remains the drug of choice for exposure. If the person is known to have isoniazid-resistant but rifampin-susceptible organisms, rifampin is the recommended drug. Children treated for exposure should receive treatment until 3 months after contact with the source case has been broken. If a skin test at this time is negative (i.e., ≤5 mm reaction), the child's treatment can be stopped; if the repeat test is positive, infection has occurred and the child should receive a 9-month course of treatment.

Newborn infants may become exposed to their mother or other family member who has previously undiagnosed pulmonary tuberculosis. In general, these infants can be treated in the same way as other exposed children. There is no reason to restrict contact with the mother or breastfeeding if the adult and child are receiving adequate, directly observed treatment and pyridoxine is given to the infant to prevent neurologic complications of isoniazid treatment.

Special circumstances can complicate treatment

TABLE 52–3. Commonly Used Drugs for the Treatment of Tuberculosis in Children

Drugs	Dosage Forms	Daily Dose, mg/kg/day	Twice-Weekly Dose, mg/kg/dose	Maximum Dose
Ethambutol	Tablets: 100 mg, 400 mg	15–25	50	2.5 gm
Isoniazid	Scored tablets: 100 mg, 300 mg Syrup: 10 mg/mL	10–15	20–30	Daily: 300 mg; twice weekly: 900 mg
Pyrazinamide	Scored tablets: 500 mg	20–40	50	2 gm
Rifampin	Capsules: 150 mg, 300 mg Syrup: formulated in syrup from capsules	10–20	10–20	600 mg
Streptomycin*	Vials: 1 gm, 4 gm	20–40	20–40	1 gm

*Administered intramuscularly.

decisions for exposed children. One of them is the presence of isoniazid and rifampin resistance, known as multidrug resistance (MDR), in the source case. Some experts attempt to treat particularly vulnerable children exposed to MDR tuberculosis with two drugs to which the organism is susceptible; others elect to withhold treatment in lieu of very close observation. The combinations used most commonly are pyrazinamide and ethambutol, or ethionamide and cycloserine. An expert in tuberculosis should always be consulted in these cases.

Tuberculosis Infection

The purpose of treating asymptomatic tuberculosis infection is to prevent the development of tuberculosis disease in the near or distant future. This treatment also has been called "preventive therapy" or "chemoprophylaxis." At present, the AAP and CDC recommend a 6- to 9-month course of isoniazid for children who have tuberculosis infection. Children who have HIV infection and tuberculosis infection should receive therapy for 1 year. Although there are no published studies that demonstrate the effectiveness of twice-weekly therapy (under DOT) for tuberculosis infection, this regimen may be justified in certain situations in which risk of progression to disease is high and adherence to the regimen is difficult. In several communities, isoniazid may be administered twice weekly to school-age children by school nurses on campus to overcome adherence problems in the home.

Rifampin treatment for 9 months is recommended for children infected with *M. tuberculosis* that is resistant to isoniazid but susceptible to rifampin. The best treatment for tuberculosis infection that is resistant to both isoniazid and rifampin is more difficult and uncertain because less effective drugs that have higher rates of adverse reactions must be used. Most experts recommend treatment with two drugs to which the organism is susceptible (i.e., the combination of pyrazinamide and ethambutol). Consultation from an expert should be sought when planning a treatment regimen for MDR tuberculosis infection or disease in children.

Treatment of tuberculosis infection in children with isoniazid has proved to be very safe. The incidence of asymptomatic elevation in serum liver enzymes is less than 2% and of clinical hepatitis, less than 1%. Routine testing of blood chemistries and serum liver enzymes is unnecessary unless the child has hepatic disease or dysfunction or is taking other potentially hepatotoxic drugs. In lieu of blood testing, frequent examinations (every 4 to 6 weeks) by the clinician are recommended to monitor for adverse reactions and adherence with treatment. Although isoniazid may lower the serum concentration of pyridoxine (vitamin B_6) in children, clinical manifestations—for example, peripheral neuritis—are very rare. Routine co-administration of pyridoxine is recommended only for breast-fed babies, pregnant women and adolescents, and persons whose diet is lacking in this vitamin.

Treatment of Tuberculosis Disease

If the child has a reactive tuberculin skin test, clinical and/or radiographic findings suggestive of tuberculosis, and previous contact with an adult who has infectious tuberculosis, the child should be treated for tuberculosis disease. The drug susceptibility test results from the source-case isolate can be used to determine the optimal treatment for the child. However, cultures should be obtained from a child who has tuberculosis when (1) the source case is unknown; (2) the likely source case has a drug-resistant organism; (3) the child has extrapulmonary disease; or (4) the child is immunocompromised, especially by HIV infection.

Currently, the AAP, CDC, and American Thoracic Society recommend that standard treatment for drug-susceptible thoracic tuberculosis in children be 6 months of isoniazid and rifampin supplemented during the first 2 months with pyrazinamide. If the risk for initial isoniazid resistance is significant, a fourth drug, usually ethambutol or streptomycin, should be given until drug susceptibility information is known. Ophthalmologic toxicity in children has not been reported at an ethambutol dose of 15 mg/kg day. As soon as isoniazid and rifampin susceptibility is established or considered likely, the fourth drug can be discontinued. Regimens using twice-weekly treatment under the direct observation of a health care worker are as safe and effective as those using daily therapy.

In general, the three-drug, 6-month regimen used for pulmonary tuberculosis appears to be effective for most forms of extrapulmonary disease. One exception may be bone and joint tuberculosis, which may require treatment for 9 to 12 months, especially if surgery is not performed. The AAP also recommends treating tuberculous meningitis for 12 months, starting initially with four drugs.

The optimal treatment of tuberculosis in HIV-infected children has not been established. Most experts believe that the initial regimens should be the same as for non–HIV-infected children but that the total treatment should be extended 9 to 12 months. However, because HIV infection and drug resistance in *M. tuberculosis* may be linked, most experts would use at least four drugs initially to treat an HIV-infected child who has suspected tuberculosis.

Treatment for drug-resistant tuberculosis in children is successful only when at least two bactericidal drugs to which the organism is susceptible are given. The specific regimen, which should be designed with the help of a tuberculosis expert, must be individualized for each patient according to available drug susceptibility information and the patient's tolerance of the various drugs and should be given for 12 to 24 months.

Follow-Up Care

The rate of adverse reactions to antituberculosis drugs is low enough in children that routine biochemical monitoring is not necessary. If the child has had hepatitis or a chronic illness, it may be advisable to obtain a baseline set of serum liver enzyme levels. If the patient or family reports any symptoms that could be caused by the drugs, a physical examination should be performed and serum liver enzyme levels determined. Serum liver enzyme elevations of two to three times normal are fairly common and do not require discontinuation of the drugs if all other findings are normal. Mild arthralgias can be caused by pyrazinamide but usually are transient, even when pyrazinamide is continued. Frequent examination of visual acuity and color discrimination is recommended when ethambutol is used. Hearing should be evaluated periodically whenever streptomycin is used.

Radiographic improvement of intrathoracic adenitis and pulmonary disease caused by tuberculosis occurs very slowly. Frequently, chest radiography is not helpful. In cases of tuberculosis infection, no repeat chest radiograph is needed unless the child develops signs and symptoms that require further evaluation. A common practice when treating tuberculosis disease is to obtain a chest radiograph at diagnosis and at 1 to 2 months into treatment to be sure that no progression or complications have occurred. If these studies are satisfactory, it is not necessary to repeat the chest radiograph until the anticipated end of treatment. However, the majority of children who have intrathoracic adenopathy caused by tuberculosis have abnormal radiographic images for 1 to 3 years, long after effective antituberculosis treatment has been stopped. A normal chest radiograph is not necessary to discontinue treatment. If improvement has occurred after 6 months of treatment, the drugs can be stopped and chest radiographs repeated at 6- to 12-month intervals until they become normal or stable.

PREVENTION AND PUBLIC HEALTH

The control of tuberculosis, for a community and for individuals, depends on close cooperation between the primary care clinician and the local health department. It is imperative that clinicians report all cases of tuberculosis to the health department as soon as possible. Public health law in all states requires that the *suspicion* of tuberculosis disease in an adult or child be reported immediately to the health department. The clinician should not wait for microbiologic confirmation of the diagnosis because it is this reporting that leads to the initiation of the contact investigation that may find infected children and allow them to be treated before disease occurs. If the clinician waits for confirmatory laboratory results, the child may progress from infection to disease before intervention. The clinician always should feel free to contact the local health department about special issues involving tuberculosis exposure, infection, or disease in a child. Not every clinical situation can be anticipated by normal guidelines, and in some cases, an unusual intervention may be warranted.

Much of the focus on tuberculin skin-testing now is on identification of risk factors for a child being in a group that has high prevalence of infection. Although some risk factors may apply nationwide, local health departments must identify those that are germane to their own area. Clinicians and their organizations must work closely with local health departments to establish which children need testing. Health departments should advise school districts whether any type of school-based skin testing is appropriate and what nature it should take. Obviously, social and political problems can occur when selective testing is suggested. What is correct from a public health point of view may not be easy to translate into a workable and generally acceptable policy. Local clinicians can be extremely helpful to health departments in advancing prudent and reasonable tuberculosis control policies, particularly when other government or public agencies are involved.

FURTHER READING

American Academy of Pediatrics. Tuberculosis. *In* Peter G (ed): 1997 Red Book: Report of the Committee on Infectious Diseases, 24th ed. Elk Grove Village, IL, AAP, 1997, p 541.

American Thoracic Society: Treatment of tuberculosis infection in adults and children. Am J Respir Crit Care Med 149:1359, 1994.

Brudney K and Dobkin J: Resurgent tuberculosis in New York City: Human immunodeficiency virus, homelessness and the decline of tuberculosis control programs. Am Rev Respir Dis 144:745, 1991.

Centers for Disease Control and Prevention: Screening for tuberculosis and tuberculosis infection in high-risk populations. MMWR 44 (RR-11):19, 1995.

Doerr CA, Starke JR, and Ong LT: Clinical and public health aspects of tuberculous meningitis in children. J Pediatr 127:27, 1995.

Huebner RE, Schein MF, and Bass JB: The tuberculin skin test. Clin Infect Dis 17:968, 1993.

Hussey G, Chisolm T, and Kibel M: Miliary tuberculosis in children: A review of 94 cases. Pediatr Infect Dis J 10:832, 1991.

Kochi A: The global tuberculosis situation and the new control strategy of the World Health Organization. Tubercle 72:1, 1991.

Lincoln EM, Davies PA, and Bovornkitti S: Tuberculous pleurisy with effusion in children. Am Rev Tuberc 77:271, 1995.

McKenna MT, McCray E, and Onorato IM: The epidemiology of tuberculosis among foreign-born persons in the United States, 1986 to 1993. N Engl J Med 332:1071, 1995.

Moehl-Boetani JC, Miller B, Halpern M, et al.: School-based screening for tuberculous infection: A cost benefit analysis. JAMA 274:613, 1995.

Morrison JB: Natural history of segmental lesions in primary pulmonary tuberculosis. Arch Dis Child 48:90, 1973.

Starke JR and Correa AG: Management of mycobacterial infection and disease in children. Pediatr Infect Dis J 14:455, 1995.

Starke JR, Jacobs RF, and Jereb J: Resurgence of tuberculosis in children. J Pediatr 120:839, 1992.

Starke JR and Smith MHD: Tuberculosis. In Feigin RD and Cherry JD (eds): Textbook of Pediatric Infectious Diseases, 4th ed. Philadelphia, WB Saunders, 1998, pp 1196–1238.

Ussery XT, Valway SE, McKenna M, et al.: Epidemiology of tuberculosis among children in the United States: 1985 to 1994. Pediatr Infect Dis J 15:697, 1996.

Vallejo JG, Ong LT, and Starke JR: Clinical features, diagnosis and treatment of tuberculosis in infants. Pediatrics 94:1, 1994.

William H. Dietz

Chapter 5 3

Obesity

Childhood obesity presents one of the most frustrating and intractable problems in pediatric practice. In this chapter, the current approach to the assessment and treatment of obesity in children and adolescents is reviewed.

ASSESSMENT

The first step in the assessment of an obese child or adolescent is to determine the degree of overweight. The body mass index (BMI: wt(kg)/ht²(m²) represents the most appropriate index for this assessment. The BMI provides a valid and reliable measure that correlates well with more basic measures of total body fat. Furthermore, use of the 95th percentile to identify adolescents who are significantly overweight has been proposed as a screening criterion by an expert committee.

An algorithm that can be used for screening children and adolescents is shown in Figure 53–1. **Use of the 95th percentile to identify an individual as overweight does not confirm that they are excessively fat. Ancillary measures such as the triceps skinfold thickness are essential to confirm that the excess weight is fat rather than frame size or muscle mass.** Furthermore, if obesity is confirmed by an increase in triceps skinfold thickness, routine laboratory tests should include (1) a fasting insulin determination and (2) a lipoprotein profile. If symptoms suggestive of sleep apnea are present, a sleep study should be performed.

Children and adolescents who are between the 85th and 95th percentiles of BMI should be considered at risk of being overweight. If children in this category have a positive family history of parental obesity, cardiovascular disease, hypercholesterolemia, or diabetes mellitus, an elevated blood pressure, a recent large change in BMI, or excessive concern about weight, they should be assessed as outlined above for individuals whose BMI is greater than the 95th percentile.

Unless obesity is contributing to other serious biologic, psychological, or social problems, the most important aspect of the assessment of overweight children and adolescents is therapeutic neutrality. Many families feel defensive about their child's obesity and anticipate that they will be held responsible for the problem. However, open-ended questions about parents' degree of concern about the child's weight and questions to children about whether their weight causes prob-

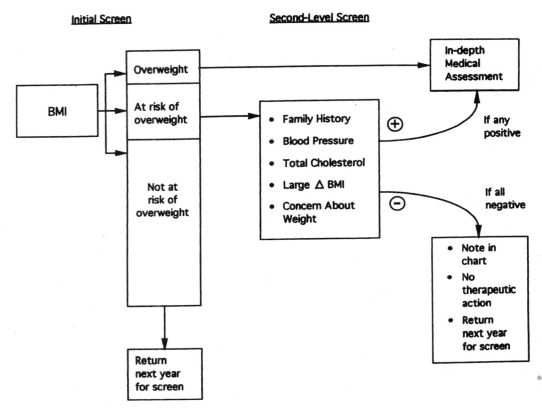

Figure 53–1. Algorithm to screen children and adolescents for treatment of obesity. BMI, body mass index. (From Himes JH, Dietz WH: Guidelines for overweight in adolescent preventive services: Recommendations from an expert committee. Am J Clin Nutr 59:307–316, 1994.)

lems for them in social situations may help establish the priority of the child's obesity within the family. If parents are not concerned about the problem, if there is no indication that the child's weight has an adverse effect on social interactions, and if the child is free of adverse health effects of obesity, the primary care clinician should share with the family his or her concerns about weight, but make no prescription for change. **Therapeutic efforts should focus on families who are concerned about their child's weight and are ready to change.** Furthermore, because the likelihood of spontaneous remission of obesity among children younger than 5 years of age is high, weight reduction efforts should probably focus on older children or on children whose weight problems are more severe.

If parents and their children are concerned about the problem, questions about what the family thinks caused the problem, what they have already done about it, or whether anything can be done about it may help establish whether the family is prepared to change.

Energy intake and activity represent the only discretionary components of energy balance. Therefore, a history of dietary intake and activity helps identify the behavioral targets necessary to achieve weight maintenance or loss. **A dietary history neither provides valid estimates of caloric intake nor indicates the reduction in calories necessary to achieve weight change. However, a brief history of the patient's usual food intake at breakfast, lunch, dinner, and snack times; the frequency over the last 7 days with which the child consumed fast food, candy, ice cream, or frozen yogurt, chips, and cookies; and the quantity of milk, juice, and soda consumed should provide several potential targets for change.** A history of time spent in vigorous play, time spent outside with friends, and the usual time spent viewing television provides a profile of the general activity level.

Virtually all of the recognized causes and consequences of childhood obesity can be identified by a careful history and physical examination. All of the recognized causes are rare compared with the usual "idiopathic" type. Sensorineural problems such as impaired vision or deafness, dysmorphic features, gonadal dysfunction, short stature, or developmental delay should prompt a careful search for one of the genetic or endocrine syndromes associated with obesity (Table 53–1). Headaches in an adolescent suggest the possibility of pseudotumor cerebri. Children at risk for sleep apnea or the obesity hypoventilation syndrome can be identified by questions regarding snoring, the number of pillows used, posture during sleep, or daytime somnolence. Shortness of breath on activity indicates a functional limitation of obesity. Abdominal pain may suggest gallbladder disease, particularly if recent weight loss has occurred, or gastroesophageal reflux owing to increased intra-abdominal pressure. Delayed menarche or oligomenorrhea may suggest polycystic ovary disease or gonadal dysfunction. Hip pain should prompt a radiograph of the hip to exclude slipped capital femoral epiphysis.

Approximately 50% of all children who have hypertension are obese. Therefore, a careful blood pressure determination with an appropriate-size cuff is essential. Inspection of the skin may reveal coarsely thickened pigmented skin at the neck, axilla, or intertriginal folds known as acanthosis nigricans. Acanthosis nigricans is associated with glucose intolerance and an increased risk of non–insulin-dependent diabetes mellitus. Papilledema found on the fundoscopic examination suggests pseudotumor. Undescended testicles in association with short stature suggests Prader-Willi syndrome. Bowing of the lower extremities occurs in Blount disease; 75% of all children who have Blount disease are overweight.

TREATMENT

The suggestions that follow apply to children or adolescents who are mildly or moderately overweight. Children who have significant morbidity

TABLE 53–1. Clinical Syndromes Associated with Childhood Obesity

Alström-Hallgren syndrome
Carpenter syndrome
Cohen syndrome
Cushing syndrome
Growth hormone deficiency
Hyperinsulinemia
Hypothalamic dysfunction or tumor
Hypothyroidism
Laurence-Moon-Biedl syndrome
Polycystic ovary disease
Prader-Labhart-Willi syndrome
Pseudohypoparathyroidism
Turner syndrome

associated with their obesity should be treated by a specialist who has the expertise necessary to implement aggressive weight reduction therapy. Such children include those who have pseudotumor, sleep apnea, primary alveolar hypoventilation, slipped capital femoral epiphysis, or Blount disease. No consensus yet exists regarding the most appropriate therapy for obese adolescents who are 200% or greater in excess of their ideal body weight.

The first goal in any overweight patient is weight maintenance. For example, the average child between the ages of 6 and 12 years gains approximately 5 kg per year. Therefore, weight maintenance is comparable to the loss of 5 kg per year. **After weight maintenance is achieved, the next goal is modest weight loss.** In cases of mild to moderate obesity, the goal again should be small quantities of weight loss. **Emphasis should be on small, incremental, permanent behavioral changes rather than major transient changes.**

Because parents usually control the food that is purchased, how food is prepared, and the times at which food is consumed, the family should become the initial focus of the assessment and treatment plan. Care of the adolescent is trickier. Involvement of the family in the initial assessment is crucial to establish the adolescent's degree of autonomy. The clinician must determine whether the adolescent's weight is a source of conflict within the family and whether the focus of therapy should be the adolescent or the family.

As indicated earlier, **only energy intake and the energy spent on activity are discretionary. Therefore, therapy must focus on energy intake and energy expenditure.** Interventions directed at energy intake should address not only the foods that are consumed, but also the pattern of eating. Reductions in dietary fat alone under conditions of ad libitum food intake show only modest effects on body weight in adults. No significant differences in growth or BMI were observed among children on low fat (30% of calories) diets for a 1-year period, compared with children whose intake of fat was unrestricted. These observations suggest that changes in dietary fat alone probably will not produce significant weight loss.

The dietary assessment should identify one or more foods that can be targeted for change. The strategy in these circumstances should acknowledge that there are no good foods or bad foods, but only foods that can be consumed frequently, in moderation, or on special occasions. Food consumed outside the home generally contains more calories and larger portions than food consumed at home. The intake of calorie-containing fluids may account for a substantial proportion of caloric intake. Children should be limited to approximately 24 ounces of low-fat or skim milk and 4 to 8 ounces of juice per day. Water consumption to satisfy thirst should be encouraged.

Both activity and inactivity also should be addressed. In general, children will play if provided the opportunity. Attention to time spent outdoors or the opportunity to play with friends may help identify potential interventions. Television time has been linked directly to obesity. In treatment programs that involved parents and reduced intake of high-calorie foods, reductions in television time achieved significantly better short-term and long-term weight losses in children than did increases in activity. Furthermore, when children were encouraged to reduce television time, their attitudes toward vigorous activity were more positive than the attitudes of children who were encouraged to increase their activity. The improved attitudes probably reflected the free choice of activity made by children who are encouraged to decrease inactivity and the forced choice made by children who are encouraged to increase their activity.

The recent use of drugs to treat obesity in adults and the approval of several new weight reduction drugs by the Food and Drug Administration has focused attention on use of medications to treat childhood and adolescent obesity. Use of phentermine and D,L-fenfluramine in adolescents has not produced weight losses of the magnitude observed in adults. Nonetheless, the cardiac effects associated with the use of phentermine and fenfluramine in adults stress the importance and safety of lifestyle modification in the prevention and treatment of obesity. **Use of the newer drugs to treat obese children and adolescents should be conducted as a clinical trial with informed consent and only by physicians who have experience in managing obese children and adolescents.**

IMPLEMENTATION

Several principles should accompany the implementation of the interventions already outlined. First, the pediatrician should help the family identify what to change, rather than attempt to implement the prescription for the family. The initial changes should focus on behavior rather than on weight. The family's choice should be manageable and limited in scope. Criteria for success should be specified and the changes monitored either daily or weekly by the family. The initial emphasis should be on behavioral change rather than on weight loss. If the family is capable of behavioral change, weight loss will follow. Accurate weights are essential to monitor progress and may not be available to families using their scales at home. Therefore, families should be invited to use the physician's office scale periodically to assess their progress.

Because obesity constitutes a chronic disease, long-term therapy is required. Therefore, mechanisms to ensure self-monitoring, including periodic interactions with the primary care clinician or another health professional, are essential.

FURTHER READING

Dietz WH: Critical periods in childhood for the development of obesity. Am J Clin Nutr 59:995–999, 1994.

Dietz WH and Robinson T: Assessment and treatment of childhood obesity. Pediatr Rev 14:337–344, 1993.

Epstein LH, Valoski A, Wing RR, and McCurley J: Ten-year follow-up of behavioral family-based treatment for obese children. JAMA 264:2519–2523, 1990.

Epstein LH, Valoski AM, Vara LS, et al.: Effects of decreasing sedentary behavior and increasing activity on weight change in obese children. Health Psychol 14:109–115, 1995.

Himes JH and Dietz WH: Guidelines for overweight in adolescent preventive services: Recommendations from an expert committee. Am J Clin Nutr 59:307–316, 1994.

Richard E. Kreipe

Chapter 54

Eating Disorders in Pediatric Practice

Primary care clinicians have an important role in the recognition and treatment of eating disorders. Unlike subspecialists, who often first see patients who have a firmly entrenched pattern of individual and familial dysfunctional habits, the primary care clinician is likely to have an established, trusting relationship with the patient and family. This facilitates the early restoration of a normal nutritional and physiologic state, involvement of the family in the treatment program, and the development of a team approach in a therapeutic partnership (Table 54–1). Unfortunately, the tradition of designating eating disorders as primarily psychiatric disturbances may lead to patients and parents delaying, or opposing, treatment because of the stigmatization of a "mental illness." We have found that **framing an eating disorder as a "developmental illness" that can be linked to normal adolescent issues (concerns about growing up or pubertal changes, difficulty with issues related to control and autonomy, or struggles with a stable sense of identity and self-esteem) results in reduced denial and resistance to treatment.** This chapter focuses on practical strategies for integrating an approach to adolescents who have eating disorders into primary care practice.

DEFINITIONS AND DIAGNOSTIC CRITERIA

Anorexia nervosa is a syndrome in which caloric intake insufficient to maintain weight or normal growth is associated with a delusion of being fat and an obsession to be thinner that persists even with weight loss. Patients who have anorexia nervosa truly believe that they are fat, even when emaciated (delusion). They are driven to lose weight (obsession) through a variety of means (compulsions), including dieting and enhancing caloric output. Exercise is used by more than 75% of patients who have anorexia nervosa; vomiting and cathartics are means used uncommonly to lose calories. A feature that differentiates simple dieting from anorexia nervosa is the inability to be satisfied with a healthy weight goal and a refusal to "give in" to eating, resulting in the relentless pursuit of thinness. Approximately 95% of patients are females; postpubertal females uniformly are amenorrheic. Children who have anorexia nervosa may present with failure to gain weight or with obsessive-compulsive traits, rather than with weight loss or obvious dieting.

Binge eating, not vomiting, is the sine qua non for *bulimia nervosa*. Awareness that the eating pattern is abnormal is associated with depressed moods and self-deprecating thoughts; temporary relief of this distress occurs with habits ridding the body of the effects of food. Over 80% of patients who have bulimia nervosa engage in self-induced vomiting and laxative or diuretic abuse. Fasting, exercise, or both may be the primary methods used to avoid weight gain. Patients who have bulimia are more likely than anorectic patients to be impulsive, not only in eating behavior but also in their use of drugs and alcohol, self-mutilation or self-harm, sexual promiscuity, lying, stealing, and other harmful habits. Approximately

TABLE 54–1. Role of the Primary Care Clinician in Eating Disorders

- Complete assessment of weight loss (intention, methods, signs, and symptoms)
- Assessment and monitoring of diet and weight loss plan
- Provision of specific guidelines for structure of daily activities:
    - Eating schedule
    - Exercise
    - Sports and recreation
- Referral to a nutritionist, if indicated, for education and meal planning
- Establishment of weight loss limit at patient's own weight goal
- Consultation with and, when appropriate, referral to specialists involved in the care of children and adolescents who have eating disorders
- Re-evaluation

40% of patients who have anorexia nervosa have a bulimic phase in the course of their illness or recovery.

PATHOGENESIS

Factors that predispose an individual to developing an eating disorder include (1) being female, especially if obese or overconcerned with thinness, in a culture, sport, or activity where thinness is highly valued; (2) being perfectionistic and eager to please others, while not considering one's own needs; (3) having difficulty communicating negative emotions such as anger, sadness, or fear; (4) having difficulty resolving conflict; and (5) having low self-esteem.

Precipitating factors tend to focus on issues related to normal adolescent development. Fears of maturation are most common in younger (<14 years old) patients and may be related to menarche and sexual development. Although sexual abuse may be a factor for some patients who have eating disorders, it should be considered primarily in chronic or resistant cases. Struggles for independence and autonomy are most common in midadolescence and may be acted out through an eating disorder. Conflicts of identity are common in older patients (>16 years old) and may be related to transitions such as graduation from high school.

Perpetuating factors serve to maintain the eating disorder once the patterns of weight control are established. Biologic as well as psychologic influences can be powerful reinforcers and sustain the eating disorder. The biologic issues that must be appreciated by the clinician include the signs and symptoms of starvation and the principles of refeeding the malnourished individual. Growing individuals have biologic needs that vary with their stage of growth and development. Psychologically, eating disorders function as coping mechanisms. In treating the illness, the clinician may threaten the homeostatic balance that has been achieved within the family. Thus, there may be denial, resistance, and anger directed at the physician treating the eating disorder. Unlike many medical conditions in which the adolescent and physician are in alliance to eliminate an illness, eating disorders may present a special challenge because the patient frequently is ambivalent—desiring, but afraid of, recovery. An appreciation of these various factors will facilitate the development of a trusting relationship between patient and clinician.

CLINICAL ASPECTS

Symptoms

The symptoms experienced by the patient are related to the various habits used to control weight (Table 54–2). Symptom checklists facilitate taking the symptom history and generally are answered honestly if patients know that there will not be retribution for their responses. Privacy and confidentiality should be respected, as in any clinical interaction with an adolescent patient. Likewise, the history should be taken to develop a plan of action to help the patient feel better physically and not merely to rule out an eating disorder.

The responses to a review of symptoms (see Appendix at end of chapter) can be interpreted as evidence that the patient is not well—although not necessarily "sick" either. Rather than trying to convince the patient that she has an eating disorder, the discussion can focus on her loss of menstrual periods (which may occur before significant weight loss), cold hands and feet, dry and flaky skin, dizziness, constipation, fatigue, irritability, depression, and weakness. The link then can be made between providing her body with enough energy and nutrients and feeling better. By acknowledging, openly and explicitly, that this may be difficult to accomplish because she is afraid of gaining weight, the clinician demonstrates an understanding of her dilemma: To feel better she must eat, but to eat may also make her feel worse emotionally. Also, by entertaining a broad differential diagnosis, the physician will be less likely to overlook other conditions that can present similarly to eating disorders. For example, a patient who has abdominal discomfort after eating could have Crohn disease, while a patient who is vomiting involuntarily could have achalasia or a brain tumor. As in all good clinical practice, the diagnosis generally is determined by the signs and symptoms.

TABLE 54–2. Symptoms of Weight Loss in Eating Disorders

Physical	Mental/Emotional
Amenorrhea	Difficulty concentrating
Cold hands and feet	Difficulty making decisions
Constipation	Irritability
Dry skin and hair	Depression
Headaches	Social withdrawal
Fainting or dizziness	Food obsessions
Lethargy, lack of energy	
Anorexia	

Signs

Regardless of how "good" a patient may look or how "normal" the weight is, a detailed physical examination is indicated whenever there is concern about an eating disorder. Patients often dress in baggy clothes to hide their thinness; they may attach weights to their underwear or drink fluids before weigh-ins to appear as if they weigh more than they do. As is true of symptoms associated with weight control habits, signs found on physical examination (Table 54–3) are evidence that the patient is not healthy. A thorough physical examination is important because it may indicate the presence of an organic condition, such as inflammatory bowel disease (right lower quadrant mass) or central nervous system lesion (papilledema). Failure to gain height or weight as expected, rather than significant loss of weight, can occur in prepubertal patients who have eating disorders and is obvious when growth is plotted on standard charts. The signs of weight loss and malnutrition characteristic of anorexia nervosa are different from the signs associated with binge eating and purging found in bulimia nervosa. Bulimia is characterized by salivary gland enlargement (from stimulation by binge eating and vomiting), dental enamel erosion (from gastric acid), and widely fluctuating body weight with intermittent edema (fluid shifts from dehydration and fluid overload). The history should guide the physical examination.

The purpose of the physical examination is not only to detect organic pathology but also to emphasize to the patient the body's adaptation to unhealthy habits. For example, patients often have slow capillary refill in their cold, blue hands and feet. This can be explained as, "Your temperature is low because your body is saving heat. Not much blood is going to your hands and feet, where a lot of heat can be lost. What little blood *is* flowing through the skin is cold and moving very slowly, so the oxygen is being removed and your skin turns blue. If you take in more energy (calories) by eating more nutritious food, you will feel

warmer and less tired." Likewise, the loss of menstrual periods, fall in blood pressure and pulse, drop in temperature, and growth of lanugo-type hair over the upper body represent physiologic adaptations to starvation, similar to the changes in a hibernating animal. This metaphor can be extended to the observation that patients who have eating disorders often withdraw from family and friends, much like animals in hibernation. Finally, **although the patient tends to focus on the loss of fat as the primary goal of weight loss, the loss of muscle mass inevitably occurs with weight loss and is associated with loss of power, strength, endurance, flexibility, and physical fitness.** This frequently provides an incentive for athletic or sports-minded adolescents to improve their nutrition and gain weight.

Laboratory Tests

There is no diagnostic laboratory test for an eating disorder; laboratory abnormalities are due to the patient's weight control habits or their complications. A routine screening battery could include a complete blood count (leukopenia common), erythrocyte sedimentation rate (normal), and chemistry panel. The results of many of these tests depend on the state of hydration. Persistently abnormal values should be followed closely and may indicate the presence of an underlying organic illness. Because many patients have normal laboratory studies, one should emphasize that tests are obtained as a baseline, not to establish the diagnosis. Imaging studies are not part of the routine evaluation of eating disorders, but an electrocardiogram may be useful to determine the nature of profound bradycardia.

MANAGEMENT

Early or Mild Stage

Although many patients whose eating is disordered may not progress to a classic eating disorder, it is advisable to intervene when any patient demonstrates dysfunctional eating or weight control habits. Health, rather than the eating disorder, becomes the focus of attention. Features of the early or mild stage include (1) mildly distorted body image; (2) weight ≤90% of average for height; (3) no symptoms or signs of excessive weight loss; and (4) use of potentially harmful weight control methods or a strong drive to lose weight. Treatment begins with the assessment of weight loss or control, including establishing a goal weight. If a

TABLE 54–3. Signs of Weight Loss in Eating Disorders

Positive	Negative
Hypothermia and acrocyanosis	Normal optic fundi and visual fields
Bradycardia and hypotension	No organomegaly
Orthostasis	No lymphadenopathy
Loss of muscle mass	No breast atrophy
Edema	
Hypoglycemia	
Leukopenia	

patient is unable to identify a target weight or seeks an unreasonably low weight (a strong "drive for thinness"), close follow-up is indicated. Referral to a nutritionist should be made if requested or if the patient has become vegetarian or has adopted unhealthy, unusual, or monotonous food choices. The role of the nutritionist is outlined in Table 54–4.

The food diaries used to evaluate nutrition can also be used to determine dysfunctional habits (e.g., eating only a piece of toast for breakfast), associated mood disturbances (e.g., refusing to eat dinner because of an argument), and accomplishments (e.g., eating high-calorie food despite anxiety). The data contained in such records assist both the adolescent and the clinician to recognize important patterns or events. Also, if the intake recorded in the food diaries is normal, further evaluation may be indicated because malabsorption could be occurring or the patient could be vomiting surreptitiously.

Re-evaluation by the physician within 1 to 2 months ensures that weight gain is proceeding in a healthy manner and that dysfunctional eating habits have not developed. Data obtained on the follow-up visit include change in eating habits, weight (in gown, without underwear, after voiding), and physical examination. Follow-up provides an opportunity to evaluate psychosocial development and adjustment.

If the patient responds to treatment by eating normally and attaining and maintaining a normal weight and health with little evidence of distress, outpatient follow-up should be for routine health maintenance and anticipatory guidance as indicated. The adolescent and parents should be aware of the warning signals of out-of-control weight loss. These include falling below the established goal weight, feeling guilty after eating (but "in control" when losing weight or not eating), ar-

TABLE 54–4. Role of the Nutritionist in Eating Disorders

Evaluate the diet and identify specific deficiencies or excesses.

Educate the patient (and family) regarding nutrient needs during adolescence and dispel dietary misconceptions frequently held by patients.

Develop a balanced meal plan within a target caloric range to achieve either weight gain or maintenance.

Apply a food exchange system to allow variety and flexibility in food selection.

Assess food diaries recorded by the patient to identify dysfunctional eating patterns that persist or arise during the course of treatment.

Provide feedback to the patient to encourage continued progress toward health.

guing over meals, and experiencing symptoms or signs of excessive weight loss. Surveillance of these patients may prevent progression to more severe phases of illness and trigger a definitive treatment response.

Established or Moderate Stage

Adolescents who progress to more advanced stages often require the additional services of professionals who have experience in treating eating disorders. Specialists in adolescent medicine, nutrition, psychiatry, and psychology each have a role in the treatment of the more-difficult-to-manage patient. Features of patients in this category include (1) distorted body image that has not diminished with weight loss; (2) weight goal less than 85% of average weight for height associated with a refusal to gain weight; (3) symptoms or signs of excessive weight loss associated with a denial that any problem exists; and (4) unhealthy means to lose weight such as eating fewer than 1000 calories per day, purging, or exercising excessively. Additional factors include evidence of family dysfunction or anticipated lack of cooperation with treatment.

An adolescent whose body image is distorted continues to feel fat despite having lost weight. Treatment of this distortion does not include challenging the patient's perceptions, and it may help to acknowledge the desire to lose weight. However, this must be balanced against the reality of being too thin, as manifested by the symptoms and signs of excessive weight loss. By noting that *feeling* fat cannot be challenged because her feelings are subjective and that *being* also thin cannot be challenged because of objective data, the clinician indicates an awareness of the dilemma facing the patient, which furthers the development of trust. In contrast, responses such as "How can you possibly feel fat, when you're so skinny?" or "Why don't you just eat?" indicate a lack of appreciation of the patient's perceptions, potentially increasing resistance to treatment.

Similarly, rational arguments for the need to gain weight, such as plotting weight for height on a growth chart, have little place in the treatment of more advanced disease. Because eating disorders are based on premises that the adolescent has regarding herself (being ineffective, inadequate, and so forth), simplistic explanations such as these usually are not compelling. Furthermore, the developmental issues over which the patient feels no control are embodied metaphorically in her struggle to lose weight. Therefore, to make eating and weight gain a battle dooms treatment to failure. If the patient wins the battle by losing weight, health is lost; if the patient loses the battle by gaining weight, her perceptions of being ineffective, powerless, and worthless are reinforced rather than reduced. There is "no way out." However, if the clinician joins with the adolescent in gaining control over the eating disorder, a healthy and growth-promoting alternative is available.

It also is not necessary to confront denial that a problem exists immediately. Frequently, such denial stems from misconceptions regarding the meaning of the diagnosis of an eating disorder. Some adolescents argue that they cannot have an eating disorder because they are not thin enough. Others fear the diagnosis means that they are "crazy," or that they will be hospitalized and "force fed." More important than labeling is the need to identify threats to health and to develop a treatment plan that addresses, monitors, and improves health status. It is necessary for the parents to understand the seriousness of the diagnosis, however, because they may need to confront the possibility of long-term treatment and hospitalization. Denial on the part of one or both parents can undermine all treatment interventions.

To restore the adolescent who has an established or moderate eating disorder to nutritional and physiologic health, it usually is necessary to provide structure to daily activities that ensures adequate caloric intake and limits caloric expenditure. This plan should take into account the present weight, the minimal goal weight for health, and the expected rate of weight gain. The development of this plan in conjunction with the patient and parents can be the responsibility of either the primary care clinician or the specialist. Behavioral "contracts" tend not to be as effective in outpatient management, especially with bulimia nervosa, because the daily monitoring of such plans generally falls to the parents. In general, the goal of outpatient treatment is to remove parents from such highly conflictual responsibilities and to shift the burden of responsibility to the adolescent to eat adequately and attain health. Then, the clinician can assume responsibility for monitoring health, and the mother and father can return to their parental roles. Negotiating a "program" or "plan" to help the patient attain and maintain health emphasizes the positive aspects of this intervention. Obviously, younger adolescents and children need closer parental involvement.

The daily structure should include eating three meals a day. In eating disorders breakfast typically is eliminated and lunch drastically reduced. Patients who have anorexia nervosa tend to continue their restriction through dinner, whereas patients who have bulimia nervosa tend to binge eat and purge after school or after dinner. Therefore, eating adequately at breakfast maximizes the likelihood of adequate daily calorie intake and should be emphasized by both the physician and the nutritionist. Eating an insufficient amount of food at meals can result in either weight loss or subsequent binge eating. Thus, parents should be encouraged to ensure that healthy food is available and that mealtimes are planned into the day, but not to assume responsibility for the patient's eating. If parents feel that it is their duty to force their adolescent to eat, eating becomes a no-win battle. If the patient gives in and eats to satisfy parents, vomiting often ensues. Power struggles can be minimized if the patient assumes responsibility for eating, with the clinician monitoring health.

In addition to increasing calorie intake, it may be necessary to limit physical activity. Restricting activity, such as participating in sports or exercise classes, has numerous advantages. It helps maintain weight by decreasing calorie output and emphasizes the seriousness of the condition to the patient and parents. It also can motivate the return to favorite activities. Parents and coaches often are relieved when the patient is restricted from excessive activity for medical reasons. It may be useful to explain the purpose of the restrictions to the coach or school nurse so that he or she can reinforce the importance of health. Also, the patient often finds it reassuring that the clinician is taking authority in a situation over which she has decreasing control.

Consultation with, or referral to, specialists in the treatment of eating disorders is often indicated at this stage of illness. The referral process can be crucial to the acceptance of complex and often difficult treatment recommendations. The trust of the patient and parents in the clinician is not readily transferred to specialists. Referral often is facilitated when specialists are identified as "consultants." A statement such as, "To provide you with the best overall care, I need the help of some people who specialize in treating eating disorders" emphasizes that the team approach has demonstrated effectiveness, while continuity of care is made explicit. This can be especially important in referral for mental health treatment: "You need to see a psychiatrist" often elicits "But I'm not crazy." A more therapeutic message would be, "You seem angry, sad, and a little hopeless about this whole situation. Many of my patients find it helpful to talk to someone about such feelings so that they can get on with their lives. I'd like you to see Dr. Smith, a psychiatrist. He can help me with this aspect of your care."

Likewise, a primary care clinician might say to the mother, "It's clear that this eating disorder is affecting your whole family. Even though Susie is the one who's losing weight, I think we need to include the rest of the family in coming up with solutions. Dr. Jones is a therapist who often helps me in working with families in such situations. Here's her phone number and address. I'll call in the referral and will see you again in 2 weeks to see how the first meeting went and to check on Susie's health."

To reinforce the importance of the referral, a follow-up appointment should be scheduled after treatment by specialists has begun. It is common for a patient or parent to resist treatment, noting "I don't like talking about it"; "They're not helping"; "It's too expensive"; or "It's not that big of a deal." To lessen conflict related to the eating disorder, parents may discontinue treatment, hoping that the issue will resolve spontaneously. Continued involvement of the clinician can prevent this. Reinforcement is often needed:

"I know how difficult it is to deal with these problems, but it will be worth it. I want you to keep up with treatment for at least another 2 months. I think you'll start to see some change soon if everybody works together." Such joining with the family emphasizes that they are not alone in their struggle.

FURTHER READING

Fisher M, Golden NH, Katzman DK, et al.: Eating disorders in adolescents: A background paper. J Adolesc Health 16:420–437, 1995.

Kreipe RE: Eating disorders in adolescents. Pediatr Rev 16:370–379, 1995.

Kreipe RE and Uphoff M: Treatment and outcome of adolescents with anorexia nervosa. Adolesc Med 3:519–540, 1992.

Satter E: Feeding dynamics: Helping children to eat well. J Pediatr Health Care 9(4): 178–184, 1995.

Steiner-Adair C: The body politic: Normal female adolescent development and the development of eating disorders. *In* Gilligan C, et al. (eds): Making Connections: The Relational Worlds of Adolescent Girls at Emma Willard School. Cambridge, MA, Harvard University Press, 1990.

Appendix : Questionnaire for Adolescents with Weight Loss

I. SYMPTOMS: Do you have any of the following symptoms?

	No	Yes
Feeling cold	☐	☐
Cold or blue hands or feet	☐	☐
Constipation	☐	☐
Problems with dry skin	☐	☐
Problems with dry hair or hair falling out	☐	☐
Dizziness	☐	☐
Fainting	☐	☐
Headaches	☐	☐
Feeling tired	☐	☐
Feeling weak	☐	☐
Feeling full after eating small amounts of food	☐	☐
Loss of appetite	☐	☐
Difficulty concentrating	☐	☐
Difficulty making decisions	☐	☐
Being irritable	☐	☐
Being sad or bored	☐	☐
Not wanting to be around friends	☐	☐
Not wanting to be around family	☐	☐
Thinking about food	☐	☐
Worrying about gaining weight	☐	☐
Loss or irregularity of menstrual periods (females)	☐	☐

II. WEIGHT AND ACTIVITY HISTORY

1. What is the *most* you have ever weighed? . . . . _____
2. What is the *least* you have weighed in the last year? . . . . _____
3. What do you weigh *now*? . . . . _____
4. What would you *like* to weigh? . . . . _____
5. Are you trying to lose weight?   ☐ No   ☐ Yes
6. How often do you weigh yourself? . . . . _____
7. Do you exercise at least once a week?   ☐ No   ☐ Yes If yes, check all that apply.

	No	Yes	Hours/Week
Running/jogging	☐	☐	_____
Aerobics/calisthenics	☐	☐	_____
Dancing/ballet	☐	☐	_____
Gymnastics	☐	☐	_____
Swimming	☐	☐	_____
Team sport(s)	☐	☐	_____
Other: _____			_____

8. Do you exercise to lose weight?   ☐ No   ☐ Yes
9. Check all the methods that you have used to try to control your weight.

Dieting	Exercising	Diet Pills	Vomiting	Laxatives
☐	☐	☐	☐	☐

Appendix continued on following page

III. EATING HISTORY

1. Rate on a scale of 0 to 5 how much you eat at each of the following times during a typical day.

Nothing = 0
Snack = 1
Small meal = 2
Meal = 3
Large meal = 4
Binge = 5

At . . .		Between . . .		After . . .	
Breakfast	_____	Breakfast and lunch	_____	Going to bed	_____
Lunch	_____	Lunch and dinner	_____	Something upsetting	_____
Dinner	_____	Dinner and bedtime	_____		

2. Please describe your typical breakfast, lunch, dinner, and snack.

	Food/Beverage	Amount
Breakfast		

	Food/Beverage	Amount
Lunch		

	Food/Beverage	Amount
Dinner		

	Food/Beverage	Amount
Snack		

IV. FAMILY HISTORY: Are there any family members with the following conditions (include aunts/uncles, cousins, grandparents, as well as immediate family)?

	No	Yes		No	Yes		No	Yes
Alcohol or drug abuse ..	☐	☐	Colitis	☐	☐	Thyroid disease	☐	☐
Anorexia nervosa	☐	☐	Depression	☐	☐	Ulcers	☐	☐
Asthma	☐	☐	Diabetes (high sugar)	☐	☐	Vomiting	☐	☐
Bulimia (binge eating) ..	☐	☐	Mental illness	☐	☐	Other	☐	☐
Cancer	☐	☐	Obesity	☐	☐			

Please explain any "yes" answers _____

_____

From Comerci GD: Eating disorders in adolescents. Pediatr Rev 10(2):37–47S, 1988.

David M. Siegel

Arthritis

The term *arthritis* is used to describe a joint in which there is inflammation. That is, **arthritis is present when there is intra-articular swelling or at least two of the following are found in a joint: (1) pain or tenderness with motion; (2) limitation of motion; or (3) warmth (and sometimes erythema).** This is to be distinguished from arthralgia, which refers only to joint pain, a symptom observed in a wide variety of conditions and much more common than true arthritis. Thus, the first task in evaluating a child who has joint pain (or as is often the case in younger children, refusal to walk or complaints of generalized extremity discomfort) is to establish whether arthritis is, indeed, present. Once this has been decided (based on physical examination), the further classification and management of joint inflammation relies on the previously gathered history of present illness (as provided by the patient and family), a thorough physical assessment, and selected laboratory data serving to confirm or refute the suspected diagnosis.

MONARTICULAR OR OLIGOARTICULAR

Arthritis can be a manifestation of many diseases, some insidious in onset and chronic in course; others develop acutely and follow a rapid evolution, often mandating prompt identification and therapeutic intervention. Diagnostic considerations begin with determining the number of affected joints; one (monarticular), several (oligoarticular, from two to four joints), or many (polyarticular, five or greater). **The finding of monarticular arthritis in a child who has fever places intra-articular bacterial infection or septic arthritis immediately at the top of the differential diagnosis. Aspiration of fluid from the joint space (arthrocentesis) becomes paramount** (Table 55–1) for synovial fluid characteristics). Expected peripheral blood abnormalities include an elevated white blood cell (WBC) count with an increased proportion of band forms and/or segmented neutrophils, as well as a markedly elevated erythrocyte sedimentation rate (ESR). Blood (and any other suspicious site of infection such as cellulitis, abscess, cerebrospinal fluid) always should be cultured, although the yield often is low. Synovial fluid culture results, however, can be negative in 20% of patients in whom blood culture results have been positive; thus, the latter can add useful information in a minority of children. The presence of active infection and purulent material in a joint signifies synovial and cartilage damage; fluid removal (with subsequent Gram stain and culture) serves not only as a diagnostic maneuver but also, when positive for bacterial infection, as the first therapeutic step. The "medical emergency" of septic arthritis should be addressed promptly and aggressively. Parenteral antibiotics should be initiated immediately, with the choice of drug based on epidemiologic and host factors. For nonimmunocompromised patients, the most common organisms to consider are *Staphylococcus aureus* and *Streptococcus* (*S. pneumoniae*, group A, and group B), although Gram stain and culture may lead to more accurate antimicrobial coverage. In the past, *Haemophilus influenzae* type B has been the most frequent cause of septic arthritis in young children, but immunization has

TABLE 55–1. Synovial Fluid Characteristics

Condition	Color/Clarity	Viscosity	WBC, mm³	PMN, %
Normal	Yellow/clear	Very high	<200	<25
Trauma	Xanthochromic/turbid	High	<2000	<25
Sepsis	Serosanguineous/turbid	Decreased	50,000–300,000	>75
Juvenile arthritis	Yellow/cloudy	Decreased	15,000–20,000	75

WBC, white blood cell count; PMN, polymorphonuclear leukocytes.
Adapted from Cassidy JT and Petty RE: Textbook of Pediatric Rheumatology, 3rd ed. Philadelphia, WB Saunders, 1995, p 585.

altered this pattern dramatically. The compromised host remains at risk for *H. influenzae,* less common bacteria, mycobacteria, and fungal organisms. Patients who have sickle cell disease have a particular propensity for *Salmonella* arthritis.

Penetration and persistence of antibiotic concentration in synovial fluid is high, accounting for the generally positive response to treatment, provided it is begun early. Minimum duration of an antimicrobial agent is somewhat organism-dependent: for example, duration of *Neisseria gonorrhoeae* is 1 week; *H. influenzae,* 2 weeks; and staphylococcus and *Enterobacter,* 3 weeks. Response is monitored by defervescence (usually 5 to 7 days) and gradual decrease in pain and warmth. Antibiotics should be continued until these symptoms have resolved and the ESR is less than 20 mm/hr. Transition from intravenous to oral therapy is guided by isolation of the organism, availability of an appropriate oral preparation, and ensurance of vigilant compliance. Most clinicians consider 1 week of parenteral treatment a minimum; patients who are placed on oral antibiotics should have peak and trough serum antibiotic levels measured weekly. Range of motion exercises and physical therapy are initiated within 2 to 3 days of starting treatment, and patients are encouraged to return to full activity as soon as tolerated following completion of drug therapy.

Onset of multiple, simultaneous, bacterially infected joints is quite unusual, but can occur. A particular variation is that of *N. gonorrhoeae* in a sexually active adolescent. In this instance, arthritis can represent primary infection in the joint or more commonly, a sterile effusion can be found in one or more joints as a consequence of a presumed immune-mediated, cross-reactivity synovitis in patients who have gonococcemia. Antibiotic therapy is warranted to treat this systemic illness, although a true septic arthritis does not exist and joint prognosis is favorable.

Whereas the question of a septic cause is the most pressing in the child who has monarticular disease, absence of fever or noninfectious synovial fluid, even with an elevated temperature, leads one to consider a range of other conditions. Obviously, if trauma is in the history, this may offer an explanation. However, **one must be wary of overinterpreting the significance of trauma as potentially causal in an episode of joint inflammation, especially in toddlers for whom daily extremity injury is virtually normal.**

Hip pain and tenderness, low-grade fever with or without an elevated WBC and ESR, and the frequent history that symptoms have been preceded by a viral upper respiratory infection represent findings that are consistent with toxic or transient synovitis of the hip. This condition occurs predominantly in 3- to 10-year-olds, 70% of whom are male; symptoms can have either a sudden or insidious onset. Virtually all of these patients require hip joint aspiration to document sterile synovial fluid; treatment then consists of rest and anti-inflammatory medication (e.g., ibuprofen or naproxen). The illness is self-limited, usually lasting approximately 6 days, although up to 1.5% of patients later develop Legg-Calvé-Perthes disease.

The child who has a coagulation defect, such as severe factor VIII or IX deficiency (hemophilia) or von Willebrand disease, experiences frequent spontaneous (no known trauma) hemarthroses ordinarily diagnosed due to an awareness of the primary disorder. Therapy consists of specific factor replacement. Similarly, patients who have sickle cell disease can experience episodes of arthritis as manifestations of vaso-occlusive crises. Other illnesses that can include monarticular (or oligoarticular) arthritis are inflammatory bowel disease; psoriasis; reactive arthritis complicating an enteral infection with *Yersinia, Campylobacter,* or *Salmonella;* and many viral illnesses. Lyme disease deserves particular mention, because 33% to 50% of cases occur in children, and it can be confused with other forms of arthritis. Although arthralgias are common in the early phase, true arthritis (typically involving the knee) is a later manifestation (from 2 to 15 months following the erythema migrans rash, when present) of the disease. Acute joint inflammation usually persists for about 1 week, but often recurs. Antibiotic treatment should be instituted at the time of diagnosis, and nonsteroidal anti-inflammatory drugs (NSAIDs) should be used for relief of symptoms.

Although not common as a presenting sign, a single inflamed joint can be the sentinel finding for certain neoplastic diseases, including leukemia, lymphoma, neuroblastoma, and primary bone malignancies. Fever often occurs in these illnesses along with other constitutional signs such as weight loss, fatigue, and sweats. Osteomyelitis can be complicated by arthritis through two possible mechanisms. Bone infection in young children most often is seeded hematogenously at the site of greatest vascularity, i.e., the growth plate, which is contiguous to the joint space (e.g., distal femur osteomyelitis and the knee). Arthritis can result from either a "sympathetic (sterile) effusion" in the neighboring joint or by direct extension of the bacterial process into the synovium and synovial fluid. In the latter, there is a septic arthritis, but the infectious process includes bone, as well. This accounts for a more prolonged prodrome of bone pain (perhaps tenderness) and fever before the appearance of arthritis. Even more unusual causes of monarticular arthritis are foreign body or plant thorn synovitis or pigmented villonodular synovitis, confirmed arthroscopically.

JUVENILE ARTHRITIS

Juvenile arthritis (JA; also called juvenile rheumatoid arthritis [JRA], juvenile chronic arthritis [JCA], and most recently, idiopathic arthritides of childhood) is characterized by three main subtypes. Monarticular disease fits in the group called pauciarticular (or oligoarticular). Onset of arthritis at 16 years old or earlier and evidence of joint inflammation on physical examination for a minimum of 6 weeks are necessary criteria for all forms of JA. In pauciarticular disease, no more than four joints are involved, and other causes of arthritis have been excluded. Affected joints tend to be those that are large (knee, elbow, ankle), and the pattern is asymmetric, the knee being the most common. Other than the arthritis, these children feel relatively well and do not present with significant fever, rash, or other organ system involvement. An important exception to this is chronic uveitis, which can complicate pauciarticular disease either before, simultaneous with, or following a flare of arthritis. Inflammation of the eye is unrelated to either the timing or severity of the joint disease. The detection of serum antinuclear antibody (ANA) in patients who have JA signifies a higher risk for uveitis and is found most frequently, but not exclusively, in girls younger than 7 years who have pauciarticular disease.

Because the uveitis is chronic and mildly, or not at all, symptomatic, it is exceedingly important that these children undergo regular ophthalmologic evaluation, including slit-lamp examination. The American Academy of Pediatrics' Section on Rheumatology has established guidelines for the frequency of these visits, based on JA subtype, ANA status, and years since disease onset. Briefly, the highest risk children (those who have ANA, both pauci- and polyarticular) require an eye examination every 3 to 4 months until 4 years after disease onset (if they have not developed uveitis). At that time they are considered medium risk (along with all other subtypes, except systemic onset) and monitoring decreases to every 6 months. Those who have systemic-onset disease, as well as patients 7 years from disease onset (or, for those children diagnosed at or after age 7, 4 years since disease onset) are low risk and require eye examinations every 12 months.

In addition to the younger, and predominantly female, patients who have pauciarticular disease, a second population consists principally of older boys (>8 years) whose joint pattern is more likely lower extremity (knees, ankles, and hips) and compounded by problems with enthesopathies. These represent inflammation (with pain and tenderness) at tendinous or ligamentous attachments to bone. Many of these children carry the major histocompatibility (MHC) locus human leukocyte antigen (HLA)-B27, and some later develop sacroileitis and ankylosing spondylitis. A family history of arthritis, especially back problems, often is present in these children. Other pauciarticular subgroups include patients who have an intermediate age of onset and absence of ANA (prognosis for these patients is good), as well as children who begin with involvement of only several joints atypically involving wrists or fingers then develop a polyarticular pattern. This latter group recently has been labeled "extended oligoarticular."

Except for the presence of ANA and HLA-B27, laboratory data in pauciarticular disease tend to be unimpressive. The ESR is modestly elevated, and there may be a slight peripheral leukocytosis and marginal anemia. Autoantibodies other then ANA are not typically found. While pauci- or oligoarticular onset accounts for approximately 50% of all children who have JA and tend to have the best prognosis with eventual remission for most, the next most common subtype is polyarticular. By definition, these children are less than 16 years of age and have had documented arthritis for at least 6 weeks, but unlike the previous group, five or more joints become inflamed. **Comprising about one third of the total JA population, polyarticular disease is subdivided further into the small minority of patients in whom IgM rheumatoid factor (RF) is found (5% to 10% of the total JA population) and the remainder in whom RF is negative.** As a whole, children who have polyarticular disease experience some degree of constitutional illness with low-grade fever, fatigue, poor growth, and a general feeling of being "unwell." Laboratory studies may be somewhat more abnormal than in pauciarticular disease, with increases of WBC and ESR accompanied by mild to moderate anemia. Those children who have positive RF are almost all female and usually present when they are older (late preadolescence, early adolescence). The disease typically affects multiple joints, is aggressive and destructive, and can be complicated by multiorgan-system vasculitis involving the lung, heart, and skin (nodules) comparable to the spectrum of disease seen in young adult women who have rheumatoid arthritis. Some also have positive ANA and are at increased risk for eye inflammation.

Although children who have polyarticular disease and are RF negative may follow a similarly inexorable and deteriorating course, overall they have a better prognosis. In both groups, joint deformities can occur with contractures, subluxations, and deviations. Cervical spine involvement most often leads to fusion and loss of motion (particularly extension and rotation), whereas the small joints of the hands and wrists can be deformed extensively. The most severely affected of these children demonstrate significant growth retardation.

Most striking in its acute and dramatic onset, systemic-onset disease is found in only 15% of the JA population. Initially arthritis is not a usual feature and in some children never occurs. **The most common presenting symptom in systemic-onset disease is daily, high, spiking fevers (40° to 41°C [104° to 105.8°F]) with a quotidian pattern (return to normal or subnormal temperature between spikes).** The febrile episodes are accompanied by a characteristically evanescent, pink (salmon colored), macular rash. The cutaneous lesions may show central clearing and often can be induced by local friction or mild trauma (Koebner phenomenon). These children commonly are most ill at the time of temperature elevations and complain of fatigue, myalgias, and arthralgias despite the frequent absence of signs of arthritis. The systemic manifestations can be numerous, including marked lymphadenopathy, hepatosplenomegaly, and polyserositis (pleuritis, pericarditis). A very high WBC count (20 to 30,000 mm³), platelets, ESR (often greater than 100 mm/hr), and C-reactive protein occur along with profound anemia (hematocrit is in the low 20s). Ferritin levels above 10,000 ng/mL have been reported as present only in systemic-onset JA. RF and ANA typically are absent. The natural history of this subtype is variable, with some patients experiencing only one episode; others have recurrences of the systemic features without development of arthritis; still others (the majority) progress to polyarticular joint disease, which can be severe and crippling.

MANAGEMENT

Children who have JA are best cared for by a team comprising the patient and family, primary care clinician, pediatric rheumatologist, nurse specialist, occupational and physical therapists, social worker, and when needed, pediatric orthopedic surgeon. Details of treatment are beyond the scope of this text, but drug therapy remains an important mainstay. Nonsteroidal anti-inflammatory drugs (aspirin now is used rarely by pediatric rheumatologists for children who have JA) help control fever as well as pain and stiffness, but many patients, especially those who have polyarticular or systemic-onset disease, require additional medication. Weekly methotrexate (oral or subcutaneous) has shown a very favorable risk-benefit ratio and has come to be used in more children earlier following onset of their symptoms. Other medications that might be selected and used based on disease subtype, patient status, and response to previous therapy include hydroxychloroquine, sulfasalazine, intramuscular gold, azathioprine, cyclophosphamide, cyclosporin A, and intravenous immune globulin. Systemic corticosteroids continue to play an important therapeutic role, especially in children who have recalcitrant systemic-onset or polyarticular disease; however, the clinician must be ever vigilant to minimize both dose and duration of exposure. Methotrexate has added a very valuable "steroid sparing" tool to the pharmaceutical armamentarium. **Intra-articular corticosteriod (specifically triamcinolone hexacetonide) is both safe and very effective in many patients who are plagued by persistence of a small number of active joints or a disease flare presenting as a single acutely inflamed joint** (e.g., an active knee joint in a child who has pauciarticular disease). In these children, joint injection can obviate the need for beginning or continuing systemic medication.

Appropriate range of motion, muscle strength-

TABLE 55–2. Types of Childhood Arthritis

Infectious	*Rheumatic*
Bacterial	Juvenile arthritis
Fungal	Systemic lupus
Viral	erythematosus
Postviral	Psoriasis
Poststreptococcal	Dermatomyositis
Traumatic	Kawasaki disease
Neoplastic	Reiter syndrome
Leukemia	Behçet disease
Lymphoma	Acute rheumatic fever
Primary bone tumor	Familial Mediterranean
Hematologic	fever
Hemophilia	Scleroderma
Von Willebrand disease	Sarcoidosis
Sickle cell disease	Vasculitis
	Congenital Syndromes
	Other
	Inflammatory bowel
	disease
	Postbacterial enteritis
	Campylobacter
	Yersinia
	Shigella
	Salmonella
	Toxic synovitis of the hip
	Cystic fibrosis
	Villonodular synovitis
	Foreign-body arthritis

ening, and splinting as assessed and implemented by occupational therapists (OT) and physical therapists (PT) are equally important as drug therapy. Long-term functional prognosis depends heavily on aggressive and ongoing OT and PT intervention. In addition to these health professional–mediated exercises, **regular involvement in physical activity (including organized athletic competition, if desired) should be encouraged. This not only serves as further range-of-motion and muscle-strengthening exercise but also promotes self-esteem and continued engagement in mainstream peer and school culture.** Only in the midst of an acute arthritis flare, when significant joint warmth, erythema, and effusion are present, should activity be restricted. Later in life, as patients age and growth plates fuse, joints severely damaged by inflammatory disease (such as hips or knees) may require replacement with prosthetic devices.

The psychosocial aspects of chronic illness in children, discussed elsewhere in this text, deserve no less an emphasis than more traditional treatment considerations for children who have JA. Family functioning, school performance, peer relations, and normal developmental progression can be affected profoundly by JA; thus, expert attention to these issues is paramount in a comprehensive, multidisciplinary treatment approach.

OTHER CONNECTIVE TISSUE DISEASES

As shown in Table 55–2, arthritis is seen in a variety of conditions other than JA that enter into the differential diagnosis. The arthritis of systemic lupus erythematosus (SLE) tends to be nondestructive but can be quite symptomatic. Whereas children who have SLE have ANA, they also have other autoantibodies (e.g., anti–ds DNA, anti-Sm, anti-SSA, anti-SSB) that are not found in JA. Dermatomyositis is a vasculitic disorder predominantly, with characteristic skin findings and muscle inflammation, but other problems can develop, including arthritis. Acute rheumatic fever (ARF) has undergone a mild resurgence over the last decade and certainly can include arthritis as one of its major manifestations. **It is important to recognize that joint inflammation can occur also following a streptococcal infection in the absence of ARF (i.e., poststreptococcal arthritis).** Consultation with a pediatric rheumatologist and/or cardiologist can help establish this important distinction.

FURTHER READING

American Academy of Pediatrics, Section on Rheumatology and Section on Ophthalmology: Guidelines for ophthalmologic examinations in children with juvenile rheumatoid arthritis. Pediatrics 92:295–296, 1993.

Fink CW: Proposal for the development of classification criteria for idiopathic arthritides of childhood. J Rheumatol 22:1566–1569, 1995.

Siegel DM and Baum J: Juvenile arthritis. Primary Care 20:883–893, 1993.

Spencer CH, Fife RZ, and Rabinovich CE: The school experience of children with arthritis: Coping in the 1990s and transition into adulthood. Pediatr Clin North Am 42:1285–1298, 1995.

Tucker LB: Nonrheumatic conditions in children including infectious diseases and syndromes. Curr Opin Rheumatol 7:419–424, 1995.

Robert H. A. Haslam

Chapter 56

The Diagnosis and Management of Seizures

Seizures are common in children. They are likely to present more often during the first year of life than at any other period, and approximately 50% of lifetime seizures occur by late adolescence. The seizure may be the result of a relatively benign process such as a fever or due to a disorder of the central nervous system (CNS), such as meningitis, which requires immediate intervention to prevent irreversible injury to the developing nervous system. In this chapter, an approach to the diagnosis of seizures and epilepsy is discussed, focusing on the child who may be managed in the ambulatory setting.

The terms *seizure* and *epilepsy* should not be used interchangeably. A *seizure* is defined as a paroxysmal involuntary discharge of cortical neurons, which may be manifested clinically by an impairment in consciousness, abnormal motor activity, behavioral and emotional abnormalities, sensory disturbances, or autonomic dysfunction. Some seizures are characterized by abnormal movements without loss of consciousness. *Epilepsy* applies to spontaneous recurrent seizures unrelated to a fever. Approximately 30,000 children and adolescents in the United States are diagnosed annually with epilepsy.

The initial seizure is a great shock to the family because it almost always is unexpected, and the actual seizure is frightening for most parents. A good place to begin the interview and subsequent management includes a brief discussion of the seizure and reassurance that in most cases the child will recover completely. Some ambulatory clinics have created educational videotapes on the common features of epilepsy and febrile seizures, which the parents can review following the history taking and examination.

CLASSIFICATION AND DESCRIPTION OF SEIZURES

The most critical step in the successful management of epilepsy is the proper classification of the seizure type. An incorrect classification likely will result in an inappropriate antiepileptic drug selection, resulting in poor seizure control, and misinformation to the patient and parents. For example, a child may present with frequent staring episodes. The differential diagnosis includes daydreaming, absence seizures, a partial seizure, or a pseudoseizure. The appropriate classification in this case is vital, because each condition requires a specific treatment plan.

The terminology used to classify seizures in the past led to confusion in the management of epilepsy. For example, diagnoses such as temporal lobe and psychomotor epilepsy are inaccurate, because seizures originating from remote areas of the brain can mimic these seizure types. In 1981 the International Classification of Epileptic Seizures (ICES) was published, which combines the clinical description of the seizure with the electroencephalograph (EEG) findings (Table 56–1). The ICES has clarified the classification of epilepsy greatly and has improved the management of af-

TABLE 56–1. International Classification of Epileptic Seizures

Partial Seizures (Focal-Onset Seizures)
Simple partial (consciousness retained)
With motor symptoms
With somatosensory or sensory symptoms
With autonomic symptoms
With psychic symptoms
Complex partial (consciousness impaired)
Simple partial developing into a complex seizure
Consciousness impaired at onset
Partial seizure with secondary generalization
Generalized Seizures
Absence seizures
Typical
Atypical
Myoclonic seizures
Clonic seizures
Tonic seizures
Tonic-clonic seizures
Atonic seizures
Unclassified Seizures

From Commission on Classification and Terminology of the International League Against Epilepsy: Proposal for revised clinical and electroencephalographic classification of epileptic seizures. Epilepsia 22:489–501, 1981.

fected children. A brief description of each seizure type follows.

Partial Seizures

Partial seizures are the most common type of epilepsy in children. *Simple partial seizures (SPS)* are brief, rarely persist longer than 10 to 20 seconds, and are unassociated with postictal phenomenon. The hallmark of SPS is that the patient remains conscious and may verbalize throughout the event. The motor component is characterized by asynchronous tonic or clonic movements, especially forced deviation of the head and eyes. The EEG typically records unilateral spike discharges or sharp waves in the anterior temporal region, but on occasion the discharges may be bilateral or multifocal. The onset of a *complex partial seizure (CPS)* may be indistinguishable from an SPS or may begin with sudden loss of consciousness. The duration of a CPS is up to 1 or 2 minutes. During the period of unconsciousness, a CPS may progress to a tonic-clonic seizure (secondary generalized seizure) owing to spread of the temporal lobe epileptogenic discharge to the cerebral hemispheres. Approximately one third of patients who have CPS experience an aura immediately preceding the seizure. **An aura always is an indication of focal onset of the seizure.** The aura may consist of abdominal discomfort or nausea and unexplained fear; frequently, the patient complains of a generalized "weird" feeling. **Automatisms are characteristic of CPS.** Automatisms are repetitive, stereotypic movements or behaviors that occur during the seizure and frequently persist into the postictal period. They are observed in approximately 50% to 75% of CPS. Automatisms in the infant may include mouthing movements, repetitive swallowing, or excessive salivation. Lip smacking and sucking or clinging to an object or parent, hand wringing, and continual picking at clothing are observed more commonly in the child. Patients who have CPS are unaware of their automatisms. The interictal (between seizures) EEG is abnormal in the majority of patients and consists of spike discharges or sharp waves originating in the anterior temporal or frontal lobes.

Generalized Seizures

Typical absence seizures are more common in the female and usually present between 5 and 7 years of age in a previously well child. They often are recognized initially by the teacher. The seizures vary in frequency from occasional to multiple episodes daily. They are brief (10 to 30 seconds) lapses of consciousness, with cessation of speech and motor activity. The child does not fall or loose balance, but automatisms may be present, including eye blinking or lip smacking. **Aura and a postictal state are never associated with typical absence seizures.** The child immediately resumes the preseizure activity at the completion of the seizure. Hyperventilation for 3 to 4 minutes in a cooperative patient usually induces a seizure. The EEG is characterized by 3 per second generalized spike and wave discharges during the duration of the seizure, with normal background activity before and after the seizure. *Atypical absence seizures* are less common and have a poorer prognosis than typical absence epilepsy. These seizures are associated with myoclonic movements of the face and may cause the child to fall. The EEG consists of 2 to 2.5 or 4 to 4.5 generalized spike and wave discharges. *Myoclonic seizures* are brief muscle contractions that usually are generalized; they may cause the child to fall. Myoclonic seizures rarely occur in isolation and usually are associated with other types of epilepsy, including partial complex and tonic-clonic convulsions. *Clonic, tonic,* and *tonic-clonic seizures* occur with loss of consciousness, perioral cyanosis, loss of sphincter control in many cases, and a 30- to 60-minutes postictal period often accompanied by vomiting and headache. *Atonic seizures* are difficult to differentiate from myoclonic seizures but tend to be associated with brief periods of unconsciousness, causing the head to drop forward; the child often falls to the floor.

CLASSIFICATION BY SYNDROME

Approximately 50% of childhood seizures can be classified into a specific syndrome determined by age, cognitive development, type of seizure, and the EEG, including the background rhythm, which is a distinct advantage over the ICES. Additional syndromes will become apparent in the future, with refined neuroimaging and molecular diagnostic techniques. A brief description of six epilepsy syndromes follows.

West Syndrome (Infantile Spasms)

West syndrome typically begins around 4 to 6 months of age, with repetitive volleys of flexor or extensor spasms involving the head and extremities. It is most common during awakening or falling asleep. The entire seizure may persist for minutes and recur several times daily. The seizure is followed by sleep or a period of decreased alertness. The seizure may be heralded by a cry or startle and can be confused with colic. Deterioration in developmental milestones is often evident at the onset of infantile spasms. The causes are protean, and before treatment, a comprehensive investigation including metabolic and structural studies is essential. The EEG is characterized by high-voltage, bilaterally asynchronous, and irregular high-voltage spike and wave discharges (hypsarrhythmia). Treatment regimens include adrenocorticotropic hormone (ACTH), corticosteroids, benzodiazepines, and vigabatrin (in Canada and Europe), especially for those children who have tuberous sclerosis and infantile spasms. A few patients display a focal EEG abnormality and can be considered for a comprehensive workup to determine if surgical removal of a circumscribed lesion is an option. Generally, the prognosis is poor, with persistent seizures and cognitive impairment in the majority. About 10% to 15% of children have an excellent prognosis. These children do not experience loss of milestones, and their diagnostic studies are normal except for the initial EEG.

Lennox-Gastaut Syndrome

This epilepsy syndrome is most common in preschool children, many of whom have a history of developmental delay preceding the onset of seizures. The child may present with status epilepticus. The syndrome is characterized by several types of seizures, including generalized tonic-clonic, myoclonic, partial complex, and absence seizures. The EEG shows a slow background and associated slow spike and wave and multifocal abnormalities. Treatment with anticonvulsants includes valproic acid and the benzodiazepines. Many children are resistant to anticonvulsants and may benefit from a ketogenic diet. The prognosis is unfavorable because of persistent recalcitrant seizures and a high incidence of mental retardation and behavioral problems.

Febrile Seizures

Febrile seizures are very common. They occur in children 6 months to 5 years of age at the time of a fever of at least 38.5°C (101.3°F). The typical convulsion is generalized tonic-clonic and rarely persists longer than 10 minutes. The primary differential diagnosis is meningitis or encephalitis, which should be considered with each presentation. Approximately 30% to 40% of children who have one febrile seizure will experience a recurrent febrile seizure. The major concern has been the possibility that repeated febrile seizures may cause epilepsy. Studies have shown a slightly increased risk of epilepsy's developing later, when several risk factors are present, including developmental delay, an abnormal neurologic examination, and a history of atypical febrile seizures (e.g., prolonged or focal seizure). Febrile seizures are managed by controlling the fever and reassuring the family. There is no role for prophylactic anticonvulsants. An EEG is not indicated, because the recording likely will be normal, and minor abnormalities common to all children will confuse the management. For those children who have recurrent febrile seizures, a course of diazepam for the duration of the fever may prevent a convulsion. One study recommends oral diazepam, 0.33 mg/kg PO every 8 hours, beginning with the first sign of a febrile illness and continuing through the duration of the illness.

Landau-Kleffner Syndrome

The Landau-Kleffner syndrome is more common in males and typically occurs between the ages of 2 and 5 years. The condition often is confused with autism, as both conditions are associated with a loss of language function. Language may deteriorate slowly or precipitously in a previously normal child. Approximately 70% have an associated seizure disorder, including focal or generalized tonic-clonic, partial complex, or atypical absence seizures. Behavioral abnormalities and academic difficulties are particularly common. The EEG may show bitemporal, multifocal, or generalized high-amplitude spike and wave discharges. Because these abnormalities may be present only during sleep, an EEG in a sleep-deprived child is essential to confirm the diagnosis. If the "sleep" EEG is normal, but a high index of suspicion for the diagnosis continues, the child should be referred to a tertiary pediatric epilepsy center for prolonged EEG recording and specific neuroimaging studies. Because the etiology of the Landau-Kleffner syndrome is unknown, the treatment is speculative. The seizures are most likely to respond to valproic acid or carbamazepine. Some children have a good response, including recovery of speech development with treatment by steroids. Language therapy often is beneficial. One center reports considerable success for selected patients with the use of multiple subpial resections of the temporal lobe. Unfortunately, many children are left with significant language dysfunction, in spite of aggressive therapy, especially if the condition began before 2 years of age.

Benign Childhood Epilepsy with Centrotemporal Spikes (Rolandic Epilepsy)

Rolandic epilepsy is the most common epilepsy syndrome in children. It has a peak onset at 9 to 10 years of age but may be observed as early as 2 years of age. The majority of seizures (75%) occur during sleep. The child is awakened due to focal facial or tongue paresthesias and associated discomfort. The seizure consists of tonic-clonic contractions localized to one side of the face and often convulsive movements of the corresponding upper extremity, which may become generalized. The seizure rarely persists longer than 1 or 2 minutes. The patient remains conscious throughout but is aphasic until the conclusion of the convulsion. The EEG characteristically demonstrates repetitive spike discharges localized to the centrotemporal area and always is associated with normal background activity. The outcome is excellent, in that the majority of children become seizure-free by adolescence. Antiepileptic drugs rarely are required for the occasional seizure. Carbamazepine is the drug of choice if the seizures are frequent and disruptive to the child.

Juvenile Myoclonic Epilepsy (Janz Syndrome)

The Janz syndrome is most common during early adolescence. Patients initially experience myoclonic jerks on awakening, which causes difficulty with combing hair, dressing, and using utensils. The myoclonus tends to disappear later in the day. Most patients present to their primary care clinician after an early morning generalized tonic-clonic convulsion. The correct diagnosis may be overlooked if the clinician does not obtain a history of myoclonic jerks preceding the generalized convulsion. The EEG characteristically shows a pattern of 4 to 6 per second irregular spike and wave discharges, which may be enhanced by photic stimulation. The seizures are well controlled by valproic acid, but in most cases the drug is required lifelong to prevent a recurrence of seizures.

DIAGNOSTIC STEPS

The first question to be addressed is, "Are these spells really seizures?" A number of nonseizure paroxysmal events that mimic epilepsy in children are treated inappropriately with anticonvulsants following an extensive and usually costly investigation. Table 56–2 provides the clinical descrip-

TABLE 56–2. Conditions That Mimic Epilepsy

Event	Distinguishing Features	Treatment
Breathholding spells	Always provoked. Brief shrill cry, followed by forced expiration, loss of consciousness, cyanosis (occasionally pallid). May be associated with generalized tonic-clonic jerks. Lethargic and sleepy for 5–10 min after the event.	Provide reassurance. Encourage parents not to reinforce behavior by briefly disregarding child during recovery.
Benign paroxysmal vertigo	Sudden onset of ataxic gait and loss of balance. Pale, frightened, and may vomit. No loss of consciousness, but dysarthric and complains of vertigo (if able to verbalize). In 25% horizontal nystagmus occurs during event.	Provide reassurance. Repetitive and persistent episodes may be prevented by dimenhydrinate 5 mg/kg/24 hr (max. 300 mg).
Simple syncope	Loss of consciousness associated with anxiety, prolonged standing, especially if overheated. Brief tonic-clonic jerks may be evident. Rare under 10 yr of age.	Tilt-table testing may distinguish from epilepsy.
Cough syncope	Follows cough paroxysms during sleep. Prolonged paroxysms lead to loss of consciousness, tonic-clonic jerks, and cyanosis. May lose control of bladder. No recollection following event. Often associated with asthma.	Control asthma.
Prolonged QT syndrome	Loss of consciousness caused by cardiac arrhythmia due to acquired or familial myocardial dysfunction. Arrhythmia precipitated by exercise, fear, or anxiety.	Teach parents CPR. Beta blockers?
Night terrors	Sudden onset of screaming during light sleep. Wild, flailing movements of extremities, unintelligible speech, dilated pupils, drooling. Most common in boys 4–6 yr of age.	Provide reassurance.
Episodic dyscontrol syndrome (rage attacks)	Always provoked. Child is physically abusive, often injuring a parent, usually the mother. Verbal threats and profanity. No loss of consciousness. Remorseful at conclusion of event.	Use behavior management.
Tics	Stereotypic, repetitive movements, unassociated with impaired consciousness.	Consider Tourette syndrome.
Masturbation	Repetitive rhythmic copulatory movements in the prone position. Stares, perspires, with plethoric facies. Unresponsive to parent's call.	Provide reassurance. Persistent masturbation requires genital examination to rule out abuse or local disorder.
Gastroesophageal reflux	Laryngospasm, bradycardia, and apnea.	Treat reflux.
Pseudoseizures	Often associated with a history of epilepsy. Most common in adolescent female. Characterized by unusual postures. Falls without injury and doesn't bite tongue. Frequent vocalizations during the event. Resists eye opening. Responsive pupils and lack of extensor plantar reflex. No urinary or fecal incontinence. A pseudoseizure may follow suggestion by examiner.	Evaluate for psychiatric disorder.

CPR, cardiopulmonary resuscitation.

tion and management of the more common non-seizure events.

A seizure is not a diagnosis, but rather a symptom of a disordered central nervous system (CNS). A thorough history and physical examination are essential to uncover clues that may lead to the cause of the seizure. Some parents are able to capture the event at home on a video recording, which later can be reviewed by the clinician. Metabolic causes of seizures, particularly in the newborn, typically are associated with anorexia, vomiting, failure to thrive, and progressive lethargy and apnea, leading to an altered state of consciousness and coma. A sibling may have died of a similar condition. Pyridoxine dependency may be the cause of seizures that begin at birth, especially if they are associated with signs of fetal distress and a history of seizures in utero. A history of hypoxic ischemic encephalopathy, developmental delay, cerebral palsy, meningitis/encephalitis, or head trauma may explain the onset of seizures, even months or years following the event. A family history of epilepsy among first-degree relatives may be elicited, especially in children whose development is normal and who have an intact neurologic examination at the time of the initial seizure. To date, the chromosome loci for three epilepsy syndromes have been identified, including juvenile myoclonic epilepsy (chromosome 6 pzi), fatal progressive myoclonic epilepsy (chromosome 21q), and benign familial neonatal convulsions (chromosomes 8q and 20q). Some children manifest changes in behavior and inattentiveness days or weeks before the seizure. A major alteration in personality associated with a loss of cognitive or motor skills or a deterioration in academic performance should raise the possibility of a CNS degenerative disease. Careful questioning may document a history before the initial seizure of brief lapses of consciousness in the form of head nodding or automatisms that were not considered significant by the parents.

A normal physical and neurologic examination is helpful, but not absolute, in ruling out an "organic" cause of the seizure. A developmental assessment may indicate cognitive delay, which is associated with a higher risk for seizures than for the normal child. A careful examination of the skin, with all clothing removed, is important to establish the diagnosis of a neurocutaneous syndrome. Although café-au-lait spots are not difficult to recognize, the small vitiliginous lesions of tuberous sclerosis often require fluorescence by a Wood lamp in a darkened room to make the diagnosis. As neurofibromatosis and tuberous sclerosis are inherited as an autosomal dominant trait, inspection of the parent's skin and retina may confirm the diagnosis, if examination of the patient is inconclusive. The head circumference is recorded (and that of the parents, if the child's measurement is abnormal), and examination of the retina is mandatory to confirm papilledema, retinal hemorrhages ("shaken baby syndrome"), or chorioretinitis, suggesting an infectious cause. The examination may be completed by searching for evidence of subtle lateralizing signs, which may indicate an indolent lesion in the contralateral hemisphere (e.g., temporal lobe glioma, hamartoma, or mesial temporal sclerosis) causing the seizure. The history might indicate that this patient had initially been right-handed but because of a left hemisphere lesion shifted to left-hand dominance. A mild hemiparesis is characterized by limb asymmetry (less muscle bulk, shortened extremities, or a smaller thumbnail) on the contralateral side. The examiner may note a decreased arm swing and circumduction of the leg, increased deep tendon reflexes, and a plantar extensor response in the affected extremity.

The EEG often is ordered to make diagnoses beyond the scope of the test. However, the routine EEG does have several important uses, including confirmation of suspected epilepsy following the history and physical examination (e.g., absence seizures or benign childhood epilepsy with centrotemporal spikes), differentiation of seizures that have similar clinical characteristics (e.g., absence seizures or CPS), detection of underlying CNS structural abnormalities (e.g., focal slow wave, absence of the corpus callosum), and confirmation of the diagnosis of pseudoseizures. **The routine interictal EEG is abnormal in approximately 60% of children who have seizures.** Infants and toddlers who have recurrent seizures are more likely to have an abnormal EEG than are older children and adolescents. An epileptogenic discharge may be enhanced by several techniques in the laboratory, including eye opening and closure, photic stimulation, hyperventilation, sleep deprivation, and special electrodes (e.g., zygomatic electrode placement). A patient taking antiepileptic drugs scheduled for an EEG should not have the medication decreased or discontinued before the study, because status epilepticus could result.

Prolonged EEG and video monitoring is used in selected patients, especially those children undergoing investigation for epilepsy surgery. The study may record ictal seizures that are not usually obtained during a routine EEG. Prolonged EEG recording is particularly helpful in determining the location and frequency of seizure discharges while simultaneously visualizing and recording alterations in consciousness and the presence of clinical signs, which is essential for classifying the seizure correctly. Finally, prolonged EEG and video recording is the "gold standard" for confirming the suspected diagnosis of pseudoseizures. Some centers use outpatient video-electroencephalography to investigate children suspected of having epilepsy and have found the procedure a useful alternative to inpatient monitoring.

Computed tomography (CT) generally is not helpful in the workup of children who have seizures. Although approximately 30% of cases demonstrate abnormalities, particularly cortical atrophy, the findings usually are nonspecific and do not alter the treatment. However, there are specific disorders associated with recurrent seizures, including tuberous sclerosis, congenital cytomegalovirus infection, and cysticercosis, in which CT may be diagnostic, due to the characteristic distribution of calcium deposits. Magnetic resonance imaging (MRI) is the neuroimaging study of choice for the investigation of selected children who have epilepsy. MRI should be obtained for patients presenting with CPS, the presence of focal neurologic signs (either during or persisting following the seizure), seizures of increasing frequency and severity, or a changing seizure pattern, and for all adolescents after a first seizure. Additional sophisticated neuroimaging studies, including functional MRI, magnetic source imaging/magnetoelectroencephalograms (MSI/MEG), single photon emission computed tomography (SPECT), and positron emission tomography (PET), are useful in the investigation of specific epilepsy syndromes (e.g., infantile spasms).

MANAGEMENT

The management of an initial seizure is based primarily on the classification of the seizure. As stated earlier, a nonseizure is not treated with an antiepileptic drug. The pediatrician may encounter a normal child who is referred following a first nonfebrile generalized tonic-clonic convulsion. These seizures often occur in the early morning and usually are related to the sleep state rather than to hypoglycemia. A normal developmental history and physical examination, a negative family history of epilepsy among first-degree relatives, and a normal EEG are associated with a good prognosis. At least 75% of these patients will remain seizure-free without antiepileptic drugs. However, if the EEG shows a significant abnormality, especially spike or sharp wave discharges in the region of the anterior temporal lobe, the initiation of medication should be considered following the first convulsion. Medications also are indicated following the initial seizure if the history

and EEG confirm a recurrent seizure disorder (e.g., absence epilepsy, infantile spasms). A more difficult decision arises when the untreated child has a second nonfebrile convulsion. Treatment at this point is somewhat empirical, but most pediatric neurologists agree that medications are indicated if the seizure recurs within a few months of the initial seizure. For those children who experience infrequent seizures (e.g., annually) and otherwise are normal, medications rarely are indicated. In this instance, the parents and child are reassured and counseled about what can promote seizures (see later section, Concerns of the Patient and Parents). Figure 56–1 provides a guide to management.

Parents are anxious to learn if their child's seizures will "develop" into epilepsy and whether medication will be necessary for a prolonged period. Several prognostic indicators are helpful in determining outcome. The age of seizure onset is important, because a first seizure in an adolescent is more likely to require lifelong therapy. The type of seizure syndrome often predicts the prognosis, and recurrent seizures that are readily controlled by antiepileptic drugs are generally associated with a favorable outcome.

Principles of Antiepileptic Drug Therapy

The goal in the management of epilepsy is to control the seizure with a single drug (monotherapy) that produces no unwanted side effects. Not infrequently, monotherapy improves seizure frequency and severity, but a second drug is added in an attempt to abolish the seizures. Polytherapy is used most often in the patient who has recalcitrant epilepsy, and it does not always improve seizure control. Polytherapy is more likely than monotherapy to be associated with adverse drug effects. A good rule of thumb is to discontinue a second drug while initiating a third. Recently developed "designer" or "add-on" drugs, including gabapentin and lamotrigine, are useful adjuncts to monotherapy, especially in the management of CPS uncontrolled by monotherapy.

Most children who have uncomplicated seizures can be managed as outpatients. The initial antiepileptic drug dose is 25% to 50% of the total recommended dose because side effects are prominent with a more aggressive drug regimen (Table 56–3). The drug dosage is increased weekly until seizures are controlled or unwanted side effects become a problem. Whether routine blood tests (complete blood count, liver function studies) are

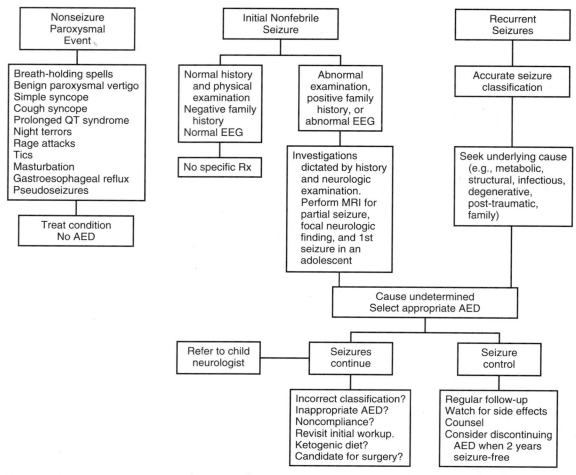

Figure 56–1. A guide to the diagnosis and management of epilepsy. AED, antiepileptic drugs; EEG, electroencephalography; MRI, magnetic resonance imaging.

indicated for the patient who has been started on an antiepileptic drug continues to be debated.

A case in point relates to the early detection of hepatotoxicity, a rare complication of valproic acid. In most reports, symptoms of impending serious liver disease including nausea, vomiting, anorexia, retching, and abdominal pain are present before abnormal liver function studies. Nonetheless, because most serious adverse drug reactions develop during the first several months of medication therapy, monthly blood screening for the initial 3 months is indicated. Thereafter, routine blood chemistries are ordered only when indicated. Hepatotoxicity as a complication of valproic acid therapy is more likely if several risk factors are present. These include an age younger than 2 years, the presence of developmental or neurologic abnormalities, polytherapy, and an underlying metabolic disorder, particularly a mitochondrial disease. Age younger than 2 years and

treatment with several drugs, including valproic acid, is associated with a 1 in 800 risk of fatal hepatotoxicity. Screening tests for a metabolic disorder are indicated for a child younger than 2 years who has a seizure disorder of unknown cause, before the initiation of valproic acid. The tests include a serum ammonia, amino acids, lactate-pyruvate ratio, blood gases, carnitine, and urinary organic acids. If any of these tests is abnormal, valproic acid should be withheld, pending further investigation. Supplemental oral L-carnitine, 30 to 100 mg/kg per day, has been advocated for the child younger than 2 years when placed on valproic acid. Unfortunately, there is no agreement that carnitine prevents hepatotoxicity; furthermore, most infants refuse the medication because of its bitter taste. Fortunately, the incidence of fatal hepatotoxicity resulting from valproic acid has decreased dramatically owing to decreased use of the drug in the child younger

TABLE 56–3. Common Antiepileptic Drugs

Drug	Seizure Type	Oral Dose	Therapeutic Serum Level, µg/mL	Common Side Effects	Serious Side Effects
ACTH	Infantile spasms	20 U IM/24 hr for 2 wk. If no response, increase to 30 U and then 40 U IM/24 hr for an additional wk	—	Hyperglycemia electrolyte abnormalities	Hypertension, infections, sudden death
Carbamazepine* Clobazam†‡	Partial, generalized tonic-clonic	Begin 5–10 mg/kg 24 hr. Increase by 5 mg/kg/24 hr every wk to 15–25 mg/kg/24 hr in 2 or 3 divided doses	4–12	Dizziness, ataxia, drowsiness, diplopia	Hepatic dysfunction, aplastic anemia
Clonazepam	Partial with secondary generalization; myoclonic infantile spasms	Begin 0.01–0.05 mg/kg/24 hr. Increase by 0.05 mg/kg/wk. Max. 0.2 mg/kg/24 hr, in 2 or 3 divided doses	—	Drowsiness, irritability, drooling, behavioral abnormalities	Leukopenia, thrombocytopenia, depression
Ethosuximide	Absence, myoclonic	Begin 10 mg/kg/24 hr in 2 divided doses; may be increased to 50 mg/kg/24 hr	40–160	Drowsiness, diplopia, nausea	Blood dyscrasias, leukopenia
Gabapentin†	Partial	Begin 10 mg/kg/24 hr, increase by 5 mg/kg/24 hr increments every 3–5 days. Max. 900–1200 mg/24 hr in 3 equally divided doses	Not established	Somnolence, dizziness, ataxia, headache, tremor, vomiting, nystagmus, fatigue	None
Lamotrigine† Nitrazepam‡	Partial, generalized tonic-clonic, Lennox-Gastaut syndrome	Begin 2 mg/kg/24 hr in 2 equal doses. Increase to maintenance dose of 5–15 mg/kg/24 hr. Begin with 0.5 mg/kg/24 hr to maintenance of 1 to 5 mg/kg/24 hr if used with valproic acid	1–4	Drowsiness, headache, blurred vision, diplopia ataxia	Severe skin rashes, especially when given in combination with valproic acid
Phenobarbital	Generalized tonic-clonic; partial with secondary generalization, status epilepticus	< 1 year: 3 to 5 mg/kg/24 hr in 1 or 2 divided doses > 1 year: 2 to 4 mg/kg/24 hr	15–40	Hyperactivity, irritability, short attention span, temper trantrums, sedation, altered sleep patterns, depression of cognitive function	Stevens-Johnson syndrome
Phenytoin	Partial, generalized tonic-clonic, status epilepticus	5–6 mg/kg/24 hr in 2 divided doses	10–20	Hirsutism, coarsening of facies, gum hypertrophy, ataxia	Stevens-Johnson syndrome, lupus-like syndrome
Primidone Topiramate Tiagabine	Generalized tonic-clonic; partial myoclonic	Begin 50 mg/24 hr in 2 divided doses. Gradually increase to 150–500 mg/24 hr divided into 3 equal doses	5–12	Aggressive behavior and personality changes	Rashes
Valproic acid*	Generalized tonic-clonic; partial with secondary generalization; absence, myoclonic, atonic	Begin 5–10 mg/kg/24 hr. Increase by 5–10 mg/kg/wk. Usual dose: 20–60 mg/kg/24 hr in 2 or 3 divided doses Enteric-coated tablets or sprinkles decrease nausea and abdominal discomfort	50–100	Weight gain, nausea, abdominal discomfort, alopecia, tremor, thrombocytopenia	Hepatotoxicity, pancreatitis
Vigabatrin†‡	Partial; infantile spasms especially with tuberous sclerosis	Begin 30 to 40 mg/kg/24 hr. Increase by 10 mg/kg/wk. Max. 80 to 100 mg/kg/24 hr in 2 equal doses	1.4–14	Agitation, drowsiness, weight gain, dizziness headache, ataxia	

*Drug of choice.
†Add-on therapy.
‡Clobazam, nitrazepam, and vigabatrin not available in the United States.
ACTH, adrenocorticotropic hormone.

than 2 years and the knowledge that monotherapy is much less likely to result in fatal liver disease.

As with most chronic diseases of childhood, drug compliance often poses a problem. In the long term, **compliance is enhanced significantly when the parents and patient (if possible) participate in the initial decision to use an antiepileptic drug.** Generally, the fewer the pills and the ease of administration (chewable tablets or sprinkles versus large tablets or capsules), the better the compliance. On occasion a drug dose(s) is overlooked and the parents are not certain how to proceed. The physician should instruct the parent to give an extra single dose on the day of discovery, along with the regular schedule.

Drug Interactions

Antiepileptic drugs may induce or inhibit liver enzyme production or they may act to displace another medication from a shared plasma protein binding site. Antiepileptic drugs capable of enzyme induction include phenobarbital, primidone, phenytoin, and carbamazepine. When these drugs are used in combination, they may lower the plasma level of each other by increasing the rate of metabolism. Conversely, enzyme inhibition tends to increase specific drug plasma levels (e.g., valproic acid causes an increased phenobarbital level) by decreasing the metabolic rate. Erythromycin inhibits microsomal enzyme systems, which results in decreased clearance of carbamazepine. When erythromycin is prescribed for a child also on carbamazepine, the pediatrician should monitor the serum levels of the antiepileptic drug during the course of antibiotic therapy, particularly if symptoms of carbamazepine toxicity become apparent. Valproic acid reduces the plasma clearance and prolongs the half-life of lamotrigine. Possibly, this interaction explains the increased incidence of severe skin rashes and the Stevens-Johnson syndrome when these two drugs are used together.

Drug Monitoring

Serum drug levels are overused by many clinicians; their routine determination is unlikely to influence patient management significantly. There are at least nine indications for therapeutic drug monitoring, including (1) at the beginning of therapy to ensure that the medication level is within the therapeutic range; (2) during accelerated growth periods; (3) for uncontrolled seizures or seizures that have changed in type; (4) for symptoms and signs of drug toxicity; (5) for patients who have hepatic or renal disease; (6) for status epilepticus; (7) for patients on polytherapy, especially valproic acid, lamotrigine, and phenobarbital, because drug interactions are common; (8) for children who have cognitive or physical handicaps in whom drug toxicity may be difficult to evaluate, especially those taking phenytoin; and (9) for noncompliant patients. Seizures can be controlled with subtherapeutic drug levels (e.g., carbamazepine). Conversely, serum drug levels above the accepted therapeutic range may have no impact on seizure control and, in fact, may increase seizure frequency and severity. Good clinical judgment is more effective in achieving seizure control than is over-reliance on therapeutic drug monitoring.

Behavioral and Cognitive Side Effects

Antiepileptic drugs are a prominent cause of behavioral abnormalities and cognitive impairment. At times, alterations in behavior and intellectual function are subtle, but aggressiveness, decreased attention span, disinterest in school, depression, and sleep disturbances are common. Children who have epilepsy are at increased risk for academic problems, which may be intensified by therapy. Phenobarbital is associated with these side effects in approximately 50% of children. In decreasing frequency the following drugs may cause similar behavior problems: ACTH, benzodiazepines, carbamazepine, phenytoin, and primidone. Valproic acid is the least likely to affect behavior and cognitive function adversely (Table 56–3). Behavioral and cognitive side effects are a common reason for a patient's being noncompliant with drugs. These complications may be decreased significantly by reducing the drug dose but may require substitution with another medication if the untoward side effects continue. Each follow-up assessment should document the presence of these common side effects, and if they are persistent in spite of drug alteration or substitution, the child should be referred to a learning center for assessment and treatment.

Recurrent and Prolonged Seizures

A few children who have epilepsy are frequent visitors to the emergency department and often require hospitalization due to frequent and prolonged seizures. These patients typically are on multiple drugs and may experience an increase in seizure activity with a low-grade fever. In some cases, a prolonged seizure can be aborted safely at home by the administration of rectal or sublingual lorazepam. Parents can be taught the procedure by a physician or nurse and often are successful in controlling the seizure and preventing hospitalization. The parent is instructed to place a lorazepam tablet (0.05 mg/kg) under the child's tongue or hold a tablet in place on the mucosal surface of the cheek by the parent's finger at the onset of increased seizure activity. The medication dissolves in seconds and has an effect within 15 minutes. A repeat dose may be administered 15 minutes later if the seizures continue. Oral medication should not be attempted during a seizure because aspiration may occur.

Duration of Antiepileptic Drug Treatment

Most studies agree that a seizure-free period of 2 years warrants a trial of discontinuing the drug. The drug is weaned slowly over 3 to 6 months (e.g., a maintenance dose of carbamazepine, 600 mg daily, may be reduced by 100 mg monthly). Approximately 70% of these children will remain seizure-free following drug withdrawal. Patients who have early morning generalized tonic-clonic seizures and absence epilepsy are most likely to remain seizure-free, whereas patients who have slowing or focal spike and wave discharges on a follow-up EEG, developmental delay, seizures that initially were difficult to bring under control, neonatal seizures, age greater than 12 years at the time of the first seizure, and CPS are at greater risk of seizure recurrence following withdrawal of the antiepileptic drug. For the seizure-free child receiving polytherapy, it is recommended that one drug be weaned at a time and the second drug discontinued only if the patient remains seizure-free. If the seizures recur following the weaning process, the same medications should be given at the dose that controlled the seizure previously for an additional 2-year period. Lifelong treatment usually is required when a second 2-year trial of drug treatment is unsuccessful.

Alternative Therapies

The *ketogenic diet* was a common treatment for children who had intractable epilepsy before the introduction of the newer antiepileptics, particularly valproic acid and the benzodiazepines. Interest in the ketogenic diet has recently been renewed, primarily by parent groups concerned about side effects of antiepileptic drugs. The diet is designed to provide a high fat content in a ratio of 4 grams of fat to 1 gram of protein to 1 gram of carbohydrate. The ketogenic diet's mode of action is unknown, but it is likely that elevated levels of β-hydroxybutyrate and acetoacetate resulting from ketosis are responsible for the suppression of seizure activity. The ketogenic diet is recommended for children who have intractable epilepsy, especially for patients who have complex myoclonic epilepsy associated with tonic-clonic convulsions in whom a trial of antiepileptic drugs was unsuccessful. As many as 50% of these children may benefit from the diet. The use of valproic acid is contraindicated in conjunction with the ketogenic diet, because the risk of hepatotoxicity is enhanced. It often is possible to wean the patient from some or all antiepileptic drugs when the seizures are controlled by the ketogenic diet, resulting in improved alertness and cognitive performance. Because the ketogenic diet may be associated with serious nutritional complications, particularly water-soluble vitamin deficiencies, it is imperative that a skilled dietitian and physician provide supervision, because many parents find the diet difficult to manage. The diet usually is maintained for a 2-year period for the seizure-free child.

Epilepsy surgery should be considered for those children who have focal seizures that do not respond to medications. The investigation and management of these children require a multidisciplinary team, including a pediatric epileptologist and a sophisticated EEG monitoring unit and modern neuroimaging equipment. Temporal lobe resections are the most common surgical procedure, but with the use of subdural EEG recording techniques and more recently MSI/MEG, focal epileptogenic lesions in nontemporal lobe regions may be removed surgically with equally excellent results.

CONCERNS OF THE PATIENT AND PARENTS

Skilled counseling is the pediatrician's most important responsibility. Poor understanding and confusion by the parents due to lack of information lead to noncompliance with antiepileptic medications. Many clinics provide excellent counseling by nurse practitioners and social workers who are available to respond to parents' concerns or questions, which are most frequent at the time of diagnosis. A letter to the parents that outlines the treatment plan is extremely effective, because the majority of parents cannot recall instructions following the initial and subsequent counseling sessions. Local and national epilepsy organizations provide support and educational material for parents, which augments the information provided by the physician and nurse.

A prominent early question is, "Will my child ever outgrow the seizures and need for medication?" The question provides an opportunity to discuss seizures and the use of an antiepileptic drug in preventing recurrent seizures. It also allows the clinician to dispel myths of epilepsy. Older children often are impressed to learn that professional athletes and celebrities who have epilepsy function well in society. Parents wish to know whether the schoolteacher should be informed. Because the child is at increased risk for a learning disability and the teacher may provide useful information about behavioral or cognitive changes following the introduction of an antiepileptic drug, it is recommended that the teacher be informed about the diagnosis and the medication prescribed to control the seizures. If the patient has a seizure at school, the informed teacher, with the parent's cooperation, can use the occasion to educate classmates about the condition.

Parents ask about what should be done during a generalized tonic-clonic seizure. They should be instructed not to put an object or finger in the patient's mouth, but to roll the child on his or her side, loosen tight clothing from around the neck, and gently restrain the patient. If the seizure persists longer than 10 minutes, an ambulance should be summoned. Some parents wish to learn cardiopulmonary resuscitation, although resuscitation rarely is required. Children who have epilepsy should not have a bath or swim unattended, because they are at risk of drowning during a seizure. An identification bracelet with "epilepsy" and the antiepileptic drug inscribed is advisable to assist in a rapid diagnosis if the child is found unconscious and alone. Parents should know that seizure frequency may be increased during an illness or when the child is overtired or under stress. Medications, including stimulants (e.g., methylphenidate), alcohol, and phenothiazines, may exacerbate seizures. Some children are more susceptible to seizure recurrence while playing video games or watching television.

The older child and adolescent will have a different set of questions, including the request to play sports. The pediatrician should encourage participation in all activities, including contact sports, as long as appropriate protective equipment is used. The clinician should be familiar with the state laws governing a driver's license, because the patient will require a medical report to be eligible. The adolescent female must be informed that antiepileptic drugs can cause birth defects. Phenobarbital is the most common medication teratogen, followed by phenytoin and carbamazepine. Although most antiepileptic drugs have been reported to cause neural tube defects, the frequency of neural tube defects with valproic acid therapy during the first trimester is 1%, a higher incidence than with other antiepileptic medications. If feasible, the epileptic patient planning a pregnancy should be weaned from the drug, under medical supervision, particularly during the first trimester.

Many parents harbor considerable guilt, particularly if there is a family history of epilepsy. Time should be reserved during each visit to reassure parents and respond to any concerns they may have, particularly relating to academic, social, or behavioral problems in the child that have become apparent since the last visit.

Most cases of epilepsy are well controlled by medication, with few if any serious side effects. The majority of patients outgrow the requirement for medication and can be expected to lead normal lives. The clinician can play a pivotal role in ensuring that the child and family learn to accept the epilepsy, while enjoying good health and living a normal lifestyle.

FURTHER READING

Devinsky O: Cognitive and behavioral effects of antiepileptic drugs. Epilepsia 36 (Suppl 2):S46–S65, 1995.

Duchowny M and Harvey AS: Pediatric epilepsy syndromes: An update and critical review. Epilepsia 37 (Suppl 1):S26–S40, 1996.

Morrell F, Whisler WW, Smith MC, et al.: Landau-Kleffner syndrome: Treatment with subpial intracortical transection. Brain 118:1529–1546, 1995.

Rosman NP, Colton T, Labazzo J, et al.: A controlled trial of diazepam administered during febrile illnesses to prevent recurrence of febrile seizures. N Engl J Med 329:79–84, 1993.

Tennison M, Greenwood R, Lewis D, and Thorn M: Discontinuing antiepileptic drugs in children with epilepsy. N Engl J Med 330:1407–1410, 1994.

Tics

Transient tics, which occur in up to 25% of children, are repeated, abrupt, rapid, and involuntary but suppressible contractions of isolated muscles or muscle groups. They do not occur during sleep, may be exacerbated by stress, and can be suppressed briefly. Symptoms include blinking of the eyelids, sniffling, wrinkling of the nose or forehead, twisting of the mouth, turning of the head to one side, shaking or nodding of the head, twisting of the neck, shrugging of the shoulders, jerking of the extremities, clearing of the throat, and vocal tics. Only a single unilateral or bilateral tic is usually noted initially, but several may occur simultaneously. Transient tic disorder usually begins between 5 and 10 years of age and disappears within 3 months thereafter; chronic simple motor or vocal tics persist for more than 12 months.

Psychogenic cough tic is characterized by recurrent, severe paroxysms of coughing that occur in older children and adolescents every few seconds or minutes. This nonproductive cough is explosive, loud, deep, barking, brassy, honking or seal-like. Ticlike mannerisms also occasionally occur in children who stutter.

Since stimulant medications for the treatment of attention-deficit hyperactivity disorder may exacerbate the frequency or severity of tics, or possibly hasten their appearance in children who have a family history of tics, their use should be carefully monitored or behavioral techniques employed.

Tourette syndrome, characterized by both motor and phonic tics, appears as early as 5 to 7 years of age and is much more frequent in boys than in girls. A family history can often be elicited. Initially, the motor tics usually involve the face or head with eye twitching and head jerking; later, they may affect the rest of the body. Tics subside during sleep, and they may wax and wane irrespective of pharmacotherapy.

Phonic tics include barking, grunting, sniffing, coughing, yelling, shrieking, crying out, throat clearing, hissing, obscenities (coprolalia), and echoing the words of others (echolalia). Other behaviors include repetition of the same word or phrase (palilalia), imitation of the movements of others (echokinesis), smelling, chewing, touching, obscene gestures (copropraxia), licking, jumping, hopping, skipping, and squatting.

Compulsive handwashing, repeatedly rubbing the same area of skin, or obsessional thinking, for example, of obscene words, may be reported. Attention-deficit hyperactivity disorder, present in 30% to 40% of these patients, may predate the onset of tics. Learning disabilities also may be identified.

TREATMENT

Other than reassurance, relaxation training, lessening of stressors or other supportive therapy, no specific treatment is generally indicated for simple transient or chronic tics. **The management of Tourette syndrome depends on its severity, the extent to which it imposes a social disability, the burden of suffering it causes, and the presence of such comorbid disorders as learning disabilities, attention-deficit hyperactivity disorder, and obsessive-compulsive disorder.** Pharmacotherapy is not necessary in all patients with Tourette syndrome, and such side effects as lethargy, sedation, dysphoria, depression, or impairment of concentration may limit its usefulness when prescribed.

Pharmacotherapeutic agents used in the treatment of Tourette syndrome include haloperidol, pimozide, and clonidine among others. Haloperidol may be prescribed in an initial dose of 0.25 to 0.5 mg at bedtime. Depending on the response, it may be increased by 0.5 mg every 4 to 5 days until either improvement or undesirable side effects ensue. The maintenance dose for haloperidol is usually 1 to 3 mg/day in divided doses. Pimozide is begun in a dosage of 0.05 mg/kg at bedtime and then increased gradually every third day, depending on symptom response, to a maximum of 0.02 mg/kg/day, not to exceed 10 mg/day. An electrocardiogram should be obtained at baseline and periodically thereafter, especially during the period of drug adjustment. Clonidine has been used in an initial dose of 0.05 mg once daily to be increased gradually until symptomatic improvement or unacceptable side effects, especially sedation, are reported. The usual maintenance dose ranges from 0.1 to 0.5 mg/day in two divided doses.

FURTHER READING

Carter AS, Pauls DL, Leckman JF, and Cohen DL: A prospective longitudinal study of Gilles de La Tourette's syndrome. J Am Acad Child Adolesc Psychiatry 33:377–385, 1994.

Lavigue JV, Davis AT, and Fauber R: Behavioral management of psychogenic cough: Alternative to the "bedsheet" and other aversive techniques. Pediatrics 87:532–537, 1991.

Peterson AL, Czmpise RL, and Azrin NH: Behavioral and pharmacological treatments for tic and habit disorders: A review. J Devel Behav Pediatr 15:430–441, 1994.

David Korones

Chapter 58

Anemia

Anemia is one of the problems encountered most frequently in pediatrics. Its causes are many, ranging from mild dietary deficiencies to severe congenital disorders; its presentation is highly variable—from the child who has no signs or symptoms to the child who is profoundly ill. Anemia is not a diagnosis; it is a laboratory finding that indicates to the pediatric clinician that a child has a reduction in red blood cell (RBC) mass. It is then incumbent on the clinician to determine why the child is anemic. **Because there are so many causes of anemia, the primary care clinician should be aware of the many ways children who have anemia present and should be well versed in how to evaluate an anemia systematically.**

DEFINITION

Although the measurement of hematocrit was defined first in 1929, almost 50 years passed before ranges of normal hematocrits were established for children of all ages and genders (Table 58–1). The hematocrit climbs gradually as the child progresses from the toddler years to adolescence. During the adolescent years, the mean hematocrit of boys climbs to 5 points above that of girls. The hematocrit of African-Americans is approximately 1 to 2 points lower than that of whites or Asians.

The clinician should be aware that definitions of normal hematocrit or hemoglobin values are guidelines. The normal range of hemoglobin values is defined arbitrarily as the mean hemoglobin ± 2 standard deviations of the population under study. Thus, the 2.5% of children who have the lowest hemoglobin values will be classified arbitrarily as anemic, when in fact some may not be. Conversely, a child may have a hemoglobin level in the normal range but be anemic. For example, a 10-year-old whose hemoglobin drops from 14.0 to 12.0 g/dL may still have a normal hemoglobin value, but such a drop in hemoglobin requires investigation. Table 58–1 gives reference values for normal hemoglobin and hematocrit according to age and gender; it is only a guideline. The hemoglobin of a given child must be evaluated in the context of the child's history, physical examination, previous laboratory studies (if available), and overall health.

HISTORY

Most children who have anemia manifest few, if any, signs or symptoms. Thus, a careful history is more likely than a physical examination to yield important clues to its etiology. A few simple questions directed at the more common causes of anemia usually are sufficient to determine its cause. **A dietary history is essential for children at any age, but it is especially important in toddlers and teenagers, the two groups of children who frequently develop iron deficiency anemia due to poor diet.** The patient should be queried about blood loss; adolescent girls should be asked about irregular or heavy menses. Ethnic background and race are important; for example, glucose-6-phosphate dehydrogenase (G6PD) deficiency is common among African-Americans and those of Mediterranean heritage. Thalassemia trait is common in people of Mediterranean, Asian, and African descent. A medication history

TABLE 58–1. Values (Mean and Lower Limits of Normal) for Hemoglobin, Hematocrit, and Mean Corpuscular Volume Determinations

Age, yr	Hemoglobin, gm/dL		Hematocrit, %		MCV, μm³	
	Mean	*Lower Limit*	*Mean*	*Lower Limit*	*Mean*	*Lower Limit*
0.5–1.9	12.5	11.0	37	33	77	70
2–4	12.5	11.0	38	34	79	73
5–7	13.0	11.5	39	35	81	75
8–11	13.5	12.0	40	36	83	76
12–14						
Female	13.5	12.0	41	36	85	78
Male	14.0	12.5	43	37	84	77
15–17						
Female	14.0	12.0	41	36	87	79
Male	15.0	13.0	46	38	86	78
18–49						
Female	14.0	12.0	42	37	90	80
Male	16.0	14.0	47	40	90	80

MCV, mean corpuscular volume.

From Oski FA, Brugnara C, and Nathan DG: A diagnostic approach to the anemic patient. *In* Nathan DG and Orkin SH: Nathan and Oski's Hematology of Infancy and Childhood, 5th ed. Philadelphia, WB Saunders, 1998, p 376.

is essential because certain drugs are precipitants of hemolytic anemias. A family history of jaundice, cholecystectomy at an early age, or splenectomy suggests a familial hemolytic anemia.

SIGNS AND SYMPTOMS

Symptoms of anemia are nonspecific. Infants and toddlers may be irritable, may exhibit changes in behavior, or may sleep longer than usual. Older children and teenagers complain of fatigue, weakness, dizziness, headaches, decreased exercise tolerance, and shortness of breath.

Findings on physical examination are few. Children whose anemias are mild often have no physical findings. Pallor is not apparent until the hematocrit is less than 25%. Detection of pallor is made more difficult by fluorescent lighting in clinicians' offices and variations of normal skin color, particularly in dark-skinned children. Pallor is assessed better by inspecting the conjunctivae, buccal mucosa, palmar creases, or nail beds. Examination of the skin or sclera may also reveal jaundice, a frequent finding in children who have hemolytic anemias. Lymphadenopathy and/or hepatosplenomegaly may indicate a more serious process such as leukemia. A pulmonary flow murmur is heard frequently in children who have anemia; a gallop or other signs of congestive heart failure are appreciated when the anemia is profound. Splenomegaly can occur in children who have autoimmune hemolytic anemia, sickle cell disease, and sickle thalassemia.

LABORATORY STUDIES

In most instances four routine laboratory tests are sufficient to diagnose an anemia and pinpoint its etiology: (1) **the hemoglobin (or hematocrit)** enables determination of whether a child is anemic; (2) **the mean corpuscular volume (MCV)** enables classification of an anemia as microcytic, normocytic, or macrocytic; (3) **the reticulocyte percentage** distinguishes a hypoproductive anemia from an anemia due to increased destruction of RBCs; **and** (4) **examination of the peripheral blood film** (the blood smear) is essential in assessing RBC morphology.

If the clinician suspects that a child has a mild or moderate anemia, a complete blood count (CBC), differential, platelet count, reticulocyte count, and blood film should be obtained. If the child is jaundiced or has a family history of hemolytic anemia, an elevated indirect bilirubin level and serum lactate dehydrogenase (LD) may confirm hemolysis. More specific tests such as serum iron, total iron-binding capacity (TIBC), ferritin, hemoglobin electrophoresis, Coombs test, or G6PD level should be reserved for the markedly anemic child or the child in whom the aforementioned tests fail to reveal an etiology.

EVALUATION AND TREATMENT

The clinician usually encounters an anemic child as follows: (1) the asymptomatic child whose anemia is detected on routine screening; (2) the symptomatic child who is not critically ill, but who manifests pallor or jaundice; and (3) the critically ill child. The following guidelines may help the clinician in the initial evaluation of these children.

THE ASYMPTOMATIC CHILD WHOSE ANEMIA IS DETECTED ON ROUTINE SCREENING. If the child has mild anemia and is at risk of iron deficiency because of age and dietary history, it is reasonable to try an empirical trial of iron supplementation. A stool guaiac test should be performed, and it is imperative to repeat the hematocrit in 1 to 2 months. If the child does not respond to iron, a more extensive evaluation is necessary. If the child has a moderate anemia or is thought not to be at risk of iron deficiency, a CBC, differential, platelet count, reticulocyte count, and peripheral blood film should be obtained. Other laboratory studies may be necessary, depending on the history and physical examination of the child.

THE SYMPTOMATIC CHILD WHO IS NOT CRITICALLY ILL. Because these children are symptomatic, their evaluation generally is more extensive. For the child who presents with pallor, a CBC, differential, platelet count, reticulocyte count, and peripheral blood film should be obtained. If the pallor is striking, additional blood for typing and screening for possible blood transfusion should be considered. Other laboratory studies should be obtained as indicated by the history and physical examination or by results of the initial CBC. For the child who presents with jaundice or scleral icterus, a serum direct and indirect bilirubin, LD, and Coombs test should be obtained in addition to the CBC. If liver disease is suspected, measuring liver function and screening for hepatitis should be considered.

THE CRITICALLY ILL CHILD. When a child presents with lethargy, obtundation, or unstable vital signs, profound or rapid-onset anemia is not the most likely cause. Nonetheless, profound anemia should be considered as a cause of this moribund state, particularly if the child manifests jaundice or striking pallor. Although initial efforts at resuscitation are directed at stabilizing the airway and circulation and administering antimicrobials, a blood type and cross match for possible immediate transfusion should be obtained. Additional tubes of blood can be ordered and held until the child is stabilized and the clinician has an opportunity to assess initial data and plan further laboratory evaluation.

CLASSIFICATION OF ANEMIAS

The evaluation of a child who has anemia will proceed more efficiently, and the anemia will be diagnosed and treated more promptly, if the clinician uses a systematic approach, such as a schema based on RBC size. With this schema, anemias are classified as microcytic, normocytic, or macrocytic based on the child's mean corpuscular volume (MCV) (Fig. 58–1). The precise type of anemia then is determined based on the child's history, physical examination, and, in some instances, further laboratory studies.

Microcytic Anemia

There are five causes of microcytic anemia for the child who presents with a low MCV (see Fig. 58–1); iron deficiency and thalassemia trait are the most common causes.

Iron Deficiency Anemia

Iron deficiency anemia is prevalent among toddlers and teenagers. Children in these two disparate age groups have similar risk factors for iron deficiency anemia: They are in a period of rapid growth, and their diets often are poor. Toddlers are weaning from iron-supplemented formula to cow's milk and table food. Adolescents may eat sporadically and may eat unbalanced meals. Teenage girls are at additional risk if they experience excessive blood loss due to frequent or heavy menses. Full-term infants are born with sufficient iron stores to maintain a normal hemoglobin for the first 6 months of life. School-age children are not in a period of rapid growth and generally eat well. Iron deficiency anemia in either of these latter two groups of children is unusual and merits a more extensive evaluation for blood loss.

Infants and toddlers who have iron deficiency anemia are irritable, sometimes disproportionately so for the level of anemia. Other symptoms specific to iron deficiency anemia include pica, ice craving, and a craving for different or unusual foods. A growing literature suggests that iron deficiency may lead to subtle but serious neurocognitive impairments that may have long-term developmental implications. The family and child should be queried about blood loss, particularly through the gastrointestinal tract. Causes of gastrointestinal bleeding include cow's milk allergy, peptic ulcer, Meckel diverticulum, bleeding polyps, or occult bleeding due to long-distance running or swimming, or to coagulopathy due to von Willebrand disease or use of aspirin. Guaiac testing of the stools should be obtained on several different occasions because occult blood loss through the gastrointestinal tract can be intermittent.

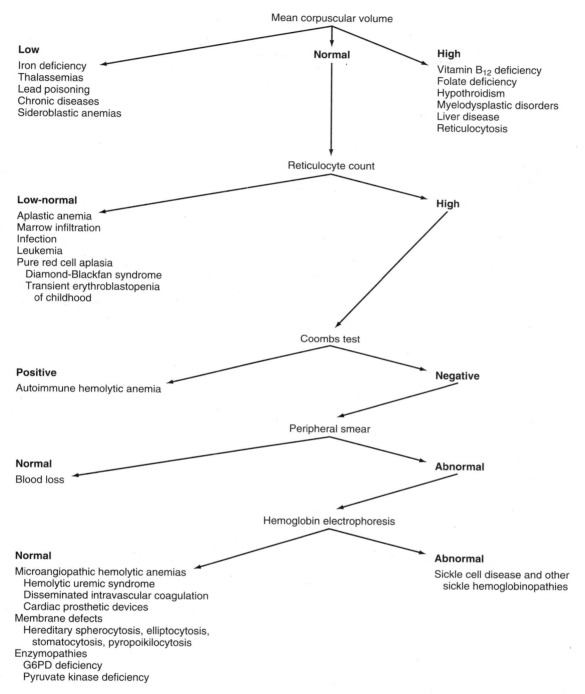

Mean corpuscular volume

Low
Iron deficiency
Thalassemias
Lead poisoning
Chronic diseases
Sideroblastic anemias

Normal

High
Vitamin B$_{12}$ deficiency
Folate deficiency
Hypothroidism
Myelodysplastic disorders
Liver disease
Reticulocytosis

Reticulocyte count

Low-normal
Aplastic anemia
Marrow infiltration
Infection
Leukemia
Pure red cell aplasia
  Diamond-Blackfan syndrome
  Transient erythroblastopenia
    of childhood

High

Coombs test

Positive
Autoimmune hemolytic anemia

Negative

Peripheral smear

Normal
Blood loss

Abnormal

Hemoglobin electrophoresis

Normal
Microangiopathic hemolytic anemias
  Hemolytic uremic syndrome
  Disseminated intravascular coagulation
  Cardiac prosthetic devices
Membrane defects
  Hereditary spherocytosis, elliptocytosis,
    stomatocytosis, pyropoikilocytosis
Enzymopathies
  G6PD deficiency
  Pyruvate kinase deficiency

Abnormal
Sickle cell disease and other
  sickle hemoglobinopathies

Figure 58–1. Diagnostic approach to anemia in the child, based on the mean corpuscular volume.

Laboratory values characteristic of iron deficiency anemia include a low MCV, low RBC number, and low reticulocyte percentage. In addition to the hypochromic, microcytic RBCs seen on the peripheral blood film, RBC size and shape may vary considerably (e.g., target cells and elliptical forms). Another clue to the presence of iron deficiency is examination of the plasma. The iron-deficient child's plasma is clear instead of its characteristic straw color. Additional laboratory studies that may be useful include serum iron, TIBC, and ferritin. In iron deficiency, the serum iron is low and the TIBC high. A low serum ferritin is diagnostic of iron deficiency anemia; however, because it is an acute-phase reactant, it sometimes is normal or elevated in the iron-deficient child who has an acute illness. These studies usually are not needed to make a diagnosis, but they may help in unclear cases or in children who do not respond to iron supplements.

It is reasonable to prescribe iron supplementation empirically to the toddler or teenager who has a low hemoglobin level and a diet low in iron. Ferrous sulfate is the formulation of iron supplementation used most widely. The oral dose is 3 to 6 mg/kg/day of elemental iron in three divided doses. It should not be given with meals because this will reduce its absorption substantially. The reticulocyte count should rise within 5 to 10 days of beginning the iron. The hemoglobin level should be two-thirds corrected within a month. Iron supplementation should be continued for 2 to 3 months after correction of the low hemoglobin so that iron stores can be repleted. If the hemoglobin again drops after iron therapy is stopped, the child should be evaluated for blood loss. The risk of iron deficiency anemia due to diet can be reduced by preventive measures such as the use of iron-fortified formula and cereals. Families also should be counseled to avoid giving infants and toddlers excessive quantities of cow's milk, a common cause of iron deficiency.

It must be emphasized that **iron deficiency anemia is not a diagnosis; it is imperative that the clinician determine its cause in any child**, even children in the typical age groups. A careful history for blood loss should be obtained in all these children. A more exhaustive history, physical examination, and evaluation for blood loss should be obtained in children whose diet appears to be adequate and in young infants and school-age children.

Thalassemia

The thalassemias are a heterogeneous group of disorders characterized by an imbalance in the production of alpha and beta chains, the two main components of the hemoglobin molecule. α-Thalassemia is characterized by a relative lack of production of α-chains, whereas β-thalassemia is due to a relative lack of β-chains. α- and β-Thalassemia trait are the mildest clinically expressed variants of this disorder. α-Thalassemia trait is common among African-Americans and Southeast Asians. A child who has this mild disorder has no signs or symptoms. Laboratory features include a mild anemia, low MCV, elevated RBC number, anisocytosis and poikilocytosis on the peripheral

blood film, and a normal hemoglobin electrophoresis. α-Thalassemia major is rare; children who have this more severe variant are markedly anemic and sometimes transfusion-dependent. β-Thalassemia trait is common in persons of Mediterranean descent. These children, too, are asymptomatic, and their laboratory findings are similar to those who have α-thalassemia trait. However, their hemoglobin electrophoresis is abnormal; an elevated hemoglobin A_2 level is diagnostic. β-Thalassemia major is uncommon.

Both thalassemia trait and iron deficiency are characterized by mild microcytic anemias; thus, it often is difficult to distinguish between these two entities; the Mentzer index (MCV/RBC number) is a useful test to distinguish between these two very common disorders. This index is based on the premise that there are greater numbers of RBCs in thalassemia trait than in iron deficiency. A quotient less than or equal to 11 is consistent with iron deficiency; a quotient greater than or equal to 13 is consistent with a thalassemia trait.

Anemia of Chronic Disease

Anemia of chronic disease or chronic inflammation is characterized by a mild to moderate anemia (hematocrit, 25 to 35%) and a low-normal MCV (65 to 75 fL). It is seldom that a child's sole manifestation of a chronic inflammatory state is anemia; the child typically will have other systemic signs or symptoms such as fatigue, malaise, or fever; he or she may have focal findings such as inflammation of the joint, as often is observed in juvenile rheumatoid arthritis or may have abdominal pain and diarrhea typical of inflammatory bowel disease. An elevated erythrocyte sedimentation rate (ESR) in a child who has a microcytic anemia of unknown cause suggests underlying inflammation. Other laboratory tests consistent with the anemia of chronic disease include a low serum iron level, low TIBC, and an elevated serum ferritin level. The asymptomatic child who has these laboratory findings should be evaluated for an underlying chronic illness such as juvenile rheumatoid arthritis, inflammatory bowel disease, chronic infection, or lupus.

Other Microcytic Anemias

Lead poisoning can cause a microcytic anemia. Now that there are comprehensive screening programs for lead poisoning, elevated serum lead levels usually are detected before a child becomes anemic. *Sideroblastic anemia,* another cause of microcytic anemia, is extremely rare in children.

Normocytic Anemia

Normocytic anemias are characterized by RBCs of normal volume but are caused by increased RBC destruction or their decreased production. Although the normocytic anemias are far less common than microcytic anemias, the causes are myriad. They may be recalled more easily if they are subdivided into anemias associated with a low reticulocyte count (predominantly hypoproductive anemias) and those associated with an elevated reticulocyte count (predominantly hemolytic anemias) (see Fig. 58–1).

Normocytic Anemia and Reticulocytopenia

The most common causes of these anemias are aplastic crisis and transient erythroblastopenia of childhood.

APLASTIC CRISIS. An aplastic crisis is the abrupt cessation of RBC production in a child who has an underlying chronic hemolytic anemia. The vast majority of aplastic crises are caused by parvovirus infection. In addition to the characteristic rash, fever, and abdominal pain caused by this virus, parvovirus selectively infects RBC precursors and causes temporary cessation of RBC production. Hemolysis continues because of the underlying hemolytic anemia, but these children have lost their ability to compensate for the increased RBC destruction. The result is a sudden, rapid, life-threatening drop in the hematocrit. Children who have known hemolytic anemias such as hereditary spherocytosis or sickle cell anemia and develop fevers or rash should be evaluated promptly. A CBC and reticulocyte count should be obtained; the child should be hospitalized and transfused if he or she appears ill or if the hematocrit is dropping and the reticulocyte count is low.

TRANSIENT ERYTHROBLASTOPENIA OF CHILDHOOD. This is a severe hypoproductive anemia that occurs most frequently in children between the ages of 1 and 4 years. The child who has transient erythoblastopenia of childhood appears remarkably well despite having a hematocrit as low as 10% or 15%. He or she usually comes to medical attention because a friend or family member who has not seen the child in several weeks notes striking pallor. The physical examination is normal except for pallor. The child may manifest signs of congestive heart failure if the hematocrit is profoundly low. Laboratory studies reveal a normocytic, normochromic profound anemia, and the reticulocyte count usually is 0.0%. The cause of this disease is unknown. Treatment is supportive. Many children recover spontaneously within a few weeks of diagnosis; others require RBC transfusion.

Other causes of normocytic anemia and reticulocytopenia are far less common. Diamond-Blackfan syndrome is a congenital pure RBC aplasia that typically manifests in the first year of life and often is associated with congenital anomalies such as thumb deformities and short stature. Renal failure can present with a hypoproductive normocytic anemia. Approximately one third of children who have autoimmune hemolytic anemia have low reticulocyte counts.

Normocytic Anemia and Reticulocytosis

The majority of children who have these laboratory findings have hemolytic anemias. These anemias can be categorized as *extrinsic* (due to a normal red blood cell in an abnormal environment) or *intrinsic* (due to an intrinsically abnormal red blood cell).

EXTRINSIC CAUSES. The two principal extrinsic causes of anemia are microangiopathic hemolytic anemia and autoimmune hemolytic anemia. *Microangiopathic hemolytic anemias* are caused by disseminated intravascular hemolysis, hemolytic uremic syndrome, prosthetic valves, or intravascular devices such as central arterial or venous catheters. The child who has this type of anemia is often quite ill, and anemia is but one component of a multisystem disorder. The diagnosis of microangiopathic hemolysis is confirmed by the presence of RBC fragments on the peripheral blood film.

Autoimmune Hemolytic Anemia. This uncommon disorder occurs in children of all ages; it may be acute and self-limited or chronic. It sometimes is associated with underlying illnesses such as lupus, human immunodeficiency virus, or lymphoma. Children typically present with jaundice or scleral icterus; 50% of these children have splenomegaly. The blood film often reveals spherocytes, and a positive direct Coombs test is diagnostic. Children who have this disorder should be evaluated for the possibility of an underlying illness. Treatment consists of prednisone, intravenous gammaglobulin, or, in refractory cases, splenectomy.

Other extrinsic causes of hemolysis include vitamin E deficiency (seen in premature infants and children who have fat malabsorption), Wilson disease, and hypersplenism.

INTRINSIC CAUSES. The RBC has only three components—the membrane, enzymes, and hemoglobin. An inherited defect in any of these components can result in a hemolytic anemia. A child who has a hemolytic anemia and a family history of anemia, jaundice, splenectomy, or cholecystectomy at an early age should be evaluated for these inherited disorders.

Membrane Disorders. *Hereditary spherocytosis* is the most common RBC membrane disorder. Although it occurs most frequently among children of Northern European descent, it can occur in any ethnic group. The disease is inherited as an autosomal dominant trait in 75% of cases. Children who have hereditary spherocytosis occasionally present with jaundice and anemia in the neonatal period, but they present more often at an older age with a history of intermittent jaundice, anemia, and splenomegaly. Laboratory evaluation reveals a mild to moderate anemia, an elevated reticulocyte percentage, an elevated mean corpuscular hemoglobin concentration (MCHC), a negative direct Coombs test, and spherocytes on the peripheral blood film. There is no standard laboratory test for the diagnosis of hereditary spherocytosis; rather, the diagnosis is based on a constellation of family history, symptoms, signs, and laboratory findings. Occasionally, a parent who has very mild hereditary spherocytosis may go undiagnosed until his or her child is diagnosed. When the diagnosis is in question in a child, it may help to examine the parents for splenomegaly and to obtain a CBC and peripheral blood film on the parents to evaluate them for subtle signs of the disease.

The major complications of this disorder are cholelithiasis, aplastic crisis, and trauma to the spleen. The child who has a hematocrit consistently less than 30 and frequent exacerbations of jaundice may have lower levels of activity and miss more school because of minor illnesses than does an unaffected child. Daily folic acid supplements are recommended for all children who have this disorder. Because RBC destruction in spherocytosis occurs in the spleen, splenectomy resolves the hemolytic anemia completely and removes the risk of the aforementioned complications. However, the benefits of splenectomy must be weighed against the risk of overwhelming sepsis due to encapsulated organisms. Whether a child who has hereditary spherocytosis should undergo splenectomy is controversial. Most pediatric hematologists recommend that the spleen not be removed from a child younger than 5 years of age because of the high risk of pneumococcal sepsis. Splenectomy generally is recommended for older children whose hematocrits are consistently less than 30% and whose energy level, school performance, and school attendance are affected by the disease.

Other membrane disorders such as hereditary elliptocytosis, stomatocytosis, and pyropoikilocytosis are far less common.

Enzymopathies. *G6PD deficiency* is the most common of the enzymopathies that cause hemolytic anemia. The defect is X-linked and thus is seen in males almost exclusively. It occurs most commonly in African-American males and in persons of Mediterranean and Southeast Asian descent. The function of the enzyme is to protect the cell against oxidant stress generated by infection, exposure to certain toxins such as naphthalene, or exposure to certain medications such as aspirin, sulfa drugs, or quinine. The deficiency in the enzyme is not absolute; rather, the enzyme has a shorter half-life. Many different mutations result in variable half-lives of the enzyme; thus, hemolysis varies in severity.

The child who has G6PD deficiency is not anemic. It is only when subject to oxidant stress that he or she experiences hemolysis and becomes anemic. When this occurs the child may manifest jaundice and other signs and symptoms of anemia. The parents of a previously healthy child who presents with these findings should be queried about any recent exposure of the child to medications, toxins, or infection; the clinician should note ethnic background in the evaluation. Laboratory studies reveal moderate normocytic anemia, reticulocytosis, and an elevated indirect bilirubin level. The G6PD level may be normal at the time of acute hemolysis; the more senescent RBCs are G6PD-deficient and break down quickly with oxidant stress, thus leaving only the younger, G6PD-replete cells at the time the test is performed. If the G6PD level is normal in a child whose presentation is consistent with G6PD deficiency, the level should be measured again several months after the acute episode. Treatment for this disease is removal of the offending agent. Transfusion usually is not necessary.

Hemoglobinopathies. The most common hemoglobinopathies are sickle cell anemia and other sickle cell syndromes such as sickle-hemoglobin C and sickle-beta thalassemia. These anemias are discussed in Chapter 59. Hemoglobin C, D, G, and a variety of other abnormal hemoglobins are rare and generally do not cause anemia.

Macrocytic Anemia

Macrocytic anemias are uncommon in children. Although vitamin B_{12} and folate deficiency usually come to mind, they are extremely rare causes of macrocytic anemia in children. Normal newborns are macrocytic; their MCVs range from 100 to 125 fL. Reticulocytosis can cause macrocytosis because reticulocytes are large. Macrocytosis occasionally is seen in children who have hypothyroidism. Children who have Down syndrome have slightly elevated MCVs. Certain medications, particularly valproic acid, can cause macrocytic anemia. Intrinsic bone marrow disorders such as aplastic anemia or myelodysplastic syndrome sometimes are associated with macrocytic anemia (due to increased production of hemoglobin F). Initial evaluation of the child who has macrocytosis should include a CBC, reticulocyte count, peripheral blood film, hemoglobin electrophoresis, and tests of thyroid function.

FURTHER READING

Dallman PR and Siimes MA: Percentile curves for hemoglobin and red cell volume in infancy and childhood. J Pediatr 94:26, 1979.

Kay R, Oski FA, and Barness LA: Core Textbook of Pediatrics, 3rd ed. Philadelphia, JB Lippincott, 1988.

Mentzer WC: Differentiation of iron deficiency anemia from thalassemia trait. Lancet 1:882, 1973.

Segel GB: Anemia. Pediatr Rev 10:77, 1988.

Wintrobe MM: Blood Pure and Eloquent, Part 6, 1st ed. New York, McGraw-Hill, 1980.

Norma B. Lerner

Chapter 59

Sickle Cell Disease

The term *sickle cell disease* is used to describe sickle cell anemia (homozygous sickle cell disease, hemoglobin SS [Hb SS]), those hemoglobinopathies in which Hb S is produced with another abnormal hemoglobin (Hb C, D, O, etc.), and the sickle β-thalassemia syndromes in which Hb S production is accompanied by either reduced or absent adult hemoglobin (Hb A). Sickle cell trait is present when the Hb S gene is inherited along with the normal Hb A gene. Children who have sickle cell trait are, except in rare circumstances, asymptomatic. In the United States, African-Americans and Hispanics from the Caribbean, Central America, and areas of South America are the groups affected most commonly by sickle cell disease.

PATHOPHYSIOLOGY

A single nucleotide change (A → T) in the glutamic acid DNA codon results in the substitution of valine for glutamic acid in the sixth position of the β-globin chain of hemoglobin. This point mutation leads to the synthesis of sickle hemoglobin (Hb S), which is responsible for the complex pathophysiology of sickle cell disease.

Our understanding of the biology of sickle cell disease and its two cardinal features, vaso-occlusion and hemolytic anemia, remains incomplete. Investigators have identified that patients' young reticulocytes express receptors that make them more adherent to vascular endothelium. Increases in certain cytokines, indicative of sickle cell dis-

ease, appear to magnify these cell-vessel interactions. Overall, the enhanced adherence may be important in slowing blood flow and increasing red blood cell (RBC) exposure to low oxygen tension in the microcirculation. When exposed to low oxygen tension, Hb S tends to polymerize within the RBC; this phenomenon results in alterations of membrane shape and function, increased cell density, and reduced deformability. Distorted "sickle"-shaped cells fail to move smoothly through small vessels, resulting in obstruction to flow, further accumulation of RBCs, and ultimately, tissue ischemia. RBC physical alterations also reduce their life span and lead to ongoing hemolysis.

Patients who have sickle cell disease also have numerous aberrations of hemostasis, such as platelet abnormalities, increased thrombin generation, and reduced anticoagulant factors. Whether this coagulopathy is primary or secondary is not fully understood, but its existence may be a consequence of, or contribute to, the well-recognized vascular abnormalities that result in such events as stroke.

CLINICAL FEATURES

Chronic Hemolytic Anemia

This problem is not detected in the newborn who has sickle cell disease, because of the early high fetal hemoglobin (Hb F) level that is present. During the first months of life, however, the proportion of Hb S (rather than Hb A) increases as the Hb F declines, leaving RBCs vulnerable to intracellular hemoglobin polymerization, membrane changes, and depressed survival. The level of anemia (7 to 10 gm/dL) and reticulocytosis (10% to 20%) typically seen in Hb SS disease usually is apparent by 4 months of age. During childhood the hemolytic anemia may be manifested by fatigue, scleral icterus, jaundice, dark urine, and less frequently, symptoms of gallbladder disease.

Several complications may intensify the anemia critically. Viral or bacterial infection may suppress erythropoiesis and produce reticulocytopenia and a fall in hemoglobin and hematocrit, known as an "aplastic crisis." This generally lasts from 5 to 10 days and most frequently is due to parvovirus B19 infection. Infants and children who have sickle cell disease also may develop an acute splenic sequestration crisis during which the spleen rapidly enlarges, pools red blood cells, and causes the hematocrit to fall, leading to potentially life-threatening anemia. Adolescents, particularly those who have Hb SC disease or $S\beta^+$-thalassemia, may have chronic splenomegaly, which results in a lower baseline hemoglobin level. Homozygosity in males for glucose-6-phosphate-dehydrogenase (G6PD) deficiency may cause increased hemolysis during periods of severe infection or exposure to high doses of oxidant medications (e.g., aspirin, sulfa drugs, antimalarials). Finally, anemia may be worsened by nutritional deficiency, such as the lack of folic acid or iron.

Susceptibility to Infection

As a result of splenic dysfunction and humoral abnormalities, children who have sickle cell disease have increased susceptibility to severe infections, particularly with encapsulated bacteria such as *Streptococcus pneumoniae* or *Haemophilus influenzae* type b. Before the use of pneumococcal vaccine and penicillin prophylaxis, *S. pneumoniae* was the major cause of death in children who had sickle cell anemia, with those below 3 years of age being at highest risk. (*H. influenzae* infection has become very rare since the introduction of the *H. influenzae* [Hib] vaccine.)

Pain

The painful "crisis" is one of the most debilitating complications of sickle cell disease. The sensation of pain is caused by the obstruction to blood flow, which produces tissue ischemia. Inflammatory cells and cytokines also contribute to the resultant discomfort. The incidence of sickle cell crisis varies considerably among patients, with one third rarely experiencing these episodes and a small percentage suffering from vaso-occlusion many times a year.

"Painful crisis" is experienced as deep, throbbing pain, usually without accompanying physical findings. Occasionally local tenderness, swelling, and erythema are seen. The pain often affects the extremities, abdomen, or back but may occur anywhere. It may migrate or encompass more sites over time. In those patients who have fever, a high white blood cell (WBC) count, and localized pain, it may be difficult to distinguish a crisis from osteomyelitis. Children younger than 5 years of age may experience a pain crisis in the form of "hand-foot syndrome" characterized by swollen, tender feet and/or hands. The hand-foot syndrome results from vaso-occlusion and infarction in the metatarsal and metacarpal bones and often is the first clinical sign of disease.

Acute Chest Syndrome

The acute chest syndrome also results from vaso-occlusion and is responsible for a large number of the hospital admissions of sickle cell disease patients. It is characterized by chest pain, cough, and tachypnea and at times by hypoxemia and fever. Pulmonary infiltrates are present on chest radiograph, raising the question of a diagnosis of infection versus infarction. Often an exact cause is not identified even after the appropriate cultures, serologies, and other laboratory tests are reviewed. Infection, intrapulmonary sickling, and infarction, as well as pulmonary bone marrow fat embolism, may play a role in causation.

Neurologic Crisis

The most common catastrophic neurologic event in sickle cell disease is cerebrovascular accident (CVA), which ultimately affects from 6% to 12% of patients. The most common cause of CVA in children is ischemic infarction, whereas hemorrhage becomes more prevalent with age. The first CVA occurs at a mean age of 8 years and is associated with a 15% mortality rate. Stroke in patients who have sickle cell disease is manifested by the same symptoms produced by other causes of CVA.

Growth and Development

Birth weights in infants who have sickle cell anemia are normal when compared with African-American controls. Delayed growth may be observed, with weight being more affected than height. Sexual development also may be delayed. Toward the end of adolescence, most patients who have sickle cell anemia ultimately attain close to adult height and sexual maturity. Patients in general, however, do not reach normal weight. A significant percentage of affected children also have microinfarcts of the nervous system, resulting in subtle but serious neurocognitive impairments.

Clinical Manifestations of Chronic Organ Damage in Sickle Cell Disease

HEART. Children who have sickle cell disease have cardiovascular symptoms compatible with chronic severe anemia, such as dyspnea, fatigue, and palpitations. On physical examination a systolic murmur frequently is appreciated. Cardiomegaly often is seen on radiographs.

LUNGS. Patients, particularly those who have repeated episodes of acute chest syndrome, ultimately may develop abnormalities of the ventilation/perfusion ratio and arterial hypoxemia. Pulmonary function tests may show depression of total lung capacity and vital capacity, abnormalities that do not correlate with a history of chest crisis.

HEPATOBILIARY SYSTEM. Chronic elevated serum bilirubin secondary to hemolysis leads to mild jaundice and often results in gallstones. Complications such as cholelithiasis, common bile duct obstruction, and acute pancreatitis may occur.

GENITOURINARY SYSTEM. The earliest defect is hyposthenuria, which usually is seen by 3 years of age. As a result, there is an obligatory urine output of greater than 2000 mL per day, as well as enuresis and nocturia. Patients also are unable to acidify urine maximally and may have mild hyperkalemia. Other manifestations of renal disease may include elevated serum uric acid, gross hematuria, papillary necrosis, urinary tract infection, hyperfiltration, nephrotic syndrome, and hypertension. Priapism, and ultimately impotence, also may occur.

NEUROLOGIC DISEASE. In addition to the residual problems after a CVA, recent cognitive testing as well as radiologic studies of some asymptomatic patients who have sickle cell disease have revealed more subtle, but progressive difficulties.

BONE. Chronic hemolytic anemia leading to erythroid hyperplasia and bone marrow expansion plus repeated infarction ultimately may result in cortical thinning and bony distortion. Debilitating aseptic necrosis of the femoral and humoral heads is seen most often in patients after age 20. The incidence of osteomyelitis is increased in the sickle cell disease population, and its differentiation from sickle cell crisis in the long bones often is difficult.

SKIN ULCERS. Recurrent chronic leg ulcers occur in patients who have sickle cell disease and may appear as early as 10 years of age.

EYES. Ophthalmologic manifestations of sickle cell disease also may be seen. Retinal neovascularization, most common in Hb SC disease, may result in blindness, vitreous hemorrhage, and retinal detachment.

LABORATORY DIAGNOSIS

When affected children are identified by newborn screening or are suspected of having sickle cell disease on the basis of clinical symptoms, the clinician should characterize the sickle cell subtype or request the aid of a hematologist to do so. A diagnosis usually can be made on the basis of a complete blood count, reticulocyte count, examination of the blood film, hemoglobin electrophoresis, and quantitative measurements of Hb A2 and F (Table 59–1). Molecular biologic techniques can establish the patient's genotype; however, such approaches generally are not necessary. An accurate classification helps to predict the symptom severity, which varies among the sickle syndromes (see Table 59–1), and permits a more informed approach to health maintenance and management of the disease.

There are, of course, times when the practitioner may need to make a diagnosis when a hemoglobin electrophoresis is not readily available. In most instances, a CBC, reticulocyte count, blood film, and solubility test (such as the Sickledex) performed on child and parents will suffice. Examples of such screening workups are presented in Figure 59–1.

MANAGEMENT

ANEMIA

Aplastic Crisis. An aplastic crisis resolves as the reticulocyte count rises. Before recovery, however, anemia may become so severe that the child

TABLE 59–1. Findings in Sickle Cell Disease Variants*

Disease Group	Clinical Severity	Electrophoresis % A	% S	% F	% A_2	Hb, gm/dL	Reticulocyte, %	MCV, fL	RBC Morphology
SS	Usually marked	0	>90	<10	<3.5	6–11	5–20	>80	Sickle cells, NRBC, target cells, Howell-Jolly bodies, normochromia, anisocytosis, poikilocytosis
Sβ⁰-thal	Marked to moderate	0	>80	<20	>3.5	6–10	5–20	<80	Sickle cells, NRBC, target cells, microcytosis, hypochromia, anisocytosis, poikilocytosis
Sβ⁺-thal	Mild to moderate	10–30	>60	<20	>3.5	9–12	5–10	<75	No sickle cells, target cells present, microcytosis, hypochromia, anisocytosis, poikilocytosis
SC	Mild to moderate	0	50	<5	(50% Hb C)	10–15	5–10	75–95	Fat sickle cells, target cells, anisocytosis, poikilocytosis
S HPFH	Asymptomatic	0	<70	>30	<2.5	12–14	1–2	<80	No sickle cells, rare target, anisocytosis, poikilocytosis

*Numbers apply to children over 5 years of age.
Hematologic values are approximate.
Hb, hemoglobin; MCV, mean corpuscular volume; NRBC, nucleated red blood cells; RBC, red blood cell.
Adapted from Reid CD, Bellevue R, Benjamine LJ: Management and Therapy of Sickle Cell Disease, 3rd ed revised. NIH Publication No. 95-2117. Bethesda, MD, National Institutes of Health, 1995.

is symptomatic. In such a case, a red cell transfusion is recommended. Because the anemia has developed over time, with a compensatory enlargement of the intravascular plasma volume, the transfusion should be delivered slowly and cautiously. In this way, volume overload and heart failure are avoided.

Splenic Sequestration. Acute splenic sequestration crisis is a major cause of mortality in the first few years of life in patients who have sickle cell disease. Older children, usually those who have Hb SC or Sβ⁺-thalassemia, may have persistently enlarged spleens and can be at risk for sequestration crisis as well. Parents should be instructed early on how to palpate the spleen. A "spleen stick," which is a tongue depressor marked at the level of the spleen when the top of the stick is held to the costal margin at the midclavicular line, is a simple but helpful aid. Its use can establish whether the spleen has acutely enlarged. It is extremely important that signs of sequestration alert families to seek help immediately because hypovolemic shock and death can ensue within hours. Children should be brought to the hospital where prompt treatment with plasma expanders and transfusions are available. Care should be taken not to overtransfuse because the spleen may respond rapidly with regression in size and deposition of much of its entrapped red cell volume into the circulation, adding to the intravascular volume. A post-transfusion hemoglobin of 6 to 7 gm/dL represents a safe goal.

After the successful treatment of the crisis, future management of the patient is somewhat controversial. Splenectomy or chronic transfusion are often chosen, with their attendant complications taken into account.

INFECTION. A febrile or ill-appearing child who has sickle cell disease should be treated as soon as possible with antibiotics and not be assumed to have a viral illness. This dictum applies even to those patients who may not have a significantly elevated temperature or systemic signs. A physical examination and appropriate laboratory tests should be performed as efficiently as possible, and an antibiotic effective against *S. pneumoniae* and *H. influenzae* should be started. In areas where organisms resistant to penicillin and cephalosporins have been identified, another antibiotic may be added empirically.

Some controversy exists regarding which febrile children should be admitted to the hospital. The National Institutes of Health recommends admission if the child has any of the following:

Parameters
    Hemoglobin (HB)/Hematocrit (Hct)—level of anemia
    Mean Corpuscular Volume (MCV)—cell volume
    Reticulocyte count (Retic)—level of cell production
    Sickledex—solubility test
    Blood film—morphology

Family One

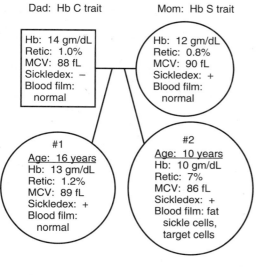

Dad: Hb C trait

Hb: 14 gm/dL
Retic: 1.0%
MCV: 88 fL
Sickledex: −
Blood film:
   normal

Mom: Hb S trait

Hb: 12 gm/dL
Retic: 0.8%
MCV: 90 fL
Sickledex: +
Blood film:
   normal

#1
Age: 16 years
Hb: 13 gm/dL
Retic: 1.2%
MCV: 89 fL
Sickledex: +
Blood film:
   normal

#2
Age: 10 years
Hb: 10 gm/dL
Retic: 7%
MCV: 86 fL
Sickledex: +
Blood film: fat
   sickle cells,
   target cells

Dx: Hb S trait   Dx: Hb SC (disease)

Family Two

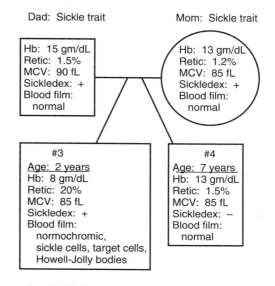

Dad: Sickle trait

Hb: 15 gm/dL
Retic: 1.5%
MCV: 90 fL
Sickledex: +
Blood film:
   normal

Mom: Sickle trait

Hb: 13 gm/dL
Retic: 1.2%
MCV: 85 fL
Sickledex: +
Blood film:
   normal

#3
Age: 2 years
Hb: 8 gm/dL
Retic: 20%
MCV: 85 fL
Sickledex: +
Blood film:
   normochromic,
   sickle cells, target cells,
   Howell-Jolly bodies

#4
Age: 7 years
Hb: 13 gm/dL
Retic: 1.5%
MCV: 85 fL
Sickledex: −
Blood film:
   normal

Dx: Hb SS (disease)   Dx: Hb AA (normal)

Family Three

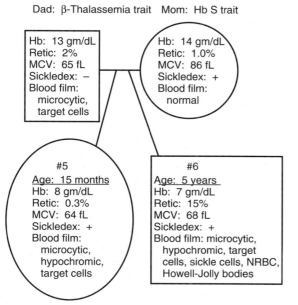

Dad: β-Thalassemia trait   Mom: Hb S trait

Hb: 13 gm/dL
Retic: 2%
MCV: 65 fL
Sickledex: −
Blood film:
   microcytic,
   target cells

Hb: 14 gm/dL
Retic: 1.0%
MCV: 86 fL
Sickledex: +
Blood film:
   normal

#5
Age: 15 months
Hb: 8 gm/dL
Retic: 0.3%
MCV: 64 fL
Sickledex: +
Blood film:
   microcytic,
   hypochromic,
   target cells

#6
Age: 5 years
Hb: 7 gm/dL
Retic: 15%
MCV: 68 fL
Sickledex: +
Blood film: microcytic,
   hypochromic, target
   cells, sickle cells, NRBC,
   Howell-Jolly bodies

Dx: Hb S trait plus iron deficiency   Dx: Hb S β-thalassemia
anemia or Hb S β-thalassemia with
an aplastic crisis

Diagnosis (Dx)/Discussion

1 Hb S trait. The child's parameters are normal
   except for the Sickledex.
2 Hb SC (disease). These findings also might be seen
   in SS, but this diagnosis would not be compatible
   with the father's negative Sickledex.
3 Hb SS (disease). These findings could be seen in SC
   disease, but this diagnosis would not be compatible
   with the parents' positive Sickledex.
4 Hb AA. All parameters are normal.
5 Hb S trait plus iron deficiency anemia or Hb S
   β-thalassemia with an aplastic crisis. The reticulocyte
   count is low; thus, these findings in this family
   are compatible with either diagnosis. Iron studies
   would help to clarify the situation.
6 Hb S β-thalassemia. Here the reticulocyte count is
   high, ruling out iron deficiency in a child who has a
   low MCV and + Sickledex findings.

Figure 59–1. Screening workups for anemia. NRBC, nucleated red blood cells.

temperature greater than 40°C (104°F), seriously ill appearance, hypotension, poor perfusion and dehydration, pulmonary infiltrate, corrected WBC count of greater than 30,000/mm³ or less than 5000/mm³, platelet count less than 100,000/mm³, hemoglobin less than 5 gm/dL, or a history of *S. pneumoniae* sepsis. A recent study compared outpatient management of children ages 6 months to 12 years who had sickle cell disease and found that by using conservative eligibility requirements, febrile children could be treated safely as outpatients with intravenous (IV) ceftriaxone at a considerable cost reduction. When a child does not present with any of the admission criteria noted previously, it is sensible to give ceftriaxone (IV or intramuscularly [IM]), obtain appropriate laboratory studies, including a blood culture, and ask the patient to return within 24 hours, or sooner if ill-appearing. A second dose of ceftriaxone should be administered at that time. If blood culture results are negative after 48 hours, antibiotics may be discontinued; in situations in which an identifiable source of infection is found (such as otitis media), oral antibiotics should be prescribed. Clearly, for now, departure from the time-honored inpatient approach to therapy should be pursued only when the clinician feels comfortable treating patients who have sickle cell disease in an ambulatory setting and when the family and clinician are able to provide excellent follow-up. Furthermore, endemic flora should be sensitive to cephalosporins.

PAIN. When painful events occur, home-based care should be instituted swiftly and include an oral intake of at least 150 mL/kg/day of electrolyte-containing fluids. Nonsteroidal anti-inflammatory medications or acetaminophen may be used initially. Codeine can be added to the regimen, if more intense pain occurs; oral morphine may ultimately be required. Emergency room care with IV hydration and narcotics, and finally hospitalization for more prolonged therapy, may be indicated. Optimally, each patient should have an individualized pain management program on file in the emergency room and inpatient service. Recently, patient-controlled analgesia (PCA) devices have provided an effective way to administer medication. Alternative approaches to pain management, such as behavior modification techniques and self-hypnosis (see Chapter 60), also are useful adjuncts to care. The schedule for administering medication should anticipate the pain by providing regularly timed doses of analgesia. Expecting the patient to ask for pain medication can only increase his or her anxiety and ultimately the level of discomfort. The possibility that pain in a child who has sickle cell disease is a symptom of an underlying infection or other condition requiring

additional investigation should be considered and explored. Studies using chronic hydroxyurea therapy to increase the Hb F level and reduce the incidence of pain in children are under way at a number of centers.

ACUTE CHEST SYNDROME. All patients who have acute chest syndrome should be admitted to the hospital where appropriate monitoring, evaluation, and management can be instituted with a hematologist in attendance. Increasing respiratory distress and hypoxemia require transfusion or exchange transfusion.

STROKE. Immediate intervention is necessary for those patients who have symptoms of CVA. They should be evaluated rapidly and admitted expeditiously to the hospital's intensive care unit where appropriate tests, monitors, and therapy can be instituted. The hematologist should be contacted and a timely exchange transfusion (or erythrocytophoresis) begun with the goal of reducing the Hb S level to below 20%. Subsequently chronic transfusion therapy, with the aim of keeping the Hb S level below 30%, should be instituted to prevent recurrence.

HEALTH MAINTENANCE

APPOINTMENTS. Services for children and adolescents who have sickle cell disease should include the routine care provided to other children. In addition, Table 59–2 outlines the more frequent visit plan needed for children who have sickle cell disease. Clearly, patients also should be attending a comprehensive sickle cell disease clinic so that these examinations can be divided between the primary clinician and a specialist. Within a short time after hospitalization or emergency room visits, plans need to be made for follow-up evaluation and chronic care.

MEDICAL HISTORY AND PHYSICAL ASSESSMENT. The history should be reviewed for signs of developing organ dysfunction associated with sickle cell disease. Common physical findings include delayed growth and sexual maturation, scleral icterus, and functional systolic heart murmur. Often, splenomegaly is appreciated in infants and young children who have Hb SS or Sβ⁰-thalassemia. This finding usually is not present beyond 6 years of age, by which time repeated infarction and fibrous tissue formation have led to splenic shrinkage. Those who have Hb SC or Sβ⁺-thalassemia syndromes often demonstrate enlarged spleens for many years. Many children whose spleens are palpable are functionally asplenic and susceptible to infection. Patients who have enlarged spleens are also predisposed to

TABLE 59–2. Sickle Cell Comprehensive Care Outline

	Age			
	< 6 mo	6 mo–1 yr	1–5 yr	5–20 yr
Provider visits: (no.)	3–6	2 or 3	3 or 4/yr	2 or 3/yr
Laboratory studies: (no.)				
CBC, reticulocyte count	2–4	1–3	1–3/yr	1 or 2/yr
Red cell antigen typing		1		
Liver function tests		1	1/yr	1/yr
Renal function tests		1	1/yr	1/yr
Urinalysis		1	1/yr	1/yr
Hepatitis/HIV screening (if transfused)	1/yr	1/yr	1/yr	1/yr
Additional studies:				
Pulmonary function tests				Every 3–5 yr
Chest radiographs				Every 3–5 yr
Ophthalmologic exam				Every 3–5 yr (ages 5–10 yrs); yearly thereafter

CBC, complete blood count; HIV, human immunodeficiency virus.

splenic sequestration (see earlier under Clinical Features). Range of motion should be tested in older children and adolescents to assess any limitation of joint movement or pain indicative of aseptic necrosis. The skin around the ankle area also should be examined carefully for ulcers.

LABORATORY STUDIES AND SPECIAL EVALUATION. Refer to Table 59–2.

IMMUNIZATIONS. Immunizations should be given according to the schedules recommended by the American Academy of Pediatrics. Patients also should receive the hepatitis B vaccine. This population is at increased risk of pneumococcal sepsis, so that the polyvalent pneumococcal vaccine must be given at age 2 and a booster between ages 4 and 6. Finally, annual influenza vaccines have been recommended; some centers administer the meningococcal vaccine as well.

PENICILLIN PROPHYLAXIS. In a randomized trial published in 1986 involving 219 children aged 3 to 36 months, the efficacy of prophylactic oral penicillin therapy in significantly reducing (84% reduction) the incidence of pneumococcal septicemia was established. It currently is recommended that oral penicillin be given twice a day to all patients who have Hb SS disease or Sβ⁰-thalassemia (125 mg twice a day to 3 years; 250 mg twice a day after 3 years). For those patients who are allergic to penicillin, erythromycin ethyl succinate (20 mg/kg) divided into two daily doses should be prescribed. The critical importance of prophylactic medication should be underscored at every visit in order to ensure continued compliance. When oral antibiotics cannot be administered reliably, injection of 1.2 million units of long-acting Bicillin every 3 weeks is a comparably effective alternative. The length of time that prophylaxis should be continued and its use in other sickle syndromes remain controversial. A recently published trial supports the safety of discontinuing prophylaxis after age 5; however, many do not find the study's conclusion compelling and recommend continued therapy. Because those who have Hb SC and Sβ⁺-thalassemia syndromes are at lower risk for overwhelming infection when compared with those who have Hb SS disease, the use of prophylaxis is controversial. Most centers do prescribe prophylaxis for these groups.

FOLIC ACID. Due to the demands of increased erythropoiesis, some clinicians supplement dietary sources by prescribing folic acid.

DENTAL CARE. An annual dental evaluation and supplemental fluoride, when not provided in the drinking water, should be advised as for any child. Routine care, fillings, and cleanings require no special attention; however, pre- and postoperative standard rheumatic antibiotic prophylaxis must be given for operative dental procedures. Hospitalization and preoperative transfusion (straight or exchange) should be employed under the supervision of a hematologist when general anesthesia is needed.

EDUCATION AND COUNSELING. A number of issues should be explored repeatedly or age appropriately during regularly scheduled visits. These are addressed in a variety of publications available through the U.S. Department of Health and Human Services. Families should be taught the use of a thermometer, and the clinician should reinforce the need to have it available. The importance of taking penicillin prophylactically and of contacting a health care professional in the event of fever also must be underscored. Parents should be instructed early how to palpate the spleen and assess its size. It is of the utmost importance that signs of sequestration alert parents and caretakers immediately to seek help. To prevent the onset of sickle cell crisis, families should be counseled to provide adequate hydration and avoid extreme cold or hypoxic conditions such as overexertion. Parents should learn to watch for signs of respiratory difficulty and also should be educated about the signs and symptoms of stroke.

Children who have sickle cell disease frequently have special needs that must be addressed. Many patients may require psychosocial counseling for problems related to their often painful and debilitating chronic illness. The clinician should advocate for special school services that allow the child to keep pace with schoolwork when it is interrupted by illness and/or hospitalization.

When a child has suffered a stroke, clinicians should help parents obtain rehabilitation services. Programs for all patients who have cognitive difficulties should also be sought.

DIAGNOSTIC TESTING AND GENETIC COUNSELING

Many states now provide universal hemoglobinopathy screening for all infants, regardless of race. These programs usually retest identified children at a later date; however, in all situations it ultimately is the responsibility of the primary care clinician to see that a definitive diagnosis is made. When help is needed, a hematologist should be consulted. Newborn screening or hemoglobin electrophoresis will generally be reported, listing the hemoglobin in highest concentration first. Newborn phenotypes are thus described as follows: Normal = FA (due to the large amount of fetal (F) hemoglobin at birth); sickle cell trait = FAS; Hb C trait = FAC; Hb SC disease = FSC; Hb SS, Hb Sβ^0-thalassemia, and Hb S HPFH = FS; Hb Sβ^+-thalassemia = FSA. Other variant hemoglobins also may be identified.

Newborn studies have the added benefit of identifying offspring bearing the Hb S, C, or other abnormal hemoglobin trait, as well as alerting families to the possibility of bearing future children affected by disease. Sickle cell trait is identified in 8% of the African-American population. Hb S trait as well as Hb C and thalassemia trait are, with a few clinical exceptions, essentially benign. Children found to have a trait should be counseled at the appropriate age regarding this diagnosis as well as the possibility of producing,

depending on their mate, a child affected by a sickle cell syndrome. In cases in which sickle cell trait is identified in a newborn, other family members, particularly parents, should be evaluated for aberrant hemoglobins, including thalassemia. When a family is found to be at risk for producing an affected offspring, the clinician should explore this possibility and the opportunities for genetic counseling in a nondirective fashion.

In the United States, currently 4000 to 5000 pregnancies each year have the potential for producing a child who has sickle cell disease. Recent advances in fetal sampling techniques as well as new molecular technologies have resulted in the ability to diagnose sickle cell disease as early as the 10th gestational week. Couples who desire prenatal diagnosis should be referred for genetic counseling and then sent to an experienced center as soon as possible, because termination of pregnancy for genetic diseases must be accomplished prior to the 24th week of gestation.

SUMMARY

Advances in care, especially early diagnosis, penicillin prophylaxis, recognition of life-threatening events, and comprehensive care planning, have resulted in greater longevity and quality of life for children who have sickle cell disease. In an age of managed care, continued cooperation between primary care clinicians and specialists is necessary if this trend is to continue. In particular, clinicians must ensure that acute events necessitating hospitalization and a hematologist's assistance are attended to expeditiously and without bureaucratic obstacles.

FURTHER READING

Lane PA: Sickle cell disease. Pediatric Clin North Am 43:639, 1996.

Platt OS, Brambilla DJ, Rosse WF, et al.: Mortality in sickle cell disease: Life expectancy and risk factors for early death. N Engl J Med 330:1639, 1994.

Reid CD, Bellevue R, Benjamine LJ, et al.: Management and Therapy of Sickle Cell Disease, 3rd ed revised. NIH Publication No. 95-2117. Bethesda, MD, National Institutes of Health; National Heart, Lung and Blood Institute, 1995.

Vichinsky EP: Comprehensive care in sickle cell disease: Its impact on morbidity and mortality. Semin Hematol 28:220, 1991.

Wilimas JA, Flynn PM, Harris S, et al.: A randomized study of outpatient treatment with ceftriaxone for selected febrile children with sickle cell disease. N Engl J Med 329:472, 1993.

Neil L. Schechter

Chapter **60**

Pain Management in Children

The past 10 years have seen a dramatic increase in knowledge about pain and its management in children and a significant shift in practice patterns. Until the mid-1980s, there was extremely limited research available in the area of pediatric pain, few sources of information for the interested clinician, and concomitant undertreatment of pain in children was normative. As late as the latter half of the 1980s, for example, it was common for newborns to undergo certain surgeries such as ductal ligations without any anesthesia, the majority of children received limited postoperative analgesia, and sedation/analgesia for painful procedures was the exception.

A variety of factors were responsible for this situation. By nature, pain is a transdisciplinary problem and as a result, no one field assumed a leadership role. Also, it is difficult to assess pain in children, and they often cannot or will not tell us if they are uncomfortable. Without adequate assessment techniques, both clinical care and research were handicapped. In addition, social attitudes against pain treatment ("no pain, no gain"; concerns about drug abuse) and limited financial incentives for the pharmaceutical industry for whom children represented a minute market, further reduced attention to children's pain.

This situation has changed dramatically however. There has been a wealth of pharmacokinetic data on children's metabolism of opioids suggesting that, for the most part, after 3 months of age, it is similar to that of adults. New assessment techniques that are developmentally appropriate allow children as young as 3 years to report their discomfort, and instruments have been developed to quantify indirect measures of pain, such as physiologic parameters and behavior. In addition, the new research has allowed for the dissipation of many myths (e.g., "infants don't feel pain"). **We now know, for example, that fetuses at the end of the second trimester prenatally have in place the neuroanatomic structures and neurochemical substrate to experience noxious stimuli.** This and other information has changed attitudes about pain management in children and has led to a significant improvement in the way children's pain is handled.

CURRENT UNDERSTANDING ABOUT PAIN

Pain is defined by the International Association for the Study of Pain as an unpleasant sensory and emotional experience associated with tissue damage or potential tissue damage. **Pain, therefore, is the individual's interpretation of nociceptor stimulation.** Nociceptors, stimulated in the periphery or viscera, transmit messages through thinly myelinated or unmyelinated afferents to the dorsal horn of the spinal column. They then are transmitted through spinothalamic tracts to the limbic system and the cerebral cortex. Each individual's interpretation of this stimulation is unique and based on a host of factors that have a role in modifying pain. In children these include age, context or meaning of the pain, affect (i.e., depression or anxiety), and individual personality differences such as temperament. In general, younger children seem to experience pain more intensely than older children. It is clear that when children are old enough to realize that short-term discomfort may have long-term benefit at preventing disease or illness, they experience procedure pain less intensely, as well. The meaning of pain for the child clearly has an impact. For example, if the child interprets that the discomfort he or she is experiencing has other implications—that is, imminent surgery or a recurrence of illness—this pain may be experienced much more intensely. Individuals who are depressed or extremely anxious also experience symptoms more intensely; thus, preparation for an upcoming procedure that reduces anxiety may affect pain. Finally, it is clear that individual differences may alter pain experience. For example, children who have a "difficult" temperament or, in particular, decreased adaptability, tend to experience the same painful stimulus more intensely than others whose personality style may be "easier."

These modifying factors should be taken into account when one is developing a treatment plan for a child who can be expected to experience pain as a part of his or her illness or treatment.

363

ASSESSMENT

Developmentally appropriate assessment is the cornerstone of adequate pain treatment. If one doesn't know how much pain an individual is experiencing, it is impossible to know how to respond to it. Current thinking suggests that the most reliable pain assessment technique is the individual's self-report of his or her discomfort. This traditionally is assessed in children over 8 years of age by use of a visual analogue scale. Children are asked to quantify their pain, where a rating of 1 is no pain and a rating of 10 is the most pain imaginable. For children under 8 years old, however, quantitative self-report is more problematic.

Recently, however, a number of modified self-report scales have been developed for children between ages 3 and 8. These instruments are more concrete in their orientation. For example, children can be asked to select a photograph or cartoon face that resembles how they feel when they're in pain. Also, color scales and pain thermometers have been developed. All of these allow children to quantify their discomfort in a manner commensurate with their developmental level so that rational treatment can be decided.

For children younger than 3 years or developmentally delayed children, however, these measures are not appropriate. As a result, proxy measures of discomfort must be used. Physiologic variables such as heart rate, respiratory rate, and blood pressure all increase when an individual is in pain, while SaO_2 and vagal tone decrease. Other physiologic measures, such as cortisol and other hormonal or metabolic markers of stress, also increase with pain and have been used for research but are not clinically useful.

In addition to physiologic variables, a number of behavioral markers correlate with pain. Facial expression (nasal labial flattening, stretched mouth, brow furrowing), crying, lack of appetite, posture, and overall irritability may all indicate increased pain. A number of rating scales that combine physiologic and behavioral variables into one instrument have been developed, but none has been accepted universally.

Regardless of the instrument chosen, it is essential that pain be measured in a scheduled manner, that it be documented in a prominent place on the medical record, and that specific protocols be developed to respond to different levels of discomfort.

TREATMENT

The treatment of pain is multimodal and as many approaches as possible should be used for each pain problem. In general, both pharmacologic and behavioral strategies should be considered.

Pharmacologic Treatment of Pain

A number of drugs have a role in the management of pain. In general, administration of pharmacologic agents should be part of an overall plan for pain management, determined by the type and severity of pain. **Local anesthetics should be used for needle procedures. When pain is mild to moderate, nonsteroidal anti-inflammatory drugs (NSAIDs) in conjunction with a weak opioid are appropriate. For more severe pain, opioids may be necessary.** These agents have potential side effects, and resuscitative drugs and reversal agents should be available when they are used. Adjuvant agents for opioid-resistant pain also are available.

Local Anesthetics

The clinician should be familiar with a number of local anesthetic agents. These should be considered whenever needle procedures are to be performed.

EMLA, a topically applied local anesthetic cream that is a mixture of prilocaine and lidocaine, produces analgesia to a depth of approximately 2 to 4 mm when left on for 60 minutes in an occlusive dressing and is extremely valuable. EMLA is appropriate for venipuncture and venous cannulation, as well as reservoir access. It also may reduce the discomfort of intramuscular injections. The hour wait makes it inappropriate for emergencies.

Lidocaine is an injectable local anesthetic agent that provides anesthesia but requires injection and burns somewhat when injected. Lidocaine can be buffered, which reduces some of the associated discomfort. An iontophoretic lidocaine preparation also is available.

TAC contains tetracaine, epinephrine, and cocaine. It can be applied topically to an open wound to produce anesthesia so that it can be sutured painlessly or allow for the painless administration of injectable lidocaine. TAC must be used with caution because of the potent vasoconstrictive effects of cocaine and therefore cannot be used near mucous membranes or in distal areas of the body. Alternatives to TAC such as LET (lidocaine, epinephrine, tetracaine), have been developed and are in use as alternatives in many institutions.

Nonsteroidal Anti-Inflammatory Drugs

NSAIDs have a role in mild to moderate pain and, in conjunction with opioids, in more severe pain (Table 60–1). In general, NSAIDs appear to act peripherally as compared with opioids, which act centrally. All NSAIDs have a "ceiling," that is, a maximal dose beyond which no further analgesia is obtained. Most of these agents, except for acetaminophen, have anti-inflammatory as well as analgesic effects. Therefore, ibuprofen is preferable to acetaminophen for pain of otitis, pharyngitis, and musculoskeletal origin. A parenteral NSAID, ketorolac, has a morphine-sparing effect and has shown efficacy in postoperative and sickle cell pain. The NSAIDs have hematopoietic, gastrointestinal, and renal effects, and these need to be considered when they are used chronically.

Opioids

Opioids are the mainstay of pain treatment for moderate to severe pain. They have a long history of use in adults and children, and their pharmacokinetics are understood well. Traditionally "weaker" opioids such as *codeine* or *oxycodone* are used in fixed-dose preparations, with acetaminophen for moderate pain and more potent opioids used for moderate to severe pain. There are a number of general principles regarding opioid administration:

1. Whenever possible, opioids should be used in a scheduled manner as opposed to on as-needed (prn) basis. It is easier to prevent pain from occurring than to ablate it once it has returned. Therefore, in predictable pain situations, opioids should be scheduled round-the-clock.

2. **Opioids have no ceiling effect. The right dose is the one that eliminates the pain.** The suggested doses are safe starting doses in opioid-naive children (Table 60–2).

3. Opioids have predictable dose-related side effects. When they are used, side effects should be anticipated. In particular, constipation and itchiness are common. Respiratory slowing and even respiratory arrest can occur; therefore, when these

agents are used, appropriate monitoring should be in place.

4. If possible, a non-noxious route of administration should be used. Therefore, intravenous or oral routes are far preferable to intramuscular, intranasal, or rectal routes.

5. Opioids should be used with caution in children under 6 months of age in a monitored setting at one fourth the per kilogram dose for older children.

Morphine is the gold standard and the drug of choice in this category. It is inexpensive and has a good safety record in pediatrics. Morphine can be administered intravenously, intramuscularly, subcutaneously, or orally. *Fentanyl* is a potent synthetic opioid that has achieved significant prominence in anesthesia practice. Fentanyl is short-acting and highly potent and, as a result, has gained popularity for short, painful procedures. It is more lipophilic than morphine and, as a result, acts transmucosally and transdermally. *Meperidine* was an opioid used commonly postoperatively in the past, but it has gone out of favor for a variety of reasons. Meperidine has a breakdown product, normeperidine, which can cause central nervous system hyperexcitability and seizures. As a result, it is not recommended except in documented morphine allergy or in situations where it has been chronically used in the past and the patient is reluctant to shift to an alternative agent.

Sedative-Hypnotics

These agents often are used in conjunction with opioids for "conscious" sedation for painful procedures or independently to reduce anxiety or to gain the child's cooperation for painless procedures such as computed tomography. Although in the past these agents were used in a cavalier way, even sometimes administered at home on the way to the hospital, significant concerns about their safety have been raised. As a result, recent guide-

TABLE 60–1. Nonopioid Drugs

Drug	Dosage	Comments
Acetaminophen	10–20 mg/kg PO, q 4–6 hr	Lacks gastrointestinal and hematologic side effects but also lacks anti-inflammatory effects
Choline magnesium trisalicylate	10–15 mg/kg PO, q 8–12 hr	May have minimal antiplatelet effect; lacks gastrointestinal effects
Ibuprofen	10 mg/kg PO, q 6–8 hr	Has anti-inflammatory activity but may have gastrointestinal and hematologic effects
Naproxen	5 mg/kg PO, q 12 hr	Has anti-inflammatory effects but may have gastrointestinal and hematologic effects
Ketorolac	0.5 mg/kg q 6 h IV	Is only parenterally available NSAID; should not be given for more than 5 days

TABLE 60–2. Opioid Analgesic Dosing*

Drug	Equianalgesic Dose Parenteral	Usual Starting Dose, IV/SC		Equianalgesic, IV/SC:PO Ratio	Usual Starting Dose, PO	
		<50 kg	>50 kg		<50 kg	>50 kg
Morphine	10 mg	Bolus dose = 0.1 mg/kg q 2–3 hr; continuous infusion = 0.03–0.05 mg/kg/hr	5–10 mg q 2–4 hr	1:3	0.3 mg/kg q 3–4 hr	30 mg q 3–4 hr
Hydromorphone	1.5 mg	0.015 mg/kg q 3–4 hr	1.0–1.5 mg q 3–4 hr	1:5	0.06 mg/kg q 3–4 hr	4–8 mg q 3–4 hr
Codeine	130 mg				0.5–1 mg/kg q 3–4 hr	60 mg q 3–4 hr
Oxycodone					0.2 mg/kg q 3–4 hr	10 mg q 3–4 hr
Meperidine†	75 mg	0.75 mg/kg q 2–3 hr	75–100 mg q 3 hr	1:4	1–1.5 mg/kg q 3–4 hr	50–75 mg q 3–4 hr
Fentanyl	100 µg	0.5–2 µg/kg/hr as continuous infusion	25–75 µg q 1 hr			
Controlled-release morphine					0.6 mg/kg q 8 hr or 0.9 mg/kg q 12 hr	30–60 mg q 12 hr
Methadone	10 mg	0.1 mg/kg q 6–8 hr	5–10 mg q 4–8 hr	1:2	0.2 mg/kg q 4–8 hr	10 mg q 4–8 hr

*Doses are for opioid-naive patient. For infants under 6 months, start at ¼ to ⅓ the suggested dose and titrate to effect.
†Use meperidine with caution; it may cause seizures and hyperexcitability with chronic dosing.

lines suggest that more cautious monitoring is necessary when sedative-hypnotic agents are used.

Chloral hydrate is the sedative-hypnotic agent used most commonly. It generally is used for imaging studies that are pain-free, but that require the child's immobility. Some children have idiosyncratic responses to chloral hydrate, and its long half-life mandates prolonged monitoring.

Midazolam is a short-acting benzodiazepine that has gained popularity for procedures either in conjunction with an opioid or independently. Midazolam has several advantages that make it useful for short painful procedures in children. It has a rapid onset of action, a short half-life, and brings with it the blessing of amnesia. As a result, in conjunction with an opioid such as fentanyl or morphine, it commonly is used to provide sedation-analgesia for children undergoing painful diagnostic or treatment procedures.

When one is engaged in conscious sedation, it is imperative that the American Academy of Pediatrics' guidelines be followed carefully. These call for sedation to take place only in a monitored setting and demand the presence of an individual who is skilled in airway management. There also must be an individual whose sole job is monitoring the patient. Failure to comply with these guidelines may result in extremely unfortunate consequences.

General Anesthetics

A number of general anesthetic agents commonly under the purview of anesthesiology are available for pain management. These agents include *propofol,* an ultra-short-acting intravenously administered general anesthetic agent; *ketamine,* an often intramuscularly administered general anesthetic agent that has less respiratory depression associated with it than some of the other agents, but has a number of emergence phenomena complicating its use; and *nitrous oxide,* which provides sedation-analgesia for children undergoing procedures, but is an environmental contaminant unless effective scavenging occurs. These agents typically are administered by anesthesiologists, although individuals who can provide anesthesia-level care, such as emergency medicine physicians and critical care physicians, may have access to them in certain institutions.

Adjuvants

These agents do not necessarily provide analgesia but may potentiate the efficacy of analgesia. These include the tricyclic antidepressants and anticonvulsants, which are classically used for neu-

ropathic pain, that is, the burning, severe pain classically associated with nerve injury that often is opioid-resistant. In particular, amytriptyline, nortriptyline, and gabapentin are used for these purposes. Stimulant medications, such as methylphenidate and dextroamphetamine, also are adjuvants. When children become sedated secondary to opioid analgesics, these agents may counteract the sedation and improve the child's sense of well-being.

Behavioral Approaches

A number of nonpharmacologic strategies have been demonstrated to reduce discomfort in children significantly (see Chapter 67). These can be used in chronic pain, but their efficacy has been demonstrated better during painful procedures. If the pain associated with the procedure is severe, they can be used in conjunction with pharmacologic approaches. If the pain is less severe, these approaches often can be used in lieu of analgesics.

PREPARATION. All children should be prepared before a painful procedure or surgery to reduce anxiety, and in a developmentally appropriate manner, by using both cognitive information about what will happen and sensory information about how it will feel.

PARENTAL INVOLVEMENT. As often as possible, parents should be present and involved in any treatment. Parents should be taught techniques that they can use to comfort their child during acute pain and during procedures. They are the individuals who are most knowledgeable about how their child will respond to pain; thus, they should be consulted in advance when a treatment plan is being developed. In addition, parents can best judge whether their child is experiencing discomfort, as they often are the only ones familiar with the child's normative patterns. As a result, they should be queried about the child's pain status. Parents can "coach" during procedures, using distraction techniques.

DISTRACTION. Any activity that distracts children from preoccupation with their pain or from impending pain is beneficial. Depending on the age of the child, different techniques are available, including specialized breathing techniques, counting, party blowers, and bubble solution. Other techniques involve having a parent read with the child, either storybooks or novelty books such as pop-up books, or having parents tell the child a favorite story. Also, parents can use visual imagery techniques in which they have the child imagine that he or she is in a more pleasant place, such as the location of a recent family vacation,

368 • MANAGEMENT OF DISEASE

than in the treatment room or emergency department.

HYPNOSIS (also see Chapter 67). Hypnosis involves more intense use of fantasy and suggestion. Therefore, hypnotic approaches involve the child in a fantasy, such as taking a magic carpet ride. Other hypnotic techniques involve focused suggestions, such as pain "switches," where children are asked to "turn off the switch" that's causing their discomfort, or "magic gloves," where children are told that a magical glove will be applied to their hand that will eliminate the pain associated with needle insertion. Many professional societies offer courses in hypnosis for children.

SELF-CONTROL. By increasing one's sense of control over illness and its treatment, pain often can be decreased. Examples of this approach include having the child help with bandage removal or select the site for venous sampling. The ultimate example of self-control in pain management is the use of patient-controlled analgesia (PCA), in which patients control their pain by administering a set amount of analgesic by pushing the button of a microprocessor. Typically, children over 7 years of age can use a PCA pump.

REHEARSAL AND MODELING. These techniques are particular to procedure-related pain. They are aimed at giving children more information about the procedure and, as a result, reducing their anxiety. This can be done by practicing the procedure on a stuffed animal or talking to other children who have undergone the procedure. Visiting the operating room or treatment room or seeing a film of the procedure also may be beneficial. Desensitization techniques may be necessary for some children who are highly anxious.

Behavioral strategies often are beneficial when used as a part of overall treatment to reduce pain in children. Children of different ages and different temperaments use them in different ways, but behavioral strategies always should be considered, especially for children who have a chronic disease, who may be subjected to multiple procedures and frequent pain throughout the course of their illness.

SPECIFIC PAIN PROBLEMS

Procedure Pain

For many children, procedures are the worst part of their medical encounters; for children who have a chronic disease, the pain of procedures often is the worst part of their illness.

The following general principles may reduce procedure pain:

1. The intervention should be tailored to the severity of the procedure and the personality of the child.
2. Individuals performing the painful procedures should have established competence if the procedure is to be performed on an awake child.
3. The child should be prepared for the procedure in a developmentally appropriate way, and parents should be present and involved during the procedure.
4. Local anesthetic should be used for all needle procedures, if at all possible.
5. For procedures that are painful, conscious sedation should be considered.
6. If conscious sedation is used, the American Academy of Pediatrics' guidelines should be followed carefully. These state clearly that there should be an individual in the room to monitor the child and an individual who is skilled in airway maintenance. They also assert that rooms should have monitoring and resuscitative equipment.
7. If procedures take place in a hospital, they should take place in a treatment room, not in the child's room.
8. Both behavioral and pharmacologic approaches should be used.
9. If a series of painful procedures will be necessary, aggressive pharmacologic approaches should be used initially so that a cycle of dread and fear of the next procedure does not develop.

Pharmacologic Approaches

LOCAL ANESTHETICS. Local anesthetics should be used whenever needles are involved. This may involve the use of EMLA or lidocaine by local infiltration that has been buffered or the use of iontophoresis.

OPIOIDS. *Morphine* and *fentanyl* are typical choices for procedures. Morphine can be administered orally or intravenously; fentanyl can be administered intravenously or transmucosally. All children who receive opioids and or benzodiazepines should be carefully monitored, as conscious sedation may inadvertently become deep sedation or general anesthesia and protective reflexes may be lost.

SEDATIVE-HYPNOTICS. *Midazolam* typically is the agent of choice, as it is short-acting and does not cause pain and local sclerosis when given intravenously. Benzodiazepines provide sedation, but no analgesia; therefore, they should be used in conjunction with an opioid for painful procedures. Because only the parenteral form of midazolam is available, flavored syrup can be added to it for oral administration. *Chloral hydrate* typically is used for painless procedures that require cooperation and no sedation.

GENERAL ANESTHETICS. These agents, which have been described previously, are typically administered by anesthesiologists. Careful monitoring is necessary, as all of these can cause lack of airway patency and loss of protective reflexes.

Nonpharmacologic Strategies

These strategies have previously been described under Behavioral Approaches.

CLINICAL ALGORITHMS. A number of clinical algorithms have been developed for painful procedures in children. For painless procedures that require only the child's cooperation and preparation, and/or in younger children, high-dose chloral hydrate is all that is necessary. For mildly painful procedures, such as intravenous cannulation or venipuncture, preparation, parental presence, the use of local anesthetic, and behavioral approaches, such as bubble-blowing or use of party blowers or other distractive techniques, are appropriate. For painful procedures such as debridement, incision and drainage, lumbar punctures, and bone marrow aspirations, parental presence and preparation are essential. In addition, local anesthetics, either topically or parenterally, should be used. If intravenous access is available, intravenous fentanyl and intravenous midazolam, 5 minutes prior to the procedure, should be considered, or as an alternative, general anesthetic agents. If there is no intravenous access, then oral morphine and oral midazolam or transmucosal fentanyl might be appropriate. Behavioral-cognitive approaches, such as distraction and hypnotic techniques, also may be of value.

It is essential that procedures be handled appropriately so that the burden of this aspect of the illness can be reduced for children and families.

Chronic Diseases

Chronic diseases that affect children often have pain as a significant component. Most often, the diagnostic and treatment procedures that are associated with chronic disease are worse than the pain associated with the disease itself. The following general principles make sense regarding the pain associated with chronic disease:

1. Behavioral and pharmacologic approaches need to be used jointly.
2. Empowering the child and parent as much as possible makes enormous sense. Parents and children often feel helpless in the face of chronic disease and the pain associated with it. If they can be made to feel competent to handle some aspects of their illness, their anxiety and concomitant pain will be reduced significantly.
3. Nighttime sleep should be ensured. If pain, discomfort, or anxiety is constraining sleep, sedative-hypnotic agents or analgesics before bedtime should be offered to ensure adequate sleep at night.
4. Noxious routes of administration should be avoided; non-noxious routes, such as orally or intravenously, should be used in their place.
5. Administration of analgesics should be scheduled when pain is predictable in order to prevent anticipated return of pain. If pain truly is episodic, then obviously this cannot occur.
6. The guidelines for doses of analgesics typically indicate the amount at which one starts. The ultimate dose should be the one that relieves the pain; therefore, continuous assessment of pain and its relief is necessary. **Increasing analgesic requirements should not be viewed as tolerance until progression of disease has been ruled out.**
7. Addiction is extremely rare, and fear of addiction should not restrict adequate opioid administration to children.

Sickle Cell Disease

Sickle cell disease (SCD) (see Chapter 59) is associated with a number of specific pain syndromes. The pain syndrome classically associated with SCD is the vaso-occlusive pain episode, which can begin as early as 6 to 9 months of age when the fetal hemoglobin has disappeared and can occur throughout the life of the individual. In 20% of children and young adults who have SCD, these occur frequently (more than three a year), whereas 50% of adolescents have few episodes of vaso-occlusive pain and 30% rarely or never have such episodes. Pain intensity can range from mild to extreme, and studies that have examined opioid requirements for this illness report that the pain is more intense than postoperative pain, perhaps because of its widespread nature. A host of precipitating factors, such as infection, hypoxemia, dehydration, fatigue, and strenuous exercise, are associated with initiation of vaso-occlusive episodes. The etiology of pain during vaso-occlusive episodes is not well understood, but most likely results from trapping of inflexible sickle hemoglobin in small vessels. This occlusion slows capillary blood flow, yielding hypoxemia and causing further sickling. As a result, ischemia, infarction, and tissue necrosis may occur. Alternative hypotheses such as centrally mediated reflexes shunting blood away from the marrow also have been offered. Pain during vaso-occlusion tends to occur primarily in the lumbar spine, abdomen, femoral shaft, ribs, and knees.

Another type of pain syndrome associated with SCD is a chronic arthritis-like pain, which occurs typically secondary to bony "infarcts" and presents in late adolescence or early adulthood. Other sources of pain in SCD are iatrogenic and occur secondary to diagnostic procedures or treatment, such as surgery.

Because of the unpredictability of pain in SCD, a crisis "mode" often occurs. There often are socioeconomic and racial differences between the patient and clinician, and because of the lack of objective evidence of pain or of vaso-occlusion, clinicians are obliged to believe the patients' reports. Differences between clinicians and patients, however, tend to promote disbelief, and as a result, patients often are undertreated.

Pain typically is managed by continuous infusion of morphine in younger children. In older children and adolescents, PCA appears to be most beneficial. In this way, patients can control their own pain. Debate remains as to whether a simultaneous, continuous-background infusion also is necessary. Recently the value of high-dose steroids as a treatment has been suggested. New treatments for sickle cell disease itself, such as hydroxyurea, which has been associated with fewer pain episodes, decreases overall pain. The development of day hospitals, alternatives to the emergency department where patients are cared for by individuals who are knowledgeable about SCD, represent a significant advance in dealing with this problem.

Cancer

The diagnosis and treatment of cancer (see Chapter 49) imposes an enormous burden on children and their families. The most frequent cancer pain syndrome found in children is procedure-related pain, secondary to the multiple bone marrow aspirations and lumbar punctures necessary for the diagnosis and treatment of cancer in children. Disease-related pain occurs less frequently and often is associated with direct tumor invasion, bone pain, nerve entrapment, or obstruction of a viscus. Neuropathic pain may occur when tumor invades local nerve tissue. Finally, treatment-related pain may result from a number of sources

such as mucositis secondary to chemotherapy or bone marrow transplantation, radiation dermatitis, or phantom limb pain from amputations.

The management of cancer pain in children requires vigilance. Children may develop many different types of pain problems; thus, a pain problem list is necessary. Ongoing assessment throughout the illness is important. Because tolerance is rarely an issue in cancer pain, increased pain may well indicate disease spread, and medication should not be increased automatically without consideration of disease progression.

The treatment of cancer pain involves a combination of behavioral and pharmacologic approaches. **Aggressive pharmacologic pain control is often critical early on. Many people are fearful that cancer is associated with inevitable pain and suffering; adequate pain control may dissuade them from this notion.** As with other chronic diseases, noxious routes of analgesic administration should be avoided. Nonopioid analgesics should be used with caution in children who have cancer because the antipyretic effects may "mask" a fever. Thoughtful opioid administration can usually control the overwhelming majority of cancer pain. If terminal care becomes necessary, the clinicians should be aware that children's primary concerns are fear of abandonment and fear of pain; these fears should be addressed directly. A supportive environment with respect for the child's and family's wishes is critical. Rapid escalation of dose sometimes is necessary, particularly with solid tumors.

Common Pain Problems

Although pain frequently accompanies many of the common childhood diseases, comfort measures have not historically been a part of routine treatment. For example, the treatment of otitis or pharyngitis emphasized elimination of the presumed underlying etiology (typically bacterial) without addressing the discomfort, which typically was the symptom that brought the child to the physician, that is, otalgia or sore throat. For many of these common pain problems, systemic and local approaches are effective.

Otitis Media

Pain associated with otitis ranges from mild to severe, with most described as moderate to severe. Antibiotics do appear to shorten the period of pain, but even with antibiotic usage pain persists for a few days. Ibuprofen appears preferable to acetaminophen because of its anti-inflammatory activity. When pain is severe, codeine also may be necessary. Local treatment involves heat to the area. The role of local anesthetic agents applied to the tympanic membrane is unresolved.

Pharyngitis

As with otitis, antibiotics appear to decrease pharyngitis pain within 48 hours. Ibuprofen appears preferable to acetaminophen with this condition, as well. Research has suggested that aspirin containing caffeine or a single injection of dexamethasone may reduce inflammation and reduce pain further. Local anesthetic sprays, lozenges, and gargles have not been studied but appear to have some efficacy.

Viral Infections of the Mouth

Herpetic gingivostomatitis and herpangina are an enormous source of distress to children, who often become dehydrated because of the discomfort associated with drinking. Avoiding dehydration through use of a straw as well as use of analgesics such as ibuprofen or acetaminophen in combination with codeine may help. Locally, viscous lidocaine in older children or used with an applicator in younger children, or a "magic mouthwash" solution containing local anesthetic and a binding agent (Kaopectate or Maalox), may have efficacy. There is anecdotal literature on the use of carafate but no formal studies at this writing.

SUMMARY

We have seen dramatic strides in the management of children's pain. At this time, the overwhelming majority of children's discomfort can be handled with available medications and behavioral approaches. What is necessary is the recognition that pain may exist in children, and with the routine implementation of developmentally appropriate assessment techniques and conscientious use of available technology children's pain may be alleviated. The time should be long past when children need to fear the pain associated with illness or associated with its treatment.

FURTHER READING

Acute Pain Management Guideline Panel: Acute Pain Management: Operative or Medical Procedures or Trauma. Clinical Practice Guideline. AHCPR Publication No. 92-0032. Rockville, MD, Agency for Health Care Policy and Research, 1992.

American Academy of Pediatrics, Committee on Drugs: Guidelines for monitoring and management of pediatric patients during and after sedation for diagnostic and therapeutic procedures. Pediatrics 89:1110–1115, 1992.

Kuttner L: A Child in Pain: How to Help, What to Do. Vancouver, Canada, Hartley and Marks, 1996.

McGrath PA: Pain in Children: Nature, Assessment, Treatment. New York, Guilford Press, 1990.

McGrath PJ and Unruh AM: Pain in Children and Adolescents. Amsterdam, Elsevier, 1987.

Schechter NL, Berde CB, and Yaster M: Pain in Infants, Children, and Adolescents. Baltimore, Williams & Wilkins, 1993.

G. Paul DeRosa

Chapter 61

Congenital, Developmental, and Nontraumatic Musculoskeletal Disorders

This chapter stresses the physical examination of the musculoskeletal system. Only topics that occur frequently, need prompt orthopedic referral, or elicit unnecessary parental anxiety are discussed. Attempts are made to alert the practitioner to potential pitfalls in diagnosis. Many of the so-called orthopedic deformities in the neonatal period are merely the result of "intrauterine packing" and have an excellent prognosis; others are transmitted genetically, so a careful family history will frequently lead to a diagnosis, and in turn, prognosis for the problem at hand.

EXAMINATION OF THE NEONATE

In the unclad newborn all four limbs should be moving in a random, purposeless fashion. If the child fails to move an upper extremity, paralysis secondary to brachial plexus injury (birth trauma) versus pseudoparalysis of the limb must be considered. The latter may be secondary to fracture of the clavicle or humerus, separation of the upper humeral epiphysis, or neonatal sepsis involving the proximal humerus and adjacent shoulder joint.

The Head, Neck, and Upper Extremities

Place a hand behind the baby's shoulders and gently lift forward. The head gently rotates backward and the neck is easily visualized. The "V" made by the two sternocleidomastoid muscles attaching to the sternum and clavicle is easily seen and palpated. The medial end of the clavicle, the sternum, and the entire anterior shoulder are easily examined in this position. Feel for the crepitus of fracture (later for the healing wad of callus of neglected clavicular fracture) and palpate for the tight band of a contracted sternocleidomastoid muscle or the "pseudotumor" in the sternocleidomastoid muscle that frequently accompanies congenital muscular torticollis. The head should be easily rotated to the right and left so that the chin touches each shoulder. Lateral inclination of the head so that the ear touches the adjacent shoulder on either side should be accomplished easily. Any resistance to motion, limited motion, or pain on attempted motion should be carefully evaluated by adequate anteroposterior (AP) and lateral cervical spine films. If one cannot incriminate a contracted sternocleidomastoid muscle for the limited motion, one must inspect the films of the cervical spine for anomalies of failure of segmentation, e.g., the Klippel-Feil syndrome, or generalized "radiographic confusion of the cervical spine."

Torticollis (wry neck) has been associated with a higher than normal incidence of developmental dislocation of the hip, so when torticollis is seen, an even closer inspection of the lower extremities is in order. Frequently children are seen who have (1) a persistence of head molding, (2) torticollis, (3) a long C-shaped scoliosis from the occiput or sacrum, and (4) asymmetry of hip abduction. Best termed the "molded baby syndrome," the prognosis is usually good for complete resolution *provided* the asymmetric hip abduction is overcome by gentle stretching of the abducted hip to prevent hip subluxation.

The shoulder and elbow should be put through a passive range of motion. Fracture separation of the upper humeral epiphysis is manifested by crepitus in the shoulder region. Radiographs are not helpful until 7 or 10 days after delivery, when the new periosteal bone formation becomes ossified.

The elbow flexion contraction of the newborn (30 to 45 degrees) may be present up to age 6 weeks, but full flexion should always be present. Pronation and supination of the forearm (not hand or wrist) should be full in the newborn. If rotation is limited, congenital synostosis of the proximal radius and ulna is the cause. This may be evident on radiographs as a bony bridge, but more than likely will be present as a cartilaginous or fibrous bridge that may ossify later.

The final part of the head and upper limb examination is inspection of the hand. Observe the grasp reflex and note that passive extension of the fingers elicits flexion of the thumb. Be certain to passively extend the thumb fully. Contracture of the interphalangeal joint may be present or the deformity may be secondary to a trigger thumb due to a discrepancy in size between the flexor tendon and its synovial sheath (Fig. 61–1). Most trigger thumbs resolve spontaneously, but those still present after 6 months of observation should be surgically released.

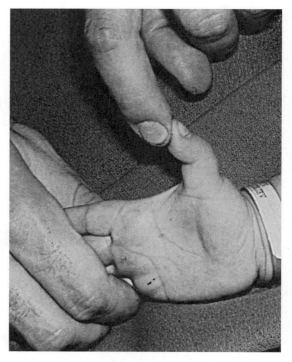

Figure 61–1. The interphalangeal joint of the thumb fails to fully extend. Palpation at the base of the thumb revealed a "node" on the flexor tendon. Surgical release of the tendon sheath allowed full function.

The Spinal Column

The child is placed prone on the examining hand with which inspection of the back from occiput to sacrum is accomplished. Each spinous process should be felt in line, to be certain that an underlying bony abnormality is not overlooked. While major malformations such as myelomeningocele are readily apparent, a hairy patch, a pigmented nevus, or a sacral dimple or pit is sometimes the only cutaneous manifestation of an underlying malformation of the vertebral column. These defects, which frequently include the spinal nerve roots as well as the osseous structures, are collectively called the *spinal dysraphism syndrome*. If the lower extremities and the sphincter function appear normal, then the cutaneous manifestations may simply be noted. Frequently, however, older children are brought to the pediatrician with the complaint of delayed continence, either bowel or bladder; a loss of continence; or a misshapen foot, either cavus or varus, that was *not* present at birth. These complaints must be considered to be due to spinal dysraphism syndrome until proved otherwise.

Children who have congenital problems of the lower extremities, foot deformities, and particularly asymmetric findings such as atrophy or hemihypertrophy should be suspected of having an underlying vertebral anomaly. The young child who has congenital scoliosis usually does not have a neurologic problem unless there is associated diastematomyelia, myelodysplasia, or sacral agenesis. **Because of the high incidence of associated kidney and bladder problems, renal ultrasound is a necessity for all children found to have vertebral anomalies.**

The Lower Extremities

For this phase of the examination the child should be placed supine on a firm examining surface with the hips and knees flexed. One should be careful not to extend the neonate's hip or knee forcibly, as flexion deformities as great as 60 degrees may be present at the hip and up to 45 to 50 degrees at the knee. Full flexion, of course, is always maintained. By placing the feet side by side with the soles on the table and flexing the hips and knees, one can ascertain the relative height of the knees. If one knee is at a lower level (a positive Galeazzi sign or Allis sign), one can assume that the shortened knee is secondary to either an ipsilateral dislocation of the hip, a congenitally short femur, or both. If the knees are at the same level, one can assume that (1) both hips are reduced and in the sockets, or (2) both hips are dislocated. If the perineum appears unusually wide and there are deep groin creases on both sides, one must suspect bilateral dislocation of the hip. After inspection for the Galeazzi sign, each hip should be examined separately to determine hip joint stability, dislocatability, and reducibility.

The Neonatal Hip Examination

In the newborn the examiner should be less concerned about range of motion of the hip joint than about the stability of the hip itself. Attempting to abduct the infant's hips to the point that the thighs touch the examining table serves no useful purpose other than to hurt the infant, cause spasm, and preclude an adequate examination. We must determine whether the hip is reduced or dislocated; if reduced, is it dislocatable or if dislocated, is it reducible?

The classical Ortolani "jerk sign" of the dislocated hip reducing into the acetabulum should be tested. The flexed hip is abducted gently, with the examiner's long finger on the greater trochanter. As abduction is increased, pressure on the trochanter from behind lifts the femoral head back into the socket with a palpable, visible, and sometimes audible "jerk." Unfortunately, the term "click" has been substituted for "jerk" in pediatric literature. It is the *movement* of the hip and not the sound that is the positive finding.

A variation of the Ortolani test has become known as the provocative maneuver of Barlow (Fig. 61–2). The examination is performed by placing the hip in the most unstable position of flexion and slight adduction (the other hand stabilizes the pelvis with the thumb on the symphysis and the fingers on the sacrum). Gentle downward pressure with the hand and lateral pressure with the thumb over the abductor region pushes the unstable hip out of the acetabulum. At this point the Ortolani maneuver of abducting the thigh and lifting on the trochanter with the long finger will reposition the femoral head into the acetabulum with the classic "jerk sign" of Ortolani. The normal hip *will not* dislocate. The femur may break, but the hip will not dislocate. (The author has treated two cases of fractured femur secondary to overenthusiastic examination.) It is a gentle test performed on a quiet infant. It does no good to overpower a screaming baby.

The incidence of the positive "jerk sign" of Ortolani is 1 to 3 per 1000 live births, whereas the incidence of a positive provocative maneuver of Barlow may be as high as 15 per 1000 live births. This lends credence to the belief that hip joint laxity is a prime factor in developmental dislocation of the hip.

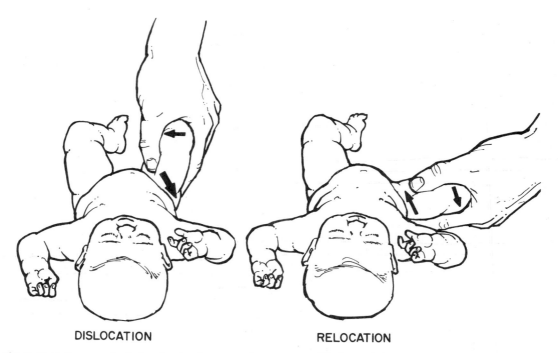

DISLOCATION   **RELOCATION**

Figure 61–2. Proper method of performing the provocative maneuver of Barlow and the accompanying Ortolani "jerk sign."

Probably there is no single cause of developmental dislocation of the hip. Rather, the etiology is multifactorial, with both mechanical and physiologic factors combining to produce instability and subsequent dislocation. That 60% of affected children are first-born suggests mechanical causes. Breech position also plays a significant role in the etiology. Postdelivery environmental factors may also contribute to the development of hip instability and dislocation. In the first months after delivery, the normal physiologic position is one of flexion and abduction. Societies in which infants customarily are wrapped onto a cradle board or swaddled to maintain hip extension have an incidence of dislocation 10 times that of normal.

TREATMENT. If simple splintage in the reduced position can be accomplished, a near-normal or normal femoral head in the acetabulum develops in 96% of cases. If the diagnosis is not made and the hip is left dislocated or becomes dislocated in the first several weeks after birth, adaptive changes quickly occur and the chances of having a normal hip greatly diminish. As the child grows, clinical evidence of the untreated dislocation becomes more obvious (Fig. 61–3). The Ortolani sign becomes negative as the child gets older (2 to 4 months). The femoral head becomes trapped outside the acetabulum and the muscle groups, especially the adductors and the flexors, become shortened about the hip. The ad-

ductor tightness is reflected in limited abduction of the thigh. The shortening is then apparent in extra skinfolds, deep thigh creases, and a positive Galeazzi sign (unequal height of knees).

Routine x-ray examination in the newborn period to detect typical developmental dislocation of the hip is *not* reliable, because x-ray studies may not reveal the dislocation. The usual bony landmarks are not visible because the infant's pelvis and the head and neck of the femur are all cartilage at this time of life. The radiolucent cartilage does not allow for accurate measurement of bony

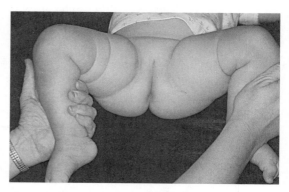

Figure 61–3. Ten-month-old infant with classic signs of hip joint dislocation: deep groin crease, extra skin folds, limited abduction, and a positive Galeazzi sign.

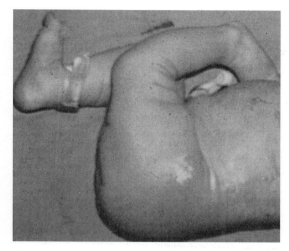

Figure 61–4. Newborn with congenital dislocation of the left knee (genu recurvatum).

landmarks. Therefore, negative findings on radiographs *do not rule out* the presence of dislocation or dislocatable hips. Reliable radiographic signs usually do not become apparent until 2 to 4 months following the dislocation. By this time the characteristic findings of a "shallow acetabulum," a laterally placed femoral neck, and a delay in the ossification of the capital femoral nucleus are all "tipoffs" to the diagnosis. It is stressed that the physical examination in the newborn period is the best test for hip joint stability. Dynamic real-time ultrasound examinations of the neonatal hip may be useful to determine whether a hip is dislocated or dislocatable. These examinations require a competent ultrasonographer, but are quite effective in experienced hands. This examination must be dynamic and in real time.

Many commercially available splints and harnesses are available today. There is no one best

design; the orthopedic surgeon should use the one with which he or she is most comfortable.

Examination of the Knee, Leg, and Foot

An uncommon problem but a true orthopedic emergency is the congenital dislocation or subluxation of the knee (Fig. 61–4). Immediate management within the first few hours after birth can usually result in a satisfactory and nearly normal knee. Delay of as little as 24 hours may render the knee irreducible and require traction and/or surgical procedures. The author's approach is that if the leg, ankle, and foot are normal and one can palpate a patella in the area anterior to the knee, reduction should be achieved immediately by gradually flexing the knee and applying gentle traction to the tibia. The knee is bent as far as possible without force. At this point an aluminum-and-foam finger splint with an elastic wrap or tape is applied. This is removed twice daily so that further flexion can be accomplished until 90 to 100 degrees of flexion is achieved. In our experience this has met with good success, provided it is accomplished in the first 6 hours after birth. In cases that have gone longer than 24 hours, we have had to resort to surgical techniques to reduce the dislocation. Frequently a dislocation of the hip exists in association with the hyperextended dislocated knee. Once the knee has been flexed and treated, care should be taken not to overlook a dislocation of the hip.

It is common for most babies who are packed in utero to have outwardly bowed, medially rotated legs, or so-called internal tibial torsion. This is the norm. The child can usually be folded into the intrauterine position and one can decide which leg was over the other by the amount of outward curving and medial rotation (Fig. 61–5). Of more

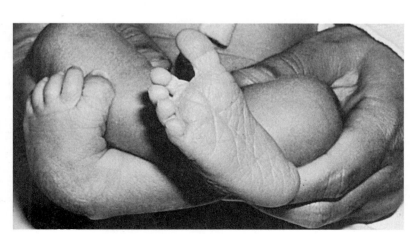

Figure 61–5. Neonate being folded into the in utero position.

importance than the outwardly curved tibia is a sharp, angular, or lateral bowing. Anterolateral bowing of the tibia has been classified as benign if a medullary canal is visible on radiograph, or at risk for fracture if a cyst is at the apex of the anterolateral bow (Fig. 61–6). Frequently these children are born with a fracture through the bowed portion of the tibia, or fracture occurs within the first year of life. Such fractures fail to unite and become congenital pseudarthroses of the tibia. These pseudarthroses are associated with neurofibromatosis in more than 90% of cases. Anterolateral bowing of the tibia with a narrow, sclerotic canal or cystic changes is an orthopedic emergency. These tibias should be protected from impending fracture by casts or braces throughout the growth of the child. In contradistinction, poste-

rior or posterior medial bowing at the junction of the middle and lower thirds of the tibia, termed *kyphoscoliosis of the tibia,* will spontaneously improve with growth. A leg-length discrepancy persists and may need surgical correction near the end of skeletal maturation.

Metatarsus adductus is a common newborn foot problem. Many of these cases are simply the result of intrauterine packing, and with gentle, passive stretching and avoidance of prone sleeping they spontaneously abate. Feet that are rigid and do not overcorrect beyond neutral on passive stretching should be vigorously manipulated and placed in serial plaster casts to stretch the contracted parts and allow for normal fitting of shoes in the future. If the foot is supple, fully overcorrectable beyond neutral, and on stimulation demonstrates all four motor groups of dorsiflexors, plantarflexors, evertors, and invertors, passive manipulation is all that is usually necessary. If the foot is rigid and incapable of being overcorrected, manipulation and serial plaster casts are mandatory.

True clubfoot, or congenital talipes equinovarus, is a frequent problem in the newborn (Fig. 61–7). The entire foot is deviated toward the midline with the heel in varus and equinus and the rest of the foot inverted. The goal of treatment is a clinically and radiographically corrected foot that is flexible and fits into conventional shoes. **In the newborn the treatment should begin at once with manipulation of the clubfoot and application of either plaster casts or adhesive strapping.** Adhesive strapping is certainly much easier to use during the newborn period, because manipulations (Fig. 61–8) can be carried out at each diaper change by the mother or caregiver. Manipulation consists of elongating the medial border of the foot, attempting to reduce the midfoot on the hindfoot, and pulling the os calcis down out of equinus. If one relies on plaster casts, these need to be changed at frequent intervals, for the correction does not come from the casts but from manipulation of the foot. Aggressive, early treatment lessens the likelihood that surgery will be required, but if a plateau is reached with no further gains made by manipulation and application of either plaster casts or splinting, surgery is indicated. The goal is to have a plantigrade foot unfettered by plaster casts and splints at the time the child begins to cruise and bear weight.

Calcaneal valgus foot position is most likely the result of intrauterine posturing. These children have a higher than normal incidence of dislocation of the ipsilateral hip. Thus, whenever a calcaneal valgus foot is seen, careful attention should be paid to the examination of the hips. Generally, passive manipulation gently stretching

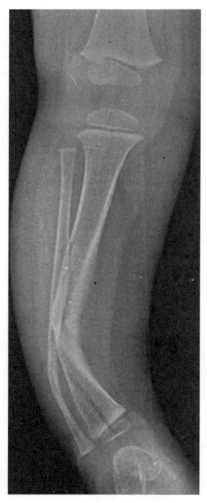

Figure 61–6. Anterior lateral bow of the tibia. No medullary canal is seen at the apex of the deformity. Sclerosis in the area indicates this tibia is at risk for fracture.

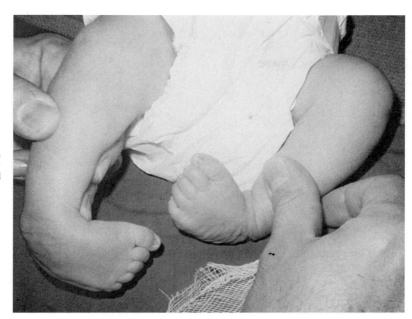

Figure 61–7. Talipes equinovarus, i.e., clubfoot deformity in the newborn. The entire foot deviates toward the midline.

out the anterior structures with or without splinting between manipulations corrects the valgus deformity. On occasion strapping or plaster may be necessary for more rigid deformities.

Care must be taken not to confuse a calcaneal valgus foot with a pes convex valgus or a rocker bottom foot deformity (Fig. 61–9). This is a difficult orthopedic problem requiring considerable expertise. The <u>talus is in vertical alignment so that the hindfoot and forefoot are both deformed</u> (Fig. 61–10). The posterior structures (capsule and tendo Achillis) are very tight, as are the anterior structures. Usually the deformity is very rigid with no motion available at the ankle joint. This birth defect may be associated with arthrogryposis, Turner syndrome, or other congenital anomalies involving the central nervous system. Orthopedic surgeons distinguish between idiopathic vertical talus and that of a neurologic basis. The great majority of these come to operative intervention. Early treatment yields a more satisfactory result than allowing the foot to remain uncorrected into the walking years.

ROTATIONAL PROBLEMS OF THE GROWING LOWER EXTREMITIES

As stated before, most babies are packed in utero with their hips and knees flexed and with one tibia overlapping the other, accounting for varying degrees of outwardly curved tibia and medially rotated feet and ankles (Fig. 61–5). In addition, the feet may wrap about the opposite member and achieve positions of marked adductus that are usually passively correctable. In general, if normal growth and development are allowed to take place, the legs begin to unwind. Longitudinal studies have shown that the bimalleolar axis (i.e., a line running from the medial malleolus through

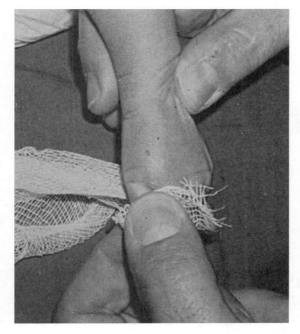

Figure 61–8. Manipulation of clubfoot. Elongation of the medial border of the foot is attempted to reduce the midfoot (navicular) on the hindfoot (talus).

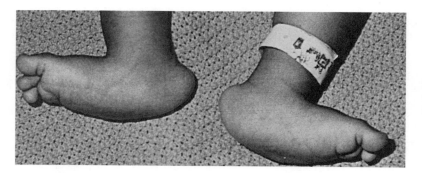

Figure 61–9. Rocker bottom foot is extremely rigid, with motion taking place only in the forefoot.

the lateral malleolus) externally rotates during the first several years of life. Many individuals, however, persist in having outwardly bowed, medially rotated legs and feet, and they are brought to the physician with the complaint of "toeing-in" or tripping while walking. If one takes a careful history and observes the child's sitting and sleeping positions, one finds that the child sits with knees flexed, the feet internally rotated, and his or her bottom resting on the feet. This perpetuates the internal rotation deformity. Likewise, the child sleeps on the abdomen with his or her knees "tucked up" under the chest and his or her bottom coming down on the internally rotated feet (Fig. 61–11). For this reason, normal growth and development or the normal evolution of external rotation cannot take place, and persistent "internal tibial torsion" or medial rotation is the rule. Treatment consists of altering the child's sleeping and sitting posture so that external rotation rather than internal rotation is encouraged.

If the child's habit of sleeping on his or her abdomen cannot be stopped, a Denis Browne splint or a detachable Fillauer bar applied to the shoes is indicated. This treatment does not correct the deformity, but merely allows normal growth and development to take place. Certain guidelines are in order for the use of these devices: (1) the width of the bar should be no wider than the width of the hips—an arbitrary rule is that no bar should be wider than 6 inches; and (2) the feet should not be forcibly externally rotated. Only 10 to 15 degrees of external rotation is needed. Extreme rotations or wide bars have the adverse effect of causing knee ligament damage, which may be irreparable. Normally, the time needed for correction is from 6 to 18 months.

Another cause for toeing-in in the ambulatory child is persistent *femoral neck anteversion.* All children are born with the femoral head and neck inclined in a more anterior direction than in the adult. As the child kicks out of the flexion deformity of the neonate and starts a sitting balance to develop a lumbar lordosis rather than the long C infantile curve, the acetabulum assumes a more vertical relationship and the femoral neck usually

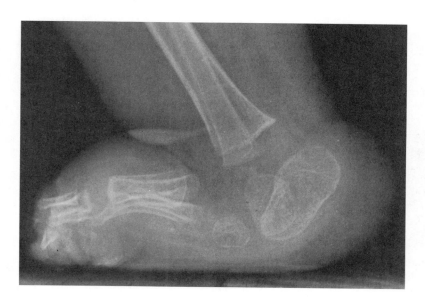

Figure 61–10. Lateral radiograph of congenital vertical talus (rocker bottom foot). The heel is in equinus, the talus is pointing directly toward the floor, and the midfoot is dislocated on the dorsum of the talus.

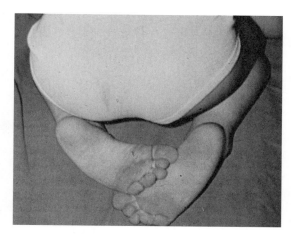

Figure 61–11. Toddler with "toe-in" gait assuming his most comfortable sleeping position. The internally rotated feet are being subjected to increased internal forces by the weight of the buttocks.

undergoes a decrease in the anteverted angle. Failure to untwist, so to speak, leads to excessive amounts of internal rotation of the hip at the expense of external rotation, the hip joint capsule being the restraint that prevents external rotation at the hip. These children classically walk with their kneecaps pointing inward, called "squinting patellae" (Fig. 61–12). When they run, their feet usually whip out to the side, giving the appearance of a clumsy, slow child. This gait is due to muscle contraction of the hip internal rotators seating the femoral head deeply into the socket for stability. The thigh, knee, and consequently, the leg and foot are internally rotated. The knee flexion and extension arc are now out of line with the forward progression of the body and, consequently, are less efficient. The child is slower because the normally smooth, coordinated mechanics of running are altered. If asked to walk slowly, most of these children can control rotation so that their feet point straight ahead. This requires conscious effort on their part and is, therefore, fatiguing. This is why their gait deteriorates near the end of the day, with increased toeing-in. Provided habits that enhance internal rotation are interrupted early (i.e., sitting in a "W" on the floor and abdominal sleeping), most toeing-in will acceptably "unwind" by age 8 or 9. There are few indications for more aggressive treatment. Shoe prescriptions with wedges or twister cable braces have no place in the treatment of anteversion of the hip or internal rotation of the tibia. What is needed is an adequate explanation of the anatomic reason why the child toes-in. This explanation plus the usually good prognosis for acceptable correction, provided that poor habits are corrected, is sufficient in most

cases. In the remainder, especially those children who have only 0 to 10 degrees of external rotation, osteotomy of the femur may be indicated.

A word of caution concerning the use of twister cable braces for femoral anteversion: These devices apply external rotation torque to the foot and ankle. While the child is in the device, he or she may indeed walk with the foot straight ahead or externally rotated. However, this external rotation force may have a deleterious effect on the medial collateral ligament of the knee or the deltoid ligament of the ankle and subtalar joint. **For this reason the use of twister braces in children who have femoral anteversion as their sole orthopedic problem is to be condemned.**

External Rotation Contracture

In contrast to those children who toe-in, there are those who "toe-out." This posture may be

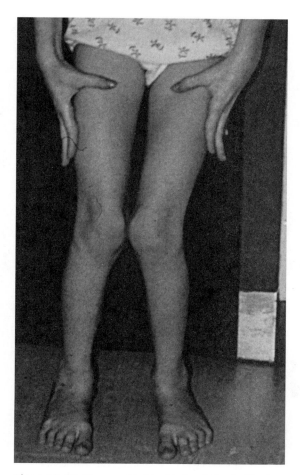

Figure 61–12. Six-year-old girl with "toe-in" gait. She demonstrates the "squinting patellae" of the excessively anteverted hips.

present at birth and diminishes as the child begins to walk. There is significant parental anxiety, as the family feels the child is crippled and doing harm to his or her foot and ankle. The physical findings are just the reverse of the anteverted hip. There is excessive *external rotation,* but limited internal rotation at the hip. Radiographs should be made to rule out a dislocation of the hips.

The etiology of toeing-out is abduction and external rotation contracture of the soft tissue around the hip secondary to intrauterine position. The treatment includes (1) adequate explanation to the family of the anatomic nature of the problem; (2) gentle, passive stretching exercises of the external rotators by internally rotating the femurs at each diaper change; and (3) avoidance of sleeping positions that perpetuate the posture, i.e., the "spread eagle" or frog prone position.

The "Noncorrective" Corrective Shoe

Much ado is made about special or corrective shoes in the treatment of common pediatric foot problems. There is no such thing as a corrective shoe. Shoes are meant to protect the foot, *not* correct it.

In general, shoes should be flexible and fitted long enough to prevent the toes from being pinched and wide enough so the forefoot is not crowded together. Rigid shoes prevent motion and should be avoided. The sole should be of a non-skid material to prevent the toddler from slipping. The upper should be soft and porous, especially in warm climates. It is best to avoid fad shoes or odd-shaped shoes that have excessive heel height and pointed toes. The shoes should not be expensive.

The altering of shoes with wedges and special heels has been a popular mode of treatment for the flexible flat-footed child or the child who toes-in or toes-out. There is no scientific basis for these altered shoe prescriptions, and the practice should be avoided.

If a child presents with a flexible foot that has a normal range of motion and is supported by normal muscles that plantarflex, dorsiflex, evert, and invert the *foot,* **the foot is normal for** *that child*! It needs to be allowed to grow and develop normally.

In contrast, **the child who presents with a painful and/or rigid foot or one that has an excessively high arch (pes cavus) should be referred for evaluation.** Rigid feet may be secondary to tarsal coalition (abnormal bony bridges between the bones), and cavus feet may be secondary to neuromuscular disease (peroneal

muscular atrophy) or the spinal dysraphism syndrome.

Knock-Knees and Bow Legs

There is a varus position of the tibia in the newborn that gradually diminishes in the first 2 years of life, called "physiologic bowing." After age 2 the tibia swings like a pendulum into a valgus position, i.e., knock-knees. This is usually present until age 4. The tibial pendulum slowly swings backward so that at about age 8, most children have the tibiofemoral alignment of the adult. Because of variation in genetic background, these fluctuations of the tibial pendulum may take excessive swings and cause parental anxiety. This anxiety may be allayed by documented serial examinations and good-quality radiographs revealing no underlying bony abnormality. If bowing persists beyond age 2, and if it is specifically confined to the tibia, one must suspect Blount disease (tibia vara), a disorder that frequently requires surgical correction (Fig. 61–13).

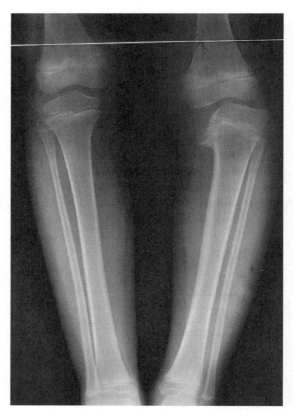

Figure 61–13. Standing anteroposterior radiographs of a 5-year-old child with normal tibiofemoral alignment in the right leg and Blount disease in the left leg.

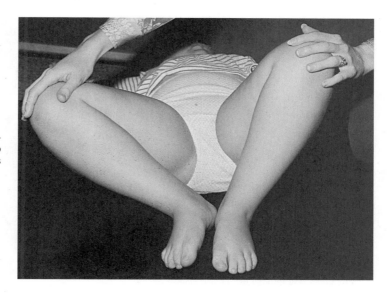

Figure 61–14. Simple abduction test demonstrating limited abduction of the left hip in the flexed position. The child has Perthes disease of the left hip.

Knock-knee that is physiologic and not secondary to underlying disease has an excellent prognosis. Secondary knock-knee is sometimes seen in overweight patients, in patients who have paralytic conditions, juvenile rheumatoid arthritis, or endocrinopathies, and following infection or injuries to the growth plates. The latter usually require surgical correction.

HIP SYNDROMES OF CHILDHOOD AND ADOLESCENCE

The child who limps alarms the family, especially if there is no history of trauma or evidence of bruising or tenderness. Excluding trauma, the toddler who limps likely has toxic synovitis of the hip or the "irritable hip" syndrome. If the child refuses to walk, one must also consider a diskitis or disk space infection in the lumbar spine.

In the child from age 4 to age 9, the limp is most likely associated with either toxic synovitis of the hip or Legg-Calvé-Perthes disease. Toxic synovitis of the hip is better termed transient synovitis or the irritable hip syndrome, thereby describing the symptoms and duration of the illness rather than its etiology. The cause remains unknown; injury, low-grade viral infection, and allergic hypersensitivity have all been incriminated, but no hard evidence supports any cause. The children are not systemically ill at the time of the synovitis. Bed rest until the signs of limited hip motion have abated is sufficient treatment. There may be several bouts of the affliction. It is tempting to consider transient synovitis as a prelude to Perthes disease, but proof of the correlation is lacking. In the case of Perthes disease, the limp predominates over the pain, which may be localized to the thigh or medial side of the knee. When the child is first seen, significant muscle atrophy of the thigh has often occurred. Any limping child requires an accurate assessment of the gait pattern and careful evaluation of the spine by palpation and range-of-motion examination.

Examination of the hip can be easily accomplished by the simple abduction test and the prone internal rotation test. With the patient lying supine on the examining table, the hips and knees are flexed, feet on the table side-by-side. The patient is asked to let his or her knees fall apart while keeping the feet together. The hip that is irritable or inflamed, for whatever cause, will have a limited range of abduction compared with the opposite noninflamed side (Fig. 61–14). Similarly, when the child is placed in the prone position with the knee flexed 90 degrees, internal rotation is markedly limited on the affected side. In my experience these two tests are most sensitive for hip joint pathology. Good-quality AP and frog lateral x-ray views of the pelvis should be made if hip pathology is suspected. Single hip x-ray studies are not as helpful as the pelvis film, especially for comparison of the affected with the uninvolved side.

In the age group from 4 to 9 years, unexplained limp without fever is considered Legg-Calvé-Perthes disease until proved otherwise. The treatment is variable depending on the locale and orthopedic surgeon, but in general, the goal is to try to preserve function by decreasing inflammation of the hip, by whatever means necessary, and restoring nearly full motion until the lesion has healed.

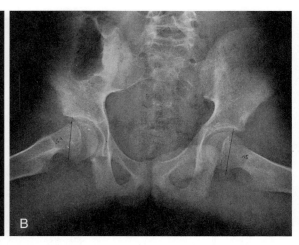

Figure 61–15. Radiographs of slipped epiphysis. Anteroposterior (AP) *(A)* and frog-position (lateral) pelvic *(B)* x-ray studies of an adolescent boy with *right* thigh pain. Note the AP view shows minimal, if any, deformity. The lateral view reveals the slipping of the femoral head through the growth plate.

The limping adolescent aged 9 to 17 must be considered to have a slipped epiphysis of the hip until proved otherwise. Many adolescents are referred to the orthopedist for a varying degree and duration of thigh or knee pain and arrive carrying a folder of normal knee radiographs. One must be aware that "hip pain" may be referred to the inner aspect of the thigh and knee and that careful hip evaluation, as described earlier, is necessary to rule out hip joint pathology. It is imperative that appropriate AP and frog lateral x-ray views of the pelvis be obtained (Fig. 61–15). The slipping of the epiphysis is best seen on the lateral film. The treatment for slipped capital femoral epiphysis is to make the diagnosis and to prevent further slippage. This can be performed by internal fixation, using threaded pins or bone grafting procedures to stimulate epiphyseal plate closure. The sequelae of severe slips and avascular necrosis secondary to severe slips is far too big a price to pay for these young people. It behooves us to pay particular attention to the adolescent who complains of thigh or knee pain.

OSGOOD-SCHLATTER DISEASE

Knee pain in the active adolescent is usually the result of direct trauma. Many young people complain of knee pain when in actuality the pain is localized to the tibial tubercle. If direct compression on the tubercle reproduces the pain or accentuates the pain, a diagnosis of Osgood-Schlatter disease may be made. This usually self-limiting lesion is related to inflammation of the attachment of the infrapatellar tendon into the tibial tubercle and, thereby, to the proximal tibial growth plate. Good-quality AP and lateral x-ray views are needed, not to diagnose Osgood-Schlatter disease, but to rule out other disorders such as a low-grade osteomyelitis or an osteosarcoma that may mimic Osgood-Schlatter disease. Once these significant problems are ruled out, attention can be given to limiting the child's activities with the advice that the lesion most likely will heal, but takes time. Many children need to be converted from running and jumping sports to swimming in order to be given an outlet for their energies.

It is stressed again that Osgood-Schlatter disease is a very common lesion of the adolescent knee and is self-limiting, not requiring treatment other than avoiding those activities that enhance the pain. Once the pain has abated, direct trauma may play a significant role in a flare-up of the condition; therefore, knee pads should be worn to prevent the second and third bouts of pain and decreased activity.

Now that physical fitness is in vogue, many adolescents are vigorously pursuing sports. In fact, overuse and abuse syndromes are becoming frequent diagnoses in children's orthopedic clinics. Anterior knee pain without antecedent trauma is a frequent adolescent complaint. After a thorough history of sports activities and pain patterns, a careful examination should include tests for meniscal injuries, ligament instabilities, compression of the tibial tubercle, and complete active and passive range of movement. Many young athletes have incomplete flexion of the knee in the prone position, thereby increasing stress on the patellofemoral joint. These children should follow a regimen of quadriceps stretching exercises to overcome the overload syndrome on the anterior knee structures. A prone passive knee flexion examination should be included in any examination of the knee joint.

SCOLIOSIS

School screening programs have encouraged the pediatrician to become more aware of scoliosis and spinal deformities. Why so much fuss about a crooked back? Long-term studies of untreated scoliosis patients have revealed an increased risk of death from cardiopulmonary causes. Many untreated adult scoliosis patients have significant back pain. Many are disabled because of symptoms of fatigue and pain. Furthermore, curves in excess of 60 degrees in the thoracic area will continue to progress after skeletal maturity, as will lumbar curves in excess of 40 degrees. For these and many other reasons, aggressive treatment of the child who has a spinal deformity is justified. Although some health officials have presented evidence that massive school screening is not cost-effective, the Scoliosis Research Society still supports the concept of school screening.

CLASSIFICATION AND ETIOLOGY. The broadest categories of scoliosis are *nonstructural* and *structural* scoliosis. Nonstructural scoliotic curves are extremely flexible and show correction on side-bending of the patient toward the convex side of the curve. In structural scoliosis, the curve fails to correct on side-bending because it is quite rigid.

After a careful history and physical examination, most scoliosis patients presenting to the pediatrician are probably categorized as idiopathic, that is, the true etiology remains obscure. If, however, we look closely at these patients and their families, we find that a great number of the families give a history of curves in other family members, so-called familial or genetic scoliosis. If a family has one child who has a curvature of the spine, all of the children in that family must be examined and observed throughout their growth period for the occurrence of scoliosis. Counseling the parents and the patient is important. Based on present knowledge, a person who has scoliosis has a one in three chance of having children who have scoliosis.

Depending on the age at the time of recognition of the curve, familial scoliosis is designated as infantile (if the child is less than 3 years of age at onset), juvenile (3 to 8 years at onset), or adolescent scoliosis. In the United States the most common form of idiopathic scoliosis is the adolescent-onset variety, which is seen in the child ages 9 to 14, just before the last rapid growth spurt. It is in this group of children that school screening is most rewarding. The overall incidence of scoliosis is variously quoted in the orthopedic literature as being between 4 and 8% of the normal population. Not all of these people need active treatment because not all scoliotic curves are progressive. Only about 2% of that population have progressive spinal curves requiring active treatment.

It is of major importance that all children be screened for scoliosis at each examination by the pediatrician. Each routine visit, each preschool and school physical, is an opportunity for the physician to examine the spine for malalignment. The examination requires only about 30 seconds, but if properly performed may yield a lifetime of dividends. In the neonatal period, the examination is performed both in the prone position and with the child suspended. In all older children the examination should be performed in the standing position.

THE EXAMINATION. Observe from the back (Fig. 61–16). Careful attention is placed on

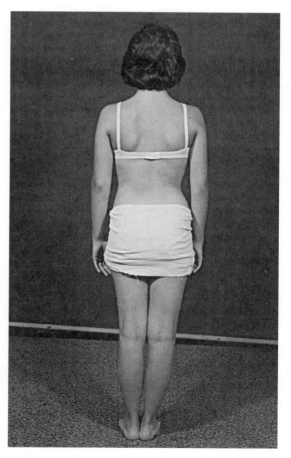

Figure 61–16. Examination of the back for scoliosis. See text for details.

the following areas: (1) Are the shoulders of unequal height? (2) Is there an obvious curve of the spine or the spinous processes? (3) Is there a prominent scapula? (4) Are there asymmetric waist creases? (5) Is there a tilt of the pelvis creating unequal leg length? (6) Does one arm hang away from the trunk farther than the other? The patient should then bend forward as if touching the toes and have the spinal alignment checked in the forward-bending position (Fig. 61–17). Both sides of the thorax and trunk should be at the same level in forward bending. If they are not, scoliosis is present. These simple observations can satisfactorily screen out most scoliotic curves. If there is concern that any of the above is present, both PA and lateral x-ray studies of the spine should be obtained in the standing position. The films should include the vertebral column in its entirety from occiput to sacrum.

MEASUREMENT OF THE CURVE. The severity of the scoliotic curve is determined by careful measurement (Fig. 61–18) of the spinal x-ray film. Curves may be of any pattern, but the most typical idiopathic adolescent curve is that of a right thoracic curve, i.e., the majority of the curvature occurs in the thoracic vertebrae and is convex to the patient's right side.

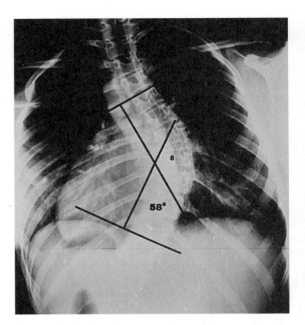

Figure 61–18. Measurement of the scoliotic curve by the Cobb method.

GUIDELINES FOR TREATMENT. The best treatment for scoliosis is early detection and prompt referral to a facility equipped to provide complete scoliosis care. Treatment of children who have scoliosis falls into three categories: (1) observation, (2) bracing and exercise programs, and (3) surgery. Although treatment must be individualized to each patient, the following generalized comments may be made. Spinal curvatures measuring less than 20 to 25 degrees in a skeletally immature patient should be observed at 6-month intervals with repeat examination, including x-ray studies. More frequent x-ray studies are not justified because curves rarely progress at a rate greater than 1 degree per month and measurement error is about 5 degrees. All subsequent x-ray studies must be compared with the original film so that true progression is not minimized by observer bias or overlooked owing to measurement error. Skeletally immature patients who have curves greater than 20 to 25 degrees, but less than 40 degrees, should be offered treatment with a brace program and an active exercise routine. The goal of all therapy in scoliosis is to prevent further deformity. If the curve is found and treatment begun early with rigid adherence to the treatment protocol, the need for spinal surgery in children who have idiopathic scoliosis may be obviated.

If brace treatment is indicated, the child must be willing to spend 18 to 22 hours each day in the brace. Brace treatment protocols are changing

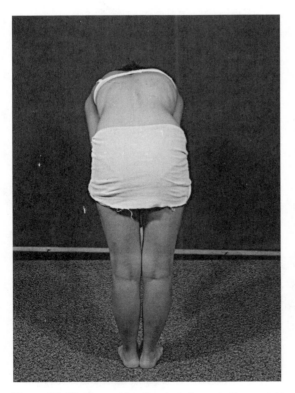

Figure 61–17. Forward-bending test demonstrating a right thoracic scoliosis.

and are not nearly as demanding as they originally were. Exercise for scoliosis falls into two categories: (1) general conditioning and spinal flexibility, and (2) in-brace exercises to extend the spinal column and isometric exercises to push against and away from the pads of the brace. The use of a mirror is encouraged for the in-brace exercises because it facilitates the visual proprioceptive feedback mechanism, i.e., the child contracts muscles and sees a result from the exercise. Patients and families must be counseled that exercises alone do not cure scoliosis. They make the child look and feel better, and they make the child aware of posture and methods to effect changes in posture. Exercises keep the spine flexible, enabling the brace to function more effectively.

Brace wearing must be continued until vertebral growth has ceased. This is usually determined by the appearance of the iliac apophysis on the x-ray studies. Families and patients should understand that growth does not cease at the same age for all patients and that wearing the brace must be continued until that individual child has reached skeletal maturity as determined radiographically.

In children whose curves are greater than 45 to 50 degrees and in whom spinal growth still remains, brace therapy is not satisfactory. These larger curves have a greater propensity for progression, hence the need for stabilization of the curve surgically.

It is hoped that through education of the public, early detection by physicians and/or school screening, and aggressive treatment, the need for surgical treatment of scoliosis will be decreased.

FURTHER READING

Hensinger R and Jones E: Neonatal Orthopaedic. New York, Grune and Stratton, 1981.

Renshaw TS: Pediatric Orthopedics. Philadelphia, WB Saunders, 1986.

Sharrad WJW: Pediatric Orthopaedics and Fractures. London, Blackwell Scientific Publications, 1993.

Wenger DR and Rang M: The Art and Practice of Children's Orthopaedics. New York, Raven Press, 1993.

Susan H. Psaila
Neil S. Prose

Chapter 62

Common Skin Disorders

ACNE

Acne vulgaris is a disorder of the hair follicle and sebaceous gland that is most prevalent during adolescence, affecting up to 90% of teenagers, with greater severity in males. Acne has a predilection for skin with high concentrations of sebaceous glands; therefore, the face, chest, and back are common sites of involvement. Given the wide range of severity among patients, acne therapy must be individualized. Treatment is important to prevent the postinflammatory pigment changes and scar formation that can result from severe or cystic acne. Equally important is the prevention of the psychologic effects for adolescents who may suffer from poor self-image or even depression as a result of their acne.

The classic lesions of acne are open and closed comedones (blackheads and whiteheads), formed by a sebum-plugged pilosebaceous follicle. The dark color of a blackhead results from oxidized lipids, melanin, and densely packed keratinocytes, not dirt. The proliferation of *Propionibacterium acnes* in noninflammatory comedones and the rupture of comedone contents into the surrounding dermis may stimulate the development of inflammatory papules, pustules, and cysts. Cystic acne is manifested by fluctuant and painful nodules and cysts that heal with postinflammatory pigment changes and scar formation.

The first step in choosing appropriate therapy is assessing the predominant lesions accurately. Mild to moderate acne can be treated with topical antibiotics (clindamycin or erythromycin) applied each morning and topical tretinoin (starting with the mildest preparation, 0.025% cream) before bed. Patients whose acne is moderately to severely inflammatory should use the aforementioned topical therapy in addition to an oral antibiotic (tetracycline, erythromycin, or minocycline). The side effects of minocycline use are known to include arthritis and autoimmune hepatitis. Patients whose acne is severely inflammatory or refractive to conventional treatments should be referred to a dermatologist for possible treatment with isotretinoin. The patient must realize that acne therapy does not result in cure and that medications may take weeks to reach full effect. Other recommendations should include the use of mild, nondrying, noncomedogenic soaps (e.g., Dove, Purpose, Neutrogena, Basis) and moisturizers (Moisturel, Cetaphil, Purpose). Patients should avoid excessive cleansing and scrubbing, which may worsen their condition. Although studies have not demonstrated a causal relationship between certain foods and acne, the patient should be advised to eat a well-balanced diet and avoid foods that consistently result in flare-ups.

INFESTATIONS

Scabies

Scabies (Fig. 62–1) is a widespread infestation caused by the mite *Sarcoptes scabiei*. It is spread primarily by skin contact, although fomite spread is possible. The characteristic skin findings, which appear 2 to 4 weeks after initial contact, are thought to represent a delayed hypersensitivity reaction. Clinically, the patient presents with severe pruritus, which is worse at night. Primary lesions include pruritic papules, vesicles, pustules, or linear burrows in the finger and toe web spaces, the axillae, flexor aspects of the wrists, genitalia, and buttocks. In infants and toddlers, the distribution of the lesions differs, with the head, neck, axillae, palms, and soles involved more prominently. This younger age group also is more likely to develop an intense nodular skin reaction to the mite.

Clinical diagnosis is aided by low-power microscopic examination of a skin scraping of a burrow. Mineral oil is applied to several lesions, which then are scraped onto a glass slide, using a sterile

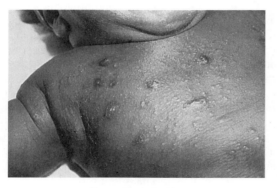

Figure 62–1. Scabies.

scalpel blade. The mites are eight-legged arachnids, which may be seen along with their eggs—smooth, oval-shaped masses approximately half the size of the mite—or clusters of reddish brown pellets (fecal matter).

Current therapy for eradication of scabies is based on topical treatment. Permethrin 5% cream (Elimite) is the treatment of choice. Therapy should be applied at bedtime to the entire skin surface below the head (including the neck), umbilicus, beneath the fingernails, and intertriginous areas and rinsed off after 8 to 12 hours. The scalps of infants and young children (<2 years of age) should also be treated. Because eggs hatch every 3 to 4 days, this treatment should be repeated in 4 to 7 days to treat any new mites. All worn clothing, towels, bedding, and stuffed animals must be washed in hot water at the time of the treatment. Alternatively, the items can be placed in a plastic bag for 3 to 4 days, because live mites can exist off a human host for only 2 to 3 days. All household members and close contacts should be treated simultaneously to prevent reinfection of the patient. Postscabetic pruritus, which may persist for days to weeks after treatment, can be treated with oral antihistamines, lubricants, and topical steroids.

Lice

Three varieties of lice produce clinical disease in humans and all can involve the scalp hair in children. Head lice (pediculosis capitis) is the most common form of louse infestation. The lice are spread through close contact and by the sharing of hats, combs, or brushes. The lice eggs (nits) are found primarily in the hairs above the ears and in the occipital regions. The nits are visible as small, whitish oval forms that are laid close to the scalp near the bottom of the hair shaft and carried outward as the hair grows. Patients present with scalp pruritus. Diagnosis can be confirmed by low-power magnification of a louse or nit. In addition, nits can be identified by Wood's light examination.

Although transmission via towels and hats does occur, crab lice *(Phthirus pubis)* are transmitted primarily by sexual contact. In adolescents and adults they typically inhabit pubic hair, and occasionally, axillary hair. In young children after close contact with infested adults, the lice may infest the scalp or eyelashes. Their bites produce bluish, pruritic macules or papules over the lower abdomen and upper thighs. A secondary eczematous rash may develop in these areas, due to scratching. Body lice (pediculosis corporis) generally live in clothing and bedding, where they lay their eggs along the seams. Bites produce pruritic papules or urticarial wheals with a characteristic hemorrhagic central punctum.

Eradication of lice requires application of permethrin 1% creme rinse (Nix) or lindane 1% shampoo (Kwell) to infested hair-bearing areas of all household members. Cleaning measures are similar to those described for scabies eradication. Nits are difficult to remove because of their firm attachment to the hair shafts. That patients treated adequately still have nonviable shells attached to the hair is a common cause of misunderstanding by school health care workers. Removal of the nits can be facilitated by soaking the hair in a solution of white vinegar mixed 1:1 with water (the acetic acid dissolves the chitin that binds the nits to the hair shafts) and then removing the nits with a fine-toothed comb. Combs and brushes may be cleaned by coating with the pediculicide for 15 minutes or soaking in rubbing alcohol for 1 hour. Because none of the treatments is completely ovicidal, a second treatment 1 week later will ensure that any new nymphs are killed. Some head lice appear resistant to traditional therapies and may be a challenge to eradicate.

FUNGAL INFECTIONS

Two types of fungal organisms produce clinical cutaneous disease: dermatophytes and yeast. Dermatophytes include the tinea fungi, and yeasts include *Candida* and *Pityrosporum* species. The distinction between these types of fungal infections is important because their treatments are different.

Tinea Corporis

Tinea corporis (ringworm) (Fig. 62–2) is a superficial fungal infection of the skin. The lesions are pruritic, annular scaly patches with central clearing and a vesicular, papular, or pustular border. The causative organism in young children usually is *Microsporum canis* or *Trichophyton tonsurans*. Diagnosis is made clinically but can be confirmed by a low-power potassium hydroxide (KOH) preparation of skin scrapings for fungal hyphae. Fungal cultures can confirm the diagnosis. Topical treatments include miconazole, clotrimazole, or ketoconazole applied once or twice a day for a minimum of 1 to 2 weeks after clinical clearing of the lesion. When lesions are severe or extensive, systemic therapy with griseofulvin may be indicated.

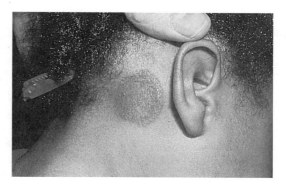

Figure 62–2. Tinea corporis.

Tinea Capitis

Tinea capitis (Fig. 62–3) is the most common fungal infection in children, and its incidence is increasing in epidemic fashion. **Today, *Trichophyton tonsurans* is responsible for more than 95% of tinea capitis in the United States.** This form of infection results most often in scattered areas of alopecia and hair loss. At times, the hairs break off at the surface, leaving short residual hairs that appear as black dots. Diffuse scaling also may simulate dandruff as the sole indication of infection. *M. canis,* now increasingly rare, generally causes round patches of scaling alopecia. Both *Microsporum* and *Trichophyton* may present with a highly inflammatory, edematous, pustular form known as a kerion.

T. tonsurans does not fluoresce; therefore, Wood's lamp examination is not helpful for diagnosis. KOH preparation or fungal culture can be obtained by plucking the hair (including the root) or scraping scale from the scalp. The only effective treatment is systemic antifungals. Current dosing recommendations for griseofulvin are 10 to 20 mg/kg/day for 6 to 8 weeks. The drug should be given with fatty foods to increase absorption.

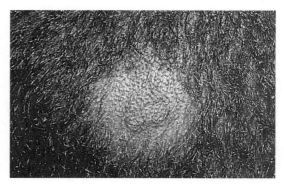

Figure 62–3. Tinea capitis.

Because most patients require only brief therapy, monitoring renal, hepatic, and hematologic function is not necessary. Concurrent treatment with topical selenium sulfide, 2.5% shampoo or ketoconazole, 2% shampoo twice a week can reduce infectivity. Superinfected lesions also should be treated with oral antibiotics. Patients who have kerions may require a 1- to 2-week course of prednisone at 1 mg/kg/day in addition to systemic antifungals to reduce the risk of permanent scarring and alopecia. Children receiving therapy may attend school.

Tinea Pedis

Tinea pedis (athlete's foot) is very common among adolescents and young adults. The infection is usually caused by the dermatophyte *Trichophyton rubrum,* and secondary bacterial infection is common. The fungus has a predilection for the toe web spaces, especially between the fourth and fifth digits. Patients complain of intense burning and itching. Scaling and fissuring predominate, but vesiculopustular lesions and maceration can be present. Clinical diagnosis can be confirmed by a KOH preparation of skin scrapings as needed. Therapy consists of twice-a-day application of topical antifungals for 3 to 6 weeks or until the infection has cleared. Powders such as 1% tolfanate (Zeasorb AF), Desenex, or talcum can be used along with light cotton socks.

Tinea Versicolor

Tinea versicolor is a common superficial fungal infection caused by a yeast, *Pityrosporum orbiculare.* Clinically, the infection presents with oval scaly patches 1 to 3 cm in diameter, usually in a guttate or raindrop pattern on the upper chest, back, and proximal upper extremities of adolescents and young adults. Lesions may be light tan, reddish, or white in color, giving rise to the term "versicolor." The rash usually is asymptomatic; however, some patients develop pruritus. Clinical diagnosis can be confirmed by a KOH preparation of the surface scale. The classic "spaghetti and meatball" pattern with rod-shaped hyphae and round spores is seen. Wood's light examination reveals white or yellow fluorescence. Treatment with selenium sulfide shampoo, 2.5% applied for 10 minutes for 7 days, may be effective. Alternatively, topical miconazole, ketoconazole, or clotrimazole can be applied once a day for 2 weeks. Normal skin color will return over a period of weeks to months.

PITYRIASIS ROSEA

Pityriasis rosea is a benign inflammatory disorder occurring most commonly in preadolescents, adolescents, and young adults. The cause is unknown. The disease sometimes begins with a single oval, erythematous, slightly scaly lesion—the "herald patch." One to 2 weeks later, similar smaller lesions appear primarily on the trunk. These generalized lesions often follow the lines of skin cleavage, creating a "Christmas tree" pattern over the trunk. Resolution of the rash may take 6 to 12 weeks. The disease is self-limited, and no treatment is required. **Because of its similar clinical presentation, secondary syphilis must be ruled out in any patient in whom pityriasis rosea is suspected.**

PSORIASIS

Psoriasis (Fig. 62–4) is a chronic disorder having a waxing and waning course. More than one third of patients who have psoriasis experience their first episode by age 20. In psoriasis, an abnormally rapid turnover of the epidermis results in the accumulation of thick scale over sites of frequent trauma and irritation, for example, the extensor surfaces of extremities and the scalp. Lesions are erythematous, sharply demarcated plaques with silvery scale. The lesions often are induced in areas of local injury, such as scratches, bites, or sunburn (the Koebner phenomenon). Children frequently have guttate or droplike lesions scattered over the body. Streptococcal pharyngitis often precedes a flare of guttate psoriasis, and antibiotic treatment of the pharyngitis sometimes resolves the skin lesions.

Patients who have severe or extensive disease

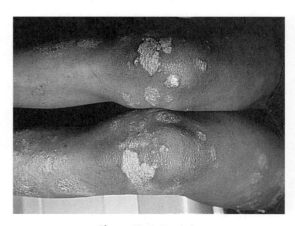

Figure 62–4. Psoriasis.

should be referred to a dermatologist. Mild cases of plaque psoriasis usually are controlled well with thick emollients, keratolytic agents, topical calcipotriene, and low-potency topical corticosteroids. Topical steroids should be applied twice a day to individual plaques for several weeks.

SEBORRHEIC DERMATITIS

Seborrheic dermatitis (Fig. 62–5) shows a predilection for areas of increased sebaceous activity such as the face, scalp, postauricular area, axillae, and groin. In infants, seborrheic dermatitis of the scalp, also known as cradle cap, begins during the first month of life and is characterized by nonpruritic salmon-colored lesions with a greasy yellow scale. In adolescents, the dermatitis may manifest as erythema and dandruff or flaking of the eyebrow, postauricular, or flexural areas. In infants, cradle cap can be treated with daily applications of a medicated shampoo, such as selenium sulfide, 2.5% for 1 to 2 weeks. The shampoo should be left on for 10 minutes and a soft washcloth used to help loosen the scales. Young adults also can use shampoos containing selenium sulfide, salicylic acid, or tar to reduce scaling. Lesions on the body can be treated with low-potency topical corticosteroids.

ATOPIC DERMATITIS

Atopic dermatitis (Figs. 62–6 and 62–7) is an inherited skin disorder that often is found in association with asthma or allergic rhinitis. Up to 75% of all patients have a family history of atopic disease. Sixty percent of children who have atopic dermatitis manifest their disease in the first year of life and 90% by age 5. The diagnosis of atopic dermatitis is based on the morphology and distri-

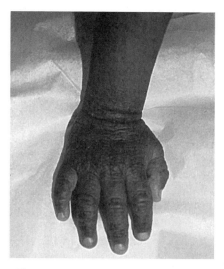

Figure 62–6. Atopic dermatitis of the hand.

bution of lesions, personal or family history of atopy, and a chronic relapsing course. Pruritus is a hallmark. Other features indicative of atopic dermatitis include xerosis, ichthyosis, allergic shiners, atopic pleats (Dennie-Morgan lines), hyperlinear palms and soles, and susceptibility to recurrent cutaneous infections.

The clinical picture of atopic dermatitis varies with the age of the patient and the disease severity. Infants typically present with symmetric, red pruritic papules and plaques that ooze and crust. Lesions are distributed over the scalp, forehead, cheeks, trunk, and extensor surfaces of the extremities. In older children, atopic dermatitis is characterized by a dry, papular, and intensely pruritic eruption. Distinct scaly patches are located on the wrists, ankles, and antecubital and popliteal fossae. The hands and feet are commonly involved with dryness, cracking, and scaling. Although more than 75% of children who have atopic der-

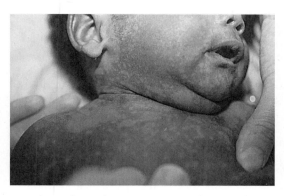

Figure 62–5. Seborrheic dermatitis.

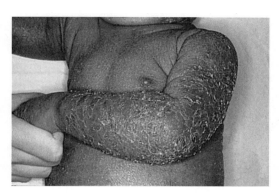

Figure 62–7. Atopic dermatitis of the arm.

matitis improve by age 14, some go on to have chronic dermatitis.

Treatment objectives include skin hydration, elimination of inflammation and infection, control of itching, and patient education. Bathing (5 to 10 minutes in lukewarm water) is potentially beneficial to dry skin as long as moisturizer is applied immediately to damp skin. A mild soap (Dove, Tone) or soap substitute (Cetaphil) should be used. Emollients should be applied two to three times a day. In general, ointments and creams are preferred. Moisturizers appropriate for atopic dermatitis include petrolatum (Vaseline), Aquaphor, Cetaphil, Moisturel, and Eucerin. Topical corticosteroids are the mainstay of controlling inflammation during an acute flare-up. For children who have relatively severe disease, medium-potency corticosteroid ointments should be applied twice daily; the potency is reduced as the disease is controlled. Secondary bacterial infection often is present during an acute flare-up. Children who have atopic dermatitis who are highly colonized with *Staphylococcus aureus* should be treated with systemic antibiotics (7- to 14-day course) such as amoxicillin-clavulanic acid or cephalexin. Sedating antihistamines (e.g., hydroxyzine, diphenhydramine) may help the child sleep and prevent itching during sleep. Parents must understand that atopic dermatitis is a condition for which there is no cure, but good control can be achieved by compliance with the treatment regimens prescribed.

CONTACT DERMATITIS

Contact dermatitis (Fig. 62–8) is an inflammatory cutaneous reaction to an exogenous substance, either an irritant or an allergen. Irritant reactions cause direct cutaneous injury, are dose related, and affect most exposed individuals. Common irritants are detergents and organic solvents. The rash associated with irritants usually is acute in onset, with well demarcated erythema, crusting, and possibly blister formation. Allergic contact dermatitis is a delayed (type IV) hypersensitivity reaction after exposure to an antigenic substance. Common allergens include the sap of poison ivy, poison oak, or poison sumac plants; nickel; rubber; glues and/or dyes in shoes; and some topical medicines such as neomycin and benzocaine. Patients develop pruritic linear edematous erythematous plaques and vesicles with irregular shapes and configurations. Swelling can be impressive with lesions that involve the skin of the face or genitals.

Avoidance of the offending agent is important. If plant dermatitis is suspected, the patient should wash exposed skin immediately. All clothes or items thought to have been in contact with the irritant or allergen also should be washed. Localized areas of dermatitis can be treated topically with an intermediate-potency corticosteroid applied twice daily for 2 to 3 weeks. If the rash is widespread or there is a significant degree of swelling, systemic corticosteroids should be considered. The usual regimen is 1 mg/kg/day (maximum 40 mg/day) for 7 to 10 days, with a slow taper to avoid a rebound exacerbation of the dermatitis. Children who have a history of plant contact dermatitis should be taught to recognize the causative plants.

DIAPER DERMATITIS

The two most common types of diaper dermatitis are irritant and candidal. Failure to change diapers frequently enough is a major predisposing factor for irritant dermatitis. Harsh soaps, chemicals, and detergents contribute to the process. Irritant diaper dermatitis usually is confined to the convex surfaces of the lower abdomen, perineum, buttocks, and proximal thighs, sparing the skin creases. The lesions vary considerably in severity; erythema, papules, and areas of ulceration may occur. Treatment consists of frequent diaper changes with gentle cleansing of the area and generous application of barrier creams (A and D ointment, Desitin, zinc oxide paste). A low-potency topical corticosteroid ointment or cream can be used to accelerate resolution of the rash. Candidal diaper dermatitis almost always involves the inguinal creases and presents with bright red plaques that have sharp borders and satellite papules and pustules. The rash commonly follows an episode of diarrhea or the use of oral antibiotics. Topical antifungal agents such as nystatin, clo-

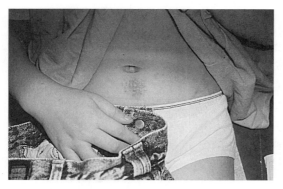

Figure 62–8. Contact dermatitis.

trimazole, or miconazole should be applied three to four times daily. Hydrocortisone 1% cream or ointment applied at the same time may help decrease erythema and inflammation. Fixed combination products such as Mycolog-II or Lotrisone should not be used because they contain very potent corticosteroids and in combination with the diaper's occlusive properties may cause side effects.

VIRAL INFECTIONS

Warts

Warts (Fig. 62–9) are benign tumors produced by human papillomavirus (HPV) infection of the skin and mucous membranes. Most warts are transmitted by skin-to-skin contact or mucous membrane contact. However, fomites also may be a source of infection. Common warts (verruca vulgaris) are skin-colored hyperkeratotic papules and nodules and occur primarily on the hands, arms, and legs. When the hyperkeratotic skin is removed, thrombosed capillaries appear as black dots. Flat warts (verruca plana) are rough, flat-topped papules ranging from 1 to 3 mm in size and occurring on the face and legs. Plantar warts usually arise on the heel and the metatarsal heads of the plantar surface of the feet. Although the possibility of sexual abuse must be considered in all children who have anogenital warts, perinatal contact through an infected birth canal and postnatal exposure by infected caretakers are likely sources of exposure.

Multiple studies have shown that more than 50% of all warts will regress without treatment in healthy patients within 2 to 3 years. As a result, the success of any therapy must be measured against the high rate of resolution without any intervention. Keratolytics (e.g., lactic

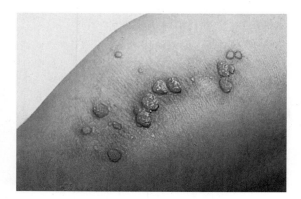

Figure 62–9. Warts on the knee.

acid, salicylic acid, tretinoin) are topical peeling agents and irritants that work by removing wart tissue and triggering an inflammatory reaction. These agents can be used at home and are inexpensive. However, they are sometimes slow to work. Destructive agents (e.g., cryotherapy, caustics, cantharidin) work by destroying the wart and surrounding normal skin. They may result in painful blister formation, require multiple treatments at 2- to 3-week intervals, and depend on patient cooperation for good results. Anogenital warts in children should be referred to a specialist for treatment.

Molluscum Contagiosum

Molluscum contagiosum is a viral infection of the skin caused by a poxvirus. It is characterized by sharply circumscribed, skin-colored, dome-shaped papules with a waxy surface and umbilicated center. Lesions are found on the face, trunk, axillae, and genitals. The number of lesions present varies from a few to hundreds. Spread by autoinoculation is common, and other members of the family can become infected by contact with the patient. Although all patients undergo spontaneous remission, the process may take months to years. Alternative therapies include destruction of lesions by curetting their cores or applying a topical irritant (e.g., tretinoin).

Herpes Simplex

The herpes simplex viruses (HSV) produce infections that primarily involve the skin and mucous membranes. After producing a primary infection, HSV may enter a latent stage in local sensory ganglia. Primary herpetic infection involving the skin typically presents with fever, malaise, localized lesions, and regional adenopathy. Lesions generally result from direct inoculation of previously traumatized skin. The lesions present as grouped vesicles on an erythematous base and progress to mucocutaneous ulcerations. They are painful and form a honey-colored crust as healing progresses. Lips (Fig. 62–10), fingers, and thumbs are the most common sites of involvement. Reactivation of the infection may be triggered by stress, local skin trauma, or systemic factors and frequently is associated with prodromal paresthesia. Clinical diagnosis can be confirmed by a Tzanck smear or viral culture. Severe primary herpetic gingivostomatitis may require treatment with oral acyclovir; symptomatic therapy usually is suffi-

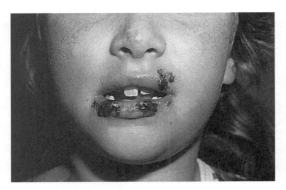

Figure 62–10. Herpes simplex lesion on the lips.

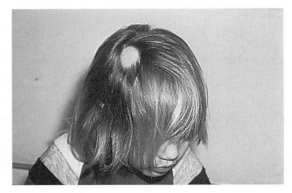

Figure 62–11. Alopecia areata.

cient for the healthy child who has recurrent cutaneous HSV infection.

Herpes Zoster

Herpes zoster (shingles) is a cutaneous viral infection due to reactivation of the varicella-zoster virus. Children who have a history of chickenpox during infancy have the highest risk for herpes zoster. Lesions consist of grouped, thin-walled vesicles of variable size on an erythematous base; they are distributed along the course of a sensory nerve root. Thoracic dermatomal involvement is most common. The lesions evolve from macule to papule to vesicle and then to a crusted stage over a few days. Nerve root pain in children is mild or nonexistent; it may precede, accompany, or follow the eruption. Only symptomatic treatment and prevention of secondary infection are required for healthy children who have herpes zoster infection.

HAIR LOSS

Alopecia Areata

Alopecia areata (Fig. 62–11) is a localized alopecia of autoimmune origin. Patients develop well-circumscribed round patches of relatively complete hair loss that may be located anywhere on the scalp, face, or body. Occasionally, hair loss involves the entire scalp (alopecia universalis) or all body hair (alopecia totalis). Clues to diagnosis include absence of inflammation or scaling in the involved area and the presence of short, easily removed hairs at the margins. Some patients who have alopecia areata also have pitting of the nails. The course of the disorder is unpredictable; in general, when the process is limited to a few areas, the prognosis for regrowth is favorable.

Hair regrowth may be patchy, and the regrowing hair may be lighter or even white in color. Therapy for alopecia areata includes topical or intralesional corticosteroids and topical irritants, such as anthralin.

Traction Alopecia

Traction alopecia is common in young girls whose hairstyles (e.g., braids or cornrows) maintain a tight pull on the hair shafts. The traction causes shaft fractures and follicular damage resulting in hair loss at the margins of the scalp or in linear areas around the part lines. Treatment consists of altering the hairstyle.

Trichotillomania

Trichotillomania (Fig. 62–12), the pulling out of one's own hair, is uncommonly seen in school-age children and adolescents. Patients present with bizarre patterns of alopecia, frequently on the ver-

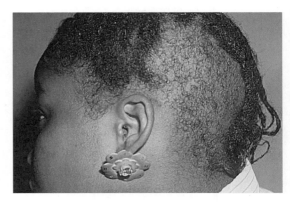

Figure 62–12. Trichotillomania.

tex or sides of the scalp. The eyebrows and eye-lashes also can be involved. The most important clinical finding is the presence of short, broken hairs with differing lengths in adjacent areas of the scalp. This disorder differs from alopecia areata in that the areas of hair loss are never completely bald. The remaining hair shafts are normal and difficult to remove from the scalp. Parents and children often deny pulling or "twirling." Although most cases are associated with situational stress or habitual behavior, in some cases psychiatric consultation is advised.

DISORDERS OF PIGMENTATION

Vitiligo

Vitiligo is an autoimmune disorder characterized by discrete areas of loss of pigmentation. The ivory-white lesions usually are bilateral and symmetric; some patients have unilateral segmental involvement. The most frequent sites are the face (periorificial), elbows, hands, genitals, and feet. Topical corticosteroids result in the return of normal skin color in some patients. Patients should be reminded that the depigmented skin is more susceptible to sunburn and that tanning accentuates the existing lesions. Vitiligo may be associated with a number of endocrine disorders, including autoimmune thyroiditis.

Pityriasis Alba

Pityriasis alba (Fig. 62–13) is a common asymptomatic skin condition, frequently occurring in patients who have atopic dermatitis. The lesions occurring primarily on the face are round to oval patches of hypopigmentation, with fine scale. Less commonly, the lesions can be seen on the neck, upper trunk, and proximal extremities. Topical corticosteroids and emollients diminish the dry skin and scaling and allow repigmentation of the involved skin.

VASCULAR LESIONS

Hemangiomas

A hemangioma (Fig. 62–14) is a benign tumor composed of proliferative and hyperplastic vascular endothelium. The majority appear during the first month of life and demonstrate rapid growth over the first 6 to 9 months, followed by slow involution over a period of years. Superficial hem-

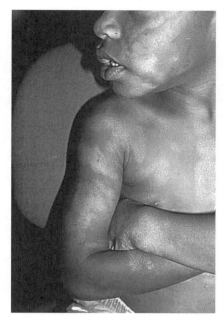

Figure 62–13. Pityriasis alba.

angiomas are soft compressible lesions that are bright red and elevated above the surrounding skin. Deep hemangiomas are bluish in color, with indistinct borders and a doughy consistency. Approximately 50% of hemangiomas disappear by age 5, and 90% are gone by age 9. Almost 50% of these children show some mild skin redundancy, with telangiectasia after resolution that can be corrected surgically. Observation and reassurance is the best approach. **When the hemangioma interferes with normal physiologic functions, treatment is indicated.** Systemic corticosteroids remain standard therapy. The usual course of therapy is 4 to 6 weeks initially at 2 to 4 mg/kg/day. Steroids are tapered once growth of the lesion has stabilized.

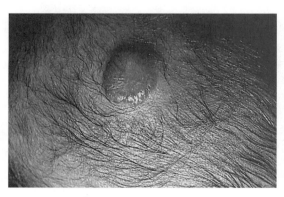

Figure 62–14. Hemangioma.

Port Wine Stains

A port wine stain (Fig. 62–15) is a vascular malformation composed of mature endothelial cells that always are present at birth and do not resolve. The lesions, pink and flat at birth, become darker and thicker with time and grow proportionally with the patient. When a port wine stain occurs over the ophthalmic branch of the trigeminal nerve, it can be associated with vascular malformations of the meninges and cerebral cortex and also seizures—the Sturge-Weber syndrome. A facial hemangioma also may be associated with glaucoma. Tunable pulse dye laser, the preferred treatment for port wine stains, is not 100% curative but can achieve significant lightening of the lesions in the majority of patients.

Salmon Patch

The salmon patch also is known as a "stork bite" or "angel kiss." This form of vascular malformation is a normal variant and is seen in 40% of newborns. Common locations are the forehead, glabella, upper eyelids, and nape of the neck. The patches are made up of distended capillaries; most tend to fade in early childhood. Neck lesions occasionally persist into adulthood. These lesions may become more prominent with crying, breathholding, or exertion. No treatment is necessary.

Pyogenic Granuloma

A pyogenic granuloma (Fig. 62–16) is a benign, rapidly growing vascular tumor that resembles a small hemangioma. The lesions are solitary, bright red, soft nodules, most often occurring on the face or an extremity. The surface is friable and bleeds

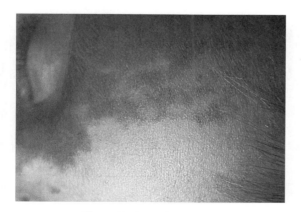

Figure 62–15. Port wine stain.

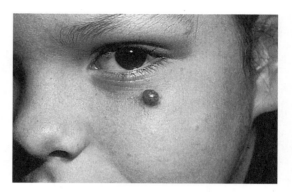

Figure 62–16. Pyogenic granuloma.

easily. Treatment consists of curettage and electrodesiccation of the blood vessels at the base.

REACTIVE ERYTHEMAS

Urticaria

Urticaria, or hives, is characterized by the acute onset of well-demarcated, intensely pruritic wheals. These erythematous and edematous lesions usually last for 1 to 2 hours but may persist up to 24 hours. Commonly, acute urticaria is caused by a hypersensitivity reaction to food, drugs, insect bites, inhaled substances, or acute infections. However, in most cases the cause is elusive. When a causative agent is identified, the treatment of choice is avoidance. Antihistamine therapy is often effective.

Erythema Multiforme/Toxic Epidermal Necrolysis

Erythema multiforme (Fig. 62–17) is an acute hypersensitivity reaction characterized by distinctive skin lesions. **Infectious diseases, especially the herpes simplex virus of erythema multiforme, and medications are the most common causes in children.** The rash is symmetric and may occur on any part of the body. The most typical locations are the hands, feet, and extensor surfaces of the extremities. In addition, the palms and soles are commonly involved. The initial lesions are dusky red macules or erythematous wheals that progress into target-shaped lesions. Any part of the lesion may develop vesicles or bullae. The eruption is self-limited but evolves in crops that last from 1 to 3 weeks. Systemic manifestations are limited to low-grade fever, malaise, and myalgia. Treatment of erythema multi-

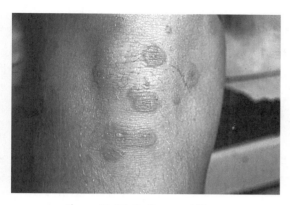

Figure 62–17. Erythema multiforme.

forme consists of identifying the causative factor if possible; symptomatic therapy depends on the severity of the disease. Stevens-Johnson syndrome, or toxic epidermal necrolysis, is a distinct disorder that almost always is due to a medication, especially sulfonamide antibiotics and phenobarbital. It is characterized by rapid and extensive epidermal necrosis. Mucous membrane involvement, particularly of the conjunctival, oral, and urethral membranes, often is severe. This syndrome has a mortality rate between 5% and 25%.

BACTERIAL INFECTIONS

Impetigo

Impetigo is a superficial bacterial infection of the skin, caused primarily by *S. aureus*. *Streptococcus pyogenes* also can be cultured from ap-proximately one third of the lesions but is the sole pathogen in only a few cases. Lesions most often form on skin that has been traumatized or is affected by an underlying disease, such as atopic dermatitis. Lesions caused by *S. aureus*, *S. pyogenes*, or both organisms are identical in appearance, beginning as a tiny vesicle or pustule and rapidly developing into honey-colored, crusted plaques that may itch but are not painful and have little surrounding erythema. Scratching may result in widespread lesions. Treatment of mild impetigo consists of topical mupirocin. Widespread impetigo must be treated with oral antibiotics.

Bullous Impetigo

Bullous impetigo is a superficial staphylococcal infection of the skin. Primary lesions are bullae filled with cloudy fluid and surrounded by a thin margin of erythema. Bullae are flaccid and short-lived; the majority of lesions are superficial and appear as shiny erosions with a collarette of scale. In infants and toddlers, the diaper area most commonly is affected. *S. aureus* is always causative; its exfoliative toxin results in bulla formation. Treatment consists of oral antistaphyloccal antibiotics.

FURTHER READING

Goldgeiger MH: Fungal infections: Tips from a dermatologist. Contemp Pediatr 13(9):21, 1996.

Hebert AA and Goller MM: Papulosquamous disorders in the pediatric patient. Contemp Pediatr 13(2):69, 1996.

Schachner LA and Hansen RC: Pediatric Dermatology. New York, Churchill Livingstone, 1995.

Weinberg S, Prose NS, and Kristal L: Color Atlas of Pediatric Dermatology. New York, McGraw-Hill, 1998.

BEHAVIOR AND DEVELOPMENT

Barbara J. Howard

Chapter 63

Behavior Problems in Infancy

Developmental changes occur so rapidly during infancy that they challenge parents' adaptability, especially first-time parents. Parents have their own developmental evolution that parallels that of their children. **Almost as soon as the parents begin to accept the huge demands resulting from the dependency of their infant, they have to begin the lifelong process of allowing their child independence.** Although infants have considerable social abilities from birth, they still rely greatly on their caregivers for modulation of their states of consciousness and expression of their emotions. Their individuality and increasing autonomy emerge quickly, however, continuously requiring readjustments in parenting. Although some infants are temperamentally more difficult even for experienced parents to understand or manage because of their very irregular, intense, or sensitive responses, most behavioral complaints in infancy are a result of difficulties parents have in adaptation rather than of infant abnormalities. When a behavioral concern arises during infancy, the primary care clinician has an opportunity to educate parents about the pertinent developmental issues, determine the meaning that the behavior has for them, elicit their ideas about solutions, strengthen their ability to communicate with each other, and increase their self-confidence in managing the current situation so that they will be more capable in mastering future concerns. The challenges of infant behavior are related to

the developmental periods discussed in the chapter.

PERIOD OF INITIAL ADAPTATION: BIRTH TO 2½ MONTHS

The first 3 months after birth have been called "the fourth trimester" because the infant is still making physiologic adjustments to life outside the uterus, and the mother still experiences the infant as part of herself. The major tasks of parents during this period include (1) becoming confident that the infant is intact or adapting to abnormalities; and (2) learning to read their infant's cues and respond specifically and appropriately as a part of coming to see the baby as a separate individual. This process of learning to understand the infant through caring for him or her is basic to establishing the attachment relationship between parent and child.

Crying

After the initial breastfeeding adjustment, crying is the greatest behavioral challenge to new parents. It causes them to question the infant's physical health, their own abilities to meet his or her needs, and even their decision to have had this baby at all. From about the age of 2 weeks, crying

396

in normal full-term infants increases to a peak median of 2¾ hours per day by 6 to 8 weeks of age; crying then begins to decline to a baseline of about 1 hour per day at 12 weeks. The crying is characteristically maximal between 5 and 10 P.M., just when the family gathers after a long work day—often having not seen the child since morning and when they are attempting to have dinner. The baby is red-faced, keeps his or her legs flexed, passes gas, thrashes about, and is difficult to console. This normal pattern of crying, which occurs similarly in all cultures studied, seems to represent a developmental process in which the child is neurologically able to progressively take in more stimulation from the environment during the day so that by evening his or her coping threshold is exceeded. After 8 weeks of age, the crying decreases as infants develop increased control over their arousal as well as more self-consoling strategies such as thumb sucking. In accord with this interpretation, the crying occurs after the longest daytime awake interval and is followed by the lengthiest sleep period.

Other theories relate the developmental course of crying to the maturational patterns of the central nervous system, gut hormones, gastrointestinal tract motility, and parent-child interaction. Some infants are considered "persistent criers" because of their pattern of fussing throughout the day. They may or may not also have colic. Swaddling and carrying for at least 1 hour of noncrying time decreases the total crying time for infants who do not meet the criteria for colic. Although recommended, it does not eliminate the peak of crying at 6 to 8 weeks of age. Since premature infants reach their peak of crying 6 to 8 weeks after their due date, they tend to cry more after 12 weeks than do full-term infants. Their crying is also perceived as being more aversive and arousing to adults. All adults, especially women, respond to infant crying with arousal. The cries of neurologically abnormal infants are interpreted as more urgent and noxious and have a different spectral pattern.

Colic

The 8% to 45% (typically cited as 23%) of infants who cry for more than 3 hours per day, more than 3 days per week for more than 3 weeks in the first 3 months, fall into the category called "colic." To qualify as colic, some investigators require that crying must occur in paroxysms, be of higher pitch, be difficult to lessen by consoling the infant, and be accompanied by tension; otherwise, infants are to be considered "excessive cri-

ers." Colicky crying does not always decrease by 3 months and may persist for 6 months or more. While temperamentally "difficult" infants with lower thresholds for response, greater intensity, and less rhythmicity are more highly represented among colicky babies, such infants have not been consistently found to have a more difficult temperament than the norm by 12 or 15 months of age, although they still cry more. Colic has been found to be more common when there has been a history of prenatal maternal stress and anxiety, but postnatal overreactivity of the parents is even more highly associated. Families of infants referred for consultation because of colic have higher rates of maternal depression, personality problems, and family conflict, but these represent the extreme. Colic is at least as common among breast-fed as formula-fed infants. In controlled studies from community populations, cow's milk formula intolerance rarely presents as colic in the absence of other symptoms. Even in highly selected cases referred for consultation, less than 10% improved with cow's milk restriction, and 25% of these also had difficulty with soy milk formula. Infants with a reaction to cow's milk protein do not always have diarrhea or blood in the stool. In the rare cases of eosinophilic esophagitis with sticky vomitus and food refusal, change to an elemental formula may be needed. Reduction in lactose or addition of fiber has not been found to be effective in decreasing crying. Increased breath hydrogen excretion at 2 months of age from lactose malabsorption correlated with the duration but not the frequency of crying. This finding is thought to be secondary to increased feeding in an attempt to console the baby, rather than being a cause. Antivacuum bottles may result in less colicky crying early on, but they show no difference after 6 weeks. No association has been found between colic and birth order, sex, race, socioeconomic status, or parental age, although mothers of first-borns more often present their infants as problematic.

The adaptation of parents undergoing the stressful early experience of infantile colic is promoted by the clinician's empathy, acknowledgement of their normal ambivalence about the infant, and monitoring to ensure adequate social support. Careful history and examination rule out unusual conditions and reassure parents whose first concern is the infant's intactness.

The differential diagnosis includes otitis media, urinary tract infection, anal fissure, acute abdomen, inguinal hernia, hair strangulation, severe constipation, glaucoma, narcotics withdrawal, and increased intracranial pressure. Gastroesophageal reflux can be painful if complicated by esophagitis. The symptoms of these conditions differ from normal crying or colic in the pattern of the infant's distress throughout the day and the presence of other signs and symptoms. Once the diagnosis of colic has been made, the parents can be informed about its course, its excellent prognosis, and suggestions for an active role in helping the baby, for example, swaddle the baby; teach the infant to find his or her thumb or suck on a pacifier to self-console; give sucrose water and provide eye contact during episodes; offer lights, music, rocking, and attention to distract; or provide white noise from a clothes drier, radio static, or vacuum, fan, or breast pump motor. All of these have been shown to be helpful and to lessen the parent's feelings of helplessness. Avoiding overstimulation during the day can decrease crying and also prompt the parents to become more perceptive of their infant's cues.

It is also important to check the appropriateness of feedings since crying can result from both under- and overfeeding. For colicky breast-fed infants, restricting maternal intake of cow's milk, cauliflower, broccoli, onions, garlic, cabbage, and chocolate may rarely be helpful. Ensuring that feedings progress to the hindmilk in the first 2 weeks by nursing to completion on at least one breast decreases subsequent colic. Formula-fed colicky infants benefit in some cases by changing to a hydrolyzed milk protein formula. The reason for the improvement may be opiate-like components, not immune reactions or lactose intolerance. It is of interest that parents who are prescribed a formula change often continue to regard their child as having gastrointestinal disease nearly 4 years later. Medications (other than herbal preparations that contain chamomile) have not been found effective beyond serving as a placebo, and they may have dangerous side effects. Recommending that parents keep a diary and also report on their infant's "best 5 minutes" each day helps them attain perspective during this stressful time.

Spoiling

Often, well-meaning relatives urge the parents not to "spoil" a crying infant by excessive attention. Although infants can be conditioned, prompt responsiveness to infant cues results in less crying later in the first year and is associated with better overall development, notably of language. Contingent responsiveness to infant cues is also thought to be the foundation for the development of a child's basic sense of trust. Encouraging parents to follow their wishes to comfort their infant and support each other through this stressful early phase often leads to very positive subsequent parenting and a high investment in the child. That one third of child abuse occurs to infants under 6 months of age and is most commonly precipitated by crying underlines the importance of monitoring family coping.

Sleep

At times, the variations in sleep patterns that occur in the newborn period lead parents to question their infant's normalcy. Parents must accept the dependency the infant has for regulation of the sleep state. The human biologic clock is set by a combination of feeding, light exposure, and social interaction. Many infants begin sleeping more during the day and staying awake at night if the family inadvertently provides mixed signals in the first 2 weeks by interacting excessively when the baby awakens at night to feed. Parents confronting this problem should be familiarized with their importance to schedule setting, including advice to minimize nighttime interaction, dim the lighting, and wait until the infant shows a clear need to feed in order to reset his or her biologic clock. Baths can be shifted to daytime if they tend to arouse the baby or given in the evenings if they produce drowsiness.

The total amount of sleep anticipated in the infant's first 3 months of life ranges from 16 to 23 hours per day, with sleep and waking alternating initially about every 2 hours. Over this period, the infant develops longer periods of waking during the day and of sleep during the night without a change in the total amount of sleep. Sleeping through the night or "settling," defined as sleeping 5 hours after midnight for 4 weeks, occurs by 3 months for 70% of full-term infants, 6 months for 83%, and 12 months for 90%. Breastfeeding tends to be associated with later settling, perhaps because of the mother's heightened responsiveness, easy digestibility of breast milk, or the characteristically frequent stools. This effect need not occur if, starting around 4 weeks, mothers wait about 10 minutes after the first signal to feed, thus lengthening the interval between feeding throughout the day and night. Premature infants tend to settle according to their age adjusted for gestation but with much greater variability. Neurologically damaged infants and older children can have substantially disrupted sleep states that may improve with administration of melatonin.

PERIOD OF RECIPROCAL EXCHANGE: 2½ TO 5 MONTHS

After initial adjustment to the infant's dependency needs in the first 3 months, parents usually enter a honeymoon period of reciprocal interaction, cooing, and laughing games. Although by now usually confident about the infant's intactness, they may still have concerns about their own ability to nurture the baby.

Feeding

The parents' chief concerns about nurturing their infant centers on feeding. Infants have a variety of feeding styles that can be confusing for new and even experienced parents. Five classic styles have been characterized as the *barracuda,* the *resters,* the *gourmet, excited ineffectives,* and *procrastinators.* Most parents have come to accept the feeding style of their infant by 3 months, but they need to adjust to subsequent changes to avoid feeding or sleep problems. Infants gain significant control over the focus of their attention and head control around 4 months of age, and this often results in their sudden turning away from the breast or bottle. These newfound abilities may be described as a feeding problem by the parent, who feels as if she were being rejected. She may benefit from a simple explanation of the infant's efforts at autonomy, and the infant may need to be fed in a nondistracting environment.

Night Waking

Parents who feed on demand may continue to feed infants who no longer require a feeding during the night at the slightest cue of restlessness. This often results in "trained night feeders." In fact, 50% of infants can sleep 8 hours without a feeding by 1.3 months of age and 95% can by 4 months of age. If fed regularly in the middle of the night, however, they become trained to awaken and be hungry. Infants may be weaned from existing middle of the night feedings by reducing breastfeeding by 1 minute per night or reducing formula-feeding by 1 ounce per night. Although parents often use feeding to put their infant to sleep, to avoid developing this habit or "sleep association" it is advisable to begin putting infants in bed in a drowsy but awake state, rearousing them if necessary, both at night and for naps by 2 months of age. If a sleep association is part of trained night waking, this must be altered as well as stretching the daytime feeding intervals by 10 minutes a day toward 4-hour intervals. To allow for resettling, parents should wait at least 1 minute before going to the infant in the middle of the night.

Infant sleep can also be disturbed by trained night waking between 4 and 8 months of age.

This problem often starts after a stress such as an illness, or a change in routine in which the infant awakens in the night and the parent attends to him or her. Subsequent nights begin to include awakenings, which the parents reinforce with attention and/or feedings. Trained night waking is twice as likely to occur in families in which the mother is depressed, perhaps because the infant is allowed to cry more during the day, is less consolable, and creates his or her own sleep schedule. Other causative factors include maternal guilt, insomnia, or adult desire for the comfort of the infant at night.

Marital tension can result in trained night waking as one parent seeks intimacy with the infant and avoids it with the spouse or goes to quiet the infant to avoid spousal disapproval. Infants who are less adaptable temperamentally are also more prone to trained night waking, especially after trips. Successful management of this problem requires the involvement of both parents. Sometimes even the neighbors need to be informed of the plan so that they will not interfere when they hear the baby crying. Precipitating stresses or illnesses need to be addressed and any existing sleep associations ended by placing the infant in bed awake. A bedtime routine should be established, including provision of a transitional object or "lovey," characteristically a soft, malleable object reminiscent of the mother, or at times, an item of intimate apparel. Naps should be limited to 2 hours. Finally, when the infant awakens in the night, he or she should be allowed to cry for 5 minutes before being checked, preferably during a lull in crying. Since one parent is likely to be better able to tolerate the crying than the other, a plan for self-restraint such as hiding in the shower or donning headphones may be needed. While brief sedation may be indicated in extreme cases, medication alone is unlikely to result in the infant's sleeping through the night. Coaching parents to teach their infant the skill of resettling at night by themselves requires that they confront the infant's growing abilities and separateness. In most cultures of the world infants sleep with their parents, and these problems do not occur.

PERIOD OF EARLY DIRECTED ACTIVITY: 5 TO 9 MONTHS

As the infant demonstrates clearer preferences after 6 months of age, parents must adapt accordingly. Suddenly, the infant's lovely simple dependency is complicated by struggles over diaper changes and dressing. Some parents need coaching to offer unique toys on the changing table and the reassurance that only dirty diapers, not wet ones, require cleansing of the skin.

Feeding Solids

Feeding of solids, generally begun before the infant is 6 months of age, is initially characterized by as much extrusion as ingestion. For some parents, this may represent not just expected messiness but subtle rejection. Others, who worry about a possible lack of adequate calories and growth, begin to restrain the child, force-feed, or introduce a series of elaborate feeding games that can later become interesting enough for the child to postpone feeding indefinitely. Conversely, the beginning of the feeding of solids may represent the end of infancy for the parent and thus be postponed. It is important to ask how the parent, usually the mother, feels about the child's self-feeding in order to elicit these underlying reactions. Parents may need to be advised to avoid creating elaborate dishes, allow the infant to participate in the feeding, feed the child unclothed, use newspapers under the high chair, plan for a bath afterward (to emphasize the expected mess), or even offer only finger foods as soon as the infant can manage them, with the parent hiding her facial reactions of concern behind a book.

Genital Play

Infant boys have erections starting prenatally as observed on ultrasound as often as 20 per hour at times. Between 6 and 8 months of age, they discover their ability to produce pleasurable sensations using their hands. Girls discover the pleasure of genital touching between 10 and 12 months. The obvious feelings and arousal associated with the infant's play upsets some parents, who may punish or criticize this normal manifestation. This anxiety is worth asking about because it causes distress to some parents but is rarely raised spontaneously as a concern. This undue parental worry may inadvertently reinforce such touching and make masturbation a problem.

PERIOD OF FOCALIZATION ON THE MOTHER: 9 TO 15 MONTHS

Infants demonstrate their assertiveness increasingly during this period of focalization, much of it directed toward the mother.

Biting

Although biting is nearly universal at the time of tooth eruption around 6 months of age, it is rarely a parenting concern then since it is not interpreted as intentional. Breastfeeding mothers respond to biting so definitively as to provide one of the rare examples of one-time learning in infancy that results in no further episodes. The 10- to 12-month-old infant may bite on the parent's neck or shoulder as part of oral exploration, often in the middle of an affectionate interaction. If the adult acts to promote this as if it were a game, it can quickly become a troublesome pattern. Showing moderately strong discomfort and immediately putting the child down will convey the real impact directly. The same principle applies to the experimental scratching and pinching common at this stage. Parents who begin to call their child "mean" need to have their perceptions of the child and their interpretation of this aggression understood. If they really think negatively of the child, it is usually projection onto the child of someone else's aggressive behavior. This misperception needs to be corrected to prevent future self-fulfilling prophecies of undesirable behavior that, otherwise, they may unconsciously reinforce.

Stranger Wariness

Around 8 months of age, infants develop the capacity to express fear of unfamiliar people—the so-called 8-month stranger anxiety. In fact, babies are able to distinguish between individuals from birth and respond differently to strangers from at least 3 months of age. The new reaction, one of fear, can be very intense and even occur in relation to the father or grandparents, much to everyone's dismay. It can worsen the parents' normal anxiety about child care providers and even raise concerns about maltreatment. This new developmental stage often results in the infant's demands for exclusive care by his or her mother, an outcome that is exhausting for her and demoralizing for others. Infants should be comforted but calmly required to accept caregiving by at least one or two other people. Some infants are temperamentally so adaptable that they approach new situations positively and have no apparent stranger anxiety; however, initial "wariness" manifested by staring at strangers reflects the same process.

Sleep Disturbance

Around 10 to 12 months of age, sleep disturbance is a common complaint, attributable to the convergence of several developmental processes. Infants are generally mobile in the crib and often able to pull themselves up to stand. They are newly aware of object permanence, i.e., things that move out of sight are still in existence, and they have a greater interest in their surroundings. In combination with stranger wariness, they may have more fearful experiences during the day. This combination results in "developmental night waking" during which the infant wakes up screaming and apparently fearful although fairly easily consoled. This occurrence occasionally starts when a babysitter who is caring for the child checks him or her during the night, resulting in a fearful experience that results in subsequent waking, then recurs nightly. **The management recommended for developmental night waking is for the parent to give the child 2 minutes to settle and then, if necessary, go to the child, reassure him or her briefly without lifting the child from the crib, and then remain for the rest of the night in view on the floor or a chair, but without talking further.** This reassurance without reinforcement takes an average of four nights before the child no longer awakens. An alternative plan is for the parents to attend to the child briefly without lifting and then leave the room for sequentially increasing periods of 5, 7, 9 minutes, etc. This strategy is also effective in about four nights; however, about one in three parents find it unacceptable. Developmental night waking due to separation fears continues to be a common reason for middle of the night problems until the preschool period, and the same solution is effective. In older children, other factors that may contribute to separation anxiety include actual separations, maternal depression, parental stress, or inadequate child care arrangements.

PERIOD OF SELF-ASSERTION: 12 TO 18 MONTHS

After 1 year of age, infants show increasingly forceful autonomy. This developmental step sometimes evokes a negative reaction on the part of parents not ready to give up their snugly, compliant baby. The toddler often appears to be driven by a motor, especially when mastering walking, and his or her single-mindedness often challenges the ability of parents to accomplish such daily activities as changing diapers, dressing, and feeding. Once on his or her feet, the toddler with newfound autonomy may struggle against lying down for naps even though exhausted or may present the nighttime problem of repeatedly standing up in the crib. Parents can be reassured that

letting the toddler hang onto the crib side until he or she drops will do no harm, but that repeated efforts to put him or her down can become an interesting game from the infant's point of view.

Tantrums

The infant's determination combined with the normal unevenness of emerging skills often results in temper tantrums, a manifestation that peaks in prevalence between 15 and 36 months of age. Tantrums represent the conflict that occurs when infants' emotions go beyond their control; tantrums are not just a maneuver to get their own way. Emotions are most labile when an infant is tired, hungry, ill, or confronted with the unfamiliar. The crying and thrashing are often difficult to interrupt and, of course, distressful to the parents, who feel helpless and angry. Some parents find these behaviors intolerable and give in to the infant's demands, thereby reinforcing tantrums as a manipulative tool. Infants with frequent temper tantrums are likely to be characterized by a poorly adaptable temperament with a low threshold for response and a high intensity. Recurrent tantrums may also occur in those who are frustrated due to an expressive language delay or fine motor delays. Accordingly, these areas need to be assessed. Although children need to learn to deal with frustration, such challenges should occur in small doses. Some parents, misinterpreting the child's increased autonomy demands as a personal rejection, react by refusing any dependency. Such parents need to be educated about the vacillation of developmental progress and the effectiveness of more flexible management. They may need their reactions explored more fully in therapy.

Other parents who have unrealistic expectations may leave valuables within reach or insist on quiet play. Both may invite conflicts. Maintaining consistent rules, routines, and caregivers; ensuring adequate and regular rest and food; and establishing a "child-friendly" environment with appropriate toys and playmates foster optimal development and help prevent tantrums. Beginning in infancy, the verbal expression of emotions should be modeled for children, their own emotions labeled, and shifting feelings into words rather than actions promoted. Whenever possible, they should be given choices within options acceptable to the adult in order to maintain a sense of control without having to struggle for it.

When a tantrum begins, the parent should attempt distraction without giving in to the demand. If this is unsuccessful, the child's safety should first be ensured, and then the adult should either stand quietly nearby or hold the child to demonstrate that the child's anger is not frightening to the adult. Caregivers who cannot deal calmly with tantrums should leave the room briefly. When the tantrum is over, the child may be briefly comforted (without giving in) and redirected to some other activity. A brief time-out, even for 10 to 15 seconds, is also effective in reducing tantrums and is definitely indicated if the child strikes the adult during the episode. Children who do not improve with these measures should be assessed for gaps in their developmental abilities, inadequate attention or inappropriate management at home, and other stressors.

Breathholding Spells

Some children start with a tantrum but progress to a breathholding spell during which they cry until they become blue, apneic, unconscious, limp, and then stiff. The other type of breathholding spell occurs with a painful experience, such as a blow to the head in a mobile infant; the child turns pale, stops breathing, and may even convulse. Mixed types also occur. Breathholding spells occur in severe form in less than 5% of children under 8 years of age but in mild form in 27%. They are inherited as an autosomal dominant trait with penetrance. Breathholding is more common in infants perceived as having a more difficult temperament with intense reactions. **Breathholding episodes are terrifying for parents, who quickly adopt strategies of distraction or indulgence in an effort to avoid them, but these usually lead to worse manipulative tantrums.** It is important to reassure parents that brain damage does not occur when a child has a breathholding spell. They should be counseled to avoid promoting secondary gain on the child's arousal from the episode. Administration of oral iron for 6 weeks decreases breathholding in 88% of cases, even without anemia.

Rhythmic Habits

Between 3% and 15% of children bang their heads during tantrums or, more often, as part of settling to sleep. Head banging during a tantrum elicits some of the same parental reactions as breathholding and requires the same behavioral treatment. Parents are often especially concerned about rhythmic habits such as head banging because they may be associated by laypersons with mental retardation or autism, conditions in which head banging is common. Head banging associated with fatigue often starts with head rolling around 6 months of age and may persist in more intense children even into adulthood. Headache, otitis media, teething, sensory deficits, or neglect should be considered in the differential diagnosis. When evaluating children with head banging, the child's daily caregiving arrangements should be assessed for adequacy of stimulation. Head banging can be ameliorated in some cases by supplementing the child with extra kinetic stimulation during the day, for example, strong rocking or dancing (not shaking) and firm holding at bedtime. Damage to the skin can be minimized by slipping a mat under the head during tantrums. Damage to the crib can be minimized by bolting it to the wall. If parents are not satisfied with behavioral measures, hydroxyzine is sometimes effective for the intense, anxious head banger.

Clinging

Another major psychologic process during the second year of life is called rapprochement. Concurrent with self-assertion, the child develops a new sense of himself or herself as being separate, a realization that can be frightening to some toddlers. This results in a clinginess that can be alarming to parents who have just adapted to their infant's independence. Such clinging is a normal developmental phase but stronger in temperamentally inhibited children. The child's tendency to react with inhibition tends to persist, but those whose parents avoid routinely rescuing them too quickly from stressful situations adapt better in the long-term. Infants who are clinging should, therefore, be comforted, then cheerfully encouraged to deal gradually with precipitating situations.

Self-Consoling Behaviors

In this age period, children may demonstrate heightened self-consoling behaviors such as thumb sucking, rocking, head banging, and masturbation that help the child cope with stress, although they may be perceived as problems by their parents. Thumb sucking bothers parents, and grandparents even more, because they see it as an indication of immaturity. This behavior is especially likely during the period of rapprochement when toddlers demonstrate other behaviors such as clinging and tantrums that may also be perceived as regressive. Of course, children in the first 2 years of life are expectedly immature, and this may need to be explained to the parents.

Sometimes there is pressure for the infant to grow up because of a second pregnancy or jealousy on the father's part because the child's demands on his wife preoccupy her. In fact, sucking on a thumb or pacifier may help a child rally the emotional strength to try new things rather than deter his or her progress; on the other hand, if the parents view the child as less mature because of the behavior, they may expect too little of the child. Pacifiers frequently become associated with falling asleep, requiring the parents to replace them in the middle of the night when the infant awakens but is too young to locate the pacifier on his or her own. In infants, sucking has important state-regulating effects under the infant's control. It is more likely to occur at times of stress, boredom, and fatigue, often in association with use of a transitional object or "lovey." Perhaps it is this connection or the obvious sensual pleasure that makes some parents associate sucking habits with sexuality, and they become more troubled about its use, especially as children get older. An infant with a sudden exacerbation of sucking or a tendency to suck rather than participate in usual activities should be assessed for excessive stressors such as separations, multiple changes in caregivers, or inadequate sleep. If these are not present, the parents can be encouraged to accept the habit as appropriate behavior.

Masturbation intensifies around 18 months with boys stimulating the penis directly and many girls using objects, table legs, or their parents' thighs, gazing into their mother's eyes and showing obvious arousal. This behavior is usually unexpected and of concern to parents. Around 21 months of age, about one third of girls stop direct masturbating while one third continue indirect stimulation. Most boys continue self-stimulation. The sudden onset of masturbation should prompt a physical evaluation for genital irritation and a careful history to identify stressors. If the child has physical evidence of trauma or other behavioral changes, the possibility of sexual misuse should be considered, but otherwise the parents should be encouraged to use matter-of-fact redirection or distraction rather than punishment.

PERIOD OF AGGRESSIVE ASSERTION: 18 TO 24 MONTHS

Aggression

The assertiveness of the toddler accelerates between 18 and 24 months, and overt aggression can present problems for parents and/or child care providers. Aggression is so common as to make the unassertive child of some concern. Toddlers, both boys and girls, almost universally use instrumental aggression during this time to get what they want from others. This can take the form of hitting, pushing, kicking, and biting. Biting is most likely to prompt a consultation with the clinician because its primitive connotation evokes outrage from caregivers and the parents of children who are bitten. Although periods of exploratory biting have occurred earlier in infancy, this later phase represents aggression to achieve an end. **All forms of aggression are more likely to occur in children who have few alternative ways of social negotiation.** These include those with expressive language delay or social learning deficits, those with underdeveloped impulse control who may be destined to meet the diagnostic criteria for attention-deficit hyperactivity disorder, those who receive inadequate attention to meet their needs as a result of poor caregiver to child ratios in child care settings, and those exposed to violence, corporal punishment, and family or media violence. Some children bite when hungry. Fathers tend to arouse their children's aggressiveness more than mothers and then expect them to settle down on their own. This pattern of interaction may be responsible for the greater abilities of children who have male caregivers to self-regulate their emotions.

Biting and other forms of aggression evoke strong feelings in adults depending on their own history of discipline. Those who were spanked as children are more likely to view spanking as appropriate and to start spanking by 9 months. On the other hand, those who perceive their own past caregivers as abusive are less likely to use physical responses to aggression in their own children. These adults may be left without an adequate model and, therefore, waver in their responses or, at times, overreact to later incidents.

Occasional instrumental aggression, including biting during infancy, can be managed with a reaction of mild shock and a brief and firm admonition, such as "No biting. Biting hurts people," and removal to time-out. The victim should then be attended to and comforted, but secondary gain for the aggressor is to be avoided. **Time-out can be effective in infants as young as 9 months of age. The child should be verbally instructed briefly, then placed on the floor, on a chair, in a playpen, or in a crib; ignored for 10 to 15 seconds until his or her crying lessens; and then redirected onto more positive activities.** Restraint on the adult's lap facing outward is also effective as long as the adult remains silent. Offering an alternative such as teething ring for biting "when mad" may also be helpful. Chronically aggressive infants should have their developmental abilities and social environment assessed for the causative factors noted previously. They may also need placement in a smaller child care setting with fewer same-aged peers with whom to cope. Aggression that is not well-managed during this period can evolve into chronic aggression in the preschool period.

Picky Eating

Feeding is a frequent concern of parents in the second year because of a child's increased selectivity and decreased caloric needs compared with the first year. The expected slimmer profile of the toddler, however, sometimes causes parental concern. Picky or selective eating is due, in part, to greater cognitive awareness of subtle differences in foods as well as greater autonomy and the toddler's understanding of his or her own power to make demands. The attention span for sitting at the table is normally less than 10 minutes until preschool. Fortunately, infants as young as 12 months will select a nutritionally balanced diet when averaged over weeks, and toddlers will take in adequate calories over a period of 48 hours if only nutritionally valuable foods are offered. The adult task is to provide the structure (of routine mealtimes and snacks with wholesome foods) in spite of the demands (for sweets and unlimited snacking), with a pleasant and calm demeanor (no matter how worried the adult is), while allowing the child as much autonomy as he or she needs (in determining how much food and in what fashion it is consumed).

Child care clinicians can assess, educate, encourage, and celebrate with parents as they progress with their children through the developmental stages of infancy, balancing nurturing with supporting developmentally appropriate autonomy.

FURTHER READING

Adair RH and Baucher H: Sleep problems in childhood. Cur Probl Pediatr 23:147–170, 1993.
Birch LL, Johnson SL, Andresen G, et al.: The variability of young children's energy intake. N Engl J Med 324:232–235, 1991.
Bremner JG: Infancy. New York, Basil Blackwell, 1988.
Lester BM: Colic and Excessive Crying. Report of the 105th Ross Conference on Pediatric Research. Columbus, OH, Ross Products Division, Abbott Laboratories, 1997.
Needlman R, Howard BJ, and Zuckerman B: Temper tantrums: When to worry. Contemp Pediatr 6(8):12–34, 1989.
Sanders LW: Issues in early mother-child interaction. J Am Acad Child Adolesc Psychiatry 1:141–166, 1962.

Paul H. Dworkin

Chapter 64

Behavior Problems of Toddlers and Preschool Children

The toddler and preschool years are a period of remarkable transformation, characterized by dramatic growth in developmental areas such as language, cognition, and interpersonal skills. By the end of this period, children are able to separate comfortably from parents and home and to begin the major occupation of childhood—attending school. The vivid contrast in behavior between the autonomous 5-year-old, who is able to adhere to the rules of the classroom, and the "selfish" 2-year-old, who typically displays separation difficulties, temper tantrums and impulsivity, illustrates the magnitude of growth during the preschool years.

DEVELOPMENTAL THEMES

Common behavior problems during the toddler and preschool years reflect developmental themes. During these years, children's development proceeds along the traditional lines of affective, cognitive, and physical growth (Fig. 64–1). Themes in *affective development* include the achievement of autonomy and independence from caregivers and family, the related lessening of attachment to parents and the alleviation of separation anxiety, the mastery of social skills and an increase in impulse control, the establishment of gender identity and the realization that gender is fixed and

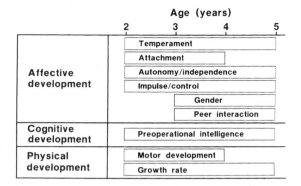

Figure 64–1. Developmental themes during the toddler and preschool years. (From Dworkin PH: The preschool child: Developmental themes and clinical issues. Curr Probl Pediatr 18:73, 1988; and modified from Telzrow RW: Anticipatory guidance in pediatric practice. J Cont Educ Pediatr 20:14, 1978. Reproduced by permission.)

stable, and the increasing importance of peer interactions and influences outside of the family. During these years, the stability of a child's behavioral style or temperament is highly evident.

Cognitive development during the preschool years has been defined by Piaget as the preoperational period. Beginning around age 2 years and lasting until approximately age 7 years, this stage of intellectual growth is perhaps most remarkable for the development of socially consensual language. The child becomes increasingly capable of integrating events over time and space, pursuing "how" and "why" questions, and distinguishing fantasy from reality. Despite these impressive accomplishments, by the culmination of the preoperational period the child is still unable to reason rationally, take the viewpoint of another person, understand that not everything is as it seems, or attend to other than the most compelling attribute of a situation. Such cognitive limitations have important implications for behavior management and discipline.

For most preschool children, language develops in a seemingly effortless but dramatic manner. By the time of school entry, most children have mastered, without formal instruction, a complex set of rules governing the proper use of language and have acquired the linguistic foundation necessary to begin to learn how to read and write.

Physical growth during the early childhood years, although perhaps less dramatic than during infancy, continues at a steady rate. The child's increasing mastery of motor skills is highly evident, as increasing gross motor abilities facilitate the child's achievement of autonomy and independence and the mastery of fine motor skills will ultimately enable the child to produce written language.

STAGE-RELATED ISSUES

Various common, stage-related behaviors may lead to parental anxiety and concerns during the preschool years. The temper tantrums, stubbornness, and aggressive behavior that are so characteristic of the "terrible twos" may well persist during the later preschool years, as the child continues the struggle for autonomy and independence while still remaining dependent on caretakers. By age 4 years, as the time for school entry approaches, greater demands for impulse control are placed on a child, and the amount of aggressive behavior generally lessens.

Temper Tantrums

Within the *Diagnostic and Statistical Manual for Primary Care (DSM-PC), Child and Adolescent Version,* temper tantrums are classified as *negative emotional behavior variation.* Such behavior reflects themes in affective development, including the child's struggle for autonomy and independence while remaining dependent on caretakers, the limited impulse control at this age, and the high visibility of such temperamental traits as adaptability, intensity, and mood.

A variety of strategies may be helpful in preventing, or at least reducing, the frequency of temper tantrums during the preschool years. Parents may be encouraged to avoid unnecessary battles by minimizing exposure to difficult situations in which the child's spontaneity must be curtailed (such as trips to the shopping mall); to encourage spontaneity and choice when feasible (e.g., offering a choice of pajamas may minimize bedtime tantrums); to make it clear when the child has no choice (e.g., when safety is involved); and to avoid attempts to control the uncontrollable (e.g., the time a child falls asleep, as opposed to staying quietly in his or her room). Parents should be encouraged to set a good example by avoiding aggression and physical punishment, to compliment good behavior (i.e., "time-in"), and to be consistent in setting reasonable and clear limits, both over time and among caretakers.

Despite such strategies, temper tantrums may be troublesome and require behavior management techniques. During the toddler and preschool years, helpful approaches include *extinction* and *time-out. Extinction* involves the systematic withdrawal of attention for certain undesirable behaviors. When correctly practiced, this technique of essentially ignoring troublesome behaviors is highly effective. **Extinction is particularly well-suited to dealing with behaviors, such as temper tantrums, that are irritating or annoying but neither dangerous nor destructive.**

Extinction has two distinct phases: a *baseline phase* and the *implementation phase*. During the baseline phase, parents record both the frequency and the consequences of the undesirable behavior. The parents then begin the implementation phase by systematically ignoring the disruptive behavior while continuing to record the behavior's frequency.

Despite the apparent simplicity of this procedure, parents must be warned of a number of potential pitfalls. Beginning implementation without the baseline phase misses the opportunity to define clearly the target behavior and accurately set expectations. Siblings or other caretakers may continue to reinforce a behavior chosen for extinction by parents. Parents must continually strive to avoid inconsistency and the perils of an intermittent reinforcement schedule. Parents should anticipate the "response burst"—an increase in the undesirable behavior—when the technique is first implemented. Extinction should be accompanied by parent's making a special effort to provide immediate attention when the child displays appropriate behavior. Finally, parents should anticipate the possibility of the spontaneous recurrence of previously diminished behaviors during illness or with other stresses.

Extinction is obviously not appropriate when dangerous or destructive behaviors arise. For such behaviors, the technique of *time-out* is highly effective. The child is removed to a dull, nonstimulating place when he or she initiates a disruptive behavior and must remain there for a predetermined length of time. For a child from 2 to 5 years of age, 5 minutes spent in a chair in a corner of a room is an ample punishment. With time-out, as with extinction, clearly defining the target behavior and determining its frequency during a baseline phase are important. A timer or clock should be used to monitor the time period for the child. The child should be warned that a behavior will result in time-out and that if he or she protests, cries, or has a tantrum, the time-out period will not begin until the protesting has stopped.

Biting

Although not included within the DSM-PC listing of presenting complaints, biting is a common problem during the toddler and preschool years, with predictable consequences. Approximately one half of all children in child care are bitten up to three times per year, with boys being more likely to bite than girls. **Although biting elicits strong emotional reactions, it does not predict later aggressive behavior, but rather reflects age-related developmental themes.** In particular, the child's lack of impulse control and limited skills and experience in peer interactions contribute to this common manifestation of frustration until around 3 years of age.

Several strategies may be helpful in preventing and managing biting and other aggressive behaviors. Caretakers should be encouraged to anticipate frustrating situations likely to elicit such responses, and redirect, as much as possible, troublesome behaviors at their outset. In particular, peer interactions should be closely monitored and positive social behaviors should be praised and reinforced. Parents should be mindful of the importance of their modeling nonaggressive behavior and refraining from physical punishment. When biting does occur, time-out is an appropriate response.

Resistance to Toilet Training

The majority of children are successfully toilet trained by age 3 years. Approximately 90% of children are bowel trained by this age, about 85% are dry during the day, and some 70% are dry at night. As is evident, 20% to 30% of normal children during the later preschool years continue to wet the bed at night, and some fecal soiling is common until 3 to 4 years of age. Delays and regressions, particularly at times of illness and family stress, are common.

An awareness of the wide range in age for achievement of bladder and bowel control and signs of developmental readiness for toilet training should help parents avoid placing undue pressure on the child. Such signs include the ability to control voluntarily the anal and urethral sphincters; the ability to sit on a potty seat for several minutes with the intent to stool or void; a desire to control the impulses to defecate and urinate, to please parents, and to become autonomous and independent; the capability of understanding the sequence of actions required to use the toilet and to understand verbal communication; and a lessening of oppositional and defiant behaviors typical of this age. In the majority of children, such physical, psychologic, and developmental readiness emerges between 18 and 30 months of age.

Toilet training is usually accomplished without difficulty when a child-oriented, developmental approach is employed. **Children may be developmentally "ready" to begin toilet training from 18 months to 3 years of age.** Timing is also influenced by the child's health and external events. Training may be postponed at times of childhood illness or family stress or when the child displays either resistance or a lack of interest.

Given the wide range in age for achievement of nighttime bladder control, a diagnosis of enuresis is not appropriate during the preschool years. Rather, use of an absorbent pad under the sheet and praise for occasional dry nights should be encouraged. Similarly, because of the relatively wide range in age for achievement of bowel control among normal children, fecal soiling is generally not equated with a diagnosis of encopresis until at least age 4 years. When resistance to toilet training does occur, parents should avoid placing undue pressure on the child by punishing, shaming, or nagging. Children may be asked periodically whether they would like to try to use the potty or imitate older siblings or adults by using the bathroom. Encouraging the child to remove soiled diapers may encourage autonomy. Ensuring soft, painless stools is helpful in avoiding discomfort caused by anal fissures. Rewards for successful training may be identified with the child, and a ceremonial discarding of diapers planned as bladder and bowel control are mastered.

CLINICAL CHALLENGES

The DSM-PC classifies behavioral manifestations that are serious enough to disrupt children's functioning in the family, in school, and with peers as *problems*, and classifies those behaviors that involve a sufficient level of severity and impairment to warrant the diagnosis of a mental illness as *disorders*. Although disorders are typically managed by mental health professionals, problems pose major clinical challenges to primary care providers.

Sleep Problems

Sleep problems may be defined as a behavior pattern of regular awakening or prolonged bedtime struggle that is stressful to parents and other caregivers and requires intervention. The DSM-PC classifies sleep problems as *sleep difficulties, sleep disturbance, sleep awakening,* and *refusing to go to sleep.* Although the typical 2- to 3-year-old child sleeps about 13 hours per day, including a 1- to 2-hour nap usually after lunch, wide variation is

found, with some children sleeping only 9 to 10 hours a night and taking no nap. Sleep problems are very common during the preschool years. For example, in some studies parents describe 70% of 2-year-old children and approximately 50% of 3- and 4-year-old children as being resistant to going to bed. Approximately 50% of children at these ages were described as awakening regularly during the night. Other common concerns of parents include nightmares, night terrors, sleepwalking, sleeptalking, and enuresis. For many such behaviors, parental expectations, cultural beliefs, and family resources and circumstances determine the extent to which they are judged problematic.

A variety of factors have been associated with sleep problems during the preschool years. Children are more likely to demonstrate such behaviors if they experienced pre- or perinatal difficulties such as asphyxia and subsequent hyperirritability; if their temperament is characteristic of the "difficult" child (i.e., nonadaptive, intense, and negative mood); if parenting practices include co-sleeping, prolonged breastfeeding, or a parenting style of permissiveness; or if children are exposed to family stressors, such as maternal depression or frequent changes in caretakers.

Anticipatory guidance during the toddler years may lessen the severity of later sleep problems. Examples of prevention strategies include encouraging the use of a transitional object and nightlight to lessen anxiety; providing a pleasant, predictable, sedate bedtime routine; encouraging the child to remain in bed after being put to sleep; and gradually delaying and minimizing the response to children's fussing and protest. Obviously, the parents must respond promptly to children's fears and nightmares.

Evaluation of sleep problems should include a thorough history, including a review of the child's sleep history and details of parent-child interactions. **Asking parents to complete a 24-hour sleep diary may be helpful in uncovering unrealistic bedtimes, late or prolonged daytime naps, insufficient limit setting, or other predisposing factors.** The physical examination should include not only a search for medical factors such as recurrent or persistent otitis media and signs of chronic upper airway obstruction and obstructive sleep apnea syndrome, but also observations of parent-child interaction.

Resistance to going to bed is a manifestation of children's desire to be more autonomous and to control their own destinies, as well as a reflection of persistent anxiety about separating from parents or other caretakers. The child may get out of bed frequently and leave the bedroom, call out repeatedly to parents for a drink or a trip to the bathroom, or cry and scream when being put to bed. A regular and predictable bedtime routine may lessen such resistance by affording the child a sense of control by knowing what to expect. A quiet activity, such as reading a story before bedtime, may ease the transition by calming the child and signaling the beginning of the routine. The need for autonomy and control may be satisfied by allowing the child to decide which pajamas to wear and what story to read. A night-light or transitional object may lessen anxiety or fears.

When resistance to going to bed becomes a problem for parents and the child, parents may opt to institute a version of extinction. The child is allowed to cry for longer time periods, while parents offer only brief and intermittent contact. For example, parents may "ignore" crying initially for several minutes, gradually delaying their response to the child over several nights, while lessening the intensity of their response. Eventually, parents may merely stand quietly in the child's doorway for several seconds. While successful as a behavior management strategy, some parents will regard this approach as unduly harsh. For those children who repeatedly leave their beds, parents may consistently escort them back to bed in a matter-of-fact manner. Resistance to bed typically lessens when the child realizes that excessive parental attention is not forthcoming.

A consistent parental response that eliminates excessive attention and reinforcement is also likely to be successful when frequent night awakening is problematic. In addition to extinction, parents may employ the technique of scheduled night awakening when frequent awakenings are troublesome. After charting the child's timing and frequency of night awakening for several days until a clear pattern is evident, parents are instructed to awaken their child at scheduled times during the evening and to do the things they normally did if the child had awakened them. Scheduled awakenings should occur 15 to 60 minutes before expected spontaneous awakenings, with the number of awakenings dependent on how often the child awoke. Scheduled awakenings are gradually eliminated, as the frequency of spontaneous awakenings decreases. The success of this approach is comparable to extinction, with improvement noted within 2 weeks and elimination of the troublesome behavior generally requiring from 6 to 8 weeks of consistent responses by parents. The extent to which parents opt for such interventions is a personal decision influenced by the extent to which such behaviors are acceptable within the family.

The inability of young children to distinguish fantasy from reality may contribute to the intensity of nightmares during early childhood. Viewing violence on television or hearing scary stories may result in frightening dreams. In contrast to night terrors, the child with a nightmare will respond to comfort and reassurance. Night terrors typically occur infrequently during the preschool years and tend to resolve spontaneously as the child grows older. The usual episode occurs some 60 to 120 minutes after the child has fallen asleep during non–rapid eye movement sleep. The child may sit upright in bed, wide-eyed and terrified, and may appear to be having hallucinations, pointing to objects or people not present. Episodes may be as brief as 30 seconds or last as long as 5 to 10 minutes and typically culminate in the child's returning rapidly to sleep. For the rare child with frequent night terrors, the technique of scheduled night awakening may be successfully applied.

Separation Anxiety

Fears are quite common during early childhood and predictable during certain developmental stages. Examples include stranger and separation anxiety during infancy and the toddler years, as well as the fear of animals, ghosts, and the dark among preschool children. In contrast to such stage-related behaviors, *separation anxiety* may be defined as developmentally inappropriate and excessive anxiety concerning separation from home or from those to whom the individual is attached. Some preschool children may display excessive fears that interfere with functioning. A particularly troublesome example is excessive anxiety when the child is expected to attend child care.

A number of strategies may be helpful to parents when child care protest is problematic. When possible, anticipating the child's need for adjustment to new child care arrangements by visiting and meeting teachers and other children prior to actual enrollment may be helpful. The transition to a new setting may be facilitated by the parent's temporarily remaining on-site with the child. Consistent arrival and departure rituals should prove comforting to the child. The child care provider may be willing to engage in favorite activities and games with the child, or even allow the child to retain a favorite transitional object, such as a blanket or toy, during the first few days of attendance. If the child's protest is particularly vehement or prolonged, then the parents should reconsider the appropriateness of their arrangements.

Atypical Behaviors and Autism

In contrast to the stage-related behaviors (i.e., *variations* and *problems* in the DSM-PC), the primary care clinician will infrequently encounter behaviors suggestive of frank *disorders.* Autism and other pervasive developmental disorders (PDD) involve deficits in social reciprocity, in communication, and in the range and breadth of interests and activities. **Because early-onset conditions of neurobiologic origin and the recognition and diagnosis of autism are often delayed, the opportunity for early intervention may be missed.** Although onset of autism occurs in the first year for 25% of affected children, during the second year for an additional 50%, and after 2 years for the remaining 25%, diagnosis is often not made until the later preschool or early school years.

Issues of formal assessment and treatment are beyond the purview of most primary care clinicians; however, awareness of the typical features should enhance early detection. Diagnostic features of autism include impaired reciprocal social interaction (e.g., the failure to seek comfort when distressed, absent or abnormal social play); impaired communication (e.g., absent verbal communication; abnormal nonverbal communication, absent imaginative activity); and a restricted repertoire of activities and interests (e.g., stereo-

typed body movements, preoccupation with objects, insistence on following routines). The lack of communication before 5 years of age is indicative of a very poor prognosis. The challenge for the primary care clinician is to distinguish typical stage-related behaviors during the first 2 to 3 years of life, such as head banging and the normal preference for solitary play, from the abnormal behavior characteristic of children with autism and PDD.

FURTHER READING

Drabman RS, Jarvie CJ: Counseling parents of children with behavior problems: The use of extinction and time-out techniques. Pediatrics 59:78–85, 1977.

Dworkin PH: The preschool child: Developmental themes and clinical issues. Curr Probl Pediatr 18:75–134, 1988.

Parker S, Zuckerman B: Behavioral and Developmental Pediatrics. Boston, Little, Brown, 1995.

Rickert VI, Johnson CM: Reducing nocturnal awakening and crying episodes in infants and young children. Pediatrics 81:203–212, 1988.

Wolraich ML (ed): The Classification of Child and Adolescent Mental Diagnoses in Primary Care. *In* Diagnostic and Statistical Manual for Primary Care (DSM-PC), Child and Adolescent Version. Elk Grove Village, IL, American Academy of Pediatrics, 1996.

Chapter 65

School Age and Adolescence

Robert S. Byrd

School Readiness

A child's academic course is often charted by his or her performance during the first few years of school. Those children with successful transitions to school fare better academically, and those with educational achievement are more likely to lead healthier lives. Although not exclusive to children living in poverty, problems at school entry are more common among socioeconomically disadvantaged children. In contrast, children grow- ing up in socially advantaged households have many experiences structured into their lives that promote readiness, sometimes to an extreme (as described by Elkind in *The Hurried Child* and *Miseducation*). This chapter describes why and how primary care clinicians should promote school readiness as part of health supervision.

Thirty-five percent of children are not "ready for school" according to a national sur-

vey of kindergarten teachers (Boyer, 1990). A fourth of these children (8%) will repeat kindergarten or first grade. Much has been advocated about promotion of school readiness, but no consistent or coordinated approach has been developed to address this problem. Schools can do little to enhance children's readiness, as their contact with students generally begins at school entry. **Primary care clinicians are the only professionals who consistently assess preschoolers' progress over stages of early development and who are in a favorable position to intervene to improve school readiness.**

To the question "What problems most restrict school readiness?" kindergarten teachers responded with one or more of the following: deficiencies in language (51%); emotional maturity (43%); general knowledge (38%); social confidence (31%); moral awareness (21%); and physical well-being (ranking sixth in importance at 6%). Thus, child health clinicians must address more than physical health when promoting school readiness. The National Education Goals Panel (1992) defined five dimensions of school readiness: (1) physical well-being and motor development, (2) social and emotional development, (3) approaches to learning, (4) language usage, and (5) cognition and general knowledge. Specific guidelines that incorporate these dimensions of readiness have yet to be developed, but many approaches to readiness promotion can be considered.

Clinical approaches to recognition of children at risk for early school failure include developmental screening, developmental surveillance, risk assessment, and anticipatory guidance. As many as 60% of pediatricians use developmental screening tests, such as the Denver Developmental Screening Test (DDST), but only 15% do so routinely. Most rely on clinical judgment, which, unfortunately, does not effectively identify problems of children who require special education services. Only 29% of children receiving special education in a five-community sample had their learning problems identified by 5 years of age. The degree to which primary care clinicians can improve identification rates of learning problems by increased use of formal screening instruments in preschoolers is unknown, but as discussed in Chapter 21, there are a number of effective strategies that can be employed.

Most pediatricians use some form of developmental surveillance rather than developmental screening in assessing children's development. *Developmental surveillance* is defined by Dworkin (1993) as a "flexible, continuous process whereby knowledgeable professionals perform skilled observations during the provision of health care. The components of developmental surveillance include eliciting and attending to parental concerns, obtaining a relevant developmental history, making accurate and informative observations of children, and sharing opinions and concerns with other relevant professionals (e.g., preschool teachers)." Formal screening tests can be used when a developmental delay is suspected. Referral to early intervention programs (as established by Public Law 99-457) can assist in both developmental testing and referral for appropriate services. In addition to the identification and referral of cognitive, speech, and hearing delays, other conditions associated with early school problems include low birth weight, frequent otitis media, and behavioral problems, and they warrant some attention to ensure that such problems do not impair a child's readiness for school.

Assessment of risk for early school problems is an approach that can augment developmental screening and surveillance. Low birth weight and other perinatal insults may heighten the risk for early school problems. However, adverse socioeconomic and familial factors play a preeminent role in producing emotional difficulties and diminution in cognitive functioning, except when a child has experienced a severe biologic insult. Factors present at birth that may impair the developmental quality of the home environment include poverty, single-parent family, low maternal education, teen parent, large family, family history of mental retardation or school problems, and parental mental health problems, such as maternal depression. Other environmental factors that may be evident later but still contribute to developmental risk include family stress, lack of age-appropriate play materials, and lack of children's books in the home. The presence of multiple risk factors greatly increases the likelihood of early school problems, and recognition of risk allows for intervention before developmental delays are evident. The effectiveness of primary care clinicians in promoting school readiness among at-risk children requires collaboration with community services or the development of support services within clinical settings. Although families of at-risk children can be referred to Head Start or other preschool compensatory education programs, these interventions for 4-year-olds are available too late for many at-risk children. Programs for younger children and their families that promote good parenting, language stimulation, and learning through play are available in many communities. Assistance in finding high quality, developmentally stimulating child care and helping a mother learn to read to her child through referral to adult education programs are useful preventive measure. Although no single universal program meets the myriad of educational needs of at-risk children, child health clinicians aware of early childhood resources and adult education services in their communities can make appropriate referrals and help parents provide a nurturing and stimulating environment for their children.

Irrespective of risk or delay, school readiness can be promoted at each health supervision visit. *Bright Futures: Guidelines for Health Supervision of Infants, Children, and Adolescents* includes recommendations for anticipatory guidance that encourage language and literacy development, curiosity, self-esteem, and social skills. The recommendations most applicable to school readiness promotion are listed in Table 65–1.

Language mastery is one of the keys to school readiness, and reading to children by parents is one of the most important readiness-promoting activities. Infants learn language interactively from parents who talk, sing, and play with them; who respond to their babbling, engaging them in "conversation" before there are words to speak; and who read to them. The Reach Out and Read program, in which infants to school-age children receive an age-appropriate book while the importance of reading is stressed to parents as part of well-child care, provides an effective model for the promotion of practice-based language/literacy.

Parenting classes and other programs that encourage language stimulation may also be helpful.

Preschoolers in the United States watch an average of 28 hours of television per week, and even more in the case of children in lower socioeconomic families. Excessive television viewing by preschoolers limits the time they spend reading, playing with peers, building with blocks, coloring with crayons, cutting with scissors, pasting and making projects, and more importantly interacting with caring adults. When discussing television limits during preschool health supervision visits, clinicians have a special opportunity to suggest activities that promote cognitive and social development.

Despite best efforts and intentions, children reach school age with differing abilities. Delay of school entry for those deemed not ready has been advocated; however, children denied entry to school remain in the same environment that failed to produce readiness. Although the youngest children in a class evidence some difficulties at school entry, little difference persists by the third or fourth grade. By adolescence, students who are older than their classmates have higher rates of parent-reported behavior problems and youth-reported health risk behaviors, including substance use.

Currently, educators recommend that children enter school along with their same-age peers, al-

---

TABLE 65–1. School Readiness: Anticipatory Guidance from *Bright Futures*

Read to the baby. Play music. (4, 6 months)
Encourage the baby's vocalizatons. Talk to him during dressing, bathing, feeding, playing, walking, and driving. (4, 6, 9 months)
Provide opportunities for exploration. (6, 9, 36 months)
Encourage exploration and initiative. (12 months)
Encourage language development by reading books to the toddler, singing her songs, and talking about what you and she are
    seeing and doing together. (12, 15, 18, 24 months)
Limit television watching to less than 1 hour per day of appropriate programs. Watch programs with your child. (12, 15, 18, 24,
    36, 48 months)
Encourage play, which is a way of learning social behavior. (15 months)
Encourage the toddler's autonomous behavior, curiosity, sense of emerging independence, and feeling of competence.
    (15 months)
Model appropriate language. (18, 24 months)
Appreciate the child's investigatory nature, and do not excessively limit his explorations. Guide him through fun learning
    experiences. (24 months)
To promote a sense of competence and control, invite the child to make choices whenever possible. (The choices should be ones
    you can live with—e.g., "Red pants or blue ones?") (24 months)
Encourage interactive reading with the child. (36, 48 months)
Encourage the child to talk with you about her preschool, friends, or observations. Answer her questions. (36, 48 months)
Give the child opportunities to make choices (e.g., which clothes to wear, books to read, places to go). (36, 48 months)
Provide opportunities for the child to socialize with other children in play groups, preschool, or other community activities.
    (36, 48 months)
Discuss with the health professional how to tell when the child is ready for school. (48 months)
Enlarge the child's experiences through trips and visits to parks and other places of interest. (48 months)

From Green M (ed): Bright Futures: Guidelines for Health Supervision of Infants, Children, and Adolescents. Arlington, VA, National Center for Education in Maternal and Child Health, 1994.

though some may require placement into a more appropriate educational setting. Some schools have an enrichment strategy for at-risk students, not a remedial one, aimed at bringing all students into the educational mainstream by the end of elementary school and performing at levels appropriate to their age group. Unfortunately, most schools set "slower" students on slower paced, remedial tracks, which over time only further distances them from their "more ready" peers. Overcoming the lack of school readiness requires more intensive efforts by parents, children, and schools, but even with these efforts, educational outcomes are generally not as good as those of children who begin ready for school.

A 5- to 6-year window of opportunity begins at birth to help enhance children's readiness for school. Developmental assessments will help identify children with developmental delays. Children at risk for school problems can be referred to early childhood programs as a preventive measure. Anticipatory guidance at each health supervision visit can assist parents in enhancing their child's readiness for school. As professionals who consistently assess preschoolers' progress over multiple stages of early development, primary care clinicians are in a unique position to intervene early so as to improve children's school readiness.

Robert S. Byrd

FURTHER READING

Boyer EL: Ready to Learn: A Mandate for the Nation. Princeton, NJ: Carnegie Foundation for the Advancement of Teaching, 1990.

Byrd RS and Weitzman ML: Predictors of early grade retention among children in the United States. Pediatrics 93:481–487, 1994.

Byrd RS, Weitzman M, and Auinger P: Increased behavior problems associated with delayed school entry and delayed school progress. Pediatrics 100:654–661, 1997.

Campbell FA and Ramey CT: Effects of early intervention on intellectual and academic achievement: A follow-up study of children from low-income families. Child Dev 65(Special No. 2):684–698, 1994.

Dworkin PH: Detection of behavioral, developmental, and psychosocial problems in pediatric primary care practice. Curr Opin Pediatr 5:531–536, 1993.

Elkind D: The Hurried Child: Growing Up Too Fast Too Soon. Reading, MA, Addison-Wesley, 1981.

Elkind D: Miseducation: Preschoolers at Risk. New York, Knopf, 1987.

Green M (ed): Bright Futures: Guidelines for Health Supervision of Infants, Children, and Adolescents. Arlington, VA: National Center for Education in Maternal and Child Health, 1994.

National Education Goals Panel: Building a Nation of Learners: The National Education Goals Report 1992. Washington, DC, National Education Goals Panel, 1992.

Needlman R, Fried L, Morely D, et al.: Clinic-based intervention to promote literacy. Am J Dis Child 145:881–884, 1991.

Palfrey JS, Singer JD, Walker DK, and Butler JA: Early identification of children's special needs: A study in five metropolitan communities. J Pediatr 111:651–659, 1987.

School Avoidance

For most children, an occasional absence from school for illnesses, real or perceived, is not a problem. Prolonged or frequent absences from school, however, may herald significant academic, social, medical, or psychologic problems that warrant prompt assessment and intervention. School absences are often attributed to illness by children and their parents and will, therefore, come to the attention of child health clinicians. Such problems are common, estimated to affect 5% of children in elementary grades and 2% of those in junior high school. **Although some children present with the chief complaint of school refusal, vague somatic complaints without any obvious source is more common.**

Despite semantic differences, the terms school avoidance, school refusal, and school phobia are often used interchangeably. **Separation anxiety is the most common cause of school avoidance.** Although many 5- and 6-year-old children demonstrate a transient separation anxiety during the start of formal school, family issues are frequently present in the more severe cases. Often, the parent-child relationship can be described as mutually dependent. Sometimes, a chronic health condition in a parent or some other stressor in the home contributes to a child's sense that he or she should stay home to care for or protect a parent. School avoidance may occur anytime during a child's school years, but anxiety-type school avoidance is more common at times of transition, such as school entry and at the start of junior high school when children change from one to multiple teachers, or when children feel their privacy is threatened in physical education class.

In addition, other conditions should be considered when assessing children with chronic school absences (Table 65–2). For example, children with an unrecognized learning disability may experience vague somatic complaints until their problem

TABLE 65–2. Differential Diagnosis for Children with Chronic School Absences

School avoidance	Chronic disease with poor
Anxiety-related type	adaptation
Secondary-gain type	Depression
Inappropriate response to minor	Obsessive-compulsive
illness	disorder
Learning disability with poor	Psychosis
adaptation	Truancy
Child-teacher conflict	Substance abuse
Family dysfunction	Teenage pregnancy
Homelessness	

is recognized and appropriate educational placement arranged. At times, fears about safety and well-being are realistic and should be assessed. Adolescents who have been poor students may be truant (neither at home nor at school during school hours), and their school absences may be a prelude to ultimately dropping out of school. Drug use, depression, poor reading skills, antisocial behavior, and pregnancy may contribute to school absence in adolescents.

Treatment for school avoidance begins with a detailed assessment. There are times when school absence is not the focus of the parents' concerns, and the child health clinician must ask how much school the child has missed. Anxiety-related school avoidance often presents with one or more anxiety-related symptoms, such as headache, abdominal pain, sleep disturbances, leg pains, fatigue, vomiting, diarrhea, dizziness, or weakness. Secondary-gain type of school avoidance often presents with fabricated symptoms, such as a sore throat. The discrepancy between how sick the child sounds and how well the child looks is a hallmark of either type of school avoidance. Symptoms may be worse at the time the child would ordinarily be leaving for school and improve later in the morning. Symptoms may also be confined to school days, worse on Mondays, in September, or after holidays. Questions that probe the motivational basis for the child's school avoidance may help direct treatment. Once organic disease has been ruled out by the history and physical

examination, the parents' specific concerns must be addressed and efforts directed at returning a child to school before such behaviors become entrenched, and academic problems ensue. Laboratory tests are usually unnecessary and may actually hamper resolution of the problem.

Primary care clinicians working with families and schools can manage most cases of school avoidance. The parents need to know that the first priority is for the child to return to school. Children should be returned to school immediately, and this expectation should not be delayed by further investigations. Somatic symptoms should be downplayed, minor symptoms ignored, and strategies for the management of more major complaints developed, such as a brief stay in the school nurse's office. The clinician, school personnel, and parents need to develop an effective plan. School attendance and classroom participation warrant positive reinforcement. For more severe cases, desensitization is required for a transitional period in returning to school. Referral to a behavioral pediatrician, psychologist, or psychiatrist may be necessary with depressed or seriously emotionally ill children or if the problem persists. In the rare case in which families are unable to send their children to school despite extensive assessment and intervention by school and clinicians, referral may be required to child protective services for educational neglect. Regular school attendance is the measure of successful treatment.

FURTHER READING

Castiglia PT: School phobia/school avoidance. J Pediatr Health Care 7:229–232, 1993.

Klerman LV: School absence—a health perspective. Pediatr Clin North Am 35(6):1253–1269, 1988.

McAnanly E: School phobia: The importance of prompt intervention. J School Health 56:433–436, 1986.

Nader PR (ed): School Health: Policy and Practice, 5th ed. Elk Grove Village, IL, American Academy of Pediatrics, 1993, pp 130–139.

Weitzman M, Klerman LV, Lamb G, et al.: School absence: A problem for the pediatrician. Pediatrics 69:739–746, 1982.

Weitzman M and Siegel DM: What we have not learned from what we know about excessive school absence and school drop out. J Dev Behav Pediatr 13:55–58, 1992.

William Lord Coleman

Learning Problems of Children and Adolescents: Assessment and Management Techniques

Success in school—learning, making friends, developing self-esteem—is a major task for children and adolescents. School success profoundly affects their future: economic, social and emotional status, career choice, and quality of life; on the other hand, learning problems impact students' ability to learn, perform, and succeed. When these problems arise, the primary care clinician is often the first professional to be consulted.

Approximately 25% of children have learning difficulties, making them the most common developmental problem of children and adolescents. Boys outnumber girls about 4:1, but this may represent a referral bias. Of these affected youth, about 5% to 10% qualify as having specific learning disabilities, a more discrete and significant disorder, that meet eligibility criteria for school-based services. This chapter briefly describes (1) several definitions of learning problems; (2) the federal laws mandating appropriate testing and provision of services; and (3) the roles of the primary care pediatrician in assessment and management. It concludes with a list of helpful readings and resources.

DEFINITIONS OF LEARNING PROBLEMS

There are many definitions of learning problems, and often clinicians, parents, and children do not understand their nature. Most clinicians do not have the time or expertise to be directly involved in the assessment and management of these problems, but they do play a key role in (1) screening; (2) referring; (3) treating the comorbid problems; (4) educating the family about the child's learning problems; (5) helping parents negotiate the maze of federal laws and eligibility criteria for special educational services; and (6) strengthening the parents' ability to advocate for their child. The child health clinician greatly enhances his or her effectiveness by being informed about definitions, laws, and eligibility criteria and imparting this knowledge to parents and children. Several definitions are listed.

The Diagnostic and Statistical Manual for Pri-

mary Care (DSM-PC), Child and Adolescent Version states: "Learning styles vary enormously among children and are reflected in differences in the rate, quality, retention, analysis, and application of what is learned. Some children learn quickly. Others require extensive repetition of material before it is retained. Some children learn best through the auditory route; others learn best visually. Similarly, children vary as to the strength of their verbal versus written responses. The method of instruction may enhance or detract from the child's ability to learn the material(s) tested."

Learning difficulties are usually considered developmental disorders and are listed in the DSM-PC as occurring at four different ages (infancy, early childhood, middle childhood, and adolescence) and manifesting at three different levels of severity (learning variation, learning problem, and learning disorder).

Diagnostic and Statistical Manual of Mental Disorders, fourth edition (DSM-IV) states that learning disorders represent inadequate development of specific academic language, speech, and motor skills not resulting from demonstrable neurologic or physical disorders, pervasive developmental disorders, mental retardation, lack of opportunity, or deficient cultural or educational experience. It subtypes the disorders into three groups (Table 65–3).

The Individuals with Disabilities Education Act, or IDEA (Public Law 101-476), defines a specific learning disability as "a disorder in one or more basic psychological processes involved in under-

TABLE 65–3. Subtypes of Learning and Learning-Related Disorders from the *DSM-IV*

Mathematics Disorder
Reading Disorder
Disorder of Written Expression
Motor Skills Disorder
Communication Disorders
  Phonologic Disorder
  Expressive Language Disorder
  Mixed Receptive-Expressive Language Disorder

From the American Psychiatric Association: Diagnostic and Statistical Manual of Mental Disorders, 4th ed (DSM-IV). Washington, DC, APA, 1994.

TABLE 65–4. Steps and Processes of a Learning Task: A Selected Outline

1. Intake
   Visual perception and auditory perception
   Selective attention and processing speed or rate
   Ability to understand vocabulary, concepts, sentence construction and meaning
2. Memory
   Sequencing abilities (letters in a word, events in a story, months of the year)
   Summarization abilities (condensing vast amounts of data, saliency determination)
   Interpretation and abstraction abilities (deriving correct meanings, making inferences)
   Organizational abilities (integrating and storing information, forming concepts)
   Retrieval abilities (rate and efficiency of retrieving information)
3. Output
   Expressive speech abilities (articulation, fluency, elaboration, vocabulary)
   (Demand speech: answering a question. Spontaneous speech: initiating a statement)
   Writing abilities (motor abilities, organization, ideation, spelling, rules of punctuation)
   Motor abilities (writing, drawing, coordination, buttoning, tying, playing sports)

standing or in using language, spoken or written, that may manifest itself in an imperfect ability to listen, speak, read, write, spell, or to do mathematical calculations. The term includes such conditions as perceptual disabilities, brain injuries, minimal brain dysfunction, dyslexia, and developmental aphasia. The term does not apply to children who have learning problems that are primarily the result of visual, hearing, or motor disabilities, of mental retardation, of emotional disturbance, or of environmental, cultural, or economic disadvantage.''

Levels of severity of learning problems vary greatly. Only those children who have moderate to severe problems qualify for school-based special services (meet eligibility criteria). Eligibility requires a specified numeric discrepancy between the Full Scale IQ score (cognitive level or potential ability) and one or more of the standardized scores (achievement level or actual ability), that is, reading, math, and writing or spelling. In North Carolina, for example, the required discrepancy is 15 points. **This discrepancy formula only determines eligibility for special services. It does not determine diagnosis or definition. It may overlook children with significant information processing problems who need services regardless of whether they are "eligible."** This is a critical distinction. Children who are eligible are categorized "learning disabled (LD)."

Another definition considers a *learning task* as involving more than one process and a *learning problem* as usually involving more than one area of dysfunction. It is helpful to separate learning into steps and processes rather than just measuring the levels of reading, mathematics, and writing or spelling. Using this model, learning problems may be described as difficulties with processing information at any of the three major steps—intake, memory, and output—and each of these steps en-

tails specific functions. For example, intake, specifically listening, entails auditory perception or receptive language abilities (phonologic awareness, vocabulary, rate of processing, sentence comprehension, and awareness of syntax and grammar) (Table 65–4).

Another variation concerns the child or adolescent who harbors several subtle neurodevelopmental dysfunctions or processes at one, two, or all three steps (e.g., weak receptive language skills, attention deficits, memory difficulties, and fine motor problems). When a learning task requires the simultaneous use of these functions (e.g., listening to a long lecture, sustaining attention, storing and integrating information, and taking notes), the cumulative effect of these dysfunctions compromises the child's learning abilities. However, due to their relatively low levels of severity individually, these dysfunctions are not readily apparent nor are they usually detected by traditional IQ and standardized achievement tests.

FEDERAL LAWS

Parents often do not fully know their rights or the schools' legal responsibilities for appropriate testing and placement options in special education. The clinician can provide information about federal laws governing programs and services for infants, children, and adolescents with learning disabilities in the public schools.

The Individuals with Disabilities Education Act (IDEA; Public Law 101-476, 1990; revised in 1997) is the current law. Essentially, IDEA amended two previous public laws: the Education for All Handicapped Children's Act (PL 94-142, 1975) and the Infants and Toddlers Handicapped Act, Part H (PL 99-457, 1987), which also designated the family as a major focus of service. IDEA

TABLE 65–5. Categories of Disabilities in the Individuals with Disabilities Education Act (IDEA)

1. Autism
2. Deaf-blindness
3. Deafness
4. Hearing impairment
5. Mental retardation
6. Multiple disabilities
7. Orthopedic impairment
8. Other health impairment (OHI): chronic illness affecting educational performance
9. Serious emotional disturbance: depression, phobia, etc., affecting educational performance
10. Specific learning disability
11. Speech or language impairment
12. Traumatic brain injury
13. Visual impairment including blindness

provides for the identification and placement of infants, children, and adolescents (ages birth to 21 years) in need of special educational services and the provision of those services. IDEA covers 13 categories of disabilities, not limited to learning disabilities. The clinician should be familiar with these categories, some of which have an impact on learning and may qualify the child for special educational services. Categories of disabilities are listed in Table 65–5. The principles of IDEA are listed in Table 65–6.

THE ROLES OF THE PEDIATRIC CLINICIAN

Pediatric clinicians are suited and expected to carry out a variety of important roles related to learning problems: (1) screen and identify; (2) conduct (or refer) an initial evaluation; (3) refer as necessary for evaluation of learning or other problems; (4) work with the teachers and other professionals in the management of the problems; (5) treat the contributing or secondary problems; (6) demystify (explain) the child's or adolescent's learning problems and educate the family about the relevant federal laws and available resources; (7) advocate; and (8) follow up.

Screening and Identification

Screening is the process of obtaining information to decide if further evaluation is needed to define the particular problems of the identified child or adolescent. Screening is best done by (1) listening to parent's concerns; (2) observing and recording the child's development, behavior, and school performance; (3) asking trigger questions (see Green, 1994); (4) and using parent and teacher questionnaires and screening tests (Table 65–7).

Initial Evaluation by the Pediatric Clinician

A complex interaction of biopsychosocial factors causes learning problems and academic underachievement. Furthermore, most children and adolescents with learning problems or disabilities experience secondary social, family, and emotional problems, including low self-esteem and

TABLE 65–6. The Principles of the Individuals with Disabilities Education Act (IDEA)

- Nonexclusion. Free and appropriate public education and related services for handicapped children regardless of the nature and severity of the problem or availability of local services and monies.
- Individualized Educational Plan (IEP). A school-based multidisciplinary team and parents formulate a comprehensive educational plan based on each child's specific needs and strengths.
- The parent must attend the IEP meeting and agree with the IEP before it can be implemented.
- Access to records. Parents have rights to view their children's educational records confidentially. Provides privacy.
- Due process. Safeguards protecting the rights of children, parents, or interested parties if disagreements arise in the provision of special education services. Parents are involved in the evaluation and decision-making process.
- Least restrictive environment. Handicapped children receive their services in a setting that approximates the setting of nonhandicapped peers given the students' needs and abilities, unless the alternative setting is more appropriate.
- Nondiscriminatory evaluation. Evaluation instruments must be valid and reliable; personnel administering tests must be trained professionals; tests must be given in child's native language or normal mode of communication.
- Lead agency. Each state designates a lead agency and forms an Interagency Coordinating Council which develops statewide multidisciplinary programs.
- Eligibility criteria. Each state develops definitions of handicaps for eligibility purposes, e.g., "biologically delayed," "environmentally at risk."
- Individualized Family Service Plan (IFSP). Each state develops a comprehensive approach including (1) the child's physical, cognitive, language, and psychosocial development; (2) the family's strengths and needs; (3) the goals for the child and family; and (4) the needed, specific services.
- The term "handicap" was changed to "disabilities."
- Written plans for adolescents making the transition from school to college or employment are required.
- The importance of assistive technology was recognized.

TABLE 65–7. Questionnaires and Screening Tests: A Selected Sample

Questionnaire
  The ANSER system (Levine)
Screening tests
  Pediatric Symptom Checklist (Jellinek)
  Denver Developmental Screening Test

loss of motivation. The pediatrician should be aware of these associated problems when generating a differential diagnosis and before implementing a treatment plan (Table 65–8).

The initial office or clinic-based evaluation includes a thorough and comprehensive history, physical and neurologic examinations, vision and hearing screening, and direct observation and interaction with the child or adolescent that may reveal problems with attention, listening or understanding, or expressing oneself clearly. The clinician should also interview parents and adolescents alone. Sometimes, children appreciate this individual time. When asked about the specific difficulties (in a supportive manner), parents and children frequently provide very helpful diagnostic information. Questions can focus on the basic academic skills, different content areas (e.g., science, history), and the three major steps plus the various processes of a learning task, as outlined in Table 65–4.

Attention deficits occur in 25% to 50% of youth with learning problems or disabilities. The clinician who suspects learning problems

should also consider attention problems and vice versa. Children with learning problems are also more likely to have social skill deficits (see Chapter 65, subchapters on Attention Deficits and Helping Children and Adolescents Make Friends: Social Skills). The clinician will save time and be more effective and comprehensive by using parent and teacher questionnaires to gather background, for example, the ANSER system. This should also include a review of previous evaluations and school records.

Referral for Learning Disabilities: Making the Diagnosis and Determining Eligibility for Special Education and Related Services

If the initial evaluation reveals a possible diagnosis of learning problems, the child should be referred for psychoeducational testing by an educational psychologist and/or educational diagnostician. Occasionally, language specialists, neuropsychologists, and occupational and physical therapists may be needed. This testing can be performed at the child's school with no cost to the parents or may be done privately and the results shared with the school. **The clinician must keep in mind that the focus of the school evaluation usually is to determine eligibility for services, not whether a child has a learning problem or other neurodevelopmental condition.** Selected information from the clinician's initial evaluation

TABLE 65–8. Factors Causing or Influencing Learning Problems: A Selected Differential Diagnosis

Biomedical
CNS illness/disorder (Tourette syndrome, meningitis, seizure disorders, perinatal complications)
Chronic illness (school absenteeism; medication; visual, auditory, physical handicaps)
Developmental
Attention deficits
Neurodevelopmental dysfunctions (language, memory, motor)
Autism
Level of intelligence/cognitive ability (mental retardation; "slow learner" range)
Behavioral
Any behavioral problem/pattern that interferes with learning (conduct disorder, truancy, chronic disorganization
  of materials and time, inadequate study/homework habits)
Emotional
Anxiety, depression, phobias
Social-Environmental
Peer influence
Excessive extracurricular activities (social, work, sports, television/music/computers)
Alcohol/substance abuse
Inadequate school environment (poor quality of teaching, indifference to academic achievement, large classes, lack
  of resources)
Family
Low level of support or appreciation for school/learning/studying
Family stress (financial, substance abuse, marital, medical, emotional)
Family history of learning, behavior, emotional, attention problems

CNS, central nervous system.

might be shared with the school or other professionals if it is helpful, if doing so will not cause embarrassment to the child, and if the parents consent.

The tests measure intelligence (IQ) and academic achievement; the most frequently used tests are listed in Table 65–9. Eligibility for special educational services is determined by comparing the scores of these tests. For example, a student with an IQ of 98, and three achievement standard scores of reading 90, writing/spelling 80, and mathematics 117, would show the following discrepancies respectively: -8, -18, and $+19$ (generally a standard score of $100 = 50$th percentile). Using the Wechsler Intelligence Scale for Children III (WISC-III), a 15-point discrepancy is required for a diagnosis of "learning disabled," so this child qualifies and deserves special education for writing/spelling with the -18 score; however, the -8 difference in reading does not qualify for special services. This means that the severity of the student's reading problem, although measurable, observable, and contributing to the learning difficulties, is not severe enough to make the child eligible for school-based special services. In this situation, the regular teacher might make accommodations or offer support, but special educational services do not appear warranted. The parents might also employ a tutor or help at home. Finally, the $+19$ score indicates that the student is achieving above expectations in mathematics.

A child with an IQ score of 70 or less can be classified as having mental retardation and can qualify for special education. However, a child with an IQ between 71 and 84 is considered a "slow learner." Although he or she cannot keep up in a regular class and does not qualify for special education, the child may be placed in a "basic" class if the school has one. If not, the teacher might make accommodations in the regular classroom, and the parents might arrange for after-school tutoring.

TABLE 65–9. Frequently Used Tests for Learning Disabilities

Psychologic Tests
Wechsler Intelligence Scale for Children III (WISC-III).
  Ages 6–16 years
Wechsler Adult Intelligence Scale (WAIS). Ages 16 and
  older
Stanford-Binet Intelligence Scale. Ages 2 years to adulthood
Achievement Tests
Wide Range Achievement Tests (WRAT)
Woodcock-Johnson Psychoeducational Battery
Metropolitan Achievement Tests
Stanford Diagnostic Achievement Tests

Working with the Teachers

The pediatric clinician should have a collegial, working relationship with the child's or adolescent's teacher(s), special education teacher, and school counselor. Treatment for learning disabilities is specialized education, provided either in the regular classroom or in a separate resource room. The clinician can be helpful by sharing the child's developmental profile (more than the psychoeducational evaluation) with the teacher and promoting the child's and parents' adaptation and work with the school, facilitating communication and good will between parents and teachers when necessary. Teachers appreciate the clinician's help and positive feedback very much. For example, the physician and teacher should work together on medication for a child's attention problems with teacher feedback on the child's responses helping to guide the dosage. The teachers need rating scales and other information from the physician so they know what to look for. Other examples include helping the child develop social skills and friendships; finding ways to foster self-esteem; and encouraging the parents to follow up on suggested study strategies and homework support. The physician and teacher should fax messages or even exchange home phone numbers, because daytime contact between the two is often so difficult.

Treat the Contributing Problems and Associated Complications

The physician must decide which comorbid problems to treat and which of the others to refer. For example, in addition to treating medical illnesses, the clinician must be alert for attentional problems and emotional-social-family complications, such as "homework wars." Helping families structure their time, reorder priorities, and reduce interruptions and distractions during homework time can be very effective. The physician can help the parents better understand the child's strengths and weaknesses and explain the impact of the disability on the child's life and how the disability affects treatment. For example, a child with a receptive language or demand-language dysfunction would not do well with listening-talk therapy (see Table 65–4). Books with specific homework strategies are much appreciated (see Frender, Metcalf, and Radenich and Schumn in Further Reading).

Demystify the Phenomenon of Learning Disabilities

Demystification is the process of constructing a narrative profile of the child that (1) explains (interprets) the phenomenon in a nonlabeling, supportive, nonstigmatizing manner using real-life examples as illustrations; (2) highlights and maintains the child's strengths; and (3) induces optimism and hope. Factual information removes blame, fosters understanding, and builds motivation. The labeling approach, for example, "LD" may be used for official billing-reimbursement purposes and for obtaining school support, but a child's self-image should be more than just a label, and that is the purpose of the descriptive, narrative approach. Educating parents about the federal laws and resources reassures parents of their rights and gives them specialized information, a chance to network with other families, and methods for working with schools.

Advocate

Advocacy has a major role in supporting the child or adolescent by going above and beyond the office visit. It may entail telephoning or writing the teacher, principal, or guidance counselor to obtain testing, special services, curriculum modifications, and classroom accommodations as mandated by various federal laws. It starts with helping the parents and child receive a welcome reception at the school, obtain a timely (cost-free) evaluation, and then receive the appropriate special education as soon as possible. Advocacy is helping make a smooth "fit" between child/parent and teacher/school. It may be finding the right school, or meeting with teachers and parents at the school to review the child's or adolescent's Individual Educational Plan (IEP). Advocacy means believing in the child or adolescent and acting on his or her behalf.

Follow-Up

Follow-up is essential, because learning is a dynamic and ongoing process as the child or adolescent is constantly encountering new challenges and expectations, learning, maturing, coping, and responding to the environment. Follow-up entails reviewing progress, monitoring compliance with recommendations, and providing anticipatory guidance, for example, planning for the challenges of a new grade or school, finding the best school, teachers, courses, and services. Follow-up supports both short- and long-term goals and is most effective when carried out in a systematic, individualized manner that provides comprehensive monitoring of the child's or adolescent's function and well-being.

FURTHER READING

For Professionals

American Academy of Pediatrics: Diagnostic and Statistical Manual for Primary Care (DSM-PC): Child and Adolescent Version. Elk Grove Village, IL, AAP, 1996.

American Psychiatric Association: Diagnostic and Statistical Manual of Mental Disorders ed 4 (DSM-IV). Washington DC, APA, 1994.

Blackman JA: Public Law 99-457: Advance or albatross? Contemp Pediatr 8:81–95, 1991.

Brooks R: Self-esteem during the school years: Its normal development and hazardous decline. Pediatr Clin North Am 39:537–550, 1992.

Casey PH and Evans LD: School readiness: An overview for pediatricians. Pediatr Rev 14:4–10, 1993.

Coleman WL, Levine MD, and Sandler AD: Learning disabilities in adolescents: Description, assessment and management. *In* Lerner RM, Petersen AC, and Brooks-Dunn J (eds): Encyclopedia of Adolescence. New York, Garland Publishing, 1991, pp 580–590.

Deshler DD, Ellis ES, and Lenz KB: Teaching Adolescents with Learning Disabilities. Denver, Dove Publishers, 1996.

Downey WS: Public Law 99-457 and the Clinical Pediatrician. Clin Pediatr 29:223–227, 1990.

Dworkin PH and Glascoe FP: Early detection of developmental delays: How do you measure up? Contemp Pediatr 14:158–168, 1997.

Dworkin PH: School failure. Pediatr Rev 10:301–312, 1989.

Green M (ed): Bright Futures: Guidelines for Health Supervision of Infants, Children, and Adolescents. Arlington VA, National Center for Education in Maternal and Child Health, 1994.

Jellinek MS and Murphy JM: The recognition of psychosocial disorders in pediatric office practice: The current status of the Pediatric Symptom Checklist. J Dev Behav Pediatr 11:273–278, 1990.

Levine MD: Developmental Variation and Learning Disorders. Cambridge MA, Educators Publishing Service, 1987.

Levine MD: The ANSER System. Cambridge, MA, Educators Publishing Service, 1996.

Palfrey JS and Rappaport LA: School placement. Pediatr Rev 8:261–271, 1987.

Purvis P and Whelan RJ: Collaborative planning between pediatricians and special educators. Pediatr Clin North Am 39:451–470, 1992.

Reed MS: Educational assessment of learning difficulties: A developmental, descriptive, and process-oriented perspective. *In* Levine MD, Carey W, and Crocker A (eds): Developmental-Behavioral Pediatrics, 2nd ed. Philadelphia, WB Saunders, 1992, pp. 638–645.

Silver LB: The controversial therapies for treating learning disabilities. Child Adoles Psychiatr Clin North Am 2:339–348, 1993.

For Professionals and Parents

Coleman WL: Learning disorders. *In* Schor EL (ed): Caring For Your School Age Child Ages 5–12. New York, Bantam, 1995, pp 483–495.

Duncan P: Getting involved in your child's schooling. *In* Schor

EL (ed): Caring For Your School Age Child Ages 5–12. New York, Bantam, 1995, pp 457–480.

Frender G: Learning to Learn. Nashville TN, Incentive Publisher, 1990. (Call 910-996-3090; Fax 910-996-8023. Write IESS, Inc, Box 432, Kernersville, NC 27285 ($16.00).

Levine MD: Keeping A Head in School. Cambridge MA, Educators Publishing Service, 1990.

Levine MD: Educational Care: A System for Understanding and Helping Children with Learning Problems at Home and in School. Cambridge MA, Educators Publishing Service, 1994.

Metcalf L: Counseling Toward Solutions: A Practical Solution-Focused Program for Working with Students, Teachers, and Parents. West Nyack, NY, The Center for Applied Research in Education, 1995.

Radenich MC and Schumn ER: How to Help Your Child with Homework. Minneapolis MN, Free Spirit Publishers, 1988 ($12.95).

Silver L: The Misunderstood Child. New York, McGraw-Hill, 1984.

LEARNING DISABILITIES RESOURCES

The American Academy of Pediatrics (AAP) has published "Learning Disabilities and Children: What Parents Need to Know" (1989) and "Learning Disabilities and Young Adults (1992). For the former, AAP members can purchase packets of 100 brochures for $24.95; nonmember cost is $29.95. For the latter, the costs are $22.50 and $27.50, respectively. Parents may obtain one free copy by sending a stamped, self-addressed envelope to AAP, Dept C, PO Box 927, Elk Grove Village, IL 60007.

Children and Adults with Attention Deficit Disorders (CHADD), 1859 North Pine Island Road, Suite 185, Plantation, FL. Phone: 954-587-3700.

The Governor's Advocacy Council. Located in the capitol of each state and territory, The Council provides free legal advice and support (including court appearances) regarding the rights of children and adolescents with special needs.

HEATH Resource Center (The National Clearinghouse on Post-secondary Education for Individuals with Disabilities), One Dupont Circle, Suite 800, Washington, DC 20036. Phone: 800-544-3284.

Learning Disabilities Association of America, 4156 Library Road, Pittsburgh, PA 15243. Phone: 412-341-1515.

National Center for Learning Disabilities, 381 Park Avenue South, Suite 1420, New York, NY 10016. Phone: 212-545-7510.

National Information Center for Children and Youths With Disabilities, PO Box 1492, Washington, DC 20013. Phone: 800-999-5599.

Office of Special Education and Rehabilitative Services, 600 Independence Ave SW, Washington, DC 20202-2641. Phone: 202-205-5507.

William Lord Coleman
Dale Sarah Sussman

Attention Deficits: Description, Diagnosis, and Management

The authors do not use attention-deficit disorder (ADD) or attention-deficit hyperactivity disorder (ADHD), because these labels imply a discrete, homogeneous disorder. The term *attention disorders* (ADs) is intended to convey the complexity, heterogeneity, and variability of this phenomenon. ADs are among the most frequently encountered neurobehavioral problems in pediatrics. They affect children of all ages, from preschool through adolescence, and they may persist into adulthood. Symptoms are chronic, pervasive (affecting more than one domain of function), and intense; the level of severity varies among individuals and across situations. Different descriptions, definitions, and diagnostic criteria, as well as comorbid problems, secondary complications, and other disorders that mimic ADs all contribute to the complexity, confusion, and controversy surrounding attention disorders.

The American Academy of Pediatrics briefly defines true ADs as "chronic neurological conditions resulting from a persisting dysfunction within the central nervous system and [they] are not related to gender, level of intelligence or cultural environment." ADs are defined in *The Diagnostic and Statistical Manual for Primary Care (DSM-PC) Child and Adolescent Version* as the inability to attend to any activity or object for any appreciable length of time indicates inattentive behaviors. The rapid shifts in attention are often accompanied by a failure to attend to or perceive details, and thus the child may miss many subtle aspects of an object or situation and is unable to bring an activity to its natural and expected conclusion. The lack of persistence is not related to frustration because of an inability to perform a particular task, but is more related to the child's marked distractibility. Other symptoms are excessive motor activity (gross movements, excessive talking, fidgeting) and impulsivity (acting or thinking quickly without thought of consequences). Hyperactivity, impulsivity, and inattention must be evaluated in the context of the child's age and developmental stage. The three subtypes are combined inattentive-hyperactive/impulsive; predominately inattentive; and predominately hyperactive/impulsive.

Prevalence estimates range from 3% to 5% of school-age children. Boys outnumber girls in a ratio ranging from 4:1 to 9:1 depending on the setting and expectations, but boys outnumber girls only 2:1 for the predominantly inattentive subtype. Of the affected school-age children, approximately two thirds experience persistent symptoms into adolescence, and approximately one third of these affected children maintain their symptoms as adults. Symptoms in adolescents and adults may be less obvious, but equally pernicious, for example, significant organizational and productivity problems.

CLINICAL MANIFESTATIONS

Clinical presentations of ADs cover a broad spectrum of severity and a wide variety of symptoms. The *DSM-PC* lists and categorizes many of the symptoms and describes three levels of severity, the different age presentations, the influence

TABLE 65–10. DSM-PC Symptoms of Hyperactivity-Impulsivity and Inattention

A. Hyperactivity-Impulsivity
  1. Often fidgets or squirms in seat
  2. Often leaves seat when remaining seated is expected
  3. Often runs or climbs excessively when it is inappropriate
  4. Often has difficulty playing or engaging in leisure activities quietly
  5. Is often "on the go" or acts as if "driven by a motor"
  6. Often talks excessively
  7. Often blurts out answers before questions are completed
  8. Often has difficulty awaiting turn
  9. Often interrupts or intrudes on others
B. Inattention
  1. Often fails to give close attention to details, makes careless mistakes
  2. Often has difficulty sustaining attention in tasks or play activities
  3. Often does not seem to listen when spoken to directly
  4. Often does not follow through on instructions and fails to finish tasks (not due to oppositional behavior or failure to understand instructions)
  5. Often has difficulty organizing tasks and activities
  6. Often avoids, dislikes, or is reluctant to engage in tasks that require sustained attention
  7. Often loses things necessary for tasks or activities
  8. Is often easily distracted by extraneous stimuli
  9. Is often forgetful in daily tasks

From Wolraich ML (ed): Diagnostic and Statistical Manual for Primary Care (DSM-PC) Child and Adolescent Version. Elk Grove Village, IL, American Academy of Pediatrics Press, 1996. Copyright American Academy of Pediatrics. Used with permission.

TABLE 65–11. Other Manifestations of Attention Deficits in Relation to Learning Processes

A. Processing control (Intake)
  1. Can't activate attention at right time
  2. Can't easily shift or modulate attention from task to task or over time
  3. Daydreams, free-associates easily and frequently
  4. Bored easily; always looking ahead; needs intense motivation
B. Mental energy control (Alertness, arousal)
  1. Trouble getting started in the morning
  2. Child yawning, feeling tired, sleep problems
  3. Child stretching, trying to stay awake, falling asleep
  4. Cognitive fatigue
  5. Inconsistent, unpredictable performance (schoolwork/behavior)
  6. Tunes in and tunes out
  7. Difficulty getting started on tasks, procrastinates
C. Production control (Output)
  1. Can't exert or sustain effort
  2. Works in hurried, unplanned manner
  3. Not prepared for next step
  4. Overfocused, slow, inefficient; output failure
  5. Difficulty with self-monitoring and monitoring quality of work

of environment, and traditional inclusive and exclusive diagnostic criteria (Table 65–10).

Attention problems affect the "attention controls" or skills required in any learning-behavioral task (i.e., processing, mental energy, and production). Processing is the ability to take in information; mental energy is the ability to be alert and aroused; production is the ability to produce or perform (Table 65–11).

ADs also affect executive functions, namely, organization (of time and materials), planning, reviewing, adaptation, self-monitoring, predicting, and making decisions based on prior experiential learning. Boys are more likely than girls to exhibit impaired executive function as well as problems with academic achievement, vigilance, sustained attention, and motor inhibition (impulsivity).

DIAGNOSIS

History

An extensive history is the centerpiece of diagnosis. Two perspectives are essential: (1) ecological: appreciating the relationship between the child and his or her social environment (family, peers, teachers); and (2) contextual: viewing the child in the context of family and community risk and protective influences (genetic, medical, developmental, psychosocial, economic, and environmental). Children and adolescents who present with symptoms of attention deficits, such as problems of inattention, inconsistent effort, impulsivity, and poor saliency determination (difficulty determining what is the most important thing on which to focus), merit a comprehensive evaluation (Table 65–12).

Attention deficits seldom exist in isolation. When taking a history, the issues of primary ADs, secondary attention deficits (secondary to medication or inappropriate expectations and demands), comorbidity (ADs and depression; ADs and learning disabilities), and complications (e.g., low self-esteem, loss of motivation, negative image or self-fulfilling prophecy, and parent frustration) need to be considered. Of children who have ADs, 25% to 50% have learning or language disabilities; 50% have impaired motor skills; 50% have externalizing behavioral problems, and 30% have affective disorders. With such a complex disorder, the physician might consider the merits of the "and-and" approach; for example, ADs *and* anxiety, versus the "either-or" approach; for example, ADs *or* anxiety. The concept of "attention deficits plus" captures this approach; for example, attention deficits *plus* a learning disability *plus* family frustration.

Diagnostic Evaluation

Parents and children should be interviewed separately as well as together. Parents often wish to share worries, fears, and family history in confidence; children also need an opportunity to share their feelings and perceptions. The primary care clinician should detail the chronicity, severity, and pervasiveness of the symptoms; assess associated or comorbid problems; and review other pertinent

---

TABLE 65–12. Problems of Control (Attention, Activity, Impulsivity): A Selected Differential Diagnosis

- Temperamental variations: e.g., the "difficult" child vs. the "easy" child
- Age: children under 4 are normally active, inattentive, impulsive; "insatiable"
- Situational: developmentally inappropriate expectations/tasks for the child
- Biologic: Tourette syndrome, fragile X, CNS infection, head trauma, seizure disorder, thyroid illness, sensory impairment, severe iron deficiency or lead poisoning, certain medications, e.g., antihistamines, phenobarbital
- Social: family chaos, environmental and economic stressors
- Emotional/psychiatric: depression, anxiety, low self-esteem, bipolar illness; also abuse and neglect
- Developmental: learning disabilities, autism, sleep disorders, problems of arousal
- Attention deficits, i.e., ADs, a chronic disorder resulting from a primary dysfunction of the CNS

AD, attention disorder; CNS, central nervous system.

---

histories, for example, perinatal, medical, development, social-emotional, and family (parenting style, beliefs and perceptions, marital discord, and environmental stresses are worth noting). The family history also should assess relatives' attention, learning, behavior, affect, temperament, and alcohol or drug use. Finally, the history should assess the family's perception and knowledge of ADs; expectations for the child; and strengths, coping abilities, and available supports (mainly relatives and friends).

Comprehensive parent and teacher questionnaires like the ANSER system supply much of the above information (Levine, 1996). They are time-efficient, useful supplements to the history that can provide the first essential input from the school. After reviewing the teachers' responses, the clinician also may need to communicate directly with school personnel (teachers, special educators, principals).

RATING SCALES. A diagnosis of ADs should never be made on the basis of any one test. Rating scales are very useful for (1) rating the severity of symptoms of inattention, overactivity, and other behaviors; (2) obtaining multirater, multisite ratings; (3) confirming indications of ADs based on an appropriate evaluation; and (4) monitoring the effectiveness of interventions (e.g., behavioral, pharmacologic). Rating scales should be completed by parents, teachers (several if possible), and other adults who interact with the child, for example, a sports coach or after-school caretaker. Frequently used rating scales (for parents and teachers) are the Conners Rating Scales (multiple versions), Achenbach/Edelbrock Child Behavior Checklist (CBCL), Jellinek Pediatric Checklist (PSC), and ADD-H Comprehensive Teacher Rating Scale (ACTERS) (teacher only). These instruments focus on a range of behavioral and emotional problems in addition to attention deficits. The (parent and teacher) Edelbrock Child Assessment Profile (CAP) covers only activity and attention. The use of only rating scales to make the diagnosis of ADs without an adequate history is inappropriate, as rating scales provide no information about etiology, associated problems, or contextual risk and protective factors.

PHYSICAL EXAMINATION. The physical and neurologic examinations, which include vision and hearing screening, provide another opportunity for direct observation and interaction. As the office visit is a brief and atypical encounter, observations of attention, activity, and mood must be interpreted with caution.

PSYCHOEDUCATIONAL EVALUATION. If learning problems coexist or are suspected, IQ (cognitive) and standardized achievement tests are indicated. The pediatric clinician needs to know that these tests and their IQ–achievement discrepancy formula only determine eligibility for special services. They may overlook children with significant learning problems who need help regardless of their eligibility status.

OTHER EVALUATIONS. Other evaluations might include a referral for genetic, speech and language, fine or gross motor, emotional, or family-social evaluation (also see subchapter, Children and Adolescents Without Friends).

Arriving at the Final Diagnosis

The diagnosis of ADs is an individualized, narrative, specific description of (1) the attention problems, specifically symptom chronicity, severity, and pervasiveness (impacted domains); (2) the affected processing controls (intake, mental energy/arousal, and production); (3) risk and protective factors in the family and environment; and (4) the child's compensating strengths and affinities. Comorbid diagnoses, associated complications, and other findings, if relevant, would complete the descriptive diagnosis. This diagnosis necessarily includes the standard terms ADD or ADHD for billing and coding purposes, but feedback to the child and parents should never be reduced to just these simplistic terms. For example, a brief descriptive diagnosis might read, as follows:

Mary is experiencing long-standing, significant attention problems. Specifically, she is slow to activate her attention at the beginning of each class, at the intake (processing) stage of a new task. She says she is "in a zone" ("Like I'm absent from class") for the first 20 minutes of each class. Her academic performance has been declining for 2 years, especially in those classes which begin promptly with long lectures that require immediate, sustained, focused attention to auditory detail. This year those classes are English, civics, biology, and history. She does better in classes that entail more active learning and less passive listening: interactive dialogues in Spanish; active participation in art and music; and daily quizzes in math. She is also having difficulties with the increased study and organizational demands of the ninth grade curriculum. In addition to her ability to benefit from active involvement in the learning process, she is still highly motivated, participates in soccer, and has several good friends. The family is supportive and actively seeking help. After Mary's initial evaluation by her physician, she was referred for a psycho-educational assessment, which did not reveal a learning disability. Her problems are consistent with a diagnosis of ADs (ADD).

MANAGEMENT AND TREATMENT

An appropriate management and treatment plan should be individualized to the particular child's strengths and weaknesses and directed to the realities and capabilities of the home and school environment. The support and collaboration of teachers and other relevant professionals often are needed, and treatment invariably is multimodal and includes medication, classroom accommodations, parenting advice, and education or demystification. The initial evaluation, diagnosis, and treatment plan may require two office visits and an evaluation or consultation, for example, a psychoeducational assessment.

Demystification

Demystification, an essential component of every child's treatment, is always the first intervention. It is the process of sharing a narrative profile of the child with the family that explains (interprets) the phenomenon of ADs in a nonlabeling, nonstigmatizing, supportive manner with nontechnical, nonmedical language, and using real-life examples as illustrations. For example, the clinician using demystification would help Mary understand how attention problems impact her ability to learn and how she could improve her attention and learning. Demystification "reframes" the problem by correcting negative beliefs and attributions, removing blame, and providing a positive and hopeful description of the child. For example, the clinician explains (in language that is appropriate for the family's level of understanding) that Mary's attention problems stem from a primary neurologic dysfunction affecting her learning skills. This clarification or "reframing" will change the possible perception that Mary makes bad grades because she is stupid or does not care.

Demystification also highlights the strengths of the child and the family and provides optimism and hope. Parents need much information about ADs in order to advocate for their child. Demystification is the beginning of this educational process. Ongoing conversations with the clinician (and other professionals), suggested readings, and information from authoritative resources greatly enhance their understanding.

Educational Support

Approximately 50% of children with ADs also have learning disabilities (LDs), which, if severe enough as measured by the psychoeducational evaluation, make the children eligible for free, federally mandated, school-based special educational services. Children with ADs whose LDs are of insufficient severity to qualify for these services are likely to experience continued academic underachievement. The clinician can be very helpful by informing parents of the different and complex federal laws that provide support for children with ADs and with LD.

Under Public Law 101-476 (1990; revised in 1997), the Individuals with Disabilities Education Act (IDEA), a child with ADs is entitled to a free, school-based psychoeducational evaluation for suspected LDs or behavioral-emotional handicaps (BEHs). If the evaluation reveals significant problems, LDs or BEHs, the child is eligible for special educational services. The clinician should be sure that accommodations for the student's ADs are included in the Individualized Educational Plan (IEP). Other Health Impaired (OHI) is a category of IDEA, and some children with ADs receive special education services under OHI (see subchapter, Learning Problems of Children and Adolescents).

Under Section 504 of the 1973 Federal Rehabilitation Act (Public Law 93-112), children with ADs are entitled to accommodations in the regular classroom so that they receive a "comparable education." These are children with ADs but without documented LDs or BEHs. Selected accommodations are listed in Table 65–13.

The pediatric clinician can help the parents obtain a proper and timely evaluation and then the indicated school support for their child. For example, to obtain accommodations under Section 504, the physician must submit a report documenting an appropriate diagnosis of ADs; the child's specific symptoms, medical history, and physical examination; and a written verification of the child's present status and continuing needs. Teacher reports must verify that the attention problems extend into the classroom and adversely affect the child's ability to learn.

Once the student has support under IDEA or Section 504, the pediatric clinician must work with school-based committees, special education teachers, and regular classroom teachers by giving them information about ADs (especially their impact on learning); suggesting specific strategies and accommodations for the individual child; communicating with teachers about the student's response to medication and other interventions; and resolving conflicts and misunderstandings between the school and parents.

Finally, children who have ADs benefit from after-school tutoring and counseling that target

TABLE 65–13. Classroom Accommodations for Children with Attention Disorders: A Selected Sample

Traditional closed classrooms are preferred (and should be requested) over an open classroom, which magnifies all auditory and visual distraction.

Preferential seating at the front of the class, close to the speaker, and away from high traffic areas (doorways, pencil sharpeners) should be arranged.

All extraneous noises and visual stimuli should be minimized, especially when giving instructions and teaching new concepts.

Teachers should always command the child's attention, if necessary by using verbal or physical cues such as lightly touching the child's shoulder or desk or using a "secret" signal. It is important not to embarrass the student.

Directions should be given in clear, well-articulated, and simply constructed sentences. Complex or compound sentences should be avoided.

Talking slower and frequently restating oral information will aid in comprehension.

Verbal instructions should be accompanied by visual aids (pictures, diagrams, outlines, models) and demonstration.

Since memory is best for real-life events or occurrences, experiental approaches to learning and concrete examples are beneficial.

Periodic feedback should be required from the child to ensure that he or she is listening to the spoken message.

Homework instructions may need to be repeated following each class on an individual basis. Assignment books are helpful.

Teachers should move into new areas of academic instruction gradually, always reviewing past material so that a child can experience some degree of success.

New concepts and vocabulary should be previewed at the beginning of a lesson, reviewed at the end of the lesson, and written on the board.

Lecture outlines should be written on the board and referred to frequently.

attention-related problems, for example, study, test taking, memory, and organizational skills. Excellent resources for parents are *Learning to Learn* by Frender (1990) and *Educational Care* by Levine (1994).

Behavior Management

Before attempting behavior management, the clinician might remind parents that their children want to be successful, gain their parents' approval, and feel loved. They generally do not intentionally want to displease or disappoint their parents. Parents' past efforts and achievements should also be specifically acknowledged. Sometimes, parents feel so angry, disappointed, and hopeless that they forget all the good things about their children and themselves.

Behavioral intervention strategies have varying degrees of success for several reasons: (1) Most behavioral and emotional problems take place within a relationship; therefore, parents need to modify their own behavior, emotional responses, and interactional patterns as they attempt to effect the same for their children; (2) the impulsivity, disinhibition, and weak feedback receptivity of children with ADs tend to minimize effects of these strategies when used in isolation; (3) the busy primary care clinician usually does not have the time or expertise to make a functional analysis of the behavior (determining the various influences), implement a set of strategies, and provide close follow-up and support.

Behavioral problems, if present, vary in severity, as do attention deficits. Children with mild to moderate problems who have compliant, capable, and caring parents may benefit from a counseling session with their primary care clinicians. The clinicians should be experienced, have adequate time, and know the family and the child. A plan of periodic follow-up visits and selected readings could be initiated. If the problems exceed the physician's capabilities or availability, the child should be referred to a behavioral pediatrician, psychologist, or other professional who can provide supplementary guidance.

General interventions for all children include (1) emphasizing positive reinforcement (e.g., contingent praise, rewards, tokens, and hugs) rather than correction procedures (e.g., mild punishments, criticism, and verbal reprimands); (2) avoiding corporal punishment; (3) using extinction techniques, that is, systematically ignoring (not reinforcing) undesirable behaviors; (4) using time-out (a brief quiet interval to stop unwanted behavior); (5) providing choices and alternatives; (6) helping the child make decisions; (7) giving the child appropriate responsibility and trust; and (8) increasing the child's motivation, confidence, and ability to self-regulate.

Children with ADs need these interventions because of their impulsivity, disinhibition, and problems adhering to rules or instructions. Consequences must be like the cause-and-effect feedback of a Nintendo or pinball game: very rapid or immediate, very specific or concrete, very frequent, and very intense (emphasizing positives). Children with ADs need schedules, routines, predictability, organization, and order. Tasks and activities should be divided into small, manageable "chunks," and directions limited to only two or three sequences. When speaking, parents and teachers should address the child by name, establish eye contact, assume a pleasant facial expression, and speak in a calm, firm, authoritative tone of voice. Parents should demonstrate the desired task or action. Goals and expectations must be realistic and continuously re-evaluated so that both parent and child experience success. Excellent recommendations are offered in the books by McCarney and Bauer and by Barkley in Further Reading at the end of the subchapter.

Other Related Interventions

Other related interventions are biofeedback, relaxation techniques, and cognitive-behavioral therapy, techniques that enhance perceptions of self-efficacy and develop self-directed coping strategies and problem-solving skills.

Social-Emotional Support

Children with ADs often have deficient social skills. Executing the tasks of a social interaction (initiation, maintenance, disagreement or conflict resolution, and closure) may be especially difficult. Peer and family relationships are often strained. Many children with ADs experience low self-esteem, depression, and anxiety. Sometimes family stresses (marital, financial, career) exacerbate the child's ADs. Social skills training, individual psychotherapy (possibly including medication), and family therapy can be very beneficial.

Maintaining Strengths and Avoiding Humiliation

Every child has strengths, interests, and affinities, sometimes unrecognized or underdeveloped, that serve as compensations for and buffers against failure and loss of motivation. They need to be rediscovered, nurtured, and given high-profile status. Parents should be aware of high-risk or humiliating situations, for example, a large, unstructured birthday party, a long religious service, or a teacher who publicly reprimands a child or refers to his or her medication in front of the class.

Medication

The success of modern medications has contributed to unrealistic expectations and overreliance on medication. This is often exacerbated by shorter office visits and managed care policies that have resulted in brief "med check" visits. Prescriptions for stimulant medication doubled every 4 to 7 years during the 1970s and 1980s.

Medications are very effective, indeed the fastest-acting, single most effective intervention, for treating the symptoms of ADs. **Medication should never be used, however, as the only treatment for ADs. Medications allow the child to better attend to and hence to appreciate and benefit from the indicated behavioral, social, emotional, and educational interventions.** Medications alone do not influence long-term academic or career/occupational outcome. Primary care clinicians should never let their role be reduced to the "prescription scribe" or the "pill pusher." The option to prescribe medication provides an opportunity to evaluate and advocate for the child.

Psychostimulants, the medications of choice, have a beneficial effect in approximately 80% of children with ADs. The most frequently prescribed stimulants are methylphenidate (90%), dextroamphetamine sulfate (Dexedrine) (8%), and pemoline (2%). They are safe and well-tolerated, and their side effects tend to be mild and transient. If a child does not respond to a particular stimulant, the physician should check patient compliance, the dose, and the schedule and consider changing to a short-acting or to a long-acting form, combining short- and long-acting forms, or changing to another stimulant. Tricyclic antidepressants are effective alternatives but they do have considerable side effects.

Alpha$_2$-adrenergic agonists are effective alone or in combination with stimulants for (1) very overactive, disruptive, and aggressive children who do not respond to stimulants alone or who experience adverse side effects; (2) children with significant "rebound" effects (irritability, hyperactivity) as the stimulant wears off; and (3) children

TABLE 65–14. Selected Medications for Attention Disorders

Name	How Supplied	Duration	Suggested Dosage	Side Effects
Psychostimulants				
Methylphenidate (Ritalin)	5-, 10-, 20-mg tablets; SR 20-mg tabs	Approx. 3–4 hr; SR 20: 6–8 hr	Usual starting dose: 0.3–0.5 mg/kg per dose not usually exceeding 2 mg/kg daily (bid, tid)	Most common: anorexia, weight loss, insomnia, rebound, abdominal pain, headaches, nausea, and tics.
Dextroamphetamine (Dexedrine)	5-mg tablets; 5-, 10-, 15-mg spansules (long-acting)	3–4 hr; spansules: 6–8 hr	Usual starting dose: Ages 3–5: 2.5 mg Over 6: 5 mg (daily, bid) not usually exceeding 40 mg daily*†	Less common: tachycardia, blood pressure elevation, nervousness, skin rashes, hives, dizziness, lowered CBC and platelet counts; abnormal liver function (Cylert).
Dextroamphetamine (Dextrostat)	5 scored and 10 double-scored tablets (short-acting)	3–4 hr	Usual starting dose: Ages 3–5: 2.5 mg Over 6: 5 mg (daily, bid) not usually exceeding 40 mg daily*†	See Dexedrine.
Dextroamphetamine and amphetamine (Adderall)	5-, 10-, 20-, 30-mg tablets (long-acting), double-scored	6–8 hr	Usual starting dose: Ages 3–5: 2.5 mg Over 6: 5 mg (daily, bid) not usually exceeding 40 mg daily	See Dexedrine.
Pemoline (Cylert)	18.75-, 37.5-, 75-mg tablets; chewable tablets, 37.5 mg	Each morning	Usual starting dose: 18.75–37.5 mg; increase by 18.75 to max. 112.5 mg	See Dexedrine.
Alpha$_2$-Adrenergic Agonists				
Clonidine (Catapres)	0.1-, 0.2-, 0.3-mg tablets; 0.1-, 0.2-, 0.3-mg transdermal	6–8 hr; transdermal: 7 days	Usual starting dose: .025–0.1 mg (daily, bid, tid); useful at bedtime; not usually exceeding 0.3–0.4 mg daily	Headaches, sedation, depression, dry mouth, hypotension; skin reaction; avoid abrupt discontinuation; do not combine tricyclic antidepressants.
Guanfacine (Tenex)	1-, 2-mg tablets	8–12 hr	0.5–1.0 mg (daily, bid); not usually exceeding 2 mg daily	See Clonidine.

CBC, complete blood cell count; SR, sustained-release; bid, twice a day; tid, three times a day.
*Usually thought to be 25%–30% more potent than methylphenidate, so 10 mg of methylphenidate is usually equivalent to 7.5 mg of amphetamines.
†If food-sensitive to Dexedrine, try Dextrostat and vice versa.

with sleep-arousal disorders (either primary or as a side effect). When added to stimulant medication, the dose of stimulant alone should be reduced by 25% to 50%. Agonists calm the child but do not necessarily enhance attention and concentration. The clinician needs to be very familiar with all aspects of these medications (Table 65–14).

Referral

Referral or consultation should be obtained from experienced behavioral-developmental pediatricians or child psychiatrists if the primary care clinician does not have the time to initiate trials of medication, to monitor responses and side effects, to educate children and parents about medication (e.g., mechanism, drug holidays, discontinuation, abuse of medications), or to answer questions about other medications (e.g., antidepressants for comorbid depression).

AN EXAMPLE OF MANAGEMENT AND TREATMENT

The treatment plan should fit the evaluation and is invariably multimodal. Using the descriptive diagnosis of Mary given above, a treatment plan might include

1. Ongoing demystification (based on a developmental perspective of ADs) and anticipatory guidance as integral parts of follow-up visits.
2. Selected accommodations under Section 504 (see Table 65–13) and having the parents discuss the evaluation with the teacher.
3. Weekly after-school tutoring to develop organizational skills, including having Mary learn how to write brief outlines of topics to be discussed in upcoming class lectures. This provides a visual aid (the outline) to enhance her listening and organizational abilities. Teachers would give her lists of weekly lecture topics and related readings. Teacher and tutor should communicate and collaborate.
4. A trial of stimulant medication: Dexedrine, 5-mg tablet, and Dexedrine, 5-mg spansule, taken together at 7:30 A.M. The tablet would give her the quick boost she needs for her first class and the spansule would cover her for the rest of the morning (when the lectures occur). It also avoids the embarrassment of taking medication at school. Pharmacologic therapy requires rating scales and teacher-physician communication and collaboration.
5. Maintenance of Mary's strengths and interests.

6. Long-term follow-up and continued advocacy.

FURTHER READING

For Professionals

Achenbach T and Edelbrock C: Manual for the Child Behavior Checklist and Revised Behavior Profile. Burlington, VT, Department of Psychiatry, University of Vermont, 1983.

Barkley R: Attention Deficit Hyperactivity Disorder. New York, Guilford Press, 1990.

Coleman WL and Levine MD: Attention deficits in adolescence: Description, evaluation, and management. Pediatr Rev 9:287–298, 1988.

Culbert TP, Banez GA, and Reiff MI: Children who have attentional problems: Interventions. Pediatr Rev 15:5–14, 1994.

Gephart HR: A managed care approach to ADHD. Contemp Pediatr 14(5):123–139, 1997.

Green M (ed): Bright Futures: Guidelines for Health Supervision of Infants, Children, and Adolescents. Arlington, VA, National Center for Education in Maternal and Child Health, 1994.

Jellinek MS and Murphy JM: The recognition of psychosocial disorders in pediatric office practice: the current status of the Pediatric Symptom Checklist. J Dev Behav Pediatr 11:273–278, 1990.

Kelly DP and Aylward GP: Attention deficits in children and adolescents. Pediatr Clin North Am 39:487–512, 1992.

Levine MD: ANSER System. Cambridge, MA, Educators Publishing, 1996.

Levine MD: Developmental Variation and Learning Disorders, 2nd ed. Cambridge, MA, Educators Publishing Service, 1998.

Reiff MI, Banez GA, and Culbert TP: Children who have attentional disorders: Diagnosis and evaluation. Pediatr Rev 14:455–465, 1993.

Wolraich ML (ed): Diagnostic and Statistical Manual for Primary Care (DSM-PC) Child and Adolescent Version. PO Box 927, Elk Grove Village, IL 60009-0927. American Academy of Pediatrics Press, 1996

For Parents

Barkley RA: Taking Charge of ADHD: The Complete Authoritative Guide for Parents. New York, Guilford, 1995.

Clark L: The Time Out Solution. Chicago, Contemporary Books, 1989.

Dreikurs R: Children: The Challenge. New York, Hawthorn-Dutton, 1964.

Faber A and Mazlish E: How to Talk So Kids Will Listen and Listen So Kids Will Talk. New York, Avon, 1980.

Frender G: Learning to Learn. Nashville TN, Incentive Publisher, 1990. (Call 910-996-3090; Fax: 910-996-8023. Write IESS, Inc, Box 432, Kernersville, NC 27285.) (An excellent source for study and organizational skills.)

Gordon T: Parent Effectiveness Training. New York, Penguin, 1970.

Kurcinka MS: Raising Your Spirited Child. New York, Harper Perennial, 1991.

Kutner L: Parent and Child: Getting Through to Each Other. New York, Morrow, 1991.

Levine MD: Educational Care. Cambridge, MA, Educators Publishing Service, 1994.

McCarney SB and Bauer AM: The Parent's Guide to Attention Deficit Disorders: Intervention Strategies for the Home. Columbia, MO, Hawthorne Press, 1995. (Call 573-874-1710.

Write Hawthorne Press, 800 Gray Oak Drive, Columbia, MO 65201.) (This is an excellent source of practical and realistic interventions.)

Schor EL (ed): Caring For Your School-Age Child Ages 5 to 12. New York, Bantam, 1995. (Sponsored by the AAP.)

Attention Disorder Resources

ADD Association, Child and Family Center, Suite C 14, 801 Encino Place, Albuquerque, NM 87102. Phone: 800-413-3902.

CHADD (Children and Adults with Attention Deficit Disor-

ders), 1859 North Pine Island Road, Suite 185, Plantation, FL. Phone: 954-587-3700

Hawthorne Educational Services, Inc., 800 Gray Oak Drive, Columbia, MO 65201. Phone: 800-542-1673 or 573-874-1710. A catalog offers a variety of books (by prominent experts) for professionals and parents on attention, learning, study, behavioral, self-esteem, and social skills problems.

Learning Disabilities Association of America, 4156 Library Road, Pittsburgh, PA 15243. Phone: 412-341-1515.

National ADD Association, Albuquerque, NM.

National Center for Learning Disabilities, 381 Park Avenue South, Suite 1420, New York, NY 10016. Phone: 212-545-7510.

Carolyn H. Frazer
Leonard A. Rappaport

Somatic Complaints in Children and Adolescents: Recurrent Headache; Abdominal, Chest, and Limb Pains

DEFINITION AND IMPACT ON CHILD'S FUNCTION

School-age and adolescent children present frequently to the pediatrician with recurrent pain complaints. **In the vast majority of cases, the pains are benign and do not represent a serious disease process. However, the impact of recurrent pain can be significant on the functioning of the child and family.** Evaluating and managing recurrent pain in children can be quite challenging for the pediatrician. Both the family and pediatrician may feel frustration with the chronic and recurrent nature of the pain and fear an underlying organic disease; however, the clinician who uses a family-centered and supportive style in concert with an organized medical approach can successfully evaluate and manage children with recurrent pain complaints in the ambulatory setting.

Traditionally, causes for pain in children have been categorized as either physical or psychosomatic. More recent formulations have suggested that the child's experience of pain is multifaceted and has physical, emotional, and functional aspects regardless of the etiology (Fig. 65–1). In the multisystem model, a physiologic pain stimulus, which in most cases we do not yet understand, is modified by the child's personal characteristics and environment to produce a unique individual

pain experience. For example, family attitudes and behavioral patterns may reinforce and even magnify a child's pain or help contain it. There may be secondary gain for a child experiencing pain, such as extra attention from a parent. The pain, in turn, impacts the child and environment, ultimately affecting the child's general functioning.

GENERAL APPROACH: FAMILY-CENTERED CARE

One of the most challenging aspects for the pediatrician in managing children with recurrent pain complaints is parents' frustration and fear that their child has a serious or even potentially fatal disease. The first step in the caring process is to create an alliance with the family by offering education and support and jointly developing an evaluation and management plan. Acknowledging from the beginning that there are multiple contributors to pain and that often a specific cause cannot be identified allows the family and clinician to have similar expectations and establish a working partnership. The clinician should obtain an understanding of the child's pain experience in the broader context of family, school, and peers. Additionally, the clinician must identify organic disease, relieve pain if possible, and support the

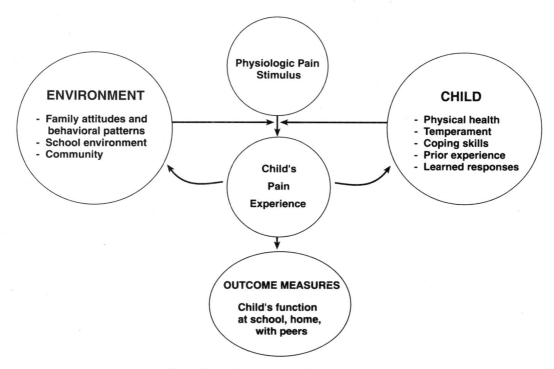

Figure 65–1. Multisystem model for recurrent pain.

child's functioning despite pain if pain relief is unlikely. **Long-term follow-up and continued support are the keys to managing recurrent pains.**

EVALUATION

History

The most important part of the evaluation is the history. Both child and parents should be interviewed, and the older child and adolescent should be interviewed alone. Through the history, information about the specific characteristics, temporal course, associated symptoms, and exacerbating or relieving factors should be obtained. A past medical history and family medical history help to identify any possible organic factors that might relate to the pain. A full review of systems related to the pain complaint is necessary, as is a wider historical review for systemic disease. The social history provides information about possible stressors, family function, and behavior patterns that may contribute to the pain. In addition, an understanding of the impact of the pain on the function of the child and family and their response to the pain is crucial. How is the pain handled at home? For example, is there any secondary gain resulting

from the pain? What is the child's function at school and home? How many days of school are missed, if any? Are there any other stressors at home or school that may be contributing to the child's ability to cope with pain? Next, find out about the family's concept of pain and prior experiences of pain. What led to the present visit? Are there any hidden fears about the pain? What are the family and child seeking from the visit?

Physical and Laboratory Examinations

A complete physical examination and, in some situations, a limited directed laboratory screening exclude most organic disease in the child with recurrent pains. **In the absence of "red flags" on history, physical examination, and laboratory tests, organic disease is very unlikely.** The physical examination should include an assessment of growth, potential signs of chronic disease, full neurologic examination, and behavioral observation. Laboratory screening is guided by the specific complaint. Refer to the guidelines and "red flags" listed with specific recurrent pain complaints.

Management

Once the clinician feels comfortable with the diagnosis of a recurrent pain syndrome, the next steps are reassuring the family that the child does not have a serious disease and explaining what is going on. A discussion of the model for pain and the numerous contributors to the child's pain help alleviate fears about the need to do further tests. **It is important to acknowledge that the child's pain is real and not give the impression that you think it is "all in his or her head."** You must also discuss the chronic and potentially recurrent nature of the pain syndrome so that the child and family have appropriate expectations. **The goal in management is to relieve pain if possible but, more importantly, to help the child maintain or regain normal functioning at school, at home, and with peers.** For example, school attendance is crucial despite the pain. The child should be encouraged to participate in regular activities, and potential behavioral patterns that may be reinforcing the pain need to be identified and changed if possible. The goal is to avoid what Barr has termed an "extended syndrome," where

the child's pain impacts more broadly on his or her overall functioning. Psychologic support should be offered to the child and the family in the form of regular follow-up visits with the clinician and formal counseling if indicated. Additional therapies such as biofeedback, hypnosis, and relaxation may help improve the child's ability to cope with pain (Fig. 65–2).

Specific Complaints

RECURRENT ABDOMINAL PAIN (RAP). RAP is the most common recurrent pain complaint in children and typically occurs in 10% to 15% of school-age children. The pain is vague and ill-defined, periumbilical, and crampy in nature. It may last for up to 30 minutes daily but is typically more sporadic and must be present for at least 3 consecutive months to make a diagnosis of RAP. Although the exact cause is not known, there are theories (with controversial support from labora-

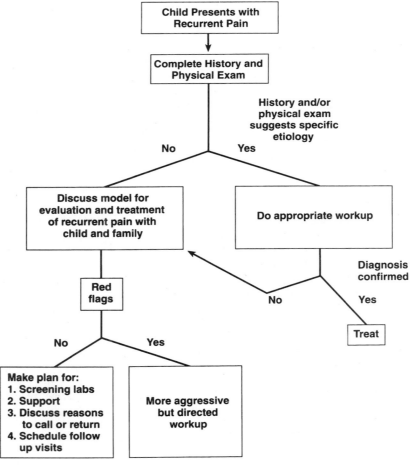

Figure 65–2. Management of recurrent pain.

tory studies) that implicate abnormalities in the autonomic system affecting gut motility or gut responses to peptides. In about 10% of cases, there is an organic cause, usually related to gastrointestinal or genitourinary disease. A small number of children with RAP may have lactose intolerance or constipation contributing to their pain. In other children, there may be *Giardia* infection. Children with symptoms of gastritis (vomiting, epigastric pain) may have *Helicobacter pylori* infection.

Workup. History, physical examination, and laboratory screening should be focused on the red flags listed below. The laboratory screening should be limited in the absence of specific symptoms: a complete blood count (CBC), erythrocyte sedimentation rate (ESR), urinalysis (UA), urine culture in girls, and in some cases *Giardia* antigen or lactose breath test.

Red Flags

Pain farther from the umbilicus or localized
Pain that is severe and wakens child from sleep
Changes in bowel or bladder function
Hematuria or hematochezia
Fever, weight loss, rash, or joint pain or swelling
Anemia
Elevated ESR or white blood cell (WBC) count
Blood or WBC on UA
Guaiac-positive stool test

Treatment. There are many suggested treatments for RAP; however, few have been studied rigorously. In a controlled trial by Feldman and coworkers (1985), adding fiber to the diet helped decrease the frequency and severity of pain in children with RAP. In cases of lactose intolerance, eliminating dairy products is helpful. Counseling and relaxation techniques may also improve a child's function and ability to cope with pain.

Prognosis. Over time, about one third of children have continuation of their pain chronically, about one third have resolution of pain, and about one third may develop other recurrent pain, such as headaches or irritable bowel syndrome, in adolescence or adulthood.

RECURRENT LIMB PAINS. Limb pains are the second most common type of recurrent pain in school-age children. These pains are commonly referred to as "growing pains" and are rarely associated with underlying disease. The pains typically present in middle childhood, occur late in the day, and may waken the child from sleep. The pain is intermittent but must be present for at least 3 months to make a diagnosis. Usually, pain is localized to the lower extremities. In addition, the pain may include but must not be local-

ized to the joints, and the physical examination must be normal.

Workup. History, physical examination, and any laboratory studies should focus on identifying any organic disease indicated by the red flags outlined below. Careful examination of the involved extremities, including skin and joint examinations, is mandatory. Laboratory screening should be guided by history and physical and may include a radiograph or other imaging.

Red Flags

Joint pain or swelling, limited range of motion
Limb deformity, swelling, bruising, redness
Focal pain reproducible on palpation
Fever
Rash
Elevated ESR or WBC
Abnormal radiograph

Treatment. Treatment is usually symptomatic in the absence of identified diseases. For example, hot baths may offer relief to some children. The most important goal is to maintain the child's normal functioning and activity. Limiting activity does not improve symptoms.

Prognosis. There is no information on the long-term prognosis for limb pains specifically. Approximately one third of children with limb pain may simultaneously have recurrent abdominal pain or headaches.

RECURRENT HEADACHES. Headaches are quite common in childhood. A subgroup of 5% to 15% of children suffer from recurrent tension or migraine headaches. Tension headaches are typically frequent, have a symmetric distribution for pain, and manifest few associated symptoms. They are thought to be secondary to muscle contraction with resultant ischemia and pain. Migraines are caused by paroxysmal vasoconstriction and vasodilation of cerebral blood vessels and may be unilateral or bilateral in children. They are frequently accompanied by nausea and visual, sensory, or motor symptoms. Children may experience an aura but have difficulty describing it. Some children may have a mixed pattern of both tension and migraine headaches. Tension and migraine headaches are benign, as there are no long-term sequelae and they are not associated with progressive disease. However, children who present with acute-onset or chronic progressive headaches are more likely to have a serious cause, such as an intracerebral hemorrhage or brain tumor.

Workup. A thorough history and complete physical examination including blood pressure, head circumference, and funduscopic and neurologic examinations identify children at risk for more serious disorders. Depending on the findings from history and physical examination, it is occasionally appropriate to obtain brain imaging studies. Unless a seizure disorder is specifically suspected from the history or physical examination, an electroencephalogram is rarely helpful.

Red Flags

Severe, focal pain that awakens child from sleep
Pain worse in early morning or when lying down
Vomiting
Papilledema, visual changes
Focal neurologic findings
Personality or behavior change
Seizures
Fever, rash, weight loss
Crescendo pattern with progressive worsening of pain

Treatment. Most adults believe that children do not get headaches; therefore, education is essential. Treatment for tension or functional headaches includes analgesics and, in some cases, tricyclic antidepressants. For the acute phase of migraines, serotonergic agents and ergotamine compounds decrease vasodilation and thus pain. Antiemetics may be needed if nausea is severe. For migraine prophylaxis, propranolol and cyproheptadine may be helpful. Diet modification (decreasing chocolate, coffee, and dairy products) may reduce episodes of migraine.

Prognosis. Most children with recurrent nonprogressive headaches can be managed successfully with behavioral and medical interventions.

RECURRENT CHEST PAIN. As with headache, chest pain in a child produces anxiety and fear in parents of a serious and dangerous condition. For the clinician, the child with acute chest pain requires prompt assessment to rule out any serious cause. The likelihood of a cardiorespiratory cause for chest pain is higher in younger children than in adolescents. However, the majority of chest pain in children is musculoskeletal or pleuritic rather than cardiac. Thus, as with other recurrent pain complaints, a careful history and physical examination either identifies or excludes most organic disease.

Workup. History and physical examination should focus on the red flags listed below with the goal being to identify serious causes such as cardiac disease, pulmonary embolus, gastric reflux, or esophagitis. A full physical examination must be completed and should include cardiorespiratory examination, blood pressure, and assessment of pulses. Cardiac arrhythmia, such as supraventricular tachycardia, may be experienced by children as brief, sharp chest pain. Reproduction of the pain with deep breathing suggests pleuritic pain, and pain reproduced with chest wall pressure is more likely musculoskeletal in origin.

Red Flags

Young age
Worse with exertion
Crushing chest pain; pain that awakens child from sleep
Hypo- or hypertension
Tachycardia
Syncope
Heart murmur, rhythm abnormality
Rales or wheezing
Systemic symptoms such as weight loss, chronic fatigue, fever
Marfanoid habitus
Family history of hypertrophic cardiomyopathy, Marfan or Ehlers-Danlos syndromes
Abnormal chest radiography or electrocardiography

Treatment. If the pain is from a benign cause, education of the family and reassurance is critical because of the frightening nature of chest pain for most families. Let the family know that chest pain in children, in contrast to adults, rarely has a serious cause or results in a long-term problem. Treatment for benign chest pain is symptomatic. For example, analgesics may be used. Counseling or relaxation therapies may be helpful.

Prognosis. As many as 45% of children presenting to the emergency room setting with acute chest pain will be experiencing the pain 6 months later, indicating that acute chest pain often becomes a more chronic or recurrent complaint.

SUMMARY

School-age children and adolescents frequently present with recurrent pain complaints such as headache or abdominal, chest, or limb pain. The majority of these complaints are benign in nature but impact significantly on the functioning of the child and family. The primary care clinician can successfully manage this group of challenging patients in the ambulatory setting using a multisystem model for pain to guide the history and physical examination, creating an alliance with the family and jointly developing an evaluation and management plan. Ongoing support and long-term follow-up are crucial to successful management. The goal is to identify any organic disease, treat the pain when possible, and avoid an "extended syndrome" by promoting normal functioning in the child at school, at home, and with peers.

FURTHER READING

Abu-Arafeh I and Russell G: Recurrent limb pain in school-children. Arch Dis Child 74:336–339, 1996.

Barr R: Recurrent abdominal pain. *In* Levine M, Carey W, Crocker A, and Gross R (eds): Developmental-Behavioral Pediatrics. Philadelphia, WB Saunders, 1983, pp 521–528.

Feldman W, McGrath P, Hodgson C, et al.: The use of dietary fiber in the management of simple, childhood, idiopathic, recurrent, abdominal, pain: Results in a prospective, double-blind, randomized, control trial. Am J Dis Child 139:1216–1218, 1985.

Frazer C and Rappaport L: Recurrent abdominal pain: Keeping it simple. Ambulatory Child Health 1:370–378, 1996.

Rothner A: Headache. *In* Swaiman K (ed): Pediatric Neurology: Principles and Practice. St. Louis, CV Mosby, 1989, pp 185–191.

Selbst S: Chest pain in children. Pediatr Rev 18:169–173, 1997.

Marc Fishman
Ann B. Bruner
Hoover Adger, Jr.

Substance Abuse Among Children and Adolescents*

Alcohol and other drug (AOD) use poses a serious threat to the health of children and adolescents. In addition to the health risks inherent with alcohol and other drug use, substance abuse often is linked with other risk behaviors such as early sexual activity, violence, academic failure, truancy or dropping out of school, and delinquency.

EPIDEMIOLOGY

In 1995 almost 40% of high school seniors reported use of some type of illicit drug in the previous 12 months, compared with 30% in 1991. Alcohol is the most common drug of abuse. In 1994 nearly 90% of high school seniors reported alcohol use, more than 50% in the past month and 5% daily. Marijuana is the illicit drug used most widely—more than 40% of 1995 high school seniors reported some use, 21% in the past month and 5% daily. Cocaine use increased during the 1980s; 6% of 1991 high school seniors reported having used cocaine, and 3% had used "crack."

The age at first use has decreased, and many adolescents use multiple drugs. Alcohol and drug use are associated with the major causes of death in teenagers—injuries, homicide, and suicide.

DEFINITIONS

The criteria for diagnosing substance abuse and dependence in *The Diagnostic and Statistical*

Manual of Mental Disorders (*DSM-IV*) recognize the variability but focus on the maladaptive patterns and impairment rather than on social positions or moral judgments (Table 65–15). The use of progressively larger amounts and preoccupation with activities necessary to access drugs are characteristic of dependence.

ETIOLOGY

No single etiology can account for all types of substance abuse. Substance abuse and dependence are examples of disorders reflecting a biopsychosocial determination. As with all behavioral disorders, the etiology of substance use disorders is multifactorial; despite all that has been learned about the heredity and neurobiology of addictions, it does not appear that a reductionist approach will ever replace a multidimensional or multifactorial view.

Substances of abuse share a unique property: All are capable of producing euphoria and changing one's perception of reality. Once initiated, addiction carries its own autonomous momentum that is not reducible to any single pathophysiology or "underlying" disorder. For adolescents, such use may decrease stress; relieve unhappiness, fear, or depression; offer peer acceptance; and provide a cheap and easy "high." All chemically dependent adolescents have many reasons for AOD use, and they can state multiple conditions that would keep them from substance use (e.g., "If only my parents would stop bugging me"), but there is no simple answer to why some develop an addiction and others do not.

---

*Adapted from Fishman M, Bruner A, and Adger H Jr: Substance abuse among children and adolescents. Pediatr Rev 18:394–403, 1997.

TABLE 65–15. Definition of Substance Abuse and Dependence from *DSM-IV*

A. Substance Abuse

A maladaptive pattern of substance use leading to clinically significant impairment or distress, as manifested by one (or more) of the following, occurring within a 12-month period:

1. Recurrent substance use resulting in a failure to fulfill major role obligations at work, school, or home.
2. Recurrent substance use in situations in which it is physically hazardous.
3. Recurrent substance-related legal problems.
4. Continued substance use despite having persistent or recurrent social or interpersonal problems caused or exacerbated by the effects of the substance.

The symptoms have never met the criteria for Substance Dependence for this class of substance.

B. Substance Dependence

A maladaptive pattern of substance use, leading to clinically significant impairment or distress, as manifested by three (or more) of the following, occurring at any time in the same 12-month period:

1. Tolerance, as defined by either of the following:
   a. Need for markedly increased amounts to achieve intoxication or desired effect.
   b. Markedly diminished effect with continued use of the same amount.
2. Withdrawal, as manifested by either of the following:
   a. The characteristic withdrawal syndrome for the substance.
   b. The same (or a closely related) substance is taken to relieve or avoid withdrawal.
3. The substance often is taken in larger amounts or over a longer period than was intended.
4. A persistent desire or unsuccessful efforts to cut down or control substance use.
5. A great deal of time is spent in activities necessary to obtain the substance, use the substance, or recover from its effects.
6. Important social, occupational, or recreational activities are given up or reduced because of substance use.
7. The substance use is continued despite knowledge of having a persistent or recurrent physical or psychologic problem that is likely to have been caused or exacerbated by the substance.

Adapted with permission from the Diagnostic and Statistical Manual of Mental Disorders, Fourth Edition. Copyright 1994, American Psychiatric Association.

Although risk factors may help to identify those who are most vulnerable, all individuals who exhibit them do not inevitably develop problems. It is helpful to look at AOD use and abuse on a continuum. For some, experimental or casual use progresses to heavy use and dependency; for others, even experimental or casual use can lead to tragic outcomes, including death. Hence, it is important to recognize that all adolescents are at risk, but some are at substantially more risk than others.

DISEASE MODEL. First formulated for alcoholism, the disease model has become increasingly popular. Its strengths have been to destigmatize addiction and encourage treatment; its weaknesses include the potential for patients to deny responsibility for their behavior and for professionals to emphasize biologic causes.

NEUROBIOLOGIC FACTORS. Each of the drugs of abuse has complex and different effects on the central nervous system. These include differential affinities and actions of the classes of opiate receptors; dopamine reuptake inhibition by cocaine at the presynaptic terminal; γ-aminobutyric acid modulation by benzodiazepines, barbiturates, and alcohol; and interaction of lysergic acid diethylamide (LSD) and other hallucinogens at serotonin and glutamate receptors. In addition, research on reward pathways that can mediate the reinforcing properties of these drugs has contributed to our understanding of the neurobiology of addiction. Endogenous opiate reward circuits may serve as a final common pathway for many drugs of abuse. This has had particular clinical relevance for naltrexone, the opiate blocker used in the treatment of alcohol and other drug dependencies.

GENETIC FACTORS. Genetics plays an important role in determining one's predisposition for developing AOD use disorders. The presence of first- and second-degree relatives who are AOD-dependent is a major risk factor for the development of addiction. Children of alcoholics are four to six times more likely to develop alcoholism than are others in the general population. Some research suggests that genetic factors account for about 30% of the variance in familial transmission of alcoholism; the extension of these results to other addictive disorders is supported by some studies.

Some work has suggested that a genetic marker, the A1 allele of the D_2 dopamine receptor on chromosome 11, may be associated with some types of alcoholism. Other promising avenues of research on the heritability of and vulnerability to alcoholism have emphasized the possible role of tolerance. Sons of alcoholic fathers have been shown to have increased alcohol tolerance regardless of their personal alcohol histories and even at their first exposure. The putative mechanism is that the lack of early aversive effects (e.g., hangover, dysphoria, and nausea) in genetically tolerant individuals may contribute to greater salience of reinforcing effects, earlier escalation of dose, and increased early exposure. It is hoped that a better understanding of both biologic and environmental factors will lead to the causes underlying these disorders.

FAMILY AND ENVIRONMENTAL FACTORS. Household drug use, especially parental use, is a major risk factor for initiation and progression of adolescent substance abuse. Exposure to and modeling of substance use and abuse behaviors, as well as exposure to the substances themselves, are likely major mechanisms. Although transient familial disruption such as divorce is not predictive of adolescent substance abuse, *ongoing* disruption of families (persistent chaos in living situations, relationships, etc.) is a major risk factor. The importance of parental attitudes toward drug use is often underestimated. Parental tolerance of drugs, independent of parental use, correlates positively with adolescent AOD use. This is true particularly for "gateway" drugs (tobacco, alcohol, marijuana), in which parents might initially think "it's not that big of a deal. . . ." Poor parental monitoring and supervision, as well as antisocial behaviors, are independent risk factors for adolescent substance abuse. Childhood physical or sexual abuse has not been shown to be an independent risk factor for adolescent AOD use, although parental substance abuse is related very strongly to child abuse and neglect. Conversely, there are protective factors: Families who have clear, parent-defined conduct norms; adolescents who have close emotional ties to their parents; adolescents who have siblings intolerant of AOD use; the continuation of consistency around important family activities or "rituals," such as vacations, mealtimes, and holidays; and the consistent presence of significant others in the life of the child or adolescent.

One of the strongest risk factors for adolescent substance abuse is AOD use in the peer group. Some authors describe the peer group metaphorically as the "vector" for transmission similar to infectious disease models; conversely, a nondrug-using peer group is a known protective factor. Discontinuity of a peer group, such as moving or changing schools, increases vulnerability transiently. The power of the peer group reflects both its influence in shaping attitudes, values, and behaviors and the selection of a peer group based on shared values and behaviors.

Research has demonstrated that age at first exposure as well as age at first intoxication are highly correlated with development and progression of substance abuse. The earlier a young person begins to drink alcohol or use other drugs, the higher the likelihood of his or her later developing AOD problems.

PERSONALITY FACTORS. The notion that there might be an "addictive personality" has not been supported; however, certain personality traits do increase vulnerability to addiction. Excitement-seeking, mood lability, easy boredom, extroversion, decreased attention span, "difficult" temperament, aggressiveness, and insecurity all have been implicated as vulnerability factors. Conversely, obsessiveness or carefulness seems to be a protective factor.

PSYCHOLOGIC FACTORS. Psychopathology and behavioral difficulties of all sorts during childhood and adolescence are associated with higher subsequent rates of addictive disorders. Antisocial, delinquent, and criminal behaviors often are predictive of and coincident with problem drug use in adolescents. For many adolescents, substance abuse is part of a broader pattern of deviant problem behaviors in numerous spheres. Cognitive disability, attention-deficit hyperactivity disorder, mood disorders, anxiety disorders, and problems of impulse control and aggression all have been linked with substance abuse. Poor academic performance, truancy, and dropping out of school are other such risk factors.

ASSESSMENT

The HEADS examination (Table 65–16) is a useful psychosocial risk behavior screening tool. With adolescents, interviewing style is extremely important. Although no single approach is best, one effective method is to begin with general health questions, establishing rapport and confidence by pursuing less controversial and less threatening subjects, using open-ended questions, and then gradually inquiring specifically about risk behaviors. "Probing" questions along the way can include such topics as peer group attitudes and behaviors, drug knowledge, social activities, and parental attitudes. The CAGE mnemonic (Table 65–17) employs useful screening questions.

A comprehensive assessment requires information about the medical, psychologic, behavioral, and social aspects of the patient's life. Because of the broad scope of a comprehensive assessment, some may prefer to make a referral to a substance abuse specialist. Because denial, defensiveness, minimization, and misrepresentation often are core features of abuse and dependence, data gathering can be challenging. Hence, the clinician must anticipate that the truth may be revealed only gradually over time and after many encounters with the adolescent and his or her family. Some sample

TABLE 65–16. The HEADS Psychosocial Screen: Sample Questions

Home
  With whom do you live? What recent changes if any have occurred in your living situation? Have you ever run away from home?

Education/**E**mployment
  Favorite/worst subjects? Any suspensions? Grades compared with those last year? Future plans? Do you have a job? Recent change in schools?

Activities
  What do you do for fun? Sports/exercise? Religious activities? Hobbies? What TV/movies do you like? Do you go to clubs/parties? Ever arrested? How do you get money for things?

Drugs
  Attitudes toward and use of drugs by peers or family? Tobacco use? Ever tried alcohol? Marijuana? Other drugs? How paid for? Ever gotten into trouble related to alcohol or other drug use?

Sexuality/**S**uicide
  Sexual orientation? Sexually experienced? History of STDs/pregnancy? Contraceptive knowledge and use? History of physical/sexual abuse?

STDs, sexually transmitted diseases.
Adapted from Goldenring JM and Cohen E: Getting into adolescent heads. Contemp Pediatr 5:75–90, 1988.

probing questions relevant to AOD use are given in Table 65–18. Finally, no assessment is complete without explicit, directed questioning about individual drugs. General questions about drinking are not sufficient; specific questions about how much beer, wine, or liquor and how often the adolescent drinks alcohol need to be asked. Specific questions about methods of use (smoked, inhaled, injected, swallowed), circumstances of use (clubs or parties, school, home, alone, with friends), subjective effects of use ("What do you like about AODs?"), and consequences of use (hangover and/or trouble with parents, school, law) are important. Questions may need to be asked repeatedly in different ways to obtain the complete history.

Irrespective of the adolescent's level of involvement with AODs, the clinician's initial task is to complete a thorough assessment, provide the adolescent and family accurate and specific infor-

TABLE 65–17. CAGE Screening Questions

Have you ever . . .
  thought about **C**utting down on your AOD use?
  felt **A**nnoyed by criticism from others about your AOD use?
  felt **G**uilty about something that you said or did during your AOD use?
  used AOD as an **E**ye opener or to feel normal?

AOD, alcohol and other drugs.

mation supporting their concerns about AOD use and its negative impact on the adolescent's life, and help the patient and family select an appropriate treatment alternative, if needed.

Urine Drug Screening

Urine drug testing has an important but often misunderstood role in the assessment of substance abuse. Drug screening is not a litmus test for addiction, but rather a spot test for the presence of certain drugs and metabolites. These tests are subject to the limitations of laboratory technical specifications as well as the usual but variable persistence of drugs and metabolites in the body after use. Another limitation of urine drug screening is that a variety of techniques can be used as a way to "beat" the tests, for example, substituting someone else's urine ("clean" urine is a marketable commodity) or masking the urine with additive agents. Although precautions may be used (direct observation, chain of custody procedures, temperature monitors, etc.), there rarely is little additional yield from the use of such cumbersome techniques in primary care. Overall, initiating a urine drug screen without taking a complete history is not very valuable; these tests must be interpreted within the appropriate clinical context. The sensitivity of urine drug tests commonly available often is overestimated, and false-negative results are common. Just because drugs are not detected in the urine does not mean that a teenager who has a suggestive history does not have a drug problem. On the other hand, just because an adolescent has a positive urine screen does not mean that he or she is chemically dependent. Obtaining a thorough history and reviewing urine drug screens as an adjunctive assessment tool that has real limitations are vital.

Special Considerations for Individual Drugs

COCAINE. Cocaine is one of the most addictive substances known. In animal self-administration models, it is the most reinforcing of all the drugs. Animals work harder for cocaine rewards than for food, water, or sex and endure electric shocks to get cocaine. Unlimited access to cocaine in laboratory primates has essentially 100% mortality; the animals continue to self-administer cocaine to the point of exhaustion, starvation, seizures, hyperthermia, and death. Similarly, cocaine-dependent patients report that cocaine, unlike other drugs, does not produce satiety; they report never feeling like they've had "enough" but

TABLE 65–18. Examples of Alcohol and Drug Use Questions for Adolescents and Their Families

For Adolescents
On what subjects do you and your parents disagree?
Do you get into arguments about rules, curfews?
What is the worst trouble you've been in recently?
Do you get into arguments often?
Have you ever been in trouble with the police?
With what kind of group do you hang out?
What do you do for fun? Do you go to parties? What types of drugs are there?
Do you ever go to clubs or concerts? What do you do there?
How's your mood? Are you often sad, angry, irritable? Do you have a temper?
Do you smoke cigarettes?
Do you know anyone who drinks alcohol or uses drugs? What about your friends?
Does anyone in your family drink alcohol or use other drugs?
What do you/parents/siblings think about drugs?
Have you had any injuries, falls, or bruises recently? Have you been to the doctor or the emergency department for any injuries?
For Parents
Have you noticed any:
   Changes in personality, mood (increased irritability or temper)? A desire for increased privacy, time alone, or isolation?
   Changes in family relationships, friends, and acquaintances?
   Changes in sleep pattern, eating and diet, hygiene?
   Changes in school performance, attendance, truancy?
   Decreased participation in household duties and activities? A decline in adherence to rules? Concerns about lying or cheating?
     Missing household money or valuables?

---

rather seeming to feel an unsatisfiable craving. Cocaine is sniffed or snorted nasally in the powdered hydrochloride form, smoked in chunks or "rocks" in pipes as the alkaloid or "freebase" form (crack), or injected intravenously. Along with its stimulant and euphoric properties, cocaine can create an overenergized, aggressive, suspicious state and cause psychosis with transient hallucinations and paranoid delusions. Acute medical sequelae of cocaine use can include hypertensive crisis, coronary vasospasm with ischemia, cardiac arrhythmia, cerebral ischemia, and rhabdomyolysis. These sequelae, especially arrhythmia, are not necessarily dose related.

HEROIN. Previously, heroin was used primarily intravenously. However, the introduction of purer forms of heroin has made nasal sniffing an increasingly popular and efficient method of use. Nasal heroin use is becoming more prevalent among younger and less experienced users. Heroin, like other opiates, typically causes sedation, and while intoxicated, heroin users often intermittently nod off to sleep. One of the most notable signs of acute opiate intoxication is pupillary miosis. Heroin users describe the sought-after feeling that they get from the drug as soothing or numbing. Opiates are direct respiratory depressants, and the most dangerous acute medical sequela is apnea or respiratory arrest, which is dose related but unpredictable owing to variations of heroin purity. Chronic medical sequelae include generalized pruritus, constipation, and bronchospasm. Cessation of chronic heroin use provokes a characteristic physiologic withdrawal syndrome lasting 3 to 5 days; withdrawal rarely is dangerous (except in very debilitated patients and infants) but is extremely uncomfortable. Symptoms of withdrawal include sweats and chills, diarrhea, nausea, insomnia, myalgias, and irritability. Milder subacute withdrawal symptoms can persist for 2 to 3 weeks.

MARIJUANA. Marijuana is one of the primary gateway drugs. Although it is relatively less toxic than other illicit drugs, with heavy use it is by no means benign. Marijuana is a depressant that has mild hallucinogenic properties; users often describe feeling relaxed or "mellow." Chronic use sometimes is characterized by apathy, decreased motivation, and flattened emotions ("burned out"). Less well characterized is a global cognitive impairment that seems to affect, particularly, cognitive speed, problem solving, and memory—which has been described as a reversible, subcortical dementia. Other medical sequelae include mild feminization (gynecomastia, testicular atrophy), galactorrhea, menstrual irregularities, and decreased sperm count.

HALLUCINOGENS. Lysergic acid diethylamide (LSD) and phencyclidine are two of the hallucinogens used most commonly. Acutely, an LSD "trip" causes somatic (dizziness, paresthesias, weakness), perceptual (altered visual or auditory senses, including hallucinations), and psychic (altered mood and sense of time, dreamlike feelings) changes. Prolonged use of LSD can cause sustained perceptual derangements (flashbacks), which can occur long after the period of acute intoxication. Flashbacks consist of perceptual distortions of actual auditory and visual stimuli; examples include motion artifacts such as trails or halos, false registration of motion (walls that move rhythmically or "breathe"), depth perception difficulties (elongation of corridors, shifting prominence of various features of geometric designs, causing the illusion of motion), distortion of ambient sounds, and mistaken and fanciful interpretations of peripheral movements. Flashbacks also can feature vivid recollections of previous periods of intoxication, either as perceptual scenes or fantasy-like scenarios. Also known as "hallucinogen-induced perceptual disorder," flashbacks can persist for weeks to months. They gradually decrease in frequency and intensity, usually resolving within 6 months of last LSD use. Frank hallucinations, although common during acute intoxication, are rare in flashbacks.

Phencyclidine (PCP) shares many of the features of LSD, although it has several other particular dangers. Acute PCP intoxication can induce aggressive, enraged, assaultive states often compounded by a false sense of confidence or power, as well as a peculiar indifference to pain. Therefore, individuals who have acute PCP intoxication are especially dangerous and often prone to violence. PCP also can produce a variety of persistent psychotic states that usually remit within weeks but can last much longer. Both of these hallucinogens can cause severe difficulties in cognitive processing, including prominent impairment of expressive and receptive language.

ALCOHOL. Acute alcohol intoxication can be severe enough to lead to respiratory depression and death. Another serious consequence of acute alcohol intoxication, which also can occur with other drugs, is the experience of an amnestic episode: loss of retrograde memory for a period of intoxication during which the patient does not subjectively know at the time that he or she is in such a state and later cannot recall the events of the episode. When the amnesia is complete, these episodes are called "blackouts"; partial amnesia is sometimes called a "brownout." Although often trivialized and minimized by problem drinkers, blackouts are quite rare in the general population and are considered by many to be clear evidence of alcoholism.

Cessation of heavy, daily drinking provokes a characteristic physiologic withdrawal syndrome. In its most severe forms, alcohol withdrawal can include delirium tremens (DTs), hallucinosis, seizures, and autonomic instability, which can be life threatening. DTs are seen rarely in adolescent patients, who have not had time to amass a sufficient alcohol history simply because of their age. Adolescents usually experience less severe forms of alcohol withdrawal, which may include sweats

and chills, tremor, tremulousness, mild hypertension, tachycardia, nausea, insomnia, and irritability. Symptoms peak about 24 hours after the last alcohol intake. The more severe medical sequelae of alcohol toxicity such as cirrhosis, peripheral neuropathy, cerebellar atrophy, and ataxia result from years of alcohol exposure and are rare in adolescents. Acute symptoms such as alcohol-related gastritis, however, are common in adolescents who ingest a significant amount of alcohol. Hence, a thorough alcohol history should be obtained from all adolescents who have gastritis, peptic ulcer disease, or recurrent, undiagnosed abdominal pain.

INHALANTS. A variety of organic solvents, fuels, and other compounds (toluene, paint thinner, glue, spray paint, gasoline, Freon [fluorinated hydrocarbons], propane) are grouped in the category of inhalants. Delivery usually is by direct inhalation from a container (leading to a pathognomonic perioral frost or pigmentation) or by a technique called "huffing," in which a cloth soaked in the substance is placed in a paper bag, from which fumes are repeatedly inhaled. Younger adolescents typically abuse inhalants because of their widespread availability and low cost. Inhalants cause a dreamlike delirious state, often accompanied by hallucinations. Heavy or prolonged use can lead to unconsciousness from either hypoxia or direct central nervous system depression. Seizures also can occur. The most common cause of death due to accidental overdose is arrhythmia. These agents are potent nervous system toxins, and acute and chronic or permanent sequelae include tremor, ataxia, and peripheral neuropathies. Cognitive and behavioral problems include hyperactivity, affective lability, expressive and receptive processing difficulties, and poorly characterized dementias.

SEDATIVES-HYPNOTICS. This class includes a variety of prescription drugs, for example, benzodiazepines (e.g., alprazolam [Zanax], lorazepam [Ativan], diazepam [Valium], and clonazepam [Klonopin]); barbiturates (amobarbital, secobarbital, phenobarbital); and miscellaneous agents such as cyclobenzaprine (Flexeril), methocarbamol (Robaxin), meprobamate, (Rophynal), and methaqualone (Quaalude). These drugs frequently are used in combination with other drugs. Their primary medicinal uses are as sedatives, anxiolytics, and muscle relaxants. Acute intoxication is very similar to drunkenness; in fact, alcohol also is a member of this class of drugs. The risk of acute overdose is increased dramatically by ingestion with alcohol. Regular use can cause physiologic dependence with a characteristic withdrawal syndrome, similar to alcohol withdrawal, with the same risks (DTs, seizure, and death). Withdrawal symptoms vary in their onset, depending on pharmacokinetics, and can be delayed as long as a week with long-acting agents. Chronic use characteristically causes cognitive deficits, motor slowing, incoordination, and mood lability. These drugs generally should not be prescribed to patients who have a history of AOD problems.

AMPHETAMINES. Pharmacologically, the amphetamines are stimulants and similar to cocaine in their effects. Several varieties are available, including pharmaceutical agents (e.g., dexedrine), over-the-counter agents (e.g., caffeine, ephedrine, and phenylpropanolamine preparations), and illicitly manufactured forms that are sniffed or smoked. Recently their use has been most prevalent on the West Coast and in the Southwest. Acute intoxication causes locomotor stimulation, increased blood pressure, tachycardia, insomnia, and anorexia, with the risk of cardiac arrhythmia, seizures, or death at high doses. Cessation of chronic use can lead to withdrawal manifested by fatigue, hypersomnolence, depression, mild hypotension, and rarely, cardiovascular collapse.

ROUTES OF DELIVERY. AODs can be ingested orally (e.g., pills, liquids, or blotter paper) or intranasally (sniffed or snorted), smoked, and injected (intravenously or subcutaneously). Each of these methods has specific acute and chronic medical sequelae. Smoking marijuana has many of the same adverse health effects as smoking cigarettes because of the heavy tars in marijuana smoke. However, crack cocaine and PCP smokers also are vulnerable to the respiratory tract injury caused by inhalation of these agents. The most frequent medical problems for those who use smoking as the route of drug delivery include reactive airway disease (either an exacerbation or new onset), recurrent bronchitis, and allergic rhinitis. Users of nasal heroin, nasal cocaine, and nasal methamphetamine are susceptible to allergic rhinitis, sinusitis, epistaxis, erosions of the nasal mucosa, and occasionally, full septal perforation. The medical sequelae of injection drug use include human immunodeficiency virus (HIV) infection, hepatitis, endocarditis, sepsis, marasmic emboli, abscesses at the injection site, cellulitis, and thrombophlebitis.

COMORBID PSYCHIATRIC DISORDERS

Psychiatric symptoms and disorders are very common among adolescents who also have a substance use disorder. This situation is complicated because it often is unclear whether a particular patient's symptoms are a consequence of AOD use or indicative of a comorbid psychiatric disorder. Moreover, it often is difficult on a single examination to distinguish between psychiatric symptoms that may resolve with abstinence and those that will persist and require specific psychiatric treatment. Serial psychiatric assessments usually are needed to determine whether comorbid psychiatric illness is present. **The most common psychiatric symptom seen in the adolescent who has a substance use disorder is depression, resulting from pharmacologic toxicity as well as demoralization from the losses, burdens, and chaos of addiction.** Usually the depression improves substantially with substance abuse treatment, abstinence, and supportive remoralization. However, a significant minority of patients also have affective disorders (major depression, dysthymia, or bipolar disorder) that may require specific psychiatric treatment. Likewise, many adolescents who have substance use disorders present with disruptive behaviors and/or attentional difficulties that persist throughout treatment and despite abstinence. Adolescents who have dual diagnoses (addiction and other psychiatric disorders) are a particularly difficult group to manage because of the difficulty in confirming diagnoses, the need for longitudinal observation and evaluation, the potential interactions between drugs of abuse and prescribed pharmacologic agents, and the potential conflict in encouraging abstinence from AODs while recommending psychotropic medications. In general, the diagnosis of a comorbid psychiatric disorder should be delayed until treatment for addiction is under way and after 2 to 4 weeks of abstinence. Patients who have persistent psychiatric symptoms after 2 to 4 weeks of abstinence generally should receive a full psychiatric assessment, as should patients who are refractory to standard interventions.

TREATMENT

Unlike most other medical treatments, AOD treatment most likely is effective only when embarked on as an ongoing rehabilitative effort and actively embraced by the patient. Available treatment modalities include short- and long-term residential therapy, group therapy, self-help groups (e.g., Alcoholics Anonymous and Narcotics Anonymous), individual outpatient therapy, structured day programs, and family counseling. Helping the patient focus on attitude and motivation is critical. The treatment process requires adolescents to make profound changes in many aspects of their lives: They must give up practiced habits, accustomed pleasures, certain social activities, and relationships with many of their friends. Patients often have to undergo a transformation in their world view and adopt a drug-free lifestyle. This generally does not happen overnight, but is accomplished gradually through education, persuasion, understanding, and change that begins with the very first discussion about their AOD use.

Adolescents should be encouraged to include their families in their treatment. Consent and confidentiality laws vary from state to state, but generally adolescents can seek and receive substance abuse services without parental participation. However, the adolescent needs to appreciate and understand that substance abuse is a serious health problem and should be encouraged to involve his or her family in the treatment. Often teens need help communicating with their parents about their situation, although family members already may have realized that there is a problem related to AOD use. Most research has shown that treatment that includes family members is more effective.

It is important to help the adolescent understand that abstinence cannot generally be achieved by willpower alone, but rather requires learning a variety of skills and techniques. These abstinence skills may include avoiding drug-using peers, learning more about the toxic effects of drugs, identifying and connecting with non–drug-using peers, and learning how to refuse drugs. The identification of specific goals (better school grades, participation in recreational activities) that can provide productive and rewarding alternatives to drug use is another helpful method. Identified goals can serve as a benchmark for the measurement of overall improvement or deterioration in general function. Urine drug screening is an important monitor of treatment compliance.

Frequently the primary care clinician who performs the initial screening and assessment is best situated to begin intervention and treatment. Negotiation of an abstinence contract (an agreement that tests the adolescent's ability to "stop anytime I want to . . .") begins the process of helping the adolescent understand that AOD use is causing him or her problems. The primary care clinician should encourage participation in after-school groups, community recreation programs, and church, hospital, or community based groups for high-risk teens as adjuncts to substance abuse treatment. Frequent follow-up is essential. Hence, the adolescent should be seen again within a week or so of the initial evaluation. Abstinence and behavior improvement should be praised and encouraged. Lack of improvement should be considered as additional evidence of a substance abuse problem that may require more intensive treatment. Discouraging results should not be seen as a failure but as an opportunity to introduce other treatments.

A multidisciplinary approach (including but not limited to medicine, psychiatry, education, social services, substance abuse prevention and treatment specialists) often provides the most comprehensive services to adolescents who have AOD problems. The primary care clinician needs to become familiar with local treatment agencies and available services and clinicians, including physicians, psychiatrists, psychologists, and others who have special expertise in adolescent addictions. These specialists should be able to provide access to a variety of treatments, including individual counseling, structured groups, 12-step self-help groups (see later), family counseling, and special school resources. With less severe or early-stage addictive disorders, it often is reasonable for primary care clinicians to initiate treatment themselves. In more complicated, advanced stages or in refractory cases, the pediatric clinician can coordinate services (i.e., referral to a specialist, inpatient treatment, or psychiatrist) and provide ongoing support, counseling, and education to the patient and family. For all patients who have substance use disorders, the primary care clinician is an essential member of the after-care (post-treatment) team.

TWELVE-STEP GROUPS. Alcoholics Anonymous (AA) and Narcotics Anonymous (NA) often are critical components of treatment. The 12 steps of NA and AA (Table 65–19) describe both the spiritual basis and the necessary actions that form the backbone of recovery for its members. Although these concepts can be conceptually difficult for some adolescents and particularly younger teens to comprehend, the core principles have tremendous power. While AA, NA, and other traditional 12-step programs do have a strong spiritual base, it is important to appreciate that they are neither religious programs nor allied with any specific religion, sect, or denomination. The 12-step recovery process is built on a basic desire to stop drinking or using drugs. The affiliative nature of the group experience, the opportunity to associate with peers who have similar problems and learn new coping behaviors from them, and the identification with an abstinent peer group can be powerful motivators. For adolescents, a particular advantage of a group is the special credibility (the authenticity of "having been there") and persuasive power of other peers that the adult professional often cannot provide. Within the group, adolescents can share their own experiences while

TABLE 65–19. The Twelve Steps of Alcoholics Anonymous and Narcotics Anonymous

1. We admitted we were powerless over alcohol/ drugs—that our lives had become unmanageable.
2. Came to believe that a Power greater than ourselves could restore us to sanity.
3. Made a decision to turn our will and our lives over to the care of a Higher Power as we understood It.
4. Made a searching and fearless moral inventory of ourselves.
5. Admitted to a Higher Power, to ourselves, and to another human being the exact nature of our wrongs.
6. Were entirely ready to have a Higher Power remove all these defects of character.
7. Humbly asked Our Higher Power to remove our shortcomings.
8. Made a list of all persons we had harmed and became willing to make amends to them all.
9. Made direct amends to such people wherever possible, except when to do so would injure them or others.
10. Continued to take personal inventory, and when we were wrong, promptly admitted it.
11. Sought through prayer and meditation to improve our conscious contact with a Higher Power as we understand It, praying only for knowledge of Its will for us and the power to carry that out.
12. Having had a spiritual awakening as the result of these steps, we tried to carry this message to alcoholics/addicts and to practice these principles in all our affairs.

learning from the experiences of others. Support groups also provide an opportunity for adolescents to observe both the difficulties others may have in attaining abstinence and the rewards that come with sobriety. The group often offers reassurance and support, as well as an avenue for supportive confrontation. Structured, supervised groups often are more useful for adolescents in the early phases of treatment before they are able to benefit from nonsupervised self-help groups. Many treatment programs use a ''facilitated'' group whereby a professional leader helps redirect the group when necessary and keeps group members on track. Support groups for substance abusers' family members also exist (Al-Anon, Nar-Anon, Alteen), and many treatment centers offer specific programs for affected family members.

INPATIENT TREATMENT. Management of adolescents as inpatients may be required in more severe cases or when patients continue to be refractory to less intensive treatments. Criteria for inpatient treatment include detoxification, failure of sufficiently intensive outpatient treatment, danger to self or others, unmanageability in the community, and severe medical or psychiatric comorbidity. Inpatient programs offer, in a structured environment, a combination of individual, group, and family therapy, along with the traditional 12-step techniques.

PREVENTION

Given the longitudinal nature of relationships that they have with their patients, primary care clinicians are critical to substance abuse prevention. By including risk behavior assessment and education as part of the routine health maintenance visit for preadolescents and adolescents, pediatric clinicians and others can provide much-needed primary and secondary prevention. Efforts at prevention should include repeated, explicit education regarding alcohol, tobacco, and other drugs, their associated health consequences, and their relation to other major risk behavior areas such as sexually transmitted diseases, HIV and the acquired immunodeficiency syndrome, pregnancy, poor school performance, truancy or dropping out of school, and violence. Displaying appropriate posters, pamphlets, and other visual aids in the waiting areas and examination rooms is just one of the many ways of helping to educate patients and their parents about AODs and promoting questions about issues and concerns.

Another important role of the primary care clinician in substance abuse prevention is advising parents, educators, and the community. This particularly is true when a drug problem has been identified, but also is invaluable for all parents who need to learn about early exposure, parental tolerance, and how to talk to their children about substance abuse. Families need to know that often their suspicions that their child is ''hanging out with the wrong crowd'' are well substantiated and that consistent supervision, monitoring, and vigilance are the best preventive tools. Parents may need reassurance about normative behaviors, encouragement regarding their role as parents, and education about the importance of providing a supportive, stable, and safe home environment.

FURTHER READING

Adger H: Problems of alcohol and other drug use and abuse in adolescents. J Adolesc Health 12:606–613, 1991.

Alderman EM, Schonberg SK, and Cohen MI: The pediatrician's role in the diagnosis and treatment of substance abuse. Pediatr Rev 8:314–319, 1992.

American Academy of Pediatrics, Committee on Substance Abuse: Role of the pediatrician in prevention and management of substance abuse. Pediatrics 91:1010–1013, 1993.

American Psychiatric Association: Diagnostic and Statistical Manual of Mental Disorders, Fourth Edition. Washington, DC, American Psychiatric Association, 1994.

Anglin TM: Interviewing guidelines for the clinical evaluation of adolescent substance abuse. Pediatr Clin North Am 34:381–398, 1987.

Bailey GW: Current perspectives on substance abuse in youth. J Am Acad Child Adolesc Psychiatry 2:151–162, 1989.

Comerci GD: Office assessment of substance abuse and addiction. Adolesc Med: State of the Art Rev 2:277–292, 1993.

Elster AB, and Kuznets NJ (eds): AMA Guidelines for Adolescent Preventive Services (GAPS). Baltimore, Williams & Wilkins, 1994.

Johnston LD, O'Malley PM, and Bachman JG: National Sur-

vey Results from Monitoring the Future Study, 1975–1995. National Institute on Drug Abuse, 1996.

Rogers PD and Adger H: Alcohol and Adolescents. Adolesc Med: State of the Art Rev 4:295–304, 1993.

Takahashi A and Franklin J: Alcohol abuse. Pediatr Rev 17:39–45, 1996.

Werner MJ and Adger H: Early identification, screening, and brief intervention for adolescent alcohol use. Arch Pediatr Adolesc Med 149:1241–1248, 1995.

William Lord Coleman

Helping Children and Adolescents Make Friends: Social Skills

Children and adolescents need friends. Friendships promote resiliency, enhance self-worth, define self-image, and help compensate for deficits in other parts of a child's or adolescent's life. Furthermore, positive social interactions fulfil deep social-emotional needs and are necessary in all aspects of a child's life: home, school, peers, the larger community, and eventually the workplace, intimate relationships, marriage, and parenthood. *Social skills* are specific cognitive functions consisting of verbal and nonverbal behaviors that facilitate social interaction and make it productive and satisfactory for all participants. *Social competence* is the ability to integrate and perform these skills. Effective social skills acquisition and competence constitute a critical developmental milestone as social interactions increase and friendship formation and peer acceptance assume ever more importance for children and adolescents.

On the other hand, chronic rejection by peers results in self-doubt, low self-esteem, sadness, and isolation, which often affect behavior or learning. Among the most poignant and challenging situations encountered by clinicians is that of the lonely child who is ignored or rejected by peers. The purpose of this chapter is to help the clinician address the presenting complaints, "My child has no friends" or "Nobody likes me."

ASSESSMENT

A biopsychosocial assessment is essential. Diagnostic information is gathered from a variety of sources: parent and teacher questionnaires, direct history taking, physical examination, and interactions with the child, noting his or her "social style" (i.e., general appearance, dress, manner of relating, social abilities, and "image"). Parent-

child interactions should also be noted. The clinician should let parent and child interact and be spontaneous rather than control or direct the interview, so that a better perspective of the child's natural behaviors and social skills may be obtained.

Background Information

Questionnaires should be comprehensive and not limited to attention-deficit hyperactivity disorder rating scales, depression inventories, or other narrowly focused forms. Questionnaires provide much information; organize the thoughts of children, parents, and teachers; and increase the likelihood of a productive and time-efficient assessment. They should cover multiple areas, such as medical health, development, behavior, emotional status, attention, social-peer interactions, school performance, and parental information (e.g., age, health, education, occupation, marital status, and family history). A good general questionnaire is the ANSER system or the Child Behavior Checklist. Additional information on the child's social abilities can be obtained with more specialized forms (Dodge and coworkers, 1985; Walker and associates, 1988).

Predisposing Conditions

Multiple ecological factors may place the child at risk for peer rejection and isolation. Predisposing conditions that cause children to be at risk for social problems fall into two general categories: intrinsic and extrinsic. Intrinsic includes biologic, developmental, and emotional factors. Extrinsic includes familial, environmental, social, cultural,

TABLE 65–20. Conditions That May Contribute to Peer Rejection

Intrinsic Conditions	Extrinsic Conditions
Biologic Factors	*Familial Factors*
Visual or hearing impairments	Inappropriate, punitive, negative parenting
Chronic illness, injuries, school absence	Parental medical or emotional illness
Unattractive appearance, obesity	Marital tension, divorce
Physical handicaps	Family conflict or chaos
Poor personal hygiene	Parental criminality, alcoholism, substance abuse
Developmental Factors	Poor parental social skills
Attention problems	Family keeps child too busy with chores, activities
Learning disabilities	Family is overly protective, limits social activities
Speech or language delays	*Cultural/Ethnic Factors*
Cognitive impairment	Different social values, customs, or language
Specific social cognition dysfunction	*Economic Factors*
Autism, Asperger's syndrome	Different class status, poverty, after-school job
Temperament (difficult, shy, aggressive)	*Peer Factors*
Personality (weird, eccentric, different)	Different standards of dress, behavior, or speech
Emotional Factors	Reputational bias
Low self-esteem, depression	*Social-Environmental Factors**
Other	Child lives in isolated area far from school
Vulnerable child syndrome	Neighborhood has few other children or resources
	Family goes away all summer; few peer activities
	Family moves frequently; child changes schools
	Danger of violence or threat of harm keep child inside

*Child may have appropriate social skills but little opportunities to form friendships.

and economic influences. Usually more than one factor or underlying problem predisposes a child to a state of unpopularity (Table 65–20).

Presentations

Children or adolescents may present directly with social-interactional problems such as difficulty in making or keeping friends or being teased or called names. Social rejection also might present indirectly as a secondary event or complication, for example, change in mood or decline in school performance (Table 65–21).

Interview

Because social rejection is a painful, sensitive, and humiliating issue, the clinician should begin the interview with indirect, nonthreatening, and nonjudgmental questions. He or she should reassure the child (and parent) that many children and adolescents experience these problems, and "there are things we can do that usually make the situation better." At some point, the child and parent should be interviewed alone so that each can share feelings and opinions. Each should be reassured of confidentiality. The interview should shift from a general, contextual view to a directed, situation-specific view, but the pace must be individualized.

The clinician can focus the interview on social competence and friendships by asking the parent and child or adolescent selected "trigger questions." For the parent of a 10-year-old: "Tell me about Sarah's relationships with other children"; and (if she plays sports), "How does she get along with the coaches?" For the child: "Tell me about your friends." "Do you have a best friend?" "What do you like to do together?" "Do your friends pressure you to do things you don't want

TABLE 65–21. Presentations of Social Skills Problems and Peer Rejection

Presentations as Social-Interactional Difficulties
Entering and joining a group or activity
Keeping same-age friends; prefers younger friends or adults
Avoiding or resolving conflicts and arguments
Maintaining group activities or conversations
Coping with failure and disappointment ("poor loser")
Handling success and victories ("ungracious winner")
Appreciating others' feelings, needs, points of view, choices
Teased; called names; bullied; teases others; bullies
Refuses to socialize; becomes solitary, isolated
Socializes with younger peers and adults; becomes dependent on parents
Is not invited to parties or events; receives no calls
Presentations as Secondary Events and Complications
Becomes tearful, sad, angry, aggressive
May "act out" (sexual promiscuity, alcohol or substance abuse, bully behavior, risky behaviors)
States, "Nobody likes me"; "Everyone hates me"
Experiences somatic pain, school phobia, or separation anxiety
Experiences decline in school performance

TABLE 65–22. "Hot Spots": The Social Settings in Which Unpopular Children Are Vulnerable

Bus stop and school bus
School bathroom
Hallways and areas around lockers
Far corners of the playground
Gym and cafeteria if teachers are not present
Home when the parents are gone

to do?" "How are you getting along with your parent(s), brother(s), sister(s)?" "Do you belong to a gang?" "Have you thought about joining one?" (Green, 1994). It is very common and to be expected for children initially to deny these unhappy and embarrassing feelings or to lack the insight or the language with which to describe them and the situations in which they occur. When the clinician or parents suspect friendship problems, they should not accept the child's initial denials or glib reassurances ("No problem," "Fine," "Everything's cool," "I have lots of friends"). He or she should gently ask again, rephrase the question, be a little more direct, or back off and try a more indirect approach: "It must be lonely for kids who don't get phone calls or who can't find anyone to sit with at lunch (the "this seat is taken" syndrome). Do you know any kids like that? What do they do? How do you think they feel?"

These trigger questions are useful in both scheduled problem-centered and regular health supervision visits.

The clinician can gain critical and specific information by inquiring, first generally and then specifically, about certain settings ("hot spots") that provide the backdrop for revealing social interaction. These data help define the general nature of the social problem, for example, active rejection ("You can't sit here"); passive rejection (ignoring, leaving out of activities, the unreturned phone call); or being bullied (verbally or physically and to what level of severity). The "hot spots" are those settings away from the eyes and ears of parents or teachers where a child is most vulnerable. They include the bus stop, the school bus, school bathrooms, hallways, the area around lockers, and any other unsupervised sites (far corners of the playground, gymnasium, lunchroom). For a sibling who experiences intense and demeaning sibling rivalry, a hot spot could be home while the parents are at work (Table 65–22).

The clinician might pose a hypothetical social task or problem or ask more specific trigger questions, for example, asking how the child might join a group of peers on the playground or respond to being called a name. "Suppose

during recess, you want to join a dodge ball game that has already started. How would you do it? How would other kids do it?" Or the question might be, "Tell me what happens on the bus ride. Do you sit alone? With whom do you sit? Do kids call you names? What kind of names?" Detailed descriptions of the setting, the child's and the other kids' behaviors, resultant feelings, and other pertinent information should be obtained.

Social Skills Abilities

Popular children demonstrate social competence comprising a variety of discrete social skills abilities or popularity subskills. At this point, the clinician must assess these specific abilities to complete the "social profile" of the child. There are numerous social skills abilities, but four of them tend to occur in most social encounters. These are easy to describe because they are observable behaviors and occur in a predictable sequence: initiation, topic selection and maintenance, conflict resolution, and closure (Table 65–23).

The clinician might begin the assessment by determining how the child employs these popularity subskills. Parent and teacher input are very valuable. "When you first see a friend at school, what do you do?" Sufficient detail should be elicited to provide a clear description of the greeting, for example, "What do you say? What is your facial expression? What does your voice sound like? How does your friend respond? What do you do next?"

Often there is only an indirect indication that the child lacks a specific ability. In that case, the clinician should selectively assess other social skills abilities that may be more subtle but, never-

TABLE 65–23. Four Social Skills Abilities: Popularity Subskills

1. *Initiation.* The greeting, eye contact, smile, addressing one by name, making appropriate "small talk." A good start sets a positive tone and increases the likelihood of a satisfactory outcome.
2. *Topic selection/maintenance.* Choosing a topic or activity, suitable to both parties, and maintaining it for an appropriate time. Requires similar levels of skill, interest, and motivation.
3. *Conflict resolution.* Resolving minor disagreements or major conflicts in an appropriate way without fighting or name-calling. Requires patience, flexibility, and "negotiation skills."
4. *Closure.* The good-bye, or ending of encounter. Ending an encounter in a pleasant and satisfactory manner. A good ending can "save" or at least improve a less-than-optimal encounter.

TABLE 65–24. Other Social Skills Abilities

Skill	Description
Adaptation	Ability to "read" a situation and adapt accordingly
Responsiveness	Ability to be receptive and reinforcing of others' agendas
Timing and staging	Ability to time and pace an encounter; knowing when to act
Indirect approach	Ability to interact in an indirect, tangential manner
Feedback receptivity	Ability to receive and respond to feedback while relating
Verbal pragmatics	Ability to understand the intention or perspective of the other and respond appropriately
Reciprocity	Ability to share, support, reinforce the other person
Social memory	Ability to recall a prior interaction and act accordingly
Social prediction	Ability to foresee the consequences of one's actions and words
Awareness of image	Ability to present oneself in a socially acceptable manner
Requesting skills	Ability to ask for something or express an opinion in a suitable way
Assertiveness skills	Ability to assert influence over peer behavior or thoughts
Recuperative strategies	Ability to compensate for social error while relating or after the interaction
Jargon fluency	Ability to use the parlance (phrases, terms) of peers in a natural and credible manner

From Levine MD: Developmental Variation and Learning Disorders, 2nd ed. Cambridge, MA, Educators Publishing Services, 1998.

theless, contribute significantly to rejection or exclusion (Table 65–24).

Other Information

In some situations, it helps to observe the child in the waiting room, at school (without embarrassing him or her), and at after-school activities. Viewing a parent's videotape of the child at a birthday party or other event may be informative.

Assessments of the peer group and its dynamics are very helpful. The child should be asked to describe the various cliques or types of children in school and other situations such as Scout meetings or athletic events. Then the child should be asked to name the characterization that probably best fits him or her and tell how a friend or acquaintance would describe him or her.

Finally, suspected predisposing conditions (e.g., learning, emotional, attentional, or family problems) warrant appropriate evaluation or referral.

MANAGEMENT

The management of the unpopular child or adolescent must take into account the various predisposing influences, the causative factors, and the resultant complications that contribute to peer rejection. The child's social skills disabilities (social cognitive dysfunction) must be presented in a way that the child can understand, acknowledge, and feel motivated to improve them. Associated problems such as attention disorders, a language disability, or emotional problems require appropriate treatment. Strengths and interests must be recognized and mobilized (Table 65–24).

For the management of discrete social skills

disabilities, the clinician might suggest and describe a five-step program and describe it to parents and teachers. The basic program could be typed and used as a handout, with handwritten, individualized comments added when it is shared with the child and parent (Table 65–25).

1. **Coach the child.** First, the child and the adult in charge discuss (a) a problematic social situation and the child's social error(s) (e.g., weak greeting skills), errors of omission, and/or errors of commission, and (b) the expectations and desired behaviors. The child should be

TABLE 65–25. What the Clinician Can Do

Provide a clear explanation of the child's social skills problems (demystification). Avoid technical terms. Illustrate real-life examples. Remove blame and shame. Induce hope.

Provide educational materials and resources.

Discuss management plans: the clinician manages problems within his or her expertise, e.g., minor social skills deficits and/or comorbid conditions; for other problems, refers to others for evaluation and/or treatment.

Enhance the child's self-esteem by maintaining affinities, interests, and strengths. Help the child find his or her niche and purpose and develop new skills that are suitable and favorably impress his or her peers.

Help the child maintain a core identity. Remind the child of his or her positive attributes. Although changes may be necessary, he or she should not feel forced to blindly conform and risk losing his or her unique individuality.

Obtain parent's and child's permission to share findings and to plan interventions with teachers and other relevant adults.

Enlist the support and active participation of the parents.

Advocate for the child. Write letters, make calls, visit the school on his or her behalf.

Follow the child or adolescent. Monitor the quality of and compliance with the interventions and evaluate the outcomes. Anticipate new social challenges and plan accordingly.

provided with at least two behaviors, an initial one and an alternative. Then the child is coached in this strategy.

2. **Stop and think.** Just before engaging in the social situation, the child pauses and previews the situation. By doing this, he or she reduces the chance of repeating errors and becomes aware and sensitive to the present situation.

3. **Focus.** The child reviews the desired behaviors, maybe generates another alternative, reflects on their outcomes, and determines the best plan of action. This allows him or her to take a more active role and increases his or her sense of control.

4. **Act.** The child carries out the plan and while doing so, monitors his or her effectiveness and mobilizes a recuperative strategy if needed.

5. **Evaluate.** The child reviews the interaction from start to finish and notes what went right or wrong. He or she reuses the successful strategies and modifies or discards the others.

The Parents

The influences of the family's social style and parental modeling are so powerful that a family-centered approach should always be considered. For example, the parents can provide a supportive home environment by using the five-step program for selected situations, providing the child with gentle reminders, and modeling good social skills.

The parents can carry out a "social engineering" activity. They carefully select a social activity for the child and one peer (acquaintance or friend) with similar interests and temperament. The time limits of the activity should be specified and adhered to, and it should be short rather than long, especially for the first encounter. If it is not appropriate or if the child is hesitant to invite the peer, the parents should call the other child's parents and offer the invitation. The parents should combine interactive activities with appropriate amounts of low-key, friendly competition and co-operation, and they should also have some parallel activities ready as an alternative or respite. The parents should discreetly monitor the situation but not control or direct the interactions. If the two children cannot resolve a conflict, the parents

TABLE 65–26. The Five-Step Program

1. Coach the child
2. Stop and think
3. Focus
4. Act
5. Evaluate

TABLE 65–27. What Parents Can Do

Provide an understanding and supportive home environment; maintain open communication.

Find the balance between empathy and responsibility; know when to remind and intervene and when to hold back and let go.

Practice the five-step program in selected, specific social situations.

Carry out a "social engineering" activity.

Allow the child to "socialize" on the phone, a "safe" and acceptable way to form friendships.

Work with schoolteachers and other adults in the child's life (e.g., relatives, coaches, Sunday school teachers).

Seek help and guidance from the child's primary care clinician or other professionals.

Seek professional help, if needed, for their own personal, parental, marital, or social problems.

should intervene early, quickly, and diplomatically without embarrassing or blaming either child. The activity should end on time (earlier if necessary), leaving both children eager for the next meeting (Tables 65–26 and 65–27).

The Teachers and Other Significant Adults

Because school is the primary arena for social interactions, teachers play a significant role in the assessment (providing data in the questionnaires), management (implementing strategies, being understanding), and follow-up (providing ongoing observations, anticipating new challenges). Coaches, bus drivers, after-school care providers, Sunday school teachers, and relatives also might be important "players" in helping these children. The clinician and parents need to gain the understanding and support of these adults (Table 65–28).

Special Professionals

Special professionals include behavioral-developmental pediatricians, psychologists, and mental

TABLE 65–28. What Teachers and Other Significant Adults Can Do

Provide guidance and feedback; advocate for the child.

Reduce high-risk situations or help the child avoid them; intervene when necessary.

Help implement the five-step program.

Carry out a "social engineering" task appropriate for a school situation.

Encourage the child to observe the behaviors of socially adept children and then discuss them.

health social workers. They may use individual or group therapy problem-solving techniques. Some professionals use formal social skills training programs. Referral to appropriate professionals for other problems (e.g., learning disorders, severe depression, family problems) is essential.

FURTHER READING

For Professionals

Achenbach TM and Edelbrock CS: Child Behavior Checklist. Available from Thomas Achenbach, Department of Psychiatry, University of Vermont, Burlington, VT.

Coleman WL and Lindsay RL: Interpersonal disabilities: Social skill deficits in older children and adolescents: Their description, assessment, and management. Pediatr Clin North Am 39:551–568, 1992.

Dodge KA, McClaskey CL, and Feldman E: A situational approach to the assessment of social competence in children. J Consult Clin Psychol 53:344–351, 1985.

Garrity C and Baris MA: Bullies and victims: A guide for pediatricians. Contemp Pediatr 13 (2):90–115, 1996.

Goldstein S and Goldstein M: Managing Attention Disorders in Children. New York, John Wiley and Sons, 1989.

Green M (ed): Bright Futures: Guidelines for Health Supervision of Infants, Children and Adolescents. Arlington VA, National Center for Education in Maternal and Child Health, 1994.

Levine MD: Developmental Variation and Learning Disorders. Cambridge MA, Educators Publishing Services, 1987, pp 240–273.

Levine MD: Unpopular children. In Parker S and Zuckerman B (eds): Behavioral and Developmental Pediatrics. Boston, Little, Brown, 1995, pp 325–328.

Levine MD: ANSER System. Cambridge MA, Educators Publishing Services, 1996.

Pelligrii DS: Psychosocial risk and protective factors in childhood. J Dev Behav Pediatr 11:201–206, 1990.

Sandler AS: Deficits in social skills. In Levine MD, Carey WB, and Crocker AC (eds): Developmental-Behavioral Pediatrics, 2nd ed. Philadelphia, WB Saunders, 1992, pp 491–494.

Walker HM, Todis B, Holmes D, et al.: The Walker Social Skillls Curriculum: The ACCESS Program. Austin, TX, Pro-Ed Publishers, 1988.

For Parents

Coleman WL: Developing Social Skills. In Schor EL (ed): Caring For Your School-Age Child Ages 5 to 12. New York, Bantam Publishers, 1995, pp 141–160.

Levine MD: Keeping a Head in School. Cambridge MA, Educators Publishing Services, 1990.

Osman B: No One to Play With: The Social Side of Learning Disabilities. New York, Random House, 1982.

David A. Brent

Mood Disorders and Suicide

Depression and suicidal behavior are important contributors to the morbidity and mortality of children and adolescents. In fact, there is evidence that the prevalence of depression, suicidal behavior, and completed suicide have all increased within the past 3 decades. As the nature of pediatric practice shifts to accommodate an emphasis on psychosocial issues, it is important for the pediatrician to be able to recognize and manage these common and serious problems of childhood and adolescence.

MOOD DISORDERS

CLASSIFICATION. One of the advances in child and adolescent psychiatry has been the development of consistent nomenclature and criteria for various psychiatric disorders. Mood disorders are classified on the basis of three factors: (1) severity, (2) course, and (3) presence or absence of mania. In terms of depressive symptoms the diagnosis of major depressive disorder requires at least 2 weeks of depressed mood more than half of the time and four additional depressive symptoms (Table 65–29). A person with a more chronic, intermittent disorder such as dysthymic disorder may have periods of depression interspersed with normal mood (Table 65–30). Adjustment disorder is a still milder disturbance of affect that follows a serious life stressor (Table 65–31). A history of manic symptoms in a person with dysthymia or major depression confers a diagnosis of bipolar affective or cyclothymic disorder, respectively (Tables 65–32 and 65–33).

DESCRIPTIVE EPIDEMIOLOGY. Mood disorders are relatively rare in prepubertal children, with estimates of point prevalences ranging from 1.8% to 2.9%. The incidence of mood disorders is estimated to be three to four times more common in adolescence (8.7%). Whereas the sex ratio for affectively ill prepubertal children approaches unity, depression among adolescents is more common in females than males.

RISK FACTORS. The most potent risk factor for developing a depressive disorder in childhood is having at least one parent with a history of depression. Anxiety disorders may also predispose to the development of depression. The increased risk of depression is greater and age of

TABLE 65–29. Criteria for Major Depressive Episode

For at least 2 weeks for more than 50% of the time:
A. Depressed mood (sad, blue, "down in the dumps," angry, bored) or loss of interest and pleasure in almost all of the usual activities.
B. Coincident with depressed mood, at least four of the following symptoms (three for children under the age of 6):
  1. Change in appetite or weight (either decreased or increased)
  2. Insomnia or hypersomnia
  3. Observable psychomotor agitation or retardation
  4. Loss of interest or pleasure, diminished libido
  5. Loss of energy, fatigue
  6. Feelings of worthlessness or inappropriate guilt
  7. Difficulty concentrating, indecision
  8. Recurrent thoughts of death, suicidal ideation, or behavior
C. Not due to organic mental disorder (e.g., medical condition, drug treatment, or substance abuse) or uncomplicated bereavement.

Adapted with permission from the Diagnostic and Statistical Manual of Mental Disorders, Fourth Edition. Copyright 1994, American Psychiatric Association.

onset of depression is younger with a greater familial loading for depression, an earlier age of onset of depression in parents, and a family history of either bipolarity or recurrent unipolar disorder. Physical or sexual abuse may also be associated with depressive symptoms. Certain medications may predispose to depression, namely, antihypertensive agents, steroids, and phenobarbital. The incidence of depression may be

TABLE 65–30. Criteria for Dysthymic Disorder

A. During past year (2 years for adults), the patient has been bothered by symptoms of major depression but of lesser severity.
B. The periods of depressive symptoms may be separated by periods of normal mood for a few days or weeks.
C. During the depressed periods, the patient has prominent depressed mood or loss of interest and pleasure.
D. During depressed periods, the patient has at least three of the following symptoms:
  1. Insomnia or hypersomnia
  2. Low energy level and fatigue
  3. Decreased productivity at school, work, or home
  4. Difficulty concentrating
  5. Feelings of inadequacy and poor self-esteem
  6. Social withdrawal
  7. Loss of interest and pleasure in usual activities
  8. Anhedonia (inability to experience pleasure)
  9. Tearfulness
  10. Suicidal thoughts
  11. Hopelessness and pessimism about the future, brooding about the past

Adapted with permission from the Diagnostic and Statistical Manual of Mental Disorders, Fourth Edition. Copyright 1994, American Psychiatric Association.

TABLE 65–31. Criteria for Adjustment Disorder with Depressed Mood

A. A reaction to an identified social stressor, characterized by depressed mood, tearfulness, and hopelessness.
B. Occurrence within 3 months of the onset of the stressor.
C. Syndrome characterized by symptoms in excess of "expectable reaction" to the stressor, the functional impairment, or both.
D. The disorder is self-limited and should remit when the stress ceases.
E. The disorder does not meet criteria for major depression or dysthymia.

Adapted with permission from the Diagnostic and Statistical Manual of Mental Disorders, Fourth Edition. Copyright 1994, American Psychiatric Association.

increased in patients with some chronic illnesses, such as epilepsy, inflammatory bowel disease, and type I diabetes (IDDM). Although the cause of depression is unknown, it is likely that biologic factors play an important role in light of familial aggregation and neuroendocrine biologic markers that have been described in early-onset depression. These findings are most consistent with disordered noradrenergic and serotonergic neurotransmission.

CLINICAL PICTURE. The clinical picture of depressive disorders in children and adolescents is similar to that described in adults. It is important to remember that "depressed mood" can refer to sadness, irritability, or boredom. Depressed children, as compared with depressed adolescents, present similarly, although depressed adolescents are more likely to have made a suicide attempt and to be using illicit drugs. However, suicidal thoughts are a very frequent symptom in both pre- and postpubertal depression. Patients with either dysthymia or major depression frequently have

TABLE 65–32. Criteria for Bipolar Disorder

Past or current history of a manic episode, characterized by:
A. At least 1 week in which mood has been primarily elevated, expansive, or irritable.
B. During this time, at least three of the following symptoms (four if mood is primarily irritable):
  1. Increase in activity (socially, at work, sexually) or physical restlessness
  2. Increased pressure of speech—"talkativeness"
  3. Flight of ideas or subjective sense of racing thoughts
  4. Inflated self-esteem (grandiosity)
  5. Diminished need for sleep
  6. Distractibility
  7. Poor judgment and impulsive reckless action (e.g., promiscuity, buying sprees, reckless driving)
C. Not due to organic mental disorder (e.g., amphetamine intoxication).

Adapted with permission from the Diagnostic and Statistical Manual of Mental Disorders, Fourth Edition. Copyright 1994, American Psychiatric Association.

TABLE 65–33. Criteria for Cyclothymic Disorder

A. During the past year (2 years for adults), periods of depressive and manic symptoms of insufficient duration or severity to meet criteria for major depressive or manic disorders.

B. The depressive and manic periods may be separated by periods of normal mood lasting a few days.

C. During the depressive periods, there is a depressed mood and loss of interest and pleasure and at least three symptoms for dysthymic disorder (see Table 65–30).

D. During the hypomanic periods, there is an expansive, elevated, or irritable mood (but of less severity than for mania) and at least three manic symptoms (see Table 65–32).

E. Absence of psychotic features (which would suggest more severe depression or mania).

Adapted with permission from the Diagnostic and Statistical Manual of Mental Disorders, Fourth Edition. Copyright 1994, American Psychiatric Association.

other comorbid-morbid psychiatric disorders simultaneously, for example, anxiety disorders, attention-deficit disorder, conduct disorder, and substance abuse. Early-onset depressive illness is frequently associated with psychotic features, specifically, mood-congruent delusions (e.g., "I am dead," "The world is coming to an end"), self-deprecatory auditory hallucinations, and paranoid ideation. The depressive picture for patients with bipolar illness often includes psychotic features along with hypersomnia, hyperphagia, and anergia.

Mood may be characterized by either expansive mood, euphoria, and grandiosity or anger and irritability. Symptoms of mania and hypomania (a milder form of mania without functional impairment) may occur separately from depressive episodes or may occur with them. The simultaneous occurrence of manic and depressive symptoms is known as a *mixed state*. This combination is a very common mode of presentation in early-onset bipolar disorder, often characterized by marked irritability and mood lability, comorbid substance abuse, and lack of clinical response to lithium. Delusions associated with either grandiosity or paranoia often accompany severe mania, particularly if prolonged sleep deprivation has occurred.

DIFFERENTIAL DIAGNOSIS. Within depressive disorders, the main differential diagnosis is among the triad of dysthymia, depression, and adjustment disorder with depressed mood. Dysthymia is both a more chronic and a more intermittent depression than major depression, although the two disorders can coexist (major depression developing on top of dysthymia). Adjustment disorder with depressed mood has less severe mood disturbance, has fewer symptoms, and is self-limited. However, if a life stressor precedes a syndrome of depression, the presence of the stressor does *not* invalidate the diagnosis of major depressive disorder. The symptoms of bereavement may be indistinguishable from depressive symptoms. The diagnosis of depression in a bereaved patient is made if bereavement is associated with severe functional impairment, suicidal ideation, psychotic features, feelings of worthlessness, or prolonged course. A previous psychiatric disorder and a family history of depression predispose to depression following bereavement.

Various other psychiatric disorders may also have associated mood disturbances. Patients with learning disabilities or attention-deficit disorder may have poor self-esteem and feel demoralized but should not be diagnosed as being depressed unless they meet criteria for the syndrome. Children with separation anxiety disorder are often quite dysphoric when separated from their parents, but in the absence of premorbid depression, the dysphoria is relieved by reunion with the parents. Patients with anorexia nervosa, particularly if malnourished, may show a markedly depressed affect. However, a diagnosis of depression should not be made until nutritional status has been normalized. Patients with drug and alcohol abuse problems often show disturbances of mood. At times, the mood disorder may antedate and even predispose to substance abuse, but often the mood disorder is secondary to substance abuse and subsides within a month of detoxification. The differential diagnosis between depression and chronic medical illness can be difficult. The incidence of depression may in fact be higher in certain illnesses, and chronic illness may have effects on sleep, appetite, and energy similar to those seen in depressed patients. Feelings of guilt, worthlessness, and hopelessness and suicidal thoughts are unlikely to be attributable to the illness itself and, if present, strongly suggest the presence of a depressive disorder.

Mania can be mimicked by stimulant abuse (e.g., cocaine, amphetamine). The irritability of mania can also be seen in depression, so that the differential diagnosis between depression and mania rests on whether the preponderance of associated symptoms are more consistent with mania or with depression. Irritability, anger, and poor judgment may also be prominent features of conduct disorder, but the lack of change in energy, sleep, sexuality, and thought patterns in conduct disorder generally excludes mania as a diagnosis. Similarly, the features of attention-deficit disorder may suggest mania, but manic patients are more likely to have mood swings and neurovegetative changes and to show hypersexuality and inappropriate joking and punning. Severe clinical deterioration in an attention-deficit–disordered patient after a trial of stimulants, particularly with some of the manic clinical features mentioned earlier or with a positive family history of mania, also suggests bipolar disorder. These guidelines for differential diagnosis notwithstanding, affective and nonaffective disorders frequently co-occur.

CLINICAL COURSE. Naturalistic studies indicate that depressive disorders in children and adolescents run a chronic and recurrent course. According to one longitudinal study, untreated major depressive disorder lasts an average of 7.2 months, and dysthymic disorder, an average of 45.9 months. Those patients with both major depressive disorder and nonaffective morbidity (e.g., additional diagnoses of conduct disorder, attention-deficit disorder) may show a more prolonged course. On the average, 40% of depressed children experience a depressive recurrence within 2 years. Earlier age of onset and co-occurrence of an underlying dysthymic disorder increase the risk of depressive recurrences. Even after recovery from depression, prepubertal children show significant social impairment. The adult sequelae of adolescent depressive symptoms include drug and alcohol use, development of antisocial behavior, and interference with interpersonal relationships. Moreover, depression confers a substantially increased risk for suicide in both male and female adolescents.

IDENTIFICATION OF DEPRESSED PATIENTS IN PEDIATRIC SETTINGS. Any disturbance in mood that is associated with functional impairment should be considered a psychiatric disorder until proved otherwise. Parents and children alike frequently have a tendency to mislabel bona fide depressive disorders as "the ups and downs" of childhood or adolescence. **Mood disorders should be a strong consideration for any child who presents with unexplained somatic complaints, drop in school performance, apathy and loss of interest, social withdrawal, increased irritability or tearfulness, sleep and appetite changes, or suicidal ideation or behavior:** Moreover, depressive illnesses frequently accompany tobacco, alcohol, and drug abuse, promiscuous sexual behavior, and risk-taking behavior. Depressive disorders may follow bereavement, particularly if the patient has a personal or family history of depression. Depression may also follow other severe stressors, such as physical or sexual assault. The pediatrician should be aware of a family history of depression, because such a history will increase the risk of depressive disorder at least threefold. A family history of bipolar disorder greatly increases the

risk that other biologic family members will develop this disorder.

Both the child and the parents contribute important information to be used by the pediatrician in diagnosing depression. The child is likely to be the most accurate reporter of symptoms that refer to an internal state, for example, depressed mood, anhedonia, guilt, worthlessness, and suicidal thoughts; the parents, by contrast, may be able to note such externally validated symptoms as irritability, decline in school performance, listlessness, withdrawal from social and other pleasurable activities, and weight loss. An important issue in the identification of mood disorders in children is to recognize that the depressed mood in children may be described as "grouchy," "mad," or "bored" rather than "sad."

MANAGEMENT. Children and adolescents with mood disorders are best managed by a child psychiatrist with clinical expertise in this area. Generally, psychiatric intervention has three components: (1) psychoeducation; (2) psychotherapy; and (3) pharmacotherapy. Most mood-disordered patients can be managed as outpatients. Inpatient referral should be reserved for those who are psychotic, acutely suicidal, acutely manic or in a mixed state, abusing substances, or refractory to less intensive intervention.

FAMILY PSYCHOEDUCATION. Family psychoeducation approaches depression as a chronic illness, with its aim to instruct family members about the nature and course of the illness. Such an approach is likely to improve compliance with treatment and reduce the risk of relapse. Psychoeducation is also aimed at reducing the tensions of living with an affectively ill person by altering familial expectations. This alteration involves parents' accepting the illness and making appropriate expectations of the patient and themselves. Finally, psychoeducation should enable the child and family to identify early signs of recurrence of the disorder and to seek treatment before the recurrent mood disorder becomes severe.

PSYCHOTHERAPY. Psychotherapy should be aimed at ameliorating the interpersonal and social deficits associated with depressive symptoms. Individual, brief cognitive-behavioral treatment, around 3 months in duration, has been shown to be more efficacious than either family or supportive treatment for the relief of adolescent depression. Group cognitive-behavioral treatment has also been shown to be helpful both in the treatment of depression and in the prevention of depression in at-risk youth. The response rates for psychotherapy and pharmacotherapy appear to be similar, although they have not been compared directly. Therefore, I generally begin with psychotherapy and add pharmacotherapy if no response is found in 4 to 6 weeks.

PHARMACOTHERAPY (also see Chapter 65, subchapter, The Use of Psychotropic Medication in Children and Adolescents). Fluoxetine, a selective serotonin reuptake inhibitor (SSRI), has been shown to be more effective than placebo for child and adolescent depression. SSRIs have a more favorable side effect profile than tricyclic antidepressants (TCAs), the most notable of which is their lack of fatality in overdose. However, SSRIs may cause agitation, sleep problems, and gastrointestinal complaints.

TCAs are no longer first-line agents for early-onset depression insofar as no study has shown a difference between TCAs and placebo, and because of their danger of fatality in overdose. However, TCAs may be useful for the treatment of attention-deficit hyperactivity disorder (ADHD) with comorbid anxiety or depression. Their use requires careful monitoring for cardiovascular side effects, with a baseline electrocardiogram, blood pressure, pulse, and regular follow-up rhythm strips and vital signs.

Treatment of bipolar disorder consists of the use of mood stabilizers for prophylaxis, as well as acute treatment of manic or depressive episodes. Traditionally, lithium has been the mainstay of mood stabilization, but this agent may be less effective than valproate or carbamazepine for those in a mixed state and who present with rapid cycling (one or more episodes of depression and/or mania per year), the latter two of which may be more common in early-onset bipolar disorder.

With regard to the use of lithium, blood levels for lithium should be monitored to check compliance and to avoid toxicity. Serious renal effects of lithium are rare, but polyuria is common and kidney function should be monitored by urinalyses, blood creatinine, and blood urea nitrogen (BUN). Hypothyroidism can complicate lithium treatment, so thyroid function tests should be performed at 4- to 6-month intervals on patients who receive maintenance lithium. Other frequent side effects of lithium include tremor, nausea, diarrhea, weight gain, acne, and psoriasis. For manic patients who do not respond to lithium alone, it may be necessary to add or substitute valproate or carbamazepine. Lithium is contraindicated in the first trimester of pregnancy, as its use is associated with congenital malformations, namely Ebstein's anomaly. Bipolar patients who experience depressive symptoms should be continued on lithium; an antidepressant should be added. In patients who present with a "bipolar-type" depression (anergia, hypersomnia, hyperphagia, psychotic symptoms),

particularly in those who have a positive family history of mania, it may be optimal to begin with lithium and then add an antidepressant to avoid precipitating mania.

Valproate has become more frequently used for the management of juvenile bipolar disorder. The most significant side effect is that of hepatotoxicity, and the drug is contraindicated in those with liver disease. The risk of liver damage is greatest in children under the age of 2 and in the first 6 months of use, necessitating the monitoring of liver function. Thrombocytopenia and other hematologic abnormalities have been reported, so that a complete blood count (CBC) should be obtained on a regular basis. Valproate is contraindicated during pregnancy due to an increased incidence of congenital malformations. Other side effects include sedation, weight gain, nausea, and vomiting, with the latter two generally transient. In girls with significant weight gain, polycystic ovarian disease has been reported. In adults, valproate was found to be superior to lithium in the treatment of mania complicated by depression.

Carbamazepine has also been used for the treatment of bipolar illness refractory to lithium. The most common side effects of carbamazepine are dizziness, drowsiness, nausea, and vomiting. The most dreaded side effects are aplastic anemia and agranulocytosis, necessitating frequent CBC monitoring at regular intervals.

SUICIDE AND SUICIDAL BEHAVIOR

Suicide is now the third-leading cause of death among adolescents and young adults aged 15 to 24. The rate of suicide among 15- to 24-year-olds has increased nearly fivefold from 2.7 per 100,000 in 1950 to 13.2 per 100,000 in 1990. This increase may be related in part to increased use and availability of alcohol and firearms among minors. Suicidal behavior (i.e., attempts) has also become increasingly common, to the point that 4% of high school students have made a suicide attempt within the previous 12 months and 8% have made a suicide attempt within their lifetime. However, only about one fourth of adolescent suicide attempts ever come to medical attention.

AGE. The biggest increase in the suicide rate has been noted among 15- to 19-year-olds, but in the last decade the suicide rate among 10- to 14-year-olds has increased over 100%. Within the child and adolescent range, the suicide rate and the rate of attempted suicide increase with age. Although prepubertal children may think about suicide, they may be protected against committing suicide by their cognitive immaturity, which prevents them from planning and attempting suicide despite impulses in that direction. When suicidal behavior is observed in preschool children, it is often associated with physical or sexual abuse.

SEX. The suicide rate is much higher among males, whereas the suicide attempt rate is much higher among females. This difference may be related to males' tendency to use more violent means when attempting suicide.

RACE AND SOCIOECONOMIC STATUS. The suicide rate is higher among whites than African-Americans, although both white and African-American males have shown a dramatic increase in recent years. Young Native Americans have a particularly high suicide rate, especially those in tribes that have experienced erosion of traditional culture and high rates of delinquency, alcoholism, and family disorganization. Suicidal behavior may be more common among lower socioeconomic groups. Among young African-American males, *higher* socioeconomic status appears to be a risk factor for completed suicide.

PRECIPITANTS. The precipitants for suicidal behavior and suicide among children and adolescents are similar, most frequently involving problems such as interpersonal conflict or interpersonal loss, legal or disciplinary crises, physical or sexual abuse, and family discord.

METHOD. In the United States, firearms are the most common method of suicide, followed by hanging, jumping, carbon monoxide asphyxiation, and self-poisoning. Suicide by firearms may be related to their availability in the home and also to a state of intoxication in the victim. By contrast, self-poisoning is the most common method of suicide attempt, with wrist cutting the next most common method.

MOTIVATION AND INTENT. Youthful suicide victims are frequently intoxicated at the time of death. Nevertheless, many adolescent suicide victims show evidence of high intent (i.e., a strong wish to die), as manifested by timing the suicide so as not to be discovered, planning ahead, leaving a note, choosing an irreversible method, and stating intent before the actual suicide. Paradoxically, suicide victims are more likely than suicide attempters to have discussed their thoughts of suicide with someone, usually a friend. This highlights the importance of taking suicide threats seriously. In contrast, only about one third of adolescents who attempt suicide actually wish to die. In fact, most adolescent suicide attempts are impulsive, with little threat to the patient's life. The motivation for most attempts appears to be the desire to influence others, gain attention, communicate love or anger, or escape a difficult or painful situation.

PSYCHIATRIC DISORDER AND PSYCHOLOGIC TRAITS. The majority of adolescent suicide victims appear to have been suffering from at least one major debilitating psychiatric disorder, predominantly disorders of mood, substance abuse, or conduct. At least half had made suicide threats or attempted suicide in the past. The constellation of depression, conduct disorder and substance abuse, and past suicidal behavior is also characteristic of adolescents who attempt suicide. Among depressed patients, those with a chronic course (duration of at least 2 years) and with comorbid substance use are most likely to be suicidal. Suicidal patients have also been shown to feel more hopeless and to show poorer problem-solving and social skills than comparable patients who had not attempted suicide.

FAMILY HISTORY. The relatives of both adolescent suicide victims and suicide attempters have high prevalences of mood disorder, alcohol and drug abuse, assaultive and antisocial behavior, suicide, and suicidal behavior.

FAMILY ENVIRONMENT. In the families of both suicide victims and suicide attempters, a high prevalence of divorce, parental absence, and abuse has been noted. The family environment of suicidal versus nonsuicidal patients has been characterized as less supportive, more conflicted, and more hostile. In community samples, suicide attempters have been exposed to family violence and have been victims of physical or sexual abuse more frequently than psychiatric or community control individuals.

EXPOSURE TO SUICIDE. Both suicide victims and suicide attempters may have been exposed to suicide more than comparable control subjects. Exposure to suicide as the result of the suicide of a schoolmate or the fictional or nonfictional representation of suicide on television may also increase the risk for suicide and suicidal behavior, particularly among the psychiatrically vulnerable.

MEDICAL ILLNESSES. Children with epilepsy have been overrepresented in series of suicides and attempted suicides. Some of this increase may be related to the iatrogenic effects of phenobarbital. In a study of American adolescents attending inner-city pediatric clinics, common presenting complaints among those with a history of suicide attempts include any psychologic concerns, having been a runaway, physical and sexual abuse, recent physical or sexual assault, problems with substance abuse, concerns about pregnancy, and presentation with a sexually transmitted disease.

RISK OF REPETITION OF SUICIDAL BEHAVIOR. In follow-up studies of adolescent

TABLE 65–34. Interviewing for Suicidal Ideation

Have you ever thought that life was not worth living?
Have you ever wished you were dead?
Have you ever tried to hurt yourself?
Do you intend to hurt yourself?
Do you have a plan to hurt yourself?
Have you ever attempted suicide?

From Brent DA: Depression and suicide in children and adolescents. Pediatr Rev 14:380, 1993.

suicide attempters ranging from 1 to almost 3 years in length, the reattempt rate was between 6% and 15% per year. The risk for repetition was greatest within the first 3 months of the initial attempt. Factors associated with reattempts were previous suicidal behavior, high suicidal intent, serious psychopathology (either depression or substance abuse), hostility and aggression, hopelessness, noncompliance with treatment, social isolation, poor school performance, family discord, abuse and neglect, and parental psychiatric illness.

RISK FACTORS FOR COMPLETED SUICIDE AMONG SUICIDE ATTEMPTERS.

Among males, the risk for suicide ranges from 0.7% among suicide attempters who present to an emergency room for a drug overdose to 10% among those who are psychiatrically hospitalized. Among females, the risk ranges from 0.1% of attempters seen in an emergency room to 2.9% on follow-up of those who are psychiatrically hospitalized. The risk factors for completed suicide are male sex, no apparent precipitant, high suicidal intent, "active" method, and bipolar or psychotic disorder. Case-control studies suggest that in addition to bipolar disorder and high intent, the risk for suicide may be related to availability of firearms in the home.

SUICIDAL IDEATION.

Suicidal ideation, or thoughts about suicide, is even more common than suicidal behavior. Suicidal ideation can be thought of as a continuum from nonspecific ideation (e.g., "Life is not worth living," "I wish I were dead"), to specific ideation (e.g., suicidal ideation with intent to die or with a suicidal plan), and finally, to actual suicidal behavior (Table 65–34). Community-based surveys indicate that between 12% and 25% of primary and high school children have some form of suicidal ideation. Specific suicidal ideation (e.g., ideation with a concrete suicidal plan), as with suicidal behavior, is associated most closely with depression, feelings of helplessness, substance abuse, and conduct disorder. Also, suicidal ideation is frequently associated with physical abuse. Given the clinical overlap between those with specific suicidal ideation and those who actually attempt suicide, it follows that those patients with specific suicidal ideation should be considered to be at high risk to act on their suicidal thoughts.

IDENTIFYING YOUTH AT RISK FOR SUICIDE AND SUICIDAL BEHAVIOR. Table 65–35 outlines the three categories of personal problems that should induce the clinician to probe further for suicidal risk: (1) psychiatric; (2) social adjustment; and (3) family or environmental. **Any child who is suspected of being at risk should be questioned about suicidal ideation (see Table 65–34), moving from nonspecific questions to more specific ones if the answers to the nonspecific queries are positive.**

After the identification of someone at risk for suicide, it is important to listen to the patient in a nonjudgmental way. The clinician should avoid making promises of confidentiality that will have to be broken to protect and properly treat the child. The patient's parents should always be given some feedback about the assessment, because parental motivation is an important predictor of compliance with treatment recommendations. **On discovering that a patient is suicidal, it is critical to obtain a no-suicide agreement, in which the patient promises to refrain from physically self-destructive behavior and to notify the clinician or a caretaking adult if he or she does feel suicidal again.** In formulation of the no-suicide agreement, the clinician should review with the patient the precipitants for the wish to commit suicide and rehearse alternative methods for coping with these stressors. **It is also important to make sure that**

TABLE 65–35. Circumstances Increasing Suicidal Risk

Psychiatric Difficulties
Depression
Bipolar disorder
Substance abuse
Conduct problems
Psychosis
Past suicidal threats or attempts
Poor Social Adjustment
School failure or dropout
Legal problems
Social isolation
Interpersonal conflict
Family or Environment
Interpersonal loss
Family problems
   Abuse or neglect
   Family history of psychiatric disorder or suicide
Exposure to suicide (in those already psychiatrically vulnerable)

From Brent DA: Depression and suicide in children and adolescents. Pediatr Rev 14:380, 1993.

potential means of suicide, such as firearms, are removed from the home.

Whether the clinician elects to manage a suicidal child or to refer him or her to a specialist depends on the clinician's level of training and comfort with this type of patient. The ideal procedure is to obtain a mental health consultation, and then the pediatric clinician, mental health specialist, and family can jointly make a decision about the next appropriate step. If mental health treatment is recommended, the pediatric clinician can play a critical role in monitoring compliance and satisfaction with treatment, because many suicidal patients and their families do not comply with treatment.

Referrals to a therapist are much more likely to go smoothly if (1) the patient and family are given a definite appointment; (2) the therapist meets the family before the first session and, preferably, is introduced to the family by the referring professional; and (3) the patient and family are seen as soon as possible from the time of the initial referral. The clinician should be familiar with the mental health resources in his or her area of practice to properly refer in the midst of a potential crisis. Consultation with and referral to a psychiatrist, as opposed to another type of mental health professional, is specifically indicated if the patient is psychotic, has a serious mood disorder, requires detoxification from drugs or alcohol, has a complicating medical condition that may be contributing to the psychiatric presentation, or requires psychopharmacologic intervention.

MANAGEMENT OF SUICIDE ATTEMPTERS. **No suicide attempter should ever be discharged directly from the emergency room without a careful psychiatric assessment.** Whereas a small number of highly suicidal and psychiatrically disturbed patients should be admitted directly to a psychiatric inpatient unit, most patients will not require such intensive or restrictive treatment. If the level of risk is unclear, a 24-hour admission to a pediatric ward may be indicated to evaluate the patient and family. Although the medical consequences alone might not warrant admission, the decision to admit to the hospital communicates to the family that the suicide attempt has been noticed and taken seriously. Many of the families of these attempters are chaotic, and a substantial minority are abusive or neglectful.

REFERRAL FOR PATIENT PSYCHIATRIC TREATMENT. Suicidal children and adolescents who are judged to be at serious risk for committing or attempting suicide are most appropriate for inpatient hospitalization. The specific indications for psychiatric hospitalization are listed in Table 65–36.

TABLE 65–36. Indications for Psychiatric Inpatient Hospitalization

Characteristics of Suicidality
Inability to maintain a no-suicide contract
Active suicidal ideation (with plan and intent)
High intent or lethality suicide attempt
Psychiatric Disorder
Psychosis
Severe depression
Substance abuse
Bipolar illness
Serious aggression
Previous attempts
Previous noncompliance or failure with outpatient treatment
Family Problems
Abuse
Severe parental psychiatric illness
Family unable or unwilling to monitor or protect patient

From Brent DA: Depression and suicide in children and adolescents. Pediatr Rev 14:380, 1993.

THERAPEUTIC INTERVENTIONS. Treatment of suicidal youngsters should proceed on three levels: (1) treatment of the underlying psychiatric illness; (2) remediation of social and problem-solving deficits; and (3) family psychoeducation and conflict resolution. For example, a depressed, suicidal patient who is socially isolated and has a severely conflicted relationship with her alcoholic mother might require antidepressant treatment for her illness, augmentation of social skills to relieve her social isolation, referral of her mother for psychiatric treatment, and family sessions to relieve the family discord and provide psychoeducation about both the parent's and child's psychiatric illness.

FURTHER READING

Birmaher B, Ryan ND, Brent D, et al.: Childhood and adolescent depression. Part I: A review of the past ten years. J Am Child Adolesc Psychiatry 35:1427, 1996.

Birmaher B, Ryan ND, Williamson DE, et al.: Childhood and adolescent depression. Part II: A review of the past ten years. J Am Acad Child Adolesc Psychiatry 35:1575, 1996.

Brent DA: Depression and suicide in children and adolescents. Pediatr Rev 14:380, 1993.

Brent DA: Practitioner review: The aftercare of adolescents with deliberate self-harm. J Child Psychol Psychiatry 38:277, 1997.

Gould MS, Fisher P, Parides M, et al.: Psychosocial risk factors of child and adolescent completed suicide. Arch Gen Psychiatry 53:1155, 1996.

Lewinsohn PM, Rohde P, and Seeley JR: Adolescent suicidal ideation and attempts: Prevalence, risk factors, and clinical implications. Clin Psychol Sci Pract 3:25, 1996.

Shaffer D, Gould MS, Fisher P, et al.: Psychiatric diagnosis in child and adolescent suicide. Arch Gen Psychiatry 53:339, 1996.

Richard F. Catalano
J. David Hawkins

Delinquent Behavior

Juvenile violent crime is a major public concern in the United States. A subset of juvenile offenders is responsible for a majority of this juvenile crime. Whether the measure is officially reported arrests or self-reported offending, a small proportion of the population of juveniles is responsible for a majority of reported offenses. These juveniles are the products of interactions among individual and environmental factors, and their lives are often characterized by the presence of other problems, including drug use, mental health and school problems. This chapter is intended as a guide to assessing the potential significance of involvement in delinquent behavior. It summarizes what is known about the developmental epidemiology of delinquency, the antecedents or risk factors as well as protective factors predictive of delinquency, and effective approaches to prevention and treatment of delinquency applicable to pediatric practice.

EPIDEMIOLOGY

Two sources of data are available: Official reports of arrest and self-reports of behavior. Juvenile arrest rates are available nationally through the Office of Juvenile Justice and Delinquency Prevention, U.S. Department of Justice. These data provide aggregate reports of arrests of juveniles over time. Changes in official delinquency rates must be interpreted carefully because "it is unclear whether an increase in the overall arrest rate reflects an increase in the proportion of all youth involved in violent behavior or an increase in the frequency of offending among active offenders or some combination of these changes" (Elliott et al., 1986). In addition, arrest data are limited to those offenders who are apprehended by the police. Research has shown that police behavior and policies are an important determinant of who gets arrested and may mask the underlying dynamics of delinquent behavior. Self-report measures provide an important epidemiologic alternative to arrest measures. The conditions that produce reliable and valid self-reports of delinquent behavior are well-established. Longitudinal collection of self-reported crime data from the same subjects allows precise examination of the developmental course of delinquent behavior and its antecedents.

Most juveniles have committed at least one delinquent act, and many are involved in some type of delinquent behavior each year. This appears to be relatively constant over time and across places. However, for most, involvement is limited to less serious offenses and low frequency offending. Despite the fact that a large majority of youth self-report involvement in chargeable offenses, only about one third of all adolescents get arrested. Even when the top 5% of the most serious violent offending juveniles are examined in self-report studies, 84% had no arrest record (Dunford and Elliott, 1984). Further, although self-report data show that roughly equal proportions of white and black juveniles are involved in all but violent crimes (Elliott, 1990), arrest data show that black juveniles are twice as likely to be arrested as white juveniles.

According to official reports of arrest, in 1992 youth aged 10 to 17 made up approximately 13% of the U.S. population and were responsible for 15% of the total arrests. This average included 35% of all property index crimes and 18% of violent index crimes. Since much of juvenile crime is committed in groups, however, several juveniles are often arrested as the result of a single crime. Since more adult crime is the act of a single perpetrator, many argue that crime clearance data are a more accurate representation of youth responsibility for crime, since such data are offense-specific rather than offender-specific. When crime clearance data are used, juveniles are responsible for a smaller percentage of crimes. For example, using these statistics, juveniles are responsible for 12.5% of all violent crimes, an amount proportionate to their percentage in the population.

Total juvenile arrests for index crimes (murder, forcible rape, robbery, aggravated assault, burglary, larceny-theft, motor vehicle theft, and arson) declined from 1980 to 1989 and then rose until 1995. Although the total increase over the period was dramatic (30%), there is evidence that the largest increase occurred before 1991, and the recent increase from 1994 to 1995 was only 2%. Serious violent youth crime declined slightly from 1980 to 1987 but increased consistently until 1994. This increase was due to increases in murder, robbery, and aggravated assault from 1988 to 1994 (Snyder, 1996). The violent crime arrest rate for juveniles decreased in 1995 and 1996.

For comparison, self-report data are available from samples of urban 14- to 18-year-olds matched on social class for the time period 1979 to 1991 (Huizinga, 1997). This analysis shows little change in the prevalence of self-reported serious property offenses (10%) and serious violence (12%) over this time. Over the period from 1979 to 1991, substantial decreases were found in rates of self-reported public disorder (44% to 26%), minor property (27% to 17%), and drug sale (12% to 5%) offenses. Despite the unchanging prevalence of serious violence across this time period, the use of weapons in violent offenses and the risk of injury from violent acts have become more prevalent. The rate of self-reported weapon use in serious assaults increased from 31% in 1979 to 82% in 1991. The prevalence of hospitalization or unconsciousness as a result of a violent act almost doubled from 33% to 58% during the same period.

Generally low levels of delinquent behavior are observed before age 10, followed by increasing prevalence from ages 10 to 15 or 16, and declining prevalence to age 21. Thus, for most forms of delinquent behavior, there is a clear pattern of growth during early adolescence and then a predictable decline into the twenties. Several researchers have discovered, however, that those children who begin their delinquency early, particularly violent delinquency, are more likely to persist (Elliott et al., 1986; Moffitt, 1993). This makes early initiation of delinquency, and violent delinquent behavior in particular, an important target for preventive interventions.

Delinquent behavior overlaps with other forms of health-compromising behaviors, including school problems, substance use, risky sexual behavior, and mental health problems. A large proportion of those engaged in delinquent behavior have additional problems. Rates of alcohol use and illicit drug use are higher for all youths who report involvement in delinquent behavior; among delinquents, these rates are higher for those who commit more serious offenses compared with those who commit minor offenses. Those who report delinquent behavior report higher rates of mental health problems, and delinquent youths also report high rates of school problems. However, it is important to note that overlap in problem behaviors should not be considered causal. Most studies of overlap are based on cross-sectional data or on studies of developmental progressions from one type of behavior to another. Neither type of data can demonstrate causal relationships among behaviors; however, it appears that many of these behaviors are predicted by common factors, described in the next section.

ETIOLOGY

Multiple predictors of delinquency have been identified in longitudinal studies. These factors either increase the likelihood of future delinquency (risk factors) or decrease the likelihood of future delinquency by either moderating or mediating risk exposure (protective factors). Risk factors and protective factors predict increased or decreased probability of delinquency, respectively. Extensive research has identified risk factors for delinquency and violence (Brewer et al., 1995; Reiss and Roth, 1993). This section briefly summarizes risk factors for delinquency and violence in four domains: community, family, school, and the individual and peer group.

Community risk factors include living in economically deprived areas, neighborhoods characterized by disorganization (high rates of crime and violence, high population density, physical deterioration of housing stock, lack of usual surveillance of public places, low levels of neighborhood attachment), high rates of mobility and school transitions, availability of firearms and drugs, and media portrayals of violence. **Family risk factors include family management problems (failure to set clear expectations and monitor behavior, as well as excessively severe, harsh, or inconsistent punishment), family conflict, favorable parental attitudes toward crime and violence, and family history of or current involvement in crime or violence.** School-related risk factors include academic failure and lack of commitment to school. Individual factors include constitutional factors (including hyperactivity, concentration problems, sensation seeking, low harm avoidance, and lack of impulse control), early and persistent antisocial behavior (including temperament problems, oppositional defiant behavior, conduct problems, truancy, and aggression), rebelliousness, favorable attitudes toward delinquency, and early initiation of delinquency and violence. Peer-related factors include having friends who engage in delinquency and violence.

Research with populations exposed to multiple risk factors has identified subgroups of individuals who negotiate risk exposure successfully without serious involvement in delinquency or violence. This research has led to studies of the factors that protect against risk exposure. Protective factors predict successful outcomes even in the face of risk. Three types of protective factors and three protective processes have been identified. Protective factors include individual factors (including female gender, high intelligence, a positive social orientation, and a resilient temperament), social bonding (warm, supportive, affective relationships in families or with other positive adults, school commitment, or investment in the future), and healthy beliefs and clear standards for behavior (including valuing educational success and healthy development, and holding norms or standards opposed to crime and violence). Protective processes include opportunities for active involvement in the socializing institutions of family, school, and community; competencies or skills (cognitive, social, emotional, and behavioral); and reinforcement for positive behavior and moderate consistent punishment for negative behavior.

Several generalizations are evident from the longitudinal research on risk factors for, and the protective factors discouraging, juvenile delinquency and violence. First, no single risk factor accounts for the majority of juvenile delinquency and violence; rather, many risk factors contribute to delinquency and violence. Second, both risk factors and protective factors are found in multiple socialization domains, that is, the community, family, school, and peer group, as well as within the individual. Third, exposure to a greater number of risk factors and a lesser number of protective factors increases the risk of crime and violence. Fourth, risk factors and protective factors become salient at different points developmentally from before conception through adolescence. Fifth, common risk factors appear to predict diverse problems (Fig. 65–3). In addition to predicting delinquency and violence, these same risk factors are found to predict other adolescent problems, including substance use, school dropout, and teen pregnancy. Sixth, risk and protective factors appear to operate in the same way in different cultural groups. Although the level of exposure to risk varies in different cultural groups, the risk factors and protective factors appear largely to operate in the same manner. Seventh, protective factors appear to act as a buffer from risk exposure.

PREVENTION

By definition, preventive efforts must occur before a problem fully develops. The most promising approach to eliminating a problem before its occurrence is to address the precursors of the problem. Although not all known risk factors have been shown to be causes of delinquency, they are the best candidates for preventive intervention since they are longitudinal predictors of delinquency. The evidence on risk factors and protective factors suggests a set of principles that should guide delinquency prevention programming (Brewer et al., 1995; Coie et al., 1993). Prevention

efforts should focus on reducing risk and enhancing protective factors. Prevention programs should explicitly connect prevention activities to their influences on risk factors and protective factors. If the preventive activities enhance protection while reducing risk factors, youths are provided with double protection. Risk reduction and protection enhancement actions should begin before the developmental point at which the targeted risk and protective factors become predictive of delinquency. Further, preventive interventions should be directed toward those individuals exposed to multiple risk factors or high levels of a single risk factor. To be most effective, risk factors and protective factors should be prioritized for preventive interventions based on a diagnosis or assessment of the individual's or community's profile of risk and protection. A continuum of preventive actions across the developmental stages of childhood that responds to the changing developmental nature of risk and protection is likely to be most successful. Once delinquent behavior has begun and has become frequent, more intensive intervention is required. However, these approaches are often not as cost-effective as prevention.

Primary care clinicians should be prepared to assess signs of early exposure to risk factors. Simple risk checklists are available that could become a routine part of primary care visits for children and adolescents (Hawkins et al., 1988). Pediatricians should encourage all parents to learn developmentally appropriate parenting skills that reduce children's risks and enhance protection against health-risk behaviors such as delinquency. Parenting programs that provide parents with information about developmental changes and appropriate ways to protect their children from risk and enhance protection, such as Preparing for the Drug (Free) Years (Hawkins et al., 1988), the Iowa Strengthening Families Program (Spoth et al., 1998), and Parents Who Care (Hawkins and Catalano, 1996) have been shown to promote developmentally appropriate parenting skills for parents of elementary through high school children, and have demonstrated positive effects. For children whose risk profiles indicate the presence of conduct problems, effective parenting programs exist, including the Parent and Child Videotape series (Webster-Stratton, 1982, 1992), appropriate for use with children at preschool and early elementary school ages, and the Adolescent Transitions program (Kavanaugh and Dishion, 1990) for parents of middle and high school youths. Once delinquent behavior has become frequent, stronger interventions are indicated that require referral to treatment or early interven-

RISK FACTORS	Substance abuse	Delinquency	Teen pregnancy	School dropout	Violence
Community					
Availability of drugs	✓				✓
Availability of firearms		✓			✓
Community laws and norms favorable toward drug use, firearms, and crime	✓	✓			✓
Media portrayals of violence					✓
Transitions and mobility	✓	✓		✓	
Low neighborhood attachment and community disorganization	✓	✓			✓
Extreme economic deprivation	✓	✓	✓	✓	✓
Family					
Family history of the problem behavior	✓	✓	✓	✓	✓
Family management problems	✓	✓	✓	✓	✓
Family conflict	✓	✓	✓	✓	✓
Favorable parental attitudes and involvement in the problem behavior	✓	✓			✓
School					
Early and persistent antisocial behavior	✓	✓	✓	✓	✓
Academic failure beginning in late elementary school	✓	✓	✓	✓	✓
Lack of commitment to school	✓	✓	✓	✓	✓
Individual/Peer					
Alienation and rebelliousness	✓	✓		✓	
Friends who engage in the problem behavior	✓	✓	✓	✓	✓
Favorable attitudes toward the problem behavior	✓	✓	✓	✓	
Early initiation of the problem behavior	✓	✓	✓	✓	✓
Constitutional factors	✓	✓			✓

Figure 65–3. Risk factors for adolescent problem behaviors. (From Hawkins JD, Catalano RF, Brown EO, et al: Preparing for the Drug [Free] Years: Workshop Leaders Manual. 1998, Developmental Research and Programs, Seattle, WA, p. 39.)

tion programs such as multisystemic family therapy.

SUMMARY

The primary care clinician can play a critical role in both prevention and early intervention for delinquency. For many families, the pediatrician is the single most credible source of information on children's health. Knowledge of those factors that place young people at risk, and of those factors that can protect against substance abuse, is the foundation for assessment, diagnosis, and preventive and early interventive action. A healthy open relationship with children and families and an understanding of normal development allow the clinician to assess existing and emerging risks for delinquency across developmental ages.

Pediatricians can also play an important role in providing knowledge and access to effective prevention programs for parents. Increasingly, effective approaches for reducing specific risks and enhancing protection have been identified and tested. These tested prevention programs are available in many forms and have been used effectively with parents in health maintenance organizations. The potential to intervene before problems arise is both the opportunity and obligation of those whose goal is to promote the health of children.

Acknowledgment

Supported in part by research grant No. 21548 from The Office of Juvenile Justice and Delinquency Prevention.

FURTHER READING

Brewer DD, Hawkins, JD, Catalano RF, and Neckerman HJ: Preventing serious, violent, and chronic juvenile offending: A review of selected strategies in childhood, adolescence, and the community. *In* Howell JC, Krisberg B, Hawkins JD, and Wilson JJ (eds): A Sourcebook: Serious, Violent, and Chronic Juvenile Offenders. Thousand Oaks, CA, Sage Publications, 1995.

Coie JD, Watt NF, West SG, Hawkins JD, et al.: The science of prevention: A conceptual framework and some directions for a national research program. Am Psychol 48:1013, 1993.

Dunford FW and Elliott D: Identifying career offenders using self-reported data. J Res Crim Delinq 21:57, 1984.

Elliott DS: Delinquent behavior. *In* Green M and Haggerty RJ (eds): Ambulatory Pediatrics, 4th ed. Philadelphia, WB Saunders, 1990.

Elliott DS, Huizinga D, and Morse B: Self-reported violent offending: A descriptive analysis of juvenile violent offenders and then offending careers. J Interpersonal Violence 1:472, 1986.

Garmezy N: Stress-resistant children: The search for protective factors. *In* Stevenson JE (ed): Recent research in developmental psychopathology. J Child Psychol Psychiatry 4(Suppl.):213–233, 1985.

Hawkins JD, Lishner DM, Jenson JM, and Catalano RF: Delinquents and drugs: What the evidence suggests about prevention and treatment programming. *In* Brown BS and Mills AR (eds): Youth at High Risk for Substance Abuse. Washington, DC, US Government Printing Office, 1987.

Hawkins JD, Catalano RF, Brown EO, et al.: Preparing for the Drug (Free) Years: A Family Activity Book. Seattle, WA, Comprehensive Health Education Foundation, 1988.

Hawkins JD, Catalano RF, and Brewer DD: Preventing serious, violent, and chronic juvenile offending: Effective strategies from conception to age six. *In* Howell JC, Krisberg B, Hawkins JD, and Wilson JJ (eds): A Sourcebook: Serious, Violent, and Chronic Juvenile Offenders. Thousand Oaks, CA, Sage Publications, 1995.

Hawkins JD and Catalano RF: Parents Who Care: A Step-By-Step Guide for Families With Teens. Seattle, WA, Developmental Research and Programs, 1996.

Huizinga DH: Over-time changes in delinquency and drug use: The 1970s to the 1990s. Unpublished report of the Office of Juvenile Justice and Delinquency Prevention (OJJDP). Presented at meetings of the Western Society of Criminology, Honolulu, HI, 1997.

Kavanaugh K and Dishion TJ: Parent Focus: A Skill Enhancement Curriculum for Parents of Young Adolescents. Eugene, OR, Independent Video Services, 1990.

Moffitt TE: Adolescence-limited and life-course-persistent antisocial behavior: A developmental taxonomy. Psychol Rev 100:674, 1993.

Reiss AJ and Roth JA (eds): Understanding and Preventing Violence. Washington DC, National Academy Press, 1993.

Snyder HN: Juvenile arrests, 1995. Office of Justice Programs Juvenile Justice Bulletin. Washington DC, Office of Juvenile Justice and Delinquency Prevention, 1996.

Spoth R, Redmond C, and Shin C: Direct and indirect latent parenting outcomes of two universal family-focused preventive interventions: Extending a public health-oriented research base. J Consult Clin Psychol 66:385, 1998.

Webster-Stratton C: The long-term effects of a videotape modeling parent-training program: Comparison of immediate and 1 year follow-up results. Behav Ther 1: 702, 1982.

Webster-Stratton C: Individually administered videotape parent training: "Who benefits?" Cognitive Ther Res 16:31, 1992.

Ellen C. Perrin

Gay and Lesbian Issues in Pediatric Care

The general topic of homosexuality has been presented to primary care clinicians with greater and greater frequency in the 1990s and is likely to continue to increase in salience in the future. There are several reasons why homosexuality has become such an important issue for pediatricians: (1) Bisexual and homosexual attraction and orientation have become considerably better understood and more accepted in mainstream society; (2) in part as a result of this, adolescents are recognizing, acknowledging, and declaring their homosexuality at increasingly younger ages; (3) the medical and psychosocial risks associated with being homosexual in our society are becoming better recognized and understood, creating an opportunity for health care clinicians to address their prevention and treatment; (4) parents who have children in the context of a heterosexual union and later recognize or declare their homosexuality are increasingly feeling empowered to declare publicly their sexual orientation and new family constellation; and (5) increasing numbers of gay men and lesbians are adopting and/or conceiving children and parenting them in the context of an ongoing same-sex relationship.

THE DEVELOPMENT OF SEXUAL ORIENTATION

The search for an explanation of individuals' sexual orientation has been persistent, but has yielded few clear-cut answers. Theories include notions of family dynamics or of intrapsychic developmental patterns that favor attractions to one or the other gender and a large number of biologic bases, such as genetic makeup, prenatal exposure to androgens, and prenatal neuroendocrinologic differences. It is likely that a combination of forces determine an individual's final sexual orientation.

Many lesbians and gay men consider themselves in some way "different" as early as the preschool period. More gay than heterosexual adult men recall playing with dolls and preferring girls as playmates, an observation that has also been corroborated by their mothers. Around the time of puberty, emotional and physical attractions toward people of the same gender may surface,

and gay and lesbian adults describe having felt "marginalized" and separate from their same-sex peers, often not sharing common interests and activities.

Gay and lesbian youth face considerable challenges in negotiating the always-complex tasks of adolescent development. They often are forced to deal directly with stigmatization and hostility. During early to middle adolescence, lesbian and gay youth begin to reflect on the idea that their feelings or behaviors are considered "homosexual," a label that often creates confusion, anxiety, and inner turmoil. The social stigma and the associated perceived need for secrecy discourage adolescent lesbians and gay males from discussing their emerging sexual desires and activities with peers and families, resulting in escalating isolation. In their distress, they may deny or seek to change their homosexual feelings, inhibit their social and sexual attractions, and avoid situations that incite or confirm their homosexual desires. They may define their homosexual attractions as temporary or situational, and sometimes even espouse explicitly antihomosexual attitudes and activities.

In middle and later adolescence, young people may come to recognize and accept their homosexual identity and start to share it with others, typically peers, gay friends or teachers, and parents. This process is termed "identity assumption." It is worrisome when same-sex attractions and activities are kept secret, avoided, or criticized, as well as when stereotypical "homosexual" behavior is paraded in an exaggerated form. Negative stereotyping, homophobia, and both verbal and physical abuse are widespread among high school and college students, school principals, teachers, coaches, and guidance counselors. During this period, escape through alcohol and other drug use, depression, and diminished self-esteem are too-common evidence of unsuccessful adaptation.

Parental reactions to the disclosure of an adolescent's homosexuality may span being affirming and supportive to being hostile and rejecting. Many lesbian and gay youths report that their parents rejected them after they disclosed their sexual orientation: only 10% of fathers and 21% of mothers were reported to be supportive, and 26% of the youths were forced to leave home because of resultant conflicts.

The individual's acceptance of his or her sexual orientation and its disclosure to others mark the final stage in the proposed developmental progression, generally occurring in late adolescence or early adulthood. With increasing disclosure and subsequent support, these young people can achieve increased self-confidence, self-esteem, and positive attitudes about their sexuality and how it interacts with the rest of their life's plans and goals.

SPECIAL RISKS FOR HOMOSEXUAL ADOLESCENTS

Risks related to sexual activity do not differ dramatically between heterosexual and homosexual youths. Because early sexual activity can include both homosexual and heterosexual experimentation, whatever the individual's predominant sexual orientation will become, sexually transmitted diseases including the human immunodeficiency virus and the acquired immunodeficiency syndrome (AIDS), as well as pregnancy, are notable risks that require preventive education and intervention by primary care clinicians. Gay and lesbian youth are vulnerable also to urethritis; anogenital, oropharyngeal, and gastrointestinal disorders; hepatitis; and anogenital trauma.

Lesbian and gay adolescents also are at increased risk for self-destructive behaviors such as prostitution, substance abuse, school failure and dropout, depression, and suicide. In some cities, 25% to 40% of "street kids" are thought to be homosexual, and large numbers (30% to 50%) of gay youths have been reported to abuse alcohol or other drugs.

The increased risk of suicide attempts and "successful" suicides among homosexual youths has been reported repeatedly. **Abundant evidence demonstrates that 50% of gay youths have seriously contemplated suicide and that close to 25% have made at least one suicide attempt during their teenage years.** Several surveys report that gay and lesbian youths are two to three times more likely to attempt suicide than are other youths and suggest that these youths account for up to 30% of adolescents who commit suicide.

The primary goal of health care for all adolescents is to promote normal adolescent development, social and emotional well-being, and physical health. This goal is no different for teenagers who are sure of their heterosexual or homosexual orientation and those who are unsure about their sexual orientation. *All* adolescents need acceptance, support, advice, and modeling from peers, family members, and professionals. It is important for all adolescents to understand that there is a large variety of responsible sexual behaviors and a wide range of sexual orientations.

Adolescents who are wondering about the complex feelings they are experiencing with regard to sexual attractions and orientation, and those who know that they are gay, lesbian, or bisexual, are a group of teenagers experiencing even more than the usual degree of upheaval and identity confusion that besets most teenagers in our society. **Many adolescents report that they would like a clinician to give them information about homosexuality, although few teens take the initiative to ask their clinician to help them with questions about their sexual orientation.**

CHILDREN WITH GAY OR LESBIAN PARENTS

Estimates are that 8 to 10 million U.S. citizens have at least one gay parent. Most were conceived in the context of a heterosexual relationship, which then changed to adapt to the recognition and/or acknowledgement of homosexuality in one or both partners. Various options of "single" parenting, recoupling, and blending families exist for these families, just as for heterosexual parents. As reproductive technologies, social acceptance of homosexuality, and legal structures reflecting increased tolerance have grown, the opportunities for lesbians and gay men to conceive and/or adopt children have expanded tremendously.

Evidence about long-term outcomes of children raised in families in which both parents are gay suggests some special strengths in these children—and no apparent risks. The strengths are predictable: they appear more tolerant of diversity and less tolerant of aggression, and they are skillful at negotiating differences with their peers. There is no evidence of special risks for physical or sexual abuse or for psychopathology of any kind, nor of increased likelihood of a homosexual orientation's developing in the children themselves. Parents' commitment to providing a safe and nurturing environment is far more important to children's development than the family's constellation of adults and children.

Pediatricians and other primary care clinicians are in a good position to identify, address, and try to help parents cope with destructive reactions both from the outside community and as a result of their own internalized self-doubts. Opportunities include, for example, (1) helping families to establish a parental and a legal role for the nonbiologic parent(s); (2) helping the child understand his or her particular family structure, its difference from the traditional family structure, and the identity and whereabouts of his or her genetic mother or father; (3) helping the child and the parents make the transition from a protected home-based or selective preschool community to the school community with its pervasive homophobic judgments; (4) helping young adolescents struggle with their issues of identity and rootedness and with the development of their own sexuality; and (5) coping with the homophobia and lack of supportive parenting that may exist on the part of an estranged partner and/or the child's grandparents.

COMMON ISSUES AND COMMON APPROACHES

In the Office

Most clinicians have relatively little experience, little training, and therefore little confidence in their ability to understand and to work effectively to address the special concerns of parents who are gay or lesbian, adolescents who are or think they might be gay or lesbian, and parents of those adolescents. Providing comprehensive and supportive medical care for gay or lesbian patients and their families may present an unfamiliar and awkward challenge. Nevertheless, the full range of human sexual orientation and behavior is an appropriate topic of clinical concern for *all* children, adolescents, and their parents, because lesbians and gay men are increasingly evident in all aspects of society.

It is not difficult for clinicians to make a tremendous impact on the lives of gay and lesbian individuals and their families. It is important that they establish a respectful relationship, with mutual rapport, with all their patients. Because gay and lesbian parents and adolescents, and those who are questioning their sexual orientation, experience such pervasive stigmatization and rejection, they are likely to be especially uncomfortable and suspicious in an office interaction. Some reassurance can be provided by stating explicitly the office policy about confidentiality and by providing written materials that describe this policy. Strict policies against homophobic and other stigmatizing remarks, jokes, or slurs should be implemented, publicly stated, and enforced. Having available books, magazines, posters, and information about community and national resources for gay and lesbian parents, youths, and their families is a powerful nonverbal statement of the office's acceptance of the wide range of sexual orientations.

It is helpful to reassure all adolescents that questions about sexuality are a routine part of the health supervision visit, whether included in a health history form or in the interview. Suggestions for gender-neutral language are included in Table 65–37. Clinicians should provide safer sex guidelines to *all* adolescents, with further screening and education as indicated for each adolescent's sexual activity. They should have available information and resources regarding lesbian and gay issues and offer support for adolescents, children, or parents faced with or anticipating conflicts with families and/or friends. In addition, primary care clinicians must ensure that physicians with whom they consult or to whom they refer gay and lesbian clients will be respectful of the range of sexual orientations, and furthermore that confidentiality will be carefully maintained.

It is *not* the responsibility of the clinician to identify adolescents who are gay or lesbian, but only to make discussion of the range of human sexual experience comfortable and acceptable to *all* adolescents. Similarly, parents must choose how much they wish to reveal about their family constellation. By making explicit their interest in the nature and quality of the child(ren)'s family environment and their support for a variety of family forms, pediatric clinicians can help parents feel comfortable in discussing their specific situations and concerns (Table 65–38).

On the Community Level

As "opinion leaders," primary care clinicians have the opportunity to model and provide opportunities for increasing awareness, knowledge, and

---

TABLE 65–37. Suggested Questions About Sexuality

Some of my patients your age are dating—some are dating boys, some girls, some both. Are you interested in dating?
Have you ever dated or gone out with someone?
Have you ever been attracted to any boys or girls?
Is there any special person in your life outside of your family?
There are many ways of being sexual with another person: petting, kissing, hugging, as well as sexual intercourse. Have you had any kinds of sexual experiences? If so, were they with boys or girls, or both?
Are you currently involved in a steady relationship with a boy or a girl?
How do you protect yourself and your partner against sexually transmitted diseases (and pregnancy)?
Do you have any concerns about your sexual feelings or the sexual things you have been doing?
Have you discussed these concerns with your parents or any other adults? Any of your friends?
Do you consider yourself to be gay/lesbian, bisexual, or heterosexual (straight)?

TABLE 65–38. Suggested Questions About Family Constellations

Who else is helping you with parenting?
Who are the important adults in this child's world?
Do you have a partner in parenting?
Could you describe who else is in your family—both children and adults?

acceptance of homosexuality among school staff, mental health professionals, and other community leaders. They can be advisers to schools regarding curriculum development and library resources, community support networks, and AIDS education and prevention programs, and they can assist in the development of continuing education opportunities for educational and health care personnel. Public support of legal and political initiatives for fair and equal treatment of gay and lesbian adolescents and of children whose parents are homosexual is an explicit choice some clinicians may want to make.

In Health Care Institutions

Clinicians can be vigilant for and address aspects of the institutional environments in which they work that may be threatening or unwelcoming to people of homosexual orientation. Examples include office brochures about adolescence that assume heterosexuality, hospital visiting policies that exclude a same-sex parent, multiple official forms that insist on signatures of "mother" and "father," absence of public evidence of pictures, brochures, and information that are inclusive of the lives of gay and lesbian individuals, and ubiquitous homophobic jokes and insults. Clinicians should insist on policies that ensure confidentiality, and these policies should be publicly displayed and reiterated. Similarly, policies against homophobic remarks should be displayed and enforced. The visible presence of books, magazines, posters, or informational pamphlets that address issues and resources relevant to families with a lesbian or gay member transmits an important message of acceptance.

FURTHER READING

Professional Books

Benkov L: Reinventing the Family. New York, Crown Publishers, 1994.
DeCrescenzo T (ed): Helping Gay and Lesbian Youth: New Policies, New Programs, New Practice. New York, Harrington Park Press, 1994.
Remafedi G: Death by Denial: Studies of Suicide in Gay and Lesbian Teenagers. Boston, Alyson Publications, 1994.

Children's Books

Elwin R and Paulse M: Asha's Mums. Toronto, Women's Press, 1990.
Greenberg KE: Zack's Story. Minneapolis, MN, Lerner Publications, 1996.
Heron A and Maran M: How Would You Feel If Your Dad Was Gay? Boston, Alyson Publications, 1991.
Newman L: Heather Has Two Mommies. Boston, Alyson Publications, 1989.
Valentine J: The Duke Who Outlawed Jelly Beans and Other Stories. Boston, Alyson Publications, 1991.
Valentine J: The Daddy Machine. Boston, Alyson Publications, 1992.

Books for Teenagers

Alyson S (ed): Young, Gay and Proud. Boston, Alyson Publications, 1991.
Bass E and Kaufman K: Free Your Mind. New York, HarperCollins Publishers, 1996.
Borhek MV: Coming Out To Parents: A Two-Way Survival Guide for Lesbians and Gay Men and Their Parents. Cleveland, OH, Pilgrim Press, 1993.
Heron A (ed): Two Teenagers in Twenty: Writings By Gay and Lesbian Youth. Boston, Alyson Publications, 1994.
Miller DA: Coping When a Parent Is Gay. New York, Rosen Publishing, 1992.

Books for Parents

Cohen S and Cohen D: When Someone You Know Is Gay. New York, Dell Publishing, 1989.
Fairchild B and Hayward N: Now That You Know: What Every Parent Should Know About Homosexuality. Orlando, FL, Harcourt Brace Publishing, 1989.
Griffin CW, Wirth AG, and Wirth MJ: Beyond Acceptance: Parents of Lesbians and Gays Talk About Their Experience. New York, St. Martin's Press, 1990.

RESOURCES FOR THE GAY AND LESBIAN COMMUNITY

Children of Lesbians and Gays Everywhere (COLAGE)
 2300 Market Street #165
 San Francisco, CA 94114
 Phone: (415) 861-5437
 email: kidsofgays@aol.com
Gay and Lesbian Parents' Coalition International
 PO Box 50360
 Washington, DC 20004
 Phone: (202) 583-8029
 email: glpcinat@ix.netcom.com
National Coalition of Gay, Lesbian, and Bisexual Youth
 PO Box 24589
 San Jose, CA 95118-4589
 Phone: (408) 269-6125
 email: info@outproud.org
National Federation of Parents and Friends of Lesbians and Gays (PFLAG).
 1012 14th Street NW, Suite 700
 Washington, DC 20005.
 Phone: (202) 638-4200
 email: pflagntl@aol.com
National Gay/Lesbian/Bisexual Youth Hotline
 Phone: (800) 347-TEEN

Conduct Disorders

The main characteristic of conduct disorder is the persistent pattern of conduct in which the basic rights of others and age-appropriate societal norms are violated by a child younger than 18 years of age (Table 65–39). Whether this condition is a true mental disorder or a variant of willful behavior that violates others' rights is debated. Conduct disorder is the most common disorder seen in children's mental health clinics, with 1-year prevalence figures varying from 1.5% to 11.9% in different countries. Conduct disorder is more common among boys than girls, and the rates for both increase with age. The majority of children who have conduct disorder also have comorbid symptoms, especially attention-deficit disorder: 41% of children who have attention-deficit disorder go on to develop symptoms of conduct disorder. Family functioning seems to be the main factor determining which route such a child will take. Families who provide a supportive, consistent environment, setting limits but allowing their children to develop social skills that let them function reasonably well in school and with peers, appear to prevent progression to diagnosable conduct disorder.

Untreated conduct disorder usually persists into adulthood. When a combination of aggression and shyness is present, drug abuse and delinquency often follow. Conduct disorder is associated in adolescence and adult life with higher rates of school failure, joblessness, and marital difficulties. When these behaviors occur in adulthood, the name of the disorder changes to *antisocial behavior*. For this diagnosis, the patient must be at least 18 years of age. Unfortunately, once the condition is diagnosed, treatment is unsatisfactory. In adulthood, society deals with many of the behaviors through the judicial system. The primary care clinician's role is that of recognizing the condition early, helping parents to set realistic limits and yet provide support, and referring the child and family to innovative preventive programs.

RISK FACTORS

Conduct disorder clearly runs in families, but how much is due to biology and how much to family factors is unclear. No twin or adoption studies have been conducted for this problem, although among adult criminals there is a higher concordance for monozygotic over dizygotic twins, suggesting some genetic loading. Some interesting physiologic differences are found among children who have conduct disorder, including low heart rate and slow recovery of skin conductance, suggesting a biologic basis for reduced anxiety and impaired passive avoidance following punish-

TABLE 65–39. *DSM-IV* **Diagnostic Criteria for Conduct Disorder**

A. A disturbance of contact lasting at least 6 months, during which at least three of the following have been present:
  (1) has stolen without confrontation of a victim on more than one occasion (including forgery)
  (2) has run away from home overnight at least twice while living in parental or parental surrogate home (or once without returning)
  (3) often lies (other than to avoid physical or sexual abuse)
  (4) has deliberately engaged in fire-setting
  (5) is often truant from school (for older person, absent from work)
  (6) has broken into someone else's house, building, or car
  (7) has deliberately destroyed others' property (other than by fire-setting)
  (8) has been physically cruel to animals
  (9) has forced someone into sexual activity with him or her
  (10) has used a weapon in more than one fight
  (11) often initiates physical fights
  (12) has stolen with confrontation of a victim (e.g., mugging, purse-snatching, extortion, armed robbery)
  (13) has been physically cruel to people

Note: The above items are listed in descending order of discriminating power based on data from a national field trial of the *DSM-IV* criteria for Disruptive Behavior Disorders.

B. If 18 or older, does not meet criteria for Antisocial Personality Disorder.

Criteria for Severity of Conduct Disorder

Mild: Few if any conduct problems in excess of those required to make the diagnosis, **and** conduct problems cause only minor harm to others.

Moderate: Number of conduct problems and effect on others intermediate between "mild" and "severe."

Severe: Many conduct problems in excess of those required to make the diagnosis, **or** conduct problems cause considerable harm to others, e.g., serious physical injury to victims, extensive vandalism or theft, prolonged absence from home.

Adapted with permission from Diagnostic and Statistical Manual of Mental Disorders, Fourth Edition (DSM-IV). Copyright 1994, American Psychiatric Association.

ment, and a perceived need for more exciting activities to achieve satisfaction. Temperamentally difficult children are more likely to be diagnosed later as having conduct disorder, but they also are more likely to be the target of parental anger and criticism as they grow up. Children who have conduct disorder often do poorly in school and are delayed in their reading; which of these factors comes first, however, is not clear. Chronic physical disorders in children occur three times more frequently among children who have conduct disorder than in the general population. Community risk factors, such as poverty, overcrowding, and racism, as well as family disorganization, are highly associated with this disorder. The more symptoms and the earlier they appear, the worse the prognosis; thus, the accumulation of risk factors and earlier onset increase the risk of conduct disorder, as they do for many other disorders.

Recently, the search for protective factors has increased with the assumption that they could provide the basis for effective preventive programs. A warm parent-child supportive relationship, prosocial groups, and good schools are all associated with reduced risk of conduct disorder, as they are for many other problems.

PREVENTION

In contrast to substance abuse prevention, most programs to prevent conduct disorders have focused on the individual rather than the community. These focus on behavioral management training for parents and improvement of communication skills for both parent and child. An especially

vulnerable time for the child at risk for conduct disorder appears to be the transition from elementary to middle school and from middle school to high school. Therefore, recent intervention programs have focused on changes in the school environment to include shared decision making and the empowering of homeroom teachers to be more central to the children's lives as counselors. Evaluation of such programs has shown decreased dropout and delinquency rates (see Chapter 65, subchapter on Delinquent Behavior).

The Institute of Medicine reported recently that conduct disorder is one of the conditions for which preventive intervention trials are now sufficiently developed to recommend large-scale, carefully evaluated interventions. If successful, such interventions should lead to optimism for a condition that generally has been unresponsive to therapy and to a more important role of the primary care clinician in early diagnosis. By and large, successful interventions will require schoolwide and community changes as well as individual family therapy.

FURTHER READING

Hawkins JD, Catalano RF, and Miller JR: Risk and protective factors for alcohol and substance abuse prevention. Psychol Bull 112:64–105, 1992.

Kazdin AE: Treatment of antisocial behavior in children: Current status and future directions. Psychol Bull 102:187–203, 1987.

McCord J and Trembly RE (eds): Preventing Antisocial Behavior: Interventions from Birth through Adolescence. New York, Guilford Press, 1992.

Mrazck PJ and Haggerty RJ: Reducing Risks for Mental Disorders: Frontiers for Preventive Intervention Research. Washington, DC, National Academy Press, 1994.

Deborah Klein Walker

Runaways

Although running away is not a new phenomenon in the United States, it has received much attention as a significant social problem in the past 3 decades. The most accepted definition of a runaway is a youth younger than 18 years of age who is gone from home at least overnight without parental permission or consent. The one finding that is consistent across all studies—regardless of definition, methodology, and theoretical approach— is that runaways experience some type of family problem. Problems with school friends, or the

police are often mentioned and are important, but they seldom are primary.

The majority of runaways leave home only once, leave on the spur of the moment, leave after an argument or fight at home, stay with friends within the community, have no contacts with police or social service agencies, and return home voluntarily. Although the majority of runaways— the one-time runaways—are no different from their "normal healthy" peers who have never run away, a small minority of runaways—the multiple-episode runaways—have problems that suggest some psychopathology or severe family disruption. Multiple-episode runaways are significantly different from one-time runaways or nonrunaways on a variety of home, school, and peer variables; this group of runaways tends to visit runaway shelters or experience sexual or physical victimization while on the run. The harsh, negative consequences experienced on the street by this small minority of runaways are often highlighted in newspaper and magazine articles about street youth.

Because running away is a family and not a court problem, both primary and secondary prevention strategies should focus on the family whenever possible. Both the runaway or youth at risk for running away and his or her family require careful consideration and continued monitoring by the primary case clinician. Referrals of youth at risk to community of school programs and fami-

lies at risk to mental health and community programs may ultimately prevent some youths from running away.

A toll-free, 24-hour nationwide telephone number (800-621-4000) can be used by youth away from home who wish to contact the parents or to request help. A good source of help for the youth who is on the run is often the community's runaway shelter. When returning the runaway to his or her family is not possible, an alternative placement (e.g., foster care, group home, independent living) should be sought.

FURTHER READING

Farrow JD, Deisher RW, Brown R, et al.: Health and health needs of homeless and runaway youth. J Adolesc Health 13:717–726, 1992.
Young RL, Godfrey W, Matthews B, and Adams G: Runaways: A review of negative consequences. Family Relations 32:275, 1983.

Lorraine V. Klerman

When the Child's Mother Is a Teenager

One of every 7.5 births in the United States is to a woman who is less than 20 years of age, and one in 20 is to a woman who is less than 18 years of age. Thus, it is very likely that most pediatricians and other clinicians who care for infants and young children are dealing with several mothers who are teenagers. Although difficult socioeconomic circumstances and poor parenting practices are found throughout the maternal age range, studies have consistently shown that, on average, young mothers and their children face more—and more difficult—problems than do older mothers.

In order to best serve the infant or child brought for care, clinicians must ask more questions about the social circumstances of a teenage mother than might be asked of an older mother. Moreover, the clinician may need to provide intensive counseling, particularly in the area of contraceptive use, or refer the mother for such help.

THE SCOPE OF THE PROBLEM OF TEENAGE PREGNANCY

In 1995, the last year for which federal data are available, there were almost 3.9 million live births

in the United States. Of these, over half a million were to women less than 20 years of age: more than 12,000 to those aged less than 15; more than 192,000 to those aged 15 through 17; and more than 300,000 to those aged 18 and 19. A majority of these teenage births were to white teenagers (69.4%). Although the rate of teenage pregnancy is higher in African-American and Hispanic women, the much larger number of white teenagers makes the actual number of teenage births higher among whites. The news media have given wide coverage to several recent cases of infanticide by white teenagers.

Teenage mothers are more likely than their older peers to experience medical and social problems during their pregnancies and in the years that follow, often with adverse consequences for their children. Pregnant teenagers seek care later in their pregnancies, often because of denial or reluctance to tell others about the pregnancy, and have higher rates of maternal complications. Their infants are more likely to be low birth weight (<2500 grams).

Teenage mothers are often unmarried (93.4% of births to women aged less than 15 and 75.2% of births to women aged 15 through 19 years of age) and face the difficulties of caring for an infant and young child without a marital partner. Teenage mothers are more likely than older mothers not to have completed high school, both because of their age and because of a tendency either to drop out of school when pregnant or to have dropped out and then become pregnant. Some pregnant teenagers remain in school, often in special classes or schools for pregnant female students, and some return to school after the birth of the infant. The greater the number of children born to the mother, however, the lesser the chances of her completing high school.

Teenage mothers are frequently poor and often receive welfare benefits. They may receive welfare payments in their own names, if they are in a living arrangement separate from their parents, or their parents' welfare check may be increased to include the infant. Nevertheless, clinicians who care for middle or working-class children should not assume that they have no children of teenage mothers in their practices or clinics.

WHAT THE CLINICIAN MUST KNOW

Certainly clinicians have no difficulty asking the mother of a new patient the date of her child's birth, but they may, at times, find it awkward to ask the date of the mother's birth. Given the increasingly early age of menarche (now about 12.5 years) and the tendency of teenage women to dress similarly to women in their twenties (or vice versa), clinicians cannot assume that they can accurately guess the age of the mother.

Once the clinician has determined that the mother is a teenager, other questions are appropriate if the child is to receive adequate care. The clinician will want to learn about the mother's living circumstances. Is she living with the father of the baby and, if so, are they married? Is she living with her parents, other relatives, or alone? The clinician will want to know who is the child's primary caretaker both during the day and at night.

Although the clinician might believe that an infant's well-being might best be served in the short-term by a full-time mother, if the teenage mother has not yet graduated high school, there may be a long-term disadvantage. The clinician will need to balance the problems involved in finding suitable child care against those that may arise for the mother and for the child if the mother has an inadequate education and few skills to offer an employer.

The clinician should discuss with the teenage mother how to select suitable child care. Many teenage mothers feel that their mothers or other female relatives are the best caretakers and may refuse initially to consider any alternative. Studies suggest, however, that children, particularly those from disadvantaged backgrounds, may benefit from the developmentally oriented programs available in well-run child care centers. **Clinicians may need to use their considerable influence to urge the mother to return to high school or seek advanced education and to place the child in a stimulating child care environment.**

Knowledge of the caretaking arrangements for the child is also essential to prevent unintentional or intentional injuries. Because teenage mothers are probably less likely to have seen or read material about child safety, the clinician should ask about potential lead paint hazards, the presence of smoke detectors and stairway guards in the home, the regulation of hot water, how the toddler is kept from toxic household substances, where infants and children sit and how they are restrained when in automobiles or trucks, and guns in the home. Questions about domestic violence are also essential, not only to protect the mother but also because child abuse is more likely in a household where an adult is being battered. Although clinicians should review all these issues with older mothers as well, they are particularly urgent with the younger, often undereducated mother.

The potential for child abuse and neglect, which has a higher incidence among young parents, should be explored. Teenage mothers may not be knowledgeable about the stages of child development and may become irritated when their children try to feed themselves and "make a mess," or when they are not toilet-trained at a young age. The normal behavior of a very young child may be even more upsetting to the child's father or to another male left in charge of the infant or child. The professional literature and the press often describe men who hit, shake, or even batter an infant or young child in order to force the baby to stop crying or to do as told. The clinician must not only counsel the mother about what to expect from her child and when but also urge her not to leave the child with anyone who does not have experience with, and tolerance of, young children.

The clinician should also discuss with the young mother the importance of interacting with the child starting in infancy. Many young mothers seem unaware of their children's potential for learning from birth or how children's future social interactions are shaped by the responses that they receive as infants. They need to learn that you cannot spoil infants by responding to their cries and that talking to children is not a waste of time but very important.

THE NEED FOR FAMILY PLANNING

A remarkably large percentage of teenage mothers are having a second or higher-order birth. In 1995, 24.3% of women aged less than 15, 12.0% of those aged 15 through 17, and 27.1% of those aged 18 and 19 had had previous live births. More than 2000 of the 18- and 19-year-olds were having a fourth or higher-order birth. This is counting only live births, excluding miscarriages, stillbirths, and induced abortions. These figures suggest that first-time teenage mothers are not receiving adequate advice about the need to wait before having another child.

The mother, the child who has already been born, and the children yet to be born can benefit from delaying subsequent pregnancies. The mother is more likely to complete her education if she waits before having another child. Also, her likelihood of marriage increases. Both additional education and marriage will lessen the possibility of welfare dependency. The child who is already born will benefit from having a mother who is not tired because of another pregnancy or who is not too busy caring for another child to give the older child the attention all children need. In addition, the children who will be born later will avoid the medical problems associated with short interpregnancy intervals and the competition for the mother's time when there are several very small children in the household.

The clinician should routinely ask the young mother about whether she wants to have any additional children and, if she does, when she wants to have them. If the mother suggests an interval between births of less than 2 years, she should be strongly advised to wait at least 2 years. More often, however, the mother will say that she plans to wait for several years, or until she finishes school and/or finds a job, or until she marries. The statistics, however, make it clear that many young mothers are unable to achieve their own child-spacing objectives.

Clinicians caring for the children of young mothers are in a unique position to assist them with family planning because they can stress the importance of family planning not only for the well-being of the mother but also for the health and well-being of the child for whom they are caring. Clinicians can ask about use of contraceptives in the context of suggesting ways to maintain the infant's health. If the young mother is using an effective method, the clinician can praise her and encourage her to continue. If she is using a method of limited effectiveness, experiencing difficulty with a method, or using no method at all, the clinician should attempt to start her on a contraceptive immediately if she is sexually active (see Chapter 65, subchapter on Contraception). Waiting for her to make an appointment on her own with a family planning clinic may result in an unintended pregnancy.

INVOLVING OTHER FAMILY MEMBERS AND AGENCIES

When the patient is the child of a teenage mother, it may be particularly important to involve other family members. If the grandmother or another older relative cares for the child much of the time, the mother should be urged to bring her to the well-child examination. The family member needs to learn about presently recommended methods of child raising, such as infants' sleeping on their backs and talking to infants. **Unless clinicians attempt to educate the grandmothers or other adult caretakers as well as the mother, they may find their messages ignored.**

If the father of the baby has remained in contact with the child, then he too should be encouraged to see the clinician during the next health supervision visit. He will need the same education as the mother, but it is particularly important that he receive the message about contraception. His child will benefit from the delay in subsequent pregnancies and he should share with the mother the responsibility for family planning.

As clinicians learn about the family circumstances of a young mother, they may identify more problems than they can optimally manage alone. It is helpful in such circumstances to have at hand a list of agencies that are willing to assist young mothers in solving their economic and social problems. These resources include public and private family services and child welfare agencies, family planning centers, organizations that deal with domestic violence, groups that provide parenting education, and agencies that offer referrals to appropriate child care placements. Because teenage mothers often do not follow through on referrals, clinicians need to incorporate in their practices a way of checking to determine that an appointment was made (or else to make it for the mother before she leaves the visit), that the mother kept her appointment, and that she is following whatever advice she received.

In some communities, health departments or other agencies have developed Teen-Tot Clinics specifically designed to treat the health problems of both teenage mothers and their children in the same setting and at the same visit, if possible. This approach makes it more likely that the impact of the mother's social circumstances will be considered when the child is treated.

Teenage motherhood is common in the United States. Although the public often hears about the consequences for the mother and for society, there seems to be less awareness of the consequences for the child. Clinicians who care for the children of young mothers are in an excellent position to minimize potential problems. Determining that a mother is a teenager and assessing her current social and economic circumstances is the first step in promoting her healthy adaptation to parenthood and preventing adverse outcomes for her child. Such an approach is especially important at this time when welfare reform limits financial assistance to many young mothers.

Acknowledgment

The preparation of this paper was made possible, in part, by a grant (MCJ 9040) from the federal Maternal and Child Health Bureau, Health Resources and Services Administration, US Department of Health and Human Services.

FURTHER READING

Alan Guttmacher Institute: Sex and America's Teenagers. New York, Alan Guttmacher Institute, 1994.
Furstenberg FF Jr, Brooks-Gunn J, and Morgan SP: Adolescent Mothers in Later Life. New York, Cambridge University Press, 1987.
Horowitz R: Teen Mothers: Citizens or Dependents? Chicago, University of Chicago Press, 1995.
Kirby D: No Easy Answers: Research Findings on Programs to Reduce Teen Pregnancy. Washington, DC, National Campaign to Prevent Teen Pregnancy, 1997.
Klerman LV and Reynolds DW: Interconception care: A new role for the pediatrician. Pediatrics 93:327–329, 1994.
Moore KA, Miller BC, Glei D, and Morrison DR: Adolescent Sex, Contraception, and Childbearing: A Review of Recent Research. Washington, DC, Child Trends, Inc, 1995.
Musick JS: Young, Poor and Pregnant: The Psychology of Teenage Motherhood. New Haven, CT, Yale University Press, 1993.
Quint JC, Musick JS, and Ladner JA: Lives of Promise, Lives of Pain: Young Mothers after New Chances. New York, Manpower Demonstration Research Corporation, 1994.

Joseph Shrand
Michael S. Jellinek

The Use of Psychotropic Medication in Children and Adolescents

Worried parents come to primary care clinicians for advice, counseling, diagnosis, and treatment of problem behaviors in their children. Psychologic issues represent 12% to 20% of primary care practice. Given the prevalence of psychologic concerns, primary care clinicians have expanded their role to include treatment of mild to moderate psychiatric disorders in an office practice. In addition, the pressure of managed and capitated care may create economic incentives that encourage clinicians to manage more directly a broad range of psychiatric conditions in their practice.

Medications are now important means of treating attention-deficit hyperactivity disorder (ADHD), depression, and anxiety disorders found in children and adolescents. Complete guidelines for diagnosis of these and other disorders can be found in the *Diagnostic and Statistical Manual of Mental Disorders,* fourth edition (*DSM-IV*) and its primary care–oriented companion manual, the *Diagnostic and Statistical Manual for Primary Care* (*DSM-IV-PC*) (see Chapter 65, subchapter on Attention Deficits). Clinicians interested in more comprehensive medical or psychiatric reviews of psychiatric disorders in children and adolescents and their treatment will find useful the references listed in Further Reading at the end of the chapter.

Diagnosis and treatment of child and adolescent psychiatric disorders is no simple task. Treatment recommendations must be accurate and work synergistically. Psychotropic medication is only one modality in the context of a comprehensive treatment plan (Table 65–40). **When medication is warranted, it should complement and enhance, but not be expected to replace, other interventions.**

GENERAL PRINCIPLES IN USING PSYCHOTROPIC MEDICATIONS

Defining, evaluating, and then tracking target symptoms is a fundamental concept of pediatric

TABLE 65–40. Elements of Comprehensive Psychiatric Treatment

Treatment	Indication
Medical management	Integrate medications with other medical issues
Pediatric counseling and support	Family support and child's self-esteem
Psychopharmacology	Manage target symptoms
Psychotherapy	
Play therapy*	Younger children: nonverbal communication
Insight-oriented therapy, interpersonal psychotherapy†	Older children, adolescents, young adults: verbal emphasis
Cognitive-behavioral therapy	Often taught to parents and to children to help with symptom reduction
Family therapy	Focus on function of family unit, conflict resolution, and set reasonable expectations for child
Substance abuse counseling	Substance abuse complicating or interfering with other treatments
Adjustments in the school setting	Ease school-related stresses, build self-esteem
Adjustments in after-school and unscheduled activities	Support normal emotional growth and self-esteem
Psychiatric day treatment settings	Severity of psychiatric illness requires daily structure and monitoring
Psychiatric partial hospital settings	Severity of psychiatric illness and degree of family conflict require both daily structure and monitoring as well as the child temporarily removed from the home (i.e., open-door residential setting)
Psychiatric inpatient settings	Severity of psychiatric illness requires locked-door setting to ensure patient safety

*Normal developmental cognitive limitations in young children make symbolic play an important inroad into understanding the child's behaviors.
†The capacity to engage in a relationship does not necessarily require the capacity for "insight," which requires a higher level of cognitive development.

psychopharmacology and largely directs ongoing treatment. Target symptoms interfering with the child's daily functioning are identified by careful interview of the patient and at least one parent or caretaker as part of the initial diagnostic process before starting medication. Appropriate target symptoms are prioritized for positive impact on the child's functioning with family, friends, school, and play and to relieve the child's emotional suffering. Target symptoms are then followed as treatment progresses.

For example, many children with untreated hyperactivity and impulsiveness from ADHD (see Chapter 65, subchapter on Attention Deficits) may cut in line at school, disrupt class, and seem disrespectful and inattentive to wishes of parents, creating negative family and social interactions. Such children often have low self-esteem, a sense of rejection, anger, and anxiety, any or all of which continue to cycle negatively in the areas of school, family, and peer relations.

ADHD symptoms of inattention, distractibility, and impulsivity can often be targeted for response to medication. As the child becomes more attentive and less impulsive in school, the teacher is likely to give the child more praise and positive attention. Self-esteem increases from this positive attention and from the child's sense of social and academic accomplishment. Productive effort is put into work, friends, and family. Social and family relations improve, as does the child's self-esteem.

By tracking the target symptoms and related consequences the clinician can assess the efficacy of medication as a positive intervention.

DISORDERS OF ACTIVITY

A boundary, blurred as it is, exists between expected and normal variations in temperament and a valid disorder of activity and attention. It is estimated that 3% to 5% of school-age children have ADHD. The diagnosis depends on a significant impairment before the age of 7 years both at home and at school (also see Chapter 65, subchapter on Attention Deficits, for details and diagnostic criteria of ADHD).

Common Target Symptoms

Hyperactivity, fidgeting, inattentiveness, impulsivity, disorganization, and difficulty finishing tasks are common target symptoms.

Medications

METHYLPHENIDATE AND DEXTROAMPHETAMINE. Stimulants such as methylphenidate (MTP) and dextroamphetamine (DPT)

are first-line treatment for ADHD. They are believed to have their biologic effects on the central and peripheral nervous systems where they prevent presynaptic reuptake of catecholamines (norepinephrine and dopamine). Comprehensive guidelines are available for the interested reader in treating children with attentional disorders (American Academy of Pediatrics, 1996).

MTP (Ritalin) is a sympathomimetic stimulant with a short duration of activity of only 2 to 5 hours. MTP may need to be given two or three times a day. For example, a 7 A.M. dose would have a beneficial effect getting the child ready for school and in morning classes. A second, noontime or later dose, would then be needed for the afternoon and homework or after-school activities. MTP or DPT should be increased, as tolerated, until either target symptoms are reduced or a total daily dose of about 1.0 mg/kg/day is administered. DPT has a similar profile to MTP with the exception that it has a slightly longer half-life. Clinicians familiar and comfortable with DPT may choose to switch from MTP to DPT if the child does not respond to the former.

MTP comes in a sustained-release form (MTP-SR), as does DPT (Dexedrine Spansules), both of which last 5 to 8 hours. However, some children have inconsistent absorption of these preparations. A child with a poor response to the sustained-release form may do well on the regular preparation. Combining sustained-release and regular preparations may be useful.

The short half-life of these stimulants makes weaning unnecessary if the medication is discontinued. Many children with ADHD take "drug holidays" during summer camp, vacation, or weekends, as these settings have different expectations and demands than school. The ultimate goal of treatment is to improve functioning and self-esteem. Therefore, if impulsive behavior interferes with social, family, and peer interactions, medication should be continued. When needed, these medications can be safely started at the previous daily effective dose.

Side Effects. The most common side effects of stimulants such as MTP and DPT are decreased appetite, sleep disturbances, and elevation of blood pressure. A less common side effect is slowing of bone growth, typically in the range of 2 to 3 cm with long-term use. Usually these correct themselves with discontinuation of the drug.

Some children experience tiredness. If this side effect occurs, simply lowering the dose by 2.5 or 5 mg may allow the child to function without the troubling sense of always being sleepy. Conversely, stimulants may interfere with nighttime sleep if given after 4 P.M., although this finding is

controversial. Children may also experience a sense of dysphoria as stimulants wear off, rarely serious enough to force discontinuation. This can be tempered by adding a small dose of the stimulant to provide a more gradual withdrawal.

ADDERALL. Adderall combines mixed salts of dextroamphetamine and amphetamine in one pill. This medication may be useful in patients with particularly refractory ADHD by combining rapid-onset and sustained-release preparations. Titration is similar to that with the other stimulants, in 5-mg increments.

ADDITIONAL MEDICATIONS USED TO TREAT ADHD. The following medications are not approved by the Food and Drug Administration for treatment of ADHD in children. Clinicians often choose to seek consultation concerning the treatment plan from a child psychiatrist before initiating these preparations.

Bupropion (Wellbutrin). Bupropion is an atypical antidepressant that selectively inhibits neuronal reuptake of dopamine; when used to treat ADHD, it has treatment efficacy comparable to the stimulants. Dosage starts at 37.5 mg twice daily and is titrated upward in 37.5-mg increments every week to 3 to 6 mg/kg/day. Wellbutrin may take up to 2 weeks to work, although some studies show an effect within 4 days. There is a higher incidence of seizures in dosages above 450 mg/day, and caution should be used in doses above this threshold.

Clonidine and Guanfacine. Clonidine and guanfacine are alpha$_2$-noradrenergic agonists with comparable efficacy to stimulants in treating ADHD. Clonidine comes in 0.1-mg, 0.2-mg, and 0.3-mg preparations, as well as a patch form. The patch gives sustained release throughout the day and lasts 1 week; oral preparations last 3 to 5 hours and may need to be administered three or four times a day. Clonidine can be sedating, so it is often started at low doses of 0.025 to 0.05 mg per dose. Its sedative properties make it an excellent sleep inducer.

Guanfacine comes in 1-mg and 2-mg preparations. It is started at 0.5 mg/day and titrated in 0.5-mg increments every 3 days to 4 mg/day if needed for target symptom reduction. The mean therapeutic dose is 0.09 mg/kg/day.

Tricyclic Antidepressants. Desipramine and nortriptyline can also be used to treat ADHD. They are discussed later in the section on antidepressants.

CAUTIONS. There is currently an active debate whether stimulants exacerbate tics. Clinicians should weigh the risk-benefit ratio in a child with ADHD and motor or phonic tics, as alternative medications can be used for ADHD if tics are present. These include desipramine (Norpramin), nortriptyline (Pamelor), clonidine (Catapres), and guanfacine (Tenex).

If the patient has not responded to MTP or DPT, a consultation with a child and adolescent psychiatrist may be helpful before initiating other medications.

DISORDERS OF MOOD

It is estimated that 1% of preschoolers, 2% of school-age children, and almost 5% of adolescents have depression in the United States. The diagnostic criteria for major depressive disorder can be found in Chapter 65, subchapter on Mood Disorders and Suicide.

Target Symptoms

Sleep, appetite, energy, concentration, enjoyment, irritability, self-esteem, and anxiety are target symptoms.

Treatment

Self-injurious, severely depressed, and suicidal children should be urgently referred for a psychiatric evaluation. Some of these children may need inpatient hospitalization to ensure their safety.

Medications

Antidepressants

Over the last decade, there has been a relative explosion of antidepressants, broadly divided into three categories: the tricyclic antidepressants (TCAs), the selective serotonin reuptake inhibitors (SSRIs), and a class called "atypical" antidepressants because they fit neither of the first two categories based on their chemical structure and often their proposed mechanism of action.

These medications are used to treat depression and other disorders. However, fluvoxamine maleate is currently the only SSRI approved for use in children and adolescents by the FDA, specifically to treat obsessive-compulsive disorder. When depression interferes with the child's functioning, however, the clinician should consider seeking potential symptom relief using psychopharmacologic treatment. Depression in children and adolescents is often a serious, recurrent disorder requiring multiple interventions and sophisticated interviewing skills. Many primary care clinicians refer or comanage those serious forms of depression with a child psychiatrist.

SELECTIVE SEROTONIN REUPTAKE INHIBITORS. Fewer side effects and comparable efficacy make SSRIs a safe and effective first choice by child and adolescent psychiatrists treating depression. They include fluoxetine (Prozac), sertraline (Zoloft), paroxetine (Paxil), trazodone (Desyrel), and fluvoxamine (Luvox). All are believed to inhibit presynaptic reuptake of serotonin but have different side effect profiles that may make one medication preferable to another in the individual patient. Sertraline is often the first choice, as it has a shorter half-life than fluoxetine (12 to 16 hours compared to >100 hours for fluoxetine), has fewer gastrointestinal side effects than paroxetine, and is less sedating than fluvoxamine.

Fluoxetine (Prozac) comes in 10-mg and 20-mg capsules, and a liquid form with 20 mg/5 mL. Younger children are often started at 5 mg/day, or 10 mg every other day, with lower doses possible using the liquid preparation. A maintenance dose of 20 mg/day is usually effective, although some patients may need doses as high as 60 to 80 mg/day. Fluoxetine and the other SSRIs should be increased every 2 weeks if target symptoms are not improved.

Sertraline (Zoloft) is prepared in 25-mg, 50-mg, and 100-mg scored tablets. It is initiated at 25 to 50 mg in the morning and increased by 25 to 50 mg every 1 to 2 weeks, with 12.5 mg titration possible for "fine-tuning." Often it is maintained at 75 to 100 mg/day and the target symptoms monitored for response. The maximum recommended dose is 200 mg/day, but doses up to 300 mg/day can be administered with close monitoring.

Paroxetine (Paxil) is available in 10-mg, 20-mg/day, and 30-mg scored tablets. It is usually initiated at 10 mg at night, as it is known to have a more sedating effect. Increases by 10 mg every 1 to 2 weeks are a safe titration of this medication up to 50 mg/day.

Trazodone (Desyrel) comes in 50-mg and 100-mg scored tablets. This SSRI has the least antidepressant properties but is safely used as a nonaddictive sleep-inducing agent. Small children respond to 25 to 50 mg qhs, while older children and adolescents may need up to 150 mg qhs. Trazodone can safely be combined with other, more stimulating antidepressants, including other SSRIs.

Fluvoxamine (Luvox), as noted, is now approved for use in children and adolescents with obsessive-compulsive disorder. It comes in a 50-mg unscored and a 100-mg scored preparation.

Fluvoxamine is initiated between 25 to 50 mg/day and is often given at night as it is somewhat sedating. Dosage ranges from 100 to 300 mg/day, with divided doses recommended if over 200 mg/day is prescribed.

Side Effects. SSRI side effects vary with the preparation. In general, they all include gastrointestinal distress, but appetite suppression, headache, fatigue, and insomnia vary. Fluoxetine and sertraline may cause insomnia and even akathesia (i.e., a sense of extreme restlessness), whereas the other SSRIs are more sedating. Sexual dysfunction is an important side effect in adolescents and can include anorgasmia, delayed orgasm, or erectile dysfunction. If side effects occur, an alternative SSRI should be tried before giving up on the entire class of medication.

Contraindications and Cautions. SSRIs cannot be safely used concomitantly with monoamine oxidase inhibitors (i.e., Parnate, Nardil). There are currently no other contraindications to the SSRIs. However, as this is a relatively new class of medication, long-term effects are not yet known.

TRICYCLIC ANTIDEPRESSANTS. Most primary care clinicians have prescribed imipramine, a tertiary amine TCA, to treat enuresis. TCAs such as desipramine and imipramine and their metabolites, nortriptyline and amitriptyline, act by inhibiting the reuptake of norepinephrine and serotonin in the central nervous system. This versatile and widely used class of medications is prescribed for depression or anxiety and is adjunctive to methylphenidate or is used alone for ADHD. TCAs are useful with many children who have both tics and ADHD. Another TCA, clomipramine (Anafranil), is discussed here, as it is the only TCA with dominant serotinergic properties and is used to treat obsessive-compulsive disorder.

The standard of care is to obtain a baseline electrocardiogram (ECG) prior to initiating a TCA. Desipramine can be started at 25 mg, and nortriptyline at 10 mg at bedtime. A steady state is reached in 5 days, and a TCA level and repeat ECG should be obtained after a week of starting medication, and after any increase in dosage. Clinically effective dosages range from 50 to 200 mg/day of desipramine and 25 to 75 mg/day of nortriptyline. A daily dose of desipramine is 2 to 5 mg/kg/day, and for nortriptyline, 1 to 3 mg/kg/day is effective.

Side Effects. TCAs have anticholinergic activity; side effects include dry mouth, constipation, urinary retention, and blurred vision. Other side effects include orthostatic hypotension, seizures, drowsiness, and ECG changes including sinus tachycardia and interference with conduction, Sudden cardiac death has aroused great concerns

and has been reported in children who had undetected cardiac conditions, in children who were taking high dosages of TCAs (over 4 mg/kg/day), and in rare case reports with no clear diagnosis. TCAs may need to be reduced or discontinued if prolongation of the QTc interval is above 420 msec compared with baseline.

As these are potentially lethal medications if taken in overdose, parents should be advised to keep them safely locked and accessible to children only with adult supervision.

Contraindications. If the child has a positive cardiac history of a murmur, an arrhythmia, or an anatomic lesion, then TCAs are contraindicated. A positive family history of cardiac disease is not a contraindication, but a signal to proceed using TCAs in that child with caution.

"ATYPICAL" ANTIDEPRESSANTS. Atypical antidepressants are generally heterocyclic compounds with diverse mechanisms of action. They include bupropion (Wellbutrin), nefazodone (Serzone), mirtazapine (Remeron), and venlafaxine (Effexor). Although none are approved for use in pediatric populations, they increase the options of clinicians when more traditional medications fail to relieve depression.

DISORDERS OF ANXIETY

Anxiety is a normal component of some developmental stages. However, even "age-appropriate" fears may grow out of proportion and seriously impair a child's ability to function and explore the world. These children are clearly distressed and frequently crippled into inaction by their apprehension, often avoiding situations that may precipitate their anxiety.

Target Symptoms

Anxiety, tachycardia, sweating, nausea, tachypnea, shortness of breath, dizziness, somatic complaints, apprehension, and avoidance of school and other social situations are target symptoms.

Treatment

Anxiety has many sources. Clinicians should be aware that some abused and neglected children may present with anxiety as the predominant symptom. If abuse is suspected as the cause of anxiety, a referral should be made to the appropriate agency. Some of these children may be in physical danger, be demonstrating signs of post-traumatic stress disorder, and need urgent protection and removal from the home.

Anxiety is frequently successfully treated with behavioral therapy. Psychotropic medication is used adjunctively, and most children do not need to stay on these medications once they have learned behavioral techniques to relieve their symptoms.

Medications

Anxiolytics

BENZODIAZEPINES. Benzodiazepines bind to γ-aminobutyric acid receptors, changing the influx of chloride ion into the neuron, hyperpolarizing it and inducing neuronal dampening, which makes it more difficult for the cell to fire. This manifests as a calming effect in the anxious patient.

Benzodiazepines differ widely in their potencies and length of action but for the most part they have similar qualities. Long-acting benzodiazepines such as clonazepam may be more useful in adolescents with separation anxiety disorder, uncomplicated simple anxiety disorder, and panic disorder with or without agoraphobia. Shorter-acting benzodiazepines such as lorazepam may be more appropriate for generalized anxiety disorder. Most benzodiazepines are taken one to three times a day, but frequency varies depending on their potency and half-life.

Clonazepam comes in 0.5-mg, 1-mg, and 2-mg preparations. It is a high-potency, long-acting benzodiazepine started at 0.25 to 0.5 mg per dose and can be safely increased to a total dose of 0.01 to 0.04 mg/kg/day. Lorazepam comes in 0.5-mg, 1-mg, and 2-mg preparations with intermediate potency and activity. Lorazepam is also started at 0.25 to 0.5 mg per dose, to a total dose of 0.04 to 0.09 mg/kg/day. Practice parameters for the assessment and treatment of anxiety disorders are available for interested practitioners (Bernstein and Shaw, 1993).

Side Effects. Benzodiazepines can be substances of abuse, and a careful substance abuse history should be obtained before prescribing these medications to adolescents suspected of using alcohol or illegal drugs. Children may complain of feeling drowsy and sedated, but in general these medicines have few side effects. They can impair schoolwork, blunting concentration and cognitive keenness. Tolerance and dependence can occur. Hence, unlike methylphenidate, these medicines must be tapered slowly because an abrupt stop can lead to withdrawal and even seizures. Some children and adolescents become disinhibited (acting as if intoxicated) with benzodiazepines, requiring the discontinuation of this intervention.

Contraindications. Given the potential for tolerance, abuse, and dependency, there is a relative contraindication to prescribing benzodiazepines to adolescents with a strong individual or family history of substance abuse.

BUSPIRONE. Buspirone (BuSpar) decreases anxiety by dampening serotonin activity while increasing norepinephrine and dopamine availability. It is unrelated to the benzodiazepines and has no addictive potential. Buspirone comes in scored 5-mg and 10-mg preparations. It may need to be given three times a day, starting with 5 mg, and increasing to 15 to 30 mg daily. Unlike the benzodiazepines, which have a rapid onset of action, buspirone may take several days or weeks to be effective. Dizziness, nausea, and drowsiness are the predominant side effects.

OTHER ANXIOLYTICS. Clonidine, diphenhydramine (Benadryl), and TCAs have anxiolytic properties. There are some excellent reviews on the growing use of psychopharmacologic treatment for anxiety in children and adolescents (see Further Reading). In addition, cognitive-behavioral therapy has excellent success in the treatment of anxiety.

OTHER PSYCHOTROPIC MEDICATIONS

Children and adolescents may present to the pediatric clinician with psychosis, bipolar disorders, Tourette syndrome, obsessive-compulsive disorder, post-traumatic stress disorder, eating disorders, substance abuse, and others. Most primary care clinicians refer these more serious disorders. Readers interested in a more comprehensive knowledge may enjoy Wiener's book on diagnosis and treatment of psychiatric disorders in children and adolescents.

Mood stabilizers such as lithium, carbamazepine (Tegretol), and divalproex sodium (Depakote) are used for bipolar illness, to augment antidepressants, and for some severe aggressive disorders. Propranolol (Inderal) has some success in treating aggression, especially in autistic and mentally retarded children. Naltrexone, an opioid antagonist, now finds use in decreasing self-abusive behaviors in autistic children, as well as self-mutilatory adolescents with character dysfunction. Neuroleptics are used for psychosis and Tourette disorder and include a wide range of medications. Clinicians may be more familiar with names like haloperidol (Haldol) and chlorpromazine (Thorazine) than olanzapine (Zyprexa) and risperidone (Risperdal). These newer antipsychotics expand treatment options for some of the sickest children. Although there is still an important place in treating psychosis for the older neuroleptics, their dopamine blockade mechanism of action often results in extrapyramidal side effects, limiting their use owing to intolerable muscle stiffness, tremor, and fear of tardive dyskinesia, a potentially irreversible involuntary movement disorder. Newer preparations are believed to have serotonergic properties with minimal and more specific dopamine blockade. As such, they appear to have fewer side effects and equivalent efficacy. Readers interested in the diagnosis, treatment, and use of neuroleptics in children are referred to assessment guidelines (McClellan and Werry, 1994) and the book edited by Richardson (1996).

SUMMARY

Accurate diagnosis of mildly to moderately impairing psychiatric disorders is essential, followed by an approach that includes selecting and tracking target symptoms. Medication side effects must be weighed in a risk-benefit ratio by the prescribing clinician. The act of prescribing medication itself may be seen as reflective of the seriousness of an emotional disorder (and at times a moral defect). When used and targeted, medication and other treatment modalities work synergistically to improve, often dramatically, the child's and family daily functioning.

Pediatric psychopharmacology is at an exciting stage of development. New medicines and new uses for old ones are changing the way in which we understand psychiatric illness. Scientific advances coupled with managed care financial pressures will encourage the use of treatments such as medications, which require the least professional time. **Given time constraints and limited training, there will also be increasing pressure to use medication in a highly focused and isolated fashion rather than in the context of a comprehensive treatment plan. Primary care clinicians and child and adolescent psychiatrists must resist this path, collaborating with child psychiatrists and others to advocate the best possible comprehensive care for children and adolescents.**

FURTHER READING

American Academy of Pediatrics, Committee on Children with Disabilities and Committee on Drugs: Medication for children with attentional disorders. Pediatrics 98 (2, Pt 1):301–304, 1996.

American Psychiatric Association: Diagnostic and Statistical Manual of Mental Disorders, 4th ed. (DSM-IV). Washington, DC, American Psychiatric Association, 1994.

American Psychiatric Association/American Academy of Pediatrics: Diagnostic and Statistical Manual of Mental Disorders, 4th ed., Primary Care Version (DSM-IV-PC). Washington, DC, American Psychiatric Association, 1995.

Barrickman LL, Perry PJ, Allen AJ, et al.: Bupropion versus methylphenidate in the treatment of attention-deficit hyperactivity disorder. J Am Acad Child Adolesc Psychiatry 34:649–657, 1995.

Bernstein GA and Shaw K: Practice parameters for the assessment and treatment of anxiety disorders. American Academy of Child and Adolescent Psychiatry. J Am Acad Child Adolesc Psychiatry 32:1089–1098, 1993.

Coffey BJ: Anxiolytics for children and adolescents: Traditional and new drugs. J Child Adolesc Psychopharmacol 1:57–83, 1990.

Institute of Medicine: Research on Children and Adolescents with Mental, Behavioral, and Developmental Disorders: Mobilizing a National Initiative. Washington, DC, National Academy Press, 1989.

Kutcher SP, Reiter S, Klein R, et al.: The pharmacotherapy of anxiety disorders in children and adolescents. Psychiatr Clin North Am 15:41–47, 1992.

Lewis M (ed): Child and Adolescent Psychiatry: A Comprehensive Textbook. Baltimore, Williams & Wilkins, 1991.

McClellan J and Werry J: Practice parameters for the assessment and treatment of children and adolescents with schizophrenia. American Academy of Child and Adolescent Psychiatry. J Am Acad Child Adolesc Psychiatry 33:616–635, 1994.

Popper CW: Psychopharmacologic treatment of anxiety disorders in adolescents and children. J Clin Psychiatry 54 (Suppl):52–63, 1993.

Practice parameters for the psychiatric assessment of children and adolescents. American Academy of Child and Adolescent Psychiatry. J Am Acad Child Adolesc Psychiatry 34:1386–1402, 1995.

Reiter S, Kutcher S, and Gardner D: Anxiety disorders in children and adolescents: Clinical and related issues in pharmacological treatment. Can J Psychiatry 37:432–438, 1992.

Richardson MA (ed): Use of Neuroleptics in Children. Washington, DC, American Psychiatric Press, 1996.

Robson KS (ed): Manual of Clinical Child and Adolescent Psychiatry, revised ed. Washington, DC, American Psychiatric Press 1994–1995.

Schatzberg AF and Nemeroff CB (eds): The American Psychiatric Press Textbook of Psychopharmacology. Washington, DC, American Psychiatric Press, 1995.

Spencer T, Wilens T, and Biederman J: Psychotropic medication for children and adolescents. Child Adolesc Psychiatr Clin North Am 4:97–121, 1995.

Wiener JM (ed): Diagnosis and Psychopharmacology of Childhood and Adolescent Disorders. New York, Wiley & Sons, 1996.

Eric A. Schaff

Contraception

One national survey reported that almost a third of ninth grade females and 44% of ninth grade males were sexually active. Half of the teenagers aged less than 17 report not using contraception at first sexual intercourse. Approximately 1 million U.S. teenagers become pregnant each year; of these pregnancies approximately 60% result in live births and 40% end in abortion. As many as 80% of these pregnancies are unintended. The consequences of early parenthood for the teen mother too often include disruption of her education, increased dependence on public assistance, and increased likelihood of living in poverty. The infants of young teen mothers are more likely to experience low birth weight with its attendant health problems and adverse social outcomes such as behavioral and educational problems in school. Contributing to the problem is that only 18% of primary care clinicians routinely ask female teenage patients about contraceptive needs.

The reasons teenagers have children are complex, but the foremost is perhaps the inability to envision future opportunities that provide a reason to delay parenting. Another significant factor relates to barriers in accessing contraception. These barriers include an inability to pay, lack of transportation, inconvenient appointment times, the perception that the health care setting is not welcoming, a lack of knowledge about family planning, a fear of a gynecologic examination, or just embarrassment or denial about admitting being sexually active. Some clinicians lack the comfort level and technical skills necessary to relate effectively to a sexually active teenager. Cultural, age, and often gender differences may further complicate this interaction.

It is standard practice to provide contraceptive services to minors confidentially and without parental approval, if necessary. Encouraging teenagers to involve their parents or other supportive adults is appropriate and desirable. Informing parents against the wishes of a teenager may discourage them from seeking needed contraceptive services.

Abstinence should be encouraged as the safest and only certain method. However, teenagers who are sexually active need advice in choosing the safest and most effective contraceptive method for their lifestyle (Table 65–41). Using two methods simultaneously and the use of emergency contraception for unprotected intercourse can significantly decrease unintended pregnancy.

Misinformation and misconceptions are an important reason for contraceptive failure. Almost all unintended pregnancies in contraceptive users are due to failure to use the method correctly and consistently. To improve compliance, clinicians should assess their teenage patient's understanding of the risks and benefits of the chosen method, their concerns about becoming pregnant and motivation to use the method, their beliefs about side effects, and their perceived barriers to using the

TABLE 65–41. Summary of Major Advantages of Different Contraceptive Methods for Teenagers

Method	STD Protection	Pregnancy Prevention*	No Estrogen	Not User-Dependent	Inexpensive
Hormonal contraceptives					
Oral contraceptives	−†	+ +	−‡	−	±
Norplant system	−†	+ +	+	+	−
Depo-Provera	−†	+ +	+	+	±
Emergency contraception	−	+ +	−	−	±
Male barrier method					
Condoms	+	+	+	−	+
Female barrier method					
Diaphragm/female condom/ cervical cap with spermicide	±	+	+	−	±
Intrauterine device§	−	+ +	+	+	−
Natural family planning	−	±	+	−	+
Coitus interruptus	−	±	+	−	+

*Used correctly and consistently.
†Hormonal methods thicken cervical mucus and decrease ascending infection (pelvic inflammatory disease).
‡Progestin-only ("minipills") are less effective and used only when estrogen is contraindicated.
§Relatively contraindicated for teenagers due to increased risk of infection and infertility.

method. In a healthy teenage population, there are no contraindications for hormonal or barrier methods. **All methods are extremely safe and both the contraceptive and noncontraceptive benefits far outweigh the rare health risk.**

HORMONAL CONTRACEPTION

Oral Contraceptives

Oral contraceptives are the most commonly used reversible family planning method in the United States. They work primarily by suppressing ovulation, but also thicken cervical mucus making it less penetrable by sperm and alter the endometrium making it less receptive for implantation of a fertilized egg. The theoretical effectiveness in preventing pregnancy is greater than 99% and the typical effectiveness is 97% (although it may be considerably lower in noncompliant teenagers). **Major advances have occurred in reversible hormonal contraceptives.**

The advantages of oral contraceptives include (1) low failure rates; (2) safety; (3) easy reversal if pregnancy is desired; (4) low cost (especially generic formulations); (5) regular menses; (6) reduction in pelvic inflammatory disease due to thickened cervical mucus preventing ascending infection; (7) less anemia due to reduced menstrual bleeding; (8) improvement of acne by suppressing ovarian and some adrenal androgen production; (9) reduced fibrocystic disease of the breast; and (10) a **40% to 50% reduction in ovarian and endometrial cancers.**

The disadvantages of oral contraceptives include (1) the need for daily compliance; (2) the cost; (3) the "minor" side effects of nausea, headaches, breakthrough vaginal bleeding, and mood changes that tend to decrease after the first few months; (4) weight gain; (5) the increased risk of chlamydia infection (possibly due to increased exposure of columnar epithelium from estrogen-induced ectopy); (6) decreased effectiveness from antiseizure medications and some antibiotics such as rifampin, ampicillin and tetracycline and, therefore, the need for a backup method; (7) the questionable role as a promoter of breast cancer in women aged less than 35 in long-term users; (8) the rare increased risk of cardiovascular disease (stroke and thromboembolic disorders) especially in heavy smokers; and (9) the decrease in lactation due to estrogen. The minor side effects have decreased over the years due to the lowering of the amount of estrogen and progestin; however, even the perception of one, such as weight gain, can be a major reason for discontinuing this method, so anticipatory guidance is essential. Switching pills

is reasonable if minor side effects persist for more than 2 or 3 months. **Cardiovascular disease from oral contraceptives is extremely rare in teenagers and less common than the risks associated with pregnancy.**

Oral contraceptives are contraindicated in patients with sickle cell disease or the rare teenager with a history of a thromboembolic disorder. Oral contraceptives also are contraindicated in active liver disease, estrogen-dependent tumors, and suspected pregnancy.

There are 21- and 28-day packs of oral contraceptives. Both have 21 days of estrogen-progestin and then there are either 7 days of no pills or 7 days of placebo before starting the next pack. Monophasic pills have a fixed combination of estrogen and progestin for 21 days, whereas in multiphasic pills the dose of either the estrogen or progestin is altered. There is no evidence to support multiphasic over monophasic pills—i.e., all oral contraceptive brands are equally effective at preventing pregnancy.

All "low-dose" oral contraceptives have the same estrogen, ethinyl estradiol, in doses from 20 to 30 μg. The progestin in oral contraceptives varies in type and dose, and has androgenic effects associated with adverse lipid changes (although clinically insignificant), weight gain, and mood swings. In 1993, two new progestins were approved, desogestrel (Desogen and Ortho-Cept) and norgestimate (Ortho-tricyclen and Ortho-Cyclen). They are potent progestins but weak androgens, and have a slightly longer half-life, so that if one pill is missed, an accidental pregnancy or light vaginal bleeding is less likely to occur. Slightly less effective, and reserved for women with contraindications to estrogen (such as breastfeeding and migraine), are progestin-only ("minipill") pills.

A gynecologic examination, including Pap test and sexually transmitted diseases testing, ideally should be performed prior to instituting oral contraceptives. This examination may be deferred at the teenager's request because there are no findings that will be a contraindication to use of hormonal contraception. A routine cholesterol screen is not indicated. Routine follow-up usually includes a visit at 3 months and then yearly, but closer monitoring may be needed when clinically indicated.

Examples of three prescribing strategies include choosing (1) an inexpensive generic brand (35 μg of ethinyl estradiol and 1 mg of norethindrone; Ortho-Novum 1/35); (2) the lowest estrogen preparation (ethinyl estradiol, 20 μg and norethindrone acetate, 1 mg; Loestrin 1/20); or (3) a weak androgen progestin, that is, desogestrel (Desogen and

Ortho-Cept), or norgestimate (Ortho-Tricyclen and Ortho-Cyclen).

Oral contraceptive pills should be started on the first Sunday after the onset of menses to ensure that the teenager is not pregnant and ovulation is effectively prevented. Pills should be taken at the same time each day linked to a routine activity. Withdrawal bleeding usually occurs 2 or 3 days after the last hormonal pill has been taken. A backup method is necessary for that cycle when any pills are missed. A missed pill should be taken as soon as possible to "catch up." If two pills are missed, take two tablets as soon as possible and two the following day. If three pills are missed, toss out the pack and restart a new pack the first Sunday after the next menses. Menses may initially be irregular and then, over time, become regular, usually lighter, and occasionally absent. If there is no menses and no pills have been missed, the pills should be continued. A pregnancy test should be obtained for reassurance or to detect the rare pregnancy. Warning signs requiring immediate medical care include severe head, chest, or leg pain. The risks of thromboembolic disorder to a healthy teenager are exceedingly rare.

Long-Acting Progestins: Subdermal Implants and Injectables

Levonorgestrel implant (Norplant, Wyeth-Ayerst, Philadelphia, PA) has been available in the United States since 1991. There have been about 630,000 users in the United States and 3 million users worldwide; approximately 20% of users have been adolescents. There has been a significant decrease in new users due to negative publicity generated around unfounded lawsuits related to side effects and difficult removals.

The implants consist of six capsules about the size of matchsticks, each containing 36 mg of levonorgestrel, a common progestin in oral contraceptives. A single skin puncture is performed under local anesthesia and the capsules are placed under the skin in a fan-shaped array in the inside of the upper arm. The levonorgestrel is released slowly through the micropores of the capsules over a 5-year period, providing continuous protection from pregnancy. Other than during the first few months of use, the progestin serum level is less than the progestin of low-dose oral contraceptives. Removal requires numbing the area with lidocaine, making a small incision, and removing the capsules with a small hemostat.

Depo-medroxyprogesterone acetate (DMPA; Depo-Provera, Pharmacia & Upjohn, Kalamazoo, MI) has been used by more than 15 million women worldwide. It is available as a single 150-mg dose vial and, after vigorous shaking of the vial, is given as a deep intramuscular injection in the deltoid or gluteal muscle. The injection area should not be massaged, which might hasten absorption and metabolism. Each injection provides 13 weeks of continuous contraception.

Long-acting progestins prevent pregnancy by suppressing ovulation, thickening the cervical mucus to prevent sperm from ascending, and causing an atrophic endometrium preventing implantation. Effectiveness is greater than 99% and success is not user-dependent. Both methods should be started within 5 days of the onset of normal menses. The continuation rate for the Norplant system at 1 year is 70% to 80%. Once the capsules are removed, ovulation and pregnancy can occur. After stopping Depo-Provera, there may be a delay in fertility up to 18 months with a mean delay of 9 months.

The contraindications to long-acting progestins include pregnancy, breast cancer, acute liver disease, and a history of idiopathic intracranial hypertension (pseudotumor cerebri). Although a thromboembolic disorder is listed as a contraindication, this is related to estrogen and should not occur with progesterone-only methods.

The cost of the Norplant system is about $365 plus the charge for insertion and removal. The initial kit includes the necessary supplies for insertion. There are insertion and removal videos and a model to help with removal available from the manufacturer. Depo-Provera costs about $30 to $50 per injection, plus the office visit cost. Managing side effects is important in supporting continued use of these methods.

The advantages of both the Norplant system and Depo-Provera include (1) no estrogen and, therefore, no risk for thromboembolic disorders; (2) decreased anemia; (3) decreased risk for ovarian and endometrial cancer and pelvic inflammatory disease; (4) reversibility; (5) minimal interference with breastfeeding; (6) possible decrease in seizures and sickling episodes from Depo-Provera; and (7) amenorrhea in 50% of women after the first year of Depo-Provera, which increases over time.

The disadvantages of these long-acting medications include (1) menstrual cycle disturbances and side effects such as hair loss, nausea, mood changes, and arm complaints from either the injection or implant, which all tend to improve over time; (2) weight gain; (3) decreased effectiveness with antiseizure medications and some antibiotics with implants but not Depo-Provera; (4) hypoestrogen state with Depo-Provera causing a decrease in bone density that has not been clinically significant and is reversible when the medication is stopped; (5) a questionable role as a promoter of breast cancer in women under age 35; and (6) delay in clearance of Depo-Provera of up to 12 months. There have been a few reports of pseudotumor cerebri (presenting as headaches, blurred vision, and papilledema) with implants requiring removal.

Emergency Contraception

Emergency high-dose estrogen and progestin contraception has been available "off-label" for more than 2 decades and received Food and Drug Administration approval in 1997. **It has been estimated that over half of the current abortions in the United States could be avoided by widely available emergency contraception.** Unfortunately, emergency contraception has been mislabeled by some as an abortifacient and the abortion controversy has prevented more widespread acceptance.

Emergency contraception is indicated in cases of rape, or when birth control fails or is not used at all. It is 75% effective in preventing pregnancy when taken within 72 hours of unprotected intercourse, which reduces the risk of a single unprotected intercourse exposure from 8% to 2% (i.e., overall it is 98% effective). High-dose estrogen-progestin is believed to work by affecting the endometrium, thereby preventing implantation of a fertilized egg and by altering fallopian tube motility to prevent fertilization from occurring. Although ovulation and therefore fertilization are most likely to occur midcycle, there is a slight pregnancy risk at other times, so emergency contraception may be offered at any point to minimize this risk.

There are also six current oral contraceptive brands approved for this indication. They all have the same estrogen, ethinyl estradiol, and either norgestrel or levonorgestrel as the progestin. Within 72 hours of unprotected intercourse, the teenager should take two tablets of the 50 µg ethinyl estradiol (Ovral) followed by two more tablets 12 hours later. An alternative therapy is four tablets of the lower dose ethinyl estradiol (Nordette, Levlen, Lo Ovral, or the yellow pills only of Tri-Levlen and Triphasil) followed by four more tablets 12 hours later.

There is a new emergency contraceptive product containing 50 µg ethinyl estradiol and norgestrel, packaged with a home pregnancy test to be performed prior to use (Preven). The costs of emergency contraception equal the cost of Preven or one package of oral contraceptives ($20 to $30)

and the cost of a medical visit if required (but it is not necessary). **Ideally, teenagers who want to avoid an unintended pregnancy should keep one dose of emergency contraceptive pills available at all times for emergency use.**

Side effects of high-dose estrogen-progestin can include nausea and vomiting. An antinausea medication may be needed orally or rectally if persistent vomiting occurs. An additional dose of the estrogen-progestin is not needed if vomiting occurs, since the vomiting indicates that the estrogen has been absorbed. Using one dose of estrogen-progestin for emergency contraception has no associated health risks. The only contraindications are a known pregnancy, a history of a thromboembolic disorder, or allergy to the medications.

Issues to be assessed by phone or at a medical visit are (1) time interval since unprotected intercourse in relationship to menstrual cycle and risk of pregnancy; (2) any medical contraindications; (3) need for medical evaluation for prior pregnancy or risk of a sexually transmitted disease (STD); (4) future contraception; and (5) need for pregnancy testing if no menses occurs within 3 to 4 weeks after using emergency contraception.

MALE BARRIER METHODS: CONDOMS

The epidemic of human immunodeficiency virus has made condoms the mainstay of all family planning efforts. Because hormonal contraceptive methods do not protect against disease, hormonal contraceptive users who are at risk for STDs should use condoms. The female teenager may need guidance to get her partner to use condoms.

Condoms are (1) inexpensive; (2) available over the counter; (3) lubricated to reduce dyspareunia; (4) associated with no side effects; (5) simple to use; (6) helpful to treat premature ejaculation by decreasing penile sensation; and (7) remediable, if broken, by using emergency contraception. The disadvantages of condoms include (1) decreased genital sensation; (2) lack of 100% protection against STDs; (3) allergy to latex or spermicide; and (4) a breakage rate of 1% to 2%.

For optimal protection, lubricated latex condoms with or without the spermicidal nonoxynol-9 offer the best protection. To prevent condom breakage, (1) avoid storing them in warm places, such as in a wallet for long periods; (2) avoid petroleum-based lubricants such as Vaseline; (3) allow room at the condom's end for the ejaculate; and (4) do not reuse them. If a condom breaks, emergency contraception should be offered.

FEMALE BARRIER METHODS: DIAPHRAGM, CERVICAL CAP, AND FEMALE CONDOM

The diaphragm is a thin rubber dome that, when inserted into the vagina, blocks sperm from entering the cervix. It must be used with spermicidal contraceptive jelly whose active ingredient is nonoxynol-9. The diaphragm's typical effectiveness rate varies from 85% to 94%. Additional advantages include (1) insertion up to 6 hours prior to coitus and (2) the woman's control. The disadvantages of the diaphragm include (1) the technical skill needed for correct placement; (2) the need to leave it in place 6 hours after intercourse; (3) the need for a second application of spermicidal jelly if intercourse is repeated; and (4) the association with vaginitis and urinary tract infections. Disadvantages for the clinician include keeping a set of sterile diaphragm rings for sizing and learning the skill to fit one when the requests are likely to be few.

The cervical cap is a thimble-shaped rubber device that fits over the cervix and can be left in place for continuous protection up to 48 hours. Its advantages and rate of effectiveness are similar to those of the diaphragm. Disadvantages include (1) the skill needed for insertion and removal (significantly more than that for the diaphragm); (2) the association of cervical dysplasia in the early months of use; and (3) the inability to fit the cervix of some women.

The female condom is available but not widely used, mainly due to the costs. It is made from polyurethane, with two flexible rings. One ring is placed inside the vagina to cover the cervix, and the open ring remains on the outside to protect the perineum from sexually transmitted diseases. The female condom should not be used with latex condoms nor be reused. It costs about $2.50.

SPERMICIDALS: VAGINAL FOAM AND VAGINAL SUPPOSITORY

Foam, gel, cream, film, and suppositories use as a spermicide nonoxynol-9 or octoxynol-9, which also has in vitro and in vivo properties against some STDs. All methods are relatively simple, effective, inexpensive, and obtained without prescription. They have effectiveness rates similar to the diaphragm and tend to have similar advantages and disadvantages. The spermicidals are important complementary methods (1) with condoms; (2) with infrequent intercourse; and (3) as an addition to other birth control methods. Vaginal suppositories must be left in place 10 to 30 minutes before intercourse to allow them to dissolve.

INTRAUTERINE DEVICE

An intrauterine device (IUD) is a stringlike piece of soft plastic that can have a copper coil wrapping. After insertion by a clinician, it conforms to the inside shape of the uterus. Exactly how the IUD works is not known. It probably causes endometrial changes that are unsuitable for implantation of a fertilized egg. Advantages of an IUD include (1) high effectiveness over multiple years; (2) reversibility; and (3) unrelatedness to sexual intercourse. Disadvantages include (1) cost; (2) skill needed for insertion; and (3) because of the increased risk of pelvic inflammatory disease and its associated infertility, the relative contraindication for teenagers.

NATURAL FAMILY PLANNING AND COITUS INTERRUPTUS

Natural family planning methods include (1) calendar charting of menstrual cycles; (2) recording of basal body temperatures; and (3) cervical mucus monitoring to detect when ovulation occurs. Coitus interruptus is the act of the male withdrawing the penis from the vagina prior to ejaculation. The advantages of these methods include the lack of side effects, acceptance by religious groups opposed to hormonal and barrier methods, and the knowledge gained about reproductive physiology. The disadvantages for young teenagers include (1) their irregular menstrual cycle, which makes predicting ovulation difficult for natural family planning; (2) the quick interval from erection to ejaculation in teen males, making coitus interruptus less reliable; and (3) the high degree of motivation required by each method.

FURTHER READING

Brown SS and Eisenberg L (eds): Committee on Unintended Pregnancy, Institute of Medicine: The Best Intentions: Unintended Pregnancy and the Well-Being of Children and Families. Washington, DC, National Academy Press, 1995.

Centers for Disease Control and Prevention: Youth Risk Behavior Surveillance—United States, 1993. MMWR 44(SS-1):1–56, 1995.

Grimes DA: The safety of oral contraceptives: Epidemiologic insights from the first 30 years. Am J Obstet Gynecol 166:1950–1954, 1992.

Hatcher RA, Trussell J, Stewart F, et al.: Contraceptive Technology, 16th revised ed. New York, Irvington Publishers, 1994.

Jick SS, Walker AM, and Jick H: Oral contraceptives and endometrial cancer. Obstet Gynecol 82:931–935, 1993.

Malone KE, Darling JR, and Weiss NS: Oral contraceptives in relation to breast cancer. Epidemiol Rev 15:80–97, 1993.

Mosher WD and McNally JW: Contraceptive use at first premarital intercourse: United States, 1965–1988. Fam Plann Perspect 23:108–116, 1991.

National Center for Health Statistics: Healthy People 2000. Publication No. PHS-95-1256-1. Hyattsville, MD, US Public Health Service, 1995.

Saleh WA, Burkman RT, Zacur HA, et al.: A randomized trial of three oral contraceptives: Comparison of bleeding patterns by contraceptive types and steroid levels. Am J Obstet Gynecol 168:1740–1747, 1993.

SECTION IV

THE PRACTICE OF CONTEXTUAL AND INTEGRATIVE CHILD CARE: NEW OPPORTUNITIES

PART A

THE PEDIATRICIAN AND THE FAMILY

Robert J. Haggerty

Chapter **66**

Integrated Child Health Services

The 20th century has seen an unprecedented improvement in child health in the United States, achieved largely through improved nutrition, immunizations, and sanitation and new medical discoveries, especially antimicrobial agents. During this time, specialized services were developed for many specific diseases, with categorical funding streams and often separate personnel and organizations to provide the services. In some ways, this approach was necessary and successful, but the complexity of the child health challenges of today have not yielded to this problem-by-problem approach. Many of the complex disorders children face today have multiple causes (e.g., substance abuse, child abuse, injuries, school-age pregnancy, and school failure), and often the same cluster of multiple causes lies behind several of these different categorical disorders. This is especially true of the interaction between chronic physical disease and problem behaviors. Several studies have demonstrated a two- to threefold increase in problem behaviors among children who have serious chronic physical illness. Rarely, however, do the categorical programs designed to treat these disorders take a comprehensive approach to both the physical and emotional problems.

For over 20 years, observers of the U.S. health care scene have deplored the plethora of categorical health programs because of their separate and narrowly defined eligibility requirements, the limited services available, and the funding streams with regulations that preclude their use for other purposes. In some cases, targeted or categorical programs have, indeed, been successful. Special

disease clinics have improved the care of children who have conditions such as myelomeningocele or cystic fibrosis, for example. On occasion, targeted immunization programs have achieved better rates of immunization, but the frustration of families and clinicians faced with a child who has multiple disorders or a disorder that does not qualify for care has now led to strong pressures to integrate and decategorize funding for child health services. Of course, advocates for special programs have been concerned that if funds and programs were integrated, bureaucracies would use the funds for purposes other than originally intended. The debate in 1997 over the use of increased federal child health funding exemplifies this. Child health advocates have wanted to keep the funds in the Medicaid program with defined and broad benefits and guaranteed use of the funds for child health services; on the other hand, governors have wanted them decategorized, to the horror of most child health advocates, who worry that these funds may be used for roads and prisons, for example. The issue is not whether all child health funds should be decategorized and integrated into a single pool, but which services should or should not be integrated.

Examples of successful, broad, integrated child health services do exist. The original Head Start program, with education, health, and social services combined for the child and family, demonstrated long-lasting effects; indeed, a 15-year follow-up study of the Perry Preschool Head Start program noted significant improvements in the health and social outcomes of children who re-

TABLE 66–1. Effect of Early Childhood Education on Head Start Group Versus Non–Head Start Group at Follow-Up at Age 19 Years

Result	Percentage
High school completion	67 vs. 49
College or job training	38 vs. 21
Welfare	19 vs. 41
Births	64 vs. 117
Arrests	31 vs. 51
Cost-benefit ratio	4.1

ceived such an integrated and comprehensive program in contrast with a comparison group (Table 66–1). The randomized clinical trial of family-focused care, carried out in the Boston Children's Hospital in the mid-1960s, also demonstrated reduced hospital and illness days among the families receiving comprehensive care. The community child health center experience in Rochester, New York, in the 1970s, also demonstrated reduced hospital days and use of emergency services among children receiving comprehensive care. A third success story is the provision of a home visit nursing program that reduced low-weight births, child abuse, and injuries.

In response to these successes, in the early 1990s The Robert Wood Johnson Foundation made another attempt at decategorization of services—the Child Health Initiative. Although nine sites were funded, all had quite different goals, populations, and programs, but they shared three common ingredients: the development of a community report card on the status of child health, the development of a care coordination program, and the melding of funding streams. Although the final evaluations are not complete, it is clear that most communities were able to develop good reporting systems and care coordination but had great difficulty in melding funding streams (see Chapter 71).

On the international scene, more targeted programs such as the United Nations Children's Fund (formerly UNICEF) GOBI Program (Growth monitoring, Oral rehydration, Breastfeeding, and Immunization), although fairly comprehensive, still did not deal with the child who has acute and chronic illnesses; indeed, separate programs often were established to care for children who had diarrhea, malaria, or acute respiratory disease. The difficulties inherent in these categorical programs have now been recognized, and the new World Health Organization–UNICEF approach is the integrated care of the sick child that combines personnel and programs for all of these diseases into one program, including the provision of preventive services.

The recognition of the need for integrated services is not limited to the health field. Educators have been especially vocal about the need for integrated services; for example, a recent annotated bibliography lists over 100 papers, monographs, and manuals on the subject. Social services and juvenile justice services also have called for more integration. **Integrated and coordinated services does not mean that all services need to be decategorized or offered in one place.** It does mean, however, that someone, including the family, is made knowledgeable about what services are being given, what are available, and what are needed. When health care is the central service, the other so-called wraparound services must be provided and coordinated. One of the major threats in the managed care environment today is the reduced attention to such wraparound services and the increased provision of limited medical services due to cost considerations. Some of the essential steps to overcome barriers to integration and coordination include

- Creating a legal authority that has the ability to pool resources from different categorical funds
- Investing in results-based outcomes rather than the number of services provided
- Investing in local capacity building with staff training and information technology that enables them to provide integrated services
- Ensuring multiyear funding
- Focusing on at-risk populations rather than on categorical services

In their review of the history of integrated services, Kahn and Kammerman (1992) list several ways in which advocates can move toward its goal (Table 66–2). It is unlikely that in any community all services for children can be integrated fully. Indeed, it is clear that not all should be integrated: The task is to decide which ones to integrate

TABLE 66–2. Categorical Versus Decategorical Programs

Policy Options
Challenge grants
Waiver strategy
State versions of decategorization
The 5% solution
Targeted high-needs communities
Selective decategorization
Negotiated decategorization
Wraparound funding

From Kahn AJ and Kammerman SB: Integrating Services Integration: An Overview of Initiatives, Issues, and Possibilities. New York, The National Center for Children in Poverty, Columbia University School of Public Health, 1992.

and in what sequence. It is important to maintain central-level administrative coordination while achieving integration at the point of delivery. The latter is the goal.

FURTHER READING

The Forgotten Half: Pathways to Success for America's Youth and Families: Final Report. Washington, DC, The William T. Grant Foundation, and Commission on Work, Family and Citizenship, 1988.

Haggerty RJ, Pless IB, and Roghmann KJ: Child Health and the Community, 2nd ed. New Brunswick, NH, Transaction Publishers, 1993.

Kahn AJ and Kammerman SB: Integrating Services Integration: An Overview of Initiatives, Issues, and Possibilities. New York, The National Center for Children in Poverty, Columbia University School of Public Health, 1992.

Olds DL, Henderson CR, Tatelbaum R, and Chamberlain R: Improving the life course of socially disadvantaged mothers: A randomized trial of nurse home visitation. Am J Public Health 78:1436–1444, 1988.

Robertson LS, Kosa J, Heagerty MC, et al.: Changing the Medical Care System. New York, Praeger Publishers, 1974.

Laurence I. Sugarman
Karen N. Olness

Chapter 67

Self-Hypnosis, Self-Care

Hypnosis, biofeedback training, and relaxation exercises help young people change maladaptive conditioned psychophysiologic responses, develop a sense of personal mastery, and become cooperative partners in health care. These cyberphysiologic* strategies have been employed successfully as primary and adjunctive therapy in pediatric medicine to help children and adolescents manage acute and chronic disease, side effects, symptoms, and behavior problems. Self-regulatory training early in life may have benefits in adulthood, particularly with respect to health and prevention.

DEFINITION OF HYPNOSIS

Hypnotic capacity is the ability to focus narrowly and intensify one's concentration and perception while decreasing awareness of peripheral stimuli. This process occurs naturally and spontaneously, for example while absorbed in reading a book or listening to music, allowing increased depth of mental activity. Hypnosis is that focused state of awareness, sometimes involving relaxation, in which one has enhanced ability to facilitate specific physiologic and behavioral outcomes. One may salivate while imagining the taste or smell of a favorite food, become tachycardic and

tachypneic while recalling an exciting event, or improve future performance with mental rehearsal.

Children are particularly endowed with the ability to use hypnosis to modify their behavior and physiology. They use their imaginative capabilities to have fun, to fantasize, to cope with fears and challenges, and to set personal goals. There is a positive correlation between the depth and creativity of children's imagery and their ability to change behavior and physiologic response in hypnosis.

The fallacy, learned from popular culture, that hypnotists magically exert mind control over passive subjects impedes the success of self-regulation training. In order to teach cyberphysiologic skills, one must dispel this misconception for colleagues, parents, and patients. Hypnosis is not magic but a natural manifestation of concentrated mental activity that can be supported by rapport with a therapist. The person in hypnosis experiences more self-control than in usual states of awareness. **All hypnosis is self-hypnosis.**

HYPNOTHERAPY

Hypnotherapy is the integration of hypnosis training into treatment. Hypnotic states themselves can be therapeutic. The youngster's purposeful practice of relaxation and mental imagery without therapeutic suggestions can help him or her to relax and reduce tension, even tension-associated pain. Therapeutic teaching in hypnosis can involve (1) development of imagery as a metaphor to help

---

*The term *cyberphysiology* has been coined to refer to this emerging discipline of self-regulation strategies. Derived from the Greek *kybernan,* the prefix *cyber-* means "to steer" or "take the helm." Cyberphysiology refers to one's ability to steer or regulate physiologic response.

change symptoms; (2) suggestions for changing behavior, including conditioned physiologic responses; and (3) exploration and understanding of feelings and relationships. **The purpose of hypnosis in therapy is to foster the mental activity that allows change to occur.**

The following example illustrates one use of hypnosis in pediatric practice.

Twelve-year-old Jonathan is on maximal medical therapy for his asthma, takes methylphenidate for attention-deficit disorder, and receives support services for his learning disabilities. He has required six courses of oral corticosteroids for exacerbations of asthma over his first 4 months of seventh grade, missing 21 days of school. He carries significant negative expectancy about his asthma and school, believing recurrent asthma episodes and poor school performance are inevitable. When asked how he helps himself when his asthma bothers him, Jonathan replies that he relaxes by reading mystery books. The primary care clinician invites him to "learn a new way to help yourself when your asthma bothers you. It can be like solving a mystery." He learns to focus his attention and imagine as he does while reading mystery books, letting a favorite place where he might relax and find comfort come to mind. His eyes close, facial muscles relax, and breathing deepens as he imagines and talks about the sights, sounds, and feelings of visiting a place in his mystery books. He notices the freshness and pleasant smell of the air at this place, as it comfortably enters and exits his lungs. While picturing and feeling this air moving through his open, relaxed airways, he is given the posthypnotic suggestion that the more he practices this exercise the more control and comfort he will find in his breathing. He is asked to enjoy and remember this experience, practice it daily, and monitor his dyspnea and asthma anxiety on a calendar. In his presence, Jonathan's parents are told that Jonathan's practice and self-monitoring are his business, so he will need no reminders.

At two 20-minute follow-up visits over the next month, Jonathan has no exacerbations of his asthma, requires no supplemental oral corticosteroids, and reduces his use of inhaled beta agonists. He continues to practice self-hypnosis most days to feel more in control of his asthma, decrease anxiety, and improve his attention in school. A telephone call 4 months later confirms that Jonathan continues to have excellent control of his asthma, using no beta agonists. He no longer practices because his sense of

control has become "automatic." He attributes his success to his ability to "use my mind." His parents notice that he has increased self-confidence and independence in his schoolwork, which has improved.

APPLICATIONS

Cyberphysiologic strategies have been used with success for a variety of problems commonly encountered in general pediatric practice (Table 67–1). Although many reports are anecdotal, in prospective, controlled, randomized clinical trials, hypnosis has reduced juvenile migraine frequency more effectively than placebo or propranolol, decreased the severity of asthma, diminished antiemetic medication use in children receiving chemotherapy for cancer, and shortened children's postoperative hospital stays.

In a series of 505 pediatric encounters using

TABLE 67–1. Problems Amenable to Hypnotherapy

Procedural Pain and Anxiety
Injections
Suturing of wounds
Pelvic examinations
Procedures related to chronic diseases
    Radiologic procedures
    Lumbar punctures
    Dialysis
    Intravenous chemotherapy
Pain Syndromes
Headaches, including migraine
Recurrent abdominal pain
Those associated with chronic disease (e.g., malignancy,
    sickle cell, hemophilia)
Reflex sympathetic dystrophy
Chronic Conditions (Adjunctive Therapy)
Asthma
Inflammatory bowel disease
Tic disorders/Tourette syndrome
Diabetes mellitus
Psychophysiologic Problems
Conditioned nausea and vomiting
Stuttering
Enuresis
Encopresis
Eczema
Vocal cord dysfunction
Anorexia nervosa/Bulimia nervosa
Habit Disorders
Trichotillomania
Thumb sucking
Tongue thrust
Nail biting
Insomnia
Habit coughs
Other
Warts
Conditioned fears
Performance anxiety

hypnotherapy for enuresis, headaches, other recurrent pain, and a variety of other problems, Kohen and coworkers (1984) reported that 83% of children and adolescents had more than a 50% reduction in symptoms; 50% showed complete resolution. There was an inverse correlation between success and the number of visits, with most children acquiring usable skills by the second visit. Less successful children were more likely not to have practiced self-hypnosis and to have been reminded by their parents to practice more. Parental reminders may have negated the autonomy required for success in self-regulation. **Successful children noted a "spillover effect" of self-efficacy into other life challenges.**

Parents of children who have chronic, complex disease or habit problems are often frustrated and "enmeshed" with their children. It is important that the clinician clarify that the success of self-regulation strategies rests in the child's drive for autonomy. For this reason it is recommended that the child be taught self-regulation without the parents present. It can be explained that these skills must be learned first by the child and, once mastered, taught to the parents by the child. Often parents are relieved to know that their children have this ability to help themselves. With very young or severely ill children, parents and children can be taught self-hypnosis as a team, enhancing their ability to find comfort together.

METHODS

Training in hypnosis (see later section, How to Get Training) helps the clinician to develop the skill and flexibility to focus the young person's awareness and to craft therapeutic suggestions with appropriately permissive language. However, many hypnotic methods can be integrated into primary care practice without formal training. By communicating carefully and attending to the child's interests and responses, the clinician can create comfort, strengthening a young person's awareness of mind-body linkage and abilities for self-regulation during most clinical encounters.

Children and adolescents often come to the primary care clinician in an altered state of awareness, conditioned by previous experiences, characterized by a narrowed focus of attention, heightened expectancy, and an enhanced responsiveness to suggestion. **Entering the clinician's office** and waiting for the doctor to come into the examination room **may be viewed as trance initiation.**

For injections, venipuncture, and short, painful procedures, the child can choose pinwheels, bubble wands, or birthday candles (unlit) to "blow away" pain and anxiety while focusing attention. For longer procedures such as the suturing of wounds and pelvic examinations, a choice of pop-up books or audiotapes of stories and music allows the young person to focus and relax while dissociating himself or herself from discomfort. **It is essential that these methods not be intended to deceive the child or adolescent, but to allow him or her to redirect his or her attention willingly toward comfort and control.**

Preschool-age children can be encouraged to bring a favorite stuffed animal, doll, or "action figure" to the office. The clinician then interacts with this surrogate as well as with the child. The object can be carefully and explicitly examined with attention paid to possible sources of anxiety for the child—the ears, mouth, and abdomen. During this inspection the clinician observes, "You know, your bear is quite cozy, isn't he?" while prompting and eliciting a nod from the child. The examiner continues, "He sure stays quiet and calm when I look in his ears, doesn't he? . . . He does not let this bother him, does he? . . . See how soft he makes his belly? . . . He sure knows how to rest while I check his body, doesn't he?" After this brief demonstration, the surrogate is handed to the child to hold while the clinician says, "You show Bear how well you will do!" This technique respects the validity of the child's imagination as a source of comfort and self-control while he or she focuses on an ally that cooperates with the examination.

While the clinician elicits the history of recurrent symptoms at an initial visit, the child's or adolescent's own imagery or metaphors for his or her experiences can both enhance the clinician's understanding of the symptoms and prepare for future teaching of self-regulation strategies. When the child is asked "What is your headache like?" the clinician can inquire about the headache's size, color, shape, and consistency, for example, in addition to the traditional descriptors. If the youngster finds this problematic, he or she can be asked to "imagine it better by letting your eyes close" or by drawing a picture of the symptom on paper with crayons. Within the framework of this induced trance, communication about the symptom complex can include the child's imagery.

Natural physical phenomena elicited during the examination can be therapeutic metaphors for such psychophysiologic problems as muscle tension headaches, recurrent abdominal pain, and conditioned fears. The patellar deep tendon reflex serves as an example of controllable subconscious reflexes that mediate muscle tension, as in muscle contraction headaches, irritable bowel syndrome, or performance anxiety. The patient learns that clenching fists, relaxing, or focusing attention elsewhere modifies the reflex and, similarly, the symptom. The adolescent who has problems getting to sleep can learn progressive relaxation during the physical examination. This same technique can ease the transition to sleep at home. Abdominal breathing taught during the physical examination can help youngsters learn that focusing on their own breathing releases tension and brings comfort. These mind-body phenomena introduce the practice of hypnosis.

Hypnosis for Pain

Hypnoanalgesia has long been reported to be a successful component of pain management. As early as 1843, John Elliotson reported on the use of hypnoanalgesia for surgery. The advent of effective chemical anesthesia and medical analgesics relegated hypnotic methods to occasional use. However, the value of hypnoanalgesia as adjunctive and primary therapy is re-emerging, as case reports and studies document its effectiveness in reducing procedural pain, augmenting operative anesthesia, and reducing the frequency and severity of recurrent or chronic pain syndromes. **Because the experience of pain is subjective, it can be altered.**

Acute Pain

Acute pain influences the child's perception. Already in a heightened state of awareness, the young person's attention is intensely focused, and he or she is highly motivated to respond to suggestions for comfort. No lengthy explanation of self-regulation in hypnosis is required. It is necessary only to capture the child's intensified attention, establish therapeutic rapport, and convey the confidence that the situation will improve. For example, one might say, "You are smart to come to the doctor [or emergency room] when part of you is hurt so that we can help you begin to get it better," or "I bet that arm really hurts right now . . . and, when it's all better, you can be proud of how well you helped it heal."

One can facilitate the child's search for comfort in a variety of ways. By asking the child where he or she would rather be, the clinician can suggest multisensory imagery to help the child dissociate from the painful experience. For example, "You can certainly enjoy your birthday party in your mind while I sew up this cut. Can you *see* all the presents? Do you *hear* your friends and family singing? Would you tell me when you make a wish and *feel* yourself *blowing* out all the candles? Can you *smell* the kind of cake you are having? Does it *taste* good?" Youngsters may find comfort in the cognitive mastery of knowing they can change sensation with relaxation and breathing; for example: "It is good to discover that you can change how your stomach feels with your breathing . . . that's right . . . simply breathing out helps your stomach relax . . . and the more you notice your breathing, in . . . then out . . . , the more comfortable you can get . . . as if you are breathing out the discomfort as it comes . . . then goes." Some children cope best by focusing on the cause of the pain and its manifestations, thereby altering the experience. One may ask the child to notice "how bright and red and healthy your blood is," and "It is good that the skin here tells you when it is hurt. It sends messages up wires to your brain," and "There have probably been other times when you have had something hurt (and then get better!). On a scale of 0 to 10, how does this compare with those times?" Several hypnotic techniques for acute pain management have been described (see Kuttner [1996], Kohen [1986], and Olness and Kohen [1996]). Used in acute settings, these methods decrease the young person's anxiety and increase comfort, self-control, and cooperation, leading to increased self-efficacy and mastery.

Chronic and Recurrent Pain

Chronic and recurrent pain differ from acute discomfort in that they are more disabling, carrying with them a sense of negative expectancy. The person who has chronic or recurrent pain learns that when the pain starts, it worsens, and when relieved, it returns. This intensifies the young person's anxiety and sense of despair, magnifying the perception of pain. **Teaching self-regulation to children and adolescents who have chronic and recurrent pain requires that the therapist help reduce both the severity of pain and the negative expectancy that accompanies it.**

Self-hypnosis is taught and practiced to reduce anxiety and to create positive expectancy. Using the young person's own descriptions of the pain and the limitations that it causes, the clinician helps him or her develop a hypnotic experience during which he or she may imagine experiencing that "pounding, dark green ball that feels like a headache softening and turning a lighter color," or "skiing on that mountain without any leg pain," or (for a child who has sickle cell disease and vaso-occlusive crises) "enjoying the nice warm blood flow with slippery, round, smooth red blood cells." During this experience, ego-strengthening suggestions for mastery, positive outcome, and reminders that "the more you practice, the better and easier it will get" help the child or adolescent develop the ability for self-control. A symptom and hypnosis practice diary can help the child and clinician monitor progress and modify the hypnotic exercise as needed.

Chronic and recurrent pain, especially when there is no clear biologic cause may be symptomatic of significant psychopathology, including post-traumatic stress disorder, sexual and physical abuse, and depression. The youngster's somatic symptoms may be protecting him or her from more severe psychologic pain. If the presenting symptom is serving a protective psychologic purpose, hypnotic techniques may be ineffective, and contraindicated, without psychotherapeutic intervention directed at the underlying psychologic condition. **It is vital that primary care clinicians carefully re-evaluate their approach** to self-regulation training for children and adolescents who have persistent symptoms, **obtaining appropriate mental health consultation.**

Hypnosis for Habits

Children often develop habits that are frustrating to themselves and to family members. These include problems such as nail biting, thumb sucking, habitual coughing, hyperventilation, hair pulling, and tongue rolling or thrusting. Some habits begin with a normal physiologic response, such as cough associated with a respiratory infection that becomes conditioned. **The most practical approach to these habits,** if the child wishes to eliminate the habit, **is to teach a self-management method that emphasizes mastery and control.** It is important for the clinician to ascertain whether the problem is of more concern to the parent than to the child. It also is important to take the time to communicate to the parents that they must "disengage" from the problem as much as possible and not remind the child to do the cyberphysiologic practice.

The training approach must take into account the child's interests, likes, learning style, and fears. Very often the use of adjunctive biofeedback is helpful. This provides graphic evidence to the child that he or she can control body responses such as electrodermal activity or peripheral temperature. An example of a typical habit problem and an approach to it follows.

Anna, a vivacious 7-year-old girl, is distressed by her nail biting. Her parents' attempt at re-wards for nail growth have not worked. Anna herself sometimes puts gloves on while watching television, a favorite nail-biting time. She does well in school, has several good friends, and enjoys reading, bicycling, and singing. She also enjoys imaginary games.

Anna listens intently as the clinician explains that she will act as a coach or a teacher to Anna but only Anna can do the exercise successfully. The clinician emphasizes that Anna's parents *cannot* remind her to practice daily. She asks Anna how she will remember, giving examples of how some children remember to do similar practice. Anna decides that she will make a poster for the door to her room and that the poster will remind her.

The clinician then suggests that Anna can relax by imagining that she is riding her bicycle to a favorite place. Anna is engaged immediately, closes her eyes, and describes her ride and where she is going. As requested by the clinician, Anna signals when she reaches a favorite place. Then Anna is asked to tell her hands to help each other. If one begins to move up toward her mouth for nail biting, the other hand gently pushes it back down. Anna practices with each hand as the helper hand. Then she is asked to imagine that she is with her friends, looks at her hands, and is happy to see that the nails are normal, beautiful, and no longer bitten. Anna is asked to repeat this exercise at home twice a day. She returns for a 15-minute review practice in 1 week. She says that she is biting her nails less. Two weeks later her nails are growing out and she is very pleased. She phones 1 month later to report that she no longer is biting her nails and has stopped the practices. Follow-up by phone and postcard is continued for 3 months.

Personal Use of Self-Hypnosis

The professional life of a primary care clinician includes many distressing situations such as the occasional requirement to give bad news to parents of a newborn, to do procedures that children perceive as an attack, to make rapid decisions over the phone in the middle of the night, and to diagnose efficiently and correctly many children in a day. Primary care clinicians often develop sleep problems that may relate to frequent interruptions at night. Many have found that investing 2 or 3 months to learn how to condition relaxation is well worth the time and effort. Not only do they benefit personally, but they improve their ability to teach these strategies to children. The child health professional may also use self-regulation to enhance his or her coping and comfort with dental or medical procedures, to overcome sleep problems, or to deal with unwanted habits. The clinician can learn these techniques for personal use from a colleague who is already skilled in them, by participating in a training workshop, or, if he or she is highly disciplined, by following the recommendations from books such as *Relaxation Response, Peak Performance,* or *Full Catastrophe Living* (see Further Reading at end of chapter).

How to Get Training

The most efficient way to get started is to immerse oneself in a 3-day introductory workshop in child hypnosis such as that sponsored by the Society for Developmental and Behavioral Pediatrics or the American Society of Clinical Hypnosis or, occasionally, under the sponsorship of a department of pediatrics, such as Rainbow Babies' and Children's Hospital in Cleveland. Alternatively, one can begin with a general beginner's workshop that will be more adult oriented. These are sponsored annually by the American Society of Clinical Hypnosis, annually by the Society for Clinical and Experimental Hypnosis, and every 3 years by the International Society of Hypnosis (see Resources listing at the end of the chapter).

Cost and Reimbursement

Increasing attention to the cost-effectiveness of medical care and practitioner reimbursement for time spent with patients raises the question: Is it practical to incorporate cyberphysiologic methods into practice? Within a general pediatric practice, the clinician bills for a certain length of visit under a coded diagnosis. The method of therapeutic intervention, whether it is medication, physical therapy, parenting advice, teaching self-hypnosis, or a combination, lies within the judgment of the clinician. For a given child, successfully teaching self-regulation can be a continuum of learning from "blowing away" needle injection pain when the child is 5 years old, to exploring imagery to cope with having sutures placed when he is age 8, to conditioning exercises for comfort and competence in test-taking at school in adolescence, to reducing stress and migraines in adulthood. Thus, in general practice, teaching self-regulation is an efficient extension of therapeutic work with young

patients that grows with them. Explicit reimbursement for "cyberphysiologic training" will have to await the acceptance by third party payers of proven cost-effectiveness. There is a great need for such outcomes-based research in this field. For the present, cyberphysiologic therapies are called "general pediatrics" and billed as such.

FURTHER READING

Benson H: Relaxation Response. New York, William Morrow and Co, 1975.

Elliotson J: Numerous Cases of Surgical Operations Without Pain in the Mesmeric State. Philadelphia, Lea and Blanchard, 1843.

Garfield CA: Peak Performance: Mental Training Techniques of the World's Greatest Athletes. Los Angeles, JP Archer and Co, 1984.

Jacknow DS, Tschann JM, Link MP, and Boyce WT: Hypnosis in the prevention of chemotherapy-related nausea and vomiting in children: A prospective study. J Dev Behav Pediatr 15:258–264, 1994.

Kabat-Zinn J: Full Catastrophe Living. New York, Delacorte Press, 1990.

Kohen DP, Olness KN, Colwell SO, and Heimel A: The use of relaxation/mental imagery (self-hypnosis) in the management of 505 pediatric behavioral encounters. J Dev Behav Pediatr 1:21–25, 1984.

Kohen DP: Applications of relaxation/mental imagery (self-hypnosis) in pediatric emergencies. Int J Clin Exp Hypn 34:283–294, 1986.

Kohen DP: Relaxation/mental imagery (self-hypnosis) for childhood asthma: Behavioral outcomes in a prospective, controlled study. Hypnosis 22:132–143, 1995.

Kuttner L: A Child in Pain: How to Help, What to Do. Point Roberts, WA, Hartley and Marks, 1996.

Lambert SA: The effects of hypnosis/guided imagery on the postoperative course of children. J Dev Behav Pediatr 17:307–310, 1996.

Olness KN, MacDonald JT, and Uden DL: Prospective study comparing propranolol, placebo, and hypnosis in management of juvenile migraine. Pediatrics 79:593–597, 1987.

Olness KN and Kohen DP: Hypnosis and Hypnotherapy with Children, 3rd ed. New York, Guilford Press, 1996.

Sugarman LI: Hypnosis in a primary care pediatric practice: Developing skills for the new morbidities. J Dev Behav Pediatr 17:300–306, 1996.

RESOURCES: ORGANIZATIONS SPONSORING PROFESSIONAL TRAINING IN HYPNOSIS

American Society of Clinical Hypnosis, 2250 East Devon Avenue, Suite 336, Des Plaines, IL 60018. Phone: 847-292-3317.

International Society of Hypnosis, Level 1, South Wing, Austin and Repatriation Medical Centre, Repat Campus, Locked Bag 1, Heidelberg West VIC 3081 Australia.

Society for Clinical and Experimental Hypnosis, 6728 Old Maclean Village Drive, Maclean, VA 22101. Phone: 703-556-9222.

Society of Developmental Behavioral Pediatrics, 19 Station Lane, Philadelphia, PA 19118. Phone: 215-248-9168.

Laurie J. Bauman

Chapter 68

Social Support

SOCIAL SUPPORT AND AMBULATORY PEDIATRICS

Social support is a key factor influencing physical and mental health status. Many studies have found that **a strong parental support system is associated with better psychologic well-being and lower morbidity and mortality. The strength of a parent's social support also is associated with parenting practices, parenting stress, and children's development and adjustment.** Therefore, the status of a parent's support system can be a meaningful indicator to the pediatric primary care clinician and bears careful monitoring. Further, clinicians who take a social support history can identify support deficits and assist parents to augment support in several ways. Finally, clinicians should not underestimate how supportive they can be to families, particularly when a medical crisis occurs or families are challenged by chronic or acute stressful life events.

WHAT IS SOCIAL SUPPORT?

Social support is a complex concept, and there is no one universally accepted definition. Psychologists believe that all people have a need for "social affiliation," for being connected in a web of relationships to others through blood, marriage, family, and community. One widely accepted definition by Sidney Cobb (1976) is that social support is information that one is loved and cared for, esteemed and valued, and part of a network of mutual obligation. When parents feel that no one loves or cares about them, when they feel that others reject them or disapprove of their behavior, or when they feel isolated, they lack this necessary web of social affiliation. They are at very high risk for a number of adverse outcomes because poor social support is associated with higher suicide rates, higher risk for drug and alcohol abuse, and poorer adherence to treatment regimens for themselves and their children. Their children also are at risk because poor parental support has been linked to higher rates of child abuse and neglect,

more reliance on the use of corporal punishment, delayed development, and more behavioral problems. Lack of parental support also has been associated with inappropriate use of health care services by children.

Variation in Social Support

Social support is a social behavior determined by norms and values, and the unspoken rules that govern supportive exchanges vary considerably by culture and gender. In general, cultures characterized by closely knit extended family groups, strong, consistently held cultural beliefs, and homogeneity have kin-dominated support systems that are stable, reliable, and "dense"—that is, everyone in the support system knows everyone else. Parents in such cultures usually have access to a large network of helpers who can assist in teaching the parent role, advise on child care issues, and provide encouragement and assistance.

Men and women differ in their social support behaviors. Women are more likely than men to confide in others about their feelings, to have larger support systems, and to feel more comfortable accessing support by making their needs known. Men tend to rely for support on their wives (more than wives do on their husbands), seek support in the form of advice or information rather than sharing feelings or concerns, and have smaller networks of supporters but larger networks of friends and acquaintances.

Often, families are separated geographically, so certain kinds of day-to-day assistance may not be possible, but data show that even when separated by hundreds and thousands of miles, families are the most important source of support in the form of money, gifts, emotional support, and advice or information; this appears consistently across culture and gender. Although grandparents may be named as supporters, it is important for the clinician to assess whether there are tensions in the relationship, since the mother's mother is most often named both as the most important supporter and as the one most likely to give too much advice or treat the parent like a child. Further, many parents, particularly mothers, are providing more support to their family members than they receive, especially when their own parents are in ill health or their supporters have many stressors. If this is true, they may be vulnerable to having inadequate support systems.

Why Do People Have Inadequate Support?

Parents who lack adequate support may present as isolated, lonely, and depressed. Some insist that their lack of a support system is their own preference and therefore not a problem. There are many reasons why parents have inadequate support, and it is a challenge for the clinician to identify the cause of the problem. For example, some parents are unwilling or uncomfortable about asking for help or accepting help because it seems to them to be an admission of weakness or failure. Some feel that the people on whom they rely for support are themselves under too much stress to be of help. Others fear that by accepting help from another they will become obligated through the norms of reciprocity to provide help in return, an obligation they may be unable or unwilling to meet. **Sometimes people are grateful for the support they receive but do not want to be on the receiving end only. They want support to be reciprocal—to support as well as to receive support.** A few deliberately keep people at arm's length because they are keeping a secret, such as domestic abuse, mental illness, or a stigmatizing condition such as the acquired immunodeficiency syndrome. Most often, though, inadequate support reflects one of two things: a deficit or weakness in the family's support system or the presence of extreme environmental demands that would overtax even "adequate" support systems. By taking a support history, one can distinguish lack of essential support resources from overwhelming acute or chronic stress.

TAKING A SOCIAL SUPPORT HISTORY

To identify a weakness in the support system, one can take a support history, which involves assessing several parameters of the social support system. **To take a social support history, one should assess (1) the size of the support network; (2) whether different kinds of support are readily available; (3) how much support** **has been provided; (4) whether the support that is received is perceived as adequate; (5) whether there are negative consequences of receiving support; (6) whether support is reciprocal; and (7) whether the parent has a confidant.** The size of the support network and availability of support can be assessed by asking the parent a few questions about whether she has people who would give her support of different types if she should need it. Practical kinds of support to ask about include whether there is anyone who would run an errand, take care of her if she were sick, or loan her money if it were needed. Ask about child care support: Are there people who would take care of her child on short notice or help regularly with child care? Emotional support can be assessed by asking if she has someone who really understands her and her life, anyone to whom she can tell her problems or confide in, someone who would be there for her if she were going through a hard time. Also, assess "esteem" support: Does she have people in her life who show her respect, who value her for who she is, who accept her as she is? As you ask about the different kinds of support she has available, try to find out who her supporters are. Does she mention the same few people over and over or does she have a large support network? Are all the supporters kin or does she mention friends and neighbors as well? Is she relying on professionals rather than on her informal support system? Is she relying too much on her children for her own support? Are there gaps in the kinds of support available?

Adequacy of support can be assessed by asking the parent whether she has the support she needs and how often she feels she could use more support. This is a very sensitive indicator of the parent's support system. Does she name many people who are supporters but feels that she is not receiving support when she needs it? Does he have too few people in his network? Is she receiving a lot of support but feels that it still isn't enough?

Negative aspects or consequences of support may interfere with a parent's willingness to use the support that is available. Parents may feel that people have disappointed them in the past by not offering to help when it was expected that they would. Parents may feel overwhelmed by too much unwanted advice or that their lives have been taken over by well-meaning people who are trying to make their decisions for them. Clinicians can ask whether there are people the parent might not want to ask for support, whether anyone has disappointed them, or whether receiving support from anyone has caused any problems.

Once the support system has been assessed, it is easier to know what solutions might be suggested for those who have problems. Those who are so distressed that even their large, responsive support system is ineffective need to be referred for counseling and professional assistance. Those who have small support systems need a different intervention than those who have large support systems that impose conditions on their support. Those who resist using support or do not know how to ask for it need different kinds of help than those who have some kinds of support but lack others.

STRESSORS AND THE SUPPORT SYSTEM

When Stressful Life Events Tax the Support System

Under some circumstances families experience a combination of stressors that taxes even their usually adequate supports. Clinicians often are witnesses to these stressors in families, including the challenges of parenting for the first time, the birth of a premature or ill infant, the diagnosis of chronic or terminal illness in a child or family member, acute catastrophic trauma, the emergence of cognitive or emotional impairments in children, marital problems and divorce, work and family conflicts, and the demands of caregiving to older parents.

Stressors can be dramatic or insidious, acute or chronic, expected or unanticipated. Some people face multiple life changes, often in a cascade following a precipitating event. For example, the death of a spouse can lead to additional problems such as loss of income, serious financial hardship, need to relocate to smaller, less adequate housing, and change in neighborhood or school. Stressors that involve loss of an important relationship through divorce, geographic separation, or death are particularly powerful because they result in not only grief over the loss but also the loss of an important support resource. When a traumatic stressful event occurs, the support system usually rallies and plays an important, if temporary, role in helping the family adjust. **Acute and chronic stress elevates the need for social support. Parents who have good social support systems are better able to cope with such stress but may need additional help. Be on the alert for parents who are experiencing many stressful life events, for example, the loss of an important relationship, those taking on a new role or losing a valued one, and those experiencing role conflict.**

Chronic, Daily Hassles Challenge Support Systems

Although the aforementioned stressors are universally perceived as challenging, it would be a mistake to underestimate the importance of daily hassles in precipitating an emotional crisis and escalating the need for support. Life is full of "broken shoelaces," frustrations that cause tension and short tempers. In addition, some of the most pernicious stressors result from the demands of the roles we occupy, particularly the parent role and its continuing conflict with work roles. It often is the everyday tensions, battles, conflicts, and demands that impose the greatest challenges to families and therefore require intense support.

The Stress of Role Changes

Changes in role are a particularly important test for support networks. Clinicians who are sensitive to role changes can support parents as they cope with role stress. Beginning a new role is common, such as beginning a new job, becoming a student, becoming a parent, or becoming the primary caregiver for an older parent or an ill or developmentally disabled child. Although most of the time the new role is desired, all roles have duties and responsibilities associated with them that can lead to stress. Similarly, loss of an important role caused by, for example, unemployment, graduation, or one's children moving out on their own, can also precipitate a crisis with associated increases in the need for support.

Most parents have "adequate" support and can manage both the daily hassles and occasional stressful events by relying on family members, friends, and occasionally professional support. However, clinicians should reassess support when parents report difficult circumstances. These parents may need extra assistance if their supporters are too far away, are under too much stress themselves, cannot meet specific support needs the parents may have, or give as much negative as positive support.

ISSUES IN AUGMENTING SUPPORT SYSTEMS

Clinicians themselves can be an important source of support to parents and can offer meaningful support to parents by being available to them, by asking them how they are doing, by listening to their concerns and normalizing their fears, and by showing that they

care about the child's overall adjustment. Clinicians who understand what emotional and affirmational support are can easily inform their patients that the people they know care about them and love them, and they can be sure to tell parents that they are doing a good job as a parent. **Just asking parents how they are doing—and really listening to them—is perceived by them to be extremely supportive.** Parents also feel very supported by health care clinicians who call the home to inquire about the progress of an ill child or to lend support around a sleeping, eating, or disciplinary problem. Sharing a personal anecdote with parents about one's own experience is also important. Simple small gestures of caring and concern are frequently remembered by parents for a long time and require little effort or time on the part of the clinician.

Clinicians also can be a liaison for parents to other sources of support. Support groups have become common and available in most communities. In addition to the usual kinds of assistance from which parents might benefit, including groups that focus on breastfeeding, discipline, or parenting, parents of children who are ill or disabled often find support groups helpful. Parents also may benefit from attending support groups focused on their own illnesses, problems with alcohol or drug use, weight regulation, depression or other mental health problems, or perhaps groups for working mothers. Support groups tend to work for members because people can share their problems and concerns with others who are going through the same situation, and the support one receives from others who really understand the problem is unique and unlikely to be found in one's own support network. In addition, people can receive and give support; many people remain in support groups because they want to help others. Support groups most often are used by people who are comfortable using support and who have minimally adequate support already. Support groups may not be able to replace a broken network—people who have inadequate support often try and drop out of support groups because they do not receive the intensity and intimacy of support that they need.

Clinicians also may help people understand their own reluctance to engage an existing support network. All some parents need is encouragement and permission to use the support they have available. Some people are not good support users and have a hard time asking for support. It is important to know that most support is not accessed by requesting it outright. One way to help people use their support systems is to suggest that they make their need known to someone they trust. That is, they need to describe their need problem—"I don't know how I can pick up Johnny at preschool when Mary is too sick to be left alone." Once the need is expressed to a loved one in the support network, usually the help is offered. When parents are offered help freely, it makes them feel cared for and makes the supporter feel good for offering.

SUMMARY

Social support is a complex social process that varies in its expression in different cultures and genders. It is a critical daily resource for families, especially in times of acute and chronic stress. Assessing a parent's support system need not take long and can give the clinician important insight into the human resources available to parents and children. It can help identify at-risk families who may need preventive intervention and alert the clinician to families who are isolated or vulnerable. The clinician can provide important kinds of support through sensitive interaction with families and be a liaison to additional resources when families are in need.

FURTHER READING

Cobb S: Social support as a moderator of life stress. Psychosom Med 38:300–313, 1976.

Cohen S and Syme SL (eds): Social Support and Health. Orlando, FL, Academic Press, 1985.

Ganster D and Victor B: The impact of social support on mental and physical health. Br J Med Psychol 61:17–36, 1988.

House JS, Landis KR, and Umberson D: Social relationships and health. Science 241:540–545, 1988.

Shumaker SA and Hill DR: Gender differences in social support and physical health. Health Psychol 10:102–111, 1991.

Vaux A: Social Support: Theory, Research and Intervention. New York, Praeger, 1991.

Chapter 69

Community Organization for Ambulatory Pediatrics

WHAT SHOULD THE PEDIATRICIAN KNOW ABOUT COMMUNITY ORGANIZATION?

"The health of children is tied to the health of communities, and both are less healthy than anyone could wish" (Palfrey, 1994). Over the past several decades many communities have awakened to the fact that changes in the economic and family structures in the U.S. have put many families and children under increased stress at the same time that the traditional support systems of the extended family and/or cohesive community have been severely weakened. There also has been a growing awareness that other Western European democracies, faced with many of these same changes, have responded in a much more supportive way to families and children and have experienced more positive child health and developmental outcomes (fewer low-birth-weight infants, infant deaths, and cases of child abuse and neglect, better readiness for school, fewer adolescent pregnancies, fewer injuries, and less community violence of all kinds).

This evolving awareness has led an increasing number of child health clinicians and other primary care clinicians to become involved with community coalitions whose goals include promoting the health and development of all children in a given geographic area. The publication of Judith Palfrey's book, *Community Child Health* (1994); the development of *Bright Futures: Guidelines for Health Supervision of Infants, Children, and Adolescents* (see Chapter 73), "founded on the principle that the health and safety of our children depends on the health and wholeness of our families, our communities, and our institution"; and the American Academy of Pediatrics' adoption of the Community Access To Child Health (CATCH) (see Chapter 73) and Healthy Tomorrows grant programs all indicate that a communitywide approach to child health and development has come into the mainstream of child health thinking. Thus, primary care clinicians need to

be aware of these trends and to understand how community coalitions come together and what roles clinicians can play in their development. Following are descriptions of two initiatives that demonstrate how community coalitions form and operate.

THE HEALTHY CITIES/HEALTHY COMMUNITIES INITIATIVE

Some groups in the United States have been influenced by the World Health Organization's Healthy Cities/Healthy Communities movement, which started in Europe in 1986 and since has spread to the United States and many other countries. This approach focuses on the quality of life for community residents of all ages and uses a top-down, bottom-up strategy for changing the ecology of a city or town. Broad-based community coalitions are formed that work with the mayor and city council to get a signed memorandum of understanding indicating that community health (defined broadly) will be put on the policy agenda and that an intersectoral council of city agencies and other service providers will be formed to coordinate programs and fill in gaps. Emphasis is placed on having equal access to services, preventing disease, promoting healthy lifestyles, and building environments that support health. **Once the "top" (mayor and city council) is engaged, the most successful programs hire a coordinator to work with the "bottom" (neighborhood groups) to develop priorities for change that best meet the needs of local residents in different parts of a city or community.** A number of these projects have been started in the cities and towns of Indiana, Colorado, California, Maine, and Massachusetts. Although families that have children benefit from these changes, they often have not been singled out specifically as a target population.

FAMILY SUPPORT COALITIONS

Other community coalitions have focused more directly on making their communities more family- and child-friendly. For instance, in New Hampshire, some of these coalitions have formed under the banner of preventing child abuse and neglect; others have come together in the "Success By Six" movement, in which the goal is to see that every child enters the school system ready to learn. The former tend to concentrate more on preventing abuse or neglect in high-risk families; the latter generally follow an ecological model, working to make community environments more supportive for all families that have young children. Regardless of the underlying motivation, communities approaching the problem from either side often end up in the middle with many similar ideas. Most have made the development of a community-based family resource center a priority and have been interested in developing home visiting for at least some of the newborn population. Other activities have included increasing access to health care for children, improving the quality of child care, increasing access to early childhood education programs, and encouraging area businesses to develop more family-friendly policies and practices.

Although these efforts have been successful in getting local programs implemented, they have not been as successful as the Healthy Cities/Healthy Communities initiative in engaging the political leadership of communities and attacking broader problems such as affordable housing, transportation, unemployment and underemployment, exposure to toxic substances, and care of the elderly that also affect families. A merger of these two movements in the same town or city is needed. The Family Resource Coalition of America based in Chicago provides information and technical assistance to community groups interested in developing local and statewide networks of family support programs.

THE EVOLUTION OF COMMUNITY COALITIONS

Community groups (see Chapter 14) generally evolve through the following steps:

1. *Building a broad-based coalition.* One or more persons concerned about what is happening to families and children in their community start talking to others. As they identify persons who have similar concerns, the coalition begins to grow. At this point they may invite a speaker to address the issue to the broader community.

2. *Assessing assets and needs.* As more people become involved, efforts are made to gather better data. Front-line providers such as physicians, school nurses, child care workers, the local elementary school principal, the police chief, a local minister, priest, or, rabbi and the visiting nurse are asked to describe what they are seeing in the community both in terms of strengths and needs. Efforts are continued to broaden the coalition.

3. *Developing an overall framework.* At this stage it often is helpful to have a "visioning" exercise to see how coalition members would like their community to be a number of years into the future. Short- and long-term priorities are identified to help the community move toward their shared goals.

4. *Implementing the vision.* This requires selling the broader community on the importance of the identified priorities and finding the necessary funding.

5. *Sustaining momentum.* Skills in program evaluation and advocacy are necessary to build and sustain the programs needed over the long periods necessary to show positive results.

ROLE OF CHILD HEALTH CLINICIANS

Although few physicians have the time to participate extensively in the many meetings required by these efforts, they can facilitate activities in a number of important ways. For example, pediatric clinicians often know and are respected by key community leaders, and their endorsement of the coalition's activities gives it legitimacy. In the data gathering phase clinicians can report what problems they are seeing in the families they serve. They also have a good knowledge of what resources for children are available in the community and what is missing. Another important activity is to help the group get access to needed baseline data such as types of preventable problems being seen in the local hospital emergency department and the immunization status at age 2 years of children entering the school system.

Program Implementation

With the help of one or more pediatric clinicians, communities have been able to obtain planning grants from the American Academy of Pediatrics' CATCH program. These have resulted in the development of a number of health and family support programs, including family resource centers, home visiting to parents of newborns, adolescent health and parenting programs, improvement of access to health care for uninsured families, and coordination of care for children who have special needs. Clinicians also can use their knowledge of growth and development to help in efforts to upgrade child care in an area by participating in continuing education programs for child care providers. Many also have participated in school health education programs.

Advocacy

Because community-based programs require a long-term investment of resources to achieve meaningful results, there will be periodic efforts by short-sighted public officials and/or agency heads to cut back or eliminate the funding of key preventive programs in times of budget restraints. Clinicians can help prevent these actions by testifying at public hearings and contacting local legislators. For example in New Hampshire, the state funds less than 10% of the cost of education in local school districts, which puts a heavy tax burden on local communities. A conservative state board of education tried to "help" local communities by lowering standards and allowing them to cut back on expenditures for early intervention and special education programs. Testimony on the importance of these programs at public hearings by pediatric clinicians and others helped head off this unwise initiative.

Some Other Specific Examples

Plymouth, New Hampshire, a small college town of about 5000 people, has developed a broad-based coalition of about 90 persons from a catchment area containing 19 surrounding small towns and a total population of about 26,000 people. They have obtained a $1 million community development block grant to build a family center that facilitates "one-stop shopping" by housing 12 area agencies that serve families. In addition, the program is being designed to strengthen all families in the catchment area by providing opportunities at the center for skills building and emotional support for parents, along with outreach activities such as home visiting for new mothers, developing toddler play groups, and promoting a sense of community where people live. The two pediatricians serving the area have been active participants in the planning, helped the coalition obtain a CATCH planning grant, and are helping to develop a medical home for children who do not have health insurance.

In another area, one pediatrician has spent a good part of his retirement working with a coalition involving the 11 small New Hampshire towns making up the Conval School District. Together they have developed a family resource center, an adolescent parenting program, a directory of community services for parents, and improved access to health care for low-income children.

Some pediatricians in full-time practice have been prime movers in the development of coalitions. A pediatrician in Webster, Massachusetts (population 16,000), has developed a community-based practice that works closely with a network of community organizations involved with families and children. This coalition has gathered data on community characteristics and on the status of area infants, children, and youths. They have used these data to develop an overall plan and implement programs that shift the community from a deficit orientation that waits until a family or child is in trouble before trying to intervene to a more proactive approach for promoting the health and development of all area children and youth and their families. **Primary prevention works by preventing medium-risk families from becoming high-risk.**

Another physician is the only pediatrician serving a six-town area in northern Maine. He is working with these communities to develop a "Healthy Futures" project. With the aid of a CATCH planning grant, he hopes to find funding for a program that eventually will coordinate health promotion home visits to families who have children in these towns with a school-based center designed to serve the children.

Making Practice Settings More Family-Friendly

Finally, pediatric clinicians can make their own practices more family-friendly by developing a bulletin board to be used by parents to share information and services, having office hours that meet the needs of working mothers, establishing support groups for families undergoing separation and divorce, and instituting programs that encourage reading to young children such as the Reach Out and Read Program started by pediatricians at Boston City Hospital. **"The single most important educational input that early childhood programs can accomplish is introducing families to the joys of reading aloud to their young children"** (Palfrey, 1994).

Implications for Training Programs

Involving pediatric and nurse practitioner trainees in these community efforts is difficult because they evolve slowly over several years and crucial meetings often are held on short notice. Conducting "show and tell" seminars in primary care training programs that highlight efforts in different local communities and having physicians and nurses adopt a site to visit and relate to over several years are possible ways to engage and provide them with the knowledge and experience necessary to work successfully with community coalitions.

Acknowledgment

I wish to thank Steve Kairys, MD, for his review of the manuscript and helpful comments for improving it.

FURTHER READING

Ashton J (ed): Healthy Cities. Philadelphia, Open University Press, 1992.

Chamberlin R: Preventing low birth weight, child abuse, and school failure: The need for comprehensive, community wide approaches. Pediatr Rev 13:64–71, 1992.

Chamberlin R: Primary prevention and the family resource movement. *In* Singer G, Powers P, and Olson A (eds): Redefining Family Support: Innovations in Public-Private Partnerships. Baltimore, Paul Brooks Publishing Co., 1995.

Kagan S and Weissbourd B (eds): Putting Families First. San Francisco, Jossey-Bass, 1994.

Palfrey JS: Community Child Health: An Action Plan for Today. Westport, CT, Praeger, 1994.

Rose G: Sick individuals and sick populations. Int J Epidemiol 114:32–38, 1985.

Deborah Klein Walker

Chapter **70**

Assessment of Community Health Needs and Services

One goal of health care, education, welfare, and social services reform is to create healthy communities in which healthy families thrive and promote the optimal functioning of every child and youth, including those who have special health care needs. In order to design, implement, and monitor a comprehensive, community-based, family-centered, culturally competent and coordinated system of care in every community, assessment of community health needs and services for children and youth must be ongoing. An ongoing assessment and reassessment of community needs and resources is most effective if it is conducted within the context of community planning and improvement. To maintain these efforts in communities over time, a maternal and child health (MCH) population-based data information system must be developed and maintained by MCH public health agencies at all levels of government.

COMMUNITY ASSESSMENT AND PLANNING

Community needs should be assessed within the context of community-based program planning and evaluation. The basic components of a community health improvement cycle include (1) mobilization of the community to come together to address health concerns; (2) collection and organization of community data; (3) determination of priorities among the numerous health issues and target groups; (4) development and implementation of interventions to address the health disparities or improvement goals desired by the community; and (5) evaluation of the interventions implemented at the community level. Once a community health improvement process is in place, it is possible to review community-based data annually and maintain a series of health improvement projects at one time.

Several guides and models exist for community assessment and planning that can be adapted for a community assessment process related to maternal and child health issues. These models include Planned Approach to Community Health (PATCH), developed by the Centers for Disease Control and Prevention as a tool for health promotion at the community level and Assessment Protocol for Excellence in Public Health (APEX-PH), a self-assessment guide designed by several public health groups to help local health entities assess and improve their capacity for examining and developing plans to overcome local health problems.

TABLE 70–1. Steps in the Community Health Improvement Process

A. Problem identification cycle
  • Form a community health coalition.
  • Collect and analyze data for a community health profile.
  • Identify critical health issues.
B. Analysis and implementation cycle
  • Analyze the health issue.
  • Inventory health resources.
  • Develop a health improvement strategy.
  • Establish accountability for activities.
  • Develop a set of performance indicators.
  • Implement the improvement strategy.
  • Monitor process and outcomes.

From Institute of Medicine, Committee on Using Performance Monitoring to Improve Community Health: Improving Health in the Community: A Role for Performance Monitoring. Washington, DC, National Academy of Sciences, 1997.

TABLE 70–3. Characteristics of a Population-Based Data System

Uses standardized definitions
Is comprehensive in scope
Is accessible via the Internet
Contains current information
Protects individual confidentiality
Provides estimates at various geopolitical entity levels

The most recent specification of a community health improvement process divides it into two distinct cycles—the problem identification cycle and the analysis and implementation cycle (Table 70–1). Finally, the Maternal and Child Health Bureau (MCHB) in the federal government has funded the development of several adaptations of these assessment and planning guides for the maternal and child health population, including a focus on children who have special health care needs.

POPULATION-BASED DATA SYSTEMS

In order to assess child health status and monitor the impact of MCH interventions, a comprehensive MCH population-based data system that operates at all levels of government and serves both consumers and providers must be implemented in every community. The advancements in computer technology and electronic highways make it possible for data to be packaged efficiently and relayed quickly to all interested consumers in a community. Consistent, effective, ongoing assessment and policy development and evaluation can be achieved only when a responsive data system is available. Information from an integrated population-based system can be used for many purposes within the community MCH improvement cycle (Table 70–2).

A data system capable of generating information to meet all of the objectives outlined in Table 70–2 must use standard definitions, be comprehensive in scope, be accessible via the Internet or other information highways in the future, be updated regularly with the most current year's data, protect individual's confidentiality, and be available for a range of geopolitical entities (e.g., census track, zip codes, town, county, city, region) (Table 70–3).

The categories of data desired in a community assessment system include the following indicators (Table 70–4): health status (e.g., measures of mortality and morbidity such as infant mortality and children who are developmentally delayed, behavioral risk (e.g., measures of adolescent risk behaviors such as smoking and drinking), sociodemographic variables (e.g., measures of parent education levels or incomes), environment (e.g., measures of crowding in housing and levels of air pollution), and service access and utilization (e.g., measures of children who are uninsured or who do not have a regular primary health care clinician).

Many sources of data are available for community assessment and planning. Potential population-based data sources include vital statistics (e.g., birth and death records), surveys (e.g., school-based Youth Risk Behavior Survey), surveillance systems and disease registries (e.g., birth defects registry or cancer registry), and program or service management information systems (e.g., hospital discharge or special education reports) (Table 70–5). Although a community assessment should begin with the existing population-based data available for a community profile, it may be

TABLE 70–2. Uses of Population-Based Community Data

Conduct local and state needs assessments
Monitor federal, state, and local mandated programs, services, and screenings
Direct program planning and management
Evaluate programs and services
Ensure follow-up services after identification

TABLE 70–4. Categories of Data Needed in Community Assessments

Health status indicators
Behavioral risk indicators
Sociodemographic indicators
Environmental indicators
Service access and utilization indicators

TABLE 70–5. Potential Population-Based Data Sources

Vital statistics
Surveys
Surveillance systems/disease registries
Program/service management information systems

necessary to collect other information from the community to complete the assessment and "prioritize" local needs. The extent to which new primary data must be collected and analyzed depends on the MCH issues being investigated and the level of resources available for data collection and analysis.

Given today's technology, a population-based data system can be designed at many levels so that billing, patient monitoring, and quality assurance data from clinician practices can be linked to population-based data systems. In addition, a pediatric clinician will be able to access all community level population-based data via the Internet. Massachusetts has implemented such a population-based electronic system, called the Massachusetts Community Health Information Profile (MassCHIP). MassCHIP has the ability to create standard or customized maternal and child health reports for several levels of geographic detail. The system is being used by a variety of persons who have modern access—local governments, school systems, health plans, hospitals, community health centers, individual health care clinicians, researchers, community agencies and organizations, and the general public.

MATERNAL AND CHILD HEALTH RESOURCES AVAILABLE

The state maternal and child health (MCH) director is an important resource for information about current needs assessments and planning processes in each community in the state. The state MCH program, funded by Title V of the 1935 Social Security Act, is required by federal statute to conduct state level needs assessments and help communities conduct their own assessments and build systems of care responsive to specific family and cultural needs. The state MCH program, in partnership with federal and local health entities (counties, towns, cities, etc.), is

committed to the improvement of the health status and well-being of *all* children and youth, regardless of the source of payment for care. The state MCH program serves as a point of accountability for the entire children and youth population by using the core public health functions of assessment, policy development, and assurance. A major priority for all state MCH Title V agencies is the development of population-based data systems and information needed by communities to do local assessments.

Pediatric clinicians have many opportunities to be involved in state or community-level needs assessment and child health planning processes. The options vary from participation in a community coalition and process to an advisory and/or consultant role as various health issues arise. Pediatric clinicians also may help collect data by offering resources from their own practice. In many communities, clinicians participate in a system of reporting diseases not part of official required disease reporting. They can identify new disorders and epidemics quickly. At a minimum, clinicians can be consumers of the population-based data systems implemented at the community level in order to improve the health status and well-being of children in their own practices as well as in the overall community.

FURTHER READING

Grayson HA and Guyer B (eds): Assessing and Developing Primary Care for Children: Reforms in Health Systems. Arlington, VA, National Center for Education in Maternal and Child Health, 1995.

Hayes M and Walker DK: The role of public health in assuring a system of health care for children. *In* Stein REK (ed): Health Care for Children: What's Right, What's Wrong, What's Next. New York, United Hospital Fund, 1997.

Institute of Medicine (US), Committee on Using Performance Monitoring to Improve Community Health. Improving Health in the Community: A Role for Performance Monitoring. Washington, DC, National Academy of Sciences, 1997.

Maternal and Child Health Bureau: Needs Assessment: Resource Handbook Washington, DC, Public Health Service, US Department of Health and Human Services, 1994.

Monahan CA, Craik D, Szpur MV, et al.: Focus on Children Community Planning Manual: Needs Assessment and Health Planning for Children, Including Children with Special Health Care Needs. Chicago, University of Illinois at Chicago and Illinois Department of Public Health, 1996.

Walker DK and Richmond JB (eds): Monitoring Child Health in the United States: Selected Issues and Policies. Boston, Division of Health Policy Research and Education, Harvard University, 1984.

Andrew S. Doniger

Chapter 71

Public Health Services for Children and Families

SHARED MISSIONS FOR PEDIATRICS AND PUBLIC HEALTH

It should not be surprising that more physicians in public health are pediatricians than any of the other medical specialties. Pediatrics and public health share common values and approaches regarding the care of children and families. This shared mission results in many opportunities for pediatricians to collaborate to improve the health of children in their local communities.

Whereas providing clinical preventive services is a relatively new development in the roles of some medical clinicians in the United States, pediatricians have a long tradition of offering preventive services such as immunizations, health education, and anticipatory guidance. This focus on primary and secondary prevention is the preeminent principle of public health practice.

Public health officials and pediatricians are highly aware of the influences of the environment on child health. Public health assesses and regulates environmental concerns. Similarly, pediatricians are concerned about the lead in paint and dust, the tobacco smoke in the air, and the fluoride in the water in the environments of children in their practices. These roles in ensuring the health of children are highly interdependent.

Pediatricians and public health clinicians recognize that the family is the most important influence in the lives of children. Both groups play an important role in ensuring that families understand normal growth and development, how to feed and nurture their children, and how to help youth avoid risky behaviors.

Public health workers and pediatricians demonstrate a sense of responsibility for the health of the populations of children they serve. Pediatricians provide community leadership by providing health services in schools and in community settings and by participating in community efforts to address child health issues.

CHANGING MISSIONS OF LOCAL HEALTH DEPARTMENTS

The public health system in the United States is comprised of a complicated web of agencies, services, and programs sponsored by government and nongovernment entities. Although federal and state governments play important roles in regulation, policy development, and the financing of public health services, most of these services are delivered by local health departments. In addition, some programs and services have been provided by private not-for-profit corporations. There is an emerging trend for some public health services to be sponsored by hospitals, managed care plans, or integrated health care delivery systems.

Local governments vary in their commitment to provide public health services. In the distant past, local health departments ran milk stations, and public health nurses assisted with childbirth in homes. In some communities, health departments have managed community hospitals and sponsored community primary care clinics with an emphasis on caring for the poor and difficult-to-serve populations.

Today's changing environment of health services has necessitated a re-examination of the role of public health and local health departments. **These changes were anticipated when the 1988 Institute of Medicine (IOM) report titled *The Future of Public Health* proposed that public health agencies emphasize three core functions: assessment, policy development, and assurance rather than medical care services.** In more concrete terms, most local health departments now offer a mix of programs in the broad areas of disease control and health promotion (Table 71–1).

In the United States, the way these responsibilities are carried out varies tremendously. In some states, each county sponsors a health department. In others, the state provides public health services, but cities and towns sponsor their own health units

TABLE 71–1. Essential Public Health Services Recommended by the National Association of County and City Health Officials

Conduct community diagnoses
Prevent and control epidemics
Provide a safe and healthy environment
Measure performance, effectiveness, and outcomes of health services
Promote healthy lifestyles and provide health education
Ensure access to laboratory testing
Provide targeted outreach and form partnerships
Provide personal health care services
Undertake research and innovation
Mobilize the community for action

From Blueprint for a Healthy Community: A Guide for Local Health Departments. Washington, DC, National Association of County Health Officials, 1994, p 6.

with services designed to meet the needs of the local population.

The services and the capacities generally vary with the size of the community being served. Urban areas have more developed services than rural settings. Larger cities generally employ physicians, epidemiologists, and public health engineers, a level of specialization that cannot be supported by smaller health departments.

In every community throughout the country one public health worker is always present—the public health nurse. The largest group of professional public health clinicians are registered nurses who have formal training or experience in community health nursing. Public health nurses play a variety of roles in local health departments, such as agency administrators, clinical service providers, and health educators.

ROLES OF LOCAL HEALTH DEPARTMENTS RELATED TO NEEDS OF CHILDREN AND FAMILIES

Although no two health departments perceive their role to be exactly the same, every health department performs certain core functions to address the needs of families and children. Perhaps the most important is *assessment of the health status of mothers and children.*

Every health department generates reports that summarize the available data on indicators such as infant mortality, low-birth-weight rates, prematurity rates, the percent of children fully immunized, rates of preventable communicable diseases, and rates of environmental health problems such as lead poisoning and other chronic diseases.

In many communities these data are contained in reports that are seen by only a small group of

planners and community officials. **Recently, many communities have created more widely circulated documents such as child or maternal and child report cards that define the health status of the community's children and families.** These report cards help mobilize the community to address child health problems. Health report cards also can be valuable in evaluating use of community resources.

Health departments also assess the adequacy of local health services for children. Where gaps are found, local health officials engage in *health services system development.* For example, gaps frequently exist in services for children living in impoverished neighborhoods in urban areas, for individuals who do not speak English, and for patients who reside in rural areas. Gaps may exist in medical services such as primary medical care (lack of availability of physicians and nurse practitioners) or in the "enabling" services.

Enabling services refer to those necessary for families to use traditional medical care services effectively, such as transportation, child care, home visiting, case management, and health education. When these are missing, patients may have a poor outcome even if the clinician care is available and affordable.

When public health officials identify gaps, they may seek to develop these services themselves or they may encourage others to do so. Because health officials are employed by governments, they frequently have access to information about government funding programs. They also have expertise in designing population-based service programs.

Because health systems are rapidly changing, public health officials may play a more important role in facilitating the changing service system than in promoting the development of new programs. For example, as managed care becomes the predominant mode of delivering health services to the poor, local health officials may be instrumental in ensuring that managed care systems include enabling services for their patients. In some states, managed care legislation specifically defines a role for local health officials in quality assurance.

The role of the local health department most easily recognized by the public is that of *disease control.* All states require the reporting of communicable diseases to public health officials. These reports trigger disease investigations and subsequent measures to limit transmission. Occasionally, the identification of larger numbers of cases results in the determination that an *outbreak* exists. Under these circumstances, local health officials may notify the public through the media, hold special clinics, and make medical recommendations to local physicians to control the outbreak.

Local health departments are increasingly involved in chronic disease control. This involves the monitoring of the prevalence of chronic diseases and risk factors for disease, the design of community interventions, and leadership in the implementation of these activities. For example, local health officials commonly enlist the help of pediatricians to develop community activities to combat childhood tobacco use. Local health departments also generally administer programs to provide financial assistance to families whose children have special health care needs.

Environmental health protection is another important area for local health departments. These programs can involve regulation and enforcement of environmental laws, leadership in efforts to improve neighborhood quality and safety, and community education about the relationship of environmental issues to personal health.

Lead poisoning in children is a critical public health issue. Local health departments frequently provide clinical services such as administering screening programs, operating laboratories that analyze children's blood samples for lead, or sponsoring clinics to manage cases of lead poisoning. These services may overlap with the roles of pediatric clinicians in some communities.

In the area of lead poisoning prevention, some activities performed by local health departments are distinct from those of pediatric clinicians. Local public health technicians inspect properties; collect and analyze paint, dust, and soil samples for lead; educate owners and landlords about safe lead removal; and take legal action against individuals who fail to comply with laws that protect children against lead poisoning.

The various roles played by different groups in a community regarding lead poisoning illustrate the need for local health departments to *coordinate community child health activities.* Public health problems exist in many community sectors, community sectors and their solutions generally include many agencies and groups. Although no rule dictates that local health officials provide the forum for the integration of efforts, it generally is accepted that this is an appropriate role for them.

For example, unintentional injuries in children continue to be a frequent cause for emergency department care and hospitalization. Certain measures protect children (such as use of car safety seats and lap and shoulder belts) and certain products put children at risk for injury (such as toys that have small parts and cribs that are poorly designed). Promoting safety measures and warning consumers about unsafe products are roles for pediatricians, store owners, parent groups, and schools, among others. Once a community decides that addressing the problem of childhood injury is a priority, some entity must coordinate activities.

LOCAL PREVENTIVE AND PRIMARY CARE SERVICES FOR CHILDREN

In every community, preventive and primary care services are provided in different ways. In almost every community, the local health department provides some direct primary care services for special populations, including immunizations, diagnosis and treatment of sexually transmitted diseases, management of tuberculosis, well-child care, and human immunodeficiency virus testing and counseling. Figure 71–1 shows the percent of local health departments that provide these services.

In 47 states, local governments are required by law to provide some direct health services to the indigent, to the uninsured, or to the "underinsured." Frequently, county governments are designated providers of last resort. To operate cost-effectively, counties generally develop programs that serve more patients and provide a broader range of services than they are legally obligated to provide.

Local health departments offer many services to improve the health of mothers and children. In most states, each of these programs is supported by separate categorical funding streams. This encourages the local health department to develop the programs separately, which often is inefficient and inconvenient for the patient.

For example, local health departments typically operate the Special Supplemental Nutrition Program for Women, Infants, and Children (WIC) food supplement and nutrition programs and immunization clinics. In many communities, these programs are offered at different sites and on different days. Yet the same families may need both services. Many local health departments have improved the efficiency of providing multiple service programs by locating them side-by-side (co-location). Other agencies have developed a common registration process. The greatest efficiencies can result from complete integration of the services ("one-stop shopping"). These service delivery system problems are common in many health and human service agencies, as well as in local health departments.

Frequently, the greatest barrier to the integration of service delivery systems is the categorical nature of the funding of these programs. In 1996, the New York State Health Department and the Monroe County Health Department in

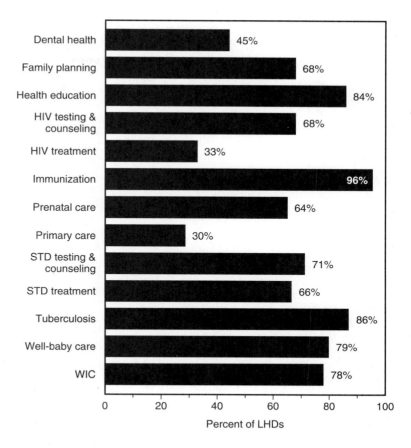

Figure 71–1. Percent of United States local health departments (LHDs) reporting activity in selected service areas, 1992–1993. HIV, human immunodeficiency virus; STD, sexually transmitted disease; WIC, Women, Infants, and Children. (From National Association of County and City Health Officials: National Profile of Local Health Departments. Washington, DC, 1995.)

Rochester, New York, entered into a unique partnership to demonstrate that the reduction of the barriers associated with the categorical funding of separate maternal-child health programs would result in a more efficient service delivery system. Eight categorical grants were molded into a single grant that removed the requirements for development of separate activities. The changes have enabled the local health department to reconfigure the services. Efficiencies achieved by the integration of these services allow for higher service volumes and better health outcomes for the patients.

Because we do not have a national system of health insurance, it is likely that this mix of private and public preventive and primary care services for children will continue into the future.

ROLES OF OTHER LOCAL GOVERNMENT AGENCIES RELATED TO CHILDREN'S HEALTH

Because so many different government agencies provide services for families and children, it is difficult for practicing pediatricians to know all of them and how to advocate for their patients.

Pediatricians often look to local health departments to help them understand these systems.

To promote the health of children and families, it is critical that pediatricians understand the mission and services of the Department of Social Services in the community. Until recently, the role of the *local Department of Social Services (LDSS)* has been to administer a mix of federal and state programs that provide direct financial support and family service programs. The financial support systems included direct cash payments (public assistance), Medicaid, and food stamps. The family service programs included child protective services, foster care services, preventive services for at-risk families, and child care.

Federal welfare reform legislation passed in 1996 created sweeping changes in these programs. The goals of the legislation were to reduce families' long-term dependence on government, reduce out-of-wedlock and teen births, and promote employment of adults. Block grants from the federal government will allow states great flexibility in providing these support services. As a result, the programs provided by LDSS are likely to change substantially in the future.

Local governments generally fund and manage

mental health, alcohol, and substance abuse services. Now often called *behavioral health services,* these reflect a greater emphasis on behaviors, and include preventive as well as treatment services. In some communities, these are provided directly by the government; in others, private agencies are the providers.

Most communities are developing managed care systems to provide behavioral health services to poor and at-risk families much in the same way that managed care systems are being designed for clinical medical services for these populations. In the future, pediatricians are likely to become the gatekeepers for behavioral health services.

Most communities plan and fund special programs for school-age children. These services, often called *youth services,* emphasize the special needs of adolescents and are designed to reduce risky behaviors and promote protective factors or assets. Almost every community funds recreational programs for youth. Many communities sponsor special programs for populations such as runaway, homeless, and drug-addicted youth. Other programs may serve adolescents who have dropped out of school or have criminal records. Many of these incorporate pediatric services as well.

Most communities or regions run *correctional services for youth.* These facilities contain children who have committed a range of crimes from theft to murder. These youth have high rates of sexually transmitted diseases, pregnancy, and mental health problems and should have access to primary health care and prevention services.

OPPORTUNITIES FOR PEDIATRICIANS TO PROVIDE PUBLIC HEALTH SERVICES TO CHILDREN AND FAMILIES

By providing high-quality care for children in offices, clinics, and schools, pediatricians are con-tributing to improving the health status of children in their community. There also are special opportunities for pediatricians to make additional public health contributions.

Local health departments often employ pediatricians as administrators, consultants, or clinicians. Although formal study of public health or preventive medicine is valuable preparation, a well-trained general pediatrician can contribute to local health departments significantly.

Local health departments often appoint advisory committees and seek physicians to serve on the Board of Health—a highly rewarding form of public service for pediatricians.

Because many health problems for children and families are multidimensional, no single agency or organization can address them successfully. Pediatricians, agency administrators, social workers, political leaders, and business executives can be most successful if they work together in a collaborative structure. Learning to collaborate with others in the community is a valuable educational goal for pediatricians to pursue.

FURTHER READING

Institute of Medicine, Committee for the Study of the Future of Public Health: The Future of Public Health. Washington, DC, National Academy Press, 1988.

Last JM and Wallace TB (eds): Maxcy-Rosenau-Last Public Health and Preventive Medicine, 13th ed. Norwalk, CT, Appleton and Lange, 1992.

National Association of County and City Health Officials: National Profile of Local Health Departments. Washington, DC, 1995.

Office of Disease Prevention and Health Promotion, US Public Health Service: Health Care Reform and Public Health. Washington, DC, US PHS, 1993.

Scutchfield E and Keck D (eds): Principles of Public Health Practice. Albany, NY, Delmar Publishers, 1997.

Abraham B. Bergman

Chapter 72

Child Advocacy: How Pediatricians Can Advocate Effectively

Pediatricians are unusual among medical specialists in that they see themselves responsible for the health of all children rather than for just those who come to them as patients. As stated in the directory of the American Academy of Pediatrics (AAP), the organization "unites pediatricians throughout the Americas to ensure for all young people the attainment of their full potential for physical, emotional, and social health." The field of pediatrics evolved in the early 1900s in response to the then major afflictions of children: malnutrition, dehydration, and communicable diseases. Control of these maladies came about because of efforts in the public realm such as improved sanitation, pasteurization of milk, and immunization. Although the specific problems are different today, the same situation pertains. Little can be done in the traditional arenas where pediatricians practice to have a major impact on such major killers as prematurity, cars, guns, drugs, alcohol, and the human immunodeficiency virus (HIV). Housing, employment, and education have a greater effect on the health of children than does medical care. Such statements are not meant to diminish the importance of clinical work, but rather to illustrate the importance of nonmedical factors on the health of children.

Children, of course, lack the economic and political power to better their own status. Compared with other population segments in the United States, the lot of children has deteriorated steadily over the past several decades. The main reason is the increased number of children raised in single-parent households headed by women. It is interesting to compare the relative status of children and senior citizens. In 1967, 30% of seniors older than 65 years of age lived in poverty, compared with 15% of children younger than age 18. In 1995 the situation was reversed: 11% of seniors lived in poverty compared with 21% of children. The reasons are not difficult to discern. Seniors constitute the highest proportion of registered voters, they

are living longer, and there are more of them. Naturally they look after their own interests, as do their children, who do not want to support them. Children, on the other hand, have no economic or political power. Those who look out for them, their parents, tend to be younger and poorer than the rest of the population. Few politicians quake in fear of children's natural advocates in the "helping professions," such as teachers, pediatricians, social workers, and other assorted groups sometimes perceived as being "bleeding hearts."

Therefore, the need for child advocates is obvious; because of tradition, training, and interest, pediatricians are qualified to serve in that capacity. This chapter seeks to outline some ways that pediatricians can function as child advocates, and how their efforts might be most effective.

Webster's dictionary defines an *advocate* as "one who supports or defends a cause or one who pleads on another's behalf." One can either advocate on behalf of individual children and families, as do all child health professionals every day, on behalf of groups of children, or on behalf of children in general. Those whose actions affect large groups of children, for example, by promoting legislation, tend to receive more public accolades. That does not mean that their activities are more worthy. In this author's pantheon of heroes, no one sits higher than the teachers of preschoolers or the foster parents of disabled children. Advocacy may involve reading to children, participating in the affairs of a school, coaching an athletic team, serving on a local school board, or simply writing a letter to the editor of a local newspaper.

ROLE MODELS

As in all spheres of medicine, we learn best by observing role models. Every community has pediatricians who set examples. Invariably these are individuals who do not view themselves in any special light. I do not think that the physicians who engage in child advocacy in my community are more numerous or do better work than those in other communities. Examples of child advocacy in this author's community, cited to illustrate the different forms that advocacy takes, include a pediatrician who works to improve health services for incarcerated youth; another, who has run a clinic for street children for over 30 years; a clinician who cares for the children of migrant farm workers; one who helps refugee and impoverished parents learn how to advocate for their children in schools; and another who helps to free the parents and foster parents of disabled children when they become enmeshed in bureaucratic red tape.

Since 1992, pediatric residents at the University of Washington have had the opportunity to spend time in a child advocacy elective. Three basic concepts are emphasized:

1. The project to be undertaken should have an attainable objective and definable end point. Residents are encouraged to "think small."
2. Success hinges more on persistent, unglamorous labor than on high profile speeches or grandiose ideas.
3. A sincere young pediatrician is perceived by the public and by politicians as an authority on children whose words will be heard (i.e, the need to assume a professional stance).

The breadth of the interests of the residents is illustrated by a list of the projects they have undertaken (Table 72–1).

SHORTAGE OF TIME

Time, of course, is the modern-day equivalent of rubies and diamonds; there is never enough of it. Between trying to fulfil personal and professional obligations, it is the rare physician who goes searching for additional activities to fill the day. Child advocacy, therefore, should not be seen as an additional burden to be undertaken, but as an activity that is fun, enriching, and gratifying. For that reason one should not feel guilty about failing to participate in a particular cause at a particular time. This is especially true for physicians in training whose idealism may clash with the overwhelming demands of a residency. If one does not jump onto a particular white horse, other horses are certain to be available.

Mention must also be made about the time a pediatrician spends with his or her own family. Relative financial poverty is not all that puts to-

TABLE 72–1. Advocacy Projects of Pediatric Residents at the University of Washington

Regulating the working hours of children in Washington State
Reducing exposure of children to passive smoke
Providing medical care to poor children in King County who have asthma
Banning infant walkers in the United States
Breaking down barriers to immunization for Hispanic children
Maintaining the free vaccine distribution program in Washington State
Developing a community program for the safe storage of handguns
Making breast pumps available through the Medicaid program
Starting a needle exchange program for "street kids"
Successfully including vitamin D in the State Medicaid formulary
Passing state legislation on early newborn hospital discharge
Identifying effects of Healthy Options (Medicaid) on children who have special needs
Providing health services for Hispanic children in the Seattle area
Reducing riding lawnmower injuries to children
Writing a political history of the Indian Health Service
Improving traffic safety practices on the Yakama Indian Reservation

day's children at a disadvantage. In an era in which both parents work out of the home, or in homes headed by a single parent, time with children, especially unscheduled time, becomes precious. Advocacy often means spending additional hours at meetings or traveling. That these hours are spent in some noble cause does not immunize against feelings of abandonment by one's own children. In fact, riding the white horse is sometimes worse than drinking, gambling or carousing. When parents are absent, children do not distinguish whether their parents are engaged in worthy or unworthy causes. With unworthy activities children can be critical; with worthy causes, children may feel guilty about voicing their protests.

SELECTING APPROPRIATE ISSUES

Selecting the appropriate issue is *the* most challenging aspect of advocacy. **The right issue is one that has an attainable objective that can be identified and in which one's personal efforts might have some effect.** The social value of the issue is less important than the amount of time and energy available to deal with it. My practice is to steer clear of global societal issues that are subject to the ebb and flow of historical forces and where my personal labor will have no impact. Examples are nuclear disarmament, educational reform, reproductive rights, and gun control. I also do not involve myself in the financing of medical care both because I have no unique contribution to make and because plenty of other physicians are perched on that branch.

The more circumscribed the issue, the more likely there is to be a satisfying outcome. As a sports lover, I view advocacy like a football game. Points are scored only when the goal line is crossed. In advocacy, the goal line is crossed only when some tangible benefit accrues to a child or children. Too many "players" get distracted by the crowd noise or by the amount of effort expended, the amount of publicity generated, the number of meetings held, or the quantity of letters written. All of these may be helpful, but can not be considered ends in themselves.

I am suspicious of those who claim to labor in the field of health policy. They often are elitists who devise wise plans in the hope that they will be sought out by politicians. The politicians never call. If one cares about a cause, it is best to take the initiative and seek out those who have the power to further that cause.

The cause should create a stirring in the heart. For example, the cause that has given me the most pleasure in the past 5 years has not been in the legislative arena, but rather in helping to create a water spray park for children as a memorial to a dear colleague. Virtually all of my advocacy projects, however, arise directly from my clinical practice. Caring for a child whose illness or injury could have been prevented provides both inspiration and energy. In the 1960s, seeing children with rotten teeth led to my participation in a successful campaign to flouridate Seattle's water; seeing children burned when their clothing ignited led to legislation mandating flame-resistant apparel; and seeing children hospitalized because of aspirin ingestion led to a poison prevention packaging law. My contacts through an epidemiology research project with families losing babies to the sudden infant death syndrome led to a campaign to "humanize" the management of that entity. For the past 15 years I have worked in a major trauma center that supplies a never-ending array of issues on which to work, such as bicycle helmets, baby walkers, drunken driving, firearm trauma, and scald burns.

SOLO VERSUS COLLECTIVE ACTIVITIES

Working in an organization that advocates for children is often the most efficient and effective means of achieving results. For physicians there is no better organization than the American Academy of Pediatrics, which has a distinguished history in child advocacy. It is at the state chapter level that one can have the greatest impact. In Washington State we are fortunate in that the state AAP chapter, the University of Washington's Department of Pediatrics, and the largest children's hospital usually speak with one voice when it comes to child health issues. There also is a warm supportive relationship between the AAP chapter and the Washington State Medical Association. Support by these organizations provides resources such as access to professional lobbyists and dissemination of information.

On the other hand, too much time sometimes is wasted seeking the endorsements of organizations when hard individual effort might be more productive. If one is not dealing with controversial ideological issues, an articulate proposal to a person who has the power to effect change might suffice. The power of a well-reasoned letter often is underestimated.

PRACTICING "POLITICAL MEDICINE"

As mentioned previously, working in the political sphere is not everyone's cup of tea. For those who are so inclined, however, the following suggestions might be helpful:

1. Avoid self-righteousness. Politicians are besieged with ideas, most of them good.

2. Use sound data in support of the cause, and when data are not available, say so. Our credibility rests on our scientific training.

3. Do not ask a politician to support an issue that will be hurtful politically; a defeated legislator is of no help. The best issues are those that combine benefit to children and to the politician.

4. Seek as wide a base of support as possible. Because legislators have to take positions on hundreds of proposals, their decisions to support or oppose depend more on the identity of the sponsors than on the merits of the proposal. The best prospects for legislative passage occur with a "trans-ideologic" coalition that is, when the most "liberal" and most "conservative" members of the body are cosponsors.

5. Never accuse politicians of being "against kids" when they do not agree with you. Epithets may soothe the psyches of the fighters, but don't help win the fray. Assume that all politicians care about children, but that they have different philosophies and approaches.

6. Work with the media. Child advocates control neither money nor votes. Our "currency,"

therefore, is public opinion. Newspapers, television, and radio stations have large news "holes" to fill every day and are attracted to stories about children. They also prefer human interest stories about individual children and families to statistics.

7. Consult the pros. Amateurs should not venture onto the political landscape without a map and compass. Professional lobbyists usually are flattered when their advice is sought.

8. Have infinite patience. Carry a good book at all times; we are supplicants and will spend much time waiting. Be brief in phone calls, letters, visits, and in testifying. When frustration sets in, as it invariably will, it is well to be reminded that we are working for our clients, the children, and not for ourselves.

9. Never underestimate staff assistants. Sometimes enlisting the aid of a junior staff member can ensure more lasting results than a handshake and pat on the back from the politician.

10. Submerge the ego. The advocate who needs credit and publicity does his or her client no favor. The politician is the one who has to face the voters. Ghost-written speeches, articles, and reports are golden, as are letters of thanks.

11. Be patient and persistent. It frequently takes several years for ideas to percolate and support to grow for legislation to be enacted.

12. The work of an advocate does not end with the passage of legislation. Enactment of a law is easy compared with seeing that it is implemented properly.

SUMMARY

Handwringing and self-pity will not improve the lot of children; effective advocacy will. When undertaken, the tasks should be taken seriously, which means learning the techniques of achieving success. I have two favorite quotes: William Gladstone said, "Indignation without action is froth." In an address to the French bishops, Albert Camus said, "You seek a world in which *no* children starve; I seek a world in which *fewer* children starve."

Thomas F. Tonniges

Chapter **73**

The Medically Underserved

In the past, many pediatricians have made an effort to serve the underserved in their communities. During the past 2 decades, however, delivering services to this population has been affected by an increase in the number of children eligible for Medicaid and the nonacceptance of Medicaid patients by a large number of clinicians. Now, with the movement toward Medicaid-managed care, the number of children moving back into pediatric practices is rising as payment for ambulatory care is making it economically feasible for pediatricians to care for these medically underserved children. This movement will have significant ramifications, as will the clinician's ability to meet their diverse needs.

Rural and inner-city areas often are thought of as being home to most of the medically underserved population. This is changing with the increasing diversity of population in the United States (due to adoption and immigration) and the emergence of special populations (due to an increased number of foster children and abused children and the recognition of children who have special health care needs). All pediatricians, whether practicing in city, suburban, or rural areas, will be challenged to serve the medically underserved.

DEFINITION

The *medically underserved child* is any infant, child, adolescent, or young adult who does not have his or her medical needs met within the context of a "medical home" or other source of pediatric specialty services. In every practice, low-income children who lack health insurance are at risk for poor health outcomes. Unfortunately, there are medically underserved children in most every practice and community in this country.

One may view the medically underserved in the same way in which children who have special health care needs are regarded, including the belief that they should have a family-centered medical home where integrated care is provided. This "home" should provide health services that are accessible, comprehensive, and compassionate. In the service of meeting the needs of the medically underserved, barriers to their appropriate care—economic, geographic, social/educational, and ethnic/cultural—must be examined and surmounted.

ECONOMIC BARRIERS

With the increasing number of children who do not have the benefit of regular and accessible care, whether because of dependency on Medicaid or the lack of health insurance, all clinicians will encounter the problem of helping families gain access to needed care. Rather than leaving this problem for others to address, the primary care clinician can do the following:

Refer patients to social services to determine their eligibility for Medicaid or Title XXI benefits and arrange with the Medicaid program to provide presumptive eligibility at the practice level.

Counsel parents to take advantage of employer health insurance programs.

Direct families to financial counseling services.

Use the old-fashioned practice of bartering to enable families to provide for their children's health expenses.

Inquire prospectively about a family's insurance and finances to alleviate future financial problems.

Advocate at the local, state, and national levels for systems that provide financial access to care for children.

Work collaboratively with local service clubs, the United Way, and religious organizations to ensure access to care at the community level.

Arrange in-service programs for office personnel about the impact of financial problems on the health of children; help them to assist families in financial problem solving.

Conduct focus groups with families who have financial problems related to access to care; solicit their suggestions for solutions.

Work with the local American Academy of Pediatrics chapter and community organizations to develop service programs such as Community Access to Child Health (CATCH).

Pediatric and other ambulatory settings need to establish policies, procedures, and collaborations that help families resolve financial issues before they become problems.

GEOGRAPHIC BARRIERS

Geographic barriers to access can affect the general health of children. For example, it may take two bus transfers to get to the doctor with a sick child or it may mean traveling hundreds of miles to a pediatrician who needs to spend only 15 to 30 minutes on a problem that could have been dealt with closer to home. It also may mean that a family has to pass through physically dangerous neighborhoods.

The concept of community-oriented primary care (COPC), if implemented in our communities, would go a long way toward eliminating geographic barriers for the medically underserved. This marriage of primary care and public health concepts encourages the primary health care clinician to visualize the needs of the whole community, rather than only the more limited numbers who come through the door to the clinic. Practices that take this approach begin by defining their community. When clinicians are working alone in very large geographic areas, they can define their role as a consultant to other primary care pediatric clinicians. Large pediatric groups can help establish satellite clinics that work in collaboration with family physicians or provide pediatric consultative services for the Title V program.

What can the primary care clinician do to decrease geographic barriers? Helpful ideas include the following:

Ask patients how difficult it is for them to access their health services.

Define your geographic area of practice.

Create a community map of various services in your service area, for example, emergency departments, urgent care centers, other primary health care facilities, school-based or school-linked services, and public health clinics.

Complete a needs assessment of your practice to determine if all needed services are provided.

If needed services are not available in your area, identify sources of information to help meet those needs.

Develop a public-private partnership with the Special Supplemental Nutrition Program for Women, Infants, and Children (WIC) clinic or a Title V clinic that can be held in your office.

Consider partnering with other clinicians by providing leadership in implementing school-based or school-linked services to address the needs of underserved school-age children.

Provide consultative services to family physicians by offering to see patients in their offices, by appointment.

Train staff to ensure that office personnel are

aware of the impact of geography on access to care.
Reduce geographic barriers by arranging convenient and dual appointment times, making each visit count (concept of missed opportunities), and allowing more than one sibling to be scheduled at a time.

Geographic barriers take many forms. It may be many miles in the case of rural and frontier areas, or it may be blocks in the case of urban areas. The clinicians, by recognizing these barriers as affecting children and contributing to our medically underserved population, can improve access to care significantly for these children and families.

Clinicians, by being sensitive to the problem of geographic barriers to care, can improve access to care for the medically underserved by becoming part of the solution.

SOCIAL AND EDUCATIONAL BARRIERS

No one feels at ease in a setting where they feel socially out of place, neglected, or at a different educational level. Depending on the location of the clinician's office, families may be placed in unfamiliar settings. With the added stress of an ill child, many patients and parents feel very uncomfortable. Primary care clinicians cannot solve all of the financial inequities of the world, but they can create an office environment where all families feel comfortable.

The attitude toward families of different social classes begins with the leadership. Office personnel can be expected to treat all patients with respect only when clinicians do the same. This may be foreign to some staff, but it is necessary if the office is to make all families feel welcome. Staff development resources may be needed for those staff having difficulty adapting to this essential practice.

Other activities that can be helpful:

Post stories of successful families; far too often the staff and public are exposed only to failures.
Create an atmosphere in which staff recognize that all children have worth and should be treated equally.
Provide an in-service program for office staff led by a Medicaid worker who is sensitive to the special needs of families.
Provide educational materials appropriate to the educational levels of the child and parent.
Provide waiting rooms and examination rooms

that are pleasant and that promote education rather than just being entertaining.
Provide an opportunity for a low-income family by hiring a family member to work in the office; the right staff member will be able not only to provide valuable service but also to serve as a model to all staff members.
Consider hiring a health educator to help address the special educational needs of the practice, thereby improving service, freeing time for the clinician, and increasing income.
Consider hiring a social worker to help with coordination of care.

CHILDREN WHO HAVE SPECIAL HEALTH CARE NEEDS

By definition, children who have special health care needs are at risk for being medically underserved. With the prevalence of managed care and third-party payers negotiating fees for service and overseeing treatment, this special population is being squeezed into a system of care that does not meet their needs. As technology and specialization have advanced over the past 30 years, these families have increasingly depended on care from many different providers and tertiary care institutions. At a time when coordination of care has become imperative, the primary care clinician and the medical home have taken on increased importance.

The primary care clinician can benefit from providing improved care and coordination to this special population not under the umbrella of the managed care system. It will be important, however, to negotiate appropriate rates and provide care of top quality for this population. How can we do this?

Tell ourselves that we are going to provide care for this population.
Provide leadership by discussing the issues related to this population with our office personnel, who frequently are the first to recognize the needs of our patients.
Most important, we must ask our patients what their needs are by conducting focus groups or surveys.
Work with our hospitals and other practices to create a community map that includes the various service agencies within the community.
Participate in the meetings of the local United Way Allocation Committee, where the needs of the community are identified.
Consider hiring a social worker to help provide case management services for this population.

Develop a "family strength assessment" of all patients and families that enter the practice.

Case management can, in the long run, help prevent family crises, improve health outcomes, increase patient and family satisfaction, and decrease expenses.

SUMMARY

The historic, economic, and societal changes taking place in the health care arena are creating many opportunities for primary care clinicians to improve service for the medically underserved children in their communities. Despite the major medical advances of the past century, the health needs of our medically underserved are not being met. This is an area in which clinicians, working with their communities, conducting needs assessments, and then incorporating public health solutions to solve primary care problems, can most likely improve child health.

Clinicians practicing the concept of community-oriented primary care can set high standards for serving the underserved population. By keeping informed of the changing health care needs of this population, mentoring medical students, and providing in-service training for office personnel, school nurses, social services workers, school psychologists, and other health professionals, primary care clinicians can provide a strong, positive model for serving this diverse population. By working collaboratively within their communities, they can demonstrate interprofessional collaboration among multidisciplinary teams. When community resources are not readily available, primary care clinicians can work with local agencies, faith healing ministries, or programs such as the CATCH program of the American Academy of Pediatrics and learn how to work with what resources are available to bring the community together to improve child health.

Whatever barriers there are within the community, the most strength comes from the families being served. By engaging and involving families in the process of improving their children's health at the practice and community level, their needs more likely will be met.

Sheryl Ryan

Chapter 74

School Health

On entry into school, the child is immersed in an environment separate from that of the family that is critically influential in the child's subsequent growth and development. In addition to being the primary site for formal education, schools provide a context for interacting with non-family adults and peers.

Education and health care traditionally have had separate financing and operational arrangements. Thus, **it is not surprising that controversy continues regarding the extent that schools should be involved in health care, when the primary goal is education.** A child's ability to learn, however, is inextricably linked to his or her health and well-being; with the changes in morbidity and mortality among children and youth that reflect not only health problems of greater complexity and behavioral dimensions but also diminished access to care, schools have needed to assume greater responsibility for the health of their students. Pediatric primary care clinicians have the unique opportunity to play critical roles in school health, by understanding the nature of school health programs within their particular communities and by working to coordinate and complement services offered in school with those provided in traditional office-based sites.

This chapter emphasizes (1) the ability of school health services to provide comprehensive primary care; (2) current efforts and strategies to integrate school health services into the larger community-based settings of health care, resulting from health care reform in the climate of managed care; and (3) the roles that clinicians can develop in moving beyond the office to address the health needs of school-age children and youth.

HISTORY

The first school health services in the United States were introduced at the end of the 19th century, when public education became mandatory under compulsory education laws. With large numbers of children brought together in cramped quarters, the control of communicable diseases was essential and resulted in the introduction of health workers at school sites. Initially, physicians visited schools to inspect for, detect, and control infectious diseases in children. Later, nurses worked on-site in schools to assist the part-time physicians, for the sole purpose of identifying children who had infectious diseases. Gradually, services were expanded to include "case-finding" of correctable defects, health education, and the provision of dental services. In the 1920s, however, the educational systems grappled with the issue of their expanding role in health and medical matters. This concern, combined with complaints by private physicians that their role as primary medical care clinicians was being infringed on by school health services, led to sharp limitations placed on these school-based services. For the next several decades, school health services were limited to narrowly defined public health services, such as disease prevention through health screening and inspection, with medical treatment needs being relegated primarily to community-based private clinicians.

In spite of this general arrangement, many school-age children were still not receiving necessary medical care. A landmark study, the Astoria Plan, conducted in New York City in 1940, revealed that large numbers of physical and mental health problems remained uncorrected in school-age children and concluded that the main reason was the lack of coordination between school health programs and traditional medical services. The Astoria Plan focused on children who had special needs, encouraged parental participation, and emphasized coordination and communication between school nurses and community physicians in order to remedy identified health problems.

Why the Astoria Plan was not replicated in other school districts is unclear, but the scope of school health remained limited throughout the next 2 decades. In part, the reluctance to expand periodic screening and physical appraisal in both primary and secondary schools may have resulted from studies at the time that failed to demonstrate significant benefit from such wide-scale efforts. For example, Yankauer and Lawrence (1955) found in their study of 1056 elementary schoolchildren that physical examinations performed in the school for screening and detection of adverse conditions were "valueless from a case-finding standpoint," because most of the conditions found had been identified already by the child's family physician. Rogers and Reese (1964) confirmed

these findings several years later in a population of high school students and concluded that the yield of discovering new significant medical disease from comprehensive screening and physical examination, beyond simple height and weight measurements, and vision, hearing, and dental evaluations was very small. However, in the late 1960s, the issue of unmet health needs of children and youth again brought pressure on school systems to expand their school health programs. Federal legislation increased the funding of nontraditional health services in schools, especially for poor children, and innovative models of health care delivery in schools were developed, most notably the comprehensive school-based clinic. The first of these was a primary care medical clinic located in an elementary school in Cambridge, Massachusetts; shortly thereafter, in 1973, the first secondary school–based comprehensive clinics opened in West Dallas, Texas, and in St. Paul, Minnesota, focusing on reproductive health care.

Since that time, the availability of comprehensive health services located in school settings has increased dramatically, as school systems and health departments have sought to provide a range of services such as expanded health education and promotion programs, mental health services, and both categorical and comprehensive medical services. Although the more traditional modes of delivering health care in schools, primarily through the work of school nurses, are found more commonly nationwide, **the past 2 decades have witnessed a major expansion of programs built on the comprehensive school-based clinic model.** By the mid-1990s, more than 620 school-based clinics were estimated to be situated in 41 states and the District of Columbia, most located within secondary schools, rather than elementary or middle schools. The expansion of such school-based services at the secondary school level has been fueled by increasing awareness that substantial numbers of youth are not receiving needed preventive or medical care within private clinicians' offices. Many of their health problems are of a behavioral, social, or mental health nature. These children frequently face access barriers, particularly for confidential services that may not be available in the traditional medical setting. For many adolescents, the school-based health center offers a more convenient and acceptable alternative to the office.

EFFECTIVENESS OF SCHOOL-BASED HEALTH SERVICES

Studies on the acceptance and use of school-based health services document their overwhelming support and use by adolescents and younger students, and especially by those who have greater health needs, greater involvement in high-risk behaviors, and less access to medical care. Few studies, however, have looked specifically at medical, social, or school performance outcomes resulting from the use of school-based services. Those that have assessed their effectiveness in changing high-risk behaviors, such as sexual activity rates or health or education outcomes (e.g., school dropout rates) have demonstrated only modest results at best. The paucity of studies demonstrating positive behavioral or school performance outcomes is a serious concern for those needing to justify the expenses involved in providing such services.

Market forces have resulted in dramatic health insurance changes in recent years, with a central focus being cost containment and managed care. One of the potential implications of these changes for school health programs and the students who rely on these services is that programs now may be evaluated in terms of their ability to provide primary health care, using the same standards that have been applied to studying other, more traditional sources of primary health care. A review by Santelli and coworkers (1996) looked at the issue of how well school-based health centers provide the key components of primary care, using the seven defining attributes of first contact, continuous, comprehensive, community-oriented, family-centered, and culturally competent care (Table 74–1). In terms of first contact, continuity, and comprehensiveness of care, school-based clinics perform well. They provide an easily identifiable point of entry, and their location on or near school grounds offers convenience and familiarity. Most centers provide a wide range of services designed to meet physical, mental health, and social services needs of children and adolescents. In this respect, they are able to meet the criteria of comprehensiveness, although many are limited in terms of the on-site reproductive health care services available. In addition to providing health services generally available in more traditional settings, school-based centers may offer more comprehensive education and health promotion services, often in classroom sites.

The attribute of primary care presenting the greatest challenge for school-based centers is that of coordination or communication. They typically operate independently of other health systems networks, and thus may not have in place either the infrastructures enabling integration or follow-up with other primary clinicians, specialists, or laboratory services; or the tradition of collaborating with community health services. Ironically, the ability of schools to coordinate their services with

TABLE 74–1. Primary Care Attributes

First contact care
    The usual entry point into the expanded health care system
Continuous care
    The longitudinal use of a regular source of care over time, regardless of any presence of disease or injury. Represented by "medical care home"
Comprehensive care
    The provision of a continuum of essential personal health services that promote and preserve health, prevent disease, injury, and dysfunction, as well as provide care for acute and chronic illnesses and disabilities
Coordinated care
    The linking of health care events and services. This requires the mechanics to transfer and incorporate that information into the health care plan
Community-oriented care
    Taking into account the needs of a defined population and the integration of a population perspective into clinical practice
Family-centered care
    The recognition that the family is the major participant in the assessment and treatment of a child or adolescent
Culturally competent care
    Considering cultural differences when providing health care

Adapted from Santelli J, Morreale M, Wigton A, et al.: School health centers and primary care for adolescents: A review of the literature. J Adolesc Health 18:357–366, 1996; by permission of Elsevier Science. Copyright 1996 by The Society for Adolescent Medicine; and Ryan S, Jones M, and Weitzman M: School-based health services. Curr Opin Pediatr 8:453–458, 1996, Copyright Rapid Science Publishers.

what may be provided by other sources of primary care in the community is now cited as one of their most important characteristics, and the one that will best enable schools to maintain their role in integrated service systems. The success of the school-based health model will be influenced greatly by the extent to which it is able to demonstrate quality and cost-effective primary care, either solely, or as one component of an integrated health care service system.

LINKAGES BETWEEN SCHOOL-BASED SERVICES AND MANAGED CARE

The emergence of managed care and the enrollment of large numbers of Medicaid recipients into managed care plans are providing a new opportunity for school health services to coordinate efforts with what is being provided at a greater community level. A variety of initiatives are taking place to develop and assess models and strategies for creating partnerships between school-based health services, managed health care organizations, and their clinicians. Table 74–2 lists a variety of models that may be used to integrate school health services with managed care plans; these range from informal ar-

TABLE 74–2. Models for Linking School-Based Health Programs with Managed Care Plans

Model	Relationship to Managed Care Health Plan
Interagency referrals	School-based providers inform parents and the managed care plan of the need for further evaluation or care. School nurses ascertain whether referrals are followed through.
Information sharing	Informal or formal sharing of medical information by school personnel with managed care providers.
Provision of follow-up care on school campuses	Specified set of services provided at schools to managed care beneficiaries, such as the monitoring of chronic diseases, through contractual arrangements.
Contractual reimbursement arrangements	
Independent primary care model	School has a formal contractual arrangement to provide range of primary care services.
Shared primary care model	Students can use both schools and assigned managed care clinic clinicians.
Satellite delivery of care	Managed care clinic clinicians deliver services at schools which serve as a satellite in its system.
Capitation	School program assumes primary risk financially to provide defined range of services to students.

Adapted from Brindis C and Wunsch B: Finding common ground: Developing linkages between school-linked/school-based health programs and managed care plans. Sacramento, CA, The Foundation Consortium for School-linked Services, 1996; Zimmerman D and Reif CJ: School-based health centers and managed care health plans: Partners in primary care. J Public Health Management Pract 1:33–39, 1995, © 1995 Aspen Publishers, Inc.; and Ryan S, Jones M, and Weitzman M: School-based health services. Curr Opin Pediatr 8:453–458, 1996, Copyright Rapid Science Publishers.

rangements, such as interagency referrals and information sharing, to formal financial contractual arrangements. These efforts have identified strategies that promote productive linkages, such as taking the time to develop collaborations with primary care clinicians in the community and developing infrastructures that allow the exchange of confidential patient information.

THE ROLE OF THE PRIMARY CARE CLINICIAN

Controversy continues around the issues of how to provide health care in a setting where the primary responsibility is to educate and how school health services can best support the primary process of education. Both educational and public health systems have traditionally assumed the fiscal responsibility for funding school-based services and already are overburdened with current responsibilities and budget constraints. However, current trends in the health care system continue to exert pressure on school systems to provide or expand school health services; **many children and adolescents still experience barriers to receiving necessary medical care.** Many of the functions previously performed by the family are now provided by other institutions, notably the schools, and ensuring the health and well-being of children now involves not just medical providers, but individuals from the disciplines of mental health, social work, and health education. The task of the school nurse also has been altered dramatically by the inclusion in schools of chil-

dren who have significant chronic and debilitating conditions.

This current climate of redefining the role of health care in the schools and the role of schools in promoting health has provided pediatric clinician once again the opportunity to shape their roles in this process of integrating school health into the greater context of primary care. **With the demand for systems to move increasingly toward integration, rather than continuing a school-community dichotomy (such as was the situation in the 1920s), primary care clinicians face the challenge of expanding their roles in schools.** Depending on the particular needs and structure of services in a particular community, they may find themselves primary clinicians at school sites, consultants, supervisors, advocates, planners, or evaluators. Many of these "new" roles may necessitate increasing their awareness and expertise about less traditional, nonclinical aspects of school health, such as program planning and evaluation, policy issues about comprehensive school programs, the functions of a school health consultant or supervisor, and the implementation of comprehensive health education or screening programs.

The American Academy of Pediatrics recently put forth its position on school health by recognizing that schools, as a focal community point for children and youth, should work toward developing the concept of "integrated school health services." This concept uses a community-based approach to assess the educational, health care, and social services needs of students and provide those services through a broad collaborative effort.

How should the primary care clinicians begin to work with a community toward implementing this integrated school health services concept? What is the model or structure existing or ideally suited for a particular community? One perspective on the state of school-based health care is shown in Figure 74–1, involving the integration of three specific models, with varying degrees of parental, community, and direct social services involvement, each with a different emphasis on the specific services to be provided by the core disciplines of nursing, medicine, health education, and social services. The school-based health center approach is typified by the free-standing comprehensive school-based health centers, with the provision of both direct medical care and disease prevention and health promotion activities. In contrast, the services integration and comprehensive school health program models include medical care as one component of a broader range of social services and health education activities (Fig. 74–1). This view that the most successful programs use school sites to provide a broad range of family resource and human services, incorporating school health as one component and including, as well, career and vocation counseling, social and mental health services, and expanded education and health promotion, has been put forth by Dryfoos (1994) in her full-service school model.

In all of these models, nursing and education are central. With the development of the school nurse practitioner, more comprehensive medical care has been provided. Health education is another core aspect of most school programs and includes formal health education in classrooms, informal education in clinical settings, in-service activities by nurses and health educators to teachers and staff, and other activities to ensure that the school is a safe and healthy environment.

By using these models, primary care clinicians can define their role in a variety of ways, in an effort to integrate their practice into the process of school health. Because many students may already have a "medical home," the school pediatric clinician may serve as the person to whom a school nurse will refer a student who has been identified as having a medical problem that requires services beyond what a school nurse can provide. When more comprehensive services are needed or provided at a school, or the expanding role of school nurses or nurse practitioners requires that they provide medically intensive services to students who have a severe or chronic illness, the clinician can function in a more expanded role. This may take the form of frequent communication with the school nurse in order to manage a medical problem more effectively so as to keep a child in school. The pediatric clinician also may supervise school nurses or nurse practitioners directly, either on site or through more informal consultation and coordination of care. Beyond a direct services provision or consultative role, the primary care clinician can educate, through classroom activities or on-service activities for nurses, health educators, teachers, and staff at a particular school. Finally, clinicians can be involved in the planning or expanding of services, in assessing health needs, or in advocating for both children and youth in school. **Pediatricians should not underestimate their ability to become an integral part of this process and these communitywide systems of care.**

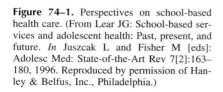

Figure 74–1. Perspectives on school-based health care. (From Lear JG: School-based services and adolescent health: Past, present, and future. *In* Juszcak L and Fisher M [eds]: Adolesc Med: State-of-the-Art Rev 7[2]:163–180, 1996. Reproduced by permission of Hanley & Belfus, Inc., Philadelphia.)

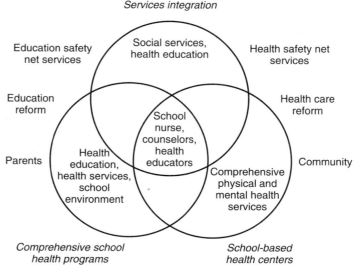

FURTHER READING

American Academy of Pediatrics, Task Force on Integrated School Health Services: Integrated school health services. Pediatrics 94:400–402, 1994.

Brellochs C, Zimmerman D, Zink T, et al. School-based primary care in a managed care environment: Options and issues. *In* Jusczak L and Fisher M (eds): Adolesc Med: State-of-the-Art Rev 7(2):207–220, 1996.

Dryfoos JG: Full Service Schools. San Francisco, Jossey-Bass, 1994.

Lear JG: School-based services and adolescent health: Past, present and future. *In* Jusczak L and Fisher M (eds): Adoles Med: State-of-the-Art Rev 7(2):163–180, 1996.

Rogers KD and Reese G: Health studies—Presumably normal high school students. Am J Dis Child 108:572–600, 1964.

Ryan S, Jones M, and Weitzman M: School-based health services. Curr Opin Pediatr 8:453–458, 1996.

Santelli J, Morreale M, Wigton A, et al.: School health centers and primary care for adolescents: A review of the literature. J Adolesc Health 18:357–366, 1996.

Yankauer A and Lawrence R: A study of periodic school medical examinations. Am J Public Health 45:71–78, 1955.

Alan E. Kohrt

Chapter 75

Rural Health in the Context of Patient, Family, and Community

The care of children in rural settings presents a number of unique challenges. For too long, medicine and health care have focused on a problem- or diagnosis-based approach to the individual. Recently, the critical value of assessing the problems and needs of the family and community also has been realized. **In order to optimize the care provided for the patient, the strengths of the child, the family, and the rural community need to be considered.** The relationship between the child health clinician and the patient, the family, and the community also needs to be considered as we look at the health care of children in rural America.

WHAT IS A RURAL COMMUNITY?

"Rural" can be determined by population, geography, and access to medical care. The federal government defines "nonmetropolitan communities" as those that have a population of less than 50,000. While this metropolitan, nonmetropolitan division has been the major source for most of the analyses of rural data, it is important to remember that rural communities can exist within a "metropolitan" area and that towns of 35,000 to 49,000 would not be considered to be rural by many. Other definitions have used towns that have a population of less than 25,000 or those communities located more than 30 minutes from a population center of greater than 50,000. The Bureau of the Census designates communities of less than 2500 people as being rural. Other communities, usually in the western United States, are defined as "frontier" when the population density is even less than that of rural communities (less than 7 people per square mile). For the child health clinician, providing health care in a community that is more than 1 hour from a tertiary pediatric hospital may be seen as providing care to a rural populations.

RURAL HEALTH CARE NEEDS

Between 20% and 25% of the total population below the age of 12 lives in nonmetropolitan communities. Although the percent of children living in rural communities has decreased over the last 20 years, the total number remained fairly constant until the late 1980s, when it decreased from 21 to 15 million children and adolescents. Family physicians provide the majority of care for rural communities: pediatricians provide care for 33% of the children and 40% of the children hospitalized. Most rural counties have a family physician: only 25% to 30% have a pediatrician, and only 35% have an obstetrician. Of all the pediatricians in the United States, only about 1 of 10 practices in a rural community, whereas 2 of 10 children live in such communities.

Rural populations have many socioeconomic factors that result in increased health needs (Table

75–1). **The most significant socioeconomic factor is the increased percent of families living in poverty** compared with those in metropolitan areas. There are more unemployed and self-employed people and, therefore, more families with no health insurance. More children are without a regular source of medical care. Health maintenance organizations with their focus on less expensive office visits and preventive care have been slower to penetrate rural areas. Thus, rural families have to pay "out of pocket" for most of their outpatient care. A higher percentage of rural children also are enrolled in Medicaid than are those in most suburban communities.

More than 700,000 children who have significant chronic illness and another 300,000 who have some limitation of daily activities live in rural America. At the same time, there are fewer physicians, especially specialists, to provide care for children who have special health care needs.

Finally, specific rural populations such as residents of Appalachia, rural African-Americans, migrant workers, and Native Americans have health status indicators such as infant mortality and average life span that are significantly worse than the average for the United States. They also have problems that are unique to or more frequently present in their population such as exposure to pesticides and tuberculosis for the migrant workers and obesity and complications of alcohol abuse in children of Native Americans.

STRENGTHS OF RURAL COMMUNITIES

The strengths of each community should be examined. Just as needs do, these will vary from one community to another. Because of a lack of anonymity and use of the same schools, businesses, religious affiliations, and service organizations, often there is a greater sense of recognition and belonging in many small towns. This sense of community is important in the development of programs and services in areas that have limited

financial and human resources. Both volunteers and employed staff receive recognition from the community, from friends and neighbors, as well as from the families that are served.

Does this sense of community, or "communality" as described by Schor (1995), affect the health of the children of rural America differently from that of children in more populated areas? According to Schor, "The primary determinants of children's health are social and originate or are experienced within the context of their families. Children's health and well-being is directly related to their families' ability to provide their essential physical, emotional and social needs. . . . Families are losing their sense of belonging to a community—communality—and with it they are losing both real and perceived access to social support and a sense of coherence in their lives." If this loss of communality does affect the health of children, as Schor states, does the opposite also apply? Does the increased sense of community in rural areas mean that rural children are healthier? In the National Health Interview Survey, satisfaction with health status was equal for children in metropolitan and rural areas. Yet, rural children have fewer visits to a clinician. Do rural families make fewer visits to the doctor's office because they are healthier or because they don't have access? And what, if any, is the effect of there being more two-parent families in rural America than in metropolitan areas? Do two-parent families improve communality and health? It is of interest that the one group less satisfied with their health was the rural poor. Do the poor have less sense of communality? The effect of "communality" on children's health is still unclear and needs further research, but it may be an important component to the health of rural communities.

RURAL HEALTH ISSUES

What are the specific child health issues for rural communities? First, just as the health problems of urban communities vary from city to city, so do they among small town and rural communities. The areas that are important for the rural child health clinician to consider are traumatic injuries, resuscitation and stabilization of critically ill newborns and children, care of the chronically ill child, and preventive care using a population-specific focus (Table 75–2). Issues of dental and mental health care are also very important but are not discussed in this chapter.

Trauma

Trauma is the leading cause of death among children after their first year of life. Mortality

TABLE 75–1. Rural Health Care Needs

Rural communities have a great need for child health care of high quality because
- 20% of America's children live in rural communities, many of which have an inadequate supply of child health clinicians.
- More rural children are poor and uninsured.
- More rural children have chronic illnesses.
- There are population-specific problems for children of migrant farmworkers, Native Americans, and minority groups.

TABLE 75–2. Rural Health Issues

Acute Care
  Increased trauma and subsequent morbidity and mortality
  Increased stabilization and care of critically ill newborns, children, and adolescents
Chronic Care
  Increased need to provide primary and secondary levels of care
  Increased need to coordinate care for chronically ill children
Preventive Care
  Increased need to educate families about the value of preventive care
  Increased need to provide anticipatory guidance, focusing on safety, injury prevention, and alcohol abuse

rates for children and adolescents from traumatic injuries are much higher in rural areas than in metropolitan areas. Although the incidence and severity of traumatic injuries may be slightly higher, the increased mortality is related more directly to the longer time required to reach the hospital from the scene of the injury. The causes of traumatic deaths vary with the age group. Burns and child abuse predominate in the younger ages, while motor vehicles and firearms are the major causes for the adolescent. Falls, pedestrian injuries, and poisonings occur among all ages. In order for the rural clinician to decrease the morbidity and mortality from rural injuries effectively, he or she has to improve the care of the injured patient, decrease the degree of injury, and most important, prevent the injury from ever occurring. To accomplish this, the primary care clinician should work with the health care team, the patient and family, and the entire community.

Patient Care Team

The importance of the community focus is well demonstrated when traumatic injuries are examined. Because of distance and topography, many if not most deaths occur before the child arrives at the emergency department. The injured child usually is stabilized initially by a volunteer emergency medical technician (EMT) who may or may not be knowledgeable about pediatric care. One of the strengths of rural communities is that because of the frequency of traumatic injuries, the emergency department physician and general surgeon often have extensive experience with traumatic injuries, but both still may need the assistance of the primary care clinician in caring for the pediatric patient. Knowing pediatric advanced life support (PALS) and judging when to transfer and when to keep the child in the community hospital are vital to the child's survival. Training

of the EMT, paramedics, and emergency department staff in PALS and pediatric trauma will be helpful. Development of improved prehospital services, including appropriate communications with emergency units, mobile intensive care units equipped with appropriate pediatric supplies, and 911 phone systems, all improve prehospital care. Regional pediatric trauma centers also can be developed. Many rural communities have already started these programs.

Family

Involvement of families in decreasing the incidence of traumatic injuries and poisonings needs to focus on prevention. Family education in the form of anticipatory guidance given at health maintenance visits and reinforced whenever appropriate helps to decrease the injuries. Age-appropriate injury prevention advice and handouts such as the American Academy of Pediatrics' TIPP program are very useful. All aspects of poisoning and all forms of traffic safety need to be addressed. In rural areas, safety regarding farm equipment, recreational vehicles (all-terrain vehicles, or ATVs), and dirt bikes must be emphasized. For adolescents, the rural clinician should emphasize the use of seatbelts, safe driving, and avoidance of alcohol and drugs while driving. It also is important to provide anticipatory guidance about gun safety. Many if not most families have hunters who own guns, especially rifles and shotguns. Many young rural adolescents are interested in hunting, and many will have taken hunter safety courses. It is important to re-emphasize to parents that all guns should be unloaded, and ammunition should be stored and *locked* in a separate location. Talking with parents about ensuring that guns are not accessible to younger siblings and their friends also is critical.

Community

The incidence, severity, and mortality of traumatic injuries cannot be decreased without a community approach. As stated earlier, the community approach starts with improving the care of injured children before they arrive in the emergency department. Only by mobilizing the entire community can many of these pre- and in-hospital patient care services be developed. A program of primary prevention includes not only anticipatory guidance for parents and families but also talks given by the rural clinician to parent-teacher associations, community service organizations, hospitals, and others. Talks about gun safety given to schools or in conjunction with hunter safety courses can be useful. Schools can develop conflict resolution programs to help children and families learn how to discuss anger and differences. As in any community, bicycle rodeos and bike safety programs also can be developed.

County-based child death review teams are being developed in several states to help communities examine causes of mortality in their areas. Using these data, the rural clinician can determine where the community needs to focus its energy and resources to decrease childhood deaths.

Working with county child and youth services to protect children and assist families in preventing child abuse also can decrease sexual and emotional as well as physical abuse. Innovative programs in Hawaii, Colorado, and other states have demonstrated the value of lay and professional home visiting services in decreasing the incidences of child abuse.

Stabilization and Care of Critically Ill Children

There is an increased demand for the rural clinician to provide stabilization and, when necessary, transfer of critically ill children. Because there are no residents or specialists available, rural clinicians perform more procedures than do their urban counterparts. Rural communities rarely have a neonatologist available, which requires the family physician or pediatrician to attend cesarean sections and complicated deliveries; therefore, the rural clinician has to maintain skills in newborn resuscitation, stabilization, and transfer of the sick neonate.

The rural physician also will need to be able to do many procedures that his or her training program may not have taught every resident, for example, suturing wounds, including facial wounds, caring for burns, treating nondisplaced fractures, and inserting gastric feeding tubes. Receiving initial and continuing education in order to perform these procedures is vital.

Chronic Care

Some studies have not reported a higher prevalence of chronic illness among children in rural areas; others have. In either case, **rural areas have to confront the reality that over 1 million children have some form of chronic illness or disability and limited resources to help them.** This again puts increased responsibility on the rural clinician. Also, some families are reluctant or do not have the resources to travel to specialty care in larger metropolitan areas and they want it provided by their primary care physician. Rural clinicians have to balance in what situations they are comfortable providing care and in what situations they need to help the family obtain a consultation with the pediatric specialist.

Patient Care Team

Rural physicians cannot know everything about every chronic illness that their patients may have. They do need to be willing to learn and to provide areas of care not provided by their metropolitan counterparts, such as intravenous chemotherapy per protocol, surgical follow-up, and chronic disease follow-up visits. Chronic care is an excellent example of where the clinical team can be used to improve care. The office can use a pediatric nurse practitioner or office nurse to help the family coordinate care. Some offices also use child or school psychologists or social workers to assist with the care of behavioral and other chronic illnesses. The pediatric specialist and the staff of the tertiary center are also part of the team. This requires a commitment by the primary care team to timely and clear communication with the tertiary care center, especially because laboratory and radiologic follow-up testing will be done in the local community.

Family

In rural areas, as in urban areas, the role of the clinician in the care of chronically ill children is changing from leader to partner-collaborator. This begins with the initial diagnosis, where it is critical to give information compassionately and respectfully, using a quiet setting with only the parents present. This helps with the child's care, the parents' coping, and the building of the therapeutic relationship. Later the primary care clinician can help the family coordinate care and is looked to by the family as the source of medical information. Although initially we may teach families, later they will teach us. Providing the family with educational, medical, and emotional support requires a commitment not just from the clinician, but from the entire office team.

The most important aspect of the patient/family/clinician therapeutic relationship is the trust that develops. Focusing on the competencies of the family and allowing them to be in control, recognizing and respecting their coping strategies, staying involved, and advocating for them help to build this trust. Partially because of a lack of providers and possibly because of their sense of loyalty, rural families and their clinicians are able to maintain the continuity of care that is basic to trust. Finally, **remembering that often we can provide care but not always a cure, the clinician's compassion is the foundation of the trusting relationship.**

Community

Although the tertiary care center may provide the medical plan for children who have special health care needs, it is in the community that the health care is delivered. One of the strengths of small towns is the very dedicated individuals and organizations who often are available to assist families who require special services. Many communities have developed early intervention programs; pediatric occupational, physical, and speech and language therapy programs; parent support groups; resource and referral centers; and respite assistance. These programs may be limited in scope because there may be only a few children who need the services or because of difficulty in finding the appropriate staff in a rural community. Sometimes there also is less financial support available in rural populations.

If the programs that are needed are not available, the rural clinician can work with the family and the community to develop them. For any health problem in the community, be it the need for resources for a child who has a chronic illness or developmental delay, adolescent pregnancy, or increased teen drinking, it is very easy, but not very beneficial, for the clinician to promote his or her own ideas of the problem and the solution. The rural community often will allow this "expert" to dictate the program, but community success will not continue without community "ownership."

The rural clinician should facilitate the development of community programs. This can be accomplished by working with community organizations or individuals to assess what they perceive as the problem or need. Together they can determine their strengths and weaknesses, set realistic goals and objectives to address the problem, obtain adequate funding, and then implement the program. Finally, a practical evaluation tool can be developed and used to improve the program and maintain funding continuously. It also is important to remember that when working with rural organizations—hospitals, community service organizations, or government agencies—the rural clinician has to be patient. During the first year in the community it is wise to listen most of the time and talk little. Rural communities often are slow to change, needing clear justification of why improvement is needed.

It is important to use all available resources in the community, the region, and the state. This can be done by developing community- or county-specific services or by helping regional or state programs to establish satellite or outreach clinics. These have been developed by state Maternal and Child Health Bureaus, tertiary care centers, and health care organizations in neighboring metropolitan areas. One example would be regional resource and referral centers that have been developed to provide information and parental support. Having one phone number to call to find out information about a disease, where the nearest parent support group is located, and who provides child and respite care is especially important in any rural area that has limited resources. These centers help families feel less isolated. The use of the Internet and World Wide Web also are addressing the lack of information for rural families.

The American Academy of Pediatrics' Community Access to Child Health (CATCH) program can help the rural community plan and implement programs to improve health care services for children.

Preventive Care (Table 75–3)

Because of the financial realities of many rural families, they often see less value in preventive care for their children. Although managed care is starting to penetrate rural areas, most families still have to pay out of pocket for their preventive visits. Therefore, the rural clinician may have a more difficult time convincing families to come in for health maintenance visits.

Although all areas of preventive care and anticipatory guidance are important for the rural family, the following deserve special focus: preventive screening for the poor, focusing on immunizations, lead poisoning, and tuberculosis; anticipatory guidance for use of fluoride, pesticide exposure,

---

TABLE 75–3. Focus for Preventive Care

Preventive screening
  Immunizations
  Lead poisoning
  Tuberculosis
Anticipatory guidance
  Fluoride
  Injury prevention
  Pesticide exposure
  Adolescent sexuality
  Alcohol abuse
Community prevention
  Injury prevention
  Adolescent pregnancy

adolescent sexuality, and alcohol abuse; and community programs for the prevention of adolescent pregnancy and child abuse. Injury prevention already has been discussed.

Patient Care

Screening for prevention, or treatment in the early stages, is the basis of pediatric care of high quality. Poor children are at a threefold increased risk for underimmunization, lead poisoning, and tuberculosis (Palfrey, 1994). In rural areas that have less access to care, these issues are even more significant.

IMMUNIZATIONS. We have learned recently that private clinicians as well as rural health clinics have been leaving many preschool children at risk for vaccine-preventable diseases. This is due, in part, to insufficient use of vaccine assessment programs, recall and reminder systems, and patient flags. Assessing immunization performance of your practice, reviewing the records of every child at every visit, calling parents to remind them of visits, giving all immunizations due at both preventive and mild sick visits, and assisting low-income families in obtaining Medicaid will help improve immunization rates.

LEAD POISONING. It is important to determine if the children in your community are at risk for lead poisoning. Poor children are at increased risk of lead poisoning. Several reports have questioned the appropriateness of the Centers for Disease Control and Prevention lead poisoning questionnaire in general and specifically in rural areas. Questions found to correlate the highest with elevated lead levels include "Are there siblings or playmates who have lead poisoning?" "Does the child live in pre-1970 housing with peeling or chipping paint?" "Does the child live near an industry that may release lead?" "Does the child live in rented or owner-occupied housing?" "Does the child have a parent who is a migrant farmworker?"

TUBERCULOSIS. As with lead poisoning, each child health clinician needs to determine if the entire community or only selected populations are at high risk for tuberculosis. Each office needs to decide when to use the tuberculosis questionnaire and when to do Mantoux testing. Children from poor families and migrant workers are at high risk.

Patient and Family Education and Community Programs

Anticipatory guidance needs to be given to pediatric patients and their families and then repeated several times to affect behavior. The many approaches to the prevention of traumatic injuries have already been discussed. Although many of these problems can be discussed in the office, the most effective way to approach them is through community action.

FLUORIDE. Many, if not most, small towns and rural communities do not have a fluoridated water supply. The rural clinician needs to ask or determine the level of natural fluoride of the water from the town water supply and surrounding wells. Fluoride then can be given at the correct dosage for age.

PESTICIDE EXPOSURE. Although all farm families may be at risk for exposure to pesticides, children of migrant workers are at especially high risk. Families and communities need to be educated about the risks and how to decrease them.

ALCOHOL ABUSE. Alcohol abuse is a problem among all adolescents, but this is especially so among Native Americans. Effective group programs have to be developed by the community, and the adolescents who will be served have to be included in that development.

ADOLESCENT SEXUALITY AND PREGNANCY. Rural communities have a higher rate of adolescent pregnancy than do metropolitan areas. Although adolescent pregnancy is a problem for all groups, it is especially high among the poor, especially in the African-American population of the rural South and the Native American population.

Anticipatory guidance is only a small portion of an overall community program. School-based programs are an important component. Lay or nurse home visiting programs have been successful in urban environments in many states.

SUMMARY

Children in rural America do not differ significantly from their metropolitan counterparts in health care needs and resources. The differences usually are of magnitude and are not related to a unique type of disease. Assessment of the child's, family's, and community's strengths and weaknesses is key to addressing the health needs of rural children.

FURTHER READING

American Academy of Pediatrics, Committee on Practice and Ambulatory Medicine: Management of Pediatric Practice, 2nd ed. Elk Grove Village, IL, American Academy of Pediatrics, 1991.

Georgetown University Child Development Center: Serving Children with Special Health Care Needs in Rural Areas:

Programs, Challenges and Strategies. Washington, DC, 1992.

Hirschfeld JA: Emergency medical services for children in rural and frontier America: Diverse and changing environments. Pediatrics 96(Suppl):179–184, 1995.

McManus MA and Newacheck PW. Rural maternal, child and adolescent health. Health Services Research 6:807–848, 1989.

Melzer SM, Grossman DC, Hart LG, and Rosenblatt RA: Hospital Services for Rural Children in Washington State. Pediatrics 99:196–203, 1997.

National Rural Health Association: Study of Models to Meet Rural Health Care Needs Through Mobilization of Health Professions' Education and Services Resources. Rockville, MD, Bureau of Health Professions, 1992.

Palfrey JS: Community Child Health: An Action Plan for Today. Westport, CT, Praeger, 1994.

Schor EL: Developing communality: Family-centered programs to improve children's health and well-being. Bull NY Acad Med 72:413–442, 1995.

Svenson JE, Spurlock C, and Nypaver M: Factors associated with the higher traumatic death rate among rural children. Ann Emerg Med 27:625–632, 1996.

Jennie A. McLaurin

Chapter 76

Health Care for Children of Migrant Farmworkers

BACKGROUND

For as long as there has been large-scale agriculture in the United States, there has been a seasonal labor force employed to cultivate and harvest it. The Office of Migrant Health estimates that nationwide migrant and seasonal farmworkers and their dependents number between 3 and 5 million. Approximately 1 million of these are classified as migrant. The term is somewhat arbitrary, as several definitions of "migrant" exist in separate programs and policies. For the federal Migrant Health Program, a migrant is one who, in the preceding 24 months, had principal employment in agriculture on a seasonal basis and who moved to seek such employment. All 50 states as well as Puerto Rico employ migrant farmworkers. Exact numbers of children of migrant farmworkers are not known, but over 600,000 school-age children are enrolled in migrant education programs in 47 of the 50 states. Table 76–1 lists the 10 states that have the greatest population of migrant farmworkers.

Children of farmworkers move with their families in three patterns of mobility (Fig. 76–1). Most are point-to-point migrants, moving from a home base (83% claim Mexico as home base) to one or more U.S. farm jobs and then back home again. U.S. farm employment constitutes the majority of the family's annual earnings, and the home base is the family's strategy to contain costs by residing in inexpensive settings during the off-season. One third of families are nomadic migrants, traveling from crop to crop, usually working for at least three employers in two locations in separate states. A small number of nomadic farmworkers travel out of the United States as part of their regular mobility pattern. The third group follows a restricted circuit within a small geographic area, such as the Central Valley in California. Farmworkers' children thus are a part of several communities in terms of schooling, housing, social relationships, and health care. The classic construct of a "medical home" must be adapted to address the needs of the child within his or her particular pattern of mobility.

The migrant farmworker labor force traditionally has been largely Hispanic. In recent years

TABLE 76–1. Ten Most Populous Farmworker States or Territories

State	Annual No. of Migrants and Dependents
California	700,233
Texas	370,815
Florida	238,247
Washington	193,437
Michigan	161,020
Oregon	147,245
North Carolina	142,144
Georgia	104,101
Puerto Rico	77,075
New York	73,423

Data from Larson AC, Plascencia L: Migrant Enumeration Project, 1993, US Public Health Service.

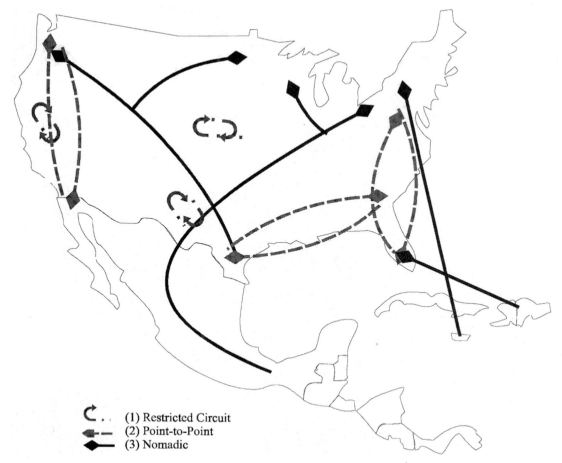

Figure 76–1. The three patterns of mobility of children of migrant farmworkers. (From Migrant Clinicians' Network, Austin, TX, 1997.)

the growth of the Hispanic sector in the migrant population has accelerated, such that 99% of migrant farmworkers are, or have family members who are, Hispanic. Forecasting of future farm labor needs indicates that harvest work will continue to be supplied by recent immigrants. Most adults (85%) are foreign-born and come from landless poor families in Latin America. The average adult foreign-born farmworker has only 7 years of formal education. Women have even fewer years of schooling, and most are unable to write (Spanish or English). Thus, language is a barrier to providing care both in terms of spoken communication and as a resource for education.

Children of farmworkers often are born in the United States and so have different citizenship from their parents and are eligible for U.S. health and human services. Although most men in farmwork are documented workers, that is, legally employed, many of the women do not have authoriza-

tion for U.S. residence. It has been shown that U.S. citizen children in families such as these experience limited access to care based on the restrictions of the undocumented family member. Children of undocumented workers also are much more likely to spend part of each year in their family's native country than are children of documented residents. The community of the migrant child may be a complex blend of two separate worlds.

Farmworker families live in conditions characterized by poverty, unstable housing, unreliable transportation, and social and cultural isolation. Most lack telephones, many have no ability to communicate with the local community, and most spend at least a third of the year unemployed. The median yearly income of a worker is $5000. Despite the presence of multiple wage earners in a family, 73% of migrant children live in poverty. Less than 20% use needs-based services, and only

25% of families have any form of third party payment for health care. In addition to living with their parents and siblings, children often live with extended family and nonfamily members. The family depends on one or more working adult male members for transportation because most women don't drive and public transportation typically is absent in rural locales. Housing may be located on farm property, exposing the child to agricultural chemicals and workplace hazards. Less than 20% of these children receive formal child care services, and an unknown number accompany their parents to the field.

There are a number of federally funded programs for migrant farmworkers and their families, including health and educational services. The Migrant Health Program, established in 1962, funds over 100 migrant health centers with 400 sites in 40 states and Puerto Rico. Many federally funded community health centers also serve farmworkers. Although the services are effective for improving the health of the clients served, less than 15% of the nation's farmworker families have access to these centers. Therefore, the wider pediatric practice community must provide a medical home to the majority of these children.

There are no national data on child health indicators in the farmworker population such as rates of infant mortality, birth defects, adolescent pregnancy, or homicides. However, a profile of the health status of farmworkers' children can be constructed. **Migrant children receive inadequate preventive medical care, are exposed to occupational illnesses and injury, have an increased rate of infectious diseases and toxic exposures, have an increased risk of family violence and mental health problems, and are subject to nutritional and educational deprivation.**

SPECIAL CONSIDERATIONS IN HEALTH CARE PROVISION

Pediatric clinicians may improve and protect the health status of these children by recognizing the special needs of the population in terms of the child's particular health history, the family's ability to facilitate care and promote health, and the local as well as the distant community's resources, supports, and protections. Consideration of the problems affecting health status will assist the clinician in developing a comprehensive care plan. **Barriers to care that must be addressed include language, literacy, transportation, hours of access, cultural differences, eligibility requirements, family mobility, and financial constraints.**

Preventive Medical Care

Children of farmworkers have delayed or absent access to preventive medical care. This delay starts in utero because migrant women are likely to enter care late and have fewer visits than are recommended by the American College of Obstetrics and Gynecology. Pregnant farmworkers are exposed to heat stress, toxins, and infectious diseases and have high rates of pregnancy loss. Birth outcomes have not been documented well, although first-generation Hispanic immigrants tend to have healthier newborns than do other women of similar socioeconomic status. There is limited use of tobacco, alcohol, and other drugs by Hispanic farmworker women.

Three fourths of migrant children have delayed immunizations at age 2 and many have an unknown status. They are at risk for both over- and underimmunization because providers do not have or do not understand current documentation. Children born to mothers who did not obtain full prenatal care are at increased risk for immunization delay. Risk of exposure to vaccine-preventable illnesses is increased by transnational migration. Measles outbreaks have been reported in migrant communities, with spread in the preschool population. Over 90% of farmworker parents do carry an immunization record when provided by a clinician. Special immunization needs, such as typhoid vaccine, may be applicable for children migrating back to high-risk areas.

Dental disease is reported as the primary problem of school-age migrant children. Over 75% of children studied have caries, with restoration incomplete in most. Nursing caries is widespread. Access to dental care is limited severely, even in migrant health centers. Children have multiple sources of drinking water as they migrate, most of it from wells that are not uniformly fluoridated. Parents have little or no experience with dental care and dental hygiene.

Injuries are a result of inadequate prevention. Farmworkers' children are endangered by poor use of car restraints, inadequate access to safe child care, exposure to farm machinery, and residence in overcrowded, poorly maintained housing. Parental expectation of the child's reasoning ability may overestimate true capacity.

Migrant children have interrupted health care provision and often receive combined care from health departments, migrant clinics, hospitals, and emergency departments. Comprehensive preventive visits may be lacking, as evidenced by the documented late diagnosis of disorders such as Down syndrome, heart defects, and developmental dysplasia of the hips in children who are up-to-

TABLE 76–2. Improving the Delivery of Preventive Care

Prenatal care	Provide information to parents about the importance and availability of prenatal care initiated in the first trimester.
Immunizations	Review the child's immunization status at every visit and offer needed vaccines without requiring a separate visit.
	Become familiar with the Mexican immunization record.
	Obtain migration history to determine length of stay and need for special immunizations due to foreign travel.
	Use the accelerated or catch-up schedule as needed.
	Offer educational resources such as the bilingual video by the AAP, "Before It's Too Late, Vaccinate."
	Provide a portable immunization record that includes the name, address, and phone number of the health care provider.
Dental health	Counsel parents of infants about nursing caries.
	Teach basic dental hygiene as part of preventive care.
	Document the child's source of drinking water and supplement fluoride as indicated.
	Seek collaboration with dental health providers.
Injury prevention	Counsel parents about car seat and seatbelt laws and proper use of restraints.
	Document child care arrangements and refer to resources such as the Migrant Head Start program where available.
	Counsel parents about dangers of farm equipment and hazards in the home.
Well-child examination	Provide a complete physical examination including developmental history on the first visit or ensure prompt follow-up for one. Provide anticipatory guidance tailored to the cultural context of the migrant family.

AAP, American Academy of Pediatrics.

date on their immunizations. Families are limited in their ability to plan for future appointments and to provide clinicians with accurate information about health care received elsewhere.

Strategies for improving the delivery of preventive care are provided in Table 76–2.

Occupational Illness and Injury

Children of farmworkers are at risk for occupational illness and injury by participating in the workforce directly, accompanying parents to the fields, or residing on farm property. At least 19% to 25% of migrant children participate as laborers. This probably is an underestimate because children often work without separate payment or documentation from that of their parents. Agriculture is one of the most dangerous occupations in the United States, with limited supports and protections for children. Most migrant workers are harvesters, so falls, overuse syndromes, and dermatitis from plants and toxins are more common than large-machinery injuries. Chemical exposures on farms may occur via drinking water, drift of wind-blown dust, or direct contact with plants. Pesticide poisoning may be either chronic or acute. Fatigue contributes to injuries as well as to poor school performance. Table 76–3 addresses the reduction of occupational illness and injury.

Infectious Diseases and Toxic Exposures

Infectious diseases and toxic exposures in migrant children are related to housing, sanitation, agriculture, and migration. Children of farmworkers have increased rates of diarrheal illness, parasitic infection, tuberculosis, lead poisoning, and agricultural chemical exposure. One third of preschoolers have been shown to have parasitic infections, mostly giardiasis but also amebiasis, malaria, trypanosomiasis, and others. Tuberculosis is six times more likely in migrant farmworkers than in other employed adults, and children have increased exposure owing to crowded living conditions and foreign travel. Most children born in Latin America receive bacille Calmette-Guérin vaccine, but this does not offer long-term protection and should not prevent the clinician from screening for tuberculosis. Lead poisoning is more common in migrant children than in other rural poor populations as a result of housing, potential exposure from housewares made abroad, and folk medicine practices. Shallow wells often contain water contaminated by fertilizer residues, increas-

TABLE 76–3. Reducing Occupational Illness and Injury

Understand the contribution of the child to the family's economy.

Identify the extent to which the child is exposed to the workplace.

Become familiar with occupational syndromes such as green tobacco illness, organophosphate poisoning, heat stress, overuse injury, pterygium, and dermatitis.

Offer educational resources such as "The Playing Fields" video produced by MCN (see Resources for the Clinician at the end of the chapter).

MCN, Migrant Clinicians' Network.

TABLE 76–4. Managing Infectious Diseases and Toxic Exposures

Teach personal hygeine to reduce diarrhea.

Understand the family's health beliefs regarding causes and cures for diarrhea.

Provide education on rehydration fluid and diet that will treat diarrhea safely.

Maintain a high index of suspicion for parasitic infection, but don't screen every child.

Screen annually for tuberculosis, placing an IPPD regardless of BCG status.

Provide parents with a portable record documenting tuberculosis screening and results.

Children 0 to 6 years should receive at least two blood lead tests, preferably at ages 1 and 2. Those who have elevations of lead levels, a family history of lead poisoning, or known exposure should be tested more frequently in collaboration with the local health department.

Encourage the use of bottled water for infant use when the family water supply is a well that has not been tested for chemical contamination.

BCG, bacille Calmette-Guérin; IPPD, intradermal purified protein derivative.

ing the potential for "blue baby syndrome" caused by nitrite poisoning. Boiling the water may destroy bacteria, but it concentrates chemicals and thus accentuates the problem. Table 76–4 describes management of infectious diseases and toxic exposures.

Family Violence and Mental Health Problems

Children of migrant farmworkers are at increased risk of witnessing violence, including domestic violence. One third of migrant women report being slapped, kicked, or punched by a household member in the previous year. Data on the prevalence of child maltreatment in the farmworker population are unclear and only substantiate educational and economic neglect. Reports of selected samples of farmworkers' children do show increased rates (64% of subjects) of mental illness, particularly of anxiety and depression. Parents are more likely to seek the counsel of clergy, family, and friends than they are to visit a professional for assistance with the child. Less than 50% of affected children receive formal treatment. Rural mental health resources are scarce, particularly those in which the workers have Spanish language competency. Table 76–5 offers an approach to the reduction of family violence and the promotion of mental health.

Nutritional and Educational Deprivation

Farmworkers' children are considered a population at special risk for malnutrition. Families spend 50% of their income on food, as compared with 10% spent by the average U.S. household. Iron deficiency anemia, vitamin A deficiency, and folate deficiency are reported commonly, even in children enrolled in supplemental food programs. Children may experience failure to thrive early in life and obesity later. Almost 50% of mothers breastfeed, although they commonly supplement with formula. The agricultural workplace makes expressing and storing human milk impractical.

Migrant children receive special educational assistance from Migrant Head Start and the Migrant Education Program. Migrant Head Start extends enrollment to children aged 2 weeks to 5 years and operates in the language of the children served. Similar to the federal health program, Migrant Head Start is able to serve less than 20% of the eligible population. The Migrant Education Program serves preschool and school-age children in all 50 states, with approximately 600,000 served annually, representing 1% of the public school population. Although 8% of public school students are classified as disabled, only 4% of migrant students are so listed. This may reflect a selection by families not to migrate when parenting a child who has special needs. Depending on their migratory pattern, children may be a regular part of two school systems year after year, having stable relationships in each. Migrant children often are not ready for school and have a diminished prospect of completing high school. Table 76–6 identifies ways to promote nutrition and education among migrant children.

GENERAL CONSIDERATIONS

In addition to the recognition of special problems related to categorical conditions, the clinician must consider some general issues affecting the health of migrant children. Barriers to care have

TABLE 76–5. Approaching Family Violence and Mental Health

Consider use of the MCN (see Resources for the Clinician at the end of the chapter) domestic violence screening tool and become informed of local resources available to farmworker families.

Screen migrant children for anxiety and depression.

Recognize the use of family, friends, and clergy in counseling parents.

Collaborate with area mental health providers and school systems to establish access to care and linkages for migrant children.

Assess parental stressors and discipline techniques and offer guidance on strategies for risk reduction and behavior modification.

MCN, Migrant Clinicians' Network.

TABLE 76–6. Promotion of Nutrition and Education

Enroll migrant children in food subsidy programs.

Check migrant children for anemia at least annually.

Obtain a diet history and provide a portable growth chart as part of routine care.

Serve as an advisor or clinician for area Migrant Head Start programs.

Develop linkages between the public schools and pediatric community to improve school enrollment and health supervision.

Offer or develop school readiness programs or counseling for migrant families that acknowledge parental literacy and family migration patterns.

Assist parents with English language competency by linking them with resources.

been noted previously, and health plans must address each of these. **The composition of the family and household, the use of child care providers, the pattern of migration, the practice of alternative medicine and home remedies, and the techniques used to discipline and encourage the child should be understood and accounted for in the prescription of treatment or education.** Translators ideally should be adults trained in medical translation. If this is not possible, the clinician should instruct the translator in matters relating to confidentiality and the role of the individual in translation rather than in the care or treatment of the patient. The dignity of the parent should be recognized at all times, with special care taken to avoid the use of children as translators. Parents should be given a portable health record with data on immunizations, anemia, growth, allergies, tuberculosis screening, medications, and chronic conditions. It should contain the clinician's address and telephone number and be updated at each visit. Finally, there are many occasions when the clinician may serve as an advocate for the child and family, whether in the local community or on a state and national level.

SUMMARY

The pediatric clinician can meet the special needs of the children of migrant farmworkers in many practical ways, including

- Establishing a medical home with continuity of care and portability of records
- Promoting education and literacy
- Reducing barriers to care by assisting with issues such as transportation, translation, and financial need
- Directing the examination for known challenges to health in this population

- Recognizing family systems and cultural issues
- Developing resources and links within the community
- Advocating for full access to health care, education, and inclusion in the community

FURTHER READING

American Academy of Pediatrias, Committee on Community Health Services; Health care for children of farmworker families. Pediatrics 5:952–953, 1995.

Johnston HL: Health for the Nation's Harvesters. Farmington Hills, MI: National Migrant Worker Council, 1985.

McLaurin JA (ed): Guidelines for the Care of Farmworkers' Children. Elk Grove Village, IL, American Academy of Pediatrics and Migrant Clinicians' Network, in press.

Mines R, Gabbard S, and Boccalandro B: Findings from the National Agricultural Workers Survey (NAWS) 1990: A Demographic and Employment Profile of Perishable Crop Farm Workers. Offices of Program Economics, Research Report No. 1. Washington, DC, US Department of Labor, 1991.

Rust GS: Health status of migrant farmworkers: A literature review and commentary. Am J Public Health 80:1213–1217, 1990.

RESOURCES FOR THE CLINICIAN

Migrant Clinicians' Network (MCN)
PO Box 164285
Austin, TX 78716
Phone: 512-327-2017
www.migrantclinician.org.

National association of health care clinicians working with migrant farmworkers. Provides educational support, research, and advocacy.

American Academy of Pediatrics (AAP)
Northwest Point Blvd
PO Box 927
Elk Grove Village, IL 60009-0927
Phone: 847-228-5005
kidsdocs@aap.org.

Provision of policy, advocacy, and educational resources. Liaison relationship with MCN (see above). Directory of migrant health providers. Publication of manual on care of farmworkers' children.

National Center for Farmworker Health
1515 Capital of Texas Hwy South, Ste 220
Austin, TX 78746
Phone: 512-328-7682
www.ncfh.org.

Operates a resource center of materials related to the health of migrant farmworkers. Catalog from agency may be obtained.

State Primary Health Care Associations

Provide technical assistance to migrant and community health centers in each state. Source of information related to resources in state for farmworkers.

Migrant Education Program and Migrant Head Start

Area information can be obtained by contacting the state office for education or from the federal Head Start office.

PART B

THE PEDIATRICIAN'S OFFICE ·

Lawrence F. Nazarian

Chapter **77**

The Well-Equipped Office

A pediatrician starting a practice or organizing a clinic is confronted with an overwhelming list of practical decisions to be made, many of which are not discussed during training. Equipping an office is one area of challenge.

Visiting well-established offices or clinics should be an initial step in planning one's own equipment list. Pick places with practice styles similar to that which will be followed in the new office. Survey several practices; people solve the same problem in different ways, and one solution may be more comfortable for you than another. This advice applies also to the established practitioner, who might profit from fresh ideas.

Another good source of information is the physician's supply house. A reliable dealer who is interested in providing personal service for many years should be found early in practice. This consultant can keep the physician abreast of new products while tailoring purchases to specific requirements. At the same time, it is wise to compare prices of different firms periodically and not automatically purchase everything from the same supplier.

As far as possible, names of specific brands or manufacturers have been omitted from this chapter to avoid endorsements or recommending outdated products. In a few instances, names are given to allow the reader to find unusual products. Previous editions of this text contained lengthy descriptions of office laboratory arrangements. Because the status of laboratory procedures in the office has been in such flux due to government regulations, this area of the office is not addressed.

TESTING OF SPECIAL SENSES

Vision Testing

Much valuable information on vision can be obtained with simple equipment. Eye charts come with letters, illiterate Es, and pictures. Letter charts should be used when possible, because picture charts do not assess as accurately. For the preschool child, however, picture charts may be the only practical means of evaluating acuity subjectively, and they do fulfil the critical function of detecting major differences in acuity between the two eyes. Eye charts require an unobstructed 20-foot hallway, although a 10-foot distance can be used and the denominator on the chart doubled. Children enjoy wearing a black "pirate" eye patch, which facilitates testing of individual eyes. More than 50% of the 3-year-olds and almost all 4-year-olds will be able to cooperate on an eye chart examination. Of particular importance in the younger child is detecting differences in visual acuity between the two eyes in order to find developing amblyopia.

The eye chart tests only distance vision. Because of their great accommodative powers, children rarely have problems with near vision. One may, however, obtain inexpensive cards for near-vision testing.

Muscle balance can be tested by way of the corneal light reflex and the cover test. Color testing requires only a book of testing plates.

An alternative way of testing vision is to use a multipurpose machine, which has the advantage of requiring only a small space. Although these machines are capable of testing a variety of functions, their main use is to evaluate distance vision, and the physician must judge if the expense is warranted.

A good overall discussion of vision testing is in Calhoun's article (see Further Reading at the end of the chapter).

Hearing Testing

Because an audiometer will receive continual use in a pediatric office, it makes sense to invest in a good machine and have it recalibrated periodically. By far the most important testing factor is a quiet room. Most 5-year-olds and many younger children will cooperate in pure-tone audiometry. The majority of 3-year-olds can be tested with an audiometer that speaks actual words at different levels of intensity. One can buy instruments that test both with words and with pure tones.

Measurement of eardrum compliance with a tympanometer adds a valuable dimension to the evaluation of middle ear function in children older than 6 months. This instrument does not require active patient participation and is not affected by cerumen, as long as the earpiece is not pushed directly into a clump of earwax. The tester must be trained in proper technique, however, and appropriate interpretation of the test patterns takes some study. Although the tympanometer is expensive, many offices consider it essential. Hand-held models are available.

The measurement of hearing in babies and developmentally disabled children requires special techniques. Brain stem–evoked potentials have been measured for years, and more recently technology has evolved that measures evoked otoacoustic emissions. It is not practical to have such equipment in the office, but one should find an audiology facility that can do this testing.

All the equipment used for hearing evaluation is expensive, complex, and subject to constant technical change. Consultation with an audiologist is strongly recommended as part of the shopping process.

Removal of cerumen is often necessary and can be accomplished with a metal irrigating syringe and a kidney basin. If several drops of wax softener are instilled and allowed to work for a few minutes, removal usually is easy. In stubborn cases, have the parent use ear drops at home for several days and bring the child back for flushing of the canals.

THE EXAMINING ROOM

The equipping of an examining room will reflect the individual style of each physician. Some general suggestions, however, apply to most situations.

Examining tables that are designed for adults are too low for the comfortable examination of a child and will cause the rapid onset of back pain in the physician. Besides being high enough, the table should be well padded and covered with a durable, washable, replaceable fabric. It is very helpful to have a large amount of built-in storage space. One should examine commercial equipment but also should consider building tables that meet the individual's needs.

The most accurate devices for measuring length are those that employ a sliding foot plate and a fixed headrest. A separate infant scale can be put on a shelf in the room or even kept in a drawer built into the examining table. Drawers can be constructed that are strong enough to hold the scale and baby safely in the open position. Add a nonstretchable tape measure for head circumference determinations.

A larger scale will be needed for older children who can stand. Height can be measured efficiently and accurately with a wooden yardstick or tape measure covered with Plexiglas that has been fixed vertically to the wall. A right-angle block is needed for proper measurement.

If examining rooms are constructed from scratch, it is extremely efficient to have in each room everything needed to prepare children for routine examinations, including a 10-foot distance for vision testing.

Anticipate which pieces of small equipment are used often and provide them for each room; the steps saved will make the expense worthwhile. For example, an otoscope and an ophthalmoscope in a wall unit that keeps the batteries charged will be used constantly. Tongue blades, culture swabs, reflex hammers, and similar tools should have their own niches within easy reach. It is helpful to have an adult stethoscope for obese children or teenagers who have thick chest walls.

Provide a wall rack for papers such as educational handouts, miscellaneous forms, and blank instruction pads. The time saved by having these resources at your fingertips will make up for any cost.

Another step saver is an intercom for communicating with the front desk. A telephone unit in each room can serve as an intercom as well as a phone. Ground rules must be established to avoid an inappropriate number of interruptions, but the entire office staff will function more efficiently when information can be exchanged this way.

Pediatricians are safety conscious and this orientation should be applied to the examining room. As much as possible, equipment should be kept out of the reach of the children. Search for sharp edges and protrusions that a toddler inevitably will find. Removable plastic plug covers for electric outlets or safety plugs not only will protect the children but also will teach parents.

Some pediatricians will construct an examining room that is significantly larger than the others for the purpose of holding conferences that involve several people or to accommodate patients who require extra room, such as those who have large wheelchairs.

THE WAITING ROOM

Great variation exists among waiting rooms of different physicians because needs are so diverse. The following suggestions have been helpful in practical experience. Some source of diversion for the waiting child is necessary. Creation of an actual play area is possible, with such items as "climbing" toys and a small table with chairs, although space limitations may make such an area impractical, or high patient flow may create unhealthy competition. One particular toy that has been highly successful in waiting rooms is the Rollercoaster (Anatex Enterprises, 14666 Titus Avenue #7, Panorama City, CA 91402), composed of colored wooden beads that are slid along twisted metal rods. This toy is unusually sturdy and captivates children over a wide age range.

Books and magazines are an excellent source of amusement and do not have some of the problems associated with toys, such as parental fear of the spread of infection. For relatively little money, the pediatrician can subscribe to a dozen magazines that cover the entire range from toddler to adult. A list of children's magazines is found at the end of this chapter. Books can be bought, obtained through children's book clubs, or brought from home when children outgrow them. Books can be carried into the examining room; it is not unusual for children to express disappointment when the story being read is interrupted by their names being called.

While deciding which books and magazines will go into the waiting room, the clinician should review strategies for encouraging parents to read to their children. **Increasing evidence confirms the long-held belief that reading is an exceptionally effective stimulant of the developing young mind.** It also is an activity that allows parents and children to share a close and comforting experience.

Talk to parents about the benefits and joys of reading even before the child's first birthday. Provide them with a list of age-appropriate magazines that will bring new material into the home regularly. Promote participation in local library hours, which will put families in contact with a children's librarian. The librarian can help you make a list of books for children of different ages that can provide fun and learning, including those that focus on specific life events, such as toileting. One pediatrician who cares for disadvantaged children gives books to his young patients—in many cases, the first book the child has ever owned—and asks about their reading experiences at subsequent visits.

Children love to watch fish in an aquarium. The fish not only amuse and occupy waiting children but also can be used in the clinical assessment of a febrile or lethargic child. The toddler who is carried over to the aquarium and reaches out toward the fish or babbles excitedly is providing valuable information. It is critical to mount the aquarium in such a way that it cannot be pulled over, because children inevitably will climb and grab.

Provision of background music need not cost a great deal. A good FM radio tuned to an easy listening station can provide a soothing influence so often welcomed in the chaos of a crowded waiting room.

Many pediatricians have a second waiting room for adolescents or for patients who are detained for a while. All physicians should provide a quiet place to allow patients who are unusually upset or have other special needs to wait. A conference room that usually is used for consultations can double as an auxiliary waiting room for these families.

Teaching aids can be put in the waiting room. A bulletin board allows the physician to display announcements that come along and may allow parents to share such information as babysitting services offered or desired.

EVENING HOURS

Parents appreciate evening hours; working parents often find it difficult or impossible to keep appointments during regular working hours. Evening visits for both health maintenance and care of illness are a boon to them and to families who have only one car or driver. Similarly, high school students who are involved in sports or jobs may not be able to come in during conventional hours.

The pediatrician also can benefit from scheduled evening sessions. All clinicians know about the glut of calls in the late afternoon. Parents are just then finding out from sitters that their youngsters are ill enough to need attention. Fevers are spiking and children who looked fine all day begin to wilt or cry. Even in an efficient office, many patients have to be worked in at the end of the day, keeping everyone in the office later, or are told to try symptomatic relief and to call the doctor if things do not improve. With evening hours, the children can be scheduled for early evening and will be seen by a doctor. The day people can get home at a reasonable hour.

Parents who call in the evening can be accommodated without the physician having to make a special trip. Children whose situations are borderline and might not be seen after the first call if the doctor is not in the office are seen more readily; thus, the number of phone calls during the night when some of those children have not improved is reduced. Performing some regular examinations in the evening can eliminate the need for well-child care on Saturdays, allowing pediatricians to concentrate on ill children and finish sooner that day. Some physicians find the evening an ideal time to schedule conferences, including prenatal visits.

The major disadvantage to evening hours is that someone has to work them! This problem can be solved by giving compensatory time off. A physician can work, for example, a 1:30 P.M. to 10:00 P.M. shift, allowing time for dinner. He or she will have no daytime hospital or overnight on-call responsibilities. The person on call after 10:00 P.M. will have worked a full day but has the evening to relax and probably will get fewer night calls because of the evening hours. In a smaller practice, the same person may need to work evenings and also be on call. He or she should be given time off the next morning to break up what could be a 36-hour shift.

It is important to have help during evening hours in the form of a nurse, receptionist, or both; the cost in salary is more than made up for by increased efficiency and reduced stress on the physician. Patient abuse of these sessions can be minimized by continuing to route calls through the answering service after regular hours and by granting evening well-child appointments only to those who have no other alternative. Being straightforward with patients at the time they call works most of the time.

The number of time slots allotted for urgent calls, nonurgent calls, and well-child visits will vary with practice needs and time of year. On days when the evening book fills up rapidly, the day people will need to work later to avoid overburdening the evening staff. Organize the evening along the same lines as the daytime schedule, but be flexible and expect to modify your original schedule as experience accumulates.

HOME VISITS (see also Chapter 16)

A home visit allows the physician to see a patient in his or her natural habitat and can lend more insight into family functioning than can innumerable office calls. Patients also appreciate the convenience and personal touch. The major drawback of these calls is inefficiency. The doctor spends valuable time driving around, and physical examinations, laboratory tests, and treatments are performed much better in the office.

Pediatricians who use the home visit selectively will find it a stimulating and informative experience that need happen only occasionally. One indication for a home visit is a chronic illness, such as neoplasia or severe neurologic disease, that renders the child bedridden. Refractory cases of illness in which the environment plays a critical role, such as asthma, often are easier to understand after a home visit. When a child's illness seems to have major emotional overtones, a trip to the home may round out the picture. Sometimes parents are incapacitated and just cannot bring the child in. The comforting value of a home visit cannot be overemphasized, especially when children are chronically ill or in the rare circumstance of a child's death.

Observation of newborn babies by hospital nurses during the critical first days of life has been reduced significantly by the current practice of sending neonates home at 1 day of age or younger. Because such problems as jaundice, infection, and feeding difficulties may arise at this time, a home visit by a pediatric clinician can be valuable, especially when the parents are inexperienced. Nurse practitioners or physician assistants can make these visits, although physicians who have the time will benefit from the additional insights gained into family functioning. In addition to increasing the chances of discovering illness in the young baby, home visits are reassuring to new parents and help to build their confidence.

The pediatrician who cares for children confined to home must be aware of community resources that can provide diagnostic, therapeutic, and support services to homes. Much of what used to occur in the hospital has been brought home, as home care agencies become more capable and insurers encourage such shifts. Laboratory work, intravenous medications, and phototherapy are among the services available at home, with many more coming.

THE TELEPHONE (see also Chapter 16)

Few physicians use the telephone as extensively as pediatricians do, and there are as many telephone systems as there are variations in practice style (see further on). A system structured to the needs of an individual office will lead to a smooth operation that is satisfying to patients and staff. Local telephone companies and private firms provide communication consultants who can present the many options available and structure an appropriate system.

Size of practice and frequency of incoming calls will determine how many lines are needed to avoid inordinate numbers of busy signals. People trained to answer the phone must be there to "staff" those lines and avoid the complaint that no one answers the calls. The cyclic nature of pediatric practice will complicate these decisions because telephone traffic varies with the incidence of infectious disease in the community. A system designed to handle a "busy average" day usually works without being wasteful, and staffing patterns can be adjusted seasonally. Periodic in-service sessions with triage telephone staff are important and can be geared to the conditions indigenous to the season.

An additional incoming line with a number known only to selected individuals is a must. One use of this line is to serve as an emergency channel if a patient has a real crisis during heavy telephone traffic on the regular lines and just cannot get through. Patients should be told that they can call the answering service in such an eventuality, and the operator then can use the unlisted line to reach the office. Although this mechanism will not be used often, it is of great comfort to parents to know that it exists.

Hospital staff and other physicians can be given the unlisted number as well so that they can get through quickly when critical information needs to be transmitted. Spouses should be discouraged from using that line for routine calls. A ring that is different from that of the regular line can be installed on the "hot line."

Still another line for outgoing calls is worthwhile. Simply marked "out" on its selection button, this line allows staff to make calls without tying up regular lines. In large practices, separate phone numbers for different functions streamline the operation. A special number for all advance appointments and another for the business office will reduce the load on the main number.

Some physicians have a calling hour that works well for them; others have found this system impractical. To record calls that must be returned, use pads of uniform preprinted call slips that have lines for the patient's name and phone number, date and time, and a phrase or two describing the problem. The best system is one in which each slip is attached to the patient's chart; for all but the most transient problems, a notation in the record can be immensely valuable later on. Recording calls in the chart leads to better care and is an essential risk-management technique.

More efficient use of the physician's time is possible when there is a personal desk or work station with a telephone near the examining rooms, where phone slips and charts can be placed, along with the mail folder and paperwork in progress. A few minutes here and there spent on various tasks between patient visits can reduce the backlog tremendously.

A tape device can be installed that activates when all lines are filled. The message will instruct the patient to call back in a little while or to call the answering service if a genuine emergency exists. The same machine can give a similar message during lunch hour if the office chooses to shut off all calls but emergencies. At night, the recording will tell the patient how to reach the physician on call.

Paging devices, some of which just beep and some of which display messages, give the clinician who is on call but away from the office an additional measure of flexibility. Add a cellular phone and the clinician has a satisfying degree of freedom.

Recent experience with after-hours nursing triage services has been encouraging. For a modest fee, sometimes paid by insurers, a trained nurse who has access to protocols and purposely stays up all night will take first call, contacting the clinician only for those few calls that truly require his or her attention. In areas where this system has been employed, a quiet revolution has occurred in the lifestyle of pediatricians, with tangible benefits in the form of more sleep and less stress. Best of all, patient satisfaction is high, and all indications are that care actually improves.

MEDICAL RECORDS

Several general principles will help the clinician who is establishing a medical record system. Each child's chart must contain the clinical information needed to facilitate proper care. Medicolegal considerations often are stressed in discussions of record keeping. If a record is written with the accuracy and completeness needed to give good care, it will stand up well in a legal proceeding. Because both functions are served by the same attention to detail, it should be pointed out that both clinical articles (see AAP, 1991) and medical liability insurance companies can provide valuable advice on constructing a record that is excellent from either perspective.

Although computerized records will become commonplace in the near future, at present the paper record predominates. Whether a traditional format or a problem-oriented approach is employed is less important than finding a system that is comfortable for individual clinicians. Legible handwriting is acceptable. Dictation of notes that are typed later will lead to a clear chart, but the notes must be transcribed quickly to make data accessible. An alternative approach employs using a word processor that can print a paper copy immediately.

Recording of data is facilitated by forms that have preprinted checklists, although finding a balance between too much and too little structure takes some experimentation. Medical records are being devised that guide the clinician through the management of complicated disorders, such as asthma. These ''care maps'' ask for specific information, reminding the clinician that certain steps should be taken. Every chart should contain a problem list, a place for prominent notation of any drug allergies or idiosyncrasies, and a location for documenting ongoing medications; all three could go on one page. Immunizations and screening tests should be recorded on an easily accessible sheet. Growth charts should be easy to find, and laboratory sheets, radiologic reports, and letters from consultants should be in a logical sequence. Flowcharts for specific conditions, such as diabetes, clarify the pattern of ongoing care. Thick records will benefit from tabbed dividers.

Documentation of telephone calls is critical and can enhance care immeasurably. If medications, particularly controlled substances, are renewed, that information must be recorded. In this day of managed care, recording of referrals made to specialists is worth the effort.

Filing systems come in many configurations. Make sure enough room is allowed for the inevitable expansion that comes with a growing practice. A tracking system that indicates where a record is located when it is not filed will save countless hours of staff time.

APPOINTMENTS, BILLING, AND REGISTRIES

Appointments and billing systems are subjects beyond the scope of this chapter. The practitioner is well advised to look at a number of existing situations for ideas and to consult freely with relevant advisers, such as an accountant. A few practical ideas may be of use to the reader.

Appointment books can fill quickly with routine examinations, especially in a busy office. Demand for this service is quite variable; when school nurses send home physical forms and when summer camp is looming, everyone wants a checkup. At other times, such as midwinter, far fewer requests come in. It is a good idea to encourage parents to make appointments for physicals in the month of the child's birthday. This arrangement will balance things considerably; forms can be filled out when necessary, using the data from the last checkup, assuming it was not too long ago.

If the appointment sheet is filled with well-child visits, ill children must be sandwiched in, and a hectic situation may ensue. One can color-code appointments in advance—either on paper or on a computer—and schedule only the number of well-child visits that will allow sufficient time for the acutely ill. For example, a green check mark can be put in front of four time slots on a given afternoon, designating those times for older children's physicals. Four more slots might be preceded by a blue check, which means for well-baby examination. The other spaces receive a red check and are used for sick and follow-up visits. When all the well-child slots are filled on a given day, no more physicals are scheduled. By trial and error, one soon can judge how many red spaces are needed at various times of the year and how many blue spaces will be required to keep the babies coming in on time. The remaining time goes to the older children. This system has the disadvantage of putting checkups on older children into the future a bit, but it has the decided advantage of allowing sufficient time for sudden illness or injury, a feature that makes good sense to parents.

It also is a good idea to put aside a block of time each week for conferences or other long visits. This block ensures that the time will be available if needed. If not filled in advance, this time can be used for last-minute illness appointments.

One feature of billing worth keeping in mind is the ''superbill.'' This form contains on it enough identifying, financial, and diagnostic data to allow it to be used as a charge slip, a submission form for insurance purposes, and a receipt for the patient, because a copy is generated. Diagnostic and procedural codes can be printed. A line can be left for recording the next appointment.

An age-gender registry will prove valuable in many ways. If the office is not computerized, every patient will have name, address, and birth date recorded on a 3- × 5-inch card, with a different color for girls and boys. The cards are filed by gender and birth date. When a new family joins the practice, new cards are made; when a family leaves, the cards are withdrawn. Naturally, it is easier to start such a registry with a new practice; but an established office can catch up by having clerical helpers, such as high school students, make cards for the patients already in the practice.

The registry allows the physician to keep a constant eye on the size of the practice. It also can be used as a research tool. One can find the names of all children of a given age who might be the subjects needed for a study.

A variation on this theme is the morbidity or disease index. If the physician codes each visit, he or she can keep track of the kinds of problems being treated and also can generate a list of all children who have a given condition. Such a tool is invaluable if, for instance, one wants to conduct an intervention study of children who are at higher risk for otitis media. The index can be simplified by including only those patients who have chronic conditions. A fair amount of clerical work is involved in these systems, although a computer will make things much easier.

TEACHING AIDS

Teaching is an important part of all medical care and assumes special importance in pediatrics, with its emphasis on prevention of problems and anticipatory guidance. Of course, teaching should occur every time the clinician discusses an element of nutrition, growth, or development or gives instructions on the care of a sick child. Certain aids can be used to reinforce or amplify oral instructions.

Written handouts can be found in infinite variety, but for routine well and illness care, the clinician should consider writing personal handouts. A one-page sheet that is custom-written for each well-baby visit contains the specific salient points each clinician feels are important for that particular age. The material reinforces what was discussed at the visit and also reflects the individual style of that clinician. The sheet given at the 4-month visit may have a large section on feeding, whereas the 18-month sheet may concentrate on discipline. Injury prevention techniques can be reinforced. Some parents refer to the handouts frequently and remark years later about how helpful they were; others drop them in the parking lot. The physician needs to know the characteristics

of the practice, but many parents profit from a later leisurely review of the doctor's instructions on, for instance, a relaxed approach to toilet training, especially if the original discussion was held while struggling with a crying toddler. One also may choose to write sheets on certain aspects of illness, such as fever and diarrhea. Good commercial handouts that one is allowed to duplicate are also available.

In the course of practice, other kinds of written material will be called for frequently. The clinician will save time if copies are readily available of instructions and advice on reducing diets, lactose-free diets, and choosing a good car seat. Pamphlets on subjects such as sex education, which require more extensive treatment than one sheet can provide, should be available to parents who request them. Bibliographies of books on subjects such as divorce or helping a child deal with death also are very helpful.

These written materials are not a substitute for the clinician's personal advice and guidance. They are useful, however, in an adjunct role and can be used to document to insurers that one is giving extensive anticipatory guidance.

Some physicians have found value in educational presentations such as self-contained slide shows or short videotape programs. A machine can be put into the waiting room that has either a fixed format or a choice of programs. Anticipatory advice can be given, or a common illness such as otitis media can be explained. As with written material, the clinician should consider putting together a personal audiovisual presentation.

One should not overlook the value of a well-placed poster or two. A brief but important point brought to the attention of a parent or older child at a receptive moment might make an impact.

THE OFFICE LIBRARY

Hardly a day passes without the clinician's needing to look something up in a reference book. A relatively small library can provide the answers to most questions immediately, especially if it is kept current. Naturally, a reference library is not a substitute for ongoing self-education. It can, however, supply a critical piece of information in the midst of a busy day.

Information about prescriptions and dosing is required frequently and is in constant need of updating. A current textbook of pediatric therapeutics can describe the treatment of an unusual disorder or supplement the physician's approach to something common. *Physicians' Desk Reference,* which is a compendium of information supplied by pharmaceutical manufacturers, readily answers questions about dosage, concentration, bottle size, adverse reactions, and similar practical matters. Another compendium of pharmaceuticals that has a great deal of clinical information is *Facts and Comparisons,* which comes in bound, looseleaf, and electronic editions. To round out the references on prescribing, the physician is well advised to subscribe to one of the brief, practice-oriented looseleaf letter-journals that come frequently and often seem to have that elusive fact needed in a given situation. Some of these journals deal exclusively with drugs and therapeutics; others are general in scope and apply to many clinical situations. Many offices find it helpful to have on hand issues of a review journal, such as *Pediatrics in Review,* which is available both in print and on CD-ROM.

Infectious diseases commonly pose questions, and many pediatricians turn first to the American Academy of Pediatrics' *Report of the Committee on Infectious Diseases,* commonly called the "Red Book." More extensive coverage of specific disorders is found in a textbook of infectious diseases, one of which is worth purchasing. County and state health departments mail infectious disease newsletters, and a file containing these updates can be invaluable.

Skin conditions are encountered frequently in pediatrics. A textbook of pediatric dermatology will be consulted often. Pictures in a textbook can be used to teach parents, especially if different phases of a condition can be demonstrated. Information on poisoning and on plant ingestion is often needed in a hurry, and books on these subjects should be part of the library. Plant books that have many pictures are especially helpful.

Dust off the atlas of anatomy from medical school days and take it to the office. Especially when dealing with injuries, the ability to demonstrate the exact structure involved in a patient's condition greatly enhances the communication.

Unusual eye findings come along often enough to warrant the acquisition of a textbook of pediatric ophthalmology, especially one written for the pediatrician.

A case can be made for specialized texts in other areas, such as orthopedics, endocrinology, and pediatric emergencies; each physician should determine his or her own specific needs. Of course, one must not overlook the general pediatric references. No office library is complete without a current textbook of general pediatrics, which will be consulted repeatedly. Current versions of the handy "peripheral brain" from residency also will see heavy use.

Finally, the pediatrician should have a file

drawer in which can be organized and stored the latest guidelines on child abuse reporting, the directory of area nursery schools, normal laboratory values from the local hospital, and the many other pieces of information that should be within reach when needed quickly.

EMERGENCY EQUIPMENT

Some physicians will need emergency equipment more often than others, depending on the nature of their practices and the proximity of a hospital or other emergency facility. Certain basic items should be considered (see Further Reading at the end of the chapter for two comprehensive references).

A bag and masks should be available to provide artificial respiration, with a small oxygen tank and proper connectors. One can buy disposable bags, making it feasible to have several sizes. Oropharyngeal airways also are necessary, and some would add a laryngoscope that has several sizes of blades and endotracheal tubes. Intravenous solutions, tubing, and needles, at least on a small scale, should be handy, as well as vials of intravenous glucose and bicarbonate solutions. In lieu of an intravenous pole, one may install an ordinary lamp hook in the ceiling. The seriously dehydrated child or the diabetic patient who is hypoglycemic may well require intravenous therapy urgently.

Several drugs should be kept with the emergency equipment, including drugs for seizures, epinephrine, and vials of antibiotics and parenteral corticosteroids. A chart of dosages should be kept in the same place.

Other drugs, tracheostomy equipment, and additional pieces of equipment may be considered by each physician. **But whatever the composition of the emergency cart, office staff must check it frequently and participate in periodic drills to make sure that things will run smoothly in an actual emergency.**

Eye injuries occur regularly, and their care is facilitated by an eye tray, on which is kept irrigating solution, fluorescein strips, mydriatic drops, antibiotic preparations, and patches. Corneal abrasions are so common that the purchase of a Wood's light is justified, to be used with fluorescein staining. Trays that contain equipment and drugs for ear problems also are helpful but should be kept separate to avoid inadvertent use of ear drops in the eye.

There are specialized surgical instruments that can be extremely helpful to the pediatrician. For example, a reverse forceps (Hegenbarth clip-applying forceps) facilitates the removal of foreign objects from the nose. When the sides are pressed together, the tips move further apart, allowing movement of the tips beyond the object. An instrument shaped like a clamp with finely pointed, angled tips makes the removal of splinters much easier (Peet splinter forceps). The physician's supply house representative can help in the selection of these and other useful surgical tools, including the proper instruments for simple suturing and a small autoclave.

In recent years a number of physicians have invested in a pulse oximeter to gauge the degree of oxygen saturation in patients who have asthma or bronchiolitis. A nebulizer for treating patients experiencing bronchospasm is a staple in many offices, and some have extra units that can be sent home with patients for temporary use until they can obtain their own. Teaching and support obviously must accompany the dispensing of a home nebulizer.

THE OFFICE COMPUTER

Computer science brings exciting promise to pediatric offices, as it does to society in general. This complex, rapidly changing field cannot be covered adequately in a textbook chapter, but certain general principles will guide the physician who is interested in computerizing the office (also see Chapter 17).

At present, many offices are using computers for billing—a necessity as managed care increases the complexity of the billing process—and for appointments. Selective data retrieval, such as the printing of a list of all patients who have asthma, also is available.

A much broader view of the capability of computers (Zurhellen, 1995) envisions an office in which a spectrum of functions are performed by the computer, ranging from an electronic medical record that can be used by more than one person at a time, to prescriptions and customized instructions for each patient that can be printed right in the examining room. No doubt even this vision will be expanded in years to come.

The first task is to *decide which functions lend themselves to computerization in your office.* Sometimes simpler systems are more efficient in a given setting; just because a job can be computerized does not mean it should. The next step is to *find out what programs are available to do those tasks.* More choices are available each year. Start with local colleagues who have had experience. Guidance can be obtained also by contacting the American Academy of Pediatrics, which stays abreast of computer applications in pediatrics.

When you know what is needed to achieve your goals, *investigate appropriate vendors.* Your local colleagues again will come in handy. For most offices, investing in a comprehensive package that includes hardware, software, and ongoing service makes sense. Thoroughly investigate the company with whom you will be working. Review the contract and include in it all the important issues you can think of. Be absolutely sure you understand what is involved in the changeover from your present system to the new one. Delays of literally months, when no bills are sent out, are not unheard of.

It is money well spent to find an independent consultant to work with you in shopping for, choosing, setting up, and troubleshooting a system. Such a resource person should not be selling anything but expertise.

Aside from the main system that performs office functions, the physician should consider having a personal computer in the office that can make use of the expanding library of educational resources, including those available on the Internet.

Finally, facsimile (fax) machines offer so many advantages for instant communication and are so reasonably priced that every office should give serious consideration to investing in this tool.

FURTHER READING

American Academy of Pediatrics (AAP), Committee on Practice and Ambulatory Medicine: Management of Pediatric Practice, 2nd ed. Elk Grove Village, IL, American Academy of Pediatrics, 1991.

Baren JM and Seidel JS: Emergency drugs. Pediatr Rev 16:229–238, 1995.

Calhoun JH: Eye examinations in infants and children. Pediatr Rev 18:28–31, 1997.

Facts and Comparisons. St. Louis, MO, Facts and Comparisons, 1998. Phone: 1-800-223-0554.

Physicians' Desk Reference. Montvale, NJ, Medical Economics Company, Inc., 1998.

Seidel JM: Preparing for pediatric emergencies. Pediatr Rev 16:467–472, 1995.

Zurhellen WM: The computerization of ambulatory pediatric practice. Pediatrics 96(Suppl):835–842, 1995.

MAGAZINES FOR CHILDREN

The first five magazines are published by Children's Better Health Institute, 1100 Waterway Boulevard, Box 567, Indianapolis, IN 46206, and all emphasize health-related themes.

Turtle. Ages 2 to 5.
Humpty Dumpty's Magazine. Ages 4 to 6.
Children's Playmate. Ages 6 to 8.
Jack and Jill. Ages 6 to 8.
Child Life. Ages 9 to 11.
Highlights for Children. Ages 2 to 12. PO Box 182167, Columbus, OH 43218-2167.

Ranger Rick. Ages 6 to 12. Nature theme. PO Box 777, Mt. Morris, IL 61054.

Contact Kids. Ages 8 to 12. Science emphasis. PO Box 7690, Red Oak, IA 51591-0690.

National Geographic World. Ages 8 to 13. Geography theme. PO Box 63001, Tampa, FL 33663-3001.

Sports Illustrated for Kids. Ages 8 to 13. Sport theme. PO Box 830609, Birmingham, AL 35283-0609.

Boy's Life. Ages 8 to 18. Primarily of interest to boys. PO Box 152079, Irving, TX 75015-2079.

Seventeen. Teen and young adult. Primarily of interest to girls. 850 Third Ave, New York, NY 10022.

Charles Homer

Chapter 78

Improving Quality in Your Practice

Clinicians caring for children want to provide the best possible care for the children they serve. Nonetheless, good intentions do not always translate into good care. Quality improvement activities are mechanisms aimed at assuring that clinicians who care for children, and the systems in which they work, are indeed meeting these intentions.

BACKGROUND

The field of quality improvement has seen great ferment, innovation, and research that directly affect the way that practice is delivered. The intense interest in quality of care derives from several sources. Research over 2 decades documents substantial variation in care. These large variations suggest that **issues other than a patient's clinical condition influence practice decisions and that practice is not linked closely to scientific data.** Other studies document gaps between desired and actual practice, for example, rates of immunization are far from 100%, and tympanostomy tube placement does not meet criteria for appropriateness in more than one out of five cases. These observations prompted finding new ways to improve quality of care.

While this positive impetus to improve care grew, the enormous cost of the health care system led to pressures to reduce health care costs. In the face of this pressure, managed care organizations had little incentive to maintain quality. In order to balance this one-sided response, both patient and provider organizations sought to develop measures of quality of care that could be used to hold health plans accountable for their performance and give employers a yardstick against which they could

assess a plan's quality. These measurement programs—most prominently the Health Employer Data and Information Set (HEDIS) of the National Commission of Quality Assurance, but also measurement sets from the Foundation for Accountability (FACCT) and others—have heightened awareness of quality. Unfortunately, the absence of good pediatric measures from these measurement sets also highlighted the vulnerability of children to initiatives that focus on care of adults. The rudimentary nature of even the adult-oriented measures raises concern about the viability of this approach as a long-term strategy to assure a quality focus. Concerted efforts are now under way to work with the organizations to develop improved measures for children's health services; meanwhile, clinicians are being assessed by these flawed indicators.

A third stream influencing the renewed focus on quality is the greater societal value placed on patient and family autonomy and decision making in health care. This trend has been accelerated by the activities of advocacy organizations emphasizing patient-centered and family-centered care, particularly for persons who have chronic conditions. These activities have led to a greater focus on the interpersonal aspects of health services and a broad acknowledgment of deficiencies in this area.

These three streams, taken together, have triggered the renewed interest in improving quality of care in general and for children in particular.

DEFINING QUALITY OF CARE

Quality of care is the extent to which health services are likely to achieve their stated goal, which is the maximization of health. For children, personal health services include health supervision, the care of acute conditions, and the management of chronic illness. These health services are made up of clinical actions and interactions with patients and families. In order for care to achieve its intended goal, these **services should be necessary (all necessary care is provided) and appropriate (no unnecessary care is delivered), of high technical quality (the right thing is done right), and delivered with dignity and respect.** These actions take place within a system of care and are intended to change the likelihood of an outcome. The challenge in improving care is how to choose which actions to change and then how to make the changes occur.

HOW TO IMPROVE

No single strategy has been shown clearly to be the best approach to improving care. Nonetheless, some concepts are broadly accepted that help shape improvement activities.

Two general themes underlie efforts at quality improvement. **First, for improvements to be of value, they must be important to patients**—the ultimate "customer" for the services that clinicians provide. **Second, most improvements require changes in systems—that is, the way people and things interact—rather than better motivation, different intent, or acquisition of knowledge alone.**

Studies of quality improvement in several industries and observations of such efforts in health care suggest several necessary prerequisites for successful efforts:

- The process of improvement requires *leadership*. Such leadership can operate at different levels—a health system, a community, or a practice. The role of leadership includes choosing a target, or targets, for improvement and then facilitating access to resources that will enable this aim to be achieved.
- A group charged with seeking improvement should choose a *measure* by which success can be assessed.
- The program should identify likely *strategies* that might achieve the intended goal.
- Finally, the program should *test* these strategies, see whether they achieve the intended results, and modify their approach depending on what they find. Many current initiatives to improve quality, including clinical practice guidelines, patient-centered care, and management of disease, can be incorporated into this framework.

IMPROVING QUALITY OF AMBULATORY CARE FOR CHILDREN

Efforts to improve ambulatory pediatrics should encompass the array of health services provided to children, including prevention and health supervision, acute care services, and management of chronic disease. These efforts should seek to affect outcomes of care, recognizing that changing outcomes requires focusing on processes of care and, to a lesser extent, the structure of care. Efforts to improve quality should not only address the technical aspects of care—whether a diagnosis is accurate or the right therapy provided, but interpersonal and equitable aspects as well. These interpersonal components of care include whether patients and families are provided opportunity to ask questions, receive understandable answers, obtain appropriate emotional support, and participate in decision making. The equitable aspects address whether all those in need of services receive them equally, as well as whether those who did not need services did not receive them.

CHOOSING AN AIM

The selection of an aim for improvement should be guided by several considerations. Aims may be imposed on a program by the need to meet external auditing requirements, such as those of HEDIS. Although such aims may be consonant with priorities of patients and staff, they often may be perceived as irrelevant or distracting from more important concerns. A better approach would be to **focus on problems that are common, ones that cause great morbidity, or ones that are the greatest importance to families.** Alternatively, a practice may seek first to address a relatively simple problem in order to achieve success and build enthusiasm for the improvement process. Clinicians may choose to poll their staff about priorities for improvement, to examine patient complaints or reasons for patients leaving a practice or even to undertake a broad baseline assessment of care. Clinicians who have advanced data systems may be able to use encounter or cost data to target areas for improvement. One particular indicator that a topic may be ripe for improvement is known variability in care and in outcomes.

Just as scientific hypotheses should state a direction and magnitude of effect, aims for improvement should not only indicate the topic, but specify the degree of improvement that is being sought. Improvement theory suggests that aims that are too small can be achieved on a short-term basis by exhortation alone and thus will not be sustained. On the other hand, aims that are too distant will appear overwhelming and may discourage initiative. If the aim is actually achieved, it can be reset at a yet higher level.

MEASUREMENT

Measurement poses one of the most vexing components of efforts to improve care. In order to assess whether changes are making a difference, some mechanism for ongoing measurement is necessary. Unfortunately, most care environments are ill-prepared for measurement. Most data systems in health care are slow, cumbersome, and inaccurate, with long delays between data collection and data reports. Many important aspects of care are challenging to measure, such as technical skill, interpersonal communication, or the failure to receive care. In addition, the culture of medical research is highly attuned to issues of bias and chance and strives to exclude these. This effort to avoid error makes measurement a costly (in time, dollars, and complexity) operation.

The pressure to produce data at a reasonable cost with a rapid turnaround time has prompted two complementary approaches to measurement for quality improvement work. In the short-term, many are seeking to develop inexpensive ways to assess care—such as through the use of small samples and the selection of proxy measures (such as the interval between adverse events). In the longer run, some sites are making long-term investments in data systems that will facilitate improvement over time. These sites include some inpatient settings, such as the Vermont Oxford Neonatal Network, as well as some managed care and integrated delivery systems.

SELECTING STRATEGIES THAT WORK

Practice Guidelines

Once an aim is selected and a measurement strategy identified, the challenge of choosing a promising approach emerges. Clinical practice guidelines are widely used to identify potential mechanisms to meet clinically oriented aims for improvement. **Practice guidelines are "systematically developed statements to assist practitioner and patient decisions about appropriate health care for specific clinical circumstances."** Such guidelines can cover simple clinical decisions such as when to order a radiograph for a particular type of injury or can seek to guide the management of an entire clinical entity, such as asthma, over time. The characteristic that distinguishes the current efforts at guideline development from previous policy and consensus statements is their reliance on rigorous assessment of published evidence and then the combination of this evidence through techniques such as meta-analysis. The use of this evidence-based approach characterized the development of guidelines at the Agency for Health Care Policy and Research, as well as the approach still in use by the American Academy of Pediatrics for their practice parameters (Table 78–1).

The process of evidence-based guideline development, particularly defining the structure of the clinical problem and identifying and reviewing the literature, is slow and expensive, beyond the capacity of most health care organizations. A more efficient mechanism for local health care systems is to build on existing evidence-based guidelines, reviewing their content and adopting them to function in the local care environment without changing their fundamental scientific basis. Such processes are widely used in managed care and community-based improvement activities.

Developing or even adapting a clinical practice guideline by itself does little to improve care. The **content of the guideline must not only be disseminated to clinicians but they must accept the validity of the recommendations and incorporate them into their daily practice.** Incorporating a new way of providing care typically entails identifying system barriers to the desired approach and changing the system so that desired practice occurs as a default. For example, the practice guidelines for the management of asthma released by the National Asthma Education and Prevention Program of the National Heart, Lung, and Blood Institute in 1991 recommended that primary care clinicians assess lung function with either peak flowmeters or spirometry at every visit. In order for clinicians to make this change in practice, they not only need to believe that it's valuable but they also need to have the equipment available in the office, accessible when needed, preferably have a space marked on the patient record to record the information, and possibly even having an office assistant obtain the measurement prior to the encounter. This approach—identification of system-based barriers to care and implementation of interventions targeting these barriers—has been applied to both preventive services and asthma treatment in pediatric practice, with both showing positive results.

Some barriers to implementing practice guidelines are embedded in systems outside the purview

TABLE 78–1. Recent and Upcoming Guidelines for Pediatrics

Guideline	Date
American Academy of Pediatrics (AAP)	
The office management of acute exacerbations of asthma in children	January 1994
Management of hyperbilirubinemia in the healthy term newborn	October 1994
Managing otitis media with effusion in young children	November 1994
Management of acute gastroenteritis in young children	March 1996
Neurodiagnostic imaging of a child who has a first simple febrile seizure	May 1996
Minor head trauma	Under development
Urinary tract infection	Under development
Moderate head trauma	Under development
Wheezing in young children	Under development
Diabetes mellitus	Under development
Treatment of febrile seizures	Under development
Developmental dysplasia of the hip	Under development
Attention-deficit hyperactivity disorder	Under development
Sinusitis	Under development
Agency for Health Care Policy and Research	
Acute pain management	1992
Sickle cell disease	1993
Evaluation and management of early HIV infection	1994
Managing otitis media with effusion in young children (same as AAP)	1994
National Institutes of Health—National Heart, Lung, and Blood Institute	
National Asthma Education and Prevention Program: Guidelines for the diagnosis and management of asthma	1991, 1997

of a particular practice. For example, while the asthma guidelines recommend extended teaching for patients about managing their asthma, financial pressures limit the amount of time clinicians can spend with each patient. In addition, clinicians may not be fully aware of a patient's actual medication use or use of acute care services and thus underestimate the patient's illness severity. **Disease management is a more global approach that seeks to improve outcomes and reduce costs through integrating the different components of the care delivery system by using information systems and clinical guidelines and assessing outcomes.**

Disease Management

Disease management attempts to address many of these barriers by applying practice guidelines to a population that has a particular condition and recasting the physician as a deliverer rather than the director of care. It posits that managing all the costs of care comprehensively, rather than seeking to minimize the costs of each component of care, will result in improvements both in health and in the financial bottom line. Disease management firms can use information technology to monitor costs and outcomes over time to assess the effectiveness of their interventions and make modifications in their program in response. The concept of

such feedback loops—between guidelines, process improvement, and outcomes—was articulated a decade ago as the promise of the "outcomes revolution" in health care.

Disease management programs often are operated by pharmacy benefits management companies, businesses that provide pharmacy services to managed care. Such companies have access to medication data and can identify patients for services based on their drug use, such as frequent beta agonist refills. Asthma has been one of the main conditions targeted by disease management. In a typical program, patients are first identified through pharmacy claims (e.g., for beta agonists or inhaled glucocorticoids) and visit encounters. Patients are categorized into different levels of costs based on similar data. Specific services may be targeted to patients in each cost group. For example, patients who have only ambulatory visits but no emergency department encounters may be sent educational materials and invited to group educational sessions. Patients who have intermediate expenditures may be offered a visit or visits by a home health agency to provide more intensive teaching and assess the home environment. Pharmacy claims for these patients may be reviewed and clinicians notified if the patient is not receiving anti-inflammatory treatment. If a patient is in a higher cost group, the clinician may be encouraged to refer the patient to a specialist or a "center of excellence," and the plan may assign a case manager.

Benchmarking

Another approach widely used in industry is the process of *benchmarking*. **Benchmarking consists of two steps. In the first step, sites compare their care and identify good performers** (so called "best practices"). **In the second step—one often overlooked in health care improvement activities—sites gain a detailed understanding of the processes of care that the better performers use.** For some aspects of care, best performers may be outside the health care industry. Disney, for example, is a commonly viewed exemplar for managing waiting time and customer service.

For some aspects of care (such as reducing waiting time), the broad concepts underlying best practices have been identified and are published in the management literature.

Benchmarking initiatives in clinical care obviously require working with health care programs. Most benchmarking activities in pediatrics have involved inpatient care—particularly both pediatric and, more extensively, neonatal intensive care. Whether such activities can be applied to ambulatory care, with fewer resources available for measurement and fewer adverse outcomes for comparison, is uncertain. One example of at least partial benchmarking in ambulatory care is the Ambulatory Care Quality Improvement Program (ACQIP) project of the American Academy of Pediatrics. In this program, subscribers self-audit practice processes on a limited basis and then send their data to the ACQIP office. Data from all participating practices are entered, and each program receives information on its performance relative to peers. In addition, practices are given general recommendations for good practice, elicited from the literature and experts.

TESTS OF CHANGE

Practice guidelines, the benchmarking of initiatives, and even disease management all provide "off the shelf" strategies that can inform a practice or system that seeks to improve care. Such strategies, nonetheless, need to be customized to a given care environment and then tested and modified according to the results. This process of repeated testing, termed PDSA, or Plan–Do–Study–Act in quality improvement jargon, appears to characterize practices and programs that improve over time.

Among the best-known applications of this approach to improving clinical care is the Breakthrough series. Organized by the Institute for Healthcare Improvement, a Boston-based program that seeks to promote quality improvement in health care, this initiative recruits organizations—typically hospitals and managed care organizations—to participate in a collaborative "improvement" activity. This activity consists of endorsing specific improvement aims; training in both the broad underpinnings of quality improvement and the successful broad strategies, or "change concepts," that apply to the clinical problem under consideration; initiating, supporting, and reporting on cycles of testing and improvement; and sharing the results of the initiatives with other participants and with a broader audience. Among participating organizations, those who implemented change cycles earlier and more often were more likely to achieve the aims of the initiative compared with organizations slower and less prolific in trying new approaches.

SUMMARY

The documentation of variability in care and gaps in performance has focused attention on the need for improvement; the study of practice change and improvement in industry has removed the personally punitive edge that long characterized quality assurance. Now that the need for improvement has been highlighted, child health clinicians need to become engaged in such activities. Researchers need to continue to develop the evidence base on which strong recommendations for care can be based. Clinicians and measurement scientists knowledgeable about children must take this knowledge and create measures of care that truly reflect what is known about the best ways to care for children. At the practice level, efforts to improve should encompass preventive- and illness-oriented care and should target technical, interpersonal, and equitable practice. Approaches in which practices might engage include adapting and implementing a practice guideline, developing a program to identify parental perspectives about care and their responses; or partnership with community agencies to improve services relevant to child health—such as violence prevention—at the community level, using these same tools. In taking these types of initiatives, clinicians caring for children cannot only regain the initiative in quality improvement from health system management, but can provide better care to the children they serve.

FURTHER READING

Bauchner H, Homer C, Salem-Schatz S, and Adams W: The status of pediatric practice guidelines. Pediatrics 99:876–881, 1997.

Bergman DA: Thriving in the 21st century: Outcome assessment, practice parameters, and accountability. Pediatrics 96:831–835, 1995.

Berwick D: Continuous improvement as an ideal in health care. N Engl J Med 320:53–56, 1989.

Berwick DM: A primer on leading the improvement of systems. BMJ 312:619–622, 1996.

Cleary P and McNeil B: Patient satisfaction as an indicator of quality of care. Inquiry 25:25–36, 1988.

Epstein R and Sherwood L: From outcomes research to disease management: A guide for the perplexed. Ann Intern Med 124:832–837, 1996.

Francis V, Korsch B, and Morris M: Gaps in doctor-patient communication. N Engl J Med 280:535–540, 1969.

Homer C, Grossman R, and Rodman J: Pediatric guidelines: Help or hindrance? Curr Opin Pediatr 8:432–435, 1996.

Plsek P: Collaborating across organizational boundaries to improve the quality of care. Am J Infect Control 25:85–95, 1997.

PART C

THE PEDIATRICIAN AND INTERNATIONAL HEALTH PERSPECTIVES

Robert J. Haggerty

Chapter **79**

The Increasingly Global Village

Just as the world is becoming a global marketplace, so too is it becoming a global village as far as child health is concerned. Few boundaries exist to the spread of disease. With rapid air travel, a child in India who has the plague can infect persons in the Western world within 24 hours. Indeed, such a potential epidemic of plague as a result of air travel occurred a few years ago, with at least 11 travelers to the United States being suspected of having plague. Drug-resistant tuberculosis and drug-resistant pneumococcus infections travel the world. Popular books and movies now paint a grim picture of the potential of infectious agents such as the Ebola virus from Africa attacking susceptible populations and causing a modern-day plague throughout the world.

Immigration and migration are occurring at unprecedented levels throughout the world, mainly from the developing world to the developed, with both Europe and the United States receiving large numbers of recent immigrants. However, in the past few years, migrations as a result of war in the former Yugoslavia and in Central Africa have made even the large-scale migration from Southeast Asia to the United States during the 1970s and 1980s, or indeed the large-scale migration to the United States in the late 19th century, seem minuscule. There are no parts of the United States unaffected by immigration, although obviously the coasts and borders as entry points experience more immigrants. Pediatric practices throughout the country have patients who speak languages other than English and who have different cultural values.

Another aspect of the globalization of health is the large number of pediatricians and other health care personnel from the United States who have served or who wish to serve in developing coun-

The Increasingly Global Village • **545**

tries. Issues of how to deal with cultural differences among a clinician's patients, whether in the United States or abroad, are covered in Chapter 22. There remains, however, the question of what the U.S. clinician's role should be in international child health. In the United States, understanding and acceptance of their language and cultural values must be the bedrock of caring effectively for children from other cultures. In working overseas we must acknowledge that broader socioeconomic issues are the major causes of illness in developing countries and overwhelm most health concerns of families in the developing world. Without a job, a home, potable drinking water, a sewer system, and adequate food, many families find health care a relatively low priority.

Female literacy is one area in which clinicians in the United States, under the "Ready to Read" program initiated at Boston University, have set a model for initiating literacy of mothers and of children within inner-city practices. The same principles can be used in developing countries, with good effect. For instance, in Sri Lanka, where the gross national product is the same as India's but female literacy is nearly 100%, the infant mortality is now lower than 20 per 1000; in India it is more than 70 per 1000, and female literacy is no more than 30%. Indeed, even within India itself, the power of literacy is shown in the province of Kerala, which has an 80% female literacy rate and an infant mortality that is under 20 per 1000. Female literacy facilitates implementation of successful family planning, early and successful prenatal and perinatal care of mother and child, and the ability to use the GOBI program successfully (Table 79–1).

That does not mean, however, that clinical care is unimportant. First, for the Western-trained clinician working abroad, the application of skilled, curative, and preventive medicine to individual patients in a dedicated and selfless way is, in itself, a major contribution. The question of what part of Western medicine should be brought to the developing world, however, is an issue of priorities. Although many in the developing world reject Western cultures, especially within nationalistic

movements, there is an almost universal acceptance of Western medicine in these countries. **The challenge is how can we as pediatricians be helpful and feel fulfilled in the arena of international health, yet recognize limited resources and ensure that what we provide emphasizes the use of appropriate technologies rather than the newest fad in Western medical armamentaria.**

Second, the clinician working abroad must understand population medicine, advocate for environmental changes that promote health, and use simplified clinical algorithms. For instance, major advances in the health of children in the developing world have occurred as a result of the implementation of the United Nations Children's Fund (formerly UNICEF) program popularly called GOBI (see Table 79–1). It was a stroke of communication genius by its director, Mr. James Grant, who emphasized in these simple terms the key ingredients of a successful child health program—ingredients that are available anywhere in the world. Recently, the World Health Organization's new comprehensive Maternal and Child Health Program, which emphasizes the care of the mother as well as of the child, has developed an integrated system of caring for the sick child. This program includes simple assessment of the patient, with the basis for initiating appropriate therapy being an understanding of the epidemiologic nature of illness in one's community, rather than a precise diagnosis of each patient's disease. For instance, in areas that have no malaria, a small child who has a fever of 39°C and a respiratory rate of 40 should be treated for pneumonia. That may sound like regression, but it has been shown that this approach is more effective in maximizing the benefits to as many patients as possible.

Third, the clinician working abroad must understand the cultural use of alternative medicines in most developing countries (and indeed in the United States) and allow their use when they are not harmful.

Many have questioned the importance of saving individual children's lives when excessive fertility is such a major problem in the developing world. It now seems clear that **in order for most parents to decide to limit their families, they must believe that most of the children will survive.** Thus, we need to combine the dedicated care to save each child with the long-term goal of reducing fertility, improving the status and literacy of women and children, and improving the environment.

Finally, there are the profound ethical issues. Some argue that as physicians we must remain committed only to the call of the individual patient. However, if we cure the baby's diarrhea only to have him or her go home to a polluted water

TABLE 79–1. UNICEF GOBI Program

G	Growth monitoring
O	Oral rehydration
B	Breastfeeding
I	Immunization
F	Family planning
F	*Haemophilus influenzae* vaccine
F	Folic acid

supply or lack of food that will induce another tragic, life-threatening episode, our treatment is insufficient. Most of us who engage in international health soon become converted to "population medicine." For those who argue that this may save those unfit for a competitive world, I have to ask: Is it any different than gene therapy? Both change the nature of future populations in ways that we cannot yet fathom.

ADVOCACY

Working in the developing world focuses the clinician's attention very quickly on the causes of illness that lie outside traditional medicine—poor sanitation, inadequate food, poverty, discrimination, war, and disasters. This must lead clinicians to become even more effective advocates for children. The United Nations Convention of the Rights of the Child is an excellent framework for directing one's advocacy. The Convention certifies the right of every child to health care and also to education, a family, and a safe environment. Clinicians who work in developing countries need to join with other groups to ensure that these rights are honored. Such rights, of course, apply to all children, in the developed world as well, and clearly are not available to all children in these countries either. Advocacy for the rights of all children is every clinician's responsibility (see Chapter 72).

WAYS IN WHICH PEDIATRICIANS CAN WORK OVERSEAS

Physicians and other clinicians work abroad as teachers and by giving direct clinical service. Although some teaching efforts can be successful in short-term visits, most efforts should aim at being organized over a long period of time. The most effective way for pediatricians to become involved in international health over time is to work through other organizations. One way is to urge your pediatric society, medical school, or religious group to develop a long-term relationship with a country in need. For instance, the American Academy of Pediatrics' (AAP) program of linkage or "twinning" a medical school in a developing country with a state AAP chapter is one good way. By doing this, exchange programs can be fostered between institutions, personal bonds can be established, and each can begin to understand the other's culture. Such long-term arrangements can avoid many of the problems of short-term visits, which generally should be discouraged. The

TABLE 79–2. Morley's Principles

- An imaginative approach, supported by local customs, must be used.
- Limited funds available must be used.
- Mother and child must not be separated.
- Services need to be near home.
- Senior pediatricians must be involved.
- Pediatricians and team should be teachers.

Data from Morley DC: Pediatric Priorities in the Developing World. London, Butterworths, 1975.

2-week look-and-see visit can do little more than interest one in a developing country and often raise unrealistic expectations. Such short visits, if necessary, should have as their main purpose the planning for an ongoing program and should not be viewed as ends in themselves. If organizations are part of an ongoing effort, individual pediatricians can be used for short periods of time, providing continuity over the long haul.

For provision of clinical services, it is even more important to organize and maintain long-term efforts, if not by one person, then by an organization that can link several clinicians together serially to provide continuity. Health Volunteers Overseas is one such ongoing program. This organization does not undertake a relationship with a particular country until it has a commitment from an organization, such as the AAP, to provide pediatricians over a long period of time, even though each pediatrician may serve no more than 1 month. In addition, such organizations have an excellent orientation course and publications to help prepare pediatricians for work overseas.

Morley (1975), with his long experience in developing countries, has listed the principles that must undergird health programs in developing countries (Table 79–2). Morley's principles should be the goals for all international programs that seek to improve child health. In the long run, in Janeway's (1957) terms, such efforts can "... promote peace by diminishing the causes of wars." As he concluded, pediatricians who participate in exchanges and international activities "will have an infinite variety of cultural adaptations which make humanity so fascinating and will enjoy the great satisfaction of having played an essential role in the creation of one world which technology has produced and that politics has not yet appreciated. In addition, they will have made lasting friendships with fine colleagues in other parts of the world."

FURTHER READING

Janeway CA: Pediatricians for peace. Ann Paediatr Fenn 3:624–634, 1957.
Morley DC: Pediatric Priorities in the Developing World. London, Butterworths, 1975.

PART D

THE ROLE OF THE PRACTITIONER IN PEDIATRIC EDUCATION

Kenneth B. Roberts

Chapter **80**

The Role of the Practitioner in Pediatric Education

A century ago, medical education and training was largely an apprenticeship, with those aspiring to be physicians learning their "trade" from experienced practitioners in the community. Osler emphasized the central role of a teaching hospital, in which the sickest patients could be cared for by teacher-clinicians, permitting multiple students to benefit simultaneously from such experiences. Abraham Flexner, a nonphysician educator, incorporated this idea into his influential report but also planted the seed for a discriminatory division that has persisted when he wrote that a clinical professor should "develop—preferably in close connection with the hospital—a consulting practice, assured thus that his time will not be sacrificed to trivial ailments." Thus began an era of university-based medical education, fueled by the development and proliferation of subspecialties and university hospital–based subspecialists, and a two-class system of physicians, in which hospital-based professors were the elite and clinicians in practice were seen as those whose time was "sacrificed to trivial ailments." Practitioners were progressively replaced as teachers of medical students and residents by full-time faculty and specialists. Indicative of this change is the current rarity, compared with even 30 or 40 years ago, of pediatric chairmen who have practiced general pediatrics at some time in their careers. Nevertheless, the ma-

jority of graduates of pediatric residency programs have entered pediatric practice directly, and many of the others have done so after additional training. **In the past decade, the need for more generalist physicians has become a national concern, and the preparation of residents to assume roles in pediatric primary care has become a focus of considerable interest.** The Pediatric Residency Review Committee, the group that determines the requirements for accreditation of residency programs, now requires a weekly continuity experience for each resident throughout the 3 years of residency. The pendulum has begun to swing back to rediscovering what those in practice have to offer trainees.

Advocates for practitioners as faculty in medical school and residency programs propose that a "complete" program include exposure to and participation with pediatric practitioners, just as it includes exposure to and participation with subspecialists. Moreover, the practitioners' "turf," the office, is important to primary care education, just as the intensive care unit helps define the role of the intensivist. Both primary care and subspecialty pediatrics are legitimate enterprises; both aspire to excellence in clinical care of patients, and both require insightful research to advance the field. University departments of pediatrics can play a valuable role by supporting both and by developing activities that model collaboration.

PRACTITIONERS AS EDUCATORS

Practitioners have much to contribute to the education and training of medical students and residents. Medical students and residents should have the opportunity to meet the members of the specialty; learn what they do; understand how the office setting affects medical decision making and the care rendered; and distinguish style from substance in primary care. Such opportunities are of benefit not only to those considering a career in primary care practice but also to those who are headed for subspecialty careers and those who are undecided. For future clinicians, the transition to practice is facilitated by understanding the role and the office setting. Future subspecialists gain insight into the referral process and collaboration between the general practitioner and the subspecialist. **The goals of establishing a relationship between practitioner and medical students or residents, beyond the content and practice of primary care, are informed career selection, improved cooperation and collaboration between subspecialists and general clinicians, and the facilitation of residents' recognizing and developing their personal clinical style.**

THE VALUE OF THE OFFICE SETTING

For years, many programs have involved practitioners as preceptors in the ambulatory clinics and inpatient services of their hospitals. Although this affords medical students and residents the opportunity to meet these clinicians, it is less successful in providing insight into what they actually do. Practitioner-preceptors in the hospital can instruct about common medical conditions, but they are at a disadvantage applying their skills to a system, population, and disorders with which they may not be that familiar. In their offices, they have a system that works for them, a population they know, and disorders that are, in general, within their expertise. Participating in the office (not merely observing) provides medical students and residents experience and insight into the daily activities of these clinicians (including well-child visits, illness visits, telephone calls, and required paperwork). The effects of the following on patient care are apparent: a relationship over time; the availability of records; high volume and rapid pace; patient expectations; physician expectations;

lack of immediate availability of hospital resources and subspecialists; and mechanism of payment. Because patients who have received hospital-based care are seen in clinicians' offices, medical students and residents gain insight into the nature of collaboration and the transition into long-term care. They experience firsthand (1) the benefit of having a written communication from the subspecialist stating the findings and recommendations from the latest visit or (2) the frustration of not having such information available. There is an opportunity to discern the different relationships between practitioners and consultants: for some children, the subspecialist provides recommendations to the practitioner, who remains the primary physician; in other instances, the disease process is such that the subspecialist, in effect, becomes the primary physician. **Practitioners' offices also afford medical students and residents the opportunity to apply what they have learned in the hospital and to identify which measures are appropriate for primary care and which require the added support of a tertiary care setting; this further eases the transition after residency.**

PRACTITIONERS AS COMMUNITY FACULTY

Practitioners can contribute to education and training at every step of medical education and training. High school and college students who are interested in medicine can relate easily to the role of the pediatrician in the health of children and to the activities of a pediatric office; they also may be excited by the opportunities to affect the health and welfare of children in the larger community, and practitioners can provide many familiar examples of such involvement.

Many medical schools have developed apprenticeship programs for first-year medical students; some continue the relationship through the second year, and some for all 4 years. These longitudinal preceptor programs afford students the opportunity to see actual examples of primary care being practiced and allow students to develop and retain a vision of what most of them went to medical school to be able to do. Some schools have recognized the potential for these programs to be a basis for developing clinical skills, such as interviewing and physical examination skills, longitudinally rather than in a short, intensive course; some use a combination of a course and longitudinal exercises. The pediatrician and his or her office have many advantages over traditional hospital-based environments for learning physical diagnosis. In a relatively brief time, children of all ages are available to students, and many children can be examined for insight into the range of normal. Although abnormalities are found more frequently in hospitalized children, the children and their families are not at their best under the stress of illness, and students may be concerned about causing further distress.

The pediatrics clerkship should provide both inpatient and outpatient experiences, and the practitioner's office is a desirable site for the outpatient portion, with the practitioner as preceptor. Many healthy children are seen, providing the opportunity to learn about well-child care, growth, and development. Children who have minor illnesses are managed as well, and the task of distinguishing children who have more serious illnesses from those who have minor illnesses becomes apparent. Students also are able to see the value of a longitudinal relationship and the critical role of the pediatrician as counselor. Elective experiences during the senior year can help confirm a student's interest in pediatrics as a career and build on previous activities to develop clinical skills further. Projects in the community can be done for experience in community-oriented primary care and public health.

Several residency programs use community practices as sites for the continuity experience of residents, and many more are pursuing this arrangement. Residents assigned to offices rather than to hospital clinics tend to see more patients in a session and to develop skills used in practice, including how to function without all of the resources of a medical center immediately available and to recognize when consultation is needed. The residents serve as links between the practices and the medical center, a benefit to both. Because the continuity experience is weekly, the practitioner-preceptor can get to know the resident's strengths and weaknesses over time and guide and foster his or her development.

In most residencies, opportunities in community practices are a 1-month assignment or an elective. The goal of such an abbreviated experience can only be exposure, rather than competency, but residents attest to the value of such experiences.

Practitioners also may participate in hospital-based activities, such as general inpatient attending rounds or precepting in outpatient activities. Practitioners can contribute to experiences in developmental and behavioral pediatrics, adolescent medicine, child advocacy, and care of handicapped children, depending on their interests; their participation underscores the role of the community practitioner in such activities, which may motivate some residents to become more involved.

Collaborative research is another valuable link, local projects and participation in the national Pediatric Research in Office Settings (PROS) network of the American Academy of Pediatrics being examples. Finally, community practitioners can play important roles on department committees, such as the Residency Education (or Curriculum) Committee.

PREPARATION OF PEDIATRIC PRACTITIONERS AS COMMUNITY FACULTY

To be respected as community faculty, practitioners must first and foremost be excellent clinicians, respected both in the community and at the university for their knowledge, skills, and attitudes. In addition, they must be interested in teaching, role modeling, and mentoring. Moreover, partners, associates, and office staff must be supportive of trainees in the office, because all are affected. Space must be available for the trainee, both to see patients (examination rooms) and for paperwork (a desk). Many medical schools provide computer linkages to offices that have medical students, and space must be available for computer-related activities, such as literature searches. The number of patients seen per day generally is not reduced by supervising medical students, but preceptors tend to spend an additional hour per day in the office. The effect on productivity of including residents is more complex. If the resident participates longitudinally for 3 years, the initial year is balanced roughly between the additional time required and the contributions of the resident to patient care; the balance is maintained during the second year, and the resident's productivity adds significantly to the practice during the third year. One-month assignments or electives are more variable, depending on the level and skill of the resident.

To help practitioners translate enthusiasm for teaching into useful skills, programs of faculty development have been devised. In such programs, practitioners can learn concepts of successful teaching and learning, various strategies to help medical students and residents learn, and skills of evaluation and feedback. **Faculty development programs benefit these practitioners directly by helping them build skills and confidence as teachers;** in addition, they foster relationships with other practitioner-teachers, providing the opportunity for group support and problem solving. Faculty development programs should acknowledge that the participants are adult learners, by using principles of adult learning theory (andragogy rather than pedagogy): Lectures should be brief and kept to a minimum; group discussion should be used to encourage participation and involvement; and the majority of the time should be devoted to practical activities, such as role playing. Developing clinical precepting skills, those skills that relate to the one-on-one interaction of faculty and student or resident who share clinical responsibility for the patient, should be emphasized.

"WHAT'S IN IT" FOR PRACTITIONERS?

Practitioners generally identify the stimulation and satisfaction derived from teaching bright, motivated learners as the primary motivation for participation in such a program. The aphorism "To teach is to learn twice" captures the essence of the benefit of questioning daily what one does and providing explanations clearly and succinctly. Students and residents also can provide the practitioner with new knowledge that helps maintain currency, and their access to resources in the medical school and medical center provides convenient linkages for community practitioners. Students and residents may attend to patients of the practitioner during hospital-based clinic visits with subspecialists, inpatient stays, or emergency department visits, creating additional linkages for the practitioner. Recognition within the professional and lay communities via faculty status may confer prestige. These appointments generally come with additional perquisites, such as access to library facilities and, increasingly, electronic access to e-mail, laboratory results, and in some centers, patient records.

THE "TOWN-GOWN" RELATIONSHIP

Involvement of pediatric practitioners in medical student and resident education creates a "town-gown" relationship of collaboration to mutual benefit rather than independence or indifference. Future practitioners have much to learn from these role models, and future subspecialists can develop valuable insight into their roles as consultants. Practitioners derive benefit from the relationship with the medical center and from involvement in education. Because the goal of all medical school and residency programs should be excellence in both primary care and subspecialty education, the participation of practitioners as community faculty can help to develop programs that provide the best of both worlds.

FURTHER READING

Roberts K and DeWitt T (eds): Pediatric residency education in community settings. Pediatrics 88:1249–1301, 1996.

Roberts K and DeWitt T: Faculty development of pediatric practitioners: Complexities in teaching clinical precepting. Pediatrics 97:389–393, 1996.

Roberts K, Starr S, and DeWitt T: The UMMC office-based continuity experience: Are we preparing pediatrics residents for primary care practice? Pediatrics 100(4):e2 1997.

Sargent J and Osborn L: Resident training in community pediatricians' offices: Not a financial drain. Am J Dis Child 144:1356–1359, 1990.

Sargent J, Osborn L, Roberts K, and DeWitt T: Establishment of primary care continuity experiences in community pediatricians' offices: Nuts and bolts. Pediatrics 91:1185–1189, 1993.

PART E

THE PEDIATRICIAN AND MANAGED CARE

Jeffrey J. Stoddard

Chapter **81**

The Pediatrician and Managed Care

The health care system in the United States has witnessed unprecedented changes over the past 2 decades. Dramatic increases in costs for medical services have led to strong countervailing efforts on the part of both the public and private sectors to restrain such costs. Escalating costs represented the major initial impetus behind federal health reform initiatives in the early 1990s. Since the demise of government-sponsored reform at the national level in 1994, private sector initiatives in health care financing and delivery have become the principal mechanisms by which the controlling of health care costs has been pursued.

Managed care, which has existed for over 50 years, has in the past 15 years become the dominant market mechanism to affect health care costs. Although the growth of managed care initially was slow, its rate of growth in the 1980s and 1990s has been astonishing, both with respect to numbers of managed care organizations and the total population enrolled in managed care plans.

WHAT IS MANAGED CARE?

Managed care describes a variety of health care plans and delivery systems that tend to share one or more of the following characteristics: control over payment for medical services, selective contracting with specific providers, case management (often via a primary care gatekeeper), and reliance on utilization review. Integration of health services delivery systems and health care financing mechanisms (insurance functions) represents the hallmark of a fully developed managed care organization.

HOW WILL MANAGED CARE AFFECT PEDIATRICIANS?

Most practicing pediatricians, whether or not they are involved directly with managed care, are likely to be significantly affected by it. As managed care has become increasingly common as a mechanism of health care financing and service delivery, it has changed many health care markets in ways that affect, directly or indirectly, all providers in those markets, including pediatricians. Few geographic areas remain entirely untouched by managed care. Many pediatricians now work exclusively for managed care organizations; others contract with them; still others retain independence from managed care organizations but face growing competitive pressures exerted by the marketplace competition that managed care brings with it. Determining one's level and type of involvement with managed care remains an individual decision. The following general questions have been suggested by the American Academy of Pediatrics' Committee on Child Health Financing as useful in determining whether managed care organizations and strategies are acceptable:

1. Will participation in the managed care plan expand or solidify the pediatrician's patient base?
2. Does the plan provide a reasonable level of reimbursement without imposing undue risk?
3. Does the plan provide patients adequate access to pediatric care, including access to pediatric specialists?
4. Will involvement with the managed care plan increase or decrease the pediatrician's administrative hassles?
5. Does the managed care plan compromise the pediatrician's ability to provide medical care of high quality?
6. Does the managed care plan contract with hospitals where the pediatrician has (or can receive) clinical privileges?

The pediatrician must consider whether the plan will enhance his or her ability to provide the type of care to the children he or she serves. As a practical matter, the crucial personal consideration for pediatricians in determining whether (or to what degree) to participate in managed care is whether the potential for expansion (or preservation) of one's patient base may be outweighed by lower reimbursement levels or by diminished autonomy.

IMPLICATIONS OF MANAGED CARE

One of the truly positive elements about managed care that appeals to many pediatricians is that many managed care organizations emphasize prevention and wellness. This emphasis is manifested by generous (prepaid) health supervision benefits and preventive service coverage. As a result of these benefits, many pediatric patients enrolled in managed care plans schedule frequent and regular health supervision visits; thus, pediatricians often are better able to monitor their patients' health. Under the traditional fee-for-service (FFS) system, such services often were not covered by indemnity insurance plans, thus resulting in out-of-pocket expenses for conscientious parents and, all too often, foregone care in other cases.

Certain characteristics of managed care plans, however, may have a somewhat detrimental impact on pediatricians and their patients. Some managed care organizations, for example, prefer to contract with small numbers of large group practices rather than with multiple solo or small groups. This obviously can result in problems for those independent pediatricians in certain market areas. In some states, "any willing provider" laws protect such physicians. The implications for pediatricians designated as "gatekeepers" within managed care plans can also be profound. Managed care plans that employ gatekeepers who have little or no training in pediatric care run the risk of serious compromises in the quality of pediatric care. On the other hand, managed care organizations that employ well-trained pediatricians as gatekeepers may provide these pediatricians with an optimal clinical role. Considerations here relate to the plans' expectations regarding the scope of services to be provided directly by the gatekeepers and the circumstances under which referrals and hospitalizations, etc., are deemed appropriate. Related to this is weighing the additional time and effort required to perform gatekeeping functions (i.e., patient care management and coordination services) against the level of additional reimbursement provided for assuming these responsibilities. It is crucial for practicing pediatricians to understand that the financial incentives under managed care are such that the pediatrician as gatekeeper may be penalized financially for providing (or arranging for) costly services and, conversely, financially rewarded for withholding such services. Such a financing arrangement is obviously contrary to traditional fee-for-service medicine, in which providers had an economic incentive to do more rather than less on their patients' behalf (without risk to themselves). Financial incentives under managed care now may create tension between pediatricians' interests in serving their patients' needs and their own financial well-being. Under managed care, tremendous pressure is felt by the gatekeepers to practice medicine prudently and cost-effectively.

Much debate but few definitive data address such concerns as relative quality of care for children in managed care settings versus that in traditional settings, especially for at-risk child populations (and the traditional providers of service to such children), including Medicaid beneficiaries and children who have special health care needs. **Available evidence indicates that children in managed care plans tend to have more office visits and may fare better in terms of receiving preventive services. However, comparisons of managed care with traditional financing systems indicate that timely access to services of high quality for special populations of children remain persistent problems** that appear to be exacerbated by some managed care structures. However, despite the absence of definitive evidence on many questions, large segments of the child population are entering managed care at an astonishing pace.

MANAGED CARE MODELS

It is important for pediatricians to understand and be familiar with the various models of managed care.

Staff Model Health Maintenance Organization

In a staff model health maintenance organization (HMO), physicians who provide care to the enrollees of the plan are full-time, salaried employees. Such physician-employees generally take care exclusively of the enrollees of the HMO and practice medicine solely at the HMO's medical facilities. Inpatient services may or may not be on-site within the HMO facilities, and medical and surgical subspecialists may or may not be represented on the staff. From the standpoint of the pediatrician, the staff model HMO offers these advantages: a predictable and secure salary (with bonus or incentive payments typically contingent on productivity); a generally well-established number of enrollees; relative freedom from many of the administrative hassles associated with private practice; consistent schedule and reduced call responsibility; and security of a large organizational structure. Disadvantages include reduced clinical autonomy, which may involve close scrutiny of practice patterns; expectations for provision of a broad scope of service; and increased emphasis on running a cost-effective practice.

Group Model Health Maintenance Organization

Under the group model arrangement, the HMO contracts with a multispecialty medical group to provide medical care to the plan's enrollees. The medical group typically is paid by the HMO on a capitation basis. The medical group may then pay its individual physicians by way of a variety of fee-for-service methods or through capitation, salary, or other methods. Advantages offered by the group model HMO include many of those seen with a staff model HMO, including predictable work schedules, freedom from business-related or administrative hassles, an established and self-contained referral network, and availability of comprehensive services on-site. Disadvantages may again include diminished physician autonomy in these settings insofar as the group is captive to the HMO for its patient base. Some independent groups, however, may have contracts with multiple HMOs as well and provide care to patients who have other (non-HMO) health insurance coverage.

Network Model Health Maintenance Organization

The network model resembles a group model HMO except that under this model, the HMO contracts with a number of multispecialty and/or single specialty group practices. Generally, these HMOs compensate the medical groups on an all-inclusive capitation basis. In contrast to the closed-panel staff and group models, network models may be either open-panel or closed-panel plans. Advantages and disadvantages to this sort of arrangement are similar to those associated with the group model HMO arrangement; however, the broader physician participation inherent in some networks may yield a marketing advantage over closed-panel plans.

Independent Practice Association Model

Under an independent practice association (IPA), an open-panel organization of independently practicing physicians is formed for the purpose of contracting with one or more HMOs. Physicians are members of the IPA, which is a separate legal entity, but continue to practice in their individual offices, with their own staffs, and also may continue to provide care to non-HMO patients. In some instances, the IPA may have exclusive contracts with one HMO; in others, the IPA may have multiple contracts with two or more HMOs. In either instance the IPA typically is paid by the HMO on an all-inclusive capitation basis. Physicians within the IPA are, in turn, most often paid on a discounted fee-for-service basis (and thereby bear some financial risk). This typically translates into some sort of "withhold" arrangement, under which some portion of payment is retained by either the HMO or the IPA and returned at year end if utilization targets are met. In some IPA arrangements, however, pediatricians (as well as other primary care physicians) are paid strictly on a capitation basis, while specialists are compensated on a fee-for-service basis. IPAs have quite a variety of relationships with hospitals, ranging from exclusivity (e.g., hospital-based IPAs) to looser arrangements involving multiple hospitals.

From the perspective of the individual patient, IPAs generally provide access to broader pools of physicians than is typical through traditional HMO arrangements, resulting in an enhanced market position. From the standpoint of the physician, IPAs provide the opportunity for more independent practice within a solo or small group setting, while simultaneously providing good access (through an organized forum) to managed care contracts and the patient populations they bring. This allows physicians relatively greater autonomy compared with the staff, group, or network models. Furthermore, physicians within IPAs can continue to provide care to patients covered by Medicaid or commercial insurance or indemnity plans, and may contract individually (outside the IPA) with other plans, allowing considerable flexibility and diversity within the physician's patient panel.

Health Maintenance Organization–Controlled Physician Network or Direct Contract Model

This model represents a variation on the IPA model, in which the HMO contracts directly with separate and autonomous physicians as opposed to an organized IPA. This type of arrangement has become common in areas where large organized HMOs and IPAs have not yet developed within the local market. Although this type of network is similar in many ways to an IPA, the absence of the physician organization component poses a potential risk to physicians insofar as no organizational forum for physician decision-making exists to represent physicians' interests.

Preferred Provider Organizations

A preferred provider organization (PPO), unlike an HMO, represents an arrangement that is not an organization per se, but rather a contractual agreement between individual providers and health insurance companies or employers. The critical element of most PPOs is a discounted fee-for-service payment arrangement under which patients are given financial incentives to use specified providers who are part of the PPO network. PPOs confer maximal flexibility to physicians to continue to provide services in a relatively traditional manner within their own offices, albeit at discounted individual rates. Moreover, PPO arrangements typically provide physicians a relatively risk-free mechanism of entering into managed care (relative to the capitation approach used by many HMOs). PPOs are often criticized for being primarily a discounting strategy, with only minimal effort being made to oversee or manage care. Some physicians entering into PPOs question

whether the flow of new patients justifies the discounting of fees that ensues.

Point of Service Plans

Point of service (POS) plans were developed to provide enrollees with the joint option of using either the HMO network or, when necessary, non-network providers. Under POS plans, enrollees must select a primary care physician from the HMO network. Care is prepaid so long as enrollees use services from this and other affiliated providers within the network (with cost-sharing kept to a minimum). If, however, the patient chooses to use providers outside of the network, then varying levels of indemnity insurance coverage exist, but cost-sharing requirements take effect. Financing of care, therefore, is variable, depending on the "point of service" where care is provided.

DEVELOPING A MANAGED CARE STRATEGY

It is important for all pediatricians who hope to remain viable in their practice to develop an individualized strategy relating to managed care, recognizing that they have a number of options. Strategic planning is essential for all pediatricians and will be shaped largely by the individual pediatrician's personal abilities, goals, aspirations, preferences, and values, as well as local market forces.

For a few pediatricians, managed care can be ignored altogether or avoided. For others, it may be viewed as a "necessary evil" that must be accommodated. Still for others, indeed for most, managed care represents a strong (if not dominant) market force that presents a range of opportunities for developing a practice and career. Thus, decisions relating to involvement in managed care by pediatricians ought to be made rationally and on an informed basis by using current, objective, and valid information. General strategies relating to involvement in managed care include the following:

1. Seek independent advice from qualified, impartial advisors knowledgeable about the local health care marketplace.
2. Understand the implications of long-term contracts, restrictions, and the fate of agreements if organizational changes ensue.
3. Understand the priorities and needs of organizational administrators, network managers, and other key stakeholders within the organizations.

4. Assess the community perception of the quality of care provided by you as an individual physician.

5. Look for special service "carve-out" opportunities that may represent competitive advantages for you or your patients.

6. Examine which pediatric colleagues you wish to affiliate with, including such factors as their abilities to deliver cost effective care of high quality.

MANAGED CARE EMPLOYMENT AND AFFILIATION ARRANGEMENTS

Full-Time Employment as a Salaried Employee

Many pediatricians, especially younger pediatricians, are very comfortable with the notion of becoming full-time salaried employees insofar as such arrangements provide them with solid salary guarantees, generous benefits, and immediate access to a well-established population base. More predictable hours, including part-time employment options, also are often feasible in these types of arrangements. The disadvantage to such employment arrangements for the pediatrician is, of course, the loss of autonomy that typically ensues. Whenever a pediatrician embarks on an exclusive employment arrangement with a single managed care organization, it becomes imperative for that pediatrician to scrutinize the employment contract, each and every facet of the health plan, the delivery system, and the organizational structure, function, leadership, market share, and philosophy.

Exclusivity

Many pediatricians increasingly are encountering the issue of exclusivity. In many communities and market areas, pediatricians can simultaneously affiliate with multiple managed care organizations or health plans. However, as markets become more competitive and mature with respect to managed care penetration and market competition, physicians increasingly are forced to select one managed care organization with which to affiliate.

Physician Practice Profiling

Just as physicians scrutinize managed care organizations, managed care organizations in-creasingly scrutinize physicians—through "profiling." Extensive data are now collected regarding physicians' practice profiles. Information related to quality of care, outcomes, numbers and duration of inpatient admissions, referral rates and patterns, use of laboratories, imaging studies, and ancillary services, comparative resource utilization, and assessment of relative cost-effectiveness of practice patterns are collected on physicians in practice. Such information is being used routinely by some large managed care organizations to monitor providers within their networks. Such data also are reviewed routinely by some prospective physician employers. It is essential for individual physicians to know and understand what such practice profiling data reflect about them.

REIMBURSEMENT

Crucial aspects with regard to managed care contracting are the *mechanisms* and the *levels* of reimbursement. There is a continuum of reimbursement methods within managed care. Such reimbursement options available in certain markets typically vary according to the extent of managed care penetration and the degree to which financing and service delivery are integrated. In those traditional markets in which fee-for-service payment remains the dominant mode, reimbursement mechanisms based on fee-for-service or modified fee-for-service payment remain largely intact. In those markets in which managed care is beginning to have an influence, discounted fee-for-service and negotiated fee rates are the typical methods of reimbursement. In those markets in which managed care has penetrated to a significant degree, capitation becomes the norm.

Capitation

Capitation is defined as reimbursement to a provider (or group of providers) via a fixed periodic payment in exchange for delivery of a defined set of health services to a specific patient population. **Under capitation, pediatricians are asked to accept a fixed capitation rate (i.e., a dollar amount per member per month) in exchange for providing the full scope of services to that patient.** Capitation rates in most instances also entail that the pediatrician be responsible for serving as the gatekeeper for all specialty and hospital services required by that patient. Capitation amounts are determined actuarially. Because revenues are fixed under capitation, such arrangements also are frequently referred to as "risk contracts."

Potential advantages of capitation to the pediatrician include ability to control use; stable, regular cash flow; and an ability to preserve or gain market share for decreased administrative costs. Potential disadvantages of capitation to the pediatrician include inability to predict and handle the risk; burdens of gatekeeper requirements relating to specialty referrals and hospitalization; requirement for efficient management of the practice; and administrative costs relating to the transition to capitation.

Full-Risk Capitation

Full-risk means that in exchange for a per-member, per-month payment, the pediatrician agrees to provide the full and comprehensive scope of services without a limit on the number of visits or the total actual cost of providing those services. Managed care organizations prefer this type of capitation because it limits their own risk, shifting it instead to the providers.

Shared-Risk Capitation

This represents an alternative to full-risk capitation. Under shared-risk plans, physicians are responsible for the delivery of and/or payment for services only if and when certain conditions are met. Such conditions might include a minimum number of enrollees, an income guarantee, a risk pool among a group of physicians or other providers, or stop-loss coverage or reinsurance for particularly high-cost cases. In general, a shared-risk plan is by far the safer choice for pediatricians who have little or no experience with capitation. It also represents a practical interim step for those physicians moving from a fee-for-service or discounted fee-for-service arrangement toward accepting greater risk.

MANAGED CARE CONTRACTING

Prior to signing a managed care contract, pediatricians need to assess their readiness individually (and the readiness of their practice) for managed care, while also assessing both the strengths and the weaknesses of the managed care plan(s) with which they are considering affiliating. Pediatricians need to review the terms and conditions of the managed care contract. The types of long-range plans and information that pediatricians need to understand include ownership; market influence, including market share, service area, covered lives, and anticipated change in patient base; administrative issues; participating providers (including physicians, ancillary providers, hospitals, and outpatient facilities); marketing strategy; management; financial data; and external evaluation and accreditation. Specific contract terms and provisions essential for the pediatrician to read carefully and understand fully include scope of covered services, authorization processes, benefit limitations and exclusions, emergency and after-hour care protocols, formulary issues, eligibility, malpractice insurance, and on-call availability.

Additional specific contract terms and provisions that warrant close attention include automatic renewals, capacity requirements, contract duration, contract assignability, provisions in the event of financial failure of the managed care organization, dispute resolution, final authority, out-of-area coverage, contract changes, termination of agreement with the plan, and gag clauses. Issues relating to selection and ongoing participation, utilization management and cost-effectiveness requirements, financial issues (including compensation methods), operational requirements, and relationships within the managed care organization (exclusivity, hold harmless clauses) also deserve careful consideration. If provisions within such contracts are not clear or well understood by the pediatrician, expert advice and clarification become essential. Although in many cases managed care organizations might be reluctant to alter the terms and conditions within their provider agreements, there typically is some degree of negotiating latitude granted to those physicians who are deemed to be attractive providers. Working with professional advisors, pediatricians should attempt to eliminate onerous or burdensome provisions from agreements, including those that might threaten their patients' interests as well as their own. Clearly, **careful attention on the part of the pediatrician to managed care organizations' benefit structure, medical management protocols, issues, provider network and delivery system, and payment formula from both the pediatrician's and the patient's perspectives is paramount.**

FURTHER READING

American Academy of Pediatrics, Committee on Child Health Financing: A Pediatrician's Guide to Managed Care. Edited by Berman S, Gross RD, and Lewak N. American Academy of Pediatrics, 1994.

American Academy of Pediatrics, Committee on Child Health Financing: Strategies for Managed Care Series. Elk Grove Village, IL, American Academy of Pediatrics, 1994–1997.

Kongstvedt PR: Essentials of Managed Health Care. Gaithersburg, MD, Aspen Publishers, 1995.

Leatherman S and McCarthy D: Opportunities and challenges for promoting children's health in managed care organizations. *In* Stein R (ed): Health Care For Children: What's Right, What's Wrong, What's Next. New York, United Hospital Fund, 1997, pp 177–198.

Rosenbaum S: Protecting children: Defining, measuring, and enforcing quality in managed care. *In* Stein R (ed): Health Care For Children: What's Right, What's Wrong, What's Next. New York, United Hospital Fund, 1997, pp 177–198.

Rowland D, Rosenbaum S, Simon L, and Chait E: Medicaid and Managed Care: Lessons from the Literature. A Report of the Kaiser Commission on the Future of Medicaid, Washington, DC, Kaiser Commission, 1995.

GLOSSARY OF MANAGED CARE TERMS

Capitation

Reimbursement to a provider (or group of providers) through the payment of a fixed, periodic payment (usually monthly) in exchange for delivering a defined set of services to a specific population of patients, thereby placing most of the financial risk for utilization with the provider.

Carve Out

In capitation payment arrangements, certain types of care "carved out" of the contract (i.e., not included) and contracted for separately through an agreement with a group of providers and, as determined by service or diagnosis, possibly compensated for on a separate basis.

Case Manager

An individual (usually a physician or nurse) acting for a managed care plan, who facilitates the care of a patient who has a complicated medical problem. The goal of case management is to optimize care while withholding unnecessary or inappropriate services.

Closed Panel

A managed care plan that contracts with physicians on an exclusive basis for services and does not allow those physicians to see patients from another managed care organization. Examples include staff and group model HMOs. This could apply to a large private medical group that contracts with an HMO.

Copayment

An amount specified in a member's contract that the member or insured is responsible for paying directly to a provider at the time services are rendered.

Exclusions

In capitation arrangements, certain high-risk and/or high-cost procedures are excluded from the capitation agreement and are paid for on a predetermined, fee-for-service basis. Also, pediatric emergencies that involve out-of-area care and ancillary diagnostic tests performed outside of the office often are excluded from the capitated formula.

Exclusivity

Selection by a provider of only one managed care organization with which to affiliate or selection by a managed care organization of one physician group with which to contract.

Gatekeeper

A primary care physician who is responsible for directly providing primary patient care as well as coordinating overall patient care. The gatekeeper determines and authorizes patient referrals to specialists, use of certain tests and procedures, and the admission of patients to hospitals.

Open Panel

A managed care plan that contracts (either directly or indirectly) with private physicians to deliver care in their own offices. Examples would include a direct contract HMO and an IPA.

Reinsurance

Special insurance coverage obtained by a provider or health plan to protect against certain unanticipated and potentially crippling financial losses incurred on covered services provided to health plan members. Such insurance may limit exposure on a per case or aggregate basis. In certain circumstances, physicians can obtain reinsurance through a contracted health plan.

Risk Sharing

Sharing the possibility for profit or loss. Typically, providers and managed care organizations, particularly HMOs, share risk through capitation payments and "withhold" pools.

Stop Loss

A provision in a managed care contract that limits a provider's financial exposure to specified dollar amounts on a per case or aggregate basis.

Withhold

The portion of the payment to physicians that is withheld by a managed care organization until the end of the year to create an incentive for the provision of efficient care. If the physician (or group of physicians) exceeds utilization targets, the withhold may not be returned or may be returned only in part. The withhold can cover all services or may be specific to hospital care, laboratory utilization, or specialty referrals.

INDEX

Note: Page numbers in *italics* refer to illustrations; page numbers followed by t refer to tables.

559

ISBN 0-7216-7401-1

90038